Exploring Psychology

Third Edition

Exploring Psychology

David G. Myers

Hope College, Holland, Michigan

WORTH PUBLISHERS

Exploring Psychology, *Third Edition*

Copyright © 1996, 1993, 1990 by Worth Publishers, Inc.

All rights reserved.

Manufactured in the United States of America

Library of Congress Catalog Card Number: 95-61216

ISBN: 1-57259-069-6 (paper)

ISBN: 1-57259-083-1 (case)

ISBN: 1-57259-096-3 (paper comp.)

Printing: 3 4 5—99 98 97

Development editor: Christine Brune

Design: Malcolm Grear Designers

Art director: George Touloumes

Production editor: Laura Rubin

Production supervisor: Patricia Lawson

Layout: Heriberto Lugo

Picture editor: Chris Migdol

Line art: Bruce P. Maddocks and Demetrios Zangos

Anatomical art: Bonnie Hofkin

Composition and separations: TSI Graphics, Inc.

Printing and binding: R.R. Donnelley & Sons Company

Cover: Celia Johnson

Illustration credits begin on page IC-1, and constitute an extension of the copyright page.

All royalties from the sale of this book are assigned to the David and Carol Myers Foundation, which exists to receive and distribute funds to other charitable organizations.

Worth Publishers

33 Irving Place

New York, New York 10003

Value Pak bundled items with corresponding ISBN numbers:

Myers: **Exploring Psychology**, 3rd (soft cover) & Straub: **Study Guide t/a Exploring Psychology**, 3rd	1-57259-112-9
Myers: **Exploring Psychology**, 3rd (soft cover) & Straub: **Study Guide for the Discovering Psychology** *Telecourse* **t/a Exploring Psychology**, 3rd	1-57259-114-5
Myers: **Exploring Psychology**, 3rd (soft cover) & Straub/Ludwig: **Computerized Study Guide t/a Exploring Psychology**, 3rd (DOS Version-3.5)	1-57259-121-8
Myers: **Exploring Psychology**, 3rd (soft cover) & Straub/Ludwig: **Computerized Study Guide t/a Exploring Psychology**, 3rd (DOS Version-5.25)	1-57259-122-6
Myers: **Exploring Psychology**, 3rd (soft cover) & Straub/Ludwig: **Computerized Study Guide t/a Exploring Psychology**, 3rd (Macintosh Version)	1-57259-123-4
Myers: **Exploring Psychology**, 3rd (soft cover) & Halonen: **Critical Thinking Companion for General Psychology**	1-57259-113-7
Myers: **Exploring Psychology**, 3rd (hard cover) & Straub: **Study Guide t/a Exploring Psychology**, 3rd	1-57259-115-3
Myers: **Exploring Psychology**, 3rd (hard cover) & Straub: **Study Guide for the Discovering Psychology** *Telecourse* **t/a Exploring Psychology**, 3rd	1-57259-117-X
Myers: **Exploring Psychology**, 3rd (hard cover) & Straub/Ludwig: **Computerized Study Guide t/a Exploring Psychology**, 3rd (DOS Version-3.5)	1-57259-124-2
Myers: **Exploring Psychology**, 3rd (hard cover) & Straub/Ludwig: **Computerized Study Guide t/a Exploring Psychology**, 3rd (DOS Version-5.25)	1-57259-125-0
Myers: **Exploring Psychology**, 3rd (hard cover) & Straub/Ludwig: **Computerized Study Guide t/a Exploring Psychology**, 3rd (Macintosh Version)	1-57259-126-9
Myers: **Exploring Psychology**, 3rd (hard cover) & Halonen: **Critical Thinking Companion for General Psychology**	1-57259-116-1

Contents in Brief

Preface   xv

Chapter 1
*Introduction: Thinking Critically With
Psychology   1*

Chapter 2
Neuroscience and Behavior   35

Chapter 3
The Developing Person   69

Chapter 4
Sensation and Perception   117

Chapter 5
States of Consciousness   163

Chapter 6
Learning   195

Chapter 7
Memory   223

Chapter 8
Thinking, Language, and Intelligence   255

Chapter 9
Motivation   297

Chapter 10
Emotions, Stress, and Health   335

Chapter 11
Personality   377

Chapter 12
Psychological Disorders   413

Chapter 13
Therapy   449

Chapter 14
Social Psychology   479

Appendix A
Statistical Reasoning   526

Appendix B
*Sample Answers to Critical Thinking
Exercises   535*

Glossary   *G-1*

References   *R-1*

Illustration Credits   *IC-1*

Name Index   *NI-1*

Subject Index   *SI-1*

Contents

Preface xv

Chapter 1

Introduction: Thinking Critically With Psychology 1

What Is Psychology? 2
Psychology's Roots 2
Psychology's Perspectives 3
Psychology's Subfields 5

Why Do Psychology? 6
The Scientific Attitude 7
What About Intuition and Common Sense? 8

How Do Psychologists Ask and Answer Questions? 10
The Scientific Method 10
Description 11
Correlation 14
THINKING CRITICALLY ABOUT *Hot and Cold Streaks—
Random Sequences That Don't Look Random* 16
Experimentation 18

Commonly Asked Questions About Psychology 23
CLOSE-UP *Human Diversity and Kinship* 25

Tips for Studying Psychology 29

Reviewing *Introduction: Thinking Critically With
Psychology* 31
Terms and Concepts to Remember 32
Rehearse It Answer Key 32
Critical Thinking Exercise 33

Chapter 2

Neuroscience and Behavior 35

Neural Communication 36
Neurons 36
How Neurons Communicate 37
How Neurotransmitters Influence Us 38

Neural and Hormonal Systems 41
The Peripheral Nervous System 41
The Central Nervous System 42
The Endocrine System 43

The Brain 45
Lower Level Brain Structures 45
CLOSE-UP *The Tools of Discovery* 46
The Cerebral Cortex 51

Brain Reorganization *58*
Our Divided Brains *58*
THINKING CRITICALLY ABOUT *Left Brain/Right Brain 64*

Reviewing *Neuroscience and Behavior 65*
Terms and Concepts to Remember 66
Rehearse It Answer Key 66
Critical Thinking Exercise 67
For Further Information 67

Chapter 3

The Developing Person 69

Prenatal Development and the Newborn *70*
From Life Comes Life *70*
The Competent Newborn *72*

Infancy and Childhood *74*
Physical Development *74*
Cognitive Development *75*
Social Development *80*
Gender and Child-Rearing *86*

Adolescence *87*
Physical Development *88*
Cognitive Development *89*
Social Development *92*

Adulthood *97*
Physical Changes *98*
Cognitive Changes *100*
Social Changes *103*

Reflections on the Major Developmental Issues *108*
Nature and Nurture *108*
Continuity and Stages *111*
Stability and Change *112*

Reviewing *The Developing Person 113*
Terms and Concepts to Remember 114
Rehearse It Answer Key 115
Critical Thinking Exercise 115

Chapter 4

Sensation and Perception 117

Sensing the World: Some Basic Principles *118*
Thresholds *118*
THINKING CRITICALLY ABOUT *Unconscious Influence: Backward Messages in Rock Albums 120*
Sensory Adaptation *122*

Vision *123*
The Stimulus Input: Light Energy *124*
The Eye *125*
Visual Information Processing *127*
Color Vision *129*

The Other Senses *131*
Hearing *131*
Touch *133*
Pain *134*
Taste *135*
Smell *136*
Body Position and Movement *138*

Perceptual Organization *139*
Form Perception *140*
Depth Perception *141*
Perceptual Constancy *145*

Interpretation *148*
Sensory Restriction and Restored Vision *149*
Perceptual Adaptation *149*
Perceptual Set *150*
CLOSE-UP *The Human Factor in Operating Machines 152*

Is There Perception Without Sensation? *153*
Claims of ESP *154*
Skepticism About ESP *155*

Reviewing *Sensation and Perception 158*
Terms and Concepts to Remember 160
Rehearse It Answer Key 160
Critical Thinking Exercise 161

Chapter 5

States of Consciousness 163

Studying Consciousness *163*
Selective Attention *164*
Levels of Information Processing *164*

Sleep and Dreams *165*
The Rhythm of Dreams *165*

Why Do We Sleep? *168*
Sleep Disorders *170*
Dreams *171*

Daydreams and Meditation *175*

Hypnosis *175*
Facts and Falsehoods *176*
THINKING CRITICALLY ABOUT *Hypnotic Age Regression: A True Story* *179*
Explaining the Hypnotized State *180*

Drugs and Consciousness *181*
Depressants *182*
Stimulants *184*
Hallucinogens *186*
Influences on Drug Use *188*

Reviewing *States of Consciousness* *191*
Terms and Concepts to Remember *192*
Rehearse It Answer Key *192*
Critical Thinking Exercise *193*
For Further Information *193*

Chapter 6

Learning *195*

Classical Conditioning *198*
Pavlov's Experiments *198*
Updating Pavlov's Understanding *202*
Pavlov's Legacy *204*
THINKING CRITICALLY ABOUT *Rape as Classical Conditioning* *205*

Operant Conditioning *206*
Skinner's Experiments *207*
Updating Skinner's Understanding *213*
Skinner's Legacy *214*
Contrasting Conditioning Techniques *216*

Learning by Observation *217*
Bandura's Experiments *218*
Applications of Observational Learning *218*

Reviewing *Learning* *220*
Terms and Concepts to Remember *221*
Rehearse It Answer Key *221*
Critical Thinking Exercise *221*

Chapter 7

Memory *223*

The Phenomenon of Memory *223*
Forming Memories: An Example *224*
Memory as Information Processing *225*

Encoding: Getting Information In *226*
How We Encode *226*

What We Encode *228*
Forgetting as Encoding Failure *231*

Storage: Retaining Information *233*
Sensory Memory Storage *233*
Short-Term Memory Storage *233*
Long-Term Memory Storage *234*
Memory's Physical Storage *235*

Retrieval: Getting Information Out *240*
Retrieval Cues *240*
Memory Construction *242*
Forgetting as Retrieval Failure *245*
THINKING CRITICALLY ABOUT *Repressed Memories of Abuse* *248*

Improving Memory *250*

Reviewing *Memory* *252*
Terms and Concepts to Remember *253*
Rehearse It Answer Key *253*
Critical Thinking Exercise *253*

Chapter 8

Thinking, Language, and Intelligence *255*

Thinking *256*
Concepts *256*
Solving Problems *257*
Making Decisions and Forming Judgments *259*
THINKING CRITICALLY ABOUT *Perceiving Risks* *261*

Language *264*
Language Development *264*
Animal Language *268*
Thinking and Language *272*

Intelligence *275*
Assessing Intelligence *275*
What Is Intelligence? *280*
THINKING CRITICALLY ABOUT *Extremes of Intelligence* *283*

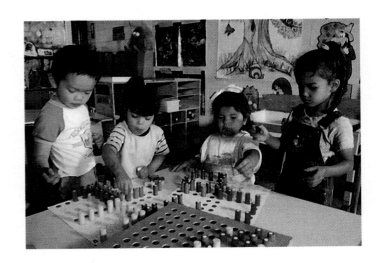

Genetic and Environmental Influences on Intelligence *285*
Group Differences *288*

Reviewing *Thinking, Language, and Intelligence 292*
Terms and Concepts to Remember 294
Rehearse It Answer Key 294
Critical Thinking Exercise 295

Chapter 9

Motivation   297

Motivational Theories *298*
Instinct Theory *298*
Drive-Reduction Theory *298*
Arousal Theory *299*
Incentive Theory *299*
A Hierarchy of Motives *299*

Hunger *301*
The Physiology of Hunger *301*
The Psychology of Hunger *303*
CLOSE-UP *Eating Disorders 304*
Obesity and Weight Control *305*
THINKING CRITICALLY ABOUT *Helpful Hints for Dieters 309*

Sexual Motivation *311*
Describing Sexual Behavior *311*
The Physiology of Sex *312*
The Psychology of Sex *314*
Sexual Dysfunctions and Therapy *315*
Gender and Sexuality *316*
Sexual Orientation *317*
Sex and Human Values *321*

Achievement Motivation *323*
Identifying Achievement Motivation *323*
Sources of Achievement Motivation *324*
Intrinsic Motivation and Achievement *324*
Motivating People *325*

The Need to Belong *328*

Reviewing *Motivation 331*
Terms and Concepts to Remember 332
Rehearse It Answer Key 332
Critical Thinking Exercise 333
For Further Information 333

Chapter 10

Emotions, Stress, and Health   335

The Physiology of Emotion *335*
Arousal *335*
THINKING CRITICALLY ABOUT *Lie Detection 337*

Physiological States Accompanying Specific Emotions *338*

Expressing Emotion *338*
Nonverbal Communication *339*
Culture and Emotional Expression *340*
The Effects of Facial Expressions *342*

Experiencing Emotion *344*
Anger *344*
Happiness *346*

Theories of Emotion *351*
The James-Lange and Cannon-Bard Theories *351*
Cognition and Emotion *353*

Stress and Health *356*
Stress and Stressors *356*
CLOSE-UP *The Wounds of War—Post-Traumatic Stress Disorder 360*
Stress, Personality, and Heart Disease *361*
Stress and Resistance to Disease *363*

Promoting Health *368*
Coping With Stress *368*

Reviewing *Emotions, Stress, and Health 374*
Terms and Concepts to Remember 375
Rehearse It Answer Key 375
Critical Thinking Exercise 375

Chapter 11

Personality   377

The Psychoanalytic Perspective *378*
Exploring the Unconscious *378*
Assessing the Unconscious *384*
Evaluating the Psychoanalytic Perspective *385*

The Trait Perspective *387*
Exploring Traits *388*
Assessing Traits *390*
Evaluating the Trait Perspective *391*

The Humanistic Perspective *393*
Exploring the Self *394*
Assessing the Self *395*
Evaluating the Humanistic Perspective *399*

The Social-Cognitive Perspective *402*
Exploring Behavior in Situations *402*
Assessing Behavior in Situations *405*
THINKING CRITICALLY ABOUT *Pseudo-Assessment—How to Be a "Successful" Astrologer or Palm Reader 406*
Evaluating the Social-Cognitive Perspective *407*

Reviewing *Personality 409*
Terms and Concepts to Remember 410
Rehearse It Answer Key 411
Critical Thinking Exercise 411

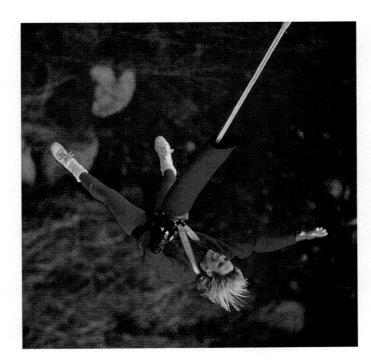

Rates of Psychological Disorders *442*

Labeling People: The Power of Preconceptions *443*

    Reviewing *Psychological Disorders 445*
    Terms and Concepts to Remember 446
    Rehearse It Answer Key 446
    Critical Thinking Exercise 447
    For Further Information 447

Chapter 13

Therapy 449

The Psychological Therapies *449*
    Psychoanalysis *450*
    Humanistic Therapies *452*
    Behavior Therapies *455*
    Cognitive Therapies *458*
    Group Therapies *462*

Evaluating Psychotherapies *463*
    Is Psychotherapy Effective? *464*
    The Relative Effectiveness of Different Therapies *466*
    Commonalities Among Psychotherapies *467*
    Culture and Values in Psychotherapy *468*
    CLOSE-UP *A Consumer's Guide to Psychotherapists 469*

The Biomedical Therapies *470*
    Drug Therapies *470*
    Electroconvulsive Therapy *473*
    Psychosurgery *474*

Preventing Psychological Disorders *474*

    Reviewing *Therapy 476*
    Terms and Concepts to Remember 477
    Rehearse It Answer Key 477
    Critical Thinking Exercise 477

Chapter 12

Psychological Disorders 413

Perspective on Psychological Disorders *414*
    Defining Psychological Disorders *414*
    Understanding Psychological Disorders *415*
    Classifying Psychological Disorders *417*

Anxiety Disorders *418*
    Generalized Anxiety Disorder *418*
    Phobic Disorders *419*
    Obsessive-Compulsive Disorder *420*
    Explaining Anxiety Disorders *421*

Somatoform Disorders *422*

Dissociative Disorders *423*
    Amnesia *423*
    Fugue *424*
    Dissociative Identity Disorder *424*

Mood Disorders *426*
    Major Depressive Disorder *427*
    Bipolar Disorder *427*
    CLOSE-UP *Suicide 428*
    Explaining Mood Disorders *429*
    CLOSE-UP *Loneliness 433*

Schizophrenia Disorders *434*
    Symptoms of Schizophrenia *434*
    Types of Schizophrenia *436*
    Understanding Schizophrenia *436*
    CLOSE-UP *Experiencing Schizophrenia 440*

Personality Disorders *440*

Chapter 14

Social Psychology 479

Social Thinking *479*
    Attributing Behavior to Persons or to Situations *479*
    Attitudes and Actions *481*

Social Influence *485*
    Conformity and Obedience *485*
    Group Influence *490*
    Cultural Influences *494*

Social Relations *496*
    Prejudice *496*
    Aggression *501*
    Conflict *509*
    Attraction *511*

Altruism *516*
Peacemaking *519*

Reviewing *Social Psychology* *522*
Terms and Concepts to Remember *524*
Rehearse It Answer Key *524*
Critical Thinking Exercise *524*
For Further Information *525*

Appendix A

Statistical Reasoning   526

Describing Data *526*
  Distributions *526*
  Central Tendencies *528*
  Variation *528*
  Correlation *530*

Statistical Inference *532*
  When Is It Safe to Generalize From a Sample? *532*
  When Is a Difference Significant? *533*

Appendix B

Sample Answers to Critical Thinking Exercises   535

Glossary *G-1*

References *R-1*

Illustration Credits *IC-1*

Name Index *NI-1*

Subject Index *SI-1*

Preface

Throughout its three editions, my vision for *Exploring Psychology* has remained the same: *to merge rigorous science with a broad human perspective in a book that engages both mind and heart.* My aim has been to create a state of the art introduction to psychology's methods and findings, written with sensitivity to students' needs and interests. I aspire to help students gain insight into, and appreciate the wonder of, important phenomena of their everyday lives. I also want to convey the inquisitive, critical, and compassionate spirit in which psychologists *do* psychology. Believing with Thoreau that "Anything living is easily and naturally expressed in popular language," I seek to communicate today's scholarship with crisp narrative and vivid storytelling.

New to the Third Edition

This new edition retains the voice, and much of the organization and content of its predecessors. It is, however, the most effortful and significant revision to date.

Enhanced "Thinking Critically" Theme

A new Chapter 1, Introduction: Thinking Critically With Psychology, takes an innovative critical thinking approach to introducing the field and to teaching the methods of psychology (see table of contents at right). This chapter shows how psychological science serves as an antidote to the pitfalls of unaided intuition. It looks at how psychology's methods can help us answer many significant questions and think more intelligently. Later chapters reinforce the "thinking critically" theme, often with boxes that model critical analysis. A Critical Thinking Exercise at the end of each chapter tests student understanding of the principles, with sample answers in an end-of-book appendix. These creative exercises use the model established by well-known critical thinking researcher Jane Halonen, whose new *Critical Thinking Companion for Introductory Psychology* is available from Worth Publishers for use with this text. By the book's end, students should not only have learned psychology's most important concepts and findings, but also how and why we play the science game.

NEW Chapter 1

Introduction: Thinking Critically With Psychology

What Is Psychology?
Psychology's Roots
Psychology's Perspectives
Psychology's Subfields

Why Do Psychology?
The Scientific Attitude
What About Intuition and Common Sense?

How Do Psychologists Ask and Answer Questions?
The Scientific Method
Description
Correlation
Experimentation

Commonly Asked Questions About Psychology

Tips for Studying Psychology

All New Anatomical Art; Improved Neuroscience Perspective

Anatomical art throughout the book has been redrawn to be as comprehensible and appealing to students as possible (for example, see Figure 2–7 below). Chapter 2 is now titled Neuroscience and Behavior and offers thoroughly updated coverage of psychology's neuroscience foundations. On the stated assumption that "everything psychological is simultaneously biological," information on the neurobiology and genetics of behavior, cognition, and emotion is integrated throughout the text, where it can be introduced in context (see cross-reference guide, page 67). This also prevents overwhelming students by packing too much into this early chapter.

Figure 2–7 The Body's Major Endocrine Glands   *The pituitary gland releases hormones that, in turn, regulate the hormone secretions of other glands.*

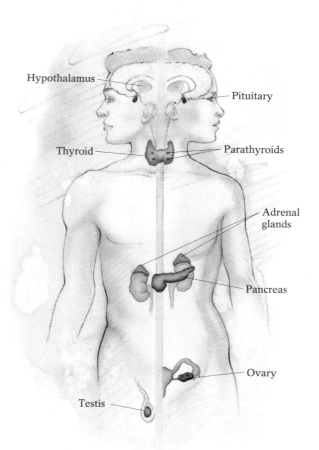

Hypothalamus
Pituitary
Thyroid
Parathyroids
Adrenal glands
Pancreas
Ovary
Testis

Fully Integrated Coverage of Culture and Gender

Integrated coverage of cultural and gender diversity permeates every chapter. This coverage begins with Chapter 1's discussions of the social-cultural perspective, of cultural and gender variations, and of "human diversity and kinship" and extends through Chapter 14's discussions of cultural and gender roles. In between are literally dozens of gender- and culture-related topics, including

Integrated Cultural Diversity

From Chapter 1 to Chapter 14 the integrated coverage of cultural diversity permeates the book in discussions of culture and:

Adolescence, pp. 87, 96–97
Aggression, pp. 501, 504–505
Aging, p. 98
Alcoholism, p. 416
Alzheimer's disease, p. 100
Anger, p. 345
Attachment, pp. 82–83
Attractiveness, p. 514
Attribution, p. 481
Behavioral effects of culture, pp. 23, 494–495
Bilingualism, pp. 272–273
Child-rearing, pp. 85–86
Cognitive development, p. 91
Conformity, p. 486
Culture shock (in learned helplessness, Ch. 11), p. 404

Depression, p. 429
Developmental similarities, pp. 85–86
Dieting, pp. 304, 308
Dissociative identity disorder (Multiple personality), p. 425
Divorce, pp. 104–105
Drugs, p. 189
Eating disorders, p. 304
Experiencing emotion, p. 344
Expressing emotion, pp. 340–341
Happiness, p. 348
Intelligence, pp. 289–290
Kinship, p. 25
Language, pp. 272–273
Learning of aggression, p. 504

Management style, p. 327
Math performance, p. 289
Menopause, p. 98
Moral development, p. 91
Norms, p. 494
Obesity, pp. 305–306, 308
Parenting, p. 83
Participative management, p. 328
Peacemaking, pp. 519–520
Perception, p. 153
Personality dimensions, p. 389
Physiology of emotion, p. 338
Prejudice, pp. 497–498
Premarital sex, p. 95
Psychological disorders, pp. 413, 416, 422–423, 429,

431–432
Roles, p. 495
Schizophrenia, pp. 434, 437
Self-serving bias, p. 397
Social responsibility norm, p. 519
Social clock, p. 104
Somatoform disorders, pp. 422–423
Study time, p. 289
Suicide, p. 428
Taste preferences, p. 303
Teen sexuality, pp. 95–96
Temperament, p. 82
Weight concern, pp. 305–306, 309
Work-related values, p. 104

Integrated Gender Diversity

The psychology of women and men is similarly integrated into the book's ongoing narrative at dozens of points throughout the text.

Abortion stress, p. 359
Adult development, pp. 98, 103–104
Alcoholism, pp. 429, 442
Body image, p. 306
Bonding, pp. 81–83
Breast cancer therapy, p. 365
Breast-feeding, p. 81
Child-rearing, pp. 86–87
Depression, pp. 429, 431, 442
Dieting, pp. 306, 308
Dreams, pp. 172, 315
Early versus late maturation, p. 89

Eating disorders, p. 304
Emotion detection, p. 339
Employment of women, p. 106
Empty nest, p. 105
Freud's views, pp. 380–381, 383, 385
Gender typing, p. 86
Generic pronoun "he," pp. 272–273
Happiness, p. 350
Heart disease, pp. 361–362
Help-receiving, p. 518
Hormones and aggression, p. 502

Hormones and sexual behavior, pp. 313–314
Hormones and sexual development, pp. 71, 88–89
Intelligence, p. 290
Intimacy and identity, pp. 93–94
Leadership, pp. 427–428
Math performance, p. 290
Menarche, p. 88
Menopause, p. 98
Moral development, p. 91
Personality disorder, pp. 440–442

Pornography, pp. 314, 506–508
Rape, pp. 506–508
Self-concept, pp. 398–399, 431
Sensitivity to smells, p. 137
Sexual abuse, p. 372
Sexual coercion, p. 182
Sexual development, p. 89
Sexual dysfunction, pp. 315–316
Sexual orientation, pp. 317–320
Sexuality, pp. 316–317
Social connectedness, p. 94
Suicide, p. 428

those indexed in the cross-reference guides above. Our illustration and photo program has been revised to make human diversity more visible. For this and succeeding editions my aim is more and more to offer a world-based psychology for a worldwide student body. Rather than covering multicultural and gender issues exclusively in boxes or special sections, all this is naturally embedded in the ongoing flow of the text.

Successful SQ3R Study Aids

1. Exploring Psychology's *complete system of learning aids includes numbered "preview questions," which appear in this format throughout the book.*

Exploring Psychology has retained its popular system of study aids, integrated into an SQ3R structure that augments the narrative without disrupting it. Each chapter opens with a chapter outline that enables students to quickly *survey* its major topics (see sample from Chapter 1 on page xv). Numbered preview *questions* at the start of each new major topic define the learning objectives that will guide students as they *read* (see sample #1 above). *Rehearse* It quizzes at the end of each major section will stimulate students to rehearse what they have learned (see sample below from Chapter 1). These test items offer a novel combination of crisp review of key ideas and practice with the multiple-choice test format. The chapter-ending *Review* answers each of the numbered preview questions and is followed by answers for each of the Rehearse It multiple-choice questions. All key terms are defined in the margins for ready reference while students are being introduced to the new term in the narrative (see sample format at left). Key terms are also listed at the end of the chapter with page references for review. Periodic "Thinking Critically About . . ." and "Close-Up" boxes encourage the development of critical thinking skills as well as application of the new concepts. Critical Thinking Exercises at the end of each chapter allow practice of new skills as well as review of important chapter topics. The "Tips for Studying Psychology" section at the end of Chapter 1 explains the SQ3R-based system of study aids, suggesting how students can survey, question, read, rehearse, and review the material for maximum retention.

In the margins of this book, students will find interesting and informative review notes, and quotes from researchers and others that will encourage them to be active learners and apply what they're learning.

key terms   Look for complete definitions of each important term in the margin near its introduction in the narrative.

! *Rehearse It**

1. Psychology is the science of behavior and mental processes. The perspective in psychology that focuses on how behavior and thought differ from situation to situation and culture to culture is the

a. cognitive perspective.
b. psychoanalytic perspective.
c. social-cultural perspective.
d. biological perspective.

2. In the history of psychology, one of the main debates has been over the nature-nurture issue. Nature is to nurture as

a. personality is to intelligence.
b. biology is to experience.
c. intelligence is to biology.
d. psychological traits are to behaviors.

3. The behavioral perspective in psychology emphasizes observable responses and how they are acquired and modified. A behavioral psychologist would be most likely to study

a. the effect of school uniforms on classroom behaviors.
b. the hidden meaning in children's themes and drawings.
c. the age at which children can learn algebra.
d. whether certain mathematical abilities appear to be inherited.

4. A psychologist who treats emotionally troubled adolescents at the local mental health agency is most likely to be a

a. research psychologist.

b. psychiatrist.
c. industrial/organizational psychologist.
d. clinical psychologist.

5. The goal of a psychologist who conducts basic research is to expand psychology's knowledge base. This psychologist would be most likely to

a. design a computer screen with limited glare and assess the effect on computer operators' eyes after a day's work.
b. treat older people who are overcome by depression.
c. observe 3- and 6-year-old children solving puzzles and analyze differences in their abilities.
d. interview children with behavioral problems and suggest treatments.

*You can use these Rehearse It questions to gauge whether you are ready for the next section. The answers are at the end of the chapter.

Goals for the Third Edition

Throughout this revision, I have steadfastly followed eight principles:

1. *To exemplify the process of inquiry* I strive to show students not just the outcome of research, but how the research process works. Throughout, the book tries to excite the reader's curiosity. It invites readers to imagine themselves as participants in classic experiments. Several chapters introduce research stories as mysteries that progressively unravel as one clue after another falls into place.

2. *To teach critical thinking* By presenting research as intellectual detective work, I exemplify an inquiring, analytical mind-set. Whether students are studying development, cognition, or statistics, they will become involved in, and see the rewards of, critical reasoning. Moreover, they will discover how an empirical approach can help them evaluate competing ideas and claims for highly publicized phenomena—ranging from subliminal persuasion, ESP, and astrology, to hypnotic age-regression, basketball streak-shooting, and repressed and recovered memories.

3. *To put facts in the service of concepts* My intention is not to fill students' intellectual file drawers with facts, but to reveal psychology's major concepts—to teach students how to think, and to offer psychological ideas worth thinking about. In each chapter I place emphasis on those concepts I hope students will carry with them long after they complete the course. Always, I try to follow Albert Einstein's dictum that "everything should be made as simple as possible, but not simpler."

4. *To be as up-to-date as possible* Few things dampen students' interests as quickly as the sense that they are reading stale news. While retaining psychology's classic studies and concepts, I also present the discipline's most important recent developments. Twenty-three percent of this edition's 1,979 references are dated 1992 to 1995.

5. *To integrate principles and applications* Throughout—by means of anecdotes, case histories, and the posing of hypothetical situations—I relate the findings of basic research to their applications and implications. Where psychology can illuminate pressing human issues—be they racism and sexism, health and happiness, or violence and war—I have not hesitated to shine its light.

6. *To enhance comprehension by providing continuity* Many chapters have a significant issue or theme that links subtopics, forming a thread that ties the chapter together. The Learning chapter conveys the idea that bold thinkers can serve as intellectual pioneers. The Thinking, Language, and Intelligence chapter raises the issue of human rationality and irrationality. The Psychological Disorders chapter conveys empathy for, and understanding of, troubled lives. "The uniformity of a work," observed Edward Gibbon, "denotes the hand of a single artist." Because the book has a single author, other threads, such as nature-nurture interaction and cultural diversity, weave throughout the *whole* book, and students hear a consistent voice.

7. *To reinforce learning at every step* Everyday examples and rhetorical questions encourage students to process the material actively. Concepts presented earlier are frequently applied, and thereby reinforced, in later chapters. Pedagogical aids augment learning without interrupting the text narrative. Major sections begin with numbered preview questions and end with Rehearse It sections for self-testing on key concepts. End-of-chapter reviews repeat the preview questions and answer them. Key terms lists with page numbers allow for further review.

8. ***To convey respect for human unity and diversity*** Time and again, readers will see evidence of our human kinship—our shared biological heritage, our common mechanisms of seeing and learning, hungering and feeling, loving and hating. They will also better understand the dimensions of our diversity—our *individual* diversity in development and aptitudes, temperament and personality, and disorder and health; and our *cultural* diversity in attitudes and expressive styles, child-rearing and care for the elderly, and life priorities.

The Supplements Package

Exploring Psychology is accompanied by widely acclaimed materials to enhance teaching and learning. For students who desire additional help mastering the text, there is Richard O. Straub's (University of Michigan, Dearborn) *Study Guide*. Each chapter uses the SQ3R method to guide students at each step of their study. For each major section of the text chapter, a list is provided of the idioms and other phrases potentially unfamiliar to students for whom English is a second language. Each word or phrase is carefully explained and related to the text material. The words and phrases are identified in the Guided Study section, and the definitions are provided at the back of the chapter. A chapter review, with fill-in and essay questions, and progress tests help students check their mastery of the material. The study guide is also computerized in an interactive program for use on IBM PC and compatibles or Macintosh computers.

The *Instructor's Resources*, created by Martin Bolt (Calvin College) for *Exploring Psychology*, has been hailed as the finest set of psychology teaching resources ever assembled. With 25 percent new items in this edition, it features dozens of ready-to-use handouts, along with learning objectives, lecture/discussion ideas, student projects, classroom exercises, and video and film suggestions. Martin Bolt's *Lecture Guides*, which come in both printed and easily modifiable IBM PC and compatibles and Macintosh formats, provide detailed outlines of each chapter, with all instructor's resources and transparencies keyed to their relevant topics. The transparency package has been carefully revised, in response to reviews, for most effective classroom use.

The award-winning computer software developed by Thomas Ludwig (Hope College) brings some of psychology's most important concepts and methods to life. *PsychSim: Interactive Graphic Simulations for Psychology* contains 19 programs, including three new to this edition, for use in the Macintosh or IBM Windows formats. Some simulations engage the student as experimenter—conditioning a rat, electrically probing the hypothalamus, or working in a sleep lab. Others engage the student as subject—responding to tests of memory or visual illusions, or interpreting facial expressions. Still others provide a dynamic tutorial/demonstration of, say, hemispheric processing or cognitive development principles. Student worksheets are provided. The *PsychSim* programs for this edition are significantly enhanced over an earlier version that received the 1990 Educom/NCRIPTAL Higher Education Software Award for "Best Psychology Software," which marked the first time that software specifically designed for introductory psychology received such acclaim.

The *Test Bank* and the *Alternate Test Bank*, by John Brink (Calvin College), provide over 3,000 multiple-choice and essay questions. Each question is keyed to a learning objective (matching those in the *Instructor's Resources*), page-referenced to the textbook, and rated in level of difficulty. (Optional questions are also included for the *PsychSim* programs and *The Brain* and *The Mind* modules, see next page.) The *Test Banks* are available in test-generation systems for IBM PC and compatibles, Macintosh, and the Apple II family of microcomputers.

Our *Psychology Videodisc* will help you bring to life for your students all of the major topics in *Exploring Psychology*, combining brief, exciting video clips and animated segments with a library of stills. This two-sided videodisc is accompanied by an extensive *Instructor's Guide*, by Martin Bolt and Richard O. Straub, complete with bar codes, descriptions of each item, suggestions for how to incorporate the material into your lecture, and a subject index that references and cross-references all items by topic across chapters. A software package by Thomas Ludwig, for use on IBM PC or Macintosh computers, includes an indexing program as well as lecture presentation programs. The indexing program makes it easy to assemble a list of relevant videodisc clips and stills for any lecture topic. Instructors may print this list for use with a remote control keypad or barcode reader, or may control the videodisc player directly from the computer to display the clips and stills in "slide show" fashion or as part of a complete computerized lecture.

In addition, Worth Publishers has produced 38 video modules from *The Mind* series, in association with WNET. These modules were edited by Frank Vattano (Colorado State University) with the consultation of Charles Brewer (Furman University) and myself. Rather than displace the instructor, as do longer films, these brief clips (which can be dubbed onto individual cassettes) dramatically enhance and illustrate lectures. They do so in ways that written and spoken words cannot—by introducing students to a split-brain patient being tested, a sleeping subject being monitored in a lab, a patient suffering the ravages of schizophrenia, and so forth. In addition to the 38 modules on video cassettes, Worth Publishers also now has a two-sided videodisc that includes 14 highlights from *The Mind* modules. This videodisc is accompanied by a bar-coded Faculty Guide.

In Appreciation

Aided by more than 300 consultants and reviewers over the last dozen years, this has become a better, more accurate book than one author alone (this author, at least) could write. My indebtedness continues to each of the teacher-scholars whose influence I acknowledged in the two previous editions.

My gratitude now extends to the colleagues who contributed criticism, corrections, and creative ideas to this new edition. For their expertise and encouragement, I thank the following reviewers:

David A. Amick, *Front Range Community College*

Ronald Baenninger, *Temple University*

Loretta Bates, *Kansas City Kansas Community College*

Barbara J. Bowman, *Washburn University*

JoAnn C. Brannock, *Fullerton College*

Joan Collins, *Sheridan College*

Mark S. Cummins, *Dawson College*

Linda E. Flickinger, *St. Clair County Community College*

Laurie E. Gallagher, *Butte Community College*

Brigitte Guetter, *Sheridan College*

Stephen Hamilton, *Mount San Antonio College*

Jane A. Howard, *University of Nebraska at Lincoln*

Sybillyn Jennings, *Russell Sage College*

Anita E. Kelly, *University of Notre Dame*

Hella L. Lange, *Normandale Community College*
Nancey Lobb, *Alvin Community College*
Elizabeth Lynch, *Glendale Community College*
Connie Manos-Andrea, *Inver Hills Community College*
Jack J. Mino, *Holyoke Community College*
David E. Neufeldt, *Hutchinson Community College*
Debra A. Poole, *Central Michigan University*
Camille M. Quinn, *Tulsa Junior College*
Tim Rampey, *Victoria College*
Janice Rank, *Victor Valley College*
Tanya Renner, *Kapi'olani Community College, University of Hawaii,*
Kay Sequeira, *Centennial College*
Margaret Thornburg, *Henry Ford Community College*
Herbert Van Schaak, *State University of New York at Oswego*
Wayne Van Zomeren, *Northwest Missouri State University*
Frank J. Vattano, *Colorado State University*
Matthew J. Zagumny, *Tennessee Technological University*

Charles Brewer (Furman University) enhanced this book with meticulous critiques, probing questions, and spirit-sustaining encouragement through its first editions, and continues to help define priorities as a special consultant.

At Worth Publishers—a company whose entire staff continues to amaze me with their devotion to the highest standards in everything they do—many people played key supportive roles. John Staley, Phil Reed, and other members of Worth's talented sales staff inspired the genesis of this book. Managing editor Anne Vinnicombe helped plan the book and oversee its first edition.

Christine Brune, chief editor for the last two editions, is a wonder worker. She offers just the right mix of encouragement, gentle admonition, and attention to detail, while coordinating the whole team of reviewers and editors. An author could not ask for more.

Other Worth staff also played essential roles. Editor Phyllis Fisher offered creative counsel on illustrations, photos, and captions. Betty Probert ably and efficiently coordinated supplements production. Freelance copyeditor Linda Strange sensitively fine-tuned the final manuscript. Production editor Laura Rubin effectively guided the transformation of manuscript into book. And Worth's gifted artistic and production team, including George Touloumes, Demetrios Zangos, Heriberto Lugo, and Patricia Lawson again crafted the elegant product before you.

At Hope College, the supporting team members for this edition included MaryLee Pikey and Ntsiki Sisulu, who researched countless bits of information and proofed hundreds of pages. In this effort, they were supported by my endlessly supportive librarian colleagues. MaryLee Pikey also prepared the name index. With infectious good cheer, Kathy Adamski composed my awkward dictation into hundreds of letters to researchers. Typesetters Phyllis and Richard Vandervelde met or exceeded all deadlines (with a passion for perfection), often by working into the wee hours.

Again, I gratefully acknowledge the influence of my writing coach, poet Jack Ridl, whose influence lingers in the voice you will be hearing in the pages that follow. He more than anyone cultivated my delight in dancing with the language and taught me to approach writing as a craft that shades into art.

After hearing countless dozens of people say that this book's supplements have taken their teaching to a new level, I reflect on how fortunate I am to be a part of a team on which everyone has produced on-time work marked by the highest professional standards. For their remarkable talents, their dedication, and their friendship, I thank Martin Bolt, John Brink, Thomas Ludwig, and Richard Straub. Martin also played a key role in inspiring and guiding the formation of the new Chapter 1. And Rick Straub authored the critical thinking exercises that appear at the end of each chapter.

Finally, my gratitude extends to the students and instructors who have written to offer suggestions, or just an encouraging word. It is for them, and those about to begin their study of psychology, that I have done my best to introduce the field I love.

When those who paint the Golden Gate Bridge finish, it is time to start over again. So with this book. The ink is barely dry before one begins envisioning the next edition. By the time you read this, I will be gathering information for the fourth edition. Letters and now electronic mail will again influence how this book continues to evolve. So, please, do share your thoughts.

David Myers

Hope College
Holland, Michigan 49422–9000
USA
E-mail: myers@hope.edu

Chapter 1

Introduction: Thinking Critically With Psychology

What Is Psychology?
Psychology's Roots
Psychology's Perspectives
Psychology's Subfields

Why Do Psychology?
The Scientific Attitude
What About Intuition and Common Sense?

How Do Psychologists Ask and Answer Questions?
The Scientific Method
Description
Correlation
Experimentation

Commonly Asked Questions About Psychology

Tips for Studying Psychology

Hoping to satisfy their curiosity about people and to remedy their woes, millions of people turn to "psychology." They listen to talk shows featuring over-the-air counseling, read magazine columns on harnessing psychic powers, attend seminars on how to stop smoking through hypnosis, and browse self-help books on the meaning of dreams, the secrets of ecstatic love, and the roots of personal happiness.

Others, intrigued by claims of psychological truth, wonder: Do mothers and infants bond in the first hours after birth? Should we trust memories of child sexual abuse "recovered" in adulthood and prosecute the alleged perpetrators? Are first-born children more driven to achieve? Does handwriting give clues to personality? Does psychotherapy help?

For many people whose exposure to psychology comes mostly from popular books, magazines, and TV, psychologists analyze personality, practice psychotherapy, and dispense child-rearing advice.

Do they? Yes, and much more. Consider some of psychology's questions, questions that from time to time you may wonder about:

▶ Have you ever found yourself reacting to something just as one of your parents would—perhaps in a way you vowed you never would—and then wondered how much of your personality you inherited? To what degree are you really like your mother or your father? *To what extent is your parents' influence transmitted through their genes? To what extent through the environment they gave you?*

▶ Have you ever played peekaboo with a 6-month-old infant and wondered why the baby finds the game so delightful? The baby reacts as though, when you momentarily move behind a door, you actually disappear—only to reappear later out of thin air. *What do babies actually perceive and think?*

▶ Have you ever awakened from a nightmare and, with a wave of relief, wondered why we have such crazy dreams? *How often, and why, do we dream?*

▶ Have you ever been to a circus and wondered how they trained the poodles to dance, the lions to jump through hoops, the chimps to ride bikes? *What are the limits on what we can train animals to do?*

A Smile Is a Smile the World Around   *Throughout this book, you will see examples of our cultural and gender diversity, but also of our similarities that define our shared human nature. Men and women in different cultures show differences in when and how often they smile, but a smile means the same thing anywhere in the world.*

▶ Do you ever get depressed or anxious and wonder whether you'll ever feel "normal"? *What triggers our bad moods—and our good ones? What is normal?*

▶ Have you ever worried about how to act among people of a different culture, race, or sex? In what ways are we alike as members of the human family? How do we differ? As citizens of multicultural countries and a shrinking global village, *how can we build community while accepting our diversity?*

Such questions provide grist for psychology's mill, for psychology is a science that seeks to answer all sorts of questions about us all: how we think, feel, and act.

What Is Psychology?

Psychology's Roots

1. How did the science of psychology develop?[1]

Psychology is a young science with roots in many countries and disciplines. Wilhelm Wundt, who founded the first psychology laboratory in 1879 at Germany's University of Leipzig, was both a physiologist and a philosopher. Ivan Pavlov, who pioneered the study of learning, was a Russian physiologist. Sigmund Freud, renowned personality theorist, was an Austrian physician. Jean Piaget, this century's most influential observer of children, was a Swiss biologist. William James, author of an important 1890 psychology textbook, was an American philosopher.

Psychology began as the science of mental life. Just over a century ago, Wundt's basic research tool was introspection—self-examination of one's own emotional states and mental processes. Wundt focused on *inner* sensations, feelings, and thoughts. Thus, until the 1920s, psychology was defined as "the science of mental life."

"I'm a social scientist, Michael. That means I can't explain electricity or anything like that, but if you ever want to know about people I'm your man."

[1]A Preview Question will appear at the beginning of each major section of a chapter. Search actively for the answer to the question as you read through the section. Answers are available in the form of a numbered chapter review at the end of the chapter.

psychology   The science of behavior and mental processes.

nature-nurture issue   The long-standing controversy over the relative contributions of genes and experience to the development of psychological traits and behaviors.

Throughout this book, important concepts are set in boldface type. As you study, you can find these terms with their definitions in a nearby margin and also at the end of the book in the Glossary section.

Information sources are cited in parentheses, with name and date, then provided fully in the References section at the book's end.

"Once expanded to the dimensions of a larger idea, [the mind] never returns to its original size."

Jurist Oliver Wendell Holmes, 1841–1935

Like Peas in a Pod *Because identical twins have the same genes, they are ideal subjects for studies designed to shed light on hereditary and environmental influences on temperament, intelligence, and other traits. Studies of identical and fraternal twins have provided a rich array of findings—described in later chapters—that underscore the importance of both nature and nurture.*

From the 1920s into the 1960s, North American psychologists redefined psychology as "the science of observable behavior." After all, they said, science is rooted in observation. You cannot observe a sensation, a feeling, or a thought, but you can observe people's *behavior* as they respond to different situations.

In the 1960s, psychology began to recapture its initial interest in mental processes through studies of how our minds process and retain information. To encompass psychology's concern both with overt behavior and with covert thoughts and feelings, **psychology** has become *the science of behavior and mental processes.*

Let's unpack this definition. *Behavior* is anything an organism *does*—any action we can observe and record. Yelling, smiling, blinking, sweating, talking, and questionnaire-marking are all observable behaviors. *Mental processes* are the internal experiences we infer from behavior—the sensations, perceptions, dreams, thoughts, beliefs, and feelings.

Yet the key word in psychology's definition is *science.* Psychology, as I will emphasize throughout this book, is less a set of findings than a way of asking and answering questions. As a *science,* psychology aims to sift opinions and evaluate ideas with careful observation and rigorous analysis. In its quest to describe and explain nature (human nature included), psychological science welcomes hunches and plausible-sounding theories. And it puts them to the test. If a theory works—if the data support its predictions—so much the better for it. If the predictions fail, the theory gets rejected or revised.

My aim in this text, then, is not merely to report results but to show you how we play the game. How do research psychologists sift contesting opinions and ideas? And how might all of us, whether scientists or simply curious people, think smarter when describing and explaining the events of our lives?

Of course, psychology also has content: Its scientific testing of ideas has produced a smorgasbord of concepts and findings, from which we can only sample the fare.

Psychology's Perspectives

2. What theoretical perspectives do psychologists take?

Knowledge transforms. Learning to read, to understand the solar system, and to comprehend the germ theory of disease alters the way people think and act. Learning psychology's findings also changes people: They no longer judge psychological disorders as a moral failing, treatable by punishment and ostracism. They less often regard and treat women as men's mental inferiors. They no longer view and rear children as ignorant, willful beasts in need of taming. "In each case," notes Morton Hunt (1990, p. 206), "knowledge has modified attitudes, and, through them, behavior."

During its short history, psychology has wrestled with some issues that will reappear throughout this book. One such issue concerns the relative contributions of biology and experience. Today's psychologists explore this **nature-nurture** debate by asking,

▸ Are intelligence, personality, obesity, and psychological disorders more influenced by heredity or by environment?

▸ How much of children's grammar is innate, and how much is shaped by experience?

▸ Are eating and sexual behavior more "pushed" by inner biology or "pulled" by external incentives?

▸ Is depression more of a brain disorder or a thought disorder?

I See You! *A biological psychologist might view this child's delighted response as evidence for brain maturation. A cognitive psychologist might see it as a demonstration of the baby's growing knowledge of his surroundings. For a cross-cultural psychologist the role of grandparents in different societies might be the issue of interest. As you will see throughout this book, different perspectives offer complementary views of behavior.*

How are humans alike (thanks to their common biology) and different (thanks to their varying cultures)?

Are gender differences biologically predisposed or socially constructed?

Over and over again we will see the nature-nurture tension dissolve: Nurture works on what nature endows. Humans, especially, are biologically endowed with an enormous capacity to learn and adapt. Moreover, every psychological event (every thought, every emotion) is simultaneously a biological event. Thus depression can be *both* a brain disorder and a thought disorder.

Whether psychologists emphasize nature or nurture depends on their theoretical perspective (Table 1–1). Take an emotion such as anger.

Someone working from a **biological perspective** might study the brain circuits that trigger the physical state of being "red in the face" and "hot under the collar."

Someone working from a **behavioral perspective** might study the facial expressions and body gestures that accompany anger, or might attempt to determine which external stimuli result in angry responses or aggressive acts.

Someone working from a **cognitive perspective** might study how our interpretation of a situation affects our anger and how our anger affects our thinking and reasoning.

Someone working from a **psychoanalytic perspective** might view an outburst as an outlet for unconscious hostility.

Someone working from a **social-cultural perspective** might explore which situations produce the most anger and how expressions of anger vary across cultural contexts.

Such perspectives needn't contradict one another. Rather, they are complementary outlooks on the same biological state. It's like explaining why grizzly bears hibernate. Is it because their inner physiology drives them to do so? Because cold environments hinder food gathering during winter? Both perspectives are useful, and they complement each other.

TABLE 1–1

Psychology's Current Perspectives

Perspective	Focus	Sample Questions
Biological	How the body and brain create emotions, memories, and sensory experiences	How do evolution and heredity influence behavior? How are messages transmitted within the body? How is blood chemistry linked with moods and motives?
Behavioral	How we learn observable responses	How do we learn to fear particular objects or situations? What is the most effective way to alter our behavior, say, to lose weight or stop smoking?
Cognitive	How we process, store, and retrieve information	How do we use information in remembering? Reasoning? Solving problems?
Psychoanalytic	How behavior springs from unconscious drives and conflicts	How are personality traits and disorders disguising unfulfilled sexual and aggressive wishes and childhood traumas?
Social-cultural	How behavior and thinking vary across situations and cultures	How are we—as Africans, Asians, Australians, or North Americans—alike as members of one human family? As products of different environmental contexts, how do we differ?

Although psychology's perspectives can shed light on many issues, we need to keep in mind psychology's limits. Don't expect psychology to answer the ultimate questions posed by Russian novelist Leo Tolstoy (1904): "Why should I live? Why should I do anything? Is there in life any purpose which the inevitable death that awaits me does not undo and destroy?" Instead, expect that psychology will help you understand why people think, feel, and act as they do. Then you should find the study of psychology both fascinating and useful.

Psychology's Subfields

3. *What are psychology's specialized subfields?*

Picturing a chemist at work, you probably envision a white-coated scientist surrounded by glassware and high-tech equipment. Picture a psychologist at work and you would be right to envision

▷ a white-coated scientist probing a rat's brain.

▷ an intelligence researcher measuring how quickly an infant becomes bored with (looks away from) a familiar picture.

▷ a consultant proposing a new "healthy life-styles" employee-training program.

▷ someone at a computer keyboard, analyzing data on whether adopted teens have temperaments more like their adoptive parents or their biological parents.

▷ a traveler en route to collecting data on human values and behaviors in different cultures.

▷ a therapist, listening carefully to a client's depressed thoughts.

The cluster of subfields that we call psychology has less unity than most other sciences. But there is a payoff: Psychology is a meeting ground for different disciplines, and thus a perfect home for those with wide-ranging interests. In their diverse activities, from biological experimentation to cultural comparisons, psychologists share a common quest: describing and explaining behavior and the mental processes that underlie it.

Psychology: A Science and a Profession *In their laboratories and consulting rooms, psychologists study and treat a wide range of human conditions. Here you can see sound-analyzing technology being used to monitor infant brain development, a graduate student running a laboratory experiment on social judgment, and a face-to-face encounter typical of psychotherapy.*

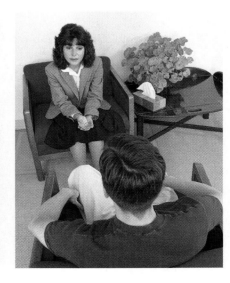

basic research Pure science that aims to increase the scientific knowledge base.

applied research Scientific study that aims to solve practical problems.

clinical psychology A branch of psychology involving the assessment and treatment of those who suffer psychological disorders.

psychiatry A branch of medicine dealing with psychological disorders; practiced by physicians and sometimes involving medical (for example, drug) treatments as well as psychological therapy.

Some psychologists conduct **basic research** that builds psychology's knowledge base. In the pages to follow we will meet a wide variety of such researchers: *biological psychologists* exploring the links between brain and mind; *developmental psychologists* studying our changing abilities from womb to tomb; *personality psychologists* investigating our inner traits.

Other psychologists conduct **applied research** that tackles practical problems. For example, *industrial/organizational psychologists* study and advise on behavior in the workplace. They use psychology's concepts and methods to help organizations select and train employees, boost morale and productivity, and design products and assess people's responses to them.

Although all introductory psychology courses focus on the methods and results of psychological science, psychology is also a helping profession devoted to such practical issues as how to have a happy marriage, how to overcome anxiety or depression, and how to raise children. **Clinical psychologists** study, assess, and treat troubled people. After graduate school training, they administer and interpret tests, provide psychotherapy, manage mental health programs, and conduct research. By contrast, **psychiatrists**, who also often provide psychotherapy, are medical doctors licensed to prescribe drugs and otherwise treat physical causes of psychological disorders.

! *Rehearse It**

1. Psychology is the science of behavior and mental processes. The perspective in psychology that focuses on how behavior and thought differ from situation to situation and culture to culture is the

a. cognitive perspective.
b. psychoanalytic perspective.
c. social-cultural perspective.
d. biological perspective.

2. In the history of psychology, one of the main debates has been over the nature-nurture issue. Nature is to nurture as

a. personality is to intelligence.
b. biology is to experience.
c. intelligence is to biology.
d. psychological traits are to behaviors.

3. The behavioral perspective in psychology emphasizes observable responses and how they are acquired and modified. A behavioral psychologist would be most likely to study

a. the effect of school uniforms on classroom behaviors.
b. the hidden meaning in children's themes and drawings.
c. the age at which children can learn algebra.
d. whether certain mathematical abilities appear to be inherited.

4. A psychologist who treats emotionally troubled adolescents at the local mental health agency is most likely to be a

a. research psychologist.

b. psychiatrist.
c. industrial/organizational psychologist.
d. clinical psychologist.

5. The goal of a psychologist who conducts basic research is to expand psychology's knowledge base. This psychologist would be most likely to

a. design a computer screen with limited glare and assess the effect on computer operators' eyes after a day's work.
b. treat older people who are overcome by depression.
c. observe 3- and 6-year-old children solving puzzles and analyze differences in their abilities.
d. interview children with behavioral problems and suggest treatments.

*You can use these *Rehearse It* questions to gauge whether you are ready for the next section. The answers are at the end of the chapter.

> "What good fortune for those in power that people do not think."
>
> Adolph Hitler, 1889–1945

Why Do Psychology?

Although in some ways we outsmart the smartest computers, our intuition often goes awry. Enter psychological science. With its procedures for gathering and sifting evidence, science restrains error. If we familiarize ourselves with its strategies and incorporate its underlying principles into our daily thinking, we can think smarter. Psychologists use the science of behavior and mental processes to *better understand why people think, feel, and act as they do.*

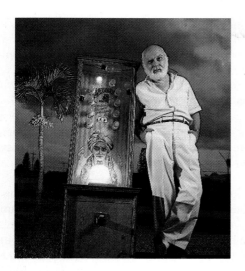

The Amazing Randi *The magician James Randi, shown here with the "Alexander the Man Who Knows" machine, is a model of skepticism. He has tested and effectively debunked a variety of psychic phenomena.*

"*A skeptic is one who is willing to question any truth claim, asking for clarity in definition, consistency in logic, and adequacy of evidence.*"

Philosopher Paul Kurtz
The Skeptical Inquirer, 1994

"*My deeply held belief is that if a god anything like the traditional sort exists, our curiosity and intelligence are provided by such a god. We would be unappreciative of those gifts . . . if we suppressed our passion to explore the universe and ourselves.*"

Carl Sagan (1979a)

critical thinking Thinking that does not blindly accept arguments and conclusions. Rather, it examines assumptions, discerns hidden values, evaluates evidence, and assesses conclusions.

The Scientific Attitude

4. What attitudes characterize scientific inquiry?

Underlying all science is a hard-headed curiosity, a passion to explore and understand without fooling or being fooled. Some questions (Is there life after death?) are beyond science. To answer them requires a leap of faith. With many other ideas, the proof is in the pudding. No matter how sensible or crazy-sounding an idea, the hard-headed question is, Does it work? When we put it to the test, can we confirm its predictions?

This scientific approach has a long history. How to evaluate a self-proclaimed prophet? Moses' answer: Put the prophet to the test. If the predicted event "does not take place or prove true," then so much the worse for the prophet (Deuteronomy 18:22). Magician James Randi uses Moses' approach when testing those claiming to see auras around people's bodies:

Randi: *Do you see an aura around my head?*
Aura-seer: *Yes, indeed.*
Randi: *Can you still see the aura if I put this magazine in front of my face?*
Aura-seer: *Of course.*
Randi: *Then if I were to step behind a wall barely taller than I am, you could determine my location from the aura visible above my head, right?*

Randi tells me that no aura-seer has yet agreed to take this simple test.

As scientists, psychologists aim to approach the world of behavior with a curious *skepticism*. They persistently ask two questions: What do you mean? and How do you know? Consider some familiar claims. Can a theater owner make you hungry by flashing an imperceptibly brief message—EAT POPCORN? Do lie detectors tell the truth? Can astrologers analyze your character and predict your future based on the position of the planets at the moment of your birth? As you will see in the chapters to follow, we can test all such claims. In the arena of competing ideas, skeptical testing can reveal which ones best match the facts. "To believe with certainty," says a Polish proverb, "we must begin by doubting."

Putting a scientific attitude into practice requires *humility*, because it means that we may have to reject our own ideas. Historians report that humility and skepticism of human authority, fueled by religious convictions, helped inspire modern science (Hooykaas, 1972; Merton, 1938). In the last analysis, what matters is not my opinion or yours, but whatever truths nature reveals in response to our questioning. If animals or people don't behave as our ideas predict, then so much the worse for our ideas. As Agatha Christie's Miss Marple explains, "It wasn't what I expected. But facts are facts, and if one is proved to be wrong, one must just be humble about it and start again."

This attitude, armed with scientific principles for sifting reality from illusion, prepares us to think smarter. Smart thinking, called **critical thinking**, examines assumptions, discerns hidden values, evaluates evidence, and assesses conclusions. Whether reading news reports or listening to conversation, critical thinkers ask questions. They wonder, How do they know that? and What axe is this person grinding? Is the conclusion based on mere anecdote and gut feelings? Or on trustworthy evidence? Does the evidence justify a cause-effect conclusion? What alternative explanations are possible? Carried to an extreme, healthy skepticism can degenerate into a negative cynicism that scorns any unproven idea. But when also applied to our own thinking, a critical attitude instead produces humility—an awareness of our own vulnerability to error and an openness to surprises and new perspectives.

What About Intuition and Common Sense?

5. What leads people to overestimate the value of common sense and underestimate the usefulness of psychological science?

Skeptical inquiry and humility before nature are well and good for science. But don't intuition and plain common sense suffice for everyday life? In separating reality from illusion, do we need the scientific attitude that drives critical thinking?

Some doubt it. They say psychology merely documents what people already know and dresses it in jargon: "You mean they pay you for using fancy methods to prove what my grandmother knew?"

Others scorn a scientific approach because of their faith in human intuition. Advocates of "intuitive management" urge us to tune into our hunches. When hiring, firing, and investing, we should distrust statistical predictors and listen to our premonitions. We should follow *Star Wars'* Luke Skywalker by trusting the force within.

Actually, notes writer Madeline L'Engle, "The naked intellect is an extraordinarily inaccurate instrument." Our intuition and common sense sometimes blunder. Like postelection commentators, we sometimes err in presuming we could have foreseen what we know happened.

Did We Know It All Along? The Hindsight Bias

Psychologist Baruch Fischhoff and others (Slovic & Fischhoff, 1977; Wood, 1979) have shown how scientific results and historical happenings can indeed seem like obvious common sense. Once people learn the outcome of an experiment or an historical episode, it suddenly seems less surprising to them than to people asked to guess the outcome. Finding out that something has happened makes it seem inevitable. Psychologists call this 20/20 hindsight vision the **hindsight bias**, also known as the *I-knew-it-all-along phenomenon*.

The phenomenon is easy to demonstrate. Give half the members of a group some purported psychological finding and the other half an opposite result. For example, imagine reading, "Psychologists have found that separation weakens romantic attraction. As the saying goes, 'Out of sight, out of mind.'" Could you imagine why this might be? Most people can, and nearly all will then regard the finding as unsurprising.

But what if you had read the opposite: "Psychologists have found that separation strengthens romantic attraction. As the saying goes, 'Absence makes the heart grow fonder.'" People given this result can also easily explain it, and they overwhelmingly see it as unsurprising common sense. Obviously, when both a supposed finding and its opposite seem like common sense, there is a problem. The point is *not* that common sense is usually wrong, but that it is after the fact. Common sense describes what's happened more easily than it predicts what will happen. As Dr. Watson says to Sherlock Holmes, "Anything seems commonplace, once explained."

Even when predicting, common sense can err. Informed by countless casual observations, our intuition may tell us that familiarity breeds contempt, that dreams predict the future, and that emotions coincide with menstrual phase. As we will see in later chapters, the available evidence suggests that these common sense ideas are wrong, wrong, and wrong. Throughout this book we will see how research has both inspired and overturned popular ideas—about aging, about sleep and dreams, about personality. And we will see how it has surprised

Looking Backward *These Soviet troops were among the last to leave Afghanistan in 1989, after a decade-long, inconclusive military intervention. With the "wisdom" of hindsight, it is hard to see how the Soviets could have made such an "obvious" policy blunder. But then, after Pearl Harbor and the Vietnam War, people asked similar questions about U.S. foreign policy.*

"Life is lived forwards, but understood backwards."

Søren Kierkegaard, 1813–1855

hindsight bias The tendency to believe, after learning an outcome, that one would have foreseen it. (Also known as the *I-knew-it-all-along phenomenon*.)

© 1988 by Sidney Harris/
American Scientist Magazine.

us with discoveries about how the brain's chemical messengers control our moods and memories, about animal abilities, about the effects of stress on our capacity to fight disease.

Overconfidence

Our everyday thinking is limited not only by our after-the-fact common sense but also by our human tendency toward overconfidence. As Chapter 8 explains, we tend to think we know more than we do. Asked how sure we are of our answers to factual questions (Is Boston north or south of Paris?), we tend to be more confident than correct.[2] Or consider these three anagrams, which Richard Goranson (1978) asked people to unscramble.

WREAT → WATER

ETRYN → ENTRY

GRABE → BARGE

Reflect for a moment: About how many seconds do you think it would have taken you to unscramble each of these?

Once people know the target word, hindsight makes it seem obvious—so much so that they become overconfident. They think they would have seen the solution in only 10 seconds or so, when in reality the average subject spent 3 minutes, as you also might, given an anagram without the solution: OCHSA (see below, left).

Are we any better at predicting our social behavior? To find out, Robert Vallone and his associates (1990) had students predict at the beginning of the school year whether they would drop a course, vote in the November election, call their parents more than twice a month, and so forth. On average, the students felt 84 percent confident of their self-predictions. Later quizzes about their actual behavior showed their predictions were correct only 71 percent of the time. Even when they were 100 percent sure of themselves, their self-predictions erred 15 percent of the time.

Overconfidence stems partly from our human tendency to seek information that *confirms* our ideas (a phenomenon that Chapter 8 will label "confirmation bias"). When assessing our ideas, we prefer to look at evidence that might confirm rather than disconfirm them. Reflecting on many experiments, P. C. Wason (1981) reports that once people have a wrong idea they often will not budge from their illogic: "Ordinary people evade facts, become inconsistent, or systematically defend themselves against the threat of new information relevant to the issue."

"It ain't so much the things we don't know that get us into trouble. It's the things we know that just ain't so."

Artemus Ward, 1834–1867

"We don't like their sound. Groups of guitars are on their way out."

Decca Records, in turning down a recording contract with the Beatles

"They couldn't hit an elephant at this dist—."

General John Sedgwick's last words, uttered during a Civil War battle, 1864

Solution to anagram: CHAOS.

[2]Boston is south of Paris.

! Rehearse It

6. As scientists, psychologists view theories with skepticism and humility. This means that they

a. approach research with a negative cynicism.

b. assume that an article published in a reputable journal must be true.

c. realize that some events are beyond proof.

d. persistently ask questions and are willing to reject ideas that cannot be verified by research.

7. A newspaper article describes how a "cure for cancer has been found." A critical thinker will most probably

a. immediately dismiss the article as untrue because there is no evidence to back up the facts.

b. accept the information as a wonderful breakthrough.

c. question the article, evaluate the evidence, and assess the conclusions.

d. question the article but quickly accept it as true due to the author's excellent reputation.

8. Psychology tells us what we already know from common sense, say some skeptics. Hindsight bias refers to our tendency to

a. perceive events as obvious or inevitable after the fact.

b. assume that events happened because we wished them to happen.

c. overestimate our abilities to predict the future.

d. make judgments that fly in the face of common sense.

How Do Psychologists Ask and Answer Questions?

Psychologists arm their scientific attitude with the scientific method: They make observations, form theories, and then refine their theories in the light of new observations.

The Scientific Method

6. What is the place of theory in the scientific method?

In everyday conversation, we sometimes use "theory" to mean "mere hunch." In science, "theory" is linked with observation. A creative **theory** *explains* through an integrated set of principles that *organize* and *predict* observable behaviors or events. By organizing isolated facts, a theory simplifies things. There are now so many known facts about behavior—Nobel-laureate psychologist Allen Newell (1988) estimated 3000, including 29 that govern behavior while typing at a keyboard—that we could never hope to remember them all. By linking observations and bridging them to deeper principles, a theory offers a useful summary. G. E. Morton (1994) likens theory construction to solving a connect-the-dots puzzle; as lines are drawn linking the isolated dots, a coherent picture emerges.

A good theory of depression, for example, will first help us organize countless observations concerning depression into a much shorter list of principles. Say we observe over and over that depressed people recall their past, describe their present, and predict their future in gloomy terms. We might therefore theorize that low self-esteem contributes to depression. So far so good: Our self-esteem principle neatly summarizes a long list of facts about depressed people.

Yet no matter how reasonable a theory may sound—and low self-esteem certainly seems a reasonable explanation of depression—we must put it to the test. A good theory implies testable predictions, called **hypotheses**. By enabling us to test and reject or revise the theory, such predictions give direction to re-

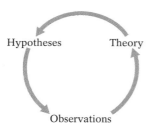

The Ongoing Process of Science *A theory implies hypotheses, which predict observations, which in turn we use to refine the theory.*

theory   An explanation using an integrated set of principles that organizes and predicts observations.

hypothesis   A testable prediction, often implied by a theory.

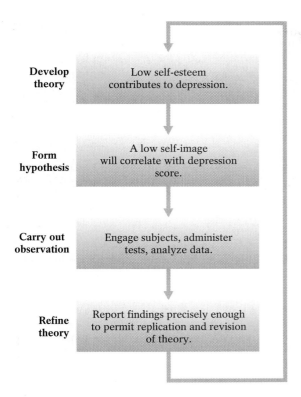

Figure 1–1 Steps in the Scientific Method *Researchers systematically follow a self-correcting process of creating, testing, and refining a theory.*

Good theories explain by

1. organizing and linking observed facts.

2. implying hypotheses that offer testable predictions and sometimes practical applications.

Research strategies:

1. Description

2. Correlation

3. Experimentation

replication   Repeating the essence of a research study, usually with different subjects in different situations, to see whether the basic finding generalizes to other subjects and circumstances.

case study   An observation technique in which one person or group is studied in depth in the hopes of revealing universal principles.

search. They specify in advance what results would support the theory and what results would disconfirm it. To test our self-esteem theory of depression we might give people a test of self-esteem and see whether, as we hypothesized, people who report poorer self-images are indeed more depressed (Figure 1–1).

In doing so, we should be aware that our theory can bias our observations. Having theorized that depression springs from low self-esteem, we may see what we expect to see. We may be tempted to perceive depressed people's comments as self-disparaging.

As one check on their biases, psychologists report their research precisely enough to allow others to **replicate** (repeat) their observations. If other researchers re-create the essence of a study with different subjects and materials and get similar results, then our confidence in the reliability of our finding grows. The first study of hindsight bias aroused psychologists' curiosity. Now, after many successful replications with differing people and questions, we feel quite sure of the phenomenon's power.

In the end, our theory will be useful if it powerfully organizes and predicts—if it (1) effectively organizes a range of observations and (2) implies clear predictions that anyone can use to check the theory or to derive practical applications. (If we boost people's self-esteem, will their depression lift?) Eventually, our research will probably lead to a revised theory (such as the one on page 431) that better organizes and predicts what we know about depression.

To describe, predict, and explain behavior and mental processes, psychologists use three methods: They *describe* behavior using *observations* from case studies, surveys, and naturalistic studies. They *predict* behavior from correlational studies. And they seek cause-effect *explanations* through *experiments* that manipulate one or more factors under controlled conditions. To think critically about popularized psychology claims, we need to recognize these designs and to know how we can use them to sharpen our everyday thinking.

Description

7. *How do psychologists observe and describe behavior?*

The starting point of any science is description. In everyday life, all of us observe and describe people, often forming hunches about why they behave as they do. Psychological scientists are doing much the same, only more objectively and systematically.

The Case Study

Among the oldest research methods is the **case study**, in which psychologists study one or more individuals in great depth in the hope of revealing things true of us all. Much of our early knowledge about the brain came from case studies of individuals who suffered a particular impairment after damage to a particular brain region. Sigmund Freud constructed his theory of personality from a handful of case studies. Developmental psychologist Jean Piaget taught us about children's thinking after carefully observing and questioning his own three children. Studies of but a handful of chimpanzees have revealed their capacity for understanding and using language. Intensive case studies are sometimes very revealing.

Although case studies can also suggest hypotheses for further study, they sometimes have a problem: Any given individual may be atypical, making the case misleading. Our tendency to leap to conclusions from unrepresentative information is a common source of mistaken judgment. Indeed, anytime a re-

The Case of the Conversational Chimpanzee   *In intensive case studies of chimpanzees, psychologists have explored the intriguing question of whether language is uniquely human. Here Nim Chimpsky signs "hug" as his trainer, psychologist Herbert Terrace, shows him the puppet Ernie. But is Nim really capable of using language? We'll explore that issue in Chapter 8.*

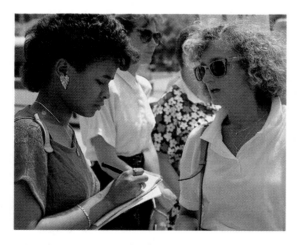

What Do You Know?   *Like this interviewer, psychologists using the survey method ask people to describe their behavior or opinions. The way the researcher frames the questions can bias answers, but accuracy also depends on respondents' memory and honesty.*

> **survey**   A technique for ascertaining self-reported attitudes or behaviors of people, usually by questioning a representative, random sample of them.

> **false consensus effect**   The tendency to overestimate the extent to which others share our beliefs and behaviors.

> **population**   A whole group under study, from which samples may be drawn.

> **random sample**   A sample that fairly represents a population because each member has an equal chance of inclusion.

searcher mentions a finding (smokers die younger: 95 percent of men over 85 are nonsmokers) someone is sure to offer a contradictory case ("Well, I had an uncle who smoked two packs a day and lived to be 89"). Anecdotal cases—dramatic stories, personal experiences, even psychological case examples—have a way of overwhelming general truths. Numbers are numbing (in one study of 1300 dream reports concerning a kidnapped child, only 5 percent correctly envisioned the child as dead—see page 156). Anecdotes are alarming ("but I know a person who dreamed her sister was in a car accident and 2 days later she was badly injured").

So, individual cases can suggest fruitful ideas. But to discern the general truths that cover individual cases requires other methods of answering questions.

The Survey

The **survey** method, which is commonly used in both descriptive and correlational studies, looks at many cases in less depth. A survey asks people to report their behavior or opinions. Questions about everything from sexual practices to political opinions are posed to the public. It's hard to think of a significant question that survey researchers have not asked. In the United States, for example, recent Harris and Gallup polls reveal that 80 percent favor equal job opportunities for homosexuals, 89 percent say they face high stress, 95 percent believe in God, and 96 percent would like to change something about their appearance. In Canada, 36 percent are "very happy," 37 percent think "often" about the meaning and purpose of life, and 45 percent attend religious services at least monthly (Inglehart, 1990.)

Wording Effects   Asking questions is tricky, because even subtle changes in the order or wording of questions can have big effects. For example, 8 in 10 Americans have agreed that "women with young children should be able to work outside the home." But 7 in 10 also agreed that "women should stay home if they have young preschool children" (*Public Opinion*, 1984, 1985). Should cigarette ads or pornography be allowed on television? People are much more likely to approve "not allowing" such things than "forbidding" or "censoring" them. They are similarly much more approving of "aid to the needy" than of "welfare." Because wording questions is such a delicate matter, critical thinkers will reflect on how the phrasing of a question might have affected the opinions respondents expressed.

Sampling   In everyday experience we are exposed to a biased sample of people. We associate mostly with those who share our attitudes and habits. Thus, when we are guessing how many people hold a particular belief, those who think as we do come to mind most readily. This tendency to overestimate others' agreement with us is the **false consensus effect** (Ross & others, 1977). Vegetarians will think more people are vegetarians than will meat-eaters, and conservatives will perceive more support for conservative views than will liberals. To restrain this bias, we can gather a more representative sample of people.

Most surveys sample a target group. If you wished to survey the students at your college you could question them all, but probably there are too many to do so. Instead, you could survey a representative sample of the total student **population**—the whole group you wanted to study and describe. How could you make your sample representative of this population? By making it a **random sample**, one in which every person in the entire group has an equal chance of participating.

To sample the students at your institution randomly, you would *not* send them all a questionnaire. (The conscientious people who return it would not represent a random sample.) Rather, you would aim for a representative sample by, say, using a table of random numbers to pick participants from a student listing and then making sure you got responses from as many as possible. Large, representative samples are better than small ones; but it is better to have a small, representative sample of 100 than a haphazard, unrepresentative sample of 500.

The random-sampling principle also works in national surveys. Imagine that you had a giant barrel containing 60 million white beans thoroughly mixed with 40 million red beans. A scoop that randomly sampled 1500 of them would contain about 60 percent white and 40 percent red beans, give or take 2 or 3 percent. Sampling voters in a national election survey is like sampling the beans; 1500 randomly sampled people provide a remarkably accurate snapshot of the opinions of a nation.

You can forecast the weather by taking a haphazard sample—by looking at the clouds and holding your finger in the wind—or you can look at weather maps based on comprehensive reporting. You can describe human experience using common sense, dramatic anecdotes, personal experience, and haphazard samples. But for an accurate picture of the experiences and attitudes of a whole population there's only one game in town—the representative survey.

The moral: Before believing survey findings, think critically: Consider the sample. You cannot compensate for an unrepresentative sample by adding more people.

We can extend the moral to everyday thinking, as we generalize from samples we observe. We meet a few students and attend a few classes during a visit to a college and infer from those instances how friendly the campus is and how good the teaching is. We observe the weather during a week-long visit to Seattle and then tell our friends about the climate there.

It is often tempting to overgeneralize from such select samples, especially so when the extremes are vivid cases. Given (1) a statistical summary of a professor's student evaluations and (2) the vivid comments of two irate students, an administrator's impression of the professor may be influenced as much by the two unhappy students as by the many favorable evaluations in the statistical summary. Driving into Chicago from the south, many people see the miles of tenement houses near the highway and think, "What an ugly city this is." Standing in the checkout line at the supermarket, George sees the woman in front of him pay with food stamps, and then watches with dismay as she drives away in a Cadillac. In each of these situations, the temptation to generalize from a few vivid but unrepresentative cases is nearly irresistible.

The moral: The best basis for generalizing is not from the exceptional cases one finds at the extremes, but from a representative sample of cases.

Naturalistic Observation

As baseball great Yogi Berra said in a moment of stunning insight, "You can observe a lot by watching." Watching and recording the behavior of organisms in their natural environment is known as **naturalistic observation**. Naturalistic observations range from watching chimpanzee societies in the jungle, to "unobtrusive measures" of parent-child interactions in different cultures, to recording students' self-seating patterns in the lunchrooms of desegregated schools.

Like the case study and survey methods, naturalistic observation does not *explain* behavior. It *describes* it. Nevertheless, description can be revealing. We once thought, for example, that only humans use tools. Then naturalistic observation revealed that chimpanzees sometimes insert a stick in a termite mound

THIS MODERN WORLD by Tom Tomorrow © 1991.

We have Berra to thank for other gems, such as "Nobody ever comes here—it's too crowded," and "If the people don't want to come out to the park, nobody's gonna stop 'em."

naturalistic observation Observing and recording behavior in naturally occurring situations without trying to manipulate and control the situation.

Naturalistic Observation *By unobtrusively watching and recording behavior in natural environments, cross-cultural psychologists have discovered significant variations in human child-rearing patterns. Here in Zaire's rain forest, psychologist Gilda Morelli and her research assistant gather data on Efe children's involvement in community routines.*

Research strategies:
1. Description
2. Correlation
3. Experimentation

correlation A statistical measure that indicates the extent to which two factors vary together and thus how well either factor predicts the other.

illusory correlation The perception of a relationship where none exists.

and withdraw it, eating the stick's load of termites. Chimps and baboons also use deception to achieve their aims. Psychologists Andrew Whiten and Richard Byrne (1988) repeatedly saw one young baboon pretending to have been attacked by another as a tactic to get its mother to drive the other baboon away from its food.

Through naturalistic observations we have also learned that culture shapes child-rearing. In Japan, children learn to "get along" and "go along" with their group. Western child-rearing more often emphasizes individual achievement and rewards assertiveness. Naturalistic observation also reveals that at school, students of different races often shun each other outside the classroom (page 519). This suggests that special efforts to engage students in cooperative play and work may be needed to foster social integration.

Correlation

8. Why do correlations permit prediction but not explanation? How accurately does the naked eye detect correlations?

Describing behavior is a first step toward predicting it. When surveys and naturalistic observation reveal that one trait or behavior accompanies another, we say the two correlate. A **correlation** is a statistical measure of relationship: It reveals how closely two things vary together and thus how well one *predicts* the other. Knowing how much high school grades *correlate* with college grades tells us how well high school grades *predict* college grades.

A *positive* correlation (ranging between 0 and a perfect +1.00) indicates a *direct* relationship, meaning that two things tend to increase together or decrease together. If amount of violence viewed on television correlates positively with aggressive social behavior (which it does), then people's TV-viewing habits will predict their aggressiveness. A *negative* correlation—equally predictive—indicates an *inverse* relationship: As one thing increases, the other decreases. Our findings on self-esteem and depression illustrate a negative correlation: People who score *low* on self-esteem tend to score *high* on depression. A negative correlation (between 0 and –1.00) means that one set of scores goes down as the other goes up.

Though informative, psychology's correlations usually leave most of the variation among individuals unpredicted. As we will see, there is a correlation between parents' abusiveness and their children's later abusiveness when they become parents. But this does not mean most abused children become abusive parents. The correlation simply indicates a statistical relationship: Although most abused children do not grow into abusers, nonabused children are even less likely to become abusive.

Illusory Correlations

Correlations make visible relationships that the naked eye would miss. They also help us stop "seeing" relationships that actually don't exist. A perceived correlation that does not really exist is an **illusory correlation**. When we *believe* there is a relationship between two things, we are likely to *notice* and *recall* instances that confirm our belief (Troilier & Hamilton, 1986).

Illusory correlations help explain many a superstitious belief, such as the presumption that more babies are born when the moon is full or that infertile couples who adopt (Figure 1–2) become more likely to conceive (Gilovich,

	Conceive	Do not conceive
Adopt	a	b
Do not adopt	c	d

Figure 1–2 Illusory Correlation in Everyday Life *Many people notice infertile couples who conceive after adopting. They are vulnerable to an illusory correlation if they ignore other pertinent information, especially from cells b and c. This information is needed to compute the likelihood of conceiving after adopting versus after not adopting. (From Gilovich, 1991.)*

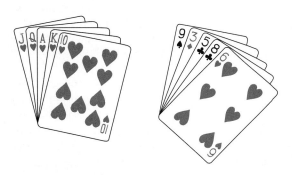

Two Random Sequences *Your chance of being dealt either of these hands is precisely the same: 1 in 2,598,960.*

BIZARRE SEQUENCE OF COMPUTER-GENERATED RANDOM NUMBERS

Bizarre-looking, perhaps. But actually no more unlikely than any other number sequence.

1991). Because we are sensitive to dramatic or unusual events, we are especially likely to notice and remember the occurrence of two such events in sequence—say, a premonition of an unlikely phone call followed by the call. When the call does not follow the premonition, we are less likely to note and remember the nonevent.

Likewise, instances of positive-thinking people being cured of cancer impress those who believe positive attitudes counter disease. But to assess whether positive thinking actually affected cancer, we need three more types of information. First, we need an estimate of how many positive thinkers *weren't* cured. And among those not trying to heal themselves through positive thinking, we need to know how many were and how many were not cured. Without these comparison figures, positive examples of a few hope-filled people tell us nothing about the actual correlation between attitudes and disease.

The moral: When we notice random coincidences, we may forget that they are random and see them as correlated. Thus, we can easily deceive ourselves by seeing what is not there.

Perceiving Order in Random Events

Illusory correlations arise from our natural eagerness to make sense of our world. Given even random data, we look for order, for meaningful patterns. And we usually find it, because *random sequences often don't look random.* If someone flipped a coin six times, would one of the following sequences of heads (H) and tails (T) be more likely than the other two: HHHTTT or HTHTHT or HHHHHH?

Daniel Kahneman and Amos Tversky (1972) found that most people believe HTTHTH would be the most likely random sequence. Actually, all possible sequences are equally likely (or, you might say, equally unlikely) to occur. A bridge or poker hand of 10 through Ace, all of hearts, would seem extraordinary; actually, it would be no more or less likely than any other specific hand of cards.

The failure to recognize random occurrences for what they are can predispose people to seek extraordinary explanations for ordinary events. Imagine that on one warm spring day 4000 college students gather for a coin-tossing contest. Their task is to flip heads. On the first toss, 2000 students do so and remain standing for a second round. As you might expect, about 1000 of these progress to a third round, 500 to a fourth, 250 to a fifth, 125 to a sixth, 62 to a seventh, 31 to an eighth, 15 to a ninth, and 8 amazing individuals, having flipped heads nine times in a row with ever-increasing displays of concentration and effort, remain standing for the tenth round.

By now, the crowd of losers is in awestruck silence as these expert coin tossers prepare to display their amazing ability yet again. The proceedings are temporarily halted so that a panel of impartial scientists can observe and document the incredible achievement of these gifted individuals. Alas, on succeeding tosses half of those remaining flip a tail, until all have been eliminated. "But, of course," their admirers say, "coin tossing is a highly sensitive skill. The tense, pressured atmosphere created by the scientific scrutiny has disturbed their fragile gift."

Some happenings, though, seem so extraordinary that we struggle to conceive an ordinary, chance-related explanation (as applies to our coin tosses). In such cases, statisticians often are less mystified. When Evelyn Marie Adams won the New Jersey lottery *twice,* newspapers reported the odds of her feat as 1 in 17 trillion. Bizarre? Actually, 1 in 17 trillion are the odds that a given person

Hot and Cold Streaks—Random Sequences That Don't Look Random

Every basketball player and every fan intuitively "knows" that players have hot and cold streaks. Players who have "hot hands" can't seem to miss, while those who have "cold" ones can't find the center of the hoop. When Thomas Gilovich, Robert Vallone, and Amos Tversky (1985) interviewed team members of the Philadelphia 76ers, the players estimated they were about 25 percent more likely to make a shot after they had just made one than after a miss. In one survey, 9 in 10 basketball fans agreed that a player "has a better chance of making a shot after having just *made* his last two or three shots than he does after having just *missed* his last two or three shots." Believing in shooting streaks, players will feed the ball to a teammate who has just made two or three shots in a row, and many coaches will bench the player who has just missed three in a row.

The only trouble is (believe it or not), it isn't true. When Gilovich and his collaborators studied detailed individual shooting records, they found that the 76ers—and the Boston Celtics, the New Jersey Nets, the New York Knicks, and Cornell University's men's and women's basketball players—were equally likely to score after a miss and after a basket. A typical 50 percent shooter averages 50 percent after just missing three shots, and 50 percent after just making three shots. It works with free throws, too. Celtic star Larry Bird made 88 percent of his free throws after making a free throw and 91 percent after missing.

Why, then, do players and fans alike believe that players are more likely to score after scoring and miss after missing? It's because in random sequences streaks *do* occur, more than people expect. In any series of 20 shots by a 50 percent shooter (or 20 flips of a coin), there is a 50-50 chance of four baskets (or heads) in a row, and it is quite possible that 1 person in 5 will have a streak of five or six. (In basketball, unlike coin tossing, other factors such as defense may predict the outcome. And some players will, of course, have a higher shooting percentage than others. This analysis deals only with streaks.) Players and fans notice these random streaks and so form the myth that "when you're hot you're hot" (Figure 1–3).

Informed of these contradictory data, many basketball fans persist in thinking that the outcome of the last few shots is a predictor of the next shot outcome. The hot hand myth survives its crash against a wall of data. In sports, such superstitious thinking is harmless fun, notes astronomer and one time sports writer Carl Sagan (1994), "but as a habitual way of thinking, it gets us into trouble in some of the other games we play."

The moral: Whether watching basketball or flipping coins, remember: Our intuition often deceives us. Random sequences frequently don't look random. Expect streaks.

Player A

Player B

Figure 1–3 Who Is the Chance Shooter? *Here are 21 consecutive shots, each scoring either a basket or a miss, by two players who each make 50 percent. Within this sample of shots, which player's sequence looks more like what we would expect in a random sequence? (See page 18) (Adapted from Barry Ross,* Discover, *1987.)*

who buys a single ticket for two New Jersey lotteries will win both times. But statisticians Stephen Samuels and George McCabe (1989) report that, given the millions of people who buy U.S. state lottery tickets, it was "practically a sure thing" that someday, somewhere, someone would hit a state jackpot twice. Indeed, say fellow statisticians Persi Diaconis and Frederick Mosteller (1989), "With a large enough sample, any outrageous thing is likely to happen."

Ron Vachon knows. At a September 1990 baseball game in Boston, Oakland A's outfielder Rickey Henderson hit two foul balls right to him, on successive pitches. That this should have happened to Vachon (who dropped them both) was incredibly unlikely. That it would eventually happen to someone was more likely. An event that happens to but 1 in 1 billion people every day occurs about six times a day, 2000 times a year.

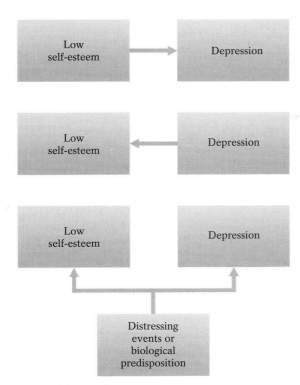

Figure 1–4 Three Possible Cause-Effect Relationships
People low in self-esteem tend to be more depressed than those high in self-esteem. One possible explanation of this correlation is that a bad self-image causes depressed feelings. But as the diagrams indicate, other cause-effect relationships are possible.

Correlation and Causation

So far we've seen that correlation enables prediction and restrains the illusions of our flawed intuition. Violence-viewing correlates with (and therefore predicts) aggression. But does it *cause* aggression? Does low self-esteem *cause* depression? If, based on the correlational evidence, you assume that they do, you have much company. Perhaps the most irresistible thinking error made both by lay people and by professional psychologists is assuming that correlation proves causation. No matter how strong the relationship, it does not! If watching TV violence correlates positively with aggressiveness, does this mean that watching TV violence influences aggressive behavior? It may. Or does it mean that aggressive people prefer violent programs?

And what about the negative correlation between self-esteem and depression? Perhaps low self-esteem does cause depression. But as Figure 1–4 suggests, we'd get the same coincidence of low self-steem and depression if depression caused people to be down on themselves or if something else—a third factor such as heredity or brain chemistry—caused both low self-esteem and depression. Among men, length of marriage correlates positively with hair loss—because both are associated with a third factor, age.

The moral: Correlation enables prediction and may hint at possible cause-effect relationships. But it does not provide a causal explanation. Knowing that two events are correlated need not tell us anything about causation. *Correlation does not prove causation.* Remember this principle and you will be wiser as you see reports of scientific studies in the news and in this book.

! *Rehearse It*

9. In psychology a good theory implies hypotheses, or predictions that can be tested. When hypotheses are tested the result is typically

a. increased skepticism.
b. rejection of the merely theoretical.
c. confirmation or revision of the theory.
d. personal bias on the part of the investigator.

10. Psychology's basic *research strategies* are description, correlation, and experimentation. Which *research design* would you use in an attempt to predict college grades from high school grades?

a. the case study
b. naturalistic observation
c. correlational research
d. experimental research

11. You wish to take an accurate poll in a certain country by questioning people who truly represent the country's adult population. Therefore, you need to make sure the people surveyed are

a. at least 30 percent urban dwellers.
b. registered voters.
c. predictable.
d. a random sample of the population.

12. Suppose a psychologist finds that the *more* natural childbirth training classes a woman attends, the *less* pain medication she requires during childbirth. The relationship between number of training sessions and amount of pain medication required is a

a. positive correlation (direct relationship).
b. negative correlation (inverse relationship).

c. cause-and-effect relationship.
d. controlled experiment.

13. Some people wrongly perceive that their dreams predict future events. This would be an example of

a. negative correlation.
b. positive correlation.
c. illusory correlation.
d. naturalistic correlation.

14. Knowing that two events are correlated does not tell us what is the cause and what is the effect. However, it does provide

a. a basis for prediction.
b. an explanation of events.
c. proof that as one increases, the other also increases.
d. an indication that an underlying third factor is at work.

experiment A research method in which the investigator manipulates one or more factors (independent variables) to observe their effect on some behavior or mental process (the dependent variable) while holding other factors constant.

Research strategies:
1. Description
2. Correlation
3. Experimentation

Answer to Figure 1–3 (page 16): Player B, whose outcomes may look more random, actually has fewer streaks than would be expected by chance. For both players, chance shooting, like chance coin tossing, should produce a change in outcome on successive shots about 50 percent of the time. But Player B's outcome changes 70 percent of the time (14 times out of 20). Player A, on the other hand, is scoring more as we would expect from a 50 percent shooter; 10 times out of 20, Player A's next outcome is different.

The color effect is not race-related. Instead, believes cross-cultural researcher John Williams (1992), it stems from our ancestors' associations with the black of night and light of day. Thus, in many African societies, "black" magic is bad magic.

Bad Guys Wear Black Hats *Since the early days of motion pictures, directors have dressed their villains in black so that viewers can easily tell the good guys from the bad. This tactic capitalizes on a common human bias that experimenters have recently documented: We see what we expect to see. When we see black, we expect aggression.*

Experimentation

9. How do experiments clarify or reveal cause-effect relationships?

Happy are they "who have been able to perceive the causes of things," remarked the Roman poet Virgil. We endlessly wonder and debate *why* people act as they do. As I write, the day's newspapers are filled with such wonderings: What caused two English schoolboys to bludgeon a 2-year-old to death? And, why do people smoke? Have babies as unmarried teens? Do stupid things when drunk? Psychology can't answer these questions directly, but it has helped us to understand what influences aggression, drug use, sexual attitudes, and thinking when drinking.

In everyday life, many factors influence behavior. To isolate cause and effect—to explain what helps cause, say, depression—psychologists conduct **experiments**. Experiments enable a researcher to focus on the possible effects of one or more factors by (1) *manipulating the factors of interest* and (2) *holding constant ("controlling") other factors.* Imagine that some researchers wanted to study the effect of alcohol consumption on thinking ability. Before giving a thinking test, they would *manipulate* alcohol consumption (by giving some people a strong-tasting drink laced with alcohol, others the same drink without alcohol). By randomly assigning people to the two conditions, which otherwise are similar, they would hold all other factors constant. This would eliminate alternative explanations for why thinking might vary with drinking.

If behavior changes when we vary an experimental factor, such as alcohol, then the factor is having an effect. To repeat, unlike correlational studies, which uncover naturally occurring relationships, an experiment manipulates a factor to see its effect. To illustrate, let's consider two actual experiments.

Do Black Sports Uniforms Affect Perceptions?

Cornell University psychologists Mark Frank and Thomas Gilovich (1988) noticed that in virtually all cultures from central Africa to the Orient to Western Europe, the color black connotes evil. In movies, the bad guys wear black. Illegal goods are bought and sold on the black market.

Summarizing these varied observations, Frank and Gilovich proposed a simple, small-scale theory: Black garb suggests evil, cuing us to *perceive* people dressed in black as evil and cuing those who wear black to *act out* their evil image. Frank and Gilovich knew that a useful theory must offer testable predictions. So they derived several hypotheses. First, they predicted that people unfamiliar with football and hockey would rate the black uniforms of National Football League and National Hockey League teams as seeming more evil than nonblack uniforms. Indeed, for both sports, people rated black uniforms as bad, mean, and aggressive.

Second, Frank and Gilovich hypothesized, and found, a positive correlation between black team uniforms and total penalties for aggressive play. In all but 1 of the 17 seasons between 1970 and 1986, the football teams with black uniforms were penalized a disproportionate number of yards. Likewise, in all 16 hockey seasons between 1970–1971 and 1985–1986, the teams wearing black uniforms spent more time in the penalty box. Moreover, when the Pittsburgh Penguins switched to black uniforms during the middle of the 1979–1980 season, their penalties increased from an average of 8 minutes per game to 12 minutes. So, in these two sports at least, there definitely has been a correlation between black uniforms and penalized play.

Remember, a correlation is simply a relationship between two factors—in this case, uniform color and penalties. Correlation cannot prove a cause-effect

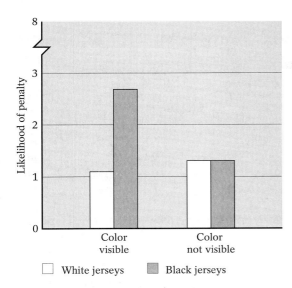

Figure 1–5 Perceptions of Violence *People judged videotaped midair tackles as more likely illegal when enacted by a player wearing black—but only when the color of the jersey was visible. (From Frank & Gilovich, 1988.)*

Note the distinction between random sampling in surveys and random assignment in experiments. Random sampling helps us generalize to a larger population. Random assignment controls extraneous influences, which helps us infer cause and effect.

experimental condition The condition of an experiment that exposes subjects to the treatment.

control condition The condition of an experiment that contrasts with the experimental treatment and serves as a comparison for evaluating the effect of the treatment.

random assignment Assigning subjects to experimental and control conditions by chance, thus minimizing preexisting differences between those assigned to the different groups.

independent variable The experimental factor that is manipulated; the variable whose effect is being studied.

dependent variable The experimental factor—in psychology, the behavior or mental process—that is being measured; the variable that may change in response to manipulations of the independent variable.

operational definition A statement of the procedures (operations) used to define research variables.

relationship. Maybe there is no cause-effect connection; maybe organizations wanting an aggressive image simply choose black outfits and hire aggressive players. (For a motorcycle gang, white outfits just won't do.) But can you imagine *possible* causes of this correlation? Frank and Gilovich suggested two: The correlation occurs because referees *perceive* acts by players in black as more violent than similar acts by players not wearing black. Or, players who wear black uniforms *enact* the expected tough image.

In experimenting to evaluate these two possibilities, Frank and Gilovich found, first, that uniform color did indeed affect perceptions. They videotaped two staged football plays in which black- or white-clad defenders either drove the ball carrier back several yards and then threw him to the ground or hit the ball carrier violently in midair. The experimenters then manipulated the jersey-color factor. People were randomly assigned to either an experimental condition or a control condition. In the **experimental condition**, raters saw the same videotape in full color. With the color on, the raters (fans and professional referees) were more likely to judge the tackles as aggressive and illegal when committed by players wearing black (Figure 1–5). For comparison, the experimenters took the color out of the picture to create a **control condition**— a condition that contrasts with the experimental treatment. When all the players' jerseys appeared dull gray, raters judged the tackles of the white- and black-clad defenders as equally illegal. Thus, the control condition of an experiment provides a baseline against which we can compare the effect of the treatment used in the experimental condition.

Note that a key feature of experiments is **random assignment**. If enough individuals of different ages and opinions are randomly assigned to two groups, the random assignment will roughly equalize the two groups in age, opinion, and every other characteristic that could possibly affect the results. With random assignment, we can therefore say that if the two groups behave or feel differently at the end of the experiment, it very probably is due to the experimental variable. Without random assignment, the groups might differ in ways that could affect the results. If the researchers asked people from one dorm to view the color video and people from another dorm to view the no-color video, they wouldn't know for sure whether the color or the dorm population made the difference.

In a second experiment, Cornell students came to a study of "the psychology of competition." Frank and Gilovich randomly assigned them to wear either black or white jerseys and then invited them to choose some games. When the students donned black rather than white jerseys, they preferred more aggressive games. On average (such findings tell us only about group trends), wearing black affected not only perceptions but behavior as well.

The Frank and Gilovich experiments were fairly simple. They manipulated just one factor, jersey color. We call this experimental factor the **independent variable** because we can vary it independently of the other factors, such as the age or size of the players. Experimenters examine the effect of one or more independent variables on some measurable behavior, called the **dependent variable** because it can vary depending on what takes place during the experiment. Both variables are given precise **operational definitions**. Operational definitions specify the procedures that create the independent variable or measure the dependent variable. Thus they answer the "what do you mean?" question with an exactness that allows others to repeat the study. In Frank and Gilovich's first experiment, the dependent variable was the subjects' ratings of illegal aggression in response to (1) the control condition (videotape with dull gray jerseys) and (2) the experimental condition (videotape showing the black versus white jerseys). Table 1–2, page 20, shows the independent and dependent variables in their second experiment.

TABLE 1-2

The Design of the Second Frank and Gilovich Experiment

	Condition	Manipulation of Independent Variable	Measurement of Dependent Variable
Random assignment of subjects	Experimental	Wear black jerseys	Aggressiveness (game choice)
	Control	Wear nonblack (white) jerseys	Aggressiveness (game choice)

Note again the importance of random assignment. If people had chosen their jersey color, the results might merely reflect a greater natural aggressiveness among those who prefer black.

"In solving one discovery we never fail to get an imperfect knowledge of others of which we had no idea before, so that we cannot solve one doubt without creating several new ones."

Joseph Priestly
Experiments and Observations on Different Kinds of Air, 1775–1786

Let's recap: An experiment has at least two different conditions, a comparison or control condition and an experimental condition. Random assignment equates the conditions before any treatment effects. In this way, the experiment tests the effect of at least one independent variable (the experimental factor) on at least one dependent variable (the response that is measured).

Note, too, that in this series of studies a very simple theory, inspired by everyday observations, generated hypotheses. These predictions were confirmed by the correlation between uniforms and penalties, which in turn stimulated experiments that examined causation. Table 1–3 compares the features of psychology's research methods.

How freely can we generalize Frank and Gilovich's findings? Surely we don't perceive Catholic priests and nuns as aggressive, nor does it seem that wearing black causes them to act aggressively. Frank and Gilovich suspect, and wonder: Do the effects occur only in situations involving competition and aggressive confrontation? As so often happens, answering one question has led to asking another. Scientific inquiry is a voyage of discovery toward a horizon, beyond which yet another horizon beckons.

These concepts—experimental and control conditions, independent and dependent variables, random assignment—are important, yet easily confused. So let's put them to work with another intriguing set of experiments.

TABLE 1-3

Comparing Research Methods

Research Method	Basic Purpose	How Conducted	What is Manipulated
Descriptive	To observe and record behavior	Case studies, surveys, and naturalistic observations	Nothing
Correlational	To detect naturally occurring relationships; to assess how well one variable predicts another	Computing statistical association, sometimes among survey responses	Nothing
Experimental	To explore cause and effect	Manipulating one or more factors and using random assignment to eliminate preexisting differences among subjects	The independent variable

Can Subliminal Tapes Improve Your Life?

A new generation of entrepreneurs would have you believe so. Mail order catalogs, cable television ads, and bookstores offer tapes with imperceptibly faint messages that will "reprogram your unconscious mind for success and happiness." While underachieving students listen to soothing music, subliminal messages (below one's threshold for hearing) persuade the unconscious that "I am a good student. I love learning." Procrastinators can be similarly reprogrammed to think "I set my priorities. I get things done ahead of time!"

Is there *anything* to these wild and sometimes wacky claims? Might positive subliminal messages help us, even a little? In Chapter 4, we will see that subliminal sensation is for real. We do process much information without conscious awareness. And under certain conditions, a stimulus too weak to recognize can subtly affect us. But does this subtle, fleeting effect extend to the powerful, enduring effects claimed by the subliminal tape merchants? Anthony Greenwald, Eric Spangenberg, Anthony Pratkanis, and Jay Eskenazi (1991) decided to find out. They randomly assigned eager university students to listen daily for 5 weeks to commercial subliminal tapes designed to improve either self-esteem or memory. Then the researchers manipulated an experimental factor. On half the tapes the researchers switched the labels. People given these tapes *thought* they were receiving affirmations of self-esteem, when, actually, they heard the memory enhancement tape. Or they got the memory tape but *thought* their self-esteem was being recharged (Figure 1–6).

Were the tapes effective? Scores on both self-esteem and memory tests, taken before and after the 5 weeks, revealed no effects. Zilch. Nevertheless, those who *thought* they had heard a memory tape *believed* their memories had improved. Same for those who thought they had heard a self-esteem tape. Although the tapes had no effects, people *perceived* they had received the benefits they expected. Reading this research, we can hear echoes of the testimonies that adorn the mail order tape catalogs. Having bought something that is not supposed to be heard, and having indeed not heard it, many customers are impressed. "I really know that your tapes were invaluable in reprogramming my mind," wrote one thankful customer.

Our natural tendencies to try new remedies when we are in an emotional down can further distort a testimony. When our emotions rebound to normal, we attribute the rebound to something we have done. If 3 days into a cold we start taking vitamin C tablets and find our cold symptoms lessening, the pills may seem more potent than they are (an illusion of control). If, after doing exceptionally poorly on the first exam, we listen to a "peak learning" subliminal tape and find our next exam score rebounds ("regresses") toward our average, we may be deceived into crediting the tape. In the 1700s, even blood-letting *seemed* effective. Sometimes people improved after the treatment; when they didn't, the practitioner inferred the disease was too far advanced to be reversed. So, whether or not a remedy is effective, enthusiastic users will probably endorse it. To find out whether it actually is effective we must experiment.

And that is precisely how we evaluate new drug treatments and new methods of psychological therapy (see Chapter 13). In many of these studies, the subjects are "blind" (uninformed) about what treatment, if any, they are receiving. One group might receive the treatment (say, a particular subliminal message or a new drug). Another group receives a pseudotreatment—an inert **placebo** (a tape without the expected message, a pill with no drug in it). Often both the subject and the research assistant who collects the data will not know which condition the subject is in. This **double-blind procedure** allows researchers to check the actual effects of a treatment apart from their subjects' and their own enthusiasm for it. In the last 10 years, 16 double-blind experiments have evaluated subliminal self-help tapes. Their results are uniform: Not one has found any therapeutic effect (Greenwald, 1992).

"There is no evidence that commercially available subliminal auditory tapes have any genuine utility. . . . We do not recommend purchasing them."

British Psychological Society
Subliminal Messages, 1992

In this experiment, what was the independent variable? The dependent variable? (See page 22.)

Subliminal tape content

	Self-esteem	Memory
Self-esteem		
Memory		

Tape label

Figure 1–6 Design of the Subliminal Tapes Experiment
Students' self-esteem and memory abilities were assessed before and after listening to subliminal tapes purporting to increase either self-esteem or memory. Half the students, however, received mislabeled tapes.

placebo [plu-see-bo] An inert substance or condition that may be administered instead of a presumed active agent, such as a drug, to see if it triggers the effects believed to characterize the active agent.

double-blind procedure An experimental procedure in which both the subject and the research staff are ignorant (blind) about whether the subject has received the treatment or a placebo. Commonly used in drug evaluation studies.

Experiments can also help us evaluate social programs. Do early childhood education programs boost impoverished children's chances for success? What are the effects of different anti-smoking appeals? Do school sex education programs reduce teen pregnancies? To answer such questions, we can experiment: If a treatment is welcomed but resources are scarce, we could use a lottery to randomly assign some people (or regions) to experience the new program and others to a control condition. If later the treated and untreated groups differ, then we can be more confident that the treatment works.

Using the principles discussed in this chapter can also help us think critically—to see more clearly what we might otherwise miss or misinterpret and to generalize more accurately from our observations. People do think smarter when they understand and use the principles of research methods and statistics (Fong & others, 1986; Lehman & others, 1988; Vander Stoep & Shaughnessy, 1991). It requires training and practice, but developing the ability to think clearly and critically is part of becoming an educated person. The report of the Project on Redefining the Meaning and Purpose of Baccalaureate Degrees (1985) eloquently asserts why there are few higher priorities in a college education:

> If anything is paid attention to in our colleges and universities, thinking must be it. Unfortunately, thinking can be lazy. It can be sloppy. . . . It can be fooled, misled, bullied. . . . Students possess great untrained and untapped capacities for logical thinking, critical analysis, and inquiry, but these are capacities that are not spontaneous: They grow out of wide instruction, experience, encouragement, correction, and constant use.

Answer to question on page 21: In the subliminal tapes experiment, the primary independent variable was the type of subliminal message, self-esteem versus memory. (This experiment actually had a second independent variable as well: people's beliefs about which tape they received.) The primary dependent variable was improvement on the self-esteem and memory measures.

! Rehearse It

15. A researcher wants to determine whether noise level affects the blood pressure of elderly subjects. In one group she varies the level of noise in the environment and records blood pressures. In this experiment the level of noise is the

a. control condition.
b. dependent variable (or the factor being measured).
c. independent variable (or the factor being manipulated).
d. cause of any blood pressure variations.

16. To test the effect of a new drug on blood cholesterol, we randomly assign subjects to control and experimental conditions. Those in the experimental condition take a pink pill containing the new medication; the control group takes a pink pill that

contains no medication. Which statement is true?

a. The medication is the dependent variable.
b. Cholesterol level is the independent variable.
c. The subjects in the control group take a placebo.
d. Neither the experimental nor the control group is told the purpose of the experiment.

17. To eliminate the biasing effect of a researcher's positive expectations on the outcome of a health clinic's research experiment,

a. subjects are randomly assigned to the control and experimental groups (random assignment).

b. the experimental subjects are carefully matched for age, sex, income, and level of education with subjects in the control group (controlled selection).
c. neither the subjects nor the researcher know whether a given subject has been assigned to the experimental or control condition (double-blind procedure).
d. experimental subjects are chosen by selecting every 10th person in an alphabetical listing of all the clinic's patients (random selection).

18. Description is to explanation as case study is to _____

a. correlation.
b. naturalistic observation.
c. experiment.
d. survey.

Commonly Asked Questions About Psychology

We have seen how case studies, surveys, and naturalistic observations allow us to describe behavior. We have noted that correlational studies assess the relationship between two factors, indicating how well we can predict one thing, knowing another. We have examined the logic that underlies experiments, which use control conditions and random assignment of subjects to isolate the effects of an independent variable on a dependent variable. And we have reflected on how a scientific approach can restrain the biases of our unaided intuition.

This is reasonable preparation for understanding what lies ahead and for thinking critically about psychological matters. Yet, knowing this much, students often approach psychology with a mixture of curiosity and apprehension. So before we plunge in, let's confront some typical questions and concerns.

How Do Laboratory Experiments Relate to Everyday Life?

When you see or hear a report of psychological research, do you ever wonder whether people's behavior in the laboratory has "external validity"—whether it predicts their behavior in real life? Does detecting the blink of a faint red light in a dark room have anything useful to say about flying a plane at night? Does our tendency to remember best the first and last items in a list of unrelated words tell us anything about how we remember the names of people we meet at a party? After viewing a violent, sexually explicit film, does an angered man's increased willingness to push buttons he thinks electrically shock a woman really say anything about whether violent pornography makes men more likely to abuse women?

Before you answer, consider the intent of laboratory experiments. Far from considering artificiality a problem, the experimenter intends the laboratory environment to be a simplified reality—one in which important features of everyday life can be simulated and controlled. Like an aeronautical wind tunnel that re-creates atmospheric forces under controlled conditions, an experiment enables a psychologist to re-create psychological forces under controlled conditions.

The experiment's purpose is not to re-create the exact behaviors of everyday life but to test theoretical principles, notes Douglas Mook (1983). *It is the resulting principles—not the specific findings—that help explain everyday behaviors.* When psychologists apply laboratory research on aggression to actual violence, they are applying theoretical *principles* of aggressive behavior, principles refined through many experiments. Similarly, it is the principles of the visual system, developed from experiments in artificial settings (such as looking at red lights in the dark), that we apply to more complex behaviors such as night flying.

The point to remember: As psychologists, our concerns lie less with particular behaviors than with general principles that help explain many behaviors.

Doesn't Behavior Depend on One's Culture and Gender?

If culture shapes behavior, what can psychological studies done with North Americans—often with white North Americans—really tell us about people in general? As we will see time and again, culture matters. Our culture influences

A Cultured Greeting *Because culture shapes people's understanding of social behavior, actions that seem ordinary to us may seem quite odd to visitors from far away. Yet, underlying these differences are powerful similarities. Schoolchildren everywhere greet their teachers with respect, although not necessarily with the formality of this young Japanese schoolgirl.*

"All people are the same; only their habits differ."

Confucius, 551–479 B.C.

our standards of promptness and frankness, our attitudes toward premarital sex and differing body shapes, our tendencies to be casual or formal, and much more. Being aware of such differences can restrain our assuming that others will, or should, think and act as we do. Given the growing mixing and clashing of cultures, the need for such awareness becomes urgent.

Yet our shared biological heritage unites us as members of a universal human family. (See "Close-Up: Human Diversity and Kinship.") The same underlying processes guide people everywhere. Varying languages—spoken and gestured—may impede communication across cultures. Yet all languages share deep principles of grammar, and people from opposite sides of the globe can communicate with a smile or a frown. People in different cultures vary in their feelings of loneliness, yet across cultures shyness and low self-esteem magnify loneliness (Jones & others, 1985). Japanese prefer their fish raw while North Americans prefer theirs cooked, but the same principles of hunger and taste influence both.

As you will see throughout this book, gender matters, too. Researchers report gender differences in what we dream, how we express and detect emotions, and in our risk of alcoholism, depression, and eating disorders. Studying such differences is not only interesting, but potentially beneficial. Many researchers believe, for example, that women converse more readily to build relationships, whereas men talk more to give information and advice (Tannen, 1990). Knowing this difference can help prevent conflicts and misunderstandings on the job and in everyday relationships.

Nevertheless, psychologically as well as biologically, women and men are overwhelmingly similar. Whether female or male, we learn to walk about the same age; experience the same sensations of light and sound; feel the same pangs of hunger, desire, and fear; and exhibit similar overall intelligence and happiness.

It is truly said that we are each in certain respects like all others, like some others, and like no other. Studying men and women of all races and cultures helps us identify our similarities and differences. Moreover, we tend to exhibit and perceive the very behaviors our culture expects of males and females. Biology determines our sex, and then culture further bends the genders.

The point to remember: Even when specific attitudes and behaviors vary across cultures, as they often do, or between the sexes, the underlying processes are much the same.

Why Do Psychologists Study Animals?

Many psychologists study animals because they find them fascinating. Psychologists also study animals to learn about people, by doing experiments that are permissible only with animals. Human physiology resembles that of many other animals. That is why animal experiments have led to treatments for human diseases—insulin for diabetes, vaccines to prevent polio and rabies, transplants to replace defective organs.

Likewise, the processes by which humans see, exhibit emotion, and become obese operate in rats and monkeys. To discover more about the basics of human learning, researchers are even studying sea slugs. To understand how a combustion engine works, you would do better to study a lawn mower's engine than a Mercedes'. Humans, like Mercedes, are more complex. But it is precisely the simplicity of the sea slug's nervous system that makes it so revealing of the neural mechanisms of learning.

Human Diversity and Kinship

Whatever our differences, we are the leaves of one tree. We in the human family share not only a common biological heritage—cut us and we bleed—but also common behavioral tendencies. Our shared brain architecture predisposes us to sense the world, develop language, and feel hunger through identical mechanisms. Coming from opposite sides of the globe, we know how to read one another's smiles and frowns. Whether our last name is Wong, Nkomo, Gonzales, or Smith, we fear strangers beginning at

"*Whatever I do or think as a black can never be more than a variant of what all people do and think. . . . All races are composed of human beings.*"

Shelby Steele
The Content of Our Character, 1990

"*Everybody is very much alike, really. But fortunately, perhaps, they don't realize it.*"

Miss Marple in Agatha Christie's *The Tuesday Club Murders*, 1933

about 8 months of age and as adults prefer the company of individuals whose attitudes and attributes are similar to our own. Regardless of our culture or gender, we regard female features that signify youth and health—and reproductive potential—as attractive. Whether we live in the Arctic or the tropics, we prefer sweet tastes to sour, we divide the color spectrum into similar colors, and we feel drawn to behaviors that produce and protect offspring. As members of one species, we affiliate, conform, reciprocate favors, punish offenses, organize hierarchies of status, and grieve a child's death. A visitor from outer space could drop in anywhere and find humans playing sports and games, dancing and feasting, singing and worshipping, laughing and crying, living in families, and forming groups. To be human is to be more alike than different. Taken together, such universal behavioral tendencies define human nature.

These behavioral similarities arise from our biological similarity. Only 6 percent of human genetic variation is differences among races. Only 8 percent is differences among tribes or nations within a race. The rest—over 85 percent—is individual variation within local groups. The average genetic difference between two Icelandic villagers or between two Kenyans is much greater than the difference between the two groups. Thus, notes geneticist Richard Lewontin (1982), if after a worldwide catastrophe only Icelanders or Kenyans survived, the human species would suffer only "a trivial reduction" in its genetic diversity.

Among our similarities, the most important—the behavioral hallmark of our species—is our enormous capacity to learn and adapt. Ironically, this fundamental likeness enables human diversity. We all are driven to eat, but depending on our culturally learned tastes, we may have a yen for fish eyes, fried insects, or chicken legs. Go barefoot for a summer and you will develop toughened, calloused feet—a biological adaptation to friction. Meanwhile, your shoed neighbor will remain a tenderfoot. Is the difference between the two of you an effect of environment? Yes, of course. Is it also the product of a biological mechanism? Yes again. Our shared biology enables our adaptive diversity (Buss, 1991).

As citizens in a multicultural world, we need to appreciate our similarities. We also need to understand our differences. At various points throughout this book we will examine our *individual differences* in traits such as temperament, intelligence, personality, psychological disorder, and health. Depending on their experiences in particular environments, one person may become aggressive, another gentle; one may value freedom, another order and control; one may prize individuality, another the social ties that bind people together. We will also glimpse a second dimension of diversity—our *group differences* in tendencies ranging from concern about body weight to expressing anger to individualism. Here again, our shared biology enables our adaptive diversity: Where famine threatens, plump seems beautiful; where food is abundant, slender is chic.

A Question of Ethics *Is it right to use animals to advance our understanding of humans? For animal rights activists, no purpose justifies hurting, frightening, or (as shown here) manipulating an animal. For most psychologists and medical researchers, animal research is ethically justified as long as researchers observe strict standards and inflict no unnecessary pain.*

"I believe that to prevent, cripple, or needlessly complicate the research that can relieve animal and human suffering is profoundly inhuman, cruel, and immoral."

Psychologist Neal Miller (1983)

"Please do not forget those of us who suffer from incurable diseases or disabilities who hope for a cure through research that requires the use of animals."

Paraplegic psychologist Dennis Feeney (1987)

Is It Ethical to Experiment on Animals?

If we share important similarities with other animals, then should we not respect them? "We cannot defend our scientific work with animals on the basis of the similarities between them and ourselves and then defend it morally on the basis of differences," notes Roger Ulrich (1991). The animal protection movement protests the use of animals in psychological, biological, and medical research—some 20 million animals annually, according to the National Academy of Sciences (1991). Researchers remind us that these 20 million animals are less than 1 percent of the 5 billion animals killed annually in the United States as a source of food (which means the average American eats 20 animals a year, without allowing for imported meat). While researchers each year conduct experiments on some 200,000 dogs and cats cared for under humane regulations, animal shelters kill 50 times that many.

Mobilization for Animals, a network of some 400 animal protection organizations, is nevertheless concerned. It has declared that in psychological experiments animals are shocked "until they lose the ability to even scream in pain, . . . deprived of food and water to suffer and die slowly from hunger and thirst, . . . put in total isolation chambers until they are driven insane or even die from despair and terror," and made "the victims of extreme pain and stress, inflicted upon them out of idle curiosity." Psychologists Caroline Coile and Neal Miller (1984) analyzed every animal research article published in the American Psychological Association's journals during the preceding 5 years. They found not one study in which any of these allegations was true. Even when researchers used shock, it usually was of a mild intensity that humans can easily endure on their fingers. Only 7 percent of psychology's studies have involved animals, 95 percent of which are rats, mice, rabbits, or birds. About 10 percent of these animal studies involved electric shock (Coile & Miller, 1984; Gallup & Suarez, 1985). In British psychology departments, where animal use has dropped by two-thirds since 1977, electric shock is used in but 4 percent of animal studies—all involving rats (Thomas & Blackman, 1991).

Moreover, say researchers, this is not the morality of good versus evil but of compassion (for animals) versus compassion (for people). How many of us would have attacked Pasteur's experiments with rabies, which in causing some dogs to suffer led to a vaccine that spared millions of people, and dogs, from agonizing death? And would we really wish to have deprived ourselves of the animal research that led to effective methods of training retarded children; of relieving fears and depression; and of controlling obesity, alcoholism, and stress-related pain and disease?

Out of the heated debate on this subject, two issues emerge. The basic one is whether it is right to place the well-being of humans above that of animals. In experiments on stress and cancer, is it right that mice get tumors so that people might not? Should some monkeys be exposed to an HIV-like virus in the search for developing an AIDS vaccine? Is the human use of other animals as natural and moral as the behavior of carnivorous hawks, cats, and whales? (Animals themselves do not assign rights to other animals lower on the food chain.) Defenders of research on animals argue that anyone who has eaten a hamburger, worn leather shoes, tolerated hunting and fishing, or supported the extermination of crop-destroying or plague-carrying pests has already agreed that, yes, it is sometimes permissible to sacrifice animals for the sake of human well-being. After all, the most fundamental right is the right not to be eaten.

Scott Plous (1993) notes that our compassion for animals varies, as does our compassion for people, based on their perceived similarity to us. As Chapter 14 explains, we feel more attraction, give more help, and act less aggressively toward similar others. Likewise, we value animals according to their perceived kinship with us. Few people equate all animals as does Ingrid Newkirk, the director of People for the Ethical Treatment of Animals: "A rat is a pig is a dog is a boy" (quoted by Baldwin, 1993). Primates and companion pets get top priority. (Western people raise or trap mink and foxes for their fur, but not dogs or cats.) Other mammals occupy the second rung on the privilege ladder, followed by birds, fish, and reptiles on the third rung, with insects at the bottom. In human-animal relations, a cockroach is not a crow is not a cow is not a collie or chimpanzee. In deciding which animals have rights we must draw a cut-off line somewhere across the animal kingdom.

If we give human life first priority, the second issue is the priority given the well-being of animals. What safeguards should protect animals? Most researchers today feel ethically obligated to enhance the well-being of captive animals and protect them from needless suffering. They also believe that humane care is good science, because pain and stress would distort animals' behavior during experiments. Thus, they welcomed national animal protection legislation updated by the United States in 1985 and Britain in 1986 and the accompanying regulations and laboratory inspections (Cherfas, 1990; Johnson, 1990). The American Psychological Association, for example, has developed extensive guidelines for the care and justified use of animals.

Ironically, animals have themselves benefitted from animal research. Studies have helped improve their care and management in laboratories, zoos, and natural habitats. By revealing our behavioral kinship with animals and the remarkable intelligence of some animals, experiments have also increased our empathy with them. At its best, a psychology that is concerned for humans and sensitive to animals can serve the welfare of both.

Is It Ethical to Experiment on People?

If the image of animals or people receiving electric shocks troubles you, you may find it reassuring that most psychological research involves no such stress. Blinking lights, flashing words, and pleasant social interactions are the rule.

Occasionally, though, researchers temporarily stress or deceive people. This is done only when judged essential to a justifiable end, such as understanding and controlling violent behavior or studying mood swings. Such experiments wouldn't work if the participants knew all there was to know about the experiment beforehand. Either the procedures would be ineffective or the participants, wanting to be helpful, might try to confirm the researchers' predictions.

Ethical principles developed by the American Psychological Association (1992) and the British Psychological Society (1993) urge investigators to (1) obtain the informed consent of potential participants, (2) protect them from harm and discomfort, (3) treat information about individual participants confidentially, and (4) fully explain the research afterward. Moreover, most universities today screen research proposals through an ethics committee that safeguards participants' well-being.

Is Psychology Free of Value Judgments?

Psychology is definitely not value-free. Values affect what we study, how we study it, and how we interpret results. Consider: Researchers' values influence their choice of research topics—whether to study worker productivity or worker morale, sex discrimination or sex differences, conformity or independence. Values can also color "the facts." Our preconceptions can bias our observations and interpretations; sometimes we see what we want or expect to see.

"The righteous know the needs of their animals."

Proverbs 12:10

"The greatness of a nation can be judged by the way its animals are treated."

Mahatma Gandhi, 1869–1948

What Do You See? *People interpret ambiguous information to fit their preconceptions. Did you see a duck or a rabbit? What influenced your first impression? (From Shepard, 1990.)*

Even the words we use to describe a phenomenon can reflect our values. Whether we label sex acts we do not practice as "perversions" or as "sexual variations" conveys a value judgment. The same holds true in everyday speech, as when one person's "terrorists" are another's "freedom fighters," or one person's "faith" is another's "fanaticism." Our labeling someone as "firm" or "stubborn," "careful" or "picky," "discreet" or "secretive" reveals our feelings. Both in and out of psychology, labels describe and labels evaluate.

Popular applications of psychology also contain hidden values. When people defer to "professional" guidance about how to live—how to raise children, how to achieve self-fulfillment, what to do with sexual feelings, how to get ahead at work—they are accepting value-laden advice. A science of behavior and mental processes can help us reach our goals, but it cannot decide them.

Is Psychology Potentially Dangerous?

If some people see psychology as mere common sense, others have an opposite concern—that it is becoming dangerously powerful. Might psychology be used to manipulate people? Might it become the tool of someone seeking to create a totalitarian *Brave New World* or *1984*?

Knowledge is a power that, like all powers, we can use for good or evil. Nuclear power has been used to light up cities—and to demolish them. Persuasive power has been used to educate people—and to deceive them. The power of mind-altering drugs has been used to restore sanity—and to destroy it.

Although it has the power to deceive, psychology strives to enlighten. Psychologists are exploring ways to enhance moral development, perceptual accuracy, learning, creativity, and compassion. And psychology speaks to many of the world's great problems—war, overpopulation, prejudice, family dysfunction, crime—all of which involve attitudes and behaviors. Psychology also speaks to humanity's deepest longings—for love, for happiness, even for food and water. Psychology cannot address all the great questions of life, but it speaks to some mighty important ones.

! Rehearse It

19. In a laboratory experiment, features of everyday life can be simulated, manipulated, and controlled. The laboratory environment is designed to help us

a. exactly re-create the events of everyday life.
b. re-create psychological forces under controlled conditions.
c. create opportunities for naturalistic observation.
d. minimize the use of animals and humans in psychological research.

20. The animal protection movement has protested the use of animals in all fields of scientific research. In defending their experimental research with animals, psychologists have noted that

a. animals' physiology and behavior can tell us much about our own.
b. they do not torture or needlessly exploit animals.
c. advancing the well-being of humans justifies animal experimentation.
d. all of the above.

21. Which of the following is true regarding gender differences and similarities?

a. Differences between the genders outweigh any similarities.
b. Despite some gender differences, the underlying processes of human behavior are the same.
c. Both similarities and differences between the genders depend more on biology than on environment.
d. Gender differences are so numerous, it is difficult to make meaningful comparisons.

Tips for Studying Psychology

The investment you are making in studying psychology may enrich your life and enlarge your vision. Although many of life's significant questions are beyond psychology, some very important ones are illuminated by even a first course in psychology. Through painstaking research, psychologists have gained insights into brain and mind, depression and joy, dreams and memories. Even the unanswered questions can enrich us, by renewing our sense of mystery about "things too wonderful" for us yet to understand. What is more, your study of psychology can help teach you *how to ask important questions*—how to think critically as you evaluate competing ideas and pop psychology's claims.

Having your life enriched and your vision enlarged (and getting a decent grade, too) requires effective study. As we will see in Chapter 7, Memory, to master any subject you must *actively process* it. Your mind is not like your stomach, something to be filled passively; it is more like a muscle, which grows stronger with exercise. Countless experiments reveal that people learn and remember material best when they put it in their own words, rehearse it, and then review and rehearse it again.

The famous **SQ3R** study method incorporates these principles (Robinson, 1970). SQ3R is an acronym for its five steps: *Survey, Question, Read, Rehearse, Review.*

To study a chapter, first *survey*, taking a bird's-eye view as you note its headings. Notice how the chapter is organized.

As you prepare to read each section, use its heading or the numbered preview question to form a *question* that you should answer. For this section, you might have asked, "How can I most effectively and efficiently master the information in this book?"

Then *read*, actively searching for the answer. At each sitting, read only as much of the chapter as you can absorb without tiring. Usually, a single main chapter section will do—the "Commonly Asked Questions" section you just finished, for example. Relating what you are reading to your own life will improve understanding and retention. Reading the occasional "Close-Up" and "Thinking Critically About . . ." boxed sections will help.

Having read a section, *rehearse* in your own words what you read. Test yourself by trying to answer your question, rehearsing what you can recall, then glancing back at what you can't recall. Take the Rehearse It self-tests.

Finally, *review:* Read over any notes you have taken, again with an eye on the chapter's organization, and quickly review the whole chapter.

Survey, question, read, rehearse, review. This book's chapters are organized to facilitate your use of the SQ3R study system. Each chapter begins with a chapter outline that aids your *survey*. Headings and preview *questions* suggest issues and concepts you should consider as you *read*. The material is organized into sections of readable length, and the end-of-section *Rehearse* It questions help gauge your readiness to read the next section. The chapter summaries *review* the chapter's essentials, repeating and answering the numbered preview questions, and list key terms to help you check your mastery of important concepts. Survey, question, read. . . .

Five additional study tips may further boost your learning:

1. *Distribute your study time.* One of psychology's oldest findings is that "spaced practice" promotes better retention than "massed practice." You'll remember material better if you space your time over several study periods rather than cram it into one long study blitz. Better to give your study

SQ3R A study method incorporating five steps: *Survey, Question, Read, Rehearse, Review.*

of this text one hour a day, with one day off a week, than six hours at a time. Doing this requires a disciplined approach to managing your time. (Richard Straub explains time management in the *Study Guide* that accompanies this text.) For example, rather than trying to read all of a chapter in a single sitting, read just one of the chapter's sections, and then turn to something else.

2. *Learn to think critically.* Whether reading or in class, note people's *assumptions and values.* What perspective or bias underlies an argument? *Evaluate evidence.* Is it anecdotal? correlational? experimental? *Assess conclusions.* Are there alternative explanations?

3. *In class, listen actively.* As psychologist William James urged a century ago, "No reception without reaction, no impression without . . . expression." Listen for the main and sub-ideas of a lecture. Write them down. Ask questions during and after class. In class, as in your private study, process the information actively and you will understand and retain it better.

4. *Overlearn.* Psychology tells us that "overlearning improves retention." Most of us are prone to overestimating how much we know. You may understand a chapter as you read it, but by devoting extra study time to testing yourself and reviewing what you think you know, you will retain your new knowledge long into the future.

5. *Be a smart test-taker.* If a test contains both multiple-choice questions and an essay question, turn first to the essay. Read the question carefully, noting exactly what the instructor is asking. On the back of a page, pencil in a list of points you'd like to make, and then organize them. Before writing, put aside the essay and work through the multiple-choice questions. (As you do so, your mind may continue to mull over the essay question. Sometimes the objective questions will bring pertinent thoughts to mind.) Then reread the essay question, rethink your answer, and start writing. When finished, proofread to eliminate spelling and grammatical errors that make you look less competent than you are. When reading multiple-choice questions, don't confuse yourself by trying to imagine how each of the alternatives might be right. Try instead to recall the answer *before* reading the alternatives given. Answer the question as if it were a fill-in-the-blank; first cover the answers and complete the sentence in your mind, and then find the alternative that best matches your own answer.

While exploring psychology, you will learn much more than effective study techniques. Psychology deepens our appreciation for how we humans perceive, think, feel, and act. By so doing it can indeed enrich our lives and enlarge our vision. Through this book I hope to help guide you toward that end. As educator Charles Eliot said a century ago: "Books are the quietest and most constant of friends, and the most patient of teachers."

Reviewing *Introduction: Thinking Critically With Psychology*

What Is Psychology?

1. **How did the science of psychology develop?**

    Beginning with the first psychological laboratory, founded in 1879 by German philosopher and physiologist Wilhelm Wundt, psychology's modern roots can be found in many disciplines and countries. Psychology's historic perspectives and current activities lead us to define the field as the science of behavior and mental processes.

2. **What theoretical perspectives do psychologists take?**

    There are many disciplines that study human nature. Psychology is one. Within psychology, the biological, behavioral, psychoanalytic, cognitive, and social-cultural perspectives are complementary. Each has its own purposes, questions, and limits; together they provide a fuller understanding of mind and behavior.

3. **What are psychology's specialized subfields?**

    Psychologists' activities are widely varied, ranging from the diagnoses and therapies of clinical psychologists and psychiatrists to the basic research conducted by biological, developmental, or personality psychologists to the applied research of industrial/organizational psychologists.

Why Do Psychology?

4. **What attitudes characterize scientific inquiry?**

    Scientific inquiry begins with an attitude—an eagerness to skeptically scrutinize competing ideas and an open-minded humility before nature. Putting ideas, even crazy-sounding ideas, to the test helps us winnow sense from nonsense. The curiosity that drives us to test ideas and to expose their underlying assumptions carries into everyday life as *critical thinking*.

What About Intuition and Common Sense?

5. **What leads people to overestimate the value of common sense and underestimate the usefulness of psychological science?**

    If intuition and common sense were trustworthy, we would have less need for scientific inquiry and critical thinking. But without such thinking we readily succumb to *hindsight bias*, or the I-knew-it-all-along phenomenon. Learning the outcome of a study (or of an everyday happening) can make it seem like obvious common sense. But things seldom seem so obvious before the fact. We also are routinely *overconfident* of our judgments, thanks partly to our bias to seek information that confirms them. Such biases lead us to overestimate our unaided intuition. Although limited by the testable questions it can address, a scientific approach can help us sift reality from illusion, taking us beyond the horizons of our intuition and common sense.

How Do Psychologists Ask and Answer Questions?

6. **What is the place of theory in the scientific method?**

    Research stimulates the construction of *theories*, which organize the *observations* and imply predictive *hypotheses*. These hypotheses (predictions) are then tested to validate and refine the theory and to suggest practical applications.

7. **How do psychologists observe and describe behavior?**

    Through individual case studies, surveys among random samples of a population, and naturalistic observations, psychologists observe and describe behavior and mental processes. In generalizing from observations, remember: Representative samples are a better guide than vivid examples.

8. **Why do correlations permit prediction but not explanation? How accurately does the naked eye detect correlations?**

    The strength of relationship between one factor and another is expressed in their *correlation*. Correlations help us to see relationships that the naked eye might miss and to discount illusory correlations and random events that might otherwise look significant. Knowing how closely two things are positively or negatively correlated tells us how much one predicts the other. But correlation is only a measure of relationship; it does not reveal cause and effect.

9. **How do experiments clarify or reveal cause-effect relationships?**

    To discover cause-and-effect relationships, psychologists conduct *experiments*. By constructing a controlled reality, experimenters can manipulate one or more factors and discover how these independent variables affect a particular behavior, the dependent variable. In many experiments, control is achieved by randomly assigning people to be either experimental subjects, who are exposed to the treatment, or control subjects, who experience no treatment or a different version of the treatment.

Commonly Asked Questions About Psychology

10. **How do laboratory experiments relate to everyday life?**

    By intentionally creating a controlled, artificial environment in the lab, researchers aim to test theoretical principles. These principles help us to understand, describe, explain, and predict everyday behaviors.

11. **Doesn't behavior depend on one's culture and gender?**

    Although attitudes and behaviors vary across cultures, the principles that underlie them vary much less. Cross-cultural psychology explores both our cultural differences and the universal similarities that define our human kinship. Gender is also a fact of life. Although gender differences tend to capture attention, it is important to remember the much greater similarities between men and women.

12. Why do psychologists study animals?

Some psychologists study animals out of an interest in animal behavior. Others do so because knowledge of the physiological and psychological processes of animals permits a better understanding of the similar processes operating in humans.

13. Is it ethical to experiment on animals?

Only about 7 percent of all psychological experiments involve animals, and under ethical and legal guidelines these animals rarely experience pain. Nevertheless, animal rights groups raise an important issue: Is an animal's temporary suffering justified if it leads to the relief of human suffering?

14. Is it ethical to experiment on people?

Occasionally researchers temporarily stress or deceive people in order to learn something important. Professional ethical standards provide guidelines for the treatment of human as well as animal participants.

15. Is psychology free of value judgments?

Psychology is not value-free. Psychologists' own values influence their choice of research topics, their theories and observations, their labels for behavior, and their professional advice.

16. Is psychology potentially dangerous?

Knowledge is power that can be used for good or evil. Applications of psychology's principles have so far been mostly for the good, and psychology addresses some of humanity's greatest problems and deepest longings.

Terms and Concepts to Remember

psychology, p. 3

nature-nurture issue, p. 3

biological perspective, p. 4

behavioral perspective, p. 4

cognitive perspective, p. 4

psychoanalytic perspective, p. 4

social-cultural perspective, p. 4

basic research, p. 6

applied research, p. 6

clinical psychology, p. 6

psychiatry, p. 6

critical thinking, p. 7

hindsight bias, p. 8

theory, p. 10

hypothesis, p. 10

replication, p. 11

case study, p. 11

survey, p. 12

false consensus effect, p. 12

population, p. 12

random sample, p. 12

naturalistic observation, p. 13

correlation, p. 14

illusory correlation, p. 14

experiment, p. 18

experimental condition, p. 19

control condition, p. 19

random assignment, p. 19

independent variable, p. 19

dependent variable, p. 19

operational definition, p. 19

placebo, p. 21

double-blind procedure, p. 21

SQ3R, p. 29

Rehearse It Answer Key

1. c.   2. b.   3. a.   4. d.   5. c.   6. d.   7. c.   8. a.   9. c.

10. c.   11. d.   12. b.   13. c.   14. a.   15. c.   16. c.   17. c.   18. c.

19. b.   20. d.   21. b.

Critical Thinking Exercise[3]

Now that you have read and reviewed Chapter 1, take your learning a step further by testing your critical thinking skills on this scientific problem-solving exercise. For an introduction to Critical Thinking Exercises, turn to Appendix B before working this exercise.

Philip, who teaches first grade, believes that educational television programs such as "Sesame Street" promote reading ability in young children. He announces his hunch to his students and tells their parents about his idea during a PTA meeting. Some parents respond enthusiastically when he asks for volunteers to participate in a 3-month experiment to test his hypothesis. Ten volunteers are assigned to the experimental group and instructed to have their children watch the 1-hour "Sesame Street" program each day after school. The parents of 10 other students, who are picked at random from the remaining members of the class, receive the same instructions except that the target program is a 1-hour, noneducational cartoon. After the 3-month period, Philip administers a standardized reading test to both groups. He is delighted to find that students in the experimental group have a substantially higher average test score than students in the comparison group.

1. What is the behavior of interest of the study?
2. What is Philip's hypothesis?
3. What is the independent variable?
4. What is the dependent variable?
5. List three variables that are controlled in the experiment.
6. List three variables that aren't controlled and explain how they might have affected Philip's findings.
7. Was the research a valid test of the hypothesis? Explain your reasoning.

Check your progress on becoming a critical thinker by comparing your answers to the sample answers found in Appendix B.

[3]The Critical Thinking Exercise at the end of each chapter was prepared by Richard O. Straub, University of Michigan, Dearborn.

Chapter 2

Neuroscience and Behavior

Neural Communication

Neurons

How Neurons Communicate

How Neurotransmitters Influence Us

Neural and Hormonal Systems

The Peripheral Nervous System

The Central Nervous System

The Endocrine System

The Brain

Lower Level Brain Structures

The Cerebral Cortex

Brain Reorganization

Our Divided Brains

1. Why do psychologists study biology?

No principle is more central to today's psychology, or to this book, than this: *Everything psychological is simultaneously biological.* Your every idea, every mood, every urge is a biological happening. You are a body. You think, feel, and act with your body. You relate to the world through your body. (Try laughing, crying, or loving without it.) Your body—your genes, your brain, your body chemistry, your inner organs, your appearance—is you. Without your body, you are, indeed, nobody. Although we find it convenient to talk separately of biological and psychological influences on behavior, let us not forget: To think, feel, or act without a body is as plausible as running without legs.

In this "decade of the brain" (as declared by the U.S. Congress) scientific attention is riveted on this chapter's focus—the most amazing part of our body: our brain and its component neural systems. The brain's ultimate challenge is to understand itself. How does the brain communicate with itself? How does experience modify it? How do its various parts process the information needed for a basketball player's jump shot? A poet's rhythm of words? A lover's memory of the first kiss?

We have come far since the early 1800s, when a German physician named Franz Gall invented *phrenology*, an ill-fated theory that bumps on the skull could reveal our mental abilities and character traits. At one point, Great Britain had 29 phrenological societies, and phrenologists traveled North America giving skull readings (Hunt, 1993). Despite its wrongheadedness, phrenology focused attention on the idea that various brain regions have particular functions. In little more than a century, we have also realized that the body is composed of cells; that among these are nerve cells that conduct electricity and "talk" to one another by sending chemical messages across a tiny gap that separates them; that specific brain systems serve specific functions (though not the functions that Gall supposed); and that from the information processed in these different brain systems we construct our experience of sights and sounds, meanings and memories, pain and passion. You and I are privileged to live in a time when discoveries about the interplay of our biology and behavior are occurring at an exhilarating pace.

A Wrongheaded Theory *Despite initial acceptance of Gall's speculations, bumps on the skull tell us nothing about how the brain works. Nevertheless, some of his assumptions have been found to hold true: Different parts of the brain do control different aspects of behavior.*

biological psychology   A branch of psychology concerned with the links between biology and behavior. (Some biological psychologists call themselves *behavioral neuroscientists, neuropsychologists, physiological psychologists,* or *biopsychologists.*)

neuron   A nerve cell; the basic building block of the nervous system.

dendrite   The bushy, branching extension of a neuron that receives messages and conducts impulses toward the cell body.

axon   The extension of a neuron, ending in branching terminal fibers through which messages are sent to other neurons or to muscles or glands.

myelin [MY-uh-lin] **sheath**   A layer of fatty cells segmentally encasing the fibers of many neurons; makes possible a vastly greater transmission speed of neural impulses.

action potential   A neural impulse; a brief electrical charge that travels down an axon.

threshold   The level of stimulation required to trigger a neural impulse.

synapse [SIN-aps]   The junction between the axon tip of the sending neuron and the dendrite or cell body of the receiving neuron. The tiny gap at this junction is called the *synaptic gap* or cleft.

"I sing the body electric."

Walt Whitman
"Children of Adam," 1855

Throughout this book you will find examples of how our biology underlies our behavior and mental processes. By studying the links between biological activity and psychological events, **biological psychologists** are gaining a better understanding of sleep and dreams, depression and schizophrenia, hunger and sex, stress and disease. We therefore begin our study of psychology with a look at its biological roots. Chapter 2 explores the neuroscience revolution, and Chapter 3 examines genetic influences on behavior.

Neural Communication

We are each a system, composed of subsystems that are parts of larger systems. Body organs such as the stomach, heart, and brain are part of larger systems for digestion, circulation, and information processing, which are part of an even larger system—you, which in turn forms a part of your family, community, and culture. Your organs, in turn, are composed of subsystems—cells—that operate biochemically. At every level, then, our existence is both part of a larger system and a combination of smaller systems. For a deep understanding of behavior, we must study how biological, psychological, and social systems work and interact.

In this chapter, we start small and begin building—up to the brain (and, by Chapter 14, to the social and cultural influences that interact with our biology). At all levels, psychologists examine how we process information—how we get information in; how we organize, interpret, and store it; and how we use it. For scientists, it is a happy fact of nature that the information systems of humans and other animals operate similarly. So similarly, in fact, that you could not distinguish between small samples of brain tissue from a person and a monkey. This similarity allows researchers to study simple animals, such as squids and sea slugs, to discover how neural systems operate, and to study mammals' brains to understand the organization of our own. Human brains are more complex, but they follow principles that govern the animal world.

Neurons

2.   *What are neurons, and how do they transmit information?*

Our body's neural information system is complexity built from simplicity. Its building blocks are **neurons,** or nerve cells. Each neuron consists of a cell body and its branching fibers (Figure 2–1). The fibers are of two types: The bushy **dendrites** receive information. The **axon** passes it along to other neurons or to muscles or glands. Unlike the short dendrites, axons may be short or may extend up to several feet. For example, the cell body and axon of a motor neuron (sending messages to muscles) are roughly on the scale of a basketball attached to a rope 4 miles long. A layer of fatty cells, called the **myelin sheath,** insulates the axons of some neurons and helps speed their impulses. For people with multiple sclerosis, the myelin sheath degenerates, communication to muscles slows, and muscle control lessens.

A neuron fires an impulse when stimulated by pressure, heat, light, or chemical messages from adjacent neurons. The impulse, called the **action potential,** is a brief electrical charge that travels down the axon, rather like a falling line of dominoes, each one tripping the next. As batteries generate electricity from chemical events, so the neuron's electrical impulse arises from chemical events.

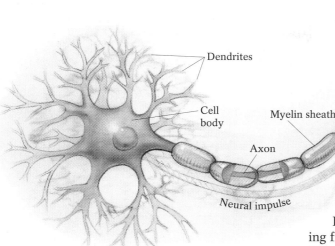

Figure 2–1 A Motor Neuron *This simplified diagram (left) shows the dendrites and cell body, which receive signals from other neurons, and the long axon. Myelin, which insulates many axons, helps speed the neuron's impulses. The photograph, taken through a microscope, shows the cell bodies and dendrites of several motor neurons in the spinal cord.*

You can remember the dendrite-axon sequence as DA—District Attorney.

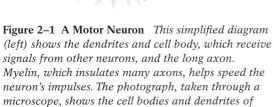

"All information processing in the brain involves neurons 'talking to' each other at synapses."

Neuroscientist Solomon H. Snyder (1984)

Depending on the type of fiber, the neural impulse travels at speeds ranging from a sluggish 2 miles per hour to, in some myelinated fibers, a breakneck 200 or more miles per hour. But even this top speed is 3 million times slower than the speed of electricity through a wire. That helps to explain why, unlike the nearly instantaneous reactions of a high-speed computer, it may take a quarter-second or more for you to react to a sudden event, such as a child darting in front of your car.

The neuron, a miniature decision-making device, receives signals on its dendrites and cell body from hundreds or even thousands of other neurons. Some of these signals are excitatory, rather like pushing a neuron's accelerator. Other signals are inhibitory, rather like pushing its brake. The combined signals trigger an impulse if excitatory signals minus inhibitory signals exceed a minimum intensity, called the **threshold**. If excitatory inputs exceed the threshold, the neuron transmits an electrical impulse down its axon, which branches into junctions with hundreds or thousands of other neurons and with muscles and glands.

Increasing the stimulus above the threshold, however, will not increase the impulse's intensity. (The neuron's reaction is an *all-or-none response*; like guns, neurons either fire or they don't.) Nor does the strength of the stimulus affect the impulse's speed.

How then do we detect the intensity of a stimulus? How do we distinguish a gentle touch from a firm hug? Although a strong stimulus cannot trigger a stronger or faster impulse in a neuron, it can trigger more neurons to fire, and to fire more often.

How Neurons Communicate

3. How do nerve cells communicate?

Neurons interweave so intricately that even with a microscope it is hard to see where one neuron ends and another begins. A hundred years ago many scientists believed that the branching axon of one cell fused with the dendrites of another in an uninterrupted fabric.

We now know that the axon terminal of one neuron is separated from the receiving neuron by a tiny gap less than a millionth of an inch wide. This junction is called the **synapse**, and the gap is called the *synaptic gap* or cleft. To the Nobel laureate, Spanish neuroanatomist Santiago Ramón y Cajal (1832–1934), these near-unions of neurons—"protoplasmic kisses," he called them—were another of nature's marvels. How does the nerve impulse execute the protoplasmic kiss? How does it cross the tiny synaptic gap? The answer is one of the important scientific discoveries of our age.

Figure 2–2 How Neurons Communicate
Electrical impulses (action potentials) travel from one neuron to another across a junction known as the synaptic gap. When a signal reaches the axon terminal, it stimulates the release of neurotransmitter molecules from the sacs, or vesicles, containing them. These molecules cross the synaptic gap and bind to receptor sites on the receiving neuron. This allows electrically charged atoms (not pictured here) to enter the receiving neuron, thereby influencing its rate of firing.

neurotransmitters Chemical messengers that traverse the synaptic gaps between neurons. When released by the sending neuron, neurotransmitters travel across the synapse and bind to receptor sites on the receiving neuron, thereby influencing whether it will generate a neural impulse.

When the action potential reaches the knoblike terminals at an axon's end, it triggers the release of chemical messengers, called **neurotransmitters** (Figure 2–2). Within 1/10,000th of a second, the neurotransmitter molecules cross the synaptic gap and bind to receptor sites on the receiving neuron—as precisely as a key fits a lock. For an instant, the neurotransmitter unlocks tiny channels at the receiving site. This allows electrically charged atoms to enter the receiving neuron, thereby either exciting or inhibiting its readiness to fire.

Most neurons have a resting rate of random firing that increases or decreases with input from other neurons and from chemicals that affect their sensitivity. Roughly speaking, the neuron is democratic: If it receives many more excitatory than inhibitory messages, the cell fires often. More electrical impulses flash down its axon, releasing more neurotransmitters, which diffuse across the synaptic gaps to other neurons.

How Neurotransmitters Influence Us

4. How do neurotransmitters influence human behavior?

The discovery of some 75 different neurotransmitters has raised a host of questions: Are certain neurotransmitters found only in specific places? What are their effects? Can we boost or diminish these effects through drugs or diet? Could such changes affect our moods, memories, or mental abilities? Such questions intrigue neuroscience researchers—stimulating reports on 3000 new neurotransmitter studies at a recent Society for Neuroscience meeting—and fascinate those of us who are spectators.

Later chapters explain the role of neurotransmitters in depression and euphoria, hunger and thinking, addictions and therapy. For now, let's glimpse how neurotransmitters influence our motions and emotions. We now know that

"When it comes to the brain, if you want to see the action, follow the neurotransmitters."

Neuroscientist Floyd Bloom (1993)

a particular neural pathway in the brain may use only one or two neurotransmitters, and that particular neurotransmitters may have particular effects on behavior and emotions. One of the best understood neurotransmitters, **acetylcholine (ACh)**, is the messenger at every junction between a motor neuron and a muscle. With powerful electron microscopes, neurobiologists can magnify thinly sliced specimens of tissue enough to see the sacs that store and release ACh molecules. When ACh is released to the muscle cells, the muscle contracts.

If the transmission of ACh is blocked, muscles cannot contract. Curare, a poison that certain South American Indians put on the tips of their hunting darts, occupies and blocks ACh receptor sites, leaving the neurotransmitter unable to affect the muscles. Struck by one of these darts, an animal becomes paralyzed. Botulin, a poison that can form in improperly canned food, causes paralysis by blocking ACh release from the sending neuron. The venom of the black widow spider causes a synaptic flood of ACh. The result? Violent muscle contractions, convulsions, and possible death.

The Endorphins

An exciting discovery about neurotransmitters occurred when Candace Pert and Solomon Snyder (1973) attached a radioactive tracer to morphine, allowing them to see exactly where in an animal's brain it was taken up. Pert and Snyder discovered that morphine, an opiate drug that elevates mood and eases pain, was taken up by receptors in areas linked with mood and pain sensations.

It was hard to imagine why the brain would contain these "opiate receptors" unless it had its own naturally occurring opiates. Why would the brain have a chemical lock, unless it also had a corresponding key? Researchers soon confirmed that the brain indeed contains several types of neurotransmitter molecules similar to morphine. Named **endorphins** (short for *end*ogenous [produced within] m*orphine*), these natural opiates are released in response to pain and vigorous exercise (Farrell & others, 1982; Lagerweij & others, 1984). They may therefore help explain all sorts of good feelings, such as the "runner's high," the pain-killing effects of acupuncture, and the indifference to pain in some severely injured people, such as David Livingstone reported in his 1857 *Missionary Travels*:

> I heard a shout. Starting, and looking half round, I saw the lion just in the act of springing upon me. I was upon a little height, he caught my shoulder as he sprang, and we both came to the ground below together. Growling horribly close to my ear, he shook me as a terrier does a rat. The shock produced a stupor similar to that which seems to be felt by a mouse after the first shake of the cat. It caused a sort of dreaminess in which there was no sense of pain nor feeling of terror, though [I was] quite conscious of all that was happening. . . . This peculiar state is probably produced in all animals killed by the carnivora; and if so, is a merciful provision by our benevolent Creator for lessening the pain of death.

How Drugs Alter Neurotransmission

If indeed the endorphins lessen pain and boost mood, why not flood the brain with artificial opiates, thereby intensifying the brain's own "feel good" chemistry? One problem is that when flooded with opiate drugs such as heroin and morphine, the brain may stop producing its own natural opiates. When the drug is withdrawn, the brain may be deprived of any form of opiate. For a drug addict, the result is agony that persists until the brain resumes production of its natural opiates or receives more of the drug. As we will see in later chapters, mood-altering drugs, from alcohol to nicotine to heroin, share a common effect: They trigger unpleasant, lingering aftereffects. For suppressing the body's own neurotransmitter production, nature charges a price.

Physician Lewis Thomas on the endorphins: "There it is, a biologically universal act of mercy. I cannot explain it, except to say that I would have put it in had I been around at the very beginning, sitting as a member of a planning committee."

The Youngest Science, 1983

acetylcholine [ah-seat-el-KO-leen] **(ACh)** A neurotransmitter that, among its functions, triggers muscle contraction.

endorphins [en-DOR-fins] "Morphine within"—natural, opiatelike neurotransmitters linked to pain control and to pleasure.

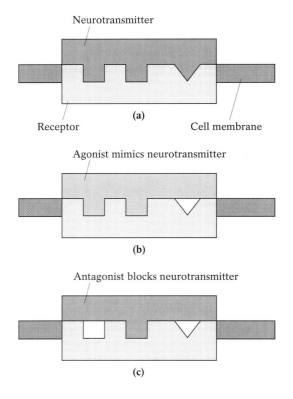

Neurotransmitter

Receptor   Cell membrane

(a)

Agonist mimics neurotransmitter

(b)

Antagonist blocks neurotransmitter

(c)

Figure 2–3 Drugs That Mimic or Block Natural Neurotransmitters *Part (a) shows a neurotransmitter molecule stimulating a receptor. Part (b) shows a drug molecule (an "agonist") similar enough to the neurotransmitter to mimic its effects. This may, for example, produce a temporary "high" by amplifying normal sensations of arousal or pleasure (as with opiate drugs). Part (c) shows a drug molecule (an "antagonist") enough like the natural neurotransmitter to occupy its receptor site and block its effect but not similar enough to stimulate the receptor. Some poisons and snake venoms paralyze by blocking acetylcholine receptors that produce muscle movement.*

The good news is that neurotransmitter research is enabling the creation of new therapeutic drugs, such as those used to alleviate depression. Some work by mimicking or blocking a particular neurotransmitter (Figure 2–3). Others work by hampering the neurotransmitter's natural breakdown or its reabsorption by the sending neuron. But designing a drug can be harder than it sounds, because some chemicals don't have the right shape to slither through the *blood-brain barrier* by which the brain fences out unwanted chemicals circulating in the blood. For example, scientists know that the tremors of Parkinson's disease result from the death of nerve cells that produce a neurotransmitter called *dopamine*. Giving patients dopamine as a drug doesn't help, though, because dopamine cannot cross the blood-brain barrier. But L-dopa, a raw material the brain can convert to dopamine, can sneak through. Given L-dopa, the patients' healthy, dopamine-making neurons produce extra dopamine, helping them regain control over their muscles.

! *Rehearse It*

1. The neuron fiber that carries messages to other neurons is the

a. dendrite.
b. axon.
c. myelin sheath.
d. synapse.

2. The neuron's response to stimulation is an *all-or-none* response. This means that the intensity of the stimulus determines

a. whether or not an impulse is generated.
b. how fast an impulse is transmitted.
c. how intense an impulse will be.
d. whether the stimulus is excitatory or inhibitory.

3. There is a minuscule space between the axon of a sending neuron and the dendrite or cell body of a receiving neuron. This small space is called the

a. axon terminal.
b. sac or vesicle.
c. synaptic gap.
d. threshold.

4. When the action potential reaches the axon terminal of a neuron, it triggers the release of chemical messengers called

a. ions.
b. synapses.
c. neural impulses.
d. neurotransmitters.

5. When the transmission of acetylcholine (ACh) is blocked,

a. death from convulsions may result.
b. the brain is flooded with substitute excitatory neurotransmitters, causing a brief "rush."
c. paralysis may result.
d. the brain starts producing antagonists, resulting in depression.

6. Endorphins are released in the brain in response to

a. morphine or heroin.
b. pain or vigorous exercise.
c. cocaine.
d. all of the above.

Neural and Hormonal Systems

5. What are the major divisions of the nervous system, and what are their basic functions?

Neurons communicating with other neurons form our body's primary information system, the **nervous system** (Figure 2–4). The brain and spinal cord form the **central nervous system**. The **peripheral nervous system** links the central nervous system with the body's sense receptors, muscles, and glands. The sensory and motor axons carrying this information are bundled into the electrical cables that we know as **nerves**. The optic nerve, for example, bundles nearly a million axon fibers into a single cable carrying the information that each eye sends to the brain.

Figure 2–4 The Functional Divisions of the Human Nervous System

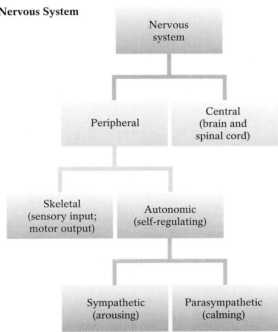

nervous system The body's speedy, electrochemical communication system, consisting of all the nerve cells of the peripheral and central nervous systems.

central nervous system The brain and spinal cord.

peripheral nervous system The neurons that connect the central nervous system to the rest of the body. It consists of the sensory neurons, which carry messages to the central nervous system from the body's sense receptors, and the motor neurons, which carry messages from the central nervous system to the muscles and glands.

nerves Neural "cables" containing many axons. These bundled axons, which are part of the peripheral nervous system, connect the central nervous system with muscles, glands, and sense organs.

sensory neurons Neurons that carry incoming information from the sense receptors to the central nervous system.

interneurons Central nervous system neurons that intervene directly between the sensory inputs and motor outputs.

motor neurons The neurons that carry outgoing information from the central nervous system to the muscles and glands.

skeletal nervous system The division of the peripheral nervous system that controls the body's skeletal muscles.

Information travels in the nervous system through three types of neurons. The **sensory neurons** send information from the body's tissues and sensory organs inward to the brain and spinal cord, which process the information. This processing involves a second class of neurons, the central nervous system's own **interneurons**, which enable its internal communication. The central nervous system then sends instructions out to the body's tissues via the **motor neurons.** Our complexity, though, resides mostly in our interneuron systems. Our nervous system has a few million sensory neurons, a few million motor neurons, and billions and billions of interneurons.

The Peripheral Nervous System

Our peripheral nervous system has two components—skeletal and autonomic. The **skeletal nervous system** controls the voluntary movements of our skeletal muscles. As you reach the bottom of this page, the skeletal nervous system will report to your brain the current state of your skeletal muscles and carry instructions back, triggering your hand to turn the page.

Figure 2–5 The Dual Functions of the Autonomic Nervous System *The autonomic nervous system controls the more autonomous (or self-regulating) internal functions, including those shown here. Its sympathetic division arouses and expends energy. Its parasympathetic division calms and conserves energy, allowing routine maintenance activity. Most organs are affected by both divisions. For example, sympathetic stimulation accelerates heartbeat, whereas parasympathetic stimulation slows it.*

SYMPATHETIC
NERVOUS SYSTEM
(arousing)

CENTRAL
NERVOUS SYSTEM

PARASYMPATHETIC
NERVOUS SYSTEM
(calming)

Brain

Dilates pupil

Contracts pupil

Heart

Accelerates heartbeat

Slows heartbeat

Spinal cord

Stomach

Inhibits digestion

Pancreas

Liver

Stimulates glucose release by liver

Stimulates digestion

Stimulates gallbladder

Adrenal gland

Kidney

Secretion of epinephrine norepinephrine

Relaxes bladder

Contracts bladder

Stimulates ejaculation in male

Stimulates erection of sex organs

autonomic [aw-tuh-NAHM-ik] **nervous system**   The part of the peripheral nervous system that controls the glands and the muscles of the internal organs (such as the heart). Its sympathetic division arouses; its parasympathetic division calms.

sympathetic nervous system   The division of the autonomic nervous system that arouses the body, mobilizing its energy in stressful situations.

parasympathetic nervous system   The division of the autonomic nervous system that calms the body, conserving its energy.

reflex   A simple, automatic, inborn response to a sensory stimulus, such as the knee-jerk response.

endocrine [EN-duh-krin] **system**   The body's "slow" chemical communication system; a set of glands that secrete hormones into the bloodstream.

hormones   Chemical messengers, mostly those manufactured by the endocrine glands, that are produced in one tissue and affect other tissues.

Our **autonomic nervous system** controls the glands and the muscles of our internal organs. Like an automatic pilot, it can be consciously overridden. But usually it operates on its own (autonomously) to influence our internal functioning, including our heartbeat, digestion, and glandular activity.

The autonomic nervous system is a dual system (Figure 2–5). The **sympathetic nervous system** arouses us for defensive action. If something alarms or enrages you, the sympathetic system will accelerate your heartbeat, slow your digestion, raise the sugar level in your blood, dilate your arteries, and cool you with perspiration, making you alert and ready for action. When the stress subsides, the **parasympathetic nervous system** produces opposite effects. It conserves energy as it calms you by decreasing your heartbeat, lowering your blood sugar, and so forth. In everyday situations, the sympathetic and parasympathetic nervous systems work together to keep us in a steady internal state.

The Central Nervous System

From the simplicity of neurons "talking" to other neurons arises the complexity of the central nervous system that enables our humanity—our thinking, feeling, and acting. Tens of billions of neurons, each in communication with thousands of other neurons, would yield an ever-changing wiring diagram that dwarfs the biggest computer.

The spinal cord is an information highway connecting the peripheral nervous system to the brain. Ascending neural "tracts" send up sensory information, and descending tracts send back motor-control information. A look at the neural pathways governing our **reflexes**, our automatic responses to stimuli, illustrates the spinal cord's work. A simple spinal reflex pathway is composed of

Figure 2-6 labels: Brain, Interneuron, Sensory neuron (incoming information), Motor neuron (outgoing information), Spinal cord, Skin receptors, Muscle

Figure 2–6 A Simple Reflex *Information from the skin receptors travels inward via a sensory neuron to a spinal cord interneuron, which sends a signal outward to the arm muscles via a motor neuron. Because this reflex involves only the spinal cord, the hand jerks away from the candle flame before the brain creates an experience of pain.*

a single sensory neuron and a single motor neuron, which often communicate through an interneuron. The knee-jerk response is one example; a headless warm body could do it.

Another such pathway makes up the pain reflex (Figure 2–6). When your fingers touch a hot stove, neural activity excited by the heat travels via sensory neurons to interneurons in your spinal cord. These interneurons respond by activating motor neurons to the muscles in your arm, causing you to jerk your hand away.

Because the simple pain reflex pathway runs through the spinal cord and out, you jerk your hand from the hot stove *before* your brain receives and responds to the information that causes you to feel pain. Information travels to and from the brain by way of the spinal cord. Were the top of your spinal cord severed, you would not feel such pain. Or pleasure. Your brain would literally be out of touch with your body. Thus, you would lose all sensation and voluntary movement in body regions whose sensory and motor neurons connect with the spinal cord below its point of injury. Male paraplegics (whose legs are paralyzed) are usually capable of an erection (a simple reflex) if their genitals are stimulated. But, depending on where and how completely the spinal cord is severed, they may have no genital feeling and be genitally unresponsive to erotic images (Kennedy & Over, 1990). To produce bodily pain or pleasure, the sensory information must reach the brain.

The other part of your central nervous system, your brain, receives information, interprets it, and decides how to respond. In doing so, the brain functions rather like a computing machine. It receives images of an object from the two eyes, computes their difference, and instantly infers how far the object must be to project such a difference. As basketball star Michael Jordan shoots a falling-away jump shot, his agile brain performs an incredible number of instant computations, adjusting for body position and movement, distance, and angle. And, as we will see, this is but one of many feats of this information-processing system that we call the brain.

The Endocrine System

6. How does the endocrine system transmit information?

Interconnected with the nervous system is the second of the body's communication systems, the slower **endocrine system** (Figure 2–7). The endocrine system's glands secrete **hormones**, chemical messengers that are produced in one tissue and travel through the bloodstream and affect other tissues, including the brain. Hormones acting on the brain influence our interest in sex, food, and aggression.

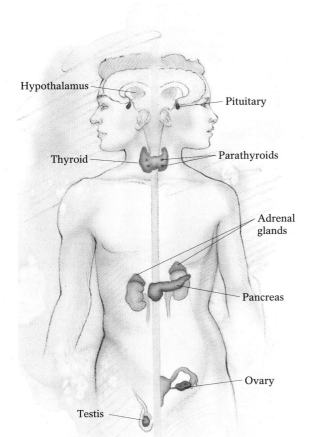

Figure 2-7 labels: Hypothalamus, Pituitary, Thyroid, Parathyroids, Adrenal glands, Pancreas, Ovary, Testis

Figure 2–7 The Body's Major Endocrine Glands *The pituitary gland releases hormones that, in turn, regulate the hormone secretions of other glands.*

Extended Growth *Most young people experience a brief period of rapid growth during adolescence—a period when their bodies take on adult size and proportions. Pituitary hormones trigger the growth spurt, which in girls typically peaks at age 12 and then slows down. For a few rare individuals, like this seven foot, seven inch woman, an excess of hormones meant that growth went on and on.*

Some hormones are chemically identical to neurotransmitters (those chemical messengers that diffuse across a synapse and excite or inhibit an adjacent neuron). The endocrine system and nervous system are therefore kindred systems: They both secrete molecules that activate receptors elsewhere. But unlike the messages of the speedy nervous system, which zip from eyes to brain to hand in a fraction of a second, endocrine messages use the slow lane. Several seconds or more may elapse before the bloodstream carries a hormone from an endocrine gland to its target tissue. But these endocrine messages are often worth waiting for, because their effects are usually longer-lasting than the effects of a neural message.

The endocrine system's hormones influence many aspects of our lives, from growth to reproduction, from metabolism to mood, keeping everything in balance while we respond to stress, exertion, and internal thoughts. In a moment of danger, for example, the autonomic nervous system will order the **adrenal glands** on top of the kidneys to release *epinephrine* and *norepinephrine* (also called *adrenaline* and *noradrenaline*). These hormones increase heart rate, blood pressure, and blood sugar, providing us with a surge of energy. When the emergency passes, the hormones—and the feelings of excitement—linger a while.

The most influential endocrine gland is the **pituitary gland**, a pea-sized structure located in the base of the brain, where it can be controlled by an adjacent brain area. The pituitary releases hormones that influence growth. Its secretions also influence the release of hormones by other endocrine glands. This makes the pituitary a sort of master gland. For example, under the brain's influence the pituitary triggers your sex glands to release sex hormones, which may in turn influence your brain and behavior.

This feedback system (brain → pituitary → other glands → hormones → brain) illustrates the intimate connection of the nervous and endocrine systems. The nervous system directs endocrine secretions, which affect the nervous system. Conducting and coordinating this whole electrochemical orchestra is that maestro we call the brain.

! Rehearse It

7. Information travels to and from the brain mostly by way of the spinal cord. The neurons of the spinal cord are called

a. motor neurons.
b. sensory neurons.
c. sending neurons.
d. interneurons.

8. The autonomic nervous system controls internal functions, such as heart rate and glandular activity. The word "autonomic" means

a. peripheral.
b. voluntary.
c. self-regulating.
d. arousing.

9. Usually, the sympathetic nervous system arouses us for action and the parasym-

pathetic nervous system calms us down. Together the two systems make up the

a. autonomic nervous system.
b. skeletal nervous system.
c. central nervous system.
d. peripheral nervous system.

10. The neurons of the spinal cord are part of the

a. skeletal nervous system.
b. central nervous system.
c. autonomic nervous system.
d. peripheral nervous system.

11. The endocrine system, the second and slower bodily communication system, produces chemical messengers that travel through the bloodstream and affect other tissues. These chemical substances are

a. hormones.
b. neurotransmitters.
c. micronutrients.
d. glands.

12. The pituitary gland releases hormones that influence growth as well as the activity of other glands. The pituitary gland is part of the

a. endocrine system.
b. peripheral nervous system.
c. sympathetic nervous system.
d. central nervous system.

The Human Brain *This small, wrinkled organ is far more complex than the most sophisticated computer. What you see here is only a portion of the brain's outer layer. Most of its surface lies hidden within its convoluted folds.*

THE FAR SIDE

"The picture's pretty bleak, gentlemen. . . . The world's climates are changing, the mammals are taking over, and we all have a brain about the size of a walnut."

adrenal [ah-DREEN-el] **glands** A pair of endocrine glands just above the kidneys. The adrenals secrete the hormones epinephrine (adrenaline) and norepinephrine (noradrenaline), which help to arouse the body in times of stress.

pituitary gland The endocrine system's most influential gland. The pituitary regulates growth and controls other endocrine glands.

brainstem The oldest part and central core of the brain, beginning where the spinal cord swells as it enters the skull; it is responsible for automatic survival functions.

medulla [muh-DUL-uh] The base of the brainstem; controls heartbeat and breathing.

The Brain

In a jar on a display shelf in Cornell University's psychology department resides the well-preserved brain of Edward Bradford Titchener, a great turn-of-the-century psychologist and proponent of the study of consciousness. Imagine yourself gazing at that wrinkled mass of grayish tissue. Is there any sense in which Titchener is still in there?[1]

You might answer that, without the living whir of electrochemical activity, there could be nothing of Titchener in his preserved brain. Consider then an experiment about which the inquisitive Titchener himself might have daydreamed. Imagine that just moments before his death, someone removed Titchener's brain from his body and kept it alive by pumping enriched blood through it as it floated in a tank of cerebral fluid. Would Titchener now still be in there? Further imagine, to carry our fantasy to its limit, that someone transplanted the still-living brain into the body of a badly brain-damaged person. To whose home should the recovered patient return?

That we can imagine such questions illustrates how convinced we are that we live in our heads. And for good reason: The brain enables the mind to see, hear, remember, think, feel, speak, dream. Indeed, say neuroscientists, the *mind is what the brain does*. But precisely where and how are mind functions tied to the brain? Let's first consider the structures that make up the brain.

Lower Level Brain Structures

If you could open the skull and look inside, the first thing you might notice is the brain's size. In dinosaurs the brain represented 1/100,000th of the body's weight, in whales it represents 1/10,000th, in elephants 1/600th, in humans 1/45th. It looks as though a principle is emerging. But keep reading. In mice the brain is 1/40th the body's weight, and in marmosets 1/25th. So there are exceptions to the rule of thumb that the ratio of brain to body weight provides a clue to a species' intelligence.

More useful clues to an animal's capacities come from the brain's structures. In primitive vertebrate (backboned) animals, such as sharks, the brain primarily regulates basic survival functions: breathing, resting, and feeding. In lower mammals, such as rodents, a more complex brain enables emotion and greater memory. In advanced mammals, such as humans, the brain processes more information, enabling us to act with foresight.

Brain evolution has not greatly altered the basic mechanisms for survival. Rather, new brain systems evolved on top of the old, much as the earth's landscape covers the old with the new. Digging down, one discovers the fossil remnants of the past—brainstem components still performing much as they did for our distant ancestors. Let's now explore the brain, starting here and working up.

The Brainstem

7. What functions do the brainstem and its associated structures serve?

The **brainstem** is the brain's oldest and innermost region. It begins where the spinal cord enters the skull and swells slightly, forming the **medulla**. Here lie the controls for your heartbeat and breathing. If the top of a cat's brainstem is severed from the rest of the brain above it, the animal will still breathe and live—and even run, climb, and groom (Klemm, 1990). But with the brainstem cut off from the brain's higher region, the cat won't purposefully run or climb to get food.

[1]Carl Sagan's *Broca's Brain* inspired this question.

The Tools of Discovery

It is exciting to consider how fast and how far the neurosciences have progressed within a lifetime. For centuries, the human brain lay largely beyond the reach of science. The neuron was too small to study with the naked eye, its impulses too faint to record with ordinary electrodes. We were able to feel bumps on the skull, dissect and analyze lifeless brains, and observe the effects of specific brain diseases and injuries. But there were no tools high-powered yet gentle enough to explore the living brain. Now, that has changed. Whether in the interests of science or medicine, we can selectively destroy tiny clusters of normal or defective brain cells, leaving their surroundings unharmed. We can probe the brain with tiny electrical pulses. We can snoop on the messages of individual neurons and on the mass action of billions. We can see color representations of the brain's energy-consuming activity. These new tools and techniques have made possible a neuroscientific revolution.

Clinical Observations

The oldest method of studying brain-mind connections is to observe the effects of brain diseases and injuries. Such observations were first recorded some 5000 years ago. But it was not until the last two centuries that physicians began systematically to record the results of damage to specific brain areas. Some noted that damage to one side of the brain often caused numbness or paralysis on the body's opposite side, suggesting that the right side of the body is wired to the brain's left side, and vice versa. Others noticed that damage to the back of the brain disrupted vision, and that damage to the left front part of the brain produced speech difficulties. Gradually, the brain was being mapped.

Manipulating the Brain

Scientists need not wait for brain injuries. They can also electrically, chemically, or magnetically stimulate various parts of the brain, noting the effects. Or they can surgically **lesion** (destroy) tissue in specific brain areas in animals. For example, a lesion in one part of the brain reduces eating, causing the rat to starve unless force-fed. Conversely, a lesion in a nearby area produces overeating.

Recording the Brain's Electrical Activity

Modern researchers have also learned to eavesdrop on the brain. Electrical activity in the brain's billions of neurons sweeps in regular waves across its surface. The **electroencephalogram (EEG)** is an amplified tracing of such waves by an instrument called an electroencephalograph. Studying an EEG of the gross activity of the whole brain is like studying the activity of a car engine by listening to the hum of its motor. However, by presenting a stimulus repeatedly and having a computer filter out electrical activity unrelated to the stimulus, one can identify the electrical wave evoked by the stimulus (Figure 2–8).

In addition, modern microelectrodes have tips so small they can detect the electrical pulse in a single neuron, making possible some astonishingly precise findings. For example, we can now detect exactly where in a cat's brain the information goes after someone strokes the animal's whisker.

---

lesion [LEE-zhuhn]   To cause tissue destruction. A brain lesion is a naturally or experimentally caused destruction of brain tissue.

electroencephalogram (EEG)   An amplified recording of the waves of electrical activity that sweep across the brain's surface. These waves are measured by placing electrodes on the scalp.

CAT (computerized axial tomograph) scan   A series of x-ray photographs taken from different angles and combined by computer into a composite three-dimensional representation of a slice through the body.

PET (positron emission tomograph) scan   A visual display of brain activity that detects where a radioactive form of glucose goes while the brain performs a given task.

MRI (magnetic resonance imaging)   A technique that uses magnetic fields and radio waves to produce computer-generated images that distinguish among different types of soft tissue; this allows us to see structures within the brain.

Figure 2–8 An Electroencephalograph Providing Amplified Tracings of Waves of Electrical Activity in the Brain   *Here it is detecting brain response to sound, making possible an early evaluation of what may be a hearing impairment.*

Brain-Imaging Techniques

Other new windows into the brain give us a Supermanlike ability to see inside the brain without lesioning it. For example, the **CAT (computerized axial tomograph) scan** examines the brain by taking x-ray photographs that can reveal brain damage. Even more dramatic is the **PET (positron emission tomograph) scan** (Figure 2–9). A PET scan depicts the activity of different brain areas by showing each area's consumption of the brain's chemical fuel, the sugar glucose (see illustration, page 56). Active neurons burn more glucose. When a person is given a temporarily radioactive form of glucose, the PET scan measures and locates the radioactivity, thereby detecting where this "food for thought" goes. In this way, researchers can see which brain areas are most active as the person performs mathematical calculations, listens to music, or daydreams.

Another new way of looking into the living brain exploits the fact that the centers of atoms, including those in our brains, spin like tops. In **MRI (magnetic resonance imaging)** the head is put in a strong magnetic field, which aligns the spinning atoms. Then a brief pulse of radio waves disorients the atoms momentarily. When the atoms return to their normal spin they release detectable signals, which become computer-generated images of their concentrations. The result is a detailed picture of the brain's soft tissues. For example, MRI scans reveal enlarged fluid-filled brain areas in some patients suffering from schizophrenia, a disabling psychological disorder (Figure 2–10).

By taking pictures less than a second apart, MRI scans can now show the brain lighting up (with increased oxygen-laden blood flow) as a person performs different mental functions (Kwong & others, 1992). As a person sees a light turn on, a *fast MRI* machine (also called *functional MRI*) detects blood rushing to the back of the brain, which processes visual information (Figure 2–17, page 54). Ask the person to solve a verbal analogy problem, and the part of the brain's left side near the front will light up. Such snapshots of the brain's mind-enabling activity may permit new insights into how and where the brain divides its labor.

What the microscope did for biology and the telescope for astronomy, these new brain-imaging instruments may do for psychological science. The tools are triggering a scientific revolution. To be learning about the neurosciences now is like studying world geography while Magellan was exploring the seas. Every year the explorers announce new discoveries, which also generate new interpretations of old discoveries. With data from different brain-imaging techniques appearing faster than anyone can read and remember them, researchers are now assembling the information in computer databases (Gibbons, 1992). This brain mapping will give all researchers instant access through electronic networks to PET or MRI studies that reveal activity in a particular brain area while a person, for example, solves math problems. Clearly, this is the decade of the brain, the golden age of brain science.

Figure 2–10 MRI Scan of a Normal Person (Left) and a Schizophrenia Patient (Right) *Note the enlarged fluid-filled brain region in the brain on the right.*

Figure 2–9 The PET Scan *To obtain a PET scan, researchers inject someone with a low and harmless dose of a short-lived radioactive sugar. Detectors around the subject's head pick up the release of gamma rays from the sugar, which has concentrated in active brain areas. A computer then processes and translates these signals into a map of the brain at work.*

Figure 2–11 Lower Brain Structures *We can imagine looking up at the brain from the bottom. First, we see the spinal cord, which then swells to form a tube (the medulla), on which rests a pair of egg-shaped structures (the thalamus), surrounding which, as we will see, are additional layers. Hanging at the back is the baseball-sized cerebellum. Sensory information, say, from your right hand, travels up the spinal cord, crosses over to the left side at the medulla, and is routed to higher brain regions through the thalamus.*

reticular formation   A nerve network in the brainstem that plays an important role in controlling arousal.

thalamus [THAL-uh-muss]   The brain's sensory switchboard, located on top of the brainstem; it directs messages to the sensory receiving areas in the cortex and transmits replies to the cerebellum and medulla.

cerebellum [sehr-uh-BELL-um]   The "little brain" attached to the rear of the brainstem; it helps coordinate voluntary movement and balance.

limbic system   A doughnut-shaped system of neural structures at the border of the brainstem and cerebral hemispheres; associated with emotions such as fear and aggression and drives such as those for food and sex.

amygdala [ah-MIG-dah-la]   Two almond-shaped neural centers in the limbic system that are linked to emotion.

Here in the brainstem is also the crossover point, where most nerves to and from each side of the brain connect with the body's opposite side. This peculiar cross-wiring is but one of many surprises the brain has to offer.

Inside the brainstem, the **reticular** ("netlike") **formation**, a finger-shaped network of neurons, extends from the spinal cord right up to the thalamus (Figure 2–11). As the spinal cord's sensory input travels up to the thalamus, some of it branches off to the reticular formation, which filters incoming stimuli and relays important information to other areas of the brain. Among its other functions, the reticular formation helps control arousal.

In 1949, Giuseppe Moruzzi and Horace Magoun discovered that electrically stimulating the reticular formation of a sleeping cat almost instantly produced an awake, alert animal. Magoun also severed a cat's reticular formation from higher brain regions without damaging the nearby sensory pathways. The effect? The cat lapsed into a coma from which it never awakened. The conclusion? The reticular formation was involved in arousal.

The Thalamus

Atop the brainstem sits a joined pair of egg-shaped structures called the **thalamus** (Figure 2–11). This is the brain's sensory switchboard: It receives information from the sensory neurons and routes it to the higher brain regions that deal with seeing, hearing, tasting, and touching. We can think of the thalamus as being to neural traffic what London is to England's train traffic: Sensory input passes through it en route to various destinations. The thalamus also receives some of the higher brain's replies, which it directs to the cerebellum and medulla.

The Cerebellum

Extending from the rear of the brainstem is the **cerebellum**, meaning little brain, which is rather what its two wrinkled hemispheres look like (Figure 2–11). The cerebellum influences learning and memory, but its most obvious function is coordinating voluntary movement. If you injured your cerebellum, you would probably have difficulty walking, keeping your balance, or shaking hands. Your movements would be jerky and exaggerated.

> *"I am a brain, Watson. The rest of me is a mere appendix."*
>
> Sherlock Holmes, in Arthur Conan Doyle *The Adventure of the Mazarin Stone*

Note that these lower brain functions all occur without any conscious effort. This illustrates another of this book's recurring themes: *Our brain processes much information outside our awareness.* We are aware of the *results* of our brain's labor (say, our current visual experience) but not of *how* we construct the visual image. Likewise, whether we are asleep or awake, our brainstem manages its life-sustaining functions, freeing our higher brain regions to dream, to think, to talk, to savor a memory.

! Rehearse It

13. The brainstem is the oldest and innermost region of the brain. The part of the brainstem that controls heartbeat and breathing is the

a. cerebellum.
b. medulla.
c. cortex.
d. thalamus.

14. The part of the brain that coordinates voluntary movement is the

a. cerebellum.
b. medulla.
c. thalamus.
d. reticular formation.

15. The lower brain structure that governs arousal is the

a. spinal cord.
b. cerebellum.
c. reticular formation.
d. medulla.

16. The thalamus receives information from the sensory neurons and routes it to the higher brain regions that control the senses. The thalamus functions like a(n)

a. memory bank.
b. pleasure center.
c. endocrine gland.
d. switchboard.

The Limbic System

> *8. What functions do the structures within the limbic system serve?*

At the border ("limbus") of the brain's older parts and the cerebral hemispheres is a doughnut-shaped neural system called the **limbic system** (Figure 2–12). We will see in Chapter 7 how one limbic system component, the *hippocampus*, processes memory. (When animals or humans lose their hippocampus to surgery or injury, they become unable to lay down new memories of facts and experiences.) For now, let's look at the limbic system's links to emotions, such as fear and anger, and to basic motives, such as those for food and sex. As we will see, the limbic system's influence on emotions and motives occurs partly through its control of the body's hormones.

The Amygdala Two almond-shaped neural clusters in the limbic system, called the **amygdala**, influence aggression and fear. In 1939, psychologist Heinrich Klüver and neurosurgeon Paul Bucy surgically lesioned part of a rhesus monkey's brain that included the amygdala. The operation transformed the normally ill-tempered monkey into the most mellow of creatures. Poke it, pinch it, do virtually anything that normally would trigger a ferocious response, and still the animal remained placid. In later studies with other wild animals, including the lynx, wolverine, and wild rat, researchers noted the same effect. What then might happen if we electrically stimulated the amygdala in a normally placid domestic animal, such as a cat? Do so in one spot and the cat prepares to attack, hissing with its back arched, its pupils dilated, its hair on end. Move the electrode only slightly within the amygdala and the cat cowers in terror when caged with a small mouse.

Hypothalamus

Pituitary gland

Amygdala

Hippocampus

Figure 2–12 The Limbic System *Although part of the endocrine system, not the brain, the pituitary gland is controlled by the hypothalamus, just above it.*

Aggression as a Brain State   *Back arched and fur fluffed, this fierce cat is ready to attack. Electrical stimulation of a cat's amygdala provokes reactions such as the one shown here, suggesting its role in emotions like rage. Which division of the autonomic nervous system is activated by such stimulation? (See page 53.)*

The Limbic System and the Hypothalamus   *Circled in this computer-enhanced MRI brain scan is the limbic system. Among its most important components is the hypothalamus (white dot). This small structure helps keep the body's internal environment in a steady state by regulating thirst, hunger, and body temperature.*

These experiments testify to the amygdala's role in such emotions as rage and fear. Still, we must be careful not to think of the amygdala as *the* control center for aggression and fear. The brain is *not* neatly organized into structures that correspond to our categories of behavior. Aggressive and fearful behaviors involve neural activity in all levels of the brain. Even within the limbic system, stimulating neural structures other than the amygdala can evoke such behavior. Similarly, if you manipulate your car's carburetor, you can affect how the car runs, but that doesn't mean that the carburetor by itself runs the car. It is merely one link in an integrated system.

The Hypothalamus   Another of the limbic system's fascinating structures lies just below (*hypo*) the thalamus, and so is called the **hypothalamus**. By lesioning or stimulating different areas in the hypothalamus, neuroscientists have isolated within it neuron networks that perform specific bodily maintenance duties. Some of these neural clusters influence hunger; still others regulate thirst, body temperature, and sexual behavior.

The hypothalamus monitors blood chemistry and takes orders from other parts of the brain. Thinking about sex (in your brain's cerebral cortex) can stimulate your hypothalamus to secrete hormones. These hormones influence the adjacent master gland, the pituitary, which influences hormone release by other glands, which the hypothalamus monitors. (Note again the interplay between the nervous and endocrine systems: The brain influences the endocrine system, which in turn influences the brain.) The powerful little hypothalamus also exerts control by triggering autonomic nervous system activity.

The story of a remarkable discovery about the hypothalamus illustrates how progress in scientific research often occurs—when curious, open-minded investigators make an unexpected observation. Two young McGill University neuropsychologists, James Olds and Peter Milner (1954), were trying to implant electrodes in the reticular systems of white rats. One day they made a magnificent mistake. In one rat, they incorrectly placed an electrode in what was later discovered to be a region of the hypothalamus (Olds, 1975). Curiously, the rat kept returning to the place on its tabletop enclosure where it had been stimulated by this misplaced electrode, as if it were seeking more stimulation. Upon discovering their mistake, the alert investigators recognized that they had stumbled upon a brain center that provides a pleasurable reward.

In a meticulous series of experiments, Olds (1958) then went on to locate other "pleasure centers," as he called them. (What the rats actually experience only they know, and they aren't telling. Not wanting to attribute human feelings to the rat, today's scientists seldom refer to "pleasure centers.") When Olds allowed rats to trigger their own stimulation in these areas by pressing a pedal,

Figure 2–13 Rat With an Implanted Electrode *With an electrode implanted in a reward center of its hypothalamus, the rat readily crosses an electrified grid, accepting the painful shocks, to press a lever that sends electrical impulses to its "pleasure centers."*

they would sometimes do so at a feverish pace—up to 7000 times per hour—until they dropped from exhaustion. Moreover, they would do anything to get this stimulation, even cross an electrified floor that a starving rat would not cross to reach food (Figure 2–13).

Similar reward centers in or near the hypothalamus were later discovered in many other species, including goldfish, dolphins, and monkeys. In fact, animal research reveals both a general reward system that triggers the release of the neurotransmitter dopamine, and specific centers associated with the pleasures of eating, drinking, and sex. Animals, it seems, come equipped with built-in systems that reward activities essential to survival.

These dramatic findings made people wonder whether humans, too, might have limbic centers for pleasure. Indeed they do. One neurosurgeon has used electrodes to calm violent patients. Stimulated patients report mild pleasure; unlike rats, they are not driven to a frenzy by it (Deutsch, 1972; Hooper & Teresi, 1986).

! Rehearse It

17. The limbic system, a doughnut-shaped structure at the border of the brain's older parts and the cerebral hemispheres, is associated with basic motives, emotions, and memory functions. Two parts of the limbic system are the amygdala and the

a. reticular formation.
b. hypothalamus.
c. thalamus.
d. medulla.

18. A ferocious response to electrical brain stimulation would lead you to suppose that the electrode had been touching the

a. medulla.
b. pituitary.
c. hippocampus.
d. amygdala.

19. The "pleasure centers" discovered by Olds and Milner were located in regions of the

a. cerebral cortex.
b. brainstem.
c. hypothalamus.
d. spinal cord.

20. The neural structure that most directly regulates eating, drinking, and body temperature is the

a. cerebellum.
b. hypothalamus.
c. thalamus.
d. amygdala.

The Cerebral Cortex

Amphibians, such as frogs, have a small cortex and operate extensively on preprogrammed genetic instructions. The larger cortex of mammals offers increased capacities for learning and thinking, enabling them to be more adaptable. Most of what makes us distinctively human arises from the complex functions of our highly developed cerebral cortex.

Structure of the Cortex

9. How is the cerebral cortex organized?

Opening a human skull and exposing the brain, we would see a wrinkled organ, shaped rather like the meat of an oversized walnut. Eighty percent of the brain's weight lies in the ballooning left and right cerebral hemispheres, which are mostly filled with axon connections between the brain's surface and its other regions. The thin surface layer of the cerebral hemispheres is the **cerebral cortex**, a ⅛-inch thick sheet of cells composed of some 30 billion nerve cells and 300 trillion synaptic connections. Being human takes a lot of nerve.

hypothalamus [hi-po-THAL-uh-muss] A neural structure lying below (*hypo*) the thalamus; it directs several maintenance activities (eating, drinking, body temperature), helps govern the endocrine system via the pituitary gland, and is linked to emotion.

cerebral [seh-REE-bruhl] **cortex** The intricate fabric of interconnected neural cells that covers the cerebral hemispheres; the body's ultimate control and information-processing center.

Speaking/
Muscle
movements
Plan ed
indgmt

Sensory
Cortex

Visual

auditory

Figure 2–14 The Basic Subdivisions of the Cortex
We can view the cortex as divided into four lobes in each hemisphere, separated by prominent fissures, or grooves.

frontal lobes The portion of the cerebral cortex lying just behind the forehead; involved in speaking and muscle movements and in making plans and judgments.

parietal [puh-RYE-uh-tuhl] **lobes** The portion of the cerebral cortex lying at the top of the head and toward the rear; includes the sensory cortex.

occipital [ahk-SIP-uh-tuhl] **lobes** The portion of the cerebral cortex lying at the back of the head; includes the visual areas, each of which receives visual information from the opposite visual field.

temporal lobes The portion of the cerebral cortex lying roughly above the ears; includes the auditory areas, each of which receives auditory information primarily from the opposite ear.

motor cortex An area at the rear of the frontal lobes that controls voluntary movements.

sensory cortex The area at the front of the parietal lobes that registers and processes body sensations.

We can view each brain hemisphere as divided into four regions, or *lobes*. Starting at the front of your brain and going around over the top, there are the **frontal lobes** (behind your forehead), the **parietal lobes** (at the top and to the rear), the **occipital lobes** (at the back of your head), and the **temporal lobes** (just above your ears). These lobes are convenient geographic subdivisions separated by prominent folds (Figure 2–14). As we will see, the lobes are not distinct operating units. Each lobe carries out many functions, and some functions require the interplay of several lobes.

Functions of the Cortex

10. What functions are served by the cerebral cortex?

More than a century ago, autopsies of partially paralyzed or speechless people revealed damage to specific areas of the cortex. But this rather crude evidence did not prove that specific parts of the cortex perform specific functions. After all, if control of speech and movement were diffused across the entire cortex, damage to almost any area might produce the same effect. Likewise, a television would go dead with its power cord cut, but we would be deluding ourselves if we were to think we had "localized" the source of the picture in the cord. This analogy suggests how easy it is to err when trying to localize brain functions.

Motor Functions In 1870, German physicians Gustav Fritsch and Eduard Hitzig applied mild electrical stimulation to the cortexes of dogs and made an important discovery: They could make different body parts move. The effects were selective: Stimulation caused movement only when applied to an arch-shaped region at the back of the frontal lobe, running roughly from ear to ear across the top of the brain. This arch we now call the **motor cortex** (Figure 2–15). Moreover, when the researchers stimulated specific parts of this region in the left or right hemisphere, specific body parts moved on the *opposite* side of the body.

Figure 2–15 The Motor and Sensory Cortex *The motor cortex controls voluntary muscle movements. The sensory cortex receives input from the skin and muscles.*

Output: Motor cortex
(Left hemisphere section
controls the body's right side)

Input: Sensory cortex
(Left hemisphere section receives
input from the body's right side)

Figure 2–16 Left Hemisphere Tissue Devoted to Each Body Part in the Motor Cortex and the Sensory Cortex *As you can see, the amount of cortex devoted to a body part is not proportional to that part's size. Rather, the brain devotes more tissue to sensitive areas and to areas requiring precise control. Thus, the fingers have a greater representation in the cortex than does the upper arm.*

The cat on page 50 is aroused via its sympathetic nervous system.

The people who first dissected and labeled the brain used the language of scholars, Latin and Greek. Their words are actually attempts at graphic description: For example, "cortex" means bark, "cerebellum" is little brain, and "thalamus" is inner chamber.

A half century ago, neurosurgeons Otfrid Foerster in Germany and Wilder Penfield in Montreal mapped the motor cortex in hundreds of wide-awake patients. The surgeons needed to know the possible side effects of removing different parts of the cortex. So, before putting the knife to the brain, they would painlessly (the brain has no sensory receptors) stimulate different cortical areas and note body responses. Like Fritsch and Hitzig, they found that when they stimulated different areas of the motor cortex at the back of the frontal lobe, different body parts moved. They were therefore able to map the motor cortex according to the body parts it controlled (Figure 2–16). Interestingly, those areas of the body requiring precise control, such as the fingers and mouth, occupied the greatest amount of cortical space.

Neuroscientist José Delgado demonstrated the mechanics of motor behavior. In one monkey, he evoked a smiling response over 400,000 times. In a human patient, stimulation of a certain spot on the left motor cortex triggered the right hand to make a fist. Asked to keep the fingers open during the next stimulation, the patient, whose fingers closed despite his best efforts, remarked, "I guess, Doctor, that your electricity is stronger than my will" (Delgado, 1969, p. 114).

Sensory Functions If the motor cortex sends messages out to the body, where do *incoming* messages reach the cortex? Penfield identified a cortical area that specializes in receiving information from the skin senses and from the movement of body parts. This area, parallel to the motor cortex and just behind it at the front of the parietal lobes, we now call the **sensory cortex** (Figure 2–15). Stimulate a point on the top of this band of tissue, and the person may report being touched on the shoulder; stimulate some point on the side, and the person may feel something on the face.

The more sensitive a body region, the greater the area of the sensory cortex devoted to it; your supersensitive lips project to a larger brain area than do your toes (Figure 2–16). Similarly, rats have a large area of the brain devoted to

Figure 2–17 New Technology Shows the Brain in Action *In this composite sketch and photograph, a fast MRI scan shows the visual cortex activated (color representation of increased blood flow) as researchers shine a light into a subject's eyes. If the light is switched off, the region instantly calms down.*

whisker sensations, owls to hearing sensations, and so forth. If a monkey or a human loses a finger, the region of the sensory cortex devoted to receiving input from that finger branches to receive sensory input from the adjacent fingers, which now become more sensitive (Fox, 1984). As this illustrates, the brain is sculpted not only by our genes (nature) but also by our experience (nurture).

Further exploration identified areas where the cortex receives input from the other senses. At this moment you are receiving visual information in the occipital lobes at the very back of your brain (Figure 2–17). Stimulated there, you might see flashes of light or dashes of color. So, in a sense, we *do* have eyes in the back of our head. From there the visual information you are now processing goes to other brain areas that specialize in tasks such as identifying words, detecting emotions, and recognizing faces.

Any sound you are hearing you processed with the auditory areas in your temporal lobes (Figure 2–18). Most of this auditory information travels a circuitous route from one ear to the auditory receiving area above your opposite ear. Stimulated there, you might hear a sound.

Visual cortex

Auditory cortex

Figure 2–18 The Visual and Auditory Cortexes *The occipital lobes at the rear receive input from the eyes. An auditory area of the temporal lobes receives information from the ears.*

Association Functions   So far we have pointed out small areas of the cortex that either receive sensory information or direct muscular responses. In humans, that leaves some three-fourths of the thin wrinkled layer, the cerebral cortex, uncommitted. Neurons in these **association areas** (the gray areas in Figure 2–19) integrate information. They associate various sensory inputs with stored memories—an important part of thinking.

Electrically probing the association areas doesn't trigger any response. So, unlike our mapping of the sensory and motor areas, we can't so neatly specify the functions of the association areas. Their silence seems to be what someone had in mind when formulating one of pop psychology's most widespread myths: that we ordinarily use only 10 percent of our brains. The myth implies that if we could activate our whole brain, we would be far smarter than those who drudge along on 10 percent brain power. But from observing surgically lesioned animals and brain-damaged humans, we know that the association areas are not dormant. Rather, they interpret, integrate, and act on information processed by the sensory areas.

association areas   Areas of the cerebral cortex that are not involved in primary motor or sensory functions; rather, they are involved in higher mental functions such as learning, remembering, thinking, and speaking.

Motor areas
Sensory areas
Association areas

Rat

Cat

Monkey

Human

Figure 2–19 Areas of the Cortex in Four Mammals *More intelligent animals have increased "uncommitted" or association areas of the cortex. These vast areas of the brain are responsible for integrating and acting on information received and processed by sensory areas.*

Phineas Gage Reconsidered *Using measurements of his skull (which was kept as a medical record) and modern neuroimaging techniques, researcher Hanna Damasio and her colleagues (1994) have reconstructed the probable path of the rod through Gage's brain. Previously scientists believed that only his left frontal lobe was injured. As you can see, however, the pathway includes the right prefrontal cortex—a finding consistent with current studies of the effects of brain damage on personality.*

aphasia Impairment of language, usually caused by left hemisphere damage either to Broca's area (impairing speaking) or to Wernicke's area (impairing understanding).

Broca's area An area of the left frontal lobe that directs the muscle movements involved in speech.

Wernicke's area An area of the left temporal lobe involved in language comprehension.

• Association areas in the frontal lobe enable judging and planning. People with damaged frontal lobes may have intact memories, score high on intelligence tests, and be able to bake a cake—yet be unable to plan ahead to begin baking the cake for a birthday party.

Frontal lobe damage can also alter personality, removing a person's inhibitions. Consider the classic case of railroad worker Phineas Gage. One afternoon in 1848, 25-year-old Gage was packing gunpowder into a rock with a tamping iron. A spark ignited the gunpowder, shooting the rod up through his left cheek and out the top of his skull, leaving his frontal lobes massively damaged. To everyone's amazement, Gage was still able to sit up and speak, and after the wound healed he returned to work. Although his mental abilities and memories were intact, his personality was not. The affable, soft-spoken Phineas Gage was now an irritable, profane, dishonest person who eventually lost his job and ended up earning his living as a fairground exhibit. This person, said his friends, was "no longer Gage." The rod had destroyed his brain's moral compass.

The association areas of the other lobes also perform mental functions. For example, an area on the underside of the right temporal lobe enables us to recognize faces. If a stroke or head injury destroyed this area of your brain, you would still be able to describe facial features and to recognize someone's sex and approximate age, yet be strangely unable to identify the person as, say, Nelson Mandela, your next-door neighbor, or even your spouse. But by and large, complex mental functions such as learning and memory don't reside in any one place. There is no one spot in a rat's small association cortex that, when damaged, will obliterate its ability to learn or remember a maze. Such functions seem spread throughout much of the cortex.

Language Complex human abilities, such as language, result from the intricate coordination of many brain areas. For example, consider the curious finding that damage to any one of several cortical areas can cause **aphasia**, an impaired use of language. It is even more curious that some aphasic people can speak fluently but are unable to read (despite good vision), while others can comprehend what they read but are unable to speak. Still others can write but not read, read but not write, read numbers but not letters, or sing but not speak. These observations are puzzling because we think of speaking and reading, or writing and reading, or singing and speaking as merely different examples of the same general ability.

Researchers began to sort out how the brain processes language after a discovery by French physician Paul Broca in 1865. Broca discovered that damage to a specific area of the left frontal lobe, later called **Broca's area**, left a person struggling to form words, yet often able to sing familiar songs with ease. A decade later, German investigator Karl Wernicke discovered that damage to a specific area of the left temporal lobe (**Wernicke's area**) would leave people able to speak words but in a meaningless way.

PET Scan Images of Language Processing
PET scans such as these detect the activity of different areas of the brain by measuring their relative consumption of a temporarily radioactive form of the brain's normal fuel, glucose. This series of side-view PET scans of a left-facing person shows levels of increased brain activity in specific areas: (a) when hearing a word—auditory cortex and Wernicke's area; (b) when seeing a word—visual cortex and angular gyrus; and (c) when repeating a word—Broca's area and the motor cortex. The red blotches show where the brain is rapidly consuming glucose.

Norman Geschwind assembled these clues into an explanation of how we use language. When you read aloud, the words (1) register in the visual area, (2) are relayed to an area that transforms the words into an auditory code that is (3) received and understood in the nearby Wernicke's area, and (4) sent to Broca's area, which (5) controls the motor cortex, creating the pronounced word (Figure 2–20). Depending on which link in this chain is damaged, a different form of aphasia occurs. Damage to the angular gyrus leaves the person able to speak and understand but unable to read. Damage to Wernicke's area disrupts understanding. Damage to Broca's area disrupts speaking. The general principle bears repeating: Complex abilities result from the intricate coordination of many brain areas.

Said differently, the brain operates by dividing its mental functions—speaking, perceiving, thinking, remembering—into subfunctions. Our conscious experience *seems* indivisible. Right now you are experiencing a whole visual scene as if your eyes were video cameras projecting the scene into your brain. Actually, as we will see, your brain breaks vision into specialized subdimensions, such as color, depth, movement, and form. (After a localized stroke that destroys one of these neural work teams, people may lose just one aspect of vision, such as the ability to perceive movement.) These specialized "neural networks," each having done its own thing, then feed their information to "higher level" networks that combine and pass the information along to progressively higher level association areas, enabling us to recognize a face as "Grandmother." The same is true of reading a word: The brain computes the word's form, sound, and meaning using different neural networks (Posner & Carr,

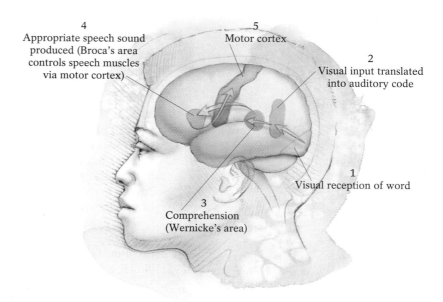

Figure 2–20 Specialization and Integration
Reading aloud requires the coordination of several brain areas. The arrows show the movement of information in the brain from the time a word is read until it is spoken.

1992). Think about it: What you experience as a continuous, indivisible stream of perception is actually but the visible tip of the information-processing iceberg, most of which lies beneath the surface of your conscious awareness.

To review, the mind's subsystems are localized in particular brain regions (Figure 2–21), yet the brain acts as a unified whole. Moving your hand; recognizing faces; even perceiving color, motion, and depth—all depend on specific neural networks. Yet complex functions such as language, learning, and loving involve the coordination of many brain areas. Both principles—specialization and integration—appear in research on the two brain hemispheres.

Figure 2–21 A Summary of Brain Structures and Their Functions

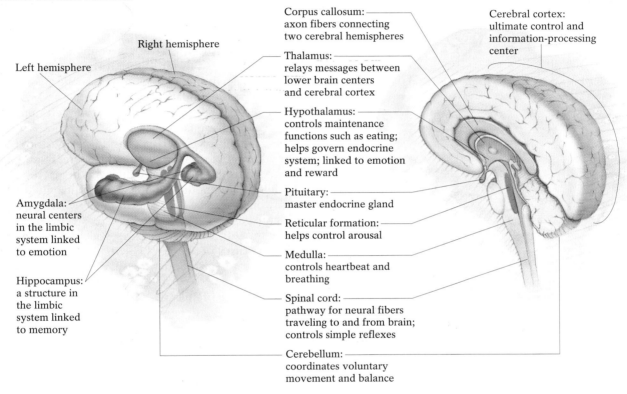

Right hemisphere

Left hemisphere

Corpus callosum: axon fibers connecting two cerebral hemispheres

Thalamus: relays messages between lower brain centers and cerebral cortex

Cerebral cortex: ultimate control and information-processing center

Hypothalamus: controls maintenance functions such as eating; helps govern endocrine system; linked to emotion and reward

Amygdala: neural centers in the limbic system linked to emotion

Pituitary: master endocrine gland

Reticular formation: helps control arousal

Medulla: controls heartbeat and breathing

Hippocampus: a structure in the limbic system linked to memory

Spinal cord: pathway for neural fibers traveling to and from brain; controls simple reflexes

Cerebellum: coordinates voluntary movement and balance

! *Rehearse It*

21. The motor cortex is the brain region that controls voluntary muscle movement. If a neurosurgeon stimulated your right motor cortex, you would most likely

a. see light.
b. hear a sound.
c. feel a touch on the right arm.
d. move your left leg.

22. The sensory cortex registers and processes body sensations, with the more sensitive body regions having the greatest representation. Which of the following has the greatest representation?

a. knee
b. toes
c. leg
d. thumb

23. About three-fourths of the cerebral cortex is not committed to any specific sensory or muscular function. The uncommitted areas are called

a. occipital lobes.
b. fissures.
c. association areas.
d. Wernicke's area.

24. Judging and planning are enabled by the

a. occipital lobes.
b. parietal lobes.
c. frontal lobes.
d. temporal lobes.

25. The area in the brain that, if damaged, might impair your speech is

a. Wernicke's area.
b. Broca's area. — speech
c. the left occipital lobe.
d. the angular gyrus.

Brain Reorganization

11. Is the brain capable of reorganizing itself if damaged?

If injury or illness destroys brain tissue, are its special functions forever lost? If you scrape your knee, new cells will generate to repair the damage. Not so with the neurons of the central nervous system. If the spinal cord is severed or if brain tissue is destroyed, the injured neurons normally will not regenerate. That's the bad news. The good news is the brain's **plasticity**, or capacity for modification. When one brain area is damaged, other areas may take over some of its functions. Nearby neurons may partly compensate for the damage by making new connections that replace the lost ones. These new connections are one way the brain struggles to recover from, say, a minor stroke.

Our brains are most plastic when we are young children—before cortical regions' functions become fixed (Kolb, 1989). If the speech areas of an infant's left hemisphere are damaged, the right hemisphere will take over much of its customary language function, apparently by making good use of the neuron surplus in a young child's brain. After age 5, however, left hemisphere damage permanently and severely disrupts language.

As an extreme example of plasticity, consider a 5-year-old boy whose severe seizures, caused by a deteriorating left hemisphere, required removing the *entire* hemisphere. Astonishingly, the individual was at last report an executive. Half his skull is filled with nothing but cerebrospinal fluid—functionally it might as well be sawdust—yet he has scored well above average on intelligence tests, completed college, and attended graduate school part-time (Smith & Sugar, 1975; A. Smith, 1987). Although paralyzed on the right side, this man (along with other such cases of "hemispherectomy") testifies to the brain's extraordinary powers of reorganization when damaged before it is fully developed.

Could we enhance the brain's self-repair by transplanting brain tissue? Even in this era of skin grafts and heart transplants, transplanting neural tissue still sounds like science fiction. But in experiments with animals, neuroscientists are now trying, with some success, to mend the brain by replacing destroyed nerve cells with healthy ones (Dunnett, 1989; Gash & others, 1986). In one dramatic experiment, Randy Labbe and her colleagues (1983) found that brain-damaged rats learned a maze twice as fast if given tissue from the corresponding brain areas of rat fetuses.

Might transplants of brain tissue someday enable neurosurgeons to repair the human brain? The tremors of Parkinson's disease and the progressive deterioration of Alzheimer's disease, for example, involve a degeneration of brain tissue that normally produces vital neurotransmitters—dopamine in Parkinson's disease, acetylcholine in Alzheimer's. If we transplanted dopamine-producing tissue into the brains of Parkinson's patients, would the tissue survive and release the needed neurotransmitters? Using such tissue from patients' own adrenal glands or from miscarried fetuses, experimental surgery on dozens of patients in Sweden, Mexico, the United States, and elsewhere has raised hopes that it might.

Our Divided Brains

For more than a century, clinical evidence has shown that the brain's two sides serve differing functions. Accidents, strokes, and tumors in the left hemisphere generally impair reading, writing, speaking, arithmetic reasoning, and under-

Question: If your Broca's area were damaged, could you write a letter? (See page 60.)

plasticity   The brain's capacity for modification, as evident in brain reorganization following damage (especially in children) and in experiments on the effects of experience on brain development.

standing. Similar lesions in the right hemisphere do not have such dramatic effects. Small wonder, then, that the left hemisphere became known as the "dominant" or "major" hemisphere, and its silent companion to the right as the "subordinate" or "minor" hemisphere. The left, verbal hemisphere is rather like the moon's facing side—the one easiest to observe and study. The other side is there, of course, but less visibly noticeable. (With some left-handers, speech is processed in the right hemisphere.) Fascinating experiments on the brain's two hemispheres reveal, however, that each hemisphere serves important functions.

Splitting the Brain

12. What is a split brain, and what does it reveal about brain functioning?

In 1961, two Los Angeles neurosurgeons, Philip Vogel and Joseph Bogen, were considering surgery for several patients who suffered from epilepsy. The surgeons speculated that major epileptic seizures were caused by an amplification of abnormal brain activity that reverberated between the two hemispheres. They therefore wondered whether they might control severe epilepsy by cutting communication between the hemispheres. To do so, the surgeons would have to sever the **corpus callosum**, the wide band of axon fibers connecting the two hemispheres (Figure 2–22).

Figure 2–22 The Corpus Callosum *This large band of neural fibers connects the two brain hemispheres. To photograph the half brain shown here, the hemispheres were separated by cutting through the corpus callosum and lower brain regions.*

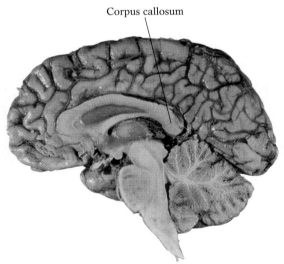

Corpus callosum

corpus callosum [KOR-pus kah-LOW-sum] The largest bundle of neural fibers connecting and carrying messages between the two brain hemispheres.

split brain A condition in which the two hemispheres of the brain are isolated by cutting the connecting fibers (mainly those of the corpus callosum) between them.

They had reason to believe such an operation would not be incapacitating. Psychologists Roger Sperry, Ronald Myers, and Michael Gazzaniga had divided the brains of cats and monkeys in this manner, without serious ill effects. So Vogel and Bogen operated. The result? The seizures were nearly eliminated and the patients were surprisingly normal, their personalities and intellect hardly affected. Waking from the surgery, one patient even managed to quip that he had a "splitting headache" (Gazzaniga, 1967).

If you chatted with one of these **split-brain** patients you probably would not notice anything unusual. You could understand why only a decade earlier neuropsychologist Karl Lashley jested that maybe the corpus callosum served only "to keep the hemispheres from sagging." But surely a broad band of 200 million nerve fibers capable of transferring more than a billion bits of information per second between the hemispheres must have a more significant purpose. It does, and the ingenious testing of these patients by psychologists Sperry and Gazzaniga revealed its purpose and provided a key to understanding the two hemispheres' special functions.

After one of the split-brain operations, the researchers placed an unseen object in a patient's left hand. He denied it was there. This came as no surprise to Sperry or Gazzaniga. They knew that information from the left hand went to the right hemisphere, and their animal experiments suggested that the right hemisphere would be unable to send this information to the left hemisphere (which in most humans controls speech). More extraordinary results came when Sperry and Gazzaniga conducted some perceptual tests.

Our eyes connect to our brains in such a way that, when we look straight ahead, the left half of our field of vision transmits through both eyes to our right hemisphere (Figure 2–23, page 60). Likewise, the right side of our field of

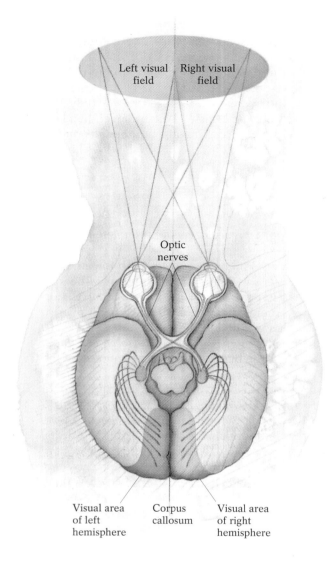

Left visual
field

Right visual
field

Optic
nerves

Visual area
of left
hemisphere

Corpus
callosum

Visual area
of right
hemisphere

Figure 2–23 The Information Highway From Eye to Brain *Information from the left half of your field of vision is received only by your right hemisphere, and information from the right half of your visual field is received only by your left hemisphere. (Note, however, that each eye receives sensory information from* both *the right and left visual fields.) The data received by either hemisphere are quickly transmitted to the other across the corpus callosum. In a split-brain patient with a severed corpus callosum, this information sharing does not take place.*

Answer to question on page 58: Yes. Broca's area produces a program for controlling the muscles of speech. If the area is damaged, a person can still understand speech and communicate through gestures or writing.

Question: If we flashed a red light to the right hemisphere of a split-brain patient and a green light to the left hemisphere, would each hemisphere observe its own color? Would the person be aware that the colors differ? What would the person report seeing? (Answers on page 63.)

vision transmits only to our left hemisphere. One woman, who had lost a vision-related part of her *right* hemisphere following a massive stroke but was otherwise normal, sometimes complained that nurses had not put dessert or coffee on her tray. A nurse would then turn the woman's head so that the tray came into view in the right half of her field of vision (where her *left* visual cortex could detect it). She then would say, "Oh, there it is—it wasn't there before" (Sacks, 1985, p. 73).

In those of us with healthy, intact brains, information presented only to our right hemisphere is quickly sent to our left hemisphere, which names it. But what happens in a person whose corpus callosum has been severed? To find out, experimenters ask a split-brain patient to look at a designated spot. Then they send information to either the left or right hemisphere (by flashing it to the spot's right or left). Finally, they quiz each hemisphere separately.

See if you can guess the results of an experiment using this procedure (Gazzaniga, 1967). While the patients stared at a dot, the word HEART was flashed across the visual field with HE in the left visual field and ART in the right. First, what did the patients *say* they saw? Second, asked to identify with their *left* hands what they had seen, did they *point* to HE or ART?

As Figure 2–24 shows, the patients *said* they saw ART and so were startled when their left hands *pointed* to HE. When given an opportunity to express itself, each hemisphere reported only what it had seen.

Similarly, when a picture of a spoon was flashed to the right hemisphere, the patients could not say what they saw; but when asked to identify what they had seen by feeling with their left hands an assortment of objects hidden behind a screen, they readily selected the spoon. If the experimenter said, "Right!" the patient might reply, "What? Right? How could I possibly pick out the right object when I don't know what I saw?" It is, of course, the left hemisphere doing the talking here, bewildered by what its other half knows. It is as if the patients have "two separate inner visual worlds," noted Sperry (1968). In a split-brain patient, each hemisphere truly has a mind of its own.

The left hemisphere, which acts as the brain's press agent, does mental gymnastics to rationalize reactions it does not understand (Figure 2–25). If the patient followed an order sent to the right hemisphere ("Walk"), the interpretive left hemisphere would offer a ready explanation ("I'm going into the house

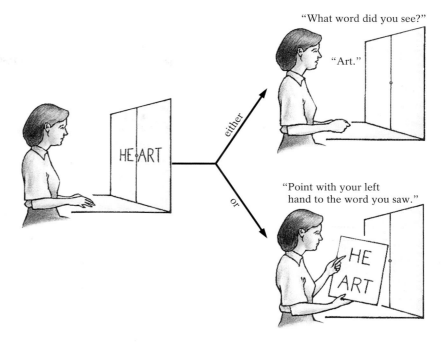

"Look at the dot."

"What word did you see?"

"Art."

either

or

"Point with your left hand to the word you saw."

Figure 2–24 Testing the Divided Brain *When an experimenter flashes the word HEART across the visual field, the split-brain patient reports seeing the portion of the word transmitted to her left hemisphere. However, if asked to indicate with her left hand what she saw, she points to the portion of the word transmitted to her right hemisphere. (From Gazzaniga, 1983.)*

"Do not let your left hand know what your right hand is doing."

Matthew 6:3

Figure 2–25 The Rationalizing Brain *When an experimenter flashes simple commands to the right hemisphere of a split-brain patient, she complies. Asked about her response, her left hemisphere, which controls speech and is unaware of what the right hemisphere has seen, invents—and seemingly believes—plausible explanations for what it does not comprehend. Thus, Michael Gazzaniga (1988) concludes that the left hemisphere is an "interpreter" that instantly constructs theories to explain our behavior. (From Gazzaniga, 1983.)*

to get a Coke"). Thus, Michael Gazzaniga (1988) concludes that the left hemisphere is an "interpreter" that instantly constructs theories to explain our behavior.

These experiments demonstrate that the right hemisphere understands simple requests and easily perceives objects. The right hemisphere's perceptual superiority is apparent in one of Sperry's films. A split-brain patient's left hand (directed by the right hemisphere) easily rearranges some blocks to match a drawing. When the right hand (directed by the left hemisphere) tries to perform the same perceptual task, it makes many errors. The bumbling performance frustrates the right hemisphere, which is observing all this. So it triggers the left hand to interrupt the bumbling right hand, but the persistent right hand pushes the left hand away. Outside the laboratory, a few split-brain patients have been for a time bothered by the unruly independence of their left hand, which would unbutton a shirt while the right hand buttoned it. It was as if each hemisphere was thinking "I've half a mind to wear my green (blue) shirt today." Indeed, said Sperry (1964), split-brain surgery leaves people "with two separate minds." (Reading these reports, I fantasize a split-brain person enjoying a solitaire game of "rocks, paper, and scissors"—left hand versus right hand.)

RUB

"What was the command?"

"Oh . . itch."

THE FAR SIDE

*You're a right-brained sort of person,
Mr. Sommersby—very creative, artistic, etc. . . .
Unfortunately, I think I also see why you're having
trouble figuring out your gas mileage."*

Tests reveal that about 95 percent of right-handers process speech primarily in the left hemisphere (Springer & Deutsch, 1994). Left-handers are more diverse. More than half process speech in the left hemisphere, as right-handers do. About one-quarter process language in the right hemisphere; the other quarter use both hemispheres more or less equally. Such left-handers may therefore require better communication between the hemispheres. This might explain the discovery that the corpus callosum averages 11 percent larger in left-handers (Witelson, 1985).

Studying Hemispheric Differences in the Intact Brain

What about the 99.99+ percent of us with undivided brains? Have scientists found our hemispheres similarly specialized? They have indeed, in several different types of studies. For example, when a person performs a *perceptual* task, brain waves, blood flow, and brain glucose consumption reveal increased activity in the *right* hemisphere; when a person speaks or calculates, activity increases in the *left* hemisphere.

On occasion, hemispheric specialization has been even more dramatically shown by briefly sedating an entire hemisphere. To check for the locus of language before surgery, a physician may inject a sedative into the neck artery that feeds blood to the hemisphere on its side of the body. Before the drug is injected, the patient is lying down, arms in the air, conversing easily. Can you predict what happens when the drug flows into the artery going to the left hemisphere? Within seconds, the right arm falls limp and, assuming the person's left hemisphere controls language, the subject becomes speechless until the drug wears off. When the drug goes into the artery to the right hemisphere, the *left* arm falls limp, but speech is still possible.

Other tests confirm hemispheric specialization. Most people recognize pictures faster and more accurately when flashed to the right hemisphere, but recognize words faster and more accurately when flashed to the left hemisphere. If a word is flashed to your right hemisphere, perception takes a fraction of a second longer—the length of time it takes to send the information through the corpus callosum to the more verbal left hemisphere.

Finally, which hemisphere would you suppose enables sign language among the deaf? Is it the right hemisphere, because of its visual-spatial superiority? Or the left, because of its preparedness to process language? Studies reveal that just as hearing people use the left hemisphere to process speech, deaf people use the left hemisphere to read signs (Corina & others, 1992). A stroke in the left hemisphere therefore disrupts a deaf person's ability to sign much as it would disrupt a hearing person's use of spoken language. To the brain, language is language, whether spoken or signed.

So, a variety of observations—of people with "split" brains and people with "normal" brains—converge beautifully. There is now little doubt that we have unified brains with specialized parts. Although language requires the left hemisphere, the right hemisphere helps us modulate our speech to make meaning clear—asking "What's that in the road ahead?" instead of "What's that in the road, a head?" (Heller, 1990). From looking at the two hemispheres, which

PET Scan Images of Hemispheric Differences
These PET scans show how active the right hemisphere becomes when the subject is listening to music (right) compared with resting (left). Red signifies the most activity, blue the least.

Answers to questions on page 60: Yes. No. Green.

look alike to the naked eye, who would suppose that they contribute so uniquely to the harmony of the whole?

We have glimpsed the truth of our overriding principle: Everything psychological is simultaneously biological. This chapter has focused on some ways in which our thoughts, feelings, and actions arise from our specialized yet integrated brain. Chapters to come will further explore the significance of the biological revolution in psychology. We will see, for example, how

- brain development underlies a child's mental development.
- genes and experience jointly influence our personality, emotions, gender, and intelligence.
- our sense organs and brains enable us to see and hear.
- the brain records memories.
- abnormal brain anatomy and chemistry influence depression and schizophrenia, and how biological treatments can alleviate these conditions.
- our brains and bodies work to create our experiences of hunger and sexuality, anger and fear, sleep and dreams.
- mind and body together influence our vulnerability to disease and our capacity for healing.
- our species' evolutionary history may predispose us to hurt, help, or sexually love certain others.

From nineteenth-century phrenology to today's neuroscience we have come a long way. Yet what is unknown still dwarfs what is known. We can describe the brain. We can learn the functions of its parts. We can study how the parts communicate. But how does this electrochemical whir give rise to a feeling of elation, a creative idea, or a memory of Grandmother's freshly baked cookies? The mind seeking to understand the brain—that is indeed the ultimate scientific challenge.

"If the human brain were so simple that we could understand it, we would be so simple that we couldn't."

Emerson M. Pugh, quoted by George E. Pugh *The Biological Origin of Human Values*, 1977

Rehearse It

26. Plasticity refers to the brain's ability to reorganize itself after damage. Especially plastic are the brains of
a. split-brain patients.
b. young adults.
c. young children.
d. right-handed people.

27. The brain structure that enables the right and left hemispheres to communicate is
a. the medulla.
b. Broca's area.
c. Wernicke's area.
d. the corpus callosum.

28. An experimenter flashes the word HERON across the visual field of a split-brain patient. HER is transmitted to his right hemisphere and ON to his left hemisphere. When asked to indicate what he saw, the patient
a. *says* he saw HER but *points* to ON.
b. *says* he saw ON but *points* to HER.
c. *says* he saw HERON but *points* to HER.
d. *says* he saw HERON but *points* to ON.

29. The study of split-brain patients has allowed us to observe the special functions of each brain hemisphere. The left hemisphere excels in

a. processing language.
b. visual perceptions.
c. recognition of emotion.
d. recognition of faces.

30. Damage to the brain's right hemisphere is most likely to reduce a person's ability to
a. recite the alphabet rapidly.
b. recognize the emotional content of facial expressions.
c. understand verbal instructions.
d. solve arithmetic problems.

Left Brain/Right Brain

"Error flies from mouth to mouth, from pen to pen, and to destroy it takes ages."

Voltaire, 1694–1778

You've heard or read it many times: Some people are "left-brained," others "right-brained." Leaping from the new research on split and intact brains, educators, management advisers, and self-help writers urge us to harness our undeveloped half brain. Are you lacking in creativity, music appreciation, or emotional empathy? Well, get your brain in balance. Awaken your dormant right hemisphere. Advocate "whole brain" education in your schools. Unleash intuitive, right-brained management from the chains of cold logic and statistics. Try *Drawing on the Right Side of the Brain* (the title of a million-copy best-seller translated into 10 languages).

What should we make of all this? By calling my friend Elsie "right-brained" have I explained why she's such a zany free spirit? And why her "left-brained" husband Bill is so coolly analytical? We've seen that research does show that each hemisphere serves special functions. But neuroscientists offer a caution flag: Beware the fad of locating complex human abilities such as science or art in either hemisphere. "The left-right dichotomy in cognitive mode is an idea with which it is very easy to run wild," warned Sperry (1982). Complex activities such as doing science or creating art require the integrated activity of both hemispheres. Even when we just read a story, both hemispheres are active—the left processing the words and finding meaning, the right appreciating humor, imagery, and emotional content (Hellige, 1993; Levy, 1985).

Why, then, do the popularizations of brain research so greatly exaggerate the findings? In *The Left-Hander Syndrome*, University of British Columbia psychologist Stanley Coren (1993) illustrates how journalism often oversimplifies and embellishes science. He recalls hearing a convention talk by Doreen Kimura, a psychologist at the University of Western Ontario in London, Ontario. Kimura reported that melodies fed to the left ear were more easily recognized than melodies fed to the right ear. Knowing that the left ear sends most of its information to the right hemisphere, she concluded that, among her right-handed student volunteers, the right brain was better at recognizing melodies.

A few days later, the *New York Times* reported that "Doreen Kimura, a psychologist from London, Ontario, has found that musical *ability* is controlled by the right side of the brain" (italics highlight the embellishment). Apparently drawing from the *Times* story, a syndicated newspaper story then reported that "London psychologist, Dr. Doreen Kimura, claims that musicians are right-brained!" (But Kimura studied university students, not musicians.) Later, a follow-up newspaper article further distorted the study: "An English psychologist has finally explained why there are so many great left-handed musicians. Dr. Doreen Kimura has found. . . ."

Knowing that Kimura is not English, did not study musicians, and did not study left-handers, Coren recalled the words of an American editor: "Everything you read in the newspaper is absolutely true, except for the rare story of which you happen to have first-hand knowledge."

What can happen is this: As information flows from scientist to reader, it gets simplified and embellished, much as gossip does in passing from one person to the next. A TV network picks up an interesting finding, reduces it to a 30-second report with an 11-second sound bite from the researcher. This alerts a major newspaper to a story angle, which in turn gets picked up by popular science magazines and, eventually, by supermarket magazines and tabloids.

At each step, notes Coren, "Ideas become more speculative and more distant from the actual research. . . . After a while, the neuropsychologist is no longer even visible in the communication chain." Eventually, the rumors grow, accumulate, and evolve into scientific myths that become "'accepted truths,' which show up in conversation and writing in sentences that begin with, 'As everybody knows . . . ,' or 'Scientists have shown that. . . .'" In the end, sighs Coren, the public myth drowns the weak voices of dissenting scientists.

The moral is not to disbelieve everything you read. Rather, beware that reporters want their stories to be newsworthy. At their best, their ideal (and mine, in writing this book) is to extract the essence—to simplify without oversimplifying. At their worst, they distort pretzel-shaped findings into a breadstick-shaped story: Some people are left-brained, others right-brained. . . .

Reviewing *Neuroscience and Behavior*

1. Why do psychologists study biology?

As a first step in understanding our behavior and mental processes, students of psychology examine the biological roots of how we think, feel, and act.

Neural Communication

2. What are neurons, and how do they transmit information?

The body's circuitry, the nervous system, consists of billions of nerve cells, called neurons. Neurons receive signals from external stimuli and from other neurons through their branching dendrites and cell bodies. They then combine these signals in the cell body and transmit electrical impulses (as an "action potential") down their axons.

3. How do nerve cells communicate?

When electrical signals reach the end of the axon, they stimulate the release of chemical messengers, called neurotransmitters. These molecules traverse the tiny synaptic gap between neurons and combine with receptor sites on neighboring neurons, thus passing on their excitatory or inhibitory messages.

4. How do neurotransmitters influence human behavior?

Dozens of different neurotransmitters have been discovered, and the functions of some have become well-understood. Learning about endorphins, the feel-good neurotransmitters, has helped us understand how drugs affect our brain chemistry.

Neural and Hormonal Systems

5. What are the major divisions of the nervous system, and what are their basic functions?

The central nervous system's neurons in the brain and spinal cord communicate with the peripheral nervous system's sensory and motor neurons. The peripheral nervous system has two main divisions. The skeletal nervous system directs voluntary movements and reflexes. The autonomic nervous system, through its sympathetic and parasympathetic divisions, controls our involuntary muscles and the glands of our endocrine system.

6. How does the endocrine system transmit information?

Hormones released by endocrine glands travel through the bloodstream and affect other tissues, including the brain. The endocrine system's master gland, the pituitary, influences hormone release by other glands.

The Brain

7. What functions do the brainstem and its associated structures serve?

Within the brainstem, the medulla controls heartbeat and breathing, and the reticular formation controls arousal. The cerebellum, which is attached to the rear of the brainstem, coordinates muscle movement. On top of the brainstem is the thalamus, the brain's sensory switchboard.

8. What functions do the structures within the limbic system serve?

The limbic system has been linked primarily to memory, emotions, and drives. For example, one of its neural centers, the amygdala, is involved in aggressive and fearful responses. Another, the hypothalamus, has been linked to various bodily maintenance functions and to pleasurable rewards. The hypothalamus also controls the endocrine system.

9. How is the cerebral cortex organized?

The cerebral cortex is a thin, wrinkled sheet of neurons with trillions of interconnections. Each of the hemispheres it covers can be viewed as having four geographical areas: the frontal, parietal, occipital, and temporal lobes, which are separated by fissures, or grooves.

10. What functions are served by the cerebral cortex?

Small, well-defined regions within the cerebral lobes control muscle movement (the motor cortex) and receive information from the body senses (the sensory cortex). However, most of the cortex—its association areas—is uncommitted to such functions and is therefore free to process other information.

Some brain regions are known to serve specific functions. In general, however, human emotions, thoughts, and behaviors result from the intricate coordination of many brain areas. Language, for example, depends on a chain of events in several brain regions.

11. Is the brain capable of reorganizing itself if damaged?

If one hemisphere is damaged early (the first 5 years) in life, the other will pick up many of its functions, thus demonstrating the brain's plasticity. Unfortunately, the brain is less plastic later in life. However, nearby neurons can often at least partially compensate for damaged ones, as when a patient recovers from a minor stroke.

12. What is a split brain, and what does it reveal about brain functioning?

A split brain is one whose corpus callosum, the bundle of nerve fibers connecting the two brain hemispheres, has been severed. Clinical observations long ago revealed that the left cerebral hemisphere is crucial for language. More recent experiments on split-brain patients have refined our knowledge of each hemisphere's special functions. By testing the two hemispheres separately, researchers have confirmed that for most people the left hemisphere is indeed the more verbal, and that the right hemisphere excels in visual perception and the recognition of emotion. Studies of normal people with intact brains confirm that each hemisphere makes unique contributions to the integrated functioning of the brain.

Terms and Concepts to Remember

biological psychology, p. 36

neuron, p. 36

dendrite, p. 36

axon, p. 36

myelin [MY-uh-lin] sheath, p. 36

action potential, p. 36

threshold, p. 37

synapse [SIN-aps], p. 37

neurotransmitters, p. 38

acetylcholine [ah-seat-el-KO-leen] (ACh), p. 39

endorphins [en-DOR-fins], p. 39

nervous system, p. 41

central nervous system (CNS), p. 41

peripheral nervous system (PNS), p. 41

nerves, p. 41

sensory neurons, p. 41

interneurons, p. 41

motor neurons, p. 41

skeletal nervous system, p. 41

autonomic [aw-tuh-NAHM-ik] nervous system, p. 42

sympathetic nervous system, p. 42

parasympathetic nervous system, p. 42

reflex, p. 42

endocrine [EN-duh-krin] system, p. 43

hormones, p. 43

adrenal [ah-DREEN-el] glands, p. 44

pituitary gland, p. 44

brainstem, p. 45

medulla [muh-DUL-uh], p. 45

lesion [LEE-zhuhn], p. 46

electroencephalogram (EEG), p. 46

CAT (computerized axial tomograph) scan, p. 47

PET (positron emission tomograph) scan, p. 47

MRI (magnetic resonance imaging), p. 47

reticular formation, p. 48

thalamus [THAL-uh-muss], p. 48

cerebellum [sehr-uh-BELL-um], p. 48

limbic system, p. 49

amygdala [ah-MIG-dah-la], p. 49

hypothalamus [hi-po-THAL-uh-muss], p. 50

cerebral [seh-REE-bruhl] cortex, p. 51

frontal lobes, p. 52

parietal [puh-RYE-uh-tuhl] lobes, p. 52

occipital [ahk-SIP-uh-tuhl] lobes, p. 52

temporal lobes, p. 52

motor cortex, p. 52

sensory cortex, p. 53

association areas, p. 54

aphasia, p. 55

Broca's area, p. 55

Wernicke's area, p. 55

plasticity, p. 58

corpus callosum [KOR-pus kah-LOW-sum], p. 59

split brain, p. 59

Rehearse It Answer Key

1. b.	2. a.	3. c.	4. d.	5. c.	6. b.	7. d.	8. c.	9. a.
10. b.	11. a.	12. a.	13. b.	14. a.	15. c.	16. d.	17. b.	18. d.
19. c.	20. b.	21. d.	22. d.	23. c.	24. c.	25. b.	26. c.	27. d.
28. b.	29. a.	30. b.						

Critical Thinking Exercise

Now that you have read and reviewed Chapter 2, take your learning a step further by testing your critical thinking skills on this pattern recognition exercise.

Playing a musical instrument is a complicated skill that involves every major aspect of behavior and cognition. To be proficient, musicians must have honed their fine motor skills. In addition, many aspects of thinking come into play, including *memory* of how to play the instrument and of musical scales and time signatures, and the planning and *decision making* inherent in translating a piece of sheet music into sound. Equally important are the musician's *motivation* and *emotion*, which influence many aspects of a musical performance.

In this exercise you will develop a map describing how various parts of the brain enable a musician to perform a piece of music. Using the following grid, identify three lower level brain structures and three brain structures of the cerebral cortex and then describe how each structure is involved in musical performance.

Brain Structures	How the Structures Are Involved in Musical Performance
Lower Level Structures	
1.	1.
2.	2.
3.	3.
Structures of the Cerebral Cortex	
1.	1.
2.	2.
3.	3.

Check your progress on becoming a critical thinker by comparing your answers to the sample answers found in Appendix B.

For Further Information

You can find more information regarding neuroscience on the following text pages:

Brain activity and
- aggression, pp. 501–503
- development, pp. 74–75
- dreams, pp. 171–174
- emotion, p. 338
- hunger, p. 302
- memory, pp. 235–239
- psychosurgery, p. 474
- sensation, Chapter 4
- sex, p. 314
- sleep, pp. 165–168
- stress and health, Chapter 10

Genes and
- aggression, p. 501
- depression, p. 430
- development, pp. 108–111, 170–171
- intelligence, pp. 285–287
- learning, pp. 202–203
- obesity, p. 307–308
- schizophrenia, pp. 438–439

Hormones and
- aggression, p. 502
- development, pp. 71, 88–89
- emotion, p. 336

- hunger, p. 302
- memory, p. 237
- sex, pp. 313–314
- stress, pp. 357–358, 361

Neurotransmitters and
- depression, p. 430
- drugs, pp. 182–187
- exercise, pp. 368–369
- hunger, p. 302
- memory, pp. 236–237
- smoking, p. 185
- therapy, pp. 471–473

Chapter 3

The Developing Person

Prenatal Development and the Newborn

From Life Comes Life

The Competent Newborn

Infancy and Childhood

Physical Development

Cognitive Development

Social Development

Gender and Child-Rearing

Adolescence

Physical Development

Cognitive Development

Social Development

Adulthood

Physical Changes

Cognitive Changes

Social Changes

Reflections on the Major Developmental Issues

Nature and Nurture

Continuity and Stages

Stability and Change

In mid-1978, the newest astonishment in medicine, covering all the front pages, was the birth of an English baby nine months after conception in a dish. The older surprise, which should still be fazing us all, is that a solitary sperm and a single egg can fuse and become a human being under any circumstance, and that, however implanted, [this multiplied] cell affixed to the uterine wall will grow and differentiate into eight pounds of baby; this has been going on under our eyes for so long a time that we've gotten used to it; hence the outcries of amazement at this really minor technical modification of the general procedure—nothing much, really, beyond relocating the beginning of the process from the fallopian tube to a plastic container.

Lewis Thomas
The Medusa and Snail, 1979

1. What are the major issues in developmental psychology?

The developing person is no less a wonder after birth than in the womb. Physically, mentally, socially, we are always in the process of becoming. As we journey through life from womb to tomb, when and how do we change? Usually we notice how we differ. To **developmental psychologists**, who study physical, mental, and social changes throughout the human life cycle, our commonalities are just as important. Virtually all of us began walking around age 1 and talking by age 2. As children we all engaged in social play in preparation for life's serious work. As adults, we all smile and cry, love and loathe, and occasionally ponder the fact that someday we will die.

Human development is a lifelong process. Psychology's developmental perspective examines how people are continually developing, from infancy through old age. Much of its research centers on three major issues:

1. *Nature/nurture:* How much is human development influenced by our genetic inheritance (our *nature*) and how much by our experience (the *nurture* we receive)?

2. *Continuity/stages:* Is development a gradual, continuous process, or does it proceed through a sequence of separate stages, like climbing separate steps?

developmental psychology A branch of psychology that studies physical, cognitive, and social change throughout the life span.

It Runs in the Family   *Whitney Houston (left), her aunt Dionne Warwick (right), and her mother Cissy Houston, a gospel singer (center), have all made their mark in the world of music. The existence of such exceptional talent across generations raises intriguing questions about the relative impact of our genes and our experience, and how they interact.*

3.   *Stability/change:* Do our early personality traits persist through life, or do we become different persons as we age?

At the chapter's end we will reflect on these three developmental issues. But first, our main agenda: to examine human development across the life span, beginning where life begins and ending where life ends.

Prenatal Development and the Newborn

From Life Comes Life

2. How does life develop before birth?

Nothing is more natural than a species reproducing itself. Yet nothing is more wondrous. Consider human reproduction. The process starts when a woman's ovary releases a mature egg, a cell roughly the size of the period at the end of this sentence, and the 200 million or more sperm deposited during intercourse begin their race upstream toward it.

Like space voyagers approaching a huge planet, the sperm approach a cell 85,000 times their own size. The relatively few sperm that make it to the egg release digestive enzymes that eat away the egg's protective coating, allowing a sperm to penetrate (Figure 3–1). But the egg is hardly passive. Rather, as soon as one sperm begins to penetrate, an electric charge shoots across the egg's surface, blocking out all other sperm during the minute or so that it takes the egg to form a protective barrier. Meanwhile, fingerlike projections sprout around the successful sperm and pull it inward. The egg nucleus and the sperm nucleus move toward each other and, before half a day elapses, fuse. The two have become one.

When egg and sperm unite, the 23 **chromosomes** carried in the egg pair up with the 23 chromosomes brought to it by the sperm. These 46 chromosomes contain the master plan for your body. Each chromosome is composed of long

chromosomes   Threadlike structures made of DNA molecules that contain the genes.

DNA (deoxyribonucleic acid)   A complex molecule containing the genetic information that makes up the chromosomes.

X chromosome   The sex chromosome found in both men and women. Females have two X chromosomes; males have one. An X chromosome from each parent produces a female.

Y chromosome   The sex chromosome found only in males. Paired with an X sex chromosome from the mother, it produces a male child.

testosterone   The most important of the male sex hormones. Both males and females have it, but the additional testosterone in males stimulates the growth of the male sex organs in the fetus and the development of the male sex characteristics during puberty.

zygote   The fertilized egg; it enters a 2-week period of rapid cell division and develops into an embryo.

Figure 3–1 The Union of Egg and Sperm *(a) A hoard of sperm cells surround a huge ovum. (b) As a sperm penetrates an egg's jelly-like outer coating, a series of chemical events begin that will cause sperm and egg to fuse into a single cell. If all goes well, that cell will subdivide again and again to emerge 9 months later as a 100-trillion-cell human being.*

(a)

(b)

threads of a molecule called **DNA (deoxyribonucleic acid)**. DNA in turn is made of thousands of *genes*, functional segments capable of synthesizing specific proteins (the biochemical building blocks of life).

Sex Chromosomes, Sex Hormones, and Gender

Males and females are variations on a single form. Eight weeks after conception, they are anatomically indistinguishable. Then, our genes activate our biological sex. Your sex is determined by your twenty-third pair of chromosomes, the sex chromosomes. The member of the pair that came from your mother was an **X chromosome**. From your father, you received either an X chromosome, making you a girl, or a **Y chromosome**, making you a boy. The Y chromosome contains a single gene that throws a master switch triggering the testes to develop and produce the principal male hormone, **testosterone**, which in turn triggers the development of external male sex organs.

What do you suppose happens when glandular malfunction or hormone injections expose a female embryo to excess testosterone? These genetically female infants are born with masculine-appearing genitals, which can be corrected surgically. Until puberty, such females typically act in more aggressive "tomboyish" ways than most girls, and they dress and play in ways more typical of boys than of girls (Berenbaum & Hines, 1992; Ehrhardt, 1987). Given a choice of toys, they (like boys) play with cars and blocks rather than with dolls and crayons.

Is their behavior due to the prenatal hormones? If so, may we conclude that biological sex differences produce behavioral gender differences? Experiments with many species, from rats to monkeys, confirm that female embryos given male hormones will later exhibit more masculine appearance and behavior (Hines & Green 1991). But these girls frequently look masculine and are known to be "different," so perhaps people also treat them more like boys. Early exposure to sex hormones thus affects us both directly (physically) and indirectly—by influencing experiences that shape us. Biological appearances have social consequences.

Prenatal Development

It was your luckiest of moments: Among 200 million sperm, the one needed to make you, in combination with that one particular egg, won the race. But even then, your destiny was not assured. Fewer than half of fertilized eggs, called **zygotes**, survive beyond the first 2 weeks (Grobstein, 1979).

But for you and me good fortune prevailed. Beginning as one cell, each of us became two cells, then four—each cell just like the first. Then, within the first week, when this cell division had produced a zygote of some 100 cells, the cells began to *differentiate*—to specialize in structure and function. About 10 days after conception, the increasingly diverse cells became attached to the mother's uterine wall, beginning approximately 37 weeks of the closest human relationship.

"From the very moment that the sperm hits the egg, a precarious trip on the thin edge of biological extinction has begun."

Ralph Blair
Nevertheless Joy!, 1989

(a)   (b)   (c)   (d)

Figure 3–2 Prenatal development. *(a) The embryo grows and develops rapidly. At 40 days, the spine is visible and the arms and legs are beginning to grow. (b) Five days later the inch-long embryo's proportions have begun to change. The rest of the body is now bigger than the head, and the arms and legs have grown noticeably. (c) By the end of the second month, when the fetal period begins, facial features, hands, and feet have formed. (d) As the fetus enters the fourth month, it weighs about 3 ounces.*

Prenatal development

zygote: conception to 2 weeks
embryo: 2 weeks through 8 weeks
fetus: 9 weeks to birth

> "You shall conceive and bear a son. So then drink no wine or strong drink."
>
> Judges 13:7

embryo   The developing human organism from about 2 weeks after fertilization through the second month.

fetus   The developing human organism from 9 weeks after conception to birth.

teratogens   Agents, such as chemicals and viruses, that can reach the embryo or fetus during prenatal development and cause harm.

fetal alcohol syndrome (FAS)   Physical and cognitive abnormalities in children caused by a pregnant woman's heavy drinking. In severe cases, symptoms include noticeable facial misproportions.

rooting reflex   A baby's tendency, when touched on the cheek, to open the mouth and search for the nipple.

The zygote's outer part attaches to the uterine wall and becomes the placenta, through which nourishment passes. In this second prenatal stage, the inner cells become the **embryo** (Figure 3–2). During the next 6 weeks, the embryo's body organs begin to form and function. The heart begins to beat and the liver begins to make red blood cells.

By 9 weeks after conception, the embryo looks unmistakably human and is now a **fetus**. By the end of the sixth month, internal organs such as the stomach have become sufficiently formed and functional to allow a prematurely born fetus a chance of survival.

At each prenatal stage, genetic *and* environmental factors affect development. The placenta screens out many potentially harmful substances, while allowing nutrients and oxygen to pass through. But nourishment isn't all that passes the placental screen. Devastating effects may follow when the placenta admits **teratogens**—harmful agents, such as certain viruses and drugs. A pregnant woman never smokes alone. When she puffs on a cigarette, she and her fetus both experience reduced blood oxygen and a shot of nicotine. If she is a heavy smoker, her newborn probably will be underweight, sometimes dangerously so. If she is a heroin addict, her baby will be born a heroin addict. If she carries the AIDS virus, her baby may do so too.

When a pregnant woman takes a drink, alcohol enters her bloodstream—and her fetus's—and depresses activity in both their central nervous systems. If she drinks heavily, her baby will be at risk for birth defects and mental retardation. For 1 in 750 infants, the effects are visible as **fetal alcohol syndrome (FAS)**, which includes a small, misproportioned head and lifelong brain abnormalities, making it now the leading cause of mental retardation (Streissguth & others, 1988). Although there is no known safe amount of alcohol for a pregnant woman, children of alcoholic mothers are especially at risk. About 4 in 10 alcoholic mothers who drink during pregnancy have babies who suffer the enduring damage of fetal alcohol syndrome.

The Competent Newborn

3. What are some of the newborn's capabilities?

Having survived prenatal hazards, newborns come equipped with reflexes ideally suited for survival. Infants will withdraw a limb to escape pain. Put a cloth over their faces, interfering with their breathing, and they will turn their heads

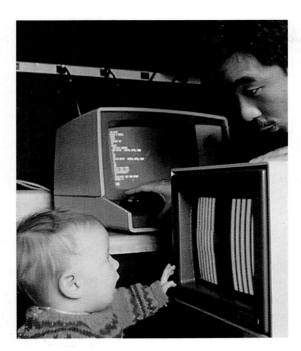

You've Come a Long Way, Baby *Studies like the one underway in this laboratory at M.I.T. are exploring infants' abilities to perceive and remember. Experiments show that young infants are capable of sophisticated visual discrimination and will look much longer at an unfamiliar than a familiar pattern. Such tests have changed psychologists' ideas of what the world looks like to a baby. The helpless infant of a generation ago has become today's "amazing newborn."*

from side to side and swipe at it. New parents are often awed by the coordinated sequence of reflexes by which babies get food. The **rooting reflex** illustrates this: When something touches their cheeks, babies will open their mouths and vigorously "root" for a nipple. Finding one, they will automatically close on it and begin sucking—which itself requires a coordinated sequence of tonguing, swallowing, and breathing. Failing to find satisfaction, the hungry baby may cry—a behavior parents are predisposed to find highly unpleasant to hear and very rewarding to relieve.

Moreover, psychologists have discovered that infants are born preferring sights and sounds that facilitate social responsiveness. Newborns turn their heads in the direction of human voices. They gaze longer at a drawing of a human face than at a bull's-eye pattern; yet they gaze more at a bull's-eye pattern—which has contrasts much like that of the human eye—than at a solid disk (Fantz, 1961). They prefer to look at objects 8 to 12 inches away, which, wonder of wonders, just happens to be the approximate distance between a nursing infant's eyes and its mother's (Maurer & Maurer, 1988).

Babies' perceptual abilities are continuously developing during the first months of life. Within days of birth, babies can distinguish their mothers' odor and voice. The infant's brain is an absorbent sponge, its neural networks stamped immediately with the smell of its mother's body. Thus, a week-old nursing baby, placed between a gauze pad from its mother's bra and one from another nursing mother, will usually turn toward the smell of its own mother's pad (MacFarlane, 1978). At 3 weeks of age, an infant who sucks on a pacifier that sometimes turns on recordings of its mother's voice and sometimes that of a female stranger will suck more vigorously when it hears its now-familiar mother's voice (Mills & Melhuish, 1974). Newborns can also learn to turn their heads to the left or right to receive a sugar solution when their forehead is stroked (Lancioni, 1980). So not only can young infants see what they need to see, and smell and hear well, but they are already using their sensory equipment to learn.

More and more, reports researcher Tiffany Field (1987), psychologists see the baby as "a very sophisticated perceiver of the world."

! *Rehearse It*

1. The life cycle begins when the egg nucleus and sperm fuse to create a new individual. The egg and sperm each contribute

a. one chromosome pair.
b. 23 chromosomes.
c. 23 chromosome pairs.
d. an XY chromosome.

2. The fertilized egg will develop into a boy if it receives

a. an X chromosome from its mother.
b. an X chromosome from its father.
c. a Y chromosome from its mother.
d. a Y chromosome from its father.

3. The 9 months of prenatal development prepare the individual for survival outside the womb. The body organs first begin to form and function during the period of the _____; within 6 months, during the period of the _____, the organs are sufficiently functional to allow a chance of survival.

a. zygote, embryo
b. zygote, fetus
c. embryo, fetus
d. placenta, fetus

4. Teratogens are chemicals that pass through the placenta's screen and may

harm an embryo or fetus. Which of the following is *not* a teratogen?

a. oxygen
b. heroin
c. alcohol
d. nicotine

5. Stroke a newborn's cheek and he or she will root for a nipple. This illustrates

a. a reflex.
b. sensorimotor learning.
c. perceptual ability.
d. a gender difference.

Infancy and Childhood

During infancy, a baby grows from newborn to toddler, and during childhood from toddler to teenager. Beginning with infancy and childhood and continuing with adolescence through old age, we will see how people of all ages develop—physically, cognitively, and socially.

Physical Development

4. How do the brain and motor skills develop during infancy and childhood?

Brain Development

While you resided in your mother's womb, your body was forming nerve cells at the rate of about one-quarter million per *minute*. On the day you were born you had essentially all the brain cells you will ever have. However, at birth the human nervous system is immature: After birth, the neural *networks* that enable us to walk, talk, and remember have a wild growth spurt (Figure 3–3). This lack of neural connections helps explain why our earliest memories seldom predate our third birthdays (Howe & Courage, 1993; Nelson, 1993).

The nervous system's development enables **maturation**, an orderly sequence of biological growth. Maturation decrees many of our commonalities: standing before walking, using nouns before adjectives. Experience, too, helps develop the brain's neural connections. Although "forgotten," early learning is not all erased. For example, the first few years are critical for learning language. Children who become deaf at age 2, after having been exposed to speech, are later more easily trained in sign language than those deaf from birth (Lenneberg, 1967).

How do early experiences leave their "marks" in the brain? Mark Rosenzweig and David Krech reared some young rats in solitary confinement and others in a communal playground (Figure 3–4). Rats living in the deprived environment usually developed a lighter and thinner brain cortex. Rosenzweig (1984; Renner & Rosenzweig, 1987) reported being so surprised by these effects of experience on brain tissue that he repeated the experiment several times before publishing his findings. These findings are consistent with what we know about the importance of active involvement for human development. These and other results have helped encourage improvement in the environments provided for laboratory, farm, and zoo animals—and for children in institutions. Several research teams have also found that infant rats and premature babies benefit from the stimulation of being touched or massaged (Field & oth-

> *"It is a rare privilege to watch the birth, growth, and first feeble struggles of a living human mind."*
>
> Annie Sullivan, in Helen Keller's *The Story of My Life*, 1903

| At birth | 3 months | 15 months |

Figure 3–3 Drawings of Human Brain Cerebral Cortex Sections *In humans, the brain is immature at birth. As the child matures, the neural networks grow increasingly more complex.*

maturation Biological growth processes that enable orderly changes in behavior, relatively uninfluenced by experience.

Figure 3–4 Experience Affects Brain Development *Mark Rosenzweig and David Krech reared rats either alone in an environment without playthings or with others in an environment enriched with playthings that were changed daily. In 14 of 16 repetitions of this basic experiment, the rats placed in the enriched environment developed significantly more cerebral cortex (relative to the rest of the brain's tissue) than did those in the impoverished environment. (From "Brain changes in response to experience" by M. R. Rosenzweig, E. L. Bennett, and M. C. Diamond. Copyright © 1972 Scientific American, Inc. All rights reserved.)*

Impoverished environment

Enriched environment

ers, 1986; Meaney & others, 1988). "Handled" infants of both species gain weight more rapidly and develop faster neurologically.

The brain's development does not end with childhood. Throughout life our neural tissue is changing. Sights and smells, touches and tugs activate and strengthen some neural pathways, while others weaken from disuse. Like pathways through a forest, less traveled paths are abandoned, popular paths are broadened. Our genes dictate our overall brain architecture, but experience directs the details. If a monkey is trained to push a lever with a finger several thousand times a day, the brain tissue that controls the finger changes to reflect the experience. Human brains work similarly. The wiring of Michael Jordan's brain reflects the thousands of hours he has spent shooting baskets. Experience nurtures nature.

Motor Development

As the infant's muscles and nervous system mature, more complicated skills emerge. With minor exceptions, the sequence of these skills is universal. Babies roll over before they sit unsupported, and creep on all fours before walking.

But there are individual differences in timing of this sequence. In the United States, one in four babies walks by age 11 months, half within a week after their first birthday, and 90 percent by age 15 months (Frankenburg & others, 1992). Nurture may influence motor development. Ugandan babies usually walk by 10 months, after experiencing more intimate and rhythmic physical contact while being carried upright on the back (Bril, 1986).

But nature (genes) plays a major role. Identical twins typically begin sitting up and walking on nearly the same day (Wilson, 1979). Biological maturation—including the rapid development of the cerebellum at the brain's rear—creates a readiness to learn walking at about 1 year of age. Experience before that time has a limited effect. This is true for other physical skills, including bowel and bladder control. Until the necessary muscular and neural maturation occurs, no amount of pleading, harassment, or punishment will produce successful toilet training.

Cognitive Development

5. How did Piaget view the mind's development?

"Who knows the thoughts of a child?" wondered poet Nora Perry. As much as anyone of his generation, developmental psychologist Jean Piaget (pronounced Pee-ah-ZHAY) knew. His interest began in 1920, when he was working in Paris to develop questions for children's intelligence tests. While administering tests to find out at what age children could answer certain questions correctly, Piaget became intrigued by children's *wrong* answers. Where others saw childish mistakes, Piaget saw intelligence at work. The errors made by children of a given age, he noted, were often strikingly similar.

The half century Piaget spent with children convinced him that the child's mind is not a miniature model of the adult's. Young children understand the world in radically different ways than adults do, a fact that we sometimes overlook when teaching children. Piaget further believed that the child's mind develops through a series of stages, in an upward march from the newborn's simple reflexes to the adult's abstract reasoning power. An 8-year-old child therefore comprehends things that a 3-year-old cannot. An 8-year-old might grasp the analogy "getting an idea is like having a light turn on in your head," but trying to teach the same analogy to a 3-year-old would be fruitless.

Piaget felt that the driving force behind this intellectual progression is our unceasing struggle to make sense of our experiences. To this end, the maturing

A Triumphant Toddler *Before 12-month-old Christopher achieved this major milestone, his motor development proceeded in the orderly sequence typical of infant locomotion. At about 6 to 7 months, most babies sit without support. At about 9 months, they stand and walk holding on. At about 1 year, they begin to walk unaided.*

Jean Piaget *"If we examine the intellectual development of the individual or of the whole of humanity, we shall find that the human spirit goes through a certain number of stages, each different from the other" (1930).*

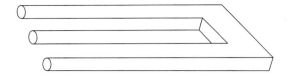

An Impossible Object *Look carefully at the "devil's tuning fork" above. Now look away—no, better first study it some more—and then look away and draw it. Not so easy, is it? Because this tuning fork is an impossible object, you have no schema for such an image.*

brain builds concepts, which Piaget called **schemas**. Schemas (or schemes) are mental molds into which we pour our experience. By adulthood we have built countless schemas that range from knowing how to tie a knot to our concept of love.

Piaget's Theory and Current Thinking on Cognitive Stages

Cognition refers to all the mental activities associated with thinking, knowing, and remembering. Piaget described cognitive development as occurring in four stages (Table 3–1). Developing children, he believed, experience spurts of change followed by greater stability as they move from one developmental plateau to the next. Each plateau has distinctive characteristics that permit specific kinds of thinking. To appreciate how the mind of a child grows, let's look at each of Piaget's stages in the light of current thinking about cognitive development.

Sensorimotor Stage During Piaget's **sensorimotor stage**, from birth to nearly age 2, babies understand the world through their sensory and motor interactions with objects—through looking, touching, mouthing, and grasping. At first they seem unaware that things continue to exist apart from their perceptions.

The Beginnings of Logical Thought *During the sensorimotor stage, from birth until about 2 years of age, children understand the world mainly through their actions and sensations. They enjoy smelling, feeling, and tasting almost anything they can get their hands on. As children reach the preoperational stage, which lasts from about 2 to 6 years of age, pretending becomes possible.*

TABLE 3–1		
Piaget's Stages of Cognitive Development		
Typical Age Range	**Description of Stage**	**Developmental Milestones**
Birth to nearly 2 years	*Sensorimotor* Experiencing the world through senses and actions (looking, touching, mouthing)	• Object permanence • Stranger anxiety
About 2 to 6 years	*Preoperational* Representing things with words and images but lacking logical reasoning	• Ability to pretend • Egocentrism
About 7 to 11 years	*Concrete operational* Thinking logically about concrete events; grasping concrete analogies and performing arithmetical operations	• Conservation • Mathematical transformations • Abstract logic
About 12 through adulthood	*Formal operational* Abstract reasoning	• Potential for mature moral reasoning

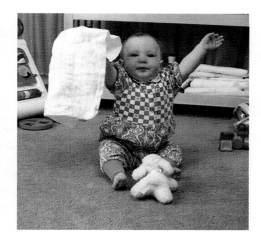

Object Permanence *Infants younger than 6 months seem not to understand that things continue to exist when they are out of sight. But for this infant, out of sight is definitely not out of mind.*

In one of his tests, Piaget would show an infant an appealing toy and then flop his beret over it to see whether the infant searched for the toy. Before the age of 6 months, they did not. They lacked **object permanence**—the awareness that objects continue to exist when not perceived. The infant lives in the present. What is out of sight is out of mind. By 8 months, infants exhibit memory for things no longer seen. Hide the toy and the infant will momentarily look for it. Within another month or two, the infant will look for it even after being restrained for several seconds.

But today's researchers wonder: Do children's cognitive abilities really grow through distinct stages? Does object permanence in fact blossom by 8 months, much as a tulip blossoms in spring? Researchers now see development more as a continuous process than a series of distinct stages as did Piaget. For example, they now view object permanence as unfolding gradually, beginning with young infants' looking for a toy where they saw it hidden a second before.

Consider a simple experiment. Karen Wynn (1992) showed 5-month-old infants one or two objects (Figure 3–5). Then she hid the objects behind a screen, sometimes removing or adding one through a trap door. When she lifted the screen, the infants sometimes did a double take, staring longer when shown a wrong number of objects.

Babies show an intuitive grasp not only of number but also of simple laws of physics. For example, they look longer when viewing an unexpected scene of a car seeming to pass through a solid object or a ball stopping in midair (Baillargeon, 1992; Spelke & others, 1992; Wellman & Gelman, 1992). Clearly, then, they are more capable of conceptual thinking than Piaget realized.

schema A concept or framework that organizes and interprets information.

cognition All the mental activities associated with thinking, knowing, and remembering.

sensorimotor stage In Piaget's theory, the stage (from birth to about 2 years of age) during which infants know the world mostly in terms of their sensory impressions and motor activities.

object permanence The awareness that things continue to exist even when not perceived.

Sequence of events 2–1 = 1 or 2

1. Objects placed in case.	2. Screen comes up.	3. Empty hand enters.	4. One object removed.

Then either: possible outcome
5. Screen drops…   revealing one object.

or: impossible outcome
5. Screen drops…   revealing two objects.

Figure 3–5 Infants' Numerical Concepts *Shown an impossible outcome, infants stare longer. (From Wynn, 1992.)*

egocentrism   In Piaget's theory, the inability of the preoperational child to take another's point of view.

preoperational stage   In Piaget's theory, the stage (from about 2 to 6 or 7 years of age) during which a child learns to use language but does not yet comprehend the mental operations of concrete logic.

conservation   The principle (which Piaget believed to be a part of concrete operational reasoning) that properties such as mass, volume, and number remain the same despite changes in the forms of objects.

Preoperational Stage   Seen through the eyes of Piaget, preschool children are still unable to reason and to take another's point of view. Although aware of themselves, of time, and of the permanence of objects, they are, he said, **egocentric**: They cannot perceive things from another's point of view. Asked to "Show mommy your picture," 2-year-old Gabriella holds up the picture, facing her own eyes. Children's conversations also reveal their egocentrism, as one young boy demonstrated (Phillips, 1969, p. 61):

> *"Do you have a brother?"*
> *"Yes."*
> *"What's his name?"*
> *"Jim."*
> *"Does Jim have a brother?"*
> *"No."*

Preschool TV-watchers who block your view of the television assume that you see what they see. Preschoolers who ask a question while you are on the phone assume that you hear nothing but what they hear. When relating to a young child, you may find it helpful to remember that such behaviors reflect a cognitive limitation: The egocentric preschooler is not intentionally "selfish" or "inconsiderate" but rather has difficulty taking another's viewpoint. Parents who abuse their children often fail to understand these limits.

Piaget believed that during this preschool period and up to about age 7, children are in what he called the **preoperational stage** of performing mental operations. For a 5-year-old, the quantity of milk that is "too much" in a tall, narrow glass may become an acceptable amount if poured into a short, wide glass. This is because the child focuses only on the height dimension and is incapable of performing the *operation* of mentally pouring it back. The child lacks the concept of **conservation**—the principle that quantity remains the same despite changes in shape.

Although Piaget did not view the stage transitions as abrupt, the rudiments of conservation can be found at an earlier age than he supposed. Preschoolers are not purely egocentric. Given very simple tasks, 4-year-olds will adjust their explanations to make them clearer to a blind-folded listener and will show a toy or picture with the front side facing the viewer. (Gelman 1979; Siegel & Hodkin, 1982). If questioned in a way that makes sense to them, 5- and 6-year-olds will exhibit some understanding of conservation (Donaldson, 1979). Likewise, more than Piaget realized, preoperational children are capable of thinking symbolically. Judy DeLoache (1987) discovered this when she showed a group of 2-year-olds a model of a room and hid a model toy in it (say, a miniature stuffed dog behind a miniature couch). The children could easily remember where to find the miniature toy. But they could not readily use that model to locate an actual stuffed dog behind a couch in a real room. Only 6

Piaget's Test of Conservation   *This preoperational child at the Ontario Science Centre does not yet understand the principle of conservation of substance. Closed flasks with identical volumes seem suddenly to hold different amounts after one is merely inverted.*

months older, 3-year-olds usually went right to the actual stuffed animal in the real room, showing that they could think of the model as a symbol for the room. Thus, the abilities to take another's perspective, to perform mental operations, and to think symbolically are not absent in the preoperational stage—and then present at some later time. Rather, these abilities begin early and develop gradually.

Preoperational children are also developing other important mental abilities. The Russian psychologist Lev Vygotsky (1932) noted that by age 7 children stop thinking aloud and instead rely on inner speech. Whether out loud or inaudible, talking to oneself merges language with activity ("out of my way!" says Jay to an object in his way). Private speech therefore helps children control their behavior and master new skills. Second-graders who mutter to themselves while doing math problems grasp third-grade math better the following year (Berk, 1994).

Concrete Operational Stage   By about 7 years of age, according to Piaget, children enter the **concrete operational stage**. Given concrete materials, they begin to grasp that a given quantity remains the same no matter how its shape changes. By age 11, children can mentally pour the milk back and forth between different-shaped glasses. They realize that change in shape does not mean change in quantity. They also enjoy jokes that allow them to use their new concepts, such as conservation:

> Mr. Jones went into a restaurant and ordered a whole pizza for his dinner. When the waiter asked if he wanted it cut into 6 or 8 pieces, Mr. Jones said, "Oh, you'd better make it 6, I could never eat 8 pieces!" (McGhee, 1976).

During the concrete operational stage, said Piaget, children fully gain the mental ability to comprehend mathematical transformations and conservation. When my daughter Laura was 6, I was astonished at her inability to reverse arithmetic operations—until considering Piaget's theory. Asked, "What is eight plus four?" she required 5 seconds to compute "twelve," and another 5 seconds to then compute twelve minus four. By age 8, she could reverse the process and answer the second question instantly.

If Piaget was correct—if children construct their understandings and think differently than adults—what are the implications for parents and teachers? Piaget contended that teachers should build on what children already know, give them concrete demonstrations, and stimulate them to think for themselves. Parents and future teachers, remember: Young children are incapable of adult logic. Understand how children think. Realize that what is simple and obvious to you—that, say, subtraction is the reverse of addition—may be incomprehensible to a 6-year-old. Accept children's cognitive immaturity as adaptive—as nature's strategy for keeping children close to protective adults and providing time for learning and socialization (Bjorklund & Green, 1992).

Formal Operational Stage   By age 12, reasoning expands from the purely concrete (involving actual experience) to encompass abstract thinking (involving imagined realities and symbols). As they approach adolescence, said Piaget, many children become capable of solving hypothetical propositions and deducing consequences: *If* this, *then* that. Systematic reasoning, which Piaget called **formal operational** thinking, is now within their grasp.

But are younger children incapable of abstract logic? Consider this simple problem:

> If John is in school, then Mary is in school. John is in school. What can you say about Mary?

Many 7-year-olds have no trouble answering correctly (Suppes, 1982). This illustrates why, once again, critics say the rudiments of Piaget's cognitive stages begin earlier than he realized.

DENNIS THE MENACE

"Cut it up into a LOT of slices, Mom. I'm really hungry!"

concrete operational stage   In Piaget's theory, the stage of cognitive development (from about 6 or 7 to 11 years of age) during which children gain the mental operations that enable them to think logically about concrete events.

formal operational stage   In Piaget's theory, the stage of cognitive development (normally beginning about age 12) during which people begin to think logically about abstract concepts.

Reflections on Piaget's Theory   Piaget's stage theory is controversial. In some ways it gets high marks. Studies around the globe, from aboriginal Australia to Algeria to North America, reveal that human cognition everywhere unfolds basically in the sequence he proposed (Segall & others, 1990). Today's researchers do, however, see development as more continuous than did Piaget. By detecting the beginnings of each type of thinking at earlier ages, they have revealed conceptual abilities that Piaget missed.

What remains of Piaget's ideas about the child's mind? Plenty. Piaget identified important cognitive milestones and stimulated interest in how the mind develops. He would not be surprised that today we are adapting his ideas to accommodate new findings—as part of our own cognitive development.

! *Rehearse It*

6. The orderly sequence of biological growth is called maturation. Maturation explains why

a. children differ greatly in temperament.
b. most children have begun walking by about 12 months.
c. enriching experiences may affect brain tissue.
d. differences between the sexes are minimal.

7. Most of us remember nothing before our third birthday because

a. we are not born with enough brain cells to form memories.
b. we were not given the extra "handling" and environmental stimulation we needed.
c. the connections between our brain cells had not yet become complex enough to form permanent memories.
d. we do not enter the memory stage until our third year.

8. As the infant's muscles and nervous system mature, more complicated skills emerge. Which of the following is true of motor-skill development?

a. It is determined solely by genetic factors.
b. The sequence but not the timing is universal.
c. Maturation has a limited effect if the environment is not right.
d. Environment creates a readiness to learn.

9. According to Piaget, the preoperational stage extends from about age 2 to 6. During this period the young child's thinking is

a. abstract.
b. negative.
c. conservative.
d. egocentric.

10. The principle of conservation explains why a pint of milk remains a pint, whether poured into a tall thin glass or a round goblet. Children acquire the mental operations necessary to understand conservation during

a. infancy.
b. the sensorimotor stage.
c. the preoperational stage.
d. the concrete operational stage.

11. Piaget's stage theory continues to inform our understanding of cognitive development in childhood. However, many researchers believe that

a. Piaget's "stages" begin earlier, and development is more continuous than Piaget realized.
b. children do not progress as rapidly as Piaget predicted.
c. few children really progress to the concrete operational stage.
d. there is no way of testing much of Piaget's theoretical work.

Social Development

6. How do the bonds of attachment form, and with what effects later in life?

Babies are social creatures from birth. In all cultures, infants develop an intense bond with those who care for them. Beginning with newborns' attraction to humans in general, infants soon come to prefer familiar faces and voices and then to coo and gurgle when given their mothers' or fathers' attention. By 8 months, object permanence emerges simultaneously with a fear of strangers, called

stranger anxiety   The fear of strangers that infants commonly display, beginning by about 8 months of age.

attachment   An emotional tie with another person; shown in young children by their seeking closeness to the caregiver and showing distress on separation.

stranger anxiety. Watch how infants of different ages react when handed over to a stranger. Beginning at 8 or 9 months, they often will cry and reach for their familiar caregivers. Is it a mere coincidence that object permanence and stranger anxiety develop together? Probably not. After about 8 months of age, children have schemas for familiar faces; when they can't assimilate a new face into these remembered schemas, they become distressed (Kagan, 1984). This illustrates an important principle: The brain, the mind, and social-emotional behavior develop together.

At 12 months many infants cling tightly to a parent when frightened or expecting separation. Reunited, they shower the parent with smiles and hugs. No social behavior is more striking than this intense and mutual infant-parent love, called **attachment**—a powerful survival impulse that keeps infants close to their caregivers. Among the early social responses—love, fear, aggression—the first and greatest is this bond of love.

Origins of Attachment

A number of elements work to create the parent-infant bond.

Body Contact   For many years, developmental psychologists reasoned that infants became attached to those who satisfied their need for nourishment. It made perfect sense. But an accidental finding revealed that this explanation of attachment is incomplete. During the 1950s, University of Wisconsin psychologist Harry Harlow bred monkeys for his learning studies. To equalize the infant monkeys' experiences and to prevent the spread of disease, he separated the monkeys from their mothers shortly after birth and raised them in sanitary, individual cages, which included a cheesecloth baby blanket (Harlow & others, 1971). Surprisingly, the infants became intensely attached to their blankets: When the blankets were taken to be laundered, the monkeys became distressed.

Harlow soon recognized that this attachment to the blanket contradicted the idea that attachment derives from the mother's association with nourishment. But could he show this more convincingly? To pit the drawing power of a food source against the contact comfort of the blanket, Harlow created two artificial mothers. One was a bare wire cylinder with a wooden head, the other a cylinder wrapped with foam rubber and terry cloth. He could associate either with nourishment by attaching a bottle.

Figure 3–6 Harlow's Mothers   *Harry Harlow reared monkeys with two artificial mothers—one a bare wire cylinder with a wooden head and an attached feeding bottle, the other a cylinder covered with foam rubber and wrapped with terry cloth but without a feeding bottle. Harlow surprised many psychologists when he reported that the monkeys much preferred contact with the comfortable cloth mother even while feeding from the nourishing mother.*

When reared with both a nourishing wire mother and a nonnourishing cloth mother, the monkeys overwhelmingly preferred the cloth mother (Figure 3–6). Like human infants clinging to their mothers, the monkeys would cling to their cloth mothers when anxious. They also used her as a secure base from which to venture into the environment, as if attached to the mother by an invisible elastic band that stretched so far and then pulled the infant monkey back. Further studies with Margaret Harlow and others revealed that other qualities—rocking, warmth, and feeding—could make the cloth mother even more appealing.

In human infants, too, attachment usually grows from body contact with parents who are soft and warm and who rock, feed, and pat. All this should reassure the fathers of breast-fed infants: Attachment does not depend on feeding alone.

Moreover, for humans, too, attachment consists of one person providing another with a *secure base* from which to explore the world and a *safe haven* in times of stress. As we mature, our attachments change. Our secure base and safe haven shift from parents to peers and partners. But at all ages we are social creatures. We gain strength when someone says to us, by words and actions, "I

Some people report that their relationship with God functions as do other attachments—by providing a secure base for exploration and a safe haven when threatened (Kirkpatrick, 1994).

THE FAR SIDE

"The Far Side" cartoon is reprinted by permission of Chronicle Features, San Francisco.

When imprinting studies go awry . . .

critical period   An optimal period shortly after birth when an organism's exposure to certain influences produces proper development.

imprinting   The process by which certain animals form attachments during a critical period very early in life.

temperament   A person's characteristic emotional reactivity and intensity.

am here. I will be here. I am interested in what you do and what you think and feel. I will actively support you" (Crowell & Waters, 1994). We are "happiest and able to deploy [our] talents to best advantage," said attachment researcher John Bowlby (1979), when we know that one or more trusted friends are standing behind us, come what may.

Familiarity   Another key to attachment is familiarity (Rheingold, 1985). In many animals, attachments based on familiarity form during a sensitive, **critical period**—an optimal period shortly after birth when certain events must take place if proper development is to occur (Bornstein, 1989). The first moving object a gosling, duckling, or chick sees during the hours shortly after hatching is normally its mother. Thereafter the young fowl trails after her, and her alone.

Konrad Lorenz (1937) explored this rigid attachment process, called **imprinting**. He wondered what ducklings would do if *he* was the first moving creature they observed. What they did was follow him around: Everywhere that Konrad went, the ducks were sure to go. Further tests revealed that although baby birds imprint best to their own species, they also will imprint to a variety of moving objects—an animal of another species, a box on wheels, a bouncing ball (Colombo, 1982; Johnson, 1992). Once formed, this attachment is difficult to reverse. Although human infants do not have such precisely timed critical periods, they too prefer familiar faces and objects. Thus, children like to reread the same books, rewatch the same movies, reenact the same family traditions. They prefer to eat familiar foods, live in the same familiar neighborhood, attend school with the same old friends. Familiarity breeds content.

Temperament   In studies the world over, some babies seem more disposed to forming a secure attachment. Placed in a strange situation (usually a laboratory playroom), some infants show *secure attachment*. In their mother's presence they play comfortably, happily exploring their new environment. When she leaves, they are distressed; when she returns, they seek contact with her. Other infants show *insecure attachment*. They are less likely to explore their surroundings and may even cling to their mother. When she leaves, they cry loudly; when she returns, they may be indifferent or even hostile toward her (Ainsworth, 1973, 1989; van IJzendoorn & Kroonenberg, 1988). What accounts for these differences?

Might the infants' differences be inborn? An infant's **temperament** includes the inborn rudiments of personality, especially the child's emotional excitability—whether reactive, intense, and fidgety, or easygoing, quiet, and placid. From the first weeks of life, "easy" babies are cheerful, relaxed, and predictable in feeding and sleeping. "Difficult" babies are more irritable, intense, and unpredictable (Chess & Thomas, 1987).

Infant monkeys also vary in temperament. Some are timid and fearful, others more relaxed. When researcher Stephen Suomi (1987) placed genetically predisposed "uptight" or "easygoing" infant monkeys with foster mothers who were themselves uptight or easygoing, heredity overrode rearing. Compared with the naturally easygoing monkeys, the uptight monkeys reacted more anxiously to the stress of separation from the mother, even when they were being raised by easygoing, nurturant foster mothers.

Physiological tests reveal that anxious, high-strung human infants (who often become shy children) have high and variable heart rates and a reactive nervous system (Kagan & others, 1992). They become more physiologically aroused when facing new or strange situations. With age, many shy, inhibited infants relax, but few fearless, spontaneous infants become shy. Heredity seems to predispose the human differences, too. Twins who share identical genes are more likely to have similar temperaments than are nonidentical twins (Emde & others, 1992; Gabbay, 1992; Robinson & others, 1992).

Figure 3–7 Social Deprivation and Fear *Monkeys raised by artificial mothers were terror stricken when placed in strange situations without their surrogate mothers.*

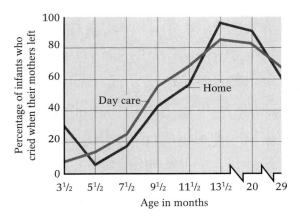

Figure 3–8 Infants' Anxiety Over Separation From Parents *In an experiment, groups of infants who had and had not experienced day care were left alone by their mothers in an unfamiliar room. In both groups, the percentage who cried when the mother left peaked at an age of about 13 months. (From Kagan, 1976.)*

Responsive Parenting But there is more to infant attachment differences than inherited temperament. Another possible influence on attachment is the mother's behavior. Mary Ainsworth (1979) observed mother-infant pairs at home during their first 6 months and then later observed the 1-year-old infants in a strange situation without their mothers. Sensitive, responsive mothers—mothers who continually noticed what their babies were doing and who responded appropriately—had infants who usually became securely attached. Insensitive, unresponsive mothers—mothers who attended to their babies when they felt like doing so but ignored them at other times—had infants who often became insecurely attached. The Harlows' monkey studies, in which the artificial mothers were the ultimate in unresponsiveness, produced even more striking effects. When put in strange situations without their artificial mothers, the deprived infants were more than distressed—they were terrified (Figure 3–7).

To see whether human infants' attachments are also a product of parenting and not just of biologically disposed temperaments, Dutch researcher Dymphna van den Boom (1990) varied parenting while controlling temperament. (Pause and think: If you were the researcher, how might you have done this?) Van den Boom's solution was to randomly assign one hundred 6- to 9-month-old temperamentally difficult infants to either an experimental condition, in which mothers received personal training in sensitive responding, or to an untreated control condition. At age one, 68 percent of the experimental condition infants were rated securely attached, as were only 28 percent of the control condition infants.

The attachments of early childhood eventually relax. Whether children are raised entirely at home or also in a day care center, whether they live in North America, Guatemala, or the Kalahari Desert, anxiety over separation from parents peaks at around 13 months and then gradually declines (Kagan, 1976) (Figure 3–8). With time, children become familiar with a wider range of situations and communicate with strangers more freely.

Does this mean that, as we develop, our need for and love of others fades away? Hardly. Yet much of the life cycle story boils down to a poignant rhythm of attachment and separation—from the attachment of fetal life to the separation of birth, from infant attachment to adolescent separation, from the attachment of marriage and parenthood to the separation of death.

Because of their attachments, parents struggle with the stresses of child-rearing. Indeed, the personal investment necessary to raise a child yields many years not only of joy and love but also of worry and irritation. Yet for most parents, a child is one's biological and social legacy—one's personal investment in the human future. To paraphrase psychiatrist Carl Jung, we reach backward into our parents and forward into our children, and through their children into a future we will never see, but about which we must therefore care.

Effects of Attachment

Does a trusting, secure attachment have lasting benefits? And does the quality of an infant's attachment predict the child's social competence in the years that follow?

Secure Attachment Predicts Social Competence At the University of Minnesota, Alan Sroufe and his colleagues (1983) identified infants who were securely attached at 12 to 18 months of age—those who used their mother as a base for comfortably exploring the world and as a haven when distressed. When Sroufe restudied these infants as 2- to 3-year-olds, he saw them functioning more confidently than other toddlers. Given challenging tasks, they were more enthusiastic and persistent. With other children they were more outgoing and responsive.

basic trust According to Erik Erikson, a sense that the world is predictable and trustworthy; said to be formed during infancy by appropriate experiences with responsive caregivers.

"Out of the conflict between trust and mistrust, the infant develops hope, which is the earliest form of what gradually becomes faith in adults."

Erik Erikson (1983)

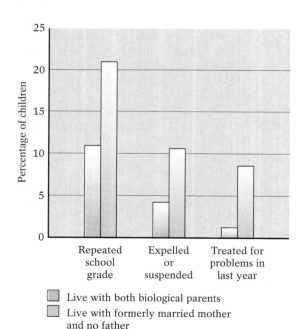

Figure 3–9 Percentage of Children Experiencing School Problems in the Previous Year *In the 1988 National Health Survey, conducted by the U.S. Census Bureau for the National Center for Health Statistics (1991), children living with both their biological parents had fewer problems. Note, however, that these problems affected a minority of children.*

Developmental theorist Erik Erikson (1902–1994) said that securely attached children approach life with a sense of **basic trust**—a sense that the world is predictable and reliable. A child who will let parents leave is a child who trusts they will return. Erikson attributed basic trust not to one's continuing positive environment or inborn temperament, but to early parenting. He theorized that infants blessed with sensitive, loving caregivers form a lifelong attitude of trust rather than fear. Erikson would not have been surprised that as adults, our romantic love styles exhibit either secure, trusting attachment; insecure, anxious attachment; or the avoidance of attachment (Feeney & Noller, 1990; Shaver & Hazan, 1993; Simpson & others, 1992). Our early attachment styles, it seems, form a foundation for our future relationships.

Deprivation of Attachment If secure attachment nurtures social competence, what happens when circumstances prevent children from forming attachments? In all of psychology, no research literature is more saddening. Children reared in institutions without the stimulation and attention of a regular caregiver, or locked away at home under conditions of abuse or extreme neglect, are often withdrawn, frightened, even speechless. Adopted during infancy or childhood into a loving home, they usually progress rapidly, especially in their cognitive development. Nevertheless, they frequently bear scars from their early mistreatment (Malinosky-Rummell & Hansen, 1993; Rutter, 1979).

So, too, did the Harlows' monkeys if reared in total isolation, without even an artificial mother. As adults they either cowered in fright or lashed out in aggression when placed with other monkeys their age. Upon reaching sexual maturity, most were incapable of mating. Artificially impregnated females often were neglectful, abusive, or even murderous toward their firstborn offspring. The unloved had become the unloving.

Most abusive human parents, too, report being neglected or battered as children (Kempe & Kempe, 1978). Many condemned murderers report the same. One study of 14 young men awaiting execution for juvenile crimes found that all but two had histories of brutal physical abuse (Lewis & others, 1988).

So, do most victims of child abuse become abusive? Is today's victim predictably tomorrow's predator? No. Most abused children do *not* later become violent criminals or abusive parents. But 30 percent of those abused do abuse their children—a rate four times higher than the national rate of child abuse (Kaufman & Zigler, 1987; Widom, 1989a,b). Moreover, young children terrorized through sexual abuse or wartime atrocities (being beaten, witnessing torture, and living in constant fear) may suffer other scars—often nightmares, depression, and a troubled adolescence (Kendall-Tackett & others, 1993).

Children and Divorce Nearly half of marriages in Western countries (slightly more than half in the United States) end in divorce. That's double the proportion of 30 years ago. This fact makes people wonder and worry: Are children casualties of divorce? Does the stress of divorce and its aftermath, or the diminished father care it usually entails, erode children's well-being?

To answer these questions, researchers have not only compared children from divided and intact families but also followed children from before divorce to after it. Mavis Hetherington and her colleagues (1989, 1992) summarize the results: Divorce places "children at increased risk for developing social, psychological, behavioral and academic problems." Consider, for example, the results of one study of more than 17,000 children by the U.S. Census Bureau for the National Center for Health Statistics (1991). The researchers knew that intact and divided families can differ in many ways (parental education, race, income, and so forth), so they statistically adjusted their results to remove such influences. Still, children of divided parents were about twice as likely to experience a variety of social, psychological, or academic problems (Figure 3–9).

Fathering a Child *Mothers and fathers both interact with their children in important ways. However, in most single-parent families, children reside with their mother and receive diminished father care. Researchers are working to understand the effects of father care on children's social development.*

Yet, children's responses are diverse. Whether children cope well after divorce or develop behavior problems depends on such factors as the child's temperament, the intensity of parental conflict before the divorce, and the continuity of other relationships, such as those with familiar friends and classmates. If the child is easygoing, if divorce enables the custodial parent to escape a traumatic or abusive situation, and if other relationships are preserved, the adjustment is most likely to go well.

Culture and Child-Rearing

7. How do parenting styles and values vary among cultures?

Parenting styles vary. Some parents spank, some reason. Some parents are strict, some are lax. Some parents seem indifferent to their children, some liberally hug and kiss them. Such differences reflect differing parental values. Social values differ not only from parent to parent but also from one culture to another. Do you prefer children who are independent or who respect authority?

If you live in Western Europe or North America, the odds are you prefer the former. Most parents in Western societies want their children to think for themselves. "You are responsible for yourself," our families and schools tell us. "Follow your conscience. Be true to yourself. Define your gifts. Satisfy your personal needs." But cultural values change over time. A half century ago, Western parents placed greater priority on obedience, respect, and sensitivity to others (Alwin, 1990; Remley, 1988). "Be true to your traditions," they taught their children. "Be loyal to your heritage and country. Show respect toward your parents and superiors."

Unlike most Westerners, who now raise their children to be independent, many Asians and Africans live in communal cultures, which focus on cultivating emotional closeness. Rather than being given their own bedrooms and sent off to day care or nursery school, infants typically sleep with their mothers and spend their days close to a family member (Morelli & others, 1992; Whiting & Edwards, 1988). Children of communal cultures grow up with a stronger sense of "family self"—a feeling that what shames the child shames the family. Compared with Westerners, people in Japanese and Chinese cultures, for example, exhibit greater shyness toward strangers and greater concern for social harmony and loyalty (Bond, 1988; Cheek & Melchior, 1990; Triandis, 1994). "My parents will be disappointed in me" is a concern of 7 percent of American and Italian teenagers, 14 percent of Australian teens, but nearly 25 percent of teens in Taiwan and Japan (Atkinson, 1988).

Mindful of how others differ from us, we often fail to notice the similarities predisposed by our shared biology. As Chapter 1 explained, cross-cultural research helps us appreciate both our cultural diversity *and* our human kinship.

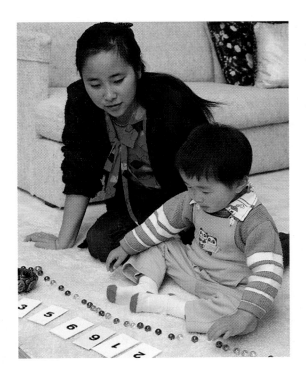

Parental Involvement Promotes Development *Parents in every culture facilitate their children's discovery of their world, but cultures differ in what they deem to be important. Asian cultures place more emphasis on school and hard work than does North American culture. This may help explain why Japanese and Taiwanese children get higher scores on mathematics achievement tests.*

Compared with person-to-person differences within groups, differences between groups are small. Thus, regardless of our culture, we humans share the same life cycle. We all speak to our infants in similar ways and respond similarly to their coos and cries (Bornstein & others, 1992a,b). Across the world, parents who are warm and supportive have children who feel better about themselves and are less hostile than do punitive and rejecting parents (Rohner, 1986; Scott & others, 1991).

"It bodes well," say researchers, "that developmental processes are alike in many subgroups of *Homo sapiens*." In surface ways we may differ, but as members together of one species we seem subject to the same psychological forces. As members of different ethnic and cultural groups, our languages vary, yet reflect universal principles of grammar (Chapter 8). Our tastes vary, yet reflect common principles of hunger (Chapter 9). Our social behaviors vary, yet reflect pervasive principles of human influence (Chapter 14).

Gender and Child-Rearing

8. What social influences help explain gender differences?

What biology initiates, environment accentuates. Society assigns each of us—even those few whose biological sex is ambiguous at birth—to a **gender**—the social category of male or female. The inevitable result is our strong **gender identity** (our sense of being male or female). To varying extents, we also become **gender-typed**. That is, some boys more than others exhibit traditionally masculine traits and interests, and some girls more than others become distinctly feminine.

Social learning theory assumes that children learn gender-linked behaviors by observing and imitating and by being rewarded or punished. "Nicole, you're such a good mommy to your dolls"; "Big boys don't cry, Alex." The modeling and rewarding is not done by parents alone, because differences in the way parents rear boys and girls aren't enough to explain gender-typing (Lytton & Romney, 1991). Even when their families discourage traditional gender-typing, children organize themselves into "boy worlds" and "girl worlds," each guided by rules for what boys and girls do.

Gender schema theory (Figure 3–10) combines social learning theory with cognition: Out of children's struggles to comprehend the world come concepts, or schemas, including a schema for their own gender (Bem, 1987, 1993). Gender becomes a lens (a schema) through which children view their experience.

> *When someone "has discovered why men on Bond Street wear black hats he will at the same moment have discovered why men in Timbuctoo wear red feathers."*
>
> G. K. Chesterton, 1874–1936

gender   The social definition of male and female.

gender identity   One's sense of being male or female.

gender-typing   The acquisition of a masculine or feminine gender identity and role.

social learning theory   The theory that we learn social behavior by observing and imitating and by being rewarded or punished.

gender schema theory   The theory that children learn from their culture a concept of what it means to be male and female and that they adjust their behavior accordingly.

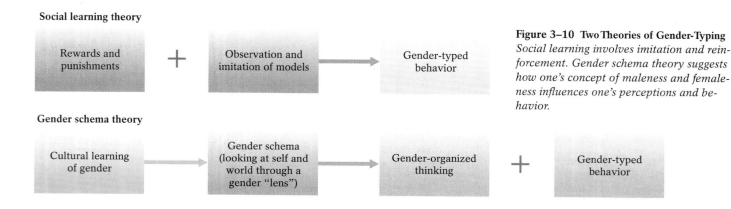

Social learning theory

Rewards and punishments + Observation and imitation of models → Gender-typed behavior

Gender schema theory

Cultural learning of gender → Gender schema (looking at self and world through a gender "lens") → Gender-organized thinking + Gender-typed behavior

Figure 3–10 Two Theories of Gender-Typing
Social learning involves imitation and reinforcement. Gender schema theory suggests how one's concept of maleness and femaleness influences one's perceptions and behavior.

By age 3, language forces them to begin organizing their worlds on the basis of gender. English, for example, uses the pronouns *he* and *she*; other languages classify objects as masculine ("*le* train") or feminine ("*la* table"). Through language, dress, toys, and songs, social learning shapes gender schemas. Children then compare themselves with their concept of gender ("I am male—thus, masculine, strong, aggressive," or "I am female—therefore, feminine, sweet, and helpful") and adjust their behavior accordingly.

! *Rehearse It*

12. Stranger anxiety and object permanence—the awareness that objects continue to exist even when not perceived—emerge about the same time. These two developments occur

a. in the first few months.
b. by about 8 months.
c. in the second year.
d. after the child has learned to think concretely.

13. Body contact facilitates attachment between infant and parent. In a famous series of experiments, Harry Harlow found that monkeys raised with artificial mothers tended when afraid to cling to

a. the wire mother.
b. the cloth mother.
c. whichever mother held the feeding bottle.
d. none of the artificial mothers.

14. From the very first weeks of life, infants differ in their characteristic emotional reactions, with some infants being intense and anxious, while others are easygoing and relaxed. These differences are usually explained as differences in

a. attachment.
b. imprinting.
c. temperament.
d. parental responsiveness.

15. Children who in infancy formed secure attachments to their parents

a. are likely to become good parents.
b. prefer the company of adults to that of their peers.
c. usually become socially competent youngsters.
d. have less stranger anxiety.

16. Social values vary from culture to culture. Western cultures are to _____ as Asian and African cultures are to

_____ .

a. obedience; social harmony
b. independence; emotional closeness
c. loyalty; interdependence
d. respect; morality

Adolescence

Among developmental psychologists, the belief that no important changes in personality occur after childhood has given way to an awareness that development is *lifelong*. As today's life-span perspective emerged, psychologists began to look at how maturation and experience shape us in infancy and childhood—*and* in adolescence and beyond. At a 5-year high school reunion, friends may be surprised at the divergence of their paths. A decade after college, two former soul mates may have trouble keeping a conversation going. As long as we live, we develop.

Adolescence is life between childhood and adulthood. It starts with the physical beginnings of sexual maturity and ends with the social achievement of independent adult status, a time period that in the Western world roughly corresponds to the teen years.

Adolescence is a time of transition. At earlier times in Western societies (and in some developing countries today), adolescence was but a brief interlude between the dependence of childhood and the responsibilities of adulthood (Baumeister & Tice, 1986). Adult status and responsibilities were bestowed shortly after sexual maturity, often marked by an elaborate initiation. The new adult worked, married, and had children.

adolescence The transition period from childhood to adulthood, extending from puberty to independence.

How will you look back on your life 10 years from now? Are you doing the things and making the choices that someday you will recollect with satisfaction?

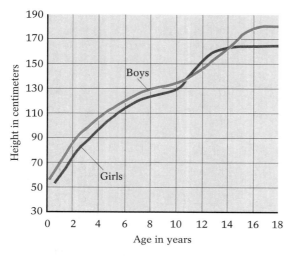

Figure 3–11 **Height Differences** *Throughout childhood, boys and girls are similar in height. At puberty, girls surge ahead briefly, but then boys overtake them at about age 14. (Data from Tanner, 1978.)*

Then, thanks to improved nutrition, sexual maturity began occurring earlier. And thanks to compulsory schooling, adult independence began occurring later. The resulting gap between biological maturity and social independence is adolescence.

To G. Stanley Hall (1904), one of the first psychologists to describe adolescence, the tension between biological maturity and social dependence creates a period of great stress. Indeed, after age 30, many people look back on their teenage years as a time they would not like to relive, a time when the social approval of peers was imperative, one's sense of direction in life was in flux, and alienation from parents was deepest (Macfarlane, 1964).

Today's psychologists note that adolescence is, indeed, often marked by mood swings. Yet for many it is also a time of vitality without the cares of adulthood, a time of rewarding friendships, a time of heightened idealism and a growing sense of life's exciting possibilities (Coleman, 1980). These psychologists would not be surprised that 9 of 10 high school seniors agree with the statement, "On the whole, I'm satisfied with myself" (*Public Opinion*, 1987).

Physical Development

9. What major physical changes occur during adolescence?

Adolescence begins at **puberty**, when one first becomes capable of reproducing. Puberty follows a surge of hormones, which may intensify moods and which trigger a 2-year period of rapid physical development that usually begins in girls at about age 11 and in boys at about age 13. About the time of puberty, boys grow as much as 5 inches a year, compared with about 3 inches for girls—propelling the average male, for the first time, to greater height than the average female (Figure 3–11). During this growth spurt, the reproductive organs, or **primary sex characteristics**, develop dramatically. So do the **secondary sex characteristics**, the nonreproductive traits of females and males, such as enlarged breasts and hips in girls, facial hair and a deepened voice in boys, pubic and underarm hair in both sexes (Figure 3–12).

The landmarks of puberty are the first ejaculation in boys, which usually occurs by about age 14, and the first menstrual period in girls, by about age 13. The first menstrual period, called **menarche** (meh-NAR-key), is a memorable event, one that is recalled by nearly all adult women. Most experience and later recall a mixture of feelings—pride, excitement, embarrassment, and apprehension (Greif & Ulman, 1982; Woods & others, 1983). For the first few months many keep it a secret from friends, and very few discuss it with their fathers (Brooks-Gunn, 1989). Girls well prepared for menarche usually experience it as a positive life transition. And a transition it is. Regardless of their age, girls afterward increasingly see and present themselves as different from boys and function more independently of their parents (Golub, 1983). Most men similarly recall their first ejaculation, which usually occurs as a nocturnal emission (Fuller & Downs, 1990).

Timing Is Everything *Some girls and boys mature relatively early or late. This variation from the norm can produce feelings of social awkwardness, especially for early-maturing girls and for late-maturing boys. As this relaxed group of fourth- and fifth-graders makes clear, however, most youngsters take their size differences for granted.*

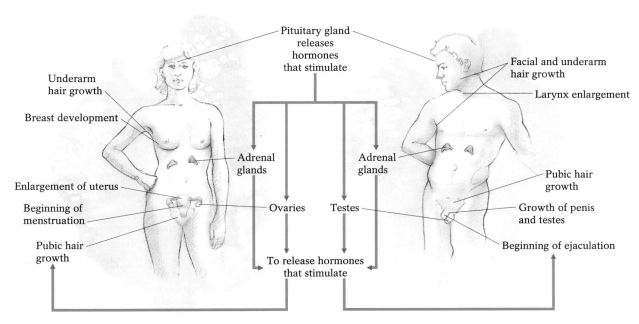

Figure 3–12 Body Changes at Puberty *At about age 11 in girls and age 13 in boys, a surge of hormones triggers a variety of physical changes.*

As in the earlier life stages, the *sequence* of physical changes (for example, breast buds before visible pubic hair before menarche) is far more predictable than their *timing*. Some girls start their growth spurt at 9, some boys as late as age 16. Such variations have little effect on height at maturity, but they may have psychological consequences. Studies performed in the 1950s by Mary Cover Jones and her colleagues revealed that early maturation pays dividends for boys. Early-maturing boys, being stronger and more athletic during their early teen years, tend to be more popular, self-assured, and independent.

For girls, early maturation can be stressful. In Sweden, North America, and New Zealand, studies of girls whose menarche comes either early (before age 12) or late (at age 14 or after) reveal that early maturation can amplify preexisting problems (Caspi & Moffitt, 1991; Simmons & Blyth, 1987; Stattin & Magnusson, 1990). If a young girl's body is out of sync with her emotional maturity and with what her friends are experiencing, she may begin associating with older friends and doing things considered out of bounds for girls her age. Moreover, the 11-year-old who towers over her classmates and becomes the object of sexual attention may temporarily suffer embarrassment and be the object of teasing (Petersen, 1987). But as her peers catch up, her postpubertal experience may help her to enjoy greater prestige and self-confidence.

puberty The time of sexual maturation, when one first becomes capable of reproducing.

primary sex characteristics The body structures (ovaries and testes) that make sexual reproduction possible.

secondary sex characteristics Nonreproductive sexual characteristics, such as female breasts and hips, male voice quality, and body hair.

menarche [meh-NAR-key] The first menstrual period.

"When the pilot told us to brace and grab our ankles, the first thing that went through my mind was that we must all look pretty stupid."

Jeremiah Rawlings, 12, after a 1989 DC-10 crash in Sioux City, Iowa

Cognitive Development

10. How did Piaget and Kohlberg describe cognitive and moral development during adolescence?

Adolescents' developing ability to reason gives them a new level of social awareness and moral judgment. As young teenagers become capable of thinking about their thinking, and of thinking about other people's thinking, they begin imagining what other people are thinking about *them*. (Adolescents might worry less about what others think of them if they knew how seldom others do, because each is worrying about the same.) As their cognitive abilities mature, many adolescents begin to think about what is ideally possible and criticize their society, their parents, and even their own shortcomings.

Drawing by Koren; ©1992
The New Yorker Magazine, Inc.

"Ben is in his first year of high school, and he's questioning all the right things."

"When I was a boy of 14 my father was so ignorant I could hardly stand to have the old man around. But when I got to be 21, I was astonished at how much he had learnt in 7 years."

Mark Twain, 1835–1910

Developing Reasoning Power

During the early teen years, reasoning is often self-focused. Adolescents may think their private experiences are unique. They assume their parents just can't understand what it feels like to be going out with the other sex or to hate school.

Gradually, though, most achieve the intellectual summit that Piaget called *formal operations*. Preadolescents reason concretely, but adolescents become more capable of abstract, logical thinking. They can reason hypothetically and deduce consequences: *If this, then that.* We can see this new reasoning power in adolescents' pondering and debating such abstract topics as human nature, good and evil, truth and justice. Having perhaps envisioned God as a person in the clouds when they were first capable of symbolic thinking in early childhood, they may now seek a deeper conception of God and existence (Elkind, 1970; Worthington, 1989). Adolescents' logical thinking also enables them to detect inconsistencies in others' reasoning and between their ideals and their actions. Indeed, their newfound ability to spot hypocrisy can lead to heated debates with parents and silent vows never to lose sight of their own ideals (Peterson & others, 1986). The new understanding of hypocrisy and possible solutions (or lack of them) to personal problems helps explain why suicide rates rise to adult levels during the teen years.

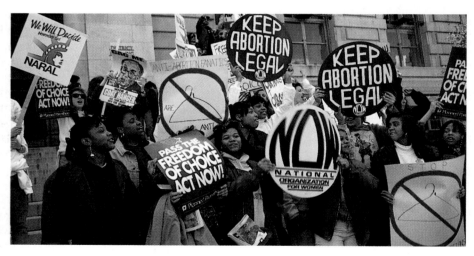

Demonstrating Their Reasoning Ability *These adolescents are on opposite sides of the abortion debate. The idealism that brings them to the picket lines is part of their newfound ability to think logically about abstract topics. According to Piaget, they are in the final cognitive stage, formal operations.*

Developing Morality

A crucial task of childhood and adolescence is learning right from wrong and developing character—the psychological muscles for controlling impulses. To be a moral person is to *think* morally and *act* accordingly. Although as the French essayist Montaigne said, "It is a delightful harmony when doing and saying go together," such harmony often eludes us. "To put one's thoughts into action," noted the German poet Goethe, is "the most difficult thing in the world."

Piaget (1932) believed that children's moral judgments build on their cognitive development. Accordingly, Lawrence Kohlberg (1981, 1984) sought to describe the development stages of *moral reasoning*, the thinking processes that occur when we consider right and wrong. In his research Kohlberg posed stories to children, adolescents, and adults in which the characters face a moral dilemma. He then analyzed their answers for evidence of different stages of moral thinking. Ponder for a moment his best-known dilemma:

In Europe, a woman was near death from a very bad disease, a special kind of cancer. There was one drug that the doctors thought might save her. It was a form of radium that a druggist in the same town had recently discovered. The drug was expensive to make, but the druggist was charging ten times what the drug cost him to make. He paid $200 for the radium and charged $2,000 for a small dose of the drug. The sick woman's husband, Heinz, went to everyone he knew to borrow the money, but he could get together only about $1,000, which was half of what it cost. He told the druggist that his wife was dying and asked him to sell it cheaper or let him pay later. But the druggist said, "No, I discovered the drug and I'm going to make money from it." Heinz got desperate and broke into the man's store to steal the drug for his wife.

What do you think: Should Heinz have stolen the drug? Why was what he did right or wrong? Kohlberg would not have been interested in whether you judged Heinz's behavior as right or wrong—either answer could be justified—but rather in the *reasoning process* by which you arrived at your judgment. We all are moral philosophers, Kohlberg proposed, and our moral reasoning helps guide our judgments and behavior. Kohlberg himself discussed with a friend the moral dilemma of suicide before, nearing 60 and racked by pain, he committed suicide (Hunt, 1993).

Kohlberg argued that as we develop intellectually we pass through three basic levels of moral thinking, moving from the simplistic and concrete toward more abstract and principled reasoning. Before age 9, most children have a *preconventional* morality of self-interest: They obey either to avoid punishment ("If you let your wife die, you will get in trouble") or to gain concrete rewards ("If you save your wife, you will be a hero").

By early adolescence, morality usually evolves to a more *conventional* level that upholds laws and social rules simply because they are the laws and rules. Being able to take others' perspectives, adolescents may approve actions that will gain social approval or that will help maintain the social order ("If you steal the drug, everyone will think you are a criminal").

Those who develop the abstract reasoning of formal operational thought may come to a third level. *Postconventional* morality affirms people's agreed-upon rights ("People have a right to live") or follows what one personally perceives as basic ethical principles ("If you steal the drug, you won't have lived up to your own ideals").

Kohlberg's controversial claim was that these levels form a moral ladder. The rungs extend from a young child's immature, preconventional morality at the bottom to, at the top, an adult's self-defined ethical principles. As with all stage theories, the sequence does not vary. We begin on the bottom rung and ascend to varying heights.

Research confirms that children in various cultures do progress from the level Kohlberg called preconventional into the stages of his conventional level (Edwards, 1981, 1982; Snarey, 1985, 1987). However, the postconventional level appears mostly in the European and North American educated middle class, which prizes individualism—giving priority to one's own goals rather than group goals (Eckensberger, 1994). Critics therefore contend the theory is biased against the moral reasoning of those in communal societies such as China and Papua, New Guinea—and also against women, whose morality may be less a matter of abstract, impersonal principles and more a matter of caring relationships.

We can stimulate children's moral reasoning through discussions of moral issues and their implications. Because morality involves *doing* the right thing, we can also teach children to restrain their impulses—to delay small gratifications now for the sake of bigger gratifications later. Those who learn to do so become more socially responsible, academically successful, and productive (Funder & Block, 1989; Mischel & others, 1988, 1989).

Martin Luther King, Jr. *Those who conform to society's rules often do not take kindly to those who seek to change those rules. Kohlberg contended that postconventional moral thinking, embodied here by Martin Luther King, Jr., may be rejected by those who do not comprehend it.*

Social Development

Theorist Erik Erikson (1963) contended that each stage of life has its own *psychosocial* task, a crisis that needs resolution. Young children wrestle with issues of *trust* (page 84), then *autonomy* (independence), then *initiative* (Table 3–2). School-age children develop *competence*, the sense that they are able and productive human beings. In adolescence, the task is to synthesize past, present, and future possibilities into a clearer sense of self. Adolescents wonder: "Who am I as an individual? What do I want to do with my life? What values should I live by? What do I believe in?" Erikson called this quest to define one's sense of self the adolescent's "search for identity."

As sometimes happens in psychology, Erikson's interests were bred by his own life experience. As the son of a Jewish mother and a Danish father, Erikson was "doubly an outsider," reports Morton Hunt (1993, p. 391). He was "scorned as a Jew in school but mocked as a Gentile in the synagogue because of his blond hair and blue eyes." Such episodes fueled his interest in the adolescent struggle for identity.

TABLE 3–2

Erikson's Stages of Psychosocial Development

Approximate age	Description of task
Infancy (1st year)	*Trust vs. mistrust* If needs are dependably met, infants develop a sense of basic trust.
Toddler (2nd year)	*Autonomy vs. shame and doubt* Toddlers learn to exercise will and do things for themselves, or they doubt their abilities.
Preschooler (3–5 years)	*Initiative vs. guilt* Preschoolers learn to initiate tasks and carry out plans, or they feel guilty about efforts to be independent.
Elementary school (6 years to puberty)	*Competence vs. inferiority* Children learn the pleasure of applying themselves to tasks, or they feel inferior.
Adolescence (teen years into 20s)	*Identity vs. role confusion* Teenagers work at refining a sense of self by testing roles and then integrating them to form a single identity, or they become confused about who they are.
Young adulthood (20s to early 40s)	*Intimacy vs. isolation* Young adults struggle to form close relationships and to gain the capacity for intimate love, or they feel socially isolated.
Middle adulthood (40s to 60s)	*Generativity vs. stagnation* The middle-aged discover a sense of contributing to the world, such as through family and work, or they may feel a lack of purpose.
Late adulthood (late 60s and up)	*Integrity vs. despair* When reflecting on his or her life, the older adult may feel a sense of satisfaction or failure.

Who Shall I Be Today?   *By varying the way they look, adolescents try out different "selves." Although we eventually form a consistent and stable sense of identity, the "self" we present may change with the situation.*

Forming an Identity

11. What is involved in the adolescent's search for identity?

To refine their sense of identity, adolescents in Western cultures usually try out different "selves" in different situations—perhaps acting out one self at home, another with friends, and still another at school and work. If two of these situations overlap—as when a teenager brings home friends with whom he is Joe Cool—the discomfort can be considerable. The teen asks, "Which self should I be? Which is the real me?" Often, this role confusion is resolved by the gradual reshaping of a self-definition that unifies the various selves into a consistent and comfortable sense of who one is—an **identity**.

But not always. Erikson noticed that some adolescents forge their identity early, simply by taking on their parents' values and expectations. (Traditional, less individualistic cultures tell adolescents who they are rather than letting them decide on their own.) Other adolescents may adopt a negative identity that defines itself in opposition to parents and society but in conformity with a particular peer group—complete, perhaps, with shaved head or pierced body parts. Still others never quite seem to find themselves or to develop strong commitments. For most, the identity question—Who am I?—continues past the teen years and reappears at turning points during adult life.

The late teen years, when many people begin attending college or working full time, provide new opportunities for trying out possible roles. As college seniors, many students have achieved a clearer identity than they had as first-year students (Waterman, 1988). Their identity typically incorporates an increasingly positive self-concept. In several nationwide studies, researchers have given young Americans tests of self-esteem. (Sample item: "I am able to do things as well as most other people.") Between ages 13 and 23, the self-concept usually becomes more positive, especially among boys and among those who belong to a satisfying peer group. A clearer, more self-affirming identity is forming, and with it comes a greater sense of control over one's future (Baumgardner, 1990; O'Malley & Bachman, 1983; Strange & Forsyth, 1993).

Developing Intimacy

Erikson contended that the adolescent identity stage is followed in young adulthood by a developing capacity for **intimacy**, the ability to form emotionally close relationships. Once you have a clear and comfortable sense of who you are, said Erikson, you are ready for close relationships.

> *"I am becoming still more independent of my parents; young as I am, I face life with more courage than Mummy; my feeling for justice is immovable, and truer than hers. I know what I want, I have a goal, an opinion, I have a religion, and love. Let me be myself and then I am satisfied. I know that I'm a woman, a woman with inward strength and plenty of courage."*
>
> Anne Frank, age 14
> *Diary of a Young Girl*, 1947

identity   One's sense of self; according to Erikson, the adolescent's task is to solidify a sense of self by testing and integrating various roles.

intimacy   In Erikson's theory, the ability to form close, loving relationships; a primary developmental task in late adolescence and early adulthood.

12. Do males and females differ in social relations?

Gender and Social Connectedness   Males and females are alike in many ways, and even in the ways they differ, they overlap. Yet it is their differences that excite interest. For example, to Carol Gilligan and her colleagues (1982, 1990), the "normal" struggle to create one's separate identity describes individualist males more than relationship-oriented females. Gilligan believes females are less concerned than are males with viewing themselves as separate individuals, and are more concerned with "making connections."

This gender difference surfaces early, in children's play. Boys typically play in large groups with an activity focus and little intimate discussion. Girls play in smaller groups, often with a single friend. Girls' play is less competitive than boys' and more imitative of social relationships (Lever, 1978). In play and in later achievement settings, females are more open and responsive to feedback than are males (Maccoby, 1990; Roberts, 1991). As teens, girls spend more time than do boys with friends and less time alone (Wong & Csikszentmihalyi, 1991).

The gender difference in connectedness carries into adulthood. Women, being more *interdependent*, use conversation to explore relationships, men use it to convey solutions (Tannen, 1990). Women emphasize caring and provide most of the care to the very young and the very old. Although 69 percent of people say they have a close relationship with their father, 90 percent say they're close to their mother (Hugick, 1989). Men, like empowered people generally, emphasize freedom and self-reliance. (That helps explain why at all ages men assign less importance to religion and pray less often than do women [Benson, 1992].)

Women also have closer relationships with each other. Study after study finds the bonds and feelings of support stronger among women than those among men (Rossi & Rossi, 1990). Women's ties, as mothers, daughters, sisters, and grandmothers, bind families together. As friends, women are more intimate than men; they talk more often and more openly (Berndt, 1992; Dindia & Allen, 1992).

When surveyed, women also are far more likely than men to describe themselves as having empathy. If you are empathic, you identify with others. You rejoice with those who rejoice and weep with those who weep. You imagine what it must feel like to live with that handicap, what it must be like to try so hard to impress people, what a thrill it must be to win that award. Physiological measures of empathy, such as one's heart rate while seeing another's distress, reveal a much smaller gender gap than reported in surveys (Eisenberg & Lennon, 1983). Nevertheless, females are more likely to *express* empathy—to cry and to report distress when observing someone in distress.

Moreover, studies consistently find females better at reading people's emotional cues (Hall, 1987). Shown a silent, 2-second film clip of an upset woman's face, women are better than men at sensing whether she is angry or discussing a divorce. Women's nonverbal sensitivity, perhaps a by-product of their roles, helps explain their greater emotional responsiveness in positive and negative situations (Grossman & Wood, 1993; Sprecher & Sedikides, 1993; Stoppard & Gruchy, 1993). It also helps explain why both men and women report their friendships with women to be more intimate, enjoyable, and nurturing (Rubin, 1985; Sapadin, 1988). When wanting understanding and someone with whom to share worries and hurts, both men and women usually turn to women.

Separating from Parents   As adolescents seek to form their own identities, they begin to separate themselves from their parents (Paikoff & Brooks-Gunn, 1991). What their friends are—what "everybody's doing"—they often become.

Family Intimacy *Relationships with parents are a vital part of adolescence. Although there may be differences over values, relationships, and responsibilities, most teenagers, like the young woman shown here, are on good terms with their parents.*

In Western cultures, adolescence is typically a time of growing peer influence and diminishing parental influence, especially on matters of personal taste and life-style. One study asked teens to report their emotions when beeped by electronic pagers at random times. Most reported feeling more free and open with friends than with family (Larson & Bradney, 1988).

For a small minority of parents and their adolescents, differences mean estrangement. But for most, disagreement at the level of bickering is not destructive. A study of 6000 adolescents in 10 countries, from Australia to Bangladesh to Turkey, found that most liked their parents (Offer & others, 1988). "We usually get along but . . .," adolescents often report (Galambos, 1992; Steinberg, 1987). In a recent Gallup Poll (1993) of American teens, 95 percent said they were more "happy" than "not that happy" with how things were going in their homes. Positive relations with parents support positive peer relations. High school girls who have the most affectionate relationships with their mothers tend also to enjoy the most intimate friendships with girlfriends (Gold & Yanof, 1985).

As identity and intimacy mature during the twenties, emotional ties between parents and children continue to loosen. During their early twenties, many still lean heavily on their parents. By their late twenties, most feel more comfortably independent of their parents and better able to empathize with them as fellow adults (Frank, 1988; White, 1983). As the twentieth century winds down, this graduation from adolescence to adulthood is taking longer. Adolescents in Europe and North America are taking longer to finish college, to leave the nest, to establish their careers. Since 1960, Americans' average age at first marriage has increased nearly 4 years (to 26 for men, 24 for women).

Adolescent Sexuality and Pregnancy

13. What factors influence teen pregnancy?

Adolescents' physical maturation fosters a sexual dimension to their emerging identity. How and when that gets expressed differs with time and culture. In the United States, the percentage of ninth- to twelfth-graders reporting having sexual intercourse rose during the 1970s and 1980s to a peak of 59 percent in 1989, then declined to 54 percent in 1991 (Kann & others, 1993). Teen intercourse rates are higher in Western Europe but much lower in Arab and Asian countries (Buss, 1989; Toufexis, 1993). These varying sexual standards help explain the changes and culture differences in rates of nonmarital childbearing (Figure 3–13).

"Will your child learn to multiply before she learns to subtract?"

Anti–teen-pregnancy poster for the Children's Defense Fund

Figure 3–13 Births to Unwed Parents *Since 1960, the percentage of babies born to unmarried Canadian, British, and American women—one-third of whom were teens—has more than quintupled. This increase stems from two trends: a decreasing birth rate among married women and a doubling of the birth rate among unmarried women. (Data from National Center for Health Statistics; Bureau of the Census, 1993, Table 1380; and British Central Statistical Office, 1993.)*

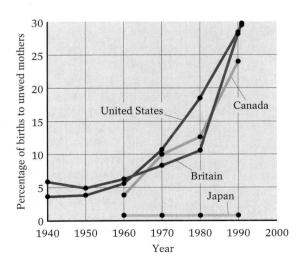

The increased adolescent pregnancy rate and the often impoverished futures of teenage mothers and of children abandoned by their biological fathers have prompted new research on teen sexuality and adolescents' use of contraceptives. Short of "just saying no," contraceptives are the surest strategy of preventing pregnancy. Although the number of American teenagers using condoms doubled during the 1980s, half of teen sexual acts were unprotected. Only one-third of sexually active male teens used condoms consistently (Sonenstein, 1992). Why? Among the contributing factors are these:

1. *Ignorance* In eight surveys, fewer than half the adolescents could correctly identify the safe and risky times of the menstrual cycle (Morrison, 1985). Thus, most unwed teen mothers report surprise at finding themselves pregnant (Brooks-Gunn & Furstenberg, 1989). They didn't choose to become pregnant; rather, they and their partners failed to prevent pregnancy.

2. *High sex guilt* Although sexual inhibitions reduce sexual activity, they also result in lack of planned birth control for those who do engage in sex (Gerrard & Luus, 1995). Not wanting to appear deliberately sexual or promiscuous, teens may hesitate to carry and produce a condom. When, as sometimes happens, passion overwhelms intentions, the result may be conception.

3. *Minimal communication about birth control* Many teenagers are uncomfortable discussing contraception with parents, partners, and peers (Kotva & Schneider, 1990; Milan & Kilmann, 1987). Teens are more likely to use contraceptives if they talk freely with friends or parents and are in an exclusive relationship with a partner with whom they communicate openly.

4. *Alcohol use* Sexually active teens are typically alcohol-using teens (National Research Council, 1987). By depressing brain centers that control judgment, inhibition, and self-awareness, alcohol tends to break down normal restraints, a phenomenon well known to sexually coercive males (page 182).

5. *Mass media norms of impulsive sex* The Planned Parenthood Federation (1986) has complained that television and movies help define sexual norms, which today are "Go for it now. . . . Don't worry about anything." An average hour of prime-time television on the three major American networks contains approximately 15 sexual acts, words, and innuendos—one every 4 minutes—nearly all involving unmarried persons and rarely communicating any concern for birth control or sexually transmitted disease (Sapolsky & Tabarlet, 1991). Planned Parenthood contends that repeated portrayals of unsafe sex, without consequence, amounts to a campaign of sex *dis*information.

With teen pregnancy rising despite increased sex education, the United States national health objectives for the year 2000 now include a dual aim: increasing condom use to 90 percent among those sexually active, and reducing the proportion of 17-year-olds who have had intercourse from approximately 70 percent to under 40 percent (Centers for Disease Control, 1992). This two-pronged emphasis on contraception ("safe sex") and abstinence ("saved sex") is reflected in changing sex education, which is shifting toward the linking of sex with commitment.

The shift responds to declining adolescent well-being (Myers, 1994). In the United States, the number of children not living with two parents has more than doubled since 1960. As elsewhere in the industrialized world, teen and young adult depression rates have soared. Teen suicide has tripled. Teen arrests for violent crime have increased sixfold. "Never before," declared a 1990 National Association of State Boards of Education report, "has one generation of

Drawing by Mankoff © 1994 *The New Yorker* Magazine, Inc.

"You'd better ask your grandparents about that, son—my generation is very uncomfortable talking about abstinence."

"All of us who make motion pictures are teachers, teachers with very loud voices."

Film producer George Lucas
Academy Award ceremonies, 1992

"We cannot renew our country when within a decade more than half of our children will be born into families where there is no marriage."

Bill Clinton
State of the Union Address, 1994

American teenagers been less healthy, less cared for, or less prepared for life than their parents were at the same age."

Throughout history, the pendulum of sexual values has swung—from the European eroticism of the early 1800s to the conservative Victorian era of the late 1800s, from the libertine flapper era of the 1920s to the family values of the 1950s. With new 1990's voices decrying family disintegration and calling for a balance between sexual expression and restraint, and with teen intercourse rates beginning to decline, the pendulum may have begun a new swing toward commitment.

! *Rehearse It*

17. Adolescence is marked by the onset of

a. an identity crisis.
b. puberty.
c. separation anxiety.
d. parent-child conflict.

18. The adolescent growth spurt is marked by dramatic developments in the sex characteristics. Primary sex characteristics relate to _____; secondary sex characteristics refer to _____.

a. ejaculation; menarche
b. breasts and facial hair; ovaries and testes
c. emotional maturity; hormone surges
d. reproductive organs; nonreproductive traits

19. According to Piaget, the ability to think logically about abstractions indicates

a. concrete operational thought.
b. egocentrism.
c. formal operational thought.
d. conservation.

20. Erik Erikson contends that each stage of life has its own special psychosocial task or challenge. At adolescence the task is to

a. attain formal operations.
b. forge an identity.
c. develop a sense of industry.
d. live independent of parents.

21. The differences among individuals of each sex are much greater than the differences between men and women. Nevertheless, women more than men exhibit a concern for

a. independence and self-reliance.
b. tending to social connections.
c. competitive achievement.
d. social stereotyping.

22. Aside from abstinence, contraception is the surest way of preventing pregnancy. More than half of all sexually active teens, however, either do not use contraceptives or do not use them regularly. Among the contributing factors to the epidemic of teen pregnancies are ignorance about reproduction and contraception, insufficient communication about contraception, and

a. the "just say no" attitude.
b. unavailability of abortion.
c. absence of guilt feelings about sexual activity.
d. alcohol use.

Adulthood

At one time, psychologists viewed adulthood, especially the center-of-life years between adolescence and old age, as one long plateau. No longer. Those who follow the unfolding of people's adult lives now believe development continues. Physically, cognitively, and especially socially, people at age 50 are different from their 25-year-old selves.

It's harder to generalize about adulthood stages than about life's early years. During adulthood, age only modestly correlates with people's traits. If you know that James is a 1-year-old and Jamal is a 10-year-old, you could say a great deal about each child. Not so with adults who differ by a similar number of years. The boss may be 30 or 60; the marathon runner may be 20 or 50; your classmates may be teenagers or grandparents. Likewise, a 19-year-old can be a parent who supports a child or a student who gets an allowance. Yet our life courses are in some ways similar. Our bodies, our minds, and our relationships undergo some changes in common with those of childhood friends, who in other ways now seem so very different.

"I am still learning."

Michelangelo's motto, 1560, at age 85

A Good Sport *Whether they choose baseball or tennis, jogging or walking, middle-aged adults who exercise maintain their physical vigor. In fact, exercise is one of the best ways to stay healthy in later life.*

Although menstruation begins earlier today than in centuries past, menopause has been occurring around age 50 for at least 1500 years (Matthews, 1992).

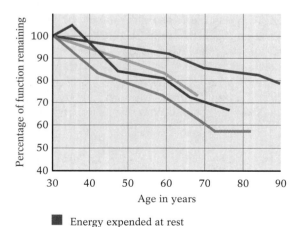

- ■ Energy expended at rest
- ■ Maximum energy expended at work
- ■ Heart's pumping capacity
- ■ Lungs' volume capacity

Figure 3–14 The Slow Decline of the Body's Physical Capacities During Adulthood *(Adapted from Insel & Roth, 1976.)*

menopause The time of natural cessation of menstruation; also refers to the biological changes experienced during a woman's years of declining ability to reproduce.

Physical Changes

14. What major physical changes occur during middle and late adulthood?

Although few of us are aware of it at the time, our physical abilities peak in early adulthood. Muscular strength, reaction time, sensory keenness, and cardiac output all crest by the mid-twenties. Like the declining daylight after the summer solstice, declining physical prowess begins imperceptibly. Athletes are often the first to notice. World-class sprinters and swimmers peak in their teens or early twenties. Women, because they mature earlier than men, also peak earlier. But most people—especially those whose daily lives do not require peak physical performance—hardly perceive the early signs of decline.

Physical Changes in Middle Adulthood

As middle-aged athletes know well, physical decline gradually accelerates (Figure 3–14). "I feel like a 15-year-old trapped in an aging 47-year-old body," said one middle-aged basketball player. But even diminished vigor is sufficient for normal activities. Moreover, during early and middle adulthood physical vigor has less to do with age than with a person's health and exercise habits. Many of today's physically fit 50-year-olds run 4 miles with ease, while sedentary 25-year-olds find themselves huffing and puffing just going up two flights of stairs.

For women, the foremost biological change related to aging is **menopause**, the ending of the menstrual cycle, usually beginning within a few years of age 50. Menopause and its occasional physical symptoms, such as hot flashes in some women, accompany a reduction in the hormone estrogen. Like the stereotype of adolescent storm and stress, the image of menopausal emotionality and depression clashes with reality: Menopause usually does *not* create psychological problems for women. One survey of 2500 middle-aged Massachusetts women, and another that followed 541 middle-aged Pennsylvania women for 3 years, found them no more or less depressed if experiencing menopause (McKinlay & others, 1987a,b; Matthews, 1992). Apart from occasional stiff shoulders and headaches, Japanese women, too, report few symptoms of menopause (Lock & others, 1988).

A woman's expectations and attitudes regarding menopause influence its emotional impact. Does she see menopause as a sign that she is losing her femininity and sexual attractiveness and beginning to grow old? Or does she look on it as liberation from contraceptives, menstrual periods, fears of pregnancy, and the demands of children?

Social psychologist Jacqueline Goodchilds (1987) appreciates the liberation: "If the truth were known, we'd have to diagnose [older women] as having P.M.F.—Post-Menstrual Freedom."

Men experience no equivalent to the menopause—no cessation of fertility, no sharp drop in sex hormones. But they do experience a more gradual decline in sperm count, testosterone level, and speed of erection and ejaculation. Some may also experience psychological distress related to their perception of decreased virility and declining physical capacities. Nevertheless, after middle age most men and women remain capable of satisfying sexual activity.

Physical Changes in Later Life

Is old age "more to be feared than death" (Juvenal, *Satires*)? Or is life "most delightful when it is on the downward slope" (Seneca, *Epistulae ad Lucilium*)? What is it like to grow old?

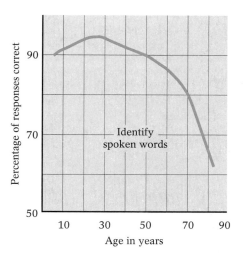

Figure 3–15 The Senses and Age *Sight, smell, and hearing all decline in later life. (From Doty & others, 1984.)*

Keeping the Biological Clock Running Smoothly *How quickly people age depends in part on their health habits. As this cheerful group makes clear, the more active people remain, the more vigor they retain.*

"Everything I've got is 93. You don't see as well. You can't kick the back of your head. Your mind doesn't get old—your body does."

George Burns, 1990

Sensory Abilities As we have seen, physical decline begins in early adult-hood, but not until later life do people become acutely aware of it. As visual sharpness diminishes and adaptation to changes in light level slows, older people have more accidents. Most stairway falls taken by older persons occur on the top step, precisely where the person typically descends from a window-lit hallway into the darker stairwell (Fozard & Popkin, 1978). By using what we know about aging when designing environments, we could reduce such accidents (National Research Council, 1990). Muscle strength, hearing, distance perception, reaction time, and stamina also diminish noticeably (Figure 3–15). In later life, the stairs get steeper, the newsprint smaller, and people seem to mumble more. After age 70, car accident rates per mile increase, reaching the relatively high teenage level by age 75 (National Research Council, 1990).

With age, the eye's pupil shrinks and its lens becomes less transparent, reducing the amount of light reaching the retina. In fact, a 65-year-old retina receives only about one-third as much light as its 20-year-old counterpart (Kline & Schieber, 1985). Thus, to see as well as a 20-year-old when reading or driving, a 65-year-old needs three times as much light—a reason for buying cars with untinted windshields. This also explains why older people sometimes ask younger people, "Don't you need better light for reading?"

Health For those growing older, there is both bad and good news about health. The bad news: The body's disease-fighting immune system weakens, making the elderly more susceptible to life-threatening ailments such as cancer and pneumonia. It's as if the very old have a very mild case of AIDS—the immune deficiency that hampers the body's ability to fight infections.

The good news: Thanks to a lifetime's accumulation of antibodies, older people *less* often suffer short-term ailments, such as common flu and cold viruses. For example, those over 65 are half as likely as 20-year-olds and one-fifth as likely as preschoolers to suffer upper respiratory infection each year (U.S. National Center for Health Statistics, 1990). This is one reason why older workers have lower absenteeism rates (Rhodes, 1983).

Aging does, however, slow neural processes. During the early years of life, up to the teen years, we process information more and more speedily (Kail, 1991). But compared with teens and young adults, older people take a bit more time to react, to solve perceptual puzzles, even to remember names (Salthouse, 1992; Schaie, 1989). Speed slows especially when the task becomes complex (Cerella, 1985; Poon, 1987). At video games, most 70-year-olds are no match for a 20-year-old. (Nor, as I discovered in play with my daughter, is a

Alzheimer's disease A progressive and irreversible brain disorder characterized by gradual deterioration of memory, reasoning, language, and, finally, physical functioning.

Figure 3–16 Incidence of Dementia (Mental Disintegration) by Age *Risk of mental loss due to Alzheimer's disease or a series of strokes doubles about every 5 years in later life. (From Jorm & others, 1987, based on 22 studies in industrial nations.)*

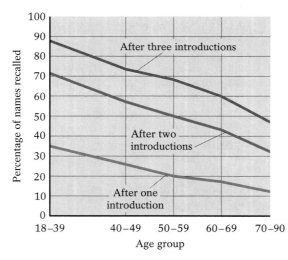

Figure 3–17 Tests of Recall *Recalling new names introduced once, twice, or three times is easier for younger adults than for older ones. (Data from Crook & West, 1990.)*

48-year-old a match for a 14-year-old at Nintendo's perceptual speed game, Tetris.) As we age, we become aware of a growing gap between what we were and what we are becoming.

Beginning in young adulthood, there is also a small, gradual loss of brain cells, contributing to a 5 percent or so reduction of brain weight by age 80. But the proliferation of neural connections, especially in people who remain active, helps compensate for the cell loss (Coleman & Flood, 1986). This helps explain the common finding that adults who remain active—physically, sexually, and mentally—retain more of their capacity for such activities in later years (Jarvik, 1975; Pfeiffer, 1977). "Use it or lose it" is sound advice. We are more likely to rust from disuse than to wear out from overuse.

Some adults do, unfortunately, suffer a substantial loss of brain cells. A series of small strokes, a brain tumor, or alcoholism can progressively damage the brain, causing that mental erosion we call senility. So, too, can the most feared of all brain ailments, **Alzheimer's disease**, which strikes 3 percent of the world's population by age 75. Up to age 95, the incidence of mental disintegration doubles roughly every 5 years (Figure 3–16). Alzheimer's symptoms are *not* the same as normal aging. (Occasionally forgetting where you placed the car keys or struggling over someone's name is no cause for alarm.) Underlying the symptoms is a deterioration of the neurons that normally produce the neurotransmitter acetylcholine. Deprived of this vital chemical messenger, memory and thinking suffer.

Alzheimer's destroys even the brightest of minds. First memory, then reasoning and language deteriorate. Robert Sayre (1979) recalls his father shouting at his afflicted mother to "think harder" when she could not remember where she had put something, while his mother, confused, embarrassed, on the verge of tears, randomly searched the house. As the disease runs its course, after 5 to 20 years, the patient becomes disoriented, then incontinent, finally mentally vacant—a sort of living death, a mere body stripped of its humanity. Caregiving family members of increasingly confused and helpless sufferers themselves often become the disease's exasperated and exhausted victims.

Cognitive Changes

15. How are memory and intelligence influenced by aging?

One of the most controversial questions in the study of the human life span is whether adult cognitive abilities, such as memory, creativity, and intelligence, parallel the gradually accelerating decline of physical abilities. Employers, for example, may wonder whether to encourage their senior workers to retire—or to capitalize on their experience. In general, people perceive the elderly as mentally less sharp (Kite & Johnson, 1988). Is this stereotype accurate? Is there truth in the old proverb, "You can't teach an old dog new tricks"? Or does truth lie with another old proverb: "You're never too old to learn"?

Aging and Memory

Early adulthood is the peak time for some types of learning and remembering. In one experiment, Thomas Crook and Robin West (1990) invited 1205 people to learn some names. Fourteen videotaped people said their names using a common format: "Hi, I'm Larry." Then the 14 individuals reappeared saying, for example, "I'm from Philadelphia"—providing a visual and voice cue to remember the person's name. As Figure 3–17 shows, everyone remembered more names after a second and third replay of the introductions, but younger adults' recall for the names consistently surpassed that of older adults. Quicker learn-

cross-sectional study A study in which people of different ages are tested or observed at the same point in time.

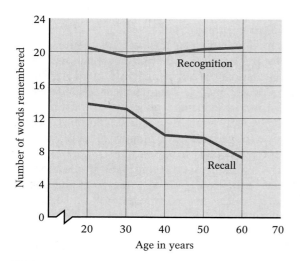

Figure 3–18 Recall and Recognition in Adulthood *In this experiment, the ability to* recall *new information declined during early and middle adulthood but the ability to* recognize *new information did not. (From Schonfield & Robertson, 1966.)*

ing by younger adults is not restricted to human beings. Aging monkeys, too, take progressively more time to master new tasks (Bachevalier & others, 1991, 1992).

But consider another experiment. David Schonfield and Betty-Anne Robertson (1966) asked adults of various ages to learn a list of 24 words. Without giving any clues, the researchers asked some to recall as many words as they could from the list. As Figure 3–18 shows, younger adults had better recall. Others, given multiple-choice questions that asked them simply to *recognize* the words they had seen, exhibited no memory decline with age. This type of memory is especially good when older adults are tested early rather than late in the day (May & others, 1993). So, how well older people remember depends: Are they being asked simply to *recognize* what they have tried to memorize (minimal decline) or to *recall* it without clues (greater decline).

Part of the memory difficulty older adults complain of may be normal forgetfulness. When a 20-year-old mislays her car keys, she gets frustrated; when her grandfather mislays his, he gets frustrated and blames his age. But forgetting—or remembering—seems also to depend on the type of information. If you are asked to recall meaningless information—remembering nonsense syllables or unimportant events—then the older you are, the more errors you are likely to make. However, if the information is meaningful, older people's rich web of existing knowledge helps them catch it. Thus, their capacity to learn and remember skills and *meaningful* material shows less decline (Graf, 1990; Labouvie-Vief & Schell, 1982; Perlmutter, 1983).

Aging and Intelligence

What happens to our broader intellectual powers as we age? Do they gradually decline, as does our ability to recall new material? Or do they remain constant, as does our ability to recognize meaningful material? The evolving answer to this question makes an interesting research story that illustrates psychology's self-correcting process (Woodruff-Pak, 1989).

Phase I: Cross-Sectional Evidence for Intellectual Decline In **cross-sectional studies**, researchers test people of various ages at the same time. When giving intelligence tests to representative samples of people, researchers consistently find that older adults give fewer correct answers than do younger adults (Figure 3–19). David Wechsler (1972), creator of the most widely used adult intelligence test, therefore concluded that "the decline of mental ability with age is part of the general [aging] process of the organism as a whole."

Figure 3–19 Cross-Sectional Comparison of Intelligence *On intelligence tests older adults get fewer questions correct than younger adults. But see Figure 3–20. (From Geiwitz, 1980.)*

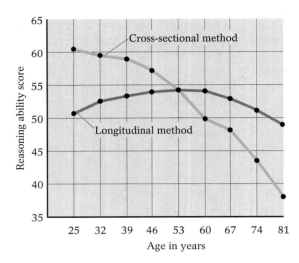

Figure 3–20 Cross-Sectional Versus Longitudinal Methods *In this test of one type of verbal intelligence (inductive reasoning), the cross-sectional method produced declining scores with age. The longitudinal method (in which the same people were retested over a period of years) produced a slight rise in scores well into adulthood. (Adapted from Schaie, 1994.)*

"In youth we learn, in age we understand."

Marie von Ebner-Eschenbach
Aphorisms, 1883

At age 70, John Rock developed the birth control pill. At age 78, Grandma Moses took up painting and was still painting after age 100. At age 81—and 17 years from the end of his college football coaching career—Amos Alozo Stagg was named coach of the year. At age 89, architect Frank Lloyd Wright designed New York City's Guggenheim Museum.

Phase II: Longitudinal Evidence for Intellectual Stability Colleges began giving intelligence tests to entering students about 1920, making it possible to retest older people who had taken an intelligence test years earlier. Several psychologists saw their chance to study intelligence **longitudinally**, by retesting the same people over a period of years. What they expected to find was a decrease in intelligence after about age 30 (Schaie & Geiwitz, 1982). What they actually found was a surprise: Until late in life, intelligence remained stable (Figure 3–20). On some tests, it even increased.

How then are we to account for the findings from the cross-sectional studies? In retrospect, researchers saw the problem. When a cross-sectional study compares 70- and 30-year-olds, it compares people not only of two different ages but of two different eras. It compares generally less educated people (born, say, in the early 1900s) with more educated people (born after 1950), people raised in large families with people raised in smaller families, people growing up in less affluent families with people raised in more affluent families.

Phase III: It All Depends But the controversy continues. For one thing, longitudinal studies have their own pitfalls. Those who survive to the end of longitudinal studies may be bright, healthy people whose intelligence is least likely to decline. If so, such studies underestimate the average decline in intelligence.

Research is further complicated by the finding that intelligence is not a single trait (see Chapter 8). Intelligence tests that assess speed of thinking may place older adults at a disadvantage because of their slower neural mechanisms for processing information. But slower need not mean less intelligent. Given other tests that assess general vocabulary, knowledge, and ability to integrate information, older adults generally hold their own. German researcher Paul Baltes (1993) has developed "wisdom" tests that assess traits such as expertise and sound judgment on important matters of life. Their results suggest that older adults more than hold their own on such tests. Thus, despite 30-year-olds' quick-thinking smarts, we usually select older people to be president of the company, the college, or the country. To be growing older is, in some ways, indeed to be still growing. Age is sage.

So, whether intelligence increases or decreases with age depends on what type of intellectual performance we measure. **Crystallized intelligence**—one's accumulated knowledge as reflected in vocabulary and analogies tests—*increases* up to old age. **Fluid intelligence**—one's ability to reason speedily and abstractly, as when solving novel logic problems—*decreases* with age (Cattell, 1963; Horn, 1982). We can see this pattern in the intelligence scores of a national sample of adults. After adjusting for education, verbal scores (reflecting crystallized intelligence) held relatively steady from ages 20 to 74, while nonverbal, puzzle-solving intelligence declined (Figure 3–21).

Figure 3–21 IQ Scores and Age *After adjustments for education, verbal intelligence scores hold steady with age, while nonverbal intelligence scores decline. (IQ scores from standardization sample of the Wechsler Adult Intelligence Scale, based on norms for 25- to 34-year-olds.) (Adapted from Kaufman & others, 1989.)*

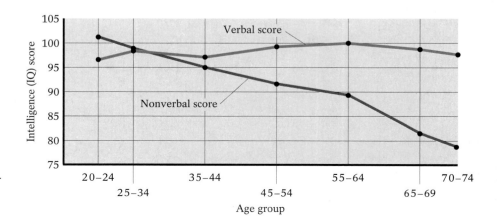

longitudinal study Research in which the same people are restudied and retested over a long time period.

crystallized intelligence One's accumulated knowledge and verbal skills; tends to increase with age.

fluid intelligence One's ability to reason speedily and abstractly; tends to decrease during late adulthood.

This helps explain why mathematicians and scientists produce much of their most creative work during their late twenties or early thirties, while those in literature, history, and philosophy tend to produce their best work later—in their forties, fifties, and beyond, after accumulating more knowledge (Simonton, 1988, 1990). History bears out this finding. For example, poets (who depend on fluid intelligence) reach their peak output earlier than prose authors (who need a deeper knowledge reservoir)—a finding observed in every major literary tradition, for both living and dead languages. So, whether intellectual performance increases or decreases with age depends on how we assess it.

Social Changes

Many differences between younger and older adults are created not by the physical and cognitive changes that accompany aging but by life events associated with family relationships and work. A new job means new relationships, new expectations, and new demands. Marriage brings the joy of intimacy and the stress of merging your life with another's. The birth of a child introduces responsibilities and significantly alters your life focus. The death of a loved one creates a sense of irreplaceable loss and a need to reaffirm your own life. Do these normal events of adult life shape a predictable sequence of life changes?

Adulthood's Ages and Stages

16. Why are age-based stage theories of adult development considered controversial?

Some psychologists describe the human journey through adulthood by intensively studying small samples of people. Daniel Levinson and others (1978, 1986) conducted lengthy interviews with 85 successful, middle-aged men and women. Based partly on their recollections, Levinson concluded that adults progress through periods of stability punctuated by times of upheaval and change. For example, he believes that as people enter their forties, they undergo a "midlife transition" to middle adulthood, which for many is a crisis, a time of great struggle or even of feeling struck down by life. They give up their dreams of fame and fortune (or the illusion that such bring happiness) and question their work and family commitments. The result, says Levinson, is often turmoil and despair. Fortyish people realize they no longer are starting out but rather are drawing closer to the end. When this painful growth period concludes at about age 45, they again settle into new or deepened attachments, set about completing their careers, and become more compassionate and reflective.

Many researchers are skeptical about such efforts to define adult life as a series of neatly packaged stages, especially stages based merely on interviews with a few selected people. To generalize from their career-oriented lives or to use their "midlife crises" to explain or justify renouncing old relationships is misleading (Gilligan, 1982). The fact—from large samples of people—is that job dissatisfaction, marital dissatisfaction, divorce, anxiety, and suicide do *not* surge during the early forties (Hunter & Sundel, 1989). Divorce, for example, is most common among those in their twenties, suicide among those in their seventies and eighties.

Are these markers of crisis too crude to detect a more subtle midlife turmoil? National Institute of Aging researchers Robert McCrae and Paul Costa (1990) gave 350 men between the ages of 30 and 60 a "Midlife Crisis Scale," assessing sense of meaninglessness and mortality, job and family dissatisfaction, and inner turmoil and confusion. They could find "no evidence at all" that

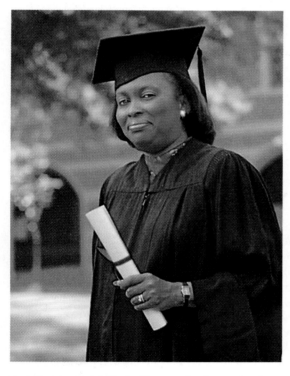

Resetting the Social Clock *To meet the demands of a changing economy, many adults have returned to school to acquire new skills. The social clock once "dictated" that college graduation should occur between ages 21 and 23. For this proud graduate, standard time is no longer the only setting.*

"Midway in the journey of our life I found myself in a dark wood, for the straight way was lost."

Dante
The Divine Comedy, 1300–1321

social clock The culturally preferred timing of social events such as marriage, parenthood, and retirement.

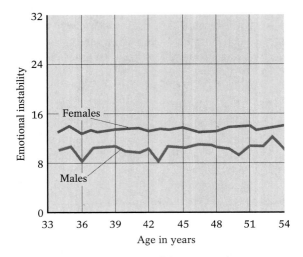

Figure 3–22 Early Forties Midlife Crises? *Among 10,000 people responding to a national health survey, there was no early forties' increase in emotional instability ("neuroticism") scores. (From McCrae & Costa, 1990.)*

"One can live magnificently in this world if one knows how to work and how to love."

Leo Tolstoy, 1856

By the late 1980s, only one-third of early 1970s newlyweds were still married and proclaiming their marriages "very happy" (Glenn, 1991).

such concerns peak at midlife. Surprised, they gave their scale to a new group of 300 men and supplemented it with a measure of emotional instability, which they gave to nearly 10,000 men and women. "The results were an exact reconfirmation: There was not the slightest evidence" that distress peaks anywhere in the midlife age range (Figure 3–22).

There is another reason skeptics question age-linked stage theories. The **social clock**—the cultural prescription of "the right time" to leave home, get a job, marry, have children, and retire—varies from culture to culture and era to era. In Jordan, 40 percent of brides are in their teens; in Hong Kong, only 3 percent are (United Nations, 1992). In Western Europe, fewer than 10 percent of men over 65 remain in the work force as do 16 percent in the United States; but 36 percent remain in the work force in Japan, and 69 percent in Mexico (Davies & others, 1991). In contemporary Western nations, the 1950s sequence from student to worker to wife to at-home mom to older worker has loosened. Modern women occupy these roles in any order or all at once. Given variations in the social clock and individual experience, the stage theory critics are suspicious of any proposed timetable of adult ages and stages.

More important than one's chronological age are life events. Marriage, parenthood, vocational changes, divorce, nest-emptying, relocation, and retirement mark transitions to new life stages whenever they occur—and increasingly they are occurring at unpredictable ages. The social clock is still ticking, but people feel freer to be out of sync with it.

Adulthood's Commitments

17. What do psychologists view as adulthood's two primary commitments?

Two basic aspects of our lives do, however, dominate adulthood. Erik Erikson called them *intimacy* (forming close relationships) and *generativity* (being productive and supporting future generations). Researchers have chosen various terms—*affiliation* and *achievement*, *attachment* and *productivity*, *commitment* and *competence*. But Sigmund Freud (1935) put it most simply: The healthy adult, he said, is one who can *love* and *work*. For most adults, love centers on family commitments toward partner, parents, and children. Work encompasses our productive activities, whether for pay or not.

Love Across time and place, human societies have nearly always included a relatively monogamous bond between men and women and a bond between parents and their children. We flirt, fall in love, and commit—one person at a time. "Pair-bonding is a trademark of the human animal," notes anthropologist Helen Fisher (1993). The arrangement makes biological sense. Parents who cooperated to nurture their children to maturity were more likely to pass their genes along to posterity than parents who didn't.

The bond of love is most satisfying and enduring when marked by a similarity of interests and values, a sharing of emotional and material support, and intimate self-disclosure (see Chapter 14). Marriage bonds are usually lasting when couples also marry after age 20 and are well-educated. Compared with their counterparts of 30 years ago, people in Western countries are better educated and marrying later.

Ironically, people are nevertheless divorcing more. When marrying, whether for the first time or the second, nearly everyone hopes for a satisfying, enduring bond. Yet marriages today are twice as likely to end in divorce as they were in 1960. To judge from the divorce rate—roughly 40 percent of Canadian marriages and half of U.S. marriages end in divorce—marriage has become a

Job Satisfaction and Life Satisfaction   *Work provides people with a sense of identity and competence and opportunities for accomplishment. Perhaps this is why a challenging and interesting occupation enhances people's happiness.*

union that often defies management. In Europe, divorce is nearly as common, after increasing 400 percent since 1960 (Inglehart, 1990).

Although rocked by increased divorce and often replaced by cohabitation, the institution of marriage endures. More than 9 in 10 adults marry. Of those who divorce, 75 percent remarry—and their second marriages are virtually as happy as the average first marriage (Vemer & others, 1989). Although the relatively few people who feel trapped in an unhappy marriage typically feel miserable, most married Europeans and North Americans generally feel happier than those unmarried, especially when compared with others who are separated and divorced (Inglehart, 1990). In the United States, for example, fewer than 25 percent of unmarried adults, but nearly 40 percent of married adults, have reported being "very happy" (Lee & others, 1991).

Marriages that last are not always devoid of conflict. Some couples fight but also shower one another with affection afterwards. Other couples never raise their voices yet also seldom praise or nuzzle. Both styles can last. After observing the interactions of 2000 couples, John Gottman (1994) reports a better indicator of likely marital success: at least a 5 to 1 ratio of positive to negative interactions. Stable marriages provide five times more smiling, touching, complimenting, and laughing than sarcasm, criticism, and insults. And if you want to predict which newlyweds will stay together, don't pay attention to how passionately they are in love. The couples who make it are more often those who restrain the number of putdowns that, unchecked, can take over a relationship (Notarius & Markman, 1993). To prevent a cancerous negativity, successful couples learn to fight fair (to state feelings without insulting) and to steer conflict away from chaos with comments like "I know it's not your fault" or "Be quiet for a moment and listen."

Often, love bears children. The most enduring of life changes, having a child, is for most people a happy event. As children begin to absorb time, money, and emotional energy, however, satisfaction with the marriage itself often declines. This is especially so among those employed women who, more than they expected, also bear the traditional burden of increased chores at home (Belsky & others, 1986; Hackel & Ruble, 1992).

Another significant event in family life happens when children leave home. If you have left home, consider your parents' experience: Did they suffer an "empty nest syndrome"—a feeling of distress focusing on a loss of purpose and relationship? Or did your parents discover renewed freedom, relaxation, and satisfaction with their own relationship?

Seven national surveys reveal that the empty nest is for most people a happy place (Adelmann & others, 1989; Glenn, 1975). Compared with middle-aged women who still have children at home, those whose nest has emptied report greater happiness and greater enjoyment of their marriage. Many parents therefore experience what sociologists Lynn White and John Edwards (1990) call a "post-launch honeymoon," especially if they maintain close relationships with their children. As Bernice Neugarten (1974) explains, "Most women are glad to see their children grow up, leave home, marry, and have their careers. The notion that they mourn the loss of their reproductive ability and their mother role does not seem to fit modern reality."

Work   For adults, a large part of the answer to "Who are you?" is the answer to "What do you do?" For most, to feel productive and competent is to raise children and to undertake a career. Career choices are hard to predict. During the first 2 years of college, most students cannot predict their later career path. Most shift from their initially intended majors while in college, many find their postcollege employment in fields not directly related to their majors, and most will change careers (Rothstein, 1980).

Does work, including a career, indeed contribute to fulfillment, as Freud supposed? One approach to answering this question has been to compare the roughly equal numbers of North American women who are or are not employed. From their studies at the Wellesley College Center for Research on Women, Grace Baruch and Rosaline Barnett (1986) conclude that what matters is not which roles a woman occupies—as paid worker, wife, and/or mother—but the quality of her experience in those roles. Happiness is having work that fits your interests and provides a sense of competence and accomplishment; having a partner who is a close, supportive companion and who sees you as special; and/or having loving children whom you like and feel proud of.

Well-Being Across the Life Span

To live is to grow older. In later life, income shrinks, work is taken away, the body deteriorates, recall fades, energy wanes, family members and friends die or move away, and the great enemy, death, looms ever closer. Small wonder that many presume the over-65 years to be the worst of times (Freedman, 1978).

Time for Fun *With the tasks of the earlier adult years behind them, many older adults have more time to enjoy pursuing their personal interests. No wonder their satisfaction with life usually remains high, especially if they are healthy and active.*

But they are not. *People of all ages report similar feelings of happiness and satisfaction with life.* Ronald Inglehart (1990) confirmed this when he amassed interviews conducted during the 1980s with representative samples of nearly 170,000 people in 16 nations. As Figure 3–23 illustrates, older people report as much happiness and satisfaction with life as younger people do. Given that growing older is one sure consequence of living, an outcome most of us prefer to its alternative, we can all take comfort in this finding.

Death and Dying

Most of us will suffer and cope with the deaths of relatives and friends. Usually, the most difficult separation is from one's spouse—a loss suffered by five times more women than men. Grief is especially severe when the death of a loved one comes suddenly and before its expected time on the social clock. The accidental death of a child or the sudden illness that claims a 45-year-old spouse may trigger a year or more of mourning flooded with memories, eventually subsiding to a mild depression that sometimes continues for several years (Lehman & others, 1987). Because AIDS so often strikes down people in midlife and younger, it has left countless family members and friends in a state of intense grief.

Figure 3–23 Age and Life Satisfaction *Does well-being align itself with any particular age group? Multinational surveys reveal that age differences in life satisfaction (and happiness) are trivial. (Data from Inglehart, 1990.)*

A Rite of Passage *In funeral rituals, mourners express their grief. Offering flowers, sharing food, and reminiscing with friends and family can help the bereaved cope with their loss.*

"How many of us older persons have really been . . . prepared for the second half of life, for old age, death and eternity?"

Carl Jung
Modern Man in Search of a Soul, 1933

The normal range of reactions to a loved one's death is wider than most people suppose. Some cultures encourage public weeping and wailing, others hide grief. Within any culture some individuals grieve more intensely and openly. Contrary to a popular myth, those who express the strongest grief immediately do not resolve their grief more quickly (Wortman & Silver, 1989).

Facing death with dignity and openness helps people complete the life cycle with a sense of life's meaningfulness and unity—the sense that their existence has been good and that life and death are parts of an ongoing cycle. Although death may be unwelcome, life itself can be affirmed even at death. This is especially so for people who review their lives not with despair but with what Erik Erikson called a sense of *integrity*—a feeling that one's life has been meaningful and worthwhile.

❗ *Rehearse It*

23. By age 75, a person has experienced losses in sight and hearing, and declining heart and muscular strength. However, this older adult is *less* likely than the young adult to suffer from

a. Alzheimer's disease.
b. accidents and falls.
c. short-term illnesses, such as the flu.
d. chronic illnesses, such as diabetes.

24. Some types of learning and remembering peak in early adulthood. By age 65, a person would be most likely to experience a decline in the ability to

a. recall and list all the items in the chapter glossary.
b. select the correct definition in a multiple-choice question.
c. evaluate whether a statement is true or false.
d. exercise sound judgment in answering an essay question.

25. In longitudinal studies the same person is retested at different ages. Longitudinal research suggests that intelligence

a. steadily declines with age.
b. peaks at age 25.
c. generally increases in later life.
d. remains stable until very late in life.

26. Most middle-age adults define themselves in terms of their career. Regarding women and work, which of the following has research shown to be true?

a. Women who work are happier than those who do not.
b. Women whose roles are wife and mother are happier than those who also work.
c. The quality of the woman's experience in her role matters more than the role the woman occupies.
d. The woman's age determines which role makes her happier.

27. Freud defined the healthy adult as one who is able to love and work. Erikson agrees; according to him the adult struggles to attain intimacy and

a. affiliation.
b. identity.
c. competence.
d. generativity.

28. Contrary to what many people assume,

a. older people are much happier than adolescents.
b. men in their forties express much greater dissatisfaction than women the same age.
c. people of all ages report similar levels of happiness.
d. those whose children have recently left home—the empty nesters—have the lowest level of happiness of all groups.

identical twins Twins who develop from a single zygote that splits in two, creating two genetic replicas.

fraternal twins Twins who develop from separate zygotes (fertilized eggs); who are genetically no closer than brothers and sisters, but shared the same fetal environment.

Curiously, twinning rates vary by race. Caucasians have twins roughly twice as often as Asians, and half as often as Africans (Diamond, 1986).

Reflections on the Major Developmental Issues

We began our survey of developmental psychology by identifying three pervasive issues: (1) whether development is steered more by genes or experience, (2) whether development is a gradual, continuous process or a discrete series of stages, and (3) whether development is characterized more by stability over time or by change. Let's conclude by taking stock of current thinking on each issue.

Nature and Nurture

18. What conclusions can we draw from research on the nature-nurture issue?

Everyone agrees: We are all influenced by genes *and* experience. The question is, how important is each? For physical attributes such as hair color, the genetic factor predominates. For psychological attributes, the answer is less obvious. In Chapter 8, we will examine the thorny debate over genetic and environmental determinants of intelligence. Here we will consider some provocative findings on how nature and nurture influence the developing personality.

Infants and young children cannot take personality tests, so investigators observe their actual behavior and infer their temperament. As we have seen, children come with differing temperaments. Are such temperamental differences hereditary? They seem to be. Animal breeders selectively mate dogs, horses, and other animals to be either high-strung or easygoing. Recall that when researcher Stephen Suomi (1987) placed genetically predisposed "uptight" versus "easygoing" infant monkeys with foster mothers who were themselves uptight or easygoing, heredity overrode rearing. Compared with the naturally easygoing monkeys, the uptight monkeys reacted more anxiously to the stress of separation from their mother, even when raised by easygoing, nurturant foster mothers. To judge from twin studies, genes influence human temperament, too (Matheny, 1989).

Studies of Twins Selective breeding varies heredity but not environment, thereby revealing an effect of heredity. Could we do the reverse—vary environment but not heredity—to see an effect of environment? Happily for our purposes, nature has given us ready-made subjects for this experiment: twins. **Identical twins**, who develop from a single fertilized egg that splits in two, are genetically identical (Figure 3-24). **Fraternal twins**, who develop from separate eggs, are genetically no more similar than ordinary brothers and sisters.

Do identical twins, being genetic replicas of one another, develop more similar personalities than fraternal twins? Studies of 13,000 pairs of Swedish identical and fraternal twins, of 7000 pairs of Finnish twins, and of 850 pairs of American twins reveal that identical twins are substantially more similar—in personality, abilities, and even interests (Floderus-Myrhed & others, 1980; Loehlin & Nichols, 1976; Rose & others, 1988). These findings suggest that there is indeed a significant genetic influence.

Separated Twins Imagine a science fiction experiment in which a mad scientist decides to separate identical twins at birth and rear them in differing environments. In reality, circumstances occasionally set up just these conditions. In 1979 when University of Minnesota psychologist Thomas Bouchard read a newspaper account of the reuniting of 39-year-old twins who had been sepa-

Figure 3–24 Same Egg, Same Genes; Different Eggs, Different Genes *Identical twins develop from a single fertilized egg, fraternal twins from two.*

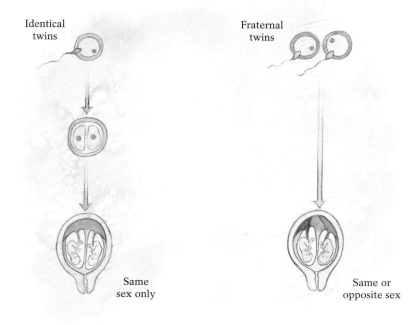

How Heritable Are Personality Traits? *Identical twins Gerald Levey and Mark Newman were separated at birth, 9 months after sharing the same fertilized egg. When reunited at age 31, they discovered that they had chosen the same vocation.*

rated from infancy, he seized the opportunity and flew them to Minneapolis for extensive tests. Bouchard was looking for differences. What "the Jim twins," Jim Lewis and Jim Springer, presented were amazing similarities (Holden, 1980a,b). Both had married women named Linda, divorced, and married women named Betty. One had a son James Alan, the other a son James Allan. Both had dogs named Toy, chain-smoked Salems, served as sheriff's deputies, drove Chevrolets, chewed their fingernails to the nub, enjoyed stock car racing, had basement workshops, and had built circular white benches around trees in their yards. They also had similar medical histories: Both gained 10 pounds at about the same time and then lost it; both suffered what they mistakenly believed were heart attacks, and both began having late-afternoon headaches at age 18.

Aided by publicity in magazine and newspaper stories, Bouchard and his colleagues (1990) have now located and studied some five dozen pairs of identical twins reared apart. They continue to be impressed by the similarities not only of tastes and physical attributes but also of personality, abilities, and even fears. In Sweden, which has a national registry of 25,000 pairs of adult twins, Nancy Pedersen and her co-workers (1988) identified 99 separated identical twin pairs and more than 200 separated fraternal twin pairs. Compared with equivalent samples of identical twins reared together, the separated identical twins had more dissimilar personalities. Still, separated twins were more alike when genetically identical rather than fraternal. And separation shortly after birth (rather than, say, at age 8) didn't amplify their personality differences.

The cute stories do not impress Bouchard's critics. They contend that if any two strangers of the same sex and age were to spend hours comparing their behaviors and life histories, they would probably discover many coincidental similarities. Even the more impressive data from the personality assessments are clouded by the reunion of many of the separated twins for some years before being tested. Moreover, adoption agencies tend to place separated twins in similar homes. When environments are similar, the impact of environment looks smaller relative to heredity. As twins age, differing experiences often make their personality differences more noticeable (McCartney & others, 1990). Nevertheless, the twin studies illustrate why scientific opinion has shifted toward a greater appreciation of genetic influences.

Coincidences are not unique to twins. Patricia Kern of Colorado was born March 13, 1941, and named Patricia Ann Campbell. Patricia DiBiasi of Oregon also was born March 13, 1941, and named Patricia Ann Campbell. Both had fathers named Robert, worked as bookkeepers, and have children ages 21 and 19. Both studied cosmetology, enjoy oil painting as a hobby, and married military men, within 11 days of each other. They are not genetically related. (From an AP report, May 2, 1983.)

It may be scary to realize the risks of having and raising children. In procreation a woman and a man shuffle their gene decks and deal a life-forming hand to their child-to-be, who is then subject to countless influences beyond their control. Keeping in mind that lives are formed by influences both under *and* beyond parents' control, we should, perhaps, be slower to credit parents for their children's achievements and slower still to blame them for their children's problems. Given our readiness to praise or blame parents, and to feel pride or shame, we do well to remember a simple principle: Within the normal range of environments, children's genetically predisposed tendencies will assert themselves. Moreover, lives also are formed by environmental influences beyond parents' control—by peer influences, by chance events, by all sorts of life experiences.

"It's a mistake to look at a child and say, 'I'm going to make this child X or Y.' I say . . . let's see what that child does well at and enjoys. Then let's reinforce those kinds of things . . . what people in the past have called gifts."

Thomas Bouchard (1990)

Adoption Studies   Adoption studies offer additional clues. For any given trait we can ask whether adopted children are more like their adoptive parents, who contribute a home environment, or their biological parents, who contributed their genes. The stunning finding from studying hundreds of adoptive families in Minnesota, Texas, and Colorado is that people who grow up together do *not* much resemble one another in personality, whether biologically related or not (Rowe, 1990).

What we have here is developmental psychology's biggest puzzle: Why are children in the same family so different? Is it because even though siblings share half their genes, each sibling has a very different combination of genes (Lykken & others, 1992)? Is it because each sibling experiences a different environment—differing peer influences, birth orders, life events (Dunn & Plomin, 1990)?

Adoption studies show that, although the personalities of adopted children do not much resemble those of their adoptive parents, adoption has many effects. First, the home environment influences adopted children's values, beliefs, and social attitudes. Second, in adoptive homes, child neglect and abuse are rare. Adopted children are less than half as likely as other children to have divorced or separated parents (Benson & others, 1994). (Adoptive parents are carefully screened; natural parents are not.) So it is not surprising that nearly all adopted children thrive. They score higher than their biological parents on intelligence tests, and many become happier and more stable people than they would have in a stressed or neglectful environment. Children need not resemble their adoptive parents to have benefitted from adoption.

A Family by Choice   *Studies of adoptive families have provided new clues to hereditary and environmental influences on development. How similar would you expect adopted children to be to their adoptive parents? To their biological parents?*

interaction effect A result in which the effect of one factor (such as genes) depends on the level of another (such as experience).

Nature and Nurture Interact To say that genes and experience are *both* important is true, but oversimplified. More precisely, they **interact**. Imagine two babies, one genetically predisposed to be attractive, sociable, and easygoing, the other less so. Assume further that the first baby attracts more affectionate and stimulating care than the second, and so develops into a warmer and more outgoing person. As the two children grow older, the more naturally outgoing one seeks activities and friends that encourage further social confidence.

What has caused their resulting personality difference? We cannot say that their personalities are *x* percent due to genes and *y* percent due to experience, for the gene-experience effect is combined. Asking which factor is more important is like asking whether the area of a soccer field is due more to its length or to its width. In fact, genes *direct* experience (Scarr & McCartney, 1983). As we grow older we *select* environments well suited to our natures. Moreover, as in our imaginary example, our genetically influenced traits *evoke* significant responses in others. This helps explain why identical twins reared in different families recall their parents' warmth as remarkably similar—almost as similar as if they had the same parents (Plomin & others, 1988). Fraternal twins recall their early family life more differently—even if reared in the same family! Thus, "children experience us as different parents, depending on their own qualities," notes Scarr (1990).

The moral: Our genes influence the experiences that shape us. It's not nature *versus* nurture, but nature *via* nurture.

Continuity and Stages

19. What conclusions can we draw from research on the issues of continuity versus stages and of stability versus change in lifelong development?

Adults are vastly different from infants. But do they differ as a giant redwood differs from its seedling—a difference created by gradual, cumulative growth? Or do they differ as a butterfly differs from a caterpillar—a difference of distinct stages?

Generally speaking, researchers who emphasize experience and learning see development as a slow, continuous shaping process. Those who emphasize biological maturation tend to see development as a sequence of genetically predetermined stages or steps; although progress through the various stages may be quick or slow, everyone passes through the stages in the same order.

Are there clear-cut stages of psychological development as there are physical stages such as crawling before walking? We have considered the stage theories of Jean Piaget on cognitive development, Lawrence Kohlberg on moral development, and Erik Erikson and Daniel Levinson on psychosocial development. And we have seen their stage theories criticized: Young children have some abilities that Piaget attributed to later stages. Kohlberg appeared biased by a worldview characteristic of educated males in individualistic cultures. The ideas of Erikson and Levinson are contradicted by research showing that adult life does not progress through a fixed, predictable series of steps.

Although research casts doubt on the idea that life proceeds through neatly defined, age-linked stages, the concept of stage remains useful. There are spurts of brain growth during childhood and puberty that correspond roughly to Piaget's stages (Thatcher & others, 1987). And stage theories contribute a developmental perspective on the whole life span, by suggesting how people of one age think and act differently when they arrive at a later age.

Stability and Change

This leads us to the final question: Over time, are people's personalities consistent, or do they change? If reunited with a long-lost grade school friend, would you instantly recognize that "it's the same old Andy"? Or does a person during one period of life seem like a different person at a later period?

Researchers who have followed lives through time have found evidence for both stability and change. There is continuity to personality and yet, happily for troubled children and adolescents, human development is lifelong: The struggles of the present may be laying a foundation for a happier tomorrow. More specifically, researchers generally agree on the following points:

1. The first 2 years of life provide a poor basis for predicting a person's eventual traits (Kagan, 1979). Even children and adolescents often change: Many confused and troubled children have blossomed into mature, successful adults (Macfarlane, 1964; Thomas & Chess, 1986). As people grow older, however, continuity of personality does gradually increase (Costa & McCrae, 1989; Stein & others, 1986).

2. Some characteristics, such as temperament, are more stable than others, such as social attitudes (Moss & Susman, 1980). But attitudes, too, become more stable with age (Krosnick & Alwin, 1989).

3. In some ways, we all change with age. Most shy, fearful toddlers begin opening up by age 4, and during adulthood most of us mellow. In the years after college, most people become calmer and more self-disciplined (McCrae & Costa, 1994). Many a 20-year-old goof-off has matured into a 40-year-old business or cultural leader. Such changes can occur without changing a person's position *relative* to others of the same age. The hard-driving young adult may mellow by later life yet still be a relatively hard-driving senior citizen.

Finally, we should remember that life contains *both* stability and change. Stability enables us to depend on others, motivates our concern for the healthy development of children, and provides our identity. Change motivates our concerns about present influences, sustains our hope for a brighter future, and enables us to adapt and grow with experience.

> *"At 70, I would say the advantage is that you take life more calmly. You know that 'this, too, shall pass!'"*
>
> Eleanor Roosevelt, 1954

! *Rehearse It*

29. Fraternal twins result when

a. a single egg is fertilized by a single sperm and then splits.

b. a single egg is fertilized by two sperm and then splits.

c. two eggs are fertilized by two sperm.

d. two eggs are fertilized by a single sperm.

30. Adoption studies seek to reveal genetic influences on personality mainly by

a. comparing adopted with nonadopted children.

b. evaluating whether adopted children more closely resemble their adoptive or biological parents.

c. studying the effect of prior neglect on adopted children.

d. studying the effect of one's age at adoption.

31. Some developmental researchers emphasize learning and experience; others emphasize biological maturation. These researchers thus believe in _____ or _____, respectively.

a. nature; nurture

b. continuity; stages

c. stability; change

d. randomness; predictability

32. Although development is lifelong, there is stability of personality over time. For example,

a. most personality traits emerge in infancy and persist throughout life.

b. temperament tends to remain stable throughout life.

c. few people change significantly after adolescence.

d. people tend to undergo greater personality changes as they age.

Reviewing *The Developing Person*

1. What are the major issues in developmental psychology?

Developmental psychologists examine our physical, mental, and social development throughout the life span. Three pervading issues create a backdrop for this study. The first is the nature-nurture issue: To what extent is development influenced by our genes and to what extent by our experiences? Second, is development a continuous process or a sequence of distinct stages? Third, are our traits stable throughout life, or do we change?

Prenatal Development and the Newborn

2. How does life develop before birth?

By studying the human life span from conception to death, developmental psychologists examine how we develop physically, cognitively, and socially. The life cycle begins when one sperm cell, out of the some 200 million ejaculated, unites with an egg to form a zygote. Attached to the uterine wall, the developing embryo begins to form body organs. By 9 weeks, the fetus becomes recognizably human. Along with nutrients, teratogens ingested by the mother can reach the developing child and place it at risk. The X (female) or Y (male) chromosome inherited from the father determines the child's sex.

3. What are some of the newborn's capabilities?

With the aid of new methods for studying babies, researchers have discovered that newborns are surprisingly competent. They are born with sensory equipment and reflexes that facilitate their interacting with adults and securing nourishment. For example, they quickly learn to discriminate the smell and sound of their mothers.

Infancy and Childhood

4. How do the brain and motor skills develop during infancy and childhood?

Within the brain, nerve cells form before birth and, sculpted by experience, their interconnections continue to multiply after birth. Infants' more complex physical skills—sitting, standing, walking—develop in a predictable sequence whose actual timing is a function of individual maturation rate.

5. How did Piaget view the mind's development?

Jean Piaget's observations of children convinced him—and almost everyone else—that the mind of a child is not that of a miniature adult. Piaget theorized that the mind develops by forming schemas that help us organize and interpret our experiences. In this way, children progress from the sensorimotor simplicity of the infant to more complex stages of thinking. For example, by about 8 months, an infant becomes aware that things still exist even when out of sight, an awareness known as object permanence.

Piaget believed that preschool children are egocentric and unable to perform simple logical operations. However, he thought that at about age 7 children become capable of performing concrete operations, such as those required to comprehend the principle of conservation. And by adolescence, most youth develop a capacity for more abstract, formal operational thinking. Recent research shows that young children are more capable, and development more continuous, than Piaget believed. The cognitive abilities that emerge at each stage have begun developing in a rudimentary form in the previous stage

6. How do the bonds of attachment form, and with what effects later in life?

Although the experiences of infancy are not consciously remembered for long and their effects may be reversed by later experiences, they can nevertheless have a lasting influence on social development. Attachment style in infancy predicts later social development. Infants become attached to their mothers and fathers not simply because mothers and fathers gratify biological needs but, more important, because they are comfortable, familiar, and responsive. If denied such care or if abused, both monkey and human infants may become pathetically withdrawn, anxious, and eventually abusive. Once an attachment forms, infants who are separated from their caregivers will, for a time, be distressed. Human infants who display secure attachment to their mothers generally become socially competent preschoolers. Infants' differing attachment styles reflect both their individual temperaments and the responsiveness of their parents and child care providers.

7. How do parenting styles and values vary among cultures?

Decisions about child-rearing involve value judgments about what traits to encourage in children. Cultural differences, such as between the communalism of Asian families and the individualism of Euro-American families, illustrate the impact of parental values.

8. What social influences help explain gender differences?

Cultural socialization through social learning and gender schemas helps explain why some children become more gender-typed than others.

Adolescence

9. What major physical changes occur during adolescence?

Adolescence begins at puberty with the onset of rapid growth and developing sexual maturity, and extends to adult independence. Boys seem to benefit from "early" maturation, girls from "late" maturation.

10. How did Piaget and Kohlberg describe cognitive and moral development during adolescence?

Piaget theorized that adolescents develop the capacity for formal operations, which enables them to reason abstractly. However, most developmentalists now believe that the rudiments of logic appear earlier than Piaget believed.

Following Piaget's lead, Lawrence Kohlberg contended that moral thinking likewise proceeds through a sequence of stages, from a preconventional morality of self-interest, to a conventional morality concerned with gaining others' approval or doing one's duty, to (in some people) a postconventional morality of agreed-upon rights or universal ethical principles. But morality also lies in actions. Moreover, say Kohlberg's critics, the postconventional level represents morality from the perspective of individualist, middle-class males.

11. What is involved in the adolescent's search for identity?

Erik Erikson theorized that a chief task of adolescence is to form one's identity, or sense of self. This often means "trying on" a number of different roles. For many people the struggle for identity continues in the adult years as new relationships emerge and new roles are assumed.

12. Do males and females differ in social relations?

Females and males differ in their social connectedness. Boys define themselves apart from their caregivers and playmates, girls through their social ties. Women typically become more caring, empathic, and sensitive to nonverbal cues, and men more independent and self-reliant.

13. What factors influence teen pregnancy?

Teens are vulnerable to pregnancy when ignorant or blindly optimistic about the risks of pregnancy, when inhibited from using birth control by guilt and minimal communication with parents and partners, and when under the influence of alcohol and mass media modeling of impulsive sex.

Adulthood

14. What major physical changes occur during middle and late adulthood?

The barely perceptible physical declines of early adulthood begin to accelerate during middle adulthood. For women, a significant physical change of adult life is menopause, which generally seems to be a smooth rather than rough transition. In men and women after 65, perceptual acuity, strength, and stamina decline, but short-term ailments are fewer. Neural processes slow, but the brain remains healthy, except for those who suffer brain disease, such as the progressive deterioration of Alzheimer's disease.

15. How are memory and intelligence influenced by aging?

As the years pass, recognition memory remains strong, although recall begins to decline, especially for meaningless information. Research on how intelligence changes with age has progressed through several phases: cross-sectional studies suggesting a steady intellectual decline after early adulthood; longitudinal studies suggesting intellectual stability until very late in life; and today's view that fluid intelligence declines in later life, but crystallized intelligence does not.

16. Why are age-based stage theories of adult development considered controversial?

Several theorists maintain that adults progress through an orderly sequence of age-related stages. Erikson proposed that after the formation of an identity, the young adult must deal with intimacy, achieve generativity in middle adulthood, and in later adulthood gain a sense of integrity. Daniel Levinson contends that moving from one stage to the next entails recurring times of crisis, such as the early-forties time of transition to midlife. Critics contend that people are not so predictable; life events involving love and work influence adult development in unanticipated ways and vary with culture. Moreover, feelings of well-being are remarkably stable across the life span.

17. What do psychologists view as adulthood's two primary commitments?

Adulthood's two major commitments are love (intimate relationships, especially with family) and work (productive activity, or what Erikson called "generativity").

Reflections on the Major Developmental Issues

18. What conclusions can we draw from research on the nature-nurture issue?

Adoption studies and studies of twins provide scientific support for the idea that genes influence one's developing personality. Developmentalists generally agree that genes *and* environment, biological *and* social factors, direct our life courses, and that their effects often interact, partly because our genetic predispositions influence our formative experiences.

19. What conclusions can we draw from research on the issues of continuity versus stages and of stability versus change in lifelong development?

Although the stage theories of Piaget, Kohlberg, and Erikson have been modified in the light of later research, the theories usefully alert us to differences among people of different ages. The discovery that people's traits continue to change in later life has helped create the new emphasis that development is lifelong. Nevertheless, research demonstrates that there is also an underlying consistency in most people's temperaments and personality traits, especially after infancy and early childhood.

Terms and Concepts to Remember

developmental psychology, p. 69

chromosomes, p. 70

DNA (deoxyribonucleic acid), p. 71

X chromosome, p. 71

Y chromosome, p. 71

testosterone, p. 71

zygote, p. 71

embryo, p. 72

fetus, p. 72

teratogens, p. 72

fetal alcohol syndrome (FAS), p. 72

rooting reflex, p. 73

maturation, p. 74

schema, p. 76

cognition, p. 76

sensorimotor stage, p. 76

object permanence, p. 77

egocentrism, p. 78

preoperational stage, p. 78

conservation, p. 78

concrete operational stage, p. 79

formal operational stage, p. 79

stranger anxiety, p. 81

attachment, p. 81

critical period, p. 82

imprinting, p. 82

temperament, p. 82

basic trust, p. 84

gender, p. 86

gender identity, p. 86

gender-typing, p. 86

social learning theory, p. 86

gender schema theory, p. 86

adolescence, p. 87

puberty, p. 88

primary sex characteristics, p. 88

secondary sex characteristics, p. 88

menarche [men-NAR-key], p. 88

identity, p. 93

intimacy, p. 93

menopause, p. 98

Alzheimer's disease, p. 100

cross-sectional study, p. 101

longitudinal study, p. 102

crystallized intelligence, p. 102

fluid intelligence, p. 102

social clock, p. 104

identical twins, p. 108

fraternal twins, p. 108

interaction effect, p. 110

Rehearse It Answer Key

1. b.	2. d.	3. c.	4. a.	5. a.	6. b.	7. c.	8. b.	9. d.
10. d.	11. a.	12. b.	13. b.	14. c.	15. c.	16. b.	17. b.	18. d.
19. c.	20. b.	21. b.	22. d.	23. c.	24. a.	25. d.	26. c.	27. d.
28. c.	29. c.	30. b.	31. b.	32. b.				

Critical Thinking Exercise

Now that you have read and reviewed Chapter 3, take your learning a step further by testing your critical thinking skills on this perspective-taking exercise.

Since he retired as a college professor 5 years ago, 65-year-old Bentley has suffered numerous health problems, including high blood pressure, chest pains, and muscle tremors. Once very active physically, Bentley has not been able to take his daily 30-minute jog for the past 3 years. For the first time in his life Bentley takes several prescription drugs daily, including one that controls his muscle tremors by blocking the neurotransmitter acetylcholine. Bentley's biggest complaint, however, is that he is bored and misses the intellectual stimulation of his former students and colleagues.

Bentley's daughter Mary recently read a magazine article on Alzheimer's disease and is worried that something may be seriously wrong with her father's mind. For a man who once prided himself on his infallible memory and the quickness of his thinking, Bentley's memory now occasionally falters, and his reactions are slower. Fearing that her father may be suffering from Alzheimer's disease, Mary decides to conduct an experiment. Pretending that she is stumped while working on a "brain teaser," she asks her father to help her identify the next letter in the series *d f i m r x e*. When Bentley becomes flustered and cannot quickly come up with the answer, Mary is crestfallen, certain that her father is in the early stages of a devastating disease.

1. State Mary's argument in your own words.
2. Describe the evidence on which Mary has based her argument.
3. State three reasons why Mary's evidence is not strong enough to support her argument.

Check your progress on becoming a critical thinker by comparing your answers with the sample answers found in Appendix B.

Chapter 4

Sensation and Perception

Sensing the World: Some Basic Principles

Thresholds

Sensory Adaptation

Vision

The Stimulus Input: Light Energy

The Eye

Visual Information Processing

Color Vision

The Other Senses

Hearing

Touch

Pain

Taste

Smell

Body Position and Movement

Perceptual Organization

Form Perception

Depth Perception

Perceptual Constancy

Interpretation

Sensory Restriction and Restored Vision

Perceptual Adaptation

Perceptual Set

Is There Perception Without Sensation?

Claims of ESP

Skepticism About ESP

In the outer world, innumerable stimuli bombard your body. In a silent, cushioned, inner world of utter darkness floats your brain. These facts raise a question that predates psychology by thousands of years and helped inspire its beginnings a century ago: *How does the world out there get in?*

To modernize the question: How do we construct our representations of the external world? How do we represent a campfire's flicker, crackle, and odor as patterns of active neural connections? And how from this living neurochemistry do we create our conscious experience of its motion and temperature, its aroma and beauty?

To represent the world in our head, we must detect physical energy from the environment and encode it as neural signals, a process traditionally called **sensation**. And we must select, organize, and interpret our sensations, a process traditionally called **perception**. In our everyday experiences, sensation and perception blend into one continuous process. In this chapter, we slow down that process to study its parts.

We will start with the sensory receptors and work up to higher levels of processing. Psychologists refer to sensory analysis that starts at the entry level and works up as *bottom-up* processing. Then we will focus on how our minds interpret what our senses detect. We construct perceptions drawing not only on sensations coming "up" to the brain but also on our unique experiences and expectations, which psychologists call *top-down* processing.

Failures of perception may occur anywhere between sensory detection and perceptual interpretation. For example, the eyes of a person born with cataracts may be unable to detect light. Without the light stimulus, the brain's higher-level visual processing equipment is useless. Studying brain-damaged patients reveals the importance of other links in the sensation-perception process. After losing a temporal lobe area essential to recognizing faces, patient "E. H." suffers from a condition called *prosopagnosia*. She has complete sensation but incomplete perception. She can sense visual information—indeed may accurately report the features of a face—yet is unable to recognize it. Shown an unfamiliar face, she is unreactive. Shown a familiar face, her autonomic nervous system responds with measurable perspiration. Still, she hasn't a clue to

What's Going on Here? *Our sensory and perceptual processes work together to help us sort out the complex images in this Bev Doolittle painting, "The Forest Has Eyes." Processing from the bottom up, our sensory systems detect the lines, angles, and colors that form the horses, rider, and surroundings. From the top down, we consider the painting's title, notice the apprehensive expressions, and then direct our attention to aspects of the painting that will give those observations meaning. (Detail, "The Forest Has Eyes" by Bev Doolittle © The Greenwich Workshop, Inc., Trumball, CT.)*

who the person is. Shown her own face in a mirror she is again stumped. Because of her brain damage, she is unable to process from the top down; she cannot relate her stored knowledge to the sensory input.

Sensing the World: Some Basic Principles

Sensory systems enable organisms to obtain the information they need to function and survive. A frog, which feeds on flying insects, has eyes with receptor cells that fire only in response to small, dark, moving objects. A frog could starve to death knee-deep in motionless flies. But let one zoom by and the frog's "bug detector" cells snap awake. A male silkworm moth has receptors so sensitive to the odor of the female sex-attractant that a single female silkworm moth need release only a billionth of an ounce per second to attract every male silkworm moth within a mile. Which is why there continue to be silkworms. We humans are similarly designed to detect what are, for us, the important features of our environments. Nature's sensory gifts suit the needs of each particular recipient. The human ear, for instance, is most sensitive to the sound frequencies of the human voice.

Thresholds

We exist in a sea of energy. At this moment, you and I are being struck by x-rays and radio waves, ultraviolet and infrared light, and sound waves of very high and very low frequencies. But to all of them we are blind and deaf. The shades on our senses are open just a crack, allowing us only a restricted awareness of this vast sea. **Psychophysics** is the study of the relationship between this physical energy and our psychological experience. What stimuli can we detect? At what levels of intensity? How sensitive are we to changing stimulation?

sensation The process by which our sense receptors and nervous system receive and represent stimulus energies from our environment.

perception The process of organizing and interpreting sensory information, enabling us to recognize meaningful objects and events.

psychophysics The study of relationships between the physical characteristics of stimuli and our psychological experience of them.

absolute threshold The minimum stimulation needed to detect a particular stimulus.

subliminal Below one's absolute threshold for conscious awareness.

Absolute Thresholds

1. What is an absolute threshold, and are we influenced by stimuli below it?

To some kinds of stimuli we are exquisitely sensitive. Standing at the top of a mountain on an utterly dark, clear night, we can, given normal senses, see a candle flame atop another mountain 30 miles away. In a silent room, we can hear a watch ticking 20 feet away. We can feel the wing of a bee falling on our cheek. We can smell a single drop of perfume in a three-room apartment (Galanter, 1962).

Our awareness of these faint stimuli illustrates our **absolute thresholds**—the minimum stimulation necessary to detect a particular stimulus (light, sound, pressure, taste, odor). Psychologists usually measure absolute threshold by recording the stimulation needed for detection 50 percent of the time. To test your absolute threshold for sounds, a hearing specialist exposes each ear to varying sound levels. For each pitch, the hearing test defines where half the time you correctly detect the sound and half the time you do not. For each of the senses, that 50–50 point defines your absolute threshold.

Subliminal Stimulation

In 1956, controversy erupted over a (false) report that New Jersey movie audiences were unwittingly being influenced by imperceptible flashed messages to DRINK COCA-COLA and EAT POPCORN (Pratkanis, 1992). Forty years later, the controversy has erupted anew. Advertisers are said to manipulate consumers by imperceptibly printing the word *sex* on crackers and by embedding erotic images in liquor ads. Rock recordings are said to contain "satanic messages" that can be heard if the recordings are played backward and that can unconsciously persuade the unwitting listener, even when played normally. Entrepreneurs offer to help us lose weight, stop smoking, or improve our memories with audiotapes of soothing ocean sounds that contain unheard messages such as, "I am thin," "Smoke tastes bad," and "I do well on tests. I have total recall of information." These claims make two assumptions: that unconsciously we can sense **subliminal** (literally, "below threshold") stimuli (Figure 4–1) and that, without our awareness, these stimuli have extraordinary suggestive powers. Can we? Do they?

(a)   **(b)**

On a Different Wavelength *Sensory capacities are not the same across species, perhaps because different ecological niches demand sensitivity to different kinds of energy. Compare, for example, the way a flower is registered by (a) a human eye and (b) a bee's eye. The bee can detect differences in ultraviolet wavelengths reflected by the flower, enabling it to see the "landing field" that makes possible more efficient food-gathering.*

How to think uncritically without psychology: James Vicary, an unemployed marketing researcher, masterminded the EAT POPCORN subliminal advertising hoax with the help of uncritical reporters and broadcasters. Vicary reportedly collected big fees from advertising firms for his promised services—and then disappeared (Rogers, 1993, 1994).

Figure 4–1 Subliminal Stimuli *Absolute threshold is arbitrarily measured as the intensity at which we perceive a stimulus 50 percent of the time. By this definition, stimuli that are perceived less than 50 percent of the time are subliminal.*

Unconscious Influence: Backward Messages in Rock Albums

The influences on how we think and act are often subtle, even unrecognized. Might it therefore be possible for unperceived backward messages, implanted on rock albums, to corrupt unwitting listeners? In the 1980s, concerns about such messages led to political efforts in the Canadian parliament and several American states to contain the supposed powers of "backmasking."

Are these concerns warranted? Assuming that such backward messages exist, could they have any influence? If indeed people are unconsciously influenced by a message they can't perceive, how might psychologists detect such influence?

Confronted with such questions and armed with the methods of psychological science, University of Alberta psychologists John Vokey and Don Read (1985) decided to investigate. They began by recording some simple sentences from Lewis Carroll's "Jabberwocky" and from the Twenty-third Psalm and then rerecorded them backward. This retained the pauses and pitches, producing a record-ing that sounded rather like a foreign language.

But it was gibberish. Listeners could not detect whether a given word was or wasn't present, whether they had heard a declarative sentence or a question, or whether the sentence was meaningful or nonsensical. When simple messages such as "Jesus loves me, this I know" were played backward, people couldn't surpass chance when guessing whether the words were Satanic, Christian, pornographic, advertising, or from a nursery rhyme.

Might meaningless backward information nevertheless have a subtle influence? Research psychologists have invented clever methods for uncovering such influences, including one that uses homophones—words that sound alike but differ in spelling and meaning. Imagine, for example, hearing the sentence, "Climbing a mountain is a remarkable *feat*." Later, even after you had forgotten the sentence, on hearing the italicized homophone you would probably be more likely to spell it as f-e-a-t rather than f-e-e-t. This effect occurs without people realizing why they have chosen a particular spelling. But you must hear the homophone normally, not backward. When Vokey and Read buried the homophone in a backward message the unconscious influence disappeared.

In continued quest of unconscious influence, Ian Begg and his McMaster University colleagues (1993) exploited "the illusory truth effect"—the tendency for repeated statements, such as "The most prevalent infection in the world today is cholera" to seem true. As usual, people became more accepting of such statements when repeatedly played forward. But the phenomenon disappeared when the researchers played the statements backward.

Once again, a popular idea collapsed when tested experimentally. Any influence of rock music lies in its forward rather than backward messages.

---

difference threshold The minimum difference that a subject can detect between two stimuli 50 percent of the time. We experience the difference threshold as a just noticeable difference (jnd).

just noticeable difference (jnd) See *difference threshold*.

Weber's law The principle that, to be perceived as different, two stimuli must differ by a constant minimum percentage (rather than a constant amount).

Can we be affected by stimuli too weak for us *ever* to notice? Recent experiments hint that, under certain conditions, the answer may be yes. One experiment subliminally flashed either emotionally positive scenes (such as kittens or a romantic couple) or negative scenes (such as a werewolf or a dead body) an instant before subjects viewed slides of nine people (Krosnick & others, 1992). Although the subjects consciously perceived only a flash of light, they gave more positive ratings to people whose photos had been associated with positive scenes. People somehow looked nicer if their photo immediately followed unperceived kittens rather than an unperceived werewolf. Chinese characters, too, get rated more positively if preceded by a flashed but unperceived smiling face rather than a scowling face (Murphy & Zajonc, 1993). Sometimes we *feel* what we do not know and cannot describe. A weak stimulus evidently triggers a weak response that evokes a feeling, though not a conscious awareness of the stimulus.

But does the fact of subliminal *sensation* verify entrepreneurial claims of subliminal *persuasion*? Can advertisers really manipulate us with "hidden persuasion"? The near-consensus among research psychologists is no. Their verdict is like that of astronomers who say that, yes, astrologers are right that stars and planets are out there, but no, they don't directly affect us. Consider: The laboratory research reveals a *subtle, fleeting* effect on *thinking*. Subliminal tape hucksters claim something different: a *powerful, enduring* effect on *behavior*. Experiments, such as the one described in Chapter 1, show that commercial subliminal tapes have no effect beyond one's belief in them (the placebo effect).

Shortly after news of the supposed EAT POPCORN effect swept North America in the mid-1950s, the Canadian Broadcasting Corporation used a popular Sunday night TV show to flash a subliminal message 352 times (*Advertising Age*, 1958). Asked to guess the message, none of the almost 500 letter-writers did so. Nearly half, however, did report feeling strangely hungry or thirsty during the show. But this was merely an effect of expectations. The actual message was TELEPHONE NOW. The effect of these 352 subliminal messages on Canadian telephone usage? Zilch.

Difference Thresholds

2. How is our threshold for detecting differences affected by the magnitude of the stimuli?

To function effectively, we need absolute thresholds low enough to allow us to detect important sights, sounds, textures, tastes, and smells. We also need to detect small differences among stimuli. A musician must detect minute discrepancies in an instrument's tuning. A wine taster must detect the slight flavor difference between two vintage wines.

The **difference threshold** (also called the **just noticeable difference**, or **jnd**) is the minimum difference a person can detect between any two stimuli 50 percent of the time. The difference threshold increases with the magnitude of the stimulus. Add 1 ounce to a 10-ounce weight and you will detect the difference; add 1 ounce to a 10-*pound* weight and you will not, because the difference threshold has increased. More than a century ago, Ernst Weber noted that regardless of their magnitude, two stimuli must differ by a constant proportion for their difference to be perceptible. This principle—that the difference in threshold is not a constant amount but some constant *proportion* of the stimulus—is so simple and so widely applicable that we still refer to it as **Weber's law**. The exact proportion varies, depending on the stimulus. For the average person to perceive their differences, two lights must differ in intensity by 8 percent, two objects must differ in weight by 2 percent, and two tones must differ in frequency by only 0.3 percent (Teghtsoonian, 1971).

Weber's law is a rough approximation that works well for nonextreme sensory stimuli. It also parallels some of our life experiences. If the price of a 50-cent candy bar goes up by a nickel, shoppers might notice the change; similarly, it might take a $5000 price hike in a $50,000 Mercedes-Benz to raise the eyebrows of its potential buyers. In both cases, the price went up by 10 percent. Weber's principle: Our thresholds for detecting differences are a roughly constant proportion of the size of the original stimulus.

The LORD is my shepherd;
I shall not want.
He maketh me to lie down
        in green pastures:
    he leadeth me
        beside the still waters.
He restoreth my soul:
    he leadeth me
        in the paths of righteousness
        for his name's sake.
Yea, though I walk through the valley
        of the shadow of death,
    I will fear no evil:
    for thou art with me;
        thy rod and thy staff
        they comfort me.
Thou preparest a table before me
        in the presence of mine enemies:
    thou anointest my head with oil,
        my cup runneth over.
Surely goodness and mercy
        shall follow me
        all the days of my life:
    and I will dwell
        in the house of the LORD
        for ever.

The Difference Threshold *In this computer-generated copy of the Twenty-third Psalm, each line of the typeface changes imperceptibly. How many lines are required for you to experience a just noticeable difference?*

The Nose Knows *An honored line of work—the profession of aroma testing—may soon be threatened by Neotronics Olfactory Sensing Equipment (a.k.a. NOSE). Using special sensors, the machine can produce a computer "fingerprint" of a rose's fragrance or any other complex odor molecules. It may outperform humans analytically, but can it possibly understand how aromas touch the heart?*

sensory adaptation Diminished sensitivity that is a consequence of constant stimulation.

"We need above all to know about changes; no one wants or needs to be reminded 16 hours a day that his shoes are on."

Neuroscientist David Hubel (1979)

For 9 in 10 people—but, curiously, for only 1 in 3 schizophrenia patients—this eye flutter turns off when the eye is following a moving target (Holzman & Matthysse, 1990).

"My suspicion is that the universe is not only queerer than we suppose, but queerer than we can suppose."

J. B. S. Haldane
Possible Worlds, 1927

Sensory Adaptation

3. What function does sensory adaptation serve?

Entering your neighbor's living room, you smell an unpleasant odor. You wonder how she tolerates the stench, but within minutes you no longer notice it. Jumping into a swimming pool, you shiver and complain how cold it is. A short while later a friend arrives and you exclaim, "C'mon in. Water's fine!" These examples illustrate **sensory adaptation**—our diminishing sensitivity to an unchanging stimulus. (To experience this phenomenon, move your watch up your wrist an inch: You will feel it—but only for a few moments.) After constant exposure to a stimulus, our nerve cells fire less frequently.

Why, then, if we stare at an object without flinching, does it not vanish from sight? Because, unnoticed by us, our eyes are always moving, quivering just enough to guarantee that retinal stimulation continually changes.

What if we could stop our eyes from moving? Would sights seem to vanish, as odors do? To find out, psychologists have devised ingenious instruments for maintaining a constant image on the retina. Imagine that we fitted a subject, Mary, with one of these instruments—a miniature projector mounted on a contact lens (Figure 4–2a). When Mary's eye moves, the image from the projector moves as well. Thus, everywhere that Mary looks the scene is sure to go.

If we project the profile of a face through such an instrument, what will Mary see? At first she will see the complete profile. But within a few seconds, as her sense receptors begin to fatigue, things get weird. Bit by bit, the image vanishes, only later to reappear and then disappear—in recognizable fragments or as a whole (Figure 4–2b).

Figure 4–2 A Stabilized Image *(a) A projector mounted on a contact lens makes the projected image move with the eye. (b) Initially the subject sees the stabilized image, but soon she sees fragments fading and reappearing. (From "Stabilized images on the retina" by R. M. Pritchard. Copyright © 1961 Scientific American, Inc. All rights reserved.)*

Although sensory adaptation reduces our sensitivity, it offers an important benefit: It enables us to focus our attention on *informative* changes in our environment without being distracted by the uninformative, constant stimulation of garments, odors, and street noise. Our sense receptors are alert to novelty; bore them with repetition and they free our attention for things more interesting and important. This reinforces a fundamental lesson: We perceive the world not exactly as it is, but as it is useful for us to perceive it.

Sensory thresholds and adaptation are not the only commonalities among the senses. All the senses receive sensory stimulation, transform it into neural information, and deliver that information to the brain. How do the senses work? How do we see? Hear? Smell? Taste? Feel pain? Let's start with vision, the sense most people prize the most.

! *Rehearse It*

1. To construct meaning out of our external environment, we select, organize, and interpret sensory information. This process is

a. sensation.
b. persuasion.
c. encoding.
d. perception.

2. Sensation is to _____ as perception is to _____.

a. absolute threshold; difference threshold
b. bottom-up processing; top-down processing
c. interpretation; detection
d. conscious awareness; persuasion

3. The absolute threshold is the minimum stimulation that a person can detect 50 percent of the time. Knowing your absolute threshold for sound tells you

a. the smallest difference you can detect between two sounds.
b. how likely you are to hear a particular faint sound.

c. why you become used to background noise.
d. whether you are being affected by subliminal stimulation.

4. People wonder whether subliminal stimuli, such as undetectably faint sights or sounds, influence us. Subliminal stimuli are

a. too weak to be processed by the brain in any way.
b. below the absolute threshold for conscious awareness.
c. consciously perceived only 50 percent of the time.
d. strong enough to affect our behavior.

5. To be perceived as different, two lights must differ in intensity by at least 8 percent. This illustrates a general principle called Weber's law, which states that for a difference to be perceived, two stimuli must differ by

a. a fixed or constant amount.
b. a constant minimum percentage.

c. a constantly changing amount.
d. more than 7 percent.

6. Confronted with an unchanging stimulus, we experience sensory adaptation. Sensory adaptation explains why

a. we perceive subliminal stimuli.
b. we notice only large differences between two stimuli.
c. we soon get used to an unpleasant smell.
d. we have difficulty keeping our eyes completely still when staring at an object.

7. Sensory adaptation reduces our sensitivity to some stimuli in the environment. However, sensory adaptation has survival benefits. It helps us focus on

a. the world as it really is.
b. underlying phenomena and stimuli.
c. important changes in the environment.
d. constant features of the environment.

Vision

Part of your taken-for-granted genius is your body's ability to convert one sort of energy to another. Our sensory systems convert stimulus energy into neural messages. Your eyes, for example, receive light energy and manage an amazing feat. They transform the energy into messages that the brain processes into what you consciously see. Let's consider how.

wavelength The distance from the peak of one light or sound wave to the peak of the next. Electromagnetic wavelengths vary from the long pulses of radio transmission to the short blips of cosmic rays.

hue The dimension of color that is determined by the wavelength of light; what we know as the color names "blue," "green," and so forth.

intensity The amount of energy in a light or sound wave, which we perceive as brightness or loudness, as determined by the wave's amplitude.

The Stimulus Input: Light Energy

4. How does the eye transform light energy into neural messages?

Scientifically speaking, what strikes our eyes is not color but pulses of electromagnetic energy that our visual system experiences as color. What we see as visible light is but a thin slice of the whole spectrum of electromagnetic radiation. As Figure 4–3 illustrates, this *electromagnetic spectrum* ranges from the imperceptibly short pulses or waves of gamma rays to the narrow band that we see as visible light to the long waves of radio transmission.

Two physical characteristics of light help determine our sensory experience of it. Its **wavelength**—the distance from one wave peak to the next—determines its **hue** (the color we experience, such as blue or green) (Figure 4–4a). **Intensity**, the amount of energy in light waves (determined by a wave's *amplitude*, or height), influences brightness (Figure 4–4b). To understand *how* we transform physical energy into a sensation of color, we first need to understand our mind's window, the eye.

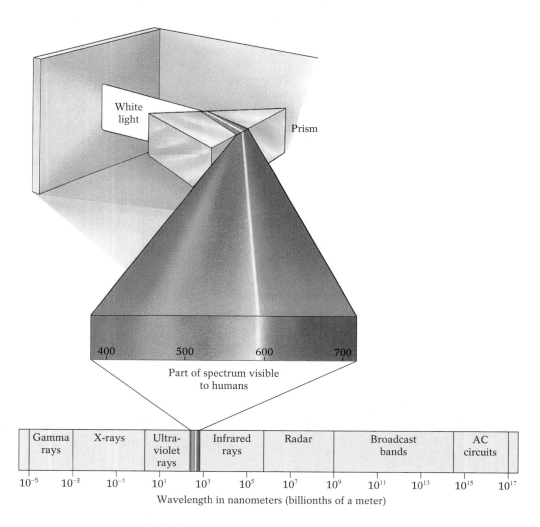

Figure 4–3   The Spectrum of Electromagnetic Energy *This spectrum ranges from gamma rays as short as the diameter of an atom to radio waves over a mile long. The narrow band of wavelengths visible to the human eye (shown enlarged) extends from the shorter waves of blue-violet light to the longer waves of red light. Other organisms are sensitive to differing portions of the spectrum. As we noted earlier (page 119), bees cannot see red but can see ultraviolet light, the part of the spectrum that causes sunburn in humans.*

Figure 4–4 The Physical Properties of Waves *(a) Waves vary in wavelength, the distance between successive peaks. Frequency, the number of complete waves that can pass a point in a given time, depends on the wavelength. The shorter the wavelength, the higher the frequency. (b) Waves also vary in amplitude, the height from peak to trough. Wave amplitude determines the intensity of colors and sounds.*

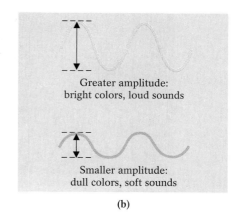

Shorter wavelength

Higher frequency:
bluish colors, high-pitched sounds

Longer wavelength

Lower frequency:
reddish colors, low-pitched sounds

(a)

Greater amplitude:
bright colors, loud sounds

Smaller amplitude:
dull colors, soft sounds

(b)

pupil The adjustable opening in the center of the eye through which light enters.

iris A ring of muscle tissue that forms the colored portion of the eye around the pupil and controls the size of the pupil opening.

lens The transparent structure behind the pupil that changes shape to focus images on the retina.

accommodation The process by which the eye's lens changes shape to focus the image of near objects on the retina.

retina The light-sensitive inner surface of the eye, containing the receptor rods and cones plus layers of neurons that begin the processing of visual information.

The Eye

Light enters the eye through the **pupil**, a small adjustable opening (Figure 4–5). The pupil's size, and therefore the amount of light entering the eye, is regulated by the **iris**, a colored muscle surrounding the pupil. Behind the pupil is a **lens** that focuses the incoming rays into an image on a light-sensitive surface. It does so by changing its curvature in a process called **accommodation**. The light-sensitive surface on which the rays focus is the **retina**, the multilayered tissue that lines the inside of the back of the eyeball.

For centuries, scientists have known that when the image of a candle passed through a small opening, its mirror image appeared inverted on a dark wall behind (like the inverted rose in Figure 4–5). This fact had scholars baffled. If the retina receives an upside-down image, how can we see the world right side up? Did the optic nerve twist the image right side up by the time it reached the cortex? Eventually scientists discovered that the retina doesn't read the image as a whole. Rather, its millions of receptor cells convert light energy into neural impulses. These impulses are sent to the brain and assembled *there* to create a perceived, upright-seeming image.

Retina
Lens
Fovea (point of central focus)
Optic nerve
Pupil
Cornea
To occipital lobe
Iris
Blind spot

Figure 4–5 The Eye *Light rays reflected from the rose pass through the cornea, pupil, and lens. The curvature and thickness of the lens change to bring either nearby or distant objects into focus on the retina. Light rays travel in straight lines. So rays from the top of the rose strike the bottom of the retina and those from the left side of the rose strike the right side of the retina. The rose's retinal image is thus upside-down and reversed.*

Rod-Shaped Rods and Cone-Shaped Cones *As the scanning electron microscope shows, rods and cones are well named. Rods are more light-sensitive than the color-sensitive cones, which is why the world looks colorless at night. Some nocturnal animals, such as toads, mice, rats, and bats, have retinas made up almost entirely of rods, allowing them to function well in dim light. These creatures probably have very poor color vision.*

Figure 4–6 The Path of Light Through the Eye *Before signals from the retina reach the brain, they pass through a switchboard of neural cells. A ray of light entering the eye triggers a photochemical reaction in the rods and cones (1) at the back of the retina behind the other neural layers. This chemical reaction in turn triggers the bipolar cells (2). The bipolar cells then activate the ganglion cells (3), which converge to form the optic nerve. The optic nerve transmits information to the brain's occipital lobe.*

TABLE 4–1		
The Human Eye		
	Cones	**Rods**
Number	6 million	120 million
Location in retina	Center	Periphery
Sensitivity in dim light	Low	High
Color sensitive?	Yes	No

Figure 4–7 The Blind Spot *Where the optic nerve leaves the eye (Figure 4–6), there are no receptor cells. This creates a blind spot in our vision. To demonstrate, close your left eye, look at the spot, and move the page to a distance from your face (about a foot) at which the car disappears. In everyday vision the blind spot doesn't impair your vision because your eyes are moving and because one eye covers what the other misses.*

The Retina

If we were to follow a single particle of light energy into the eye, we would see that it first makes its way through the retina's outer layer of cells to its buried receptor cells, the **rods** and **cones** (Table 4–1 and Figure 4–6). When light energy strikes the rods and cones chemical changes generate neural signals that activate the neighboring *bipolar cells*, which in turn activate the neighboring *ganglion cells*. The axons from the network of ganglion cells converge like the strands of a rope to form an **optic nerve** that carries information to the brain. Nearly a million messages can be sent by the optic nerve at once, through nearly 1 million ganglion fibers. (The auditory nerve, which enables hearing, carries much less information through its mere 30,000 fibers.) Where the optic nerve leaves the eye there are no receptor cells—creating a **blind spot** (Figure 4–7).

Rods enable black-and-white vision; cones enable you to see color. As illumination diminishes, the cones become ineffectual. The rods, however, remain sensitive in dim light, because several rods will funnel their faint energy from dim light onto a single bipolar cell. That is why you don't see colors in dim light. When you enter a darkened theater or turn off the light at night, your pupils dilate to allow more light to reach the rods in the retina's periphery. Typically it takes 20 minutes or more before our eyes fully adapt.

You can demonstrate dark adaptation by closing or covering one eye for up to 20 minutes, then making the room light not quite bright enough to read this

rods Retinal receptors that detect black, white, and gray; necessary for peripheral and twilight vision, when cones don't respond.

cones Receptor cells concentrated near the center of the retina that function in daylight or in well-lit conditions. The cones detect fine detail and give rise to color sensations.

optic nerve The nerve that carries neural impulses from the eye to the brain.

blind spot The point at which the optic nerve leaves the eye, creating a "blind" spot because no receptor cells are located there.

feature detectors Nerve cells in the brain that respond to specific features of the stimulus, such as movement, angle, or shape.

book with your open eye. Now open the dark-adapted eye and read. This period of dark adaptation is yet another instance of the remarkable adaptiveness of our sensory systems, for it parallels the natural twilight transition between the sun's setting and darkness.

Visual Information Processing

5. How is visual information processed in the brain?

We process visual information at progressively more abstract levels. At the entry level, the retina's neural layers encode and analyze the sensory information before routing it to the cortex. The information from the retina's nearly 130 million receptor rods and cones is received and transmitted by the million or so ganglion cells, whose fibers make up the optic nerve. But most information processing occurs in the brain. Any given area of the retina relays its information to a corresponding location in the visual cortex at the back of the brain (Figure 4–8).

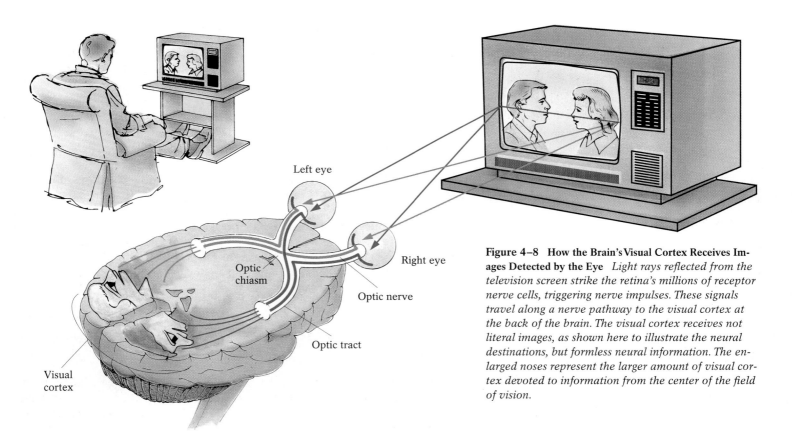

Figure 4–8 How the Brain's Visual Cortex Receives Images Detected by the Eye *Light rays reflected from the television screen strike the retina's millions of receptor nerve cells, triggering nerve impulses. These signals travel along a nerve pathway to the visual cortex at the back of the brain. The visual cortex receives not literal images, as shown here to illustrate the neural destinations, but formless neural information. The enlarged noses represent the larger amount of visual cortex devoted to information from the center of the field of vision.*

Turn your eyes to the left, close them, and then gently rub the right side of your right eyelid with your fingertip. Note the patch of light to the left, moving as your finger moves. Why do you see light? Why at the left? (See page 135.)

Feature Detection

When individual ganglion cells register information in their region of the visual field, they send signals to the visual cortex. Nobelists David Hubel and Torsten Wiesel (1979) demonstrated that when certain cortical neurons, called **feature detectors**, receive this information, they respond to specific features of a scene—to particular edges, lines, and angles. From these elements the brain assembles the perceived image.

Figure 4–9   Electrodes Record How Individual Cells in This Monkey's Visual Cortex Respond to Different Visual Stimuli *Hubel and Wiesel won the Nobel prize for their discovery that most cells in the visual cortex respond only to particular features—for example, to the edge of a surface, or to a line at a 30-degree angle in the upper right part of the field of vision. More complex features trigger higher-level detector cells, which integrate information from these simpler ones.*

Scene

↓

Retinal processing:
Receptor rods and cones → bipolar cells → ganglion cells

↓

Feature detection:
Brain's detector cells respond to elementary features—bars, edges, or gradients of light

↓

Abstraction:
Brain's higher-level cells respond to combined information from feature detector cells

↓

Recognition:
Brain matches the constructed image with stored images

Figure 4–10   A Simplified Summary of Visual Information Processing

For example, Hubel and Wiesel report that a given brain cell might respond maximally to a line flashed at a particular tilt (Figure 4–9). If the line is tilted further—say, from a 2 o'clock to a 3 o'clock or 1 o'clock position—the cell quiets down. Thus, the feature detector cells record amazingly specific features taken in by the eye. Feature detector cells pass this information to other cells that respond only to more complex patterns. The basic idea then is that perceptions arise from the interaction of many neuron systems, each performing a simple task.

Parallel Processing

Neural impulses travel a million times slower than a computer's internal messages, yet the brain humbles any computer by recognizing a familiar face instantly. Unlike most computers, which do step-by-step serial processing, we do **parallel processing**, which means we can do several things at once. Our brain divides a visual scene into subdimensions such as color, depth, movement, and form and works on each aspect simultaneously (Livingstone & Hubel, 1988).

The distribution of visual tasks to different neural work teams explains a strange phenomenon. After a stroke, people may lose just one aspect of vision. A person may perceive color but not movement. If something moves, it disappears until it stops. Other brain-damaged patients can tell you all about the subdimensions of an object—the size and color of a rose, for instance—without recognizing the object or the person. This reminds us of an important truth: Our brains do many things at once, automatically and without our awareness.

The other senses process information with similar speed and intricacy. Opening the back door, you recognize the aroma wafting from the kitchen even before you step inside. Answering the phone, you recognize the friend calling from the moment she says "Hi." Within a fraction of a second after such events stimulate the senses, millions of neurons have simultaneously coordinated in extracting the essential features, comparing them with past experience, and identifying the stimulus (Freeman, 1991).

This emerging scientific understanding of sensation illustrates neuropsychologist Roger Sperry's (1985) reflection: The "insights of science give added, not lessened, reasons for awe, respect, and reverence." Think about it: As you look at someone, the visual information is sent to your brain as millions of neural impulses, then reassembled into its component features, and finally, in some as yet mysterious way, composed into a consciously perceived, meaningful image (Figure 4–10). That all of this happens instantly, effortlessly, and continuously is indeed awesome.

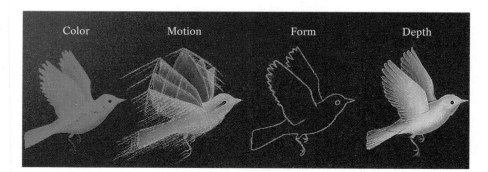

Parallel Processing *Studies of brain-damaged patients suggest that the brain delegates the work of processing color, motion, form, and depth to different areas. After taking a scene apart, how does the brain integrate these subdimensions into the perceived image? The answer to this question is the Holy Grail of vision research.*

parallel processing Information processing in which several aspects of a problem are processed simultaneously. The brain's natural mode of information processing for many functions, including vision; contrasts with the step-by-step (serial) processing of most computers and of conscious problem solving.

Young-Helmholtz trichromatic (three-color) theory The theory that the retina contains three different color receptors—one most sensitive to red, one to green, one to blue—which when combined can produce the perception of any color.

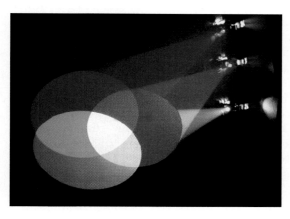

Figure 4–11 The Three Primary Colors of Light *The primary colors mix to create other colors. For example, red and green combine to create yellow. All three—red, green, and blue—combine to create white.*

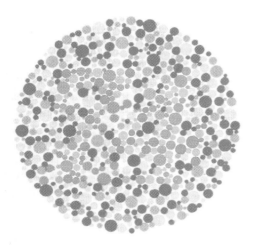

Figure 4–12 Color-Deficient Vision *People who suffer red-green blindness have trouble perceiving this number within this design.*

Color Vision

6. What theories contribute to our understanding of color vision, and how are we affected by color constancy?

People talk as if objects possess color. We say, "The tomato is red." Perhaps you have pondered the old question, "If a tree falls in the forest and no one hears it, does it make a sound?" We can ask the same of color: If no one sees the tomato, is it red?

The answer is no. First, the tomato is everything *but* red, because it *rejects* (reflects) the long wavelengths of red. Second, the tomato's color is our mental construction. As Isaac Newton (1704) noted, "The [light] rays are not coloured." Color, like all aspects of vision, resides not in the object but in the theater of our brains. Even while we are dreaming, we may perceive things in color.

In the study of vision, one of the most basic and intriguing mysteries is how we see the world in color. How, from the light energy striking the retina, does the brain manufacture our experience of color—and of such a multitude of colors? Our difference threshold for colors is so low that we can discriminate some 7 million different color variations (Geldard, 1972).

At least most of us can. For about 1 person in 50, vision is color-deficient— and that person is probably male, because the defect is genetically sex-linked. To understand why some people have color-deficient vision we must first understand how normal color vision works.

Modern detective work on the mystery of color vision began in the nineteenth century when Hermann von Helmholtz built on the insights of an English physicist, Thomas Young. Both recognized a clue in the fact that any color can be created by combining the light waves of three primary colors—red, green, and blue (Figure 4–11). Young and Helmholtz inferred that the eye must have three types of receptors, one for each primary color.

Many years later, researchers measured the response of various cones to different color stimuli and confirmed the **Young-Helmholtz trichromatic (three-color) theory**, which simply states that the retina has three types of color receptors, each especially sensitive to one of three colors. And surprise! Those colors are, indeed, red, green, and blue. When we stimulate combinations of these cones, we see other colors. For example, there are no receptors especially sensitive to yellow. Yet when both red- and green-sensitive cones are stimulated, we see yellow.

Most color-deficient people are not actually "color blind." Rather, they simply lack functioning red- or green-sensitive cones. Their vision is dichromatic instead of trichromatic, making it difficult to distinguish red and green, as in Figure 4–12 (Boynton, 1979). Dogs, too, lack receptors for the wavelengths of red, giving them only limited, dichromatic color vision (Neitz & others, 1989).

Soon after Young and Helmholtz proposed the trichromatic theory, physiologist Ewald Hering pointed out that other parts of the color vision mystery remained unsolved. For example, we see yellow when mixing red and green light. But how is it that people blind to red and green can often still see yellow? And why does yellow appear to be a pure color and not a mixture of red and green, as purple does of red and blue?

Hering found a clue in the well-known occurrence of *afterimages*. When you stare at a green square for a while and then look at a white sheet of paper, you see red, green's "opponent color." Stare at a yellow square and you will later see its opponent color, blue, on the white paper (as in the flag demonstration in Figure 4–13, page 130). Hering surmised that there were two additional

Figure 4–13   Afterimage Effect *Stare at the center of the flag for a minute and then shift your eyes to the dot in the white space beside it. What do you see? (After tiring your neural response to black, green, and yellow, you should see their opponent colors.)*

color processes, one responsible for red versus green perception, and one for blue versus yellow.

A century later, researchers confirmed Hering's **opponent-process theory**. *After* leaving the receptor cells, visual information is analyzed in terms of the opponent colors red and green, blue and yellow, and also black and white. In the retina and in the thalamus (where impulses from the retina are relayed en route to the visual cortex) some neurons are turned "on" by red but turned "off" by green. Others are turned on by green but off by red. Opponent processes explain afterimages, such as in the flag demonstration, in which we tire our green response by staring at green. When we then stare at white (which contains all colors, including red), only the red part of the green/red pairing will fire normally.

The present solution to the mystery of color vision is therefore roughly this: Color processing occurs in two stages. The retina's red, green, and blue cones respond in varying degrees to different color stimuli, as the Young-Helmholtz trichromatic theory suggested. Their signals are then processed by the nervous system's opponent-process cells, en route to the visual cortex.

"Is it not stirring to understand how the world actually works—that white light is made of colors, that color measures light waves, that transparent air reflects light . . . ? It does no harm to the romance of the sunset to know a little about it."

Carl Sagan
Skies of Other Worlds, 1988

Color Constancy

Our experience of color depends on something more than the wavelength information received by our trichromatic cones and transmitted through the opponent-process cells of our thalamus.

That something more is the surrounding *context*. If you view only part of a tomato, without knowing what it is, its color will seem to change as the light changes. But if you see the whole tomato as one item in a bowl of fresh vegetables, its color will remain roughly constant as the lighting shifts—a phenomenon known as **color constancy**. Dorothea Jameson (1985) notes that a green leaf hanging from a brown branch may, when the illumination changes, now reflect the same light energy that formerly came from the brown branch. Yet to us the leaf stays greenish and the branch stays brownish.

We take this color constancy for granted, but the phenomenon is remarkable. It demonstrates that our experience of color comes not just from the object—the color is not in the isolated leaf—but from everything around it as well. You and I see color thanks to our brains' computations of the light reflected by any object *relative to its surrounding objects*.

In an unvarying context, we maintain color constancy. But what if we change the context? Because the brain computes the color of an object relative to its context, the perceived color changes (as is dramatically apparent in Figure 4–14). This principle—that we perceive objects not in isolation but in their environmental context—is especially significant for artists, interior decorators, and clothing designers. The color of a wall or of a swatch of paint on a canvas is determined not just by the paint in the can but by the surrounding colors.

Figure 4–14   Color Depends on Context *In this painting by Josef Albers, the unchanging line seems to vary from gray to yellow as its surrounding context changes.*

Rehearse It

8. Two physical characteristics of light help determine our sensory experience of it. The characteristic that determines the color we experience is

a. intensity.
b. amplitude.
c. wavelength.
d. hue.

9. The blind spot is located in the area of the retina

a. where there are rods but no cones.
b. where there are cones but no rods.
c. where the optic nerve leaves the eye.
d. where the bipolar cells meet the ganglion cells.

10. Rods and cones are the eye's receptor cells. Cones are especially sensitive to _____ light and are responsible for our _____ vision.

a. bright; black-and-white
b. dim; color

c. bright; color
d. dim; black-and-white

11. According to Hubel and Wiesel, the brain includes cells that respond maximally to certain bars, edges, and angles. These cells are called

a. rods and cones.
b. feature detectors.
c. bug detectors.
d. ganglion cells.

12. Unlike most computers, the brain is capable of simultaneously processing separate aspects of an object. We call this ability

a. parallel processing.
b. feature detection.
c. recognition.
d. accommodation.

13. Researchers today believe that the Young-Helmholtz and opponent-process theories together account for color vision.

The Young-Helmholtz theory shows that the eye contains _____, and the opponent-process theory accounts for the brain's having _____.

a. opposing retinal processes; three pairs of color receptors
b. opponent-process cells; three types of color receptors
c. three pairs of color receptors; opposing retinal processes
d. three types of color receptors; opponent-process cells

14. We perceive tomatoes and string-beans as consistently red and green, even though shifting illumination may alter their reflective wavelengths. This demonstrates the phenomenon of

a. afterimages.
b. color constancy.
c. trichromatic vision.
d. color processing.

The Other Senses

For humans, vision is the major sense. More of our brain cortex is devoted to vision than to any other sense. Moreover, when there is a conflict between visual and other sensory information, vision tends to dominate or "capture" the other senses. This phenomenon of **visual capture** is an everyday experience. When viewing a movie for which the projector provides the sound, we nevertheless perceive the sound as coming from the screen, where we *see* the actors talking. While viewing a roller coaster ride on a giant wraparound movie screen, we may brace ourselves, even though our other senses tell us we're not moving. In both cases, vision has captured the other senses.

Yet without our senses of hearing, touch, taste, smell, and body motion and position, our capacities for experiencing the world would be vastly diminished.

Hearing

7. How does the ear transform sound energy into neural messages?

Like our other senses, our hearing, or **audition**, is highly adaptive. We hear a wide range of sounds, but we are best able to hear sounds having frequencies within a range that corresponds to the range of the human voice. We also are remarkably sensitive to faint sounds, an obvious boon to our ancestors' survival when hunting or being hunted. (If our ears were much more sensitive, we

opponent-process theory   The theory that opposing retinal processes (red-green, yellow-blue, white-black) enable color vision. For example, some cells are stimulated by green and inhibited by red; others are stimulated by red and inhibited by green.

color constancy   Perceiving familiar objects as having consistent color, even if changing illumination alters the wavelengths reflected by the objects.

visual capture   The tendency for vision to dominate the other senses; we perceive voices in films as coming from the screen we see rather than from the projector behind us.

audition   The sense of hearing.

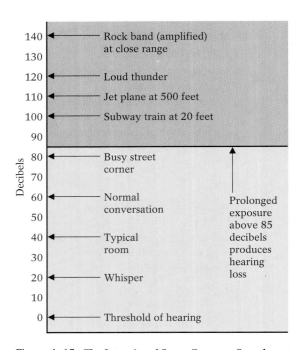

Figure 4–15 **The Intensity of Some Common Sounds, Measured in Decibels**

The Middle Ear *This remarkable photo of the middle ear (see Figure 4–16) shows the eardrum (at left, curving in a bit), the round window (black spot at far right), the stirrup (just left of the round window), and the oval window (covered by the stirrup). The actual distance from eardrum to oval window is less than 1 centimeter.*

would hear a constant hiss from the movement of air molecules.) Moreover, we are acutely sensitive to differences in sounds. We can easily detect differences among thousands of human voices, which helps us instantly recognize the voice of almost anyone we know.

For hearing as for seeing, the fundamental question is: How do we do it? How do we transform sound energy into neural messages that the brain interprets as a particular sound coming from a particular place?

The Stimulus Input: Sound Waves

Hit a piano key and the resulting stimulus energy is sound waves—jostling molecules of air, each bumping into the next, like a shove being transmitted through the crowded exit tunnel of a football stadium. The resulting waves of compressed and expanded air are like the ripples on a pond circling out from where a tossed stone has broken the surface of the water. The strength, or amplitude, of sound waves determines their *loudness*. Waves also vary in length, and therefore in **frequency** (recall Figure 4–4, page 125). Their frequency determines their **pitch**: The longer the waves (thus, the lower their frequency), the lower the pitch; the shorter the waves (thus, the higher their frequency), the higher the pitch. A piccolo produces much shorter sound waves than does a kettledrum.

Decibels are the measuring unit for sound energy. The absolute threshold for hearing is arbitrarily defined as 0 decibels. Every 10 decibels corresponds to a tenfold increase in sound. Thus, normal conversation (60 decibels) is about 100 times louder than a whisper (40 decibels). And a tolerable 90 decibel sound is a trillion times louder than the faintest detectable sound. (For light, too, we can tolerate a stimulus a trillion times more intense than a barely noticeable glimmer.) When prolonged, however, exposure to sounds above 85 decibels can produce hearing loss (Figure 4–15).

The Ear

To hear, we must somehow convert sound waves into neural activity. The human ear accomplishes this feat through an intricate mechanical chain reaction (Figure 4–16). First, the visible outer ear channels sound waves through the auditory canal to the *eardrum*, a tight membrane that vibrates with the waves. The **middle ear** transmits the eardrum's vibrations through a piston made of three tiny bones (the *hammer, anvil,* and *stirrup*) to a snail-shaped tube in the **inner ear** called the **cochlea** (KOHK-lee-uh). The incoming vibrations cause the cochlea's membrane (the *oval window*) to vibrate the fluid that fills the tube. This motion causes ripples in the *basilar membrane*, which is lined with *hair cells*, so named because of their tiny hairlike projections. At the end of this sequence, the rippling of the basilar membrane bends these hair cells, rather like the wind bending a wheat field. The hair cell movement triggers impulses in the adjacent nerve fibers, which converge to form the auditory nerve. Through this mechanical chain of events, sound waves cause the hair cells of the inner ear to send neural messages up to the temporal lobe's auditory cortex. From vibrating air to moving piston to fluid waves to electrical impulses to the brain: We hear.

Brief exposure to extremely intense sounds, such as gunfire near one's ear, and prolonged exposure to intense sounds, such as amplified music, can damage receptor cells (Backus, 1977; West & Evans, 1990). Although rock and roll may be here to stay, the sad truth for some rock musicians is that their hearing may not be. For others, hearing loss, especially for the higher frequencies, accompanies the biology of aging. To many older adults, chirping birds seem quieter and soft conversation becomes frustratingly unintelligible.

Figure 4–16 How We Transform Sound Waves Into Nerve Impulses That Our Brain Interprets *(a) The outer ear funnels sound waves to the eardrum. The bones of the middle ear amplify and relay the eardrum's vibrations through the oval window into the fluid-filled cochlea. (b) The resulting pressure changes in the cochlear fluid cause the basilar membrane to ripple, bending the hair cells on the surface. Hair cell movements trigger impulses at the bases of the nerve cells, whose fibers converge to form the auditory nerve. (For clarity, the cochlea is shown partially uncoiled.)*

frequency The number of complete wavelengths that pass a point in a given time (for example, per second).

pitch A tone's highness or lowness; depends on frequency.

middle ear The chamber between the eardrum and cochlea containing three tiny bones (hammer, anvil, and stirrup) that concentrate the vibrations of the eardrum on the cochlea's oval window.

inner ear The innermost part of the ear, containing the cochlea, semicircular canals, and vestibular sacs.

cochlea [KOHK-lee-uh] A coiled, bony, fluid-filled tube in the inner ear through which sound waves trigger nerve impulses.

How Do We Locate Sounds?

As the placement of our eyes allows us to sense depth visually (page 142), the placement of our two ears allows us to enjoy stereophonic ("three-dimensional") hearing. For at least two reasons, two ears are better than one. If a car to the right honks, your right ear receives a more *intense* sound slightly *sooner* than your left ear. Because sound travels 750 miles per hour and our ears are but 6 inches apart, the loudness difference and time lag are extremely small. But our auditory system is so sensitive that our two ears can detect such minute differences (Brown & Deffenbacher, 1979; Middlebrooks & Green, 1991). A just noticeable difference in the direction from which two sounds come corresponds to a time difference of just 0.000027 second! With auditory as with visual information, the brain uses parallel processing—by putting specialized neural teams to work simultaneously on different subtasks. Owls (and probably humans, too) process timing differences in one neural pathway and intensity differences in another before converging their information to pinpoint a sound's location (Konishi, 1993).

Touch

8. How do we sense touch and feel pain?

If you had to give up one sense, which would it be? If you could retain only one sense, which would it be?

Touch would be a good candidate for retention. Right from the start, touch is strangely essential to our development. As we noted in Chapter 3, premature babies gain weight faster and go home sooner if stimulated by hand massage. Infant rats deprived of their mothers' grooming touch produce less growth hor-

The Precious Sense of Touch   *As William James wrote in his* Principles of Psychology *(1890), "Touch is both the alpha and omega of affection."*

A Professional Firewalker   *What's the most painful thing you can imagine? Walking on hot coals is surely high on the list. But as physicist John Campbell demonstrates, this particular feat is grounded in our gullibility. Burning substances that conduct heat poorly are safe to touch quickly. That's why Campbell's wet feet can quick-step across hot coals without being burned and why your fingers can painlessly touch a baking cake, although not the pan.*

"When belly with bad pains doth swell, It matters naught what else goes well."

Sadi
The Gulistan, 1258

mone and have a lower metabolic rate—a good way to keep alive until the mother returns, but a reaction that will lead to stunted growth if she's delayed. Infant monkeys allowed to see, hear, and smell—but not touch—their mothers are desperately unhappy; much less so are those separated by a screen with holes that allow touching. As lovers, we yearn to touch—to kiss, to stroke, to snuggle like spoons.

Columnist Dave Barry is perhaps right to say of the skin that it "keeps people from seeing the inside of your body, which is repulsive, and it prevents your organs from falling onto the ground." But skin does more. Our "sense of touch" is actually a mix of at least four distinct skin senses—pressure, warmth, cold, and pain. Touching various spots on the skin with a soft hair, a warm or cool wire, and the point of a pin reveals that some spots are especially sensitive to pressure, others to warmth, others to cold, still others to pain. Within the skin are different types of specialized nerve endings.

Surprisingly, there is no simple relationship between what we feel at a given spot and the type of specialized nerve ending found there. Only pressure has identifiable receptors. The relationship between warmth, cold, and pain and the receptors that respond to them remains a mystery. Other skin sensations are variations of the basic four (pressure, warmth, cold, and pain):

- Stroking adjacent pressure spots creates a tickle.
- Repeated gentle stroking of a pain spot creates an itching sensation.
- Touching adjacent cold and pressure spots triggers a sense of wetness, which you can experience by touching dry, cold metal.

Pain

Be thankful for occasional pain. Pain is your body's way of telling you that something has gone wrong. It draws your attention to a burn, a break, or a rupture and tells you to change your behavior immediately. The rare people who are born without the ability to feel pain may experience severe injury without ever being alerted by pain's danger signals. Usually, they die by early adulthood. Without the discomfort that makes us occasionally shift position, their joints fail from excess strain. Without pain, the effects of unchecked infections and injuries accumulate (Neese, 1991). More numerous are those who endure chronic pain. The suffering of people with persistent or recurring backaches, arthritis, headaches, and cancer-related pain prompts us to try to understand pain.

Pain is a property not only of the senses—of the region where we feel it—but of the brain as well. As the dreamer sees with eyes closed and the listener hears a ringing during utter silence, so some 7 in 10 amputees may feel pain or movement in their nonexistent limbs (Melzack, 1992). An amputee may try to step off a bed onto a phantom foot or to lift a cup with a phantom hand. These *phantom limb sensations* indicate that with pain, as with sights and sounds, the brain can misinterpret the spontaneous central nervous system activity that occurs in the absence of normal sensory input. To see, hear, and feel, we require not a body but a brain.

Unlike vision, however, the pain system is not located in a simple neural cord running from a sensing device to a definable area in the brain. Moreover, there is no one type of stimulus that triggers pains (as light triggers vision), and there are no special receptors (like the retina's rods and cones) for pain. At low intensities, the stimuli that produce pain cause other sensations, including warmth or coolness, smoothness or roughness.

Although no theory of pain explains all the available findings, psychologist Ronald Melzack and biologist Patrick Wall's (1965, 1983) **gate-control theory** provides a useful model. Melzack and Wall believe that the spinal cord contains

gate-control theory Melzack and Wall's theory that the spinal cord contains a neurological "gate" that blocks or allows pain signals to pass on to the brain. The "gate" is opened by the activity of pain signals traveling up small nerve fibers and closed by activity in larger fibers or by information coming from the brain.

"Pain is increased by attending to it."

Charles Darwin
Expression of Emotions in Man and Animals, 1872

"From there to here, from here to there, funny things are everywhere."

Dr. Seuss
One Fish, Two Fish, Red Fish, Blue Fish

Although Lamaze training reduces labor pain, most Lamaze patients request a local anesthetic during labor. Some—having expected a "natural, painless birth"—feel needless guilt and failure (Melzack, 1984). Melzack therefore advocates—as does the Lamaze program itself—childbirth training that prepares a woman "to cope with an event which is often extremely painful and, at the same time, one of the most fulfilling peak experiences in her life."

Answer to question on page 127: Your retinal cells are so responsive that even pressure triggers them. But your brain interprets their firing as light. Moreover, it interprets the light as coming from the left—which is where light normally comes from when it activates the right side of the retina.

a sort of neurological "gate" that either blocks or allows pain signals to pass on to the brain. The spinal cord contains small nerve fibers that conduct most pain signals, and larger fibers that conduct most other sensory signals. When tissue is injured, the small fibers activate and open the neural gate, and you feel pain. Large-fiber activity closes the pain gate, turning pain off.

Thus, one way to treat chronic pain is to stimulate (electrically, by massage, or even by acupuncture) "gate-closing" activity in the large neural fibers. Rubbing the area around your stubbed toe creates competing stimulation that will block some of the pain messages. Placing ice on a bruise serves not only to control swelling but also to trigger cold messages that close the gate on the pain signals. Some arthritic patients wear a small portable electrical stimulation unit next to a painful area. When the unit stimulates nerves in the area, the patient feels a vibrating sensation rather than pain (T. Murphy, 1982).

Melzack and Wall believe the pain gate can also be closed by information from the brain. These brain-to-spinal cord messages help explain some striking psychological influences on pain. When distracted from pain signals and soothed by the release of endorphins, our experience of pain may be greatly diminished. Sports injuries may be unnoticed, until taking the after-game shower. During a 1989 basketball game, Ohio State University guard Jay Burson broke his neck—and kept playing. Clearly, there is more to pain than what stimulates the sense receptors.

There is also more to our memories of pain than the pain we experience. In experiments, and after medical procedures, people overlook a pain's duration. Their memory snapshots instead record its peak moment and how much pain they felt at the end. Daniel Kahneman and his co-researchers (1993) discovered this when they asked people to immerse one hand in painfully cold water for 60 seconds, and then the other hand in the same painfully cold water for 60 seconds followed by a slightly less painful 30 seconds more. Curiously, when asked which trial they would prefer to repeat, most preferred the longer trial, with more net pain—but less pain at the end. When patients recalled the pain of a colon examination a month later, their memories were similarly dominated by the final (and the worst) moments, not by how long the pain lasted. It's better, it seems, for medical personnel to taper down a painful procedure than to switch it off abruptly.

If pain is indeed a physical and a psychological phenomenon, then it should be treatable both physically and psychologically. For example, the widely practiced Lamaze method of childbirth combines several of these pain control techniques. Among them are relaxation (through deep breathing and muscle relaxation), counterstimulation (through gentle massage), and distraction (through focusing attention on, say, a pleasant photograph).

Distracting people with pleasant images ("Think of a warm, comfortable environment") or drawing their attention away from the painful stimulation ("Count backward by 3's") is an especially effective way to increase pain tolerance (Fernandez & Turk, 1989; McCaul & Malott, 1984). No wonder a well-trained nurse will distract needle-shy patients with chatter and may ask them to look away when inserting the needle.

Taste

9. How do we experience taste and smell?

Our sense of taste involves four basic sensations—sweet, sour, salty, and bitter (McBurney & Gent, 1979). All other tastes are mixtures of these. Investigators have, however, been frustrated in their search for specialized nerve fibers for each of the four basic taste sensations.

sensory interaction The principle that one sense may influence another, as when the smell of food influences its taste.

Taste is a chemical sense. Inside the little bumps on the top and sides of your tongue are 200 or more taste buds. Each contains a pore that catches food chemicals. These molecules are sensed by 50 taste receptor cells that project antennalike hairs into the pore. Some of these receptors respond mostly to sweet-tasting molecules, others to salty- , sour- , or bitter-tasting ones. It doesn't take much to trigger a response. When a stream of water is pumped across the tongue, the addition of a concentrated salty or sweet taste for but one-tenth of a second gets noticed (Kelling & Halpern, 1983). When a friend asks for "just a taste" of your soft drink, you can squeeze off the straw after a mere fraction of a second.

Taste receptors reproduce themselves every week, so if you burn your tongue with hot food it matters little. However, as you grow older, the number of taste buds decreases, as does taste sensitivity (Cowart, 1981). (No wonder adults enjoy strong-tasting foods that children resist.) Heavy smoking and alcohol use accelerate the decline in taste buds and sensitivities.

Although taste buds are essential for taste, there is more to taste than meets the tongue. Hold your nose, close your eyes, and have someone feed you various foods. A piece of apple may then be indistinguishable from a piece of raw potato; a piece of steak may taste like cardboard. To savor a taste, we normally breathe the aroma through our nose—which is why eating is not much fun when you have a bad cold, and why people who lose their sense of smell may think they have also lost their sense of taste. Smell not only adds to our perception of taste, it also changes it. A drink's strawberry odor enhances our perception of its sweetness. This is **sensory interaction** at work—the principle that one sense may influence another. Smell plus taste equals flavor. Similarly, we correctly perceive the location of the voice directly in front of us partly because we also see that the person is in front of us, not behind, above, or beneath us.

Smell

Breaths come in pairs—inhale, exhale—except at two moments: birth and death. Each day, as you inhale and exhale nearly 20,000 breaths of life-sustaining air, you bathe your nostrils in a stream of scent-laden molecules. More than you may realize, your resulting experiences of smell (*olfaction*) are intimate ones. To smell someone you inhale something of the person.

Like taste, smell is a chemical sense. We smell something when air-carried molecules of a substance reach a tiny cluster of 5 million receptor cells at the top of each nasal cavity (Figure 4–17).

These olfactory receptor cells, waving like sea anemones on a reef, respond selectively to the aroma of brownies baking, to a wisp of smoke, to a friend's fragrance, and instantly alert the brain. Even nursing infants and mothers have a literal chemistry to their relationship, as they quickly learn to recognize each others' scents (McCarthy, 1986). Aided by smell, a mother fur seal returning to a beach crowded with pups will find her own. Yet, unlike that of the mother fur seal, our sense of smell is less impressive than the acuteness of our seeing and hearing (within the stimulus ranges we detect). Looking out across a garden we see its forms and colors in exquisite detail and hear its singing birds, yet smell little of it without jamming our nose into the flowers.

Precisely how olfactory receptors work is a mystery. Unlike light, which can be separated into its spectral colors, an odor cannot be separated into more elemental odors. Thus, the olfaction system has no parallel to the retina, which detects myriad colors with sensory cells dedicated to red, green, or blue. Olfactory receptors recognize odors individually.

Figure 4–17 The Sense of Smell *To smell a rose, molecules of its fragrance must reach receptors at the top of the nose. Sniffing swirls air up to the receptors, enhancing the aroma.*

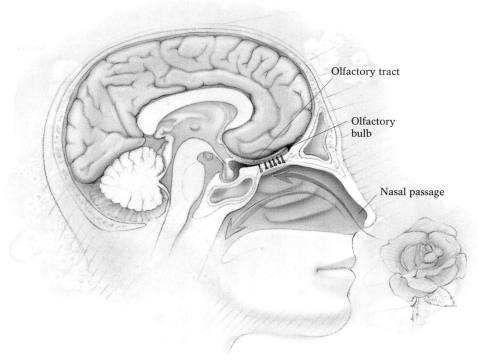

Olfactory tract

Olfactory bulb

Nasal passage

Odor molecules come in so many shapes and sizes that it takes lots of different receptors to detect them. A large family of genes design receptor proteins that recognize particular molecules (Buck & Axel, 1991). As a key slips into a lock, so odor molecules slip into these receptors. Yet we seem not to have a distinct receptor for each of the some 10,000 odors we can detect. This suggests that some odors trigger a combination of receptors. The ability to identify scents peaks in early adulthood and gradually declines thereafter (Figure 4–18).

As any dog or cat with a good nose could tell us, we each have our own identifiable chemical signature. (One noteworthy exception: A dog will follow the tracks of one identical twin as though they had been made by the other [Thomas, 1974].) Animals that have many times more olfactory receptors than we do also use their sense of smell to communicate and navigate. Long before the shark can see its prey, or the moth its mate, odors direct the way.

Figure 4–18 Age, Sex, and Sense of Smell *Among the 1.2 million people who responded to a National Geographic scratch and sniff survey, women and younger adults most successfully identified six sample odors. (From Wysocki & Gilbert, 1989.)*

The Olfactory Brain *Information from the taste buds (orange arrow) travels to an area of the temporal lobe not far from that where olfactory information is received. The brain's circuitry for smell (magenta arrow) also connects with areas involved in memory storage, which helps explain why a smell can trigger a memory explosion.*

kinesthesis [kin-ehs-THEE-sehs] The system for sensing the position of individual body parts.

vestibular sense The sense of the head's movement and position, including the sense of balance.

gestalt An organized whole. Gestalt psychologists emphasize our tendency to integrate pieces of information into meaningful wholes.

Odors also have the power to evoke memories and feelings. In *Remembrance of Things Past*, the French novelist Marcel Proust described how the aroma and flavor of a bit of cake soaked in tea resurrected long-forgotten memories of his aunt's bedroom in the old family house. "The smell and taste of things," he noted, "bears unfaltering, in the tiny and almost impalpable drop of their essence, the vast structure of recollection."

Laboratory studies confirm that, though it's difficult to recall odors by name, we do indeed have a remarkable capacity to recognize long-forgotten odors and their associated personal episodes (Engen, 1987; Schab, 1991). Students who do a word exercise while smelling the aroma of chocolate remember the words better the next day if the chocolate aroma is again present (Schab, 1990). And pleasant odors evoke pleasant memories (Ehrlichman & Halpern, 1988). The smell of the sea, the scent of a perfume, or an aroma like the floor-wax smell in Grandma's kitchen bring to mind happy memories.

Body Position and Movement

10. How do we sense our body's position and movement?

With only the five familiar senses we have so far considered, we would be helpless. We could not put food in our mouths, stand up, or reach out and touch someone. To know just how to move your arms to grasp someone's hand, you first need to know the current position of your arms and hands and then be aware of their changing positions as you move them. To take just one step requires feedback from and instructions to some 200 muscles.

Humans come equipped with millions of such position and motion sensors. They are all over our bodies—in the muscles, tendons, and joints—and they are continually providing our brains with information. If we twist our wrists 1 degree, the sensors immediately report it. This sense of our body parts' position and movement is **kinesthesis** (kin-ehs-THEE-sehs).

Have you ever considered life without kinesthesis, without, say, being able to sense the positions of your limbs when awakening during the night? Such is the experience of Christina, whose nerve fibers carrying information from muscles, tendons, and joints were destroyed by disease, leaving her floppy as a rag doll (Sacks, 1985). What does it feel like? Like she is disembodied, her body dead, not real, not hers. Against all odds, Christina has, however, learned to walk and eat—by visually attending to her limbs and directing them accordingly.

A companion **vestibular sense** monitors the head's (and thus the whole body's) position and movement. The biological gyroscopes for this sense are in the inner ear. In the *semicircular canals*, which look like a three-dimensional pretzel (Figure 4–16a, page 133), and the *vestibular sacs*, which connect the canals with the cochlea, are substances that move when the head rotates or tilts. This movement stimulates hairlike receptors in these organs of the inner ear. The receptors then send to the brain messages that enable us continually to sense our body position and maintain our balance.

If you've been twirling around and come to an abrupt halt, the fluid in your semicircular canals and your kinesthetic receptors does not immediately return to its neutral state. The aftereffect fools your dizzy brain with the sensation that you're still spinning. This illustrates a principle that underlies perceptual illusions. Mechanisms that normally give us an accurate experience of the world can, under special conditions, fool us. Understanding how we get fooled provides clues to how our perceptual system works.

! *Rehearse It*

15. The amplitude of a light wave determines our perception of brightness. The amplitude of a sound wave determines our perception of

a. loudness.   **c.** audition.
b. pitch.   **d.** frequency.

16. The frequency of sound waves determines their pitch. The _____ the waves are, the lower their frequency is and the _____ their pitch.

a. shorter; higher
b. longer; lower
c. lower; longer
d. higher; shorter

17. Sound waves pass through the auditory canal to a tight membrane. Vibrations of this membrane are transmitted by three tiny bones to a snail-shaped tube in the inner ear, where the waves are converted into neural activity. This tube is called the

a. anvil.
b. basilar membrane.
c. cochlea.
d. eardrum.

18. At least four skin senses—pressure, warmth, cold, and pain—make up our sense of touch. Of all the skin senses, the only one that has its own identifiable receptor cells is

a. pressure.
b. warmth.
c. cold.
d. pain.

19. There is no one type of stimulus that triggers pain and no one definable spot in the brain that interprets pain. Although no theory fully explains our experience of pain, the gate-control theory is useful. According to this theory,

a. special pain receptors send signals directly to the brain.

b. pain is a property of the senses, not the brain.
c. small nerve fibers in the spinal cord conduct most pain signals.
d. the stimuli that produce pain are unrelated to other sensations.

20. The taste of the food we eat is greatly enhanced by its smell or aroma. One sense influencing another is

a. sensory adaptation.
b. chemical sensation.
c. gate-control theory.
d. sensory interaction.

21. Kinesthesis is the body's way of sensing its position. The receptors for our companion vestibular sense are in the

a. skin.
b. brain.
c. inner ear.
d. skeletal muscles.

Perceptual Organization

11. What did the Gestalt psychologists contribute to our understanding of perception?

We have examined the processes by which we sense sights and sounds, tastes and smells, touch and movement. Now our central question is, how do we see not just shapes and colors, but a rose in bloom, a familiar face, a sunset? How do we hear not just a mix of pitches and rhythms, but a child's cry of pain, the hum of distant traffic, a symphony? In short, how do we *organize* and *interpret* our sensations so that they become meaningful perceptions?

Early in this century, a group of German psychologists became intrigued with how the mind organizes sensations into perceptions. Given a cluster of sensations, the human perceiver organizes them into a **gestalt**, a German word meaning a "form" or a "whole." The Gestalt psychologists provided compelling demonstrations of gestalt perception. Look at Figure 4–19. Note that the individual elements of the figure are really nothing but eight blue circles, each containing three converging white lines. But when we view them all together, we see a *whole* form, a "Necker cube." As the Gestalt psychologists were fond of saying, in perception the whole may exceed the sum of its parts. There is far more to perception than meets the senses.

Such demonstrations led the Gestalt psychologists to describe principles by which we organize our sensations into perceptions. As you read about these or-

Figure 4–19 A Necker Cube *What do you see: circles with white lines, or a cube? If you stare at the cube, you may notice that it reverses location, moving the tiny X in the center from the front edge to the back. At times the cube may seem to float in front of the page, with circles behind it; at other times the circles may become holes in the page through which the cube appears, as though it were floating behind the page. (From Bradley & others, 1976.)*

ganizational principles, keep in mind the fundamental truth they illustrate: Our brains do more than merely register information about the world. Perception is not just opening a shutter and letting a picture print itself on the brain. Always, we are filtering sensory information and inferring perceptions in ways that make sense to us. Mind matters.

Form Perception

12. How do the principles of figure-ground and grouping contribute to our perception of form?

Imagine that you wanted to design a video/computer system that, like your eye/brain system, could read handwritten addresses or recognize faces at a glance. (The U.S. Postal Service is, in fact, investing millions of dollars hoping to develop such a scanner.) What abilities would it need?

Figure and Ground

To start with, the system would need to recognize the addresses and faces as distinct from their backgrounds. Likewise, our first task in perception is to perceive any object, called the *figure*, as distinct from its surroundings, called the *ground*. Among the voices you hear at a party, the one you attend to becomes the figure, all others part of the ground. As you read, the words are the figure; the white paper, the ground. In Figure 4–20, the **figure-ground** relationship continually reverses—but always we organize the stimulus into a figure seen against a ground. (Is it a vase, or the profiles of two faces?) Such reversible figure and ground illustrations demonstrate again that the same stimulus can trigger more than one perception.

Figure 4–20   Reversible Figure and Ground
Vase or two faces?

Grouping

Having discriminated figure from ground, we (and our video/computer system) must then organize the figure into a meaningful form. Some basic features of a scene—such as color, movement, and light-dark contrast—we process instantly and automatically (Treisman, 1987). To bring order and form to these basic sensations, our minds follow certain rules for **grouping** stimuli together. These rules, identified by the Gestalt psychologists, illustrate their idea that the perceived whole differs from the mere sum of its parts (Rock & Palmer, 1990):

Proximity   We group nearby figures together. We see not six separate lines, but three sets of two lines.

Similarity   If figures are similar to each other, we group them together. We see the triangles and circles as vertical columns of similar shapes, not as horizontal rows of dissimilar shapes.

Continuity   We perceive smooth, continuous patterns rather than discontinuous ones. This pattern could be a series of alternating semicircles, but we perceive it as a wavy line and a straight line.

figure-ground   The organization of the visual field into objects (the *figures*) that stand out from their surroundings (the *ground*).

grouping   The perceptual tendency to organize stimuli into coherent groups.

proximity   The perceptual tendency to group together visual and auditory events that are near each other.

similarity   The perceptual tendency to group together similar elements.

continuity   The perceptual tendency to group stimuli into smooth, continuous patterns.

Proximity   Similarity   Continuity

Figure 4–21 Grouping Principles *You probably perceive this doghouse as a gestalt—a whole (though impossible) structure. As the photo on page 149 shows, gestalt grouping principles are at work here. (Reprinted from GAMES Magazine [810 Seventh Avenue, New York, NY 10019]. Copyright © 1983 PSC Games Limited Partnership.)*

closure The perceptual tendency to fill in gaps, thus enabling one to perceive disconnected parts as a whole object.

connectedness The perceptual tendency to perceive features, such as dots, as a single unit when uniform and linked.

depth perception The ability to see objects in three dimensions although the images that strike the retina are two-dimensional; allows us to judge distance.

visual cliff A laboratory device for testing depth perception in infants and young animals.

Closure If a figure has gaps, we complete it, filling in the gaps to create a complete, whole object. We easily fill the gaps in this figure's outline and see a complete triangle.

Connectedness We perceive spots, lines, or areas as a single unit when uniform and linked.

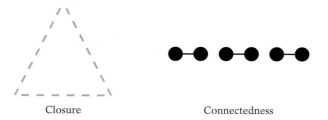

Closure   Connectedness

The grouping principles usually help us perceive reality, but sometimes they lead us astray, as when viewing the doghouse in Figure 4–21.

Depth Perception

13. Why do we see the world in three dimensions?

From the two-dimensional images that fall on our retinas we somehow organize three-dimensional perceptions. Seeing objects in three dimensions, called **depth perception**, allows us to estimate their distance from us. At a glance, we estimate the distance of an oncoming car or the height of a cliff. This ability is partly innate. Eleanor Gibson and Richard Walk (1960) discovered this using a miniature cliff with a drop-off covered by sturdy glass. The inspiration for these experiments occurred to Gibson as she was eating a picnic lunch on the rim of the Grand Canyon. She wondered: Would a toddler peering over the rim perceive the dangerous drop-off and draw back?

Back in their Cornell University laboratory, Gibson and Walk placed 6- to 14-month-old infants on the edge of a **visual cliff** (Figure 4–22). Their mothers then coaxed them to crawl out on the glass. Most refused to do so, indicating that they could perceive depth. Perhaps by crawling age they had *learned* to perceive depth. Yet newborn animals with virtually no visual experience—including young kittens, a day-old goat, and newly hatched chicks—respond similarly. What is more, during the first month of life, human infants turn to

Figure 4–22 Visual Cliff *Eleanor Gibson and Richard Walk devised this miniature cliff with a glass-covered drop-off to determine whether crawling infants and newborn animals can perceive depth. Even when coaxed, infants are reluctant to venture onto the glass over the cliff.*

binocular cues   Depth cues, such as retinal disparity and convergence, that depend on the use of two eyes.

monocular cues   Distance cues, such as linear perspective and interposition, available to either eye alone.

retinal disparity   A binocular cue for perceiving depth; the greater the disparity (difference) between the two images the retina receives of an object, the closer the object is to us.

convergence   A binocular cue for perceiving depth; the extent to which the eyes turn inward when looking at an object.

relative size   A monocular cue for perceiving distance; when we assume two objects are the same size, the one that produces the smaller image appears more distant.

avoid objects coming directly at them but are unbothered by objects approaching at an angle that would not hit them (Ball & Tronick, 1971).

Although nature predisposes our wariness of heights, experience amplifies it. Infants' wariness increases with crawling experience, at whatever age crawling begins. Given the enhanced locomotion made possible by a walker, infants become even more wary of heights (Campos & others, 1992).

How do we do it? How do we transform two-dimensional retinal images into three-dimensional perceptions? Some depth cues require both eyes—**binocular cues**. Others are available to each eye separately—**monocular cues**.

Binocular Cues

Because our eyes are about 2½ inches apart, our retinas receive slightly different images of the world. When the brain compares these two images, their **retinal disparity** (the difference in the two images) provides an important cue to the relative distance of different objects. When you hold your finger directly in front of your nose, your retinas receive quite different views. (You can see this if you close one eye and then the other, or create a finger sausage as in Figure 4–23.) At greater distance—say, when you hold your finger at arm's length—the disparity is smaller.

Figure 4–23   The Floating Finger Sausage
Hold your two index fingers about 5 inches in front of your eyes, with their tips half an inch apart. Now look at the other side of the room, beyond them, and note the weird result. Move your fingers out farther and the retinal disparity—and the finger sausage—will shrink.

The creators of 3-D movies and "Viewmaster" 3-D scenes simulate retinal disparity by photographing a scene with two cameras placed a few inches apart (a feature we might want to build into our video/computer). When viewed through spectacles or a device that allows the left eye to see only the image from the left camera and the right eye the image from the right camera, the 3-D effect mimics normal retinal disparity.

Another binocular cue to distance is **convergence**, a neuromuscular cue from the greater inward turn when the eyes view a near object. By noting the angle of convergence, the brain can compute whether you are focusing on this printed page or on the person across the room.

Monocular Cues

With both eyes open, we can readily and precisely touch the tip of a pen held in front of us; with one eye closed, the task becomes noticeably more difficult. This demonstrates the importance of binocular cues in judging the distance of nearby objects. Two eyes are better than one. How then do we judge whether a person is 100 feet or 100 yards away? In both cases, the retinal disparity while looking straight ahead is slight. At such distances we depend on monocular cues such as the following:

Relative size   If we assume that two objects are similar in size, we perceive the one that casts the smaller image on the retina as farther away.

Relative size

interposition A monocular cue for perceiving distance; nearby objects partially block our view of more distant objects.

relative height A monocular cue for perceiving distance; higher objects appear more distant.

relative motion A monocular cue for perceiving distance; when we move, objects at different distances change their relative positions in our visual image, with those closest moving fastest.

linear perspective A monocular cue for perceiving distance; we perceive the converging of what we know to be parallel lines as indicating increasing distance.

Relative height

Linear perspective

Interposition

Interposition If one object partially blocks our view of another, we perceive it as closer. We perceive the interposed young deer as closer than its partially obscured mother.

Relative height We perceive objects higher in our field of vision as farther away. This may contribute to the illusion that vertical dimensions are longer than identical horizontal dimensions. To most people, the St. Louis Gateway Arch appears taller than it is wide. Actually, the height and width of its outer edges are equal. Measure the photograph and see.

Relative motion As we move, stable objects appear to move relative to us. If while riding in a train you fix your gaze on some object—say, a tree—you see the objects closer than the tree (the fixation point) appear to move backward. The nearer an object is, the faster it seems to move. Objects beyond the fixation point appear to move with you at a decreasing speed as the object gets farther away. Your brain uses these speed and direction clues to compute the objects' relative distances.

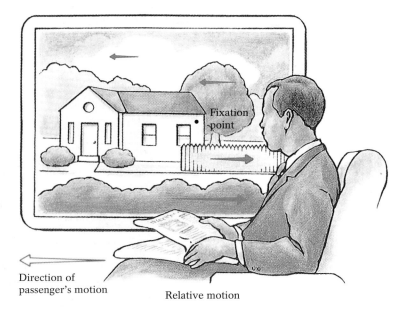
Direction of passenger's motion
Fixation point
Relative motion

Linear perspective Parallel lines, such as railroad tracks, appear to converge with distance. The more the lines converge, the greater their perceived distance. Linear perspective can contribute to rail-crossing accidents, by leading people to overestimate a train's distance (Leibowitz, 1985). (A train's massive size also makes it appear to be moving more slowly than it is.)

Morning fog

Midday sunshine

Relative brightness

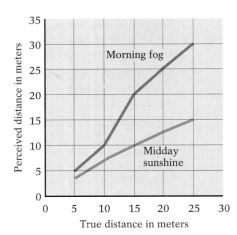

Relative brightness) Nearby objects reflect more light to our eyes. Thus, given two identical objects, the dimmer one seems farther away. Psychologist Helen Ross (1975) asked passersby to estimate the distances of white disks she had placed on the lawn at Britain's Hull University. Those who judged the distance in the thick morning fog perceived the disks to be farther away than did those who made their estimates in the midday sunshine. This illusion contributes to accidents, as when a fog-shrouded vehicle, or one with only its parking lights on, seems farther away than it is.

To convey depth on a flat canvas (Figure 4–24), artists use some of these monocular cues, as do people who must gauge depth with but one eye. In 1960, the University of Washington football team won the Rose Bowl, thanks partly to the superb passing of quarterback Bob Schloredt. Schloredt, who was obviously skilled at judging his receiver's distance, must be supersensitive to monocular cues for distance, because he is blind in his left eye.

Figure 4–24 Perspective Techniques *By the time that "Bristol, Broad Quay" was painted (c. 1730, Anonymous), the techniques for showing perspective were well established. Note the effective use of distance cues such as interposition, linear perspective, and relative size and height.*

relative brightness   A monocular cue for perceiving distance; dimmer objects appear more distant.

perceptual constancy   Perceiving objects as unchanging (having consistent lightness, color, shape, and size) even as illumination and retinal images change.

Perceptual Constancy

14. How do perceptual constancies help us to organize our sensations into meaningful perceptions?

So far we have noted that our video/computer system must first perceive objects as we do—as having a distinct form and location. Its next task is even more challenging: to recognize the object without being deceived by changes in its size, shape, brightness, or color. **Perceptual constancy** allows us to perceive an object as unchanging while the stimuli we receive from it change. You glance at someone ahead of you on the sidewalk and instantly recognize a classmate. In less time than it takes to draw a breath, the information reaching your eyes has been sent to your brain, where work teams comprising millions of neurons have extracted the essential features, compared them with stored images, and identified the person.

Shape and Size Constancies

Sometimes an object's actual shape is unchanging, but the object *seems* to change shape with our viewing angle (Figure 4–25). More often, thanks to *shape constancy*, we perceive familiar objects as having a constant form even while our retinal images of them change. When a door opens, it casts a changing shape on our retinas, yet we manage to perceive the door as having a constant doorlike shape (Figure 4–26).

Figure 4–26   Shape Constancy *A door casts an increasingly trapezoidal image on our retinas as it opens, yet we still perceive it as rectangular.*

Box A   Box B

Figure 4–25 -Perceiving Shape *Do the tops of boxes* A *and* B *have different dimensions? They appear to. But—believe it or not—they are identical. (Measure and see.) With both boxes we adjust our perceptions relative to our viewing angle. (From Shepard, 1981.)*

Thanks to *size constancy* we perceive objects as having a constant size, even while our distance from them varies. Size constancy allows us to perceive a car as big enough to carry people, even when we see its tiny image from two blocks away. This illustrates the close connection between an object's perceived *distance* and perceived *size*. Perceiving an object's distance gives us cues to its size. Likewise, knowing its general size—that the object is, say, a car—provides us with cues to its distance.

Size-Distance Relationship   The marvel of size perception is how effortlessly it occurs. Given the perceived distance of an object and the size of its image on our retinas, we instantly and unconsciously infer the object's size. Although the monsters in Figure 4–27a (page 146) cast the same retinal images, the linear perspective tells our brain that the monster in pursuit is farther away. We therefore perceive it as larger.

Figure 4–27   The Interplay Between Perceived Size and Distance *(a) The monocular cues for distance make the pursuing monster look larger than the pursued. It isn't. (From Shepard, 1990.) (b) The Ponzo illusion. The two identical orange bars cast identical images on our retinas. But our experience tells us that a more distant object can create the same-sized image only if it is larger. Thus, we perceive the bar that seems more distant as larger.*

(a)   (b)

This interplay between perceived size and perceived distance helps explain several well-known illusions. For example, can you imagine why the moon looks up to 50 percent larger near the horizon than when high in the sky? For at least 22 centuries, scholars have wondered and argued about the causes of the *moon illusion* (Hershenson, 1989). Researchers have not yet found a fully satisfactory explanation. A suggested partial reason is that cues to objects' distances at the horizon make the moon behind them seem farther away (Kaufman & Rock, 1962). Thus, the moon on the horizon seems larger (like the distant monster in Figure 4–27a and the distant bar in Figure 4–27b. Take away these distance cues by looking at the horizon moon (or the monsters) through a paper tube and it immediately shrinks.

The size-distance relationship helps us understand a famous illusion: To the left is an adaptation of a classic illusion created in 1889 by Franz Müller-Lyer. Does either line segment, *AB* or *BC*, appear longer? To most people the two segments appear the same length. Surprise! They are not. As your ruler can verify, line *AB* is a full one-third longer than line *BC*. One explanation of this illusion is that our experience with the corners of rooms or buildings affects our perceptions of distance and size. Thus, we perceive the vertical line on the ticket booth in Figure 4–28 as closer to us and therefore shorter, and the vertical line by the door as farther away and therefore longer.

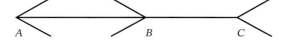

Figure 4–28   The Müller-Lyer Illusion *Richard L. Gregory (1968) suggested that the corners in our rectangularly carpentered world teach us to interpret "outward" or "inward" pointing arrowheads at the ends of a line as a cue to the line's distance from us and so to its length. The red line defined by the corner at the ticket booth looks shorter than the red line defined by the corner to the right. But if you measure them, you will see that both are the same length.*

Figure 4–29 The Ames Room *When viewed through a peephole with one eye, this distorted room, designed by Adelbert Ames, appears to have a normal rectangular shape. The girl in the near corner appears disproportionately large because we judge her size based on the false assumption that she is the same distance away as the girl in the far corner.*

Size-distance relationships also explain why in Figure 4-29 the two same-aged girls seem so different in size. As the diagram reveals, the girls are actually about the same size, but the room is distorted. Viewed with one eye through a peephole, the trapezoidal walls produce the same images as those of a normal rectangular room viewed with both eyes. Presented with the peephole's one-eyed view, the brain makes the reasonable assumption that the room is normal and perceives the girls as very different in size.

Our occasional misperceptions demonstrate the workings of our normally effective perceptual processes. The perceived relationship between distance and size is generally valid, but under special circumstances it can lead us astray—as when helping to create the moon illusion, the Müller-Lyer illusion, and the Ames room illusion. Using distance cues to assess perceived size triggers illusions only if we aren't familiar with the object or if the distance cues are misleading. When we correctly interpret the distance cues—which we normally do—we perceive the size of objects correctly.

Lightness Constancy

White paper reflects 90 percent of the light falling on it; black paper, only 10 percent. In sunlight the black paper may reflect 100 times more light than does the white paper indoors, but it still looks black (McBurney & Collings, 1984). This illustrates *lightness constancy* (also called *brightness constancy*), our perceiving an object as having a constant lightness even while its illumination varies. Perceived lightness depends on *relative luminance*—the amount of light an object reflects relative to its surroundings. If you view sunlit black paper through a narrow tube so nothing else is visible, it may look gray, because in bright sunshine it reflects a fair amount of light. View it without the tube and it is again black, because it reflects much less light than the objects around it. The phenomenon is similar to that of color constancy (page 130). A red apple in a fruit bowl retains its redness as the light changes, because our brain computes the light reflected by any object relative to its surrounding objects.

If perceived lightness stays roughly constant, given an unchanging context, what happens when the surrounding context changes? As Figure 4–30 shows, the brain computes brightness and color relative to surrounding objects. Thus, perceived lightness changes with context.

Figure 4–30 Lightness Contrast *Although they are in fact identical, the perceived lightness of the interior rectangles differs depending on their surroundings. Like color constancy (page 130), this phenomenon has great significance for artists and interior designers.*

Form perception, depth perception, and perceptual constancy illustrate how we organize our visual experiences. Perceptual organization applies to other senses, too. It explains why we perceive the clock's steady tick not as a tick-tick-tick, but group it as, say TICK-tick, TICK-tick. Listening to an unfamiliar language, we have trouble hearing where one word stops and the next one begins. Listening to our own language, we automatically hear distinct words. This, too, is a form of perceptual organization. But it is more, for we even organize a string of letters—THEDOGATEMEAT—into words that make a meaningful phrase, more likely "The dog ate meat" than "The do gate me at" (McBurney & Collings, 1984). This process involves not only organization but interpretation—finding meaning in what we perceive.

! *Rehearse It*

22. Gestalt psychologists identified the principles by which we organize our perceptions. Our tendencies to fill in the gaps and to perceive a pattern as continuous are two different examples of the organizing principle called

a. figure-ground.
b. depth perception.
c. shape constancy.
d. grouping.

23. In their experiments, Gibson and Walk used a visual cliff to test depth perception in infants and young animals. Their results suggest that

a. infants have not yet developed depth perception.
b. crawling infants perceive depth.
c. depth perception depends on experience.
d. humans differ significantly from animals in being able to perceive depth in infancy.

24. The images that fall on our retinas are two-dimensional, or flat. Yet we perceive the world as having three-dimensional depth. Depth perception underlies our ability to

a. discriminate figure from ground.
b. perceive objects as having a constant shape or form.
c. judge distances.
d. fill in the gaps in a figure.

25. In estimating distances we use both binocular cues, which depend on both eyes, and monocular cues, which are available to either eye alone. Examples of monocular cues are interposition and

a. closure.
b. retinal disparity.
c. linear perspective.
d. convergence.

26. In the Müller-Lyer illusion we misperceive the length of the lines between arrowheads. We do so partly because

a. distance cues do not help us assess size.
b. the visual distance cues (implied by the arrowheads) mislead us.
c. the perceived relationship between distance and size is generally illusory.
d. of our linear perspective.

27. Form perception and perceptual constancy are organizing principles that apply to hearing as well as vision. For example, in listening to a concerto, you follow the solo instrument and perceive the orchestra as accompaniment; this illustrates the organizing principle of

a. figure-ground.
b. shape constancy.
c. grouping.
d. depth or distance perception.

Interpretation

Philosophers have debated the origin of our perceptual abilities: Is it nature or nurture? German philosopher Immanuel Kant (1724–1804) maintained that knowledge comes from our *inborn* ways of organizing sensory experiences. Indeed, we come equipped to process sensory information. But British philosopher John Locke (1632–1704) argued that through our experiences we *learn* to perceive the world. Indeed, we learn to link an object's distance with its size. But just how important is experience? How radically does it shape our perceptual interpretations?

Sensory Restriction and Restored Vision

15. What does research on sensory restriction and restored vision reveal about the effects of experience on perception?

Writing to John Locke in 1690, William Molyneux wondered whether "a man *born* blind, and now adult, taught by his *touch* to distinguish between a cube and a sphere" could, if made to see, visually distinguish the two. Locke's answer was no, because the man would never have *learned* to see the difference.

Molyneux's hypothetical case has since been put to the test with dozens of adults who, though blind from birth, have gained sight (Gregory, 1978; von Senden, 1932). Most were people born with cataracts—clouded lenses that enabled them to see only diffused light, rather as you or I might see a diffuse fog through a Ping-Pong ball sliced in half. When their cataracts were surgically removed, the patients could distinguish figure from ground and could sense colors—suggesting that these aspects of perception are innate. But much as Locke supposed, the formerly blind patients often could not visually recognize objects that were familiar by touch.

Seeking to gain more control than is provided by clinical cases, researchers have conducted Molyneux's imaginary experiment with animals, by outfitting them with goggles through which they see only diffuse, unpatterned light (Wiesel, 1982). After infancy, when their visual impairments were removed, these animals exhibited perceptual limitations much like those of humans born with cataracts. Their eyes had not degenerated; their retinas still relayed signals to their visual cortex. But lacking stimulation, the cortical cells had not developed normal connections. Thus, the animals remained functionally blind to shape.

In both humans and animals, a similar period of sensory restriction does no permanent harm if it occurs later in life. Cover the eye of an animal for several months during adulthood, and vision will be unaffected after removing the eye patch. Remove cataracts that develop *after* early childhood, and a human, too, will enjoy a return to normal vision. The effects of visual experiences during infancy in cats, monkeys, and humans suggest there is a *critical period* (page 82) for normal sensory and perceptual development. Experience guides the organization of the brain's neural connections.

Perceptual Adaptation

16. How adaptable is our perception?

Given a new pair of glasses, we may feel slightly disoriented and dizzy. Within a day or two, we adjust. Our **perceptual adaptation** to changed visual input makes the world seem normal again. Now imagine a far more dramatic new pair of glasses—one that shifts the apparent location of objects 40 degrees to the left. When you first put them on and toss a ball to a friend, it sails off to the left. Walking forward to shake hands with the person, you veer to the left.

Could you adapt to this distorted world? Chicks cannot. When fitted with such lenses, they continue to peck where food grains *seem* to be (Hess, 1956; Rossi, 1968). But humans adapt to distorting lenses quickly. Within a few minutes your throws would again be accurate, your stride on target. Remove the lenses and you would experience an aftereffect: At first your throws would err in the *opposite* direction, sailing off to the right; but again, within minutes you would readapt.

> *"Let us then suppose the mind to be, as we say, white paper void of all characters, without any ideas: How comes it to be furnished? . . . To this I answer, in one word, from EXPERIENCE."*
>
> John Locke
> *An Essay Concerning Human Understanding*, 1690

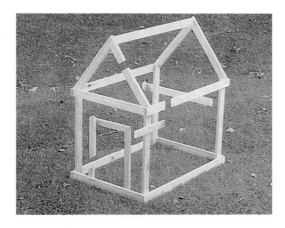

The Solution *Another view of the impossible doghouse in Figure 4–21 (page 141) reveals the secrets of this illusion. From the photo angle in Figure 4–21, the grouping principle of closure leads us to perceive the boards as continuous. (Reprinted from GAMES Magazine [810 Seventh Avenue, New York, NY 10019]. Copyright © 1983 PSC Games Limited Partnership.)*

perceptual adaptation In vision, the ability to adjust to an artificially displaced or even inverted visual field.

Perceptual Adaptation *Dr. Hubert Dolezal views the world through inverting goggles. Remarkably, people can learn to adapt to an upside-down visual world.*

Indeed, given an even more radical pair of glasses—one that literally turns the world upside down—you could still adapt. Turn-of-the-century psychologist George Stratton (1896) experienced this when he invented and for 8 days wore optical headgear that flipped left to right *and* up to down, making him the first person to experience a right-side-up retinal image while standing upright.

At first, Stratton was disoriented. When he wanted to walk, he had to search for his feet, which were now "up." Eating was nearly impossible. He became nauseated and depressed. But Stratton persisted, and by the eighth day he could comfortably reach for something in the right direction and walk without bumping into things. When Stratton finally removed the headgear, he readapted quickly.

In later experiments people wearing the optical gear have even been able to ride a motorcycle, ski the Alps, and fly an airplane. Is this because through experience they perceptually reinvert their upside-down world to an upright position? No, the street, ski slopes, and runway still seem above their heads. But by actively moving about in this topsy-turvy world, they adapt to the context and learn to coordinate their movements.

Perceptual Set

17. How do our assumptions, expectations, and contexts affect our perceptions?

As everyone knows, to see is to believe. As many people also know, but do not fully appreciate, to believe is to see. Our experiences, assumptions, and expectations may give us a **perceptual set**, or mental predisposition, that greatly influences what we perceive. Is the image in the center picture of Figure 4–31 a man playing the saxophone or a woman's face? What we see in such a drawing can be influenced by first viewing either of two unambiguous versions (Boring, 1930).

Figure 4–31 Perceptual Set *Which do you see in the center picture: the male saxophonist or the woman's face? Glancing first at one of the two unambiguous versions of the picture is likely to influence your interpretation. (From Shepard, 1990.)*

Everyday examples of perceptual set abound. In 1972, a British newspaper published genuine, unretouched photographs of a "monster" in Scotland's Loch Ness—"the most amazing pictures ever taken," stated the paper. If this information creates in you the same perceptual set it did in most of the paper's readers, you, too, will see the monster in the photo reproduced in Figure 4–32a. But when Steuart Campbell (1986) approached the photos with a different perceptual set, he saw a curved tree trunk—very likely the same tree trunk others had seen in the lake the day the photo was shot. Moreover, with this different perceptual set, you may now notice that the object is floating motionless, without any water disturbance or wake around it—hardly what we would expect of a lively monster.

perceptual set A mental predisposition to perceive one thing and not another.

(a)   (b)

Figure 4–32 Believing is Seeing *(a) Is this the Loch Ness monster or a log? (b) Are these flying saucers or clouds? We often see what we expect to see.*

Our perceptual set can influence what we hear as well as what we see. Witness the kindly airline pilot who, on a takeoff run, looked over at his depressed co-pilot and said, "Cheer up." The co-pilot heard the usual "Gear up" and promptly raised the wheels—before they had left the ground (Reason & Mycielska, 1982). When listening to rock music played backward, people often perceive an evil message *if* specifically told what to listen for (Vokey & Read, 1985). When observing presidential campaign debates, most Americans perceive their favorite candidate as being the better debater (Gallup, 1992). Clearly, much of what we perceive comes not just from the world "out there" but also from what's behind our eyes and between our ears.

What determines our perceptual set? Our concepts of male saxophonists and women's faces, of monsters and tree trunks, of clouds and UFOs, all help us interpret ambiguous sensations with top-down processing.

Context Effects

A given stimulus may trigger radically different perceptions, partly because of our differing expectations, but also because of the immediate context. A few examples:

Did the speaker say "cults and sects" or "cults and sex"? Did the critic advocate "attacks" or "a tax" on our politicians? We must discern from the surrounding words.

Did the pursuing monster in Figure 4–27 on page 146 look aggressive? Did the pursued one seem frightened? If so, you are experiencing a context effect. The two monsters are the same.

Is the "Magician's Cabinet" in Figure 4–33 sitting on the floor or hanging from the ceiling? How we perceive it depends on the context defined by the bunnies.

Figure 4–33 Context Effects *Is the box in the far left frame lying on the floor or hanging from the ceiling? The context defined by the inquisitive bunnies guides our perceptions. (From Shepard, 1990.)*

When I worked in Seattle's county hospital, we occasionally faced the task of transporting a dead body through crowded hallways without alarming the patients or their visitors. Our solution was to create a context that matched people's schemas for sleeping and sedated patients: With the body's face uncovered and the sheet turned down in normal fashion, we could wheel an apparently "sleeping" body past the unsuspecting.

The Human Factor in Operating Machines

At the 1991 Cal Tech commencement, then-President George Bush proposed a national goal: "By the turn of the century, Americans must be able to get their VCRs to stop flashing 12:00." Democrat Tipper Gore could agree with Republican Bush on that much: She finally covered her VCR clock with black masking tape to hide the relentless blinking. Like her ABC-News colleague Peter Jennings, Barbara Walters also can't program any of her three VCRs. "I'm reduced to asking friends to tape for me," she has said. "I am deeply ashamed" (Zoglin, 1992).

I love our VCR, though I still haven't figured out how to make it "express record." Our stove is wonderful, except for the moments I spend puzzling over which control works which burner. The push-bar doors on our campus buildings are safe and easy, though occasionally frustrating when I push the wrong end. The extra buttons on my computer-linked phone are handy, though when transferring a call I still must look up which button to press.

Human factors psychologists help to design appliances, machines, and work settings that harness rather than confound our natural perceptions. Psychologist

Donald Norman (1988) suggests how simple design changes could reduce some of our frustrations. For example, by exploiting "natural mapping," we could design stove controls that require no labels.

Understanding human factors can do more than design for reduced frustration; it can help avoid disaster. After beginning commercial flights in the late 1960s, the Boeing 727 was involved in several landing accidents caused by pilot error. Psychologist Conrad Kraft (1978) noted a common setting for these accidents: All took place at night and involved landing short of the runway after crossing a dark stretch of water or unilluminated ground. Beyond the runway, city lights would project a larger retinal image if on a rising terrain. This would make the ground seem farther away than it was. By re-creating these conditions in flight simulations, Kraft discovered that pilots were deceived into thinking they were flying safely higher than they were (Figure 4–34). Aided by Kraft's finding, the airlines began corrective measures (such as requiring the co-pilot to monitor the altimeter and call out altitudes) and the accidents diminished.

(a) Traditional labeling

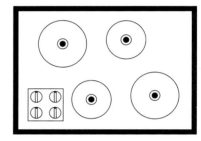

(b) Natural map

Good Design *Common stove controls require labeling, as in (a). By using a natural map (b), we needn't read labels. (From Norman, 1988.)*

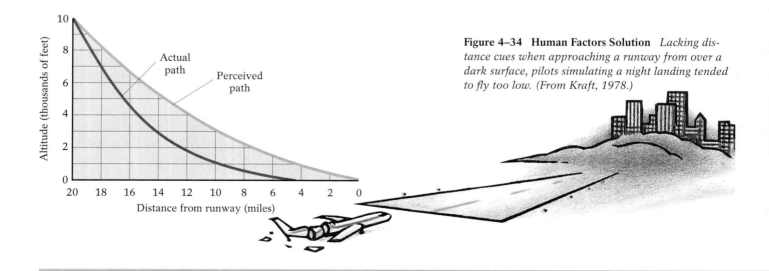

Figure 4–34 Human Factors Solution *Lacking distance cues when approaching a runway from over a dark surface, pilots simulating a night landing tended to fly too low. (From Kraft, 1978.)*

Culture and Context Effects *What is above the woman's head? In this experiment, nearly all the participants from East Africa thought she was balancing a metal box or can on her head and that the family was sitting under a tree. Westerners, to whom corners and box-like architecture are more common, were more likely to perceive the family as being indoors, with the woman sitting under a window. (Adapted from Gregory & Gombrich, 1973.)*

The effects of perceptual sets and context show how experience helps us construct perception. Simple perceptions are hardly simple. They are the brain's creative products. "We hear and apprehend only what we already half know," said Thoreau. The river of perception is fed by two streams, sensation and cognition. To return to the question, Is perception innate or learned? we can answer simply: It's both.

Rehearse It

28. In some cases, surgeons have restored vision to patients who have been blind from birth. The newly sighted individuals were able to sense colors but had difficulty

a. recognizing objects by touch.
b. recognizing the shapes of objects.
c. distinguishing figure from ground.
d. distinguishing between bright and dim light.

29. Experiments in which subjects wear glasses that displace or invert their visual fields show that, after a period of disorien-

tation, they learn to function quite well. This ability is called

a. perceptual constancy or visual capture.
b. perceptual set.
c. sensory restriction.
d. perceptual adaptation.

30. Our perceptual set influences what we perceive. This mental predisposition reflects our

a. experiences, assumptions, and expectations.
b. perceptual adaptation.

c. objectivity, realism, and intelligence.
d. perceptual constancy.

31. Locke and other empiricists believed that our perception of the world is learned through experience. Support for their view can be found in

a. the writings of Immanuel Kant.
b. research on depth perception.
c. research on perceptual set and context.
d. theories of color vision.

Is There Perception Without Sensation?

Can we perceive only what we sense? Or, without sensory input, are we capable of extrasensory perception? Half of Americans say they believe in **extrasensory perception (ESP)** and another quarter aren't sure (Gallup & Newport, 1991). The media overflow with reports of psychic wonders: crimes solved, dreams come true, futures foretold. Paranormal television (such as "Unsolved Mysteries" and "Sightings") and movies (such as *Close Encounters* and *The Exorcist*) are big business. Dial-a-psychic 900 numbers have become a $100

extrasensory perception (ESP) Perception that occurs without sensory input. A controversial notion, said to include telepathy, clairvoyance, and precognition.

parapsychology The study of paranormal phenomena including ESP and psychokinesis.

Which supposed psychic ability does the sportscaster claim? (See page 156.)

"A man does not attain the status of Galileo merely because he is persecuted; he must also be right."

Stephen Jay Gould
Ever Since Darwin, 1977

million-a-year industry (ABC News, 1993). Are there indeed *any* people who can read minds, see through walls, or foretell the future?

In laboratory experiments, **parapsychologists**—those who study paranormal (literally, beyond the normal) happenings—have sometimes been astonished at psychics who seem capable of discerning the contents of sealed envelopes, influencing the roll of a die, or drawing a picture of what someone else is viewing at an unknown remote location. But other research psychologists and scientists—including 96 percent of scientists in the National Academy of Sciences—are skeptical (McConnell, 1991). If ESP is real, we would need to overturn the scientific understanding that we are creatures whose minds are tied to our physical brains and whose perceptual experiences of the world are built of sensations. Sometimes new evidence does overturn our scientific preconceptions. So let's look at some claims for ESP, and then see why scientists remain dubious.

Claims of ESP

18. What types of ESP have been proposed, and why are most research psychologists skeptical?

Claims of paranormal phenomena include astrological predictions, psychic healing, reincarnation, communication with the dead, and out-of-body frequent flyer programs. Of these, the most respectable, testable, and—for a chapter on sensation and perception—relevant claims are for three varieties of ESP:

▸ *Telepathy*, or mind-to-mind communication—one person sending thoughts to another or perceiving another's thoughts.

▸ *Clairvoyance*, or perceiving remote events, such as sensing that a friend's house is on fire.

▸ *Precognition*, or perceiving future events, such as a political leader's death or a sporting event's outcome.

Closely linked with these are claims of *psychokinesis*, or "mind over matter," such as levitating a table or influencing the roll of a die.

Consider one careful experiment conducted by Bruce Layton and Bill Turnbull (1975) at the University of North Carolina. Layton and Turnbull had a computer generate a randomized 100-item list of the digits 1, 2, 3, 4, and 5 for each of their 179 student participants. They gave each student such a list in a sealed envelope and asked the student to guess which number was in each of the 100 positions.

By chance, 1 guess in 5, or 20 guesses out of the 100, should be correct. When told beforehand that ESP was beneficial, subjects averaged 20.66 correct out of 100. When told that ESP was harmful, they averaged only 19.49 correct. The difference might seem trivial—indeed, you would never notice so small an effect while observing an experiment. But a statistical analysis revealed that a difference that large among so many participants would seldom occur by chance. So Layton and Turnbull concluded that an ESP effect had occurred.

Bolstered by such experiments, believers in ESP accuse research psychologists of the same sort of skepticism that led eighteenth-century scientists to scoff at the idea that meteorites come from outer space. Novelist Arthur Koestler, who on his death in 1983 left more than $700,000 to fund a British professorship in parapsychology, once complained that today's skeptical scientists resemble the Italian philosophers who refused to look at Jupiter's moons through Galileo's telescope—because they "knew" that such moons did not exist. Stubborn skepticism sometimes blinds people to surprising truth.

Skepticism About ESP

The skeptics reply that an uncritical mind is a gullible mind. Time and again, they point out, so-called psychics have exploited unquestioning audiences with amazing performances in which they *appeared* to communicate with the spirits of the dead, read minds, or levitate objects—only to have it revealed that their acts were a hoax, nothing more than the illusions of stage magicians. Indeed, many psychic deceptions have been exposed by magicians, who resent the exploitation of their arts in the name of psychic powers.

Even scientists get hoodwinked. A notable case involved two teenage magicians, Steve Shaw and Michael Edwards (Randi, 1983a,b). In 1979, this young pair approached Washington University's new parapsychology laboratory, offering to demonstrate their "psychic powers." Over the next 3 years, the two pretended to defy the laws of nature. They appeared to project mental images onto film, cause clocks to slide across a table, effortlessly bend metal objects, and move objects in sealed jars. Although forewarned against trickery by James Randi, the youngsters' magician-adviser, the laboratory director ignored the warnings and for a time proclaimed that "these two kids are the most reliable of the people that we've studied" ("Psychic Abscam," 1983). This parapsychologist's gullibility illustrates how tempting it is to label phenomena *we* don't understand as beyond explanation: "What other explanation could there possibly be but ESP?" the awestruck observer asks.

Premonitions or Pretensions?

Can psychics see into the future? Although one might wish for a psychic stock forecaster, the tallied forecasts of "leading psychics" reveal meager accuracy. Between 1978 and 1985, the New Year's predictions of the *National Enquirer*'s favorite psychics yielded 2 accurate predictions out of 486 (Strentz, 1986). During the early 1990s, tabloid psychics were all wrong in predicting surprising events (Madonna did not become a gospel singer, a UFO base was not found in the Mexican desert, Queen Elizabeth did not abdicate her throne to enter a convent). And they missed all the significant unexpected events, such as the dissolution of the Soviet Union, Saddam Hussein's assault on Kuwait, and the O. J. Simpson case. Before 1994, psychics offered many predictions about Michael Jackson—that he would marry Oprah Winfrey, become a traveling evangelist, and have a sex-change operation—but missed their chance to predict his marriage to Lisa Marie Presley (CSICOP, 1994).

Examination of psychic visions offered to police departments reveals that these, too, are no more accurate than guesses made by others (Reiser, 1982). Psychics working with the police do, however, generate dozens or even hundreds of predictions; this increases the odds of an occasional correct guess, which psychics can then report to the media. As a Spanish proverb says, "A person who talks a lot is sometimes right." Moreover, vague predictions provide a perceptual set and can later be interpreted to match events. Nostradamus, a sixteenth-century French psychic, explained in an unguarded moment that his ambiguous prophecies "could not possibly be understood till they were interpreted after the event and by it." Police departments are wise to all this. When Jane Ayers Sweat and Mark Durm (1993) asked the police departments of America's 50 largest cities whether they ever used psychics, 65 percent said they never had. Of those that had, not one had found it helpful.

Are the spontaneous "visions" of ordinary people any more accurate? Consider our dreams. Do they foretell the future, as about half of university students believe (Messer & Griggs, 1989)? Or do they only seem to because we are more likely to recall or reconstruct dreams that seem to have come true? Sixty years ago, two Harvard psychologists (Murray & Wheeler, 1937) tested

> *"A psychic is an actor playing the role of a psychic."*
>
> Psychologist-magician Daryl Bem (1984)

> *"The most eminent scientist, untrained in magic, is putty in the hands of a clever charlatan."*
>
> Martin Gardner (1983)

BIZARRO

The "Bizarro" cartoon by Dan Piraro is reprinted by permission of Chronicle Features.

More recent experiments in which people attempted to send mental images to dreamers produced some intriguing initial results, but these could not be replicated even with the same subjects. Dream telepathy experiments therefore were discontinued (Hyman, 1986).

"There comes a point where one has to accept the message of the data, that absence of evidence is evidence of absence."

Frank Close
Too Hot to Handle: The Race for Cold Fusion, 1991

Answer to question on p. 154: Precognition.

"At the heart of science is an essential tension between two seemingly contradictory attitudes—an openness to new ideas, no matter how bizarre or counterintuitive they may be, and the most ruthless skeptical scrutiny of all ideas, old and new."

Carl Sagan (1987)

the prophetic power of dreams. After aviator Charles Lindbergh's baby son was kidnapped and murdered but before the body was discovered, the researchers invited the public to report their dreams about the child. Of the 1300 dream reports submitted, how many accurately envisioned the child dead? A mere 5 percent. And how many also correctly anticipated the body's location—buried among trees? Only 4 of the 1300. Although this number was surely no better than chance, to those 4 dreamers the accuracy of their *apparent* precognitions must have seemed uncanny.

Every day each of us imagines many events. Occasionally an unlikely imagined event is bound to occur and to astonish us when it does. If you tell everyone in a group of 100 people to think "heads" before each tosses six coins, someone is likely to get all heads (whether thinking heads or not) and to feel eerie afterwards. As Chapter 1 explained, random sequences will sometimes contain weird conjunctions or streaks. Given the billions of events that occur in the world each day, and given enough days, some stunning coincidences are sure to occur. "Time converts the improbable to the inevitable," notes Stephen Jay Gould.

Finally, consider this, say the skeptics: After tens of thousands of experiments, *there has never been discovered a reproducible ESP phenomenon, nor any individual who can convincingly demonstrate psychic ability* (Marks, 1986). A National Research Council investigation of ESP similarly concludes that "the best available evidence does not support the contention that these phenomena exist" (Druckman & Swets, 1988).

One skeptic, magician James Randi, has offered $10,000 to anyone who can demonstrate "*any* paranormal ability" before a group of competent experts. Other similar offers total more than a third of a million dollars (Jones, 1985–1986; Karr, 1993). To anyone whose claims could be authenticated, the scientific seal of approval would be worth far more. Randi's offer has been publicized for well over two decades, and dozens of people have been tested, sometimes under the scrutiny of an independent panel of judges. To refute those who say there is no ESP, one need only produce a single person who can demonstrate a single reproducible ESP phenomenon. As yet, no one has exhibited any such power.

Lacking such evidence, and faced with increasing skepticism, the Parapsychological Association has recently been losing membership, and several major parapsychological laboratories lost their funding and closed during the 1980s (Hess, 1993). Even while fascination with ESP grows in some parts of the world, doubts about ESP are increasing among American teens: 67 percent told the 1978 Gallup Youth Survey they believed in ESP, but this declined to 43 percent in 1992.

Thinking Critically About ESP

In times past, there have been all kinds of crazy ideas—that bumps on the head reveal character traits, that bloodletting is a cure-all, that each sperm cell contains a miniature person inside. When faced with such claims—or with claims of mind-reading or out-of-body travel or mind-over-matter—how can we separate crazy ideas from those that sound crazy but are true? At the heart of science we find a simple answer: Test them to see if they work. If they do, so much the worse for our skepticism. If they don't, so much the worse for the ideas.

This scientific attitude appears in the agreement of believers and skeptics that what parapsychology needs to give it credibility is a reproducible phenomenon and a theory to explain it. Could the Layton and Turnbull clairvoyance experiment (in which students beat chance in guessing numbers in sealed envelopes) provide such a reproducible phenomenon? The skeptical editor of the *Journal of Experimental Social Psychology*, to which Layton and Turnbull submitted their results for publication, wondered. So he and the authors reached an unusual agreement: The researchers would repeat their experiment, and the journal would then publish the results of both, regardless of the new outcome. (As this illustrates, both ESP researchers and skeptics genuinely seek truth.) The result of the second experiment? Layton and Turnbull summarized honestly and succinctly: "No [statistically] significant effects were present."

Knowing how easily people are deceived, and lacking reproducible results, most research psychologists remain skeptical. Indeed, they are dismayed by all the shows, books, and magazines on paranormal topics. But some are newly intrigued by findings recently published by social psychologist Daryl Bem and parapsychologist Charles Honorton (1994) using the "ganzfeld procedure." The procedure places the subject in a reclining chair, plays hissing white noise through headphones, and shines diffuse red light through translucent Ping-Pong ball halves taped over the eyes. Ostensibly, this reduction of external distractions improves subjects' ability to hear still small voices within. Building on earlier studies using this procedure, Bem and Honorton isolated a "sender" and "receiver" in separate, shielded chambers and had the sender concentrate on a randomly selected visual image. Over 11 studies, the receivers beat chance by a small but reliable margin (32 percent versus 25 percent chance) when rating which of four images best matched the images they experienced during the session.

Recall that psychology-based critical inquiry asks two questions: What do you mean? And how do you know (what's your evidence)? Parapsychologists say these ganzfeld tests of ESP offer clear answers to both questions. Skeptic Ray Hyman (1994) grants that their methodology surpasses that of previous ESP experiments, but he questions certain procedural details that may have introduced bias. Intrigued, other researchers are now at work replicating these experiments. Will this be the first reliable ESP phenomenon? Or one more dashed hope, one more "phenomenon" that later will be refuted and abandoned? Stay tuned, and remember: The scientific attitude blends curious skepticism with open-minded humility. It demands that extraordinary claims be supported by clear and reliable evidence; given such evidence, it is open to nature's occasional surprises.

As critical thinkers, this can be our attitude, too. We, too, can be skeptical, but without closing ourselves to all startling claims. We can be open to new ideas without being gullible, discerning without being cynical. We can be critical thinkers; yet, knowing that our understanding of nature is incomplete, we can agree with Shakespeare's Hamlet that "there are more things in heaven and earth, Horatio, than are dreamt of in your philosophy."

Why are so many people predisposed to believe that ESP exists? Why do sensational claims so often race ahead of simple facts? In part, such beliefs may stem from understandable misperceptions, misinterpretations, and selective recall. But for some people there also exists an unsatisfied hunger for wonderment, an itch to experience the magical. In Britain and the United States, the founders of parapsychology were mostly people who, having lost their religious faith, were searching for a scientific basis for believing in the meaningfulness of life and the possibility of life after death (Alcock, 1985; Beloff, 1985). In the upheaval since the collapse of autocratic rule in Russia, there has come an "avalanche of the mystical, occult and pseudoscientific" (Kapitza, 1991). "Extrasensorial" healers, astrologers, and seers fascinate the awestruck public.

To feel awe and to gain a deep reverence for life, we need look no further than our own perceptual system and its capacity for organizing formless nerve impulses into colorful sights, vivid sounds, and evocative smells. Within our ordinary perceptual experiences lies much that is truly extraordinary—surely much more than has so far been dreamt of in our psychology. A century of research has revealed many of the secrets of sensation and perception, but for future generations of researchers there remain profound and genuine mysteries to solve.

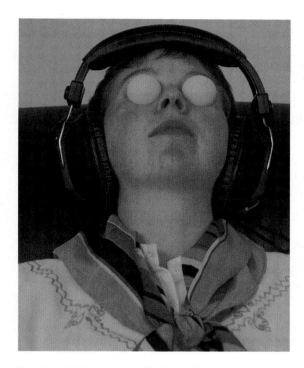

The Ganzfeld Procedure *Hoping to detect faint telepathy signals, parapsychologists are using sensory deprivation to minimize distractions.*

"*I have uttered what I did not understand, things too wonderful for me.*"

Job 42:3

"*The most commonplace crime is often the most mysterious. . . . Life is infinitely stranger than anything which the mind of man could invent.*"

Sherlock Holmes, in Arthur Conan Doyle's
A Study in Scarlet, 1888

Rehearse It

32. More than half of Americans believe in the reality of ESP (extrasensory perception). The response of psychologists to these claims has been to

a. deny the possibility of perception apart from sensation.

b. doubt the existence of mysteries and extraordinary phenomena.

c. test and critique ESP claims.

d. devise a theory that explains why ESP exists.

33. The most testable varieties of ESP involve perceiving future events, mind-to-mind communication, and perceiving remote events. In order, these refer to

a. clairvoyance, telepathy, and precognition.

b. telepathy, clairvoyance, and precognition.

c. precognition, telepathy, and clairvoyance.

d. precognition, clairvoyance, and telepathy.

Reviewing *Sensation and Perception*

Sensing the World: Some Basic Principles

1. What is an absolute threshold, and are we influenced by stimuli below it?

Each species comes equipped with sensitivities that enable it to survive and thrive. We sense only a portion of the sea of energy that surrounds us, but to this portion we are exquisitely sensitive. Our absolute threshold for any stimulus is the minimum stimulation that is detectable 50 percent of the time. Although recent experiments reveal that we can process some information from subliminal (subthreshold) stimuli, the restricted conditions under which this occurs would not enable unscrupulous opportunists to exploit us with subliminal messages.

2. How is our threshold for detecting differences affected by the magnitude of the stimuli?

To survive and thrive, an organism must have difference thresholds low enough to detect minute changes in important stimuli. In humans, a difference threshold (also called a just noticeable difference, or jnd) is a constant proportion of the magnitude of the stimulus—a principle known as Weber's law.

3. What function does sensory adaptation serve?

The phenomenon of sensory adaptation helps to focus our attention on informative changes in stimulation by diminishing our sensitivity to constant or routine odors, sounds, and so forth.

Vision

4. How does the eye transform light energy into neural messages?

Each of our senses receives stimulation, transforms it into neural signals, and sends these neural messages to the brain.

The energies we experience as visible light are a thin slice from the broad spectrum of electromagnetic radiation. The perceived hue and brightness of light depend on the wavelength and intensity. After entering the eye and being focused by a cameralike lens, light waves strike the retina. The retina's light-sensitive rods and color-sensitive cones convert the light energy into neural impulses, which travel along the optic nerve to the brain.

5. How is visual information processed in the brain?

Nerve cells in the retina process information before routing it to the brain. Within the cortex, individual feature detector cells respond to specific aspects of the visual stimulus, and their information is pooled by higher level brain cells for interpretation. Subdimensions of vision (color, movement, depth, and form) are processed separately and simultaneously, illustrating our brain's capacity for parallel processing.

6. What theories contribute to our understanding of color vision, and how are we affected by color constancy?

Research on how we see color supports two nineteenth-century theories. First, as the Young-Helmholtz trichromatic (three-color) theory suggests, the retina contains three types of cones. Each is most sensitive to the wavelengths of one of the three primary colors (red, green, or blue). Second, as opponent-process theory maintains, the nervous system codes the color-related information from the cones into pairs of opponent colors, as demonstrated by the phenomenon of afterimages and as confirmed by measuring opponent processes within the retina and within visual neurons of the thalamus. The phenomenon of color constancy under varying illumination shows that our brains construct our experience of color.

The Other Senses

7. How does the ear transform sound energy into neural messages?

The pressure waves we experience as sound vary in frequency and amplitude, and correspondingly in perceived pitch and loudness. Through a mechanical chain of events, these sound waves traveling down the auditory canal cause minuscule vibrations in the eardrum. Transmitted via the bones of the middle ear to the fluid-filled cochlea, these vibrations create movement in tiny hair cells, triggering neural messages to the brain. We localize sound by detecting minute differences in the loudness and timing of the sounds received by each ear.

8. How do we sense touch and feel pain?

Our sense of touch is actually four senses—pressure, warmth, cold, and pain—that combine to produce other sensations, such as a tickle. One theory of pain is that a "gate" in the spinal cord either opens in response to pain signals traveling up small nerve fibers, which then pass on to the brain, or closes to prevent their passage. Because pain is both a physiological and psychological phenomenon, it often can be controlled through a combination of physical and psychological treatments.

9. How do we experience taste and smell?

Taste, a chemical sense, is a composite of four basic sensations—sweet, sour, salty, and bitter—and of the aromas that interact with information from the taste buds. Like taste, smell is a chemical sense, but there are no basic sensations for smell.

10. How do we sense our body's position and movement?

Our effective functioning requires a kinesthetic sense, which notifies the brain of the position of body parts, and a vestibular sense, which monitors the position and movement of the head.

Perceptual Organization

11. What did the Gestalt psychologists contribute to our understanding of perception?

The early Gestalt psychologists were impressed with the seemingly innate way in which we organize fragmentary sensory data into whole perceptions. They studied how our minds structure the information that comes to us.

12. How do the principles of figure-ground and grouping contribute to our perception of form?:

To recognize an object, we must first perceive it (see it as a figure) as distinct from its surroundings (the ground). We must also organize the figure into a meaningful form. Several gestalt principles—proximity, similarity, continuity, closure, and connectedness—describe this process.

13. Why do we see the world in three dimensions?

Research using a visual cliff has revealed that many species perceive the world in three dimensions at, or very soon after, birth. We transform two-dimensional retinal images into three-dimensional depth perceptions by use of binocular cues (such as retinal disparity and convergence) and monocular cues (such as interposition; the relative size, height, and brightness of objects; and linear perspective).

14. How do perceptual constancies help us to organize our sensations into meaningful perceptions?

Because of size, shape, and lightness constancy, objects appear to have unchanging characteristics regardless of their true distance from us or their actual shape or illumination. These constancies explain several of the well-known visual illusions.

Interpretation

15. What does research on sensory restriction and restored vision reveal about the effects of experience on perception?

For many species, infancy is a critical period during which experience must activate the brain's innate visual mechanisms. If cataract removal restores eyesight to adults who were blind from birth, they remain unable to perceive the world normally. Generally, they can distinguish figure from ground and can perceive colors, but they are unable to recognize shapes and forms. In controlled experiments, infant animals have been reared with severely restricted visual input. When their visual exposure is returned to normal, they, too, suffer enduring visual handicaps.

16. How adaptable is our perception?

Human vision is remarkably adaptable. Given glasses that shift the world slightly to the left or right, or even turn it upside down, people manage to adapt their movements and, with practice, to move about with ease.

17. How do our assumptions, expectations, and contexts affect our perceptions?

Clear evidence that perception is influenced by our learned assumptions and beliefs as well as by sensory input comes from the many demonstrations of perceptual set. Contexts plus the ideas we have stored in memory help us to interpret otherwise ambiguous stimuli. This helps explain why some of us "see" monsters, faces, and UFOs that others do not.

Is There Perception Without Sensation?

18. What types of ESP have been proposed, and why are most research psychologists skeptical?

Parapsychologists have tried to document several forms of ESP—telepathy, clairvoyance, and precognition. But for several reasons, especially the lack of a reproducible ESP effect, most research psychologists remain skeptical. New studies using the ganzfeld procedure have recently raised hopes of a measurable telepathy phenomenon. Follow-up studies should soon indicate the phenomenon's reliability.

Terms and Concepts to Remember

sensation, p. 117
perception, p. 117
psychophysics, p. 118
absolute threshold, p. 119
subliminal, p. 119
difference threshold, p. 121
just noticeable difference (jnd), p. 121
Weber's law, p. 121
sensory adaptation, p. 122
wavelength, p. 124
hue, p. 124
intensity, p. 124
pupil, p. 125
iris, p. 125
lens p. 125
accommodation, p. 125
retina, p. 125
rods, p. 126
cones, p. 126
optic nerve, p. 126
blind spot, p. 126

feature detectors, p. 127
parallel processing, p. 128
Young-Helmholtz trichromatic (three-color) theory, p. 129
opponent-process theory, p. 130
color constancy, p. 130
visual capture, p. 131
audition, p. 131
frequency, p. 132
pitch, p. 132
middle ear, p. 132
inner ear, p. 132
cochlea [KOHK-lee-uh], p. 132
gate-control theory, p. 134
sensory interaction, p. 136
kinesthesis [kin-ehs-THEE-sehs], p. 138
vestibular sense, p. 138
gestalt, p. 139
figure-ground, p. 140
grouping, p. 140
proximity, p. 140

similarity, p. 140
continuity, p. 140
closure, p. 141
connectedness, p. 141
depth perception, p. 141
visual cliff, p. 141
binocular cues, p. 142
monocular cues, p. 142
retinal disparity, p. 142
convergence, p. 142
relative size, p. 142
interposition, p. 143
relative height, p. 143
relative motion, p. 143
linear perspective, p. 143
relative brightness, p. 144
perceptual constancy, p. 145
perceptual adaptation, p. 149
perceptual set, p. 150
extrasensory perception (ESP), p. 153
parapsychology, p. 154

Rehearse It Answer Key

1. d.	2. b.	3. b.	4. b.	5. b.	6. c.	7. c.	8. c.	9. c.
10. c.	11. b.	12. a.	13. d.	14. b.	15. a.	16. b.	17. c.	18. a.
19. c.	20. d.	21. c.	22. d.	23. b.	24. c.	25. c.	26. b.	27. a.
28. b.	29. d.	30. a.	31. c.	32. c.	33. c.			

Critical Thinking Exercise

Now that you have read and reviewed Chapter 4, take your learning a step further by testing your critical thinking skills on the following passage.

Your college roommate, who has been your closest friend since grade school, is convinced she has psychic ability. For years she has claimed to be able to "read your mind," and often does seem to know what you are about to say or do in certain situations. She recently claimed to have experienced a precognitive "vision" a week before you were involved in an automobile accident, although she was too embarrassed to warn you of the impending danger. When pressed for the details of her "vision," she says, "I just felt that something awful was going to happen to you." To prove her psychic ability, she asks you to pick a card at random from a deck of ordinary playing cards and concentrate on its suit (hearts, diamonds, clubs, or spades) while she attempts to read the suit telepathically from your mind. Much to your amazement, and your friend's delight, she correctly identifies the card's suit.

Understand the Assertion

1. State your roommate's assertion in your own words. Define all important concepts and terms as they are used in this example.

Consider the Evidence

2. Is the evidence for your roommate's assertion based on trustworthy research?

Evaluate the Explanation

3. Evaluate the proposed explanation.

   a. Restate it in your own words.

   b. Determine whether the explanation makes sense based on the evidence.

   c. State an alternative explanation.

Check your progress on becoming a critical thinker by comparing your answers to the sample answers found in Appendix B.

Chapter 5

States of Consciousness

Studying Consciousness

Selective Attention

Levels of Information Processing

Sleep and Dreams

The Rhythm of Sleep

Why Do We Sleep?

Sleep Disorders

Dreams

Daydreams and Meditation

Hypnosis

Facts and Falsehoods

Explaining the Hypnotized State

Drugs and Consciousness

Depressants

Stimulants

Hallucinogens

Influences on Drug Use

Now playing at an inner theater near you: the premiere showing of some sleeping person's vivid dream. This never-before-seen mental movie features captivating characters wrapped in a plot so original and unlikely, yet so intricate and real-seeming, that the viewer later marvels at its creation. Awakening from a troubling dream, wrenched by its emotions, who among us has not wondered about this weird state of consciousness? How does our brain so creatively, colorfully, and completely construct this alternative conscious world? In the shadowland between our dreaming and waking consciousness, we may even wonder for a moment which realm represents reality. And what shall we make of other altered states of consciousness—of daydreaming, hypnosis, and drug-altered hallucinations?

But first questions first: What is consciousness? In every science there are concepts so fundamental they are nearly impossible to define. Biologists agree on what is alive but not on precisely what life is. In physics, matter and energy elude simple definition. To psychologists, consciousness is similarly a fundamental yet slippery concept.

Studying Consciousness

1. What is consciousness and how does it function?

At its beginning, psychology was sometimes defined as "the description and explanation of states of consciousness" (Ladd, 1887). But the difficulty of scientifically studying consciousness led many psychologists during the first half of this century to turn to direct observations of behavior—an approach favored by an emerging school of psychology called *behaviorism* (page 198). At mid-century, psychology was no longer defined as the study of consciousness or "mental life" but rather as the science of behavior. Psychology had almost lost consciousness. Consciousness was viewed like a car's speedometer: "It doesn't make the car go, it just reflects what's happening" (Seligman, 1991, p. 24).

By 1960, mental concepts began to reenter psychology. Advances in neuroscience made it possible to relate brain activity to various normal mental states—waking, sleeping, dreaming. Researchers were also beginning to study altered states of consciousness induced by hypnosis and drugs. Psychologists of

> *"Psychology must discard all reference to consciousness."*
>
> Behaviorist John B. Watson (1913)

all persuasions were affirming the importance of mental processes (cognition). Psychology was regaining consciousness.

For most psychologists today, **consciousness** is our awareness of ourselves and our environment. When we learn a complex concept or behavior—say, driving a car—consciousness focuses our concentration on the car and the traffic. This awareness varies with our attentional spotlight. With practice, driving becomes automatic and does not require our undivided attention—freeing our consciousness to focus on other tasks.

Selective Attention

Awareness comes to us moment by moment, one perception vanishing as the next appears. When you were looking at the Necker cube and figure-ground demonstrations in Chapter 4, you could *know* that two interpretations were possible, yet at any moment you consciously experienced only one of them. This illustrates an important principle: Our conscious attention is *selective*.

Selective attention means that at any moment we focus our awareness on only a limited aspect of all that we are capable of experiencing. Until reading this sentence, you have been unaware that your shoes are pressing against your feet or that your nose is in your line of vision. Now, suddenly, your attentional spotlight shifts and your feet feel encased, your nose stubbornly intrudes on the page before you. While attending to these words, you've also been blocking from awareness information coming from your peripheral vision. But you can change that. While staring at the X below, notice what surrounds the book (the edges of the page, your desk top, and so forth).

X

Another example of selective attention is the *cocktail party effect*—the ability to attend selectively to only one voice among many. Imagine hearing two conversations over a headset, one in each ear, and being asked to repeat the left-ear message as it is spoken. When you pay attention to what's being said in your left ear, you won't perceive what is said in your right ear. If later you are asked what language your right ear heard, you may draw a blank (though you could report the speaker's sex and loudness). At the level of conscious awareness, whatever has your attention has your undivided attention.

Levels of Information Processing

Psychological research on perception, learning, memory, thinking, and emotion reveals that we also process much information *outside* our awareness. We register and react to stimuli we do not consciously perceive. We perform well-learned tasks automatically, as when typing without attending to where the letters are on the keyboard. We change our attitudes and reconstruct our memories with no awareness of doing so. We are influenced by our past in ways we don't know (Greenwald & Banaji, 1995). *Conscious* awareness is but the tip of the information-processing iceberg.

Beneath the surface, subconscious information processing occurs simultaneously on many parallel tracks. When we look at a flying bird, we are consciously aware of the result of our cognitive processing but not of our subprocessing of the bird's color, form, movement, distance, and identity.

Unlike the parallel processing of subconscious information, conscious processing takes place in sequence (serially), is relatively slow, and has limited capacity. Consciousness is like a chief executive officer. Its many assistants automatically take care of routine business without bothering the CEO. This allows the CEO to monitor the whole system and deal with new challenges. Thus, when traveling a familiar route we can talk politics while driving "on automatic."

Attention *With experience, tasks such as driving become mostly automatic, freeing our conscious attention for other matters. However, in an emergency, a driver immersed in a phone conversation may run into trouble.*

For a recap of serial and parallel processing, see page 128.

consciousness Our awareness of ourselves and our environment.

selective attention The focusing of conscious awareness on a particular stimulus, as in the *cocktail party effect*.

circadian [ser-KAY-dee-an] **rhythm** The biological clock; regular bodily rhythms (for example, of temperature and wakefulness) that occur on a 24-hour cycle.

Less habitual tasks require our conscious attention. When first arriving in a country where cars go on the other side of the road, driving commands one's full attention. Or try this: You can move your right foot in a smooth counterclockwise circle, and you can write the number 3 repeatedly with your right hand—but not at the same time. (If you are musically inclined, try something equally difficult: Tap a steady three beats with your left hand while tapping four beats with your right hand.) Both tasks require conscious attention, which can only be in one place at a time. If time is nature's way of keeping everything from happening at once, then consciousness is nature's way of keeping us from thinking and doing everything at once.

Consciousness occurs in varied states. We have not only normal seeing and hearing, reasoning and remembering, but also the altered consciousness of sleep dreams and daydreams, hypnotic states, chemically induced hallucinations, and near-death visions.

"I love to sleep. Do you? Isn't it great? It really is the best of both worlds. You get to be alive and unconscious."

Comedian Rita Rudner, 1993

Sleep and Dreams

Sleep—sweet, renewing, mysterious sleep. Sleep—the irresistible tempter to whom we must all succumb. Sleep—the mantle that covers human thought. What is it? Why must we have it? Why do we spend a third of our lives—some 25 years, on average—sleeping? Why do we dream?

Such questions have intrigued humans for centuries. Now, some of these mysteries are being solved. In laboratories throughout the world, thousands have slept attached to recording devices while others observe. By recording sleepers' brain waves and muscle movements, by observing and awakening them from time to time, the sleep-watchers glimpse things that a thousand years of common sense never told us. Perhaps you can anticipate some of their discoveries. Are the following statements true or false?

1. When people dream of performing some activity, their limbs often move in concert with the dream (page 168).
2. Older adults sleep more than young adults (page 169 and Figure 5–6).
3. After 2 or 3 sleepless days, a person's performance on a brief but demanding intellectual task suffers (page 169).
4. Sleepwalkers are acting out their dreams (page 167).
5. Sleep experts recommend treating insomnia with an occasional sleeping pill (page 170).
6. The dreams we have just before awakening in the morning are similar to those we have soon after falling asleep (page 171).
7. Some people dream every night; others seldom dream at all (page 168).

All these statements (adapted from Palladino & Carducci, 1983) are false. Let's see why.

The Rhythm of Sleep

2. What is the biological rhythm we experience, and how does it affect the stages of our sleep?

The rhythm of the day parallels the rhythm of life—from our waking to a new day's birth to our nightly return to what Shakespeare called "death's counterfeit." Our bodies synchronize with the 24-hour cycle of day and night through a biological clock called the **circadian rhythm** (from the Latin *circa*,

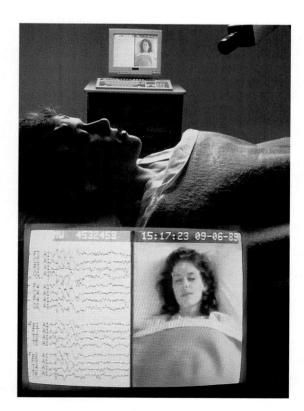

A Study in Sleep *In a sleep laboratory, recording equipment monitors a woman's physiological state. Electrodes pasted to her face and scalp pick up electrical signals from her brain, while the television camera records her facial expression and eye movements. These patterns will vary with her sleep rhythm.*

REM sleep   Rapid eye movement sleep; a recurring sleep stage during which vivid dreams commonly occur. Also known as paradoxical sleep because the muscles are relaxed (except for minor twitches) but other body systems are active.

alpha waves   The relatively slow brain waves of a relaxed, awake state.

delta waves   The large, slow brain waves associated with deep sleep.

If our natural circadian rhythm was attuned to a 23-hour cycle, would we instead need to discipline ourselves to stay up later at night and sleep in longer in the morning?

"about," and *dies*, "day"). Our body temperature, for example, rises as morning approaches, peaks during the day, and then begins to drop before we go to sleep. Awake at 4:00 A.M. with a depressed body temperature, we may fret over concerns: Does a lovers' spat signal a split? Does a child's moodiness mean more trouble ahead? By midday, our body energized, we fret less. Pulling an all-nighter, we feel groggiest about 4:00 A.M., but we feel a second wind as our normal wake-up time arrives.

A transcontinental flight disrupts our circadian rhythm and we experience jet lag, mainly because we are awake when our circadian rhythm cries, "Sleep!" If we stay up late and sleep in on weekends, our biological clock begins to reset itself. When the weekend ends, the result may be "Sunday night insomnia" and "Monday morning blues." (Those who sleep till noon on Sunday and then go to bed just 11 hours later in preparation for the new workweek often find sleep elusive.)

Mysteriously, young adults isolated without clocks or daylight typically adopt a 25-hour day. This helps explain why many people find it easier to jet west, with an extended day, than east; why rotating shift workers adapt better to progressively later shifts than to earlier shifts; why until our later years we must discipline ourselves to get to bed on time and force ourselves to get up. When placed under constant illumination, most animals, too, exceed a 24-hour day.

There is also a biological rhythm during our sleep. About every 90 or 100 minutes we pass through a cycle of five distinct sleep stages. This elementary fact was unknown until 8-year-old Armond Aserinsky went to bed one night in 1952. His father, Eugene, a University of Chicago graduate student, needed to test an electroencephalograph he had been repairing during the day (Aserinsky, 1988; Seligman & Yellen, 1987). He placed electrodes near Armond's eyes to record the rolling eye movements believed to occur during sleep. Before long, the machine went wild, tracing deep zigzags on the graph paper. Aserinsky thought the machine was still broken. But as the night proceeded, the activity periodically recurred, indicating, Aserinsky finally realized, fast, jerky eye movements accompanied by energetic brain activity. When he awakened Armond during one such episode of *r*apid *e*ye *m*ovement sleep (**REM sleep**), the boy reported he was having a dream.

To find out if similar cycles occur during adult sleep, Nathaniel Kleitman (1960) and Aserinsky pioneered procedures that have now been used with thousands of volunteers. To appreciate both their methods and findings, imagine yourself as a subject. As the hour grows late you yawn in response to reduced brain metabolism. Yawning stretches your neck muscles and increases your heart rate, thus increasing the blood flow to your brain, and your alertness

Left eye movements

Right eye movements

EMG (muscle tension)

EEG (brain waves)

Figure 5–1 Measuring Sleep Activity *Sleep researchers measure brain-wave activity, eye movements, and muscle tension by electrodes that pick up electrical signals from the brain, eye, and facial muscles. (From Dement, 1978.)*

(Moorcroft, 1993). When you are ready for bed, the researcher glues electrodes to your scalp (to detect your brain's electrical waves), just outside the corners of your eyes (to detect eye movements), and on your chin (to detect muscle tension) (Figure 5–1). Other devices allow the researcher to record your heart rate, your respiration rate, and even the degree of your genital arousal.

When you are in bed with your eyes closed, the researcher in the next room sees on the EEG the relatively slow **alpha waves** of your awake but relaxed state (Figure 5–2). As you adapt to all this equipment and grow tired, you slip into sleep and begin your dive toward deeper and deeper levels. Your breathing rate slows and your brain waves slow further and show the irregular waves of Stage 1 sleep. During this light sleep, which lasts about 2 minutes, you may experience fantastic images. You may have a sensation of falling (at which moment your body may suddenly jerk) or of floating weightlessly.

Soon, you relax more deeply and begin about 20 minutes of Stage 2 sleep, characterized by the periodic appearance of *sleep spindles*—bursts of rapid, rhythmic brain-wave activity. Although you can still be awakened without too much difficulty during this phase, you are now clearly asleep. Sleeptalking— usually garbled or nonsensical—can occur during any sleep stage but seldom appears during deep sleep. More often it occurs during Stage 2 sleep or in the Stage 1 borderline between sleeping and waking.

Then for the next few minutes you go through the transitional Stage 3 to the deep sleep of Stage 4. Starting in Stage 3 and increasingly in Stage 4, your brain emits large, slow **delta waves**. These stages together are therefore called *slow-wave sleep*. They last for about 30 minutes, during which you are hard to awaken. Curiously, it is during the deep sleep of Stage 4 that we may begin walking in our sleep, or (as children) wet the bed. Moreover, even when we are deeply asleep, our brains somehow process the meaning of certain stimuli. We move around on our beds, but we manage not to fall out of them. The occasional roar of passing vehicles may leave deep sleep undisturbed, but the cry from a baby's nursery quickly interrupts it. EEG recordings confirm that our brain's auditory cortex responds to sound stimuli even while we sleep (Kutas, 1990).

About an hour after you first fall asleep, a strange thing happens. Rather than continuing in deep slumber, you ascend from your initial sleep dive. Returning through Stage 3 and Stage 2 (where you spend about half your night), you enter the most intriguing sleep phase of all—REM sleep (Figure 5–3). For about 10 minutes, your brain waves become rapid and saw-toothed, more like those of the nearly awake Stage 1 sleep. But unlike Stage 1 sleep, REM sleep is a time when your heart rate rises, your breathing becomes more rapid and ir-

Awake, relaxed

◄ Alpha waves ►

Stage 1 sleep

Stage 2 sleep

Spindle (burst of activity)

Stage 3 sleep

Stage 4 sleep

◄ Delta waves ►

REM sleep

Figure 5–2 Brain Waves and Sleep Stages *The regular alpha waves of an awake, relaxed state are quite different from the slower, larger delta waves of deep Stage 4 sleep. Although the rapid REM sleep waves resemble the waves of near-waking Stage 1 sleep, the body is more aroused during REM sleep than during Stage 1 sleep. (From Dement, 1978.)*

Figure 5–3 The Stages in a Typical Night's Sleep *Most people pass through a cycle of the five sleep stages several times, with the periods of Stage 4 sleep and then Stage 3 sleep diminishing and REM sleep periods increasing in duration. (From Cartwright, 1978.)*

"Boy are my eyes tired! I had REM sleep all night long."

People rarely snore during dreams. When REM starts, snoring stops.

regular, and every half minute or so your eyes dart around in a momentary burst of activity behind closed lids. Because anyone watching a sleeper's eyes can notice these REM bursts, it is amazing that science was ignorant of REM sleep until 1952.

During REM sleep, your genitals become aroused and you have an erection or increased vaginal lubrication. The common "morning erection" stems from the night's last REM period, often just before waking. Except during very scary dreams, genital arousal always occurs, regardless of whether the dream's content is sexual (Karacan & others, 1966). In young men, sleep-related erections outlast REM periods, lasting 30 to 45 minutes on average (Karacan & others, 1983; Schiavi & Schreiner-Engel, 1988). A typical 25-year-old man therefore has an erection during nearly half his night's sleep, a 65-year-old man for one-quarter. Many men troubled by "erectile disorder" (impotence) have morning erections, which suggests that their problem is not with their genitals.

Although your brain's motor cortex is active during REM sleep, your brainstem blocks its messages, leaving your muscles relaxed—so relaxed that, except for an occasional finger, toe, or facial twitch, you are essentially paralyzed. Moreover, you cannot easily be awakened. Thus, REM sleep is sometimes called *paradoxical* sleep because internally the body is aroused while externally it appears calm.

Even more intriguing than the paradoxical nature of REM sleep is what the rapid eye movements announce: the beginning of a dream. Even those who claim they never dream will, more than 80 percent of the time, recall a dream after being awakened during REM sleep. Unlike the fleeting images of Stage 1 sleep, REM sleep dreams are often emotional and usually storylike. (People occasionally recall dreams when awakened from stages other than REM sleep, but these dreams usually contain a single vague image, such as, "I was trying to borrow something from someone.")

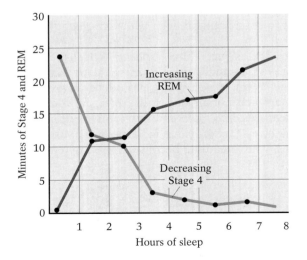

Figure 5–4 The Progression of Stage 4 and REM Sleep Across a Night's Sleep *(Data averaged from 30 young adults by Webb, 1992.)*

As the night wears on, this sleep cycle repeats itself about every 90 minutes. During the night, deep Stage 4 sleep gets progressively briefer and then disappears, and the REM sleep period gets longer (Figure 5–4). By morning, 20 to 25 percent of our average night's sleep—some 100 minutes—has been REM sleep. This means that those who say, "I never dream," actually spend about 600 hours a year experiencing some 1500 dreams, or more than 100,000 dreams over a typical lifetime.

Why Do We Sleep?

3. What is the function of sleep?

Sleep commands roughly one-third of our lives. Deprived of it, we begin to feel terrible; our bodies yearn for it. You can know you are sleep-deprived—as many college students are (Levine & others, 1988)—if most of the following are true: You need an alarm clock to shorten your natural sleep pattern; you feel sleepy while sitting in class or you lack vigor needed for peak performance; you collapse into sleep almost immediately after your head hits the pillow. How much sleep do you need? The answer is simple, says sleep researcher William Moorcroft (1993): enough so you will not feel tired the next day.

Obviously, we need sleep. But why? It seems an easy question to answer: Just keep people awake for several days and note how they deteriorate. If you were a subject in such an experiment, how do you think it would affect your body and mind?

Of course, you would become terribly drowsy at times—especially during the hours when your biological clock programs you to sleep. But could lack of sleep physically damage you? Would it noticeably alter your biochemistry or body organs? Would you become emotionally disturbed? Intellectually disoriented?

The major effect, as fatigued college students know, is sleepiness, and sometimes a general malaise (Mikulincer & others, 1989). Owing to modern light bulbs, TV, shift work, and social diversions, people today more than ever suffer from sleep patterns that thwart their having an energized feeling of well-being. Teenagers typically need 8 or 9 hours sleep but now average nearly 2 hours less sleep a night than their counterparts of 80 years ago (Holden, 1993). Many fill this need by using home room for their first siesta and after-lunch study hall for a slumber party. As sleep researcher William Dement (1990) laments, "The national sleep debt is larger and more important than the national debt."

Other effects are more subtle: impaired creativity and concentration, diminished immunity to disease, slight hand tremors, irritability, slowed performance, occasional misperceptions on monotonous tasks (Horne, 1989; Koslowsky & Babkoff, 1992). With some tasks, such as truck driving and controlling air traffic, these effects can be devastating. "Rest. That's what I need is rest," said Eastern Airlines Captain James Reeves to the control tower on a September 1974 morning—30 minutes before crashing his airliner at low altitude, killing the crew and all 68 passengers (Moorcroft, 1993). The *Exxon Valdez* oil spill; Union Carbide's Bhopal, India, disaster; and the Three Mile Island and Chernobyl nuclear accidents all occurred after midnight, when operators were likely to be drowsiest.

On short, highly motivating tasks, however, sleep deprivation has little effect. When 17-year-old Randy Gardner made his way into the *Guinness Book of World Records* by staying awake for 11 days, he at times had to keep moving to stay awake. Nevertheless, during his final night of sleeplessness, Gardner managed to beat researcher Dement 100 straight times in a pinball game. He then slept 15 hours and awoke feeling fine (Gulevich & others, 1966).

Why, then, must we sleep? We have few answers, but sleep may have evolved for at least two reasons: First, it hides us out of harm's way. Our ancestors were safer if asleep at night. Animals with the least reason to fear predation or the most need to graze tend to sleep less. For instance, elephants and horses sleep only 3 to 4 hours a day. Second, sleep helps us recuperate. It helps restore body tissues, especially those of the brain. As we sleep, our brain is actively repairing and reorganizing itself and consolidating memories. Our lowered body temperature during sleep also conserves energy for the daytime hours.

Sleep may also play a role in the growth process. During deep sleep, the pituitary gland releases a growth hormone. As adults grow older, they release less of this hormone, and they spend less time in deep sleep (Pekkanen, 1982). These physiological discoveries are only beginning to solve the ongoing riddle of sleep. As researcher Dement (1978, p. 83) deadpanned, "We have miles to go before we sleep."

A few of the unanswered questions about sleep: Why do we sleep more when we are young? Why do some animals sleep most of the day, others not at all? Why, when REM sleep paralyzes our muscles, do we twitch and jerk? Most important, what is sleep's function? (Adapted from UCLA Brain Research Institute, 1989.)

The current record holder, Robert ("Ramblin Rob") McDonald, reportedly stayed awake for 18 days, 22 hours, in a 1986 rocking chair marathon.

"Sleep faster, we need the pillows."
Yiddish proverb

Sleep Disorders

4. What are the major sleep disorders?

1993 Time/CNN poll of adults:

"How many hours do you sleep each night?"

Under six	12%
Six	26
Seven	30
Eight	28
Over eight	3

"The lion and the lamb shall lie down together, but the lamb will not be very sleepy."

Woody Allen in the movie
Love and Death, 1975

The idea that "everyone needs 8 hours of sleep" is untrue. Newborns spend nearly two-thirds of their day asleep, most adults no more than one-third. Age-related differences in average time spent sleeping are rivaled by differences in the normal amount of sleep among individuals at any age. Some people thrive with fewer than 6 hours of sleep per night; others regularly sleep 9 hours or more. Sleep patterns may be genetically influenced. When Wilse Webb and Scott Campbell (1983) checked the pattern and duration of sleep among fraternal and identical twins, only the identical twins were strikingly similar.

Whatever their normal need for sleep, some 10 to 15 percent of adults complain of **insomnia**—persistent problems in falling or staying asleep. True insomnia is not the occasional inability to sleep that we experience when anxious or excited. When stressed, alertness is a natural and adaptive response. We commonly underestimate the amount of sleep we get on restless nights. Even if we've been awake only an hour, we may *think* we've had insomnia much of the night, because that's the part we remember. From middle age on, sleep is seldom uninterrupted. Occasional awakenings become the norm, not something to fret over or treat with medication.

The most common quick fixes for true insomnia, sleeping pills and alcohol, can aggravate the problem. Both reduce REM sleep and can leave a person with next-day blahs. With continued use it takes bigger doses to get an effect, and when the drug is discontinued the insomnia may worsen. Sleep experts offer other alternatives:

1. Relax before bedtime.
2. Avoid caffeine (this includes chocolate) after late afternoon and avoid rich foods before bedtime. A glass of milk may help. (Milk provides raw materials for the manufacture of serotonin, a neurotransmitter that facilitates sleep.)
3. Sleep on a regular schedule (rise at the same time even after a restless night) and avoid naps.
4. Exercise regularly but not in the late evening (best in the late afternoon).
5. Reassure yourself that the temporary loss of sleep causes no great harm, certainly nothing worth losing sleep over. "Sleep is like love or happiness," notes Wilse Webb (1992, p. 170). "If you pursue it too ardently it will elude you." One experimenter offered subjects $10 for every minute they fell asleep faster than the night before. Not a single person made money.
6. If nothing else works, aim for less sleep; go to bed later or get up earlier.

Rarer but more severe than insomnia are the sleep disorders narcolepsy and sleep apnea. People with **narcolepsy** (from *narco*, "numbness," and *lepsy*, "seizure") suffer periodic, overwhelming sleepiness, sometimes at the most inopportune times, perhaps just after taking a terrific swing at a softball or when laughing loudly or shouting angrily (Dement, 1978). The person collapses directly into a brief period of REM sleep, with its accompanying loss of muscular tension. Those who suffer from narcolepsy—1 in 1000 people, estimates the National Commission on Sleep Disorders Research—must live with extra caution. As a traffic menace, "snoozing is second only to boozing," says the American Sleep Disorders Association, and those with narcolepsy are especially at risk (Aldrich, 1989).

insomnia   A sleep disorder involving recurring problems in falling or staying asleep.

narcolepsy   A sleep disorder characterized by uncontrollable sleep attacks in which the sufferer lapses directly into REM sleep, often at inopportune times.

sleep apnea   A sleep disorder characterized by temporary cessations of breathing during sleep and consequent momentary reawakenings.

night terrors   A sleep disorder characterized by high arousal and an appearance of being terrified; unlike nightmares, night terrors occur during Stage 4 sleep, within 2 or 3 hours of falling asleep, and are seldom remembered.

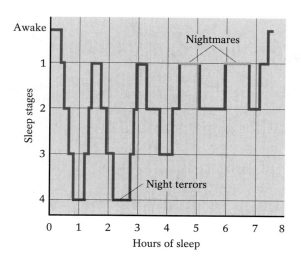

Figure 5–5 Night Terrors and Nightmares *Night terrors occur within 2 or 3 hours of falling asleep, during Stage 4 sleep. Nightmares occur toward morning, during REM sleep. (From Hartman, 1984.)*

The National Heart, Lung, and Blood Institute reports that 1 in 25 people (mostly overweight men) suffer from **sleep apnea**—a disorder that was unknown before modern sleep research. They intermittently stop breathing during sleep. (*Apnea* means "stopping respiration.") After an airless minute or so, decreased blood oxygen arouses the sleeper to awaken and snort in air for a few seconds. The process can repeat more than 400 times a night, depriving the person of slow-wave sleep. Apnea sufferers complain of sleepiness and irritability during the day (and their mates complain about their loud "snoring") but are often unaware of their disorder.

Still other sleepers, mostly children, experience **night terrors**. The person might sit up or walk around, talk incoherently, experience a doubling of heart and breathing rates, and appear terrified (Hartmann, 1981). The night-terror sufferer very seldom awakens fully and recalls little or nothing the next morning—at most, a fleeting, frightening image. Night terrors are not nightmares, which typically occur during early morning REM sleep. Like sleepwalking, night terrors usually occur during the first few hours of sleep and begin during Stage 4 sleep (Figure 5–5). Family members will usually guide a sleepwalker back to bed or try to awaken and reassure the person. As we grow older we have less of the deep Stage 4 sleep, but for some this also means an end to sleepwalking and night terrors.

! *Rehearse It*

1. Consciousness involves selective attention to ongoing perceptions. An example of selective attention is the "cocktail party effect," which is the ability to

a. drink without becoming intoxicated.
b. follow many voices simultaneously.
c. attend to but one voice among many other voices.
d. be affected by unnoticed stimuli.

2. Stage 1 sleep is a twilight zone of light sleep that lasts about 2 minutes. During Stage 1 sleep, a person is most likely to experience

a. sleep spindles.
b. fantastic images.
c. night terrors or nightmares.
d. rapid eye movements.

3. In the deepest stage of sleep—surprisingly, the stage when people sleepwalk—the brain emits large, slow delta waves. This deep stage of sleep is called

a. Stage 2.
b. Stage 4.
c. REM sleep.
d. paradoxical sleep.

4. An electroencephalograph shows that several times a night we pass through a cycle of five sleep stages, each with characteristic brain waves. As the night progresses the REM stage

a. gradually disappears.
b. becomes briefer and briefer.
c. remains about the same.
d. becomes progressively longer.

5. Two relatively rare sleep disorders are narcolepsy and sleep apnea. With narcolepsy, the person _____; with sleep apnea, the person _____
_____.

a. has persistent problems falling asleep; experiences a doubling of heart and breathing rates during sleep
b. experiences a doubling of heart and breathing rates; has persistent problems falling asleep during sleep
c. intermittently stops breathing during sleep; suffers periodic, overwhelming sleepiness
d. suffers periodic, overwhelming sleepiness; intermittently stops breathing during sleep

Dreams

Discovering the link between REM sleep and dreaming opened a new era in dream research. Instead of relying on someone's hazy recall hours or days after having a dream, researchers could catch dreams as they happen. They could awaken their subjects during a REM sleep period, or within 3 minutes afterward, and hear a vivid account of the dream.

"*I do not believe that I am now dreaming, but I cannot prove that I am not.*"

Philosopher Bertrand Russell, 1872–1970

Would you suppose that people dream if blind from birth? Studies of blind people in France, Hungary, and Egypt all found them dreaming of using their nonvisual senses—hearing, touching, smelling, tasting (Buquet, 1988; Taha, 1972; Vekassy, 1977).

A popular sleep myth: If you dream you are falling and hit the ground (or if you dream of dying), you die. Unfortunately, those who could confirm these ideas are not around to do so. Some people, however, have had such dreams and are alive to report them.

Nocturnal Mysteries *Everyone dreams, and the content is sometimes as bizarre as these images from Francisco de Goya's "The Dream of Reason Produces Monsters." Our fascination with dreams has led to some interesting theories about their function.*

What We Dream

5. What do we dream?

REM dreams are vivid, emotional, and bizarre. Several times a night, you are the creator and producer of a surrealistic mental movie, in which events frequently occur in a jumbled sequence, scenes change suddenly, people appear and disappear, and physical laws, such as gravity, may be violated. Yet dreams are so vivid we may confuse them with reality. Occasionally, we may be sufficiently aware during a dream to wonder whether we are, in fact, dreaming. When experiencing such *lucid dreams*, some people are able to test their state of consciousness. If they can perform some absurd act, such as floating in the air, then they know they are dreaming.

Although we are more likely to be awakened by and to remember our most emotional dreams, many dreams are rather ordinary. When awakened during REM sleep, people report dreams with sexual imagery less often than you might think. In one study, only 1 in 10 dreams among young men and 1 in 30 among young women had sexual overtones (Hall & Van de Castle, 1966).

More commonly, we dream of daily life events, such as a meeting at work or taking an exam. In the month after the 1989 San Francisco earthquake, 4 in 10 college students in the area (but only 1 in 20 students elsewhere) had one or more nightmares about an earthquake (Wood & others, 1992). Six years of our life we spend dreaming, most of which is anything but sweet: People commonly dream of repeatedly failing in an attempt to do something; of being attacked, pursued, or rejected; or of experiencing misfortune (Hall & others, 1982).

The story line of our dreams—what Sigmund Freud called their **manifest content**—often incorporates experiences and preoccupations from the day's events, especially in our first dreams of the night. The sensory stimuli of our sleeping environment may also intrude. A particular odor or the telephone's ringing may be instantly and ingeniously woven into the dream story. In one experiment, William Dement and Edward Wolpert (1958) lightly sprayed cold water on dreamers' faces. Compared with sleepers who did not get the cold water treatment, these subjects were more likely to dream about water—about waterfalls, leaky roofs, or even about being sprayed by someone. Even while in REM sleep, focused on internal stimuli, we maintain some awareness of changes in our external environment.

So, could we learn a foreign language by listening to tapes during sleep? If only it were so easy. While sleeping we can learn to associate a sound with a mild electric shock (and to react to the sound accordingly). But we do not remember taped information played while we are soundly asleep (Eich, 1990; Wyatt & Bootzin, 1994). In fact, experiences that occur during the 5 minutes just before falling asleep are typically lost from memory (Roth & others, 1988). This helps explain why dreams that momentarily awaken us are mostly forgotten by morning. To remember a dream, get up and stay awake for a while.

Why We Dream

6. What is the function of dreams?

In his landmark book *The Interpretation of Dreams*, published in 1900, Freud argued that by fulfilling wishes a dream is a psychic safety valve that harmlessly discharges otherwise unacceptable feelings. According to Freud, a dream's manifest content is but a censored, symbolic version of its **latent content**, which consists of unconscious drives and wishes that would be threatening

manifest content According to Freud, the remembered story line of a dream (as distinct from its latent content).

latent content According to Freud, the underlying but censored meaning of a dream (as distinct from its manifest content). Freud believed that a dream's latent content functions as a safety valve.

if expressed directly. Although most dreams have no overt sexual imagery, Freud nevertheless believed that most adult dreams can be "traced back by analysis to *erotic wishes*." In Freud's view, a gun, for example, might be a disguised representation of a penis.

Although Freud considered dreams the key to understanding our inner conflicts, his critics say that dream interpretation leads down a blind alley. Some contend that even if dreams are symbolic, they can be interpreted almost any way one wishes. Others maintain there is nothing hidden in dreams. A dream about a gun, they say, is a dream about a gun. Legend has it that even Freud, who loved to smoke cigars, acknowledged that "sometimes, a cigar is just a cigar."

Freud's theory of dreams is giving way to newer theories. One of these sees dreams as *information processing*: Dreams may help sift, sort, and fix in memory our day's experiences. Following stressful experiences or intense learning periods, REM sleep increases (Palumbo, 1978). What is more, there is "consistent and compelling evidence" that REM sleep facilitates memory (McGrath & Cohen, 1978). In one experiment, people heard unusual phrases before bedtime and then were given a memory test the next morning. If awakened every time they began REM sleep, they remembered less than if awakened during other sleep stages (Empson & Clarke, 1970; Karni & Sagi, 1994). A night of solid sleep (and dreaming) does, it seems, have an important place in a student's life. As we sleep, our busy brains are consolidating the day's important memories.

Another explanation of dreams proposes that they may also serve a physiological function. Perhaps dreams—or the associated brain activity of REM sleep—provide the sleeping brain with periodic stimulation. As you may recall from Chapter 3, stimulating experiences develop and preserve the brain's neural pathways. This theory makes sense from a developmental point of view. Infants, whose neural networks are just developing, spend a great deal of time in REM sleep (Figure 5–6).

Still other physiological theories propose that dreams erupt from neural activity that spreads upward from the brainstem (Antrobus, 1991; Hobson, 1988). According to one version, this neural activity is random, and dreams are the brain's attempt to make sense of it. Much as a neurosurgeon can produce

Figure 5–6 Sleep Across the Life Span *As we age, our sleep patterns change. During our first few months, we spend progressively less time in REM sleep. During our first 20 years, we spend progressively less time asleep. (Adapted from Snyder & Scott, 1972.)*

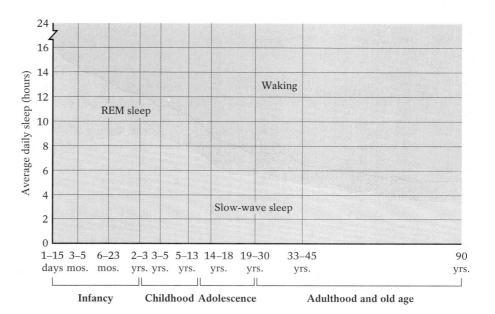

REM rebound The tendency for REM sleep to increase following REM sleep deprivation (created by repeated awakenings during REM sleep).

hallucinations by stimulating different parts of a patient's cortex, so can stimulation originating within the brain. Psychologists Martin Seligman and Amy Yellen (1987) note that the seconds-long bursts of rapid eye movements during REM sleep coincide with bursts of activity in the visual cortex. If awakened during one of these bursts of brain activity, people report vivid experiences, usually dramatic hallucinations.

Given these visual scenes, our cognitive machinery weaves a story line. The emotion-related limbic system also becomes active during REM sleep. Add its activity to the brain's commotion and—voila!—we dream.

The theory, then, is that dreams spring from the mind's relentless effort to make sense of unrelated visual bursts, which are given their emotional tone by the limbic system. This would help explain many of our dream experiences, such as the sudden and bizarre changes in scene (triggered by a new visual burst). Dream reports by Seligman's University of Pennsylvania students confirm that the most vivid dream images are the surprising, discontinuous aspects of the dream; other, less vivid images we presumably conjure up to string the visual bursts together.

The function of dreams provokes vigorous debate, but the disputants all agree that we *need* REM sleep. Deprived of it by repeated awakenings, people return more and more quickly to the REM stage after falling back to sleep. When finally allowed to sleep undisturbed, they literally sleep like babies, with increased REM sleep—a phenomenon called **REM rebound**. The withdrawal of REM-suppressing sleeping medications also increases REM sleep, but with accompanying nightmares. Most other mammals also experience REM sleep and REM rebound. Animals' need for REM sleep suggests that its causes and functions are deeply biological. That REM sleep occurs in mammals (and not in animals such as fish, whose behavior is less influenced by learning) also fits the information-processing theory of dreams. All of which serves to remind us once again of a basic lesson: Biological and psychological explanations of behavior are partners, not competitors.

But if dreams serve physiological functions and lack the disguised meanings that Freud supposed, are they psychologically meaningless? Perhaps, but not necessarily. Every psychologically meaningful experience involves an active brain. Moreover, say advocates of dream reflection, dreams may be akin to abstract art—amenable to more than one meaningful interpretation, and illuminating to ponder.

! Rehearse It

6. According to Sigmund Freud, dreams are the key to the understanding of our inner conflicts. In interpreting dreams, Freud was most interested in their

a. information-processing function.
b. physiological function.
c. manifest content, or story line.
d. latent content, or symbolic meaning.

7. Some theories of dreaming propose that dreams serve a physiological purpose. One such theory suggests that dreams

a. are the brain's attempt to make sense of random neural activity.
b. help sift, sort, and fix in memory our day's experiences.
c. are manifestations of the sensory stimuli that intrude on our sleep.
d. prevent the brain from being disturbed by periodic stimulations.

8. The tendency for REM sleep to increase following REM sleep deprivation is referred to as

a. paradoxical sleep.
b. deep sleep.
c. REM rebound.
d. slow-wave sleep.

Daydreams and Meditation

7. What is the function of daydreams and meditation?

From interview and questionnaire studies with hundreds of adults, clinical psychologist Jerome L. Singer (1975) reported that nearly everyone has daydreams or waking fantasies every day—on the job, in the classroom, walking down the street—in fact, almost anywhere at any time. Compared with older adults, young adults spend more time daydreaming and admit to more sexual fantasies (Cameron & Biber, 1973; Giambra, 1974). Daydreaming mostly involves the familiar details of our lives—perhaps imagining an alternative approach to a task we are performing, or picturing ourselves explaining to an instructor why a paper will be late, or replaying in our minds personal encounters that we relish or wish had gone differently.

Are the hours we spend in fantasy merely a way of escaping rather than facing reality? At times, they are. But daydreaming can also be adaptive. Some daydreams help us prepare for future events by keeping us aware of unfinished business and serving as mental rehearsals. Playful fantasies enhance the creativity of scientists, artists, and writers. For children, daydreaming in the form of imaginative play is important to social and cognitive development—a fact that makes the diversion of television watching a matter of concern to some child psychologists (Singer, 1986).

Daydreams may also substitute for impulsive behavior. People prone to delinquency and violence or who seek the artificial highs of dangerous drugs have fewer vivid fantasies (Singer, 1976).

A more focused, yet fully conscious state of awareness comes through *meditation*. Meditators assume a comfortable position in a quiet environment and adopt a receptive, serene attitude. Then they focus on their breathing, on a word (in Eastern meditation, a mantra such as *Om*), or on a phrase (in Christianity, perhaps a short prayer). Experienced meditators exhibit blood pressure, heart rate, brain wave, and metabolism levels like those of deeply relaxed people (Alexander & others, 1987; Holmes, 1984; Wallace & Benson, 1972). Like relaxation, or even more so, meditation can help relieve pain, anxiety, and stress-related illnesses (Eppley & others, 1989). One astonishing recent study assigned 73 residents of homes for the elderly either to daily meditation or to no treatment. After 3 years, one-fourth of the nonmeditators had died, while all the meditators were still alive (Alexander & others, 1989).

Looking Into the Inner World   *Daydreams and fantasies are a constructive part of everyone's repertory of behavior. For these Dutch commuters, daydreams may release tension, increase creativity, illuminate solutions to problems—and even lessen boredom.*

Hypnosis

8. What do hypnotized people experience, and how do they behave?

Imagine you are about to be hypnotized. The hypnotist invites you to sit back, fix your gaze on a spot high on the wall, and relax. In a quiet, low voice the hypnotist suggests, "Your eyes are growing tired. . . . Your eyelids are becoming heavy . . . now heavier and heavier. . . . They are beginning to close. . . . You are becoming more deeply relaxed. . . . Your breathing is now deep and regular. . . . Your muscles are becoming more and more relaxed. Your whole body is beginning to feel like lead."

After a few minutes of this hypnotic induction, your eyes are probably closed and you may undergo **hypnosis**—a state of apparently heightened suggestibility that enables a hypnotist's coaxings and directions to trigger specific behaviors, perceptions, and perhaps even memories. When the hypnotist sug-

hypnosis   An apparently heightened suggestibility in which some people narrow their focus of attention and claim to experience imaginary happenings as if they were real.

Subject to Influence   *As a deeply hypnotized subject sits before a TV screen, researcher David Spiegel asks her to imagine that a cardboard box is blocking the screen. When a stimulus appears on the screen, her brain waves do not display the normal response to the stimulus. Findings like this, Spiegel argues, suggest that hypnosis can alter brain functioning.*

How Does It Smell?   *Only a person with highly developed hypnotic abilities could remain outwardly unperturbed over an open bottle of ammonia. Researchers have found a range of hypnotic responsiveness, with fantasy-prone people being among the best subjects.*

gests, "Your eyelids are shutting so tight that you cannot open them even if you try," your eyelids may seem beyond your control and may remain closed. Told to forget the number 6, you may be puzzled when you count 11 fingers on your hands. Invited to smell a sensuous perfume that is actually ammonia, you may linger delightedly over its pungent odor. Asked to describe a nonexistent picture the hypnotist claims to be holding, you may talk about it in detail. Told that you cannot see a certain object, such as a chair, you may indeed report that it is not there, although, curiously, you may manage to avoid the chair when walking around.

And if instructed to forget all these happenings once you are out of the hypnotic state, you may later report **posthypnotic amnesia**, a temporary memory loss rather like being unable to recall a familiar name. Although people *say* they don't remember "forgotten" material, subtle tests lead skeptics to doubt their reported amnesia (Coe, 1989a). The material must be "in there," for it can affect later behavior and be recalled at a prearranged signal (Kihlstrom, 1985; Spanos & others, 1985).

Let's consider whether the hypnotic state is actually an *altered* state of consciousness. We can ponder two perplexing questions: What is hypnosis? What does hypnosis tell us about human consciousness?

Facts and Falsehoods

Can Hypnosis Work for Anyone?

Those who study hypnosis agree that its power resides not in the hypnotist but in the subject's openness to suggestion (Bowers, 1984). To some extent, nearly everyone is suggestible. When people standing upright with their eyes closed are told repeatedly that they are swaying back and forth, most will indeed sway a little. In fact, postural sway is one of the items on the Stanford Hypnotic Susceptibility Scale that assesses a person's hypnotizability. During the assessment, a hypnotist gives a brief hypnotic induction and then presents a series of suggested experiences that range from easy (one's outstretched arms will move together) to difficult (with eyes open one will see a nonexistent person).

The Curious History of Mesmerism *The modern history of hypnosis begins with the work of Franz Anton Mesmer in eighteenth century France. His views on animal magnetism, which scientists refuted, were popular with the public, and hypnotism became a kind of parlor game like the one shown here.*

See Chapter 7 for more discussion of how people may construct false memories.

Those who are highly hypnotizable—say, the 20 percent who can carry out a suggestion not to smell or react to a bottle of ammonia held under their nose—are still likely to be the most hypnotizable 25 years later (Piccione & others, 1989). These hypnotically susceptible people are often fantasy-prone. They frequently become deeply absorbed in imaginative activities (Lynn & Rhue, 1986; Silva & Kirsch, 1992). They easily become absorbed in the imaginary events of a novel or movie.

Can Hypnosis Enhance Recall of Forgotten Events?

Can hypnotic procedures enable people to relive earlier experiences? To recall kindergarten classmates? To retrieve forgotten or suppressed details of a crime? Should testimony obtained under hypnosis be admissible in court?

Most university students agree that "under hypnosis a person [can] recall childhood events with very high accuracy" (Furnham, 1993). Testimonies to this come from **age regression** demonstrations, in which subjects supposedly relive experiences from their childhood. But 60 years of research dispute claims of age regression: Hypnotized people are *not* more genuinely childlike than unhypnotized people who are asked to feign childlike behavior (Nash, 1987). Age-regressed people act as they *believe* children would, but they typically miss the mark by outperforming real children of the specified age (Silverman & Retzlaff, 1986). Age-regressed people may, for example, *feel* childlike and may print much as they know a 6-year-old would, but they sometimes do so with perfect spelling and typically without any change in their adult brain waves, reflexes, and perceptions.

Because researchers have found that "hypnotically refreshed" memories combine fact with fiction, many courts ban testimony from witnesses who have been hypnotized. Hypnosis has unpredictable effects, sometimes boosting recall, but sometimes contaminating memory with false recollections or increasing confidence in false memories (McConkey, 1992). Without either person being aware of what is going on, the hypnotist's hints—"Did you hear loud noises?"—can become the subject's memory. Thus, previously hypnotized witnesses may end up testifying confidently to events they never experienced (Laurence & Perry, 1988).

posthypnotic amnesia Supposed inability to recall what one experienced during hypnosis; induced by the hypnotist's suggestion.

age regression In hypnosis, the supposed reliving of earlier experiences, such as those of early childhood; greatly susceptible to false recollections.

posthypnotic suggestion A suggestion, made during a hypnosis session, to be carried out after the subject is no longer hypnotized; used by some clinicians to help control the symptoms of certain ailments.

dissociation A split in consciousness, which allows some thoughts and behaviors to occur simultaneously with others.

It distresses memory researchers that the unreliability of hypnotically induced memories is unappreciated by many therapists. When hypnosis researcher Michael Yapko (1994) surveyed 869 therapists attending various therapy conventions, 47 percent agreed that "Psychotherapists can have greater faith in details of a traumatic event when obtained hypnotically than otherwise." And 54 percent agreed that "Hypnosis can be used to recover memories of actual events as far back as birth." Such ignorance "of the facts" left Yapko aghast: "I am deeply concerned that psychotherapy patients will be led to believe destructive ideas that are untrue . . . all in the name of 'psychotherapy.'"

Can Hypnosis Force People to Act Against Their Will?

Researchers Martin Orne and Frederick Evans (1965) demonstrated that hypnotized subjects *could* be induced to perform an apparently dangerous act. For example, the subjects followed a request to dip a hand briefly in fuming acid and then throw the "acid" in a research assistant's face. When interviewed a day later, they exhibited no memory of their acts and emphatically denied they would follow orders to commit such actions.

Had hypnosis given the hypnotist a special power to control these people against their will? To find out, Orne and Evans unleashed that enemy of so many illusory beliefs—the control group: Orne asked some additional subjects to *pretend* they had been hypnotized. The laboratory experimenter, unaware that these control subjects had not been hypnotized, treated all subjects in the same manner. The result? All the *un*hypnotized subjects performed the same acts as the hypnotized ones. Similarly, most hypnotized subjects can be induced to cut up their country's flag or deface a Bible, and a few will even cooperate in stealing an exam or selling illegal drugs. But people asked to simulate hypnosis are no less likely to perform the same acts (Levitt, 1986).

Can Hypnosis Be Therapeutic?

The clinical use of hypnosis has mushroomed. Hypnotherapists do nothing magical. Rather, they try to help patients harness their own healing powers (Baker, 1987). **Posthypnotic suggestions** (suggestions to be carried out after the hypnosis session has ended) have helped alleviate headaches, asthma, warts, and stress-related skin disorders.

Is hypnosis the therapeutic agent? Do its benefits surpass those of merely encouraging people to relax and form positive images? The answer remains in doubt. For example, hypnosis speeds the disappearance of warts. But in controlled studies, so do the same positive suggestions given without hypnosis (Spanos, 1991).

Hypnosis can, however, relieve pain. When unhypnotized subjects put their arms in an ice bath, they feel intense pain within 25 seconds. When hypnotizable subjects do the same after being given suggestions to feel no pain, they indeed report feeling little pain. As some dentists know, even light hypnosis can reduce fear, and thus hypersensitivity to pain. And some 10 percent of us can become so deeply hypnotized that even surgery can be performed without anesthesia.

How can this be? One theory of hypnotic pain relief involves **dissociation**, a split between different levels of consciousness. Hypnosis, it suggests, dissociates the sensation of the pain stimulus (of which the subject is still aware) from the emotional suffering that defines our pain experience. The ice water therefore feels very cold but not painful.

Another theory proposes that hypnotic pain relief is due to selective attention, as when an injured athlete, caught up in the competition, feels little or no pain until the game ends. Support for this view comes from several studies

The Lamaze Method of Childbirth *Like hypnosis, the Lamaze method involves breathing and concentration techniques that draw attention away from pain. Women for whom the method works tend to have high hypnotic ability (Venn, 1986).*

Hypnotic Age Regression: A True Story

Remembrances of Christmases Past?

What shall we make of a clever study by Robert True (1949)? He *age-regressed* hypnotized volunteers back to their Christmases and birthday parties at ages 10, 7, and 4. In each case, he asked them what day of the week it was. Without hypnosis, the odds that a person could name offhand the day of a long-ago date are but 1 in 7. Remarkably, the hypnotized subjects' answers were 82 percent correct. Other investigators were unable to replicate True's results. When Martin Orne (1982) asked True why, he replied that *Science*, the journal that published his article, had shortened his key question to "What day is this?" Actually, he had asked his age-regressed subjects, "Is it Monday? Is it Tuesday?" and so forth until the subject stopped him with a yes. When Orne asked True if he knew the actual day of the week while posing the questions, True granted that he did but was puzzled why Orne would ask. Can you see why? True's experiment appears to be a beautiful example of how hypnotists can subtly influence their subjects' memories (and, more generally, of how experimenters can subtly communicate their expectations). "Given the eagerness of the hypnotized subject to fulfill the demands placed upon him," surmised Orne, it takes only the slightest change of inflection (in asking "Is it Wednesday?") for the subject to respond, "Yes."

The final blow to True's experiment came when Orne simply asked ten 4-year-olds what day of the week it was. To his surprise, none knew. If 4-year-olds typically do not know the day of the week, then True's adults were reporting information they probably didn't know when they were 4.

Remembrances of Lives Past?

If people's hypnotic regressions to childhood are partly imagined, then how believable are claims of hypnotic "regression to past lives"? Can the 1 in 5 Americans who believe in reincarnation (*Gallup Poll Monthly*, 1991) find support in such reports? Nicholas Spanos (1987–1988; Spanos & others, 1991) reports that when hypnotized, fantasy-prone people who believe in reincarnation will offer vivid details of "past lives." But they nearly always report being their same race—unless the researcher has informed them that different races are common. They often report being someone famous rather than one of the countless "nobodies." Some contradict one another by claiming to have been the same person, such as King Henry VIII (Reveen, 1987–1988). Moreover, they typically do not know things that any person of that historical time would have known. One subject who "regressed" to a "previous life" as a Japanese fighter pilot in 1940 could not name the emperor of Japan and did not know that Japan was already at war. Hypnotic regressions to past lives thus offer no credible evidence of reincarnation.

Drawing by M. Stevens; © 1987 The New Yorker Magazine, Inc.

showing that hypnosis relieves pain no better than does merely relaxing and distracting people (Chaves, 1989). With their attention distracted during hypnosis, some women can experience childbirth with minimal pain; but so can some women without hypnosis, especially if given childbirth training (D'Eon, 1989).

The unanswered question of how hypnosis relieves pain—by *dissociating* the pain sensation from conscious awareness, or merely by focusing *attention* on other things—brings us to the basic issue: Is hypnosis a unique psychological state?

Explaining the Hypnotized State

9. Should hypnosis be considered an extension of normal consciousness or an altered state?

We have seen that hypnosis involves heightened suggestibility. We have also seen that hypnotic procedures do not endow a person with special powers. But they can sometimes enhance recall of real (and unreal) past events, aid in overcoming psychologically influenced ailments, and help alleviate pain. So, just what is hypnosis? Does it qualify as an altered—out-of-the-ordinary—state of consciousness?

Hypnosis as a Social Phenomenon

Skeptics note that hypnosis is not a unique physiological state. Moreover, behaviors produced through hypnotic procedures can also be produced without them. This suggests that hypnotic phenomena may be nothing more than the workings of normal consciousness (Lynn & others, 1990; Spanos & Coe, 1992).

In Chapter 4 we saw how powerfully our interpretations influence ordinary perceptions. Especially in the case of pain, for which the effects of hypnosis seem most dramatic, our perceptions follow our attention. Moreover, imaginative people can manufacture vivid perceptions without hypnosis. Perhaps, then, "hypnotized" people are just acting the role of "good hypnotic subjects" and allowing the hypnotist to direct their fantasies.

It's not that people are consciously faking hypnosis. Rather, they're doing and reporting what's expected of them. Like actors who get caught up in their roles, they begin to feel and behave in ways appropriate to the hypnotic role. The more they like and trust the hypnotist and feel motivated to demonstrate hypnotic behavior, the more they do so (Gfeller & others, 1987). If an experimenter eliminates the motivation for acting hypnotized—by stating that hypnosis reveals "gullibility"—subjects become unresponsive. If told later to scratch their ear when they hear the word *psychology*, subjects will likely do so only if they think the experiment is still under way (and scratching is therefore expected).

Based on such findings, advocates of the *social influence theory* contend that hypnotic phenomena are *not* unique to hypnosis. They argue that, like other supposed altered states such as multiple personality (page 424) and spirit or demon possession, hypnotic phenomena are instead an extension of everyday social behavior (Spanos, 1994). Hypnotic subjects, say skeptics, are imaginative actors caught up in playing the role of hypnotic subject.

Hypnosis as Divided Consciousness

Most hypnosis researchers grant that normal social and cognitive processes play a part in hypnosis, but they believe hypnosis is more than imaginative acting. For one thing, hypnotized subjects will *sometimes* carry out suggested behaviors on cue, even when they believe no one is watching. Their doing so shows that more may be at work than merely trying to be a "good subject." Moreover, many practitioners remain convinced that certain phenomena *are* unique to hypnosis. What else explains hypnotic experiences such as pain reduction (Bowers, 1990)? Skeptics reply that hypnotists' livelihoods depend on maintaining an aura of mysterious power (Coe, 1989b).

To veteran researcher Ernest Hilgard (1986, 1992), hypnosis is a special state of *dissociated consciousness*. Hilgard views hypnotic dissociation as a more extreme form of everyday mind splits. Putting a child to bed, we might

Demonstrating Dissociation *A hypnotized subject being tested by Ernest Hilgard exhibits no pain when her arm is placed in an ice bath. But asked to press a key if some part of her feels the pain, she does so. To Hilgard, this suggests that hypnosis divides consciousness into one part that is unaware of pain and another part—a "hidden observer"—that is aware of it.*

read *Goodnight Moon* for the fourteenth time while mentally organizing a busy schedule for the next day. With practice, it is even possible to read and comprehend a short story while copying dictated words, much as you can doodle while listening to a lecture, or much as a skilled pianist can converse while playing a familiar piece (Hirst & others, 1978). Thus, when hypnotized subjects write answers to questions about one topic while talking or reading about a different topic, they display an accentuated form of normal cognitive dissociation.

Although the *divided-consciousness theory* of hypnosis is controversial this much seems clear: You and I process much information without conscious awareness. We have seen examples of unconscious information processing in the chapter on sensation and perception, and we will see more in later chapters on learning, memory, and thinking. Without doubt, there is more to thinking than we are conscious of.

Then again, there is little doubt that social influences do play an important role in hypnosis. So, might the two views—social influence and divided consciousness—be bridged? Researchers John Kihlstrom and Kevin McConkey (1990) believe the two approaches may eventually converge into a "unified account of hypnosis." Until then, they suggest, we can understand hypnosis as an extension *both* of normal principles of social influence *and* of everyday splits in consciousness.

! *Rehearse It*

9. Most people daydream every day. These daydreams serve several functions: They provide an escape from reality, they help us prepare for the future, they enhance creativity, and they may substitute for

a. a rich, complete life.
b. impulsive behavior.
c. night dreams.
d. meditative time.

10. Hypnotism is a temporary state of apparently heightened suggestibility, usually induced by a hypnotist. Subjects who are hypnotizable and will carry out a hypnotic suggestion usually

a. are fantasy-prone.
b. have low self-esteem.
c. are good at playing a role.
d. are female.

11. Although experts differ in their understandings of hypnotism, most agree that hypnotism can be effectively used to

a. elicit testimony about a "forgotten" event.
b. re-create childhood experiences.
c. relieve pain.
d. alter personality.

12. Ernest Hilgard believes hypnosis is not merely an extension of normal social influence but involves dissociation, which means

a. nonconformity to social pressure.
b. a state of paradoxical sleep.
c. a state of divided consciousness.
d. conscious enactment of a hypnotic role.

Drugs and Consciousness

10. What are psychoactive drugs?

If there is controversy about whether hypnosis alters consciousness, there is little dispute that drugs do. **Psychoactive drugs** are chemicals that change perceptions and moods. An imaginary drug user's day dramatizes the widespread use of legal psychoactive drugs: It begins with a wake-up cup of strong coffee. By midday, several cigarettes and a prescription tranquilizer have calmed the nerves. An early exit from work makes time for a happy-hour cocktail, providing a relaxing and sociable prelude to a dental appointment, where nitrous oxide makes an otherwise painful experience mildly pleasurable. A diet pill be-

psychoactive drug   A chemical substance that alters mood and perceptions.

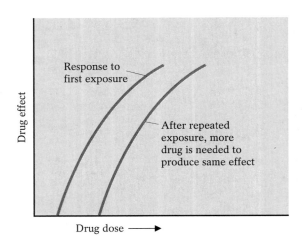

Figure 5–7 Drug tolerance *With repeated exposure to a psychoactive drug, the drug effect lessens. Thus, it takes bigger doses to get the desired effect.*

tolerance The diminishing of a drug's effect with regular use of the same dose, requiring the user to take larger and larger doses before experiencing the drug's effect.

withdrawal The discomfort and distress that follow the discontinued use of addictive drugs.

physical dependence A physiological need for a drug, with unpleasant withdrawal symptoms when use is discontinued.

psychological dependence A psychological need to use a drug, such as to relieve negative emotions.

depressants Drugs (such as alcohol, barbiturates, and opiates) that reduce neural activity and slow body functions.

stimulants Drugs (such as caffeine, nicotine, and the more powerful amphetamines and cocaine) that excite neural activity and speed up body functions.

hallucinogens Psychedelic ("mind-manifesting") drugs, such as LSD, that distort perceptions and evoke sensory images in the absence of sensory input.

fore dinner helps stem the appetite, and its stimulating effects can later be partially offset with a sleeping pill. Before drifting off into REM-depressed sleep, our hypothetical drug user is dismayed by a news report of "rising drug abuse."

Continued use of a psychoactive drug produces **tolerance**: The user requires larger and larger doses to experience the drug's effect. A person who rarely drinks alcohol might get tipsy on one can of beer, but an experienced drinker may not feel the effects until the second six-pack (Figure 5–7). Despite the connotations of "tolerance," heavy drinkers' brains, hearts, and livers suffer damage from the excessive alcohol they are "tolerating."

Users who stop taking psychoactive drugs may experience the undesirable side effects of **withdrawal**. As the body responds to the drug's absence, the user may feel physical pain and intense cravings for a dose. This indicates a **physical dependence** on the drug. People can also develop **psychological dependence**, particularly for drugs used to relieve stress. Although the drug may not be physically addictive, it nevertheless becomes an important part of the user's life, often as a way of relieving negative emotions. With either physical addiction or psychological dependence, the user's primary focus becomes obtaining and using the drug.

There are three types of psychoactive drugs: **depressants**, or "downers," which calm neural activity and slow down body functions; **stimulants**, or "uppers," which temporarily excite neural activity and arouse body functions; and **hallucinogens**, which distort perception and evoke sensory images without sensory input. Drugs in all three categories do their work at the brain's synapses by stimulating, inhibiting, or mimicking the activity of neurotransmitters, the brain's chemical messengers.

Depressants

11. What are depressants, and what are their effects?

Let's look first at drugs such as alcohol, tranquilizers, and opiates, which slow down body functions.

Alcohol

True or false? In large amounts, alcohol is a depressant; in small amounts, it is a stimulant.

False. Small doses of "spirits" may, indeed, enliven a drinker, but they do so by slowing brain activity that controls judgment and inhibitions. If provoked, people under alcohol's influence respond more aggressively than usual. If asked to help, people under alcohol's influence respond more helpfully than usual. In everyday life, alcohol *increases* both harmful tendencies—as when sexually coercive college men try to disinhibit their dates by getting them to drink (Abbey, 1991; Mosher & Anderson, 1986)—and helpful tendencies—as when restaurant patrons tip more when tipsy (M. Lynn, 1988). Thus, alcohol makes us more aggressive or helpful, or self-disclosing or sexually daring, when such tendencies are present. Whatever urges you feel when sober, you are more likely to act upon if intoxicated.

Low doses of alcohol relax the drinker by slowing sympathetic nervous system activity. With larger doses, reactions slow, speech slurs, and skilled performance deteriorates. These physical effects, combined with the lowering of inhibitions, contribute to alcohol's worst consequences—to several hundred thousand lives claimed annually worldwide in alcohol-related accidents and violent crime. Accidents occur despite drinkers' belief (when sober) that it is wrong to drive impaired and despite their insisting they wouldn't do so. Yet under alcohol's influence, people's moral judgments become more immature,

Don't Drink and Drive *Mothers Against Drunk Driving (MADD) has raised awareness of the appalling consequences of driving under the influence of alcohol. Here, relatives look over photographs on the MADD "victim board" set up on the steps of the Capitol.*

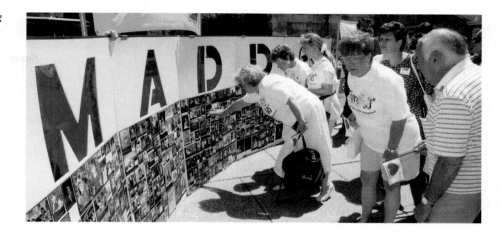

Fact: College students drink more alcohol than their noncollege peers, and fraternity and sorority members drink three times as much as other students (Atwell, 1986; Malloy & others, 1994). Although few university students believe they have an alcohol problem, many meet the criteria for alcohol abuse (Marlatt, 1991).

Fact: Binge drinking—the consumption of five or more drinks on some occasion during the last month—is reported by 22 percent of American adults. The highest rate of binge drinking—52 percent—is among 18- to 24-year-old males (Centers for Disease Control, 1983).

Fact: A survey of 56,000 college students found that D and F students imbibe three times as much as A students (Presley & Meilman, 1992).

Fact: In a Harvard School of Public Health survey of 18,000 students at 140 colleges and universities, almost 9 in 10 students reported abuse by intoxicated peers, including sleep and study interruption, insults, sexual advances, and property damage (Wechsler & others, 1994).

Fact: Alcohol kills more people than all illegal drugs combined. So does tobacco (Siegel, 1990).

their qualms about drinking and driving lessen—and virtually all will drive home from a bar, even if given a breathalyzer test and told they are intoxicated (Denton & Krebs, 1990).

Alcohol has an intriguing effect on memory. It impairs neither short-term recall for what just happened nor existing long-term memories. Rather, it disrupts the *processing* of recent experiences into long-term memories. Thus, the day after being intoxicated, heavy drinkers may not recall whom they met or what they said or did the night before. This memory blackout stems partly from an inability to transfer memories from the intoxicated to the sober state (Eich, 1980). Blackouts after drinking may also result from alcohol's suppression of REM sleep. (Recall that people deprived of REM sleep have difficulty fixing their day's experiences into permanent memories.)

Alcohol has another intriguing effect on consciousness: It reduces self-awareness (Hull & others, 1986). Compared with people who feel good about themselves, those who want to suppress their awareness of failures or shortcomings are more likely to drink. The Nazi doctors who selected "unfit" concentration camp inmates for the gas chambers often did so while drunk, or got drunk afterwards (Lifton, 1986). By focusing attention on the immediate situation and away from future consequences, alcohol also facilitates urges that the individual might otherwise resist (Steele & Josephs, 1990). Thus, sexually active university students are less likely to use condoms when intoxicated (MacDonald & others, 1994a,b).

As with other psychoactive drugs, alcohol's behavioral effects stem not only from its alteration of brain chemistry but also from the user's expectations. Many studies have found that when people *believe* that alcohol affects social behavior in certain ways, and *believe*, rightly or wrongly, that they have been drinking alcohol, they will behave accordingly (Leigh, 1989). One experiment by David Abrams and Terence Wilson (1983) gave Rutgers University men who volunteered for a study on "alcohol and sexual stimulation" either an alcoholic or a nonalcoholic drink. (Both drinks had a strong taste that masked any alcohol.) In each group, half the subjects thought they were drinking alcohol and half thought they were not. Regardless of what they drank, after being shown an erotic movie clip, the men who *thought* they had consumed alcohol were more likely to report having strong sexual fantasies and feeling guilt-free. Being able to *attribute* their sexual responses to alcohol released their inhibitions—whether they actually had drunk alcohol or not.

This research illustrates an important principle: A drug's psychological effects are powerfully influenced by the user's expectations. And that explains why drug experiences vary with culture (Ward, 1994). If one culture assumes that a particular drug produces euphoria (or aggression or sexual arousal) and another does not, each culture may find its expectations fulfilled.

"Just tell me where you kids get the idea to take so many drugs."

Cost analysis shows that smokers repay society for the health, disability, and fire-risk costs of their habit by dying earlier, saving Social Security and retirement pension payments (Manning & others, 1989).

Barbiturates

The **barbiturate** drugs, or *tranquilizers*, mimic the effects of alcohol. Because they depress sympathetic nervous system activity, barbiturates such as Nembutal and Seconal are sometimes prescribed to induce sleep or reduce anxiety. In larger doses, they can lead to impaired memory and judgment. In combination with alcohol—as when people take a sleeping pill after an evening of drinking—the total depressive effect on body functions can be lethal. With sufficient doses, barbiturates by themselves can also cause death, which makes them the drugs often chosen by those attempting suicide.

Opiates

The **opiates**—opium and its derivatives, morphine and heroin—also depress neural functioning. The pupils constrict, the breathing slows, and the user becomes lethargic. For a few hours, blissful pleasure replaces pain and anxiety. But for pleasure one pays a price, which for the heroin user is the gnawing craving for another fix, the need for progressively larger doses, the week-long physical anguish of withdrawal—and for some the ultimate price, death by overdose.

The pathway to addiction is treacherous. When repeatedly flooded with artificial opiates, the brain eventually stops producing its own opiates, the endorphins. Then, when the drug is withdrawn, the brain lacks the normal level of these painkilling neurotransmitters. The result is the agony of withdrawal.

Stimulants

12. What are the stimulants, and what are their effects?

The most widely used stimulants are caffeine, nicotine, the powerful **amphetamines**, and the even more powerful cocaine. Stimulants speed up body functions, hence the nickname "speed" for amphetamines. Strong stimulants increase heart and breathing rates. The pupils dilate, appetite diminishes (because blood sugar rises), and energy and self-confidence rise. For these reasons, people use stimulants to stay awake, lose weight, or boost mood or athletic performance. As with other drugs, the benefits come with a price. When drug stimulation ends, the user experiences a compensating slowdown and may "crash" into tiredness, headaches, irritability, and depression. Like the depressants, stimulants—including the caffeine found in coffee, tea, certain sodas, chocolate, and diet aids—can be addictive (Silverman & others, 1992).

Nicotine

Each year throughout the world, the tobacco industry kills some 3 million of its best customers—equivalent to 20 loaded jumbo jets daily (Peto & others, 1992, 1994). And the worst is yet to come. Given present trends, estimates a 1994 World Health Organization report, *half a billion* people alive today will be killed by tobacco. Thus, the elimination of smoking would do more to increase life expectancy than any other preventive measure. Smoking's addictiveness and destructiveness have prompted psychologists to study why people smoke and how they might be helped to quit.

Each year, millions of people try to lick their addiction, and only 8 percent succeed, according to a 1994 Centers for Disease Control report. Once addicted to nicotine it is hard to quit, because tobacco is as addictive as heroin or cocaine. The smoking habit is tough to break because the craving, hunger, and irritability that accompany nicotine withdrawal are aversive states that a ciga-

barbiturates Drugs that depress the activity of the central nervous system, reducing anxiety but impairing memory and judgment.

opiates Opium and its derivatives, such as morphine and heroin; they depress neural activity, temporarily lessening pain and anxiety.

amphetamines Drugs that stimulate neural activity, causing speeded-up body functions and associated energy and mood changes.

The recipe for Coca-Cola originally included an extract of the coca plant, creating a cocaine tonic for tired elderly people. Between 1896 and 1905, Coke was indeed "the real thing."

Figure 5–8 Cocaine Euphoria and Crash *After neurotransmitters carry a message across a synapse (a), the sending nerve cell normally reabsorbs excess neurotransmitters (a process called reuptake) (b). Cocaine blocks reuptake of three neurotransmitters: dopamine, norepinephrine, and serotonin (Ray & Ksir, 1990.) The extra neurotransmitter molecules therefore remain in the synapse, intensifying their normal mood-altering effects and producing a euphoric rush (c). When cocaine level drops, the absence of these neurotransmitters produces a crash. Amphetamines act differently— by stimulating the release of excess norepinephrine.*

rette relieves. After an hour or a day without smoking, the habitual smoker finds a cigarette powerfully reinforcing. Given low-nicotine cigarettes, the smoker will smoke more of them to maintain a roughly constant level of nicotine in the blood.

Smoking not only terminates the aversive craving, it also is pleasurable. Nicotine triggers the release of epinephrine and norepinephrine, which in turn diminish appetite and boost alertness and mental efficiency. More important, nicotine stimulates the central nervous system to release neurotransmitters that calm anxiety and reduce pain sensitivity (Pomerleau & Pomerleau, 1984). These rewards of smoking, combined with the relief smoking provides from the discomfort of withdrawal, keep people smoking even when they wish they could stop—indeed, even when they know they are committing slow-motion suicide. However, a 1990 report by the Centers for Disease Control found that half of Americans who have ever smoked have quit. More than 90 percent did so on their own, often after repeated attempts.

Cocaine

In national surveys, 3 percent of adults and 4 percent of high school seniors reported having tried cocaine during the past year (Johnston & others, 1994; National Institute on Drug Abuse, 1992). Of the seniors, 1.5 percent said they had smoked *crack*, a potent form of cocaine. By the early 1990s the decade-long cocaine epidemic began subsiding. Credit goes partly to increased treatment and awareness but also to the impoverishment, imprisonment, and deaths of so many cocaine victims (Hamid, 1992).

When animals and people chew coca leaves, small amounts of cocaine enter the bloodstream gradually, without any apparent ill effects (Siegel, 1990). But when extracted cocaine is sniffed ("snorted"), and especially when smoked ("free-based") or injected, it enters the bloodstream quickly. The result: a "rush" of euphoria that lasts 15 to 30 minutes. Because the rush depletes the brain's supply of the neurotransmitters dopamine, norepinephrine, and serotonin, a crash of agitated depression occurs as the drug's effect wears off (Figure 5–8). Crack works even faster and produces a briefer but more intense high, a more intense crash, and a craving for more crack, which wanes after several hours and then returns several days later (Gawin, 1991).

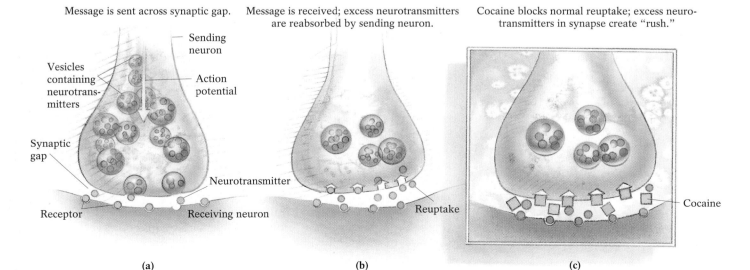

Message is sent across synaptic gap.

Message is received; excess neurotransmitters are reabsorbed by sending neuron.

Cocaine blocks normal reuptake; excess neurotransmitters in synapse create "rush."

Sending neuron

Vesicles containing neurotransmitters

Action potential

Synaptic gap

Neurotransmitter

Reuptake

Cocaine

Receptor

Receiving neuron

(a)　　　(b)　　　(c)

186   Exploring Psychology

hallucinations False sensory experiences, such as seeing something without any external visual stimulus.

LSD (*lysergic acid diethylamide*) A powerful hallucinogenic drug; also known as "acid."

near-death experience An altered state of consciousness reported after a close brush with death (such as through cardiac arrest); often similar to drug-induced hallucinations.

THC The major active ingredient in marijuana; triggers a variety of effects, including mild hallucinations.

Regular cocaine users become addicted. Monkeys have become so strongly addicted that they will press a lever more than 12,000 times to gain each cocaine injection (Siegel, 1990). Human and animal cocaine users may experience emotional disturbance, suspiciousness, convulsions, cardiac arrest, or respiratory failure. In situations that often trigger aggression, ingesting cocaine may increase aggressive reactions. Caged rats fight when given foot shocks, and they fight even more when given foot shocks and cocaine. Asked to determine how much electric shock one's opponent will receive in a laboratory competition, those who have ingested high-dose cocaine rather than a placebo set higher levels (Licata & others, 1993).

As with all psychoactive drugs, cocaine's psychological effects depend not only on the dosage and form in which one takes the drug but also on one's expectations, one's personality, and the situation—a mix of factors. Given a placebo, cocaine users who *think* they are taking cocaine often have a cocaine-like experience (Van Dyke & Byck, 1982).

Hallucinogens

13. What are the hallucinogens, and what are their effects?

Hallucinogens are psychoactive drugs that distort perceptions and evoke **hallucinations**, vivid images without sensory input (which is why these drugs are also called *psychedelics*, meaning "mind-manifesting"). Some hallucinogens are natural substances, such as marijuana, a mild hallucinogen. Others are synthetic. Of the synthetics, the two best known are PCP ("angel dust"), a potent and illegal pain killer that has highly unpredictable and sometimes devastating psychological effects, and LSD.

LSD

The first "acid trip" was taken in 1943 by chemist Albert Hofmann, the creator of **LSD** (*lysergic acid diethylamide*). After accidentally ingesting some of the chemical, Hofmann reported that he "perceived an uninterrupted stream of fantastic pictures, extraordinary shapes with intense, kaleidoscopic play of colors" (Siegel, 1984). LSD and other powerful hallucinogens are chemically similar to (and therefore block the actions of) a subtype of the neurotransmitter serotonin (Jacobs, 1987). The emotions of an LSD trip vary from euphoria to detachment to panic.

As with all drug use, a person's current mood and expectations color the LSD experience. Yet despite emotional variations, the resulting perceptual distortions and hallucinations have commonalities. The experience typically begins with simple geometric forms, such as a lattice, a cobweb, or a spiral. The next phase consists of more meaningful images; some may be superimposed on a tunnel or funnel, others may involve the replay of past emotional experiences. When the hallucinogenic experience peaks, people frequently feel separated from their bodies and experience dreamlike scenes as if they were real—so real that users may become panic-stricken or may harm themselves.

These hallucinatory sensations are strikingly similar to the **near-death experience** reported by about one-third of those who survive a brush with death, as when revived from cardiac arrest (Moody, 1976; Ring, 1980; Schnaper, 1980). Psychologist Ronald Siegel (1980) reports that one may experience visions of tunnels and bright lights or beings of light (Figure 5–9), a replay of old memories, and out-of-body sensations. Siegel (1982) notes that whether you provoke your brain to hallucinate by loss of oxygen, sensory deprivation, or drugs, "it will hallucinate in basically the same way."

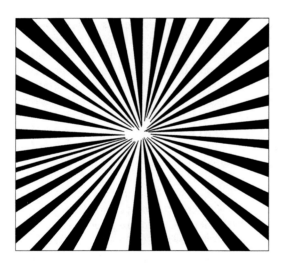

Figure 5–9 Near-Death Vision or Hallucination? *Psychologist Ronald Siegel (1977) reports that people under the influence of hallucinogenic drugs often see "a bright light in the center of the field of vision. . . . The location of this point of light create[s] a tunnel-like perspective." Susan Blackmore (1991, 1993) offers an explanation of similar light during a near-death experience: As oxygen deprivation turns off the brain's inhibitory cells, neural activity increases in the visual cortex. The result is a growing patch of light, which looks much like what you would see moving through a tunnel. (From "Hallucinations" by R. K. Siegel. Copyright © 1977 Scientific American, Inc. All rights reserved.)*

Given that oxygen deprivation and other insults to the brain are known to produce hallucinations, it is difficult to resist wondering whether near-death experiences are manufactured by the brain under stress. Patients who have experienced temporal lobe seizures have reported similarly profound mystical experiences, as have solitary sailors and polar explorers while enduring monotony, isolation, and cold (Suedfeld & Mocellin, 1987). Fantasy-prone persons are especially susceptible—or should we say *open*—to near-death and other out-of-body experiences, such as believing one has encountered or been abducted by aliens (Ring, 1992; Wilson & Barber, 1983).

Marijuana

Marijuana consists of the leaves and flowers of the hemp plant, which for 5000 years has been cultivated for its fiber. Marijuana's major active ingredient is **THC**, the everyday name of the complex organic molecule delta-9-tetrahydrocannabinol. Whether smoked or eaten in such foods as brownies, THC produces a mix of effects that makes the drug difficult to classify. (Smoking gets the drug into the brain in about 7 seconds; this produces a greater effect than does eating the drug, which causes its peak concentration to be reached at as lower, unpredictable rate.) Like alcohol, marijuana relaxes, disinhibits, and may produce a euphoric high. But marijuana also acts as a mild hallucinogen by amplifying sensitivity to colors, sounds, tastes, and smells.

As with other drugs, the marijuana user's experience varies, depending on the situation. If the person feels anxious or depressed, taking the drug may intensify these feelings. In other situations, using marijuana can be not only pleasurable but therapeutic. For those who suffer the pain of glaucoma (caused by pressure within the eyeball) or the nausea that sometimes accompanies cancer chemotherapy, marijuana may spell relief. In acknowledging such benefits, a review of marijuana research published by the National Academy of Sciences (1982) also identified some not-so-pleasant consequences. Like alcohol, marijuana impairs the motor coordination, perceptual skills, and reaction time necessary for safe driving and machine operation. "THC causes animals to misjudge events," reports Ronald Siegel (1990, p. 163). "Pigeons wait too long to respond to buzzers or lights that tell them food is available for brief periods; and rats turn the wrong way in mazes." Marijuana also disrupts memory formation and interferes with immediate recall of information learned only a few minutes before. Clearly, being stoned is not conducive to learning.

Unlike alcohol, which the body eliminates within hours, THC and its by-products linger in the body for a month or more. Thus, contrary to the usual tolerance phenomenon, regular users may achieve a high with smaller amounts of the drug than occasional users would take to get the same effect.

Uncertainty persists about marijuana's physical effects, but medical research suggests that long-term marijuana use may depress male sex hormone and sperm levels and damage the lungs more than cigarette smoking (Wu & others, 1988). Large doses hasten the loss of brain cells (Landfield & others, 1988). Although marijuana is not as addictive as cocaine or nicotine, one study that followed 654 junior high students into their early twenties found that adolescents who heavily used marijuana developed more health and family problems than did nonusers (Newcomb & Bentler, 1988).

Despite their differences, the psychoactive drugs summarized in Table 5–1 (page 188) share a common feature: They trigger negative aftereffects that offset their immediate positive effects. The aftereffects illustrate the more general principle that emotions tend to produce opposing emotions, which linger after the original emotions disappear. With repetition, the opposing emotions grow stronger. This emotions-trigger-opposing-emotions principle parallels that of

TABLE 5-1

A Guide to Selected Psychoactive Drugs

Drug	Type	Pleasurable Effects	Adverse Effects
Alcohol	Depressant	Initial high followed by relaxation and disinhibition	Depression, memory loss, organ damage, impaired reactions
Heroin	Depressant	Rush of euphoria, relief from pain	Depressed physiology, agonizing withdrawal
Cocaine	Stimulant	Rush of euphoria, confidence, energy	Cardiovascular stress, suspiciousness, depressive crash
Nicotine	Stimulant	Arouses and relaxes, sense of well-being	Heart disease, cancer (from tars)
Marijuana	Mild hallucinogen	Enhances sensation, relieves pain, distorts time, relaxed high	Lowered sex hormones, disrupted memory, lung damage

"How strange would appear to be this thing that men call pleasure! And how curiously it is related to what is thought to be its opposite, pain! . . . Wherever the one is found, the other follows up behind."

Plato
Phaedo, fourth century B.C.

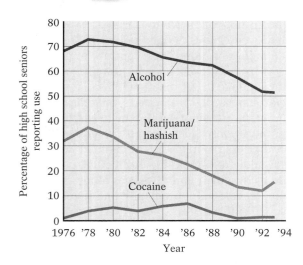

Figure 5-10 Trends in Drug Use *The percentage of high school seniors who report having used alcohol, marijuana, or cocaine during the past 30 days has declined since the late 1970s. (From Johnston & others, 1994.)*

drug-induced pleasures; the pleasures wane as the drug exacts its compensatory price. That helps explain both tolerance and withdrawal. Because the opposing, negative aftereffects are getting stronger, it takes larger and larger doses to produce the desired high (tolerance), causing the aftereffects to worsen in the drug's absence (withdrawal). This in turn creates a need to switch off the withdrawal symptoms by taking still more of the drug.

Influences on Drug Use

14. Why do people use psychoactive drugs?

Drug use by North American youth increased during the 1970s and declined during the 1980s. In the University of Michigan's annual survey of 16,000 high school seniors, the proportion who believed there is "great risk" in regular marijuana use rose from 35 percent in 1978 to 78 percent in 1991, then dropped to 65 percent in 1994 (Johnston & others, 1994). After peaking in 1978, marijuana use by this age group declined until 1992 (Figure 5–10). In the UCLA/American Council on Education annual survey of new college students, support for the legalization of marijuana dropped from 53 percent in 1977 to 32 percent in 1994 (Astin & others, 1987, 1994). Similar attitude and usage changes appear in surveys of Canadian teens. Between the late 1970s and early 1990s, Ontario teens, for example, became less and less likely to report using marijuana, tobacco, and alcohol (Smart & others, 1991).

Other studies reveal a changing national attitude toward alcohol. More than at any time since prohibition, health- and safety-conscious people see alcohol less as a cheerful beverage than as a drug to be shunned. The number of new American collegians who reported abstinence from beer during the past year has nearly doubled from 25 percent in 1981 to 47 percent in 1994. Effectively inform people about the health hazards of using cocaine, marijuana, alcohol, or tobacco and—without therapy, support groups, or medicines—many will simply stop.

Some warning signs of alcoholism:

- Drinking binges
- Regretting things done or said when drunk
- Feeling low or guilty after drinking
- Failing to honor one's resolve to drink less
- Drinking to alleviate depression or anxiety
- Avoiding family or friends when drinking

In the real world, alcohol accounts for one-sixth or less of beverage use. In television's world, alcohol drinking occurs more often than the combined drinking of coffee, tea, soft drinks, and water (Gerbner, 1990).

Still, many people continue to use psychoactive drugs. For some adolescents, occasional drug use represents thrill-seeking. Other adolescents become regular drug users. Why?

In the case of alcohol, some people may be biologically vulnerable. For example, evidence accumulates that heredity influences alcoholic tendencies. Consider:

- Adopted individuals are more susceptible to alcoholism if one or both of their biological parents is alcoholic (Mirin & Weiss, 1989).
- Having an alcoholic identical twin puts a male at increased risk for alcohol problems by age 20 (Heath & others, 1989; McGue & others, 1992).
- Compared with children of nonalcoholics, children of alcoholics have a higher tolerance for multiple alcoholic drinks over an hour or two (Schuckit, 1994).
- Researchers have bred rats that prefer alcoholic drinks to water (Holden, 1991).
- Molecular geneticists have recently identified a gene on chromosome 11 that is more common among alcoholics, especially severe alcoholics (Noble, 1993).

Psychological and social factors may also have an important influence. In their studies of New Jersey and California youth and young adults, Michael Newcomb and L. L. Harlow (1986) found that one psychological factor is the feeling that one's life is meaningless and directionless, a common feeling among school dropouts who subsist without job skills, without privilege, with little hope.

Other studies reveal that heavy users of alcohol, marijuana, and cocaine often have experienced significant stress or failure and are depressed. As we noted earlier, alcohol temporarily dulls the pain of self-awareness; by so doing, it may offer a way to avoid having to cope with depression, anger, anxiety, or insomnia. The relief may be temporary, but as Chapter 6 explains, behavior is often controlled more by its immediate than by its later consequences.

Especially for teenagers, drug use also has social roots, evident in differing rates of drug use across cultural groups. Alcohol and other drug addiction rates are extremely low among the Amish, Mennonites, Mormons, and orthodox Jews (Trimble, 1994). And what do you suppose is the rate of drug usage among African-American students—low or high? One of psychology's best-kept secrets is that, contrary to popular stereotypes, African-American high school seniors "report the lowest rates of use for virtually all drugs" (Johnston & others, 1994). For example, nearly a third of white seniors, but only 13 percent of black seniors, report recent heavy drinking. Monthly smoking rates are 33 percent among white seniors but only 10 percent among black seniors. Although these data exclude high school dropouts, independent government studies of drug use in households nationwide and among 12,272 high schoolers in all 50 states confirms the finding: African-American teens have sharply lower rates of drinking, smoking, and cocaine use (Bass & Kane-Williams, 1993; Kann & others, 1993).

Social influences are transmitted largely through the peer culture. By their words and examples, peers influence attitudes about drugs. They also provide the drugs and the parties for their use. If an adolescent's friends use drugs, the odds are that he or she will, too. If the friends don't, the temptation may not even arise. As always with correlations, the traffic between friends' and one's own drug use may be two way: Our friends influence us, but we also select as friends those who share our likes and dislikes.

Peer influence is a matter not just of what friends do and say but also of what adolescents *believe* their friends are doing and favoring. Young adoles-

Nic-a-teen *Aware that virtually all smokers start as teenagers, cigarette companies often target their ads at a young audience. By portraying tough, appealing, socially adept smokers, they entice teens to imitate such models.*

If you have always been a nonsmoker, you are almost certain to remain so forever.

cents consume more alcohol when, as often happens, they overestimate their friends' use (Aas & Klepp, 1992; Graham & others, 1991). At the university level, drinking dominates social occasions partly because students overestimate their fellow students' enthusiasm for alcohol use (Prentice & Miller, 1993; Self, 1994). Thinking that few students share their concerns about the risks associated with alcohol, most students surrender to the perceived norm.

Those who use drugs are more likely to stop if their drug use was peer influenced (Kandel & Raveis, 1989). When the friends stop or the social network changes, usage typically ceases. Teenagers who come from close-knit families and do well in school seldom use drugs, largely because they rarely associate with those who do (Oetting & Beauvais, 1987, 1990).

Smoking, for example, usually begins during early adolescence and is especially common among those whose friends, parents, and siblings smoke (Chassin & others, 1987; Schulenberg & others, 1994). Among teens whose parents and best friends are *non*smokers, the smoking rate is close to zero (Moss & others, 1992). Adolescents learn behaviors through the models they imitate and the social rewards they receive. Teens who start smoking typically have friends who model smoking, suggest its pleasures, and offer cigarettes (Evans & others, 1988). Self-conscious adolescents, who think the world is watching their every move, may begin smoking to imitate those models, to receive the social reward of being accepted by them, and to project a mature image (Covington & Omelich, 1988).

The findings suggest three possible channels of influence for drug prevention and treatment programs: (1) education about the long-term costs of a drug's temporary pleasures, (2) efforts to boost people's self-esteem and sense of purpose in life, and (3) attempts to modify peer associations or to "inoculate" youth against peer pressures, by training "refusal skills." People are very unlikely to abuse drugs if they understand the physical and psychological costs, feel good about themselves and the direction their lives are taking, and are in a peer group that disapproves of drug use.

❗ *Rehearse It*

13. Depressants are drugs that reduce neural activity and slow body functions. The depressants include alcohol, barbiturates,

a. and opiates.
b. cocaine, and morphine.
c. caffeine, nicotine, and marijuana.
d. and amphetamines.

14. Alcohol is a depressant that, in significant doses, powerfully affects behavior. For example, drinking alcohol may make a person more helpful or more self-disclosing; conversely, it may make a person more aggressive or more sexually daring. These alcohol effects result from

a. alcoholic blackouts or memory losses.
b. deprivation of REM sleep.

c. sensory arousal and hallucinations.
d. the lowering of inhibitions.

15. Nicotine, caffeine, amphetamines, and cocaine stimulate neural activity, speed up body functions, and

a. induce sensory hallucinations.
b. interfere with memory.
c. induce a temporary sense of well-being.
d. lead to heroin use.

16. About one-third of those who have survived a brush with death have reported near-death experiences, which are strikingly similar to the hallucinations evoked by

a. amphetamines.
b. barbiturates.
c. LSD.
d. marijuana.

17. Smoking marijuana can relieve certain kinds of pain and nausea. It also

a. impairs motor coordination, perception, reaction time, and memory.
b. inhibits people's emotions.
c. increases male sex hormone levels.
d. stimulates brain cell development.

18. Drug use by young North Americans generally declined during the 1980s and early 1990s. *Social* explanations for drug use today focus on the powerful effect of peer influence. An important *psychological* contributor to drug use is

a. inflated self-esteem.
b. the feeling that life is meaningless and directionless.
c. academic and job pressures.
d. overprotective parents.

Reviewing *States of Consciousness*

Studying Consciousness

1. What is consciousness and how does it function?

Psychology has returned to the study of consciousness—our awareness of ourselves and our behavior. At any moment our selective attention makes us conscious of a very limited amount of all that we are capable of experiencing, as when we attend to one voice among many at a party. Speedy, parallel processing handles subconscious information; conscious processing is serial and much slower.

Sleep and Dreams

2. What is the biological rhythm we experience, and how does it affect the stages of our sleep?

Our daily schedule of waking and sleeping is timed with a body clock known as circadian rhythm. Each night's sleep also has a rhythm of its own, cycling from transitional Stage 1 sleep to deep Stage 4 sleep and back up to the more internally active REM sleep stage about every 90 minutes. Periods of Stage 4 sleep progressively shorten and periods of dream-laden REM sleep lengthen through the night.

3. What is the function of sleep?

Depriving people of sleep has not conclusively revealed why, physiologically, we need sleep. Recent research reveals that sleep is linked with the release of pituitary growth hormone and that it may help to restore brain tissues and consolidate memories.

4. What are the major sleep disorders?

The disorders of sleep include insomnia (recurring wakefulness), narcolepsy (uncontrollable lapsing into REM sleep), sleep apnea (the temporary cessation of breathing while sleeping), and night terrors (high arousal and terrified appearance occurring during Stage 4 sleep).

5. What do we dream?

Although conscious thoughts can occur during any sleep stage, waking people up during REM sleep yields predictable "dreamlike" reports; waking them up during other sleep stages only occasionally yields a fleeting image. Our dreams are mostly of ordinary events; they often relate to everyday experiences and more frequently involve anxiety or misfortune than triumphant achievements.

6. What is the function of dreams?

Freud believed that a dream's manifest content, or story line, is a censored version of its latent content, which gratifies our unconscious wishes. Newer explanations of why we dream suggest that dreams (1) help process information from the day and fix it in memory, (2) serve a physiological function, and/or (3) are the brain's efforts to string periodic hallucinations (from activity bursts in the visual cortex) into a story line. Despite their differences, most theorists agree that REM sleep and its associated dreams serve an important function, as shown by the REM rebound that occurs following REM deprivation.

Daydreams and Meditation

7. What is the function of daydreams and meditation?

Virtually everyone daydreams, especially in times when attention can be freed from the tasks at hand. Daydreaming can be adaptive; it can help us prepare for future events and may substitute for impulsive behavior. Meditation, like deep relaxation, can help relieve stress-related symptoms and illnesses.

Hypnosis

8. What do hypnotized people experience, and how do they behave?

Although hypnosis was historically linked with quackery, it has more recently become the subject of serious research. Psychologists now agree that hypnosis is a state of heightened suggestibility to which people are subject in varying degrees, and that, although hypnotic procedures may help someone to recall past events, the hypnotist's beliefs frequently work their way into the subject's recollections. They also agree that hypnotized people can no more be made to act against their will than can nonhypnotized people. Hypnosis can be at least temporarily therapeutic, and hypnotizable people can enjoy significant pain relief.

9. Should hypnosis be considered an extension of normal consciousness or an altered state?

There is debate on whether hypnosis is a by-product of normal social and cognitive processes or an altered state of consciousness, perhaps involving a dissociation between levels of consciousness.

Drugs and Consciousness

10. What are psychoactive drugs?

Psychoactive drugs are perception- and mood-altering substances. A surprising number of these drugs, such as caffeine, nicotine, and alcohol, are legal and a part of everyday life. The use of psychoactive drugs often leads to tolerance and physical and/or psychological dependence. Users who are physically dependent will experience withdrawal when they try to stop taking the drug. The three types of psychoactive drugs are depressants, stimulants, and hallucinogens.

11. What are depressants, and what are their effects?

Alcohol, barbiturates, and the opiates are examples of depressants, which dampen neural activity and slow body functions. Alcohol seems to enliven by disinhibiting both harmful and helpful tendencies and by impairing judgment. Alcohol also disrupts the processing of recent experiences into long-term memory and reduces self-awareness. User expectation strongly influences alcohol's behavioral effects. Barbiturates can be especially dangerous in combination with alcohol. The harmful aftereffects of opiates oppose and offset the temporary pleasure they induce.

12. What are the stimulants, and what are their effects?

Caffeine, nicotine, the amphetamines, and cocaine are examples of stimulants, which stimulate neural activity and arouse body functions. The reinforcing effects of nicotine make smoking a difficult habit to kick, but increased knowledge of its devastating health effects has led to a decreasing percentage of Americans who smoke. All stimulants, but especially cocaine and crack, produce a crash of agitated depression as the drug wears off. This reinforces the use of more drug to get out of the depression, leading regular cocaine and crack users to become addicted. As with nearly all psychoactive drugs, stimulants act at the synapses by influencing the brain's neurotransmitters, and their effects depend on dosage and the user's personality and expectations.

13. What are the hallucinogens, and what are their effects?

LSD and marijuana are examples of hallucinogens, which distort perception and evoke sensory images without sensory input. Both LSD and marijuana can distort the user's judgments of time and, depending on the setting in which they are taken, can alter sensation and perception. Similar hallucinations are reported in near-death experiences, perhaps as a result of oxygen deprivation in the brain. Although marijuana can be therapeutic for those enduring glaucoma or chemotherapy, it has detrimental effects on health, judgment, and memory.

14. Why do people use psychoactive drugs?

Drug use among teenagers and young adults declined during the 1980s, as attitudes changed. Nevertheless, psychological factors (such as stress, depression, and hopelessness) and social factors (such as peer pressure) combine to lead many people to experiment with—and become dependent on—drugs. Some people also appear to have a greater biological susceptibility to dependence on drugs such as alcohol.

Terms and Concepts to Remember

consciousness, p. 164

selective attention, p. 164

circadian [ser-KAY-dee-an] **rhythm**, p. 165

REM sleep, p. 166

alpha waves, p. 167

delta waves, p. 167

insomnia, p. 170

narcolepsy, p. 170

sleep apnea, p. 171

night terrors, p. 171

manifest content, p. 172

latent content, p. 172

REM rebound, p. 174

hypnosis, p. 175

posthypnotic amnesia, p. 176

age regression, p. 177

posthypnotic suggestion, p. 178

dissociation, p. 178

psychoactive drug, p. 181

tolerance, p. 182

withdrawal, p. 182

physical dependence, p. 182

psychological dependence, p. 182

depressants, p. 182

stimulants, p. 182

hallucinogens, p. 182

barbiturates, p. 184

opiates, p. 184

amphetamines, p. 184

hallucinations, p. 186

LSD, p. 186

near-death experience, p. 186

THC, p. 187

Rehearse It Answer Key

1. c. **2.** b. **3.** b. **4.** d. **5.** d. **6.** d. **7.** a. **8.** c. **9.** b.

10. a. **11.** c. **12.** c. **13.** a. **14.** d. **15.** c. **16.** c. **17.** a. **18.** b.

Critical Thinking Exercise

Now that you have read and reviewed Chapter 5, take your learning a step further by testing your critical thinking skills on the following passage.

Consider the following hypnosis "experiment." "Geraldo the hypnotist" is invited to demonstrate hypnosis to your psychology class. He brings along three volunteers currently enrolled in his hypnosis certification course. Geraldo claims that hypnotists can trigger specific behaviors, perceptions, and memories in subjects because hypnosis involves a unique physiological and psychological state. He then hypnotizes the volunteers and begins a demonstration of age regression. The volunteers are "regressed" back to their first day of kindergarten. Remarkably, their behavior and speech seem childlike. After instructing them to forget everything that happened, Geraldo brings the subjects out of the hypnotic state and invites you and your classmates to question them. To your amazement, the subjects report no memory of the incident. Geraldo concludes that his presentation demonstrates that hypnotic age regression actually causes subjects to relive earlier experiences, while the suggestion of posthypnotic amnesia erases memories from the brain.

Understand the Assertion

1. State the hypnotist's assertion in your own words. Define all important concepts and terms as they are used in this example.

Consider the Evidence

2. Is the evidence for the hypnotist's assertion based on trustworthy research?

Evaluate the Explanation

3. Evaluate the explanation for the hypnotist's conclusion.
   a. Restate the explanation in your own words.
   b. Determine whether the explanation makes sense based on the evidence.
   c. State an alternative explanation.
   d. Suggest a more valid test of hypnosis.

Check your progress on becoming a critical thinker by comparing your answers to the sample answers found in Appendix B.

For Further Information

You can find further information regarding drugs on the following text pages:

Alcohol and aggression, pp. 502–503

Alcohol and memory, p. 237

Alcohol treatment, pp. 202, 457

Drugs and the fetus, p. 72

Drugs and neurotransmitters, pp. 39–40

Drug therapies, pp. 470–473

Learning

Classical Conditioning

Pavlov's Experiments

Updating Pavlov's
Understanding

Pavlov's Legacy

Operant Conditioning

Skinner's Experiments

Updating Skinner's
Understanding

Skinner's Legacy

Contrasting Conditioning
Techniques

Learning by Observation

Bandura's Experiments

Applications of Observational
Learning

1. What is learning?

When a chinook salmon first emerges from its egg in the gravel bed of a stream, its genes provide many of the behavioral instructions it needs for life. It instinctively knows how and where to swim, what to eat, and how to protect itself from predators. Following this built-in plan, the young salmon soon begins a trek to the sea. After some 4 years in the ocean, instinct drives the mature salmon back to its birthplace. It navigates hundreds of miles to the mouth of its home river and then, guided by the scent of its home stream, begins an upstream odyssey to its ancestral spawning ground. Once there, the salmon seeks out the exact conditions of temperature, gravel, and water flow that will facilitate its breeding, and then mates and dies.

Unlike the salmon, we are not born with a genetic blueprint for life. Much of what we do we must learn from experience. Although we must struggle to find the life direction a salmon is born with, our learning gives us more flexibility. We can learn how to build igloos or grass huts or submarines and thereby adapt to almost any environment. Indeed, nature's most important gift to us may be our *adaptability—our capacity to learn new behaviors that enable us to cope with ever-changing circumstances.*

No topic is closer to the heart of psychology than **learning**, *a relatively permanent change in an organism's behavior due to experience.* In earlier chapters we considered the learning of moral ideas, of visual perceptions, of a drug's expected effects. In later chapters we will consider how learning shapes our thought and language, our motivations and emotions, our personalities and attitudes.

Learning in all such realms breeds hope. What is learnable we can potentially teach—a fact that encourages parents, educators, athletic coaches, and animal trainers. What has been learned we can potentially change by new learning—an assumption that underlies counseling, psychotherapy, and rehabilitation. No matter how unhappy, unsuccessful, or unloving we are, that need not be the end of our story. Of all the world's creatures, we humans are the most capable of changing our behavior through learning.

©1984 by Sidney Harris; American Scientist Magazine.

"Actually, sex just isn't that important to me."

learning A relatively permanent change in an organism's behavior due to experience.

associative learning   Learning that certain events occur together. The events may be two stimuli (as in classical conditioning) or a response and its consequences (as in operant conditioning).

"Learning is the eye of the mind."

Thomas Drake
Bibliotheca Scholastica Instructissima, 1633

By definition, experience is key to learning. More than 2000 years ago, the Greek philosopher Aristotle concluded that we learn by association. Our minds naturally connect events that occur in sequence: We *associate* them. If, after seeing and smelling freshly baked bread, you eat some and find it satisfying, then the next time you see and smell fresh bread, your experience will lead you to expect that eating some will be satisfying again. And if you associate a sound with a frightening consequence, then your fear may be aroused by the sound itself. As one 4-year-old exclaimed after watching a TV character get mugged, "If I had heard that music, I wouldn't have gone around the corner!" (Wells, 1981).

Simple animals can learn simple associations. When disturbed by a squirt of water, the sea snail *Aplysia* will protectively withdraw its gill. If the squirts continue, as happens naturally in choppy water, the withdrawal response diminishes. But if the sea snail repeatedly receives an electric shock just after being squirted, its withdrawal response to the squirt alone becomes stronger. Somehow the animal learns to associate the squirt with the impending shock. More complex animals can learn more complex associations, especially those that bring favorable consequences. Sea lions in an aquarium will repeat behaviors, such as slapping and barking, that prompt people to toss them a herring.

By linking two events that occur close together, both the sea snail and the sea lion exhibit **associative learning**. The sea snail associates the squirt with impending shock; the sea lion associates slapping and barking with receiving a herring. In both cases, the animals learned something important to their survival: to associate the past with the immediate future.

Conditioning is the process of learning associations. In *classical conditioning*, we learn to associate two stimuli (as when we learn that a nearby flash of lightning signals an impending crack of thunder) (Figure 6–1).

Two related events:

Stimulus 1

Lightning

+

Stimulus 2

Thunder

Result after repetition:

Stimulus

We see lightning

Response

We anticipate impending thunder

Figure 6–1 Classical Conditioning

In *operant conditioning*, we learn to associate a response and its consequence (as when we learn that pushing a vending machine button relates to the delivery of a candy bar) (Figure 6–2).

To simplify things, we will consider these two types of associative learning separately. Often, though, they occur together in the same situation. A clever Japanese rancher reportedly herds cattle by outfitting them with electronic

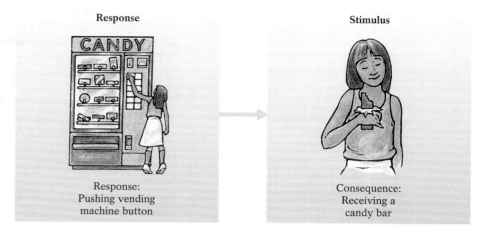

Figure 6–2 Operant Conditioning

Most of us would be unable to name the order of the songs on our favorite CD. Yet hearing the end of one piece cues (by association) an anticipatory mental representation of the next. Likewise, when singing your national anthem, you associate the end of each line with the beginning of the next. (Pick a line out of the middle and notice how much harder it is to recall the *previous* line.)

pagers, which he calls from his portable phone. After a week of training, the cows learned to associate two stimuli—the beep on their pager and the arrival of food (classical conditioning). But they also learned to associate their hustling to the food trough with the pleasure of eating (operant conditioning).

This, however, leaves many questions: What principles influence the learning and the loss of associations? How can we apply these principles? And what really are the associations: Does the beep on the cow's pager evoke a cognitive representation of food, to which the cow responds by coming to the trough? Or does it make little sense to explain conditioned associations in terms of cognitive processes?

Conditioning is not the only form of learning. Complex animals, such as chimpanzees, sometimes learn behaviors merely by observing others perform them. If one animal learns to solve a puzzle that gains a food reward while another watches, the second animal may perform the trick more quickly. We humans learn in all these ways—by learning to associate events (as in classical and operant conditioning) and by observation. Through language, we also learn things we have neither experienced nor observed.

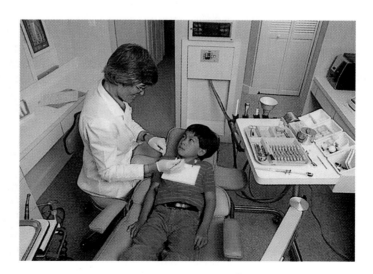

Conditioned Fear *The dentist's smile does nothing to allay the apprehension of this young patient. Because of pain experienced during previous visits in the dentist's chair, he has learned to expect discomfort.*

behaviorism   The view that psychology (1) should be an objective science that (2) studies behavior without reference to mental processes. Most research psychologists today agree with (1) but not (2).

classical conditioning   A type of learning in which an organism comes to associate events. A neutral stimulus that signals an unconditioned stimulus (UCS) begins to produce a response that anticipates and prepares for the unconditioned stimulus. (Also known as *Pavlovian conditioning*.)

unconditioned response (UCR)   In classical conditioning, the unlearned, naturally occurring response to the unconditioned stimulus (UCS), such as salivation when food is in the mouth.

unconditioned stimulus (UCS)   In classical conditioning, a stimulus that unconditionally—naturally and automatically—triggers a response.

conditioned response (CR)   In classical conditioning, the learned response to a previously neutral conditioned stimulus (CS).

conditioned stimulus (CS)   In classical conditioning, an originally neutral stimulus that, after association with an unconditioned stimulus (UCS), comes to trigger a conditioned response.

Ivan Pavlov   *"Experimental investigation . . . should lay a solid foundation for a future true science of psychology" (1927).*

All these ways of learning enable us to adapt to our environments. As this chapter will explain, we learn to expect and prepare for significant events such as food or pain (classical conditioning). We also learn to repeat acts that bring good results and to avoid acts that bring bad results (operant conditioning). And by watching others, we gain new behaviors indirectly (observational learning).

In searching for laws underlying such learning, psychologist John B. Watson (1913) urged his colleagues to discard reference to inner thoughts, feelings, and motives. Forget the mind, said Watson. Psychology should instead study how organisms respond to stimuli in their environments. "Its theoretical goal is the prediction and control of behavior." Simply said, psychology should be an objective science based on *observable behavior*. This view, which influenced North American psychology during the first half of this century, Watson called **behaviorism**.

Classical Conditioning

2. How does classical conditioning demonstrate learning by association?

Although the idea of learning associations had long generated philosophical discussion, it was not until this century that psychology's most famous research verified it. For many people, the name Ivan Pavlov (1849–1936) rings a bell. His experiments are classics, and the phenomenon he explored we justly call **classical conditioning** (or *Pavlovian conditioning*).

Pavlov was driven by a lifelong passion for research. After receiving a medical degree at age 33, he spent the next two decades studying the digestive system, work that earned him Russia's first Nobel prize in 1904. But it was his novel experiments on learning, to which he devoted the last three decades of his life, that earned this feisty scientist his place in history.

Pavlov's Experiments

Pavlov's new direction came when his creative mind seized on an incidental finding. After studying salivary secretion in dogs, he knew that when he put food in a dog's mouth the animal would invariably salivate. He also noticed that when he worked with the same dog repeatedly, the dog began salivating to stimuli associated with food—to the mere sight of the food, to the food dish, to the presence of the person who regularly brought the food, or even to the sound of that person's approaching footsteps. Because these "psychic secretions" interfered with his experiments on digestion, Pavlov considered them an annoyance—until he realized they pointed to a simple but important form of learning. From that time on, Pavlov studied learning, which he hoped might enable him to understand better the brain's workings.

At first, Pavlov and his assistants tried to imagine what the dog was thinking and feeling as it drooled in anticipation of the food. This only led them into fruitless debates. So to attack the phenomenon more objectively, they experimented. They paired various neutral stimuli with food in the mouth to see if the dog would begin salivating to the neutral stimuli alone. To eliminate the possible influence of extraneous stimuli, they isolated the dog in a small room, secured it in a harness, and attached a device that diverted its saliva to a measuring instrument (Figure 6–3). From an adjacent room they could present food—at first by sliding in a food bowl, later by blowing meat powder into the

Figure 6–3 Pavlov's Device for Recording Salivation
The isolated dog's saliva was collected drop by drop in a tube. (Adapted from Goodwin, 1991.)

dog's mouth at a precise moment. If a neutral stimulus—something the dog could see or hear—now regularly signaled the arrival of food, would the dog associate the two stimuli? If so, would it begin salivating to the neutral stimulus in anticipation of the food?

The answers proved to be yes. Just before placing food in the dog's mouth to produce salivation, Pavlov would sound a tone. After several pairings of tone and food, the dog began salivating to the tone alone in anticipation of the meat powder. Using this procedure, Pavlov conditioned dogs to salivate to other stimuli—a buzzer, a light, a touch on the leg, even the sight of a circle.

Because salivation in response to food in the mouth was unlearned, Pavlov called it an **unconditioned response (UCR)**. Food in the mouth automatically, *unconditionally*, triggers a dog's salivary reflex (Figure 6–4). Thus, Pavlov called the food stimulus an **unconditioned stimulus (UCS)**.

Salivation in response to the tone was *conditional* upon the dog's learning the association between the tone and the food. This learned response we therefore call the **conditioned response (CR)**. The previously neutral tone stimulus that now triggered the conditional salivation we call the **conditioned stimulus (CS)**. It's easy to distinguish these two kinds of stimuli and responses. Just remember: conditioned = learned; *un*conditioned = *un*learned.

If this demonstration of associative learning was so simple, what did Pavlov do for the next three decades? He and his associates explored the causes and effects of classical conditioning. Their experiments identified five major conditioning processes: acquisition, extinction, spontaneous recovery, generalization, and discrimination.

BEFORE CONDITIONING

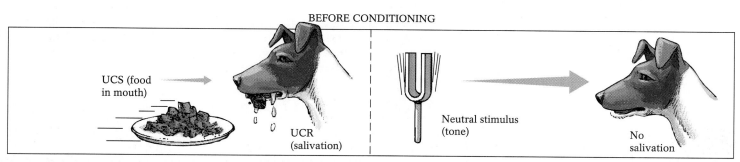

An unconditioned stimulus (UCS) produces an unconditioned response (UCR). A neutral stimulus produces no response.

The unconditioned stimulus is presented just after a neutral stimulus. The unconditioned stimulus continues to produce an unconditioned response.

The neutral stimulus now produces a conditioned response (CR), thereby becoming a conditioned stimulus (CS).

Figure 6–4 Pavlov's Classic Experiment
When a neutral stimulus (a tone) is presented just before an unconditioned stimulus (food in mouth), the neutral stimulus becomes a conditioned stimulus. The previously neutral stimulus, now a conditioned stimulus, produces a conditioned response.

Acquisition

3. How do the processes of acquisition, extinction, spontaneous recovery, generalization, and discrimination affect a CR?

Check yourself: If the aroma of brownies baking sets your mouth to watering, what is the UCS? The CS? The CR? (See page 202.)

Remember:

UCS = UnConditioned Stimulus
UCR = UnConditioned Response
 CS = Conditioned Stimulus
 CR = Conditioned Response

Regarding the **acquisition**, or initial learning, of the response, there was first a question of timing: How much time should elapse between presenting the neutral stimulus (the tone, the light, the touch, or whatever) and the unconditioned stimulus? In most cases, not much. With many species and procedures, half a second works well. What do you suppose would happen if the food (UCS) appeared *before* the tone (CS) rather than after? Do you think conditioning would occur?

Not likely. Although there are exceptions, conditioning seldom occurs when the CS comes after the UCS. This finding fits the presumption that classical conditioning is biologically adaptive. It helps organisms *prepare* for good or bad events. Pavlov's tone (CS) signals an important biological event—the arrival of food (UCS). To a deer in the forest, the sound of a snapping twig (CS) may come to signal a predator (UCS). If the good or bad event had already occurred, the CS would probably not signal anything significant.

Michael Domjan (1992) showed how this works by conditioning the sexual arousal of male Japanese quail. The researchers turned on a red light before presenting an approachable female. Over time, as the red light continued to herald a female's impending arrival, the male quail became excited (and began copulating with her more quickly). Moreover, the quail developed a general liking for their cage's red-light district.

The Quail's Sexual Conditioning *As in Figure 6–4, the top row indicates events* before *conditioning, and the bottom row* after *conditioning.*

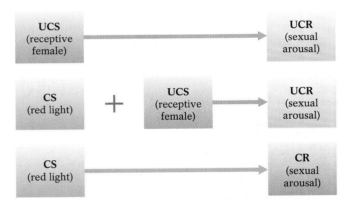

In humans, too, objects, smells, and sights associated with sexual pleasure become conditioned stimuli for sexual arousal. Psychologist Michael Tirrell (1990) recalls: "My first girlfriend loved onions, so I came to associate onion breath with kissing. Before long, onion breath sent tingles up and down my spine. Oh what a feeling!" (Questions: What is the unconditioned stimulus here? What is the conditioned response?) In laboratory experiments, even a geometric figure can become sexually arousing if repeatedly associated with an erotic stimulus (Byrne, 1982). (Note that in this case the figure is a CS, which gains its power to arouse by repeated pairing with a naturally erotic stimulus.)

Extinction and Spontaneous Recovery

acquisition The initial stage of learning, during which a response is established and gradually strengthened. In classical conditioning, the phase in which a stimulus comes to evoke a conditioned response. In operant conditioning, the strengthening of a reinforced response.

extinction The diminishing of a response when, in classical conditioning, an unconditioned stimulus (UCS) does not follow a conditioned stimulus (CS); or when, in operant conditioning, a response is no longer reinforced.

After conditioning, what happens if the CS occurs repeatedly without the UCS? Will the CS continue to elicit the CR? Pavlov found that when he sounded the tone again and again without presenting food, the dogs salivated less and less. Their declining salivation illustrates **extinction**, which occurs when the CS (tone) no longer signals an impending UCS (food).

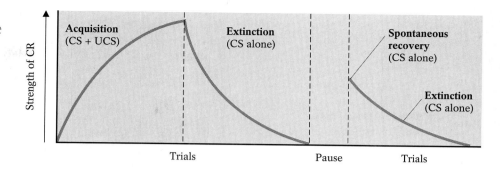

Figure 6–5 Idealized Curve of Acquisition, Extinction, and Spontaneous Recovery *The rising curve shows that the CR rapidly grows stronger as the CS and UCS are repeatedly paired (acquisition), then wanes as the CS is presented alone (extinction). After a rest pause the CR reappears (spontaneous recovery).*

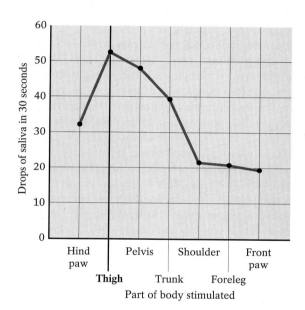

Figure 6–6 Generalization *Pavlov demonstrated generalization after attaching miniature vibrators to various parts of a dog's body. After conditioning salivation to stimulation of the thigh, he stimulated other areas. The closer they were to the original site of stimulation, the stronger the conditioned response. (From Pavlov, 1927.)*

spontaneous recovery The reappearance, after a rest period, of an extinguished conditioned response.

generalization The tendency, once a response has been conditioned, for stimuli similar to the conditioned stimulus to evoke similar responses.

discrimination In classical conditioning, the ability to distinguish between a conditioned stimulus and similar stimuli that do not signal an unconditioned stimulus. In operant conditioning, responding differently to stimuli that signal a behavior will be reinforced or will not be reinforced.

Pavlov found, however, that if he allowed several hours to elapse before sounding the tone again, the salivation to the tone would reappear spontaneously (Figure 6–5). This **spontaneous recovery**—the reappearance of a (weakened) CR after a rest pause—suggested to Pavlov that extinction was suppressing the CR rather than eliminating it.

After breaking up with his fire-breathing heartthrob, Tirrell also experienced extinction and spontaneous recovery. He recalls that "the smell of onion breath (CS), no longer paired with the kissing (UCS), lost its ability to shiver my timbers. Occasionally, though, after not sensing the aroma for a long while, smelling onion breath awakens a small version of the emotional response I once felt."

Generalization

Pavlov and his students noticed that a dog conditioned to the sound of one tone also responded somewhat to the sound of a different tone or even to a buzzer never paired with food. Likewise, a dog conditioned to salivate when rubbed would also salivate some when scratched (Windholz, 1989) or when stimulated on a different body part (Figure 6–6). This tendency to respond to stimuli similar to the CS is called **generalization**. Generalization can be adaptive, as when toddlers taught to fear moving cars in the street respond similarly to trucks and motorcycles, or as when a child bitten by one dog may fear all dogs.

Because of generalization, stimuli that are similar to naturally disgusting or appealing objects will, by association, evoke some disgust or liking. Normally desirable foods, such as fudge, are unappealing when presented in a disgusting form, as when shaped to resemble dog feces (Rozin & others, 1986). We perceive adults with childlike facial features (round face, large forehead, small chin, large eyes) as having childlike warmth, submissiveness, and naiveté (Berry & McArthur, 1986). In these cases, people's emotional reactions to one stimulus generalize to similar stimuli.

Discrimination

Pavlov's dogs also learned to respond to the sound of a particular tone and *not* to other tones. This learned ability to *distinguish* between a conditioned stimulus and similar but irrelevant stimuli is **discrimination**. Like generalization, discrimination has survival value. Slightly different stimuli are at times followed by vastly different consequences. Being able to recognize these differences is adaptive. Confronted by a pit bull, your heart may race; confronted by a cocker spaniel, it does not. Facing an approaching group of skinheads, you may cross the street; approaching some bald gentlemen, you don't.

Updating Pavlov's Understanding

4. What cognitive processes and biological constraints affect classical conditioning?

Pavlov's and Watson's disdain for "mentalistic" concepts such as consciousness has given way to a growing realization that they underestimated the importance of cognitive processes (thoughts, perceptions, expectations) and of biological constraints on an organism's capacity for learning.

Cognitive Processes

The early behaviorists believed that the learned behaviors of various organisms could be reduced to mindless stimulus-response mechanisms. The idea that rats and dogs exhibit cognition therefore struck many psychologists as silly. No longer. Classical conditioning experiments by Robert Rescorla and Allan Wagner (1972) revealed that when two significant events occur close together in time, an animal learns the *predictability* of the second event, given the first. What matters is not how *often* an electric shock, say, follows a tone, but how predictably. The more predictable the association, the stronger the conditioned response. It's as if the animal learns an *expectancy*, an awareness of how likely it is that the UCS will follow the CS.

These findings help explain why classical conditioning treatments that ignore cognition often have limited success. For example, therapy for alcoholics sometimes includes giving them alcohol spiked with a nauseating drug. Will they then associate alcohol with sickness? If classical conditioning were merely a matter of "stamping in" stimulus-response associations, we might hope so, and—to some extent—this does occur (as we will see on page 457). However, alcoholics are aware that they can blame their nausea on the drug, not on the alcohol. This cognition often weakens the association between alcohol and sickness. So, even in classical conditioning, it is not only the simple stimulus-response association but also the thought that counts.

Biological Predispositions

Ever since Darwin, scientists have assumed that animals share both a common evolutionary history and resulting commonalities in their make-up and functioning. Pavlov and Watson, for example, believed the basic laws of learning were essentially similar in all animals. So it should make little difference whether one studied pigeons or people. Moreover, it seemed that any natural response could be conditioned to any neutral stimulus. As learning researcher Gregory Kimble proclaimed in 1956, "Just about any activity of which the organism is capable can be conditioned and . . . these responses can be conditioned to any stimulus that the organism can perceive" (p. 195).

Twenty-five years later, Kimble (1981) humbly acknowledged that "half a thousand" scientific reports had proven him wrong. More than the early behaviorists realized, an animal's capacity for conditioning is constrained by its biology. The biological predispositions of each species dispose it to learn the particular associations that enhance its survival.

John Garcia and Robert Koelling (1966) demonstrated the importance of biological predispositions. They gave rats a particular taste, sight, or sound (CS) and later also gave them radiation or drugs (UCS) causing nausea (UCR). Two startling findings emerged: First, even if sickened as late as several hours after

"*All brains are, in essence, anticipation machines.*"

Daniel C. Dennett
Consciousness Explained, 1991

Answer to questions on page 200: Brownies (and their taste) are the UCS. The associated aroma is the CS. Salivation to the aroma is the CR.

John Garcia *As the laboring child of California farm-workers, Garcia's early schooling occurred in the off-season. After entering junior college in his late twenties, and earning his Ph.D. in his late forties, he received the American Psychological Association's Distinguished Scientific Contribution Award "for his highly original, pioneering research in conditioning and learning."*

"Once bitten, twice shy."

G. F. Northall
Folk-Phrases, 1894

tasting a particular flavor, the rats thereafter avoided that flavor. This appeared to violate the notion that for conditioning to occur, the UCS must follow the CS immediately.

Second, the sickened rats developed aversions to the tastes but not to the sights or sounds. This contradicted the behaviorists' idea that any perceivable stimulus could serve as a CS. But it made adaptive sense, because for rats the easiest way to identify tainted food is to taste it. Birds, which hunt by sight, appear biologically primed to develop aversions to the *sight* of tainted food (Nicolaus & others, 1983).

Humans, too, seem biologically prepared to learn some things rather than others. We more readily learn to fear snakes and spiders than to fear flowers (Cook & others, 1986). Again, it makes sense: Such animals harm us more frequently than do flowers.

All these cases support Darwin's principle that natural selection favors traits that aid survival. Nature prepares the members of each species to learn those things crucial to its survival. Someone who readily learns a taste aversion is unlikely to eat the same toxic food again and is more likely to survive and leave descendants. Indeed, all sorts of bad feelings, from nausea to anxiety to pain, serve good purposes. Like the low-oil light on a car dashboard, each alerts the body to a threat (Neese, 1991).

Garcia and Koelling's provocative findings stimulated new research, which confirmed their surprising findings and extended them to other species. When coyotes and wolves were tempted into eating sheep carcasses laced with a sickening poison, they developed an aversion to sheep meat (Gustavson & others, 1974, 1976). Two wolves later penned with a live sheep seemed actually to fear it. Such research suggests possible humane ways for controlling predators and agricultural pests.

Similarly, cancer patients who suffer nausea and vomiting beginning more than an hour following chemotherapy often develop classically conditioned nausea to stimuli associated with taking the drug. (Under normal circumstances, such revulsion to sickening stimuli is adaptive.) The conditioned stimuli evoke a cognitive representation of the unconditioned stimulus and the associated nausea. Thus, merely returning to the clinic or seeing the nurses can provoke sick feelings (Burish & Carey, 1986; Davey, 1992).

Has research on biological constraints compelled researchers to abandon the search for universal principles of learning that generalize across species? No; biological predispositions affirm a deeper principle: *Learning enables organisms to adapt to their environments.* Adaptation shows us why animals would be responsive to stimuli that announce significant events, whether delayed as sickness or immediate as food or pain. Adaptation also helps explain why in the taste-aversion experiments, cause need not precede effect immediately.

Nausea Conditioning Among Cancer Patients

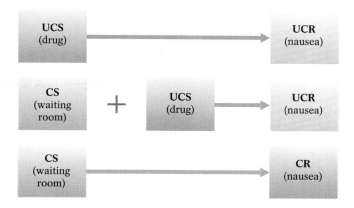

Pavlov's Legacy

5. Why is Pavlov's work important?

What, then, remains of Pavlov's ideas about conditioning? A great deal. All the researchers we have met so far in this chapter agree that classical conditioning is a basic form of learning. Judged by today's knowledge of cognitive processes and biological predispositions, Pavlov's ideas were incomplete. But if we see further than Pavlov did, it is because we stand on his shoulders.

Why is Pavlov's work so important? If he had taught us only that old dogs can learn new tricks, his experiments would have long ago been forgotten. Why should anyone care that a dog can be conditioned to drool at the sound of a tone? The importance lies first in this fact: Many other responses to many other stimuli can be classically conditioned in many other organisms—in fact, in every species tested, from earthworms to fish to dogs to monkeys to people (Schwartz, 1984). Thus, classical conditioning is one way that virtually all organisms learn to adapt to their environment.

Second, Pavlov showed us how an internal process such as learning can be studied objectively. Pavlov was proud that his methods involved virtually no subjective judgments or guesses about what went on in the dogs' minds. The salivary response is an overt behavior measurable as so many drops or cubic centimeters of saliva. Pavlov's success therefore suggested a scientific model for how the young discipline of psychology might proceed—by isolating the elementary building blocks of complex behaviors and studying them with objective laboratory procedures.

Applications of Classical Conditioning

In later chapters on motivation, emotions, psychological disorders, and therapy we will see how Pavlov's principles of classical conditioning apply to human health and well-being. For example, former crack cocaine users often feel a craving when they again encounter cues (people, places) associated with previous highs. Thus, drug counselors advise addicts to steer clear of settings associated with the euphoria of previous drug use. Classical conditioning even works on the body's disease-fighting immune system. When, say, a particular taste accompanies a drug that influences immune responses, the taste by itself may come to produce an immune response (page 366).

Pavlov's work provided a basis for John Watson's (1878–1958) idea that human behavior, though biologically influenced, is mainly a bundle of conditioned responses. In one famous though ethically troublesome study, Watson and Rosalie Rayner (1920; Harris, 1979) showed how specific fears might be conditioned. Their subject was an 11-month-old infant named Albert. Like most infants, "Little Albert" feared loud noises but not white rats. Watson and Rayner presented him with a white rat and, as he reached out to touch it, struck a hammer against a steel bar just behind his head. After seven repetitions of seeing the rat and then hearing the frightening noise, Albert burst into tears at the mere sight of the rat. What is more, 5 days later Albert showed generalization of his conditioned response by reacting with fear to a rabbit, a dog, and a sealskin coat, but not to dissimilar objects such as toys.

Although Little Albert's fate is unknown, Watson's is not. After losing his professorship at Johns Hopkins University over an affair with Rayner (whom he later married), he became the J. Walter Thompson advertising agency's resident psychologist. There he used his knowledge of associative learning to conceive many successful campaigns, including one for Maxwell House that helped make the "coffee break" an American custom (Hunt, 1993).

John B. Watson *In 1924, Watson admitted to "going beyond my facts" when offering his famous boast: "Give me a dozen healthy infants, well-formed, and my own specified world to bring them up in and I'll guarantee to take any one at random and train him to become any type of specialist I might select—doctor, lawyer, artist, merchant-chief, and, yes, even beggar-man and thief, regardless of his talents, penchants, tendencies, abilities, vocations, and race of his ancestors."*

Rape as Classical Conditioning

"A burnt child dreads the fire," says a medieval proverb. Experiments with dogs reveal that, indeed, if a painful stimulus is sufficiently powerful, a single event is sometimes enough to traumatize the animal when it again faces the situation. The human counterparts to these experiments can be tragic, as illustrated by one woman's experience of being attacked and raped, and thereby conditioned to many years of fear. Her fear (CR) is most powerfully associated with particular locations and people (CS), but it generalizes to other places and people. Note, too, how her traumatic experience robbed her of the normally relaxing associations with such stimuli as home and bed.

Four months ago I was raped. In the middle of the night I awoke to the sound of someone outside my bedroom. Thinking my housemate was coming home, I called out her name. Someone began walking slowly toward me, and then I realized. I screamed and fought, but there were two of them. One held my legs, while the other put a hand over my mouth and a knife to my throat and said, "Shut up, bitch, or we'll kill you." Never have I been so terrified and helpless. They both raped me, one brutally. As they then searched my room for money and valuables, my housemate came home. They brought her into my room, raped her, and left us both tied up on my bed.

We never slept another night in that apartment. We were too terrified. Still, when I go to bed at night—always with the bedroom light left on—the memory of them entering my room repeats itself endlessly. I was an independent person who had lived alone or with other women for 4 years; now I can't even think about spending a night alone. When I drive by our old apartment, or when I have to go into an empty house, my heart pounds and I sweat. I am afraid of strangers, especially men, and the more they resemble my attackers the more I fear them. My housemate shares many of my fears, and is frightened when entering our new apartment. I'm afraid to stay in the same town, I'm afraid it will happen again, I'm afraid to go to bed. I dread falling asleep.

Eleven years later this woman could report that her conditioned fears are gradually extinguishing:

The frequency and intensity of my fears have subsided. Still, I remain cautious about personal safety and occasionally have nightmares about my experience. But more important is my renewed ability to laugh, love, and trust—both old friends and new. Life is once again joyful. I have survived. (From personal correspondence, with permission.)

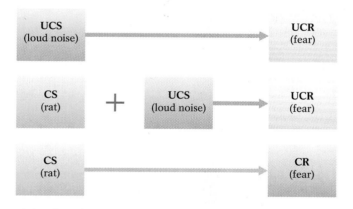

Little Albert's Conditioning

Although some psychologists had difficulty repeating Watson and Rayner's findings with other children, the work with Little Albert has had legendary significance for many psychologists. Some have wondered if each of us might not be a walking repository of conditioned emotions. Might our less adaptive emotions be controlled by the application of extinction procedures or by conditioning new responses to emotion-arousing stimuli? One therapist told a patient, who for 30 years had feared going into an elevator alone, to force himself to enter 20 elevators a day. Within 10 days, his fear nearly vanished (Ellis & Becker, 1982). In Chapter 13, Therapy, we will see more examples of how psychologists use behavioral techniques to treat emotional disorders.

! Rehearse It

1. Associative learning involves learning that certain events occur together. Two forms of associative learning are classical conditioning, in which the organism associates _____, and operant conditioning, in which the organism associates _____.

a. two responses; a response and a consequence
b. two stimuli; two responses
c. two stimuli; a response and a consequence
d. two responses; two stimuli

2. Learning is defined as "a relatively permanent change in behavior due to

a. instinct."
b. mental processes."
c. experience with the environment."
d. education or schooling."

3. Working with dogs, Pavlov paired a tone or other neutral stimulus with food in the mouth. The dogs came to salivate when presented with the neutral stimulus alone. Salivation in response to food in the mouth occurs naturally in dogs, without conditioning; food is therefore the unconditioned

stimulus (UCS). Salivation in response to a tone must be learned; the tone is therefore a

a. conditioned stimulus.
b. unconditioned stimulus.
c. conditioned response.
d. unconditioned response.

4. Dogs can learn to respond to one kind of stimulus and not to another—for example, to salivate at the sight of a circle (the CS) but not a square. Distinguishing between a CS and an irrelevant stimulus is

a. generalization.
b. discrimination.
c. acquisition.
d. spontaneous recovery.

5. Early behaviorists believed that for conditioning to occur the unconditioned stimulus (UCS) must immediately follow the conditioned stimulus (CS). _____ demonstrated this was not always so.

a. The Little Albert experiment
b. Pavlov's experiments with dogs
c. Watson's behaviorism theory
d. Garcia and Koelling's taste-aversion studies

6. Research by Garcia and Koelling showed that rats developed aversions to certain tastes but not to sights or sounds, thus supporting

a. Pavlov's demonstration of discrimination.
b. Darwin's principle that natural selection favors traits that aid survival.
c. Watson's view that study should be limited to observable behavior.
d. Kimble's original view that organisms can be conditioned to any stimulus.

7. Watson and Rayner classically conditioned fear of a white rat in a small child named Albert. After Watson paired the rat with a frightening noise, Little Albert acted fearful in the presence of the rat (even without the noise). The child later was fearful when presented with a rabbit, a dog, and a sealskin coat. Little Albert's fear of objects resembling the rat illustrates

a. extinction.
b. generalization of the conditioned response.
c. spontaneous recovery.
d. discrimination between two stimuli.

DENNIS THE MENACE

"I think Mom's using the can opener."

Operant Conditioning

6. What is operant conditioning, and how does it differ from classical conditioning?

Classical conditioning associates neutral stimuli with important stimuli that produce responses. But it's one thing to teach an animal to salivate at the sound of a tone or a child to fear cars in the street; it's quite another to teach an elephant to walk on its hind legs or a child to say please. Through **operant conditioning** subjects associate *behaviors* with their *consequences*. Thus, they become more likely to repeat rewarded (reinforced) behaviors and less likely to repeat punished behaviors.

Classical and operant conditioning both involve acquisition, extinction, spontaneous recovery, generalization, and discrimination. Yet their difference is straightforward: Classical conditioning cognitively associates stimuli (a CS and the UCS it signals). It also involves **respondent behavior**—behavior that occurs as an *automatic* response to some stimulus (such as salivating in response to meat powder and later in response to tone). Operant conditioning involves **op-**

Respondent behavior <u>responds</u> to stimuli.

Operant behavior <u>operates</u> to produce stimuli.

erant behavior, so-called because the act *operates* on the environment to produce rewarding or punishing stimuli. We can therefore distinguish classical from operant conditioning by asking: *Is the organism learning associations between events that it doesn't control (classical conditioning)? Or is it learning associations between its behavior and resulting events (operant conditioning)?*

Skinner's Experiments

B. F. Skinner (1904–1990) was a college English major and aspiring writer who, seeking a new direction, entered graduate school in psychology and went on to become modern behaviorism's most influential and controversial figure. Skinner's work elaborated a simple fact of life that turn-of-the-century psychologist Edward L. Thorndike called the *law of effect*: Rewarded behavior is likely to recur. Using Thorndike's law of effect as a starting point, Skinner developed a "behavioral technology" that enabled him to teach pigeons such unpigeonlike behaviors as walking in a figure eight, playing Ping-Pong, and keeping a missile on course by pecking at a target displayed on a screen.

For his pioneering studies with rats and later with pigeons, Skinner designed the now famous **Skinner box** (Figure 6–7). The box is typically a soundproof chamber with a bar or key that an animal presses or pecks to release a food or water reward, and with a device that records these responses. Experiments by Skinner and other operant researchers did far more than teach us how to pull habits out of a rat. They explored the precise conditions that foster efficient and enduring learning.

Figure 6–7 A Skinner Box *Inside the box, the rat presses a bar for a food reward. Outside, a measuring device records the animal's accumulated responses.*

---

operant conditioning A type of learning in which behavior is strengthened if followed by reinforcement or diminished if followed by punishment.

respondent behavior Behavior that occurs as an automatic response to some stimulus; Skinner's term for behavior learned through classical conditioning.

operant behavior Behavior that operates on the environment, producing consequences.

Skinner box A chamber containing a bar or key that an animal can manipulate to obtain a food or water reinforcer, with attached devices to record the animal's rate of bar pressing or key pecking. Used in operant conditioning research.

shaping An operant conditioning procedure in which reinforcers guide behavior toward closer and closer approximations of a desired goal.

Shaping

In his experiments, Skinner used **shaping**, a procedure in which rewards, such as food, gradually guide an animal's behavior toward a desired behavior. Imagine that you wanted to condition a rat to press a bar. After observing how the animal naturally behaves before training, you would build on its existing behaviors. You might give the rat a food reward each time it approaches the bar. Once the rat is approaching regularly, you would require it to move closer before rewarding it; then closer still, and finally to touch the bar before giving it the food. With this method, you reward responses that are ever-closer to the final desired behavior and ignore all other responses. In this way, researchers and animal trainers gradually *shape* complex behaviors.

By shaping nonverbal organisms to discriminate between stimuli, a psychologist can also determine what they perceive. Can a dog distinguish colors? Can a baby discriminate sounds? If we can shape them to respond to one stimulus and not to another, then obviously they can perceive the difference. For example, if an experimenter reinforces a pigeon for pecking after seeing a human face, but not after seeing other images, the pigeon will learn to recognize a face (Herrnstein & Loveland, 1964). After being trained to discriminate between flowers, people, cars, and chairs, pigeons can usually identify in which of these categories a new pictured object belongs (Bhatt & others, 1988; Wasserman, 1993). With training, pigeons have even been taught to discriminate between Bach's music and Stravinsky's (Porter & Neuringer, 1984).

HI AND LOIS

In the shaping procedure, the trainer builds on the individual's existing behaviors by expecting and immediately rewarding successively closer approximations of a desired behavior. In everyday life we continually reward and shape the behavior of others, said Skinner, but we often do so unintentionally. Sometimes we even reward offensive behavior. Billy's whining annoys his mystified parents. But look how they typically deal with Billy—by rewarding the very behavior they find so annoying:

Billy: *Could you tie my shoes?*

Father: *(Continues reading paper.)*

Billy: *Dad, I need my shoes tied.*

Father: *Uh, yeah, just a minute.*

Billy: *DAAAAD! TIE MY SHOES!*

Father: *How many times have I told you not to whine? Now, which shoe do we do first?*

We might also compare the way psychologists shape behavior—by rewarding small improvements—to the way some teachers use rewards. On a wall chart, the teacher pastes gold stars after the names of children scoring 100 percent on spelling tests. All children take the same tests. As everyone can then see, some children, the academic all-stars, easily get 100 percent. The others, no matter how hard they try or how much they improve, get no reward. The teacher would be better advised to reward poor spellers for gradual improvement (successive approximations toward their potential).

Principles of Reinforcement

7. What are the basic types of reinforcers?

So far, we have referred rather loosely to the power of "rewards." This idea gains a more precise meaning in Skinner's concept of the **reinforcer**, any event that increases the frequency of a preceding response. A reinforcer may be a tangible reward. It may be praise or attention. Or it may be an activity—being able to use the car when the dishes are done or to have recess after an hour of study (Timberlake & Farmer-Dougan, 1991). Again, anything that increases behavior (whether it seems positive or not) is a reinforcer.

Most people think of reinforcers as rewards. Actually there are two basic kinds of reinforcers. One type (positive reinforcer) strengthens a response by presenting a positive stimulus after a response. Food is a positive reinforcer for animals; attention, approval, and money are positive reinforcers for most people. The other type (negative reinforcer) strengthens a response by reducing or *removing* an aversive (unpleasant) stimulus. Imagine that alien invaders put you in an electrified cage, but that you could reduce or remove the electric shock by pressing a bar. You would surely press the bar, and feel (negatively) reinforced for doing so. When a barely awake person pushes the snooze button, the silencing of the annoying alarm is similarly a reinforcer. When someone

A Discriminating Creature *University of Windsor psychologist Dale Woodyard uses a food reward to train this manatee to discriminate between objects of different shapes, colors, and sizes. A manatee can remember such responses for as long as a year.*

reinforcer In operant conditioning, any event that *strengthens* the behavior it follows.

primary reinforcer An innately reinforcing stimulus, such as one that satisfies a biological need.

secondary reinforcer A conditioned reinforcer; a stimulus that gains its reinforcing power by association with a primary reinforcer.

Positive Reinforcement   *The trophy has positively rein-forced these youngsters for the work involved in per-fecting their drill routines. Praise from friends and family may further reinforce their disciplined efforts.*

stops nagging or whining, that, too, is a reinforcer. (Note that contrary to popu-lar usage, a negative reinforcer is not a punishing event; it is the *removal* of a punishing event.)

So imagine that whenever a child throws a tantrum, the parent gives in for the sake of peace and quiet. The child's tantrums will be reinforced when the parent gives in (positive reinforcement). And the parent's behavior will be rein-forced when the child stops screaming (negative reinforcement). Or imagine a worried student who, after goofing off and getting a bad exam grade, studies harder for the next exam. The student may be reinforced by reduced anxiety and by a better grade. Whether it works by giving something positive or by re-ducing something negative, *a reinforcer always strengthens behavior.*

Primary and Secondary Reinforcers   **Primary reinforcers**—getting food or being relieved of electric shock—are innately satisfying. We need not learn to like them. **Secondary reinforcers** are learned. They get their power through association with primary reinforcers. If a rat in a Skinner box learns that a light reliably signals that food is coming, the rat will work to turn on the light. The light has become a secondary reinforcer associated with food. Our lives are filled with secondary reinforcers—money, good grades, a pleasant tone of voice, a word of praise—each of which has been linked with more basic re-wards. Secondary reinforcers greatly enhance our ability to influence one an-other.

Immediate and Delayed Reinforcers   Consider a typical shaping exper-iment. Before performing a "wanted" behavior such as pressing the bar, an an-imal will engage in a sequence of "unwanted" behaviors—scratching, sniffing, and moving around. Whichever of these behaviors immediately precedes the reinforcer becomes more likely to recur. If we delay the reinforcer for bar pressing for as long as 30 seconds, allowing other behaviors to intervene and be reinforced, virtually no learning of the bar pressing occurs.

Humans, though, do respond to reinforcers that are greatly delayed: the paycheck at the end of the week, the grade at the end of the semester, the tro-phy at the end of the season. Indeed, to function effectively we must learn to postpone immediate rewards for greater long-term rewards. Four-year-old chil-dren who in laboratory testing show an ability to delay gratification—who'd sooner have a big reward tomorrow than a small one right now—become more socially competent and more likely to be high achievers as adolescents (Mischel & others, 1989).

Drawing by Cheney; © 1993 *The New Yorker* Magazine, Inc.

"Oh, not bad. The light comes on, I press the bar, they write me a check. How about you?"

The immediacy of reinforcement does influence our behavior, however. Smokers, heavy drinkers, and other drug users may know that their immediate pleasure—the effect that often comes within seconds—is more than offset by future ill effects. Still, immediate reinforcement prevails. Indeed, drugs such as nicotine and cocaine that provide the most immediate reinforcement are the most strongly addictive (Marlatt, 1991). Likewise, for many teens the immediate gratification of risky, unprotected sex in passionate moments prevails over the delayed gratifications of sex after commitment (Loewenstein & Furstenberg, 1991). And the hour-long enjoyment of staying up to watch another TV show may seem to outweigh the prospect of tomorrow's day-long sluggishness. To our detriment, small but immediate reinforcements are sometimes more alluring than big but delayed reinforcements.

8. How do partial reinforcement schedules affect behavior?

Reinforcement Schedules   So far, most of our examples have assumed **continuous reinforcement**: The desired response is reinforced every time it occurs. Under such conditions, learning occurs rapidly. But when the reinforcement stops—when we disconnect the food delivery chute—extinction also occurs rapidly. The rat soon stops pressing the bar. If a normally dependable candy machine fails to deliver a candy bar twice in a row, we stop putting money into it (although a week later we may exhibit spontaneous recovery by trying again).

In real life, continuous reinforcement is rare. A salesperson does not make a sale with every pitch, nor does an angler get a bite with every cast. But they persist because their efforts have occasionally been rewarded. Researchers have explored several **partial reinforcement** schedules in which responses are sometimes reinforced, sometimes not (Nevin, 1988). Initial learning is typically slower with partial reinforcement, which makes continuous reinforcement preferable until a behavior is mastered. But partial reinforcement produces greater persistence—greater *resistance to extinction*—than is found with continuous reinforcement. Imagine a pigeon that has learned to peck a key to obtain food. When the experimenter gradually fades out the delivery of food until it occurs only rarely and unpredictably, pigeons may peck 150,000 times without a reward (Skinner, 1953). With partial reinforcement, hope springs eternal.

Corresponding human examples come readily to mind. Slot machines reward gamblers occasionally and unpredictably. This partial reinforcement affects them much as it affects pigeons: They keep trying, sometimes interminably. A valuable lesson for parents: *Occasionally* giving in to children's tantrums for the sake of peace and quiet puts the child on a partial reinforcement schedule. That's the very best procedure for making a behavior persist.

Skinner (1961) and his collaborators compared four schedules of partial reinforcement. Some are rigidly fixed, some unpredictably variable.

Fixed-ratio schedules reinforce behavior after a set number of responses. Like people paid on a piecework basis—say, for every 30 pieces—laboratory animals may be reinforced on a fixed ratio of, say, one reinforcer for every 30 responses. Once conditioned, the animal will pause only briefly after a reinforcer and will then return to a high rate of responding (Figure 6–8). Because resting while on a fixed-ratio schedule reduces rewards, employees often find such arrangements tiring. Unions have therefore pressured employers to replace piecework pay with hourly wage schedules.

Variable-ratio schedules provide reinforcers after an unpredictable number of responses. This is what gamblers and fly casters experience—unpredictable reinforcement—and what makes gambling and fishing behavior so hard to extinguish. Like the fixed-ratio schedule, it produces high rates of responding, because reinforcers increase as the responding increases.

continuous reinforcement   Reinforcing the desired response every time it occurs.

partial reinforcement   Reinforcing a response only part of the time; results in slower acquisition of a response but much greater resistance to extinction than does continuous reinforcement.

fixed-ratio schedule   In operant conditioning, a schedule of reinforcement that reinforces a response only after a specified number of responses.

variable-ratio schedule   In operant conditioning, a schedule of reinforcement that reinforces a response after an unpredictable number of responses.

fixed-interval schedule   In operant conditioning, a schedule of reinforcement that reinforces the first response after a specified time.

variable-interval schedule   In operant conditioning, a schedule of reinforcement that reinforces a response at unpredictable time intervals.

punishment   An aversive event that *decreases* the behavior it follows.

Figure 6–8 Partial Reinforcement Schedules *Skinner's laboratory pigeons produced these response patterns to each of four reinforcement schedules. For people as for pigeons, reinforcers (diagonal marks on the graph) linked to responses—whether to a fixed number (a) or a variable number (b)—produce higher response rates than reinforcers linked to time intervals—either fixed (c) or variable (d). Fixed schedules produce higher response rates than the related variable schedules. (Adapted from "Teaching Machines" by B. F. Skinner. Copyright © 1961 Scientific American, Inc. All rights reserved.)*

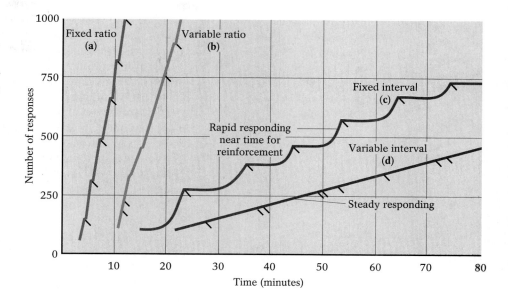

> "The charm of fishing is that it is the pursuit of what is elusive but attainable, a perpetual series of occasions for hope."
>
> Scottish author John Buchan, 1875–1940

Fixed-interval schedules provide an equal pause after each reinforcer. During this time no reinforcers are available. When the fixed interval ends, the next response is reinforced. Like people checking more frequently for the mail as the delivery time approaches, pigeons on a fixed-interval schedule peck a key more frequently as the anticipated time for reward draws near, producing a choppy stop-start pattern.

Variable-interval schedules reinforce the first response after *varying* time intervals. Like the unpredictable pop quiz that reinforces studying or the "hello" that finally rewards persistence in redialing a busy phone number, variable-interval schedules tend to produce slow, steady responding. This makes sense, because there is no knowing when the waiting will be over. Should the pop quiz become predictable, students will begin the stop-start work pattern that characterizes fixed-interval schedules.

Animal behaviors differ, yet Skinner (1956) contended that these reinforcement principles of operant conditioning are universal. It matters little, he said, what response, what reinforcer, or what species you use. The effect of a given reinforcement schedule is pretty much the same: "Pigeon, rat, monkey, which is which? It doesn't matter. . . . Behavior shows astonishingly similar properties."

Punishment

9. How does punishment affect behavior?

The effect of **punishment** is opposite to that of reinforcement. Reinforcement increases a behavior; punishment decreases it. Thus, a punisher is an aversive consequence that *decreases* the frequency of a preceding behavior. Swift and sure punishers can powerfully restrain unwanted behavior. A dog that learns to come running at the sound of the electric can opener will learn to hide if its master starts operating the can opener to catch it and banish it to the basement. A rat that is shocked after touching the forbidden object and a child who loses a treat after running into the street will learn not to repeat the behavior.

Nevertheless, punishment has drawbacks. Punished behavior is not forgotten; it is suppressed. This temporary suppression may reinforce the people who do the punishing. But if the punishment is avoidable, the punished behavior may reappear in safe settings. The child who learns through spankings not to

Question: Airline frequent-flyer programs that offer a free flight after every 25,000 miles of travel use which reinforcement schedule? Door-to-door sales people are reinforced by which schedule? (See page 213.)

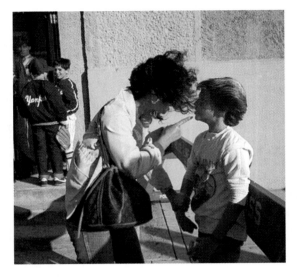

The Problem With Punishment *Swift and sure punishment can decrease unwanted behavior, but it can also evoke undesired responses, such as anger, fear, or resistance.*

swear around the house may swear elsewhere. The driver who is hit with a couple of speeding tickets may buy a radar detector and speed freely when no radar patrol is around.

Punishment may also increase aggressiveness by demonstrating that aggression is a way to cope with problems. This helps explain why so many aggressive delinquents and abusive parents come from abusive families (Straus & Gelles, 1980). Moreover, punishment can create fear; the person receiving the punishment may associate the fear not only with the undesirable behavior but also with the person who administers it or with the situation in which it occurs. Thus, a child may come to fear the punitive teacher and want to avoid school. Worse, when punishments are unpredictable and inescapable, both animals and people may develop the sense that events are beyond their control. As a result, they may come to feel helpless and depressed. For these reasons, most European countries have banned hitting children in schools and child care institutions (Leach, 1993, 1994). The Scandinavian countries and Austria have further outlawed physical punishment by parents (thus extending to children the same legal protection given to spouses).

Even when punishment suppresses unwanted behavior, it often does not guide one toward more desirable behavior. Punishment tells you what *not* to do; reinforcement tells you what *to* do. The teacher whose feedback on a paper says, "No, but try this . . . " and "Yes, that's it!" reduces unwanted behavior by reinforcing alternative behaviors. Most psychologists therefore favor an emphasis on reinforcement rather than punishment. Catch people doing something right and affirm them for it.

Parents of delinquent youth often lack this awareness of how to reinforce desirable behavior without screaming or hitting (Patterson & others, 1982). Training programs for such parents help them reframe contingencies from dire threats to positive incentives—from "You clean up your room this minute or no dinner!" to "You're welcome at the dinner table after you get the room cleaned up." When you stop to think about it, many threats of punishment are just as forceful, and perhaps more effective, if rephrased positively. Thus, "If you don't get your homework done, there'll be no TV" would better be phrased as . . .

! *Rehearse It*

8. Thorndike's "law of effect" states that "rewarded behavior is likely to recur." This law became the basis for operant conditioning and the "behavioral technology" developed by

a. Ivan Pavlov.
b. B. F. Skinner.
c. John Garcia.
d. John B. Watson.

9. B. F. Skinner taught rats to press a bar to obtain a food pellet. To guide the rat's natural behavior toward the desired behavior, he used

a. punishment.
b. shaping.
c. taste aversion.
d. discrimination.

10. A reinforcer is any stimulus presented after a response that increases the frequency of that response. Imagine that your dog barks at every noise it hears. The barking disturbs you, so you put the dog outside when it starts to bark. The stopping of the barking is for you the termination of an aversive stimulus, or a

a. positive reinforcer.
b. negative reinforcer.
c. punishment.
d. primary reinforcer.

11. Continuous reinforcement—reinforcement of the desired response every time it occurs—makes for rapid learning and for rapid extinction when reinforcement

stops. A partial reinforcement schedule that reinforces a response at unpredictable times is a

a. fixed-interval schedule.
b. variable-interval schedule.
c. fixed-ratio schedule.
d. variable-ratio schedule.

12. A medieval proverb notes that "a burnt child dreads the fire." In behavioral terms, the burning is an example of a

a. primary reinforcer.
b. negative reinforcer.
c. punisher.
d. positive reinforcer.

cognitive map A mental representation of the layout of one's environment. For example, after exploring a maze, rats act as if they have learned a cognitive map of it.

latent learning Learning that occurs but is not apparent until there is an incentive to demonstrate it.

For more information on animal behavior, see books by (I am not making this up) Robin Fox and Lionel Tiger.

Answer to question on page 212: Frequent-flyer programs use a fixed-ratio schedule. Door-to-door sales people are reinforced on a variable-ratio schedule (after varying numbers of rings).

Updating Skinner's Understanding

Although Skinner granted both the existence of private processes and the biological underpinnings of behavior, many psychologists criticized him for discounting the importance of these factors.

Cognition and Operant Conditioning

10. What cognitive processes and biological constraints influence operant conditioning?

A mere 8 days before dying of leukemia, Skinner (1990) stood before the American Psychological Association convention for one final blast at "cognitive science," which he viewed as a throwback to turn-of-the-century introspectionism. Skinner died resisting the growing belief that cognitive processes—thoughts, perceptions, expectations—have a necessary place in the science of psychology and even in our understanding of conditioning. Yet we have seen several hints that cognitive processes are at work in operant learning. For example, animals on a fixed-interval reinforcement schedule respond more and more frequently as the time approaches when a response will produce a reinforcer. The animals behave as if they expect that repeating the response will soon produce the reward.

Other evidence of cognitive processes comes from studies of rats in mazes. Rats exploring a maze, with no obvious reward, are like people driving around a new town. The rats develop a **cognitive map**, a mental representation of the maze. This occurs even if the rats are carried passively through the maze in a wire basket. When an experimenter then places a reward in the maze's goal box, the rats immediately perform as well as rats that have been reinforced with food for running the maze. During their explorations, the rats seemingly experience **latent learning**—learning that becomes apparent only when there is some incentive to demonstrate it. The unavoidable conclusion: Learning can occur without reinforcement. As the cognitive mapping experiments suggest, there is more to learning than associating a response with receiving a tangible consequence. There is also cognition. In Chapter 8, Thinking, Language, and Intelligence, we will encounter striking evidence of animals' cognitive abilities in solving problems and using aspects of language.

Biological Predispositions

As with classical conditioning, an animal's natural predispositions constrain its capacity for operant conditioning. When you reinforce its behavior with food, you can easily condition a golden hamster to dig or to rear up, because these actions are among the animal's natural behaviors when searching for food. But it's much harder to use food reinforcers to shape hamster behaviors, such as face washing, that aren't normally associated with food or hunger (Shettleworth, 1973). Pigeons easily learn to flap their wings to avoid shock and to peck to obtain food, because they naturally flee with their wings and eat with their beaks. But they have a hard time learning to peck to avoid shock or to flap to obtain food. Biological constraints predispose organisms to learn associations that are naturally adaptive.

A Natural Athlete *Animals can most easily learn and retain behaviors that draw on their biological predispositions, such as a raccoon's inborn tendency to manipulate objects with its paws.*

B. F. Skinner   "*I am sometimes asked, 'Do you think of yourself as you think of the organisms you study?' The answer is yes. So far as I know, my behavior at any given moment has been nothing more than the product of my genetic endowment, my personal history, and the current setting*" (1983).

"*You mene I've bin spending this whol term with a defektiv reeding machin?*"

Skinner's former associates, Keller Breland and Marian Breland (1961), came to appreciate biological predispositions while using operant procedures to train animals for circuses, TV shows, and movies. The Brelands had originally assumed that operant principles would work on almost any response that any animal could make. But after training 6000 animals of 38 different species, from chickens to whales, they concluded that biological predispositions were more important than they had supposed. In one act, they trained pigs to pick up large wooden "dollars" and deposit them in a piggy bank. After learning this behavior, however, the animals began to drift back to their natural ways. They would drop the coin, push it with their snouts as pigs are prone to do, pick it up again, and then repeat the sequence—delaying their food reinforcer. As this "instinctive drift" illustrates, "misbehaviors" occurred when the animals reverted to their biologically predisposed patterns.

Skinner's Legacy

B. F. Skinner was one of the most controversial intellectual figures of our time. He stirred a hornet's nest by repeatedly insisting that external influences, not internal thoughts and feelings, shape behavior and by urging the use of operant principles to influence people's behavior at school, work, and home. Recognizing that behavior is shaped by its consequences, we should administer rewards in ways that promote more desirable behavior.

Skinner's critics objected: They said he dehumanized people by neglecting their personal freedom and by seeking to control their actions. Skinner's reply: People's behavior is already haphazardly controlled by external consequences, so why not administer those consequences for human betterment? In place of the punishments used in homes, schools, and prisons, would not reinforcers be more humanitarian? And if it is humbling to think that we are shaped by our histories, this very idea also gives us hope that we can shape our future.

Applications of Operant Conditioning

11. How might educators, business managers, and other individuals apply operant conditioning?

We have seen applications of operant conditioning principles, and in later chapters we will see how psychologists apply these principles to problems ranging from high blood pressure to social withdrawal. Reinforcement technologies are also at work in schools, businesses, and homes.

At School   A generation ago, Skinner and others advocated teaching machines and textbooks that would shape learning in small steps and provide immediate reinforcement for correct responses. These machines and texts, they said, would revolutionize education and free teachers to concentrate on each student's individual needs.

To envision Skinner's dream, imagine two math teachers. Faced with a class of academically diverse students, Teacher *A* gives the whole class the same math lesson. The teacher knows that some students already understand the concepts and that others will be frustrated by their inability to comprehend. But with so many different children, how can one teacher guide them individually? When test time comes, the whiz kids breeze through unchallenged, and the slower learners again experience failure. Faced with a similar class, Teacher *B* paces the material according to each student's rate of learning and provides prompt feedback with positive reinforcement to slow and fast learners. Does the individualized instruction of Teacher *B* sound like an impossible ideal?

Token Reinforcement *Operant conditioning has proved to be a powerful tool in teaching people with severe mental disabilities. At the Brooklyn Development Center (New York), clients receive tokens for learning, maintaining, or improving a skill. They can then take the tokens to the Center's "store," where volunteers "sell" them different items.*

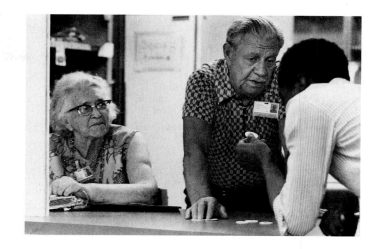

Although the predicted revolution has not occurred, to the end of his life Skinner (1986, 1988, 1989) believed the ideal was achievable. "Good instruction demands two things," he said. "Students must be told immediately whether what they do is right or wrong and, when right, they must be directed to the step to be taken next." To do this, and to free teachers for uniquely human tasks, computers were his final hope. For reading and math drills, the computer could be Teacher *B*—engaging the student actively, pacing material according to the student's rate of learning, quizzing the student to find gaps in understanding, providing immediate feedback, and keeping flawless records for the supervising teacher.

Experiments comparing computer-assisted instruction (CAI) with traditional classroom instruction suggest that, for some drill and practice tasks, the computer can indeed be more effective (Kulik & others, 1980, 1985). As personal computers have become more widely available, so too have new techniques of CAI. A computer can effectively train students to type or play the piano, while tracking progress and providing positive reinforcements. Educational games and simulations can entice students to explore and discover principles on their own. Instructional software and online learning allow students to work at their own pace.

At Work Believing that reinforcers influence productivity, business managers have capitalized on psychological research. Many companies now enable their employees to share profits, or even to participate in company ownership. When workers' productivity boosts rewards for all, their motivation, morale, and cooperative spirit often increase (Deutsch, 1991). Reinforcement for jobs well done is especially effective in boosting productivity when the desired performance is *well-defined and achievable*. Reward specific behaviors, not vaguely defined merit. Criticism, too, triggers the least resentment and the greatest performance boost when it is considerate and specific (Baron, 1988).

It's also a good idea to make the reinforcement *immediate*. Thomas Watson, who led IBM during its tremendous growth, would write out a check on the spot for achievements he observed (Peters & Waterman, 1982). But rewards need not be material, nor should they be so big that they become political and a source of discouragement to those who don't receive them. An effective manager may simply walk the floor and praise people for good work, or write unexpected notes of appreciation for a completed project. As Skinner said, "How much richer would the whole world be if the reinforcers in daily life were more effectively contingent on productive work?"

At Home   In homes, as elsewhere, immediate consequences most effectively influence behavior. We can use operant conditioning on ourselves, by reinforcing our most desired behaviors and extinguishing those undesired. To take charge of your own behavior, psychologists suggest these step-by-step procedures:

1. State your goal—say, to stop smoking, eat less, or study or exercise more—in measurable terms, and make it public. You might, for example, aim to boost your study time by an hour a day. Announce your goal to friends.

2. Record how often you engage in the behavior you wish to promote and note how this behavior is being reinforced. You might log your current study time, noting under what conditions you do and don't study. (When I began writing textbooks, I logged my time and was astonished to discover how much time I was wasting.)

3. Begin systematically to reinforce the desired behavior. To increase your study time, allow yourself a snack (or some other reinforcing activity) only after specified periods of study. Agree with your friends that you will join them for weekend activities only if you have met your weekly studying goal.

4. As your new behaviors become more habitual, gradually reduce the incentives while giving yourself a mental pat on the back.

Contrasting Conditioning Techniques

The last three decades of research have changed psychologists' views of both classical and operant conditioning (summarized in Table 6–1). Learning, like so much else, depends on both nature and nurture. Biological predispositions make learning some associations easier than learning others, yet animals exhibit more sophisticated cognitive processes than once seemed likely.

> "O! This learning, what a thing it is."
>
> William Shakespeare
> *Taming of the Shrew*, 1597

TABLE 6–1

Comparison of Classical and Operant Conditioning

	Classical Conditioning	Operant Conditioning
Acquisition	Associating events; CS announces UCS.	Associating response with a consequence (reinforcer or punisher).
Extinction	CR decreases when CS is repeatedly presented alone.	Responding decreases when reinforcement stops.
Cognitive processes	Subjects develop expectation that CS signals the arrival of UCS.	Subjects develop expectation that a response will be reinforced or punished; they also exhibit latent learning without reinforcement.
Biological predispositions	Natural predispositions constrain what stimuli and responses can easily be associated.	Organisms best learn behaviors similar to their natural behaviors; unnatural behaviors instinctively drift back toward natural ones.

observational learning   Learning by observing and imitating the behavior of others.

modeling   The process by which a behavior is observed and imitated.

"Children need models more than they need critics."

Joseph Joubert
Pensées, 1842

Learning by Observation

12. What is observational learning?

From drooling dogs, running rats, and pecking pigeons we have learned much about the basic processes of learning. But conditioning principles alone do not tell us the whole story. Among higher animals, especially humans, learning need not occur through direct experience. **Observational learning**, in which we observe and imitate others' behaviors, also plays a big part.

An example: Susan Mineka (1985) wondered why nearly all monkeys reared in the wild fear snakes, yet lab-reared monkeys do not. Surely, most wild monkeys do not actually suffer snake bites. Might they learn their fear through observation? To find out, Mineka experimented with six wild-reared monkeys (all strongly fearful of snakes) and their lab-reared offspring (virtually none of which feared snakes). After repeatedly observing their parents or peers refusing to reach for food in the presence of a snake, the younger monkeys developed a similar strong fear of snakes. When retested 3 months later, their learned fear persisted. This suggests that our fears reflect not only our own past traumas but also the fears of our parents and friends.

Moreover, we may be biologically prepared to learn by observation some fears more quickly than others. Monkeys learn to fear snakes even by watching videotapes of monkeys reacting fearfully to a snake; but they *don't* learn to fear flowers when video-splicing transposes the seemingly feared stimulus into a flower (Cook & Mineka, 1991). We humans quickly learn to fear snakes, spiders, and cliffs—fears that probably helped our ancestors survive. We are less predisposed to fear cars, electricity, bombs, and environmental warming, which in modern society are far more dangerous (Lumsden & Wilson, 1983; McNally, 1987). Stone Age fears leave us unprepared for high-tech dangers.

The process of observing and imitating a specific behavior is often called **modeling**. By observing and imitating models we learn all kinds of social behaviors. By 9 months of age, infants will imitate novel play behaviors, and by age 14 months will imitate acts modeled on television (Meltzoff, 1988a,b,c) (Figure 6–9). To persuade children to smoke, expose them to parents and older youth who smoke. To encourage children to read, read to them and surround them with books and people who read them. To increase the odds of your children practicing your religion, worship and attend other religious activities with them.

Figure 6–9 Learning From Observation *This 14-month-old boy in Andrew Meltzoff's laboratory is imitating behavior he has seen on TV. In the top photo the infant leans forward and carefully watches the adult pull apart a toy. In the middle photo he has been given the toy. In the bottom photo he pulls the toy apart, imitating what he has seen the adult do.*

Albert Bandura *"Learning would be exceedingly laborious, not to mention hazardous, if people had to rely solely on the effects of their own actions to inform them what to do"* (1977).

Bandura's Experiments

Picture this scene from a famous experiment devised by Albert Bandura, the pioneering researcher of observational learning (Bandura & others, 1961). A preschool child is at work on a drawing. An adult in another part of the room is working with some Tinker Toys. The adult then gets up and for nearly 10 minutes pounds, kicks, and throws a large inflated Bobo doll around the room, while yelling such remarks as, "Sock him in the nose. . . . Hit him down. . . . Kick him."

After observing this outburst, the child is taken to another room where there are many appealing toys. Soon the experimenter interrupts the child's play and explains that she has decided to save these good toys "for the other children." She now takes the frustrated child to an adjacent room containing a few toys, including a Bobo doll. Left alone, what does the child do?

Compared with children not exposed to the adult model, children who observed the aggressive outburst were much more likely to lash out at the doll. Apparently, observing the adult model lowered their inhibitions. But something more than lowered inhibitions is at work, for the children also imitated the very acts they observed and used the identical words they heard.

Applications of Observational Learning

The bad news from such studies is that antisocial models—in one's family or neighborhood, or on TV—may have antisocial effects (pages 503–508). This helps us understand how abusive parents might have aggressive children and why men who batter their wives often had wife-battering fathers. The lessons we learn as children are not easily unlearned as adults, and they are sometimes visited on future generations.

The good news is that **prosocial** (positive, helpful) models can have prosocial effects. People who exemplify nonviolent, helpful behavior can prompt similar behavior in others. Mahatma Gandhi and Martin Luther King, Jr., both drew on the power of modeling, making nonviolent action a powerful force for social change. Parents are powerful models. European Christians who risked their lives to rescue Jews from the Nazis and American civil rights activists of a generation ago usually had a close relationship with at least one parent who modeled a strong moral or humanitarian concern (London, 1970; Oliner & Oliner, 1988).

Models are most effective when their actions and words are consistent. Sometimes, however, models say one thing and do another. Many parents seem to operate according to the principle "Do as I *say*, not as I do." Experiments suggest that children learn to do both (Rice & Grusec, 1975; Rushton, 1975). When exposed to a hypocrite, they tend to imitate the hypocrisy by doing what the model did and saying what the model said.

What determines whether we will imitate a model? Bandura believes part of the answer is reinforcements and punishments—those received by the model as well as by the imitator. We look and we learn. By looking, we learn to anticipate a behavior's consequences in situations like those we are observing. By watching TV programs, children may "learn" that physical intimidation is an effective way to control others, that free and easy sex brings pleasure without the misery of unwanted pregnancy or disease, or that men are supposed to be tough and women gentle. We are especially likely to imitate those we respect and admire, those we perceive as similar to ourselves, and those we perceive as successful. (For more on media models, see Chapter 14.)

prosocial behavior Positive, constructive, helpful behavior. The opposite of antisocial behavior.

A Model Grandma   *This boy is learning to cook by observing his grandmother. As the sixteenth-century proverb states, "Example is better than precept."*

Although our knowledge of learning principles comes from the work of thousands of investigators, this chapter has focused on the ideas of a few pioneers—Pavlov, Watson, Skinner, and Bandura. They illustrate the impact that can result from single-minded devotion to a few well-defined problems and ideas. These researchers defined the issues and impressed on us the importance of learning. As their legacy demonstrates, intellectual history is often made by people who, at the risk of overstatement, pursue ideas to their limits.

! *Rehearse It*

13. Although Skinner disputed the idea, most researchers today believe that cognitive processes can play an important role in learning. Evidence for the effect of cognition (thoughts, perceptions, and expectations) comes from studies in which rats

a. spontaneously recover previously learned behavior.
b. develop cognitive maps.
c. exhibit respondent behavior.
d. generalize responses.

14. Animals, like people, can learn from experience, with or without reinforcement. After being carried passively through a maze without reward, rats offered a food reward at the end of the maze quickly demonstrated their prior learning of the maze by immediately doing as well as rats that had been reinforced for running the maze. The rats that had learned without reinforcement demonstrate

a. modeling.
b. biological predisposition.
c. shaping.
d. latent learning.

15. Children learn many social behaviors by imitating parents and other models. This type of learning is called

a. observational learning.
b. reinforced learning.
c. operant conditioning.
d. classical conditioning

16. Parents are powerful models of behavior. They are *most* effective in getting their children to imitate them if

a. their words and actions are consistent.
b. they have outgoing personalities.
c. the father works and the mother stays home to care for the children.
d. they carefully explain why a behavior is acceptable in adults but not in children.

17. Bandura believes that modeling is not automatic. Whether a child will imitate a model depends in part on the

a. child's closeness to the model.
b. child's ability to distinguish right from wrong.
c. rewards and punishments received by the model and by the imitator.
d. child's age in relation to that of the model.

Reviewing *Learning*

1. **What is learning?**

   All animals, especially humans, adapt to their environments aided by learning. The process of learning associations between events is called conditioning. Through classical conditioning, we learn to anticipate important events, such as impending food or pain. Through operant conditioning, we learn to repeat acts that bring desired results and to avoid acts that bring punishment. Through observational learning, we learn from the experience and example of others.

   Pavlov's work laid a foundation for John B. Watson's emerging belief that, to be an objective science, psychology should study only overt behavior, without considering unobservable mental activity. Watson called this position *behaviorism*.

Classical Conditioning

2. **How does classical conditioning demonstrate learning by association?**

   Although learning by association had been discussed for centuries, it remained for Ivan Pavlov to capture the phenomenon in his classic experiments on conditioning. Pavlov repeatedly presented a neutral stimulus (such as a tone) just before an unconditioned stimulus (UCS, food) triggered an unconditioned response (UCR, salivation). After several repetitions, the tone alone (now the conditioned stimulus, CS) began triggering a conditioned response (CR, salivation). Further experiments on acquisition revealed that classical conditioning was usually greatest when the CS was presented just before the UCS, thus preparing the organism for what was coming.

3. **How do the processes of acquisition, extinction, spontaneous recovery, generalization, and discrimination affect a CR?**

   Learned responses undergo an initial establishment (acquisition); subsequent weakening if not reinforced (extinction); a reappearance after a rest pause (spontaneous recovery); and triggering by stimuli similar to the conditioned stimulus (generalization) but not by dissimilar stimuli (discrimination).

4. **What cognitive processes and biological constraints affect classical conditioning?**

   The behaviorists' optimism that learning principles would generalize from one response to another and from one species to another has been tempered. Conditioning principles, we now know, are cognitively and biologically constrained. In classical conditioning, animals learn when to "expect" an unconditioned stimulus. Moreover, rats are biologically predisposed to learn associations between, say, a peculiar taste and a sickness-producing drink, which they will then avoid. But they don't learn to avoid a sickening drink announced by a noise.

5. **Why is Pavlov's work important?**

   Pavlov's conditioning principles generalize to many species and are applicable to humans, especially to the learning of emotions such as fear. His objective methods illustrated how psychology could proceed as a science.

Operant Conditioning

6. **What is operant conditioning, and how does it differ from classical conditioning?**

   Through classical (Pavlovian) conditioning, an organism associates different stimuli that it does not control. Through operant conditioning, the organism associates its behaviors with consequences. When rats or pigeons are placed in a Skinner box, researchers can shape their behavior by rewarding closer and closer approximations of the desired behavior. When followed by positive or negative reinforcement, the behavior is strengthened; when followed by punishment, the occurrence of the behavior diminishes.

7. **What are the basic types of reinforcers?**

   Reinforcers can be positive (when presented after a response) or negative (when an aversive stimulus is withdrawn); primary (unlearned) or secondary (learned through association with primary reinforcers); and immediate or delayed. Regardless of type, all reinforcers strengthen the behaviors that they follow.

8. **How do partial reinforcement schedules affect behavior?**

   Partial reinforcement schedules (fixed-interval, fixed-ratio, variable-interval, and variable-ratio) produce slower acquisition of the target behavior than does continuous reinforcement, but greater resistance to extinction.

9. **How does punishment affect behavior?**

   Like reinforcement, punishment is most swiftly effective when strong, immediate, and consistent. Although punishment decreases the frequency of the behavior it follows, it is not simply the logical opposite of reinforcement, for punishment can result in several undesirable side effects, such as increased aggression, fear of the punisher, and feelings of helplessness and depression.

10. **What cognitive processes and biological constraints influence operant conditioning?**

    Many psychologists have criticized behaviorists, such as Skinner, for underestimating the importance of cognitive and biological processes in operant conditioning. Research on cognitive mapping and latent learning points to the importance of cognitive processes in learning. Research has also made it clear that biological predispositions constrain what an animal can be taught.

11. **How might educators, business managers, and individuals apply operant conditioning?**

    Operant principles are applied successfully in schools, in the workplace, and at home. Computer-assisted instruction both shapes and reinforces learning; immediate reinforcement boosts worker productivity; individuals can strengthen their own desired behavior and extinguish unwanted behavior.

Learning by Observation

12. What is observational learning?

Observational learning results from watching others' behavior and imitating it. In experiments, children tend to imitate what a model both does and says, whether the behavior is prosocial or antisocial. Such experiments have stimulated research on social modeling in the home, on television, and within peer groups.

Terms and Concepts to Remember

learning, p. 195

associative learning, p. 196

behaviorism, p. 198

classical conditioning, p. 198

unconditioned response (UCR), p. 199

unconditioned stimulus (UCS), p. 199

conditioned response (CR), p. 199

conditioned stimulus (CS), p. 199

acquisition, p. 200

extinction, p. 200

spontaneous recovery, p. 201

generalization, p. 201

discrimination, p. 201

operant conditioning, p. 206

respondent behavior, p. 206

operant behavior, p. 206

Skinner box, p. 207

shaping, p. 207

reinforcer, p. 208

primary reinforcer, p. 209

secondary reinforcer, p. 209

continuous reinforcement, p. 210

partial reinforcement, p. 210

fixed-ratio schedule, p. 210

variable-ratio schedule, p. 210

fixed-interval schedule, p. 211

variable-interval schedule, p. 211

punishment, p. 211

cognitive map, p. 213

latent learning, p. 213

observational learning, p. 217

modeling, p. 217

prosocial behavior, p. 218

Rehearse It Answer Key

1. c.   **2.** c.   **3.** a.   **4.** b.   **5.** d.   **6.** b.   **7.** b.   **8.** b.   **9.** b.

10. b.   **11.** b.   **12.** c.   **13.** b.   **14.** d.   **15.** a.   **16.** a.   **17.** c.

Critical Thinking Exercise

Now that you have read and reviewed Chapter 6, take your learning a step further by testing your critical thinking skills on the following passage. You may find it helpful to review the text material in the section "Pavlov's Experiments" before completing this exercise.

Psychologists believe that children learn to control their bladders during sleep through classical conditioning, a type of learning in which an organism comes to associate different events. Normally, a wet bed or diaper causes a child to awaken. Through repeated pairings, bladder tension becomes associated with the sensation of wetness and children wake up when they sense full bladders. But some children do not learn the connection between bladder tension and wetness, probably because wetting the bed or diaper does not awaken them. Psychologists have attempted to control bed wetting through classical conditioning by developing a special sheet containing fine electric wires. When the sleeping child wets the bed, the urine (which conducts electricity) immediately completes an electrical circuit and causes a loud bell to ring, awakening the child. Over time, bladder tension becomes associated with the bell and the child wakes up before actually wetting the bed.

Understand the Assertion

1. State the psychologists' assertion in your own words. Define all important concepts and terms as they are used in this example.

Consider the Evidence

2. Identify the CS, CR, UCS, and UCR for children who learn to wake up without special training, and for children who are conditioned with the special sheet and bell.

Evaluate the Explanation

3. Evaluate the theoretical explanation for the psychologists' conclusion.

    a. Restate the explanation in your own words.

    b. Determine whether the explanation makes sense based on the evidence.

    c. State an alternative explanation.

Check your progress on becoming a critical thinker by comparing your answers to the sample answers found in Appendix B.

Memory

The Phenomenon of Memory

Forming Memories:
An Example

Memory as Information
Processing

**Encoding: Getting
Information In**

How We Encode

What We Encode

Forgetting as Encoding Failure

**Storage: Retaining
Information**

Sensory Memory Storage

Short-Term Memory Storage

Long-Term Memory Storage

Memory's Physical Storage

**Retrieval: Getting
Information Out**

Retrieval Cues

Memory Construction

Forgetting as Retrieval Failure

Improving Memory

Imagine your life without memory. There would be no savoring the remembrances of joyful moments, no guilt or misery over painful recollections. Each moment would be a fresh experience. But each person would be a stranger, every language foreign, each task—dressing, cooking, biking—a novel challenge.

Your memory is your mind's storehouse, the reservoir of your accumulated learning. To the Roman statesman Cicero, memory was "the treasury and guardian of all things." To a psychologist, **memory** is any indication that learning has persisted over time.

The Phenomenon of Memory

Conversing with John, a former graduate student, you would be impressed by his wit, his intelligence (he might explain his master's thesis), and his skill at tasks such as typing. It might be some time before you noticed that John suffers a tragic defect, caused by a brain injury suffered in a motorcycle accident. John has **amnesia** and cannot form new memories. Although he remembers his life before the accident, John otherwise lives in an eternal present. Each morning when his rehabilitation therapist greets him she must reintroduce herself. She must listen patiently as over and over he retells anecdotes from his preaccident life. Each time the need arises, he inquires, "Where is the bathroom?" and is told anew.

At the other extreme are some special people who would be medal winners in a memory Olympics, such as Russian journalist, Shereshevskii, or S, as psychologist Alexander Luria (1968) called him. S's memory not only allowed him merely to listen while other reporters were scribbling notes, it also earned him a place in virtually every modern book on memory. You and I can repeat back a string of about seven digits—almost surely no more than nine. S could repeat up to 70 digits or words, provided they were read about 3 seconds apart in an otherwise silent room. Moreover, he could recall them backward as easily as forward. His accuracy was unerring, even when asked to recall a list as much as 15 years later, after having memorized hundreds of other lists. "Yes, yes," he might recall. "This was a series you gave me once when we were in your apartment. . . . You were sitting at the table and I in the rocking chair. . . . You were wearing a gray suit and you looked at me like this. . . ."

memory The persistence of learning over time via storage and retrieval of information.

amnesia Loss of memory.

Memory Lost and Found *Larry Treadgold, an engineer, invented a paging system that serves as a kind of artificial memory for his son Adrian. Brain-injured in an auto accident, the young man can speak, understand, and retain information for as long as he pays attention. But as soon as he is distracted, the information fades away. The paging system allows a central computer to take over memory functions, reminding him, for example, to "take your 8 A.M. medications, call 123–4567 to confirm." If he fails to do so, the computer continues to repage him or contacts an emergency number.*

THE FAR SIDE

More facts of nature: All forest animals, to this very day, remember exactly where they were and what they were doing when they heard that Bambi's mother had been shot.

Do these memory feats make your own memory seem feeble? If so, consider your capacity for remembering countless voices, sounds, and songs; tastes, smells, and textures; faces, places, and happenings. Imagine viewing more than 2500 slides of faces and places, for only 10 seconds each, and later seeing 280 of these slides one at a time, paired with a previously unseen slide. If you are like the subjects in an experiment by Ralph Haber (1970), you would recognize 90 percent of those you saw before.

Or consider the vividness of your memories of unique and highly emotional moments in your past—perhaps a car accident, your first romantic kiss, your first day as an immigrant in a new country, or where you were when you heard some tragic news. Most Americans over 50 feel sure of exactly what they were doing when they heard the news of President Kennedy's assassination (Brown & Kulik, 1982). Few San Francisco Bay Area residents will hesitate in recalling exactly where they were when the 1989 earthquake struck. This clarity for our memories of surprising, significant events leads some psychologists to call them **flashbulb memories**, because it's as if the brain commands, "Capture this!"

How do we accomplish such memory feats? How can we remember things we have not thought about for years, yet forget the name of someone we met a minute ago? How are memories stored in our brains? Why can even our flashbulb memories sometimes prove dead wrong? (Hours after the space shuttle *Challenger* explosion, people reported where they had heard the news—and were sometimes wildly inaccurate when recalling their whereabouts 1 to 3 years later [McCloskey & others, 1988; Neisser & Harsch, 1992].) Does what we know about memory give us clues to how we can improve our memories? These will be our questions as we review a century of research on memory.

Forming Memories: An Example

History is sometimes determined by what people can remember about events. On June 17, 1972, police caught five men trying to tap the telephones of the Democratic National Committee in the Washington, D.C., Watergate Office Building. In 1973, when President Nixon's legal counselor, John Dean, testified before a U.S. Senate committee investigating White House involvement in what came to be called "the Watergate scandal," his recall of conversations with the President was so impressive that some writers called him "the human tape recorder." Ironically, it was later revealed that a secret taping system had actually recorded the conversations that Dean recounted, providing a rare opportunity to compare an eyewitness's recollections with the actual event. Dean's recollection of the essentials proved correct. The highest-ranking members of the White House staff went to prison for doing what John Dean said they did, and President Nixon was forced to resign.

However, when Ulric Neisser (1981) compared the details in the tapes with the testimony, he discovered that John Dean was far from a human tape recorder. For example, Dean recalled that entering a September 15 meeting with President Nixon and his chief-of-staff, Robert Haldeman,

> the President asked me to sit down. Both men appeared to be in very good spirits and my reception was very warm and cordial. The President then told me that Bob—referring to Haldeman—had kept him posted on my handling of the Watergate case. The President told me I had done a good job and he appreciated how difficult a task it had been and the President was pleased that the case had stopped with [his reelection committee's attorney] Liddy.

But almost every detail Dean recalled was wrong. The tape of the meeting revealed that the President did not ask Dean to sit down. He did not say Dean had done a good job. He did not say anything about Liddy or the indictments.

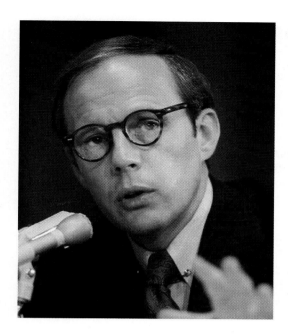

A Human Tape Recorder *John Dean is shown here testifying before the Senate Watergate Committee. When his testimony was compared with the White House tapes, Dean's memory was found to be accurate for the substance of most conversations but not for the details.*

Dean's memory was better for a March 15 conversation during which he delivered a well-prepared report to the President on the unraveling of the White House cover-up. The tape caught Dean actually saying, "We have a cancer within, close to the presidency, that is growing. It is growing daily . . . because (1) we are being blackmailed, (2) people are going to start perjuring themselves. . . ." In his later congressional testimony, Dean *recalled* "telling the President that there was a cancer growing on the presidency and . . . that it was important that this cancer be removed immediately because it was growing more deadly every day."

How could John Dean have been so right in his basic understanding of the Watergate discussions, yet, except for the March 15 conversation, so wrong in recalling the details of most conversations? Why are you likely when I quiz you later in this chapter to misrecall a sentence such as, "The angry rioter threw the rock at the window"? To understand Dean's memory (and our own), we need a model of memory.

Memory as Information Processing

1. How do psychologists describe the human memory system?

To remember any event requires that we *get information into our brain* (**encoding**), *retain it* (**storage**), and later *get it back out* (**retrieval**). Consider how a computer encodes, stores, and retrieves information. First, it translates input (keystrokes) into an electronic language, much as the brain encodes sensory information into a neural language. The computer permanently stores vast amounts of information on a disk. From this information storehouse it can retrieve a file or document into a working memory, which also can receive new information from the keyboard. Part of this working memory is visible on the screen.

Similarly, we store vast amounts of information in **long-term memory**. From our memory storehouse we can retrieve information into an active working memory, part of which is displayed on our mental screen as **short-term memory**. We can't focus on everything at once. So we shine the flashlight beam of attention on certain incoming stimuli, often novel or changing stimuli, which may fill our on-screen, short-term memory (Figure 7–1).

flashbulb memory   A clear memory of an emotionally significant moment or event.

encoding   The processing of information into the memory system, for example by extracting meaning.

storage   The retention of encoded information over time.

retrieval   The process of getting information out of memory storage.

long-term memory   The relatively permanent and limitless storehouse of the memory system.

short-term memory   Activated memory that holds a few items briefly, such as the seven digits of a phone number while dialing, before the information is stored or forgotten.

Figure 7–1 A Simplified Model of Human Memory
Sensory memory registers incoming information, part of which gets encoded and displayed "on screen" as short-term memory. We also retrieve information from long-term memory into short-term memory.

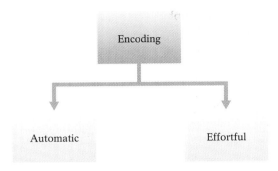

How Do We Process? *We process information either automatically or effortfully.*

Encoding: Getting Information In

2. How do the sights, sounds, and other sensations we experience get selectively encoded and transferred into the memory system?

Some encoding occurs automatically, freeing your attention to simultaneously process information that requires effort. Thus, your memory for the route you walked to class yesterday you handled by **automatic processing**. Your learning this chapter's concepts requires **effortful processing**.

How We Encode

Automatic Processing

With little or no effort, you encode an enormous amount of information about *space*, *time*, and *frequency*: During an exam, you may recall the place on the textbook page where the forgotten material appears. To guess where you left your coat, you can re-create a sequence of the day's events. You may realize that "this is the third time I've run into you this afternoon." Memories like these form almost automatically. In fact, not only does automatic processing occur effortlessly, it is difficult to shut off. When you hear or read a word in your native language, whether an insult or a friendly greeting, it is virtually impossible not to register its meaning automatically.

Some types of automatic processing we learn. For example, learning to read reversed sentences at first requires effort:

citamotua emoceb nac gnissecorp luftroffE

After practice, effortful processing becomes more automatic, much as reading from right to left becomes easy for students of Hebrew (Kolers, 1975).

Ready, Set, Go! *Riding a bicycle, rolling out pie dough, or diving are all complex motor skills that require practice. As they are executed again and again, however, they take less and less effort and gradually become automatic. We can carry them out while thinking about other things.*

Effortful Processing

3. How much does rehearsal aid in forming memories?

We encode and retain vast amounts of information automatically, without any intentional effort. Other types of information we remember only with effort and attention. With novel information such as names, **rehearsal**, or conscious repetition, boosts memory. This was shown long ago by the pioneering researcher of verbal memory, German philosopher Hermann Ebbinghaus (1850–1909). Ebbinghaus did for the study of memory what Ivan Pavlov did for the study of conditioning. Impatient with philosophical speculations about memory, Ebbinghaus wanted to study it scientifically. To do so, he decided to study his own learning and forgetting of novel verbal materials.

Where could Ebbinghaus find verbal material that was not familiar? His solution was to form a list of all possible nonsense syllables created by sandwiching a vowel between two consonants. Then, for a particular experiment, he would randomly select a sample of the syllables. To get a feel for how Ebbinghaus tested himself, rapidly read aloud, eight times over, the following list. Then recall the items (from Baddeley, 1982):

JIH, BAZ, FUB, YOX, SUJ, XIR, DAX, LEQ, VUM, PID, KEL, WAV, TUV, ZOF, GEK, HIW.

After learning such a list, Ebbinghaus could recall few of the syllables the following day. But were they entirely forgotten? As Figure 7–2 portrays, the more frequently he repeated the list aloud on day 1, the fewer repetitions he required to relearn the list on day 2. Here, then, was a simple beginning principle: *The amount remembered depends on the time spent learning.* Even after we learn material, additional rehearsal (*overlearning*) increases retention. Thus, John Dean almost perfectly recalled his "cancer on the presidency" remarks, because he had written them out and rehearsed them several times before uttering them to President Nixon.

The moral is that for novel verbal information, practice—effortful processing—does indeed make perfect. And that helps us understand some other interesting phenomena:

▶ The *next-in-line effect*: When people go around a circle reading words or saying their names, their poorest memories are for what was said by the person just before them (Bond & others, 1991; Brenner, 1973). When we are next in line, we focus on our own performance and often fail to process the last person's words.

▶ Information presented in the seconds just before sleep seldom is remembered (Wyatt & Bootzin, 1994). When our consciousness fades before we've processed the information, all is lost.

▶ Taped information played during sleep is registered by the ears but is not remembered (Wood & others, 1992). Without opportunity for rehearsal, "sleep learning" doesn't occur.

We also retain information better when rehearsal is distributed over time (as when learning classmates' names), a phenomenon called the **spacing effect** (Dempster, 1988). Harry Bahrick and Lynda Hall (1991) noted the effect of spaced rehearsal in a study of adults' memory of high school algebra. Those who took algebra only once forgot most of what they learned over the next half century. Others—after doing no better in high school—rehearsed their algebra knowledge while taking higher level math courses. For the rest of their lives these people remembered most of their high school algebra, especially if their college math was spaced over several semesters rather than massed into 1 year. In the first century, the Roman philosopher Seneca anticipated the finding that spaced study beats cramming: "The mind is slow in unlearning what it has been long in learning."

A phenomenon you have surely experienced further illustrates the benefits of rehearsal. Experimenters have shown people a list of items (words, names, dates) and then immediately asked them to recall the items in any order. As people struggle to recall the list, they often demonstrate the **serial position effect**: They remember the last and first items better than they do those in the middle (Figure 7–3, page 228). Perhaps because they are still in short-term

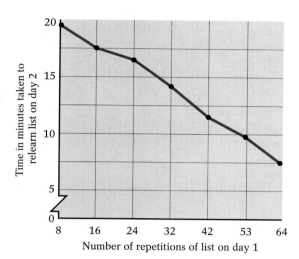

Figure 7–2 Ebbinghaus's Retention Curve *Ebbinghaus found that the more times he practiced a list of nonsense syllables on day 1, the fewer repetitions he required to relearn it on day 2. Said simply, the more time we spend learning novel information, the more we retain. (From Baddeley, 1982.)*

automatic processing Unconscious encoding of incidental information, such as space, time, and frequency, and of well-learned information, such as word meanings.

effortful processing Encoding that requires attention and conscious effort.

rehearsal The conscious repetition of information, either to maintain it in consciousness or to encode it for storage.

spacing effect The tendency for distributed study or practice to yield better long-term retention than is achieved through massed study or practice.

serial position effect Our tendency to recall best the last and first items in a list.

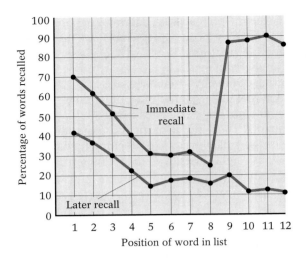

Figure 7–3 The Serial Position Effect *After being presented with a list of words, people immediately recall the last and first items most accurately. But later they recall only the first items best—even if they had repeated the last items for a few moments to keep them "on screen." (From Craik & Watkins, 1973.)*

imagery Mental pictures; a powerful aid to effortful processing, especially when combined with a meaningful context.

mnemonics [nih-MON-iks] Memory aids, especially those techniques that use vivid imagery and organizational devices.

memory, the last items are briefly recalled especially quickly and well. But after a delay—after attention has shifted from the last items—recall is best for the first items. As an everyday parallel, imagine that as you are being introduced to several people, you repeat (rehearse) all their names from the beginning as you meet each person. By the end, you will have spent more time rehearsing the earlier names than the later names; thus, the next day you will probably recall the earlier names better. Also, learning the first few names may interfere with your learning the later ones.

Rehearsal will not encode all information equally well. Sometimes merely repeating information, such as the new phone number we are about to dial, is not enough to store it for later recall (Craik & Watkins, 1973; Greene, 1987). How, then, do we process information into long-term memory? Processing our sensory input is like sorting through the day's mail: Some items we instantly discard. Others we process more thoughtfully: We open, read, and retain them. Our memory system processes information not just by repetitive rehearsal, but by encoding its significant features.

What We Encode

4. What methods of effortful processing aid in forming memories?

We process information in three key ways—by encoding its meaning, by visualizing it, and by mentally organizing it. To some extent we do so automatically. But in each case there are effortful strategies for enhancing memory.

Encoding Meaning

Do you recall (from page 225) the sentence about the rioter? Can you complete the sentence: "The angry rioter threw . . ."?

When processing verbal information for storage, we usually encode its meaning. For example, we associate it with what we already know or imagine. Whether we hear "eye-screem" as "ice cream" or "I scream" depends on how the context and our experience guide us to interpret the sounds.

Perhaps, then, like the subjects in an experiment by William Brewer (1977), you recalled the rioter sentence as the meaning you encoded when you read it (for example, "The angry rioter threw the rock through the window") and not as written ("The angry rioter threw the rock *at* the window"). As such recall indicates, we tend not to remember things exactly as they were. Rather, *we remember what we encoded.* Studying for an exam, you may remember your lecture notes rather than the lecture itself. Likewise, as we hear or read about a situation, our minds construct a model of it. Gordon Bower and Daniel Morrow (1990) liken our minds to theater directors who, given a raw script, imagine a finished stage production. Asked later to recall what we heard or read, we recall not the literal text but the mental model we constructed from it. This helps us understand John Dean's misrecollections of precisely what President Nixon said and did, and Dean's better recall of the *meaning* that he encoded from his conversations with the President.

To experience the importance of meaning for verbal memory, put yourself in the place of the students whom John Bransford and Marcia Johnson (1972) asked to remember the following recorded passage:

The procedure is actually quite simple. First you arrange things into different groups. Of course, one pile may be sufficient depending on how much there is to do. . . . After the procedure is completed one arranges the materials into different groups again. Then they can be put into their appropriate places. Eventually they will be used once more and the whole cycle will then have to be repeated. However, that is part of life.

How many *F*s are in the following sentence? FINISHED FILES ARE THE RESULTS OF YEARS OF SCIENTIFIC STUDY COMBINED WITH THE EXPERIENCE OF YEARS. (See page 231.)

> "A thing when heard, remember, strikes less keen on the spectator's mind than when 'tis seen."
>
> Horace
> *Ars Poetica*, 8 B.C.

When the students heard the paragraph you have just read, without a meaningful context, they remembered little of it. When told that the paragraph was about washing clothes (something meaningful to them), they remembered much more of it—as you probably could now after rereading it.

Such research suggests the futility of trying to remember words we do not understand and the benefits of rephrasing into meaningful terms what we read and hear. From his experiments on himself, Ebbinghaus estimated that, compared with learning nonsense material, learning meaningful material required but one-tenth the effort. Further, as memory researcher Wayne Wickelgren (1977, p. 346) noted, "The time you spend thinking about material you are reading and relating it to previously stored material is about the most useful thing you can do in learning any new subject matter."

Encoding Imagery

We struggle to memorize formulas, definitions, and dates, yet we can easily picture where we were yesterday, who was with us, where we sat, and what we wore. Your earliest memories—probably of something that happened at around age 3 or 4—almost surely involve visual **imagery**, or mental pictures.

In a variety of experiments, researchers have documented the benefits of mental images. For example, we remember words that lend themselves to picture images better than we remember abstract, low-imagery words. (When I quiz you later, which three of these words will you most likely recall: *typewriter, void, cigarette, inherent, fire, process*?) Similarly, you probably still recall the sentence about the rock-throwing rioter, not only because of the meaning you encoded but also because the sentence lent itself to a visual image. As these examples suggest, and as some memory experts believe, memory for concrete nouns is aided by encoding them *both* meaningfully and visually (Marschark & others, 1987; Paivio, 1986). Two codes are better than one.

Imagery is at the heart of many memory aids. **Mnemonic** (nih-MON-ik) devices (so named after the Greek word for memory) were developed by ancient Greek scholars and orators as aids to remembering lengthy passages and speeches. Using the "method of loci," they imagined themselves moving through a familiar series of locations, associating each place with a visual representation of the to-be-remembered topic. Then, when speaking, the orator would mentally revisit each location and retrieve the associated image.

A variation on this method uses vivid stories to organize words to be memorized. Gordon Bower and Michael Clark (1969) used lists of unrelated nouns, asking one group simply to study the lists and another group to invent stories using the nouns. (A sample made-up story: "A LUMBERJACK DARTed out of a forest, SKATEd around a HEDGE past a COLONY of DUCKs. He tripped on some FURNITURE, tearing his STOCKING while hastening toward the PILLOW where his MISTRESS lay.") After working through 12 lists of 10 words each, the group that merely studied each list struggled to recall 13 percent of the words; the group that invented vivid stories recalled an astounding 93 percent.

Other mnemonic devices involve both acoustic (sound) and visual codes. For example, the "peg-word" system requires that you first memorize a jingle:

> One is a bun; two is a shoe;
> Three is a tree; four is a door;
> Five is a hive; six is sticks;
> Seven is heaven; eight is a gate;
> Nine is swine; ten is a hen.

Without much effort, you will soon be able to count by peg-words instead of numbers: bun, shoe, tree . . . and then to visually associate the peg-words with to-be-remembered items. Now you are ready to challenge anyone to give you a grocery list to remember. Carrots? Imagine them stuck into a bun. Milk? Fill the

"You simply associate each number with a word, such as 'table' and 3,476,029."

Figure 7–4 Effects of Chunking on Memory *When we organize information into meaningful units, such as letters, words, and phrases, we recall it more easily. (From Hintzman, 1978.)*

Figure 7–5 An Example of Chunking—for Those Who Read Chinese *After looking at these characters, can you reproduce them exactly? If so, you are almost certainly literate in Chinese.*

chunking Organizing items into familiar, manageable units; often done automatically.

shoe with it. Paper towels? Drape them over the tree branch. Think "bun, shoe, tree" and you see their associated images: carrots, milk, paper towels. With few errors (Bugelski & others, 1968), you will be able to recall the items in any order and to name any given item. Such mnemonic systems are often the secret behind the feats of memory experts who repeat long lists of names and objects.

Organizing Information for Encoding

Meaning and imagery enhance memory partly by helping us organize information. When the laundry paragraph became meaningful, its sentences formed a sequence. Mnemonic devices help organize material for later retrieval. To experience the importance of organization, glance for a few seconds at row 1 of Figure 7–4, then look away and try to reproduce what you saw. It's nearly impossible. But you can easily reproduce the second row, which is no less complex. Similarly, row 4 is much easier to remember than row 3, although both contain the same letters. And the sixth cluster is more easily remembered than the fifth, although both contain the same words.

Chunking As this demonstrates, we organize easily remembered information into meaningful units, or chunks. **Chunking** information into meaningful units occurs so naturally that we take it for granted. Consider your ability to reproduce perfectly the 150 or so line segments that make up the sixth cluster of phrases in Figure 7–4. Surely it would astonish an illiterate person or someone unfamiliar with the English language.

You or I might feel similar admiration for the ability of someone literate in Chinese to glance at the characters in Figure 7–5 and then to reproduce all the strokes; or for chess masters who, after a 5-second look at the board during a game, can recall the exact positions of most of the pieces (Chase & Simon, 1973); or for varsity basketball players who, given a 4-second glance at a basketball play, can recall the positions of the players (Allard & Burnett, 1985). Like the experienced chess masters and athletes, we all remember information best when we can organize it into personally meaningful arrangements.

Chunking also aids our recall of unfamiliar material. One mnemonic technique organizes it into a more familiar form by creating words (called acronyms) or sentences from the first letters of words to be remembered. Should you ever need to recall the names of the five Great Lakes, just remember HOMES (*H*uron, *O*ntario, *M*ichigan, *E*rie, *S*uperior). Want to remember the colors of the rainbow in order of wavelength? Think of ROY G. BIV (*r*ed, *o*range, *y*ellow, *g*reen, *b*lue, *i*ndigo, *v*iolet).

Hierarchies When people develop expertise in an area, they process information not only in chunks but also in hierarchies composed of a few broad concepts divided and subdivided into narrower concepts and facts. By organizing their knowledge in such ways, experts can retrieve information efficiently. This chapter therefore aims not only to teach you the elementary facts of memory but also to help you organize these facts around broad principles, such as encoding; subprinciples, such as automatic and effortful processing; and still more specific concepts, such as meaning, imagery, and organization (Figure 7–6).

Gordon Bower and his colleagues (1969) demonstrated the benefits of hierarchical organization by presenting words either randomly or grouped into categories. When the words were hierarchically organized, recall was two to three times better. Such results show the benefits of organizing what you study—of giving special attention to chapter outlines, headings, topic sentences (or, in this book, the italicized "preview questions" at the beginning of each major section), and summary paragraphs. If you can master a chapter's concepts with their overall organization, the odds are that your recall will be good

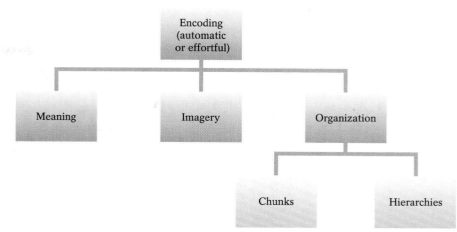

Figure 7–6 Organization Benefits Memory *When we see words organized into hierarchical groups, as here, we remember them better than when we see the same words presented randomly.*

Answer to question on page 229: Partly because your initial processing of the letters was primarily acoustic rather than visual, you probably missed some of the six *F*s, especially those that sound like a *V* rather than an *F*.

at test time. Taking lecture and text notes in outline format—a type of hierarchical organization—may also prove effective.

Forgetting as Encoding Failure

Amidst all the applause for memory—all the efforts to understand it, all the books on how to improve it—have any voices been heard in praise of forgetting? William James (1890, p. 680) was such a voice: "If we remembered everything, we should on most occasions be as ill off as if we remembered nothing." To discard the clutter of useless or out-of-date information—where we parked the car yesterday, a friend's old phone number, restaurant orders already cooked and served—is surely a blessing (Bjork, 1978). The Russian memory whiz S, whom we met at the beginning of the chapter, was haunted by his junk heap of memories, which continually dominated his consciousness. He had difficulty in thinking abstractly—generalizing, organizing, evaluating. A good memory is helpful, but so is the ability to forget.

What causes forgetting? One answer is that we failed to encode the information. Thus, it never entered the memory system.

Indeed, among the myriad sights and sounds that bombard us, we can attend to very little. Consider something you've looked at countless times: What letters accompany the number 5 on your telephone? If you live in North America, Britain, or Australia, you have probably also looked at thousands of pennies in your lifetime. You can surely recall the features (color and size) you use to identify coins. But can you recall what the side with the head looks like? If not, let's make the memory test easier: If you are familiar with U.S. coins, can you recognize the real thing in Figure 7–7 (page 232)? Raymond Nickerson and Marilyn Adams (1979) found that most people cannot. Likewise, few British

Why Do We Forget? *Forgetting can occur as a result of failure to encode information for entry into our long-term memory system.*

Figure 7–7 Test Your Memory *Which one of these pennies is the real thing? (If you live outside the United States, what does your country's penny look like?) (From Nickerson & Adams, 1979.) (See page 234.)*

people can draw from memory the one-pence coin they have seen thousands of times (Richardson, 1993). The details of a penny are not very meaningful—nor are they essential for distinguishing pennies from other coins—and few of us have made the effort to encode them. As we noted earlier, we encode some information automatically; other types of information require effortful processing. Without effort, many memories never form.

! *Rehearse It*

1. Many people have vivid memories of highly emotional moments—for example, what they were doing when they heard the news of an assassination; what kind of morning it was when they brought the new baby home from the hospital. These clear memories of emotional moments are called

a. short-term memories.
b. flashbulb memories.
c. automatic memories.
d. effortful memories.

2. Human memory involves information processing. We take information in, retain it, and later get it back out. In psychological terms, these steps are

a. retrieval, encoding, and storage.
b. encoding, storage, and retrieval.
c. storage, encoding, and retrieval.
d. retrieval, storage, and encoding.

3. In his research on verbal memory, Hermann Ebbinghaus would test his ability to recall a list of nonsense syllables. He found that the more often he repeated the list aloud, the fewer repetitions he required to relearn the list. This increase in retention was due to additional rehearsal, or

a. automatic processing.
b. retrieval.
c. overlearning.
d. the flashbulb effect.

4. Rehearsal is the conscious repetition of information a person wants to remember, either in the short or long term. Rehearsal is part of

a. automatic processing.
b. effortful processing.
c. forgetting.
d. retrieval.

5. Psychologists have found that when people are shown a list of words and are immediately tested, they tend to recall the first and last items on the list more readily than those in the middle (called the serial position effect). When people are *retested* after a delay, they are most likely to recall

a. the first items on the list.
b. the first and last items on the list.
c. a few items at random.
d. the last items on the list.

6. Many people use visual imagery to help them remember material that would

otherwise be difficult to master. Memory aids that use visual imagery, peg-words, or other organizational devices are called

a. acronyms.
b. nonsense material.
c. mental pictures.
d. mnemonics.

7. Chunking is a way of organizing information into familiar and manageable units. A related technique involves organizing material into broad categories, which are then divided into the subcategories. This technique, used in chapter outlines and organizational charts, is called

a. serial position.
b. peg-words.
c. hierarchial organization.
d. mental pictures.

8. In some cases, forgetting may be due to encoding failure. That is, meaningless information may not be transferred from

a. the environment into sensory memory.
b. sensory memory into short-term memory.
c. long-term memory into short-term memory.
d. short-term memory into long-term memory.

Storage: Retaining Information

If you experience something that you later recall, you must, somehow, have stored and retrieved it. What is stored in long-term memory lies dormant, waiting to be reawakened by a cue. What is our memory storage capacity? Let's start with the first memory store noted in Figure 7–1, our fleeting sensory memory.

Sensory Memory Storage

5. How does sensory memory work?

Consider what one intriguing memory experiment revealed about our **sensory memory**—the initial recording of sensory information in the memory system. As part of his doctoral research, George Sperling (1960) showed people three rows of three letters, each for only 1/20th of a second (Figure 7–8). It was harder than reading by lightning flashes. After the nine letters disappeared from the screen, the subjects could recall only about half of them.

Why? Was it because they had insufficient time to glimpse them? No, Sperling cleverly demonstrated that even at faster than lightning-flash speed, people actually *can* see and recall all the letters, but only momentarily. Rather than ask them to take time to recall all nine letters at once, Sperling would sound a high, medium, or low tone immediately *after* flashing the nine letters. This cue directed the subject to report only the letters of the top, middle, or bottom row, respectively. Now the subjects rarely missed a letter, showing that all nine letters were momentarily available for recall.

Sperling's experiment revealed that we have a fleeting photographic memory called **iconic memory**. For an instant, the eyes register an exact representation of a scene and we can recall any part of it in amazing detail. But only for a few tenths of a second. If Sperling delayed the tone signal by as much as a second, the iconic memory was gone and the subjects once again recalled only about half the letters. The visual screen clears quickly, as it must, lest new images be superimposed over old ones. The auditory sensory image, called **echoic memory**, also dies quickly (Cowan, 1988; Lu & others, 1992). But a partially interpreted auditory echo disappears more slowly. The last few words spoken seem to linger for 3 or 4 seconds. Sometimes, just as you ask, "What did you say?" you can hear in your mind the echo of what was said.

Short-Term Memory Storage

6. What are the limits of short-term memory?

Among the vast amounts of information registered by our sensory memory, we illuminate some with our attentional flashlight. We also retrieve information from long-term storage for "on screen" display. But unless we *work* with that information to encode it meaningfully or to rehearse it, it quickly disappears. Thus, short-term memory is often referred to as *working memory*. During your finger's trip from the phone book to the phone, your memory of a telephone number will disappear unless you work to maintain it in consciousness.

To find out how quickly it will disappear, Lloyd Peterson and Margaret Peterson (1959) asked people to remember three consonants, such as *CHJ*. To prevent subjects' rehearsal of the letters by their working memory, the researchers asked them to begin immediately counting aloud backward by threes from some number. With the help of a friend, you can demonstrate the result

How many of the six quiz words on page 229 can you now recall? Of these, how many are high-imagery words? How many are low-imagery?

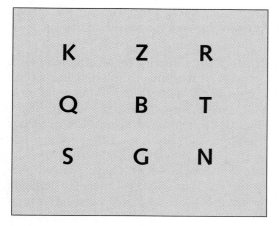

Figure 7–8 Momentary Photographic Memory *When George Sperling flashed a group of letters similar to this for 1/20th of a second, people could recall only about half of the letters. But when signaled to recall a particular row* immediately *after the letters had disappeared, they could do so with near-perfect accuracy.*

sensory memory The immediate, initial recording of sensory information in the memory system.

iconic memory A momentary sensory memory of visual stimuli; a photographic or picture-image memory lasting no more than a few tenths of a second.

echoic memory A momentary sensory memory of auditory stimuli; if attention is elsewhere, sounds and words can still be recalled within 3 or 4 seconds.

Figure 7–9 Short-Term Memory Decay *Unless rehearsed, verbal information may be quickly forgotten. (From Peterson & Peterson, 1959.)*

Answer to question on page 232: The first penny (a) is the real penny.

Clark's Nutcracker *Among animals, one contender for champion memorist would be a mere birdbrain—the Clark's nutcracker—which during winter and early spring can locate up to 6000 caches of buried pine seeds (Shettleworth, 1993).*

shown in Figure 7–9. After 3 seconds people recalled the letters only about half the time; after 12 seconds they seldom recalled them at all. Without active processing, short-term memories have a limited life.

The short-term memory store also has limited capacity. It typically stores but seven or so chunks of information (give or take two), a recall capacity that has been enshrined in psychology as "the Magical Number Seven, plus or minus two" (Miller, 1956). Adults, especially younger adults, have greater memory spans than children (Chi, 1976; Salthouse, 1992). Yet both children and adults have short-term recall for roughly as many words as they can speak in 2 seconds (Cowan, 1994; Hulme & Tordoff, 1989).

Long-Term Memory Storage

7. *How large and durable is our long-term memory?*

In Arthur Conan Doyle's *A Study in Scarlet*, Sherlock Holmes offers a popular but misleading theory of memory capacity:

> I consider that a man's brain originally is like a little empty attic, and you have to stock it with such furniture as you choose. . . . It is a mistake to think that that little room has elastic walls and can distend to any extent. Depend upon it, there comes a time when for every addition of knowledge you forget something that you knew before.

Contrary to Sherlock Holmes's belief, our capacity for storing long-term memories is essentially limitless. By one careful estimate, the average adult has about a billion bits of information in memory. Allowing for all the brain must do to encode, store, retrieve, and manipulate this information, its storage capacity is probably a thousand to a million times greater (Landauer, 1986). So our brains are *not* like attics, which once filled can store more only by discarding old items.

The point is vividly illustrated by those whose efforts have enabled phenomenal memory feats. Rajan Mahadevan, a Florida State University graduate student from India, would be the current gold medalist of memorists. At last report, he had correctly recited the first 99,000 digits of pi. Moreover, in answer to questions from researcher Charles Thompson and his colleagues (1993), Rajan can give, say, the 9382nd digit. Or give him any string of 10 digits and, after a few moments of mental search for the string, he'll pick up the series from there, firing numbers like a machine gun. He also can repeat 50 random digits—backwards. It's no genetic gift, he says; anyone could learn to do it. But given the genetic influence on so many human traits, and knowing that Rajan's father memorized Shakespeare's complete works, one wonders.

How precise and durable are our stored memories? Ebbinghaus (1885) learned lists of nonsense syllables and measured how much he retained when relearning each list, from 20 minutes to 30 days later. His famous "forgetting curve" (Figure 7–10) indicates that much of what we learn we may quickly forget. Many later experiments allow us to state the forgetting curve as one of psychology's laws: The course of forgetting is initially rapid, then levels off with time (Wixted & Ebbesen, 1991).

Harry Bahrick (1984) confirmed Ebbinghaus's finding. He examined the forgetting curve for Spanish learned in school. By using the cross-sectional method (page 101), he compared the knowledge of Spanish among people who had just taken Spanish classes with the knowledge of those who had studied it up to 50 years before. Compared with those just completing a high school or college Spanish course, those who had been out of school for 3 years had forgotten much of what they had learned (Figure 7–11). However, after roughly 3 years, forgetting leveled off; what people remembered then, they still remembered 25 years later, even if they had not used their Spanish at all.

Figure 7–10 Ebbinghaus's Forgetting Curve *After learning lists of nonsense syllables, Ebbinghaus studied how much he retained up to 30 days later. He found that memory for novel information fades quickly, then levels off. (Adapted from Ebbinghaus, 1885.)*

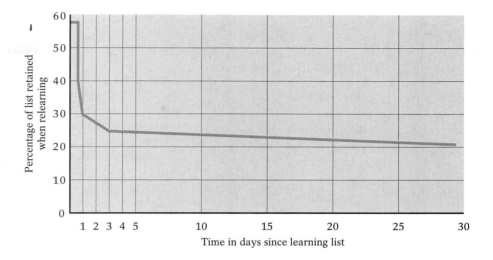

Is the forgotten Spanish gone—lost from storage—or merely inaccessible? If we could somehow uncover them, would we find our past experiences intact, like long-lost books in a dusty attic? Sigmund Freud thought so. If only we could recover and resolve the painful repressed memories of our childhood, he thought, emotional healing would follow. When "age-regressed" under hypnosis, some people do offer detailed reports of childhood experiences. But as we noted in Chapter 5, such reports are unreliable and typically contain fabricated material.

Figure 7–11 The Forgetting Curve for Spanish Vocabulary *Compared with people just completing a Spanish course, those 3 years out of Spanish classes remembered much less. Compared with the 3-year group, however, those who studied Spanish even longer ago did not forget much more. (Adapted from Bahrick, 1984.)*

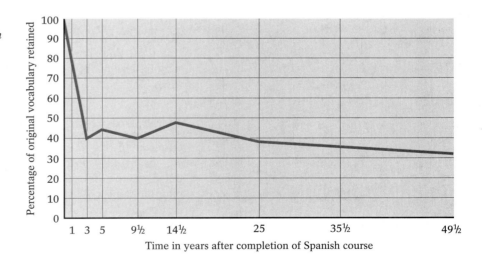

Memory's Physical Storage

8. How are memories recorded in the brain?

For a time, it was thought that brain stimulation during surgery provided evidence that our past is "in there," in complete detail, just waiting to be relived. As you may recall from page 53, to predict possible side effects of surgery, brain surgeon Wilder Penfield helped map the brain's motor cortex by electrically stimulating wide-awake patients. Occasionally, Penfield's patients would report hearing things, such as "a mother calling her little boy." Penfield (1969) assumed he was activating long-lost experiences etched permanently on the brain.

Scrutinizing these famous reports, memory researchers Elizabeth Loftus and Geoffrey Loftus (1980) discovered that these flashbacks were extremely rare, occurring in only a handful of Penfield's 1100 stimulated patients. Moreover, the content of these few recollections suggested that the experiences were not being relived but were being invented. As if they had been dreaming, people would recall being in locations they had never visited. Although the brain's storage capacity may be essentially unlimited, Penfield's evidence did *not* suggest that we store most information with the exactness of a tape recorder. Rather, say memory researchers, forgetting occurs as new experiences interfere with our retrieval (page 246) and as the physical memory trace gradually decays.

But what exactly is the "memory trace"? Since 1980, new clues to the physical basis of long-term memory have surfaced rapidly. While cognitive psychologists study our memory "software," neuroscientists are gaining new insights into our memory "hardware"—how and where we physically store information in our brains.

For several decades, neuroscientists have searched the brain for physical evidence of memory. The search has at times been exasperating. One psychologist, Karl Lashley (1950), trained rats to solve a maze, then cut out pieces of the rats' cortexes and tested their memory of the maze. Eventually, he hoped to locate where memory of the maze was stored. Alas, no matter what part of the cortex he removed, the rats retained at least a partial memory of how to solve the maze. Lashley's conclusion: Memories do not reside in single, specific spots.

Are memories instead rooted in the brain's ongoing electrical activity? If so, then temporarily shutting down that activity should eliminate them, much as a power failure eliminates the settings on an electronic clock. To test this, Ralph Gerard (1953) trained hamsters to turn right or left to get food. Then he lowered their body temperature until the brain's electrical activity ceased. When the hamsters were revived and their brains were active again, would they remember which way to turn? Yes. Their long-term memories survived the electrical blackout.

Synaptic Changes

Other neuroscientists are analyzing memory on a finer scale, by exploring changes within and between single neurons. Memories begin as neural impulses whizzing through brain circuits, which somehow cause permanent neural changes. Where does the neural change occur that makes memories permanent? The available clues point to the synapses—the sites where nerve cells communicate with one another through their neurotransmitter messengers (Alkon & others, 1991). Chapter 3 notes how experience modifies the brain's neural networks. Given increased activity in a particular pathway, neural interconnections form or strengthen.

Eric Kandel and James Schwartz (1982) observed actual changes in the sending neurons. By observing sea snails' neural connections before and after being conditioned to retract their gills, the researchers pinpointed changes. When learning occurs, the snails release more of the neurotransmitter serotonin at certain synapses, and these synapses become more efficient at transmitting signals.

Increased synaptic efficiency makes for more efficient neural circuits. In experiments, rapidly stimulating certain memory-circuit connections has increased their sensitivity for hours or even weeks to come. (The sending neuron now needs less prompting to release its neurotransmitter, and receptor sites may increase.) This prolonged strengthening of potential neural firing, called **long-term potentiation (LTP)**, provides a neural basis for learning and remem-

long-term potentiation (LTP)   An increase in a synapse's firing potential after brief, rapid stimulation. Believed to be a neural basis for learning and memory.

bering associations. Drugs that block LTP interfere with learning (Lynch & Staubli, 1991). Mutant mice engineered to lack an enzyme needed for LTP can't learn their way out of a maze (Silva & others, 1992). Rats given a drug that enhances LTP will learn a maze with half the usual number of mistakes, raising hopes for a drug that may someday enhance human memory (Service, 1994).

Passing an electric current through the brain won't disrupt old memories after long-term potentiation has occurred. But very recent experiences will be wiped out. Such is the experience both of laboratory animals and of depressed people given electroconvulsive therapy (page 473). A blow to the head can do the same. When football players who have been dazed or momentarily knocked unconscious are interviewed a few minutes later, they typically cannot recall the name of the play during which the incident occurred (Yarnell & Lynch, 1970). Likewise, a boxer knocked out in round 2 may have no memory of that round. (They are like sleepers who can't remember what they heard just before losing consciousness.) The information in short-term memory before the blow just didn't have time to consolidate into long-term memory. Drugs that block neurotransmitters also disrupt information storage (Squire, 1987). For example, alcohol impairs memory formation by disrupting serotonin's messenger activity (Weingartner & others, 1983). Waking up after a night of heavy drinking, a person may have trouble remembering the previous evening.

The naturally stimulating hormones that humans and animals produce when excited or stressed have an opposite effect: They boost learning and retention. Emotion-triggered hormonal changes help explain why we long remember exciting or shocking events, such as our first kiss, a political assassination, a major earthquake. People who have suffered personal traumatic experiences often relive the experience with vivid flashbacks. And people who *experienced* the 1989 San Francisco Bay earthquake had perfect recall a year and a half later of where they were and what they were doing when the earthquake began (they had recorded the details a day or two after the quake). Others' memories for the circumstances under which they *heard* about the quake were prone to errors (Neisser & others, 1991; Palmer & others, 1991). (A second reason for the greater durability of actual experiences is our reliving and rehearsing them.)

Storing Implicit and Explicit Memories

After a memory-to-be enters the cortex through the senses, it winds its way into the depths of the brain. Where it goes depends on the type of information, as strikingly illustrated in the special cases of amnesic patients similar to John, whom we met at the beginning of this chapter.

Neurologist Oliver Sacks (1985, pp. 26–27) describes another such patient. Jimmie, a brain-damaged man, had no memories—thus, no sense of elapsed time—beyond his injury in 1945. Asked to name the President, he replied, "FDR's dead. Truman's at the helm."

When Jimmie gave his age as 19, Sacks thrust a mirror at him: "Look in the mirror and tell me what you see. Is that a 19-year-old looking out from the mirror?"

Jimmie turned ashen, gripped the chair, cursed, then became frantic: "What's going on? What's happened to me? Is this a nightmare? Am I crazy? Is this a joke?" When his attention was diverted to some children playing baseball, his panic ended, the dreadful mirror swiftly forgotten.

Flipping through a *National Geographic*, Sacks showed Jimmie a photo. "What is this?" he asked.

"It's the moon," Jimmie replied.

"No, it's not," Sacks answered. "It's a picture of the earth taken from the moon."

What's Next? *In the early stages of Alzheimer's disease, a loss of brain tissue that secretes important neurotransmitters results in a considerable mental impairment. In recent years, social agencies have begun offering day care services. At centers like the one shown here, patients are kept busy and their caretakers get a break.*

implicit memory   Retention without conscious recollection (of skills, preferences, and dispositions). (Also called *nondeclarative memory*.)

explicit memory   Memory of facts and experiences that one can consciously know and "declare." (Also called *declarative memory*.)

hippocampus   A neural center located in the limbic system that helps process explicit memories for storage.

The two-track memory system reinforces an important principle introduced in Chapter 4's description of parallel processing: Mental feats such as vision, thinking, and memory may seem to be single abilities, but they are not. Rather, we split information into different components for separate and simultaneous processing.

"Doc, you're kidding? Someone would've had to get a camera up there!"
"Naturally."
"Hell! You're joking—how the hell would you do that?" Jimmie's wonder was that of a bright young man from 40 years ago reacting with amazement to his travel back to the future.

Careful testing of these unique people reveals something even stranger: Although incapable of recalling new facts or anything they have recently done, Jimmie and other similarly amnesic people can learn. They can be classically conditioned, and with practice they can learn to read mirror-image writing or do a jigsaw puzzle (Schacter, 1992; Squire, 1987). They do all these things with absolutely no memory of having learned them. Or consider what happens when such patients have learned to solve a Tower of Hanoi puzzle, which requires moving rings from one pole to another until they are stacked in order of size. Amnesia victims will deny having seen the puzzle before, insist it is silly for them to try, and then, like a practiced expert, proceed to solve it.

These curious findings make it hard to argue that memory is a single, unified system. Whatever has destroyed the amnesics' conscious recall has not destroyed their unconscious capacity for learning. They can learn *how* to do something—**implicit memory** (*nondeclarative memory*). But they cannot know and declare *that* they know—**explicit memory** (*declarative memory*). Having read a story once, they will read it faster a second time through, showing implicit memory. However, they cannot recall having seen the story before, showing their lack of explicit memory. Having played golf on a new course, they will forget it completely, yet their game will improve with experience on the course. If repeatedly shown the word *perfume*, they wouldn't recall having seen it. But if asked the first word that comes to mind in response to the letters *per*, they surprise themselves by readily displaying their learning. Strangely, they retain their past but do not explicitly recall it (Figure 7–12).

Our explicit and implicit memories involve separate brain systems. Brain scans and autopsies reveal that amnesic patients usually have suffered damage to the **hippocampus**, a limbic system structure that plays a vital role in the gradual processing of our explicit memories for names, images, and events into long-term memory (Figure 7–13). When people recall words (using explicit memory) the hippocampus lights up on a PET scan (Squire & Ojemann, 1992). Chickadees and other birds can store food in hundreds of places and return to these unmarked caches months later, but lose this ability if their hippocampus has been removed (Sherry & Vaccarino, 1989). Among older humans, recall for new words and pictures is impaired if the hippocampus has shrunk (Golomb & others, 1993, 1994).

Your hippocampus is a temporary processing site for your explicit memories, but you could lose it and still lay down memories for skills and conditioned associations. Hoping to locate such implicit memories, psychologist

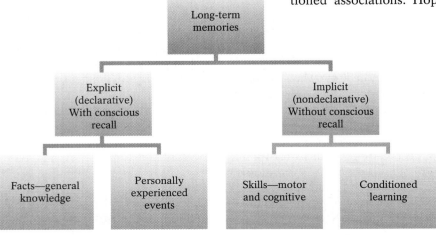

Figure 7–12 Memory Subsystems *Explicit and implicit memories are processed and stored separately. Thus, one may lose explicit memory (becoming amnesic), yet display implicit memory for what can't be explicitly recalled.*

Hippocampus

Figure 7–13 The Hippocampus *Explicit memories for facts and episodes are processed in the hippocampus (blue) and fed to other brain locations for permanent storage.*

Richard Thompson and his fellow sleuths David Krupa and Judith Thompson studied how a rabbit's brain learns to associate a tone with an impending air puff in the eye (and thus to blink in anticipation of the puff). First, they discovered that the pathway connecting the brain's reception of the tone with the blink response runs through a part of the cerebellum (at the back of the head) to the brainstem. If they cut the pathway, the learned response was lost. That was like cutting the cords to your stereo speakers, which would confirm the cord's part in the electronic path but might still leave you wondering where the music is stored. Their next step was to administer a drug during the rabbits' eye-blink training that could temporarily deaden different parts of the neural pathway. This pinpointed the implicit memory—in the cerebellum. The rejuvenated rabbits failed to display the learned response only when the cerebellum was deactivated during training (Krupa & others, 1993).

This dual explicit-implicit memory system helps explain infantile amnesia. The reactions and skills we learned during infancy reach far into our future. Yet as adults we recall nothing (explicitly) of our first 3 years. Our conscious minds are blank, not only because we index so much of our explicit memory by words that nonspeaking children have not learned, but also because the hippocampus is one of the last brain structures to mature.

! *Rehearse It*

9. Sensory information is initially recorded in our sensory memory. This memory may be visual (_____ memory) or auditory (_____ memory).

a. implicit; explicit
b. iconic; echoic
c. declarative; nondeclarative
d. long-term; short-term

10. Our capacity for storing long-term memories is essentially limitless. However, our short-term memory for new information is limited. When confronted with a list of novel items, most people can immediately recall

a. only the first items on the list.
b. a series of about 20 items.
c. a series of about 7 items.
d. only meaningful items.

11. The average adult probably has about 1 billion bits of information in long-term memory, which has a capacity perhaps a thousand to a million times greater than that. Evidence suggests that the best way to learn and remember new information is to

a. undergo hypnosis.
b. undergo electrical stimulation of the motor cortex.
c. systematically forget or discard old memories.
d. relate new information to old.

12. Ebbinghaus found that retention of novel information such as nonsense syllables drops off quickly; 3 days after such a learning session, we have forgotten much of what we learned. Ebbinhaus's forgetting curve shows that as time goes on, our retention of nonsense syllables tends to

a. increase slightly.
b. decrease slightly.
c. decrease greatly.
d. level out.

13. Researchers have found that long-term potentiation (LTP) provides a neural basis for learning and memory. LTP refers to

a. emotion-triggered hormonal changes.
b. the role of the hippocampus in processing explicit memories.
c. an increase in a synapse's firing potential after brief, rapid stimulation.
d. the creation of a memory trace as experiences are processed through the memory system.

14. An amnesic patient who has suffered damage to the hippocampus typically has difficulties in learning new facts and recalling recent events. However, the person may well be able to recall the more distant past and certain well-learned skills, such as how to ride a bicycle or hem a dress. Memories of skills are

a. explicit memories.
b. implicit memories.
c. iconic memories.
d. echoic memories.

15. The physical basis of memory—how and where memories are physically stored in the brain—is not yet well understood. However, research suggests that the hippocampus, a neural center in the limbic system of the brain, plays an important role. The hippocampus may function like

a. a way station between short- and long-term explicit memories.
b. a computer's hard disk.
c. the cortex.
d. a processing center for implicit memories.

Retrieval: Getting Information Out

9. How do we get information out of memory storage?

To most people, memory is **recall**, the ability to retrieve information not in conscious awareness. To a psychologist, memory is any sign that something learned has been retained. So *recognizing* or more quickly *relearning* information also indicates memory.

Long after you cannot recall most of the people in your high school graduating class, you may still recognize their yearbook pictures from a photographic lineup and pick their names out from a list of names. Harry Bahrick and his colleagues (1975) reported that people who graduated 25 years earlier could not *recall* many of their old classmates, but they could *recognize* 90 percent of their pictures and names.

Relearning speed can reveal memory. If you once learned something and then forgot it, you probably will relearn it more quickly than when you learned it originally. When you study for a final exam or resurrect a language used in early childhood, the relearning is easier. Tests of **recognition** and of time spent **relearning** reveal that we remember more than we can recall.

The speed and vastness of our recognition memory dwarfs any librarian's ability to call up information. "Is your friend wearing a new or old outfit?" "Old." "Is this seconds-long movie clip from a film you've ever seen?" "Yes." "Have you ever before seen this person? "No." Before the mouth can form our answer to any of millions of such questions, the mind knows, and knows that it knows.

Retrieval Cues

To retrieve a fact from a library, you need a way to access it. In recognition tests, retrieval cues (such as photographs) provide reminders of information (classmates' names) we could not otherwise recall. Retrieval cues also are guides to where to look. If you want to know what the pyramid on the back of a dollar bill signifies, you might look in *Collier's Encyclopedia* under "dollar," "currency," or "money." But your efforts would be futile. To get the information you want, you would have to look under "Great Seal of the United States" (Hayes, 1981). Like information stored in encyclopedias, memories are inaccessible unless we have the right cues for retrieving them. The more and better learned the retrieval cues, the more accessible the memory.

You can think of a memory as held in storage by a web of associations (J. R. Anderson, 1983). To retrieve a specific memory, you first need to identify one of the strands that leads to it, a process called **priming** (Bower, 1986). Often our associations are activated, or primed, without our awareness. Hearing or seeing the word *rabbit* can unconsciously prime people to spell the spoken word *hair* as *h-a-r-e*. As Figure 7–14 indicates, *rabbit* primes associations with *hare* even though we may not recall having seen or heard *rabbit*.

Remembering Things Past *Even if Madonna and Paul Newman had not become famous, their high school classmates would most likely still recognize their yearbook photos.*

Multiple-choice questions test our:
(a) recall.
(b) recognition.
(c) relearning.
Fill-in-the-blank questions test our _____.
(See page 244.)

Figure 7–14 Priming—Another Type of Implicit Memory
The spreading of associations can unconsciously activate related associations. After seeing or hearing rab-bit, we are later more likely to spell the spoken word hair as h-a-r-e. (Adapted from Bower, 1986.)

Seeing or hearing the word *rabbit* → Activates concept → Primes spelling the spoken word *hair/hare* as *h-a-r-e*

Retrieval cues often prime our memories for earlier experiences. The best retrieval cues come from the associations formed at the time we encode a memory. Before the Watergate hearings, John Dean refreshed his memory "by going through every single newspaper article outlining what had happened and then placing myself and what I had done in a given sequence in time" (Neisser, 1981). Mnemonic devices provide us with handy retrieval cues: ROY G. BIV; HOMES; bun, shoe, tree.

Context Effects

It does help to put yourself back in the context where you experienced something. Duncan Godden and Alan Baddeley (1975) discovered this by having scuba divers listen to a list of words in two different settings, either 10 feet underwater or sitting on the beach. As Figure 7–15 illustrates, the divers recalled more words when they were retested in the same place.

You have probably experienced similar context effects. Returning to where you once lived or to the school you once attended may flood you with retrieval cues and memories. Taking an exam in the same room where you are taught may help a little.

Sometimes, being in a context similar to one we've been in before may trigger the experience of **déjà vu**—that eerie sense that "I've been in this exact situation before." People who pose the question as, "How could I recognize a situation that I'm experiencing for the first time?" may suppose that something paranormal is occurring. Could it be reincarnation ("I must have experienced this in a previous life") or precognition ("I viewed this scene in my mind before experiencing it")? If we pose the question differently ("Why do I feel as if I recognize this situation?"), we can see how our memory system might produce the déjà vu feeling (Alcock, 1981). If we have previously been in a similar situation, although we can't recall what it was, the current situation may be loaded with cues that unconsciously help us to retrieve the earlier experience. Thus, if in such a context you see a stranger who looks and walks like one of your friends, the similarity may give rise to an eerie feeling of recognition. Because the feeling conflicts with your knowing that the person is a stranger, you may think, "I've seen that person in this situation before."

Moods and Memories

Associated words, events, and contexts are not the only retrieval cues. Events in the past may have aroused a specific emotion, which later can prime us to recall its associated events. Cognitive psychologist Gordon Bower (1983) explains: "A specific emotional state is like a specific room in a library into which the subject places memory records, and he can most easily retrieve those records by returning to that same room or emotional state." The things we learn in one state—be it joyful or sad, drunk or sober—are sometimes more easily recalled when we are again in the same state, a subtle phenomenon called *state-dependent memory*. What is learned when drunk, high, or depressed is not recalled well in *any* state (drugs and depression interfere with encoding), but it's recalled slightly better when again drunk, high, or depressed. Someone who hides money when drunk may forget the location, until drunk again.

More striking is a mood's effect on memories (Ellis & Ashbrook, 1989; Matt & others, 1992). We seem to associate good or bad events with their accompanying emotions. Thus, the emotions become retrieval cues; when again feeling good or bad, we more easily recall associated good or bad times. If people are put in a buoyant mood—whether under hypnosis or just by the day's events (a World Cup soccer victory for the German subjects of one study)—they recall the world through rose-colored glasses (Forgas & others, 1984;

Figure 7–15 The Effects of Context on Memory *Words heard underwater are best recalled underwater; words heard on land are best recalled on land. (Adapted from Godden & Baddeley, 1975.)*

recall A measure of memory in which the person must retrieve information learned earlier, as on a fill-in-the-blank test.

recognition A measure of memory in which the person need only identify items previously learned, as on a multiple-choice test.

relearning A memory measure that assesses the amount of time saved when relearning previously learned information.

priming The activation, often unconscious, of particular associations in memory.

déjà vu (A French expression meaning "already seen.") That eerie sense that "I've experienced this before." Cues from the current situation may subconsciously trigger retrieval of an earlier experience.

Schwarz & others, 1987). They judge themselves to be competent and effective, other people to be benevolent, life in general to be wonderful. Put in a bad mood by negative events, the very same people suddenly recall and predict everything more negatively.

So it shouldn't surprise us that in some studies *currently* depressed people recall their parents as having been rejecting, punitive, and guilt-promoting, whereas *formerly* depressed people describe their parents much as do those who have never suffered depression (Lewinsohn & Rosenbaum, 1987; Lewis, 1992). Our memories are somewhat **mood-congruent**. Being depressed sours memories by priming negative associations, which we use to explain our current mood. No wonder Robert Bornstein and others (1991) report that adolescents' ratings of parental warmth give little clue to how the same adolescents will rate their parents 6 weeks later. When teenagers are down, their world, including their parents, seems inhuman; as their mood brightens, their parents metamorphose from devils into angels. You and I may nod our heads knowingly. Yet, in a good or bad mood, we persist in attributing our changing judgments and memories to reality.

Moods also influence how we *interpret* other people's behavior. In a bad mood, we read someone's look as a glare; in a good mood we encode the same look as interest. How we perceive the world depends on our mood. Passions exaggerate.

Your mood's effect on encoding and retrieval helps explain why moods persist. When happy, you recall happy events, which helps prolong the good mood. When depressed, you recall depressing events, which in turn feeds depressing interpretations of current events. As we will see in Chapter 12, this process maintains depression's vicious cycle.

Memory Construction

10. How accurate are our memories?

Picture yourself having the following pleasant experience:

> You enter a restaurant and are seated at a table with a white tablecloth. You study the menu. You tell the waiter that you want prime rib, medium rare, a baked potato with sour cream, and a salad with blue cheese dressing. You also order some red wine from the wine list. A few minutes later the waiter returns with your salad. Later he brings the rest of the meal, which you enjoy, except that the prime rib is a bit overdone.

Were I immediately to quiz you on this paragraph (from Hyde, 1983), you could surely retrieve considerable detail. For example, without looking back, answer the following questions:

1. What kind of salad dressing did you order?
2. Was the tablecloth red checked?
3. What did you order to drink?
4. Did the waiter give you a menu?

You were probably able to recall exactly what you ordered, and maybe even the color of the tablecloth. Does retrieval therefore consist merely of "reading" the information stored in our brain's library? We do have an enormous capacity for storing and reproducing the incidental details of our daily experience. But as we have seen, we often construct our memories as we encode them, and we may also alter our memories as we withdraw them from the memory bank. Like a scientist who infers a dinosaur's appearance from its remains, we infer our past from stored information plus what we now assume.

"When a feeling was there, they felt as if it would never go; when it was gone, they felt as if it had never been; when it returned, they felt as if it had never gone."

George MacDonald
What's Mine's Mine, 1886

---

mood-congruent memory   The tendency to recall experiences that are consistent with one's current good or bad mood.

misinformation effect   After witnessing an event and receiving misleading information about it, incorporating the "misinformation" into one's memory of the event.

Accident

Leading question:
"About how fast
were the cars going
when they *smashed*
into each other?"

Memory construction

Figure 7–16 Memory Construction *When people who saw the film of a car accident were asked a leading question, they recalled a more serious accident than they had witnessed. (From Loftus, 1979.)*

"*Memory is insubstantial. Things keep replacing it. Your batch of snapshots will both fix and ruin your memory. . . . You can't remember anything from your trip except the wretched collection of snapshots.*"

Annie Dillard
"To Fashion a Text," 1988

Did the waiter give you a menu? Not in the paragraph given. Nevertheless, many people answer yes. By filtering information and filling in missing pieces, their schemas for restaurants direct their memory construction.

In many dozens of experiments, involving more than 20,000 people, Elizabeth Loftus has shown how eyewitnesses similarly reconstruct their memories when questioned. In one experiment with John Palmer, Loftus showed a film of a traffic accident and then quizzed the viewers about what they saw (Loftus & Palmer, 1974). Those asked, "How fast were the cars going when they *smashed* into each other?" gave higher speed estimates than those asked, "How fast were the cars going when they *hit* each other?" A week later, the researchers asked the viewers if they recalled seeing any broken glass. Compared with those who had been asked the question with *hit*, those asked the question with *smashed* were more than twice as likely to recall broken glass (Figure 7–16). In fact, there was no broken glass.

In many follow-up experiments around the world, people have witnessed an event, received or not received misleading information about it, and then taken a memory test. The repeated result is a **misinformation effect**: After exposure to subtle misinformation, many people misremember. They have misrecalled a yield sign as a stop sign, hammers as screwdrivers, Coke cans as peanut cans, *Vogue* magazine as *Mademoiselle*, "Dr. Henderson" as "Dr. Davidson," breakfast cereal as eggs, and a clean-shaven man as a man with a mustache (Loftus & others, 1989). As a memory fades with time following an event, the injection of misinformation becomes easier (Loftus, 1992).

So unwitting is the misinformation effect that people later find it nearly impossible to discriminate between their memories of real and suggested events (Schooler & others, 1986). This difficulty was strikingly true among those who 3 years later misrecalled their whereabouts on hearing of the space shuttle *Challenger*'s explosion (Neisser & Harsch, 1992). When shown their own handwritten accounts from the day after, many were surprised. Some were so sure of their made-up memories that they insisted their original version must have been flawed.

As people recount an experience, they fill in their memory gaps with plausible guesses and assumptions. After more retellings, they often recall these guessed details, now absorbed into their memories, as if they actually observed them (Roediger & others, 1993). Others' vivid retellings may also implant false memories. The psychologist Jean Piaget was startled as an adult to learn that his vivid, detailed memory of his nursemaid's thwarting his kidnapping was utterly false. Piaget apparently constructed the memory from the many retellings of the story he had heard (later confessed by the nursemaid to have been false).

Note that Piaget remembered, but misattributed his memory to the wrong source (to his own experiences rather than to his nursemaid's stories). When we encode memories, we distribute different aspects of them to different parts of our brains. One of the frailest parts of a memory is its source. Thus we may recognize someone but have no idea where we have seen the person. We retain the image, but not the context in which we acquired it.

Debra Poole and Stephen Lindsay (1995) replicated Piaget's "source amnesia" by having preschoolers interact with Mr. Science, who engaged them in demonstrations such as blowing up a balloon with baking soda and vinegar. Three months later, their parents, on three successive days, read them a story about themselves and Mr. Science, describing some things they had experienced and some they had not. When asked by a new interviewer what Mr. Science had done with them, 4 in 10 children spontaneously recalled Mr. Science doing things that were only mentioned in the story.

The moral: Memory is reconstruction as well as reproduction. You therefore can't be sure whether a memory is real by how real it feels. Unreal memories feel like real memories. In experiments on eyewitness testimony, researchers have repeatedly found that the most confident eyewitnesses are the most persuasive, but they often are not the most accurate. Eyewitnesses, whether right or wrong, express roughly similar self-assurance (Bothwell & others, 1987; Cutler & Penrod, 1989; Wells & Murray, 1984).

Memory construction helps explain why John Dean's recollections of the Watergate conversations were a mixture of real and imagined events. It explains why "hypnotically refreshed" memories of crimes so easily incorporate errors, some of which originate with the hypnotist's leading questions. ("Did you hear loud noises?") And it explains why dating partners who fall in love *over*estimate their first impressions of one another, while those who break up *under*estimate their earlier liking (McFarland & Ross, 1987).

Recognizing that the misinformation effect can occur as police and attorneys ask questions framed by their own understandings of an event, Ronald Fisher, Edward Geiselman, and their colleagues (1987, 1989) train police interviewers to ask less suggestive, more effective questions. To activate retrieval cues, the detective first asks witnesses to visualize the scene—the weather, time of day, lighting, sounds, smells, positions of objects, and their mood. Then the witness tells in detail, and without interruption, every point recalled, no matter how trivial. Only then does the detective ask evocative follow-up questions: "Was there anything unusual about the person's appearance or clothing?" Using this "cognitive interview" technique, Fisher and Geiselman report that accurate recall increases by some 50 percent.

Children's Eyewitness Recall

If memories can be sincere, yet so sincerely wrong, might children's recollections of sexual abuse err? Who is most often victimized—abused children whose recollections are disbelieved, or those falsely accused whose reputations are ruined? Both sides in this emotional debate agree that

- child sexual abuse occurs and can leave a person scarred—more vulnerable to low self-image, sexual promiscuity, anxiety, and depression (Briere & Runtz, 1993; Trickett & Putnam, 1993).
- some innocent people, occasionally those caught in a child custody conflict, suffer the injustice of false accusations.
- some perpetrators hide their guilt by casting doubt on their truth-telling accusers.

At issue is the credibility of children's reports. By asking leading questions, can interviewers plant false memories of a story they expect to hear? Are children credible eyewitnesses in cases of murder, assault, and robbery? Research—most of it conducted in just the last decade—suggests that the truth lies between the two extremes (Brooks & Siegal, 1991; Ceci & Bruck, 1993a,b; Doris, 1991). Children are not, as some believe, as reliable and resistant to suggestion as are adults. In 15 of 18 studies, preschoolers were more suggestible than were older children or adults. In one study of nearly 2000 people who had watched a film clip while visiting a San Francisco science museum, younger children were especially susceptible to the misinformation effect (Loftus & others, 1992). But children also do not, as others believe, routinely confuse reality with fantasy. If questioned about their experiences in words they understand, they often freely recall what happened and who did it. Children are especially credible when their disclosure is made in a first interview with a neutral person who asks nonleading questions, when involved adults have not talked with them prior to the interview, and when their story is consistent over time.

As a father of a young child, Stephen Ceci (1993) thinks "it would be truly awful to ever lose sight of the enormity of child abuse." Yet his and Maggie

"Memory isn't like reading a book: It's more like writing a book from fragmentary notes."

Psychologist John F. Kihlstrom (1994)

Answers to questions on page 240: Multiple-choice questions test recognition. Fill-in-the-blank questions test recall.

Bruck's (1993a,b) studies of children's memories have sensitized them to children's suggestibility. In one study, 3-year-olds were asked to show on anatomically correct dolls where a pediatrician had touched them. Fifty-five percent of the children who had not received genital examinations showed either genital or anal touching.

In another study, a child chose a card from a deck of possible happenings and an adult then read from the card. For example, "Think real hard, and tell me if this ever happened to you. Can you remember going to the hospital with the mousetrap on your finger?" After 10 weekly interviews, with the same adult repeatedly asking children to think about several real and fictitious events, a new adult asked the same question. The stunning result: 58 percent of preschoolers produced false (often vivid) stories regarding one or more events they had never experienced. Here is one from a boy who initially had denied the mousetrap incident (Ceci & others, 1994):

> My brother Colin was trying to get Blowtorch [an action figure] from me, and I wouldn't let him take it from me, so he pushed me into the wood pile where the mousetrap was. And then my finger got caught in it. And then we went to the hospital, and my mommy, daddy, and Colin drove me there, to the hospital in our van, because it was far away. And the doctor put a bandage on this finger.

Given such detailed stories, professional psychologists who specialize in interviewing children were often fooled. They could not reliably separate real from false memories. Nor could the children themselves. One child, reminded that his parents had several times told him that the mousetrap incident never happened—he had only imagined it—protested, "But it really did happen. I remember it!"

Forgetting as Retrieval Failure

11. What causes retrieval failure?

We have seen that forgetting occurs when we fail to encode information and when our stored memories decay. Forgotten events are like books you can't find in your library—some because you never acquired them, others because they were discarded.

There is a third possibility: Even if the book is stored and available, it may be inaccessible. Perhaps you don't have the information needed to look it up and retrieve it. Information sometimes gets into our brain and, though we know it is there, we cannot get it out. A person's name may lie poised on the *tip of the tongue*, waiting to be retrieved. When people who cannot recall information get retrieval cues ("It begins with an *m*"), they often remember what they could not recall. Retrieval problems lie behind the occasional memory failures of older adults. (As Chapter 3 noted, older people tend to recall less than younger adults do, but they usually remember as well if given reminders or a recognition test.)

"[The] research leads me to worry about the possibility of false allegations. It is not a tribute to one's scientific integrity to walk down the middle of the road if the data are more to one side."

Stephen Ceci (1993)

How Do We Forget? *Forgetting can occur as a result of failure to retrieve information from long-term memory.*

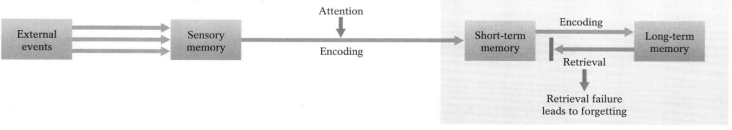

*Pro*active means forward-acting.

*Retro*active means backward-acting.

French, learned **beforehand**, interferes proactively

Proactive interference

Spanish, learned **afterwards**, interferes retroactively

Retroactive interference

Figure 7–17 Proactive and Retroactive Interference

Figure 7–18 Retroactive Interference *More forgetting of the syllables occurred when a person stayed awake and experienced other new material. (From Jenkins & Dallenbach, 1924.)*

Interference

Learning some items may interfere with retrieving others, especially when the items are similar. If someone gives you a phone number to remember, you may be able to recall it later. But if two more people give you their numbers, each successive number will be more difficult to recall. Such **proactive interference** occurs when something you learned earlier disrupts recall of something you experienced later. As you collect more and more information, your mental attic never fills, but it certainly gets cluttered.

For example, after buying a new combination lock or receiving a new phone number, the old one may interfere. Benton Underwood (1957) explored this phenomenon. He found that people who learn different lists of words on successive days have more and more difficulty remembering each new list the next day. This proactive interference explains why Ebbinghaus, after memorizing countless lists of nonsense syllables during his career, could remember only about one-fourth of a new list of syllables on the day after he learned it—far fewer than you as a novice could remember after learning a single list.

Retroactive interference occurs when new information makes it harder to recall something you learned earlier. For example, the learning of new students' names typically interferes with a professor's recall of names learned in previous classes. Figure 7–17 illustrates both types of interference.

You can minimize retroactive interference by reducing the number of interfering events—say, by going to sleep shortly after learning new information. This is what John Jenkins and Karl Dallenbach (1924) found in a classic experiment. Day after day, two people each learned some nonsense syllables, then tried to recall them after up to 8 hours of being awake or asleep at night. As Figure 7–18 shows, forgetting occurred more rapidly after being awake and involved with other activities. The investigators surmised that "forgetting is not so much a matter of the decay of old impressions and associations as it is a matter of interference, inhibition, or obliteration of the old by the new" (p. 612). Later experiments have confirmed that the hour before a night's sleep (though not the minute before sleep) is a good time to commit information to memory (Fowler & others, 1973).

Although interference is an important cause of forgetting, we should not overstate the point. Sometimes old information facilitates our learning of new information. Knowledge of Latin may aid one's learning of French—a phenomenon called *positive transfer*. It's when the old and new information compete with each other that interference occurs.

proactive interference The disruptive effect of prior learning on the recall of new information.

retroactive interference The disruptive effect of new learning on the recall of old information.

repression In psychoanalytic theory, the basic defense mechanism that banishes anxiety–arousing thoughts, feelings, and memories from consciousness.

"[It is] necessary to remember that events happened in the desired manner. And if it is necessary to rearrange one's memories . . . then it is necessary to forget that one has done so. The trick of doing this can be learned like any other mental technique. . . . It is called doublethink."

George Orwell *1984*, 1948

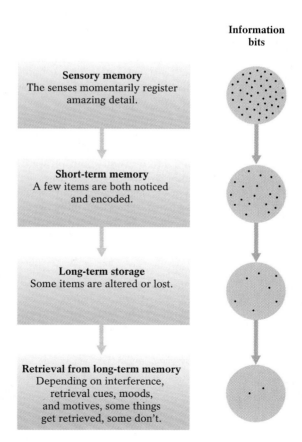

Information bits

Sensory memory
The senses momentarily register amazing detail.

Short-term memory
A few items are both noticed and encoded.

Long-term storage
Some items are altered or lost.

Retrieval from long-term memory
Depending on interference, retrieval cues, moods, and motives, some things get retrieved, some don't.

When Do We Forget? *Forgetting can occur at any memory stage. As we process information, we filter, alter, or lose much of it.*

Motivated Forgetting

The huge cookie jar in our kitchen was jammed with freshly baked chocolate chip cookies. Still more spread across the cooling racks on the counter. Twenty-four hours later, not a crumb was left. Who had taken them? My wife, three children, and I were the only people in the house during that time. So while memories were still fresh, I immediately conducted a little memory test. Andy acknowledged wolfing down as many as 20. Peter admitted eating 15. Laura guessed that she had stuffed her then-6-year-old body with 15 cookies. My wife, Carol, recalled eating 6, and I remembered consuming 15 and taking 18 more to the office. Collectively, we sheepishly accepted responsibility for 89 cookies. Still, we had not come close; 160 cookies had been baked.

In experiments that parallel the cookie-memory phenomenon, Michael Ross and his colleagues (1981) found that people unknowingly revise their own histories. After Ross persuaded a group of people that frequent toothbrushing is desirable, they (more than other people) recalled having frequently brushed their teeth in the last 2 weeks. Having taken a highly touted study skills course, students later inflated their estimates of self-improvement. By *de*flating their evaluations of their previous study habits they convinced themselves that they had really benefitted (Conway & Ross, 1984). To remember our past is often to revise it. By recalling events in a desired manner we protect and enhance our self-images.

Why do our memories fail us? Why did my family and I not encode, store, and retrieve so many of the instances of our cookie-eating? As noted earlier, we encode information about frequency fairly automatically. So was it a storage problem? Might our memories of cookies, like Ebbinghaus's memory of nonsense syllables, have vanished almost as fast as the cookies themselves? Or might the information still be intact but irretrievable because it would be embarrassing to remember?

With his concept of **repression**, Sigmund Freud proposed that with more painful information our memory systems are indeed self-censoring. To protect our self-concepts and to minimize anxiety, we supposedly repress painful memories. But the submerged memory still lingers, said Freud, and with patience and effort may be retrieved during therapy or by some later cue. One reported case involved a woman with an intense, unexplained fear of running water. An aunt solved the mystery one day by whispering, "I have never told." The words cued the woman's memory of an incident when, as a disobedient young child, she wandered away from a family picnic and became trapped under a waterfall—until being rescued by her aunt, who promised not to tell her parents (Kihlstrom, 1990).

Stories such as this have persuaded most clinicians that repression of painful memories can indeed occur. There are also anecdotes of stressed battlefield survivors who, for a time afterward, cannot remember their horror-filled experience. But not all memory researchers are convinced. "Repression folklore is . . . partly refuted, partly untested, and partly untestable," says Elizabeth Loftus (1995). After analyzing case reports of temporary battlefield amnesia, David Holmes (1994) reports that most "recovered memories" were unconfirmed and occurred during hypnosis, with drugs, or with role-playing suggested by the therapist. Physiological causes of memory loss, such as concussions, were not ruled out. In laboratory experiments, people have not been more likely to forget unpleasant experiences than pleasant ones. And in real life, most people remember horrible experiences all too well (see "Thinking Critically About Repressed Memories of Abuse"). Holocaust survivors and those who suffer other traumatic stresses seldom forget. "The things we remember best," noted Spanish philosopher Baltasar Gracián in 1647, "are those better forgotten."

Repressed Memories of Abuse

Serious questions lie at the heart of an intense controversy over reports of repressed and recovered memories of childhood sexual abuse. Without disputing the all-too-common reality and horror of such abuse, critics use principles of memory construction to question the reality of repressed memories.

In 1974, 4-year-old Rachel (not her real name) and two others were molested by Rachel's uncle. Rachel told her mother, who informed the mother of one of the others, who proceeded to stab and kill the uncle. Seventeen years later, psychologist Linda Meyer Williams (1995) tracked down Rachel and 128 other women who were recorded as having experienced child sex abuse (sexual intercourse or fondling). When asked whether she had ever been sexually abused as a child or whether any family members had ever gotten into trouble for their sexual behavior, Rachel calmly said no, then added: "Oh wait a minute. . . . My uncle sexually assaulted someone. . . . I never met my uncle (my mother's brother), he died before I was born. You see, he molested a little boy. When the little boy's mother found out that her son was molested, she took a butcher knife and stabbed my uncle in the heart, killing him."

Rachel was but one of 49 victims—38 percent of those interviewed—who did not spontaneously recall the specific reported incident of their own abuse (although most did recall other traumatic sexual experiences). Elsewhere, scores of alleged victims have come forward claiming to have *recovered* memories of abuse. Ellen Bass and Laura Davis (1988), authors of the popular incest-recovery manual *The Courage to Heal*, have even offered a long list of incest survivor characteristics, including feelings of shame, powerlessness, unworthiness, vulnerability, perfectionism, and deficient goals and motivation. If you have some of these feelings, don't be sur-

prised if you have no memory of sexual abuse, some therapists have said, because "denial" and "repression" are common. "If you are unable to remember any specific instances . . . but still have a feeling that something abusive happened to you, it probably did," say Bass and Davis (pp. 21–22). "If you think you were abused and your life shows the symptoms, then you were."

Believing this, some therapists have reasoned with patients that "people who've been abused often have your symptoms, so you probably were abused. Let's see if, aided by hypnosis or drugs, or helped to dig back and visualize your trauma, you can recover it." In one recent survey of British and American doctoral-level therapists, 7 in 10 said they had used such techniques to help clients recover suspected repressed memories of childhood sexual abuse (Poole & others, 1995).

Often, the patient then does form an image of a threatening person. With further visualization, the image grows more vivid, leaving the patient stunned, angry, and ready to confront or sue the equally stunned and devastated parent or other relative, who, as the therapist has predicted, vigorously denies the accusation. One woman in her 32nd therapy session recalled that her father had abused her at age 15 months. After such aided recall, actress Roseanne Barr Arnold (1991) claimed to recall sexual abuse beginning in infancy.

Persuading adult women that their fathers were incestuous is understandably tearing families apart, thousands of which have sought advice from the "False Memory Syndrome Foundation," established in 1992. Without questioning the professionalism of most therapists, the skeptics say that the uncorroborated accusations suggested by some therapists are a 1990s reenactment of the Salem witch trials. The trouble with working from symptoms to cause, notes Carol

Tavris (1993), is that the symptom list is "general enough to include everybody at least sometimes. Nobody doesn't fit it." Moreover, people feel unworthy, ashamed, and perfectionistic for so many reasons that the symptoms hardly prove any one cause.

Psychologists committed to protecting abused children and those committed to protecting wrongly accused adults agree on the following:

- Incest happens, more often than we once supposed. Although there is no characteristic "survivor syndrome" (Kendell-Tackett & others, 1993), sexual abuse can leave its victims predisposed to problems ranging from sexual dysfunction to depression.

- Forgetting happens. Like Rachel, notes Elizabeth Loftus (1995), many of the women interviewed by Linda Meyer Williams were very young when abused or may not have understood the meaning of their experience—circumstances under which forgetting is "utterly common." Forgetting of isolated past events, both negative and positive, is an ordinary part of everyday life.

- Recovered memories are commonplace. Cued by a remark or an experience, we recover memories of long-forgotten events, both pleasant and unpleasant. The debate concerns whether the unconscious mind sometimes forcibly represses painful experiences and, if so, whether these can be retrieved by certain therapist-aided techniques.

- Memories "recovered" under hypnosis or the influence of drugs are unreliable. (Recall from Chapter 5 the ease with which "regressed" hypnotized subjects incorporate suggestions into their memories, even memories of "past lives.")

- Memories of things happening before age 3 are also unreliable, because people don't reliably recall happenings of any sort from their first 3 years—a phenomenon called *infantile amnesia*.

- Memories, whether real or false, can be emotionally upsetting. If a false memory of abuse becomes a real part of one's history, the client as well as the family may suffer. But then real traumas, too, can cause lasting suffering.

- Although repression has not been confirmed experimentally, most clinicians continue to believe that repression (or at least not thinking about a painful experience) happens.

TODAY'S SPECIAL GUEST

BRUNDAGE MORNALD, OF BATTLE CREEK, MONTANA

UNDER HYPNOSIS, MR. MORNALD RECOVERED LONG-BURIED MEMORIES OF A PERFECTLY NORMAL, HAPPY CHILDHOOD.

Drawing by Lorenz; © 1993
The New Yorker Magazine, Inc.

Without knowing a person's initial experience (as we do in memory experiments) it is difficult to assess the person's memory. Nevertheless, to many memory researchers, the idea that people literally record, then repress, then recover painful experiences is scientifically naive. There just isn't evidence, notes David Holmes (1990, 1994), that an event can be repressed for years, and then accurately reproduced. With rare exceptions, most negative emotional events are actually remembered well (Christianson, 1992). In one study of 5- to 10-year-old children who had witnessed a parent's murder, not one repressed the memory; to the contrary, the unforgettable experience haunted them, like a flashbulb memory (Malmquist, 1986). Holocaust survivors remember all too well the Nazi atrocities (Helmreich, 1992, 1994). And in most child abuse cases that are substantiated with corroborating photos, diaries, testimony, or admitted guilt, victims never forget their horrific experiences. The family secret may be undisclosed, but it is not forgotten.

Moreover, 20 years of research on the misinformation effect reveals how easily and unwittingly people can fabricate false memories. Elizabeth Loftus and James Coan (in press) have demonstrated this by experimentally implanting false childhood memories. They had a trusted family member recall for a teenager three real childhood experiences and a false one—a vivid account of the child's being lost for an extended time in a shopping mall at age 5 until being rescued by an elderly person. Two days later, one subject, Chris, said, "That day I was so scared that I would never see my family again." Two days after that he began to visualize the flannel shirt, bald head, and glasses of the old man who supposedly had found him. Told the story was made up, Chris was incredulous: "I thought I remembered being lost . . . and looking around for the guys. I do remember that, and then crying, and Mom coming up and saying, 'Where were you? Don't you . . . ever do that again.'" Such is the memory construction process by which people can recall being abducted by UFOs, victimized by a satanic cult, molested in a crib, or having lived a past life.

Loftus knows firsthand the phenomenon she studies. At a recent family reunion, an uncle told her that at 14, she found her mother's drowned body. Shocked, she denied it. But the uncle was adamant, and over the next few days she began to wonder if *she* had a repressed memory. "Maybe that's why I'm so obsessed with this topic." As the now-upset Loftus pondered her uncle's suggestion, she "recovered" an image of her mother lying in the pool, face down, and of herself finding the body. "I started putting everything into place. Maybe that's why I'm such a workaholic. Maybe that's why I'm so emotional when I think about her even though she died in 1959."

Then her brother called and said there was a mistake. The uncle had double-checked his story. Loftus had not found the body after all (Monaghan, 1992).

But then again, after being molested by a male baby-sitter at age 6 (and not forgetting), Loftus also knows firsthand the reality of sexual abuse. And that makes her wary of those whom she sees as trivializing real abuse by suggesting and probing for uncorroborated traumatic experiences, then accepting them uncritically as fact. The enemies of the truly victimized are not only those who prey and those who deny, she says, but those whose writings and allegations "are bound to lead to an increased likelihood that society in general will disbelieve the genuine cases of childhood sexual abuse that truly deserve our sustained attention" (Loftus, 1993).

Elizabeth Loftus *"People in general and jurors in particular have a lot of misconceptions about the way memory works"* (quoted by Monaghan, 1992).

! *Rehearse It*

16. To measure long-term memory, psychologists test a person's ability to *recall* information. They also test ability to *recognize* what has been learned and they measure *relearning* time. A psychologist who asks you to write down as many objects as you can remember having seen a few minutes earlier is testing your

a. recall.
b. recognition.
c. recall and recognition.
d. relearning.

17. To gain access to a memory, a person activates an association that leads to that memory. The association may be activated by a specific odor, visual image, or mnemonic; all of these are examples of

a. relearning.
b. déjà vu.
c. declarative memories.
d. retrieval cues.

18. In order to retrieve a memory, it is sometimes helpful to return to the setting where the event occurred. In some cases, retrieval may be enhanced by a context similar to one you have already experienced. The resulting feeling that "you've been there before" is referred to as

a. déjà vu.
b. mood-congruent memory.
c. relearning.
d. the misinformation effect.

19. When happy, we tend to recall happy times. When depressed, we more often recall depressing events. This tendency to recall experiences that are consistent with our current emotions is called

a. mnemonics.
b. chunking.
c. repression
d. mood-congruent memory.

20. Because we often alter information as we encode it and because we tend to fill in memory gaps with our assumptions about events, our memories are generally not exact reproductions of events. One reason for this memory reconstruction is

a. proactive interference.
b. the misinformation effect.

c. retroactive interference.
d. the eyewitness recall effect.

21. Experiments show that the hour before sleep is a good time to memorize information. For example, studying a vocabulary list before going to sleep minimizes the disrupting effects of all the other new words and terms that might, in the course of a school day, claim our attention. Going to sleep after learning new material minimizes

a. the misinformation effect.
b. amnesia.
c. retroactive interference.
d. proactive interference.

22. People unknowingly revise or rearrange their memories of events. According to Sigmund Freud, painful or unacceptable memories are self-censored, or blocked from consciousness, through a mechanism called

a. repression.
b. proactive interference.
c. anxiety.
d. physical decay of the memory trace.

Improving Memory

12. How might we apply memory principles to everyday situations, such as remembering a person's name, or even the material of this chapter?

Now and then we are dismayed at our forgetfulness—at our embarrassing inability to recall someone's name, at forgetting to bring up a point in conversation, at forgetting to bring along something important, at finding ourselves standing in a room unable to recall why we are there (Herrmann, 1982). What can we do to minimize such lapses? Much as biology benefits medicine and botany benefits agriculture, can the psychology of memory benefit education? Sprinkled throughout this chapter and summarized here for easy reference are concrete suggestions for improving memory. The SQ3R—*S*urvey, *Q*uestion, *R*ead, *R*ehearse, *R*eview—study technique introduced in Chapter 1 incorporates several of these strategies.

▶ ***Study repeatedly to boost long-term recall.*** Overlearn. To learn a name, say it to yourself after being introduced; wait a few seconds and say it again; wait longer and say it again. To provide many separate study sessions, make use of life's little intervals—riding on the bus, walking across campus, waiting for class to start.

▶ *Spend more time rehearsing or actively thinking about the material.* Speed-reading (skimming) complex material—with minimal rehearsal—yields little retention. Rehearsal and critical reflection help more. It pays to study actively!

▶ *Make the material personally meaningful.* To build a network of retrieval cues, take thorough text and class notes in your own words. Mindlessly repeating information is relatively ineffective. Better to form images, understand and organize information, relate the material to what you already know or have experienced, and put it in your own words. Without such cues, you may be stuck when a question uses phrasing different from the rote forms you memorized. To increase retrieval cues, form as many associations as possible.

▶ *To remember a list of unfamiliar items, use mnemonic devices.* Associate items with peg-words. Make up a story that incorporates vivid images of the items. Chunk information into acronyms.

▶ *Refresh your memory by activating retrieval cues.* Mentally re-create the situation and the mood in which the original learning occurred. Return to the same location. Jog your memory by allowing one thought to cue the next.

▶ *Minimize interference.* Study before sleeping. Don't study in close proximity topics that are likely to interfere with each other, such as Spanish and French.

▶ *Test your own knowledge, both to rehearse it and to help determine what you do not yet know.* If you must later *recall* information, do not be lulled into overconfidence by your ability to *recognize* it. Test your recall. Outline sections on a blank page. Define concepts before reading their marginal definitions. Take practice tests; the study guides that accompany many texts, including this one, can help, as will the periodic "Rehearse It" sections.

> *"Knit each new thing on to some acquisition already there."*
>
> William James
> *Principles of Psychology,* 1890

Thinking and Memory   *Most of what we know is not the result of efforts to memorize. We learn because we're curious and because we spend time thinking about our experiences. Actively thinking as we read often yields the best retention.*

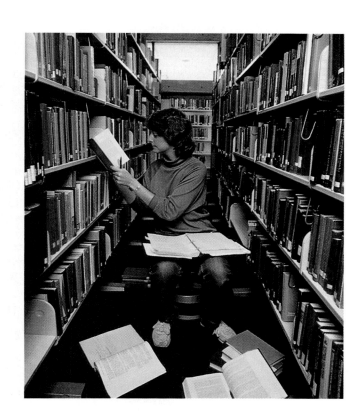

Reviewing *Memory*

The Phenomenon of Memories

1.   How do psychologists describe the human memory system?

Memory is the persistence of learning over time. The computer is one convenient model for thinking about human memory. Both systems must encode, store, and retrieve information. Both feature long-term storage, from which we can activate information into a working memory; in computers, part of this working memory is displayed on screen. On-screen memory is similar to our short-term memory; unless used or rehearsed, it quickly disappears.

Encoding: Getting Information In

2.   How do the sights, sounds, and other sensations we experience get selectively encoded and transferred into the memory system?

Some types of information, notably concerning space, time, and frequency, we encode mostly automatically. Other types of information, including much of our processing of meaning, imagery, and organization, require effort.

3.   How much does rehearsal aid in forming memories?

Without rehearsal, much information (such as a new phone number) is lost within 3 seconds. The more we rehearse information, the better we retain it—especially if our rehearsal is spaced out over time rather than massed. When learning a list of words or names, our later recall is often best for those learned first, which we may have rehearsed more.

4.   What methods of effortful processing aid in forming memories?

Effortful encoding of meaning, imagery, and organization enhances long-term retention. Mnemonic devices exploit the memorability of visual images and of information that is organized into chunks. Organizing information into hierarchies also aids memory.

Storage: Retaining Information

5.   How does sensory memory work?

We have a precise but fleeting iconic (photographic) memory for visual stimuli and a slightly longer-lasting echoic memory for auditory stimuli.

6.   What are the limits of short-term memory?

In the short run, our memory span for information just presented is very limited—up to about seven or eight items, depending on the information and how it is presented.

7.   How large and durable is our long-term memory?

Our capacity for storing information permanently is essentially unlimited. Nevertheless, most of what we learn is soon forgotten; the brain does not store information with the durabilty and exactness of a tape recorder.

8.   How are memories recorded in the brain?

The search for the physical basis of memory has recently focused on brain circuits, synapses, neurotransmitters, and hormones. One brain structure, the hippocampus, processes explicit memories; implicit memories involve different brain mechanisms.

Retrieval: Getting Information Out

9.   How do we get information out of memory storage?

To be remembered, information that is "in there" must be retrieved, with the aid of associations (cues) that serve as reminders. Even mood can be a retrieval cue, leading us to recall happy times when happy, sad times when sad.

10.   How accurate are our memories?

Memories are not stored as exact copies, and they certainly are not retrieved as such. Rather, we construct our memories, using both stored and new information. Thus, when eyewitnesses are subtly exposed to misinformation after an event, they often believe they saw the misleading details as part of the event. This seems especially true of young children.

11.   What causes retrieval failure?

One explanation of forgetting is that we fail to encode information for entry into our memory system. Without effortful processing, much of what we sense we never notice or process. Some of what we encode is altered or lost in memory storage. Retrieval failure may be caused by proactive or retroactive interference, by insufficient cues, or even by motivated forgetting (repression).

Improving Memory

12.   How might we apply memory principles to everyday situations, such as remembering a person's name, or even the material of this chapter?

The psychology of memory suggests concrete strategies for improving memory. These include repeated, spaced study; active rehearsal; encoding of well-organized, vivid, meaningful associations; mnemonic techniques; the return to contexts and moods that are rich with associations; minimizing interference; and self-testing and rehearsal.

Terms and Concepts to Remember

memory, p. 223

amnesia, p. 223

flashbulb memory, p. 224

encoding, p. 225

storage, p. 225

retrieval, p. 225

long-term memory, p. 225

short-term memory, p. 225

automatic processing, p. 226

effortful processing, p. 226

rehearsal, p. 226

spacing effect, p. 227

serial position effect, p. 227

imagery, p. 229

mnemonics [nih-MON-iks], p. 229

chunking, p. 230

sensory memory, p. 233

iconic memory, p. 233

echoic memory, p. 233

long-term potentiation (LTP), p. 236

implicit memory, p. 238

explicit memory, p. 238

hippocampus, p. 238

recall, p. 240

recognition, p. 240

relearning, p. 240

priming, p. 240

déjà vu, p. 241

mood-congruent memory, p. 242

misinformation effect, p. 243

proactive interference, p. 246

retroactive interference, p. 246

repression, p. 247

Rehearse It Answer Key

1. b.   **2.** b.   **3.** c.   **4.** b.   **5.** a.   **6.** d.   **7.** c.   **8.** d.   **9.** b.

10. c.   **11.** d.   **12.** d.   **13.** c.   **14.** b.   **15.** a.   **16.** a.   **17.** d.   **18.** a.

19. d.   **20.** b.   **21.** c.   **22.** a.

Critical Thinking Exercise

Now that you have read and reviewed Chapter 7, take your learning a step further by testing your critical thinking skills on the following passage.

Danny just happened to be driving into the parking lot of a convenience store the night it was held up and the attendant was killed. He caught a quick glimpse of a man running from the store, carrying what appeared to be a handgun. When the police arrived at the scene, Danny was unable to provide much detail about the gunman's appearance. Nevertheless, they took him to headquarters and showed him hundreds of mug book photographs. Believing that a man named Raymond had committed the crime, the investigator showed Danny Raymond's photograph several times. After many frustrating hours, during which Danny was unable to identify the killer conclusively, the investigator handed Danny the photograph of Raymond, saying "We know this man visited the convenience store the night of the crime. Is that the man you saw running from the store?" When Danny said he wasn't sure, he was allowed to leave and asked to think more carefully about what he had seen that night.

Three weeks later, Danny was asked to pick the killer from a line-up of five men, one of whom was Raymond. Although he remembered feeling uncertain of the identity of the man when he was first questioned, Danny was surprised at how easily and confidently he picked Raymond from the line-up now.

1.   Why couldn't Danny identify the gunman right after he witnessed him fleeing from the store?

2.   Why was Danny able to identify Raymond from the line-up several weeks later?

Check your progress on becoming a critical thinker by comparing your answers to the sample answers found in Appendix B.

Chapter 8

Thinking, Language, and Intelligence

Thinking

Concepts

Solving Problems

Making Decisions and Forming Judgments

Language

Language Development

Animal Language

Thinking and Language

Intelligence

Assessing Intelligence

What Is Intelligence?

Genetic and Environmental Influences on Intelligence

Group Differences

Throughout history, we humans have deplored our foolishness and celebrated our wisdom. In a moment of humility the psalmist wondered, "What are human beings that you are mindful of them?" but in the next breath rhapsodized that human beings were "little lower than God." The poet T. S. Eliot was struck by "the hollow men . . . Headpiece filled with straw." But Shakespeare's Hamlet extolled the human species as "noble in reason! . . . infinite in faculties! . . . in apprehension how like a god!" In the preceding chapters, we, too, have sometimes marveled at our capabilities, sometimes at our propensity to err.

We have studied the human brain—a mere 3 pounds of tissue containing circuitry far more complex than the planet's telephone networks. We have marveled at the competence of newborn infants. We have appreciated the human sensory system, which disassembles visual stimuli into millions of nerve impulses, distributes them for parallel processing, and then reassembles them into clear and colorful perceived images. We have acknowledged the seemingly limitless capacity of human memory and the ease with which we process information, consciously and unconsciously. Little wonder, then, that our species has the genius to invent the camera, the car, and the computer; to unlock the atom and crack the genetic code; to travel into space and probe the oceans' depths.

At the same time, we have seen that our species is kin to the other animals, influenced by principles that produce learning in rats and pigeons. We have noted that we form-fit reality into our preconceptions and succumb to perceptual illusions. We have seen how easily we deceive ourselves about pseudopsychic claims, hypnotic regression, and constructed memories. Little wonder, then, that we sometimes imagine we can read minds and travel outside our bodies; that we form distorted images of other ethnic, age, and gender groups; that we are subject to the same biological impulses as other creatures.

In this chapter, we encounter further instances of these two images of the human condition—the rational and the irrational. We will see how we form concepts, solve problems, and make judgments. We will look at our flair for language and ask whether our species alone is capable of language. We will consider the roots of our intelligence. In the end, we will reflect on how deserving we are of our name, *Homo sapiens*—wise human.

Thinking

Previous chapters explained how we receive, perceive, store, and retrieve information. Now we consider how our cognitive system uses this information. Thinking, or **cognition**, is the mental activity associated with processing, understanding, and communicating information. *Cognitive psychologists* study these mental activities, including the logical and sometimes illogical ways in which we create concepts, solve problems, make decisions, and form judgments. We begin this chapter with the building blocks of thinking.

Concepts

1. What functions do concepts serve?

To think about the countless events, objects, and people in our world, we simplify things. We group them into **concepts**, mental groupings of similar objects, events, and people. The concept *chair* sums up a variety of items—a baby's high chair, a wing chair, the chairs around a dining room table, a dentist's chair.

Imagine life without concepts. We would need a different name for every object and idea. We could not ask a child to "throw the ball" because there would be no concept of ball. Instead of saying, "They were angry," we would have to describe facial expressions, vocal intensities, gestures, and words. Concepts such as *ball* and *anger* provide much information with a minimum of cognitive effort.

To simplify things further, we organize concepts into hierarchies. Cab drivers organize their cities into geographical sectors, which subdivide into neighborhoods and again into blocks. The earliest naturalists simplified and ordered the overwhelming complexity of some 5 million living species by clustering them into two basic categories—the plant kingdom and the animal kingdom. Then they divided these basic categories into smaller and smaller subcategories—vertebrates, bony fish, and Atlantic salmon, for instance, in order of increasing specificity. Classifying the world into hierarchies of concepts makes for cognitive efficiency.

We use definitions to form some concepts. Told the rule that a triangle has three sides, we thereafter classify all three-sided geometric forms as triangles. By definition, a bird is an animal that has wings and feathers and hatches from an egg. More often, though, we form our concepts by developing **prototypes**—a best example of a particular category (Rosch, 1978). The more closely objects match our prototype of a concept, the more readily we recognize them as examples of the concept. A robin and a goose both satisfy our rule for *bird*. Yet people agree more quickly with the statement "A robin is a bird" than with the statement "A goose is a bird." For most of us, the robin is the birdier bird; it more closely resembles our bird prototype. Likewise, "maternal love" and "self-love" both qualify as love. But people more instantly agree that "maternal love is a type of love," because it better matches their love prototype (Fehr & Russell, 1991).

If something fails to match our prototype, we may have trouble classifying it. Thus, we might be slow to recognize nonflying penguins and kiwis as birds.

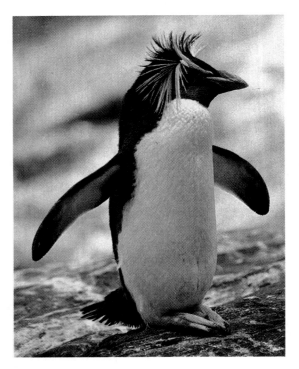

A Bird and a . . . ? *If asked to imagine a bird, most people quickly come up with a mental picture that is something like this robin. It takes them a bit longer to conceptualize a penguin as a bird because it doesn't match their prototype of a small, feathered, flying creature.*

When our symptoms don't fit one of our disease prototypes, we are slow to perceive an illness (Bishop, 1991). People whose heart attack symptoms don't match their prototype of a heart attack are often slow to seek help.

Solving Problems

2. By what strategies do we solve problems, and what obstacles hinder our problem solving?

One tribute to our rationality is our ability to form and use concepts. Another is our skill at solving problems—at coping with novel situations for which we have no well-established response. Some problems we solve through trial and error. Thomas Edison tried thousands of light bulb filaments before stumbling upon one that worked. For other problems, we may follow an **algorithm**, a step-by-step procedure that guarantees a solution. Told to find a word using all the letters in SPLOYOCHYG, we could try each letter in each position, but generating and examining the 907,200 resulting combinations would take too long. Because step-by-step algorithms can be laborious (well-suited to computers), we often solve problems with simple rule-of-thumb strategies, called **heuristics**. Thus, in rearranging the letters of SPLOYOCHYG, we might exclude letter combinations such as two *y*'s together. By using rule-of-thumb heuristics and then applying trial and error, you may hit upon the answer (page 259).

Sometimes we are unaware of using any problem-solving strategy; the answer just comes to us. We can all recall occasions when we puzzled over a problem for some time. Then, suddenly, the pieces fell together and we perceived the solution. This facility for sudden flashes of inspiration we call **insight**. Ten-year-old Johnny Appleton displayed insight in solving a problem that had stymied construction workers: how to rescue a young robin that had fallen into a narrow 30-inch-deep hole in a cement block wall. Johnny's solution: to slowly pour in sand, giving the bird enough time to keep its feet on top of the constantly rising sand (Ruchlis, 1990).

We humans aren't the only creatures that display insight. German psychologist Wolfgang Köhler (1925) observed apparent insight while studying chimpanzees placed on an island off the coast of Africa. In one experiment with a caged chimp named Sultan, Köhler placed a piece of fruit and a long stick well beyond reach, and a short stick inside the cage. Spying the short stick, Sultan grabbed it and tried to reach the fruit with it. But the stick, by design, was too short. After several unsuccessful attempts, the chimp dropped the stick and paused to survey the situation. Then suddenly, as if thinking "Aha!," Sultan jumped up, seized the short stick again, and this time used it to pull in the longer stick—which he then used to reach the fruit. Sultan's actions displayed animal cognition, claimed Köhler, and showed that there is more to learning than conditioning.

In their natural environment, chimpanzees exhibit a variety of insightful tool uses. Some can break off a reed or a stick, strip the twigs and leaves, carry it to a termite mound, fish for termites by twisting it just so, and then carefully remove it without scraping off many termites. One anthropologist, trying to mimic the chimpanzee's deft termite fishing, failed miserably.

In human experience, insight provides a sense of satisfaction. After solving a difficult problem or discovering how to resolve a conflict, we feel happy. The joy of a joke may similarly lie in our capacity for insight—our sudden comprehension of an unexpected ending or a double meaning. We find double meaning in the story of Professor Smith, who complained to his colleagues that student interruptions had become a problem: "The minute I get up to speak, some fool begins to talk."

To search for horseradish in a supermarket you could search every aisle (an algorithm) or check the mustard, spice, and gourmet sections (heuristics).

cognition The mental activity associated with processing, understanding, and communicating information.

concept mental grouping of similar objects, events, or people.

prototype The best example of a category; matching new items to the prototype provides a quick and easy method for including items in a category (as when comparing feathered creatures to a prototypical bird, such as a robin).

algorithm A methodical, logical rule or procedure that guarantees solving a particular problem; may be contrasted with the usually speedier but also more error-prone use of *heuristics*.

heuristic A rule-of-thumb strategy that often allows us to make judgments and solve problems efficiently; usually speedier but also more error-prone than *algorithms*.

insight A sudden and often novel realization of the solution to a problem; it contrasts with strategy-based solutions.

Obstacles to Problem Solving

A major obstacle to problem solving is our eagerness to search for information that confirms our ideas, a phenomenon known as **confirmation bias**. In an experiment with British university students, P. C. Wason (1960) demonstrated our reluctance to seek information that might disprove our beliefs. Wason gave students the three-number sequence, 2-4-6, and asked them to guess the rule he had used to devise the series. (The rule was simple: any three ascending numbers.) Before submitting their answers, the students generated their own sets of three numbers, and each time Wason told them whether or not their sets conformed to his rule. Once they had done enough testing to feel *certain* they had the rule, they were to announce it.

The result? Seldom right but never in doubt: Most people convinced themselves of a wrong rule. Typically, they formed a wrong idea ("Maybe it's counting by twos") and then searched only for confirming evidence (by testing 6-8-10, 100-102-104, and so forth). Such experiments reveal that we seek evidence that will verify our ideas more eagerly than we seek evidence that might refute them (Klayman & Ha, 1987; Skov & Sherman, 1986). Business managers, for example, are more likely to follow the successful careers of those they once hired than to track the achievements of those they rejected, which helps them confirm their perceived hiring ability.

Another obstacle to problem solving is **fixation**—the inability to see a problem from a fresh perspective. Once we incorrectly represent the problem, it's hard to restructure how we approach it. Can you overcome fixation in arranging the six matches shown in Figure 8–1 so that they form four equilateral triangles? Next, explain how you would use the materials in Figure 8–2 to mount the candle on a bulletin board. Try both these problems before reading on.

If your attempts to solve the matchstick problem were fixated on two-dimensional solutions, then the three-dimensional solution shown in Figure 8–3 (page 260) will have eluded you.

Flexible, rational thinking becomes even more difficult in times of stress and tension (Janis, 1989). During international crises, views of an enemy become fixed in simplified good-versus-bad terms. During personal crises, too, thinking often becomes rigid. One Korean War paratrooper readying for a mission was given the last parachute—a left-handed one. "It's the same as the oth-

Figure 8–1 The Matchstick Problem *How would you arrange six matches to form four equilateral triangles? (From "Problem Solving" by M. Scheerer. Copyright © 1963 by Scientific American, Inc. All rights reserved.)*

Figure 8–2 The Candle-Mounting Problem *Using these materials, how would you mount the candle on a bulletin board? (From Duncker, 1945.)*

confirmation bias A tendency to search for information that confirms one's preconceptions.

fixation The inability to see a problem from a new perspective; an impediment to problem solving.

functional fixedness The tendency to think of things only in terms of their usual functions; an impediment to problem solving.

representativeness heuristic A rule of thumb for judging the likelihood of things in terms of how well they seem to represent, or match, particular prototypes; may lead one to ignore other relevant information.

ers," explained the ordnance sergeant, "but the rip cord hangs on the left side of the harness." At 8000 feet, the soldiers jumped one by one, and all went well—except for this one man who fell straight to his death. Investigators discovered that under the stress of the jump the man had become fixated on the familiar way to open a chute. The right side of his uniform, where normally he found the rip cord, was completely torn off. Even his chest flesh had been gouged by his bloody right hand. Inches to the left was the rip cord, apparently untouched (Csikszentmihalyi, 1990).

One type of fixation goes by the awkward but appropriate label **functional fixedness**. This is our tendency to perceive the functions of objects as fixed and unchanging. A person may ransack the house for a screwdriver when a dime would have done the job. Perhaps you experienced functional fixedness when you tried to solve the candle-mounting problem. If you thought of the matchbox as having only the function of holding matches, you may have overlooked its use shown in Figure 8–4 (page 260).

Making Decisions and Forming Judgments

3. How are our decisions and judgments influenced by heuristics, overconfidence, and framing?

When making each day's hundreds of tiny judgments and decisions—Is it worth the bother to take an umbrella? Can I trust this person? Should I shoot the basketball or pass to the player who's hot?—we seldom take the time and effort to reason systematically. Usually, we follow our intuition. After interviewing policymakers in government, business, and education, social psychologist Irving Janis (1986) concluded that they "often do not use a reflective problem-solving approach. How do they usually arrive at their decisions? If you ask, they are likely to tell you . . . they do it mostly by the *seat of their pants*."

Using and Misusing Heuristics

Those mental shortcuts we call heuristics often help us make reasonable seat-of-the-pants judgments. But the price we pay for their efficiency can sometimes be costly bad judgments. To gain an idea of how heuristics determine our intuitive judgments—and how they can lead smart people into dumb decisions—consider two heuristics identified by cognitive psychologists Amos Tversky and Daniel Kahneman (1974): *representativeness* and *availability*.

"In creating these problems, we didn't set out to fool people. All our problems fooled us, too."

Amos Tversky (1985)

The Representativeness Heuristic To judge the likelihood of things in terms of how well they represent particular prototypes is to use the **representativeness heuristic**. To illustrate, consider:

> A stranger tells you about a person who is short, slim, and likes to read poetry, and then asks you to guess whether this person is more likely to be a professor of classics at an Ivy League university or a truck driver. Which would be the better guess? (Adapted from Nisbett & Ross, 1980.)

If you are like most people, you answered "a professor" because the description seems more *representative* of Ivy League scholars than of truck drivers. The representativeness heuristic enabled you to make a snap judgment. But it also led you to ignore other relevant information, such as the total number of classics professors versus truck drivers. When I help people think through this question, their own reasoning usually leads them to an answer that contradicts their immediate intuition. The typical conversation goes something like this:

Answer to SPLOYOCHYG anagram on page 257: PSYCHOLOGY.

Figure 8–3 Solution to the Matchstick Problem *To solve this problem, you must break the fixation of limiting your considerations to two-dimensional solutions. (From "Problem Solving" by M. Scheerer. Copyright © 1963 by Scientific American, Inc. All rights reserved.)*

Bulletin board

Thumbtack pushed through empty matchbox

Figure 8–4 Solution to the Candle-Mounting Problem *Solving this problem requires recognizing that a box need not always serve as a container. (From Duncker, 1945.)*

> *"The human understanding is most excited by that which strikes and enters the mind at once and suddenly, and by which the imagination is immediately filled and inflated. It then begins almost imperceptibly to conceive and suppose that everything is similar to the few objects which have taken possession of the mind."*
>
> Francis Bacon *Novum Organum*, 1620

Question: *First, let's figure out how many professors fit the description. How many Ivy League universities do you suppose there are?*

Answer: *Oh, about 10, I suppose.*

Question: *How many classics professors would you guess there are at each?*

Answer: *Maybe four.*

Question: *Okay, that's 40 Ivy League classics professors. What fraction of these are short and slim?*

Answer: *Let's say half.*

Question: *And, of these 20, how many like to read poetry?*

Answer: *I'd say half—10 professors.*

Question: *Okay, now let's figure how many truck drivers fit the description. How many truck drivers do you suppose there are?*

Answer: *Maybe 400,000.*

Question: *What fraction are short and slim?*

Answer: *Not many—perhaps 1 in 8.*

Question: *Of these 50,000, what percentage like to read poetry?*

Answer: *Truck drivers who like poetry? Maybe 1 in 100—oh, oh, I can see where this is going—that leaves me with 500 short, slim, poetry-reading truck drivers.*

Question: *Yup. So, although the person I described may be much more representative of classics professors than of truck drivers, this person is still (even accepting your stereotypes) 50 times more likely to be a truck driver.*

This example illustrates people's illogical use of the representativeness heuristic. To judge the likelihood of something, we intuitively compare it with our mental representation of that category—of, say, what truck drivers are like. If the two match, then that fact usually overrides other considerations of statistics or logic.

The Availability Heuristic The **availability heuristic** operates when we base our judgments on the availability of information in our memories. If instances of an event are easily available—if they come to mind readily—we presume such events are common. The faster people can remember an instance of some event ("a broken promise"), the more they expect it to recur (MacLeod & Campbell, 1992). Usually, cognitively available events *are* more likely to recur—but not always. To see this, make a guess: Does the letter *k* appear more often as the first or third letter in English words?

Because words beginning with *k* come to mind more easily than words having *k* as their third letter, most people guess that *k* occurs more frequently as the first letter. Actually, *k* is three times more likely to appear as the third letter. So far in this chapter, words such as *know*, *kingdom*, and *kin* are outnumbered 45 to 18 by words such as *make*, *likely*, *asked*, and *acknowledged*.

The availability heuristic affects our social judgments, as Ruth Hamill and her co-workers demonstrated (1980). They presented people with a single, vivid case of welfare abuse, in which a long-term welfare recipient had several unruly children fathered by different men. The statistical fact is that this case was exceptional: Most people who received welfare did so for 4 years or less (Duncan & others, 1988). Yet when the statistical reality was pitted against the single vivid case, the memorable case had greater influence on people's opinions about welfare recipients.

In everyday life, too, a memorable picture sometimes overwhelms a thousand statistics. When a little girl named Jessica McClure fell into a Texas well, the attention of hundreds of millions of people worldwide was riveted on her 3-day rescue. During those 3 days, more than 100,000 invisible children—mere statistics on some world health ledger—died of preventable starvation, diarrhea, and disease (Gore, 1992).

Perceiving Risks

"Most people reason dramatically, not quantitatively," said Oliver Wendell Holmes. With horrific television and magazine images of air crashes in mind, many people, petrified of air travel, prefer the safety of their own cars. Of those who do fly, 44 percent report feeling fearful (*Gallup Report*, 1989).

Ironically, the statistical reality is that, mile for mile, U.S. travelers during the 1980s were 26 times more likely to die in a car crash than on a commercial flight (National Safety Council, 1991). In the 27 months following March 22, 1992, major U.S. airlines carried more than 1 billion passengers on *16 million* flights without a single death (Tolchin, 1994). For most air travelers, the most dangerous part of the journey is the drive to the airport.

Still, when overall statistics vie with vivid images of helpless crash victims, many people find the memorable instances more persuasive. It's like judging the likelihood of shark attacks after watching *Jaws*: Regardless of statistics, memorable images have a way of heightening swimmers' feelings of risk. Or it's like judging, from seeing the faces of missing children on milk cartons, your child's risk of being abducted by a stranger—which the U.S. Justice Department reports actually happens to fewer than 1 in 100,000 children a year nationwide (Bonner, 1990). (Almost all child snatchings are family related.)

In 1988, a terrorist bomb that exploded Pan Am Flight 103 over Scotland caused many would-be international vacationers to stay home and brave the more dangerous highways. The same fearful public continues to drive without seatbelts, smoke billions of cigarettes a year, guz- zle alcohol, and devour foods that put people at risk for the greatest of killers— heart disease. All because people's *perceptions* of risk are virtually unrelated to actual risk (Slovic, 1987)—a phenomenon due partly to our greater fear of things we cannot control and partly to our overestimating the likelihood of dreaded, publicized, and cognitively available events. Thus, the public dreads a catastrophic nuclear accident (which after the 1986 Chernobyl disaster we can readily visualize), yet accepts the less dramatic risks of coal-generated power, which quietly fuels acid rain and global warming.

The moral: Whether making travel plans or choosing foods, defining safety standards or evaluating environmental hazards, rational people should define risks based not on mentally available media images but on statistical reality.

Vivid Events Are More Available to Memory *Photos of this July 1994 crash etched a sharper image in many minds than did the 16 million consecutive fatality-free flights on U.S. airlines during the preceding 27 months. Because such vivid happenings are more available to memory, they seem more common than they really are.*

Overconfidence

Our use of intuitive heuristics when forming judgments, our eagerness to confirm the beliefs we already hold, and our facility for explaining away failures combine to create **overconfidence**, a tendency to overestimate the accuracy of our knowledge and judgments. Asked factual questions—"Is absinthe a liqueur or a precious stone?"—people's answers are more confident than correct. When 60 percent of people answer such a question correctly, they, on average, feel 75 percent sure of their answer (Fischhoff & others, 1977). (Absinthe is a licorice-flavored liqueur.)

Overconfidence plagues decisions outside the research laboratory, too. People are more confident than correct whether trying to predict the stock market, predict other people's behavior based on interviewing them, or predict their own future actions (will you drop a course this year? call your home more than twice next month?) (Dunning & others, 1990; Malkiel, 1985; Vallone & others, 1990).

Overconfidence has adaptive value. Failing to appreciate one's potential for error when making military, economic, or political judgments can have devas-

availability heuristic A rule of thumb for estimating the likelihood of events based on their availability in memory; if instances come readily to mind (perhaps because of their vividness), we presume such events are likely.

overconfidence The tendency to be more confident than correct—to overestimate the accuracy of one's beliefs and judgments.

"*When you know a thing, to hold that you know it; and when you do not know a thing, to allow that you do not know it; this is knowledge.*"

Confucius, 551–479 B.C.
Analects

tating consequences, but so can lack of self-confidence. People who err on the side of overconfidence live more happily and find it easier to make tough decisions (Baumeister, 1989; Taylor, 1989). Moreover, when given prompt and clear feedback on the accuracy of their judgments—as weather forecasters are after each day's predictions—people soon learn to assess their accuracy more realistically (Fischhoff, 1982). The wisdom to know when we know a thing and when we do not is born of experience.

Framing Decisions

A further test of rationality is whether the same issue, presented in two different but logically equivalent ways, will elicit the same answer. For example, whether a surgeon tells someone that 10 percent die during a particular surgery or that 90 percent survive, the information is the same. But the effect is not. The risk seems greater to people who hear that 10 percent will die (Marteau, 1989). This impact of the way we present an issue is called **framing**.

Similarly, consumers respond more positively to ground beef described as "75 percent lean" rather than "25 percent fat" (Levin & Gaeth, 1988). A new medical treatment strikes people as more successful and recommendable if framed as having a "50 percent success rate" rather than a "50 percent failure rate." People are more bothered by an incident of student cheating if told that 65 percent of students had cheated than if told that 35 percent had not cheated (Levin & others, 1988). And 9 in 10 college students rate a condom as effective if it supposedly has a "95 percent success rate" in stopping the AIDS virus; only 4 in 10 think it successful when given a "5 percent failure rate" (Linville & others, 1992).

Consider how the framing effect influences economic and business decisions:

"*This CD player costs less than players selling for twice as much.*"

- Merchants mark up their "regular prices" to appear to offer huge savings on "sale prices." A $100 coat marked down from $150 by Store *X* can seem like a better deal than the same coat priced regularly at $100 by Store *Y* (Urbany & others, 1988).

- Many people find a 7 percent pay cut in a period of zero inflation much more objectionable than a 5 percent pay raise when inflation is 12 percent—though the effect is basically the same (Kahneman & others, 1986).

- If your dentist offers a 5 percent discount for immediate cash payment, you may not feel particularly unhappy paying the full fee 30 days later. But you probably would be irritated if the same fee were framed differently—say, if the basic fee were lowered 5 percent with an equivalent surcharge for late payment. Somehow, a 5 percent surcharge is more irritating than a forfeited 5 percent discount, although they add up to the same thing.

That people's judgments flip-flop so dramatically is startling. It suggests that our judgments and decisions may not be well reasoned, and that those who understand the power of framing can use it to influence important decisions—for example, by framing survey questions to support or reject a particular viewpoint. (Recall from Chapter 1 the potentially powerful effects of subtle wording differences in surveys.)

The Belief Perseverance Phenomenon

4. How do our preexisting beliefs influence our decision making?

An additional source of irrationality is our tendency, called **belief perseverance**, to cling to our beliefs in the face of contrary evidence. Belief persever-

framing   The way an issue is posed; how an issue is framed can significantly affect decisions and judgments.

belief perseverance   Clinging to one's initial conceptions after the basis on which they were formed has been discredited.

"Once you have a belief, it influences how you perceive all other relevant information. Once you see a country as hostile, you are likely to interpret ambiguous actions on their part as signifying their hostility."

Political scientist Robert Jervis (1985)

Belief Perseverance   *Do risk-prone or cautious people make better fire fighters? Once we've formed opinions on a question like this and developed reasons for our views, we tend to cling to our beliefs—even if presented with contradictory evidence.*

"I'm happy to say that my final judgment of a case is almost always consistent with my prejudgment of the case."

ance often fuels social conflict. Charles Lord and his colleagues (1979) revealed how this happens when they studied people with opposing views of capital punishment. People on both sides studied two supposedly new research findings, one supporting and the other refuting the claim that the death penalty deters crime. Each side was impressed by the study that supported its beliefs, and each readily disputed the other study. Thus, showing the pro- and anti-capital-punishment groups the *same* mixed evidence actually *increased* their disagreement.

For those who wish to rein in the belief perseverance phenomenon, a simple remedy exists: *Consider the opposite.* When Lord and his colleagues (1984) repeated the capital-punishment study, they asked some of their subjects to be "as *objective* and *unbiased* as possible." The plea did nothing to reduce the biased evaluation of evidence. They asked another group, however, to consider the opposite—to ask themselves "whether you would have made the same high or low evaluations had exactly the same study produced results on the *other* side of the issue." Having imagined and pondered opposite findings, these people were much less biased in their evaluations of the evidence.

If ambiguous evidence gets interpreted as supporting a person's preexisting belief, would the belief be demolished by information that clearly discredited its basis? Not necessarily. Craig Anderson and Lee Ross discovered that it can be surprisingly difficult to change a false belief once a person has in mind ideas that support it. In one such study with Mark Lepper (1980), they asked subjects to consider whether risk-prone people or cautious people are better fire fighters. Then they told half the subjects about a risk-taker who was an excellent fire fighter and about a cautious person who was a poor fire fighter. From these cases, the subjects surmised that risk-prone people tend to be better fire fighters. "Risk-takers are braver," was a typical explanation. The researchers gave the other subjects two cases suggesting the opposite conclusion, that cautious people are better fire fighters. Subjects typically reasoned, "Cautious people think before they act. They're less likely to make foolish mistakes."

The researchers then discredited the basis for the beliefs by informing both groups that the cases were simply made up for the experiment. Did discrediting the evidence undermine the subjects' newly formed beliefs? Not by much, because the subjects held onto their explanations for why these new beliefs made sense. Although the evidence was gone, their theory survived.

The more we come to appreciate why our beliefs might be true, the more tightly we cling to them. Once people have explained to themselves why they believe that a child is "gifted" or "learning disabled," or that presidential candidate *X* or *Y* will be more likely to preserve peace or start a war, or that women or men are naturally superior, they tend to ignore evidence undermining that belief.

We have seen how our irrational thinking can plague our efforts to solve problems, make wise decisions, form valid judgments, and reason logically. From this we might conclude that our heads are indeed filled with straw. All in all, these and many other findings suggest "bleak implications for human rationality" (Nisbett & Borgida, 1975). Still, let us not forget that our cognition is effective and efficient: It enables our survival and our inventive genius. Moreover, even the most sophisticated computers are dwarfed by the most ordinary of human mental abilities—recognizing a face, distinguishing a cat from a dog, knowing whether the word *line* refers to a rope or a fragment of poetry or a social come-on. A computer's capabilities exceed our own at tasks that use its unique strengths—vast memory and precise logic and retrieval. But computers have not duplicated the wide-ranging intelligence of a human mind, a mind that can *all at once* converse naturally, perceive the environment, use common sense, experience emotion, and consciously reflect on its own existence.

! *Rehearse It*

1. We use the concept "bird" to think and talk about a variety of creatures, all of which have wings and feathers. A concept is

a. a mental grouping of similar things.
b. an example of insight.
c. a fixation on certain characteristics.
d. another word for "prototype."

2. Sometimes we solve problems through trial and error, trying hundreds or even thousands of solutions before finding one that works. At other times we are more methodical or systematic. The most systematic procedure for solving a problem is

a. heuristics.
b. an algorithm.
c. insight.
d. intuition.

3. A major obstacle to problem solving is confirmation bias, the tendency to search for information that confirms our preconceptions, while ignoring information that might prove us wrong. Another obstacle to problem solving is fixation, which is

a. an error we make when basing our judgments on certain vivid memories.
b. the art of framing the same question in two different ways.
c. the inability to view a problem from a new perspective.
d. a rule of thumb for judging the likelihood of an event in terms of our mental image of it.

4. You move into a new neighborhood and notice that your next-door neighbor is very neatly dressed, wears glasses, and is reading a Greek play. Given a choice between her being a librarian and a store clerk, you incorrectly guess that she is a librarian. Your incorrect judgment is probably due to

a. the availability heuristic.
b. confirmation bias.
c. overconfidence.
d. the representativeness heuristic.

5. After a New York City bombing by foreign-born terrorists in 1993, many observers incorrectly assumed that the 1995 bombing of a federal building in Oklahoma City was probably the work of foreign-born terrorists. This assumption illustrates

a. belief perseverance.
b. the availability heuristic.
c. functional fixedness.
d. confirmation bias.

6. The way an issue is posed can affect our decisions and judgments. For example, one study found that people perceived student cheating to be worse if told that 65 percent of students had cheated than if told that 35 percent of students had not cheated. In this case people's reactions were influenced by

a. belief perseverance.
b. fixation.
c. confirmation bias.
d. framing.

Language

The most tangible indication of our thinking power is **language**—our spoken, written, or gestured words and the ways we combine them as we think and communicate. Humans have long and proudly proclaimed that language sets us above all other animals. "When we study human language," asserted linguist Noam Chomsky (1972), "we are approaching what some might call the 'human essence,' the qualities of mind that are, so far as we know, unique" to humans. To cognitive scientist Steven Pinker (1990), language is "the jewel in the crown of cognition." When the human vocal tract evolved the capacity to utter the commonest vowels (which chimps cannot), our capacity for language exploded. Complex vocalization boosted our ancestors' ability to communicate information, catapulting our species forward (Diamond, 1989). Whether spoken, written, or signed, language enables us to communicate complex ideas from person to person and to transmit civilization's accumulated knowledge across generations.

Language Development

5. When do children acquire language, and how does it develop?

Make a quick guess: How many words did you learn each day, on average, during the years between your first birthday and your high school graduation?

Language Transmits Culture *The actual words and grammar may differ from culture to culture, but every society has a history that it transmits in story form to its children. Here, a group of Ivory Coast boys listen as an elder retells a tribal legend.*

language Our spoken, written, or gestured words and the ways we combine them to communicate meaning.

babbling stage Beginning at 3 to 4 months, the stage of speech development in which the infant spontaneously utters various sounds at first unrelated to the household language.

Although you probably know more than 80,000 words, you use only 150 words for about half of what you say.

The average high school graduate knows some 80,000 words (Miller & Gildea, 1987). That averages (after age 1) to nearly 5000 words learned a year, or 13 a day! How you did it—how the 5000 words a year you learned could so far outnumber the roughly 200 words a year that your schoolteachers consciously taught you—is one of the great human wonders. Before children can add 2 + 2, they are creating their own original and grammatically appropriate sentences. Most parents would have trouble stating the rules of syntax. Yet their preschoolers comprehend and speak with a facility that puts to shame a college student struggling to learn a foreign language or a scientist struggling to simulate natural language on a computer. How does our astonishing facility for language unfold, and how can we explain it?

Acquiring Language

Children's language development moves from simplicity to complexity. By 4 months of age, babies can read lips and discriminate speech sounds. They prefer to look at a face that matches a sound, so we know they can recognize that *ah* comes from wide open lips and *ee* from a mouth with corners pulled back (Kuhl & Meltzoff, 1982). At about this age, babies enter a **babbling stage** in which they spontaneously utter a variety of sounds such as *ah-goo*. Babbling is not the imitation of adult speech, for it includes sounds from various languages, even sounds that do not occur in the household's language. From this early babbling, a listener could not identify an infant as being, say, French, Korean, or Ethiopian. Deaf infants babble (repeat syllable-like gestures), too, and they obviously are not imitating speech (Petitto & Marentette, 1991). It seems, then, that before nurture molds our speech, nature enables a wide range of possible sounds.

Babbling eventually comes to resemble the characteristic sounds and intonations of the household language. By about age 10 months, a trained ear can identify the language of the household by listening to an infant's babbling (de Boysson-Bardies & others, 1989). Sounds outside the infant's native tongue begin to disappear. And infants gradually lose their ability to discriminate sounds they never hear. Clever experiments by Janet Werker (1989) reveal that at 6 months infants can perceive sound differences in other languages, but by 12 months they cannot (Figure 8–5). Thus, by adulthood an English-speaker cannot discriminate certain Japanese speech sounds nor can a Japanese adult

Figure 8–5 Testing for Speech Sound Perception *We are all born with the ability to recognize speech sounds from all the world's languages. (a) In Janet Werker's lab, an infant is reinforced with applause and by activating toy animals when he looks to the right after hearing a changed sound (as in ba, ba, ba, ba, da, da). (b) Adult Hindi-speakers and young infants from English-speaking homes can easily discriminate two Hindi* t *sounds not spoken in English. By about age 1, however, English-speaking listeners rarely perceive the sound difference. (Adapted from Werker, 1989.)*

(a)

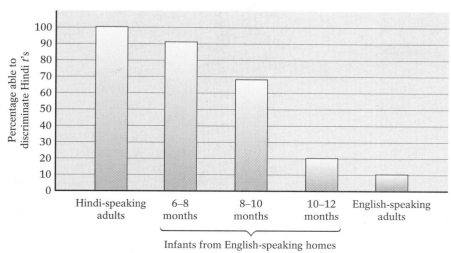

(b)

TABLE 8-1

Summary of Language Development

Month (approximate)	Stage
4	Babbles many speech sounds.
10	Babbling reveals household language.
12	One-word stage.
24	Two-word, telegraphic speech.
24+	Language develops rapidly into complete sentences.

"Got idea. Talk better. Combine words. Make sentences."

© 1994 by Sidney Harris.

with no training in English distinguish between the English *r* and *l* (Japanese has a consonant midway between *r* and *l*). Japanese also has no *p* or *f*. Thus, *please* sounds very much like *freeze*, which may explain why Yoshihiro Hattori, a Japanese exchange student mistaken for a burglar, failed to understand a gun-toting Louisiana homeowner's order to *freeze* and was tragically shot to death.

Around the first birthday (the exact age varies from child to child), most children enter the **one-word stage**. Having already learned that sounds carry meanings, they begin to use sounds to communicate meaning. Their first words usually contain only one syllable—*ma* or *da*, for instance—and may be barely recognizable. But family members quickly learn to understand the infant's language, and gradually it conforms more and more to the family's language.

Most of the child's first words refer to things that move or can be played with—a dog or a ball, for example, rather than the table or crib that just sits there (Nelson, 1973). At this one-word stage, an inflected word may equal a sentence. "Doggy!" may mean "Look at the dog out there!"

Children typically use more and more single words during their second year and, by about their second birthday, enter the **two-word stage**, when they start uttering two-word sentences (Table 8–1). Language at this stage is characterized by **telegraphic speech**: Like telegrams (TERMS ACCEPTED. SEND MONEY.), it contains mostly nouns and verbs (*Want juice*). Also like telegrams the words are in a sensible order. The English-speaking child typically says adjectives before nouns—*big doggy* rather than *doggy big*.

There seems to be no "three-word stage." Once children move out of the two-word stage, they quickly begin uttering longer phrases (Fromkin & Rodman, 1983). Although the sentences may still sound like a telegraphed message, they continue to make grammatical sense (*Mommy get ball*). By early elementary school, the child understands complex sentences and begins to enjoy the humor conveyed by double meanings: "You never starve in the desert because of all the sand-which-is there."

Explaining Language Development

Those who study language acquisition inevitably wonder how we do it. Attempts to answer this question have sparked a spirited intellectual controversy. The nature-nurture debate surfaces again and, here as elsewhere, appreciation for innate predisposition has grown.

Behaviorist B. F. Skinner (1957) believed we can explain language development with familiar learning principles, such as association (of the sights of things with the sounds of words); imitation (of the words and sentence order modeled by others); and reinforcement (with success, smiles, and hugs when the child says something right). Thus, Skinner argued, babies learn to talk in many of the same ways that animals learn to peck keys and press bars. "Verbal behavior evidently came into existence when, through a critical step in the evolution of the human species, the vocal musculature became susceptible to operant conditioning," Skinner (1985) surmised.

Linguist Noam Chomsky (1959, 1987) thinks Skinner was naive. Surely, says Chomsky, a Martian scientist observing children in a single-language community would conclude that language is almost entirely inborn. It isn't, because children learn the language used in their environment. But the rate at which they acquire words and grammar without being taught is too extraordinary to be explained solely by learning principles. Children create all sorts of sentences they have never heard and, therefore, could not be imitating. Moreover, many of their errors result from overgeneralizing logical grammatical rules, such as adding *-ed* to make the past tense (from de Cuevas, 1990):

one-word stage   The stage in speech development, from about age 1 to 2, during which a child speaks mostly in single words.

two-word stage   Beginning about age 2, the stage in speech development during which a child speaks mostly two-word statements.

telegraphic speech   Early stage of speaking in which the child's speech is like a telegram—"go car"—using mostly nouns and verbs and omitting "auxiliary" words.

Child: *My teacher holded the baby rabbits and we petted them.*
Mother: *Did you say your teacher held the baby rabbits?*
Child: *Yes.*
Mother: *What did you say she did?*
Child: *She holded the baby rabbits and we petted them.*
Mother: *Did you say she held them tightly?*
Child: *No, she holded them loosely.*

Chomsky (1987) likens the behaviorist view of how language develops to filling a bottle with water. He views language development as "helping a flower to grow in its own way." It is, he believes, akin to sexual maturation—given adequate nurture, it just "happens to the child." Thanks to their inborn "universal grammar," children readily learn the grammar of whatever language they hear. Other worlds may have languages that, for us humans, are unlearnable, but our world does not. Chomsky maintains that our language acquisition capacity is like a box—a "language acquisition device"—in which grammar switches are thrown as children experience their language. Thus, English-speaking children learn to put the object of a sentence last ("She ate an apple"). Japanese-speaking children put the object before the verb ("She an apple ate"). We are born with the hardware and an operating system; experience writes the software (Figure 8–6).

Figure 8–6 Nature and Nurture   *Genes design the mechanisms for a language, and experience fills them as it modifies the brain. Grow up in Paris and you will speak French (environment matters), but not if you are a cat (genes matter).*

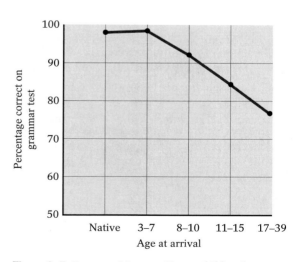

Figure 8–7 Grammar Mastery   *Young children have a readiness to learn language. Ten years after coming to the United States, Asian immigrants took a grammar test. Those who arrived before age 8 understood grammar as well as native speakers. Those who arrived later did not. (From Johnson and Newport, 1989.)*

Cognitive scientists still debate how much of our language capacity is inborn (Shanks, 1993). With experience (but with no "inborn" linguistic rules), computer neural networks can learn to form past-tense verbs appropriately. They can learn, for example, to change words ending in *ow* to *ew*, as in *throw/threw*. To some scientists, this suggests the brain could be a blanker slate than Chomsky believes.

The scholars agree, however, that for language development life's first years are critical. Those who learn a second language as adults usually speak it with the accent of their first language. Do they master the foreign *grammar* better than the accent? To find out, Jacqueline Johnson and Elissa Newport (1989) gave Korean and Chinese immigrants to the United States a grammar test, requiring them to identify each of 276 sentences ("Yesterday the hunter shoots a deer") as grammatically correct or incorrect. Some subjects had immigrated in early childhood, others as adults. Regardless of their age at immigration, each of the participants had been in the United States for approximately 10 years. Nevertheless, as Figure 8–7 reveals, those who learned their second language early learned it best. Chomsky would say that once the grammar switches are thrown during a child's developing years, mastering another grammar becomes more difficult.

The impact of early experience is also evident among the deaf. Hearing children of hearing-speaking parents, and deaf children of deaf-signing parents, have much in common. Both groups babble as infants—hearing children by repeating sounds, deaf children by repeating elementary sign gestures (Petitto &

The Game of Language Acquisition   *The first language of millions of children is not the dominant culture's language. This second language they learn when they reach school. For the children at this Berkeley, California, bilingual preschool, such learning flowers naturally with the aid of games and other kinds of play.*

No Means NO! No Matter How You Say It   *Deaf children of deaf-signing parents and hearing children of hearing parents have much in common. They develop language skills at about the same rate, and they are equally effective at opposing parental wishes and demanding their way.*

Marentette, 1991). Both groups develop vocabularies, at comparable rates (Meier, 1991). For both groups, later-than-usual exposure to language (at age 2 or 3) unleashes their brain's idle language capacity, producing a rush of language. But consider the 90+ percent of deaf children born to hearing-nonsigning parents. These children typically do not experience language during their early years. Compared with deaf children exposed to sign language from birth, those who learn to sign as teens or adults are like immigrants who learn English after childhood. They can master the basic words and how to order them, but they never become as fluent as native signers in producing and comprehending subtle grammatical differences (Newport, 1990).

To summarize, children are biologically prepared to learn language as they interact with their caregivers. Skinner's emphasis on learning helps explain why infants acquire the language they hear and how they add new words to their vocabularies. Chomsky's emphasis on our built-in readiness to learn grammar rules helps explain why preschoolers acquire language so readily and use grammar so well. Once again, we see biology and experience working together.

Returning to our debate about humanity's thinking powers, let's pause to issue a report card. On decision making and judgment, our error-prone species might rate a C+. On problem solving, where humans are inventive yet vulnerable to fixation, we would probably receive better marks, perhaps a B+. On cognitive efficiency, our fallible but quick heuristics earn us an A. And when it comes to learning and using language, the awestruck experts would surely award the human species an A+.

Animal Language

6. *Is language unique to humans, or do animals also have language?*

If in our use of language we humans are, as the psalmist rhapsodized, "little lower than God," where do other animals fit in the scheme of things? Are they "little lower than human"? In part, the answer lies in the extent to which animals share our capacity for language.

Without doubt, animals communicate. Vervet monkeys have different alarm cries for different predators: a barking call for a leopard, a coughing for an eagle, and a chuttering for a snake. Hearing the leopard alarm they climb the nearest tree. Hearing the eagle alarm they rush into the bushes. Hearing the snake chutter they stand up and scan the ground (Byrne, 1991). But do animals' communications make up a language?

The Case of the Apes

The greatest challenge to humanity's claim to be the only language-using species has come from reports of apes that "talk" with people. Genetically speaking, our closest relatives are the chimpanzees, and the chimpanzees' closest relatives are not other apes, but us (Sagan & Druyan, 1992). Knowing that chimpanzees could not vocalize more than a few words, University of Nevada researchers Allen Gardner and Beatrice Gardner (1969) tried to teach sign language words to a chimp named Washoe, as though she were a deaf human child. After 4 years, Washoe could use 132 signs. By 1993, 27-year-old Washoe had a vocabulary of 240 signs (Geranios, 1993). The Gardners' announcement of the success of their efforts aroused enormous scientific and public interest.

But Is This Language?   *The ability of chimpanzees to express themselves in American Sign Language (ASL) raises questions about the very nature of language. Here, the trainer is asking, "What is this?" The sign in response is "Baby." Does the response constitute language?*

Another "Talking" Chimpanzee   *Lana has learned to speak by punching word symbols on a computer keyboard. When she presses a key, the symbol lights up.*

One *New York Times* reporter, having learned sign language from his deaf parents, visited Washoe and exclaimed, "Suddenly I realized I was conversing with a member of another species in my native tongue."

During the 1970s, further evidence of "ape language" surfaced. Although apes usually signed just single words, they sometimes strung signs to form intelligible sentences. Washoe signed, "You me go out, please." Apes even appeared to combine words creatively. Washoe designated a swan as a "water bird." Koko, a gorilla trained by Francine Patterson (1978) in California, reportedly described a long-nosed Pinocchio doll as an "elephant baby." Lana, a chimpanzee that "talks" by punching buttons wired to a computer that translates her punchings into English, wanted her trainer's orange. She had no word for *orange*, but she did know her colors and the word for *apple*, so she improvised: "? Tim give apple which-is orange" (Rumbaugh, 1977).

Seeing a doll floating in her water, Washoe signed, "Baby in my drink."

As ape language reports accumulated, it seemed that apes might indeed be "little lower than human." Their vocabularies and sentences were simple, rather like those of a 2-year-old child. Yet the apes did seem to share what we humans have considered our unique ability.

But Can Apes Really Talk?   By the late 1970s, the claims of "talking apes" raised a question: Were the chimps language champs or were the researchers chumps? The ape language researchers were making monkeys out of themselves, said the skeptics, who raised the following arguments:

- Apes gain their limited vocabularies only with great difficulty. They are hardly like speaking or signing children, who effortlessly soak up dozens of new words a week. Saying that apes can learn language because they can sign words is like saying humans can fly because they can jump.

- Chimps can make signs or push buttons in sequence to get a reward, but so can pigeons—by pecking a sequence of keys to get grain (Straub & others, 1979). No one says the pigeon is "talking."

- Apes can certainly use symbols meaningfully, but the evidence is far from convincing that they can equal even a 3-year-old's ability to order words with proper syntax. To the child, "you tickle" and "tickle you" communicate different ideas. A chimp might sign the phrases interchangeably.

- After training a chimp whom he named Nim Chimsky, Herbert Terrace (1979) concluded that much of chimpanzees' signing is nothing more than their imitating their trainers' signs.

- Presented with ambiguous information, people tend to see what they want or expect to see. (Recall the demonstrations of perceptual set in Chapter 4.) Interpreting chimpanzee signs as language may be little more than wishful thinking on the part of their trainers, claimed Terrace. (When Washoe signed "water bird," she perhaps was separately naming "water" and "bird.")

"Although humans make sounds with their mouths and occasionally look at each other, there is no solid evidence that they actually communicate with each other."

© 1979 by Sidney Harris; *American Scientist Magazine.*

In science as in politics, controversy stimulates progress. The provocative claim that "apes share our capacity for language" and the skeptical rejoinder that "apes no use language" (as Washoe might have put it) have moved psychologists toward a greater appreciation of apes' remarkable capabilities and of our own. Everyone agrees that humans alone possess language, if by the term we mean verbal or signed expression of complex grammar. If we mean, more simply, the ability to communicate through a meaningful sequence of symbols, then apes are indeed capable of language.

"[Our] egocentric view that [we are] unique from all other forms of animal life is being jarred to the core."

Duane Rumbaugh and Sue Savage-Rumbaugh (1978)

Although chimpanzees do not have our facility for language, their thinking and communicating abilities continue to impress their trainers. After her second infant died, a depressed Washoe repeatedly asked "Baby?" and became withdrawn when told "Baby dead, baby gone, baby finished." Two weeks later, caretaker Roger Fouts (1992) had better news for Washoe: "I have baby for you." Washoe reacted to the signed news with instant excitement, her hair on end, swaggering and panting while signing over and again, "Baby, my baby." When Fouts then introduced the foster infant, Loulis, it took several hours for them to warm to each other, whereupon Washoe broke the ice by signing "Come baby" and cuddling Loulis. In the months that followed, Loulis picked up 68 signs simply by observing Washoe and three other language-trained chimps.

Moreover, Washoe, Loulis, and the others now sign spontaneously, as when asking one another to *chase, tickle, hug, come,* or *groom.* People who sign can eavesdrop on these chimp-to-chimp conversations with near-perfect agreement about what the chimps are saying, 90 percent of which pertains to social interaction, reassurance, or play (Fouts & Bodamer, 1987). Moreover, the chimps are modestly bilingual; they can translate spoken English words into signs (Shaw, 1989–1990).

Also impressive is the discovery by Savage-Rumbaugh and her colleagues (1993) that pygmy chimpanzees can learn to comprehend the nuances of spoken English. Kanzi, one such chimp with the grammatical abilities of a 2½-year-old, knows the spoken words *snake, bite,* and *dog.* Given stuffed animals and asked, for the first time, to "make the dog bite the snake," he put the snake to the dog's mouth. (See also Figure 8–8.) For chimps as for humans, early life is a critical time for learning language. If raised without early exposure to speech or word symbols, the chimps are unable as adults to gain language competence (Rumbaugh & Savage-Rumbaugh, 1994).

So, trained apes' language capabilities are modest by human standards. Yet their impressive cognitive powers seem indeed to make them "little lower than human." If Kanzi "had a vocal tract, he would be talking," exclaims Duane Rumbaugh (1994). Realizing this, we see once again how animal research can increase our respect for the creatures studied. Believing that animals could not think, Descartes and other philosophers argued that they were living robots without moral rights. But some animals, including apes and dolphins, do show remarkable abilities to think, to feel family loyalty, even to display altruism. Working out the moral implications of all this is an unfinished task for our own thinking species.

Figure 8–8 Language? *Asked to "feed your ball some tomato," Kanzi picked up a tomato and a pumpkin-faced spongeball, then placed the tomato to the ball's mouth. (From Savage-Rumbaugh & others, 1993.)*

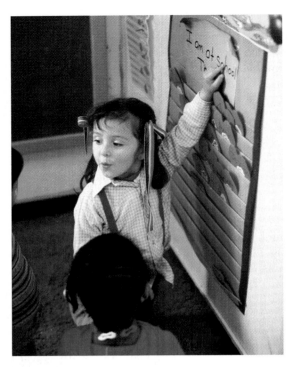

It Pays to Increase Your Word Power *This girl's efforts to increase her vocabulary will expand her capacity to think.*

"All words are pegs to hang ideas on."

Henry Ward Beecher
Proverbs from Plymouth Pulpit, 1887

"To call forth a concept, a word is needed."

Antoine Lavoisier
Elements of Chemistry, 1789

linguistic relativity   Whorf's hypothesis that language determines the way we think.

Thinking and Language

7. What is the relationship between thinking and language?

Thinking and language intricately intertwine. Asking which comes first is one of psychology's chicken-and-egg questions. Do our ideas come first and wait for words to name them? Or are our thoughts conceived in words and unthinkable without them?

Language Influences Thinking

Linguist Benjamin Lee Whorf contended that language determines the way we think. According to Whorf's (1956) **linguistic relativity** hypothesis, different languages impose different conceptions of reality: "Language itself shapes a man's basic ideas."

Whorf's idea seldom occurs to people who speak but one language. To them, language seems only a vehicle for thought. But to those who speak two dissimilar languages, such as English and Japanese, it seems obvious that one thinks differently in different languages (Brown, 1986). Unlike English, which has a rich vocabulary for self-focused emotions such as anger, Japanese has many words for interpersonal emotions such as sympathy (Markus & Kitayama, 1991). Many bilinguals report that they even have a different sense of self, depending on which language they are using (Matsumoto, 1994). After immigrating from Asia to North America, bilinguals may reveal different personalities when taking the same personality test in their two languages (Dinges & Hull, 1992). Learn a language and you learn about a culture. When a language becomes extinct—the likely fate of most of the world's 6000 remaining languages—the world loses the culture and thinking that hangs on that language.

Another example: In English, there is one word for *snow*. The Eskimo language has many. This, said Whorf, allows Eskimos to *perceive* differences in snow that would be unnoticed by people who speak another language. The language-thought link also occurs at the level of grammar—the Hopi Indians, for example, have no past tense for their verbs. Therefore, Whorf contended, the Hopi cannot so readily *think* about the past.

Critics claim that words *reflect* rather than create the way we think. The Eskimos *need* words to describe sticky, powdery, and packed snow. We may lack the Eskimos' rich vocabulary for describing snow, but that does not mean we cannot perceive these differences. My language lacks the dozen words with which the sea-hunting Makaw Indians could describe varying tides. But having grown up near them on Washington's coastal waters, I can understand what their words refer to. Likewise, a New Guinean without our words for shapes and colors nevertheless perceives them much as we do (Rosch, 1974).

Although it is too strong to say that language *determines* the *way* we think, our words certainly can *influence what* we think (Hardin & Banaji, 1993). We therefore do well to choose our words carefully. When people referred to women as *girls*—as in "the girls at the office"—it perpetuated a view of women's having lower status, did it not? Or consider the generic use of the pronoun *he*. Does it make any difference whether I write "A child learns language as *he* interacts with *his* caregivers" or "Children learn language as *they* interact with *their* caregivers"? Some argue that it makes no difference because every reader knows that "the masculine gender shall be deemed and taken to include females" (as the British Parliament declared in 1850).

But is the generic *he* always taken to include females? Twenty studies have consistently found that it is not (Henley, 1989). For example, Janet Hyde (1984) asked children to finish stories for which she gave them a first line such as, "When a kid goes to school, _____ often feels excited on the first day." When Hyde used *he* in the blank, the children's stories were nearly always about males. *He or she* in the blank resulted in female characters about one-third of the time. Studies with adolescents and adults in North America and New Zealand have found similar effects of the generic *he* (Hamilton, 1988; Martyna, 1978; Ng, 1990). Sentences about "the artist and his work" tend to conjure up images of a man.

Consider, too, that people use generic pronouns selectively, as in "the doctor . . . he" and "the secretary . . . she" (MacKay, 1983). If *he* and *his* were truly gender-free, we shouldn't skip a beat when hearing that "a nurse must answer his calls" or that "man, like other mammals, nurses his young." That we are startled indicates that the *his* carries a gender connotation that clashes with our ideas of *nurse*.

The power of language to influence thought makes vocabulary building a crucial part of education. To expand language is to expand the ability to think. In young children thinking develops hand in hand with language (Gopnik & Meltzoff, 1986). What is true for preschoolers is true for everyone: *It pays to increase your word power.* That is why most textbooks, including this one, introduce new words—to teach new ideas and new ways of thinking.

Increased word power helps explain what McGill University researcher Wallace Lambert (1992; Lambert & others, 1993) calls the "bilingual advantage." Bilingual children in Canada, Switzerland, Israel, South Africa, and Singapore outperform monolinguals on intelligence tests. Knowing this, Lambert helped devise a Canadian program that enables English-speaking children to be immersed in French. For most of their first three school years they are taught by a French-speaking teacher; not until the fifth and sixth grades do they receive half their instruction in English. Not surprisingly, the children attain a natural French fluency unrivaled by other methods of language teaching. Moreover, compared with similarly capable children in control conditions, they do so without detriment to their English fluency, and with increased aptitude scores, math scores, and appreciation for French Canadian culture.

Increasing their word power through sign language has also had great benefits for deaf people, who for thousands of years were viewed as incompetent to inherit property, marry, be educated, or have challenging work (Sacks, 1990). Since the spread of signed instruction, the deaf have shown that, when exposed to signing as preschoolers and then schooled in their language, they become fully literate. Deaf children with native sign fluency (as children of signing deaf parents) outperform other deaf children on measures of intelligence and academic achievement (Isham & Kamin, 1993). For both the deaf and the hearing, language transforms experience. Language connects us to past and future. Language fuels our imagination. Language links us to one another.

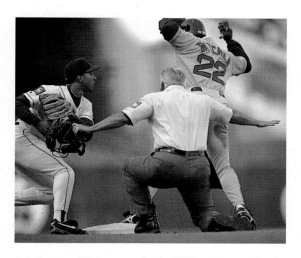

A Safe Sign   *We have outfielder William Hoy to thank for baseball sign language. The first deaf player to join the major leagues in 1892, he invented hand signals for "Strike!" "Safe!" (shown here) and "Yerr Out!" (Pollard, 1992). Such gestures worked so well that referees in all sports now use invented signs, and fans are fluent in sports sign language.*

Thinking Without Language

When you are alone, do you talk to yourself? Is "thinking" simply conversing with yourself? Without a doubt, words convey ideas. But are there not times when ideas precede words? To turn on the cold water in your bathroom, in which direction do you turn the handle?

To answer this question, you probably thought not in words but with a mental picture. Indeed, we often think in images. Artists think in images. So do composers, poets, mathematicians, athletes, and scientists. Albert Einstein reported that he achieved some of his greatest insights through visual images and only later put them into words.

Liu Chi Kung placed second in the 1958 Tchaikovsky competition—the piano Olympics—and was imprisoned a year later during China's cultural revolution. Soon after his release, after 7 years without touching a piano, he was back on tour and critics judged his musicianship better than ever. How did he do it without practice? "I did practice," said Liu, "every day. I rehearsed every piece I had ever played, note by note, in my mind" (Garfield, 1986).

A Thoughtful Sport *Karate involves control and development of the mind as well as the body. These students are defending themselves from an imaginary opponent in preparation for real self-defense.*

Closely Connected *Thinking affects our language, which then affects our thought.*

Many successful athletes prepare for contests by imagining themselves performing their events (Suinn, 1986; Whelan & others, 1991). Golf great Jack Nicklaus has said that he would "watch a movie" in his head before each shot. Georgia Nigro (1984) demonstrated the wisdom of mental practice in a laboratory test. She had subjects make 24 actual dart throws at a target, then had half the subjects throw 24 darts mentally, and, finally, had all the subjects again make 24 throws. Only those who had mentally practiced showed any improvement. A National Research Council committee of psychologists investigated claims of performance-enhancement techniques for the U.S. Army and concluded that most techniques (including ESP and "neurolinguistic programming") were of no value (Druckman & Swets, 1988). Based on experiments such as Nigro's, however, they deemed the mental practice of motor skills useful.

What, then, should we say about the relationship between thinking and language? We have seen that language influences thinking. But if thinking did not also affect language, there would never be any new words. New words express new ideas. The basketball term *slam dunk* was coined after the act itself had become fairly common. So, let us simply say that *thinking affects our language, which then affects our thought.*

Psychological research on thinking and language mirrors the mixed reviews given our species in literature and religion. The human mind is simultaneously capable of striking intellectual failures and of vast intellectual power. In an age when misjudgments can have disastrous consequences, we do well to appreciate our capacity for error. Yet our heuristics often serve us well, and they certainly are efficient. Moreover, our ingenuity at problem solving and our extraordinary power of language surely, among the animals, rank humankind as almost "infinite in faculties."

7. Children progress from babbling to sentences of two and then four, five, six or more words. The one-word stage of speech development is usually reached at about

a. 4 months.   **b.** 6 months.
c. 1 year.   **d.** 2 years.

8. According to Noam Chomsky, we are biologically prepared to acquire language and are born with a readiness to learn the grammatical rules of the language we hear. He believes that all we need to acquire language is

a. instruction in grammar.
b. exposure to language in early childhood.
c. reinforcement for babbling and other early verbal behaviors.
d. imitation and drill.

9. B. F. Skinner believed that we learn language the same way we learn other behaviors—through association, imitation, and reinforcement. Skinner's behaviorist view is most helpful in explaining

a. the onset of babbling.
b. the speech behavior of deaf infants.
c. the seemingly effortless mastery of grammatical rules by very young children.
d. why children learn their household's language.

10. There is much controversy over whether apes can be taught to use language in the way that humans do. However, most researchers of ape sign language agree that apes can

a. communicate through symbols.
b. reproduce most human speech sounds.
c. create new sentences and meanings.
d. surpass a human 3-year-old in language skills.

11. According to Benjamin Lee Whorf, the language we speak determines the way we perceive and think about the world. His linguistic relativity hypothesis suggests an explanation for why

a. a person who learns a second language thinks differently in that language.
b. children have a built-in readiness to learn grammatical rules.
c. apes are able to communicate through sign language.
d. artists, athletes, and others are able to think in visual images.

Intelligence

So far, we have considered how humans, in general, think and communicate. But do we humans not differ from one another in our intellectual capacities? No controversy in psychology has been more heated than the question of whether there exists in each person a general intellectual capacity that can be measured and quantitifed as a number. School boards, courts, and scientists debate the usefulness and fairness of intelligence and aptitude tests. Should such tests be used to rank individuals and to determine whether to admit them to a particular college or to hire them in a particular job? Do groups differ in native intelligence?

Let's therefore consider: What is intelligence? How is it assessed? And, to what extent does it result from nature (heredity) rather than nurture (environment)? Is intelligence testing society's best means of identifying those who would benefit from special opportunities? Or is intelligence testing a potent discriminatory weapon camouflaged as science?

Assessing Intelligence

8. How are modern intelligence tests classified, and when and why were they created?

intelligence The capacity for goal-directed and adaptive behavior; involves the abilities to profit from experience, solve problems, reason, and successfully meet challenges and achieve goals.

Intelligence is a concept intended to explain why some people perform better than others on cognitive tasks. In the *Handbook of Human Intelligence*, Robert Sternberg and William Salter (1982, p. 3) reported that most experts view **intelligence** as a person's capacity for "goal-directed adaptive behavior." Intelligent behavior reflects a capacity to adapt, by learning from experience, solving problems, and reasoning clearly. To understand the concept of intelligence, it helps first to know the history of intelligence testing.

aptitude tests   Tests designed to predict a person's future performance; aptitude is the capacity to learn.

achievement tests   Tests designed to assess what a person has learned.

mental age   A measure of intelligence test performance devised by Binet; the chronological age that most typically corresponds to a given level of performance. Thus, a child who does as well as the average 8-year-old is said to have a mental age of 8.

Stanford-Binet   The widely used American revision (by Terman at Stanford University) of Binet's original intelligence test.

intelligence quotient (IQ)   Defined originally as the ratio of mental age (ma) to chronological age (ca) multiplied by 100 (thus, IQ = ma/ca × 100). On contemporary intelligence tests, the average performance for a given age is assigned a score of 100.

Wechsler Adult Intelligence Scale (WAIS)   The current revision (WAIS-R) is the most widely used intelligence test; contains verbal and performance (nonverbal) subtests.

Alfred Binet   *"The scale, properly speaking, does not permit the measure of intelligence, because intellectual qualities . . . cannot be measured as linear surfaces are measured"* (Binet & Simon, 1905).

By this point in your life, you've faced dozens of different tests of your mental abilities: elementary school tests of basic reading and math skills, course examinations, intelligence tests, driver's license examinations, and college entrance examinations, to mention just a few. Psychologists classify such tests as either **aptitude tests**, intended to *predict* your ability to learn a new skill, or **achievement tests**, intended to *reflect* what you have learned. Thus, a college entrance exam, which seeks to predict your ability to do college work, is an aptitude test. Exams covering what you have learned in this course are achievement tests.

The actual differences between aptitude tests and achievement tests are not so clear-cut. Your achieved vocabulary influences your score on most aptitude tests. Similarly, your aptitudes for learning and test-taking influence your grades on tests of your course achievement. Most tests, whether labeled aptitude or achievement, assess both ability and its development. Distinguishing aptitude and achievement is a practical matter: We use aptitude tests to predict future performance and achievement tests to assess current performance.

The Origins of Intelligence Tests

The best known example of aptitude testing is an intelligence test.

Alfred Binet: Predicting School Achievement   The modern intelligence-testing movement began at the turn of the century when the French government passed a law requiring that all children attend school. Teachers soon faced a distressing range of individual differences. Some children seemed incapable of benefitting from the regular school curriculum and in need of special classes. But how could the schools objectively identify children with special needs?

The government was justifiably reluctant to trust teachers' subjective judgments of children's learning potential. Academic slowness might merely reflect inadequate prior education. Also, teachers might prejudge children on the basis of their social backgrounds. To minimize bias, France's minister of public education in 1904 commissioned French psychologist Alfred Binet and others to study the problem.

Binet and his collaborator, Théodore Simon, began by assuming that all children follow the same course of intellectual development but that some develop more rapidly. On tests, therefore, a "dull" child should perform as does a typical younger child, and a "bright" child as does a typical older child.

So, Binet and Simon set out to measure what came to be called a child's **mental age**, the chronological age that typically corresponds to a given level of performance. The average 9-year-old has a mental age of 9. But many 9-year-olds have mental ages below or above 9. Children below average, such as 9-year-olds who perform at the level of typical 7-year-olds, would struggle with normal schoolwork for their age.

To measure mental age, Binet and Simon developed varied reasoning and problem-solving questions that might predict school achievement. By testing "bright" and "backward" Parisian schoolchildren on these questions, Binet and Simon succeeded: They found items that did predict how well the children handled schoolwork. Binet hoped his test would be used to improve children's education, but he also feared it would be used to label children and limit their opportunities (Gould, 1981).

Lewis Terman: The Innate IQ   What Binet viewed as merely a practical guide for identifying slow learners who needed special help was soon seen by others to be a numerical measure of inherited intelligence. After Binet's death in 1911, Stanford University professor Lewis Terman decided to use Binet's

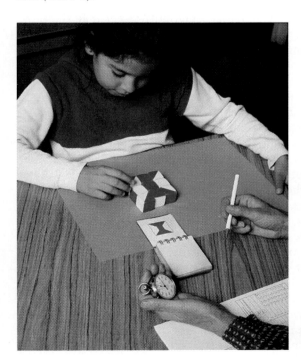

"You did very well on your IQ test. You're a man of 49 with the intelligence of a man of 53."

test. He soon found, however, that the Paris-developed age norms worked poorly with California schoolchildren. So Terman revised the test. He adapted some of Binet's original items, added others, established new age norms, and extended the upper end of the test's range from teenagers to "superior adults." Terman gave his revision the name it retains today—the **Stanford-Binet**.

For such tests, German psychologist William Stern derived the famous **intelligence quotient**, or **IQ**. The IQ was simply a person's mental age divided by chronological age and multiplied by 100 to get rid of the decimal point:

$$IQ = \frac{\text{mental age}}{\text{chronological age}} \times 100$$

Thus, an average child, whose mental and chronological ages are the same, has an IQ of 100. But an 8-year-old who answers questions as would a typical 10-year-old has an IQ of 125.

Most current intelligence tests, including the Stanford-Binet, no longer compute an IQ. The original IQ formula works fairly well for children but not for adults. Consider: Should a 40-year-old who does as well on the test as an average 20-year-old be assigned an IQ of only 50? Obviously, something is out of whack. Today's intelligence tests therefore produce a mental ability score based on the test-taker's performance relative to the average performance of others the same age. As on the original Stanford-Binet, current tests define this score so that 100 is average, with about two-thirds of all people scoring between 85 and 115. Although there is no longer any intelligence *quotient*, the term "IQ" still lingers in everyday vocabulary as a shorthand expression for "intelligence test score."

Matching Patterns   *As psychometrists time their work, this girl and man concentrate on solving Block Design puzzles, which test the ability to analyze patterns. Wechsler's individually administered intelligence test comes in forms suited for adults (WAIS-R) and children (WISC-R).*

The Most Widely Used Intelligence Test: The WAIS-R

With Terman's help, the U.S. government used intelligence testing to evaluate newly arriving immigrants, many of whom were unfamiliar with the culture assumed by the test. Among the supposedly "feeble-minded" Eastern European immigrants of the early 1900s was a 6-year-old Romanian boy, David Wechsler. Ironically, three decades later *psychologist* David Wechsler created today's most widely used intelligence test, now known as the **Wechsler Adult Intelligence Scale— Revised (WAIS-R)**. Later he developed a similar test for school-age children called the Wechsler Intelligence Scale for Children (WISC), and still later a test for preschool children. The WAIS-R consists of 11 subtests, as illustrated in Figure 8–9 (page 278). It yields not only an overall intelligence score, as does the

VERBAL

General Information
What day of the year is Independence Day?

Similarities
In what way are *wool* and *cotton* alike?

Arithmetic Reasoning
If eggs cost 60 cents a dozen, what does 1 egg cost?

Vocabulary
Tell me the meaning of corrupt.

Comprehension
Why do people buy fire insurance?

Digit Span
Listen carefully, and when I am through, say the numbers right after me.

7   3   4   1   8   6

Now I am going to say some more numbers, but I want you to say them backward.

3   8   4   1   6

PERFORMANCE

Picture Completion
I am going to show you a picture with an important part missing. Tell me what is missing.

'85

SUN	MON	TUE	WED	THU	FRI	SAT
1	2	3	4	5	6	7
8	9	10	11	12	13	14
15	16	17	18	19	20	21
22	23	24	25	26	27	28
29	30					

Picture Arrangement
The pictures below tell a story. Put them in the right order to tell the story.

Block Design
Using the four blocks, make one just like this.

Object Assembly
If these pieces are put together correctly, they will make something. Go ahead and put them together as quickly as you can.

Digit-Symbol Substitution

Code

△	○	▱	×	8
1	2	3	4	5

Test

△	8	×	○	△	▱	8	×	△	8

Figure 8–9 Sample Subtest Items From the Wechsler Adult Intelligence Scale—Revised (WAIS-R) Subtests *(From Thorndike & Hagen, 1977.)*

"The IQ test was invented to predict academic performance, nothing else. If we wanted something that would predict life success, we'd have to invent another test completely."

Social psychologist Robert Zajonc (1984b)

Stanford-Binet, but also separate "verbal" and "performance" (nonverbal) scores. Striking differences between the two scores alert the examiner to possible learning problems. For example, a verbal score much lower than the same person's performance score might indicate a reading or language disability. The tests also provide clues to cognitive strengths that a teacher or an employer might build upon.

College Aptitude Tests: The SAT   Large-scale group testing is now efficiently accomplished through multiple-choice tests, such as the Scholastic Assessment Test (SAT), which is taken annually by 1 million Americans seeking college admission. (Most other countries, including Canada, have no such exam for college admission; instead, they evaluate an applicant's prior academic record, which reflects both aptitude and motivation.) Like the original Binet test, the SAT attempts to predict academic performance. Unlike the Stanford-Binet and Wechsler tests, however, the SAT yields no overall intelligence score. Rather, it separately assesses verbal and mathematical aptitudes.

The SAT is a good example of an aptitude test that also assumes some prior achievement. More than half of its 60 mathematical questions, for example, presume a basic knowledge of either algebra or geometry. The American College Testing (ACT) exam, also taken annually by a million college-bound high school students, is even more of an achievement test. On the ACT, the average high school student today would probably outscore Aristotle and other geniuses of the distant past because the test measures students' "educational development" in English usage, mathematics, reading, and science reasoning.

standardization Defining meaningful scores by comparison with the performance of a pretested "standardization group."

normal curve The symmetrical bell-shaped curve that describes the distribution of many physical and psychological attributes in a group of people. Most intelligence scores fall near the average, and fewer and fewer scores lie near the extremes.

reliability The extent to which a test yields consistent results, as assessed by the consistency of scores on two halves of the test, on alternative forms of the test, or on retesting.

Principles of Test Construction

9. What three principles of test construction apply in evaluating a psychological test?

To be widely accepted, psychological tests must meet three criteria: They must be *standardized, reliable,* and *valid.* The Stanford-Binet and the Wechsler tests meet these requirements.

Standardization Knowing how many questions you got right on an intelligence test would tell us almost nothing. To evaluate your performance, we need a basis for comparing it with others' performance. To enable meaningful comparisons, test-makers first give the test to a representative sample of people. When other individuals take the test, we can then compare their scores with the standards defined by this group. This process of defining meaningful scores relative to a pretested group is called **standardization**.

Recall that Terman and his colleagues recognized that a scale standardized on Parisians did not provide a satisfactory standard for evaluating Americans. So they revised the test and standardized the new version by testing 2300 native-born, white Americans of differing socioeconomic levels. Ironically, they then evaluated nonwhite American and immigrant groups based on this standard (Van Leeuwen, 1982).

Standardized test results typically form a *normal distribution,* a bell-shaped pattern of scores that forms the **normal curve** (Figure 8–10). Whether we are measuring people's heights, weights, or mental aptitudes, most scores tend to cluster around the average. On an intelligence test, we call this average score 100. As we move out from the average (toward either extreme) we find fewer and fewer people. Within each age group, the Stanford-Binet and the Wechsler tests assign any person a score according to how much that person's performance deviates above or below the average. As Figure 8–10 shows, a performance higher than all but 2 percent of all scores earns an intelligence score of 130. A performance that is comparably *below* 98 percent of all the scores earns an intelligence score of 70.

Figure 8–10 The Normal Curve *Scores on aptitude tests tend to form a normal, or bell-shaped, curve. For example, the Wechsler scale calls the average score 100. It defines other scores to make about 68 percent of them fall within 15 points above or below 100. About 95 percent fall within 30 points above and below 100.*

Reliability A good test must yield dependably consistent scores; in a word, it must have **reliability**. To check a test's reliability, researchers retest people using the same test or another form of it. If the two scores generally agree, or *correlate,* the test is reliable. Alternatively, the researcher may split a test in half and see whether scores derived from odd and even questions agree.

validity The extent to which a test measures or predicts what it is supposed to.

The higher the correlation between the *test-retest* or the *split-half* scores, the higher the test's reliability. Recall from Chapter 1 that the lowest correlation, –1.0, represents perfect disagreement between two sets of scores—as the first score goes up, the second goes down. A correlation of zero represents no consistency. The highest correlation, +1.0, represents perfect consistency—as the first score goes up, so does the second. The tests we have considered so far—the Stanford-Binet, the WAIS-R, and the SAT—all have reliabilities of about +.9, which is very high. When retested, people's scores tend to match their first score closely.

Validity High reliability does not ensure a test's **validity**—the extent to which the test actually measures what it is supposed to measure or predicts what it is supposed to predict. If you use a shrunken tape measure to measure people's heights, your data would have high reliability (consistency) but low validity. How, then, can we determine whether a test is valid? For some tests, it is enough that they tap the pertinent behavior. The road test for a driver's license has content validity because it samples the tasks a driver routinely faces. Your course exams have content validity if they assess your mastery of a representative sample of course material. Other tests are evaluated in terms of how well they predict future achievement.

Are general aptitude tests as predictive as they are reliable? As critics are fond of noting, the answer is plainly no. The predictive power of aptitude tests is fairly strong in the early grades, but later it weakens. A better predictor of future grades is past grades, which reflect both aptitude and motivation. More generally, the best predictor of future behavior is a large sample of past behaviors of the same sort.

What Is Intelligence?

10. Is intelligence a single general ability, or is it formed from several distinct abilities?

Reading conflicting ideas about intelligence can leave you feeling as Alice in Wonderland felt after reading "Jabberwocky": "Somehow it seems to fill my head with ideas—only I don't exactly know what they are." So let's see if we can refine the concept. Is intelligence one dimension or many?

Is Intelligence One General Ability or Several Specific Abilities?

We all know some people talented in mathematics, others in creative writing, and still others in art, music, or dance. Perhaps you have known a talented artist who is dumbfounded by the simplest mathematical problems, or a brilliant math student who has little aptitude for literary discussion. We may therefore wonder whether people's mental abilities are too diverse to justify labeling them with the single word *intelligence* or quantifying them with a number from some single scale.

The Factor Analysis Approach To find out whether there might be a general ability factor that runs throughout our specific mental abilities, psychologists study how various abilities relate to one another.

A statistical method called *factor analysis* allows researchers to identify clusters of test items that measure a common ability. For example, people who do well on vocabulary items often do well on paragraph comprehension. This cluster helps define a verbal intelligence factor. Psychologists have identified

general intelligence (*g*) A general underlying intelligence factor believed by Spearman and others to be measured by every task on an intelligence test.

savant syndrome A condition in which a person otherwise limited in mental ability has an amazing specific skill, such as in computation or drawing.

several such clusters, including a spatial ability factor and a reasoning ability factor.

Charles Spearman (1863–1945), who helped develop factor analysis, believed there is also a **general intelligence**, or *g*, factor that underlies the specific factors. People often have special abilities that stand out, Spearman allowed. But those who score high on one factor, such as verbal intelligence, typically score higher than average on other factors, such as spatial or reasoning ability. So there is at least a small tendency for different abilities to come in the same package. Spearman believed that this commonality, the *g* factor, underlies all of our intelligent behavior, from excelling in school to navigating the sea.

Psychologist Howard Gardner (1983, 1993) supports the idea that intelligence comes in *different* packages. He notes that brain damage may diminish one type of ability but not others. Gardner has also studied reports of people with exceptional abilities, including those who excel in only one. People with **savant syndrome**, for example, score at the low end on intelligence tests but have an island of brilliance—some incredible ability, as in computation, drawing, or musical memory (Figure 8–11). These people may have virtually no language ability, yet may be able to compute numbers as quickly and accurately as an electronic calculator, or identify almost instantly the day of the week that corresponds to any given date in history.

Figure 8–11 Savant Syndrome *Although hardly able to talk coherently, Britain's Stephen Wiltshire can draw intricate scenes after just one good look. This drawing is of St. Mark's in Venice, Italy. By age 13, Stephen was famous throughout Britain for his ability to "draw, with greatest ease, any street he had seen; but he could not, unaided, cross one by himself" (Sacks, 1995).*

Using such evidence, Gardner argues that we do not have *an* intelligence, but instead have *multiple* intelligences, each independent of the others. In addition to the verbal and mathematical aptitudes assessed by standard tests, he identifies distinct aptitudes for musical accomplishment, for spatially analyzing the visual world, for mastering movement skills (as in dance), and for insightfully understanding ourselves and others. According to Gardner, the computer programmer, the poet, the street-smart adolescent who becomes a crafty executive, and the point guard on the basketball team exhibit different kinds of intelligence. A general intelligence score is therefore like the overall rating of a city—which doesn't give you much specific information about its schools, roads, or nightlife.

creativity   The ability to produce novel and valuable ideas.

Drawing by Reilly; © 1988
The New Yorker Magazine, Inc.

"You're wise, but you lack tree smarts."

On his way home from picking up a Nobel prize in Stockholm, physicist Richard Feynman stopped in Queens, New York, to look at his high school record. "My grades were not as good as I remembered," he reported, "and my IQ was [a good, though unexceptional] 124" (Faber, 1987).

Wouldn't it be wonderful if the world were so just, responds intelligence researcher Sandra Scarr (1989), that being weak in any area would be compensated by genius in some other area? Alas, the world is not just, for there remains some tendency for different skills to correlate. For example, people with mental disadvantages often have lesser physical abilities as well; thus, we hold Special Olympics to give them a chance to enjoy fair competition.

Robert Sternberg and Richard Wagner (1993) agree with Gardner's idea of multiple intelligences but distinguish more simply among three intelligences: the *academic* problem-solving skills assessed by intelligence tests (presenting well-defined problems having a single right answer), the *practical* intelligence often required for everyday tasks (often ill-defined, with multiple solutions), and the *creative* intelligence demonstrated in reacting to novel situations. Intelligence tests predict school grades reasonably well but predict vocational success less well. Managerial success, for example, depends less on the academic abilities assessed by an intelligence test score (assuming the score is average or above) than on a shrewd ability to manage oneself, one's tasks, and other people. People who demonstrate keen practical intelligence may or may not have distinguished themselves in school. Likewise, Stephen Ceci and Jeffrey Liker (1986) report that racetrack fans' expertise in handicapping horses—a practical but complex cognitive task—is unrelated to their intelligence scores. So personal competence in everyday living requires much that traditional intelligence tests do not measure.

We might, then, liken mental abilities to physical abilities. Athleticism is not one thing but many. The ability to run fast is distinct from brute strength, which is distinct from the eye-hand coordination required to throw a ball on target. A champion weightlifter rarely has the potential to be a skilled ice skater. Yet there remains some tendency for good things to come packaged together—for running speed and throwing accuracy to correlate, thanks to general athletic ability. Likewise, intelligence involves several distinct abilities, which cluster together in the same individual often enough to define a small general intelligence factor.

Creativity and Intelligence

11. What factors affect creativity?

Creativity is the ability to produce ideas that are both novel and valuable. The outlets for creativity vary by culture. Samoan culture encourages creativity in dance, Balinese culture in music, the African Ashanti culture in wood carvings (Lubart, 1990). In each, creativity means expressing familiar themes in novel ways.

Results from tests of intelligence and creativity suggest that a certain level of aptitude is necessary but not sufficient for creativity. In general, people with high intelligence scores do well on creativity tests. ("How many uses can you think of for a brick?") But beyond a certain level—a score of about 120—the correlation between intelligence scores and creativity disappears. Exceptionally creative architects, mathematicians, scientists, and engineers usually score no higher on intelligence tests than do their less creative peers (MacKinnon & Hall, 1972). So there is clearly more to creativity than intelligence scores.

Studies of creative people suggest five other components of creativity (Sternberg, 1988; Sternberg & Lubart, 1991, 1992). The first is *expertise*—a well-developed base of knowledge. "Chance favors only the prepared mind," observed Louis Pasteur.

Extremes of Intelligence

One way to glimpse the validity and significance of any test is to compare people who score at the two extremes of the normal curve. The two groups should differ noticeably, and they do.

In one famous project begun in 1921, Lewis Terman studied more than 1500 California schoolchildren with IQ scores over 135. Contrary to the popular myth that intellectually gifted children are frequently maladjusted because they are "in a different world" from their nongifted peers, Terman's high-scoring children were unusually healthy, well adjusted, and academically successful. When restudied over the next six decades (Goleman, 1980), most of these people had attained

mental retardation A condition of limited mental ability, as indicated by an intelligence score below 70, that produces difficulty in adapting to the demands of life; varies from mild to profound.

Down syndrome A condition of retardation and associated physical disorders caused by an extra chromosome in one's genetic makeup.

high levels of education. Their vocational success varied, yet the group included many doctors, lawyers, professors, scientists, and writers. Terman's whiz kids remind one of Jean Piaget, who by age 7 was devoting his free time to studying birds, fossils, and machines; who by age 15 began publishing scientific articles on mollusks; and who later went on to become this century's most famous developmental psychologist (Hunt, 1993).

At the other extreme are people whose intelligence test scores fall below 70. To be labeled as having **mental retardation**, a child must have both a low test score *and* difficulty adapting to the normal demands of living independently. Only about 1 percent of the population meets both criteria, with males outnumbering females by 50 percent (American Psychiatric Association, 1994). As Table 8–2 indicates, most such mentally challenged individuals can, with support, live in mainstream society.

Mental retardation sometimes results from known physical causes. **Down syndrome**, a disorder attributed to an extra chromosome in the person's genetic makeup, is one such cause (although most people with Down syndrome are

not severely retarded).

During the last two centuries the pendulum of opinion about how best to care for the mentally challenged has made a complete swing. Until the mid-nineteenth century, they were cared for at home. Those with the most severe disabilities often died, but people with milder forms of retardation found a place in a farm-based society. Then, residential schools for slow learners were established. By the twentieth century, many of these institutions had become warehouses providing residents no privacy, little attention, and no hope. Parents often were told to separate themselves permanently from a retarded child before they became attached.

Now, in the last half of this century, the pendulum has swung back to normalization—allowing mentally impaired people to live in their own communities as normally as their functioning permits. We educate such children in less restrictive environments and we integrate, or *mainstream*, many into regular classrooms. Most grow up with their own families until moving into a protected living arrangement, such as a group home. The hope, and often the reality, is a happier and more dignified life.

TABLE 8-2

Degrees of Mental Retardation

Level	Typical Intelligence Scores	Percentage of the Retarded	Adaptation to Demands of Life
Mild	50–70	85	May learn academic skills up to sixth-grade level. Adults may, with assistance, achieve self-supporting social and vocational skills.
Moderate	35–49	10	May progress to second-grade level academically. Adults may contribute to their own support by labor in sheltered workshops.
Severe	20–34	3–4	May learn to talk and to perform simple work tasks under close supervision but are generally unable to profit from vocational training.
Profound	Below 20	1–2	Require constant aid and supervision.

Source: Adapted from the American Psychiatric Association (1994).

Reprinted with permission of Paul Soderblom.

Everyone held up their crackers as David threw the cheese log into the ceiling fan.

The second is *imaginative thinking skills*—an ability to see things in new ways, to recognize patterns, to make connections. To be creative you must first master the basic elements of a problem, then redefine or explore the problem in a new way. Copernicus first developed expertise regarding the solar system's sun and planets and then defined the system as revolving around the sun, not the earth.

Creativity's third ingredient is a *venturesome personality*—one that tolerates ambiguity and risk, perseveres in overcoming obstacles, and seeks new experiences rather than following the pack. Inventors, for example, have a knack for persisting after failures, as Thomas Edison did in trying countless substances for his light-bulb filament.

The fourth component is what psychologist Teresa Amabile calls the *intrinsic motivation* principle of creativity: "People will be most creative when they feel motivated primarily by the interest, enjoyment, satisfaction, and challenge of the work itself—rather than by external pressures" (Amabile & Hennessey, 1992). Creative people focus not so much on extrinsic motivators—meeting deadlines, impressing people, or making money—as on the intrinsic pleasure and challenge of their work.

The final component is a *creative environment* that sparks, supports, and refines creative ideas. After studying the careers of 2026 prominent scientists and inventors, Dean Keith Simonton (1992) noted that the most eminent among them were not lone geniuses. Rather they were mentored, challenged, and supported by their relationships with colleagues.

! *Rehearse It*

12. Aptitude and achievement tests are tests of mental abilities. Aptitude tests are designed to _____, whereas achievement tests are designed to _____.

a. predict ability to learn; reflect what has been learned
b. assess adaptive behavior; identify level of intelligence
c. uncover undeveloped skills; objectively evaluate adaptability
d. measure performance; differentiate slow learners from all others

13. Intelligence quotient, or IQ, was originally defined as the ratio of mental age to chronological age multiplied by 100. By this definition, a 6-year-old with a measured mental age of 6, would have an IQ of 100. Likewise, a 6-year-old with a measured mental age of 9 would have an IQ of

a. 67.
b. 133.
c. 86.
d. 150.

14. The Wechsler Adult Intelligence Scale—Revised (WAIS-R) yields an overall intelligence score as well as separate verbal and performance (nonverbal) scores. The WAIS-R is best able to tell us

a. what part of an individual's intelligence is determined by genetic inheritance.
b. whether the test-taker will succeed in a job.
c. how the test-taker compares with other adults in vocabulary and arithmetic reasoning.
d. whether the test-taker has specific skills for music and the performing arts.

15. The Stanford-Binet, WAIS-R, and WISC are known to have very high reliability (about +.9). This means that

a. a pretest has been given to a representative sample.
b. the test yields consistent results, for example on retesting.
c. the test measures what it is supposed to measure.
d. the results of the test will be distributed on a bell-shaped curve.

16. Savant syndrome is retardation combined with incredible ability in one specific area. The existence of savant syndrome seems to support

a. Terman's ideas on "superior adults."
b. Spearman's notion of general intelligence, or *g* factor.
c. Gardner's theory of multiple intelligences.
d. Binet's conception of mental age.

17. Creativity is the ability to produce novel and valuable ideas. Which of the following is *not* a characteristic of a creative person?

a. expertise
b. extrinsic motivation
c. a venturesome personality
d. imaginative thinking skills

Genetic and Environmental Influences on Intelligence

12. Is intelligence influenced more by heredity or environment?

Intelligence seems to run in families. But why? Are intellectual abilities mostly inherited? Or are they molded more by one's environment?

Few of psychology's issues arouse such passion. Consider: If we mainly inherit our differing mental abilities, and if success reflects those abilities, then people's socioeconomic standing will correspond to their inborn differences. Thus, those on top may believe their innate mental superiority justifies their social position.

If, on the other hand, mental abilities are primarily nurtured by the environments that raise and school us, then children from disadvantaged environments will often lead disadvantaged lives. In this case, people's socioeconomic standings will result from unequal opportunities, a situation that many regard as basically unjust. Setting aside such political implications as best we can, let's examine the evidence.

Genetic Influences

Do people who share the same genes also share comparable mental abilities? As you can see from Figure 8–12, which summarizes many studies, the answer is clearly yes. In support of the genetic contribution to intelligence, researchers note that:

- The IQ scores of identical twins are virtually as similar as those of the same person taking the same test twice. Fraternal twins, who share only half their genes, are much less similar in IQ scores.

- Even identical twins whose parents do not dress or treat them identically are virtual carbon copies of one another in IQ score (Loehlin & Nichols, 1976). Likewise, identical twins who have been reared separately have similar IQ scores (Bouchard, 1993).

On the other hand, some evidence points to an effect of environment. Fraternal twins, who are genetically no more alike than any other siblings but who are treated more alike because they are the same age, tend to score more alike than other siblings. As new data accumulate, assessments of the extent to which

> *"I am, somehow, less interested in the weight and convolutions of Einstein's brain than in the near certainty that people of equal talent have lived and died in cotton fields and sweatshops."*
>
> Stephen Jay Gould
> *The Panda's Thumb*, 1980

Figure 8–12 Intelligence: Nature and Nurture *The most genetically similar people have the most similar intelligence scores. But the correlations also reveal an effect of environment: Identical twins reared apart test somewhat less alike than those reared together. Remember: 1.0 indicates a perfect correlation; zero indicates no correlation at all. (From Bouchard, 1982.)*

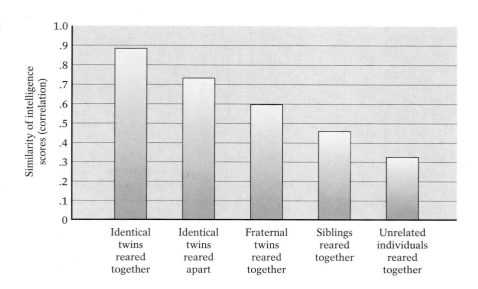

heritability The proportion of variation among individuals that we can attribute to genes. The heritability of a trait may vary, depending on the range of populations and environments studied.

variation in IQ scores can be attributed to heredity have dropped from earlier estimates of around 80 percent to newer estimates of between 50 percent (Plomin & Rende, 1991) and 60 percent (Bouchard & Segal, 1988).

Seeking to disentangle genes and environment, researchers have also asked whether adopted children and their adoptive siblings, thanks to their shared environment, share similar aptitudes. During childhood, the intelligence test scores of adoptive siblings correlate modestly. But with age, the effect of common rearing wanes; by adulthood, the correlation is roughly zero (McGue & others, 1993).

Researchers have also asked whether adopted children have intelligence test scores more like those of their biological parents, from whom they received their genes, or of their adoptive parents, who provide their home environment. As Figure 8–13 illustrates, adopted children's scores more closely resemble those of their biological parents than those of their adoptive parents. It matters whether one is adopted into an impoverished or an enriched environment (Turkheimer, 1991). Yet being reared "together in the same adoptive home does not make you intellectually similar to your brothers and sisters," notes Sandra Scarr (1989); "being genetically related by half of your genes does."

To say that the **heritability** of intelligence—the variation in intelligence test scores attributable to genetic factors—is roughly 50 to 60 percent does *not* mean that your genes are responsible for 50 to 60 percent of your intelligence and your environment for the rest. (Likewise, saying that the heritability of height is 90 percent does not mean that a 60-inch-tall woman can credit her genes for 54 inches and her environment for the other 6 inches.) Rather, it means that we can attribute to heredity 50 to 60 percent *of the variation in intelligence within a group of people.* This point is so often misunderstood that I repeat: We can never say what percentage of an *individual's* intelligence is inherited. Heritability refers instead to the extent to which *differences among people* are attributable to genes.

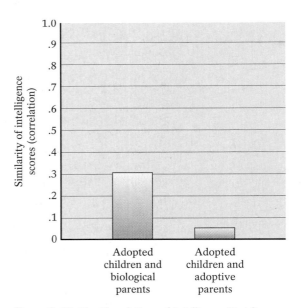

Figure 8–13 The Correlations of Intelligence Test Scores Between 245 Adopted Colorado Children and Their Adoptive and Biological Parents *By age 7, the adopted children had intelligence test scores more like those of their biological parents. (From Fulker & others, 1988.)*

Even this conclusion must be qualified, because heritability can vary from study to study. If we were to follow Mark Twain's proposal to raise boys in barrels to age 12, feeding them through a hole, they would emerge with lower-than-normal intelligence scores. Yet their (equal) environments would not account for the differences between them. Thus, despite their deprived environments, heritability for their IQ score *differences* would be near 100 percent. *As environments become more equal, heredity as a source of differences necessarily becomes more important.* On the other hand, compare people with similar heredities who are raised in drastically different environments (barrels versus advantaged homes), and heritability—differences due to genes—will be low.

Remember, too, that genes and environment intertwine. For example, students with a natural aptitude for mathematics are more likely to select math courses in high school, and later to score well on math aptitude tests—thanks *both* to their natural math aptitude *and* to their math experience. Our genes shape the experiences that shape us.

Environmental Influences

We have seen that our genes make a difference. Even if we were all raised in the same intellectually stimulating environment, we still would not have the same aptitudes. But we have also seen that heredity doesn't tell the whole story. Within the limits dictated by our genes, our life experiences matter.

Human environments are rarely so impoverished as the dark and barren cages inhabited by deprived rats that develop thinner-than-normal brain cortexes (as described in Chapter 3). Yet severe life experiences do leave marks on humans, as psychologist J. McVicker Hunt (1982) observed in a destitute Iranian orphanage in Tehran, where the typical child could not sit up unassisted at age 2 or walk at age 4. What care the infants received was not in response to their crying, cooing, or other behaviors. The infants were therefore not developing any sense of personal control over their environment, and so were becoming passive "glum lumps." Extreme deprivation was bludgeoning native intelligence.

Aware of the benefits of responsive caregiving, Hunt began a program of "tutored human enrichment." For instance, he trained caregivers to play vocal games with the infants. First, they imitated the babies' babbling. Then they led the babies in vocal follow-the-leader by shifting from one familiar sound to another. Then they began to teach sounds from the Persian language.

The results were dramatic. All 11 infants who received these language-fostering experiences could name more than 50 objects and body parts by 22 months. So charming had the infants become that most were adopted—an unprecedented success for the orphanage.

Hunt's findings testify to the importance of environment. Severe disadvantage takes a toll on children (Ramey & Ramey, 1992). But do such findings indicate a way to "give your child a superior intellect"? Some popular books claim that with intensive preschool training this is possible, but most experts are doubtful (Phillips & Stipek, 1993). Sandra Scarr (1984) agrees that neglectful upbringing can have grave long-term consequences. However, she also believes that "as long as an infant has normal human contact and normal exposure to sights, sounds, human speech, and so forth, the baby will thrive." As for future intelligence, "Parents who are very concerned about providing special educational lessons for their babies are wasting their time."

Hunt would probably agree with Scarr that extra instruction has little effect on the intellectual development of children from stimulating environments. But he was optimistic when it came to children from disadvantaged environments.

"There is a large body of evidence indicating that there is little if anything to be gained by exposing middle-class children to early education."

Developmental psychologist Edward F. Zigler (1987)

Indeed, his 1961 book, *Intelligence and Experience*, helped launch Project Head Start in 1965. Head Start is a U.S. government–funded preschool program serving 700,000 children, most of whom come from families below the poverty level (Kramer, 1993). It aims to enhance children's chances for success in school and beyond by boosting their cognitive and social skills.

Does it succeed? Researchers have studied Head Start and other preschool programs by comparing equivalent groups of children who do versus those who don't experience the intervention. Their findings indicate that high-quality programs for disadvantaged children produce at least short-term cognitive gains, even on intelligence tests (Haskins, 1989). Quality programs also increase school readiness, decreasing the likelihood of a child's repeating a grade or being placed in special education. Although the aptitude benefits dissipate over time (reminding us that life experience *after* Head Start matters, too), psychologist Edward Zigler, the program's first director, believes there are other long-term benefits (Zigler & Muenchow, 1992). High-quality preschool programs improve attitudes toward learning, and they reduce school dropouts and criminality. So, the effect of education on aptitude doesn't end with the preschool years.

Getting a Head Start *To increase readiness for schoolwork and expand children's notions of where school might lead them, Project Head Start offers educational activities. Here preschool children in a classroom learn about colors and those on a field trip learn what fire fighters do.*

Group Differences

13. How, and why, do ethnic and gender groups differ in aptitude test performance?

If there were no group differences in aptitude scores, psychologists could politely debate hereditary and environmental influences in their ivory towers. But if school environments favor certain groups, then tests that predict school performance must also favor those groups. Indeed, there are group differences. What are they? And what shall we make of them?

Race Differences

We can all wish it were otherwise, but it is an agreed-upon fact that (1) the races differ in average IQ score, and (2) high-scoring people (and races) are more likely to attain high levels of education and income. A statement by 52 intelligence researchers explains: "The bell curve for whites is centered roughly around IQ 100; the bell curve for American blacks roughly around 85; and those for different subgroups of Hispanics roughly midway between those for whites and blacks" (Avery & others, 1994). Comparable results come from other academic aptitude tests, such as the SAT.

Everyone agrees that there are other group differences as well. European New Zealanders outscore native Maori New Zealanders. Israeli Jews outscore Israeli Arabs. Most Japanese outscore the stigmatized Japanese minority, the Burakumin. And hearing people outscore those born deaf (Braden, 1994; Steele, 1990a; Zeidner, 1990).

Everyone further agrees that such *group* differences provide little basis for judging individuals. Women outlive men by 6 years, but knowing someone's sex doesn't tell us with any precision how long that person will live. Even Charles Murray and Richard Herrnstein (1994), whose writings have drawn attention to black-white differences, remind us that "millions of blacks have higher IQs than the average white."

If heredity contributes to individual differences in intelligence, does it also contribute to group differences? It's conceivable, and a few psychologists speculate that different climates and survival challenges could have led to racial differences in aptitudes (Lynn, 1991; Rushton, 1990). But it's also clear that, as in our earlier barrel-versus-home-reared boys example, group differences in a heritable trait may be entirely environmental. Consider one of nature's experiments: Allow some children to grow up hearing their culture's dominant language, while others do not. Then give them an intelligence test rooted in that language, and (no surprise) the hearing will outscore the deaf. Although individual performance differences may be substantially genetic, the group difference is not.

So, is there evidence that the racial gap may be similarly environmental? Consider:

- Genetics research reveals that under the skin the races are remarkably alike (Cavalli-Sforza & others, 1994; Lewontin, 1982). Individual differences within a race are much greater than between-race differences. The average genetic difference between two Icelandic villagers or between two Kenyans greatly exceeds the difference between their groups. Moreover, looks can deceive. Europeans and Africans are genetically closer than are Africans and Aboriginal Australians.

- Asian students outperform North American students on math achievement and aptitude tests. But this difference may reflect conscientiousness rather than competence. Asian students also attend school 30 percent more days per year and spend much more time in and out of school studying math (Stevenson, 1992).

- The IQ test performance of today's better fed and educated population exceeds that of the 1930s population by the same margin that the average white today exceeds the average black—demonstrating a generational group difference that no one attributes to genetics.

- When black children are adopted early in life into white families and "reared in the culture of the schools and the IQ tests," their later intelligence scores approach those of the average white child (Weinberg & others, 1992).

> White and black infants have scored equally well on an infant intelligence measure (preference for looking at novel stimuli)—a predictor of future intelligence scores (Fagan, 1992).

> In different eras, different ethnic groups have experienced golden ages—periods of remarkable achievement. Twenty-five hundred years ago it was the Greeks and the Egyptians, then the Romans; in the eighth and ninth centuries genius seemed to reside in the Arab world; 500 years ago it was the Aztec Indians and the peoples of Northern Europe. Today, people marvel at Asians' technological genius. Cultures rise and fall over centuries; genes do not. That fact makes it difficult to attribute a natural superiority to any race.

Gender Differences

In science, as in everyday life, differences, not similarities, excite interest. Compared with the anatomical and physiological similarities between men and women, our sex differences are relatively minor. Yet it is the differences we find exciting. Similarly, in the psychological domain, gender similarities dwarf gender differences, but the differences often capture our attention. To some, it is news that there is no gender gap in average verbal ability as assessed by tests of vocabulary, reading comprehension, and solving analogies (Hyde & Linn, 1988). But most people find differences more newsworthy. Girls are better spellers: At the end of high school, only 30 percent of males spell better than the average female (Lubinski & Benbow, 1992). Boys outnumber girls at the low extremes. Boys are more often slow to talk. In remedial reading classes, boys outnumber girls three to one (Finucci & Childs, 1981). In high school, underachieving boys outnumber girls by two to one (McCall & others, 1992).

In math grades, the average girl typically equals or surpasses the average boy (ETS, 1992; Kimball, 1989). And on math tests given to more than 3 million representatively sampled people in 100 independent studies, males and females have obtained nearly identical average scores (Hyde & others, 1990). But again—despite much greater diversity within the genders than between them—group differences make the news. Although females have an edge in math computation, males in various cultures score higher in math problem solving (Hedges & Nowell, 1995; Lummis & Stevenson, 1990). For example, male high school seniors average 45 points higher on the SAT math test (literally meaning they average four more correct answers on the 60-question test). Because U.S. National Merit Scholarships are based on SAT scores, only about 35 percent of these awards have gone to girls (despite girls' generally higher grades).

The score differences are sharpest at the extremes. Among precocious 12-year-olds scoring above 700 on SAT math, boys outnumber girls 13 to 1 (Lubinski & Benbow, 1992). In other Western countries, virtually all math prodigies participating in the International Mathematics Olympiad have been males. Female math prodigies have, however, reached the top levels in non-Western countries such as China (Halpern, 1991). The average male edge seems most reliable in tests involving speedily rotating three-dimensional objects in one's mind (Halpern, 1986; Linn & Peterson, 1986; Sanders & Soares, 1986) (Figure 8–14). Such spatial ability helps when fitting suitcases into a car trunk, playing chess, or doing certain types of geometry problems.

Do natural sex differences therefore explain why most mathematicians and more than 9 in 10 rated chess players and American architects, engineers, and mapmakers are men? Before concluding yes, consider how social expectations shape boys' and girls' interests and abilities (Eccles & others, 1990). Traditionally, math and science were considered masculine subjects. For example, many parents would send their sons to computer camps and give their daughters more encouragement in English. As you might expect, the male edge in math problem solving grows with age, becoming detectable only after elementary

> "Do not obtain your slaves from Britain, because they are so stupid and so utterly incapable of being taught."
>
> Cicero, 106–43 B.C.

Figure 8–14 The Mental Rotation Test *This is a test of spatial abilities. Which two responses show a different view of the standard? (See page 292 for answers.) (From Vandenberg & Kuse, 1978.)*

Which two circles contain a configuration of blocks identical to the one in the circle at the left?

Standard

Responses

school. But as more and more girls are encouraged to develop their abilities in math and science, the gender gap is narrowing. Among representative national samples of high school juniors taking the Preliminary Scholastic Assessment Test (PSAT), the male edge has nearly disappeared since 1960 (Linn & Hyde, 1991).

The Question of Bias

14. Are intelligence tests biased and discriminatory?

Are intelligence tests biased? How we answer depends on what we mean by *bias*. One meaning is that the tests detect not only innate differences in intelligence but also differences caused by cultural experiences. In this sense, everyone agrees that intelligence tests are biased. No one claims that heritability is 100 percent responsible for any test score. An intelligence test measures a person's developed abilities at a particular time. These abilities necessarily reflect that person's experiences *and* environment. If people's experiences and backgrounds are unequal, the test's results will reflect those inequalities. Intelligence tests, say their advocates, are biased in the same sense that yardsticks are biased—because their measurements detect the nutritional effect that has led to people being, on average, 3 inches taller than a half century ago (Angoff, 1987; Lynn, 1987).

Another meaning of *bias* hinges on whether a test is less valid for some groups than for others. If the SAT accurately predicts the college achievement of one race but not that of another, then the test would be biased. The near-consensus among psychologists, as summarized by the National Research Council's Committee on Ability Testing, is that the major aptitude tests are *not* biased in this statistical meaning of the term (Rowe & others, 1994; Wigdor & Garner, 1982). The predictive validity of the SAT or of a standard intelligence test is roughly the same for blacks and whites and for rich and poor. If an IQ score of 95 predicts *C* grades, the rough prediction usually applies to all ethnic and economic groups.

So, aptitude tests seem biased in one sense (sensitivity to performance differences caused by cultural experience) but not in another (statistical prediction for different groups).

Are tests discriminatory? Again, the answer can be yes or no. In one sense, yes, their purpose is to discriminate—to distinguish among individuals. In another sense, their purpose is to reduce discrimination by reducing reliance on the subjective criteria that once were more crucial for school and job placement—criteria such as who you know, what you look like, or how much the interviewer happens to like "your kind of person." Banning aptitude tests would force the people who decide on admissions and jobs to rely more on other considerations, such as their personal opinions. Civil service tests, for example, were devised to discriminate more fairly and objectively, by reducing the political, racial, and ethnic discrimination that preceded their use. So perhaps our aim should be to realize the benefits that Alfred Binet foresaw for intelligence tests—to enable schools to recognize who might best benefit from early inter-

Answers to the mental rotation test on page 291: the first and fourth alternatives.

> *"Almost all the joyful things of life are outside the measure of IQ tests."*
>
> Madeleine L'Engle
> *A Circle of Quiet*, 1972

vention—while being alert to Binet's fear that test scores may be misinterpreted as literal measures of a person's worth and fixed potential.

Finally, we must remember that *intelligence test scores reflect only one aspect of personal competence*. Other attributes—motivation, character, social skills, artistic talent, athletic ability, sensitivity, emotional maturity—matter. The competence that intelligence tests sample is important but far from all-inclusive. The spatial ability of the carpenter differs from the logical ability of the computer programmer, which differs from the verbal ability of the poet. Differences are not deficits. Because there are many ways of being successful, our personal and cultural differences—regardless of their origins—are valuable variations on the human theme of adaptability. Human traits and gifts come in many flavors.

! Rehearse It

18. A current view is that between 50 and 60 percent of intelligence score variation among individuals can be attributed to heredity. The strongest support for the hereditary influence on intelligence is the finding that

a. identical twins, but not other siblings, have nearly identical IQ scores.

b. the correlation between IQ scores of fraternal twins is higher than that for other siblings.

c. unrelated people living in the same environment tend not to have similar IQ scores.

d. the IQ scores of adopted children do not closely correlate with those of their biological or adoptive parents.

19. The heritability of a trait may vary, depending on the range of populations and environments studied. To say that the heritability of intelligence is 60 percent means that 60 percent of

a. intelligence is due to genetic factors.

b. the similarities among groups of people are attributable to genes.

c. the variation in intelligence within a group of people is attributable to genetic factors.

d. intelligence is due to the mother's genes and the rest is due to the father's genes.

20. Within the limits set by heredity, experiences help shape intelligence. The experience that has the clearest, most profound effect on intellectual development is

a. being enrolled in a Head Start program.

b. growing up in an economically disadvantaged home or neighborhood.

c. being raised in a very neglectful home or institution.

d. being exposed to very stimulating toys and lessons in infancy.

Reviewing *Thinking, Language, and Intelligence*

Our cognitive system receives, perceives, and retrieves information, which we then use to think and communicate, sometimes wisely, sometimes foolishly. In this chapter we have explored how we form concepts, solve problems, make decisions and judgments, use language, and exhibit intelligence.

Thinking

1. What functions do concepts serve?

Concepts are one of the building blocks of thinking. They serve to simplify and order the world by organizing it into a hierarchy of categories. Concepts often form around prototypes, or best examples of a category.

2. By what strategies do we solve problems, and what obstacles hinder our problem solving?

When faced with new situations for which no well-learned response suffices, we may use any of several strategies, such as trial and error, algorithms, and rule-of-thumb heuristics. Insight, a sudden and often novel realization, can also offer solutions to problems. We do, however, face certain obstacles to successful problem solving. The confirmation bias predisposes us to verify rather than challenge our hypotheses. And fixations such as functional fixedness may prevent our taking a needed fresh perspective on a problem.

3. **How are our decisions and judgments influenced by heuristics, overconfidence, and framing?**

Our use of heuristics, such as the representativeness and availability heuristics, provides highly efficient but occasionally misleading guides for making quick decisions and forming intuitive judgments. Our tendencies to seek confirmation of our hypotheses and to use quick and easy heuristics can blind us to our vulnerability to error, a phenomenon known as overconfidence. Framing—the way a question is presented—can significantly affect our thinking.

4. **How do our preexisting beliefs influence our decision making?**

As the belief perseverance phenomenon indicates, we sometimes cling to our ideas after their basis has been discredited, because the explanation for their apparent validity lingers in our minds. In general, people tend to accept as more logical those conclusions that agree with their beliefs.

Language

5. **When do children acquire language, and how does it develop?**

Among the marvels of nature is a child's ability to acquire language. The ease with which children progress from the babbling stage through the one-word stage to the telegraphic speech of the two-word stage and beyond has sparked a lively debate concerning how they do it. Behaviorist B. F. Skinner explained that we learn language by the familiar principles of imitation and reinforcement. Challenging this claim, linguist Noam Chomsky argues that children are biologically prepared to learn words and use grammar. For mastery of grammar, the learning that occurs during life's first few years is, however, critical.

6. **Is language unique to humans, or do animals also have language?**

Another vigorously debated issue is whether language is a uniquely human ability. Several teams of psychologists provoked enormous interest by teaching various apes, including a number of chimpanzees, to communicate with humans by using sign language or by pushing buttons wired to a computer. The animals have developed considerable vocabularies and are able to string words together to express meaning and requests. Skeptics point out significant differences between apes and humans in their facility with language, especially in their respective abilities to order words grammatically. Nevertheless, these studies have revealed that apes possess considerable cognitive ability.

7. **What is the relationship between thinking and language?**

Language facilitates and expresses our thoughts. There is no disputing that words convey ideas and that different languages can embody different ways of thinking. Although the linguistic relativity hypothesis suggests that language *determines* thought, it is more accurate to say that language *influences* thought. Studies of the effects of using the generic pronoun *he* and the ability of vocabulary enrichment to enhance thinking reveal the influence of words.

However, some ideas, such as the ability to perceive and remember different colors, do not depend on language. We sometimes think in images rather than in words, and we invent new words to describe new ideas. So we might say that our thinking affects our language, which then affects our thought.

Intelligence

8. **How are modern intelligence tests classified, and when and why were they created?**

Today, intelligence tests are commonly classified as either aptitude tests (designed to predict ability to learn a particular skill) or achievement tests (designed to assess current competence). In the early 1900s, French psychologist Alfred Binet and his colleague Théodore Simon developed questions in an attempt to help predict children's future progress in the Paris school system. Lewis Terman of Stanford University adapted Binet's test and offered his Stanford-Binet as a way to direct people toward occupations for which they were deemed well suited. Later, David Wechsler developed the most widely used intelligence test, the Wechsler Adult Intelligence Scale—Revised (WAIS-R).

9. **What three principles of test construction apply in evaluating a psychological test?**

A good test must be *standardized*, so that any person's performance can be meaningfully compared with others'; *reliable*, so it yields dependably consistent scores; and *valid*, so it measures what it is supposed to measure. Test scores usually fall into a bell-shaped distribution, the normal curve. The average score is assigned an arbitrary number (such as 100 on an intelligence test). Aptitude tests are highly reliable, but their validity is more modest (as judged by their predictions of academic success).

10. **Is intelligence a single general ability, or is it formed from several distinct abilities?**

Psychologists agree that people have specific abilities, such as verbal and mathematical aptitudes. However, they debate whether a general intelligence (*g*) factor runs through all these specific abilities. Factor analysis and studies of special conditions, such as the savant syndrome, have identified clusters of mental aptitudes.

11. **What factors affect creativity?**

Intelligence correlates weakly with creativity. Creative people generally have a reasonable level of intelligence, but also a developed expertise, imaginative thinking skills, a venturesome personality, intrinsic motivation, and a supportive environment.

12. **Is intelligence influenced more by heredity or environment?**

Studies of twins, family members, and adopted children together point to a significant hereditary contribution to intelligence scores. Heritability, differences attributable to genes, increases as environmental differences decrease. These studies, plus others that compare children reared in extremely impoverished or in enriched environments or in different cultures, indicate that life experiences also significantly influence intelligence test performance.

13. **How, and why, do ethnic and gender groups differ in aptitude test performance?**

Like individuals, groups vary in intelligence test scores. Hereditary variation *within* a group need not signify a hereditary explanation of *between*-group differences. In the case of the racial gaps in test scores, the evidence suggests that environmental differences are largely, perhaps entirely, responsible.

Girls have tended to score higher on spelling tests, boys on math aptitude tests (though not in math grades). Although some psychologists believe that a gender difference in spatial ability explains the gender gap in math test perfor-mance, the difference is shrinking as more girls develop their math ability.

14. **Are intelligence tests biased and discriminatory?**

If by "biased" one means sensitive to differences caused by cultural experience, then aptitude tests are necessarily bi-ased. But if one means what psychologists commonly mean—that a test predicts less validly for one group than for another—then the current tests considered in this chap-ter seem not to be biased. Indeed, tests are designed specifi-cally to avoid more subjective forms of discrimination.

Terms and Concepts to Remember

cognition, p. 256

concept, p. 256

prototype, p. 256

algorithm, p. 257

heuristic, p. 257

insight, p. 257

confirmation bias, p. 258

fixation, p. 258

functional fixedness, p. 259

representativeness heuristic, p. 259

availability heuristic, p. 260

overconfidence, p. 261

framing, p. 262

belief perseverance, p. 262

language, p. 264

babbling stage, p. 265

one-word stage, p. 266

two-word stage, p. 266

telegraphic speech, p. 266

linguistic relativity, p. 272

intelligence, p. 275

aptitude tests, p. 276

achievement tests, p. 276

mental age, p. 276

Stanford-Binet, p. 277

intelligence quotient (IQ), p. 277

Wechsler Adult Intelligence Scale (WAIS), p. 277

standardization, p. 279

normal curve, p. 279

reliability, p. 279

validity, p. 280

general intelligence (*g*), p. 281

savant syndrome, p. 281

creativity, p. 282

mental retardation, p. 283

Down syndrome, p. 283

heritability, p. 286

Rehearse It Answer Key

1. a.   2. b.   3. c.   4. d.   5. b.   6. d.   7. c.   8. b.   9. d.

10. a.   11. a.   12. a.   13. d.   14. c.   15. b.   16. c.   17. b.   18. a.

19. c.   20. c.

Critical Thinking Exercise

Now that you have read and reviewed Chapter 8, take your learning a step further by completing the following exercise. Circle the correct answer to each of the following questions and rate your confidence from 50% ("it's a toss up") to 100% ("I'm certain").

1. What is the tallest building in the world?
   a. The Sears Tower   b. The World Trade Center

   Confidence: _____

2. Which country has the largest population?
   a. South Africa   b. Vietnam

   Confidence: _____

3. What color is taupe?
   a. yellowish pink   b. brownish gray

   Confidence: _____

4. Who was the last president of the U.S.S.R.?
   a. Boris Yeltsin   b. Mikhail Gorbachev

   Confidence: _____

5. Of what country is Canberra the capital?
   a. Australia   b. Bolivia

   Confidence: _____

6. Which is the largest planet in our solar system?
   a. Saturn   b. Jupiter

   Confidence: _____

7. Which language is used by more people?
   a. Mandarin   b. English

   Confidence: _____

8. Which country is the world's largest oil producer?
   a. Saudia Arabia   b. The former Soviet Union

   Confidence: _____

9. In which country is the Krone used as the monetary unit?
   a. Finland   b. Greenland

   Confidence: _____

10. What is the most frequent cause of death in the United States?
    a. Heart disease   b. Cancer

    Confidence: _____

Determine your average confidence level by adding the percentages and dividing by 10, then check your answers with those found in Appendix B.

Average Confidence Level _____

9

Motivation

Motivational Theories

Instinct Theory

Drive-Reduction Theory

Arousal Theory

Incentive Theory

A Hierarchy of Motives

Hunger

The Physiology of Hunger

The Psychology of Hunger

Obesity and Weight Control

Sexual Motivation

Describing Sexual Behavior

The Physiology of Sex

The Psychology of Sex

Sexual Dysfunctions and Therapy

Gender and Sexuality

Sexual Orientation

Sex and Human Values

Achievement Motivation

Identifying Achievement Motivation

Sources of Achievement Motivation

Intrinsic Motivation and Achievement

Motivating People

The Need to Belong

In everyday conversation, the question "What motivated you to do that?" is a way of asking "What *caused* your behavior? *Why* did you act that way?" To psychologists, a **motivation** is a need or desire that serves to *energize* behavior and to *direct* it toward a goal. Like intelligence, motivation is a hypothetical concept. We infer motivation from behaviors we observe. Consider motivation in these situations:

- David Mandel (1983), a former Nazi concentration camp inmate, recalls how a starving "father and son would fight over a piece of bread. Like dogs." One father, whose 20-year-old son stole his bread from under his pillow while he slept, went into a deep depression, asking over and again how his son could do such a thing. The next day the father died. "Hunger does something to you that's hard to describe. I can't believe it myself today, so how can I expect anyone else to understand it?"

- In the Old Testament's *Song of Solomon* love poems, a man and a woman express their intense sexual passion for one another. "I am sick with love," she declares. "O that his left hand were under my head, and that his right hand embraced me!" He, in turn, pronounces her "delectable." "You are stately as a palm tree, and your breasts are like its clusters. I say I will climb the palm tree and lay hold of its branches."

- In Texas, a school truant officer discovers Alfredo Gonzales, age 14, picking fruit and sends him off to the first day of school in his life. Although placed at the lowest skill level and paddled for asking questions in Spanish—he knows no English—Alfredo decides "I could do better." Indeed, today he is a highly educated college administrator who works to motivate youth to wake up, as he did, to "their own potential and to gain a desire to achieve it."

- Separated from friends or family—isolated in prison, alone at a new school, living in a foreign land—most people feel keenly their lost connections with important others. Wrenched from the only family she has ever known, 2½-year-old Jessica DeBoer sobs en route to her biological parents' home hundreds of miles away. As social animals, we all have something of Jessica within us—a sense of who we belong to, who is "us."

motivation   A need or desire that energizes and directs behavior.

In this chapter, we will explore motivation by focusing on these four motives—hunger, sex, achievement, and belonging. Although other identifiable motives exist (including thirst, curiosity, and a need for approval), a close look at these four reveals the interplay between nature (the physiological "push") and nurture (the cognitive and cultural "pulls").

Motivational Theories

1. What theoretical perspectives have helped psychologists understand motivation?

Instinct Theory

Early in this century, as the influence of Charles Darwin's evolutionary theory grew, it became fashionable to classify all sorts of behaviors as instincts. If people criticized themselves, it was because of their "self-abasement instinct." If they boasted, it reflected their "self-assertion instinct." After scanning 500 books, one sociologist in 1924 compiled a list of 5759 supposed human instincts! Before long, the instinct-naming fad collapsed under its own weight. For rather than *explaining* human behaviors, the early instinct theorists were simply *naming* them. It was like "explaining" a bright child's low grades by labeling the child an "underachiever." To name a behavior is *not* to explain it.

To qualify as an **instinct**, a complex behavior must have a fixed pattern throughout a species and be unlearned (Tinbergen, 1951). Such behaviors are common in other species (recall imprinting in birds and the return of salmon to their birthplace). Human behavior, too, exhibits certain innate tendencies, including simple fixed patterns such as an infant's rooting and sucking. Most psychologists, though, view human behavior as directed by physiological needs *and* psychological wants.

Although instinct theory failed to explain human motives, the underlying assumption that genes predispose species-typical behavior is as strong as ever. We saw this in Chapter 6's discussion of our biological predisposition to learn certain aversions. And we will see this in later discussions of how evolution might influence our gender differences; our helping behavior; and our attraction to certain people.

Drive-Reduction Theory

When the instinct theory of motivation collapsed, it was replaced by **drive-reduction theory**—the idea that a physiological need creates an aroused psychological state that *drives* the organism to reduce the need by, say, eating or drinking. With few exceptions, when a physiological need increases, so does a psychological drive.

The physiological aim of drive reduction is **homeostasis**—the maintenance of a steady internal state. An example of homeostasis (literally "staying the same") is the body's temperature-regulation system, which works like a thermostat. Both systems operate through feedback loops: Sensors feed room temperature to a control device. If room temperature cools, the control device switches on the furnace. Likewise, if body temperature cools, blood vessels constrict to conserve warmth, and we feel driven to put on more clothes or seek a warmer environment. Similarly, if the water level in our cells drops, sensors detect our need for water and we feel thirsty.

Same Motive; Different Wiring *The more complex the nervous system, the more adaptable the organism. Both the weaver bird and the woman satisfy their need for shelter in ways that reflect their inherited capacities. The bird's behavior pattern is fixed; it can build only this kind of nest. The woman's behavior is flexible; she can learn whatever skills she needs to build many different kinds of houses.*

Driven by Curiosity *Young people and baby monkeys are fascinated by things they've never handled before. Their drive to explore the relatively unfamiliar is one of several motives that do not fill any obvious physiological need.*

Arousal Theory

Rather than reduce a physiological need or minimize tension, some motivated behaviors *increase* arousal. Monkeys will monkey around trying to figure out how to unlock a latch that opens nothing, or how to open a window that allows them to see outside their room (Butler, 1954). The motivation to explore drives the 9-month-old infant who investigates every accessible corner of the house. It drives the scientists whose work this text discusses. And it drove the voyagers who first ventured across and beneath the oceans. Asked why he wanted to climb Mount Everest, George Mallory answered, "Because it is there." Those who, like Mallory, enjoy high arousal are most likely to enjoy intense music, novel foods, and risky behaviors (Zuckerman, 1979).

Experiments on sensory restriction in a monotonous chamber reveal our need for stimulation. Despite having all our biological needs satisfied, we feel driven to experience stimulation. Without it, we feel bored and look for a way to increase arousal to some optimum level. With too much stimulation, we feel stressed and look for a way to decrease arousal.

Incentive Theory

Not only are we *pushed* by our "need" to reduce drives and achieve optimum arousal, we are also *pulled* by **incentives**—positive or negative stimuli that lure or repel us. This is one way our individual learning histories influence our motives. Depending on our learning, the aroma of fresh roasted peanuts (or toasted ants), the sight of someone we find attractive, and the threat of disapproval can all motivate our behavior. Our internal needs energize and direct our behavior, but so do these external incentives. When there is both a need and an incentive, we feel driven. The food-deprived person who smells baking bread feels a hunger for it. For each motive, we can therefore ask, "How is it pushed by our inborn physiological needs and pulled by incentives in the environment?"

A Hierarchy of Motives

2. What is the basic idea behind Maslow's hierarchy of needs?

Some needs take priority over others. At this very moment, with your needs for air and water satisfied, other motives—such as your desire to achieve—energize

instinct A complex behavior that is rigidly patterned throughout a species and is unlearned.

drive-reduction theory The idea that a physiological need creates an aroused tension state (a drive) that motivates an organism to satisfy the need.

homeostasis A tendency to maintain a balanced or constant internal state; the regulation of any aspect of body chemistry, such as the level of glucose sugar in the blood, around a particular level.

incentives Positive or negative environmental stimuli that motivate behavior.

| Self-actualization needs |
| Need to live up to one's |
| fullest and unique potential |

Self-actualization needs
Need to live up to one's fullest and unique potential

Esteem needs
Need for self-esteem, achievement, competence, and independence; need for recognition and respect from others

Belongingness and love needs
Need to love and be loved, to belong and be accepted; need to avoid loneliness and alienation

Safety needs
Need to feel that the world is organized and predictable; need to feel safe, secure, and stable

Physiological needs
Need to satisfy hunger and thirst

Figure 9–1 Maslow's Hierarchy of Needs *If our lower-level needs are met, we are prompted to satisfy our higher-level needs. (From Maslow, 1970.)*

hierarchy of needs Maslow's pyramid of human needs, beginning at the base with physiological needs that must first be satisfied before higher-level safety needs and then psychological needs become active.

and direct your behavior. Let your need for water go unsatisfied and your thirst will preoccupy you. But if you were deprived of air, your thirst would disappear.

These examples illustrate how the particular needs that motivate our behavior depend on which needs are not met. Abraham Maslow (1970) proposed one such **hierarchy of needs** (Figure 9–1). At its base are our physiological needs, such as food and water. Only if these needs are met are we prompted to meet our need for safety, and then to meet the uniquely human needs to give and receive love and to enjoy self-esteem. Beyond this, said Maslow (1971), lies the highest of human needs: to actualize one's full potential. (More on self-esteem and self-actualization in Chapter 11, Personality.)

Maslow's hierarchy is somewhat arbitrary. Moreover, the order of such needs is not universally fixed. People have starved themselves to make a political statement. Nevertheless, the simple idea that some motives are more compelling than others provides a framework for thinking about motivation. Let's now consider the four representative motives, beginning at the basic, physiological level with hunger and working up through sexual motivation to the higher-level motives of achievement and belonging. At each level, we will see how psychological factors such as learning interact with what is physiologically given.

! *Rehearse It*

1. Although instinct theory fails to explain most human behavior, the existence of simple fixed patterns such as an infant's rooting and sucking suggests some innate tendencies in humans. Indeed, the underlying assumption of instinct theory—that____—is as strong as ever.

a. physiological needs arouse psychological states
b. genes predispose species-typical behavior
c. physiological needs increase arousal
d. external needs energize and direct behavior

2. Drive reduction motivates many behaviors necessary for survival. A need, or deprivation (for example, a lack of water), leads to an aroused state or drive; and this in turn motivates the organism to act to reduce this drive (drink a glass of water) and restore internal stability. Drive reduction also motivates behaviors such as

a. eating and breathing.
b. satisfaction of curiosity.
c. nest building and other instincts.
d. pursuit of stimulation.

3. The aim of drive reduction is internal stability. For example, if we are too hot, we perspire; if we are dehydrated, we feel thirsty—and drink. The maintenance of a balanced internal state is called

a. instinct.
b. sensory restriction.
c. a hierarchy of needs.
d. homeostasis.

4. Motivated behaviors satisfy a variety of needs. Experiments on sensory restriction indicate that one such need can be to

a. reduce physiological needs.
b. minimize tension.
c. increase arousal.
d. ensure stability.

5. Behavior is also influenced by incentives in the environment. For example, a pile of leaves in the driveway may motivate you to get out the rake; your neighbor's disapproval may motivate you to turn down your radio. To explain the effects of external incentives, we must refer to

a. biological needs.
b. instinct.
c. individual learning histories.
d. homeostasis.

6. According to Abraham Maslow, we are not prompted to satisfy psychological needs, such as the need to be accepted or loved, until we have satisfied more basic needs. The most basic needs are physiological needs, including the need for food, water, and oxygen; just above these are

a. safety needs.
b. self-esteem needs.
c. belongingness needs.
d. psychological needs.

Hunger

"You're my best student, Beth, but I think this diet is having a negative effect on your work."

A vivid demonstration of the supremacy of physiological needs followed reports of starvation in prison camps and occupied areas during World War II. To learn more about the results of semistarvation, scientist Ancel Keys and his colleagues (1950) solicited volunteers for an experiment. From among the more than 100 conscientious objectors to the war who applied, they selected 36 men. First, they fed the men just enough to maintain their initial weight. Then, for 6 months, they cut this food level in half.

The effects soon became visible. Without thinking about it, the men began conserving energy; they appeared listless and apathetic. Their body weights dropped rapidly, eventually stabilizing at about 25 percent below their starting weights. The psychological effects were even more dramatic. Consistent with Maslow's idea of a need hierarchy, the men became obsessed with food. They talked food. They daydreamed food. They collected recipes, read cookbooks, and feasted their eyes on delectable forbidden foods. Meanwhile, they lost their former interests in sex and social activities. They became preoccupied with their unfulfilled basic need. As one subject reported, "If we see a show, the most interesting part of it is contained in scenes where people are eating. I couldn't laugh at the funniest picture in the world, and love scenes are completely dull."

The Physiology of Hunger

3. What physiological factors cause us to feel hungry?

Keys' semistarved subjects felt hunger in response to a homeostatic system designed to maintain normal body weight and an adequate supply of nutrients. But precisely what is it that triggers hunger? Is it the pangs of an empty stomach? So it feels. And so it seemed after A. L. Washburn, working with Walter Cannon (Cannon & Washburn, 1912), intentionally swallowed a balloon. When inflated in his stomach, the balloon transmitted his stomach contractions to a recording device (Figure 9–2). While his stomach was being monitored, Washburn pressed a key each time he felt hungry. The result: Washburn was having stomach contractions whenever he felt hungry. (Some diet aids reduce this empty stomach feeling by filling the stomach with indigestible fibers that swell as they absorb water.)

Figure 9–2 Monitoring Stomach Contractions *Using this procedure, Washburn showed that stomach contractions (transmitted by the stomach balloon) accompany our feelings of hunger (indicated by a key press). (From Cannon, 1929.)*

glucose The form of sugar that circulates in the blood and provides the major source of energy for body tissues. When its level is low, we feel hunger.

set point The point at which an individual's "weight thermostat" is supposedly set. When the body falls below this weight, an increase in hunger and a lowered metabolic rate may act to restore the lost weight.

metabolic rate The body's base rate of energy expenditure.

Alas, there is more to hunger than the pangs of an empty stomach. Researchers discovered this a quarter-century later when they removed some rats' stomachs and attached their esophagi to their small intestines (Tsang, 1938). Without stomach pangs, did hunger persist? Did the rats continue to eat regularly? Indeed they did. Hunger persists similarly in humans whose ulcerated or cancerous stomachs have been removed. In fact, one can feel hungry even on a full stomach. Animals that fill their stomachs by eating low-calorie food will eat more than animals that consume a less filling, high-calorie diet (McHugh & Moran, 1978). If the pangs of an empty stomach are not the only source of our hunger, what else is involved?

Body Chemistry

Changes in body chemistry also affect hunger. People and other animals automatically regulate their caloric intake to maintain a stable body weight. This suggests that the body is somehow, somewhere, keeping tabs on its available resources. One such resource is the blood sugar, **glucose**. Increases in the hormone *insulin* diminish blood glucose, partly by converting it to stored fat, thus causing hunger to increase.

Body chemistry also influences taste preferences. When feeling tense or depressed, do you crave sweet or starchy carbohydrate-laden foods? Carbohydrates help boost levels of the neurotransmitter serotonin, which has calming effects. Given the drug fenfluramine, which similarly increases serotonin, carbohydrate cravers lose their cravings. This suggests that stress-related cravings might be treatable by providing food substitutes that mimic biochemical effects (Hall, 1987).

The Brain and Set Point

Low blood glucose is a source of hunger. But you do not consciously feel your blood chemistry. Rather, the brain automatically monitors information on your body's internal state. Signals from the stomach, the intestines, and the liver (indicating whether glucose is being deposited or withdrawn) all signal the brain to motivate eating or not. But where in the brain are these messages integrated? During the 1940s and 1950s, researchers located hunger controls within the hypothalamus, a small but complex neural traffic intersection buried deep in the brain (Figure 9–3).

Actually, there are two distinct hypothalamic areas that help control eating. Activity along the sides of the hypothalamus, known as the *lateral hypothalamus*, or *LH*, brings on hunger. When electrically stimulated there, a well-fed animal will begin to eat; when the area is destroyed, even a starving animal has no interest in food. Activity in the lower middle of the hypothalamus, known as the *ventromedial hypothalamus*, or *VMH*, depresses hunger. Stimulate this area and an animal will stop eating; destroy it and the animal's stomach and intestines will process food more rapidly, causing it to eat more often and to become grossly fat (Duggan & Booth, 1986; Hoebel & Teitelbaum, 1966).

How do these complementary areas of the hypothalamus work? One theory is that they influence how much glucose is converted to fat and how much is left available to fuel immediate activity (thus minimizing hunger). After VMH lesions, rats produce more fat and use less fat energy, rather like a miser who runs a bit of extra money to the bank and resists taking any out (Pinel, 1993).

An older theory is that manipulating these two areas of the hypothalamus alters the body's "weight thermostat," which predisposes us to keep our body at a particular weight level, called its **set point** (Keesey & Corbett, 1983). When semistarved rats fall below their normal weight, biological pressures act to re-

Hypothalamus

Figure 9–3 The Hypothalamus *As we saw in Chapter 2, the hypothalamus performs various body maintenance functions, including control of hunger. The hypothalamus responds to our current blood chemistry as well as to incoming neural information about the body's state.*

Evidence for the Brain's Control of Eating *A lesion near the ventromedial (middle) area of the hypothalamus caused this rat's weight to triple. At 92.05 grams, it weighs about three times more than normal.*

store the lost weight: Hunger increases and energy expenditure decreases. If body weight rises—as happens when rats are force-fed—hunger decreases and energy expenditure increases. The stable weight toward which semistarved and overstuffed rats return is their set point.

Some researchers believe that slow, sustained changes in body weight can, however, alter one's set point. Other researchers now doubt that the body has a precise set point that drives hunger. Hunger, they say, is determined by too many factors, including learned incentives, for that to be true. Body weight settles around a level at which all these factors reach an equilibrium.

Despite the day-to-day variations in our eating, our bodies are astonishingly good at regulating our weight, much better than we could be through conscious efforts to control food intake precisely. Over the next 40 years you will eat about 20 tons of food. If during those years you increase your daily intake by just 0.01 ounce more than required for your energy needs, you will gain 24 pounds (Martin & others, 1991). With astonishing precision, our bodies automatically balance energy intake and expenditure.

Our bodies regulate weight much as rats' bodies do—through the control of food intake and energy output. If our body weight rises above our set point, we tend not to feel so hungry; if our weight drops below, we tend to eat more. To maintain its set-point weight, the body also adjusts its **metabolic rate**—its resting rate of energy expenditure. By the end of their 24 weeks of semistarvation, the subjects in the World War II experiment had stabilized at three-quarters of their normal weight—while eating half what they previously did. The stabilization resulted from reduced energy expenditure, achieved partly by physical lethargy and partly by a 29 percent drop in their resting metabolic rate.

The Psychology of Hunger

4. What psychological factors contribute to hunger?

Our eagerness to eat is both pushed by our physiological state—our body chemistry and hypothalamic activity—and pulled by our learned responses to external stimuli.

Culture and Hunger

Our preferences for sweet and salty tastes are genetic and universal. Other tastes are conditioned, as when people given highly salted foods develop a liking for excess salt (Beauchamp, 1987) or when people develop an aversion to a food eaten before becoming violently ill. (The frequency of children's illnesses provides many chances for them to learn food aversions.)

Culture affects taste, too. Bedouins enjoy eating the eye of a camel, which most North Americans would find repulsive. Similarly, most North Americans shun dog, rat, and horse meat, all of which are prized elsewhere, but welcome beef, which Hindus wouldn't think of eating. Such preferences vary with exposure (Pliner & Pelchat, 1991; Rozin, 1976). We humans have a natural dislike of many things unfamiliar, including novel foods (especially novel animal-based rather than vegetarian foods). This "neophobia" surely was adaptive for our ancestors, serving to protect them from potentially toxic substances. In experiments, people have tried novel fruit drinks or unfamiliar ethnic foods. With repeated exposure, their appreciation for the new taste typically increases; moreover, exposure to one set of novel foods increases willingness to try another (Pliner, 1982; Pliner & others, 1993).

An Acquired Taste *For Alaskan Eskimos, but not for most other North Americans, whale blubber is a tasty treat. People everywhere learn to enjoy the fatty, bitter, or irritating foods that are prescribed by their culture.*

Eating Disorders

Psychological influences on eating behavior are strikingly evident in those for whom normal homeostatic pressures are overwhelmed by a motive for thinness. Consider two eating disorder cases.

Mary is a 5' 3", 15-year-old who, upon reaching 100 pounds, decided she needed to lose weight to enhance her attractiveness. After gradually reducing her food intake to a few vegetables a day and adding a vigorous exercise program, she now weighs a mere 80 pounds. Yet she still feels "fat" and plans to continue dieting. Mary has been having difficulty sleeping, has at times been depressed, and no longer has regular menstrual periods. She is socially inactive and seldom dates, but she is very successful academically. Mary does not regard herself as ill or needing treatment.

Alice is a 5' 9", 160-pound 17-year-old who says she has always been a little chubby. For the last 5 years, she has often eaten in binges, followed by vomiting. She will eat a quart of ice cream or an entire pie and then, to control her weight, make herself vomit in secret. Alice wants to date, but she doesn't because she is ashamed of her looks. She has at times taken diet pills to try to lose weight.

Mary is diagnosed as having **anorexia nervosa**—a disorder in which a person becomes significantly underweight (typically, 15 percent or more) yet feels fat and fears becoming obese. Even when emaciated, the person continues to limit food intake. The disorder usually develops in adolescence, 9 times out of 10 in females.

anorexia nervosa An eating disorder in which a normal-weight person (usually an adolescent female) diets and becomes significantly (15 percent or more) underweight, yet, still feeling fat, continues to starve herself.

bulimia nervosa An eating disorder characterized by private, "binge-purge" episodes of overeating, usually of highly caloric foods, followed by vomiting or laxative use.

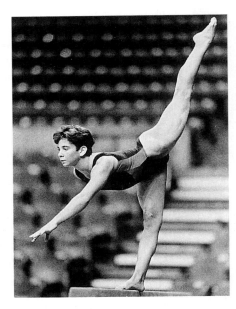

A Diet Gone Berserk *Champion U.S. gymnast Christy Henrich, shown here at the 1989 World Games, was plagued by anorexia and bulimia. She was at times training 9 hours a day and eating one apple. "My life is a horrifying nightmare. It feels like there's a beast inside of me," she explained before dying in 1994, a 60-pound tragedy who barely dented her hospital mattress (Deardorff, 1994).*

Alice's condition, which is more common, is **bulimia nervosa**—a disorder marked by repeated binge-purge episodes of overeating followed by vomiting or laxative use. Bulimia patients eat as some alcoholics drink—in spurts, sometimes under the influence of friends who also are binging (Crandall, 1988). Most binge-purge eaters are women in their late teens or twenties. Like those with anorexia, they are preoccupied with food, are fearful of becoming overweight, and are depressed or anxious (Hinz & Williamson, 1987). The depression and shame are felt most keenly during and following binges. About half of those with anorexia also display the binge-purge-depression symptoms of bulimia. But unlike anorexia, bulimia is marked by weight fluctuations within or above normal ranges. This makes the condition easy to hide.

Researchers report that the families of bulimia patients have a higher-than-usual incidence of alcoholism, obesity, and depression. Anorexia patients often come from a middle- or upper-class family that is competitive, high-achieving, and protective (Pate & others, 1992; Yates, 1989, 1990). They set high standards, fret about falling short of expectations, and are intensely concerned with how others perceive them (Heatherton & Baumeister, 1991; Striegel-Moore & others, 1993).

Genetics also may influence susceptibility to eating disorders. When one twin has bulimia, the chances of the other twin's sharing the disorder are much greater if they are identical rather than fraternal twins (Fichter & Noegel, 1990). People with eating disorders may also have abnormal supplies of certain neurotransmitters that put them at risk for anxiety or depression (Fava & others, 1989).

There is, however, a cultural explanation for the fact that anorexia and bulimia occur mostly in women and mostly in weight-conscious cultures. Mothers of girls with eating disorders are themselves often focused on their own weight and on their daughter's weight and appearance (Pike & Rodin, 1991). Anorexia nervosa always begins as a weight-loss diet, and the self-induced vomiting of bulimics nearly always begins after a dieter has broken diet restrictions and gorged. Although ideals of beauty have varied over the centuries, women in every era have struggled to make their bodies conform to the ideal of their day. Thus, the sickness of today's eating disorders lies not just within the victims but also within their weight-obsessed culture—a culture that says, in countless ways, "Fat is bad," that motivates millions of women to be "always dieting," and that encourages eating binges by pressuring women to live in a constant state of semistarvation. "You can't be too rich or too thin," declared the Duchess of Windsor. As obesity researchers Susan Wooley and Orland Wooley (1983) noted, "An increasingly stringent cultural standard of thinness for women has been accompanied by a steadily increasing incidence of serious eating disorders in women."

PEANUTS

External Incentives and Hunger

Like Pavlov's dogs, people learn to salivate in anticipation of food cues. Some people are especially responsive to appealing foods. When food is abundant, such people tend to gain the most weight.

Consider the 9- to 15-year-old girls studied by Judith Rodin and Joyce Slochower (1976) at an 8-week summer camp. During the first week of camp, some girls could not resist munching readily visible M&Ms even after a full meal. These girls were typical of a category the researchers called *externals*—people whose eating is triggered more by the presence of food than by internal factors. In the 7 weeks that followed, the "external" girls gained the most weight.

In a delicious demonstration of how internal and external factors interact, Rodin (1984) invited other research subjects to her laboratory for lunch after they had gone 18 hours without food. While blood samples were being taken, a large, juicy steak was wheeled in, crackling as it finished grilling. As the hungry subjects sat watching, hearing, and smelling the soon-to-be-eaten steak, Rodin monitored their rising blood insulin levels and their accompanying feelings of hunger. When stimulated by the sight, sound, and aroma of the steak, "externals" had the greatest insulin increase and accompanying hunger response. This illustrates how certain individuals' psychological experiences of an external incentive (the steak) can affect their internal physiological state.

Obesity and Weight Control

5. What factors predispose some people to become and remain obese?

As the weight loss during Keys' semistarvation experiment demonstrated, calories matter. Yet there is more to weight than calories eaten—otherwise why do some people gain while others who eat the same amount remain slim? Why do so few overweight people win the battle of the bulge? And what hope is there for the one-third of Americans who, according to a 1994 report of the National Center for Health Statistics, are overweight?

First, the good news about fat. Fat is an ideal form of stored energy that provides the body with a high-caloric fuel reserve to carry it through periods when food is scarce—a common occurrence in the feast-or-famine existence of our prehistoric ancestors. Eating three or more meals every day is a relatively recent phenomenon and a luxury hundreds of millions of people still do not enjoy. In circumstances of alternating feast and famine, overeating and storing the excess as fat is adaptive; it prepares the body to withstand famine. This may explain why in most developing societies today, as in Europe in earlier centuries—in fact, wherever people face famine—obesity is a sign of affluence and social status (Furnham & Baguma, 1994).

The Female Ideal *The female ideal of 1637 was a rounded contrast to today's thin fashion models. There was biological wisdom in this: A plump woman stored more of the energy and nutrients needed to nourish a fetus and nurse an infant through a famine. However, to many people today, thinness connotes fitness, vitality, and self-control.*

The bad news is that in those parts of the world where food and sweets are now abundantly available, the adaptive tendency to store fat has become maladaptive. Being slightly overweight poses no health risks. But the National Institutes of Health reports that genuine obesity increases the risk of diabetes, high blood pressure and heart disease, gallstones, arthritis, and certain types of cancer. This is more true for apple-shaped people who carry their weight in pot bellies than for pear-shaped people with ample hips and thighs (Greenwood, 1989).

Obesity is not just a threat to physical health. Being perceived as obese can affect how you are treated and how you feel about yourself. People often stereotype the obese as slow, lazy, and sloppy (Ryckman & others, 1989). The obese—sometimes victims of ridicule and job discrimination—know it. In studies of patients who were especially unhappy with their weight—those who had lost an average of 100 pounds after short-cutting digestion with intestinal bypass surgery—4 in 5 said their children had asked them not to attend school functions. Nine in ten said they would rather have a leg amputated than be obese again (Rand & Macgregor, 1990, 1991). Another study followed 370 obese 16- to 24-year-olds (Gortmaker & others, 1993). When restudied 7 years later, two-thirds of the women were still obese—and were less likely to be married and were making less money than a comparison group of some 5000 other women. Even after correcting for aptitude test scores, race, and parental income, the obese women's incomes were $7000 a year below average.

Body Image Issues: Not Just for Women Only *While many contemporary women aspire to an ideal of thinness, their male peers often aim for a denser "muscled look." Such beliefs about what is attractive have varied over time. How might the dapper Victorian gentleman on the right have responded to our sweaty modern hero? Probably with amazement and dismay.*

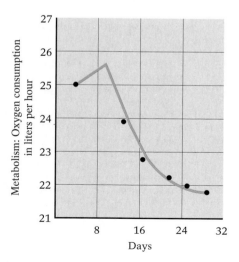

Figure 9–4 **The Effects of a Severe Diet on Obese Patients' Body Weight and Metabolism** *After 7 days on a 3500-calorie diet, six obese patients were given only 450 calories a day for the next 24 days. Body weight declined only 6 percent and then leveled off, because metabolism dropped about 15 percent. (From Bray, 1969.)*

The Physiology of Obesity

Many people think fat people are gluttons. They see obesity as a matter of choice or as reflecting a personality problem. If being obese signifies either a lack of self-discipline or a personality problem, then who would want to hire, date, or associate with such people? And if obese people believe such things about themselves, how could they feel anything but unworthy and undesirable?

Research on the physiology of obesity challenges these ideas. Consider the arithmetic of weight gain: People get fat by consuming more calories than they expend, and the energy equivalent of a pound of fat is 3500 calories. Dieters have therefore been told that they will lose a pound for every 3500-calorie reduction in their diet. Surprise: This conclusion turns out to be false. To see why, consider the physiology of fat.

Fat Cells The immediate determinants of body fat are the size and number of fat cells. A typical adult has about 30 billion of these miniature fuel tanks, half of which lie near the skin's surface. A fat cell can vary from relatively empty, like a deflated balloon, to overly full. In the obese, fat cells may swell to two or three times their normal size and then divide. Once the number of fat cells increases—due to genetic predisposition, early childhood eating patterns, or adult overeating—it never decreases. On a diet, fat cells may shrink, but they do not disappear (Sjöstrum, 1980).

The unyielding nature of our fat cells is but one way in which, once we become fat, our bodies maintain fat. Another way is that fat tissue has a low metabolic (energy expenditure) rate. Compared with other tissue, fat takes less food energy to maintain. Thus, once we become fat, we require less food to maintain our weight than we did to attain it.

Set Points and Metabolism Many scientists believe there is another reason why most obese people find it so difficult to lose weight permanently. Their bodies' "weight thermostats" are set to maintain body weight within a higher than average range. When weight drops below the set point range, hunger increases and metabolism decreases.

As many a dieter can testify, the drop in resting metabolic rate can be particularly frustrating. After the rapid weight losses that occur during the initial 3 weeks or so of a rigorous diet, further weight loss comes slowly. In one experiment (Bray, 1969), obese patients whose daily food intake was reduced from 3500 to 450 calories lost only 6 percent of their weight—partly because their metabolic rates dropped about 15 percent (Figure 9–4). Thus, the body adapts to starvation by burning off fewer calories, and to extra calories by burning off more. That is why reducing your food intake by 3500 calories may not reduce your weight by 1 pound. And that is why when a diet ends and the body is still conserving energy, amounts of food that only maintained weight before the diet may now increase it.

Individual differences in resting metabolism explain why—contrary to the stereotype of the overweight glutton—it is possible for two people of the same height, age, and activity level to maintain the same weight, even if one of them eats much more than the other does. Or why it is possible for a person to eat less than another similarly active person, yet weigh more (Rose & Williams, 1961). This appears true despite findings that people—obese people, especially—tend to overestimate their physical activity and underestimate their caloric intake (Brownell & Wadden, 1992; Lichtman & others, 1992).

The Genetic Factor Studies of adoptees and twins reveal a genetic influence on body weight. Despite shared family meals, the body weights of adopted children are not correlated with their adoptive parents' and siblings' weights:

The Lean Look *Contemporary clothing ads and films present an ideal of thinness that most women cannot attain. The message is so pervasive in our culture that even those of flawless appearance are often worried about their bodily "imperfections."*

The Barbie fashion doll's proportions: 36–18–33 (*Life*, 1991).

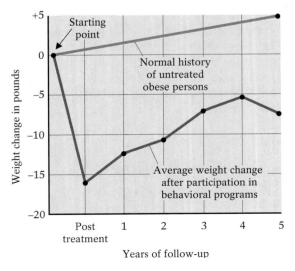

Figure 9–5 Weight Change and Weight Loss Programs
Behavior-management weight loss programs promote weight loss, but most lost weight is regained. (From Brownell & Jeffery, 1987.)

Rather, people's weights resemble those of their biological parents (Grilo & Pogue-Geile, 1991). Moreover, identical twins have closely similar weights, even when reared apart (Stunkard & others, 1990).

New experiments reveal a mechanism for weight-control in mice. As a normal mouse's fat cells become bloated, its genes produce a protein (leptin) that signals its brain to curb eating and increase activity. When obese mice receive daily leptin injections, they lose weight (Halaas & others, 1995). This discovery excites wondering: might leptin also make fat humans thinner?

Being overweight is therefore *not* simply a matter of scarfing too many hot fudge sundaes. And losing weight is not simply a matter of mind over platter.

Genes are not the whole story, however. Diet or exercise rather than genes must explain why obesity is six times more common among lower-class than among upper-class women, more common among Americans than among Europeans, and more common among Americans today than in 1900. (Compared with their counterparts in the early 1900s, people are eating a higher fat diet and expending fewer calories.) Ironically, the growing pudginess of Americans coincides with an increasing idealization of the thin and fit look. Consider:

- American models of a generation ago weighed 8 percent less than the average woman; today they weigh 23 percent less—which makes the average model thinner than 95 percent of women (Wolf, 1991). Most of today's models and actresses have hardly more than half the 22 to 26 percent body fat of an average woman (Brownell, 1991). When young women view magazine pictures of ultra-thin models, they report increased feelings of shame, guilt, and body dissatisfaction (Stice & Shaw, 1994).

- In 1950, department-store mannequins looked nearly like real women. Since then, they have lost about 3 inches around their hips, which now average only 31 inches—quite unlike today's average young adult woman's 37 inches. In fact, women with as little body fat as these mannequins likely would not menstruate (University of California, 1993).

- Whereas the average North American woman weighs *more* than her counterpart of 40 years ago, today's average Miss America contestant weighs about 15 pounds *less*.

Losing Weight

Perhaps you shake your head in sympathy with obese people: "Slim chance they (or we) have of becoming and staying thin. If they lose weight on a diet, their metabolism slows and their hungry fat cells cry out, 'Feed me!'" Indeed, the condition of an obese person's body reduced to average weight is much like that of a semistarved body. Held under its normal set point, each body "thinks" it is starving. Having lost weight, formerly obese people look normal, but their fat cells may be abnormally small, their metabolism slower, and, like the semistarved subjects we met earlier, their minds are obsessed with food.

All this explains why most people who succeed on a weight loss program eventually gain it nearly all back (Garner & Wooley, 1991; Wing & Jeffery, 1979). One study followed 207 obese patients who had lost large amounts of weight during a 2-month hospital fast (Johnson & Drenick, 1977). Half gained back all the lost weight within 3 years, and virtually all were again obese within 9 years. Programs that modify life-style and ongoing eating behavior have better carryover to postdiet weight management. Yet participants in these programs, too, typically regain much of their lost weight (Figure 9–5). When cultural ideals of slimness collide with hunger, hunger usually wins. Commercial weight loss programs can justifiably proclaim that they help people lose weight, *temporarily*. For most people, however, the only long-term result is a thinner wallet.

Helpful Hints for Dieters

Minimize exposure to tempting food cues. Keep tempting foods out of the house or out of sight, stay out of the candy shops, and go to the supermarket only on a full stomach.

Take steps to boost your metabolism. Inactive people are often overweight (Figure 9–6). Sustained exercise, such as brisk walking, running, and swimming, not only empties fat cells, builds muscle, and makes you feel better, it can also

temporarily speed up metabolism (Kolata, 1987; Thompson & others, 1982).

Modify both your metabolic rate and your hunger by changing the food you eat. Findings suggest that complex carbohydrates (pasta, grains, potatoes) increase metabolism and are less readily converted to body fat than are the same calories eaten as fats (Rodin, 1979, 1985). Complex carbohydrates and fructose (the sugar in fruits) stimulate

less of a hunger-producing insulin jump than refined sugar (sucrose).

Don't starve all day and eat one big meal at night. This eating pattern, common among overweight people, slows metabolism.

Beware of the binge. Among people who consciously restrain their eating, drinking alcohol or feeling anxious or depressed can unleash the urge to eat (Herman & Polivy, 1980). Once the diet is broken, the person often thinks "what the heck" and then binges (Polivy & Herman, 1985, 1987): A lapse becomes a full collapse. Remember, most people occasionally lapse. Remind yourself that you've succeeded before and continue with your plan.

Set realistic goals. Targeting an ambitiously low weight usually dooms a dieter to eventual defeat, but setting a realistic objective—such as walking several times a week—can promote effort and persistence.

Figure 9–6 Couch Potatoes Beware: A Correlational Study of TV Watching and Obesity *In one study of 6671 12- to 17-year-olds, obesity was more common among those who watched the most television. Of course, overweight people may avoid activity, preferring to sit and watch TV. But the association between TV watching and obesity remained when many other factors were controlled, suggesting that inactivity and snacking while TV watching contribute to obesity. (From Dietz & Gortmaker, 1985.)*

Janet Polivy and Peter Herman (1987) believe that widespread, chronic dieting among basically normal-weight girls and women represents the seeds of eating disorder on a massive scale.

Nonetheless, the bulge battle rages as intensely as ever. It is especially intense in North America, where weight concern and dieting are a greater preoccupation than in, say, Australia or Third World countries (Rothblum, 1990; Tiggemann & Rothblum, 1988). Americans spend about $40 billion a year trying to lose weight (Brownell & Rodin, 1994). In a 1991 poll, 32 percent of men and 44 percent of women said they were trying to lose weight (Burros, 1994). The gender difference is even larger for teenagers: 15 percent of boys and 44 percent of girls are trying to lose weight (Centers for Disease Control, 1991). With fat cells, set points, metabolism, and genetic factors all tirelessly conspiring to make losing weight a big problem, what advice can we offer to those who wish to shed excess pounds?

Begin a diet only if you feel motivated and self-disciplined enough to restrict your eating permanently. For most people, permanent weight loss requires making a career of staying thin—a lifelong change in eating habits combined with gradually increased exercise. In fact, sustained exercise can be a weapon against the body's normal metabolic slowdown when dieting. One of the few predictors of successful long-term weight loss is exercise during and after dieting (Brownell & Wadden, 1991, 1992; Foreyt & Goodrick, 1994) (see "Thinking Critically About Helpful Hints for Dieters").

Although preserving weight loss is a constant challenge, Stanley Schachter (1982) is not as pessimistic as most obesity researchers about the likelihood of doing it successfully. He recognizes the overwhelming rate of failure among people in structured weight loss programs. But he also notes that these are a special group of people, probably people who have been unable to help themselves. Moreover, the failure rates recorded for these programs are based on single attempts at weight loss. Perhaps when people try repeatedly to lose weight, more of them do eventually succeed. When Schachter interviewed a haphazard sample of people, he found that one-fourth of them had at one time been significantly overweight and had tried to slim down. Of these, 6 out of 10 had *succeeded*: They weighed at least 10 percent less than their maximum prediet weight (an average loss of 35 pounds) and were no longer obese. And a survey of 90,000 *Consumer Reports* (1993) readers found 25 percent of dieters claiming enduring weight loss.

Two other studies reveal less encouraging results: Fewer than a third of formerly overweight people were no longer overweight (Jeffery & Wing, 1983; Rzewnicki & Forgays, 1987). But the findings do hint that prospects for losing weight may be somewhat brighter than the dismal conclusions we draw from following patients who undergo a single weight loss program.

There is, however, another option for overweight people, the one chosen by 13 percent of the people Schachter interviewed—simply to accept one's weight. We all do well to note what researchers have *not* identified as causes of obesity: guilt, hostility, oral fixation, or any similar personality maladjustment. Nor is obesity simply a matter of a lack of willpower. If dieters are more likely to binge when under stress or after breaking their diets, this may be largely a consequence of their constant dieting. "Fat is not a four-letter word," proclaims the National Association to Aid Fat Acceptance. Although this motto disregards the health risks linked with significant obesity, it does convey a valid point: It is surely better to accept oneself as a little chubby than to diet and binge and feel continually out of control and guilty. Fans loved Oprah Winfrey before she lost 67 pounds and they loved her after she, for a time, put most of them back on.

! *Rehearse It*

7. The hypothalamus, a structure deep within the brain, controls feelings of hunger and satiety, in part by evaluating changes in blood chemistry. Hunger occurs in response to high blood insulin and

a. high blood glucose.
b. low blood glucose.
c. decreased energy expenditure.
d. stimulation of any part of the hypothalamus.

8. Our bodies tend to stay at a particular weight level, or set point. Changes in the metabolic rate help keep us at this weight. For example, when our weight falls below the set point, we feel hungrier (and eat more) and lethargic (and reduce our en-

ergy expenditure). The operation of this "weight thermostat" is an example of

a. homeostasis.
b. an eating disorder.
c. individual learning.
d. binge-purge episodes.

9. Obese people find it very difficult to lose weight permanently. This is due to several factors, including the fact that

a. with dieting fat cells shrink, then disappear.
b. the set point of obese people is lower than average.
c. with dieting, resting metabolic rate increases.
d. there is a genetic influence on body weight.

10. Both anorexia nervosa and bulimia nervosa are eating disorders characterized by excessive weight loss. Which of the following is true regarding bulimia nervosa?

a. Bulimics continue to want to lose weight even when underweight.
b. Bulimia is marked by weight fluctuations within or above normal ranges.
c. Bulimia patients often come from middle-class families that are competitive, high-achieving, and protective.
d. If one twin is diagnosed as bulimic, the chances of the other twin's sharing the disorder is more likely if they are fraternal rather than identical twins.

Sexual Motivation

Sex is part of life. Had this not been so for all your ancestors, you would not be reading this book. Sexual motivation is nature's clever way of making people procreate, thus enabling our species' survival. When two people feel attracted, they hardly stop to think of themselves as guided by their genes. As the pleasure we take in eating is nature's method of getting our body nourishment, so the pleasure of sex is our genes' way of preserving and spreading themselves.

Describing Sexual Behavior

Before looking at what energizes and directs sexual arousal, let's consider the behavior patterns that a theory of sexual motivation must explain.

Unable to answer his students' questions about people's sexual practices, Indiana University biologist Alfred Kinsey and his colleagues (1948, 1953) set out to find some answers. Kinsey's confidential interviews with 18,000 people—85 percent conducted by himself or his associate Wardell Pomeroy—asked more than 350 rapid fire questions. Social scientists were quick to point out what Kinsey readily acknowledged—that his nonrandom sample contained an overrepresentation of well-educated, white urbanites. Nevertheless, his statistics-laden volumes became best-sellers. Here readers learned the surprising news that most of the men and nearly half the women reported having had premarital sexual intercourse; that a majority of women and virtually all men reported masturbating; and that women who reported masturbating to orgasm before marriage seldom had difficulties experiencing orgasm after marriage.

Because we do not know whether Kinsey's sample accurately represented the nation's sexual practices in the 1940s, let alone those of today, it can be misleading to report his precise findings. Moreover, Kinsey and Pomeroy's questioning encouraged (some say, demanded) admission of sexual activity. They never asked subjects *whether* they had engaged in a particular activity, they asked them *when* they had first engaged in it (thus making it easier for people to divulge their behavior). Pomeroy (1972, pp. 113, 124, 127) reported that he and Kinsey "went on the broad assumption that everybody had done everything." If Kinsey or Pomeroy doubted a subject's denial, they might respond, "Yes, I know you have never done that, but how old were you the *first* time you did it?" or even "Look, I don't give a damn what you've done, but if you don't tell me the straight of it, it's better that we stop this history right here. Now, how old were you the first time this or that happened?"

By today's standards of random sampling and nonleading questioning, Kinsey's tactics, and thus his results, are suspect. Yet his surveys were surely less misleading than some of the haphazard sexual surveys that have been reported more recently in the popular press. When popular "sex reports" begin with a biased sample of people (such as subscribers to selected magazines) and receive replies from, say, only 3 percent of this nonrandom sample, there is good reason to doubt the generality of their findings.

Better information is now becoming available. In the United States, for example, four new surveys of randomly sampled adults counter the media image of rampant marital infidelity—an image reinforced by media psychologist Joyce Brothers' (1990) pronouncement that two-thirds of married men and half of married women have affairs. Actually, nearly 9 in 10 married adults claim (even when responding anonymously) to have had sex only with their spouse during their present marriage. And 94 to 98 percent say they have been faithful during the past year (Greely, 1991; Laumann & others, 1994; Leigh & others, 1993; Smith, 1990). Faithful attractions greatly outnumber fatal attractions. And disapproval of extramarital sex, at 91 percent, runs as high as ever among adult Americans (Smith, 1994).

Alfred Kinsey *The eminent biologist, shown here conducting one of his interviews, did not begin with sexually explicit questions. Rather, he first helped people feel at ease by asking nonthreatening questions about family background, health, and education.*

Eager to understand why the AIDS virus has spread more among some groups than others, researchers undertook new sex surveys at the beginning of this decade. The World Health Organization, for example, is conducting the first-ever global survey of human sexuality, based on interviews with some 2000 people in each of 20 countries. Researchers hope that results from such surveys will help us better understand the behaviors that spread AIDS and other sexually transmitted diseases.

The Physiology of Sex

Like hunger, sexual arousal depends on the interplay of internal and external stimuli. To understand sexual motivation, we must consider both.

The Sexual Response Cycle

6. What stages mark the human sexual response?

The headlines created by Kinsey's 1940s surveys reappeared after some 1960s studies in which scientists recorded the physiological responses of volunteers who masturbated or had intercourse. With the help of 382 female and 312 male volunteers—a somewhat atypical sample, consisting only of people able and willing to display arousal and orgasm while being observed in a laboratory— gynecologist-obstetrician William Masters and his collaborator Virginia Johnson (1966) monitored or filmed more than 10,000 sexual "cycles."

Their description of the **sexual response cycle** identified four stages, similar in men and women. During the initial *excitement phase*, the genital areas become engorged with blood, causing the man's penis to become partially erect and the woman's clitoris to swell and the inner lips covering her vagina to open up. Her vagina also expands and secretes lubricant, and her breasts and nipples may enlarge.

In the *plateau phase*, excitement peaks as breathing, pulse, and blood pressure rates continue to increase. The penis becomes fully engorged and some fluid (frequently containing enough live sperm to enable conception) may appear at the tip of the penis. Vaginal secretion continues to increase, the clitoris retracts, and orgasm feels imminent.

Masters and Johnson observed muscle contractions all over the body during *orgasm*; these were accompanied by further increases in breathing, pulse, and blood pressure rates. A woman's arousal and orgasm facilitate conception by helping propel semen from the penis, positioning the uterus to receive sperm, and drawing the sperm further inward (Sarnoff & Sarnoff, 1989). In the excitement of the moment, men and women are hardly aware of all this but are more aware of their rhythmic genital contractions that create a pleasurable feeling of sexual release. The feeling apparently is much the same for both sexes. In one study, a panel of experts could not reliably distinguish between descriptions of orgasm written by men and those written by women (Vance & Wagner, 1976).

After orgasm, the body gradually returns to its unaroused state as the engorged genital blood vessels release their accumulated blood—relatively quickly if orgasm has occurred, relatively slowly otherwise. (It's like the nasal tickle that goes away rapidly if you have sneezed, slowly otherwise.) During this *resolution phase*, the male enters a **refractory period**, lasting from a few minutes to a day or more, during which he is incapable of another orgasm. A female does not have so lengthy a refractory period, which may make it possible for her to have another orgasm if restimulated during or soon after resolution.

sexual response cycle The four stages of sexual response described by Masters and Johnson—excitement, plateau, orgasm, and resolution.

refractory period A resting period after orgasm, during which a man cannot achieve another orgasm.

estrogen A sex hormone, secreted in greater amounts by females than by males. In nonhuman female mammals, estrogen levels peak during ovulation, promoting sexual receptivity.

Hormones and Sexual Behavior

7. What role do hormones play in human sexuality?

Sex hormones have two effects: They direct the development of male and female sex characteristics, and (especially in nonhuman animals) they activate sexual behavior. In most mammals, nature neatly synchronizes sex with fertility. The female becomes sexually receptive ("in heat") when production of the female hormone **estrogen** peaks at ovulation. (In experiments, researchers simulate this by injecting female animals with estrogen.) Male hormone levels are more constant, and researchers cannot so easily manipulate the sexual behavior of male animals by hormone treatments (Feder, 1984). Nevertheless, castrated male rats—having lost their testes, which manufacture the male sex hormone testosterone—gradually lose much of their interest in receptive females, and they gradually regain it if injected with testosterone.

Hormones don't so neatly control human sexual behavior. Women's sexual desire is only slightly higher at ovulation (Harvey, 1987; Meuwissen & Over, 1992). Women's sexuality also differs from that of other mammalian females in being more responsive to testosterone than to estrogen (Kaplan, 1979; Morris & others, 1987).

In men, normal fluctuations in testosterone levels, from man to man and hour to hour, have little effect on sexual drive (Byrne, 1982). Indeed, hormone fluctuations are partly a response to sexual stimulation. When James Dabbs and his colleagues (1987) had male collegians converse separately with a male and with a female student, the men's testosterone levels rose with the social arousal, but especially after talking with the female. Like the effect of the crackling steak on insulin level, sexual arousal can be a cause as well as a consequence of increased testosterone levels.

Although normal short-term hormonal changes have little effect on desire, large hormone shifts have a bigger effect over the life span. A person's interest in dating and sexual stimulation usually increases with the pubertal surge in sex hormones. If the hormonal surge is precluded—as happened with prepubertal boys who were castrated during the 1700s and 1800s to preserve their soprano voices for Italian opera—the normal development of sex characteristics and sexual desire does not occur (Peschel & Peschel, 1987). Among adult men who suffer castration, sex drive typically falls along with declining testosterone levels (Hucker & Bain, 1990). Likewise, male sex offenders lose much of their sexual urge when voluntarily taking Depo-Provera, a drug that reduces testosterone levels to that of a prepubertal boy (Money & others, 1983). And in later life, the typical frequency of intercourse declines as sex hormone levels decline.

"Fill'er up with testosterone."

Drawing by Mankoff; © 1993 *The New Yorker* Magazine, Inc.

Hormones influence sexual arousal via the hypothalamus, which both monitors variations in blood hormone levels and activates the appropriate neural circuits. In rats, destroying a key area of the hypothalamus may end sexual activity; stimulating this area, either electrically or by directly inserting minute quantities of hormones, may activate sexual behavior.

To summarize, we might compare human sex hormones, especially testosterone, to the fuel in a car. Lacking fuel, the car will not run. But if the fuel level is minimally adequate, adding more fuel to the gas tank won't change how the car runs. The analogy is imperfect, because the interaction between hormones and sexual motivation is two-way. However, the analogy correctly suggests that biology is a necessary but not sufficient explanation of human sexual behavior. The hormonal fuel is essential, but so are the psychological stimuli that turn on the engine and shift it into high gear.

The Psychology of Sex

8. How do internal and external factors interact to stimulate sexual arousal?

Hunger and sex are different sorts of motives. Hunger responds to a *need*. If we do not eat, we die. Sex is not in this sense a need. If we do not have sex, we may feel like dying, but we do not die. There are nevertheless similarities between hunger and sexual motivation. Both depend on internal physiological factors. And both are influenced by external stimuli.

External Stimuli

Many studies confirm that men become aroused when they see, hear, or read erotic material. More surprising to many people (because sexually explicit materials are sold mostly to men) is that most women—at least the less inhibited women who volunteer to participate in such studies—report nearly as much arousal to the same stimuli (Stockton & Murnen, 1992).

In one such study, psychologist Julia Heiman (1975) attached instruments that detected arousal (changes in penis circumference or in vaginal color) to sexually experienced university volunteers. Then the students listened to either a sexually explicit erotic tape, a romantic tape (of a couple expressing love without physical contact), a combined erotic-romantic tape, or a neutral control tape. Which do you suppose the men were most aroused by? And the women? Both found the tape of explicit sex most arousing, especially when a woman initiated the sex and the depiction centered on her responses.

People may find such arousal either pleasing or disturbing. (Those who find it disturbing often limit their exposure to such materials, just as those wishing to control hunger limit their exposure to tempting cues.) Some sexually explicit materials can have adverse effects. First, depictions of women being sexually coerced—and enjoying it—tend to increase viewers' acceptance of the false idea that women enjoy rape, and they tend to increase male viewers' willingness to hurt women (see pages 506–507). Second, images of sexually attractive women and men may lead people to devalue their own partners and relationships. After male collegians view TV or magazine depictions of sexually attractive women, they often find an average woman, or their own girlfriends or wives, less attractive (Gutierres & others, 1985; Kenrick & Gutierres, 1980; Weaver & others, 1984). Viewing X-rated sex films similarly tends to diminish people's satisfaction with their sexual partners (Zillmann, 1989). Some sex researchers fear that reading or viewing erotica may create expectations that few men and women can hope to live up to.

"Ours is a society which stimulates interest in sex by constant titillation. . . . Cinema, television, and all the formidable array of our marketing technology project our very effective forms of titillation and our prejudices about man as a sexy animal into every corner of every hovel in the world."

Germaine Greer (1984)

Imaginative Stimuli

Sexual motivation arises from the interplay of physiology and environment. But the stimuli inside our heads—our imaginations—also influence sexual arousal and desire (Figure 9–7). The brain, it has been said, is our most significant sex organ. People who, because of a spinal cord injury, have no genital sensation, can still feel sexual desire (Willmuth, 1987). Consider, too, the erotic potential of dreams. As noted in Chapter 5, genital arousal accompanies all types of dreams, even though most dreams have no sexual content. But in nearly all men and some 40 percent of women (Wells, 1986), dreams sometimes do contain sexual imagery that leads to orgasm. In men, these nocturnal emissions ("wet dreams") are more likely when orgasm has not occurred recently.

Figure 9–7 Forces Affecting Sexual Motivation *Sexual motivation results from the interplay of physiology, environment, and imagination. (From Byrne, 1982.)*

Wide-awake people become sexually aroused not only by memories of prior sexual activities but also by fantasies. Fantasies need not correspond to actual behavior. In one survey of masturbation-related fantasies (Hunt, 1974), 19 percent of women and 10 percent of men reported imagining someone forcing them to have sex. Fantasy is not reality, however. To paraphrase Susan Brownmiller (1975), for women there's a big difference between fantasizing that supermodel Fabio just won't take no for an answer and having a hostile stranger actually force himself on you.

> *"There is no difference between being raped and being run over by a truck except that afterward men ask if you enjoyed it."*
>
> Marge Piercy
> "Rape Poem," 1976

Sexual Dysfunctions and Therapy

Masters and Johnson sought not only to describe the human sexual response cycle but also to understand and treat the inability to complete it. **Sexual dysfunctions** are problems that consistently impair sexual functioning. Some involve sexual motivation, especially lack of sexual energy and arousability. Men, for example, may experience *premature ejaculation* (before they or their partners wish) or *impotence* (the inability to have or maintain an erection). Women more often than men experience low sexual desire or *orgasmic dysfunction* (infrequently or never experiencing orgasm).

What causes such problems? The idea that personality disorders are to blame has been largely discounted. Men who experience premature ejaculation are similar, even in their sexual arousal patterns, to men who do not; they simply ejaculate at lower levels of sexual arousal—something that often occurs with young men who have had long periods of sexual abstinence (Spiess & others, 1984).

When Barbara Andersen (1983) reviewed research on the diagnosis and treatment of orgasmic dysfunction in women, she too could find no associated personality traits. Furthermore, she reported that treating orgasmic dysfunction through traditional psychotherapy (as though it were a disorder of personality)

sexual dysfunction A problem that consistently impairs sexual arousal or functioning.

has been unsuccessful. She did, however, report a nearly 100 percent success rate with a behavioral treatment that trains women to enjoy their bodies and to give themselves orgasms, with a vibrator if necessary. Some of these women can then generalize their new sexual responsiveness to interactions with their mates (LoPiccolo & Stock, 1986; Wakefield, 1987). Success has also been reported in training men to control their premature ejaculations by repeatedly stimulating the penis and then stopping stimulation (or even firmly squeezing the head of the penis) when the urge to ejaculate arises.

Gender and Sexuality

9. How do men's and women's sexual attitudes and behaviors differ?

"With few exceptions anywhere in the world," report cross-cultural psychologist Marshall Segall and his colleagues (1990, p. 244), "males are more likely than females to initiate sexual activity." Across 177 studies of some 130,000 people, men are much more accepting of casual sex and they report masturbating much more often (Oliver & Hyde, 1993). This is among the largest of gender differences. A few examples:

- In a Canadian survey of 2350 Adults Only video store customers, 80 percent were males (though half claimed to engage a partner in watching the movies) (Jenish, 1993).

- In a 1994 survey of 238,000 new American college students, 56 percent of men but only 32 percent of women agreed that "If two people really like each other, it's all right for them to have sex even if they've known each other for a very short time" (Astin & others, 1994).

- In a careful survey of 3432 18- to 59-year-old Americans, 48 percent of women but only 25 percent of men cited affection as a reason for first intercourse. And how often do they think about sex? "Every day" or "several times a day," acknowledged 54 percent of men and 19 percent of women (Laumann & others, 1994).

Such attitudes carry over to behavior. Casual hit-and-run sex is most frequent among males with traditional masculine attitudes (Pleck & others, 1993). Russell Clark and Elaine Hatfield (1989) observed the striking gender difference in sexuality when in 1978 they sent some average-looking student research assistants strolling across the Florida State University quadrangle. Spotting an attractive person of the other sex, a researcher would approach and say, "I have been noticing you around campus and I find you to be very attractive. Would you go to bed with me tonight?" The women all declined, some with obvious irritation. ("What's wrong with you, creep, leave me alone.") But 75 percent of the men readily agreed, often with comments such as "Why do we have to wait until tonight?" Somewhat astonished by their result, Clark and Hatfield repeated their study in 1982 and twice more during the late-eighties AIDS era (Clark, 1990). Each time, virtually no women, but half or more of the men, agreed to go to bed with a stranger.

Men also have a lower threshold for perceiving someone's warmth as a sexual come-on. In study after study, men more often than women attribute a woman's friendliness to sexual interest (Abbey, 1987; Johnson & others, 1991). Such "misattribution" of a woman's cordiality as a "come on" helps explain men's greater sexual assertiveness (Kenrick & Trost, 1987). The unfortunate results can range from sexual harassment to date rape (Kanekar & Nazareth, 1988; Muehlenhard, 1988; Shotland, 1989).

sexual orientation An enduring sexual attraction toward members of either one's own gender (homosexual orientation) or the other gender (heterosexual orientation).

Sexual Orientation

10. What factors do and don't appear linked with sexual orientation?

To motivate is to energize and direct behavior. So far, we have considered the energizing of sexual motivation but not its direction. We express the direction of our sexual interest in our **sexual orientation**—our enduring sexual attraction toward members of a particular gender. Cultures vary in their attitudes toward homosexuality. Yet as far as we know, all cultures in all times have been predominantly heterosexual (Bullough, 1990). Whether a culture condemns and punishes homosexuality or views it as an acceptable alternative, homosexuality survives and heterosexuality prevails.

Homosexual people often recall childhood play preferences like those of the other sex (Bailey & Zuker, 1995). But most report not becoming aware of same-gender sexual feelings until during or shortly after puberty, and not thinking of themselves as gay or lesbian until nearer to or after age 20 (Garnets & Kimmel, 1990).

How many people are exclusively homosexual? Until recently, the popular press assumed a homosexuality rate of 10 percent. But in both Europe and the United States, a dozen national surveys have recently explored sexual orientation, using methods that protect the respondent's anonymity. Their results agree in suggesting that a more accurate figure is about 3 or 4 percent of men and 1 percent of women (Johnson & others, 1992; Laumann & others, 1994; National Center for Health Statistics, 1991; Rogers & Turner, 1991). Less than 1 percent of people report being actively bisexual. But more adults report having had an isolated homosexual experience. And most people have an occasional homosexual fantasy.

Although health experts find it helpful to know sexual statistics, numbers don't decide issues of human rights. Similarly, it's helpful in manufacturing school desks to know that about 10 percent of people are left-handed. But whether left-handers are 3 percent or 10 percent of the population doesn't answer the moral question of whether lefties should enjoy equal rights. Whether a minority is 3 percent of the population or nearer 10 percent is irrelevant to issues of justice.

"It has been maintained for years that we each use only about 10 percent of our brain capacity; that the condom failure rate is 10 percent; and until just last year, that 10 percent of Americans are homosexual. Such statistics are partly artifacts, I suspect, of our decimal system; in a base 12 system, we'd no doubt show a similar affinity for statistics that were multiples of 8.333 percent."

John Allen Paulos
"Counting on Dyscalculia," 1993

AIDS Awareness *The AIDS threat has prompted safer sex among homosexuals. Gay men, especially, report fewer sexual partners (Joseph & others, 1987; Winkelstein & others, 1987). Yet there remains a streak of unrealistic optimism, which explains why so many homosexual men still seldom use condoms (Baumann & Siegel, 1987; Fineberg, 1988). Grand Rapids, Michigan, artist Mark Heckman created a billboard—pasted with 2000 condoms—that people could not ignore—to focus attention on AIDS and one way to reduce exposure to the virus.*

What does it feel like to be homosexual in a heterosexual culture? One way for heterosexual people to understand is to imagine how they would feel if they were to be ostracized or fired for openly admitting or displaying their feelings toward someone of the other sex; if they were to overhear people making crude jokes about heterosexual people; if most movies, TV shows, and advertisements portrayed (or implied) homosexuality; and if their family members were pleading with them to change their heterosexual life-style and to enter into a homosexual marriage.

Facing such reactions, homosexual people often struggle with their sexual orientation. At first, they may try to ignore or deny their desires, hoping they will go away; but they don't. Then they may try to change, through psychotherapy, will power, or prayer. But the feelings typically persist, as do those of heterosexual people—who are similarly incapable of becoming homosexual (Haldeman, 1994). Eventually, homosexuals may accept their orientation—by electing celibacy (as do some heterosexuals); by engaging in promiscuous sex (a choice more commonly made by men than by women); or by entering into a committed, long-term love relationship (a choice more often made by women than by men) (Peplau, 1982; Weinberg & Williams, 1974).

Most psychologists today view sexual orientation as neither willfully chosen nor willfully changed. Sexual orientation in some ways is like handedness: Most people are one way, some the other. A very few are truly ambidextrous. Regardless, the way one is endures. Nor is sexual orientation linked with psychological disorder or sexual crime, such as being a child molester. Some homosexuals do abuse children, but most child molesters are heterosexual males (Gonsiorek, 1982). These facts led the American Psychiatric Association in 1973 to drop homosexuality from its list of "mental illnesses."

Understanding Sexual Orientation

If our sexual orientation is indeed something we do not choose and cannot change, then how does a person move toward either a heterosexual or a homosexual orientation?[1] Some consensus has emerged from hundreds of research studies on sexual orientation (Storms, 1983):

1. Homosexuality is not linked with problems in a child's relationships with parents, such as with a domineering mother and an ineffectual father, or a possessive mother and a hostile father.

2. Homosexuality does not involve a fear or hatred of people of the other gender.

3. Sexual orientation is not linked with levels of sex hormones currently in the blood.

4. Sexual victimization of children by an adult homosexual or others is not a factor in homosexual orientation.

Consider the findings of lengthy Kinsey Institute interviews with nearly 1000 homosexuals and 500 heterosexuals (Bell & others, 1981; Hammersmith, 1982). The investigators assessed nearly every imaginable psychological cause of homosexuality—parental relationships, childhood sexual experiences, peer relationships, dating experiences, even number of brothers and sisters. Their findings: Homosexuals were no more likely than heterosexuals to have been smothered by maternal love, neglected by their father, or sexually abused. The

---

[1]Note that the scientific question is not "What causes homosexuality?" (or "What causes heterosexuality?") but "What causes differing sexual orientation?" In pursuit of answers, psychological science compares the backgrounds and physiology of people whose sexual orientations *differ.*

Erick Has Two Moms *Maria Christina Vlassidis (left) and Marie Tatro (center) tell playmates of their son Erick, 8, that they are both his moms. Both women, who are lesbians, attend school conferences and are equally active in supporting other aspects of his life.*

sons of homosexual men are not more likely to become gay if they live with their gay dad (Bailey & others, 1995).

So, what determines sexual orientation? One theory proposes that people develop same-sex erotic attachments if segregated by gender at the time their sex drive matures (Storms, 1981). But even in a tribal culture in which homosexual behavior is expected of all boys before marriage, heterosexuality prevails (Money, 1987). (As this illustrates, homosexual *behavior* does not always indicate a homosexual *orientation*.) Another theory proposes the opposite: that people develop romantic attachments to those who *differ* from, and thus are more fascinating than, the peers they associated with while growing up (Bell, 1982). The bottom line from a half century's theory and research: If there are environmental factors that influence sexual orientation, we do not yet know what they are. If someone were to ask me, "What can I do to influence my child's sexual orientation?," my answer would have to be: "I haven't a clue."

The Brain and Sexual Orientation New research indicates that sexual orientation may be at least partly physiological. Researcher Simon LeVay (1991) discovered this while studying sections of the hypothalamus taken from deceased heterosexual and homosexual people. As a gay scientist, LeVay wanted to do "something connected with my gay identity," but he knew he had to avoid biasing the results. So he did the study "blind," without knowing which donors were gay. After 9 months peering through his microscope at a cell cluster he thought might be important, LeVay sat down one morning and broke the codes. His discovery: The cell cluster was reliably larger in heterosexual men than in women and homosexual men. As the brain difference became apparent, "I was almost in a state of shock. . . . I took a walk by myself on the cliffs over the ocean. I sat for half an hour just thinking what this might mean" (LeVay, 1994).

It should not surprise us that brains differ with sexual orientation. Remember our maxim: Although we find it convenient to talk separately of psychological and biological explanations, *everything psychological is simultaneously biological.* The critical question is, when did the brain difference begin? At conception? In the womb? During childhood or adolescence? Did experience produce the difference? Or did genes or prenatal hormones?

LeVay does not view this little neural center as a sexual orientation center; rather, he sees it as an important part of the neural pathway engaged in sexual behavior. Moreover, he acknowledges that it's possible that sexual behavior patterns influence the brain's anatomy. (In fish, birds, and humans, brain structures are known to vary with experience.) But he believes it more likely that brain anatomy influences sexual orientation. Laura Allen and Roger Gorski (1992) offered a similar conclusion after discovering that a section of the fibers connecting right and left hemispheres is one-third larger in homosexual men than in heterosexual men. "The emerging neuroanatomical picture," notes Brian Gladue (1994), "is that, in some brain areas, homosexual men are more likely to have female-typical neuroanatomy than are heterosexual men."

"Gay men simply don't have the brain cells to be attracted to women."

Simon LeVay
The Sexual Brain, 1993

Genes and Sexual Orientation   The evidence suggests that genetic influence plays a role. One research team studied the twin brothers of homosexual men. Among their identical twin brothers, 52 percent were homosexual, as were 22 percent of fraternal twin brothers (Bailey & Pillard, 1991). In a follow-up study of homosexual women, a similar 48 percent of their identical twins were homosexual, as were 16 percent of their fraternal twins (Bailey & others, 1993). With half the identical twin pairs differing, we know that genes aren't the whole story. Still, this is the sort of pattern we expect to see when genes are having an *influence*. Moreover, with a single transplanted gene, scientists can now cause male fruit flies to display homosexual behavior (Zhang and Odenwald, 1995).

Prenatal Hormones and Sexual Orientation   The elevated rate of homosexual orientation even in fraternal twins might also result from their sharing the same prenatal environment. In animals and some exceptional human cases, sexual orientation has been altered by abnormal prenatal hormone conditions. Female sheep, for example, will show homosexual behavior if their pregnant mothers are injected with testosterone during a critical gestation period (Money, 1987). With humans, a critical period for the brain's neural-hormonal control system may exist between the middle of the second and fifth months after conception (Ellis & Ames, 1987; Gladue, 1990). It seems that exposure to the hormone levels typically experienced by female fetuses during this time may predispose the person (whether female or male) to be attracted to males in later life. Some tests reveal that homosexual men have spatial abilities like those typical of heterosexual women—a pattern consistent with the hypothesis that homosexuals were exposed to atypical prenatal hormones (Gladue, 1994; McCormick & Witelson, 1991).

> "Biological theories of sexual orientation are far more promising than any current alternatives."
>
> J. Michael Bailey and Richard C. Pillard (1994)

Because the physiological evidence is preliminary and controversial, some scientists remain skeptical. Rather than specifying sexual orientation, perhaps biological factors predispose a temperament that influences sexuality "in the context of individual learning and experience" (Byne & Parsons, 1993). Nevertheless, the consistency of the genetic, prenatal, and brain findings has swung the pendulum toward a physiological explanation. If these influences prove critical (perhaps especially in certain environmental contexts), it would explain why sexual orientation is so difficult to change.

Still, some people wonder: Should the cause of sexual orientation matter? Maybe it shouldn't, but people's assumptions matter. Those who believe, as do most homosexual people, that sexual orientation is a biological given—an enduring identity, not a choice—express more accepting attitudes toward homosexual persons (Furnham & Taylor, 1990; Whitley, 1990). Others respond that diabetes, alcoholism, and schizophrenia are also biologically influenced—but are not considered desirable or normal (Krauthammer, 1993). Nevertheless, in American surveys, agreement that homosexuality is "something that people are born with" doubled from 16 to 31 percent between 1983 and 1993. Over roughly the same time period, support for equal job rights for homosexuals increased from 59 to 80 percent (Moore, 1993). Disapproval of homosexual behavior remains strong, however (NORC, 1993).

To gay and lesbian activists, the new biological research is a double-edged sword (Diamond, 1993). If sexual orientation, like skin color and sex, is genetically influenced, that offers a further rationale for civil rights protection. Moreover, it may alleviate parents' concerns about their children having gay teachers and role models. It does, however, raise the haunting possibility that genetic markers of sexual orientation could someday be identified through fetal testing, and the fetus aborted. This new research on sexual orientation may be raising as many questions as answers.

Sex and Human Values

11. What roles do personal values play in sex research and sex education?

Recognizing that values are both personal and cultural, most sex researchers and educators strive to keep their writings on sexuality value-free.

But can the study of sexual behavior and what motivates it really be free of values? Those who think not say that the very words we use to describe behavior often reflect our personal values. When sex researchers label sexually restrained individuals as "erotophobic" and as having "high sex guilt," they express their own values. Whether we label sexual acts we do not practice as "perversions," "deviations," or part of an "alternative sexual life-style" depends on our attitudes toward the behaviors. Labels both describe and evaluate.

When educational information about sex is separated from the context of human values, some students may get the idea that sexual intercourse is merely recreational activity. Diana Baumrind (1982), a University of California child-rearing expert, suspects that adolescents interpret sex education that pretends to be "value-free" as meaning that adults are neutral about adolescent sexual activity. She feels that such an implication is unfortunate, because "promiscuous recreational sex poses certain psychological, social, health, and moral problems that must be faced realistically."

Nevertheless, researchers have found that teenagers who have had sex education classes are no more likely to engage in premarital sex than those who have not (Furstenberg & others, 1985; Zelnik & Kim, 1982). Moreover, we enrich our lives by knowing ourselves, by realizing that others share our feelings, by understanding what is likely to please or displease our loved one. Witness the crumbling of falsehoods about homosexuality. Witness the growing realization that some types of sexually explicit material can lead people to devalue or hurt others.

Perhaps we can agree that the knowledge provided by sex research is preferable to ignorance, yet also agree that researchers' values should be stated openly, enabling us to debate them and to reflect on our own values. We might

The mathematics of sexually transmitted disease: Imagine an island on which, up to now, all people are virgins. Now assume that Pat has sex with nine people, each of whom over the same time period has sex with nine people, who in turn have sex with nine others. How many "phantom" sex partners (past partners of partners) will Pat have? Laura Brannon and Timothy Brock (1994) report that the actual number—511—is more than five times the average student's guess.

A Sharing of Love *For most adults, a sexual relationship fulfills not only a biological motive, but a social need for intimacy.*

also remember that scientific research on sexual motivation does not aim to define the personal meaning of sex in our lives. One can know every available fact about sex—that the initial spasms of male and female orgasm come at 0.8-second intervals, that the female nipples expand 10 millimeters at the peak of sexual arousal, that systolic blood pressure rises some 60 points and the respiration rate to 40 breaths per minute—but fail to understand the human significance of sexual intimacy.

Surely one significance of sexual intimacy is its expression of our deeply social nature. Sex is a socially significant act. Men and women can achieve orgasm alone, yet most people find greater satisfaction while embracing their loved one. Although the yearning for closeness was not part of our description of sexual motivation, sex at its human best is a life-uniting and love-renewing experience.

> *"The relationship between women and men should be characterized not by patronizing behavior or exploitation, but by love, partnership, and trustworthiness. . . . Sexuality should express and reinforce a loving relationship lived by equal partners."*
>
> *Towards a Global Ethic*
> 1993 Parliament of the World's Religions

! Rehearse It

11. In the 1940s, Alfred Kinsey and his colleagues used questionnaires to investigate human sexual behavior. His results have been criticized because

a. his sample was not large enough.
b. his sample was not representative of the population as a whole.
c. he asked leading questions.
d. both b. and c. are true.

12. The sexual response cycle in men and women consists of four stages: excitement, plateau, orgasm, and resolution. The sexual response cycle was first clinically observed and described by

a. Alfred Kinsey and his colleagues.
b. William Masters and Virginia Johnson.
c. Simon Le Vay.
d. Abraham Maslow.

13. Daily and monthly fluctuations in hormone levels do not greatly affect sexual desire in humans. Over the life span, however, hormonal changes are significant. A striking effect of hormonal change on human sexual behavior is the

a. arousing effects of erotic materials.
b. sharp rise in sexual interests at puberty.

c. increase in women's sexual desire at the time of ovulation.
d. increase in testosterone levels in castrated males.

14. Sexual behavior is motivated by internal biological factors, by external stimuli, and by imaginative stimuli. An example of an external stimulus that might influence sexual behavior is

a. blood level of testosterone.
b. the onset of puberty.
c. a sexually explicit film.
d. an erotic fantasy or dream.

15. Sexual dysfunctions are problems that consistently impair sexual functioning. In some cases, they involve sexual motivation, especially lack of arousability. The cause of such problems is

a. personality traits, because psychotherapy has been used successfully to treat such problems.
b. genetic factors, because no treatment has successfully eliminated the problem.
c. physiological factors, because exercise has been found to help people with such problems.
d. unknown, although behavioral therapy has been used successfully to treat such problems.

16. One of the largest of gender differences involves attitudes and behaviors related to sexual activity. Which of the following is true regarding this gender difference?

a. Women are more likely than men to cite affection as a reason for first intercourse.
b. Men are less likely than women to rent "adult only" videos.
c. Women are more likely than men to perceive warmth as a sexual come-on.
d. Men are less likely than women to agree that sex is acceptable between two people even if they know each other only a short time.

17. Sexual orientation refers to our enduring sexual attraction to members of a particular gender. Current research suggests several possible physiological contributors to sexual orientation, including all but which of the following?

a. certain cell clusters in the hypothalamus
b. gender segregation during the time the sex drive matures
c. a section of fibers connecting right and left hemispheres of the brain
d. exposure to hormone levels typically experienced by female fetuses

achievement motivation A desire for significant accomplishment: for mastery of things, people, or ideas; for attaining a high standard.

The Image of Achievement *Her Emmy Award–winning talk show and the millions of dollars she has earned have not dampened Oprah Winfrey's achievement motivation. She constantly seeks new ways to actualize her great energy and talent. "I've been blessed—but I create the blessings," she says.*

Figure 9–8 What Is This Boy Daydreaming About? *By analyzing responses to ambiguous photos like this, motivation researchers seek clues to people's levels of achievement motivation.*

Achievement Motivation

12. Who has the greatest need to achieve? Why?

The biological perspective on motivation—the idea that physiological needs drive us to satisfy those needs—provides only a partial explanation of what energizes and directs our behavior. Hunger and sex have both social and physiological components. Moreover, there are motives that, unlike hunger and sex, seem not to satisfy any physical need. Millionaires may be motivated to make ever more money, movie stars to become ever more famous, politicians to achieve ever more power, daredevils to seek ever greater thrills. Such motives seem not to diminish when they are fed. The more we achieve, the more we may need to achieve.

Identifying Achievement Motivation

Think of someone you know who strives to succeed by excelling at any task where evaluation is possible. Now think of someone who is less disciplined and driven. Psychologist Henry Murray (1938) defined the first person's high need for achievement, or **achievement motivation**, as a desire for significant accomplishment, for mastering skills or ideas, for control, and for rapidly attaining a high standard.

To study this motive, we first need a way to measure it. But how? Recall from the semistarvation studies that people driven by hunger begin to fantasize about food. Our sexual orientation is similarly reflected in our sexual fantasies. Do these examples suggest a way to assess a person's need to achieve?

Murray and investigators David McClelland and John Atkinson presumed that people's fantasies would reflect their achievement concerns. So they asked subjects to invent stories about ambiguous pictures. If, when shown the daydreaming boy in Figure 9–8, a subject commented that the boy was preoccupied with his pursuit of a goal, that he imagined himself performing a heroic act, or that he was feeling pride in some success, the story was scored as indicating achievement concerns. McClelland and Atkinson regarded those people whose stories consistently included such themes as having a high need for achievement.

Would you expect people whose stories express high achievement to prefer tasks that are easy, moderately challenging, or very difficult? People whose stories suggest low achievement motivation tend to choose either very easy or very difficult tasks, where failure is either unlikely or not embarrassing (Geen, 1984). Those whose stories express high achievement motivation tend to prefer moderately difficult tasks, where success is attainable yet attributable to their skill and effort. In a ring toss game, for instance, they often stand at an intermediate distance from the stake; this enables some successes, yet provides a suitable challenge. People with a strong need to achieve are also more likely to persist in a task when things get difficult (Cooper, 1983). By contrast, high school underachievers are less persistent in completing college degrees, holding on to jobs, and maintaining their marriages (McCall, 1994).

As you might expect from their persistence and eagerness for realistic challenge, people with high achievement motivation do achieve more. One study followed the lives of 1528 California children whose intelligence scores were in the top 1 percent. When researchers 40 years later compared the men whose occupational lives were most and least successful, they found a difference in motivation level. Those most successful were more ambitious, energetic, and persistent. As children, they had more active hobbies. As adults, they participated in more groups and favored participating in sports over passively watch-

What is your greatest achievement to date? What is your greatest future ambition—to attain fame? Fortune? Creative accomplishment? Security? Love? Power? Wisdom? Spiritual wholeness?

"They can because they think they can."

Virgil
Aeneid, 19 B.C.

Remember the two people you chose, one who consistently strives to succeed, the other who is less concerned with achievement? Is either a first-born (or only) child? Such children are more likely than their later-born siblings to become "distinguished" in their fields or be named Rhodes or National Merit Scholars. Later-borns, however, tend to be more socially skilled and creative (Falbo & Polit, 1986; Sulloway, 1990).

intrinsic motivation A desire to perform a behavior for its own sake and to be effective.

extrinsic motivation A desire to perform a behavior due to promised rewards or threats of punishment.

ing (Goleman, 1980). Another study of outstanding athletes, scholars, and artists found that all were highly motivated and self-disciplined, willing to dedicate hours every day to the pursuit of their goals (Bloom, 1985). These superstar achievers were distinguished not so much by their extraordinary natural talent as by their extraordinary daily discipline. For them preparation plus opportunity equalled success.

Analysis of the life histories of great scientists, philosophers, political leaders, writers, and musicians confirms the importance of disciplined motivation. Great achievers, consumed by a passion to perfect their gift, often are continuously productive from an early age, notes Dean Keith Simonton (1994). So much so that a small proportion of contributors to any field produce most of its achievements. Although intelligence is distributed like a bell curve, achievements are not—and that tells us that achievement involves much more than raw ability.

Sources of Achievement Motivation

Why, despite similar potentials, does one person become more motivated to achieve than another? Highly motivated children often have parents who encourage their independence from an early age and praise and reward them for their successes (Teevan & McGhee, 1972). Such parents encourage their children to dress and feed themselves and to do well in school, and they express delight when their children achieve. Theorists speculate that the high achievement motivation displayed by such children has *emotional* roots, as children learn to associate achievement with positive emotions. There may also be *cognitive* roots, as children learn to attribute their achievements to their own competence and effort and to develop higher expectations (Dweck & Elliott, 1983).

Intrinsic Motivation and Achievement

13. *What is intrinsic motivation, and how can it be nurtured?*

In the classroom, at the workplace, and on the athletic field, two types of achievement motivation operate. **Intrinsic motivation** is the inner desire to be effective and to perform a behavior for its own sake. **Extrinsic motivation** is seeking external rewards and avoiding punishments.

To sense the difference between extrinsic and intrinsic motivation, you might reflect on your own current experience. Are you feeling pressured to get this reading finished before a deadline? Worried about your course grade? Eager for rewards that depend on your doing well? If your answers are yes, then you are extrinsically motivated (as, to some extent, almost all students are). Are you also finding the course material interesting? Does learning it enable you to feel more competent? If there were no grade at stake, might you be curious enough to want to learn the material for its own sake? If your answers are yes, intrinsic motivation also fuels your efforts.

In sports, as in other activities, excessive external pressures and incentives can undermine intrinsic enjoyment. One researcher, Dean Ryan (1980), studied college football players. He found that those on athletic scholarships (who were, in a sense, playing for pay) enjoyed their play less than did the nonscholarship players. Apparently, pay and pressure turn play into work. However, rewards can increase intrinsic motivation if their effect is to inform the players of their athletic competence (as with a "most improved player" award).

So, should coaches emphasize extrinsic pressures, rewards, and competition? It depends on the goal, report motivation researchers Edward Deci and Richard Ryan (1985, 1992). For some, as for professional football coach Vince

The Reverend Jesse Jackson *The civil rights leader's high level of intrinsic motivation has driven him to seek new and more difficult challenges. A phrase from his speech at the 1983 civil rights march on Washington, D.C., sums it up: "If my mind can conceive it and my heart can believe it, I know I can achieve it."*

Lombardi, "Winning isn't everything; it's the only thing." If so, it may pay to control the players with pressures and rewards for winning. But what if the goal is—as it should be for most programs of physical education, fitness, and amateur sports—the promotion of an enduring interest and participation in physical activity? Then, say Deci and Ryan, "External pressures, competitive emphasis, and evaluative feedback are in contradiction to this goal." Thus, if Little League coaches want their players to continue playing baseball after Little League, they should focus not on the urgency of winning but on the joy of playing one's best.

Researchers in the psychology of religion have also explored intrinsic versus extrinsic motivation (Bergin, 1991; Gorsuch, 1988). Some religiously active people score high on tests of extrinsic religious motivation, by reporting their religion is a means to other ends. (They might agree, for example, that "a primary reason for my interest in religion is that my church is a congenial social activity.") Others score high on *intrinsic* religious motivation, by reporting their religion is an end in itself. ("My religious beliefs are what really lie behind my whole approach to life.") Compared with the extrinsically religious, intrinsically religious people tend to score lower on tests of prejudice and anxiety. They also tend to live with a greater sense of control over their lives and a clearer sense of purpose (Wulff, 1991).

Motivating People

14. What motivational strategies are most effective at home, school, and work?

The growing field of **industrial/organizational psychology** includes studies of how managers might best:

- match people with jobs, by identifying motivated, well-suited personnel.

- make jobs suit people, by creating work environments that boost morale and output.

- evaluate performance and create incentives for excellence.

- promote teamwork and group achievement.

What every leader (manager, coach, or teacher) wants to know is "How can I manage in ways that enhance people's motivation, productivity, satisfaction?" (Satisfied workers aren't always more productive, but they are less likely to be absent or to quit.) Four factors known to improve a leader's effectiveness are cultivating intrinsic motivation, attending to people's motives, setting goals, and choosing an appropriate leadership style.

Cultivate Intrinsic Motivation

If intrinsic motivation stimulates achievement, especially in situations where people work independently (as students, executives, and scientists often do), then how might we encourage it? The consistent answers, from hundreds of studies: First, provide tasks that challenge and trigger curiosity (Malone & Lepper, 1986). Second, avoid snuffing out people's sense of self-determination with an overuse of controlling extrinsic rewards (Deci & Ryan, 1987).

Note that we can use extrinsic rewards in two ways: to *control* ("If you clean up your room, you can have some ice cream") or to *inform* someone of successes ("That was outstanding—we congratulate you"). Attempts to *control* people's behaviors through rewards and surveillance may be successful as long as these controls are present. If taken away, interest in the activity often drops.

industrial/organizational psychology
A subfield of psychology that studies and advises on workplace behavior. Industrial/organizational (I/O) psychologists help organizations select and train employees, boost morale and productivity, and design products and assess responses to them.

Rewards *The type of reward affects motivation.*

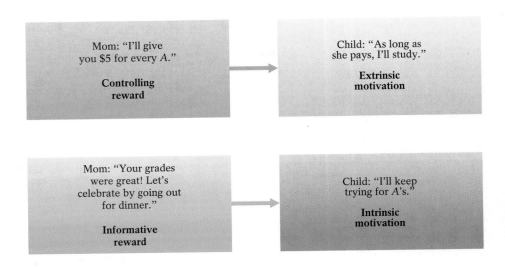

Ironically, teachers who try hardest to boost their students' achievement on competency tests tend to be most controlling, thus undermining their students' intrinsic interest. On the other hand, rewards that *inform* people they are doing well can boost their feelings of competence and intrinsic motivation.

There is an important practical principle here. Because the controlling use of rewards undermines intrinsic motivation (and creativity—see page 284), parents, teachers, and managers should take care not to be overcontrolling. It is important to expect, support, challenge, and inform, but if you want to encourage internally motivated, self-directed achievements, do not overly control.

Attend to People's Motives

Effective managerial styles vary with the people managed. To motivate people, Martin Maehr and Larry Braskamp (1986; Braskamp, 1987) advise managers to assess their people's motives and adjust their managerial style accordingly. Challenge employees who value *accomplishment* to try new things and to exhibit excellence. Give those who value *recognition* the attention they desire. Place those who value *affiliation* in a unit that has a family feeling and shares decision making. Motivate those who value *power* with competition and opportunities for triumphant success. Different strokes for different folks, but for each a way to motivate.

Toys "R" Everywhere *Hiring Japanese top executives who know their own culture and listening to what they have to say has enabled Toys "R" Us and other Western firms to succeed in Japanese markets. Here ladened shoppers leave the flagship store—one of 10 planned for Japan.*

task leadership Goal-oriented leadership that sets standards, organizes work, and focuses attention on goals.

social leadership Group-oriented leadership that builds teamwork, mediates conflict, and offers support.

"Good leaders don't ask more than their constituents can give, but they often ask—and get—more than their constituents intended to give or thought it was possible to give."

John W. Gardner
Excellence, 1984

Set Specific, Challenging Goals

In study after study, specific, challenging goals have motivated higher achievement, especially when combined with progress reports (Locke & Latham, 1990; Mento & others, 1987; Tubbs, 1986). Clear objectives, such as those you might set in planning your course work, serve to direct attention, promote effort, and stimulate creative strategies. So, to motivate high productivity, effective leaders work with people to define explicit goals, elicit commitments, and provide feedback on progress.

Choose an Appropriate Leadership Style

Whether a directive or a democratic leadership style works best depends on the situation and the leader. The best leadership style for leading a discussion is not the best style for leading troops on a charge (Fiedler, 1981). Some people excel at **task leadership**—setting standards, organizing work, and focusing attention on goals. Being goal-oriented, task leaders are good at keeping a group centered on its mission. Typically, they have a directive style, which can work well if the leader is bright enough to give good orders (Fiedler, 1987).

Other managers excel at **social leadership**—mediating conflicts and building the sort of team spirit that makes for high performance (Evans & Dion, 1991). Social leaders often have a democratic style: They delegate authority and welcome the participation of team members. Many experiments show that social leadership is good for morale. Subordinates usually feel more satisfied and motivated when they can participate in decision making (Burger, 1987; Spector, 1986).

Imagine, suggest John Williams and Deborah Best (1990, p. 15), hearing about two people: One is "adventurous, autocratic, coarse, dominant, forceful, independent, and strong." The other is "affectionate, dependent, dreamy, emotional, submissive, and weak." If you find it easy to picture the first person as a man, and the second as a woman, you are not alone. The world around, people perceive the first set of traits as more descriptive of men, the second set as more descriptive of women. As leaders, men indeed tend to be directive, even autocratic, and women tend to be more democratic (Eagly & Johnson, 1990). When people interact, men are more likely to utter opinions, women to express support (Aries, 1987; Wood, 1987). In everyday behavior, men are more likely to act as powerful people do—to talk assertively, to interrupt, to initiate touching,

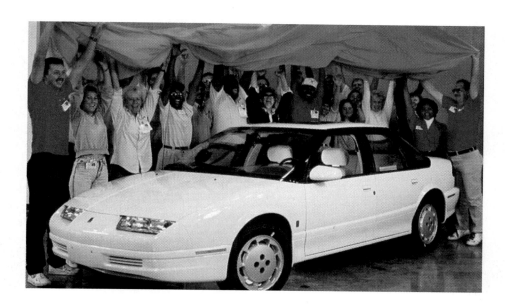

Participative Management *General Motors' Saturn plant in Tennessee has 10-member "teams" of employees. Each work team helps decide such things as new hires for their team and how to run their own area. Part of their salary depends on resulting car quality and company profits.*

Drawing by Anthony; © 1988 *The New Yorker Magazine, Inc.*

to smile less, to stare (J. Hall, 1987; Major & others, 1990). Thus women more often excel at social leadership, men at task leadership (Eagly & Karau, 1991).

In recent years many businesses have begun to increase employee participation in making decisions, a management style common in Sweden and Japan (Naylor, 1990; Sundstrom & others, 1990). Ironically, a major influence on the "Japanese-style participative management," now increasingly popular in North America, was MIT social psychologist Kurt Lewin. Lewin and his students demonstrated the effects of worker participation on productivity in laboratory and factory experiments. Shortly before World War II, Lewin visited Japan and explained his findings to industrial and academic leaders (Nisbett & Ross, 1991).

Because effective leadership styles vary with the situation and the person, the once-popular "great person" theory of leadership—that all great leaders share certain traits—fell out of favor. However, Peter Smith and Monir Tayeb (1989) report from recent studies in India, Taiwan, and Iran that effective managers in coal mines, banks, and government offices often exhibit a high degree of *both* task and social leadership. As achievement-minded people, they care about how work is progressing, yet they are sensitive to their subordinates' needs. Effective leaders of laboratory groups, work teams, and large corporations also tend to exude a self-confident "charisma" (House & Singh, 1987; Shamir & others, 1993). Their charisma involves a *vision* of some goal, an ability to *communicate* it clearly and simply, and enough optimism and faith in their group to *inspire* others to follow. Such leadership motivates others to identify with and commit themselves to the group's mission.

The Need to Belong

15. Why and when do we feel the need to belong?

We humans feel motivated to eat, to have sex, and to achieve. But being what Aristotle called "the social animal," we also need to feel connected with certain others in enduring, close relationships. Human beings, contend Roy Baumeister and Mark Leary (1995), "are fundamentally and pervasively motivated by a **need to belong**."

Aiding Survival

Social bonds boosted our ancestors' survival rate. For both children and adults, bonding was adaptive. By keeping children close to their caregivers, attachments served as a powerful survival impulse. As adults, those who formed attachments were more likely to come together to reproduce and to stay together to nurture their offspring to maturity.

need to belong A motivation to form and maintain enduring, close personal relationships.

Cooperation in groups also enhanced survival. In solo combat, our ancestors were not the toughest predators. But as hunters they learned that six hands were better than two. Those who foraged in groups also gained protection from predators and enemies. If those who felt a need to belong survived and reproduced most successfully, their genes would in time predominate. The inevitable result: an innately social creature. People in every society on earth belong to groups (and, as Chapter 14 explains, prefer and favor "us" over "them").

Wanting to Belong

The need to belong colors our thoughts and emotions. People spend much time thinking about their actual and hoped-for relationships. When relationships form, we often feel joy. Falling in mutual love, people have been known to get cheek-aches from their irrepressible grins. Asked, "What is necessary for your happiness?" or "What is it that makes your life meaningful?" most people mention—before anything else—satisfying close relationships with family, friends, or romantic partners (Berscheid, 1985). As C. S. Lewis said, "The sun looks down on nothing half so good as a household laughing together over a meal." Happiness hits close to home.

Increasing Social Acceptance

Much of our social behavior aims to increase our belonging—our social acceptance and inclusion. To avoid rejection, we generally conform to group standards and seek to make favorable impressions. (More on this in Chapter 14, Social Psychology.) To win friendship and esteem, we monitor our behavior, hoping to create the right impressions. Seeking love and belonging, we humans spend billions on clothes, cosmetics, and diet and fitness aids—all motivated by our quest for acceptance.

Like sexual motivation, which feeds both love and exploitation, the need to belong feeds both deep attachments and menacing threats. Out of our need to define a "we" come loving families, faithful friendships, and team spirit, but also teen gangs, ethnic hostilities, and fanatic nationalism. So it goes with basic motives, which have multiple and strong effects on how we think, feel, and act.

Maintaining Relationships

People resist breaking social bonds. For most of us, familiarity breeds liking, not contempt. Thrown together at school, at summer camp, on a cross-country bus tour, people resist the group's dissolution. Hoping to maintain the relationships, they promise to call, to write, to come back for reunions. Parting, they

Positive Attachment *Older women from Asian groups have traditionally been highly involved with their grandchildren. This relationship pattern may satisfy a need to belong that can be harder for the elderly in other cultures to fulfill.*

feel distress. At the end of a mere vacation cruise, people may hug their waiter or cry when saying goodbye forever to their cabin attendant. Attachments can even keep people in abusive relationships; the fear of being alone may seem worse than the pain of emotional or physical abuse.

When something threatens or dissolves our social ties, negative emotions overwhelm us. Exile, imprisonment, and solitary confinement are progressively more severe forms of punishment. Recently bereaved people often feel that life is empty and pointless. Children reared in institutions without a sense of belonging to anyone, or locked away at home under extreme neglect, become pathetic creatures—withdrawn, frightened, speechless. Adults who are denied others' acceptance and inclusion may feel depressed. Anxiety, jealousy, loneliness, and guilt all involve threatened disruptions of our need to belong. People suffer even when bad relationships break. In one 16-nation survey, separated and divorced people were half as likely as married people to declare themselves "very happy" (Inglehart, 1990). After such separations, feelings of loneliness and anger are commonplace.

Fortifying Health

Do you have close friends—people with whom you freely disclose your ups and downs? As we will see in Chapter 10, Emotions, Stress, and Health, people who feel supported by close relationships live with better health and at lower risk for psychological disorder and premature death than do those who lack social support. Married people, for example, are less at risk for depression, suicide, and early death than are unattached people. Such evidence confirms the other indications that we humans have a deep need to belong.

In this chapter we have seen that identifiable physiological mechanisms drive some motives, such as hunger (though external incentives and learned tastes matter, too). Other motives, such as achievement, are more obviously driven by psychological factors, such as an intrinsic quest for mastery and the external rewards of recognition. What unifies all such motives is their common effect: the energizing and directing of behavior. Without motivation—without hunger, thirst, sex, curiosity, a drive to achieve, an urge to belong—life would be dull and aimless. Motivation adds purpose—and zing—to life.

! Rehearse It

18. Achievement motivation is defined as a desire for significant accomplishment, for mastering skills or ideas, for control, and for rapidly attaining a high standard. Given a choice of tasks, high-achievers would select one that is

a. very difficult so they have an excuse for failure.

b. very easy in order to avoid failure.

c. moderately challenging because success will be attributed to their skill and effort.

d. extremely difficult, so that when they do complete the task, they can feel superior to others performing the same task.

19. Psychologists identify two types of achievement motivation: extrinsic and intrinsic. Intrinsic motivation is a desire to perform a behavior because it is enjoyable and leads to feelings of mastery. For a violinist, an example of an intrinsic motive is the desire to

a. earn enough to maintain an extravagant life-style.

b. be promoted to concertmaster.

c. perfect a difficult passage.

d. obtain a positive grade or evaluation.

20. Task leadership is goal-oriented, while social leadership is group-oriented. Research indicates that effective managers exhibit

a. only task leadership.

b. only social leadership.

c. both task and social leadership, depending on the situation and the person.

d. task leadership for building teams and social leadership for setting standards.

Reviewing *Motivation*

Motivation is the energizing and directing of our behavior, as exemplified in our yearning for food, our longing for sexual intimacy, our desire to achieve, and our need to belong.

Motivational Theories

1. What theoretical perspectives have helped psychologists understand motivation?

Under Darwin's influence, early theorists viewed behavior as controlled by biological forces, such as *instincts*. But when it became clear that people were naming, not explaining, various behaviors by calling them instincts, psychologists turned to a drive-reduction theory of motivation. Most physiological needs create aroused psychological states that drive us to reduce or satisfy those needs. The aim of *drive reduction* is internal stability, or homeostasis. Thus, drive reduction motivates survival behaviors, such as eating and drinking. Rather than reducing a physiological need or tension state, some motivated behaviors increase *arousal*. Curiosity-driven behaviors, for example, suggest that too little as well as too much stimulation can motivate people to seek an optimum level of arousal. Not only are we pushed by our internal drives, we are pulled by external *incentives*. Depending on our personal and cultural experiences, some stimuli (for example, certain foods or erotic images) will arouse our desires.

2. What is the basic idea behind Maslow's hierarchy of needs?

Maslow's hierarchy of needs expresses the idea that, until satisfied, some motives are more compelling (that is, more basic) than others.

Hunger

3. What physiological factors cause us to feel hungry?

Hunger's inner push primarily originates not from the stomach's contractions but from variations in body chemistry. For example, we are likely to feel hungry when our blood glucose levels are low. This information is monitored by the hypothalamus, which regulates the body's weight as it influences our feelings of hunger and satiety. To maintain weight, the body also adjusts its metabolic rate of energy expenditure.

4. What psychological factors contribute to hunger?

Our preferences for certain tastes are partly genetic and universal, but also partly learned in a cultural context. Especially in "external" people, the sight and smell of food can trigger hunger and eating, partly by stimulating a rise in insulin level.

5. What factors predispose some people to become and remain obese?

Fat is a concentrated fuel reserve stored in fat cells. Under genetic influence, the number and size of these cells determine one's body fat. Obese people find it difficult to lose weight permanently because the number of fat cells is not reduced by a diet, because the energy expenditure necessary for tissue maintenance is lower in fat than in other tissues, and because the overall metabolic rate decreases when body weight drops below the set point. Those who nevertheless wish to diet should minimize exposure to food cues, boost energy expenditure through exercise, and make a lifelong change in eating patterns.

Sexual Motivation

6. What stages mark the human sexual response?

Biologically, the human sexual response cycle normally follows a pattern of excitement, plateau, orgasm, and resolution. During the resolution phase, males enter a refractory period during which another orgasm is not possible.

7. What role do hormones play in human sexuality?

Sex hormones help our bodies develop and function as either male or female. In many nonhuman animals, hormones also help to stimulate sexual activity, but in humans, they influence sexual behavior more loosely, especially once minimally sufficient hormone levels are present.

8. How do internal and external factors interact to stimulate sexual arousal?

External stimuli can trigger sexual arousal in both men and women. Sexually explicit materials may also lead people to perceive their partners as comparatively less appealing and to devalue their relationships. In combination with the internal hormonal push and the external pull of sexual stimuli, imagined stimuli (fantasies) help trigger sexual arousal. Some sexual dysfunctions respond well to behavioral treatment, which assumes that people can learn to modify their sexual responses.

9. How do men's and women's sexual attitudes and behaviors differ?

One of the largest reported gender differences is women's generally greater disapproval of and lesser willingness to engage in casual, uncommitted sex.

10. What factors do and don't appear linked with sexual orientation?

One's heterosexual or homosexual orientation seems neither willfully chosen nor able to be willfully changed. Evidence discounts certain environmental explanations of sexual orientation. Preliminary new evidence links sexual orientation with genetic influences, prenatal hormones, and the size of certain brain structures.

11. What roles do personal values play in sex research and sex education?

Sex research and education are not value-free. Sex-related values should therefore be discussed openly, recognizing the social significance of sexual expression.

Achievement Motivation

12. Who has the greatest need to achieve? Why?

Some human behaviors are energized and directed without satisfying any apparent biological need. Achieving personal goals, for example, may be motivated by a person's social needs for competence and independence. People with a high need to achieve tend to prefer moderately challenging tasks and to persist in accomplishing them. Many achievement-oriented children have parents and teachers who encourage and affirm independent achievement rather than overly controlling them with external rewards and threats.

13. What is intrinsic motivation, and how can it be nurtured?

Intrinsic motivation is the desire to be effective and to perform a behavior for its own sake. Rewards that boost people's sense of competence or inform them of improvement may increase intrinsic motivation. Rewards used to control behavior (extrinsic motivation) do not.

14. What motivational strategies are most effective at home, school, and work?

People's performance can be improved by increasing their intrinsic motivation, by adjusting leadership style to complement individual motives, by setting specific, challenging goals, and by practicing effective, goal-oriented task leadership and group-oriented social leadership.

The Need to Belong

15. Why and when do we feel the need to belong?

Although motivated to individual achievement, no one is an island. Our need to belong—to feel connected and identified with others—boosted our ancestors' chances for survival and is therefore part of our human nature. We experience our need to belong when suffering the breaking of social bonds, when feeling the gloom of loneliness or the joy of love, and when seeking social acceptance.

Terms and Concepts to Remember

motivation, p. 297

instinct, p. 298

drive-reduction theory, p. 298

homeostasis, p. 298

incentives, p. 299

hierarchy of needs, p. 300

glucose, p. 302

set point, p. 302

metabolic rate, p. 303

anorexia nervosa, p. 304

bulimia nervosa, p. 304

sexual response cycle, p. 312

refractory period, p. 312

estrogen, p. 313

sexual dysfunction, p. 315

sexual orientation, p. 317

achievement motivation, p. 323

intrinsic motivation, p. 324

extrinsic motivation, p. 324

industrial/organizational psychology, p. 325

task leadership, p. 327

social leadership, p. 327

need to belong, p. 328

Rehearse It Answer Key

1. b.	2. a.	3. d.	4. c.	5. c.	6. a.	7. b.	8. a.	9. d.
10. b.	11. d.	12. b.	13. b.	14. c.	15. d.	16. a.	17. b.	18. c.
19. c.	20. c.							

Critical Thinking Exercise

Now that you have read and reviewed Chapter 9, take your learning a step further by testing your critical thinking skills on the following passage.

Janet and Sheila have been good friends since meeting in an introductory psychology class in their freshman year. They are about the same height and age but vary in weight. Janet, both of whose parents are obese, has always struggled with her weight, which fluctuates between 15 and 20 percent above normal. Acquaintances assume she is lazy and gluttonous, but Janet's friends know that she is neither. Sheila is of normal weight, as is her family.

Janet and Sheila have decided to conduct an experiment, with themselves as the subjects, for their final health psychology project. For a month, they eat the same total number of calories per day, spread across several small, healthy meals that are low in fat and include whole grains, fruits, and vegetables. They also add a brisk 30-minute walk to their daily routine. At the end of the month, Janet and Sheila weigh themselves for the first time since the experiment began. Although Janet is pleased to find that she has lost some weight, Sheila has lost more. Several students, after hearing the results of the experiment, speculate that perhaps Janet simply hadn't employed the willpower that Sheila had, and that was why Sheila lost more weight.

1. What factors in Janet's background might have contributed to her obesity?

2. What factors in Sheila's background might have contributed to her being of normal weight?

3. Why did Sheila lose more weight than Janet, even though they consumed the same number of calories and the same types of food and did the same amount of exercise?

Check your progress on becoming a critical thinker by comparing your answers with the sample answers found in Appendix B.

For Further Information

You can find further information on industrial/organizational psychology on the following pages:

Absenteeism and age, p. 99

Assessing job performance, pp. 397, 405–407

Conflict management, pp. 519–521

Consumer decisions, p. 262

Creativity encouragement, p. 284

Economic decision making, pp. 509–510

Employee evaluation, p. 481

Executive/subordinate stress, pp. 360–361

Group decision making, pp. 492–493

Human factors psychology, p. 152

Job interviews, pp. 339–340

Lie detection, p. 337

Loafing, pp. 490–491

Management aptitude, p. 282

Motivating workers, p. 215

Odor and performance, p. 138

Pay schedules, pp. 210–211

Personnel work (see Employee evaluation and Job interviews)

Predicting job performance, pp. 405–407

Risk assessment, p. 261

Shift work and sleep, p. 166

Stress, pp. 356–373

Subliminal ads, pp. 21, 119–121

Work motivation, pp. 105–106

Chapter 10

Emotions, Stress, and Health

1. What are the components of an emotion?

Feelings—powerful, spontaneous, sometimes unforgettable. Where do feelings come from? Of all the species, we humans seem the most emotional (Hebb, 1980). More often than any other creature, we express fear, anger, sadness, joy, and love. No one needs to tell you that emotions add color to your life, that in times of stress they can disrupt your life or save it. But what are the ingredients of emotion?

Imagine that, while walking home along a deserted street late at night, you hear the rumble of an engine and think that someone on a motorcycle is following you. Your heart begins to race, your pace quickens, you wonder about the cyclist's intent, and you feel scared. As this illustrates, **emotions** are a mix of (1) physiological arousal (heart pounding), (2) expressive behavior (quickened pace), and (3) conscious experience (interpreting the person's intent and feeling fearful). The puzzle is how these three pieces fit together: Did you first notice your heart racing, your speeded-up walking, and then feel afraid? Or did your sense of fear come first, stirring your heart and legs to respond?

In this chapter we will consider how emotions affect our health, and how to cope with the emotions that cause us to experience stress. But first, let's study the individual pieces of the emotion puzzle—its physiology, expression, and conscious experience.

The Physiology of Emotion

2. What physiological changes accompany emotional arousal?

Arousal

When experiencing emotion you are physically aroused. Some physical responses are so obvious that you easily notice them. As you hear the motorcycle's rumble behind you, your muscles tense, your stomach develops butterflies, your mouth becomes dry.

The Physiology of Emotion

Arousal

Physiological States Accompanying Specific Emotions

Expressing Emotion

Nonverbal Communication

Culture and Emotional Expression

The Effects of Facial Expressions

Experiencing Emotion

Anger

Happiness

Theories of Emotion

The James-Lange and Cannon-Bard Theories

Cognition and Emotion

Stress and Health

Stress and Stressors

Stress, Personality, and Heart Disease

Stress and Resistance to Disease

Promoting Health

Coping With Stress

---

emotion   A response of the whole organism, involving (1) physiological arousal, (2) expressive behaviors, and (3) conscious experience.

335

Your body also mobilizes for action in less noticeable ways. To provide energy, your liver pours extra sugar into your bloodstream. To help burn the sugar, your respiration increases to supply needed oxygen. Your digestion slows, diverting blood from your internal organs to your muscles. Your pupils dilate, letting in more light. To cool your stirred-up body, you perspire. If you were wounded, your blood would clot more quickly. Think of this after your next crisis: Without any conscious effort, your body's response to danger was wonderfully coordinated and adaptive—preparing you to fight or flee.

As we learned in Chapter 2 (page 42), our *autonomic nervous system* controls our arousal (Figure 10–1). Its sympathetic division activates arousal by directing the adrenal glands atop the kidneys to release the stress hormones epinephrine (adrenaline) and norepinephrine (noradrenaline). The surge in epinephrine and norepinephrine increases heart rate, blood pressure, and blood sugar levels. When the crisis passes, the parasympathetic neural centers become active, calming the body. Even after the parasympathetic division inhibits further release of stress hormones, those already in the bloodstream linger awhile, so arousal diminishes gradually.

One explanation of sudden death caused by a voodoo "curse" is that the terrified person's parasympathetic nervous system, which calms the body, overreacts to the extreme arousal by slowing the heart to a stop (Seligman, 1974).

Sympathetic (arousing)		Parasympathetic (calming)
Pupils dilate	EYES	Pupils contract
Decreases	SALIVATION	Increases
Perspires	SKIN	Dries
Increases	RESPIRATION	Decreases
Accelerates	HEART	Slows
Inhibits	DIGESTION	Activates
Secrete stress hormones	ADRENAL GLANDS	Decrease secretion of stress hormones

Figure 10–1 Emotional Arousal *Physiological arousal is controlled by our autonomic nervous system. The sympathetic division activates. The parasympathetic calms.*

Prolonged arousal, produced by sustained stress, taxes the body. Yet in many situations arousal is adaptive. Too little arousal (say, sleepiness) can be as disruptive as extremely high levels of arousal. When you're taking an exam, it pays to be moderately aroused—alert but not trembling with nervousness.

Although performance is usually best when arousal is moderate, the level of arousal for optimal performance varies for different tasks. With easy or well-learned tasks, peak performance comes with relatively high arousal. With more difficult or unrehearsed tasks, the optimal arousal is somewhat less (Figure 10–2). Thus, runners, who are performing a well-learned task, usually achieve their peak performances when highly aroused by competition. Basketball players shooting free throws—a less routine skill—may perform slightly less well if a packed fieldhouse makes them hyperaroused (Sokoll & Mynatt, 1984). Likewise, students who feel great anxiety during exams perform more poorly than equally able but more confident students. Training anxious students how to relax before an exam often enables them to perform better (Hembree, 1988).

Figure 10–2 Arousal and Performance *Performance peaks at lower levels of arousal for difficult tasks, and at higher levels for easy or well-learned tasks.*

Given the physical indicators of emotion, might we, like Pinocchio, give some tell-tale sign whenever we lie? The *lie detector*, or **polygraph**, was once used mainly in law enforcement and national security work. But by the mid-1980s, 2 million Americans annually were reportedly being tested, usually by corporations trying to screen applicants for honesty or to uncover employee theft (Holden, 1986a).

Just what does the polygraph do? It does not literally detect lies. Rather, it measures several of the arousal responses that accompany emotion, such as changes in breathing, pulse rate, blood pressure, and perspiration. While you try to relax, the examiner measures your physiological responses as you answer questions. Some of these, called control questions, are designed to make anyone a little nervous. If asked, "In the last 20 years, have you ever taken something that didn't belong to you?" many people will tell a white lie and say no, causing arousal that the polygraph would detect. If your physiological reactions to the critical questions ("Did you ever steal anything from your previous employer?") are weaker than to the control questions,

polygraph A machine, commonly used in attempts to detect lies, that measures several of the physiological responses accompanying emotion (such as perspiration, heart rate, blood pressure, and breathing changes).

Who's Lying? *Can polygraph tests like this identify liars, or are its promoters putting something over on a gullible public? To learn more about this disputed issue, read on.*

the examiner infers you are telling the truth. The assumption is that only a thief becomes agitated when denying a theft.

But there is a problem: An innocent person might also respond with heightened tension to the accusations implied by the relevant questions. When a Yakima, Washington, mother of a 4-year-old boy was accused by her ex-husband's new wife of sexually abusing her son, she gladly accepted a police offer of a polygraph test "to prove her innocence." Asked, "Did you take Tommy's penis in your mouth?" the accused mother understandably reacted with greater perspiration and blood pressure than when asked "Have you

ever told a lie to get out of trouble?" (Physiologically, the fear of being disbelieved looks a lot like the fear of being caught lying.) This revealed her guilt, explained the police sergeant-turned-polygrapher to the jury. (Fortunately her attorney managed to locate a scientific expert who persuaded the jury that, by itself, this was not credible evidence of guilt.) Many rape victims similarly "fail" lie detector tests when reacting emotionally while telling the truth about their assailant (Lykken, 1991).

The major adversary of lie detector tests is University of Minnesota psychologist David Lykken (1983, 1991). He notes that because physiological response is much the same from one emotion to another, the polygraph cannot distinguish among anxiety, irritation, and guilt. They all appear as arousal. Thus, these tests err about one-third of the time. They more often label the innocent guilty—when the relevant question upsets the honest person—than the guilty innocent (Figure 10–3). Good advice, then, would be never to take a lie detector test if you are innocent.

Although too error-prone for use in testing employees, the polygraph can serve as a tool in criminal investigation. Police sometimes use the polygraph to induce confessions by criminals whom they scare into thinking that any lies will be transparent. A more honest approach uses the *guilty knowledge test*, which assesses a suspect's physiological responses to details of a crime known only to the police and the guilty person. If a camera and money were stolen, the polygraph examiner could see whether the suspect reacts strongly to such details as the specific brand name of the camera and the dollar amounts. Presumably, only a guilty person would. Given enough such specific probes, an innocent person will seldom be wrongly accused.

Nevertheless, critics and advocates alike disapprove of commercial use of the polygraph. The truth is that lie detectors can lie. The U.S. Congress recognized this when it passed the Employee Polygraph Protection Act of 1988, prohibiting most nongovernmental polygraph testing.

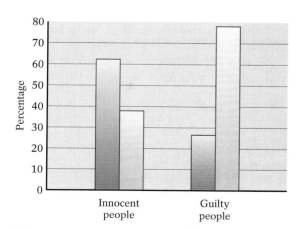

Figure 10–3 How Often Do Lie Detectors Lie? *Benjamin Kleinmuntz and Julian Szucko (1984) had polygraph experts study the polygraph data of 50 theft suspects who later confessed to being guilty and 50 suspects whose innocence was later established by someone's confession. Had the polygraph experts been the judges, more than one-third of the innocent would have been declared guilty, and almost one-fourth of the guilty would have been declared innocent.*

■ Judged innocent by polygraph   □ Judged guilty by polygraph

Physiological States Accompanying Specific Emotions

Imagine conducting an experiment exploring physiological signs of arousal. In each of four rooms, you have someone watching a movie: In the first is a horror show; in the second, an anger-provoking film; in the third, a sexually arousing film; in the fourth, an utterly boring film. From the control center you monitor each person's physiological responses. By examining the perspiration, breathing, and heart rates of the viewers, could you tell who was frightened, who was angry, who was sexually aroused, and who was bored?

With training, you could probably pick out the bored viewer from the other three. Discerning physiological differences among fear, anger, and sexual arousal is much harder (Zillmann, 1986). Fear and anger accelerate the heart rate more than happiness does (Levenson, 1992). Still, apart from the breathing disruption caused by laughter, experts even have difficulty distinguishing viewers' physiological responses to sad versus funny movies (Averill, 1969).

Fear, anger, sexual arousal, and sadness certainly *feel* different (and, as we will see, cognitively they *are* different). A terrified person may feel a clutching, sinking sensation in the chest and a knot in the stomach. An angry person may feel "hot under the collar" and will probably experience a pressing, inner tension. The sexually stimulated person will experience a genital response. The sad person may be choked up and have an empty, drained feeling (Epstein, 1984). Moreover, despite their similar physiological arousal, frightened, angered, and saddened people often *look* different—"paralyzed with fear," "ready to explode," or "down in the dumps." Knowing this, can we pinpoint some distinct physiological indicators of each emotion?

Fear and rage are accompanied by differing finger temperatures and hormone secretions (Ax, 1953; Levenson, 1992). Different emotions also arise through different brain circuits (Kalin, 1993; Panksepp, 1982). As we saw on page 50, stimulate one area of a cat's limbic system and it will pull back in terror at the sight of a mouse. Stimulate another limbic area and the cat will look enraged—pupils dilated, fur and tail erect, claws out, hissing furiously. As people experience negative emotions, such as disgust, the right hemisphere becomes more electrically active. The left hemisphere activates when processing positive emotions (Davidson & others, 1990, 1992). For some infants and adults, the left frontal lobe shows more activity than the right. These individuals are typically more cheerful and less readily threatened or depressed than those with more active right frontal lobes.

So, although emotions as varied as fear and anger involve a similar general autonomic arousal (thanks to the sympathetic nervous system), there are real, if subtle, physiological differences that help explain why we experience them so differently. Moreover, the physical accompaniments of emotion appear innate and universal—the same in a Sumatran village as in North America (Levenson & others, 1991).

> "No one ever told me that grief felt so much like fear. I am not afraid, but the sensation is like being afraid. The same fluttering in the stomach, the same restlessness, the yawning. I keep on swallowing."
>
> C. S. Lewis
> *A Grief Observed*, 1961

In 1966, a young man named Charles Whitman killed his wife and mother and then climbed to the top of a tower at the University of Texas and shot 38 people. An autopsy later revealed a tumor in his limbic system.

Expressing Emotion

3. How do we communicate nonverbally? Are nonverbal expressions of emotion universally understood?

There is another method of deciphering people's emotions: We "read" their bodies, listen to their voices, and look at their faces.

Nonverbal Communication

All of us communicate nonverbally as well as verbally. If irritated, we may tense our bodies, press our lips together, and turn away. With a gaze, an averted glance, or a stare we can communicate intimacy, submission, or dominance (Kleinke, 1986). Among couples passionately in love, eye-gazing is typically prolonged and mutual (Rubin, 1970). Would intimate gazes stir such feelings between strangers? To find out, Joan Kellerman, James Lewis, and James Laird (1989) asked unacquainted male-female pairs to gaze intently for 2 minutes either at one another's hands or into one another's eyes. After separating, the eye-gazers reported feeling a greater tingle of attraction and affection.

Most of us are good enough at reading nonverbal cues to decipher the emotions in an old silent film. We are especially good at detecting nonverbal threats. In a crowd of faces, a single angry face will "pop out" faster than a single happy one (Hansen & Hansen, 1988). Some of us are more sensitive to these cues than others are. Robert Rosenthal, Judith Hall, and their colleagues (1979) discovered this by showing hundreds of people brief film clips of portions of a person's emotionally expressive face or body, sometimes with a garbled voice added. For example, after a 2-second scene revealing only the face of an upset woman, the researchers would ask whether the woman was criticizing someone for being late or talking about her divorce. Rosenthal and Hall reported that some people are much better emotion detectors than others, and that women are better at it than men.

Armed with high-tech equipment, psychologists are now linking various emotions with specific facial muscles (Figure 10–4). Hard-to-control facial muscles reveal signs of emotions you may be trying to conceal. Lifting just the inner part of your eyebrows, which few people do consciously, reveals distress or worry. Eyebrows raised and pulled together signal fear. A feigned smile, such as one we make for a photographer, often continues for more than 4 or 5 seconds, by which time most authentic expressions have faded. Feigned smiles also get switched on and off more abruptly than a genuine smile (Bugental, 1986).

Our brains are rather amazing emotion-detectors. Elisha Babad, Frank Bernieri, and Robert Rosenthal (1991) discovered just *how* amazing after videotaping teachers talking to unseen schoolchildren. A mere 10-second clip of either the teacher's voice or face provided enough clues for both young and old viewers to determine whether the teacher liked and admired the child he or she was addressing. Although teachers may think they can conceal their feelings and stay objective, their students can sense what their expressions and gestures reveal.

Subtle facial indicators of emotion may someday enable a new behavioral approach to lie detection. For example, given mild emotional stimuli, electrodes attached to your facial muscles can now detect your hidden reactions (Tassinary & Cacioppo, 1992). Your face may not look any different, but voltage changes on the skin reveal underlying micromuscular smiles or frowns.

The growing awareness that we communicate through the body's silent language has led to studies of how job applicants and interviewers communicate (or miscommunicate) nonverbally. Popular guidebooks and articles offer advice on how to interpret nonverbal signals when negotiating a business deal, selling a product, or flirting with someone. It pays to be able to read feelings that "leak

> *"Your face, my thane, is a book where men may read strange matters."*
>
> William Shakespeare's Lady Macbeth to her husband

(a)　　　　　　**(b)**

(c)　　　　　　**(d)**

Figure 10–4 Smiles as Indicators of Emotions *Paul Ekman's system for classifying a particular smile consists of a specific code for each of the 80 facial muscles used to create it. Notice how different these smiles are. (a) A smile that masks anger (the woman has just been told she is being dismissed). (b) An overly polite smile (the man is telling a patient to enjoy her hospital stay). (c) A smile softening verbal criticism ("I'd appreciate it if you wouldn't come to rehearsal drunk"). And (d) a reluctant, compliant smile ("I guess I don't have any choice, so OK").*

A Silent Language of Emotion *The art of nonverbal communication reached a pinnacle early in the century as silent films became widely available. For a nickel, enraptured audiences could watch performers mime a wide range of unmistakable emotions. Here Chester Conklin woos a woman on horseback while Louise Fazenda fumes.*

"For news of the heart ask the face."
Guinean proverb

Figure 10–5 Culture-Specific or Culturally Universal Expressions? *As people of differing cultures and races, do our faces speak differing languages? Which face expresses disgust? Anger? Fear? Happiness? Sadness? Surprise? The answers are on page 343.*

through" via subtle facial expressions, body movements, and postures. Fidgeting, for example, may reveal anxiety or boredom. More specific interpretations of postures and gestures are risky. Different expressions may convey the same emotion: Either a cold stare or the avoidance of eye contact may signify hostility. And a given expression can convey very different emotions: Folded arms, for example, can signify irritation or relaxation.

Such gestures, facial expressions, and tones of voice are all absent in computer-based communication. Experienced electronic mail users sometimes insert sideways "emoticons," such as ;-) for a knowing wink and :-(for a frown. But e-mail letters and group discussions otherwise lack nonverbal cues to status, personality, age, and emotion. Thus, when first meeting an e-mail pen pal face to face, people are often surprised at the personality they encounter.

Culture and Emotional Expression

The meaning of gestures varies with the culture. Some years ago, psychologist Otto Klineberg (1938) observed that in Chinese literature people clapped their hands to express worry or disappointment, laughed a great "ho-ho" to express anger, and stuck out their tongues to show surprise. Similarly, the North American "thumbs up" and "A-OK" signs would be interpreted as insults in certain other cultures. (When U.S. President Nixon made the latter sign in Brazil he didn't realize he was saying "Let's have sex.") Just how important cultural definitions of gestures can be was demonstrated in 1968, when North Korea photographed supposedly happy officers from a captured U.S. Navy spy ship. In the photo, three of the men made the obscene middle-finger gesture; they had explained to their captors it was a "Hawaiian good luck sign" (Fleming & Scott, 1991).

Do facial expressions also have different meanings in different cultures? To find out, two investigative teams—one led by Paul Ekman and Wallace Friesen (1975, 1987, 1994), the other by Carroll Izard (1977, 1994)—showed photographs of different facial expressions to people in different parts of the world and asked them to guess the emotion. You can try this yourself. Match the six emotions with the six faces of Figure 10–5.

You probably did pretty well. How do you suppose people from Brazil or Japan did when judging these pictures? About the same as North Americans, it turns out. A smile's a smile the world around. Ditto for the other basic expressions. Despite some differences, cultures and languages also share many similarities in how they categorize emotions—as anger, fear, and so on (Russell, 1991). The physiological indicators of emotion also cross cultures (Levenson & others, 1992; Mesquita & Frijda, 1992).

(a)

(b)

(c)

(d)

(e)

(f)

While weightless, astronauts' fluids move toward their upper body, and their faces become puffy. This makes nonverbal communication more difficult, increasing the risks of misunderstanding, especially among multinational crews (Gelman, 1989).

Do people from different cultures make and interpret facial expressions similarly because they experience similar influences, such as American movies and CNN? Apparently not. Ekman and his team asked isolated people in New Guinea to display various emotions in response to such statements as, "Pretend your child has died." When the researchers showed videotapes of the New Guineans' facial reactions to North American collegians, the students could easily read them. Children's facial expressions—even those of blind children who have never seen a face—are also universal (Eibl-Eibesfeldt, 1971). The world over, children cry when distressed, shake their heads when defiant, and smile when happy.

The discovery that the facial muscles speak a universal language would have come as no surprise to pioneering emotion researcher Charles Darwin (1809–1882). He speculated that in prehistoric times, before our ancestors communicated in words, their ability to convey threats, greetings, and submission with facial expressions helped them survive. That shared heritage, he believed, is why all humans express the basic emotions by similar facial expressions. A sneer, for example, retains elements of an animal's teeth-baring snarl. Smiles, too, are a form of social communication, not just emotional reflexes. Bowlers don't smile when they score a strike—they smile when they turn to face their companions (Jones & others, 1991; Kraut & Johnston, 1979).

Although cultures share a universal facial language, they differ in how, and how much, they express emotion. In cultures that encourage individuality, as in Western Europe, Australia, New Zealand, and North America, emotional displays often are intense and prolonged. People focus on their own goals and attitudes and express themselves accordingly. Watching a film of someone's hand being cut, Americans grimace (whether alone or with other viewers). In the presence of others, Japanese viewers hide their emotions (Triandis, 1994). In Asian and other cultures that emphasize social connections and interdependence, displays of emotions such as sympathy, respect, and shame are more common than in the West. Moreover, Asians rarely and only briefly display self-aggrandizing or negative emotions that might disrupt communal feeling within close-knit groups (Markus & Kitayama, 1991; Matsumoto & others, 1988).

A Universal Language   *You know the meaning of each facial expression, and each of these people would understand the same expression on your face. Charles Darwin believed this universal facial language reflects our shared evolutionary heritage.*

  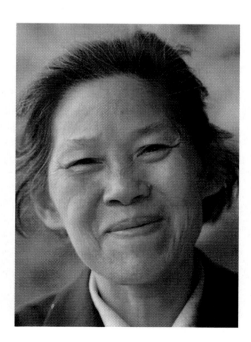

The Effects of Facial Expressions

4. Do our facial expressions influence our feelings?

Expressions not only communicate emotion, they also amplify and regulate it. In his 1872 book, *The Expression of the Emotions in Man and Animals*, Darwin contended that "the free expression by outward signs of an emotion intensifies it. . . . He who gives way to violent gestures will increase his rage."

Was Darwin right? I was driving in my car one day when the song "Put On a Happy Face" came on the radio. How phony, I thought. But I tested Darwin's hypothesis anyway, as you can, too. Fake a big grin. Now scowl. Can you feel the difference?

The subjects in dozens of experiments have felt a difference. For example, when James Laird and his colleagues (1974, 1984, 1989) subtly induced students to make a frowning expression—by asking them to "contract these muscles" and "pull your brows together" (supposedly to help the researchers attach facial electrodes). The results? The students reported feeling a little angry. Students similarly induced to smile felt happier, found cartoons more humorous, and recalled happier memories than did the frowners. People instructed to express other basic emotions also experienced them. For example, they reported feeling more fear than anger, disgust, or sadness when made to construct an expression of fear: "Raise your eyebrows. And open your eyes wide. Move your whole head back, so that your chin is tucked in a little bit, and let your mouth relax and hang open a little" (Duclos & others, 1989). Going through the motions awakens the emotions.

The effect is subtle, yet detectable in the absence of competing emotions. Consider these findings:

- If subtly manipulated into furrowing their brows (see Figure 10–6), people feel sadder while looking at sad photos.

- Saying the speech sounds *e* and *ah*, which activate smiling muscles, puts people—believe it or not—in a better mood than saying the German *ü* (rather like saying the English "e" and "u" together), which activates muscles associated with negative emotions (Zajonc & others, 1989).

- Just activating one of the smiling muscles by holding a pen in the teeth (rather than with the lips, which activates a frowning muscle) is enough to make cartoons seem more amusing (Strack & others, 1988). A heartier smile, made not just with the mouth but with raised cheeks as well, works even better (Ekman & others, 1990).

> *"Refuse to express a passion and it dies. . . . If we wish to conquer undesirable emotional tendencies in ourselves, we must . . . go through the outward movements of those contrary dispositions which we prefer to cultivate."*
>
> William James
> *Principles of Psychology*, 1890

Figure 10–6 How to Make People Frown Without Telling Them To Frown *Randy Larsen, Margaret Kasimatis, and Kurt Frey's (1992) solution: Attach two golf tees above the eyebrows and ask the subjects to make the tee tips touch. With "sad face" muscles activated, subjects felt sadder while viewing scenes of war, sickness, and starvation.*

Which Smile Makes Paul Ekman Feel Happy? *The smile on the right, which engages the face muscles of a natural smile.*

Answers to the questions in Figure 10–5: (a) happiness, (b) anger, (c) sadness, (d) surprise, (e) disgust, (f) fear.

Smile warmly on the outside and you feel better on the inside. Scowl and the whole world seems to scowl back. Why might this be so? Paul Ekman and his colleagues (1983) designed an experiment to find out. Their subjects were professional actors trained in the Stanislavsky method, in which they physically (and psychologically) "become" the characters they are playing. The actors would assume an expression and then hold it for 10 seconds while the researchers measured changes in their heart rates and finger temperatures. When they made a fearful expression, their heart rate increased some 8 beats per minute and finger temperature was steady. When making an angry expression, both heart rate and finger temperature increased as though the actor were indeed "hot-headed." Our facial expressions, it seems, send signals to our autonomic nervous system, which then responds accordingly. This experiment shows how facial feedback affects our emotions, and it provides further evidence that different emotions accompany subtly different body states.

If assuming an emotional expression triggers a feeling, then imitating others' expressions should help us feel what they are feeling. Again, the laboratory evidence is supportive. Kathleen Burns Vaughn and John Lanzetta (1981) asked some students but not others to make a pained expression whenever an electric shock was apparently delivered to someone they were watching. With each apparent shock, the grimacing observers perspired more and had a faster heart rate than the other observers. So one small way to become more empathic—to feel what others feel—is to let your own face mimic the other person's expression. Acting as another acts helps us feel what another feels.

! *Rehearse It*

1. Emotions such as fear and anger involve a general autonomic arousal that is orchestrated by the sympathetic nervous system. In many situations, arousal is adaptive. For example, with a challenging task, such as taking an exam, performance is likely to be best given

a. very high arousal.
b. moderate arousal.
c. low arousal.
d. diminishing arousal.

2. The emotions of fear and anger involve a similar general autonomic arousal. However, different brain areas are involved.

For example, stimulate one area of a cat's _____ and the cat draws back in terror; stimulate another area and the cat hisses with rage.

a. cortex
b. hypothalamus
c. reticular activating system
d. limbic system

3. We can successfully interpret nonverbal threats and certain other silent messages regardless of the national origin of the sender. However, some nonverbal behaviors are *not* universal. People in different cultures are most likely to differ in their interpretations of

a. adults' facial expressions.
b. children's facial expressions.
c. smiles.
d. postures and gestures.

4. When people are induced to assume fearful expressions, they will feel their heart rates increase. This suggests that the autonomic nervous system responds to

a. signals from the facial muscles.
b. conscious feelings of emotion.
c. physiological responses involved in deception.
d. electrical stimulation.

Figure 10–7 Infants' Naturally Occurring Emotions *To identify the emotions present from birth, Carroll Izard analyzed the facial expressions of very young infants. Shown here are (a) joy (mouth forming smile, cheeks lifted, twinkle in eye); (b) anger (brows drawn together and downward, eyes fixed, mouth squarish; (c) interest (brows raised or knitted, mouth softly rounded, lips may be pursed); (d) disgust (nose wrinkled, upper lip raised, tongue pushed outward; (e) surprise (brows raised, eyes widened, mouth rounded in oval shape); (f) sadness (brow's inner corners raised, mouth corners drawn down); and (g) fear (brows level, drawn in and up, eyelids lifted, mouth corners retracted).*

Experiencing Emotion

The ingredients of emotion include not only physiological arousal and expressive behavior but also our conscious experience. Psychologists have asked people to report their experiences of different emotions. Estonians, Poles, Greeks, Chinese, and Canadians all seem to place emotions along two dimensions—pleasant versus unpleasant, and intensely aroused versus sleepy (Russell & others, 1989). On the intensity scale, for example, terrified is more frightened than afraid, enraged is angrier than angry, delighted is happier than happy. To these two dimensions, we might add a third: duration. Among Americans and Japanese, at least, the emotions of joy and sadness typically endure longer than anger and guilt, which outlast fear and disgust (Matsumoto & others, 1988).

Other psychologists have sought to identify emotions that are physiologically, facially, and experientially distinct. Carroll Izard (1977) believes there are 10 such basic emotions (joy, interest-excitement, surprise, sadness, anger, disgust, contempt, fear, shame, and guilt), most of which are present in infancy (Figure 10–7). Other emotions, he says, are combinations of these. Love, for instance, is a mixture of joy and interest-excitement.

Let's now examine two important emotions: anger and happiness. What functions do these emotions serve? And what influences our experience of them?

Anger

5. What are the causes and consequences of anger?

Anger is said by the sages to be "a short madness" (Horace, 65–8 B.C.) that "carries the mind away" (Virgil, 70–19 B.C.) and can be "many times more hurtful than the injury that caused it" (Thomas Fuller, 1654–1734). But other sages say "noble anger" (William Shakespeare, 1564–1616) "makes any coward brave" (Cato, 234–149 B.C.) and "brings back . . . strength" (Virgil).

What makes us angry? To find out, James Averill (1983) asked many people to recall or keep careful records of their experiences with anger. Most reported becoming at least mildly angry several times a week; some became angry several times a day. Often the anger was a response to friends' or loved ones' perceived misdeeds. Anger was especially common when another person's act seemed willful, unjustified, and avoidable. But blameless annoyances—foul odors, high temperatures, aches and pains—also have the power to make us angry (Berkowitz, 1990).

What do people do with their anger? And what *should* they do with it? When anger fuels physically or verbally aggressive acts that we later regret, it is maladaptive. But Averill's subjects recalled that when they were angry they often reacted assertively rather than hurtfully. Their anger frequently led them

"Anger will never disappear so long as thoughts of resentment are cherished in the mind."

Buddha, 500 B.C.

One problem with chronic hostility is its link with heart disease (page 361).

catharsis Emotional release. In psychology, the catharsis hypothesis maintains that "releasing" aggressive energy (through action or fantasy) relieves aggressive urges.

to talk things over with the offending person, thereby lessening the aggravation. Such controlled expressions of anger are more adaptive than either hostile outbursts or internalizing the angry feelings.

Popular books and articles on aggression sometimes advise that even hostile outbursts can be better than keeping anger pent up. When irritated, should we go ahead and curse, tell a person off, or retaliate? Was Ann Landers (1969) right that "youngsters should be taught to vent their anger"?

Such advice is typical of individualized cultures, but it would seldom be heard in cultures where people's identity is more group-centered. People who keenly sense their interdependence see anger as a threat to group harmony (Markus & Kitayama, 1991). In Tahiti, for instance, people learn to be considerate and gentle. From infancy on in Japan, expressions of anger are less common than in Western cultures.

The "vent your anger" advice presumes that emotional expression provides emotional release, or **catharsis**. The catharsis hypothesis maintains that we reduce anger by releasing it through aggressive action or fantasy. Experimenters report that this sometimes occurs. When people retaliate against someone who has provoked them, they may indeed calm down—*if* their counterattack is directly against the provoker, *if* their retaliation seems justifiable, and *if* their target is not intimidating (Geen & Quanty, 1977; Hokanson & Edelman, 1966). In short, expressing anger can be *temporarily* calming *if* it does not leave us feeling guilty or anxious.

But expressing anger can also breed more anger. For one thing, it may provoke retaliation, thus escalating a minor conflict into a major confrontation. For another, expressing anger can magnify anger. (Recall Darwin's suggestion that violent gestures increase anger.) Ebbe Ebbesen and his colleagues (1975) saw this when they interviewed 100 frustrated engineers and technicians just laid off by an aerospace company. Some were asked questions that released hostility, such as, "What instances can you think of where the company has not been fair with you?" When these people later filled out a questionnaire that assessed their attitudes toward the company, did this opportunity to "drain off" their hostility reduce it? Quite the contrary. Compared with those who had not vented their anger, those who had let it all out exhibited more hostility.

Thus, although "blowing off steam" may temporarily calm an angry person, it may also amplify underlying hostility. When angry outbursts do calm us, they may be reinforcing and therefore habit forming. If basketball coaches can drain off some of their tension by berating referees, then the next time they feel tense with irritation they may be more likely to explode again. Similarly, the next time you are angry you are likely to do whatever has relieved your anger in the past.

A Cool Culture *Caregivers who turn abusive against other family members are rare in Micronesia. This photo of community life on Pulap Island suggests one reason why. Family life takes place in the open in the South Pacific, so relatives and neighbors can witness angry outbursts and step in before the emotion gets out of hand and turns into child, spouse, or elder abuse.*

feel-good, do-good phenomenon People's tendency to be helpful when already in a good mood.

So what's the best way to handle anger? Experts offer two suggestions. First, bring down the physiological arousal of anger by waiting. "It is true of the body as of arrows," notes Carol Tavris (1982), "what goes up must come down. Any emotional arousal will simmer down if you just wait long enough." Second, deal with anger in a way that involves neither being chronically angry over every little annoyance nor passively sulking, which is merely rehearsing your reasons for anger. Don't be like those who, stifling their feelings over a series of provocations, finally overreact to a single incident (Baumeister & others, 1990). Vent the anger by exercising, playing an instrument, or confiding your feelings to a friend or a diary.

Anger can benefit relationships when it expresses a grievance in ways that promote reconciliation rather than retaliation. Civility means not only keeping silent about trivial irritations but also communicating important ones clearly and assertively. A nonaccusing statement of feeling—perhaps letting one's partner know that "I get irritated when you leave your dirty dishes for me to clean up"—can help resolve the conflicts that cause anger.

Happiness

6. What are the causes and consequences of happiness?

"How to gain, how to keep, how to recover happiness is in fact for most [people] at all times the secret motive for all they do," observed William James (1902, p. 76). Understandably so, for one's state of happiness or unhappiness colors everything else. People who are happy perceive the world as safer (Johnson & Tversky, 1983), make decisions more easily (Isen & Means, 1983), rate job applicants more favorably (Baron, 1987), and report greater satisfaction with their whole lives (Schwarz & Clore, 1983). When your mood is gloomy, life as a whole seems depressing. Let your mood brighten, and suddenly your relationships, your self-image, and your hopes for the future all seem more promising.

Moreover—and this is one of psychology's most consistent findings—when we feel happy we are more willing to help others. In study after study, a mood-boosting experience (such as finding money, succeeding on a challenging task, or recalling a happy event) made people more likely to give money, pick up someone's dropped papers, volunteer time, and so forth. It's called the **feel-good, do-good phenomenon** (Salovey, 1990).

Despite the significance of happiness, psychology has more often focused on negative emotions. From 1967 to 1994, *Psychological Abstracts* (a summary of the psychological literature) included 5099 articles mentioning anger, 36,851 mentioning anxiety, and 46,380 mentioning depression. But for every 17 abstracts on these topics, only one mentioned the positive emotions of joy (405), life satisfaction (2340), or happiness (2389). There is, of course, good reason to focus on negative emotions, which can make our lives miserable and drive us to seek help. But researchers are becoming increasingly interested in positive emotions as well. During the 1980s, annual research output on positive well-being nearly quadrupled (Myers, 1993).

On this subject, as on so many others, whatever psychological research reveals will have been anticipated by someone. The sages of the ages have given us any number of contradictory maxims: that happiness comes from living a virtuous life, but also that it comes from getting away with evil; that it comes from knowing the truth, and from preserving illusions; that it comes from restraint, and from purging ourselves of pent-up rage and misery. They also have told us that happiness comes from living for the present, and living for the future; from making others happy, and from enjoying our enemies' misery; from

"Everything important has been said before."
Philosopher Alfred North Whitehead, 1861–1947

being with others, and from living in peaceful solitude (Tatarkiewicz,1976). The list goes on, but the implication is clear: The scientist's task is to ask which of these competing ideas fit reality. To sift the actual predictors of happiness from the merely plausible hunches requires research.

In their research on happiness, psychologists have studied influences upon both our temporary moods and our long-term life satisfaction. Studying people's reports of daily moods confirms that stressful events—an argument, a sick child, a car problem—trigger bad moods. No surprise there. But by the next day, the gloom nearly always lifts (Affleck & others, 1994; Bolger & others, 1989; Stone & Neale, 1984). If anything, people tend to rebound from bad days to a *better*-than-usual good mood the following day. When in a bad mood, can you usually depend on rebounding within a day or two? Are your times of elation similarly hard to sustain? In the long run, our emotional ups and downs tend to balance.

Apart from prolonged grief over the loss of a loved one or continuing anxiety after a traumatic stress, such as child abuse, rape, or the terrors of war, even tragedy is not permanently depressing. The finding is surprising but reliable. People who become blind or paralyzed usually recover near-normal levels of day-to-day happiness. For example, able-bodied University of Illinois students described themselves as happy 50 percent of the time, unhappy 22 percent of the time, and neutral 29 percent of the time. To within 1 percentage point, students with disabilities rated their emotions identically (Chwalisz & others, 1988). Moreover, students perceive their friends with disabilities as just as happy as their other friends (Allman, 1989).

The effect of dramatically positive events is similarly temporary. Once their rush of euphoria wears off, state lottery winners typically find their overall happiness unchanged (Brickman & others, 1978). Other research confirms that there is much more to well-being than being well-off. Many people (including most new collegians, as Figure 10–8 hints) believe they would be happier if they had more money. They probably would be—temporarily. But in the long run, increased affluence hardly affects happiness. People with lots of money are not much happier than those with just enough money to afford life's necessities. Wealth is like health: Its utter absence breeds misery, yet having it is no guarantee of happiness.

"Weeping may tarry for the night, but joy comes with the morning."

Psalms 30:5

"If I couldn't know the joy of dancing, I could know the ecstasy of creating."

Christy Brown
My Left Foot, 1954

Figure 10–8 Are Today's Collegians Materialistic? *From 1970 through most of the 1980s, annual surveys of more than 200,000 entering American college students revealed an increasing desire for wealth. (From Astin & others, 1994; Dey & others, 1991.)*

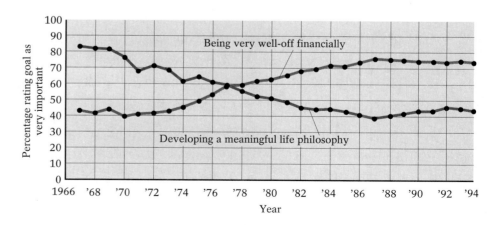

During the last three decades, the average U.S. citizen's buying power doubled. The 1957 per-person income, inflated to 1990 dollars, was approximately $8000; by 1994, thanks partly to the rich getting richer and to women's increasing employment, it was over $16,000. Did this increased wealth—enabling twice as many cars per capita, and color TVs, VCRs, home computers, microwave ovens, cellular phones, and answering machines galore—also buy

Figure 10–9 Does Money Buy Happiness? *It surely helps us to avoid certain types of pain. Yet, though buying power has doubled since the 1950s, the average American's reported happiness has remained almost unchanged. (Happiness data from Niemi & others, 1989, and T. Smith, 1994; income data from* Historical Statistics of the U.S. *and* Economic Indicators.)

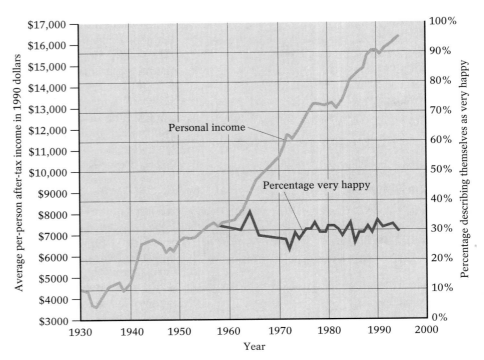

"No happiness lasts for long."

Seneca
Agamemnon, A.D. 60

Adaptation researcher Allen Parducci (in press) recalls a striking example: "On the Micronesian island of Ponope, which is almost on the equator, I was told of a bitter night back in 1915 when the temperature dropped to a record-breaking 69 degrees!"

more happiness? As Figure 10–9 shows, the average American is now twice as rich but no happier. In 1957, 35 percent said they were "very happy," as did slightly fewer—29 percent—in 1994. Indeed, judging by the doubled divorce rate, tripled teen-suicide rate, sixfold increased juvenile violence arrest rate, and increasing depression (page 427)—all since 1960—Americans are more often miserable. The same is true of the European countries and Japan: In all these countries, people enjoy better nutrition, health care, education, and technology, and are somewhat happier than people in very poor countries, yet their rising real incomes have *not* been accompanied by rising happiness. The findings lob a bombshell at our culture's materialism: *Economic growth in affluent countries provides no apparent boost to morale or social well-being.*

Two psychological principles explain the surprising findings that for all but the very poor, more money buys no more than a temporary surge of happiness, and why our emotions seem attached to elastic bands that pull us back from highs or lows. In its own way, each principle suggests that happiness is relative.

The Adaptation-Level Principle: Happiness Is Relative to Our Prior Experience

The **adaptation-level principle** describes this tendency to judge various stimuli relative to what we have previously experienced. We adjust our "neutral" levels—the points at which sounds seem neither loud nor soft, temperatures neither hot nor cold, events neither pleasant nor unpleasant—based on our experience. We then notice and react to variations up or down from these levels. Thus, if our income, grade-point average, or social prestige increases, we feel an initial surge of pleasure. We then adapt to this new level of attainment, come to see it as normal, and require something even better to give us another surge of happiness. Yesterday's luxury can become today's necessity.

So, could we ever create a permanent social paradise on earth? Donald Campbell (1975) argued no: If you woke up tomorrow to your utopia—perhaps a world with no bills, no ills, all *A*s, someone who loves you unreservedly—you would, for a time, feel euphoric. But before long you would soon recalibrate your adaptation level and would again sometimes feel gratified (when achievements surpass expectations), sometimes deprived (when they fall

The Pursuit of Happiness *For some people happiness is a walk in the woods, a sunny view of a waterfall, or some other experience of the tranquility and beauty of unspoiled places. Such settings may free us from stress that triggers bad moods or may put us in touch with a place in ourselves that is beyond unhappiness.*

"I've got the bowl, the big yard, I know I should be happy."

Drawing by M. Twohy;
© 1992 The New Yorker Magazine, Inc.

adaptation-level principle Our tendency to form judgments (of sounds, of lights, of income) relative to a "neutral" level defined by our prior experience.

relative deprivation The perception that one is worse off relative to those with whom one compares oneself.

below), and sometimes neutral. That helps explain why, despite the realities of triumph and tragedy, million-dollar lottery winners and paraplegics report similar levels of happiness. *The moral*: Satisfaction and dissatisfaction, success and failure—all are relative to our recent experience.

The Relative Deprivation Principle: Happiness Is Relative to Others' Attainments

Happiness is relative not only to our past experience, but also to our comparisons with others. We are always comparing ourselves with others. And whether we feel good or bad depends on who those others are.

An example: To explain the frustration expressed by U.S. Air Corps soldiers during World War II, researchers formulated the concept of **relative deprivation**—the sense that we are worse off than others with whom we compare ourselves. Despite a relatively rapid promotion rate for the group, many soldiers were frustrated about their own promotion rates (Merton & Kitt, 1950). Apparently, seeing so many others being promoted inflated the soldiers' expectations. And when expectations soar above attainments, the result is disappointment. When the Oakland Athletics signed outfielder Jose Canseco to a $4.7 million annual salary, his fellow outfielder Rickey Henderson became openly dissatisfied with his $3 million salary and refused to show up on time for spring training (King, 1991).

Such comparisons help us understand why the middle- and upper-income people in a given country tend to be slightly more satisfied with life than the relatively poor, with whom the better-off can compare themselves (Diener, 1984). Nevertheless, once a person reaches a moderate income level, further increases do little to increase happiness. Why? Because as people climb the ladder of success they mostly compare themselves with those who are at or above their current level (Gruder, 1977; Suls & Tesch, 1978). For Rickey Henderson, Jose Canseco was the standard of comparison. For many American physicians, earning an average $170,000, the higher salaries of professional athletes and corporate CEOs become a point of comparison (Associated Press, 1993). As Bertrand Russell (1930, pp. 68–69) observed, "Napoleon envied Caesar, Caesar envied Alexander, and Alexander, I daresay, envied Hercules, who never existed. You cannot, therefore, get away from envy by means of success alone, for

The effect of comparison with others helps us understand why students of a given level of academic ability tend to have a higher academic self-concept if they attend a school where most other students are not exceptionally able (Marsh & Parker, 1984). If you were near the top of your class in high school, you might feel inferior upon entering a college where everyone was near the top of their class.

When Downward Comparisons Lead Upward *Comparing ourselves with those worse off can sometimes prompt us not only to count our blessings but to share them. Self-made millionaire Eugene Lang (center) did just that during an address to the graduating class of the public grade school he had attended in Harlem. After reflecting on their poverty, he suddenly offered to pay the college costs of any who graduated from high school. (With his active support during the next 4 years, most did graduate from high school and over half went on to college.)*

there will always be in history or legend some person even more successful than you are."

By "counting our blessings" when we compare ourselves with those less fortunate, we can, however, increase our satisfaction. As comparing ourselves with those better-off creates envy, so comparing ourselves with those less well-off boosts contentment. Marshall Dermer and his colleagues (1979) demonstrated this by asking University of Wisconsin–Milwaukee women to study others' deprivation and suffering. After viewing vivid depictions of how grim life was in Milwaukee in 1900, or after imagining and then writing about various personal tragedies, such as being burned and disfigured, the women expressed greater satisfaction with their own lives. Similarly, when mildly depressed people read about someone who is even more depressed, they feel somewhat better (Gibbons, 1986).

Predictors of Happiness

If, as the adaptation-level principle implies, our emotions tend to balance around normal, then why do some people seem so filled with joy and others so gloomy day after day? What makes one person normally happy and another less so? Reviews of research indicate there are several predictors of happiness (Table 10–1). Remember, though, that knowing that two variables correlate does not tell us whether one causes the other. For example, many studies indicate that religiously active people tend to report greater happiness and life satisfaction. Is happiness conducive to faith? Or does faith enhance happiness?

Whether at work or leisure, most of us derive greatest enjoyment from engaging, challenging activities. Mihaly Csikszentmihalyi (pronounced chick-SENT-me-hi) (1990) and his colleagues discovered this after interrupting subjects several times a day with an electronic paging device. When beeped, the people would note what they were doing and how they were feeling. Usually, they felt happier if mentally engaged by work or active leisure than if passively vegetating. Ironically, the less expensive (and usually more involving) a leisure activity is, the more absorbed and happier people are while doing it. People are happier gardening than sitting on a power boat. They're happier when talking to friends than when watching TV. Indeed, happy are those whose work and leisure absorb them, enabling them unself-consciously to "flow" in focused activity.

TABLE 10–1

Happiness Is . . .

Researchers Have Found That Happy People Tend to	However, Happiness Seems Only Minimally Related to Other Factors, Such as
Have high self-esteem	Age
Be optimistic and outgoing	Race
Have close friendships, or a satisfying marriage	Gender (women are more often depressed, but also more often joyful)
Have work and leisure that engage their skills	Educational level
Have a meaningful religious faith	Parenthood (having or not having children)

Source: Summarized from Myers (1993) and Myers and Diener (1995).

! Rehearse It

5. After graduating from college, you get a job and move to a large metropolitan city. At first, you find the street noise irritatingly loud. But after awhile, it no longer bothers you, thus illustrating the

a. relative deprivation principle.
b. adaptation-level principle.
c. happiness predictors.
d. catharsis principle.

6. In some situations, venting anger—"blowing up"—seems to calm a person temporarily. In other cases, acting angry increases hostility. Experts suggest that to bring down anger, a good first step is to

a. retaliate verbally or physically.
b. wait or "simmer down."

c. express anger in action or fantasy.
d. review the grievance silently.

7. A philosopher notes that one cannot escape envy by means of success alone: There will always be someone more successful, more accomplished, or richer with whom to compare oneself. In psychology this observation is embodied in the

a. relative deprivation principle.
b. adaptation-level principle.
c. list of predictors of happiness.
d. feel-good, do-good phenomenon.

8. When happy and unhappy people are compared, researchers find that happy people are optimistic, outgoing, and likely to have satisfying close relationships. One

of the most consistent findings of psychological research is that happy people are also

a. more likely to express anger.
b. generally luckier than others.
c. concentrated in the wealthier nations.
d. more likely to help others.

9. Age, race, and gender seem not to be predictably related to subjective feelings of happiness or well-being. However, researchers have found that happy people tend to

a. have children.
b. score high on intelligence tests.
c. have a meaningful religious faith.
d. have completed high school and have some college education.

Theories of Emotion

We have seen that emotions arise from the interplay of physiological arousal, expressive behavior, and conscious experiences. But there are two controversies over this interplay. The first is an old debate: Does your heart pound because you are afraid, or are you afraid because you feel your heart pounding? The second concerns the link between our thinking and feeling: Does cognition always precede emotion?

The James-Lange and Cannon-Bard Theories

7. What issue distinguishes the James-Lange and Cannon-Bard theories of emotion?

Common sense tells most of us that we cry because we are sad, lash out because we are angry, tremble because we are afraid. However, to pioneering psychologist William James the common sense view of emotion was 180 degrees out of line. According to James, "We feel sorry because we cry, angry because we strike, afraid because we tremble" (1890, p. 1066). After you evade an oncoming car in your lane, you may then *notice* your racing heart and feel shaken with fright. Your feeling of fear follows your body's response (Figure 10–10).

Figure 10–10 The James-Lange Theory of Emotion *To experience an emotion is to be aware of our physiological reactions.*

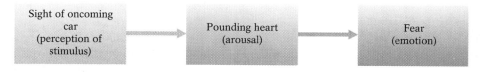

Sight of oncoming car (perception of stimulus) → Pounding heart (arousal) → Fear (emotion)

James-Lange Theory

James's idea, which was also proposed by Danish physiologist Carl Lange (1834–1900) and is therefore called the **James-Lange theory**, struck American physiologist Walter Cannon (1871–1945) as implausible. For one thing, Cannon thought the body's responses were not distinct enough to evoke the different emotions. Does a racing heart signal fear, anger, or love? For another, changes in heart rate, perspiration, and body temperature seemed to occur too slowly to trigger sudden emotion. Cannon, and later another physiologist, Philip Bard, concluded that physiological arousal and the emotional experience occur simultaneously: The emotion-arousing stimulus is routed simultaneously to the brain cortex, causing the subjective awareness of emotion, and to the sympathetic nervous system, causing the body's arousal. Thus, this **Cannon-Bard theory** implies that your heart begins pounding *as* you experience fear but that one does not cause the other (Figure 10–11).

As long as the evidence suggested that the arousal of one emotion is much the same as another, the James-Lange assumption that we experience our emo-

Figure 10–11 The Cannon-Bard Theory of Emotion
Emotions occur independent of physiology.

Sight of oncoming car (perception of stimulus) → Pounding heart (arousal)

Sight of oncoming car (perception of stimulus) → Fear (emotion)

Cannon-Bard Theory

tions through differing body states seemed improbable. With new evidence showing subtle physiological distinctions among the emotions, the James-Lange theory became more plausible. As James struggled with his own feelings of depression and grief, he came to believe that we can control emotions by going "through the outward motions" of whatever emotion one wants to experience. "To feel cheerful," he advised, "sit up cheerfully, look around cheerfully, and act as if cheerfulness were already there." The new findings concerning emotional effects of facial expressions (page 339) are precisely what James might have predicted.

To check your understanding of the James-Lange and Cannon-Bard theories, imagine that your brain could not sense your heart pounding or your stomach churning. According to each theory, how would this affect your experienced emotions?

Cannon and Bard would have expected you to experience emotions normally, because they believed emotions occur separately from (though simultaneously with) the body's arousal. James and Lange would have expected greatly diminished emotions because they believed that to experience emotion you must first perceive your body's arousal.

The condition you imagined actually exists in people with severed spinal cords. Psychologist George Hohmann (1966) interviewed 25 soldiers who received such injuries in World War II. He asked them to recall emotion-arousing incidents that occurred before and after their spinal injuries. Those with injuries in the lower part of the spine, who had lost sensation only in their legs, reported little change in their emotions. Those who could feel nothing below the neck reported a considerable decrease in emotional intensity (as James and Lange would have expected). These soldiers said they might act much the same as before in emotion-arousing situations, but as one confessed about his anger, "It just doesn't have the heat to it that it used to. It's a mental kind of anger."

"Whenever I feel afraid
I hold my head erect
And whistle a happy tune . . ."

Richard Rodgers and Oscar Hammerstein
The King and I, 1958

James-Lange theory   The theory that our experience of emotion is our awareness of our physiological responses to emotion-arousing stimuli.

Cannon-Bard theory   The theory that an emotion-arousing stimulus simultaneously triggers (1) physiological responses and (2) the subjective experience of emotion.

two-factor theory   Schachter's theory that to experience emotion one must (1) be physically aroused and (2) cognitively label the arousal.

On the other hand, emotions expressed mostly in body areas above the neck are felt more intensely by those with spinal cord injury. Virtually all the men Hohmann interviewed reported increases in weeping, lumps in the throat, and getting choked up when saying good-bye, worshipping, or watching a touching movie.

Although such evidence breathed new life into the James-Lange theory, most researchers agree with Cannon and Bard that our experienced emotions also involve cognition (Averill, 1993). Whether we fear the man behind us on the dark street depends entirely on whether we interpret his actions as hostile or friendly. So with James and Lange we can say that arousal is an important ingredient of emotion. And with Cannon and Bard we can say that there is more to the experience of emotion than reading our physiology.

Cognition and Emotion

8. What is the relationship between thinking and feeling?

Now, the second and newer controversy: Put simply, what is the connection between what we *think* and how we *feel*? Which is the chicken and which the egg? Do emotions always grow from thoughts? Are our feelings always subject to our mind's appraisal of a situation? Or can we experience emotion apart from thinking? This issue has practical implications for self-improvement.

Schachter's Two-Factor Theory of Emotion

Most psychologists believe that our cognitions—our perceptions, memories, and interpretations—are an essential ingredient of emotion. One such theorist has been Stanley Schachter, whose **two-factor theory** proposes that emotions have two ingredients: physical arousal and a cognitive label (Figure 10–12). Like James and Lange, Schachter presumes that our experience of emotion grows from our awareness of our body's arousal. But he also believes, like Cannon and Bard, that emotions are physiologically similar. Thus, he argues, an emotional experience requires a conscious interpretation of the arousal.

Figure 10–12 Summary of Schachter's Two-Factor Theory of Emotion   *To experience emotion, we must be aroused and must cognitively label the arousal.*

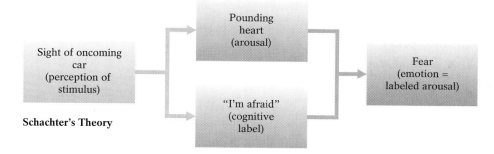

Schachter's Theory

It is often hard to disentangle our arousal response to an event from our interpretation of the event. Imagine that after an invigorating run you arrive home to find a message that you got the longed-for job. With arousal lingering from the run, would you feel more elated than if you received this news after awakening from a nap?

To find out, Schachter and Jerome Singer (1962) aroused college men with injections of the hormone epinephrine. Picture yourself as one of their subjects: After receiving the injection, you go to a waiting room, where you find yourself with another person (actually an accomplice of the experimenters) who is acting either euphoric or irritated. As you observe this person, you begin to feel your heart race, your body flush, and your breathing become more rapid. If told to expect these effects from the injection, what would you feel? Schachter and Singer's subjects felt little emotion—because they attributed their arousal to the drug. But if told the injection would produce no effects, what would you feel? Perhaps you would react, as another group of subjects did, by "catching" the apparent emotion of the person you are with—becoming happy if the accomplice is acting euphoric, and testy if the accomplice is acting irritated.

This discovery—that a stirred-up state can be experienced as one emotion or another very different one, depending on how we interpret and label it—has been replicated in dozens of experiments. Although emotional arousal is not as undifferentiated as Schachter believed, arousal can intensify just about any emotion (Reisenzein, 1983; Sinclair & others, 1994). Insult people who have just been aroused by pedaling an exercise bike or watching a rock concert film and they will find it easy to misattribute their arousal to the provocation. Their feelings of anger will be greater than those of similarly provoked people who were not previously aroused. Arousal from emotions as diverse as anger, fear, and sexual excitement can spill from one emotion to another (Zillmann, 1986). In anger-provoking situations, sexually aroused people react with more hostility. Similarly, the arousal that lingers after an intense argument or a frightening experience may intensify sexual passion (Palace & Gorzalka, 1990). Arousal fuels emotion and cognition channels it.

Must Cognition Precede Emotion?

So, to experience an emotion, must we first label our arousal? Robert Zajonc (pronounced ZI-yence) (1980, 1984a) contends the answer is no. He argues that our emotional reactions are sometimes quicker than our interpretations of a situation; we therefore feel some emotions *before* we think. For example, in earlier chapters, we noted that when people repeatedly view stimuli flashed too briefly for them to perceive and recall, they nevertheless come to prefer these stimuli. Without being consciously aware of having seen the stimuli, they rather like them. (Can you recall liking something or someone immediately without at first knowing why?)

Figure 10–13 The Brain's Shortcut for Emotions *Sensory input may be routed both to the cortex and directly to the amygdala for a more instant emotional reaction. (Adapted from Joseph LeDoux, "Emotion, Memory and the Brain," June 1994, p. 56. Copyright 1994 by* Scientific American, *Inc. All rights reserved.)*

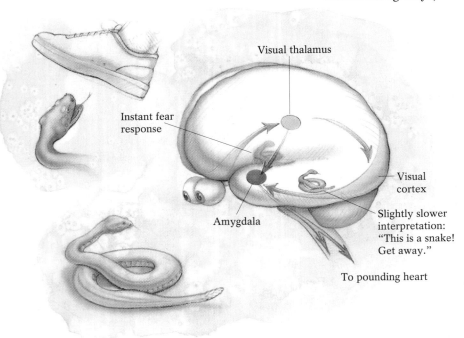

Visual thalamus

Instant fear response

Visual cortex

Amygdala

Slightly slower interpretation: "This is a snake! Get away."

To pounding heart

Research on neurological processes supports the idea that we can experience emotion before cognition. Some neural pathways involved in emotion bypass the cortical areas involved in thinking. One such pathway runs from the eye or ear via the thalamus to one of the brain's emotional control centers, the amygdala (LeDoux, 1994). This enables a quick, automatic emotional response, which may then be modified after the cortex has further interpreted a threat (Figure 10–13). In the forest, we jump at a nearby rustling sound, leaving the cortex to decide later whether it was made by a predator or just the wind. Such evidence convinces Zajonc that *some* of our emotional reactions involve no deliberate thinking. Cognition, he believes, is not always necessary for emotion.

Emotion researcher Richard Lazarus (1984, 1991) disagrees. He concedes that our brains process and react to vast amounts of information without our conscious awareness, and he willingly grants that some emotional responses do not re-

Experienced emotion

Cognition

Figure 10–14 Emotion and Cognition Feed Each Other
But which is the chicken and which the egg? Lazarus believes that, although emotions influence thinking, our cognitive appraisal of a situation always precedes emotion. Zajonc contends that some of our emotional reactions precede cognitive processing.

quire *conscious* thinking. Nevertheless, he says, even instantaneously felt emotions require some sort of quick cognitive appraisal of the situation; otherwise, how do we *know* what we are reacting to? The appraisal may be effortless and we may not be conscious of it, but it is still a function of the mind (Figure 10–14). Emotions arise when we appraise an event as beneficial or harmful to our well-being.

For us, the important conclusion concerns what Lazarus and Zajonc agree on: Some emotional responses—especially simple likes, dislikes, and fears—involve no conscious thinking. We may fear the spider, even if we "know" it is harmless. After conditioning, Little Albert was afraid of furry objects (Chapter 6). Such responses are hard to alter by changing our thinking.

Other emotions—including moods such as depression and complex feelings such as hatred and love—are greatly affected by our interpretations, memories, and expectations. For these emotions, as we will see in Chapter 13 (Therapy), learning to *think* more positively about ourselves and the world around us makes us *feel* better. Regardless of the origins of our emotional responses, how we feel matters to our body. Nervous about a speech or performance, we frequent the bathroom. Smoldering over a family conflict, we get a splitting headache. When such stress endures, as we will see next, it may trigger a skin rash, an asthma attack, or an ulcer, or even put us at risk for heart disease, cancer, and strokes.

❗ *Rehearse It*

10. Two important theories of emotion are the James-Lange theory and the Cannon-Bard theory. The James-Lange theory states that our experience of an emotion is a consequence of our physiological response to a stimulus; we are afraid because our heart pounds. The Cannon-Bard theory, on the other hand, proposes that the physiological response (like heart pounding) and the subjective experience of, say, anger

a. are unrelated.
b. occur simultaneously.
c. occur in the opposite order (with feelings of fear first).
d. are regulated by the thalamus.

11. Given the following situation—you have just spent an hour on a treadmill and

you receive a letter saying that your scholarship to college has been approved—the two-factor theory of emotion would predict that your physical arousal will

a. weaken your happiness.
b. intensify your happiness.
c. transform your happiness into relief.
d. have no particular effect on your happiness.

12. Research suggests that we can experience an aroused state as one of several different emotions, depending on how we interpret and label the arousal. If physically aroused by swimming, then heckled by an onlooker, we may interpret our arousal as anger and

a. become less physically aroused.
b. feel angrier than usual.
c. feel less angry than usual.
d. feel sexually aroused.

13. Robert Zajonc maintains that some of our emotional reactions occur before we have had the chance to label or interpret them. Richard Lazarus disagrees. The two psychologists differ about whether or not emotional responses occur in the absence of

a. physical arousal.
b. conscious thought.
c. cognitive processing.
d. learning.

The Faces of Stress   *Challenging positive events, such as graduating into the working world, can be stressful. But most stresses arise from negative events that threaten our well-being, such as a child's sudden death from a stray bullet.*

Worldwide, reports the World Health Organization, nearly a quarter of health care contacts are prompted by psychological problems (Sartorius, 1994).

behavioral medicine   An interdisciplinary field that integrates and applies behavioral and medical knowledge to health and disease.

health psychology   A subfield of psychology that provides psychology's contribution to behavioral medicine.

stress   The process by which we perceive and respond to certain events, called stressors, that we appraise as threatening or challenging.

general adaptation syndrome (GAS)   Selye's concept of the body's adaptive response to stress as composed of three stages—alarm, resistance, exhaustion.

Stress and Health

Walking along the path toward his Rocky Mountain campsite, Karl hears a rustle at his feet. As he glimpses a rattlesnake, his body mobilizes for fight or flight: His muscles tense, his adrenaline flows, his heart pounds. Then flee he does, racing to the security of camp. Once there, Karl's muscles gradually relax and his heart rate and breathing ease.

Karen leaves her suburban apartment one morning and, delayed by road construction, arrives at the parking lot of the commuter train station just in time to see the 8:05 pull away. Catching the next train, she arrives in the city late and elbows her way through crowds of rush-hour pedestrians. Once at her bank office, she apologizes to her first client, who wonders where Karen has been and why her quarterly investment report is not ready. Karen does her best to mollify the client. Afterward, she notices signs of her pent-up emotion—her tense muscles, clenched teeth, and churning stomach.

Karl's response to stress saved his life; Karen's, if chronic, could increase her risk of heart disease, high blood pressure, and other stress-linked health problems. Moreover, feeling under pressure, she might sleep and exercise less and smoke and drink more, further endangering her long-term health.

If we could understand and modify such behavioral sources of illness, we might lessen people's suffering and increase their life expectancy and quality of life. To pursue these goals, psychologists and physicians created the interdisciplinary field of **behavioral medicine**, integrating behavioral and medical knowledge. **Health psychology** provides psychology's contribution to behavioral medicine. This new subfield of psychology assumes that illness results from the interaction of our biological, psychological, and social systems. Health psychologists ask: How do our emotions and stress responses influence our risk of disease? How do our attitudes and behaviors affect our well-being? How can we reduce or control stress?

Stress and Stressors

9. What is stress?

Stress is a slippery concept. People sometimes use the word *stress* to describe threats or challenges ("Karen was under a lot of stress"), other times to describe our responses ("When Karl saw the rattler he experienced acute stress"). Most psychologists would define Karen's missed train as a "stressor," Karl's

Figure 10–15 The Stress Process *How we react to stressors depends on who we are and how we appraise and cope with them. For example, criticism that an easygoing optimist perceives as a challenge may seem a dire threat to a temperamental pessimist.*

physical and emotional responses as a "stress reaction," and the process by which Karen and Karl related to their environments as **stress**. Thus, stress is not just a stimulus or a response. It is the process by which we appraise and cope with environmental threats and challenges (Figure 10–15).

When perceived as challenges, stressors can have positive effects by arousing and motivating us to conquer problems. Championship athletes, successful entertainers, and great teachers and leaders all thrive and excel when aroused by a challenge. But more often stressors threaten our resources—our status and security on the job, our loved ones' health or well-being, our deeply held beliefs, our self-image (Hobfoll, 1989). And when such stress is severe or prolonged, it may also harm.

The Stress Response System

Although medical interest in stress dates back to Hippocrates (460–377 B.C.), it was not until the 1920s that Walter Cannon (1929) confirmed that the stress response is part of a unified mind–body system. He observed that extreme cold, lack of oxygen, and emotion-arousing incidents all trigger an outpouring of epinephrine (adrenaline) and norepinephrine (noradrenaline). These stress hormones enter the bloodstream from sympathetic nerve endings in the inner part of the adrenal glands. This is but one part of the sympathetic nervous system's response. As we saw in Figure 10-1 (p. 336), when alerted by any of a number of brain pathways, the sympathetic nervous system increases heart rate and respiration, diverts blood to skeletal muscles, and releases fat from the body's stores—all to prepare the body for what Cannon called *fight or flight*. All in all, this stress response struck Cannon as wonderfully adaptive.

Canadian scientist Hans Selye's (1936, 1976) 40 years of research on stress extended Cannon's findings and helped make stress a major concept in both psychology and medicine. Selye studied animals' reactions to various stressors, such as electric shock, surgical trauma, and immobilizing restraint. He discovered that the body's adaptive response to stress is so general—like a single burglar alarm that sounds no matter what intrudes—that he called it the **general adaptation syndrome (GAS)**.

Selye saw the GAS as having three phases (Figure 10–16). Let's say you suffer a physical or emotional trauma. In Phase 1, you experience an *alarm reaction* due to the sudden activation of your sympathetic nervous system. Your heart rate zooms, blood is diverted to your skeletal muscles, and you feel the faintness of shock. With your resources mobilized you are now ready to fight the challenge during Phase 2, *resistance*. Your temperature, blood pressure, and respiration remain high, and there is a sudden outpouring of hormones. If persistent, the stress may eventually deplete your body's reserves during Phase 3, *exhaustion*. With exhaustion, you are more vulnerable to illness or even, in extreme cases, collapse and death.

Figure 10–16 Selye's General Adaptation Syndrome

Newer research reveals subtle differences in the body's reactions to different stressors. Nevertheless, few medical experts today quarrel with Selye's basic point: Prolonged stress can produce physical deterioration. This leads to the practical concerns of today's health psychologists: What causes stress? What are the effects of stress? And how can we alleviate those effects?

Stressful Life Events

10. What provokes stress?

How stressed we feel depends on how we appraise events. One person alone in a house dismisses its creaking sounds and experiences no stress; someone else suspects an intruder and becomes alarmed. One person regards a new job as a welcome challenge; someone else appraises it as risking failure. Research has focused on our responses to three types of stressors: catastrophes, significant life changes, and daily hassles.

Catastrophes   Catastrophes are unpredictable, large-scale events such as war and natural disasters that nearly everyone appraises as threatening. Although people often provide one another with aid and comfort after such events, the health consequences can be significant. Two examples:

> In the year following the crash of a 747 jumbo jet at Lockerbie, Scotland, police officers—after being pressed into recovering human remains and patrolling the disaster zone—suffered a 38 percent increase in short-term illnesses (Paton, 1992).

> In the Republic of Belarus, where the worst fallout rained down from the nearby Chernobyl nuclear disaster, those who have left their native homes and friends and those who have stayed to live in a threatening environment have all suffered severe stress. Stress-related ailments such as hypertension and heart disease have reportedly tripled (Kolominsky & Parkhomenko, 1993).

Do community disasters usually produce effects this great? After digesting data from 52 such studies of catastrophic floods, hurricanes, and fires, Anthony Rubonis and Leonard Bickman (1991) found the typical effect more modest but nonetheless genuine. In disaster's wake, rates of psychological disorders, such as depression and anxiety, rose an average 17 percent. The nuclear accident at Three Mile Island produced similar stress symptoms in area residents (Baum & Fleming, 1993). Refugees fleeing their homeland also suffer increased rates of psychological disorder. Their stress stems from the trauma of uprooting and family separation and from the challenges of adjusting to a foreign culture, with its differing language, ethnicity, climate, and social norms (Williams & Berry, 1991). In all these cases, the health consequences often come only after prolonged stress.

Significant Life Changes   The second type of life event stressor is personal life changes—the death of a loved one, the loss of a job, a marriage or divorce. Some psychologists study the health effects of life changes by following people over time to see if such events precede illnesses. Others compare the life changes recalled by those who have or have not suffered a specific health problem, such as a heart attack. A review of these studies commissioned by the National Academy of Sciences revealed that people recently widowed, fired, or divorced are more vulnerable to disease (Dohrenwend & others, 1982). A Finnish study of 96,000 widowed people confirmed the phenomenon: Their risk of death doubled in the week following their partner's death (Kaprio & others, 1987). Experiencing a cluster of crises puts one even more at risk.

Why, then, do some people feel stressed after a major life change while others do not? Because what matters more than the situation itself is our appraisal of it. Retirement may be viewed by one person as a time to relax and enjoy, by another person as a threat to identity and income. Having an abortion creates stress for women who morally oppose abortion and who lack their partner's or parents' support. Yet most women who appraise abortion differently do not experience severe distress after abortion (Adler & others, 1990; Major & others, 1990; Russo, 1992). The events of our lives flow through a psychological filter.

Daily Hassles As we noted earlier, our happiness stems less from enduring good fortune than from our response to daily events—a longed-for date, a gratifying letter, your team's winning the big game. The principle works for negative events, too. Everyday annoyances may be the most significant sources of stress (Kohn & Macdonald, 1992; Lazarus, 1990; Ruffin, 1993). These daily hassles include rush-hour traffic, aggravating housemates, long lines at the bank or store, too many things to do, and misplacing things. Although some people can simply shrug them off, others are "driven up the wall" by such inconveniences. Thus, 6 in 10 people say they feel "great stress" at least once a week (Harris, 1987).

"It's not the large things that send a man to the madhouse . . . no, it's the continuing series of small tragedies . . . not the death of his love but the shoelace that snaps with no time left."

Charles Bukowski, 1983

Patience Is a Virtue *Learning to handle everyday hassles calmly can reap dividends. Experiencing stress from daily inconveniences—far more common than life's occasional crises—can take its toll on health and well-being.*

Over time, these little stressors can add up and take a toll on health and well-being. Hypertension (high blood pressure) is common among the residents of urban ghettos, who endure the daily stresses that accompany poverty, unemployment, single parenting, crime, and overcrowding. There is a correspondingly low rate of heart attacks among those who live the relatively peaceful monastic life (Henry & Stephens, 1977).

The Wounds of War—Post-Traumatic Stress Disorder

During the fighting in Vietnam, Jack's platoon was repeatedly under fire. In one ambush, his closest friend was killed while standing a few feet away. Jack himself killed a young Vietcong soldier by bludgeoning him with a rifle butt. Years later, images of these events intrude as flashbacks and nightmares. He still jumps at the sound of a cap gun or the backfire of a car. When annoyed by family or friends, he lashes out in ways he seldom did before Vietnam. To calm his continuing anxiety, he drinks more than he should.

Such has been the experience of many combat veterans and sexual assault victims. Traumatic stress—experiencing or witnessing severely threatening events with a sense of fear, helplessness, or horror—can produce a *post-traumatic stress disorder*, symptoms of which include haunting memories and nightmares, social withdrawal, and anxiety or depression (Goodman & others, 1993; Kaylor & others, 1987; Wilson & others, 1988). After witnessing atrocities or living in life-threatening circumstances, children of the world's war zones and violent neighborhoods show similar symptoms (Garbarino, 1991, 1992). Their sense of basic trust erodes; many experience fearful wariness, troubled sleep, nightmares, and a sense of hopelessness about their future.

To pin down the frequency of post-traumatic stress disorder, the Centers for Disease Control (1988) compared 7000 Vietnam combat veterans with 7000 noncombat veterans who served during the same years. Combat stress more than doubled a veteran's risk of suffering alcohol abuse, depression, or anxiety.

Studies of Israeli and American soldiers reveal that the more terrifying and prolonged the battle experience, the greater the psychological casualties (King & King, 1991; Solomon, 1990). Among Vietnam veterans, the roughly 15 percent overall rate of post-traumatic stress symptoms was halved among those who never saw combat and tripled among those who experienced heavy combat. For example, more than a decade after the war, one study located 2095 identical twins among Vietnam-era veterans (Goldberg & others, 1990). Compared with co-twins who served noncombat roles in Vietnam, those who experienced heavy combat were 5.4 times more likely to be suffering post-traumatic stress disorder.

Researchers have also found that psychological disorders and suicide attempts were most common among vets who felt responsible for a trauma, because they had either killed someone or failed to prevent a death (Fontana & others, 1992). Many still experience nightmares, have trouble sleeping and concentrating, and find themselves easily startled. This is especially so for those exposed to savage mutilation, torture, or the sight of a friend's death. Much as they might wish to supress or repress the memory, it intrudes.

Despite such symptoms, most combat-stressed veterans live productive lives. So have most American Jews who survived the Holocaust trauma—starvation, beatings, lost freedom, and the murders of loved ones—although they, too, often suffered lingering post-traumatic stress symptoms. In fact, compared with other American Jews of the same age, these survivors have been *less* likely to have seen a psychotherapist (18 percent versus 31 percent) and *more* likely to have had stable marriages (83 percent versus 62 percent). Moreover, virtually none have committed criminal acts. Researcher William Helmreich (1992, p. 276) reflects on their successes:

The story of the survivors is one of courage and strength, of people who are living proof of the indomitable will of human beings to survive and of their tremendous capacity for hope. It is not a story of remarkable people. It is a story of just how remarkable people can be.

Perceived Control

Catastrophes, important life changes, and daily hassles and conflicts are especially stressful when we appraise them as both negative *and* uncontrollable. If two rats receive simultaneous shocks, but one of them can turn a wheel to stop the shocks, the helpless rat becomes more susceptible to ulcers and lowered immunity to disease (Laudenslager & Reite, 1984) (Figure 10–17).

So it goes in humans: Perceiving a loss of control, we are vulnerable to ill health. Elderly nursing home patients who have little perceived control over their activities tend to decline faster and die sooner than do those given more control over their activities (Rodin, 1986). Given control over their work environments—by being able to adjust office furnishings and control interruptions and distractions—workers, too, experience less stress (O'Neill, 1993).

A related factor that influences our stress vulnerability is optimism. Psychologists Michael Scheier and Charles Carver (1992) report that optimists—people who agree with statements such as, "In uncertain times, I usually expect the best"—cope better with stressful events and enjoy better health. During

Figure 10–17 Health Consequences of a Loss of Control
The "executive" rat at the left can switch off the tail shock by turning the wheel. Because it has control over the shock, it is no more likely to develop ulcers than is the unshocked control rat on the right. The "subordinate" rat in the center receives the same shocks as the executive rat. But because the subordinate rat has no control over the shocks, it is more likely to develop ulcers. (Adapted from Weiss, 1977.)

"Executive" rat　　　"Subordinate" rat　　　Control rat

To shock control　　To shock source　　　No connection to shock source

the last month of a semester, students previously identified as optimistic report less fatigue and fewer coughs, aches, and pains. Optimists also respond to stress with smaller increases in blood pressure, and they recover faster from heart bypass surgery.

Why do perceived loss of control and pessimism predict health problems? Animal studies show—and human studies confirm—that losing control provokes an outpouring of stress hormones. When rats cannot control shock or when humans feel unable to control their environment, stress hormone levels rise and immune responses drop (Rodin, 1986). Captive animals therefore experience more stress and are more vulnerable to disease than are wild animals (Roberts, 1988). The crowding that occurs in high-density neighborhoods, prisons, and college dorms is another source of diminished feelings of control—and of increased levels of stress hormones and blood pressure (Fleming & others, 1987; Ostfeld & others, 1987).

Stress, Personality, and Heart Disease

11. Who is most vulnerable to heart disease?

Although infrequent before this century, **coronary heart disease**—the narrowing of the vessels that nourish the heart muscle—had become North America's leading cause of death by the 1950s. In the United States alone, more than 700,000 people die annually from heart disease.

Many factors increase the risk of heart disease—smoking, obesity, family history of the disease, high-fat diet, physical inactivity, elevated blood pressure, and elevated cholesterol level. But even when all these factors are considered, a large number of instances of heart disease remain unexplained. Many inactive, overweight smokers are free of the disease and many active, slender nonsmokers suffer heart attacks.

So what else might be involved? In 1956, cardiologists Meyer Friedman, Ray Rosenman, and their colleagues stumbled upon an idea (Friedman & Ulmer, 1984). While studying the eating behavior of white, San Francisco Junior League women and their husbands, Friedman and Rosenman discovered that the women consumed as much cholesterol and fat as their husbands did, yet they were far less susceptible to heart disease. Was it because of their female sex hormones? No, the researchers surmised, because African-American

coronary heart disease The clogging of the vessels that nourish the heart muscle.

Type A Friedman and Rosenman's term for competitive, hard-driving, impatient, verbally aggressive, and anger-prone people.

Type B Friedman and Rosenman's term for easygoing, relaxed people.

TYPE A PERSONALITY / TYPE B PERSONALITY

"The fire you kindle for your enemy often burns you more than him."

Chinese proverb

women with the same sex hormones but facing more stress are as prone to heart disease as their husbands are.

The Junior League president thought she knew the answer. "If you really want to know what is going to give our husbands heart attacks, I'll tell you. It's stress," she said sadly, "the stress they have to face in their businesses, day in, day out. Why, when my husband comes home at night, it takes at least one martini just to unclench his jaws."

To test the idea that stress increases vulnerability to heart disease, Friedman and Rosenman measured the blood cholesterol level and clotting speed of 40 tax accountants. From January through March, both of these coronary warning indicators were completely normal. Then, as the accountants began scrambling to finish their clients' tax returns before the April 15 filing deadline, their cholesterol and clotting measures rose to dangerous levels. In May and June, with the deadline past, the measures returned to normal. The researchers' hunch had paid off: Stress predicted heart attack risk.

The stage was set for what was to become Friedman and Rosenman's classic 9-year study of more than 3000 healthy men aged 35 to 59. At the start of the study, they interviewed each man for 15 minutes about his work and eating habits. During the interview, they noted the man's manner of talking and other behavioral patterns. Those who seemed the most reactive, competitive, hard-driving, impatient, time-conscious, supermotivated, verbally aggressive, and easily angered they called **Type A**. A roughly equal number who were more easygoing they called **Type B**. Which group do you suppose turned out to be the most coronary-prone?

By the time the study was complete, 257 of the men had suffered heart attacks, 69 percent of whom were Type A. Thus, compared with the Type B men, the Type As were more than twice as vulnerable. Moreover, not one of the "pure" Type Bs—the most mellow and laid-back of their group—had suffered a heart attack.

As often happens in science, this exciting discovery provoked enormous public interest. But after the honeymoon period, in which the finding seemed definitive and revolutionary, other researchers began asking, Is the finding reliable? If so, what is the toxic component of the Type A profile—the time-consciousness? The competitiveness? The anger?

Why may Type A people be more prone to heart disease? Further research found that reactive Type A individuals are more often "combat ready." When harassed or challenged, their active sympathetic nervous system redistributes blood flow to the muscles and away from the internal organs—including the liver, which removes cholesterol and fat from the blood. Thus, their blood may contain excess cholesterol and fat that is later deposited around the heart. Further stress—sometimes conflicts triggered by their own abrasiveness—may then trigger the altered heart rhythms that, in those with weakened hearts, can cause sudden death (Kamarck & Jennings, 1991). In such ways, the hearts and minds of people interact.

Newer research reveals that the Type A's toxic core is not a fast-paced life but is negative emotions—especially the anger associated with an aggressively reactive temperament (Matthews, 1988; Williams, 1993). The effect of an anger-prone personality appears most noticeably in studies in which interviewers assess verbal assertiveness and emotional intensity. (If you pause in the middle of a sentence, an intense, anger-prone person may jump in and finish it for you.) Among young and middle-aged adults, those who react with anger over little things are the most coronary-prone. One study followed Duke University law students over 25 years. Those inclined to be hostile and cynical were five times more likely than their gentler, trusting classmates to die by middle age (Williams, 1989). As Charles Spielberger and Perry London (1982) put it, rage "seems to lash back and strike us in the heart muscle."

psychophysiological illness Literally, "mind–body" illness; any stress-related physical illness, such as hypertension, ulcers, and headaches. Note: This is distinct from hypochondriasis— misinterpreting normal physical sensations as symptoms of a disease.

lymphocytes The two types of white blood cells that are part of the body's immune system: one type releases antibodies that fight bacterial infections; the other attacks cancer cells, viruses, and foreign substances, among other duties.

Anger isn't the only toxic emotion. Depression, too, can be lethal. Centers for Disease Control researchers studied adults who were feeling a sense of hopelessness or at least mild depression. Compared with those without such feelings, these downhearted people were more vulnerable to heart disease in the ensuing 12 years. This was true even after controlling for differences in age, sex, smoking, and other factors linked to heart ailments (Anda & others, 1993). The depression that follows a spouse's death also increases one's risk of having a heart attack or stroke (National Academy of Sciences, 1984).

Stress and Resistance to Disease

12. How does stress make us vulnerable to disease?

Not so long ago, the term *psychosomatic* described psychologically caused physical symptoms. To laypeople, the term implied that the symptoms were unreal—they were "merely" psychosomatic. To avoid such connotations and to describe better the genuine physiological effects of psychological states, most experts today refer instead to **psychophysiological** ("mind–body") **illnesses**. These illnesses, which include certain forms of hypertension, ulcers, and headaches, are stress-related. In people with reactive temperaments, chronic stress produces various changes. In one person, prolonged resentment, anger, or anxiety may stimulate an excess of digestive acids that eats away parts of the lining of the stomach or small intestine—one cause of ulcers. Another person under stress may retain excess sodium and fluids, which, together with constriction of the arteries' muscle walls, contributes to increased blood pressure (Light & others, 1983).

Stress and the Immune System

Evidence that psychophysiological ailments are real comes from hundreds of new experiments that reveal the nervous and endocrine systems' influence on the immune system. The immune system is a complex surveillance system that defends the body by isolating and destroying bacteria, viruses, and other foreign substances. It includes two types of white blood cells, called **lymphocytes**. One type releases antibodies that fight bacterial infections. The other attacks cancer cells, viruses, and other foreign substances—even "good" ones, such as transplanted organs. Another agent of the immune system is the *macrophage* ("big eater"), which identifies, pursues, and ingests harmful invaders. Age, nutrition, genetics, body temperature, and stress all influence the immune system's activity.

The immune system can err in two directions. Responding too strongly, it may attack the body's own tissues, causing arthritis or an allergic reaction. Or it may underreact, allowing, say, cancer cells to multiply.

The immune system is not a headless horseman. Rather, it exchanges information with the brain and the hormone-secreting endocrine system. The brain regulates the secretion of stress hormones, which in turn suppress the disease-fighting lymphocytes. Thus, when animals are physically restrained, given unavoidable electric shocks, or subjected to noise or crowding, they become more susceptible to disease (Jemmott & Locke, 1984). One study monitored immune responses in 43 monkeys over 6 months (Cohen & others, 1992). Twenty-one were stressed by being housed with new roommates—three or four new monkeys—each month. (To empathize with the monkeys, recall the stress of leaving home to attend school or summer camp, and imagine having to repeat this experience weekly.) Compared with monkeys left in stable groups, the socially disrupted monkeys developed suppressed immune systems.

The Immune System in Action *A large macrophage (at top) is about to trap and ingest a tiny bacterium (lower right). Macrophages constantly patrol the body in a search for invaders, such as this* Escherichia coli *bacterium, and for debris, such as worn-out red blood cells.*

Does stress similarly suppress the immune system of humans? Consider:

▷ Accumulating evidence shows that stress lowers the body's resistance to upper respiratory infections as well as to herpes (Cohen & Williamson, 1991).

▷ In three separate *Skylab* missions, the immune systems of the astronauts showed reduced effectiveness immediately after the stress of reentry and splashdown (Kimzey, 1975; Kimzey & others, 1976).

▷ Marital spats are not good for health. As 90 healthy newlywed couples spent a half hour discussing problem areas in their marriage, some became angrier than others—and suffered more immune system suppression during the next day (Kiecolt-Glaser & others, 1993).

▷ Students' disease-fighting mechanisms are weaker during high-stress times, such as exam weeks and on days when they are upset (Jemmott & Magloire, 1988; Stone & others, 1987). In one experiment, a stressful experience increased the severity of symptoms experienced by volunteers who were knowingly infected with a cold virus (Dixon, 1986). In another, 47 percent of subjects living stress-filled lives developed colds after a virus was dropped in their noses, but only 27 percent of those living relatively free of stress caught colds (Cohen & others, 1991, 1993, 1995).

▷ The National Academy of Sciences (1984) reports that the grief and depression that follow the death of a spouse decrease immune defenses (which helps explain the increase in disease among those recently widowed). In fact, depression of any sort tends to suppress the immune system (Herbert & Cohen, 1993; Weisse, 1992). Thus, in one study of leukemia patients preparing to undergo bone marrow transplants, 12 of 13 depressed patients died within a year. Among the many more who were not depressed, 39 percent were still alive after 2 years (Colon & others, 1991).

Stress and Cancer

Stress and negative emotions such as depression also have been linked to cancer. To explore a possible connection between stress and cancer, experimenters have given rodents tumor cells or cancer-producing substances. Those rodents also exposed to uncontrollable stress, such as inescapable shocks, are more prone to cancer (Sklar & Anisman, 1981). With their immune systems weakened by stress, their tumors develop sooner and grow larger.

Several investigators report that people, too, are at increased risk for cancer a year or so after experiencing depression, helplessness, or bereavement. For example, cancer occurs more often than usual among those widowed, divorced, or separated. One study of the husbands of women with terminal breast cancer pinpointed a possible reason: During the first 2 months after their wives' deaths, the bereaved men's lymphocyte responses dropped (Schleifer & others, 1979).

Another study gave a personality test to 2018 middle-aged men employed by the Western Electric Company in 1958. During the next 20 years, 7 percent of those not depressed and 12 percent of those somewhat depressed died of cancer (Persky & others, 1987). A large Swedish study revealed that people with a history of workplace stress had a 5.5 times greater risk of colon cancer than those who reported no such problems (Courtney & others, 1993). In both these studies, the cancer difference was not attributable to differences in age, smoking, drinking, or physical characteristics.

In the first weeks after receiving their diagnosis, cancer patients and those carrying the HIV virus are understandably anxious and depressed (Andersen, 1989; Antoni & others, 1991). Might promoting their fighting spirit aid their

"*When the heart is at ease, the body is healthy.*"
Chinese proverb

"*A cheerful heart is a good medicine, but a downcast spirit dries up the bones.*"
Proverbs 17:22

Supporting Survival *This "Sharing Group" is part of California's Wellness Community program, which promotes stress reduction and optimism as possible boosts for its cancer-patient participants.*

"I didn't give myself cancer."

Barbara Boggs Sigmund, 1939–1990
Mayor of Princeton, New Jersey

When organic causes of illness are unknown, it is tempting to invent psychological explanations. Before the germ that causes tuberculosis was discovered, personality explanations of TB were popular (Sontag, 1978).

survival? Can hope boost the body by alleviating negative emotions that suppress the cancer-fighting immune system?

With cancer patients, several studies offer hope. Mastectomy patients who display a determination to conquer their breast cancer survive longer than do those who are stoic or feel hopeless (Hall & Goldstein, 1986; Pettingale & others, 1985). A study of 86 women undergoing breast cancer therapy at Stanford University Medical School found that those who participated in weekly group therapy survived an average of 37 months, double the 19-month average survival rate among the nonparticipants (Spiegel & others, 1989). The investigator, psychiatrist David Spiegel (1993), was stunned. He expected the support groups to alleviate cancer-related emotional distress, but he was intending to show that more positive emotions would *not* influence the course of cancer. At least half a dozen research teams are now repeating his study. If Spiegel's finding proves reliable, it will surely reinforce efforts to train physicians to communicate with patients in ways that minimize resignation and sustain hope.

One danger in publicizing reports on attitudes and cancer is that they may lead some patients to blame themselves for their cancer—"If only I had been more expressive, relaxed, and hopeful." A corollary danger is a "wellness macho" among the healthy, who credit their health to their healthy character and lay a guilt trip on the ill: "She has cancer? That's what you get for holding your feelings in and being so nice." Dying thus becomes "the ultimate failure."

In noting the link between emotions and cancer, we must remember that stress does not create cancer cells. Rather, it affects their growth by weakening the body's natural defenses against a few proliferating, malignant cells. Although a relaxed, hopeful state may enhance these defenses, we must be aware of the thin line that divides science from wishful thinking. The physiological processes at work in advanced cancer or AIDS are not likely to be derailed by avoiding stress or by a relaxed but determined spirit (Kessler & others, 1991).

We must also remember that our emotional reactivity is partly inherited (recall page 82). As theologian Reinhold Niebuhr recognized in his "serenity prayer," we do well to accept those things about ourselves that we cannot change, to change those things that we can, and to seek wisdom to discern the difference. By studying the interplay among emotions, the brain, and the immune system, health psychologists seek the wisdom needed to distinguish between pseudoscientific hocus-pocus and the genuine effects of emotions on health.

Conditioning the Immune System

A hay fever sufferer sees the flower on the restaurant table and, not realizing it is plastic, begins to sneeze. Such experiences hint that stress is not the only psychological influence on the body's ailments. Simple classical conditioning may be an added influence. This raises an intriguing question: If conditioning affects the body's overt physiological responses, might it affect the immune system as well?

Psychologist Robert Ader and immunologist Nicholas Cohen (1985) discovered that the answer is yes. Ader came upon this discovery while researching taste aversion in rats. He paired the rats' drinking of saccharin-sweetened water with injections of a drug that happened to suppress immune functioning. After repeated pairings, sweetened water alone triggered immune suppression as if the drug had been given (Figure 10–18). Such conditioned immune suppression can triple an animal's likelihood of growing a tumor when fed a carcinogen (Blom & others, 1994).

Figure 10–18 The Conditioning of Immune Suppression *After Ader and Cohen associated sweetened water with a drug that causes immune suppression in rats, the inert substance alone triggered the conditioned immune response.*

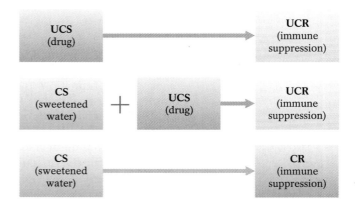

Many questions about the role of the immune system and how to harness its healing potential remain unanswered. If it is possible to condition the immune system's suppression, should it not also be possible to condition its enhancement? Might this be one way in which placebos—treatments that have no biochemical effect—promote healing? Can a placebo sometimes elicit the same healthful state produced by an actual drug? Research now under way may soon answer such questions.

For now, we can view the toll that stress sometimes takes on our resistance to disease as a price we pay for the adaptive benefits of stress (Figure 10–19). Stress invigorates our lives by arousing and motivating us. An unstressed life would hardly be challenging or productive. Moreover, spending our resources in fighting or fleeing an external threat aids our immediate survival. But it does

Figure 10–19 Negative Emotions Can Have a Variety of Health-Related Consequences *This is especially so when experienced by "disease-prone" angry, depressed, or anxious persons. Of course, disease also results from many other factors.*

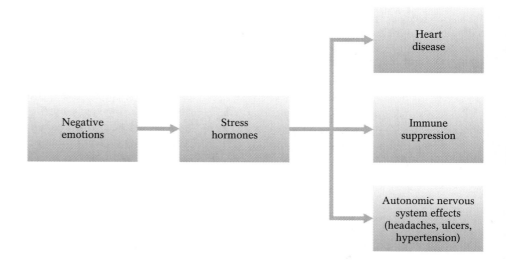

so at the cost of diminished resources for fighting internal threats to our body's health. When the stress is momentary, the cost is negligible. When uncontrollable aggravations persist, however, the cost may become considerable.

All this new behavioral medicine research provides yet another reminder of one of contemporary psychology's overriding themes. Mind and body continuously interact. Everything psychological is simultaneously biological. And because psychological states are biological events, they influence other parts of our biological system. As the Indian sage Santi Parva recognized more than 4000 years ago, "Mental disorders arise from physical causes, and likewise physical disorders arise from mental causes."

! *Rehearse It*

14. The physiologist Walter Cannon described the role of the sympathetic nervous system in preparing the body for fight or flight. Hans Selye extended Cannon's findings by describing the body's adaptive response to stress in general. Selye's general adaptation syndrome (GAS) consists of an alarm reaction followed by

a. fight or flight.
b. resistance and exhaustion.
c. challenge and recovery.
d. stressful life events.

15. In the months following a catastrophe, such as an earthquake or nuclear accident, there is a higher than usual number of short-term illnesses and stress-related psychological disorders. Following widowhood, there is an increased risk of illness and death. These findings suggest that

a. daily hassles have adverse health consequences.
b. experiencing a very stressful event increases one's vulnerability to illness and death.
c. the amount of stress felt is directly related to the number of stressors involved.
d. having a negative outlook has an adverse effect on recovery from illness.

16. Stressors are events that we appraise as threatening or challenging. Research suggests that the most significant sources of stress are

a. catastrophes.
b. traumatic events, such as the loss of a loved one.
c. daily hassles.
d. threatening events that we witness.

17. The stress we experience depends on how we perceive the events of our lives. A person (or animal) is most likely to find an event stressful and to suffer reduced immunity and other adverse health effects if the event seems

a. painful or harmful.
b. predictable and negative.
c. uncontrollable and negative.
d. both repellent and attractive.

18. Cardiologists Meyer Friedman, Ray Rosenman, and their colleagues observed that heart attacks were more frequent in Type A men—in those who appeared to be hard-driving, verbally aggressive, and anger prone. The component of Type A behavior linked most closely to coronary heart disease is

a. living a fast-paced life-style.
b. working in a competitive area.
c. meeting deadlines and challenges.
d. feeling angry and negative much of the time.

19. Evidence suggests that disease-fighting mechanisms are weakened during times of high stress, for example, following the death of a loved one. Stress hormones suppress the lymphocytes, which ordinarily attack bacteria, viruses, cancer cells, and other foreign substances. The stress hormones are released mainly in response to a signal from the

a. lymphocytes and macrophages.
b. brain.
c. upper respiratory tract.
d. adrenal glands.

20. Research has shown that people are at increased risk for cancer a year or so after experiencing depression, helplessness, or bereavement. In describing this link between emotions and cancer, researchers are quick to point out that

a. accumulated stress that is not relieved by positive emotions poses the greatest threat to people who are genetically vulnerable to cancer.
b. anger is the negative emotion most closely linked to cancer.
c. stress does not create cancer cells, but it weakens the body's natural defenses against them.
d. feeling optimistic about chances of survival ensures that a cancer patient will get well.

21. In testing taste aversion in rats, researchers paired the rats' drinking of saccharin-sweetened water with injections of a drug that suppressed immune functioning. After repeated pairings, sweetened water *alone* triggered immune suppression. These results suggest that

a. the immune system is under direct control of the hypothalamus.
b. classical conditioning may influence the body's ailments.
c. placebos are as effective as actual drugs in treating the body's ailments.
d. external threats diminish our body's ability to fight internal threats.

Promoting Health

Traditionally, people have sought out medical doctors for the diagnosis and treatment of disease. That, say the advocates of behavioral medicine, is like ignoring a car's maintenance and going to a mechanic only when the car breaks down. Now that we realize that our attitudes and behaviors affect our health, attention is focusing more and more on health maintenance—on ways of coping with stress, preventing illness, and promoting well-being.

Coping With Stress

13. How do people cope with stress, and what stress management techniques are effective?

Coping with stress can mean confronting or escaping the problem and taking steps to prevent its recurrence. Coping can involve fight or flight, repelling the challenge or avoiding it, solving the problem or mentally distancing oneself from it. Yet stressors are an unavoidable part of life. This fact, coupled with the growing awareness that recurring stress correlates with heart disease, lowered immunity, and other bodily ailments, gives us a clear message. If the stress cannot be eliminated by changing or ignoring the situation, we had best learn to manage it. Stress management includes aerobic exercise, biofeedback, relaxation, and social support networks.

Aerobic Exercise

Studies suggest that **aerobic exercise**—sustained exercise that increases heart and lung fitness—can reduce stress, depression, and anxiety. The third of people who regularly exercise cope with stressful events better, exhibit more self-confidence, and are less often depressed than those who exercise less (Brown, 1991; Hogan, 1989; *Prevention*, 1995). But when stated the other way around—stressed and depressed people exercise less—cause and effect become unclear.

Experiments resolve the ambiguity by randomly assigning stressed, depressed, or anxious people either to aerobic exercise treatments or to other treatments. In one such experiment, Lisa McCann and David Holmes (1984) assigned one-third of a group of mildly depressed female college students to a program of aerobic exercise and another third to a treatment of relaxation exercises; the remaining third, a control group, received no treatment. As Figure 10–20 shows, 10 weeks later the women in the aerobic exercise program reported the greatest decrease in depression. Many of them had, quite literally, run away from their troubles.

More than 100 other studies confirm that exercise reduces depression and anxiety (Petruzzello & others, 1991; Scott & Pepperell, 1992). Repeated surveys, some by government agencies, reveal that Canadians and Americans are more self-confident, self-disciplined, and psychologically resilient if physically fit (Stephens, 1988). Even a 10-minute walk stimulates 2 hours of increased well-being by raising energy levels and lowering tension (Thayer, 1987, 1993).

Other research reveals that exercise also benefits health. One 16-year study of 17,000 middle-aged Harvard alumni found that those who exercised regularly were likely to live longer (Paffenbarger & others, 1986). A study of 15,000 Control Data Corporation employees found that those who exercised averaged 25 percent fewer hospital days than those who didn't (Anderson & Jose, 1987). And a digest of data from 43 studies revealed that, compared with inactive adults, people who exercise suffer half as many heart attacks (Powell & others, 1987). The "movement movement" is reaping dividends. So off your duffs, couch potatoes!

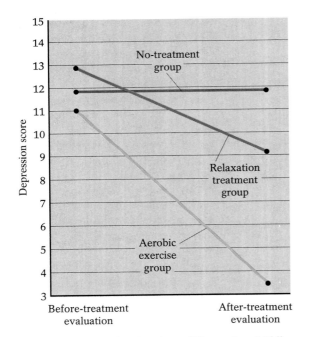

Figure 10–20 Aerobic Exercise and Depression *Mildly depressed college women who participated in an aerobic exercise program showed markedly reduced depression compared with those who did relaxation exercises or received no treatment. (From McCann & Holmes, 1984.)*

aerobic exercise Sustained exercise that increases heart and lung fitness; may also alleviate depression and anxiety.

biofeedback A system for electronically recording, amplifying, and feeding back information regarding a subtle physiological state, such as blood pressure or muscle tension.

Researchers are now wondering *why* aerobic exercise alleviates the effects of stress and negative emotions. They know that exercise strengthens the heart and lowers both blood pressure and the blood pressure reaction to stress (Perkins & others, 1986; Roviario & others, 1984). Perhaps exercise also orders up chemicals from our body's internal pharmacy by increasing production of mood-boosting neurotransmitters such as norepinephrine, serotonin, and the endorphins. Perhaps the emotional benefits of exercise are a side effect of increased body warmth or of the muscle relaxation and sounder sleep that occur afterward. Or perhaps a sense of accomplishment and an improved physique enhance one's emotional state. Such possibilities help explain why exercise relieves stress and boosts well-being (Martinsen, 1987).

Biofeedback

When a few psychologists started experimenting with ways to train people to bring their heart rate and blood pressure under conscious control, many of their colleagues thought them foolish. These functions are, after all, controlled by the autonomic ("involuntary") nervous system. Then, in the late 1960s, ingenious experiments by respected psychologists began to make the doubters wonder. Neal Miller, for one, found that rats could modify their heartbeat if given pleasurable brain stimulation when their heartbeat increased or decreased. Later research revealed that some paralyzed humans (who cannot use their skeletal muscles) could also learn to control their blood pressure (Miller & Brucker, 1979).

Miller was experimenting with **biofeedback**, a system of recording, amplifying, and feeding back information about subtle physiological responses. Biofeedback instruments have been likened to a mirror (Norris, 1986). The instruments no more control one's body than a mirror combs one's hair. Rather, by reflecting the results of a person's own efforts, they allow the person to assess which techniques are most effective in controlling a particular physiological response.

In the example in Figure 10–21, a sensor records tension in the forehead muscle of a headache sufferer. A computer processes this physiological information and instantly feeds it back to the person in some easily understood image. As a person relaxes the forehead muscle, a pointer on a screen may go lower or a light may grow brighter. The patient's task is to learn to control the pointer or the light and thereby learn to control the tension in the forehead muscle and the accompanying headaches.

Initially, biofeedback researchers and practitioners reported that people could learn to increase their production of alpha brain waves, warm their hands, and lower their blood pressure—all signs of a more relaxed state. These reports triggered both excitement and some 4000 studies, including more than

Figure 10–21 Biofeedback Systems *Biofeedback systems, such as this one, which records tension in the forehead muscle of a headache sufferer, allow people to monitor their subtle physiological responses.*

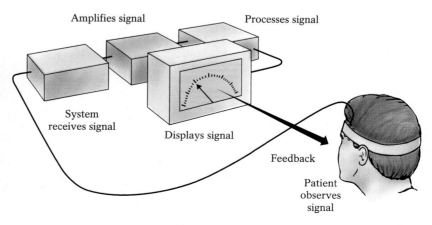

Amplifies signal

Processes signal

System receives signal

Displays signal

Feedback

Patient observes signal

400 in Russia (Sokhadze & Shtark, 1991). A decade later, when researchers stepped back to assess the results, they decided the initial claims for biofeedback were overblown and oversold (Miller, 1985). Biofeedback does enable some people to influence their finger temperature and forehead-muscle tension, and it can help somewhat in reducing the intensity of migraine headaches and chronic pain (King & Montgomery, 1980; Qualls & Sheehan, 1981; Turk & others, 1979). But other, simpler methods of relaxation, which require no expensive equipment, produce many of the same benefits.

Relaxation

If relaxation is an important part of biofeedback, then might relaxation exercises alone be a natural antidote to stress? Cardiologist Herbert Benson (1976, 1984, 1987, 1992) became intrigued with this possibility when he found that experienced meditators could decrease their blood pressure, heart rate, and oxygen consumption and raise their fingertip temperature. You can experience the essence of this *relaxation response*, as Benson calls it, right now: Assume a comfortable position, breathe deeply, and relax your muscles from foot to face. Now, concentrate on a single word or a phrase—perhaps, as for 80 percent of Benson's patients, a favorite prayer. Close your eyes and let other thoughts drift away when they intrude as you repeat this phrase continually for 10 to 20 minutes. Simply by setting aside a quiet time or two each day, many people report enjoying greater tranquility and a spiritual sense of closeness to a power beyond themselves. Stress worsens pain, infertility, and insomnia, and it also suppresses the immune system. Meditative relaxation counteracts all these effects, reports Benson. One astonishing study assigned 73 residents of homes for the elderly either to daily meditation or to none. After 3 years, one-fourth of the nonmeditators had died, whereas all the meditators were still alive (Alexander & others, 1989).

If Type A heart attack victims could be taught to relax, might their risk of another attack be reduced? To find out, Meyer Friedman and his colleagues randomly assigned hundreds of middle-aged heart attack survivors in San Francisco to one of two groups. The first group received standard advice from cardiologists concerning medications, diet, and exercise habits. The second group received similar advice plus continuing support and counseling on how to slow down and relax—by walking, talking, and eating more slowly; smiling at others and laughing at themselves; admitting mistakes; taking time to enjoy

Meditation—a modern phenomenon with a long history: "Sit down alone and in silence. Lower your head, shut your eyes, breathe out gently, and imagine yourself looking into your own heart. . . . As you breathe out, say 'Lord Jesus Christ, have mercy on me.'. . . Try to put all other thoughts aside. Be calm, be patient and repeat the process very frequently" (Gregory of Sinai, died 1346).

Learning the "Relaxation Response" *Relaxation training is a component of many stress-reduction programs. At Boston's Deaconess Hospital, hypertension patients learn meditation techniques that counteract stress.*

Figure 10–22 Recurrent Heart Attacks and Life-Style Modification *The San Francisco Recurrent Coronary Prevention Project offered heart attack survivors counseling from a cardiologist. Those who were also guided in modifying their Type A life-style suffered fewer repeat heart attacks. (From Friedman & Ulmer, 1984.)*

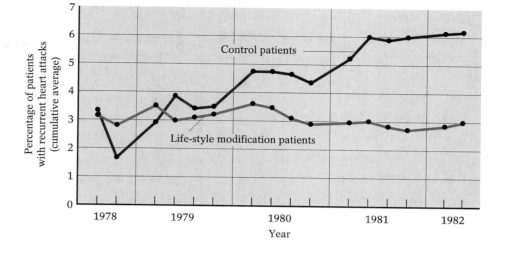

The United States spends three times more per person on health care than does Great Britain (partly because the average income of a U.S. doctor is nearly four times that of a British doctor). In the United States, average life expectancy is 75; in Britain it is also 75 *(Fein, 1992; Information Please Almanac; Roemer, 1991).*

life; and renewing their religious faith. As Figure 10–22 indicates, during the ensuing 3 years the second group experienced half as many repeat heart attacks as the first group. This, wrote the exuberant Friedman, is an unprecedented, spectacular reduction in heart attack recurrence. A smaller-scale British study similarly divided heart attack-prone people into control and life-style modification groups (Eysenck & Grossarth-Maticek, 1991). During the next 13 years, it also found a 50 percent reduction in death rate among those trained to alter their thinking and life-style.

Social Support

Linda and Emily had much in common. When interviewed for a study conducted by UCLA social psychologist Shelley Taylor (1989), both Los Angeles women had married, raised three children, suffered comparable breast tumors, and recovered from surgery and 6 months of chemotherapy. But there was a difference. Linda, a widow in her early fifties, was living alone, her children scattered in Atlanta, Boston, and Europe. "She had become odd in ways that people sometimes do when they are isolated," reported Taylor. "Having no one with whom to share her thoughts on a daily basis, she unloaded them somewhat inappropriately with strangers, including our interviewer."

Interviewing Emily was difficult in a different way. Phone calls interrupted. Her children, all living nearby, were in and out of the house, dropping things off with a quick kiss. Her husband called from his office for a brief chat. Two dogs roamed the house, greeting visitors enthusiastically. All in all, Emily "seemed a serene and contented person, basking in the warmth of her family."

Three years later the researchers tried to reinterview the women. Linda, they learned, had died 2 years before. Emily was still lovingly supported by her family and friends and was as happy and healthy as ever.

Because no two cancers are identical, we can't be certain that different situations led to Linda's and Emily's fates. But they do illustrate a conclusion drawn from several large studies: Social support—feeling liked, affirmed, and encouraged by intimate friends and family—promotes happiness and health.

Humans aren't the only source of stress-buffering comfort. After stressful events, Medicare patients who have a dog or other companionable pet are less likely to visit their doctor (Siegel, 1990).

If this result seems obvious, imagine why close relationships could contribute to *illness*. Relationships are often fraught with stress, especially in crowded living conditions lacking privacy (Evans & others, 1989). "Hell is others," wrote Jean-Paul Sartre. Peter Warr and Roy Payne (1982) at the University of Sheffield asked a representative sample of British adults what, if anything, had emotionally strained them the day before. "Family" was their most frequent answer. Even when well-meaning, family intrusions can be stressful. And stress, as we have seen, contributes to heart disease, hypertension, and a suppressed immune system.

On balance, however, close relationships more often contribute to health and happiness. Asked what prompted yesterday's times of pleasure, the same British sample, by an even larger margin, again answered "family." For most of us, family relationships provide not only our greatest heartaches, but also our greatest comfort and joy.

Moreover, seven massive investigations, each following thousands of people for several years, reveal that close relationships affect health. Compared with those having few social ties, people are less likely to die prematurely if supported by close relationships with friends, family, or fellow members of church, work, or other support groups (Cohen, 1988; House & others, 1988; Nelson, 1988). Some recent examples:

> Recall the study that followed leukemia patients preparing to undergo bone marrow transplants. Two years later, only 20 percent of those who said they had little social support from their family or friends were still alive. Among those who felt strong emotional support, the 2-year survival rate was 54 percent (Colon & others, 1991).

> A study of 1234 heart attack patients found a near-double rate of a recurring attack within 6 months among those living alone (Case & others, 1992).

> A study of 1965 heart disease patients revealed a 5-year survival rate of 82 percent among those married or having a confidant, but only 50 percent among those not (Williams & others, 1992).

> A 70-year study following 1528 high-IQ score California children found that those who had the support of two married parents throughout their childhood outlived children of divorce by about 4 years (Friedman & others, 1995).

Close relationships provide the opportunity to confide painful feelings. In one study, health psychologists James Pennebaker and Robin O'Heeron (1984) contacted the surviving spouses of people who had committed suicide or died in car accidents. Those who bore their grief alone had more health problems than those who openly expressed it. Talking about our troubles can be "open-heart therapy."

In a simulated confessional, Pennebaker asked volunteers to share with a hidden experimenter some upsetting events that had been preying on their minds. He asked some of the volunteers to describe a trivial event before they divulged the troubling one. Physiological measures revealed that their bodies remained tense the whole time they talked about the trivial event; they relaxed only when they later confided the cause of their turmoil. Even writing about personal traumas in a diary can help. When volunteers in other experiments did this, they had fewer health problems during the ensuing 4 to 6 months (Pennebaker, 1990). As one subject explained, "Although I have not talked with anyone about what I wrote, I was finally able to deal with it, work through the pain instead of trying to block it out. Now it doesn't hurt to think about it." Suppressed traumas sometimes eat away at us and affect our physical health. Consider:

> When Pennebaker surveyed more than 700 undergraduate women, he found that about 1 in 12 reported a traumatic sexual experience in childhood. Compared with women who had experienced nonsexual traumas, such as parental death or divorce, the sexually abused women—especially those who had kept their secret to themselves—reported more headaches and stomach ailments.

"Woe to one who is alone and falls and does not have another to help."

Ecclesiastes 4:10

"I get by with a little help from my friends."

John Lennon and Paul McCartney
Sgt. Pepper's Lonely Hearts Club Band, 1967

Friendships Are Good Medicine *Several long-term studies of thousands of people have found that individuals with close supportive relationships are less likely than socially isolated people to die prematurely.*

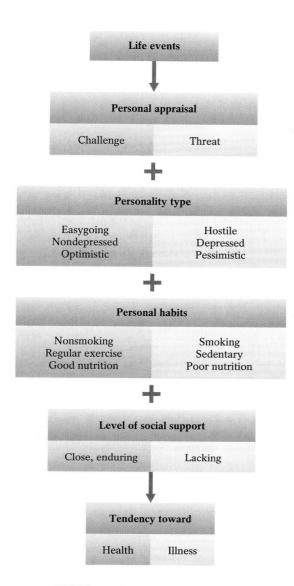

Life events

↓

Personal appraisal

Challenge	Threat

+

Personality type

Easygoing Nondepressed Optimistic	Hostile Depressed Pessimistic

+

Personal habits

Nonsmoking Regular exercise Good nutrition	Smoking Sedentary Poor nutrition

+

Level of social support

Close, enduring	Lacking

↓

Tendency toward

Health	Illness

Figure 10–23 Coping With Stress *Life events can be debilitating or not. It all depends on how we appraise them and whether the stresses are buffered by a stress-resistant disposition, healthy habits, and enduring social support.*

⇨ After the 1989 San Francisco Bay Area earthquake, residents talked nonstop about the upheaval for about 2 weeks. Then the talking died down as people tired of hearing others' opinions and feelings. ("Thank you for not sharing your earthquake experience," read one popular T-shirt.) But for another month people kept thinking about the quake. During this inhibition phase—when people kept ruminating but with less disclosure of their anxieties and feelings—hostility, nightmares, and health problems peaked (Pennebaker & Harber, 1993).

⇨ Pennebaker and his colleagues (1989) also invited 33 Holocaust survivors to spend 2 hours recalling their experiences. Many did so in intimate detail never before disclosed. Most watched and showed family and friends a videotape of their recollections in the weeks following. Again, those who were most self-disclosing had the most improved health 14 months later. Although talking about a stressful event can temporarily arouse people, it calms them in the long run (Mendolia & Kleck, 1993). Confiding is good for the soul.

Sustained emotional reactions to stressful events can be debilitating. However, the level of stress experienced depends on the person and the environment. Nothing is stressful until we appraise it as such. Thus, our personalities and interpretations influence how we react emotionally when stressful things happen. Moreover, the toxic impact of stressful events can be buffered by a relaxed, healthy life-style and by the comfort and aid provided by supportive friends and family (Figure 10–23).

❗ *Rehearse It*

22. A number of studies reveal that aerobic exercise raises energy levels and helps alleviate depression and anxiety. The reasons for these emotional effects of exercise are unclear. One explanation is that exercise triggers the release of mood-boosting neurotransmitters such as norepinephrine, serotonin, and

a. the placebos.
b. the endorphins.
c. epinephrine.
d. acetylcholine.

23. Neal Miller found that rats could learn to control their heart rate when they were rewarded with pleasurable brain stimulation for doing so. Later research has shown that humans can also learn to control blood

pressure through biofeedback. Biofeedback teaches people to exercise control over functions that are usually controlled by

a. the autonomic nervous system.
b. conscious thought.
c. the immune system.
d. external stimuli.

24. Biofeedback is a system for electronically recording, amplifying, and feeding back information about physiological states that we are usually not conscious of—including finger temperature and forehead-muscle tension. Using a biofeedback system to control finger temperature is most similar to

a. programming a computer to control appliances.

b. using an automatic pilot to fly a plane.
c. using a mirror to practice a dance.
d. using training wheels to learn to ride a bicycle.

25. Long-term studies of thousands of people have shown that people who have close relationships—a strong social support system—are less likely to die prematurely than those who do not. These studies provide evidence that

a. social ties can be a source of stress.
b. people who lose a close relationship are at risk for illness.
c. Type A behavior is responsible for many premature deaths.
d. social support has a beneficial effect on health.

Reviewing *Emotions, Stress, and Health*

1.   What are the components of an emotion?

Emotions are psychological responses of the whole organism that involve an interplay among (1) physiological arousal, (2) expressive behaviors, and (3) conscious experience.

The Physiology of Emotion

2.   What physiological changes accompany emotional arousal?

In an emergency, the sympathetic nervous system automatically mobilizes the body for fight or flight, directing the adrenal glands to release hormones that in turn increase heart rate, blood pressure, and blood sugar level. Other changes include tensed muscles, dry mouth, dilated pupils, slowed digestion, and increased sweating. In day-to-day life, our performance on a task is usually best when arousal is moderate, though this varies with the difficulty of the task. The physical arousal that occurs with one emotion is in most ways indistinguishable from that which occurs with another. However, scientists have discovered subtle differences in the brain pathways and hormones associated with different emotions.

Expressing Emotion

3.   How do we communicate nonverbally? Are nonverbal expressions of emotion universally understood?

Much of our communication is through the silent language of the body. Even very thin (seconds-long) videotaped slices of behavior can reveal feelings. Gestures appear to be culturally determined, but facial expressions, such as those of happiness and fear, are common the world over.

4.   Do our facial expressions influence our feelings?

Expressions not only communicate emotion to others, they also amplify our own emotions and signal our bodies to respond accordingly.

Experiencing Emotion

5.   What are the causes and consequences of anger?

Anger is most often aroused by events that are not only frustrating or insulting but also interpreted as willful, unjustified, and avoidable. Other negative emotions, such as depression, can also feed anger. Although blowing off steam may be temporarily calming, it does not, in the long run, reduce anger. Expressing anger can actually arouse more anger.

6.   What are the causes and consequences of happiness?

A good mood boosts people's perceptions of the world and their willingness to help others. The moods triggered by the day's good or bad events seldom last beyond that day. Even significant good events, such as a substantial raise in income, seldom increase happiness for long. We can explain the relativity of happiness with the adaptation-level principle and relative deprivation principle. Nevertheless, some people are usually happier than others, and researchers have identified factors that predict such happiness.

Theories of Emotion

7.   What issue distinguishes the James-Lange and Cannon-Bard theories of emotion?

One of the oldest theoretical controversies regarding emotion is whether we feel emotion after we notice our body responses (as James and Lange proposed) or at the same time that our bodies respond (as Cannon and Bard believed).

8.   What is the relationship between thinking and feeling?

A more recent controversy among emotion researchers concerns whether we can experience human emotions apart from cognition. Can we feel before we think? Stanley Schachter's two-factor theory of emotion contends that the cognitive labels we put on our states of arousal are an essential ingredient of emotion. Richard Lazarus agrees that cognition is essential: Many important emotions arise from our interpretations or inferences. Robert Zajonc, however, believes that some simple emotional responses occur instantly, not only outside our conscious awareness but before any cognitive processing occurs. The issue has practical implications: To the degree that emotions are rooted in thinking, we can hope to change them by changing our thinking.

Stress and Health

9.   What is stress?

Stress is the process by which we appraise and respond to events that challenge or threaten us. Walter Cannon viewed stress as a "fight or flight" system. Hans Selye saw it as a three-stage, general adaptation syndrome (alarm/resistance/exhaustion).

10.   What provokes stress?

Modern research on stress has assessed the health consequences of cataclysmic events, significant life changes, and daily hassles. Events are especially stressful when perceived as both negative and uncontrollable. Optimists cope more successfully with stress and enjoy better health.

11.   Who is most vulnerable to heart disease?

Coronary heart disease, North America's number one cause of death, has been linked with the competitive, hard-driving, impatient, and (especially) anger-prone Type A personality. Under stress, the body of a reactive, hostile person secretes more of the hormones that accelerate the narrowing of the heart's artery walls.

12.   How does stress make us vulnerable to disease?

In addition to contributing to heart disease and a variety of psychophysiological illnesses, stress can suppress the immune system, making a person more vulnerable to infections and cancer. New experiments indicate that the immune system's responses can be influenced by conditioning.

Promoting Health

13. How do people cope with stress, and what stress management techniques are effective?

Among the components of stress management programs are aerobic exercise, biofeedback, and relaxation. Although the degree of mind control over the body that can be gained through biofeedback has fallen short of early expectations, biofeedback has become one accepted method for helping people control ailments such as tension headaches and high blood pressure. Simple relaxation exercises offer some of the same benefits. Counseling Type A heart attack survivors to slow down and relax has helped them lower their rate of recurring attacks. Social support also helps people cope, partly by buffering the impact of stress.

Terms and Concepts to Remember

emotion, p. 335

polygraph, p. 337

catharsis, p. 345

feel-good, do-good phenomenon, p. 346

adaptation-level principle, p. 348

relative deprivation, p. 349

James-Lange theory, p. 352

Cannon-Bard theory, p. 352

two-factor theory, p. 353

behavioral medicine, p. 356

health psychology, p. 356

stress, p. 357

general adaptation syndrome (GAS), p. 357

coronary heart disease, p. 361

Type A, p. 362

Type B, p. 362

psychophysiological illness, p. 363

lymphocytes, p. 363

aerobic exercise, p. 368

biofeedback, p. 369

Rehearse It Answer Key

1. b.	**2.** d.	**3.** d.	**4.** a.	**5.** b.	**6.** b.	**7.** a.	**8.** d.	**9.** c.
10. b.	**11.** b.	**12.** b.	**13.** c.	**14.** b.	**15.** b.	**16.** c.	**17.** c.	**18.** d.
19. b.	**20.** c.	**21.** b.	**22.** b.	**23.** a.	**24.** c.	**25.** d.		

Critical Thinking Exercise

Now that you have read and reviewed Chapter 10, take your learning a step further by testing your critical thinking skills on the following passage. You may find it helpful to review the text material in the section "Theories of Emotion" before completing this exercise.

Subjects in a recent study were shown an erotic movie while they were in each of three phases of recovery from aerobic exercise. Subjects first pedaled an exercise bicycle intensely enough to produce significant physical arousal. During each of the three recovery phases, the subjects were asked (1) whether they still felt physically aroused from the exercise and (2) how sexually excited they felt by the film. The subjects' actual physical arousal (heart rate) was measured throughout the experiment. During the first two phases of recovery, all of the subjects still showed signs of actual physical arousal—although by the second phase, they said they no longer *felt* physically aroused from the exercise. By the third phase, the subjects no longer showed signs of physical arousal from the exercise. The subjects reported feeling significantly more sexually excited by the film during the second phase of exercise recovery than during the first and third phases.

1. How well would the James-Lange theory explain the results of this experiment? What variations in reported feelings of sexual excitement would this theory have predicted in the three phases of exercise recovery?

2. How well would the Cannon-Bard theory explain the results of this experiment? What variations in reported feelings of sexual excitement would this theory have predicted in the three phases of exercise recovery?

3. How well would Schachter's two-factor theory explain the results of this experiment? What variations in reported feelings of sexual excitement would this theory have predicted in the three phases of exercise recovery?

Check your progress on becoming a critical thinker by comparing your answers with the sample answers found in Appendix B.

Personality

The Psychoanalytic Perspective

Exploring the Unconscious

Assessing the Unconscious

Evaluating the Psychoanalytic Perspective

The Trait Perspective

Exploring Traits

Assessing Traits

Evaluating the Trait Perspective

The Humanistic Perspective

Exploring the Self

Assessing the Self

Evaluating the Humanistic Perspective

The Social-Cognitive Perspective

Exploring Behavior in Situations

Assessing Behavior in Situations

Evaluating the Social-Cognitive Perspective

1. What is personality?

Novelist William Faulkner was a master at creating characters with vivid personalities.[1] One of his creations, Ike McCaslin, appears at various ages in more than a dozen novels and short stories. Ike is highly principled, and consistently so. At age 10 he feels a deep reverence for the wilderness and its creatures. At 21 he forfeits a "tainted" inheritance. In his late seventies he counsels his nephew to use his land responsibly. Ike the adult is an extension of Ike the child.

Another Faulkner character, Jason Compson, is a selfish, whining 4-year-old in the opening section of *The Sound and the Fury*, and a selfish, screaming 34-year-old as the novel closes. As head of the Compson household, he verbally abuses family members and household servants. Lying, threatening, conniving, he is a self-centered child who becomes a self-centered adult.

Faulkner's characters, as they appear and reappear throughout his fiction, exhibit the distinctiveness and consistency that define personality. The preceding chapters have emphasized how we are similar—how we all develop, perceive, learn, remember, think, and feel. This chapter emphasizes our individuality. Your individual **personality** is your characteristic pattern of thinking, feeling, and acting. If your behavior pattern is unusually distinctive and consistent—if, say, you are strikingly outgoing, whether at a party or in a classroom—people are likely to say that you have a "strong" personality.

Actually, much of this book deals with personality. We have considered biological influences on personality, personality development across the life span, and personality-related aspects of learning, motivation, health, and emotion. In later chapters we will study disorders of personality and social influences on personality.

In this chapter we will explore and evaluate four major perspectives on personality:

▶ Sigmund Freud's *psychoanalytic* theory proposes that childhood sexuality and unconscious motivations influence personality.

personality An individual's characteristic pattern of thinking, feeling, and acting.

[1]Faulkner scholar Nancy Nicodemus assisted with these examples.

free association In psychoanalysis, a method of exploring the unconscious in which the person relaxes and says whatever comes to mind, no matter how trivial or embarrassing.

psychoanalysis The technique of treating psychological disorders by seeking to expose and interpret unconscious tensions. Freud's psychoanalytic theory of personality sought to explain what he observed during psychoanalysis.

unconscious According to Freud, a reservoir of mostly unacceptable thoughts, wishes, feelings, and memories. According to contemporary research psychologists, information processing of which we are unaware.

preconscious A store of information that is not conscious, but is retrievable into conscious awareness.

Sigmund Freud (1856–1939) *"I was the only worker in a new field."*

"Two passengers leaned against the ship's rail and stared at the sea. 'There sure is a lot of water in the ocean,' said one. 'Yes,' answered his friend, 'we've only seen the top of it.'"

Psychologist George A. Miller (1962)

- *Trait* researchers identify specific dimensions of our personality.
- The *humanistic* approach focuses on our inner capacities for growth and self-fulfillment.
- *Social-cognitive* psychologists emphasize how we shape and are shaped by our environment.

The Psychoanalytic Perspective

Well before entering the University of Vienna in 1873, the youthful Sigmund Freud showed signs of the independence and brilliance that often mark people of eminence. He had a prodigious memory. He so loved serious reading that he once ran up a bookstore debt beyond his means, feeding his insatiable interest in plays, poetry, and philosophy. As a teen he often took his evening meal in his tiny bedroom, to lose no time from his studies.

After medical school, Freud began a private practice, specializing in nervous disorders. Before long, however, he faced patients whose disorders made no neurological sense. A patient might have lost all feeling in her hand—yet there is no sensory nerve that when damaged would numb the entire hand and nothing else. Noting that hypnosis could also produce such symptoms, Freud wondered whether they might be psychologically rather than physiologically caused. His wonderings set his mind running in a direction that was destined to change human self-understanding.

Exploring the Unconscious

2. What role do unconscious dynamics play in Freud's theory of personality?

While experimenting with hypnosis, Freud decided that the loss of feeling in one's hand might be caused by the fear of touching one's genitals; that blindness or deafness might be caused by not wanting to see or hear something that aroused intense anxiety. In time, Freud began to see patients with a variety of symptoms. Given patients' uneven capacity for hypnosis, he turned to **free association**—in which he merely told the patient to relax and say whatever came to mind, no matter how embarrassing or trivial. Freud believed that free association produced a chain of thought leading into the patient's unconscious, thereby retrieving and releasing painful unconscious memories, often from childhood. Freud called the process **psychoanalysis**.

Underlying Freud's psychoanalytic conception of personality was his belief that the mind is like an iceberg—mostly hidden. Our conscious awareness is the part of the iceberg that floats above the surface. Below the surface is the much larger, **unconscious** region containing thoughts, wishes, feelings, and memories, of which we are largely unaware. Some of these thoughts we store temporarily in a **preconscious** area, from which we can retrieve them at will into conscious awareness. Of greater interest to Freud was the mass of unacceptable passions and thoughts that he believed we *repress*, or forcibly block from our consciousness because they would be so painful to acknowledge. Freud believed that, although we are not consciously aware of them, these troublesome feelings and ideas powerfully influence us. In his view, our unacknowledged impulses express themselves in disguised forms—the work we choose, the beliefs we hold, our daily habits, our troubling symptoms. In such ways, the unconscious seeps into our thoughts and actions.

"Good morning, beheaded—uh, I mean beloved."

Freud believed he glimpsed the unconscious not only in people's free associations, beliefs, habits, and symptoms but also in their dreams and slips of the tongue and pen. He called dreams the "royal road to the unconscious." By analyzing people's dreams, Freud believed he could reveal the nature of their inner conflicts and release their inner tensions. Slips while reading, writing, and speaking suggested to Freud that what we say and do may reflect the workings of our unconscious minds. Consider his example of a financially stressed patient who, not wanting any large pills, said, "Please do not give me any bills, because I cannot swallow them." For Freud, something more than random error explains the new apartment occupant who misspoke "It suits my needs" as "It seats my nudes." Jokes, too, he viewed as a way to express repressed sexual and aggressive tendencies. For Freud the determinist, nothing was ever accidental.

Personality Structure

3. How did Freud view personality structure and development, and what were the defense mechanisms he proposed?

For Freud, human personality—including its emotions and strivings—arises from a conflict between our aggressive, pleasure-seeking biological impulses and the social restraints against them. In his view, personality results from our efforts to resolve this basic conflict—to express these impulses in ways that bring satisfaction without also bringing guilt or punishment.

Freud theorized that the conflict centers on three interacting systems, id, ego, and superego. These concepts are, said Freud, "useful aids to understanding" the mind's dynamics (Figure 11–1).

Figure 11–1 Freud's Idea of the Mind's Structure *Consciousness is like an iceberg's visible tip. Note that the id is totally unconscious, but ego and superego operate both consciously and unconsciously. (Adapted from Freud, 1933, p. 111.)*

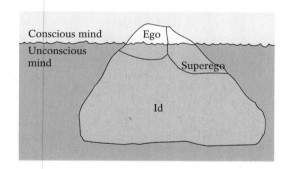

The **id** is a reservoir of unconscious psychic energy that constantly strives to satisfy basic drives to survive, reproduce, and aggress. The id operates on the **pleasure principle**: If unconstrained by reality, it seeks immediate gratification. Think of newborn infants, who, governed by the id, cry out for satisfaction the moment they feel a need, caring nothing for the outside world's conditions and demands.

As the **ego** develops, the young child learns to cope with the real world. The ego operates on the **reality principle**, which seeks to gratify the id's impulses in realistic ways that will bring long-term pleasure rather than pain or destruction. Imagine what would happen if, lacking an ego, we expressed our unrestrained sexual or aggressive impulses whenever we felt them. The ego, which contains our partly conscious perceptions, thoughts, judgments, and memories, is the personality "executive." It decides on our actions as it intervenes among the impulsive demands of the id, the restraining demands of the superego, and the real-life demands of the external world.

id A reservoir of unconscious psychic energy that, according to Freud, strives to satisfy basic sexual and aggressive drives.

pleasure principle The id's demand for immediate gratification.

ego The largely conscious, "executive" part of personality that, according to Freud, mediates among the demands of the id, superego, and reality.

reality principle The ego's tendency to satisfy the id's desires in ways that will realistically bring pleasure rather than pain.

"Fifty is plenty."

"Hundred and fifty."

superego The part of personality that, according to Freud, represents internalized ideals and provides standards for judgment (the conscience) and for future aspirations.

psychosexual stages The childhood stages of development (oral, anal, phallic, latency, genital) during which, according to Freud, the id's pleasure-seeking energies focus on distinct erogenous zones.

oral stage The first of Freud's psychosexual stages, from birth to about 18 months, during which sensual pleasure centers on the mouth through sucking, biting, and chewing.

anal stage The second of Freud's psychosexual stages, from about 18 months to 3 years, during which pleasure focuses on bowel and bladder elimination, retention, and control.

phallic stage The third of Freud's psychosexual stages, from about ages 3 to 6, during which the pleasure zone is the genitals and sexual feelings arise toward the parent of the other sex.

Oedipus [ED-uh-puss] complex According to Freud, a boy's sexual desires toward his mother and feelings of jealousy and hatred for the rival father. According to some other psychoanalysts, a parallel Electra complex occurs in girls.

Beginning around age 4 or 5, a child's ego recognizes the demands of the newly emerging **superego**. The superego is a voice of conscience that forces the ego to consider not only the real but the ideal. Its sole focus is on how one *ought* to behave. The superego develops as we internalize the morals and values of parents and culture, thereby providing both our sense of right and wrong and our ideals. It strives for perfection and judges our actions, producing positive feelings of pride or negative feelings of guilt. Someone with an exceptionally strong superego may be continually upright yet, ironically, guilt-ridden; another with a weak superego may be wantonly self-indulgent and remorseless. Because the superego's demands often oppose the id's, the ego struggles to reconcile the two. The chaste student who is sexually attracted to someone satisfies both id and superego by, say, joining a volunteer organization to work next to the desired person.

Personality Development

Analysis of his patients' histories convinced Freud that personality forms during life's first few years. Again and again his patients' symptoms seemed rooted in unresolved conflicts from early childhood. He concluded that children pass through a series of **psychosexual stages** during which the id's pleasure-seeking energies focus on distinct pleasure-sensitive areas of the body called *erogenous zones*.

During the **oral stage**, which lasts throughout the first 18 months, the infant's sensual pleasures focus on sucking, biting, and chewing.

During the **anal stage**, from about 18 months to 3 years, the sphincter muscles become sensitive and controllable, and bowel and bladder retention and elimination become a source of gratification.

During the **phallic stage**, from roughly 3 to 6 years, the pleasure zone shifts to the genitals. Freud believed that during this stage boys seek genital stimulation and develop both unconscious sexual desires for their mother and jealousy and hatred for their father, whom they consider a rival. Boys also were said to feel guilt and a lurking fear that their father would punish them, such as by castration. Freud called this collection of feelings the **Oedipus complex** after the Greek legend of Oedipus, who unknowingly killed his father and married his mother. Although some psychoanalysts believed that girls experience a parallel *Electra complex*, Freud (1931, page 229) said no: "It is only in the male child that we find the fateful combination of love for the one parent and simultaneous hatred for the other as a rival."

Children eventually cope with these threatening feelings, said Freud, by repressing them and by identifying with (trying to become like) the rival parent. It's as if something inside the child decides, "If you can't beat 'em (the parent of the same sex), join 'em." Through this **identification** process children's superegos gain strength as they incorporate many of their parents' values. Freud believed that identification with the same-sex parent provides our **gender identity**—our sense of being male or female.

With their sexual feelings repressed and redirected, children enter a **latency stage**. Freud maintained that during latency, extending from around age 6 to puberty, sexuality is dormant and children play mostly with peers of the same sex.

At puberty, latency gives way to the final stage, the **genital stage**, as youths begin to experience sexual feelings toward others.

In Freud's view, maladaptive behavior in the adult results from conflicts unresolved during earlier psychosexual stages. At any point in the oral, anal, or phallic stage, strong conflict can lock, or **fixate**, the person's pleasure-seeking energies in that stage. Thus, people who were either orally overindulged or deprived (perhaps by abrupt, early weaning) might fixate at the oral stage. Orally

identification The process by which, according to Freud, children incorporate their parents' values into their developing superegos.

gender identity One's sense of being male or female.

latency stage The fourth of Freud's psychosexual stages, from about age 6 to puberty, during which sexual impulses are repressed.

genital stage The last of Freud's psychosexual stages, beginning in puberty, during which sexuality matures and the person seeks pleasure through sexual contact with others.

fixation According to Freud, a lingering focus of pleasure-seeking energies at an earlier psychosexual stage, where conflicts were unresolved.

defense mechanisms In psychoanalytic theory, the ego's protective methods of reducing anxiety by unconsciously distorting reality.

repression In psychoanalytic theory, the basic defense mechanism that banishes anxiety-arousing thoughts, feelings, and memories from consciousness.

regression In psychoanalytic theory, an individual's retreat, when faced with anxiety, to a more infantile psychosexual stage where some psychic energy remains fixated.

reaction formation In psychoanalytic theory, a defense mechanism by which the ego unconsciously switches unacceptable impulses into their opposites. Thus, people may express feelings that are the opposite of their anxiety-arousing unconscious feelings.

fixated adults are said to exhibit either passive dependence (like that of a nursing infant) or an exaggerated denial of this dependence—perhaps by acting tough and uttering biting sarcasm. They might also continue to seek oral gratification through smoking and excessive eating. Those who never quite resolve the anal conflict, between the desire to eliminate at will and the demands of toilet training, may be either messy and disorganized (*anal expulsive*) or highly controlled and compulsively neat (*anal retentive*). In such ways, believed Freud, the twig of personality is bent at an early age.

Defense Mechanisms

To live in social groups, we cannot act out our sexual and aggressive impulses willy-nilly. We must control them. When the ego fears losing control of the inner war between the demands of the id and the superego, the result is anxiety. Anxiety, said Freud, is the price we pay for civilization.

Unlike specific fears, the dark cloud of anxiety is unfocused. Anxiety is therefore hard to cope with, as when we feel unsettled but are not sure why. Freud proposed that the ego protects itself against anxiety with ego **defense mechanisms**. Defense mechanisms reduce or redirect anxiety in various ways, but always by distorting reality. Some examples:

Repression banishes anxiety-arousing thoughts and feelings from consciousness. According to Freud, repression underlies the other defense mechanisms, all of which disguise threatening impulses and keep them from reaching consciousness. Freud believed that repression explains why we do not remember our childhood lust for our parent of the other sex. However, he also believed that repression is often incomplete, with the repressed urges seeping out in dream symbols and slips of the tongue.

We also cope with anxiety through **regression**—retreating to an earlier, more infantile stage of development where some of our psychic energies still fixate. Thus, when facing the anxious first days of school, a child may regress to the oral comfort of thumb-sucking. Juvenile monkeys, when anxious, retreat to infantile clinging to their mothers or to one another (Suomi, 1987). Even homesick new college students may long for the security and comfort of home.

In **reaction formation**, the ego unconsciously makes unacceptable impulses look like their opposites. En route to consciousness, the unacceptable proposi-

Regression *Faced with a mild stress, children and young monkeys will regress, retreating to the comfort of earlier behaviors.*

Freud's Consulting Room *Freud's office was rich with antiquities from around the world, including art work related to his ideas about unconscious motives. His famous couch, piled high with pillows, placed patients in a comfortable reclining position facing away from him to help them focus inward.*

projection In psychoanalytic theory, the defense mechanism by which people disguise their own threatening impulses by attributing them to others.

rationalization In psychoanalytic theory, a defense mechanism that offers self-justifying explanations in place of the real, more threatening, unconscious reasons for one's actions.

displacement In psychoanalytic theory, the defense mechanism that shifts sexual or aggressive impulses toward a more acceptable or less threatening object or person, as when redirecting anger toward a safer outlet.

sublimation In psychoanalytic theory, the defense mechanism by which people rechannel their unacceptable impulses into socially approved activities.

collective unconscious Carl Jung's concept of a shared, inherited reservoir of memory traces from our species' history.

tion "I hate him" becomes "I love him." Timidity becomes daring. Feelings of inadequacy become bravado. According to the principle behind this defense mechanism, vehement social crusaders, such as those who fervently campaign against gay rights, may be motivated by the very sexual desires against which they crusade.

Projection disguises threatening impulses by attributing them to others. Thus, "He hates me" may be a projection of the actual feeling "I hate him" or "I hate myself." An El Salvadoran saying captures the idea: "The thief thinks everyone else is a thief." According to Freudian theory, racial prejudice, too, may be the result of projecting one's own unacceptable impulses or characteristics onto members of another group. (As you can imagine, reaction formation and projection have sometimes provided a handy way to ridicule other people's motives.)

The familiar mechanism of **rationalization** lets us unconsciously generate self-justifying explanations so we can hide from ourselves the real reasons for our actions. Thus, habitual drinkers may say they drink with their friends "just to be sociable." Students who fail to study may rationalize, "All work and no play makes Jack [or Jill] a dull person."

Displacement diverts one's sexual or aggressive impulses toward an object more psychologically acceptable than the one that aroused them. Children who can't express anger against their parents may displace their anger onto the family pet. Students upset over an exam may snap at a roommate.

Sublimation is the transformation of unacceptable impulses into socially valued motivations. Sublimation is therefore socially adaptive and may even be a wellspring for great cultural and artistic achievements. Freud suggested that Leonardo da Vinci's paintings of the Madonna were a sublimation of his longing for intimacy with his mother, who was separated from him at an early age.

Note again that all these defense mechanisms function indirectly and unconsciously. They reduce anxiety by disguising our threatening impulses. We never say, "I'm feeling anxious; I'd better project my sexual or hostile feelings onto someone else." Defense mechanisms would not work if we recognized them. As the body unconsciously defends itself against disease, so also, believed Freud, does the ego unconsciously defend itself against anxiety.

Freud's Descendants and Dissenters

4. How did Freud's followers differ from him?

Freud's writings soon attracted followers, mostly young, ambitious physicians who formed an inner circle around their strong-minded leader. These pioneering psychoanalysts and others, whom we now call neo-Freudians, accepted Freud's basic ideas: the personality structures of id, ego, and superego; the importance of the unconscious; the shaping of personality in childhood; and the dynamics of anxiety and the defense mechanisms. But they veered away from Freud in two important ways. First, they placed more emphasis on the role of the conscious mind in interpreting experience and coping with the environment. What's more, they doubted that sex and aggression were all-consuming motivations. Instead, they placed more emphasis on loftier motives and on social interaction, as the following examples illustrate.

Alfred Adler and Karen Horney agreed with Freud that childhood is important. But they believed that childhood *social*, not sexual, tensions are crucial for personality formation. Adler, who himself struggled to overcome childhood illnesses and accidents, said that much of our behavior is driven by an effort to conquer childhood feelings of inferiority, feelings that trigger strivings for superiority and power. (It was Adler who proposed the still-popular idea of the "inferiority complex.") Horney said that childhood anxiety, caused by the dependent child's sense of helplessness, triggers the desire for love and security. In countering Freud's assumptions that women have weak superegos and suffer "penis envy," Horney sought to balance the bias she detected in this masculine view of psychology.

Unlike other neo-Freudians, Carl Jung—Freud's disciple-turned-dissenter—placed less emphasis on social factors and agreed with Freud that the unconscious exerts a powerful influence. But to Jung (pronounced Yoong), the unconscious contains more than a person's repressed thoughts and feelings. There is also a **collective unconscious**, he believed, a common reservoir of images derived from our early ancestors' universal experiences. Jung said that the collective unconscious explains why, for many people, spiritual concerns are

> *"The female . . . acknowledges the fact of her castration, and with it, too, the superiority of the male and her own inferiority; but she rebels against this unwelcome state of affairs."*
>
> Sigmund Freud
> *Female Sexuality*, 1931

Alfred Adler *"The individual feels at home in life and feels his existence to be worthwhile just so far as he is useful to others and is overcoming feelings of inferiority"* (Problems of Neurosis, 1964).

Karen Horney *"The view that women are infantile and emotional creatures, and as such, incapable of responsibility and independence is the work of the masculine tendency to lower women's self-respect"* (Feminine Psychology, 1932).

Carl Jung *"We can keep from a child all knowledge of earlier myths, but we cannot take from him the need for mythology"* (Symbols of Transformation, 1912).

deeply rooted and why people in different cultures share certain myths and images, such as that of mother as a symbol of nurturance.

Assessing the Unconscious

5. How do projective tests assess personality, and are they considered valid?

Those who study personality or provide therapy need ways to evaluate personality characteristics. Different personality theories imply different methods of assessment.

Freud's theory maintains that the significant influences on our personalities arise from the unconscious, which contains residues from early childhood experiences. Psychoanalysts therefore dismiss objective assessment tools, such as agree-disagree or true-false questionnaires, as merely tapping the conscious surface. Their tool of choice would be a sort of psychological x-ray—a test that can see through our surface pretensions and reveal our hidden conflicts and impulses.

Projective tests aim to provide such a view by providing people with an ambiguous stimulus and then asking them to describe it or tell a story about it. The stimulus has no inherent meaning, so any meaning people read into it presumably reflects their interests and conflicts. Henry Murray (1933) demonstrated a possible basis for such a test at a house party hosted by his 11-year-old daughter. Murray got the children to play a frightening game called "Murder." When shown some photographs after the game, the children perceived the photos as more malicious than they had before the game.

These children, it seemed to Murray, had *projected* their inner feelings onto the pictures. A few years later, Murray introduced the **Thematic Apperception Test (TAT)**—ambiguous pictures about which people make up stories. As you may recall from page 323, one use of the TAT has been to assess achievement motivation. Shown a daydreaming boy, those who imagine him fantasizing an achievement are presumed to be projecting their own concerns.

There are now a variety of projective tests. These tests ask subjects to draw a person, to complete sentences ("My mother . . ."), or to provide the first word that comes to mind after the examiner says a test word. Most widely used is the famous **Rorschach inkblot test**, introduced in 1921 by Swiss psychiatrist Hermann Rorschach (ROAR-shock). The test assumes that what we see in its 10 inkblots reflects our inner feelings and conflicts. If we see fierce animals or weapons, the examiner may infer we have aggressive tendencies.

Is this a reasonable assumption? If so, can a psychologist use the Rorschach to understand one's personality and diagnose an emotional disorder? Recall from Chapter 8's discussion of intelligence tests that the two primary criteria of a good test are reliability (consistent results) and validity (predicting what it's supposed to). On those criteria, how good is the Rorschach?

Most researchers have considered it not very good (Peterson, 1978). There has been no one accepted system for scoring and interpreting the test. So unless two raters were trained in the same scoring system, their agreement on the results of any given test would be minimal. Nor has the test been very successful at predicting behavior or at discriminating between groups (for example, identifying who is suicidal and who is not).

Although not as popular as it once was, the Rorschach remains one of the most widely used psychological instruments (Lubin & others, 1984; Piotrowski & Keller, 1989). Some clinicians continue to be confident of the test's validity—not as a device that by itself can provide a diagnosis, but as a source of suggestive leads that supplement other information. Other clinicians believe the test is still an icebreaker and a revealing interview technique. A new

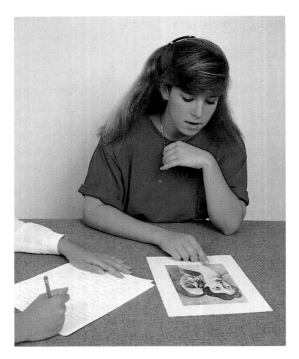

The TAT *This psychologist presumes that the hopes, fears, and interests expressed in this young woman's descriptions of a series of ambiguous pictures in the Thematic Apperception Test (TAT) are projections of her inner feelings.*

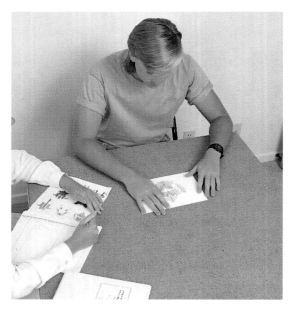

The Rorschach Test *In this projective test, people say what a series of symmetrical inkblots look like. In psychoanalytic terms, tests like this are useful because the interpretation of ambiguous stimuli reveals unconscious aspects of the test-taker's personality.*

"The forward thrust of the antlers shows a determined personality, yet the small sun indicates a lack of self-confidence. . . ."

research-based, computer-aided scoring and interpretation tool is improving agreement among raters and enhancing the test's validity (Exner, 1986; Shontz & Green, 1992). This scoring system, however, assumes the blots actually do look like certain things—the opposite of the test's rationale (Dawes, 1994). Moreover, Freud himself would probably have been uncomfortable with trying to assign each patient a test score and more interested in the therapist–patient interactions that take place during the test.

Evaluating the Psychoanalytic Perspective

6. How do Freud's ideas hold up today?

Knowing what you do about Freud's ideas, listen now to his critics. Bear in mind that we critique Freud from the perspective of the late twentieth century, a perspective that is itself subject to revision. Freud died in 1939 without the benefit of all that we have since learned about human development, thinking, and emotion and without today's research tools. To criticize Freud's theories by comparing them with current concepts is a bit like comparing Henry Ford's Model T with today's Escort.

Freud's Ideas in the Light of Modern Research

Recent theories and research contradict many of Freud's specific ideas. Research indicates that human development is lifelong, not fixed in childhood. Developmental psychologists also question Freud's idea that conscience and gender identity form as the child resolves the Oedipus complex at age 5 or 6. Children gain their gender identity earlier and become strongly masculine or feminine even without a same-sex parent present (Frieze & others, 1978). Freud's ideas about childhood sexuality arose from his rejection of stories of childhood sexual abuse told by his female patients—stories he thought were an expression of their own childhood sexual wishes and conflicts. Today we take reports of sexual abuse seriously. Freud's ideas about the natural superiority of men are widely discounted and considered sexist.

As we saw in Chapter 5, new ideas about why we dream dispute Freud's belief that dreams disguise and fulfill wishes. Even slips of the tongue can be explained as competition between similar verbal choices in our memory network. Researchers find little support for Freud's idea that people protect themselves against painful self-knowledge by projecting their own unrecognized negative impulses onto others (Holmes, 1978, 1981). And Jerome Kagan (1989b) notes that history has been equally unkind to another of Freud's ideas—that sexual repression causes psychological disorder. From Freud's time to ours, sexual repression has diminished, but psychological disorders have not.

Finally, as explained in Chapter 7, more and more memory researchers believe that repression—a cornerstone of Freud's theory—rarely if ever occurs. The skeptical researchers are actually beginning to sound like those skeptical of ESP. "After a hundred years of research," observed parapsychology critic Mark Hansel (1980), there is no objective evidence of ESP. "Despite seventy years of research, there is no objective evidence to support the concept of repression," argues David Holmes (1994).

History has been kinder to Freud's "iceberg" view of the mind, at least in part. We now know that we indeed have limited access to all that goes on in our minds (Erdelyi, 1985, 1988; Kihlstrom, 1990; Lewicki & others, 1992). However, the "iceberg" notion held by today's research psychologists differs from Freud's—so much so, argues Anthony Greenwald (1992), that it is time to abandon Freud's view of the unconscious. As we saw in earlier chapters, many researchers think of the unconscious not as seething passions and repressive

projective tests Personality tests, such as the Rorschach and TAT, that provide ambiguous stimuli designed to trigger projection of one's inner dynamics.

Thematic Apperception Test (TAT) A projective test in which people express their inner feelings and interests through the stories they make up about ambiguous scenes.

Rorschach inkblot test The most widely used projective test, a set of 10 inkblots, designed by Hermann Rorschach; seeks to identify people's inner feelings by analyzing their interpretation of the blots.

censoring but as blander information processing that occurs without our awareness. To them, the unconscious involves the schemas that automatically control our perceptions and interpretations; the processing of stimuli to which we have not consciously attended; the right-hemisphere activity that enables the split-brain patient's left hand to carry out an instruction the patient cannot verbalize; the parallel processing of different aspects of vision and thinking; the implicit memories that operate without conscious recall; the conditioned emotions that activate instantly. This understanding of unconscious information processing is more like the pre-Freudian view of an unconscious underground stream of thought from which spontaneous creative ideas surface.

Freud's Ideas as Scientific Theory

Psychologists also criticize Freud's theory for its scientific shortcomings. Recall from Chapter 1 that good scientific theories explain observations and offer testable hypotheses. Freud's theory, say the critics, rests on few objective observations and offers few hypotheses to verify or reject. (For Freud, his own recollections and interpretations of patients' free associations, dreams, and slips were evidence enough.)

The most serious problem with Freud's theory, according to critics, is that it offers after-the-fact explanations of any characteristic (of one person's smoking, another's fear of horses, another's sexual orientation) yet *fails* to predict such behavior and traits. If you feel angry at your mother's death, you illustrate the theory because "your unresolved childhood dependency needs are threatened." If you do not feel angry, you again illustrate the theory because "you are repressing your anger." That, said Calvin Hall and Gardner Lindzey (1978, p. 68), "is like betting on a horse after the race has been run."

Such criticisms of Freud's specific concepts and after-the-fact interpretations have led some modern critics to scorn his theory. Peter Medawar (1982, pp. 71–72) compared it to "a dinosaur . . . one of the saddest and strangest of all landmarks in the history of twentieth-century thought." Perhaps we can evaluate Freud less harshly, for three reasons:

1. To criticize Freudian theory for not making testable predictions is like criticizing baseball for not being an aerobic exercise. Is it fair to fault something for not being what it was never intended to be? Freud never claimed that psychoanalysis was predictive science. He merely claimed that, looking back, psychoanalysts could find meaning in our state of mind (Rieff, 1979).

2. Some of Freud's ideas are enduring. It was Freud who drew our attention to the unconscious and the irrational, to anxiety and our struggle to cope with it, to the importance of human sexuality, and to the tension between our biological impulses and our social well-being. It was Freud who challenged our self-righteousness, punctured our pretensions, and reminded us of our potential for evil. Few dispute that Freud's ideas were creative, courageous, and comprehensive.

3. Correctly or incorrectly, Freud influenced our view of human nature. Rightly or wrongly, some ideas that many of us assume to be true—that childhood experiences mold personality, that many behaviors have disguised motives, that dreams have symbolic meaning—are Freud's legacy. His early 1900s concepts penetrate our 1990s language. Without realizing their source we may speak of ego, repression, projection, complex (as in "inferiority complex"), sibling rivalry, and fixation. As Peter Drucker (1982) remarked, "[Many] psychologists have no use for Freud, and I have some grave doubts about him, but he is the only one who created vision and insight and changed our view of ourselves and of the world." For that, Sigmund Freud continues to rank as one of modern history's towering intellectual figures.

"We are arguing like a man who should say, 'If there were an invisible cat in that chair, the chair would look empty; but the chair does look empty; therefore there is an invisible cat in it.'"

C. S. Lewis
Four Loves, 1958

! *Rehearse It*

1. According to Freud, we block thoughts, wishes, feelings, and memories that are unacceptable or unbearably painful from consciousness. The blocked material surfaces in disguised forms, for example, in physical symptoms, dreams, or slips of the tongue. This unconscious blocking of unacceptable thoughts is

a. free association.
b. repression.
c. anxiety.
d. reaction formation.

2. Freud described the personality as consisting of three interacting systems, the id, ego, and superego. A term such as "ego" or "id" is best understood as a

a. useful aid in explaining the mind's workings.
b. name for a region of the brain.
c. description of a stage in psychosexual development.
d. testable hypothesis.

3. Freud proposed an Oedipus complex, which is resolved through a process called identification, during which the child incorporates parental values. This process is closely associated with the development of the "voice of conscience," the part of the

personality that internalizes ideals and that Freud called the

a. ego.
b. superego.
c. reality principle.
d. sublimation.

4. According to the psychoanalytic view of development, the oral, anal, and phallic stages are followed by a latency stage during which sexuality is largely dormant or submerged. The latency stage extends roughly through

a. the preschool years.
b. the elementary school years.
c. adolescence.
d. infancy.

5. Defense mechanisms identified by Freud include regression (in which a person copes with anxiety by retreating to an earlier stage of development) and projection (in which a person disguises threatening impulses by attributing them to others). There are many other defense mechanisms. All of them have in common some distortion or disguising of reality, and all of them are

a. conscious.

b. unconscious.
c. preconscious.
d. rationalizations.

6. Projective tests are personality tests that present test-takers with an ambiguous stimulus and ask them to respond to it, for example, by describing it or telling a story about it. One well-known projective test, which uses inkblots as stimuli, was created by

a. the neo-Freudians.
b. Freud and his circle.
c. Carl Jung.
d. Hermann Rorschach.

7. Many of Freud's specific ideas—for example, his ideas on the formation of gender identity and the function of dreams—have been modified by the neo-Freudians or challenged by recent research. However, most psychologists would agree with Freud about

a. the existence of unconscious mental processes.
b. the Oedipus and Electra complexes.
c. the predictive value of Freudian theory.
d. adult psychological problems being the result of inadequate psychosexual development.

The Trait Perspective

7. How do trait theorists view personality?

Psychoanalytic theory explains personality in terms of the dynamics that underlie behavior. It peers beneath the surface in search of hidden motives. In 1919, Gordon Allport, a curious 22-year-old psychology student, interviewed Freud in Vienna and discovered just how preoccupied the founder of psychoanalysis was with finding hidden motives, even in Allport's own behavior during the interview. That experience ultimately led Allport to do what Freud did not do—to describe personality in terms of fundamental **traits**—people's characteristic behaviors and conscious motives. Meeting Freud, said Allport (1967), "taught me that [psychoanalysis], for all its merits, may plunge too deep, and that psychologists would do well to give full recognition to manifest motives before probing the unconscious." Allport therefore defined personality in terms of identifiable behavior patterns. He was less concerned with *explaining* and more with *describing* individual traits.

trait A characteristic pattern of behavior or conscious motive; assessed by self-report inventories and peer reports.

Whoopi Whoops It Up! *On stage, Whoopi Goldberg seems as outgoing and enthusiastic as her name implies. While few of us carry such apt names, trait terms can describe our temperaments and typical behaviors.*

How do psychologists describe and classify personalities? An analogy may help. Imagine that you want to describe and classify apples. Someone might correctly say that every apple is unique. Still, you might find it useful to begin by classifying apples as distinct *types*—Delicious, Granny Smith, McIntosh, and so forth. Based on children's physiological and psychological reactivity, Jerome Kagan (1989b) classifies children's temperaments as either shy-inhibited or fearless-uninhibited types. Some health psychologists have classified people as intense, *Type A*, or as laid back, *Type B*, personalities (pages 362–363).

Also popular today, especially in business and career counseling, is an effort to classify people based on their responses to 126 questions written by Isabel Briggs Myers (1987) and her mother, Kathleen Briggs. The *Myers-Briggs Type Indicator* is quite simple. It offers its 2 million annual takers choices, such as "Do you usually value sentiment more than logic, or value logic more than sentiment?" Then it counts their preferences, labels them as indicating, say, a "feeling" or "thinking" type, and describes each type in complimentary terms. Feeling types, for example, are told they are sensitive to values and "sympathetic, appreciative, and tactful"; thinking types are told they "prefer an objective standard of truth" and are "good at analyzing." Most people therefore readily embrace their announced type profile, which merely mirrors their declared preferences. They may also accept it as a basis for being matched with work partners and tasks that supposedly suit their temperaments. A National Research Council report, however, noted that the test's use has outrun research on its value as a predictor of job performance, and that "the popularity of this instrument in the absence of proven scientific worth is troublesome" (Druckman & Bjork, 1991, p. 101).

Exploring Traits

If classifying people as one or another distinct personality type fails to fully capture their individuality, how else could we describe their personalities? To return to our apple analogy, we might describe an apple along several trait dimensions—as relatively large or small, red or yellow, sweet or sour. By placing people on several trait dimensions simultaneously, psychologists can describe countless individual personality variations. (Remember from Chapter 4 that variations on just three color dimensions—hue, saturation, and brightness—create many thousands of colors.)

What trait dimensions describe personality? Allport and his associate H. S. Odbert (1936) literally counted all the words in an unabridged dictionary with which one could describe people. The list numbered almost 18,000! How, then, could psychologists condense the list to a manageable number of basic traits?

One way has been to propose traits, such as anxiety, that some theory regards as basic. A newer technique is *factor analysis*, the statistical procedure described in Chapter 8 to identify clusters of test items that tap basic components of intelligence (such as spatial ability, reasoning ability, or verbal skill). Imagine that people who describe themselves as outgoing also tend to say they like excitement and practical jokes, and that they do not like quiet reading. Such a statistically correlated cluster of behaviors reflects a basic trait, or factor—in this case, a trait called *extraversion*.

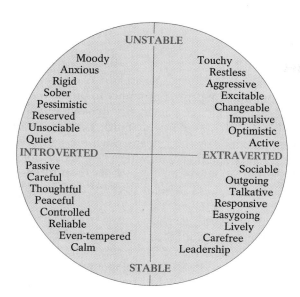

Figure 11–2 Two Personality Factors *As mapmakers can tell us a lot by using two axes (north-south and east-west), so can the Eysencks by using two primary personality factors—extraversion-introversion and stability-instability. Varying combinations define other, more specific traits. (From Eysenck & Eysenck, 1963.)*

British psychologists Hans Eysenck and Sybil Eysenck believe that we can reduce many of our normal individual variations to two or three genetically influenced dimensions, including *extraversion-introversion* and *emotional stability-instability* (Figure 11–2). Their *Eysenck Personality Questionnaire* has been given to people in 35 countries around the world, from China to Uganda to Russia. When people's answers are analyzed, the extraversion and emotionality factors inevitably emerge as basic personality dimensions (Eysenck, 1990, 1992). Extraverts, they contend, seek stimulation because their normal levels of brain arousal are relatively low. Emotionally stable people react calmly because their autonomic nervous systems are not so reactive as those of unstable people.

Many other trait theorists, too, view personality traits as biologically rooted. Jerome Kagan attributes differences in children's shyness and inhibition to their autonomic nervous system reactivity. Twin and adoption studies of genetic influences on personality traits (pages 108–109) further remind us that behavior patterns form as a person's genetic endowment interacts with a particular environment.

Most researchers believe that the Eysencks' dimensions are important but that they don't tell the whole story of someone's personality. They offer a slightly expanded set of factors—dubbed the *Big Five* (Goldberg, 1993; John, 1990; Noller & others, 1987). If a test specifies where you are on the five dimensions of Table 11–1, it has said much of what there is to say about your personality. Around the world, people describe others in terms roughly consistent with the Big Five—how agreeable they are, how extraverted they are, and so forth. The Big Five may not be the last word: But it's currently our best approximation of the basic trait dimensions. If you could ask five questions about the personality of a stranger—say, a blind date you were soon to meet—querying where the person is on these five dimensions would be most revealing.

TABLE 11–1	
The "Big Five" Personality Factors	
Trait Dimension	**Description**
Emotional stability	Calm versus anxious Secure versus insecure Self-satisfied versus self-pitying
Extraversion	Sociable versus retiring Fun-loving versus sober Affectionate versus reserved
Openness	Imaginative versus practical Preference for variety versus preference for routine Independent versus conforming
Agreeableness	Soft-hearted versus ruthless Trusting versus suspicious Helpful versus uncooperative
Conscientiousness	Organized versus disorganized Careful versus careless Disciplined versus impulsive

Source: Adapted from "Clinical assessment can benefit from recent advances in personality psychology" by R. McCrae & P.T. Costa, Jr., 1986, *American Psychologist*, 41, p. 1002.

personality inventory   A questionnaire (often with true-false or agree-disagree items) on which people respond to items designed to gauge a wide range of feelings and behaviors; used to assess selected personality traits.

Minnesota Multiphasic Personality Inventory (MMPI)   The most widely researched and clinically used of all personality tests. Originally developed to identify emotionally troubled people (still considered its most appropriate use), this test is now used for many other screening purposes.

empirically derived test   A test (such as the MMPI) developed by testing a pool of items and then selecting those that discriminate groups of interest.

Assessing Traits

8. How do we assess traits?

Assessment techniques derived from trait concepts aim simply to profile a person's behavior patterns, not to reveal the hidden personality dynamics (which is the intent of projective tests). Many trait scales provide quick assessments of a single trait, such as extraversion, anxiety, or self-esteem. Such measures are commonly used in studies of personality and behavior. Alternatively, psychologists can assess several traits at once by administering **personality inventories**— longer questionnaires on which people respond to items covering a wide range of feelings and behaviors.

The personality inventory that psychologists have most extensively researched and widely used is the **Minnesota Multiphasic Personality Inventory (MMPI)**. Although it assesses psychological disorders rather than "normal" personality traits, the MMPI illustrates a good way to develop a personality inventory. One of its creators, Starke Hathaway (1960), compared his effort to that of Alfred Binet. As we learned in Chapter 8, Binet developed the first intelligence test by selecting items that discriminated children who would have trouble progressing normally in French schools. The MMPI items, too, were **empirically derived**. That is, from a large pool of items Hathaway and his colleagues selected those that discriminated particular groups.

They initially gave hundreds of true-false statements ("No one seems to understand me"; "I get all the sympathy I should"; "I like poetry") to groups of psychologically disordered patients and to "normal" people. They retained any statement—no matter how silly it sounded—on which the patient group's answer differed from that of the normal group. "Nothing in the newspaper interests me except the comics" may seem senseless, but it just so happened that depressed people were more likely to answer "true." (Nevertheless, pundits have had fun spoofing the MMPI with their own mock items, such as: "Weeping brings tears to my eyes"; "As a child I often suffered from bubonic plague"; "I think oatmeal is erotic"; "Frantic screams make me nervous"; "I stay in the bathtub until I look like a raisin" [Frankel & others, 1983].)

Today's new MMPI-2, renormed on a full cross-section of Americans and containing revised items, still contains 10 clinical scales (Figure 11–3). It also retains several validity scales, including the so-called lie scale that assesses the extent to which a person is faking a good impression (by responding "false" to statements such as "I get angry sometimes"). And it has 15 content scales assessing, for instance, work attitudes, family problems, and anger. Scores are converted to a "*T*-scale," such that an average score is called 50 and about two-thirds of people fall between 40 and 60.

In contrast to the subjectivity of projective tests, personality inventories are scored objectively—so objectively that a computer can administer and score them. (The computer can also provide descriptions of people who previously responded similarly.) Objectivity does not, however, guarantee validity. Sophisticated test-takers can fake a good impression if taking the MMPI for employment purposes (by answering in socially desirable ways, except on those items for which nearly anyone would admit to being imperfect). Moreover, the ease of computerized testing tempts untrained administrators—including many personnel officers, educational admissions officers, and physicians—to use the test in ways for which it has not been validated (Matarazzo, 1983). Nevertheless, for better or worse, the objectivity of the MMPI contributes to its rising popularity (Piotrowski & Keller, 1989) and to its translation into more than 100 languages.

Figure 11–3 Minnesota Multiphasic Personality Inventory (MMPI-2) Test Profile *High scores suggest a psychological disorder. This graph plots the scores of Ed, a depressed and anxious young man, before and after psychotherapy. Scores are converted to a "T-scale," such that an average score is called 50 and about two-thirds of people fall between 40 and 60. (Adapted from Butcher, 1990.)*

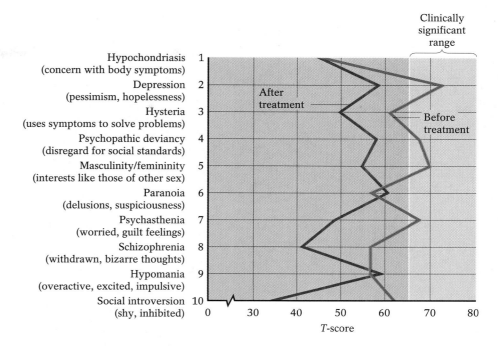

"There is as much difference between us and ourselves, as between us and others."

Michel de Montaigne
Essays, 1588

Roughly speaking, the temporary, external influences on behavior are the focus of social psychology, and the enduring, inner influences are the focus of personality psychology. In actuality, behavior always depends on the interaction of persons with situations.

Evaluating the Trait Perspective

9. Does research support the consistency of personality traits?

Are our personality traits stable and enduring? Or does our behavior depend on where we are and whom we're with? William Faulkner (1897–1962) strove to mirror reality in fiction by creating characters, like the self-centered Jason Compson, whose personality traits were consistent across various times and places. The Italian playwright Luigi Pirandello (1867–1936) had a different view. For him, personality was ever-changing, tailored to the particular role or situation. In one of Pirandello's plays Lamberto Laudisi describes himself to Signora Sirelli: "I am really what you take me to be; though, my dear madam, that does not prevent me from also being really what your husband, my sister, my niece, and Signora Cini take me to be—because they also are absolutely right!" To which she responds, "In other words you are a different person for each of us."

Who best represents human personality, Faulkner's consistent Jason Compson or Pirandello's inconsistent Laudisi? Most of us agree that this is not an either/or question: Our behavior is influenced by the interaction of our inner disposition with our environment. Still, the question lingers: Which is *more* important? Are we *more* as Faulkner or as Pirandello imagined us to be? Forced to choose, most people would probably side with Faulkner. Until the late 1960s, most psychologists would have, too. Isn't it obvious that some people are dependably conscientious and others unreliable, some cheerful and others dour, some outgoing and others shy?

Remember, to be a genuine personality trait a characteristic must persist over time *and* across situations. If friendliness is a trait, friendly people must act friendly at different times and places. Do they? In Chapter 3, we considered research that has followed lives through time. We noted that some scholars are impressed with personality change (especially those who study infants); others are struck by personality stability during adulthood. If people's personalities

*"Mr. Coughlin over there was the founder of
one of the first motorcycle gangs."*

are assessed in young adulthood and then assessed again several decades later, their characteristics persist. Interests may change—the avid tropical fish collector may become the avid gardener. Careers may change—the determined salesperson may become a determined social worker. Relationships may change—the hostile spouse may start over with a new partner. But most people recognize their traits as their own, note Robert McCrae and Paul Costa (1994), "and it is well that they do. A person's recognition of the inevitability of his or her one and only personality is . . . the culminating wisdom of a lifetime." Faulkner would not have been surprised.

The consistency of specific behaviors from one situation to the next is another matter. As Walter Mischel (1968, 1984) points out, people do not act with predictable consistency. In one of the first studies to reveal this, Hugh Hartshorne and Mark May (1928b) gave thousands of children opportunities to lie, cheat, and steal while at home, at play, and in the classroom. Were some children consistently honest, others dishonest? Generally not. "Most children will deceive in certain situations and not in others," the researchers reported. A child's "lying, cheating, and stealing as measured by the test situations used in these studies are only very loosely related" (p. 411). More than a half-century later, Mischel's studies of college students' conscientiousness revealed a similar finding. There was virtually no relation between a student's being conscientious on one occasion (say, showing up for class on time) and being similarly conscientious on another occasion (say, turning in assignments on time). Pirandello would not have been surprised.

Mischel also points out that people's scores on personality tests only mildly predict their behaviors. For example, people's scores on an extraversion test do not neatly predict how sociable they actually will be on any given occasion. If we remember such results, says Mischel, we will be more cautious about labeling and pigeonholing individuals. We will be more restrained when asked to predict whether someone is likely to violate parole, commit suicide, or be an effective employee. Years in advance, science can tell us the phase of the moon for any given date, but we're a long way from being able to predict how you will feel and act tomorrow.

In defense of traits, Seymour Epstein (1983a,b) maintained that trying to predict a specific act on the basis of a personality test is like trying to predict your answer to a single test question on the basis of an intelligence test. Your answer to any given question is unpredictable because it depends on so many variables (your reading of the question, your understanding of the topic, your concentration level at the moment, luck). Your *average* accuracy over many questions on several tests is more predictable. Similarly, says Epstein, people's *average* outgoingness, happiness, or carelessness over *many* situations is predictable. When rating someone's shyness or agreeableness, this consistency enables people who know someone well to agree (Kenrick & Funder, 1988). As our best friends can verify, we *do* have personality traits. Moreover, our traits are socially significant. They influence our health, our thinking, and our job performance (Deary & Matthews, 1993; Jackson & Rothstein, 1993).

In unfamiliar, formal situations—perhaps when eating in a strange home—our traits may remain hidden as we attend carefully to social cues. In familiar, informal situations—just hanging out with friends—we feel less constrained, allowing our traits to emerge (Buss, 1989). In such situations, our expressive styles are impressively consistent. Thus, we often form lasting impressions within a few moments of meeting someone and noting the person's animation, manner of speaking, and gestures. Nalini Ambady and Robert Rosenthal (1992, 1993) videotaped 13 Harvard University graduate students teaching undergraduate courses. Observers then viewed three thin slices of each teacher's behavior—mere 10-second clips from the beginning, middle, and end of a class—and rated each teacher's level of confidence, activeness, warmth, and so forth. These behavior ratings, based on 30 *seconds* of teaching from an entire semester, predicted amazingly well the teacher's average student ratings at the semester's end. Observing even thinner slices—three 2-second clips—yielded ratings that still correlated as high as +.72 with the student evaluations. Some people's first impressions, derived from expressive behavior, predicted other people's lasting impressions!

To sum up, we can say that at any moment the immediate situation powerfully influences a person's behavior, especially when the situation makes clear demands. We can better predict drivers' behavior at traffic lights from knowing the color of the lights than from knowing their personalities. However, averaging people's behavior across many occasions reveals that they do have distinct personality traits. Moreover, individual differences in some traits such as expressiveness can be quickly perceived.

! Rehearse It

8. Trait theory describes personality in terms of characteristic behaviors, or traits, such as agreeableness or extraversion. A pioneering trait theorist was

a. Sigmund Freud.
b. Alfred Adler.
c. Gordon Allport.
d. Henry Murray.

9. Hans and Sybil Eysenck define personality in terms of two primary factors—extraversion-introversion and stability-instability. Most researchers today believe that the Eysenck's dimensions are too limiting and prefer the so-called "Big Five" personality factors. These include all but which of the following?

a. conscientiousness
b. anxiety
c. extraversion
d. agreeableness

10. Trait theorists assess the personality by developing a profile of a person's traits. For example, they administer long questionnaires called personality inventories, which ask people to report their characteristic feelings and behaviors. The most widely used of all personality inventories is the

a. extraversion-introversion scale.
b. TAT.
c. MMPI-2.
d. Rorschach.

11. The items of the MMPI were empirically derived. This means, for example, that the designers of the test figured out which responses indicated schizophrenia by

a. taking case histories before and after the test.
b. analyzing the content of the items in light of their understanding of the disorder.

c. comparing the responses of known schizophrenia patients with those of normal people.
d. assessing the degree of deception, using validity scales.

12. People's scores on personality tests are only mildly predictive of their behavior. Such tests best predict

a. a person's behavior on a specific occasion.
b. a person's average behavior across many situations.
c. behavior involving a single trait, such as conscientiousness.
d. behavior that depends on situation or context.

The Humanistic Perspective

10. What is the central focus of the humanistic perspective?

By 1960, some personality psychologists became discontented with Freud's negativity and with trait psychology's objectivity. In contrast to Freud's study of the base motives of "sick" people, these *humanistic psychologists* focused on the strivings of "healthy" people for self-determination and self-realization. In contrast to trait psychologists' profiles, they viewed whole persons as beyond encapsulation as so many test scores. Two pioneering theorists illustrate these emphases on human potential and seeing the world through the person's (not the experimenter's) eyes: Abraham Maslow (1908–1970) and Carl Rogers (1902–1987).

Abraham Maslow *"Any theory of motivation that is worthy of attention must deal with the highest capacities of the healthy and strong person as well as with the defensive maneuvers of crippled spirits"* (Motivation and Personality, 1970).

Rogers believed that genuineness, acceptance, and empathy nurture growth not only in the relationship between therapist and client but also between parent and child, leader and group, teacher and student, administrator and staff member—in fact, between any two human beings.

---

self-actualization According to Maslow, the ultimate psychological need that arises after basic physical and psychological needs are met and self-esteem is achieved; the motivation to fulfill one's potential.

unconditional positive regard According to Rogers, an attitude of total acceptance toward another person.

self-concept All our thoughts and feelings about ourselves, in answer to the question, "Who am I?"

Exploring the Self

Abraham Maslow's Self-Actualizing Person

Maslow proposed that we are motivated by a hierarchy of needs (page 300). If our physiological needs are met, we become concerned with personal safety; if we achieve a sense of security, we then seek to love, to be loved, and to love ourselves. Given self-esteem, we ultimately seek **self-actualization**, the process of fulfilling our potential.

Unlike many theorists before him, Maslow (1970) developed his ideas by studying healthy, creative people rather than troubled, clinical cases. He based his description of self-actualization on a study of people who seemed notable for their rich and productive lives—Abraham Lincoln, Thomas Jefferson, and Eleanor Roosevelt among them. These people shared certain characteristics. Maslow reported they were self-aware and self-accepting, open and spontaneous, loving and caring, and not paralyzed by others' opinions. Secure in their sense of who they were, their interests were problem-centered rather than self-centered. Often they focused their energies on a particular task, which they regarded as their mission in life. Most enjoyed a few deep relationships rather than many superficial ones. Many had been moved by spiritual or personal *peak experiences* that surpassed ordinary consciousness.

These are mature adult qualities, said Maslow, ones found in those who have learned enough about life to be compassionate, to have outgrown their mixed feelings toward their parents, to have found their calling, to have "acquired enough courage to be unpopular, to be unashamed about being openly virtuous, etc." Maslow's work with college students led him to speculate that those likely to become self-actualizing adults were likable, caring, "privately affectionate to those of their elders who deserve it," and "secretly uneasy about the cruelty, meanness, and mob spirit so often found in young people."

Carl Rogers' Person-Centered Perspective

Fellow humanistic psychologist Carl Rogers agreed with much of Maslow's thinking. Rogers believed that people are basically good and are endowed with self-actualizing tendencies. Each of us is like an acorn, primed for growth and fulfillment, unless thwarted by an environment that inhibits growth. Rogers (1980) surmised that a growth-promoting climate required three conditions—genuineness, acceptance, and empathy.

According to Rogers, people nurture our growth by being *genuine*—by being open with their own feelings, dropping their facades, and being transparent and self-disclosing.

People also nurture growth by being *accepting*—by offering us what Rogers called **unconditional positive regard**. This is an attitude of grace, an attitude that values us even knowing our failings. Have you ever experienced the relief of having dropped your pretenses, confessed your worst feelings, and discovered that you were still accepted? We sometimes enjoy this gratifying experience in a good marriage, a close family, or an intimate friendship in which we no longer feel a need to explain ourselves and are free to be spontaneous without fear of losing the other's esteem.

Finally, people nurture growth by being *empathic*—by nonjudgmentally reflecting our feelings and meanings. "Rarely do we listen with real understanding, true empathy," said Rogers. "Yet listening, of this very special kind, is one of the most potent forces for change that I know."

Genuineness, acceptance, and empathy are the water, sun, and nutrients that enable people to grow like vigorous oak trees, according to Rogers. For "as persons are accepted and prized, they tend to develop a more caring attitude

The Picture of Empathy *Being open and sharing confidences is easier when the listener shows real understanding. Within such relationships people can relax and fully express their true selves.*

Possible Selves *By giving them a chance to try out many possible selves, pretend games offer children important opportunities to grow emotionally, socially, and cognitively. Although this young boy may not grow up to be a physician, playing adult roles will expand his vision of what he might become.*

What possible future selves do you envision? To what extent do these imagined selves motivate you now?

toward themselves" (Rogers 1980, p. 116). As persons are empathically heard, "it becomes possible for them to listen more accurately to the flow of inner experiencings." Rogers would have been pleased by a finding published shortly after his death: Preschool children whose parents exhibit such attitudes usually become creative adolescents (Harrington & others, 1987).

For Maslow, and even more for Rogers, a central feature of personality is one's **self-concept**—all the thoughts and feelings we have in response to the question, "Who am I?" If our self-concept is positive, we tend to act and perceive the world positively. If it is negative—if in our own eyes we fall far short of our "ideal self"—said Rogers, we feel dissatisfied and unhappy. A worthwhile goal for parents, teachers, and friends is, therefore, to help others know, accept, and be true to themselves.

Assessing the Self

Humanistic psychologists sometimes assess personality with questionnaires that evaluate people's self-concepts. One questionnaire, inspired by Carl Rogers, asks people to describe themselves both as they ideally would like to be and as they actually are. When the ideal and the actual self are nearly alike, said Rogers, the self-concept is positive. Thus, to assess his clients' personal growth during therapy he looked for successively closer ratings of actual and ideal self.

Other humanistic psychologists believe that any standardized assessment of personality is depersonalizing, that even a questionnaire detaches the psychologist from the living human. Rather than forcing the person to respond to narrow categories, these humanistic psychologists believe that interviews and intimate conversation enable a better understanding of each person's unique experiences.

Research on the Self

11. What have we learned from research on the self?

Psychology's concern with people's sense of self dates back at least to William James, who devoted more than 100 pages to the topic in his 1890 *Principles of Psychology*. By 1943, Gordon Allport lamented that the self had become "lost to view." Although humanistic psychology's emphasis on the self did not instigate much scientific research, it did help renew the concept of self and keep it alive. Now, a century after James, the self is one of Western psychology's most vigorously researched topics. Every year new studies galore appear on self-esteem, self-disclosure, self-awareness, self-schemas, self-monitoring, and so forth. One example of the new thinking about self is the concept of *possible selves* put forth by Hazel Markus and her colleagues (Inglehart & others, 1989; Markus & Nurius, 1986). Your possible selves include your visions of the self you dream of becoming—the rich self, the thin self, the loved and admired self. They also include the self you fear becoming—the unemployed self, the alcoholic self, the academically failed self. Such possible selves motivate us by laying out specific goals and the energy to work toward them. Olympian Carl Lewis concentrated on the achievements of Olympic hero Jesse Owens to give form to his aspirations. Similarly, University of Michigan students in a combined undergraduate/medical school program earn higher grades if they undergo the program with a clear vision of themselves as successful doctors. Those who dream most, achieve most.

Underlying this research is an assumption (shared by humanistic psychologists) that the self, as organizer of our thoughts, feelings, and actions, is a pivotal center of personality. More often than not, unhappiness and despair

self-esteem   One's feelings of high or low self-worth.

self-serving bias   A readiness to perceive oneself favorably.

> *"To love oneself is the beginning of a life-long romance."*
>
> Oscar Wilde
> *An Ideal Husband*, 1895

> *"It is only our bad temper that we put down to being tired or worried or hungry. We put our good temper down to ourselves."*
>
> C. S. Lewis, 1898–1963

coexist with a negative self-image. Research studies confirm the benefits of positive self-esteem but also hint at the hazards of pride.

The Benefits of Self-Esteem   High **self-esteem**—a feeling of self-worth—pays dividends. People who feel good about themselves (who strongly agree with self-affirming questionnaire statements) have fewer ulcers and fewer sleepless nights, succumb less easily to pressures to conform, are less likely to use drugs, are more persistent at difficult tasks, and are just plain happier (Brockner & Hulton, 1978; Brown, 1991).

People with low self-esteem don't necessarily see themselves as worthless or wicked, but they do lack good things to say about themselves. Such low self-esteem exacts costs. More often than not, unhappiness and despair coexist with low self-esteem. People who feel they are falling short of their hopes are vulnerable to depression. Those whose self-image falls short of what they think they *ought* to be are vulnerable to anxiety (Higgins, 1987).

These correlational links between low self-esteem and life problems have other possible interpretations. Maybe life problems cause low self-esteem. Maybe self-esteem reflects reality. However, an *effect* of low self-esteem appears in experiments. Temporarily deflate people's self-image (say, by telling them they did poorly on an aptitude test or by disparaging their personality) and they will be more likely to disparage other people or to express heightened racial prejudice. People who are negative about themselves also tend to be thin-skinned and judgmental (Baumeister, 1993; Baumgardner & others, 1989; Pelham, 1993). Although some "love their neighbors as themselves," others loathe their neighbors as themselves. In experiments, those made to feel insecure often become excessively critical, as if to impress others with their own brilliance (Amabile, 1983). Such findings are consistent with Maslow's and Rogers' presumptions that a healthy self-image pays dividends. Accept yourself and you'll find it easier to accept others.

The Pervasiveness of Self-Serving Bias   Carl Rogers (1958) once objected to the religious doctrine that humanity's problems arise from excessive self-love, or pride. He noted that most people he had known "despise themselves, regard themselves as worthless and unlovable." Mark Twain had the idea: "No man, deep down in the privacy of his heart, has any considerable respect for himself."

Actually, most of us have a good reputation with ourselves. In studies of self-esteem, even low-scoring people respond in the midrange of possible scores (Baumeister & others, 1989). (A "low" self-esteem person responds to statements such as "I have good ideas" with qualifying adjectives such as *somewhat* or *sometimes*.) Moreover, one of psychology's most provocative yet firmly established recent conclusions concerns our potent **self-serving bias**—our readiness to perceive ourselves favorably (Brown, 1991; Myers, 1996). Consider:

> *People accept more responsibility for good deeds than for bad, and for successes than for failures.* Athletes often privately credit their victories to their own prowess and their losses to bad breaks, lousy officiating, or the other team's exceptional performance. After receiving poor exam grades, most students in a half dozen studies criticized the exam, not themselves. On insurance forms, drivers have explained accidents in such words as: "An invisible car came out of nowhere, struck my car, and vanished." "As I reached an intersection, a hedge sprang up, obscuring my vision, and I did not see the other car." "A pedestrian hit me and went under my car." The question "What have I done to deserve this?" is one we ask of our troubles, not our successes—those we assume we deserve.

PEANUTS

PEANUTS reprinted by permission of UFS, Inc.

⬛ ***Most people see themselves as better than average.*** This is true for nearly any subjective and socially desirable dimension. In national surveys, most business executives say they are more ethical than their average counterpart. In several studies, 90 percent of business managers and more than 90 percent of college professors rated their performance as superior to their average peer. In Australia, 86 percent of people rate their job performance as above average, and only 1 percent as below average. Although the phenomenon is less striking in Asia, where modesty is valued, self-serving biases have been observed worldwide: among Dutch, Australian, and Chinese students; Japanese drivers; Indian Hindus; and French people of all walks of life. The world, it seems, is Garrison Keillor's Lake Wobegon writ large—a place where "all the women are strong, all the men are good-looking, and all the children are above average."

Self-serving bias flies in the face of today's pop psychology. "All of us have inferiority complexes," insists John Powell (1989, p. 15). "Those who seem not to have such a complex are only pretending." But additional evidence removes any doubts: We remember and justify our past actions in self-enhancing ways. We exhibit an inflated confidence in the accuracy of our beliefs and judgments. We overestimate how desirably *we* would act in situations where most people behave less than admirably. We are quicker to believe flattering descriptions of ourselves than unflattering ones, and we are impressed with psychological tests that make us look good. We exhibit group pride—a tendency to see our group (our school, our country, our race) as superior.

Moreover, pride does often go before a fall. Self-serving perceptions underlie conflicts ranging from other-blaming marital discord to self-promoting ethnic snobbery. It was "Aryan pride" that fueled Nazi atrocities. It was national self-righteousness that led both the Americans and Soviets during the arms race to say, "Your weapons threaten us, ours are only for defense." No wonder religion and literature so often warn against the perils of excessive pride.

Still, people object to the idea of self-serving bias. They think of those who do seem to despise themselves, who feel worthless and unlovable. If self-serving bias prevails, why do so many people disparage themselves? For at least two reasons. Sometimes people's self-directed put-downs are subtly strategic: They elicit reassuring strokes. Saying "No one likes me" may at least elicit "But not everyone has met you!" At other times, such as before a game or an exam, self-disparaging comments prepare us for possible failure. The coach who extols the superior strength of the upcoming opponent makes a loss understandable, a victory noteworthy.

Even so, it's true: All of us some of the time, and some of us much of the time, *do* feel inferior—especially when we compare ourselves with those who are a step or two higher on the ladder of status, grades, looks, income, or agility. The deeper and more frequently we have such feelings, the more unhappy, even depressed, we are. But for most people—the 98 percent who at anytime are *not* suffering depression (Diener, 1993; Gotlib, 1992)—thinking has a natural positive bias.

We can therefore affirm what humanistic psychologists rightly emphasize:

individualism Giving priority to one's own goals over group goals, and defining one's identity in terms of personal attributes rather than group identifications.

collectivism Giving priority to the goals of one's group (often one's extended family or work group) and defining one's identity accordingly.

Like athletes who take more pleasure in their team's victory than in their own performance, collectivists find satisfaction in advancing their groups' interests, even at the expense of personal needs.

No wonder, says Harry Triandis (1989b), that modern world colonization was led not by Asians, who were reluctant to cut social and family ties, but by the more individualist Europeans. And no wonder that countries colonized by Europeans willing to leave friends and family are today highly individualistic.

For the individual, self-affirming thinking is generally adaptive. To a point, even our positive illusions are beneficial. They maintain our self-confidence, protect against anxiety and depression, and sustain our sense of well-being. "Life is the art of being well-deceived," observed the English essayist William Hazlitt. Recognizing both the perils of self-righteousness and the dividends of positive self-esteem, psychologists Roy Baumeister (1989), Jonathan Brown (1991), and Shelley Taylor (1989) all suggest that humans function best with modest self-enhancing illusions.

Culture and the Self

12. What distinguishes the individualist and collectivist views of self?

If someone were to rip away your social connections, making you a solitary refugee in a foreign land, how much of your identity would remain intact? The answer might depend in large part on whether your culture nurtures **individualism** or **collectivism**.

For individualists, a great deal of their identity would remain intact—the very core of their being, their sense of "me," their awareness of their personal convictions and values. Although individualism varies from person to person, cross-cultural psychologists have mostly studied how it varies by culture, ranging from the extreme collectivism of rural Asia to the extreme individualism of the United States (Hofstede, 1980; Triandis, 1994). Individualistic persons and cultures give priority to personal goals and define their identity mostly in terms of their personal attributes. They strive for personal control and individual achievement.

For collectivists, being set adrift in a foreign land might entail a much greater loss of identity. Cut off from family, groups, and loyal friends, collectivists would lose connections that have defined who they are. In a collectivist culture, a social network provides one's bearings. What's important is not "me" but "we." Collectivists give priority to the goals of their groups—often their family, clan, or work group—and define their identity accordingly. By their group identifications, collectivists gain a sense of belonging, a set of values, a network of caring individuals, an assurance of security.

The contrast between these two types of cultures is apparent even in the way members are named. Individualist cultures give priority to personal identity, by putting the personal name first ("John Brink"). Collectivist cultures give priority to one's family identity ("Hui Harry"). Compared with American students, students in Japan and China are much less likely to complete the sentence "I am . . ." with personal traits ("I am sincere," "I am confident") and are much more likely to declare their social identities ("I am a Keio University student," "I am the third son in my family") (Cousins, 1989; Triandis, 1989a,b). For Westerners, individual identity is primary; for Japanese, collective identity is more often primary.

Individualists easily move in and out of social groups. They feel relatively free to switch churches, leave one job for another, or even to leave their extended families and migrate to a new place. In contrast, collectivists may act shy in new groups. They have deeper, more stable attachments to their familiar groups and friends. Relationships are long term. Thus, loyalties run strong between employer and employees.

Because they value communal solidarity, people in collectivist cultures place a premium on maintaining harmony and allowing others to save face. Direct confrontation and blunt honesty are rare, as are expressions of personal egotism. What people say reflects not just what they feel (their inner attitudes) but what they presume others feel (Kashima & others, 1992). Elders and superiors command respect. To preserve group spirit, people avoid touchy topics,

TABLE 11-2

Individualist and Collectivist Values

	Individualism	Collectivism
Concept of self	Independent (identity from individual traits)	Interdependent (identity from belonging)
Life task	Discover and express one's uniqueness	Maintain connections, fit in
What matters	Me—personal achievement and fulfillment; rights and liberties	We—group goals and solidarity; social responsibilities and relationships
Coping method	Change reality	Accommodate to reality
Morality	Defined by individuals (self-based)	Defined by social networks (duty-based)
Relationships	Many, often temporary or casual; confrontation acceptable	Few, close and enduring; harmony required
Attributing behavior	Behavior reflects one's personality and attitudes	Behavior reflects social norms and roles

Source: Adapted from Thomas Schoeneman (1994) and Harry Triandis (1994).

defer to others' wishes, and display a polite, self-effacing humility (Kitayama & Markus, in press; Markus & Kitayama, 1991). People remember those who have done them favors and make reciprocation a social art. The collectivist self is not independent but *inter*dependent (Table 11–2). Among collectivists, no person is an island.

Individualism and collectivism each offers benefits—at a cost. People in competitive, individualist cultures have more personal freedom, take more pride in personal achievements, are less geographically bound to their families, and enjoy more privacy. Their less unified cultures offer a smorgasbord of life-styles and invite individuals to construct their own identities. But compared with collectivists, individualists are also lonelier; more alienated; more homicidal; more vulnerable to stress-related diseases, such as heart attacks; and more likely to divorce (Popenoe, 1993; Triandis & others, 1988). Collectivists demand less romance and personal fulfillment in marriage, which puts the marriage relationship under less pressure (Dion & Dion, 1993). In one survey, "keeping romance alive" was rated as important to a good marriage by 78 percent of American women and 29 percent of Japanese women (*American Enterprise*, 1992). In recent decades, Western individualism has increased and the priority placed on social obligations and family ties has decreased (Yankelovich, 1993). Reflecting on such findings, Martin Seligman (1988) notes that "rampant individualism carries with it two seeds of its own destruction. First, a society that exalts the individual to the extent ours now does will be ridden with depression. . . . Second, and perhaps most important, is meaninglessness [which occurs when there is no] attachment to something larger than you are."

Evaluating the Humanistic Perspective

13. What impact has the humanistic perspective had on psychology?

One thing said of Freud can also be said of the humanistic psychologists: Their impact has been pervasive. Their ideas have influenced counseling, education, child-rearing, and management. They have also influenced—sometimes in ways they did not intend—much of today's popular psychology.

"We do pretty well when you stop to think that people are basically good."

Through popular psychology many of us absorb some of what Maslow and Rogers so effectively taught—that a positive self-concept is the key to happiness and success, that acceptance and empathy help nurture positive feelings about oneself, and that people are basically good and capable of self-improvement. The National Opinion Research Center (1985) reported that by a 4 to 1 margin, Americans believe "human nature is basically good" rather than "fundamentally perverse and corrupt." Humanistic psychologists also take satisfaction in the dramatic difference between today's response to one of the MMPI statements and the response given 50 years ago. Among those in the 1930s normal standardization sample, only 9 percent agreed that "I am an important person"; in the mid-1980s, more than half of the new sample agreed with the statement (Holden, 1986b). Responding to a 1989 Gallup Poll, 85 percent of Americans rated "having a good self-image or self-respect" as *very* important; 0 percent rated it unimportant. And 89 percent of people responding to a 1992 *Newsweek* Gallup Poll rated self-esteem as very important for "motivating a person to work hard and succeed." Humanistic psychology's message has been heard.

Perhaps one reason humanistic psychology's message has been so well received is that its emphasis on the individual self reflects and reinforces Western cultural values. As self-reliant individualism has grown, with increased priority given to personal identity and aspirations, the popular media have celebrated the rugged individual. Movie plots feature rugged heroes who, true to themselves, buck social convention or take the law into their own hands. Popular songs proclaim that "I Did it My Way" and "I Gotta Be Me" and remind us that to love yourself is "The Greatest Love of All" (Schoeneman, 1994).

The prominence of the humanistic perspective set off a backlash of criticism. First, said the critics, its concepts are vague and subjective. Consider the description of self-actualizing people as open, spontaneous, loving, self-accepting, and productive. Is this really a scientific description? Or is it merely a description of Maslow's personal values and ideals? What Maslow did, noted M. Brewster Smith (1978), was to offer impressions of his own personal heroes. Imagine another theorist who began with a different set of heroes—perhaps Napoleon, Alexander the Great, and John D. Rockefeller, Sr. This theorist would likely describe self-actualizing people as "undeterred by the needs of others," "motivated to achieve," and "obsessed with power."

Second, some critics object to the idea that, as Carl Rogers put it, "The only question which matters is, 'Am I living in a way which is deeply satisfying to me, and which truly expresses me?'" (quoted by Wallach & Wallach, 1985). They fear that the individualism encouraged by humanistic psychology—trusting and acting on one's feelings, being true to oneself, fulfilling oneself—promotes self-indulgence, selfishness, and an erosion of moral restraints (Campbell & Specht, 1985; Wallach & Wallach, 1983). Indeed it is those who focus not on themselves but beyond themselves who are most likely to experience social support, to enjoy life, and to cope effectively with stress (Crandall, 1984).

Humanistic psychologists rebut such objections. They counter that belligerence, hostility, and insensitivity are often traceable to a poor self-concept. Moreover, they argue, a secure, nondefensive self-acceptance is actually the first step toward loving others.

Finally, the humanistic psychologists have been accused of failing to appreciate the reality of our human capacity for evil. Faced with assaults on the environment, overpopulation, and threats of nuclear war, apathy can develop from either of two rationalizations. One is a naive optimism that denies the threat ("People are basically good; everything will work out"). The other is a dark despair ("It's hopeless; why try?"). Action requires enough realism to fuel concern and enough optimism to provide hope. Humanistic psychology, say the critics, encourages the needed hope but not the equally necessary realism about evil.

However, even within humanistic psychology there is debate over whether people are basically good. Carl Rogers clearly thought so. Although aware of the "incredible amount" of cruel, destructive behavior in today's world, he did "not find that this evil is inherent in human nature." Given growth-promoting conditions, "I have never known an individual to choose the cruel or destructive path" (Rogers, 1981). Evil, in his view, springs not from human nature but from toxic cultural influences, including "the constricting, destructive influence of our educational system, the injustice of our distribution of wealth, [and] our cultivated prejudices against individuals who are different."

Fellow humanistic psychologist Rollo May dissented from Rogers' optimism. Of course the cultural context matters, he said. But "Who makes up the culture except persons like you and me? The culture is evil as well as good because we, the human beings who constitute it, are evil as well as good." May agreed with critics who see people joining the humanistic movement to find "a community of like-minded persons who also are playing possum to the evils about us." Accepting the reality of human evil requires "the age-old religious truths of mercy and forgiveness," he said, "and it leaves no place for self-righteousness" (R. May, 1982).

! *Rehearse It*

13. Abraham Maslow theorized that human beings are motivated by a hierarchy of needs. When basic physiological and psychological needs are satisfied, he wrote, people become motivated to fulfill their potential through self-actualization. Maslow based his ideas on

a. Freudian theory.
b. his experiences with patients.
c. a series of laboratory experiments.
d. his study of healthy, creative people.

14. According to Carl Rogers, a growth-promoting environment is one that offers genuineness, acceptance, and empathy. The total acceptance Rogers advocated is called

a. self-concept.
b. unconditional positive regard.
c. self-actualization.
d. the "ideal self."

15. Researchers have found that high self-esteem is beneficial, noting that people who feel good about themselves have fewer ulcers, are less likely to use drugs, and are happier, for example. On the other hand, low self-esteem is linked with life problems. How should this link between low self-esteem and life problems be interpreted?

a. Life problems cause low self-esteem.
b. The answer isn't clear because the link is correlational and does not indicate cause and effect.
c. Low self-esteem leads to life problems.
d. Because of the self-serving bias, we must assume that external factors cause low self-esteem.

16. Researchers have found that people tend to accept responsibility for their successes or good qualities, and blame circumstances or luck for their failures. This is an example of

a. low self-esteem.
b. self-actualization.
c. self-serving bias.
d. empathy.

17. Individualists and collectivists have differing identities. Compared to collectivists, individualists more often define themselves in terms of their

a. family connections.
b. nationality.
c. social roles.
d. personal achievements.

18. The humanistic perspective is most concerned with the potential for human growth and self-fulfillment; ideas of the humanistic psychologists have found their way into counseling, education, child-rearing, and popular psychology. The humanistic perspective has been so well received because

a. its emphasis on the individual fits well with the erosion of moral restraints in modern society.
b. it feeds people's optimism about the good in human nature.
c. it negates the idea that humans have basic capacity for evil.
d. its emphasis on the individual self reflects and reinforces Western cultural values.

The Social-Cognitive Perspective

14. What factors does the social-cognitive perspective emphasize?

Our fourth major perspective on personality derives from psychological principles of learning, cognition, and social behavior. Called the **social-cognitive perspective** by psychologist Albert Bandura (1986), its proponents emphasize the importance of external events. Like learning theorists, they believe that we learn many of our behaviors either through conditioning or by observing others and modeling our behavior after them. They emphasize the importance of mental processes: What we think about our situations affects our behavior. So instead of focusing solely on how our environment controls us (behaviorism), social-cognitive theorists focus on how we and our environment interact: How do we interpret and respond to external events? How do our schemas, our memories, and our expectations influence our behavior patterns?

Exploring Behavior in Situations

Reciprocal Influences

Bandura (1986) calls the process of interacting with our environment **reciprocal determinism**. "Behavior, internal personal factors, and environmental influences," he says, "all operate as interlocking determinants of each other" (Figure 11–4). For example, children's TV-viewing habits (past behavior) influence their viewing preferences (internal personal factor), which influence how television (environmental factor) affects their current behavior. The influences are mutual.

Personal/cognitive
factors

Behavior   Environment

Figure 11–4 Reciprocal Determinism *The social-cognitive perspective proposes that our personalities are shaped by the interaction of our situations, our thoughts and feelings, and our behaviors. (From Bandura, 1978.)*

Chill or Thrill *Bungee jumping is not an activity for timid people, but for a thrill-seeker it's just right. Our individual personalities are expressed in the situations we choose and how we react to our experiences.*

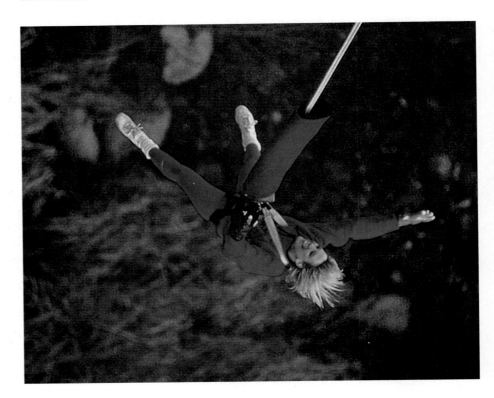

social-cognitive perspective Applies interactive principles of social learning and cognition to study how the environment shapes people's behavior and beliefs, and how these in turn influence people's situations.

reciprocal determinism The interacting influences between personality and environmental factors.

personal control Our sense of controlling our environments rather than feeling helpless.

external locus of control The perception that chance or outside forces beyond one's personal control determine one's fate.

internal locus of control The perception that one controls one's own fate.

Consider three specific ways in which persons and environments interact:

1. **Different people choose different environments.** The school you attend, the reading you do, the television programs you watch, the music you listen to, the friends you associate with—all are part of an environment you have chosen, based partly on your dispositions. You choose it and it shapes you.

2. **Our personalities shape how we interpret and react to events.** Anxious people, for example, are more likely to be attuned to potentially threatening events than are nonanxious people (Eysenck & others, 1987). Thus, anxious people perceive the world as more threatening, and they react accordingly.

3. **Our personalities help create situations to which we react.** Many experiments reveal that how we view and treat our families, roommates, and friends influences how they in turn treat us. If we expect someone to be angry with us, we may give the person a cold shoulder, touching off the very behavior we expect.

In such ways, we are both the products and the architects of our environments. If all this has a familiar ring, it may be because it parallels and reinforces a pervasive theme in psychology and in this book: Behavior emerges from the interplay of external and internal influences. Boiling water turns an egg hard and a potato soft. A threatening environment turns one person into a hero, another into a scoundrel. *At every moment*, our behavior is determined by our genes, our experiences, and our personalities.

Personal Control

14. What are the causes and consequences of personal control?

One important aspect of personality is our sense of **personal control**—whether we learn to see ourselves as controlling, or as controlled by, our environments. Studies of people's sense of personal control demonstrate that behavior is affected by whether people perceive the control of their lives as internal (in themselves) or external (at the mercy of the outside world).

Psychologists have two basic ways to study the effect of personal control (or any personality factor). One: *Correlate* people's feelings of control with their behaviors and achievements. Two: *Experiment*, by raising or lowering people's sense of control and noting the effects.

Locus of Control Consider your own feelings of control. Do you feel that your life is beyond your control? That the world is run by a few powerful people? That getting a good job depends mainly on being in the right place at the right time? Or do you more strongly believe that what happens to you is your own doing? That the average person can influence government decisions? That being a success is a matter of hard work, not luck?

Hundreds of studies have compared people who perceive what psychologist Julian Rotter calls an **external locus of control** (that chance or outside forces determine their fate) with those who perceive an **internal locus of control** (that to a great extent they control their own destinies). In study after study, "internals" achieve more in school, act more independently, and feel less depressed than do "externals" (Benassi & others, 1988; Findley & Cooper, 1983; Lefcourt, 1982). Moreover, they are better able to delay gratification and cope with various stresses, including marital problems (Miller & others, 1986).

learned helplessness The hopelessness and passive resignation learned when an animal or human is unable to avoid repeated aversive events.

Learned Helplessness Versus Personal Control Helpless, oppressed people often perceive control to be external, and this perception may deepen their feelings of resignation. This is precisely what researcher Martin Seligman (1975, 1991) and others found in experiments with both animals and people. When dogs were strapped in a harness and given repeated shocks, with no opportunity to avoid them, they learned a sense of helplessness. When later placed in another situation where they *could* escape the punishment by merely leaping a hurdle, they cowered without hope. Faced with repeated traumatic events over which they have no control, people, too, come to feel helpless, hopeless, and depressed. This passive resignation is called **learned helplessness** (Figure 11–5). In contrast, animals that are able to escape the shocks in the first situation learn personal control and easily escape shocks in the new situation.

Figure 11–5 Learned Helplessness *When animals and people experience no control over repeated bad events, they often learn helplessness.*

Uncontrollable bad events (dog receives inescapable shock) → Perceived lack of control → Generalized helpless behavior (dog passively accepts escapable shock)

In concentration camps, in prisons, even in factories, colleges, and well-meaning nursing homes, people given little control experience a similar lowering of morale and increased stress. In a new place, part of the culture shock is a sense of lowered control when we are unsure how people in the unfamiliar environment will respond (Triandis, 1994). Increasing control—allowing prisoners to move chairs and control room lights and the TV, workers to participate in decision making, nursing home patients to make choices about their environment—noticeably improves health and morale (Miller & Monge, 1986; Ruback & others, 1986; Wener & others, 1987). In one famous study of nursing home patients, 93 percent of those encouraged to exert more control became more alert, active, and happy (Rodin, 1986). As researcher Ellen Langer (1983, p. 291) concluded, "Perceived control is basic to human functioning." She recommended that "for the young and old alike," we create environments that enhance a sense of control and personal efficacy.

To those who worry that the behavioral sciences might undermine traditional values, the verdict of these studies is reassuring: People thrive under conditions of democracy, personal freedom, and empowerment. Small wonder that the citizens of stable democracies report higher levels of happiness (Inglehart, 1990). Shortly before the democratic revolution in the former East Germany, psychologists Gabriele Oettingen and Martin Seligman (1990) compared the telltale body language of working-class men in East and West Berlin bars. Compared with their counterparts on the other side of the Wall, the empowered West Berliners much more often laughed, sat upright rather than slumped, and had upward rather than downward turned mouths. To paraphrase the Roman philosopher Seneca, happy are those who choose their own business.

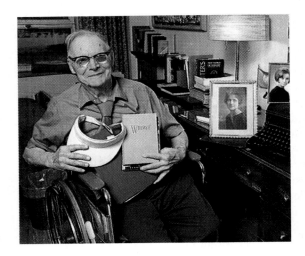

Control Affects Well-Being *Nursing home residents who can arrange their own possessions, control other aspects of their daily lives, and pursue their own interests are more vigorous and happy than those who do not have these opportunities.*

Optimism One measure of how helpless or effective you feel is where you stand on the trait dimension of optimism/pessimism. How do you characteristically explain negative and positive events? Perhaps you have known students who blame poor grades on their lack of ability ("I can't do this") or on situations beyond their control ("bad" teachers, textbooks, or exam questions). Such students are more likely to persist in getting low grades than are students who adopt the more hopeful attitude that effort, good study habits, and self-discipline can make a difference (Noel & others, 1987; Peterson & Barrett, 1987). Similarly, Martin Seligman and Peter Schulman (1986) compared new life insurance representatives who were more or less optimistic in their outlooks. Those who put an optimistic spin on setbacks—by seeing them as flukes or as suggesting a new approach rather than viewing them as signs of incompetence—sold more policies during their first year and were half as likely to quit. Seligman's finding came to life for him when Bob Dell, one of the optimistic recruits who began selling for Metropolitan Life after taking Seligman's optimism test, later dialed him up and sold him a policy.

If positive thinking in the face of adversity pays dividends, so, too, can a realistic dash of pessimism. Anxiety over contemplated failure can actually fuel energetic efforts to avoid the dreaded fate (Cantor & Norem, 1989; Goodhart, 1986; Showers, 1992). Overconfident students often perform less well than their equally able peers who, fearing they are going to bomb on the upcoming exam, proceed to study furiously and get fabulous grades. Success requires enough optimism to provide hope, but also enough pessimism to prevent complacency.

Health, too, benefits from a basic optimism. As we saw in Chapter 10, a depressed hopelessness dampens the body's disease-fighting immune system. In repeated studies, optimists have been found to outlive pessimists or to live with fewer illnesses.

Excessive optimism can, however, blind us to real risks. Neil Weinstein (1980, 1982) has shown how our natural positive-thinking bias can promote "an unrealistic optimism about future life events." Most college students perceive themselves as less likely than their average classmate to develop drinking problems, drop out of school, or have a heart attack by age 40. Most late adolescents see themselves as much less vulnerable than their peers to the AIDS virus (Abrams, 1991).

Given such illusory optimism, people may fail to take sensible precautions. Most young Americans know that half of U.S. marriages end in divorce, but they are confident that *theirs* will not (Lehman & Nisbett, 1985). Most cigarette smokers smoke hazardous high-tar brands, but only 17 percent believe their brand to have a more hazardous tar level than most others (Segerstrom & others, 1993). Sexually active undergraduate women perceive themselves, compared with other women at their university, as much *less* vulnerable to unwanted pregnancy, especially if they do *not* consistently use effective contraception (Burger & Burns, 1988). Those who optimistically shun seat belts, deny the effects of smoking, and venture into ill-fated relationships remind us that, like pride, blind optimism may go before a fall.

Assessing Behavior in Situations

16. How do social-cognitive researchers evaluate personality?

Social-cognitive researchers explore the effect of differing situations on people's behavior patterns and attitudes. They study, for example, how viewing aggressive or nonaggressive models affects behavior. They assess the impact of dehumanizing situations on people's attitudes. And they examine the consistency of people's personalities in varying circumstances.

An ambitious example that predates social-cognitive theory is the U.S. Army's World War II strategy for assessing candidates for spy missions. Rather than using paper-and-pencil tests, army psychologists subjected the candidates to simulated undercover conditions. They tested their ability to handle stress, solve problems, maintain leadership, and withstand intense interrogation without blowing their covers. Although time-consuming and expensive, the assessment of behavior in a realistic situation helped predict later success on real spy missions (OSS Assessment Staff, 1948).

"O God, give us grace to accept with serenity the things that cannot be changed, courage to change the things which should be changed, and the wisdom to distinguish the one from the other."

Reinhold Niebuhr
"The Serenity Prayer," 1943

Pseudo-Assessment—How to Be a "Successful" Astrologer or Palm Reader

How should we evaluate alternative ways of assessing personality? Does the alignment of the stars and planets at the time of one's birth give a clue? Is one's handwriting revealing? Do our palms expose deep secrets? While astronomers scoff at the naiveté of astrology, psychologists ask a different question: Does it work? Are birth dates correlated with character traits? Given someone's birth date, can astrologers surpass chance when asked to identify the person from a short lineup of different personality descriptions? Can people pick out their own horoscopes from a lineup of horoscopes? The consistent answers have been: no, no, no, and no (British Psychological Society, 1993; Carlson, 1985). Graphologists, who make predictions from handwriting samples, have similarly been found to do no better than chance when trying to guess people's occupations, based on several pages of their handwriting (Beyerstein & Beyerstein, 1992; Dean & others, 1992).

How, then, do astrologers and the like persuade thousands of newspapers worldwide and millions of people to buy their advice? Ray Hyman (1981), palm reader turned research psychologist, helps us to see why people get suckered, by revealing the methods of astrologers, palm readers, and crystal-ball gazers.

Their first technique, the "stock spiel," builds on the observation that each of us is in some ways like no one else and in other ways like everyone. That some things are true of us all enables the "seer" to offer statements that seem impressively accurate: "I sense that you're nursing a grudge against someone; you really ought to let that go." "You worry about things more than you let on, even to your best friends." "You are adaptable to social situations and your interests are wide-ranging."

Such generally true statements can be combined into a personality description. Imagine that you take a personality test and then receive the following character sketch:

You have a strong need for other people to like and to admire you. You have a tendency to be critical of yourself. . . . You pride yourself on being an independent thinker and do not accept other opinions without satisfactory proof. You have found it unwise to be too frank in revealing yourself to others. At times you are extraverted, affable, sociable; at other times you are introverted, wary, and reserved. Some of your aspirations tend to be pretty unrealistic (Forer, 1949).

In experiments, college students have received stock assessments like this one. When they think the bogus feedback was prepared just for them and when it is generally favorable, they nearly always rate the description as either "good" or "excellent." Peter Glick and his co-workers (1989) found that even skeptics of astrology, when given a flattering description attributed to an astrologer, begin to think that "maybe there's something to this astrology business after all."

French psychologist Michael Gauguelin placed an ad in a Paris newspaper offering a free personal horoscope. Ninety-four percent of those receiving the horoscope later praised the description as accurate. Actually, all had received the horoscope of France's Dr. Petiot, a notorious mass murderer (Kurtz, 1983).

This acceptance is called the Barnum effect, named in honor of master showman P. T. Barnum's dictum, "There's a sucker born every minute." So powerful is the Barnum effect that, given a choice between this stock spiel and an individualized personality description actually based on a real test, most people choose the phony description as being more accurate. Astrologers and palm readers sprinkle their assessments with stock statements (as in the description quoted, which was drawn from statements in a newsstand astrology book).

Another of Hyman's techniques is to "read" the person's clothing, physical features, nonverbal gestures, and reactions to what you are saying. Imagine yourself as the character reader who was visited by a young woman in her late twenties or early thirties. Hyman describes the woman as "wearing expensive jewelry, a wedding band, and a black dress of cheap material. The observant reader noted that she was wearing shoes which were advertised for people with foot trouble." Do these clues suggest anything?

Drawing on these observations, the character reader proceeded to amaze his client with his insights. He assumed that the woman had come to see him, as did most of his female customers, because of a love or financial problem. The black dress and the wedding band led him to reason that her husband had died recently. The expensive jewelry suggested that she had been financially comfortable during marriage, but the cheap dress suggested that her husband's death had left her impoverished. The therapeutic shoes signified that she was now standing on her feet more than she was used to, implying that she had been working to support herself since her husband's death.

If you are not as shrewd as this character reader (who correctly guessed that the woman was wondering if she should remarry in hope of ending her economic hardship), no matter, says Hyman. Just tell people what they want to hear. Memorize some Barnum statements from astrology and fortune-telling manuals and use them liberally. Tell people it is their responsibility to cooperate by relating your message to their specific experiences. Later they will recall that you predicted the specifics. Phrase statements as questions, and when you detect a positive response assert the statement strongly. Be a good listener, and later, in different words, reveal to people what they earlier revealed to you.

Better yet, beware of fortune-tellers, who, by exploiting people with these techniques, become fortune-takers.

Business, military, and educational organizations are continuing this strategy in their evaluations of several hundred thousand persons each year in some 2000 assessment centers (Bray & Byham, 1991). AT&T observes prospective managers doing simulated managerial work. Many colleges assess potential faculty members' teaching abilities by observing them teach. The army assesses its soldiers by observing them during military exercises.

These procedures exploit the principle that the best means of predicting people's future behavior is not a personality test or an interviewer's intuition. Rather, it is their past behavior patterns in similar situations (Mischel, 1981). As long as the situation and the person remain much the same, the best predictor of future job performance is past job performance; the best predictor of future grades is past grades; the best predictor of future aggressiveness is past aggressiveness; the best predictor of drug use in young adulthood is high school drug use. If you can't check the person's past behavior, the next-best thing is to create an assessment situation that simulates the task demands so you can see how the person handles them.

Evaluating the Social-Cognitive Perspective

17. How does the social-cognitive perspective hold up under criticism?

The social-cognitive perspective on personality sensitizes researchers to how situations affect, and are affected by, individuals. More than the other perspectives, we can also credit it with building from psychological research on learning and cognition.

One criticism is that the theory works *too* well, after the fact. In hindsight, we can explain anything as a product of cognition and the social environment. Another criticism is that the theory focuses so much on the situation that it fails to appreciate the person's inner traits. Where is the person in this view of personality, ask the dissenters (Carlson, 1984). And where are human emotions? True, the situation guides our behavior. But in many instances our unconscious motives, our emotions, and our pervasive traits shine through, say the critics. Percy Ray Pridgen and Charles Gill faced the same situation: They jointly won a $90 million lottery jackpot (Harriston, 1993). Upon learning the winning numbers, Pridgen began trembling uncontrollably, then huddled with a friend behind a bathroom door while confirming the win, then sobbed. Gill told his wife, and then went to sleep.

And that brings us back to where we began our review of these personality theories: Each of the perspectives summarized in Table 11–3 (page 408) can teach us something. The psychoanalytic perspective draws our attention to the unconscious and irrational aspects of human existence. The trait perspective systematically describes and classifies important personality components. The humanistic perspective reminds us of the pivotal importance of our sense of self and of our healthy potential. The social-cognitive perspective applies psychology's basic concepts of learning and thinking and teaches us that we always act in the context of situations that we help to create.

Seldom in life does a single perspective on any issue give us the complete picture. Human personality reveals its different aspects when we view it from different perspectives. Each perspective enlarges our vision of the whole person.

TABLE 11-3

The Four Perspectives on Personality

Perspective	Behavior Springs From	Assessment Techniques	Evaluation
Psychoanalytic	Unconscious conflicts between pleasure-seeking impulses and social restraints	Projective tests aimed at revealing unconscious motivations	A speculative, hard-to-confirm theory with enormous cultural impact
Trait	Expressing biologically influenced dispositions, such as extraversion or introversion	(a) Personality inventories that assess the strength of different traits (b) Peer ratings of behavior patterns	A descriptive approach criticized as sometimes underestimating the variability of behavior from situation to situation
Humanistic	Processing conscious feelings about oneself in the light of one's experiences	(a) Questionnaire assessments of self-concept (b) Empathic interviews	A humane theory that reinvigorated contemporary interest in the self; criticized as subjective and sometimes naively self-centered and optimistic
Social-cognitive	Reciprocal influences between people and their situations, colored by perceptions of control	(a) Questionnaire assessments of people's feelings of control (b) Observations of people's behavior in particular situations	An interactive theory that integrates research on learning, cognition, and social behavior; criticized as underestimating the importance of the unconscious, of emotions, and of enduring traits

! *Rehearse It*

19. Albert Bandura, a social-cognitive theorist, believes that interacting with our environment involves reciprocal determinism, or mutual influences among personal factors, environmental factors, and behavior. An example of an environmental factor is

a. the presence of books in a home.
b. a preference for outdoor play.
c. the ability to read at a fourth-grade level.
d. the fear of violent action on television.

20. Researchers have found that when elderly patients are given an active part in the management of their care and surroundings, their morale and health tend to improve. The assumption is that the patients do better when they perceive

a. learned helplessness.
b. an external locus of control.

c. an internal locus of control.
d. reciprocal determinism.

21. Martin Seligman described an attitude of passive resignation, which he called learned helplessness. Working with animals and people, Seligman identified the circumstances under which learned helplessness develops. For example, a dog will respond with learned helplessness if it has received repeated shocks and has had

a. the opportunity to escape.
b. no control over the shocks.
c. pain or discomfort.
d. no food or water prior to the shocks.

22. We have reviewed four perspectives on personality: the psychoanalytic, trait, humanistic, and social-cognitive perspectives. Which perspective describes person-

ality as a collection of predispositions and behaviors that can be scored on a personality test?

a. psychoanalytic
b. trait
c. humanistic
d. social-cognitive

23. A goal of many personality theories is to be able to predict a person's behavior in a particular situation. A theory that is very sensitive to the way people affect, and are affected by, particular situations, but says little about enduring traits, is the _____ theory.

a. psychoanalytic
b. trait
c. humanistic
d. social-cognitive

Reviewing *Personality*

1. **What is personality?**

   Like intelligence, personality is an abstract concept that cannot be seen, touched, or directly measured. To psychologists, personality is one's relatively distinctive and consistent pattern of thinking, feeling, and acting. We have examined four major perspectives on personality, each valuable for the light it sheds on our complex behavior patterns.

The Psychoanalytic Perspective

2. **What role do unconscious dynamics play in Freud's theory of personality?**

   Sigmund Freud's treatment of emotional disorders led him to believe that they resulted from unconscious dynamics of personality, dynamics which he sought to analyze through the techniques of free associations and dreams.

3. **How did Freud view personality structure and development, and what were the defense mechanisms he proposed?**

   Freud saw personality as composed of a reservoir of pleasure-seeking psychic impulses (the id), a reality-oriented executive (the ego), and an internalized set of ideals (the superego).

   Freud believed that children develop through several formative psychosexual stages, which he labeled the oral, anal, phallic, latency, and genital stages. He suggested that people's later personalities were influenced by how they resolved conflicts associated with these stages and whether they remained fixated at any stage.

   To cope with anxiety caused by the tensions between the demands of id and superego, the ego has protective, reality-distorting defense mechanisms: repression, regression, reaction formation, projection, rationalization, displacement, and sublimation. Of these, repression is the most basic.

4. **How did Freud's followers differ from him?**

   Neo-Freudians, among them Alfred Adler and Karen Horney, accepted many of Freud's ideas but placed more emphasis on conscious experience and on social motivations other than sex and aggression, such as feelings of inferiority and anxiety. Carl Jung expanded Freud's concept of the unconscious to include a collective unconscious inherited by all humans.

5. **How do projective tests assess personality, and are they considered valid?**

   Psychoanalytic assessment aims to reveal the unconscious aspects of personality. Although some critics question the reliability and validity of projective tests, such as the Rorschach inkblots, many clinicians continue to use the Rorschach.

6. **How do Freud's ideas hold up today?**

   Critics say many of Freud's specific ideas are implausible, unvalidated, or contradicted by new research, and that his theory offers only after-the-fact explanations. Nevertheless, Freud drew psychology's attention to the unconscious, to the struggle to cope with anxiety and sexuality, and to the conflict between biological impulses and social restraints. His cultural impact has been enormous.

The Trait Perspective

7. **How do trait theorists view personality?**

   Rather than explain the hidden aspects of personality, trait theorists have described the predispositions that underlie our actions. Through factor analysis, these theorists have isolated distinct dimensions of personality: for example, the "Big Five" trait dimensions—emotional stability, extraversion, openness, agreeableness, and conscientiousness.

8. **How do we assess traits?**

   To assess traits, psychologists have devised objective personality inventories such as the empirically derived MMPI. Computerized testing has made these inventories widely available; however, they are still most helpful when used to assess those who are emotionally troubled.

9. **Does research support the consistency of personality traits?**

   Critics of trait theory question the consistency with which traits are expressed. Although people's traits do seem to persist through time, human behavior varies widely from situation to situation. Nevertheless, people's average behavior across different situations is fairly consistent.

The Humanistic Perspective

10. **What is the central focus of the humanistic perspective?**

    Humanistic psychologists have sought to turn psychology's attention to the growth potential of healthy people, as seen through the individual's own experiences and self-concept. Abraham Maslow believed that if basic human needs are fulfilled, people will strive to actualize their highest potential. To describe self-actualization, he studied some exemplary personalities and summarized his impressions of their qualities. To nurture growth in others, Carl Rogers advised being genuine, accepting, and empathic. In such a climate, people can develop a deeper self-awareness and a more realistic and positive self-concept. Humanistic psychologists assess personality through questionnaires that rate self-concept and by seeking to understand others' subjective personal experiences in therapy.

11. **What have we learned from research on the self?**

Through studies of self-esteem and self-serving bias, we know that self-esteem is an adaptive quality and that most people do perceive and explain themselves favorably.

12. **What distinguishes the individualist and collectivist views of self?**

Individuals and cultures vary in whether they give priority to "me" or "we"—to personal control and individual achievement or to social connections and solidarity. Self-reliant *individualism* defines identity in terms of personal goals and attributes; socially connected *collectivism* gives priority to group goals and to one's social identity and commitments.

13. **What impact has the humanistic perspective had on psychology?**

Humanistic psychology's critics complain that its concepts are vague and subjective, its values self-centered, and its assumptions naively optimistic. Nevertheless, humanistic psychology has helped to renew psychology's interest in the concept of self.

The Social-Cognitive Perspective

14. **What factors does the social-cognitive perspective emphasize?**

The social-cognitive perspective applies principles of social learning and cognition to personality, with particular emphasis on the ways in which our personalities are influenced by our interaction with the environment. Bandura's recipro-

cal determinism emphasizes how personal-cognitive factors interact with the environment.

15. **What are the causes and consequences of personal control?**

By studying variations among people in their perceived locus of control and in their experiences of learned helplessness or mastery and competence, researchers have found that an inner locus of control helps people to cope with life.

16. **How do social-cognitive researchers evaluate personality?**

Social-cognitive researchers study how people's behaviors and beliefs both affect and are affected by their situations. They have found that the best way to predict someone's behavior in a given situation is to observe that person's behavior in similar situations.

17. **How does the social-cognitive perspective hold up under criticism?**

Though faulted for underemphasizing the importance of unconscious dynamics and inner traits, the social-cognitive perspective builds on psychology's well-established concepts of learning and cognition and reminds us of the power of social situations.

Terms and Concepts to Remember

personality, p. 377

free association, p. 378

psychoanalysis, p. 378

unconscious, p. 378

preconscious, p. 378

id, p. 379

pleasure principle, p. 379

ego, p. 379

reality principle, p. 379

superego, p. 380

psychosexual stages, p. 380

oral stage, p. 380

anal stage, p. 380

phallic stage, p. 380

Oedipus [ED-uh-puss] complex, p. 380

identification, p. 380

gender identity, p. 380

latency stage, p. 380

genital stage, p. 380

fixation, p. 380

defense mechanisms, p. 381

repression, p. 381

regression, p. 381

reaction formation, p. 381

projection, p. 382

rationalization, p. 382

displacement, p. 382

sublimation, p. 382

collective unconscious, p. 383

projective tests, p. 384

Thematic Apperception Test (TAT), p. 384

Rorschach inkblot test, p. 384

trait, p. 387

personality inventory, p. 390

Minnesota Multiphasic Personality Inventory (MMPI), p. 390

empirically derived test, p. 390

self-actualization, p. 394

unconditional positive regard, p. 394

self-concept, p. 395

self-esteem, p. 396

self-serving bias, p. 396

individualism, p. 398

collectivism, p. 398

social-cognitive perspective, p. 402

reciprocal determinism, p. 402

personal control, p. 403

external locus of control, p. 403

internal locus of control, p. 403

learned helplessness, p. 404

Rehearse It Answer Key

1. b.   **2.** a.   **3.** b.   **4.** b.   **5.** b.   **6.** d.   **7.** a.   **8.** c.   **9.** b.

10. c.   **11.** c.   **12.** b.   **13.** d.   **14.** b.   **15.** b.   **16.** c.   **17.** d.   **18.** d.

19. a.   **20.** c.   **21.** b.   **22.** b.   **23.** d.

Critical Thinking Exercise

Now that you have read and reviewed Chapter 11, take your learning a step further by testing your critical thinking skills on the following passage.

Darren is a first-year college student who has a biting, sarcastic manner. He is quite pessimistic and feels that the world is run by a few powerful people. When he received a poor grade on a recent exam, Darren blamed the instructor and claimed the test was unfair. He no longer attends lectures or studies for the course and will probably drop it. He is experiencing similar difficulties in his other courses.

Darren always dreamed of doing well in college. Now he is despondent over his failure and believes his professors hate him. Most of all, he is concerned that if he fails in school his parents will no longer love him. Deciding that he needs guidance, Darren begins weekly counseling sessions with Dr. Roitman, a psychoanalyst. After several weeks, Dr. Roitman decides that Darren's maladaptive behavior and attitude stems from unresolved childhood conflicts. He believes that Darren was orally overindulged and is fixated at this stage of psychosexual development. He also feels that Darren's ego is using the defense mechanisms of projection and rationalization to reduce anxiety. Thus, Darren is unconsciously distorting reality by projecting his own self-hatred onto his professors, and is rationalizing his academic failure with a self-justifying explanation in place of its real, more threatening reason.

Understand the Assertion

1. State the psychoanalyst's assertion in your own words. Define all important concepts and terms as they are used in this example.

Consider the Evidence

2. Is the evidence for the psychoanalyst's assertion empirical (observable)? Is the evidence based on trustworthy research?

Evaluate the Explanation

3. Evaluate the theoretical explanation for the psychoanalyst's conclusion.

   a. Restate it in your own words.

   b. Determine whether the explanation makes sense based on the evidence.

   c. State alternative explanations for Darren's problems.

Check your progress on becoming a critical thinker by comparing your answers with the sample answers found in Appendix B.

Chapter 12

Psychological Disorders

Perspectives on Psychological Disorders

Defining Psychological Disorders

Understanding Psychological Disorders

Classifying Psychological Disorders

Anxiety Disorders

Generalized Anxiety Disorder

Phobic Disorders

Obsessive-Compulsive Disorder

Explaining Anxiety Disorders

Somatoform Disorders

Dissociative Disorders

Mood Disorders

Major Depressive Disorder

Bipolar Disorder

Explaining Mood Disorders

Schizophrenia Disorders

Symptoms of Schizophrenia

Types of Schizophrenia

Understanding Schizophrenia

Personality Disorders

Rates of Psychological Disorders

Labeling People: The Power of Preconceptions

People are fascinated by the exceptional, the unusual, and the abnormal. "The sun shines and warms and lights us and we have no curiosity to know why this is so," observed Ralph Waldo Emerson, "but we ask the reason of all evil, of pain, and hunger, and mosquitoes and silly people."

Why a fascination with disturbed people? Perhaps in them we see something of ourselves. At various moments, all of us feel, think, or act as disturbed people do much of the time. We, too, get anxious, depressed, withdrawn, suspicious, deluded, or antisocial, although less intensely and enduringly. Studying psychological disorders may therefore at times evoke an eerie sense of self-recognition that illuminates our own personality dynamics. "To study the abnormal is the best way of understanding the normal," proposed psychologist William James (1842–1910).

Another reason for our curiosity is that so many of us have felt, either personally or through friends or family members, the bewilderment and pain of a psychological disorder. In all likelihood, you or someone you care about has been disabled by unexplained physical symptoms, overwhelmed by irrational fears, or paralyzed by the feeling that life is not worth living. Each year there are nearly 2 million inpatient admissions to U.S. mental hospitals and psychiatric units (Bureau of the Census, 1994). Some 2.4 million others, often troubled but not disabled, seek help as outpatients from mental health organizations and clinics. Many more—15 percent of Americans, according to one government study—are judged to need such help (Robins & Regier, 1991). Such problems are not peculiar to the United States. No known culture is free of the two terrible maladies this chapter examines in depth—depression and schizophrenia (Draguns, 1990a,b). Due in part to brain dysfunctions, some 400 million people worldwide suffer psychological disorders, reports the World Health Organization's mental health director (Sartorius, 1994). As members of the human family, few of us go through life unacquainted with the reality of psychological disturbance.

Perspectives on Psychological Disorders

1. What criteria are used to judge a person's behavior as disordered?

Most people would agree that someone who is too depressed to get out of bed for weeks at a time suffers a psychological disorder. But what about those who, having experienced a loss, are unable to resume their usual social activities? Where should we draw the line between normality and abnormality? How should we *define* psychological disorders? Equally important, how should we *understand* disorders—as sicknesses that need to be diagnosed and cured, or as natural responses to a troubling environment? Finally, how might we *classify* disordered personalities? Can we do so in a way that allows us to help disturbed people and not merely stigmatize them with labels?

Defining Psychological Disorders

James Oliver Huberty had been hearing voices. He "talked with God," his wife reported. Although he had never been to Vietnam, he strode into a San Ysidro, California, McDonald's restaurant one summer day in 1984, screaming, "I've killed a thousand in Vietnam and I'll kill a thousand more." In the next few minutes, before police gunned him down, Huberty murdered 21 people.

At the end of World War II, James Forrestal, the first U.S. secretary of defense, became convinced that Israeli secret agents were following him. His suspiciousness struck his physicians as bizarre. They diagnosed him as mentally ill and confined him to an upper floor of Walter Reed Army Hospital. From there he plunged to his death. Although Forrestal had problems, it was later discovered that he was, in fact, being followed by Israeli agents, who feared he might secretly negotiate with representatives of Arab nations (Sagan, 1979b). As Woody Allen once said, even paranoids can have enemies.

Both the voices that Huberty heard and the degree of anxiety and depression that Forrestal experienced were deviations from the normal. These were "*ab*normal" (atypical) perceptions. Being different from most other people in one's culture is *part* of what it takes to define a psychological disorder.

But there is more to a disorder than being atypical. Olympic gold medalists are abnormal in their physical abilities, and they are heroes. To be considered disordered, other people must find the atypical behavior *disturbing*. Certainly the atypical behavior of a James Oliver Huberty is disturbing.

Standards of acceptability for behaviors vary. In some cultures, people routinely behave in ways (such as going about naked) that in other cultures would be grounds for arrest. In at least one cultural context—wartime—even mass killing may be viewed as heroic. One person's homicidal "terrorist" is another person's "freedom fighter." Standards of acceptability also vary over time. Sex experts William Acton, writing in the late 1800s, and William Masters and Virginia Johnson, writing in the late 1900s, all knew that some women have orgasms during intercourse while others don't (Wakefield, 1992). For Acton, orgasm was the disorder (resulting from overstimulation); for Masters and Johnson, lack of orgasm was the disorder (resulting from inadequate stimulation). Two decades ago, the American Psychiatric Association dropped homosexuality as a disorder (because it was no longer believed connected with psychological problems). Later it added tobacco dependence (because it deemed smoking both addictive and self-destructive).

A Benign Obsession *Although British street cleaner Snowy Farr's eccentric behavior may indeed be atypical, clinicians would not label it disordered because it is neither particularly disturbing nor maladaptive.*

psychological disorder A condition in which behavior is judged atypical, disturbing, maladaptive, and unjustifiable.

"If a man is in a minority of one, we lock him up."

Oliver Wendell Holmes, 1841–1935

Atypical and disturbing behaviors are more likely to be considered disordered when judged as harmful. Indeed, many clinicians define disorders as behaviors that are *maladaptive*—as when a smoker's nicotine dependence produces physical damage. Accordingly, even typical behaviors, such as the occasional despondency that many college students feel, may signal a psychological disorder if they become disabling. For those who define disorder, maladaptiveness is a key; the behaviors must be distressing or disabling or put one at greatly increased risk of suffering or death.

Finally, abnormal behavior is most likely to be considered disordered when others find it rationally *unjustifiable*. Doctors attributed Forrestal's suspicions to his imagination—and declared him disordered. Had he managed to convince others of his suspicions, he might have been helped, not merely labeled. James Oliver Huberty claimed to hear voices and to talk with God, and we presume he was deranged. But Shirley MacLaine can wear a crystal on her neck and say, "See the outer bubble of white light watching you. It is part of you," and she is not considered disordered because enough people take her seriously (Friedrich, 1987).

So, mental health workers label behavior **psychologically disordered** when they judge it *atypical, disturbing, maladaptive*, and *unjustifiable*. Huberty's behavior met these criteria, so we have few doubts in judging him a disordered man.

Understanding Psychological Disorders

Imagine yourself living hundreds or thousands of years ago. How might you have accounted for the behavior of a James Oliver Huberty? To explain puzzling behavior, our ancestors often presumed that strange forces—the movements of the stars, godlike powers, or evil spirits—were at work. "The devil made him do it," you might have said. The cure might have been to get rid of the evil force—by exorcising the demon or even by chipping a hole in the skull to allow the evil spirit to escape (Figure 12–1). Until the last two centuries, "mad" people were sometimes caged in zoolike conditions or given "therapies" appropriate to a demon. Disordered people have been beaten, burned, and castrated. They have had teeth pulled, lengths of intestines removed, and the clitoris cauterized. They have had their own blood removed and replaced with transfusions of animal blood (Farina, 1982). We have fortunately come a long way since the days of such brutal treatment.

Figure 12–1 An Ancient Cure *The hole chipped in this ancient skull found in Peru may have been designed to open the cranium to allow evil spirits to escape. One wonders whether the patient survived the cure.*

The Medical Perspective

2. What is the medical model of psychological disorders, and why do critics question it?

Reformers such as Philippe Pinel (1745–1826) in France insisted that madness was not demon possession but a sickness in response to severe stresses and inhumane conditions. For Pinel and other reformers, treatment meant boosting patients' morale by unchaining them, talking with them, and replacing brutality with gentleness, isolation with activity, and filth with fresh air and sun.

When it was later discovered that an infectious brain disease, syphilis, produced a particular psychological disorder, people also came to believe in physical causes for disorders and to search for medical treatments. Today, this medical perspective is familiar to us in the medical terminology of the mental *health* movement: A mental *illness* (also called a psycho*pathology*) needs to be *diagnosed* on the basis of its *symptoms* and *cured* through *therapy*, which may include *treatment* in a psychiatric *hospital*. In the 1800s, the assumption of this **medical model**—that psychological disorders are sicknesses—provided the impetus for much-needed reform. The "sick" were unchained, and hospitals replaced asylums.

The medical perspective gains credibility from recent discoveries. Genetically influenced abnormalities in brain biochemistry contribute to some disorders. Two of the most troubling, depression and schizophrenia, are often treated medically. As we will see, psychological factors, such as traumatic stress, also play an important role.

Social-Cultural Perspectives

Equating psychological disorders with sickness does, however, have its critics, among them psychiatrist Thomas Szasz. Szasz believes that mental "illnesses" are socially, not medically, defined. When, for many years, Soviet psychiatrists diagnosed dissident citizens as "psychotic," they were using medical metaphors to disguise their contempt for these people's political ideas. Szasz (1984, 1987) concludes that in North America, too, mental health practitioners have too much authority in today's society. When they demean people with the label "mentally ill," their patients may begin to view themselves as "sick" and therefore give up taking responsibility for coping with their problems. Many critics respond similarly to the idea that alcohol abuse, overeating, gambling, and sexual promiscuity are addictive diseases—purely uncontrollable compulsions that require sympathy and treatment. Labels, as we will see, can be self-fulfilling fables.

Psychologists who reject the "sickness" idea typically contend that *all* behavior, whether called normal or disordered, arises from the interaction of nature (genetic and physiological factors) and nurture (past and present experiences). To presume that a person is "mentally ill" attributes the condition solely to an internal problem—to a "sickness" that must be found and cured. Maybe there *is* no deep, internal problem. Maybe there is instead a growth-blocking difficulty in the person's environment, in the person's current interpretations of events, or in the person's bad habits and poor social skills.

When Native Americans were banished from their ancestral lands, forced to live in poverty on more barren reservations, and deprived of personal control, the result was a rate of alcoholism more than five times that of other Americans (May, 1986). Because only some Native Americans become alcoholic, the medical model would attribute such alcoholism to individual "sickness." A psychological perspective would emphasize the interaction between an individual's vulnerability and a hope-eroding environment.

Evidence of environmental effects comes from links between disorder and culture. Some major disorders such as depression and schizophrenia are universal. From Asia to Africa and across the Americas, the core symptoms of schizophrenia include irrationality and incoherent speech (Brislin, 1993; Draguns, 1990b). Other disorders are culture-bound (Beardsley, 1994; Carson & others, 1988). Different cultures have different stresses and produce different ways of coping. Anorexia nervosa and bulimia, for example, are disorders mostly of Western cultures (page 304). *Susto*, marked by severe anxiety, restlessness, and fear of black magic, is a disorder found in Latin America. *Taijin-kyofusho*, which combines social anxiety with easy blushing and fear of eye contact, appears in Japan. Such disorders may share an underlying dynamic (anxiety), yet culturally differ in the symptoms that surface (eating problem or type of fear).

Most mental health workers today assume that disorders are indeed influenced by genetic predispositions and physiological states. And by inner psychological dynamics. And by social circumstances. To get the whole picture, we would do best to rely upon an interdisciplinary "bio-psycho-social" perspective.

> *"It's no measure of health to be well adjusted to a profoundly sick society."*
>
> Krishnamurti (Indian spiritual teacher), 1895–1986

medical model The concept that diseases have physical causes that can be diagnosed, treated, and, in most cases, cured. When applied to psychological disorders, the medical model assumes that these "mental" illnesses can be diagnosed on the basis of their symptoms and cured through therapy, which may include treatment in a psychiatric hospital.

DSM-IV The American Psychiatric Association's *Diagnostic and Statistical Manual of Mental Disorders (Fourth Edition)*, a widely used system for classifying psychological disorders.

Classifying Psychological Disorders

3. Why are psychological disorders classified, and what system is used?

In biology and the other sciences, classification creates order. To classify an animal as a mammal says a great deal—that it is warm-blooded, has hair or fur, and nourishes its young with milk. In psychiatry and psychology, too, classification orders and describes clusters of symptoms. To classify a person's disorder as "schizophrenia" suggests that the person talks incoherently, hallucinates or has delusions (bizarre beliefs), shows either little emotion or inappropriate emotion, or is socially withdrawn. Thus, the diagnostic term provides a handy shorthand for describing a complex disorder.

In psychiatry and psychology, diagnostic classification ideally aims to describe a disorder, to predict its future course, to imply appropriate treatment, and to stimulate research into its causes. Indeed, to study a disorder we must first name and describe it. The current authoritative scheme for classifying psychological disorders is the American Psychiatric Association's *Diagnostic and Statistical Manual of Mental Disorders (Fourth Edition)*, nicknamed **DSM-IV**. This 1994 volume and accompanying case illustrations provide the basis for much of the material in this chapter. DSM-IV was developed in coordination with the tenth edition of the World Health Organization's *International Classification of Diseases* (ICD-10).

For the DSM-IV categories to be valid, they must first be reliable. If one psychiatrist or psychologist diagnoses someone as having, say, a "catatonic schizophrenia disorder," what are the chances that another mental health worker will independently give the same diagnosis? With the DSM-IV's diagnostic guidelines, the chances are good. The guidelines work by asking clinicians a series of objective questions about observable behaviors, such as, "Is the person afraid to leave home?" In one study, 16 psychologists used this structured-interview procedure to diagnose 75 psychiatric patients as suffering either (1) depression, (2) generalized anxiety, or (3) some other disorder (Riskind & others, 1987). Without knowing the first psychologist's diagnosis, another psychologist viewed a videotape of each interview and offered a second opinion. For 83 percent of the patients, the two opinions agreed.

Let us now consider a few of the most prevalent and perplexing disorders, remembering that the people we will meet are not sideshow curiosities but real people—troubled people whose loved ones are troubled for them.

"I'm always like this, and my family was wondering if you could prescribe a mild depressant." :

© 1992 by Sidney Harris.

Rehearse It

1. Each year there are almost 2 million admissions to U.S. psychiatric hospitals—and 2.4 million more seek treatment for psychological disorders at mental health organizations and clinics. According to one U.S. government study, the percentage of people who probably need such help is about

a. 1 percent.
b. 5 percent.
c. 15 percent.
d. 60 percent.

2. To be labeled "disordered," a behavior must usually be atypical, disturbing, unjustified, and maladaptive. For example, we all wash our hands; physicians may well wash their hands 100 times a day. But if a person washes his or her hands 100 times a day for no apparent reason and is unable to do much else, the behavior will be labeled disordered because it is, among other things,

a. unjustified and maladaptive.
b. not explained by the medical model.
c. harmful to others.
d. untreatable.

3. In the past, people considered to be mad or insane were beaten, punished, or caged. The more modern approach is to equate psychological disorders with sickness and to refer the "mentally ill" to hospitals, where they can be treated as patients. This more modern approach is called the

a. social-cultural perspective.
b. psychological model.
c. medical model.
d. diagnostic model.

4. Many psychologists adhere to the idea that mental illness is a sickness arising from an internal problem. Others contend that other factors may be involved—for example, a growth-blocking difficulty in the person's environment or the person's bad habits and poor social skills. Psychologists who take this approach to mental illness are said to be advocates of the _____ perspective.

a. medical
b. biomedical
c. social-psychological
d. social-cultural

5. The American Psychiatric Association's system of classifying psychological disorders is found in the *Diagnostic and Statistical Manual of Mental Disorders (Fourth Edition)*, or DSM-IV. The DSM-IV system is more reliable than its predecessors; one study found that psychologists using the manual's structured-interview procedure agreed on a diagnosis for more than 80 percent of patients. The DSM-IV has improved reliability because it helps mental health workers base their diagnoses on

a. a few well-defined categories.
b. in-depth histories of the patients.
c. the patients' observable behaviors.
d. the theories of Pinel, Freud, and others.

Anxiety Disorders

4. What behaviors characterize anxiety disorders?

Anxiety is part of our everyday experience. When speaking in front of a class, when peering down from a ledge, when waiting for a big game to begin, any one of us might feel anxious. And, at one time or another, most of us feel enough anxiety that we fail to make eye contact or we avoid talking to someone—"shyness," we call it. Fortunately for most of us, our occasional uneasiness is not intense and persistent. If it becomes so, we may have one of the three important **anxiety disorders**: **generalized anxiety disorder**, in which a person feels unexplainably tense and uneasy; **phobic disorder**, in which a person feels irrationally afraid of a specific object or situation; and **obsessive-compulsive disorder**, in which a person is troubled by repetitive thoughts or actions.

Generalized Anxiety Disorder

Tom, a 27-year-old electrician, seeks help, complaining of dizziness, sweating palms, heart palpitations, and ringing in his ears. He feels edgy and sometimes finds himself shaking. With reasonable success he hides his symptoms from his family and co-workers. Nevertheless, he has had few social contacts since the symptoms began 2 years ago. Worse, he occasionally has to leave work. His

anxiety disorders Psychological disorders characterized by distressing, persistent anxiety or maladaptive behaviors that reduce anxiety.

generalized anxiety disorder An anxiety disorder in which a person is continually tense, apprehensive, and in a state of autonomic nervous system arousal.

phobic disorder An anxiety disorder marked by a persistent, irrational fear of a specific object or situation.

obsessive-compulsive disorder An anxiety disorder characterized by unwanted repetitive thoughts (obsessions) and/or actions (compulsions).

panic attack An anxiety disorder marked by a minutes-long episode of intense dread in which a person experiences terror and accompanying chest pain, choking, or other frightening sensations.

family doctor and neurologist can find no physical problem, and a diet for those with low blood sugar has not helped.

Tom's unfocused, out-of-control, threatened feelings suggest a generalized anxiety disorder. The symptoms of this disorder are commonplace; their persistence is not. The sufferers are continually tense and jittery, worried about bad things that might happen, and experience all the symptoms of autonomic nervous system arousal (racing heart, clammy hands, stomach butterflies, sleeplessness). The tension and apprehension may leak out through furrowed brows, twitching eyelids, or fidgeting.

One of the worst characteristics of a generalized anxiety disorder is that the person cannot identify, and therefore cannot avoid, its cause. To use Sigmund Freud's term, the anxiety is "free-floating." As some 1 in 75 people know, for no apparent reason the anxiety may at times suddenly escalate into a terrifying **panic attack**—a minutes-long episode of intense fear that something horrible is about to happen to them. Heart palpitations, shortness of breath, choking sensations, trembling, or dizziness typically accompany the panic. The experience is unpredictable and so frightening that the sufferer often comes to fear the fear itself and to avoid situations where panic has struck.

Phobic Disorders

Fear is normally an adaptive response. Fear prepares our bodies to flee danger. Fear of real or imagined enemies binds people together as families, tribes, and nations. Fear of injury protects us from harm. Fear of punishment or retaliation constrains us from harming one another.

Phobias are irrational fears that are maladaptive. Phobias focus anxiety on some specific object, activity, or situation. (See Figure 12–2 for a ranking of some common fears.) Phobias are a common psychological disorder that people often accept and live with. Some phobic disorders are incapacitating, however. Marilyn, a 28-year-old homemaker, so fears thunderstorms that she feels anxious as soon as a weather forecaster mentions possible storms later in the week. If her husband is away and a storm is forecast, she sometimes stays with a close relative. During a storm, she hides from windows and buries her head to avoid seeing the lightning. She is otherwise healthy and happy.

Other people with phobic disorders suffer from irrational fears of specific animals or of airplanes or elevators or even public places such as department stores. Sometimes it is possible to avoid the fear-arousing stimulus: One can

> "He who fears all snares falls into none."
>
> Publilius Syrus
> *Sententiae,* 43 B.C.

Figure 12–2 Some Common and Uncommon Fears *This national survey ranks the relative fear levels of Americans in response to some sources of anxiety. A fear becomes a phobia if it provokes a compelling but irrational desire to avoid the dreaded object or situation. (From* Public Opinion, *1984.)*

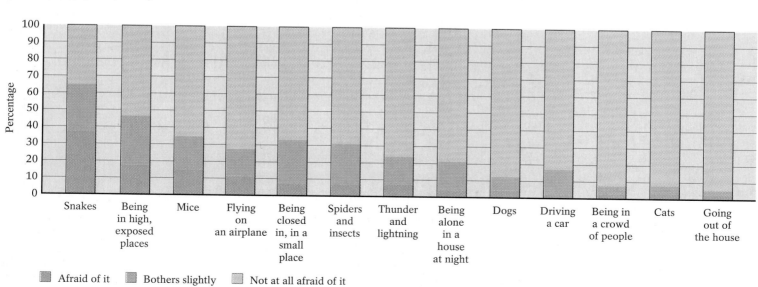

Afraid of it   Bothers slightly   Not at all afraid of it

hide during thunderstorms or avoid air travel. With other phobias, such as an intense fear of being scrutinized by others (*social phobia*) or of being in open or public places (*agoraphobia*), avoiding fear-arousing situations may dictate never leaving home. Compared with the other disorders discussed in this chapter, phobias appear at a younger age—often by the early teens (Burke & others, 1990).

Obsessive-Compulsive Disorder

As with the generalized anxiety and phobic disorders, we can see aspects of ourselves in the obsessive-compulsive disorder. We may at times be obsessed with senseless or offensive thoughts that will not go away. Or we may engage in compulsive, rigid behavior—rechecking a locked door, stepping over cracks in the sidewalk, or lining up our books and pencils "just so" before studying.

Obsessive thoughts and compulsive behaviors cross the fine line between normality and disorder when they become so persistent that they interfere with the way we live or when they cause distress. Checking to see that the door is locked is normal; checking the door 10 times is not. Hand washing is normal; hand washing so often that one's skin becomes raw is not. (Table 12–1 offers more examples.) At some time during their lives, often during their late teens or twenties, 2 to 3 percent of people cross that line from normal preoccupations and fussiness to debilitating disorder (Karno & others, 1988). The thoughts become so haunting, the rituals so senselessly time-consuming, that effective functioning becomes impossible.

One such person was billionaire Howard Hughes. Hughes would compulsively dictate the same phrases over and over again. Under stress, he developed an obsessive fear of germs. He became reclusive and insisted that his assistants carry out elaborate hand-washing rituals and wear white gloves when handling documents he would later touch. He ordered tape around doors and windows and forbade his staff to touch or even look at him. "Everybody carries germs around with them," he explained. "I want to live longer than my parents, so I avoid germs" (Fowler, 1986).

Drawing by Richter; © 1983 The New Yorker Magazine, Inc.

"He always times '60 Minutes.'"

TABLE 12–1	
Common Obsessions and Compulsions*	
	Percentage Reporting Symptom
Obsessions (repetitive thoughts)	
Concern with dirt, germs, or toxins	40
Something terrible happening (fire, death, illness)	24
Symmetry, order, or exactness	17
Compulsions (repetitive behaviors)	
Excessive hand washing, bathing, tooth brushing, or grooming	85
Repeating rituals (in/out of a door, up/down from a chair)	51
Checking doors, locks, appliances, car brake, homework	46

*Seventy children and adolescents suffering obsessive-compulsive disorder reported their symptoms.

Source: Adapted from Rapoport, 1989.

Explaining Anxiety Disorders

5. How do psychologists explain anxiety disorders?

In seeking to understand anxiety disorders, psychologists have emphasized three familiar perspectives—psychoanalytic, learning, and biological.

The Psychoanalytic Perspective

Psychoanalytic theory assumes that, beginning in childhood, intolerable impulses, ideas, and feelings get repressed. This submerged mental energy nevertheless influences our actions and emotions, sometimes producing feelings of anxiety, depression, or other maladaptive symptoms that mystify even the sufferer. One of Freud's classic cases concerned a 5-year-old boy known as Little Hans, whose phobia of horses (in those days before cars) prevented his going outdoors. Freud's controversial speculation was that Little Hans's fear of horses expressed his underlying fear of his father, whom Hans viewed as a rival for his mother's affections.

Alternatively, the forbidden impulses may break through as thinly disguised thoughts, which may provoke acts aimed at suppressing the associated anxiety. The result: obsessions and compulsions. Repetitive hand washing, for instance, supposedly helps suppress anxiety over one's "dirty" urges.

The Learning Perspective

Learning researchers link general anxiety with learned helplessness (page 404). In the laboratory, researchers can create chronically anxious, ulcer-prone rats by giving them unpredictable electric shocks (Schwartz, 1984). Like the rape victim who reported feeling anxious when entering her old neighborhood (page 205), the animals are apprehensive in their lab environment. For many victims of post-traumatic stress disorder (page 360), anxiety swells with any reminder of their trauma. Such experiences might help explain why anxious people are hyperattentive to possible threats (Mineka & Sutton, 1992).

When experimental shocks become predictable—when preceded by a particular conditioned stimulus—the animals' fear focuses on *that* stimulus and they relax in its absence. Recall from Chapter 6, Learning, that dogs learn to fear neutral stimuli associated with shock, that infants come to fear furry objects associated with frightening noises, and that adults can become terrified of incidental stimuli linked with traumatic experiences. As infants become mobile they experience falls and near-falls—and become increasingly afraid of heights (Campos & others, 1992).

Through such conditioning, the short list of naturally painful and frightening events can multiply into a long list of human fears—fear of spiders, fear of closed spaces, fear of driving. Recently, my car was struck by another whose driver missed a stop sign. For months afterward, I felt a twinge of unease with the approach of any car from a side street. Perhaps Marilyn's phobia was similarly conditioned during a terrifying or painful experience associated with a thunderstorm.

Conditioned fears may remain long after we have forgotten the experiences that produced them (Jacobs & Nadel, 1985). Moreover, some fears arise from stimulus generalization. A person who fears heights after a fall may be afraid of airplanes without ever having flown. Fearing panic attacks, a person may just stay inside (Antony & others, 1992). Someone might also learn fear through observational learning—by observing others' fears. As we saw in Chapter 6, wild monkeys transmit their fear of snakes to their offspring; similarly,

An Emotional High   *Although we humans seem biologically predisposed to fear heights—certainly an adaptive response—this construction worker seems fearless. The biological perspective helps us understand why most people would be terrified in this situation.*

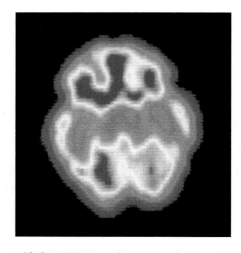

Figure 12–3 A PET Scan of the Brain of a Person With Obsessive-Compulsive Disorder   *This scan reveals abnormally high metabolic activity (red areas) in the frontal lobes, seen at the top of the photo. This is visible in a region of the left hemisphere's frontal lobe involved in directing attention.*

human parents transmit their fears to their children. Avoiding or escaping the feared situation reduces anxiety, thus reinforcing the phobic behavior.

Compulsive behaviors similarly reduce anxiety. If washing your hands relieves your feelings of unease, you will likely wash your hands again when the feelings return.

The Biological Perspective

Other researchers explain our anxiety-proneness in evolutionary, genetic, and physiological terms.

We humans seem biologically prepared to develop fears of heights, storms, snakes, and insects—dangers our ancestors faced. Compulsive acts typically exaggerate behaviors that contributed to our species' survival. Grooming gone wild becomes hair pulling. Washing up becomes ritual hand washing. Checking territorial boundaries becomes checking and rechecking a door known to be locked (Rapoport, 1989).

Some people more than others seem genetically predisposed to particular fears and high anxiety. Identical twins often develop similar phobias, in some cases even when raised separately (Carey, 1990; Eckert & others, 1981). One pair of 35-year-old identical female twins independently developed claustrophobia. They also became so fearful of water that each would gingerly wade backward into the ocean, only up to the knees. Among monkeys, fearfulness runs in families. Individual monkeys react more strongly to stress if their close relatives are anxiously reactive (Suomi, 1986). Among humans, the risk of anxiety disorder rises when the afflicted relative is an identical twin (Kendler & others, 1992).

General anxiety disorder, panic, and even obsessions and compulsions are biologically measurable as an overarousal of brain areas involved in impulse control and habitual behaviors. PET scans of persons with obsessive-compulsive disorder reveal unusually high activity in an area of the frontal lobes just above the eyes (Figure 12–3) and in a more primitive area deep in the brain (Rauch & Jenike, 1993; Resnick, 1992). Some antidepressant drugs control obsessive-compulsive behavior by dampening this activity through affecting the availability of the neurotransmitter serotonin, one of the messenger molecules that shuttle signals between nerve cells.

Somatoform Disorders

6. What characterizes the somatoform disorders?

Ellen becomes dizzy and nauseated in the late afternoon—shortly before she expects her husband home. Her doctor and a neurologist cannot identify a physical cause. They suspect the symptoms have an unconscious psychological origin, possibly triggered by her mixed feelings about her husband. In **somatoform disorders**, such as Ellen's, the distressing symptoms take a somatic (bodily) form, without apparent physical causes. One person may have a variety of complaints—vomiting, dizziness, blurred vision, difficulty in swallowing. Another may experience severe and prolonged pain.

In China, where people less often express the emotional aspects of distress, bodily complaints are common (Draguns, 1990a). Because psychological explanations of anxiety and depression are socially less approved, the Chinese appear more sensitive to, and more willing to report, the bodily symptoms of their distress. Mr. Wu, a 36-year-old technician in Hunan, illustrates one of

China's most common psychological disorders (Spitzer & others, 1989). He finds work difficult because of his insomnia, fatigue, weakness, and headaches. Chinese herbs and Western medicines provide no relief. To his Chinese clinician, he is "exhausted," not depressed. Similar, generalized bodily complaints have often been observed in African cultures (Binitie, 1975).

Even to people in the West, somatic symptoms are familiar. To a lesser extent, we have all experienced inexplicable physical symptoms under stress. It is little comfort to be told that the problem is "all in your head." Although the symptoms may be psychological in origin, they are nevertheless genuinely felt.

One type of somatoform disorder, more common in Freud's day than ours, is **conversion disorder**, so called because anxiety was presumed to be converted into a physical symptom. (As we noted in Chapter 11, Freud's effort to treat and understand psychological disorders stemmed from his puzzlement over ailments that had no physiological basis.) A patient with a conversion disorder might lose sensation in a way that makes no neurological sense. Yet the physical symptoms would be real; one could stick pins in the affected area and get no response. Others experience unexplained paralysis, blindness, or an inability to swallow, and they are strangely indifferent to their problems.

As you can imagine, somatoform disorders send people not to a psychologist or psychiatrist but to a physician. This is especially true of those who experience **hypochondriasis**. In this relatively common somatoform disorder, people interpret normal sensations (a stomach cramp today, a headache tomorrow) as symptoms of a dreaded disease. Sympathy or temporary relief from everyday demands may reinforce such complaints. No amount of reassurance by any physician convinces the patient not to worry. So the patient moves on to another physician, seeking and receiving more medical attention but failing to confront the disorder's psychological root.

"He was a dreadful hypochondriac."

Dissociative Disorders

7. What are dissociative disorders, and why are they controversial?

Among the most intriguing disorders are the rare **dissociative disorders**, in which a person appears to experience a sudden loss of memory or change in identity. When a situation becomes too stressful, people may dissociate themselves from it. Their conscious awareness becomes separated from painful memories, thoughts, and feelings. (Note that this presumes the existence of repressed memories, which as Chapter 7 explained, have recently been questioned.)

Certain symptoms of dissociation are not so rare. Now and then, many people may have a sense of being unreal, of being separated from one's body, of watching oneself as if in a movie. Facing trauma, such detachment may actually protect a person from being overwhelmed by emotion. Only when such experiences are severe and prolonged do they suggest a dissociative disorder.

Amnesia

Amnesia, the failure to recall events, can be caused by head injuries or alcoholic intoxication. But dissociative amnesia, some psychologists believe, usually begins as a response to intolerable psychological stress. One 18-year-old victim was rescued from his sailboat by the Coast Guard and brought to a hospital. He knew he had gone sailing with friends and that he was a college student, but said he could not recall what had happened to his friends. Moreover, he kept

somatoform disorders Psychological disorders in which the symptoms take a somatic (bodily) form without apparent physical cause.

conversion disorder A rare somatoform disorder in which a person experiences very specific, genuine physical symptoms for which no physiological basis can be found.

hypochondriasis A somatoform disorder in which a person misinterprets normal physical sensations as symptoms of a disease.

dissociative disorders Disorders in which conscious awareness becomes separated (dissociated) from previous memories, thoughts, and feelings.

amnesia Loss of memory. Dissociative amnesia is selective memory loss often brought on by extreme stress.

fugue [fewg]   A dissociative disorder in which flight from one's home and identity accompanies amnesia.

dissociative identity disorder   A rare dissociative disorder in which a person exhibits two or more distinct and alternating personalities. Also called *multiple personality disorder.*

forgetting he was in a hospital; each reminder surprised him. Later, aided by a drug that relaxed him, he formed a memory: A ferocious storm had washed his companions overboard.

As this case illustrates, the forgetfulness of amnesia is selective: The young man supposedly forgot what was intolerably painful. Those with amnesia may be somewhat disoriented and may forget who they are, but they will remember how to drive, count, and talk. Typically, the amnesia vanishes as abruptly as it began and rarely recurs.

Fugue

Like amnesia, **fugue** (pronounced fewg, meaning "flight") involves presumed forgetting, but it also involves fleeing one's home and identity for days, months, or years. Gene Smith, a mid-level manager, had been passed over for promotion, faulted by his supervisor, and rejected by his 18-year-old son, who during a violent argument called him a "failure." Two days later, Smith disappeared. A month later and 200 miles away, police brought a man who said he was "Burt Tate" to the emergency room. Tate had been hurt in a fight at a diner, where he had been working as a short-order cook since drifting into town a month earlier. He claimed not to recall where he had lived or worked before that. He admitted that was strange but did not seem upset by it. After a missing-person's check, Mrs. Smith confirmed that Burt Tate was Gene Smith. Though noticeably anxious when faced with his wife, he denied recognizing her. When "awakening" from a fugue state, people such as Gene Smith remember their old identities but typically deny remembering what occurred during the fugue. Skeptics wonder if such patients may be feigning memory loss for strategic reasons.

Dissociative Identity Disorder

Even more mysterious and controversial is the massive dissociation of self from ordinary consciousness in those with multiple personality disorder, now called **dissociative identity disorder.** These people have two or more distinct personalities. The first is usually restrained and dull, the second more impulsive and uninhibited. The person may be prim and proper one moment and loud and flirtatious the next. Each personality has its own voice and mannerisms, and the original one typically denies awareness of the other(s).

Although people diagnosed as having multiple personalities are usually not violent, there have been cases in which the person reportedly became dissociated into a "good" and a "bad" or aggressive personality—a modest version of the Dr. Jekyll/Mr. Hyde split immortalized in Robert Louis Stevenson's story. Freud would say that, rid of the original "good" personality's awareness, the wanton second personality is free to discharge forbidden impulses. One unusual case that for a time seemed to support this interpretation involved Kenneth Bianchi, who was convicted of the "Hillside Strangler" rapes and murders of 10 California women. During a hypnosis session with Bianchi, psychologist John Watkins (1984) "called forth" a hidden personality:

> **Watkins:** *I've talked a bit to Ken, but I think that perhaps there might be another part of Ken that I haven't talked to, another part that maybe feels somewhat differently from the part that I've talked to. . . . Would you talk with me, Part, by saying, "I'm here"?*

Bianchi answered "Yes" and engaged in the following interchange:

> **Watkins:** *Part, are you the same thing as Ken, or are you different in any way?*
> **Bianchi:** *I'm not him.*
> **Watkins:** *You're not him? Who are you? Do you have a name?*
> **Bianchi:** *Steve. You can call me Steve.*

The "Hillside Strangler"   *Kenneth Bianchi is shown here at his trial.*

When speaking as Steve, Bianchi stated that he hated Ken because Ken was nice and that he (Steve), aided by a cousin, had murdered women. He also claimed that Ken knew nothing about his existence and that Ken was innocent of the murders.

Was Bianchi's second personality a ruse, simply a way of disavowing responsibility for his actions? Bianchi, a practiced liar who had read about multiple personality in psychology books, was later convicted of the crimes. Even normal people sometimes act as if they had a multiple personality, as when displaying a goofy, loud-mouthed self while hanging out with friends, and a subdued, respectful self around grandparents. Exploring our capacity for personality shifts, Nicholas Spanos (1986, 1994) asked college students to pretend they were accused murderers being examined by a psychiatrist. When given the same hypnotic treatment Bianchi received, most spontaneously expressed a second personality.

This discovery made Spanos wonder: Are dissociative identities simply a more extreme version of our normal human capacity to shift moods and to vary the "selves" we present in different situations? Are clinicians who discover multiple personalities merely triggering fantasy-prone people's enactment of a role? If so, can such people then convince themselves of the authenticity of their own role enactments? Are they like actors, who commonly report "losing themselves" in their roles? (Recall from Chapter 5 that Spanos also raised these questions about the hypnotic state. Given that most multiple personality patients are highly hypnotizable, whatever explains one condition—dissociation or role playing—may help explain the other.)

Those who accept dissociative identity as a genuine disorder find support in the distinct brain and body states associated with differing personalities (Putnam, 1991). Handedness, too, sometimes switches with personality (Henninger, 1992).

Skeptics nevertheless find it suspicious that the disorder has just recently become rather popular, with an estimated 7000 diagnosed cases in North America alone (Shulruff, 1990). That means that the number of cases reported just since 1980 is 35 times greater than the 200 cases reported until that year (Humphrey & Dennett, 1989). This is just what one might expect now that the role of multiple personality has been well publicized in books and films, such as *The Three Faces of Eve* and *Sybil*. Moreover, most clinicians have never encountered a case of dissociative identity, and the disorder is almost nonexistent outside North America, although in other cultures some people are said to be "possessed" by an alien spirit (Aldridge-Morris, 1989; Kluft, 1991). In Britain, the diagnosis is rare, and in India and Japan it is essentially nonexistent. In North America, not only has the number of such diagnoses exploded, from only 2 reported cases per decade from 1930 to 1960, but so has the average number of personalities displayed—from 3 to 12 per patient (Goff & Sims, 1993).

To skeptics, that sounds like a cultural phenomenon—a disorder created by therapists in a particular social context (Merskey, 1992). Skeptics note how some therapists go fishing for it: "Have you ever felt like another part of you does things you can't control? Does this part of you have a name? Can I talk to the angry part of you?" Once patients permit a therapist to "talk to the part of you that says those angry things" they have begun acting out the fantasy. Moreover, say skeptics, "It is no coincidence" that multiple personality studies began among hypnosis practitioners (Goff, 1993).

With the dissociative disorders, as with the anxiety and somatoform disorders, the psychoanalytic and learning perspectives view the symptoms as ways of dealing with anxiety. Psychoanalysts see them as defenses against the anxiety caused by the eruption of unacceptable impulses. Learning theorists see them as behaviors reinforced by anxiety reduction.

"Pretense may become reality."
Chinese proverb

"Though this be madness, yet there is method in 't."

William Shakespeare
Hamlet, 1600

Others view dissociative disorders as hypnotic-like states into which people lapse as a protective response to traumatic childhood experiences. People diagnosed as having dissociative identity disorder increasingly are women, most of whom reportedly suffered physical, sexual, or emotional abuse as children (Coon & others, 1988; Goff & Sims, 1993; Kluft, 1991). Perhaps, then, multiple personalities are the desperate efforts of the traumatized to flee inward. Maladaptive as they may be, are such psychological disorders expressions of our human struggle to cope with and survive the stresses of life?

! Rehearse It

6. When anxiety is so distressing, uncontrollable, or persistent that it results in maladaptive behavior, the person is said to have an anxiety disorder. If a person's anxiety takes the form of an irrational fear of a specific object or situation—for example, an irrational fear of dogs, thunderstorms, or closed spaces—the disorder is called

a. a phobic disorder.
b. a panic attack.
c. generalized anxiety.
d. an obsessive-compulsive disorder.

7. The experience of anxiety often involves physical symptoms, such as trembling, dizziness, chest pains, or choking sensations. An episode of intense dread, which is typically accompanied by such symptoms and by feelings of terror, is called

a. generalized or chronic anxiety.
b. a social phobia.
c. a panic attack.
d. an obsessive fear.

8. Jennifer has always been concerned with cleanliness and neatness. Her mother never had to remind her to clean up her room. When Jennifer became consumed with the need to clean the entire house and refused to participate in any other activities, her family consulted a therapist, who diagnosed her as having _____ disorder.

a. obsessive-compulsive
b. generalized anxiety
c. phobic
d. conversion

9. Rats subjected to unpredictable shocks in the laboratory become chronically anxious. To the learning researcher this suggests that anxiety is a response to

a. a phobia.
b. biological factors.
c. the pressures of the superego.
d. helplessness.

10. Psychologists have different ideas about the causes of phobic disorders. For example, some psychologists stress the importance of biological predispositions, noting that we seem predisposed to fear certain stimuli. Psychologists of the learning perspective, on the other hand, maintain that phobias are

a. the result of individual genetic makeup.
b. a way of repressing unacceptable impulses.
c. conditioned fears.
d. a symptom of having been abused as a child.

11. A person with a somatoform disorder experiences bodily symptoms that seem to have a psychological, rather than physical, origin. A relatively common somatoform disorder today is

a. conversion disorder.
b. hypochondriasis.
c. unexplained blindness.
d. amnesia.

12. Amnesia, fugue, and dissociative identity (multiple personality) involve gaps in awareness, for example, sudden loss of memory or change of identity. These psychological disorders are called

a. anxiety disorders.
b. dissociative disorders.
c. mood disorders.
d. memory disorders.

Mood Disorders

8. What behaviors characterize mood disorders?

The emotional extremes of **mood disorders** come in two principal forms: (1) **major depressive disorder**, in which the person experiences prolonged hopelessness and lethargy until eventually rebounding to normality; and (2) **bipolar disorder** (often called manic depressive disorder), in which the person alternates between depression and *mania*, an overexcited, hyperactive state.

mood disorders Psychological disorders characterized by emotional extremes.

major depressive disorder A mood disorder in which a person, for no apparent reason, experiences 2 or more weeks of depressed moods, feelings of worthlessness, and diminished interest or pleasure in most activities.

bipolar disorder A mood disorder in which a person alternates between the hopelessness and lethargy of depression and the overexcited state of mania.

mania A mood disorder marked by a hyperactive, wildly optimistic state.

"My life had come to a sudden stop. I was able to breathe, to eat, to drink, to sleep. I could not, indeed, help doing so; but there was no real life in me."

Leo Tolstoy
My Confession, 1887

"All the people in history, literature, art, whom I most admire: Mozart, Shakespeare, Homer, El Greco, St. John, Chekhov, Gregory of Nyssa, Dostoevsky, Emily Brontë: not one of them would qualify for a mental-health certificate."

Madeleine L'Engle
A Circle of Quiet, 1972

Major Depressive Disorder

Perhaps you know what depression feels like. If you are like most college students, at some time during this year—more likely the dark months of winter than the bright days of summer—you will probably experience a few of the symptoms of depression (Beck & Young, 1978). You may feel deeply discouraged about the future, dissatisfied with your life, or isolated from others. You may lack the energy to get things done or even to force yourself out of bed; be unable to concentrate, eat, or sleep normally; or even wonder if you would be better off dead. Perhaps academic success came easily to you in high school, and now you find that disappointing grades jeopardize your goals. Maybe conflicting parental and peer pressures seem intolerable. Perhaps social difficulties, such as loneliness or the breakup of a romance, have plunged you into despair. And maybe your brooding has at times only worsened your self-torment.

If so, you are not alone. Along with the phobias, depression is considered the "common cold" of psychological disorders—an expression that effectively describes its pervasiveness, but not its seriousness. Although phobias are more common, depression is the number one reason why people seek the help of mental health professionals.

The line between life's normal "downs" and major depression is difficult to define. Joy, contentment, sadness, and despair are different points on a continuum, points at which any of us may be found at any given moment. Depression can be an appropriate response to profoundly sad events, such as a significant loss or bereavement. To feel bad in reaction to painful events is to be in touch with reality. In such times, depression is like a car's low-oil-pressure light—a signal that warns us to stop and take protective measures. Depression is a sort of psychic hibernation: It slows us down, avoids attracting predators, and evokes support. To grind to a halt and ruminate, as depressed people do, is to reassess one's life when feeling threatened. Biologically speaking, the purpose of life is not happiness but survival and reproduction. From this perspective, there is sense to suffering (Neese, 1991).

Major depression occurs when signs of depression (poor appetite, insomnia, lethargy, feelings of worthlessness, or loss of interest in family, friends, and activities) last 2 weeks or more without any notable cause. The difference between a blue mood after bad news and a mood disorder is like the difference between gasping for breath after exercising and being chronically short of breath.

Bipolar Disorder

With or without therapy, depressive episodes usually end. Depressed people typically rebound—usually by returning to their previous behavior patterns. However, some people rebound to or from the opposite emotional extreme—a euphoric, hyperactive, wildly optimistic state of **mania**. If depression is living in slow motion, mania is fast forward. Alternating between depression and mania signals *bipolar disorder*. During the manic phase of a bipolar disorder, the person is typically overtalkative, overactive, elated (though easily irritated if crossed), has little need for sleep, and shows fewer sexual inhibitions. Speech is loud, flighty, and hard to interrupt.

One of mania's maladaptive symptoms is grandiose optimism and self-esteem, which may lead to reckless spending and investment sprees. Although people in a manic state find advice irritating, they need protection from their own poor judgment. In milder forms, however, the energy and free-flowing thinking of mania can fuel creativity. Bipolar disorder is especially common among poets, artists, and playwrights (Jamison, 1993, 1995). Handel composed his nearly 4-hour-long *Messiah* during 3 weeks of intense, creative energy.

Suicide

"But life, being weary of these worldly bars,
Never lacks power to dismiss itself."
William Shakespeare
Julius Caesar, 1599

Each year some three-quarters of a million wearied, despairing people worldwide will say no to life by electing a permanent solution to what may be a temporary problem (Retterstøl, 1993). In retrospect, their families and friends may recall signs they now believe should have forewarned them—the suicidal talk, the giving away of possessions, or the withdrawal and preoccupation with death. Most of those who kill themselves have been depressed. One-third have tried suicide before.

Few of those who talk suicide or think suicidal thoughts (a number that includes one-third of all adolescents and college students) actually attempt suicide, and few of these succeed in killing themselves (Centers for Disease Control, 1989; Westefeld & Furr, 1987). Still, most individuals who do commit suicide have talked of it. And any who do talk suicide are at least sending a signal of their desperate or despondent feelings.

To find out who commits suicide, researchers have compared the suicide rates of different groups.

- **National differences** The suicide rates of England, Italy, and Spain are little more than half those of Canada, Australia, and the United States; Austrian, Danish, and Swiss suicide rates are nearly double (Bureau of the Census, 1993).

- **Racial differences** In the United States, whites are twice as likely as blacks to kill themselves (Figure 12–4).

- **Gender differences** Women are much more likely than men to attempt suicide. Depending on the country, however, men are two to four times more likely to succeed. (Men are more likely to use foolproof methods, such as putting a bullet into the brain, the method of choice in 6 of 10 U.S. suicides.)

White males
Black males
White females
Black females

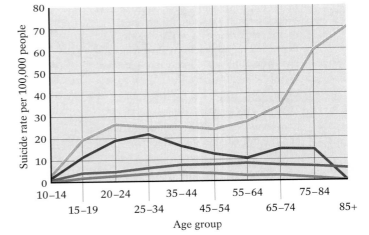

Figure 12–4 Suicide Rate by Gender, Race, and Age *In the United States, suicide rates are higher among whites than blacks, and higher among males than among females. (From Bureau of the Census, 1993.)*

- **Age differences** Due partly to improved reporting (Gist & Welch, 1989), the known suicide rate among 15- to 19-year-olds has more than doubled since 1950. It now nearly equals the traditionally higher suicide rate among adults (Figure 12–5). In both the United States and Australia, the teen suicide surge is almost entirely among males (Hassan & Carr, 1989.)

- **Other group differences** Suicide rates are much higher among the rich, the nonreligious, and those who are single, widowed, or divorced (Hoyer & Lund, 1993; Stack, 1992; Stengel, 1981).

People who commit suicide often do so not while in the depths of depression, when energy and initiative are lacking, but when they begin to rebound and become capable of following through. Teenage suicides may follow a traumatic event, such as a romantic breakup or a guilt-provoking antisocial act; they are often linked with drug and alcohol abuse (Fowler & others, 1986; Kolata, 1986). Compared with people who suffer no disorder, alcoholics are roughly 100 times more likely to commit suicide, as some 3 percent of them do (Murphy & Wetzel, 1990). Even among those who have attempted suicide, alcoholics are five times more likely than nonalcoholics eventually to kill themselves (Beck & Steer, 1989). Among the elderly, suicide is sometimes chosen as an alternative to future suffering. In people of all ages, suicide is not necessarily an act of hostility or revenge, as many people think, but may be a way of switching off unendurable pain (Shneidman, 1987).

Social suggestion may trigger the final act. Following highly publicized suicides and TV programs featuring suicide, known suicides increase. So do fatal auto "accidents" and private airplane crashes.

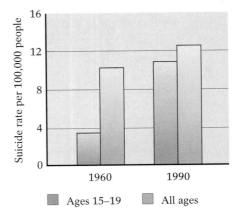

Figure 12–5 Increasing U.S. Rates of Teen Suicide *Teen suicide has soared since 1960. (From National Center for Health Statistics.)*

It is as true of emotions as all else: What goes up comes down. Before long, the elated mood either returns to normal or plunges into a brief depression. Though equally maladaptive as major depression, bipolar disorder is much less common, occurring in about 1 percent of the population. Unlike major depression, it afflicts as many men as women.

Explaining Mood Disorders

9. What causes mood disorders?

For some people, recurring depression during winter's dark months constitutes a *seasonal affective disorder*.

Because depression profoundly affects many people, it has been the subject of thousands of studies. Psychologists are working to develop a theory of mood disorders that will suggest ways to treat or prevent them. Researcher Peter Lewinsohn and his colleagues (1985) summarized the facts that any theory of depression must explain. Among them are the following:

▶ *Many behavioral and cognitive changes accompany depression.* Depressed people are inactive and unmotivated. They also are especially sensitive to negative happenings, expect negative outcomes, and are more likely to recall negative information. When the depression lifts, these behavioral and cognitive accompaniments disappear.

▶ *Depression is widespread.* Its commonality suggests that its causes, too, must be common.

▶ *Compared with men, women are twice as vulnerable to major depression, even more so if they have been depressed before.* In general, women are most vulnerable to passive disorders—things internal, such as depression, anxiety, and inhibited sexual desire. Men's disorders are more active—alcohol abuse, antisocial conduct, lack of impulse control (see Table 12–2, page 442). Curiously, though, the gender difference in depression rates does not exist among college students or bereaved persons (Goodman & Koenig, 1992; Nolen-Hoeksema, 1990).

▶ *Most depressive episodes last less than 3 months.* Although therapy can speed recovery, most people suffering major depression return to normal without professional help. Depression comes and, a few weeks or months later, it goes.

About 50 percent of those who recover from depression will suffer another episode within 2 years. Recovery is more likely to be enduring the longer patients stay well, the fewer their previous episodes, the less stress they experience, and the more social support they have (Belsher & Costello, 1988).

▶ *Stressful events related to work, marriage, and close relationships often precede depression.* A family member's death, a wage cut, or a physical assault increase one's risk of depression (Shrout & others, 1989). National samples of Israelis, whose tiny nation is a living stress laboratory, revealed greater feelings of depression after the outbreak of the 1982 Israel-Lebanon war (Hobfoll & others, 1989).

To these facts we can add one more: With each new generation, the rate of depression is increasing and the disorder is striking earlier (now often in the late teens). It's true in Canada and the United States—and in Germany, Italy, France, Lebanon, New Zealand, Taiwan, and Puerto Rico (Cross-National Collaborative Group, 1992). In North America, today's young adults are three times as likely as their grandparents to report having recently—or ever—suffered depression (despite the grandparents' having had many more years at risk). In one National Institute of Mental Health study of 18,244 Americans, only 1 percent of those born before 1905 had suffered major depression by age 75. Of those born since 1955, 6 percent had been depressed by age 25. The increase appears genuine, *not* primarily a result of younger adults' greater willingness to admit depression. The increasing rate of depression helps explain a dramatic

They Know the Pain of Depression *Actress Patty Duke spent years suffering from bipolar disorder before she was finally treated. Now she spends her free time educating others about mental illness in thanks "for having been saved from that pit." CBS correspondent Mike Wallace became debilitated by severe depression during a tough libel trial. "Depression is palpable," he says. "You begin to feel like a fake and a fraud. You second-guess everything about everything."*

rise in the proportion of psychiatric patients with mood disorders. In a survey of North American psychiatric teaching hospitals, mood disorder diagnoses rose from 10 percent of patients in 1972 to 44 percent in 1990 (Stoll & others, 1993).

As you might expect, researchers understand and interpret these facts in ways that reflect their different perspectives.

The Psychoanalytic Perspective

To explain depression, psychoanalytic theory applies Freud's ideas about the importance of early childhood experiences and unconscious impulses. It suggests that depression occurs when significant losses evoke feelings associated with losses experienced in childhood. Loss of a romantic relationship or a job might evoke feelings associated with the loss of the intimate relationship with one's mother. Unresolved anger toward one's parents is also a factor, Freud believed. Some losses, such as a loved one's death, may evoke the anger once felt toward parents who were similarly "abandoning" or "rejecting." This anger is unacceptable to the superego, so the emotion turns inward against the self. Combined with the sense of loss, this internalized anger is said to produce depression.

The Biological Perspective

Most of the mental health research dollars of late have funded explorations of physiological influences on mood disorders. Depression is a whole-body disorder, involving genetic predispositions, biochemical imbalances, melancholy mood, and negative thoughts.

Genetic Influence   We have long known that mood disorders run in families. The risk of major depression and bipolar disorder increases if you have a parent or sibling who became depressed before age 30 (Pauls & others, 1992; Weissman & others, 1986). If one identical twin is diagnosed as suffering major depressive disorder, the chances are about 1 in 2 that at some time the other twin will be, too. If one identical twin has bipolar disorder, the chances are 7 in 10 that the other twin will at some point be diagnosed similarly. (Led by James Watson, Nobel laureate for determining the structure of DNA, a collaborative search for the genes that put people at risk for bipolar disorder is now under way. Stay tuned.) Among fraternal twins, the corresponding odds are just under 1 in 5 (Tsuang & Faraone, 1990). Moreover, adopted people who suffer a mood disorder often have close biological relatives who suffer mood disorders, become alcoholic, or commit suicide (Wender & others, 1986).

The Depressed Brain   Genes act by directing biochemical events that, down the line, influence behavior. One biochemical key is the neurotransmitters, those chemical messenger molecules. Norepinephrine, a neurotransmitter that increases arousal and boosts mood, is overabundant during mania and scarce during depression. A second neurotransmitter, serotonin, appears scarce during depression. Drugs that alleviate mania reduce norepinephrine; drugs that relieve depression tend to increase norepinephrine or serotonin supplies by blocking either their reuptake by neurons (as Prozac does with serotonin) or chemical breakdown.

Using the new scanning machines, researchers are also spotting neurological signs of depression. In recent studies, the brains of depressed people have been found to be less active, indicating a slowed-down state (Figure 12–6). The left frontal lobe, which serves functions related to positive emotions, is especially likely to be relatively inactive (Davidson, 1992). MRI scans have even shown the frontal lobes to be 7 percent smaller in severely depressed patients (Coffey & others, 1993).

Figure 12–6 The Ups and Downs of Bipolar Disorder
These PET scans show that brain energy consumption rises and falls with the patient's emotional switches. The red areas show where the brain is rapidly consuming glucose. (PET scans courtesy of Drs. Lewis Baxter and Michael E. Phelps, UCLA School of Medicine.)

Depressed state
(17-May-83)

Manic state
(18-May-83)

Depressed state
(27-May-83)

Brain chemistry → Cognition → Mood → Brain chemistry

Figure 12–7 Depression—An Ailing Mind in an Ailing Body *Altering any one component of the chemistry-cognition-mood circuit can alter the others.*

"I have learned to accept my mistakes by referring them to a personal history which was not of my making."

B. F. Skinner (1983)

The Social-Cognitive Perspective

Biological factors do not operate in a social vacuum. As Figure 12–7 suggests, they accompany psychological reactions to experience. The mind's negative thoughts somehow influence biochemical events that in a vicious cycle amplify depressing thoughts.

Recent research reveals how *self-defeating beliefs* feed the vicious cycle. Depressed people view life through dark glasses. Their intensely negative assumptions about themselves, their situations, and their futures lead them to magnify bad experiences and minimize good ones. As one occasionally depressed young woman put it:

> My thoughts become negative and pessimistic. As I look into the past, I become convinced that everything that I've ever done is worthless. Any happy period seems like an illusion. My accomplishments appear as genuine as the false facade of a Western movie. I become convinced that the real me is worthless and inadequate. I can't move forward with my work because I become frozen with doubt (Burns, 1980, pp. 28–29).

Self-defeating beliefs may arise from *learned helplessness*. As we saw in Chapter 11, both dogs and humans act depressed, passive, and withdrawn after experiencing uncontrollable painful events. Women more often than men have been abused or made to feel helpless, which helps explain why women have been twice as vulnerable to depression as have men (Nolen-Hoeksema, 1990, and see page 429). (Another explanation is that men more often suppress their negative feelings, act them out, or drown them in alcohol.)

Maladaptive Explanations Feed Depression Why do life's unavoidable failures lead some people, but not others, to become depressed? The difference lies partly with people's *attributions* of blame. We have some choice of whom or what to blame for our failures. If you fail a test and blame yourself, you may feel stupid and depressed. If you externalize the blame—perhaps attributing your failure to an unfair test—you are more likely to feel angry.

Depressed people tend to explain bad events in terms that are *stable* ("It's going to last forever"), *global* ("It's going to affect everything I do"), and *internal* ("It's all my fault"). Lyn Abramson, Gerald Metalsky, and Lauren Alloy (1989) theorize that the result of these pessimistic, overgeneralized, self-blaming attributions is a depressing sense of hopelessness.

Martin Seligman (1991) argues that depression is now common among young Westerners because of epidemic hopelessness, which stems from the rise of individualism and the decline of commitment to religion and family. When facing failure or rejection, contends Seligman, the self-focused individual takes on personal responsibility for problems and has nothing to fall back on for hope. In non-Western cultures, where close-knit relationships and cooperation are the norm, major depression is less common and less tied to guilt and self-blame over perceived failure. In Japan, for example, depressed people instead tend to report feeling shame over letting down their family or co-workers (Draguns, 1990a).

Depression's Vicious Cycle "A recipe for severe depression is preexisting pessimism encountering failure," notes Martin Seligman (1991, p. 78). Depression is often brought on by stressful experiences—losing a job, getting divorced or rejected, physical trauma—anything that disrupts your sense of who you are and why you are a worthy human being (Hamilton & others, 1993; Kendler & others, 1993). Such brooding after failure can be adaptive; insights gained during times of depressed inactivity may later enable better strategies for interacting with the world. But depression-prone people respond to bad events in an especially self-focused, self-blaming way (Pyszczynski & others, 1991; Wood & others, 1990a,b). Their self-esteem fluctuates more rapidly up with boosts and down with threats (Butler & others, 1994). When down, their brooding amplifies negative feelings, which in turn trigger depression's other cognitive and behavioral symptoms.

None of us is immune to the bad feelings, diminished self-esteem, and negative thinking brought on by rejection or defeat. As Edward Hirt and his colleagues (1992) demonstrated, even small losses can temporarily sour our thinking. They studied some Indiana University basketball fans who seemed to regard the team as an extension of themselves. After the fans were depressed by watching their team lose, or elated by a victory, the researchers asked them to predict the team's future performance, and their own. After a loss, the fans offered bleaker assessments not only of the team's future, but also of their own likely performance at throwing darts, solving anagrams, and getting a date. When things aren't going our way, it may seem as though they never will.

New evidence suggests there is two-way traffic between depressed mood and negative thinking. Depression causes self-focused negative thinking, and a self-focused, self-blaming style of explaining events puts one at risk for depression when bad events strike. If you tend to see bad grades, social rejection, and work problems as inevitable and your own fault, and if you ruminate about such things, then when bad events happen you will experience a bad case of the blues. In research demonstrating this effect, Susan Nolen-Hoeksema and Jannay Morrow (1991) happened to assess Stanford University students' moods and ruminations 2 weeks before the 1989 earthquake devastated much of their area. Those identified as prone to brood over negative events showed more symptoms of depression both 10 days and 7 weeks after the earthquake. If you have an optimistic way of interpreting events, a failure or stress is unlikely to provoke depression (Seligman, 1991). Even if you do get depressed, you are more likely to recover quickly (Metalsky & others, 1993; Needles & Abramson, 1990).

Another source of depression's vicious cycle is its social consequences. Being withdrawn, self-focused, and complaining elicits rejection (Gotlib & Hammen, 1992; Segrin & Dillard, 1992). In one study, researchers Stephen Strack and James Coyne (1983) noted that "depressed persons induced hostil-

"Man never reasons so much and becomes so introspective as when he suffers, since he is anxious to get at the cause of his sufferings."

Luigi Pirandello
Six Characters in Search of an Author, 1922

Loneliness

Loneliness—the painful awareness that one's social relationships are deficient—is both a contributor to depression and its own problem. The deficiency stems from a mismatch between one's actual and desired social contacts. One person may feel lonely when isolated and another may feel lonely in a crowd.

Aloneness often breeds loneliness. People who are alone—unmarried, unattached, and often young—are more likely to feel lonely. Dutch psychologist Jenny de Jong-Gierveld (1987) speculates that the current emphasis on individual fulfillment and the downgrading of stable relationships and commitment to others are "loneliness-provoking factors."

People commonly experience one or more of four types of loneliness (Beck & Young, 1978). To be lonely is to feel *excluded* from a group you would like to belong to; to feel *unloved* and uncared about by those around you; to feel *constricted* and unable to share your private concerns with anyone; or to feel *alienated*, or different, from those in your community.

Like depressed people, lonely people tend to blame themselves, attributing their deficient social relationships to their own inadequacies (Snodgrass, 1987). There may be a basis for this self-blame: Chronically lonely people tend to be shy, self-conscious, and lacking in self-esteem, and to be perceived as less socially competent and attractive (Cheek & Melchior, 1990; Lau & Gruen, 1992; Vaux, 1988). They often find it hard to introduce themselves, make phone calls, and participate in groups (Rook, 1984; Spitzberg & Hurt, 1987). In addition, their belief in their social unworthiness restricts their noticing and remembering positive feedback and from taking steps that would reduce their loneliness (Frankel & Prentice-Dunn, 1990). Thus, factors that work to create and maintain the cycle of depression can also produce a cycle of loneliness.

Drawing by Cheney; © 1989 *The New Yorker Magazine, Inc.*

---

ity, depression, and anxiety in others and got rejected. Their guesses that they were not accepted were not a matter of cognitive distortion." Weary of the depressed person's fatigue, hopeless attitude, and lethargy, a spouse may threaten to leave or a boss may begin to question the person's competence. Indeed, depressed people are at high risk for divorce and job loss, thus compounding their depression. Misery may love another's company, but company does not love another's misery.

We can now assemble the pieces of the depression puzzle (Figure 12–8): (1) Stressful events interpreted through (2) a pessimistic explanatory style create (3) a hopeless, depressed state that (4) hampers the way the person thinks and acts. This, in turn, fuels (1) more negative, stressful experiences. On the brighter side, we can break the cycle of depression at any of these points—by moving to a different environment, by reversing our self-blame and negative attributions, by turning our attention outward, or by engaging in more pleasant activities and more competent behavior. The several points at which the cycle can be broken enable several different therapeutic methods (Chapter 13).

Winston Churchill called depression a "black dog" that periodically hounded him. Poet Emily Dickinson was so afraid of bursting into tears in public that she spent much of her adult life in seclusion (Patterson, 1951). Abraham Lincoln was so withdrawn and brooding as a young man that his friends feared he might take his own life (Kline, 1974). As each of these lives reminds us, people can and do struggle through depression. Most regain their capacity to love, to work, and even to succeed at the highest levels.

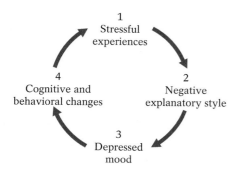

Figure 12–8 The Vicious Cycle of Depression *This cycle can be broken at any point. The next chapter describes some therapeutic techniques. (Adapted from Lewinsohn & others, 1985.)*

! Rehearse It

13. Conversion disorder and dissociative identity are relatively rare psychological disorders. An example of a disorder that is so common it has been called "the common cold" of psychological disorders is

a. amnesia.
b. depression.
c. bipolar disorder.
d. schizophrenia.

14. With bipolar disorder, the person alternates between the lethargy of depression and the overexcited state of mania. Although bipolar disorder is as maladaptive as depression, it is much less common and it affects

a. all ethnic groups equally.
b. primarily scientists and doctors.
c. as many men as women.
d. younger people more than older people.

15. Depression affects many people, often following a stressful event, such as divorce or job change. In a depressive episode, a person tends to be inactive and unmotivated and overly sensitive to negative happenings. In most cases, the depressive episode lasts

a. less than 3 months.
b. 6 months.
c. 6 months to a year.
d. 2 years.

16. Depression tends to run in families. It can often be alleviated by drugs that block the reuptake of the neurotransmitters norepinephrine and serotonin. These statements suggest that an explanation for depression may well be found in

a. psychoanalytic theory.
b. learned helplessness.

c. stressful events.
d. biological factors.

17. Depressed people are more likely than others to blame themselves, rather than external factors, for their failures. Such self-defeating beliefs often arise from feelings of helplessness or futility. Psychologists who emphasize the importance of negative perceptions, beliefs, and thoughts in depression are working within the _____ perspective.

a. psychoanalytic
b. biological
c. behavioral
d. social-cognitive

Schizophrenia Disorders

10. What behaviors characterize schizophrenia disorders?

If depression is the common cold of psychological disorders, chronic schizophrenia is the cancer. About 1 in 100 people will develop schizophrenia, joining the millions who have suffered one of humanity's most dreaded disorders. It typically strikes during adolescence or young adulthood. It knows no national boundaries, and it affects males and females about equally.

Symptoms of Schizophrenia

Literally translated, **schizophrenia** means "split mind." It refers not to a multiple-personality split but rather to a split from reality that shows itself in disorganized thinking, disturbed perceptions, and inappropriate emotions and actions.

Disorganized Thinking

Imagine trying to communicate with Maxine Mason, a young woman whose thoughts spilled out in no logical order. Her biographer, Susan Sheehan (1982, p. 25; 1995), observed her saying aloud to no one in particular,

> This morning, when I was at Hillside [Hospital], I was making a movie. I was surrounded by movie stars. The X-ray technician was Peter Lawford. The security guard was Don Knotts. That Indian doctor in Building 40 was Lou Costello. I'm Mary Poppins. Is this room painted blue to get me upset? My grandmother died four weeks after my eighteenth birthday.

schizophrenia A group of severe disorders characterized by disorganized and deluded thinking, disturbed perceptions, and inappropriate emotions and actions.

delusions False beliefs, often of persecution or grandeur, that may accompany schizophrenia.

As this strange monologue illustrates, the schizophrenia patient's thinking is fragmented, bizarre, and distorted by false beliefs, called **delusions** ("I'm Mary Poppins"). Jumping from one idea to another may occur even within sentences, creating a sort of "word salad." One young man begged for "a little more allegro in the treatment," and suggested that "liberationary movement with a view to the widening of the horizon" would "ergo extort some wit in lectures." Those with *paranoid* schizophrenia have delusions of persecution or grandeur. They may therefore be suspicious or angry about supposed tormentors and enemies.

Many psychologists believe disorganized thoughts result from a breakdown in selective attention. Recall from Chapter 5 that we normally have a remarkable capacity for selective attention—for, say, giving our undivided attention to one voice at a party while filtering out competing sensory stimuli. Schizophrenia sufferers have impaired attention (Gjerde, 1983). Thus, an irrelevant stimulus or an extraneous part of the preceding thought easily distracts them. Minute stimuli, such as the grooves on a brick or the inflections of a voice, may distract attention from the whole scene or from the speaker's meaning. As one former schizophrenia patient recalled, "What had happened to me . . . was a breakdown in the filter, and a hodge-podge of unrelated stimuli were distracting me from things which should have had my undivided attention" (MacDonald, 1960, p. 218).

Disturbed Perceptions

The schizophrenia victim may also perceive things that are not there. Such *hallucinations* (sensory experiences without sensory stimulation) are usually auditory. The person may hear voices that seem to come from outside the head and that make insulting statements or give orders. The voices may tell the patient that she is bad or that he must burn himself with a cigarette lighter. Less commonly, people see, feel, taste, or smell things that are nonexistent. Such halluci-

Art by People Diagnosed With Schizophrenia *Commenting on the kind of artwork shown here, poet John Ashbery wrote: "The lure of the work is strong, but so is the terror of the unanswerable riddles it proposes."*

nations have been compared to dreams breaking into waking consciousness. When the unreal seems real, the resulting perceptions are at best bizarre and at worst terrifying.

Inappropriate Emotions and Actions

The emotions of schizophrenia are often utterly inappropriate. Maxine Mason's emotions seemed split off from reality. She laughed after recalling her grandmother's death. On occasion, she became angry for no apparent reason or cried when others laughed. Other victims of schizophrenia sometimes lapse into *flat affect*, a zombie-like state of apparent apathy.

Motor behavior also may be inappropriate. The person may perform senseless, compulsive acts, such as continually rocking or rubbing an arm. Those who exhibit *catatonia* may remain motionless for hours on end and then become agitated.

As you can imagine, disorganized thinking, disturbed perceptions, and inappropriate emotions and actions disrupt social relationships. During their most severe periods, schizophrenia sufferers live in a private inner world, preoccupied with illogical ideas and unreal images. Although some people suffer from schizophrenia only intermittently, others remain socially withdrawn and isolated throughout much of their lives. Rarely is schizophrenia a one-time episode that is "cured," never to return.

Types of Schizophrenia

We have described schizophrenia as if it were a single disorder. Actually, it is a cluster of disorders that have common features but also some distinguishing symptoms. Schizophrenia patients with *positive symptoms* are disorganized and deluded in their talk or prone to inappropriate laughter, tears, or rage. Schizophrenia patients with *negative symptoms* have toneless voices, expressionless faces, or mute and rigid bodies.

Sometimes, as in the case of Maxine Mason, schizophrenia develops gradually, emerging from a long history of social inadequacy (which partially explains why those predisposed to schizophrenia often end up in the lower socioeconomic levels, or even as homeless people). Other times it appears suddenly, seemingly as a reaction to stress. There is a rule that holds true around the world (World Health Organization, 1979): When the schizophrenia is a slow-developing process (called *chronic*, or *process* schizophrenia), recovery is doubtful. When, in reaction to particular life stresses, a previously well-adjusted person develops schizophrenia rapidly (*acute*, or *reactive* schizophrenia), recovery is much more likely. Those with chronic schizophrenia often exhibit the negative symptoms of withdrawal. The outlook is better for those exhibiting positive symptoms, who more often have a reactive condition that responds to drug therapy (Fenton & McGlashan, 1991, 1994; Fowles, 1992).

Understanding Schizophrenia

11. What causes schizophrenia?

Schizophrenia is not only the most dreaded psychological disorder but also one of the most heavily researched. At the 1993 International Congress on Schizophrenia, more than 70 percent of the new research studies explored the biology of schizophrenia (Iacono & Grove, 1993). Important new discoveries link schizophrenia with brain abnormalities and genetic predispositions.

Brain Abnormalities

The idea that imbalances in brain chemistry might underlie schizophrenia has long intrigued scientists. Strange behaviors, they knew, could have strange chemical causes. The saying "mad as a hatter" refers to the psychological deterioration of British hatmakers whose brains, it was later discovered, were slowly poisoned as they moistened the brims of mercury-laden felt hats with their lips (Smith, 1983). Scientists are beginning to understand the mechanism by which chemicals such as LSD produce hallucinations. These discoveries hint that schizophrenia might have a biochemical key.

One such key to schizophrenia involves the neurotransmitter dopamine. When researchers examined schizophrenia patients' brains after death, they found an excess of receptors for dopamine—in fact, a sixfold excess for the so-called D4 dopamine receptor (Seeman & others, 1993; Wong & others, 1986). Such a high level may intensify brain signals, the researchers speculate, creating schizophrenia's positive symptoms. As we might therefore expect, drugs that block dopamine receptors often lessen schizophrenia symptoms. Drugs that increase dopamine levels, such as amphetamines and cocaine, sometimes intensify schizophrenia symptoms (Swerdlow & Koob, 1987). Such dopamine overactivity may be what makes schizophrenia victims overreact to irrelevant external and internal stimuli.

Modern brain-scanning techniques reveal that many chronic schizophrenia patients have abnormal brain tissue. Schizophrenia patients have been found to have a smaller thalamus—a structure deep in the brain that filters and directs incoming sensation (Andreason & others, 1994). Patients, especially male patients, also often have enlarged, fluid-filled areas and a corresponding shrinkage of cerebral tissue (Gur & others, 1991; Van Horn & McManus, 1992). The greater the shrinkage, the worse the thought disorder often is (Cannon & Marco, 1994; Shenton & others, 1992).

Naturally, scientists wonder what causes these brain abnormalities. One possibility is a prenatal problem, such as a midpregnancy viral infection that might impair development of the fetal brain (Waddington, 1993). Can you imagine some ways to test this fetal virus idea? Scientists exploring this possibility have asked the following questions:

▶ *Are people at increased risk of schizophrenia if, during the middle of their fetal development, their country experienced a flu epidemic?* The repeated answer is yes (Mednick & others, 1994; Murray & others, 1992).

▶ *Are those born during the winter and spring months—after the fall-winter flu season—also at increased risk?* The answer is yes, at 5 to 15 percent increased risk (Pulver & others, 1992; Torrey & others, 1977, 1993; Wright & Murray, 1993).

▶ *In the southern hemisphere, where the seasons are the reverse of the northern hemisphere, are the months of above-average schizophrenia births similarly reversed?* Again, the answer is yes. In Australia, for example, people born between August and October are at greater risk—unless they migrated from the northern hemisphere, in which case their risk is greater if born between January and March (McGrath & others, 1994).

▶ *As infectious disease rates have declined, has there been a correlated decline in the later incidence of schizophrenia?* Once again, the answer is yes (Eagles, 1991).

Although schizophrenia has other causes as well (as genetics research makes plain), these converging lines of evidence suggest that prenatal viral infections do play a contributing role.

Genetic Factors

Might people also inherit a predisposition to certain brain abnormalities? The evidence strongly suggests that some do. The 1 in 100 odds of any person's being diagnosed with schizophrenia become 1 in 10 among those who have an afflicted sibling or parent, and close to 1 in 2 among those who have an afflicted identical twin (Figure 12–9). Although there are only a dozen such known cases, it appears that an identical twin of a schizophrenia victim retains that 1 in 2 chance whether they are reared together or apart.

Figure 12–9 Risk of Developing Schizophrenia *The lifetime risks of suffering from schizophrenia vary with one's genetic relatedness to someone having this disorder. (From family and twin studies conducted between 1920 and 1987 in Europe, from Irving Gottesman, 1991.)*

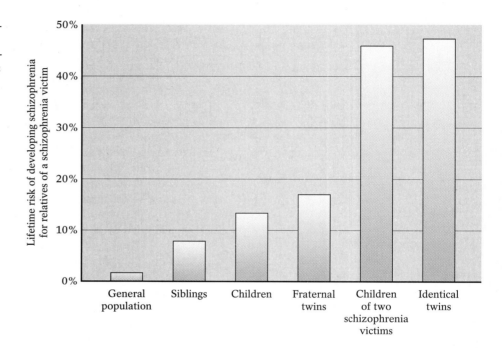

Adoption studies confirm a genetic link (Gottesman, 1991). Children adopted by someone who develops schizophrenia are unlikely to "catch" the disorder. Rather, adopted children have an elevated risk if a biological parent is diagnosed with schizophrenia.

The genetic contribution to schizophrenia is beyond question. But the genetic role is not so straightforward as the inheritance of eye color. After all, about half the twins who share identical genes with a schizophrenia sufferer do *not* develop the disorder. Thus, behavior geneticists Susan Nicol and Irving Gottesman (1983) concluded that some people "have a genetic predisposition to the disorder but that this predisposition by itself is not sufficient for the development of schizophrenia."

Given the genetic influences upon disorders such as schizophrenia and bipolar disorder, might scientists develop genetic tests that reveal who is at risk? (We do know, for example, that genes influence the excess of one type of dopamine receptor [Anderson, 1994].) If so, might it be possible to prescribe treatments that prevent the disorder? Although hopes for such tests grow, the patterns of inheritance seem too complex to hope that a single gene abnormality will prove predictive (Gottesman, 1993). But given the explosion in gene and brain research technologies, scientists are optimistic that schizophrenia will be much better understood before this "decade of the brain" is over.

Schizophrenia in Twins *When twins differ, only the one afflicted with schizophrenia typically has enlarged, fluid-filled cranial cavities (Suddath & others, 1990). The difference between the twins implies some non-genetic factor, such as a virus, is also at work.*

No schizophrenia   Schizophrenia

Psychological Factors

If, by themselves, genetically predisposed physiological abnormalities do not cause schizophrenia, neither do psychological factors alone. As Nicol and Gottesman report, "No environmental causes have been discovered that will invariably, or even with moderate probability, produce schizophrenia in persons who are not related to a schizophrenic."

Nevertheless, if genes predispose some people to *react* to particular experiences by developing schizophrenia, then there must be identifiable triggering experiences. Researchers have asked: Can stress trigger schizophrenia? Can difficulties in family communications be a contributing factor?

The answer to each question is a strong maybe. The psychological triggers of schizophrenia have proved elusive, partly because they may vary with the type of schizophrenia and whether it is a slow-developing, chronic schizophrenia, or a sudden, acute reaction to stress. It is true that young people with schizophrenia tend to have unusually disturbed communications with their parents. But is this a cause or a result of their disorder? It is true that stressful experiences, biochemical abnormalities, and schizophrenia's symptoms often occur together. But the traffic between brain biochemistry and psychological experiences runs both ways, so cause and effect are difficult to sort out. It is true that schizophrenic withdrawal often occurs in adolescence or early adulthood, coinciding with the stresses of having to become independent, assert oneself, and achieve social success and intimacy. So is schizophrenia the maladaptive coping reaction of biologically vulnerable people?

The Genain Quadruplets *The odds of any four people picked at random all being diagnosed with schizophrenia are 1 in 100 million. But Nora, Iris, Myra, and Hester Genain all have the disease. Two of the sisters have more severe forms of the disorder than the others, suggesting the influence of environmental as well as biological factors.*

Most of us can relate more easily to the ups and downs of mood disorders than to the strange thoughts, perceptions, and behaviors of schizophrenia. Sometimes our thoughts do jump around, but we do not talk nonsensically. Occasionally we feel unjustly suspicious of someone, but we do not fear that the world is plotting against us. Often our perceptions err, but rarely do we see or hear things that are not there. We have felt regret after laughing at someone's misfortune, but we rarely giggle in response to bad news. At times we just want to be alone, but we do not live in social isolation. However, millions of people around the world do talk strangely, suffer delusions, hear nonexistent voices, see things that are not there, laugh or cry at inappropriate times, or withdraw into their private imaginary worlds. Because this is true, the quest to solve the cruel puzzle of schizophrenia continues.

These recollections by a recovered schizophrenia patient illustrate the symptoms often experienced by those who suffer the positive symptoms of schizophrenia. Note the hallucinations and the delusions of persecution and grandeur.

One night I was invited to listen to a talk by a worker in the foreign service. I was suspicious of him and thought he thought I was a Communist spy. I didn't say anything. I just leaned over and stared at him.

I thought the Government was spying on my room with a telescope in a building across the street. I thought people were loading down my food in the cafeteria with salt. In criminology class I thought the professor and the other students were laughing about me. I thought they were directing the poisoning of my food in the cafeteria. When I went to the cafe-

teria my hand shook as the waitress poured what I thought was poisonous coffee into my cup. I thought everyone in the cafeteria knew I was going to die. They all thought it was too bad but I was so evil it was necessary.

On a Saturday I drank lemonade to try to neutralize the poison. Then I would take showers to try to sweat the poison out. I was so nervous I could hardly think. I thought I might only have hours left to live. I thought of taking a bus home to my parents. But no, I thought, it was too late for that.

One day when my strange behavior landed me in a jail cell, the walls began to buzz like bees. I felt there were thousands of bees in the walls buzzing. The buzzing went on and on. There was no relief. It was maddening. Finally, I felt my father's hand rest on my head and I felt

peace. Then voices, like the roar of a crowd came. I felt like Jesus; I was being crucified. Night settled in. It was dark. I just continued to huddle under the blanket, feeling weak, laid bare and defenseless in a cruel world I could no longer understand.

When someone asks me to explain schizophrenia I tell them, you know how sometimes in your dreams you are in them yourself and some of them feel like real nightmares? My schizophrenia was like I was walking through a dream. But everything around me was real. At times, today's world seems so boring and I wonder if I would like to step back into the schizophrenic dream, but then I remember all the scary and horrifying experiences. (Excerpted with permission from S. Emmons and C. Geiser, *Adventures in Schizophrenia*, unpublished manuscript.)

Personality Disorders

12. What characteristics are typical of personality disorders?

Does a full moon trigger "madness" in some people? James Rotton and I. W. Kelly (1985) examined data from 37 studies that related lunar phase to crime, homicides, crisis calls, and mental hospital admissions. Their conclusion: There is virtually no evidence of "moon madness." Nor does lunar phase correlate with suicides, assaults, emergency room visits, or traffic disasters (Byrnes & Kelly, 1992; Kelly & others, 1990; Martin & others, 1992).

Personality disorders—inflexible and enduring patterns of behavior that impair one's social functioning—sometimes coexist with one of the other psychological disorders, but they need not involve anxiety, depression, or loss of contact with reality. A person with a *histrionic personality disorder* displays a shallow, attention-getting emotionality. Histrionic individuals go to great lengths to gain others' praise and reassurance. Those with *narcissistic personality disorder* exaggerate their own importance, aided by success fantasies. They find criticism hard to accept, often reacting with rage or shame. Those with *borderline personality disorder* have an unstable identity, unstable relationships, and unstable emotions. If personality is one's enduring pattern of thinking, feeling, and acting, then a markedly unstable sense of self defines a "borderline personality."

The most frequent of these disorders, and the most troubling to society, is the **antisocial personality** disorder. The person (formerly called a *sociopath* or a *psychopath*) is typically a male whose lack of conscience becomes plain before age 15, as he begins to lie, steal, fight, or display unrestrained sexual behavior. About half of such children become antisocial adults—unable to keep a job, irresponsible as a spouse and parent, and assaultive or otherwise criminal (Farrington, 1991). When the antisocial personality combines a keen intelligence with amorality, the result may be a charming and clever con artist—or worse.

Despite their antisocial behavior, most criminals do not fit the description of antisocial personality disorder. Most criminals show responsible concern for

personality disorders Psychological disorders characterized by inflexible and enduring behavior patterns that impair social functioning.

antisocial personality A personality disorder in which the person (usually a man) exhibits a lack of conscience for wrongdoing, even toward friends and family members. May be aggressive and ruthless or a clever con artist.

their friends and family members; antisocial personalities feel little and fear little. In extreme cases, the results can be tragic. Henry Lee Lucas reported that at age 13 he strangled a woman who refused to have sex with him. He at one time confessed to having bludgeoned, suffocated, stabbed, shot, or mutilated some 360 women, men, and children during his 32 years of crime. During the last 6 years of his reign of terror, Lucas teamed with Elwood Toole, who reportedly slaughtered about 50 people whom he "didn't think was worth living anyhow." It ended when Lucas confessed to stabbing and dismembering his 15-year-old common-law wife, who was Toole's niece.

The antisocial personality expresses little regret over violating others' rights. "Once I've done a crime, I just forget it," said Lucas. Toole was equally matter-of-fact: "I think of killing like smoking a cigarette, like another habit" (Darrach & Norris, 1984).

As with mood disorders and schizophrenia, the antisocial personality disorder is woven of biological as well as psychological strands. Although there is no single gene that codes for a complex behavior such as crime, twin and adoption studies reveal that biological relatives of certain individuals are at increased risk for criminality (Brennan & Mednick, 1991; DiLalla & Gottesman, 1993). Their genetic vulnerability surfaces as minimal arousal under stress, which makes for a rather fearless approach to life. When they await aversive events, such as electric shocks or loud noises, they show little autonomic nervous system arousal (Hare, 1975). Even as youngsters, before committing any crime, they react with lower levels of stress hormones than do others their age (Figure 12–10). If channeled in more productive directions, such fearlessness may lead to courageous heroism or adventurism. Lacking a sense of social responsibility, the same disposition produces a cool con artist or killer (Lykken, 1982).

Perhaps a biologically based fearlessness, as well as early environment, helps explain the reunion of long-separated sisters Joyce Lott, 27, and Mary Jones, 29—in a South Carolina prison where both were sent on drug charges. After a newspaper story about their reunion, their long-lost half-brother Frank Strickland called. He explained it would be a while before he could come see them—because he, too, was in jail, on drug, burglary, and larceny charges (Shepherd & others, 1990).

Figure 12–10 Arousability and Risk of Crime *Levels of the stress hormone adrenaline were measured in two groups of 13-year-old Swedish boys. In both stressful and nonstressful situations, those who were later convicted of a crime (as 18- to 26-year-olds) showed relatively low arousal. (From Magnusson, 1990.)*

Rehearse It

18. People who suffer from schizophrenia often show disorganized thinking and disturbed perceptions. They may speak illogically and may hear voices urging self-destruction. Hearing voices in the absence of any auditory stimulation is an example of a(n)

a. delusion or false belief.
b. inappropriate emotion.
c. word salad.
d. hallucination.

19. Stressful events, faulty family communications, and, especially, inherited abnormalities in brain chemistry and structure are all possible factors in the development of schizophrenia. Chances for recovery are best when

a. onset is sudden, in response to stress.
b. deterioration occurs gradually, during childhood.
c. no environmental causes can be identified.
d. there is a detectable brain abnormality.

20. Unlike other psychological disorders, personality disorders need not involve any apparent anxiety, depression, or loss of contact with reality. A personality disorder, such as antisocial personality, is characterized by

a. the presence of multiple personalities.
b. bodily symptoms that have psychological causes.
c. enduring and maladaptive personality traits.
d. mood disturbances.

Rates of Psychological Disorders

13. How common are the psychological disorders we've discussed?

How prevalent are the various disorders discussed in this chapter? Who is most vulnerable to them? At what times of life? To answer such questions, the National Institute of Mental Health (NIMH) undertook during the 1980s a short census of psychological disorders in the United States. In five different regions of the country researchers conducted lengthy, structured interviews with a representative sample of people—all told, nearly 20,000 people—and then projected their findings to the entire U.S. population. After asking hundreds of questions that probed for symptoms—"Has there ever been a period of 2 weeks or more when you felt like you wanted to die?"—the researchers estimated both the current and the lifetime prevalence of various disorders.

How many people suffer, or have suffered, a psychological disorder? More than most of us suppose. Reporting on the NIMH study, Lee Robins and Darrel Regier (1991, p. 329) note that "one or more of the psychiatric disorders . . . had been experienced at some time in their lives by 32 percent of American adults, and 20 percent had an active disorder." These surprisingly high rates reflect the inclusion of institutionalized as well as community samples, and surely also reflect how well many people manage to hide disorders such as a phobia, alcohol abuse, or depression. Table 12–2 shows the relative prevalence of most of the disorders we have considered among three ethnic groups and among men and women. As you can see, despite differences in their rates of various psychological disorders, all these groups are vulnerable.

The incidence of serious psychological disorders is doubly high among those below the poverty line (Centers for Disease Control, 1992). Like so many other correlations, the poverty-disorder association raises a chicken-and-egg

TABLE 12-2

Percentage of Americans Who Have Ever Experienced Psychological Disorders

	Ethnicity			Gender		
	White	Black	Hispanic	Men	Women	Totals
Alcohol abuse or dependence	13.6%	13.8%	16.7%	23.8%	4.6%	13.8%
Generalized anxiety	3.4	6.1	3.7	2.4	5.0	3.8
Phobic disorder	9.7	23.4	12.2	10.4	17.7	14.3
Obsessive-compulsive disorder	2.6	2.3	1.8	2.0	3.0	2.6
Mood disorder	8.0	6.3	7.8	5.2	10.2	7.8
Schizophrenia disorders	1.4	2.1	0.8	1.2	1.7	1.5
Antisocial personality	2.6	2.3	3.4	4.5	0.8	2.6

Source: Data from Robins & Regier, 1991. Similar gender differences, though with somewhat higher rates of disorder, come from the U.S. National Comorbidity Survey (Kessler & others, 1994).

question: Does poverty cause disorders? Or do disorders cause poverty? It's both, though the answer varies with the disorder. Schizophrenia understandably leads to poverty. Yet the stresses and demoralization of poverty can also precipitate disorders, especially depression in women and antisocial personality and substance abuse in men (Dohrenwend & others, 1992).

Those who experience a psychological disorder usually do so by early adulthood. "Over 75 percent of our sample with any disorder had experienced its first symptoms by age 24," report Robins and Regier (1991, p. 331). The symptoms of antisocial personality and of phobic disorder appear earliest, by a median age of 8 and 10, respectively. Symptoms of alcohol abuse, obsessive-compulsive disorder, bipolar disorder, and schizophrenia appear at a median age near 20. Major depression often hits somewhat later, at a median age of 25. Such findings make clear the need for research and treatment to help the growing number of people, especially youth and young adults, who suffer the bewilderment and pain of a psychological disorder.

Labeling People: The Power of Preconceptions

14. Why do clinicians label patients with different diagnoses? Why do some psychologists criticize such labeling?

As noted earlier, the practice of attaching diagnostic labels to people is controversial. Most clinicians believe that classification helps in describing, treating, and researching the causes of psychological disorders. Critics, however, say that these labels are at best arbitrary and at worst value judgments that masquerade as science. It is better, they say, to study the roots of specific symptoms, such as delusions or hallucinations, than to study catchall categories, such as schizophrenia (Persons, 1986). Moreover, once we label a person, we view that person differently (Farina, 1982). Labels create preconceptions that can bias our perceptions and interpretations. For example, Ellen Langer and her colleagues (1974, 1980) had people rate an interviewee they thought was either normal (a job applicant) or out of the ordinary (a psychiatric or cancer patient). All subjects saw the identical videotape. Those who watched unlabeled interviewees (supposed job applicants) perceived them as normal; those who watched supposed patients perceived them as "different from most people." Therapists (who thought they were evaluating a psychiatric patient) perceived the interviewee as "frightened of his own aggressive impulses," a "passive, dependent type," and so forth.

Labels can also stigmatize people in others' eyes. U.S. Senator Thomas Eagleton experienced this in 1972, when he was dumped as the Democratic party's vice-presidential candidate after it was discovered he had been treated for depression with electroshock therapy. The same stigma surfaced when a female associate of psychologist Stewart Page (1977) called 180 people in Toronto who were advertising furnished rooms for rent. When she merely asked if the room was still available, the answer was nearly always yes. When she said she was about to be released from a mental hospital, the answer three times out of four was no (as it was when she said she was calling for her brother who was about to be released from jail). When some of those who answered no were called by a second person who simply asked if the room was still available, the advertiser nearly always revealed that it was. Surveys in Western Europe have uncovered similar attitudes toward those labeled mentally ill.

"One of the unpardonable sins, in the eyes of most people, is for a man to go about unlabelled. The world regards such a person as the police do an unmuzzled dog, not under proper control."

T. H. Huxley
Evolution and Ethics, 1893

If people form their impressions of psychological disorder from the media, such findings are hardly surprising. Television researcher George Gerbner (1985) reports that 1 in 5 prime-time and daytime programs depicts a psychologically disordered person, and 7 in 10 such programs portray this character as violent or criminal. Movies, too, stereotype mental patients, sometimes as homicidal (Anthony Hopkins' role in *Silence of the Lambs*), or as "zoo specimens" (Woody Allen as *Zelig*) (Hyler & others, 1991; Wahl, 1992). A few schizophrenia-prone people do commit crimes, and some disordered people are amoral and antisocial (Monahan, 1992; Phillips & others, 1988; Silverton, 1988). However, at least 9 in 10 disordered people are *not* dangerous; instead, they are anxious, depressed, or withdrawn.

Labels not only bias perceptions, they can also change reality. When teachers are told certain students are "gifted," when students expect someone to be "hostile," or when interviewers check to see whether someone is "extraverted," they may act in ways that elicit the very behavior expected (Snyder, 1984). Someone who was led to think you are nasty may treat you coldly, provoking you to respond as a nasty person would. Labels can serve as self-fulfilling prophecies.

But let us also remember the benefits of diagnostic labels. As Robert Spitzer (1975), a chief author of the current diagnostic system explains:

> There is a purpose to psychiatric diagnosis. It is to enable mental health professionals to (a) communicate with each other about the subject matter of their concern, (b) comprehend the pathological processes involved in psychiatric illness, and (c) control psychiatric outcomes.

We need not dismiss psychological labels in order to be encouraged by the many successful people—including Leonardo da Vinci, Isaac Newton, and Leo Tolstoy—who pursued brilliant careers while enduring psychological difficulties. The bewilderment, fear, and sorrow caused by psychological disorders are real. But, as the next chapter shows, hope is also real.

! *Rehearse It*

21. Based on an NIMH report, researchers note that 32 percent of American adults have experienced a psychiatric disorder at some time in their lives. Despite differences in the prevalence of disorders among ethnic groups and among men and women, all groups are vulnerable. One factor that crosses ethnic and gender lines and is closely correlated with serious psychological disorder is

a. age.
b. education.
c. poverty.
d. religious faith.

22. Labels such as "schizophrenia" and "hypochondriasis" may be useful in clinical situations. In other contexts, however, labels create preconceptions and biases. From watching television dramas you would never guess that most schizophrenia-prone people, when encountered in the real world, seem

a. antisocial and amoral.
b. violent or homicidal.
c. accomplished in the arts and literature.
d. anxious, depressed, or withdrawn.

Reviewing *Psychological Disorders*

Perspectives on Psychological Disorders

1. What criteria are used to judge a person's behavior as disordered?

Between normality and abnormality lies not a gulf, but a fine and somewhat arbitrary line. Where we draw the line depends on how atypical, disturbing, maladaptive, and unjustifiable a person's behavior is.

2. What is the medical model of psychological disorders, and why do critics question it?

The medical model's assumption that psychological disorders are mental "illnesses" has displaced earlier views that demons and evil spirits were to blame. However, critics question the medical model's labeling of psychological disorders as sicknesses. They argue that the disorders are socially defined and that some disorders are found only in certain cultures. Most mental health workers today believe that disorders are influenced by genetic predisposition, physiological states, psychological dynamics, and social circumstances.

3. Why are psychological disorders classified, and what system is used?

Many psychiatrists and psychologists believe that a system for naming and describing psychological disorders facilitates treatment and research. The current edition of the *Diagnostic and Statistical Manual of Mental Disorders* (DSM-IV) provides an authoritative classification scheme.

Anxiety Disorders

4. What behaviors characterize anxiety disorders?

Those who suffer an anxiety disorder may for no apparent reason feel uncontrollably tense and uneasy (generalized anxiety disorder). They may be irrationally afraid of a specific object or situation (phobic disorder), or troubled by repetitive thoughts and actions (obsessive-compulsive disorder).

5. How do psychologists explain anxiety disorders?

The psychoanalytic perspective views anxiety disorders as the discharging of repressed impulses. The learning perspective sees them as a product of learned helplessness or fear conditioning. The biological perspective considers possible evolutionary, genetic, and physiological influences.

Somatoform Disorders

6. What characterizes the somatoform disorders?

The somatoform disorders involve a somatic (bodily) symptom—a physiologically unexplained but genuinely felt ailment. Freud was particularly fascinated by conversion disorder, in which anxiety seem to be converted to a physical symptom that had no physiological basis. Today, hypochondriasis (interpreting one's normal sensations as symptoms of a dreaded disease) is a much more common disorder.

Dissociative Disorders

7. What are dissociative disorders, and why are they controversial?

Under stress, a person's conscious awareness may become dissociated (separated) from previous memories, thoughts, and feelings. Dissociative amnesia can be caused by head injuries or alcoholic intoxication. It usually involves selective forgetting in response to stress. Fugue involves not only forgetting one's identity but also fleeing one's home. Most mysterious of all dissociative disorders are cases of dissociative identity (multiple personality). The afflicted person is said to have two or more distinct personalities, with the original typically unaware of the other(s). Skeptics question whether this disorder may be a cultural phenomenon, finding it suspicious that the disorder has just recently become popular and is virtually nonexistent outside North America.

Mood Disorders

8. What behaviors characterize mood disorders?

In major depression, the person—without apparent reason—descends for weeks or months into deep unhappiness, lethargy, and feelings of worthlessness before rebounding to normality. In the less common bipolar disorder, the person alternates between the hopelessness and lethargy of depression and the hyperactive, wildly optimistic, impulsive phase of mania.

9. What causes mood disorders?

Current research on depression is vigorously exploring two sets of influences. The first focuses on genetic predispositions and neurotransmitter abnormalities. The second views the cycle of depression from a social-cognitive perspective, in the light of a vicious cycle of self-defeating beliefs, learned helplessness, negative attributions, and stressful experiences.

Schizophrenia Disorders

10. What behaviors characterize schizophrenia disorders?

Schizophrenia shows itself in disorganized thinking (nonsensical talk and delusions, which may stem from a breakdown of selective attention); disturbed perceptions (including hallucinations); and inappropriate emotions and actions. It is rarely a one-time episode. Schizophrenia is a set of disorders that emerge either gradually from a chronic history of social inadequacy (in which case the outlook is dim) or suddenly in reaction to stress (in which case the prospects for recovery are brighter).

11. What causes schizophrenia?

As they have for depression, researchers have identified brain abnormalities (such as in receptors for the neurotransmitter dopamine) that seem linked with certain forms of schizophrenia. Prenatal viral infections are one possible cause. Twin and adoption studies also point to a genetic predisposition that, in conjunction with environmental factors, may bring about a schizophrenia disorder.

Personality Disorders

12. What characteristics are typical of personality disorders?

Personality disorders are enduring, maladaptive personality traits. For society, the most troubling of these is the remorseless and fearless antisocial personality.

Rates of Psychological Disorders

13. How common are the psychological disorders we've discussed?

A 1980s National Institute of Mental Health survey of nearly 20,000 institutionalized and community residents revealed that 1 in 3 American adults has at some time experi-enced a psychological disorder, and that 1 in 5 does so currently. The three most common disorders are phobic disorder and mood disorder (with women outnumbering men 2 to 1) and alcohol abuse or dependence (with men outnumbering women 5 to 1).

Labeling People: The Power of Preconceptions

14. Why do clinicians label patients with different diagnoses? Why do some psychologists criticize such labeling?

Diagnostic labels facilitate mental health professionals' communications and research. Critics point out that for these benefits we pay the price of stigmatizing people and creating self-fulfilling prophecies. Labels also create preconceptions that bias our perceptions of people's past and present behavior and unfairly stigmatize them.

Terms and Concepts to Remember

psychological disorder, p. 415

medical model, p. 416

DSM-IV, p. 417

anxiety disorders, p. 418

generalized anxiety disorder, p. 418

phobic disorder, p. 418

obsessive-compulsive disorder, p. 418

panic attack, p. 419

somatoform disorders, p. 422

conversion disorder, p. 423

hypochondriasis, p. 423

dissociative disorders, p. 423

amnesia, p. 423

fugue [fewg], p. 424

dissociative identity (multiple personality) disorder, p. 424

mood disorders, p. 426

major depressive disorder, p. 426

bipolar disorder, p. 426

mania, p. 427

schizophrenia, p. 434

delusions, p. 435

personality disorders, p. 440

antisocial personality, p. 440

Rehearse It Answer Key

1. c.	2. a.	3. c.	4. c.	5. c.	6. a.	7. c.	8. a.	9. d.
10. c.	11. b.	12. b.	13. b.	14. c.	15. a.	16. d.	17. d.	18. d.
19. a.	20. c.	21. c.	22. d.					

Critical Thinking Exercise

Now that you have read and reviewed Chapter 12, take your learning a step further by testing your critical thinking skills on the following passage.

Since her divorce 3 months ago, 65-year-old Phyllis has constantly felt tired, has had difficulty sleeping and eating, and has lost all interest in family, friends, and her usual activities. Once proud of her accomplishments and optimistic about her future, Phyllis is now convinced that everything she has ever done, or will do, is worthless. Although her husband was far from a perfect partner, Phyllis has convinced herself that the divorce really was her fault. Her once close friends, who have grown weary of Phyllis's self-absorbed and hopeless attitude, have stopped calling on her. The family physician referred Phyllis to a psychiatrist, who prescribed an antidepressant drug. The drug seemed to help somewhat, but Phyllis was worried that she would become addicted, so she stopped taking it regularly. Phyllis's son-in-law has grown concerned about her dejected attitude. However, his wife assures him there is no cause for alarm. She says her mother is simply growing old, noting that her mother's listlessness is reminiscent of her deceased maternal grandmother's behavior at that age.

1. Should Phyllis's daughter be more concerned about her mother's behavior, or is she correct in attributing it to aging? Explain your reasoning.

2. How might Phyllis's behavior be classified by a clinical psychologist?

3. How might Phyllis's behavior be explained according to the psychoanalytic, biological, and social-cognitive perspectives?

Check your progress on becoming a critical thinker by comparing your answers with the sample answers found in Appendix B.

For Further Information

You can find further information on psychological disorders on the following pages:

Alcoholism, pp. 182–183
Alzheimer's disease, pp. 100, 237
Amnesia, pp. 223–224, 237–238
Brain damage, Chapter 2

Color blindness, p. 129
Eating disorders, p. 304
Illness, Chapter 10
Mental retardation, p. 283

Post-traumatic stress disorder, p. 360
Sexual dysfunction, pp. 315–316
Sleep disorders, pp. 170–171
Substance abuse, pp. 182–188

Therapy

The Psychological Therapies

Psychoanalysis

Humanistic Therapies

Behavior Therapies

Cognitive Therapies

Group Therapies

Evaluating Psychotherapies

Is Psychotherapy Effective?

The Relative Effectiveness of Different Therapies

Commonalities Among Psychotherapies

Culture and Values in Psychotherapy

The Biomedical Therapies

Drug Therapies

Electroconvulsive Therapy

Psychosurgery

Preventing Psychological Disorders

The history of treating psychological disorders reveals how mystifying and intractable these problems are. We have treated psychological disorders with a bewildering variety of methods, harsh and gentle: by cutting holes in the head and by giving warm baths and massages; by restraining, bleeding, or "beating the devil" out of people; by placing them in sunny, serene environments; by administering drugs and electric shocks; and by talking—talking about childhood experiences, about current feelings, about maladaptive thoughts and behaviors.

The transition from brutal to gentler treatments occurred thanks to the efforts of reformers such as Philippe Pinel in France and Dorothea Dix in the United States, Canada, and Scotland. Both advocated the construction of mental hospitals offering more humane methods of treatment. As we will see, the introduction of therapeutic drugs and community-based treatment programs has, however, largely emptied mental health hospitals since the mid-1950s.

Today's favored treatment depends on the therapist's viewpoint. Those who believe that psychological disorders are learned tend to favor psychological therapies. Those who view disorders as biologically rooted are likely to advocate medication as well. Those who believe that disorders are responses to social conditions will, in addition, want to reform the "sick" environment.

We can classify therapies into two main categories: The *psychological therapies* involve structured interaction (usually verbal) between a trained professional and a client with a problem. The *biomedical therapies* directly affect the nervous system.

The Psychological Therapies

Psychological therapy, or **psychotherapy**, is "a planned, emotionally charged, confiding interaction between a trained, socially sanctioned healer and a sufferer" (Frank, 1982). From among the 250 or more types of psychotherapy (Parloff, 1987), we will consider the most influential techniques. These derive from psychology's major personality theories: psychoanalytic, humanistic, be-

Dorothea Dix (1802–1887) *"I . . . call your attention," she said, "to the state of the Insane Persons confined within this Commonwealth, in cages."*

The History of Treatment   *William Hogarth's (1697–1764) engraving (left) of St. Mary of Bethlehem hospital in London (commonly called Bedlam) depicts the treatment of mental disorders in the eighteenth century. Visitors paid to gawk at the patients as if they were viewing zoo animals. The chair above was designed by Benjamin Rush (1746–1813) "for the benefit of maniacal patients." Rush, a founder of the movement for more humane treatment of the mentally ill, believed that they required restraint to regain their sensibilities.*

havioral, and cognitive. We will also consider the use of these techniques in group therapies.

Although each technique is distinctive, common threads run through them. Therapists who view disorders as an interplay of bio-psycho-social influences may welcome a combination of treatments. Indeed, half of all psychotherapists describe themselves as taking an **eclectic approach**—as using a blend of therapies (Beitman & others, 1989; Smith, 1982). Depending on the client and the problem, an eclectic therapist will use a variety of techniques.

Psychoanalysis

1. What are the aims and methods of psychoanalysis?

Although most of today's therapists do not practice as Sigmund Freud did, his psychoanalytic techniques survive. **Psychoanalysis** is part of our modern vocabulary, and its assumptions influence many other therapies.

Aims

As we noted when considering Freud's theory in Chapters 11 and 12, psychoanalysis assumes that many psychological problems are fueled by childhood's residue of supposedly repressed impulses and conflicts. Psychoanalysts try to bring these repressed feelings into conscious awareness where the patient can deal with them. By gaining insight into the origins of the disorder—by fulfilling the ancient imperative to "know thyself" in a deep way—the patient "works through" the buried feelings. The theory presumes that healthier, less anxious living becomes possible when patients release the energy previously devoted to id-ego-superego conflicts.

Methods

Psychoanalysis is historical reconstruction. It unearths the past in hopes of unmasking the present. But how?

When Freud discarded hypnosis as unreliable, he turned to *free association*. Imagine yourself as a patient using the free association technique. The analyst invites you to relax, perhaps by lying on a couch. He or she will probably sit out of your line of vision, helping you focus attention on your internal

psychotherapy An emotionally charged, confiding interaction between a trained therapist and someone who suffers a psychological difficulty.

eclectic approach An approach to psychotherapy that takes advantage of techniques from the various forms of therapy, depending on the client's problems.

psychoanalysis Sigmund Freud's therapeutic technique, in which the patient's free associations, resistances, dreams, and transferences—and the therapist's interpretations of them—release previously repressed feelings, allowing the patient to gain self-insight.

resistance In psychoanalysis, the blocking from consciousness of anxiety-laden material.

interpretation In psychoanalysis, the analyst's assisting the patient to note and understand resistances and other significant behaviors in order to promote insight.

transference In psychoanalysis, the patient's transfer to the analyst of emotions linked with other relationships (such as love or hatred for a parent).

thoughts and feelings. Beginning with a childhood memory, a dream, or a recent experience, you say aloud whatever comes to your mind from moment to moment. It sounds easy, but soon you notice how often you edit your thoughts as you speak, omitting material that seems trivial, irrelevant, or shameful. Even in the safe presence of the analyst, you may pause momentarily before uttering an embarrassing thought. You may make a joking remark or change the subject to something less threatening. Sometimes your mind may go blank or you may find yourself unable to remember important details.

To the psychoanalyst, these blocks in the flow of your free associations are **resistances**. They hint that anxiety lurks and that you are repressing sensitive material. The analyst will want to explore these sensitive areas by making you aware of your resistances and by helping you interpret their underlying meaning. The analyst's **interpretations**—suggestions of underlying wishes, feelings, and conflicts—aim to provide people with *insight*. If offered at the right moment, the analyst's interpretation—of, say, your not wanting to talk about your mother—may illuminate what you are avoiding. You may then discover what your resistances mean and how they fit with other pieces of your psychological puzzle.

Freud believed that another clue to repressed impulses is our dreams' *latent content* (page 172). Thus, after inviting you to report a dream, the analyst may suggest its hidden meaning, thereby adding yet another piece to your developing self-portrait.

During many such sessions you will probably disclose more of yourself to your analyst than you have ever revealed to anyone. Because psychoanalytic theory emphasizes the formative power of childhood experiences, much of what you reveal will pertain to your earliest memories. You will also probably find yourself experiencing strong positive or negative feelings for your analyst. Such feelings may express the dependency or mingled love and anger that you earlier experienced toward family members or other important people in your life. When this happens, Freud would say you are actually *transferring* your strongest feelings from those other relationships to the analyst. Analysts and other therapists believe that this **transference** exposes long-repressed feelings, giving you a belated chance to work through them with your analyst's help. By examining your feelings toward the analyst you may also gain insight into your current relationships.

Note how much of psychoanalysis therapy is built on the assumption that repressed memories exist. That assumption, as we noted in Chapter 7, is now being challenged. This challenge to an assumption that is basic to so much of professional and popular psychology is provoking a new and intense debate.

Critics also say that psychoanalysts' interpretations are hard to refute. If, in response to the analyst's suggested interpretation, you say, "Yes! I see now,"

Classical Psychoanalysis *The placement of the analyst's chair out of view is thought to minimize distraction and make it easy for the patient—relaxed on a couch—to verbalize whatever comes to mind.*

your acceptance confirms the analyst's interpretation. If you emphatically say, "No! That doesn't ring true," your denial may be taken to reveal more resistance, which would also confirm the interpretation. Psychoanalysts acknowledge that it's hard to prove or disprove their interpretations. But they insist that interpretations often are a great help to patients.

Traditional psychoanalysis is slow and expensive. It requires up to several years of several sessions a week with a highly trained and well-paid analyst. (Three times a week for just 2 years at $100 per hour comes to about $30,000.) Only those with a high income can afford such treatment.

Although there are relatively few traditional psychoanalysts, psychoanalytic assumptions influence many therapists, especially those who make *psychodynamic* assumptions. Psychodynamic therapists try to understand patients' current symptoms by exploring their childhood experiences. They probe for repressed, emotion-laden information. They seek to help people gain insight into the unconscious roots of problems and work through newly resurrected feelings. Although influenced by psychoanalysis, these therapists may talk to people face to face (rather than out of the line of vision), once a week (rather than several times weekly), and for only a few weeks or months (rather than several years).

No brief therapy excerpt can exemplify the lengthy process of probing the past. But we can illustrate psychoanalysts' goal of enabling insight via their interpretations. In the following interaction, therapist David Malan responds to all that he has heard from a depressed patient by suggesting insights into her problems. Note how Malan interprets the woman's earlier remarks and suggests that her relationship with him reveals a characteristic pattern of behavior (1978, pp. 133–134).

Malan: *I get the feeling that you're the sort of person who needs to keep active. If you don't keep active, then something goes wrong. Is that true?*

Patient: *Yes.*

Malan: *I get a second feeling about you and that is that you must, underneath all this, have an awful lot of very strong and upsetting feelings. Somehow they're there but you aren't really quite in touch with them. Isn't this right? I feel you've been like that as long as you can remember.*

Patient: *For quite a few years, whenever I really sat down and thought about it I got depressed, so I tried not to think about it.*

Malan: *You see, you've established a pattern, haven't you? You're even like that here with me, because in spite of the fact that you're in some trouble and you feel that the bottom is falling out of your world, the way you're telling me this is just as if there wasn't anything wrong.*

Humanistic Therapies

2. What are the basic themes of humanistic therapy, such as Rogers' person-centered approach?

As we noted in Chapter 11, the humanistic perspective emphasizes people's inherent potential for self-fulfillment. Not surprisingly, then, humanistic therapists aim to boost self-fulfillment by helping people grow in self-awareness and self-acceptance. Unlike psychoanalytic therapists, humanistic therapists tend to focus on

▶ the present instead of the past;

▶ awareness of feelings as they occur rather than achieving insights into the childhood origins of the feelings;

Face-to-Face Therapy   *In this type of therapy session the couch has disappeared. But the influence of psychoanalytic theory probably has not, especially if the therapist probes for the origin of the patient's symptoms by analyzing repressed information from the past.*

person-centered therapy A humanistic therapy, developed by Carl Rogers, in which the therapist uses techniques such as active listening within a genuine, accepting, empathic environment to facilitate clients' growth.

active listening Empathic listening in which the listener echoes, restates, and clarifies. A feature of Rogers' person-centered therapy.

> *"We have two ears and one mouth that we may listen the more and talk the less."*
>
> Zeno, 335–263 B.C.
> *Diogenes Laertius*

- conscious rather than unconscious thoughts;
- taking immediate responsibility for one's feelings and actions rather than uncovering hidden determinants;
- promoting growth and fulfillment instead of curing illness. Thus, those in therapy are called "clients" rather than "patients."

The most widely used humanistic technique is Carl Rogers' (1961, 1980) **person-centered therapy**. Person-centered therapists focus on the client's conscious self-perceptions rather than on their own interpretations as therapists. The therapist listens, without judgment or interpretation, and refrains from directing the client toward certain insights. This strategy has earned person-centered therapy the label *nondirective* therapy.

Believing that most people already possess the resources for growth, Rogers encouraged therapists to exhibit *genuineness*, *acceptance*, and *empathy*. When therapists drop their facades and genuinely express their true feelings, when they enable their clients to feel unconditionally accepted, and when they empathically sense and reflect their clients' feelings, the clients may increase in self-understanding and self-acceptance. Rogers (1980, p. 10) explained:

> Hearing has consequences. When I truly hear a person and the meanings that are important to him at that moment, hearing not simply his words, but him, and when I let him know that I have heard his own private personal meanings, many things happen. There is first of all a grateful look. He feels released. He wants to tell me more about his world. He surges forth in a new sense of freedom. He becomes more open to the process of change.
>
> I have often noticed that the more deeply I hear the meanings of the person, the more there is that happens. Almost always, when a person realizes he has been deeply heard, his eyes moisten. I think in some real sense he is weeping for joy. It is as though he were saying, "Thank God, somebody heard me. Someone knows what it's like to be me."

"Hearing" refers to Rogers' technique of **active listening**—echoing, restating, and seeking clarification of what the person expresses—verbally or nonverbally—and acknowledging the expressed feelings. Active listening is now an accepted part of therapeutic counseling practices in many schools, colleges, and clinics. The counselor listens attentively and interrupts only to restate and confirm the client's feelings, to accept what the client is expressing, or to seek clarification. In his counseling of a 28-year-old male client, Rogers illustrates active listening:

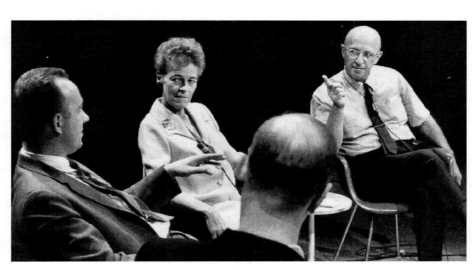

Active Listening *The late Carl Rogers (right) empathizes with a client during a group therapy session.*

Client: *I just ain't no good to nobody, never was, and never will be.*

Rogers: *Feeling that now, hm? That you're just no good to yourself, no good to anybody. Never will be any good to anybody. Just that you're completely worthless, huh?—Those really are lousy feelings. Just feel that you're no good at all, hm?*

Client: *Yeah. (Muttering in low, discouraged voice) That's what this guy I went to town with just the other day told me.*

Rogers: *This guy that you went to town with really told you that you were no good? Is that what you're saying? Did I get that right?*

Client: *M-hm.*

Rogers: *I guess the meaning of that if I get it right is that here's somebody that— meant something to you and what does he think of you? Why, he's told you that he thinks you're no good at all. And that just really knocks the props out from under you. (Client weeps quietly.) It just brings the tears. (Silence of 20 seconds)*

Client: *(Rather defiantly) I don't care though.*

Rogers: *You tell yourself you don't care at all, but somehow I guess some part of you cares because some part of you weeps over it (Meador & Rogers, 1984, p. 167).*

As this brief excerpt illustrates, the person-centered counselor seeks to provide a psychological mirror that helps clients see themselves more clearly. But can a therapist be a perfect mirror, without selecting and interpreting what is reflected? Rogers conceded that one cannot be *totally* nondirective. Nevertheless, he believed that the therapist's most important contribution is to accept and understand the client. Given a nonjudgmental, grace-filled environment that provides *unconditional positive regard*, people may accept even their worst traits and feel valued and whole.

If you wish to practice active listening in your own relationships, three hints may help: (1) *Paraphrase*. Check your understanding by summarizing the speaker's words in your own words. (2) *Invite clarification*. "What might be an example of that?" may encourage the speaker to say more. (3) *Reflect feelings*. "That must be frustrating," might mirror what you're sensing from the speaker's body language and intensity.

"You say, 'Off with her head,' but what I'm hearing is, 'I feel neglected.'"

! Rehearse It

1. All of the psychological therapies involve verbal interactions between a trained professional and a client with a problem. A therapist who encourages clients to relate their dreams and searches for the unconscious roots of their problems is drawing from

a. psychoanalysis.
b. humanistic therapies.
c. person-centered therapy.
d. nondirective therapy.

2. According to psychoanalytic theory, a patient's emotional relationship with the therapist mirrors other important relationships in the patient's life—for example, an early relationship with a parent. In psychoanalysis, the development of strong feelings for the therapist is an important part of the therapeutic process and is called

a. transference.
b. resistance.
c. interpretation.
d. empathy.

3. Humanistic therapists focus on present experience—on becoming aware of feelings as they arise and taking responsibility for them. Compared with psychoanalytic therapists, humanistic therapists are more likely to emphasize

a. hidden or repressed feelings.
b. childhood experiences.
c. psychological disorders.
d. self-fulfillment and growth.

4. Especially important to Carl Rogers' person-centered therapy is the technique of active listening. The therapist who practices active listening

a. engages in free association.
b. exposes the patient's resistances.
c. restates and clarifies the client's statements.
d. directly challenges the client's self-perceptions.

Behavior Therapies

3. What are the assumptions and techniques of the behavior therapies?

All the therapies we have considered so far assume that, for rational (nonpsychotic) people at least, psychological problems diminish as self-awareness grows. The psychoanalyst expects problems to subside as people gain insight into their unresolved and unconscious tensions. So does the humanistic therapist, as people "get in touch with their feelings." Behavior therapists, however, doubt that self-awareness is the key. They assume that the problem behaviors *are* the problems. You can, for example, become aware of why you are highly anxious during exams and still be anxious. Instead of trying to alleviate distressing behaviors by resolving a presumed underlying problem, **behavior therapy** applies well-established learning principles to eliminate the unwanted behavior. To treat phobias or sexual dysfunctions, behavior therapists do not delve deep below the surface looking for inner causes. Rather, they try to replace problem thoughts and maladaptive behaviors with more constructive ways of thinking and acting.

Classical Conditioning Techniques

One cluster of behavior therapies derives from principles developed in Pavlov's conditioning experiments (pages 198–201). As Pavlov and others showed, we learn various behaviors and emotions through classical conditioning. So, are maladaptive symptoms conditioned responses? If, say, a claustrophobic fear of elevators is a learned response to the stimulus of being in an enclosed space, then might one unlearn the fear by counterconditioning the fear response? **Counterconditioning** pairs the trigger stimulus with a new response that is incompatible with fear. For example, if we repeatedly pair the enclosed space of the elevator with a relaxed response, the fear response may be displaced. Two such counterconditioning techniques are *systematic desensitization* and *aversive conditioning*.

Systematic Desensitization   Picture this scene reported in 1924 by Mary Cover Jones, an associate of the behaviorist John B. Watson: Three-year-old Peter is petrified of rabbits and other furry objects. (Unlike Little Albert's laboratory-conditioned fear of white rats, described in Chapter 6, Peter's fear arose during the course of his life at home and is more intense.) Jones aims to replace Peter's fear of rabbits with a conditioned response that is incompatible with fear. Her strategy is to associate the fear-evoking rabbit with the pleasurable, relaxed response associated with eating.

As the hungry child begins eating his midafternoon snack, Jones introduces a caged rabbit on the other side of the huge room. Peter hardly notices as he eagerly munches his crackers and milk. On succeeding days, she gradually moves the rabbit closer and closer. Within 2 months, Peter tolerates the rabbit in his lap and strokes it while he eats. Moreover, his fear of other furry objects subsides as well, having been "countered" or replaced by a relaxed state that cannot coexist with fear (Fisher, 1984; Jones, 1924).

Unfortunately for those who might have been helped by her counterconditioning procedures, Jones's story of Peter and the rabbit did not immediately become part of psychology's lore. It was not until more than 30 years later that psychiatrist Joseph Wolpe (1958, 1982) refined her technique into what has become the most widely used method of behavior therapy: **systematic desensitization**. Wolpe assumed, as did Jones, that you cannot simultaneously be anxious and relaxed. Therefore, if you can repeatedly relax when facing anxi-

behavior therapy   Therapy that applies learning principles to the elimination of unwanted behaviors.

counterconditioning   A behavior therapy procedure that conditions new responses to stimuli that trigger unwanted behaviors; based on classical conditioning.

systematic desensitization   A type of counterconditioning that associates a pleasant relaxed state with gradually increasing anxiety-triggering stimuli. Commonly used to treat phobias.

THE FAR SIDE

Professor Gallagher and his controversial technique of simultaneously confronting the fear of heights, snakes and the dark.

Figure 13–1 Systematic Desensitization of a Phobia
Beverly, who is terribly afraid of spiders, is gradually able to relax—as shown by her decreasing pulse rate—first at the sight of a spider, then in the presence of a toy spider, a dead spider, and a live one. (From Gilling & Brightwell, 1982.)

ety-provoking stimuli, you can gradually eliminate your anxiety. The trick is to proceed gradually.

Let's see how this might work with a common phobia. Imagine yourself afraid of public speaking. A behavior therapist might first ask your help in constructing a hierarchy of anxiety-triggering speaking situations. Your anxiety hierarchy could range from mildly anxiety-provoking situations, such as speaking up in a small group of friends, to panic-provoking situations, such as having to address a large audience.

The therapist would then train you to relax. Using *progressive relaxation*, you learn to relax one muscle group after another, until you achieve a drowsy state of complete relaxation and comfort. Then, with your eyes closed, the therapist asks you to imagine a mildly anxiety-arousing situation: You are having coffee with a group of friends and are deciding whether to speak up. If imagining the scene causes you to feel any anxiety, you signal your tension by raising your finger, and the therapist instructs you to switch off the mental image and go back to deep relaxation.

This imagined scene is repeatedly paired with relaxation until you can feel no trace of anxiety while imagining it. The therapist progresses up your anxiety hierarchy, using the relaxed state to desensitize you to each imagined situation. After several therapy sessions, you practice the imagined behaviors in actual situations, beginning with relatively easy tasks and gradually moving to more anxiety-filled ones (Figure 13–1). Conquering your anxiety in an actual situation, not just in your imagination, raises your self-confidence (Foa & Kozak, 1986; Williams, 1987). Eventually, you may even become a confident public speaker.

Therapists sometimes combine systematic desensitization with other techniques. For clients with phobias, they may have someone model appropriate behavior in a fear-arousing situation. If you were afraid of snakes, you would first observe someone handling a snake. Then you would be coaxed in gradual steps to approach, touch, and handle it yourself (Bandura & others, 1969). By applying this principle of observational learning, therapists have helped people overcome disruptive fears of snakes, spiders, and dogs.

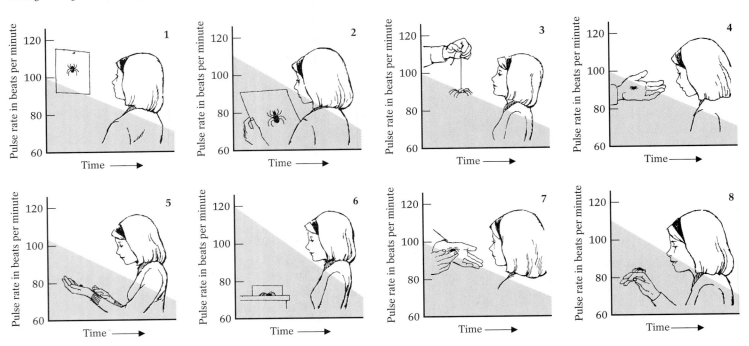

Notice that the systematic desensitization and modeling procedures make no attempt to help you achieve insight into your fear's underlying cause. If you are afraid of heights, the therapist will not spend much time probing when you first experienced this fear or what may have caused it. Nor do behavior therapists worry that eliminating your fear of heights will leave an underlying problem that may now be expressed as, say, a fear of elevators. On the contrary, they find that overcoming maladaptive behaviors helps people feel better about themselves.

Aversive Conditioning   In systematically desensitizing a patient, the therapist seeks to substitute a positive (relaxed) response for a negative (fearful) response to a harmless stimulus. In **aversive conditioning**, the therapist tries to replace a positive response to a harmful stimulus with a negative (aversive) response. Thus, aversive conditioning is the reverse of systematic desensitization.

The procedure is simple: It associates unwanted behavior with unpleasant feelings. In treating an alcoholic, aversion therapists offer appealing drinks laced with a drug that produces severe nausea. By linking the drinking of alcohol with violent nausea, the therapist seeks to transform the alcoholic's reaction to alcohol from positive to negative (see Figure 13–2, and recall the taste aversion experiments with rats and coyotes in Chapter 6). Similarly, by giving child molesters electric shocks as they view photos of naked children, aversion therapists aim to eliminate the molesters' sexual response to children. And by giving withdrawn and self-abusing autistic children harmless "aversives," such as a spray of cold water in the face, therapists hope to suppress self-injury while reinforcing more appropriate behavior. Because this therapy involves an unpleasant experience, it is practiced sparingly and only with the appropriate consent.

Does aversive conditioning work? In the short run it may. Arthur Wiens and Carol Menustik (1983) studied 685 alcoholic patients who completed an aversion therapy program at a Portland, Oregon, hospital. One year later, after returning for several booster treatments of alcohol-sickness pairings, 63 percent were still successfully abstaining. But after three years, only 33 percent remained abstinent. As we saw in Chapter 6, the problem is that cognition influences conditioning. People know that outside the therapist's office they can drink without fear of nausea or engage in sexually deviant behavior without fear of shock. The person's ability to discriminate between the aversive conditioning situation and all other situations can limit the treatment's effectiveness.

A milder form of aversive conditioning, developed by learning theorist O. H. Mowrer, exists for chronic bedwetters. The child sleeps on a liquid-sensitive pad connected to an alarm. Moisture on the pad triggers the alarm, awakening the child. With repetition, this association of urinary relaxation with awakening stops the bedwetting. In three out of four cases the treatment is effective and the success provides a boost to the child's self-image (Christophersen & Edwards, 1992).

Operant Conditioning

As we saw in Chapter 6, voluntary behaviors are strongly influenced by their consequences. This simple fact enables behavior therapists to reinforce desired behaviors and to withhold reinforcement for undesired behaviors. Using operant conditioning to solve specific behavior problems has raised hopes for some cases thought to be hopeless. Retarded children have been taught to care for themselves. Socially withdrawn autistic children have learned to interact. People with schizophrenia have been helped to behave more rationally in their hospital ward.

Figure 13–2 Aversion Therapy for Alcoholics *After repeatedly imbibing an alcoholic drink mixed with a drug that produces severe nausea, some patients develop at least a temporary conditioned aversion to alcohol.*

What might a psychoanalyst say about this therapy for bedwetting? How might a behavior therapist reply?

aversive conditioning   A type of counterconditioning that associates an unpleasant state (such as nausea) with an unwanted behavior (such as drinking alcohol).

token economy An operant condition- ing procedure that rewards desired behav- ior. A patient exchanges a token of some sort, earned for exhibiting the desired be- havior, for various privileges or treats.

cognitive therapy Therapy that teaches people new, more adaptive ways of think- ing and acting; based on the assumption that thoughts intervene between events and our emotional reactions.

In extreme cases, the treatment must be intensive. For 19 withdrawn, un- communicative, 3-year-old autistic children in one study, it involved a 2-year, 40-hour-a-week shaping program by their parents (Lovaas, 1987). The combi- nation of positive reinforcement of desired behaviors and the ignoring or pun- ishing of aggressive and self-abusive behaviors worked wonders. By first grade, 9 of the 19 children were functioning successfully in school and exhibiting nor- mal intelligence. Only 1 of 40 comparable children who did not undergo this treatment showed similar improvement.

The rewards used to modify behavior vary. With some people the reinforc- ing power of attention or praise is sufficient. Others require more concrete re- wards, such as food. In institutional settings, therapists may create a **token economy**. When patients display appropriate behavior, such as getting out of bed, washing, dressing, eating, talking coherently, cleaning up their rooms, or playing cooperatively, they receive a token or plastic coin. Later, they can ex- change their accumulated tokens for various rewards, such as candy, television watching, trips to town, or better living quarters. Therapists use tokens to shape behavior in the step-by-step manner described on page 207. Token economies have been successfully applied in various settings (classrooms, hospitals, homes for the delinquent) and with various populations (disturbed children, those with mental disabilities, schizophrenia patients).

Critics of such *behavior modification* express two concerns. One concern is practical: What happens when the reinforcers stop, as when the person leaves the institution? Might the person have become so dependent on the extrinsic rewards that the appropriate behaviors quickly disappear? If so, how can be- havior therapists make the appropriate behaviors durable? First, they may wean patients from the tokens by shifting them toward rewards, such as social approval, more typical of life outside the institution. They may also train pa- tients to behave in ways that are intrinsically rewarding. For example, as a with- drawn person becomes more socially competent, the intrinsic satisfactions of social interaction may help maintain the behavior.

The second concern is ethical: Is it right for one human to control another's behavior? Those who set up token economies typically deprive people of some- thing they desire and then decide which behaviors they will reinforce. To critics, the whole behavior modification process has a totalitarian taint. Advocates reply that control already exists; rewards and punishers are already maintaining destructive behavior patterns. So why not reinforce adaptive behavior instead? They argue that treatment with positive rewards is more humane than being in- stitutionalized or punished, and that the right to effective treatment and to an improved life justifies temporary deprivation.

Cognitive Therapies

4. *What are the goals and techniques of the cognitive therapies?*

We have seen how behavior therapists treat specific fears and problem behav- iors. But how do they deal with major depression or general anxiety? One can reinforce healthier behaviors and train people to avoid "high risk" situations. Still, when anxiety has no focus, making a hierarchy of anxiety-triggering situ- ations is difficult. The cognitive revolution that has so changed psychology dur- ing the last 3 decades has influenced how therapists treat these less clearly defined psychological problems (Figure 13–3).

The **cognitive therapies** assume that our thinking colors our feelings (Fig- ure 13–4). As we noted in Chapter 12, self-blaming and overgeneralized expla- nations of bad events are an integral part of the vicious cycle of depression. The depressed person interprets a suggestion as criticism, disagreement as dislike, praise as flattery, friendliness as pity. Ruminating on such thoughts sustains the

Figure 13–3 The Cognitive Revolution *Half of all fac- ulty in accredited clinical psychology Ph.D. programs now align themselves with a cognitive or cognitive-be- havioral therapy orientation (Data from Mayne & others, 1994.)*

Figure 13–4 A Cognitive Perspective on Psychological Disorders *The person's emotional reactions are produced not directly by the event, but by his or her thoughts in response to the event.*

bad mood. (That explains why distracting oneself, perhaps by getting absorbed in a task, can alleviate a bad mood [Erber & Tesser, 1992; Lyubomirsky & Nolen-Hoeksema, 1994].) If depressing thinking patterns are learned, then surely they can be replaced. Thus, cognitive therapists try in various ways to teach people new, more constructive ways of thinking.

Rational-Emotive Therapy

According to Albert Ellis (1962, 1987, 1993), the creator of **rational-emotive therapy** (also called *rational-emotive behavior therapy*), many problems arise from irrational thinking. For example, he describes a disturbed woman and suggests how therapy might challenge her illogical, self-defeating assumptions (1984, p. 198):

> [She] does not merely believe it is *undesirable* if her love partner is rejecting. She tends to believe, also, that (1) it is *awful*; (2) she *cannot stand* it; (3) she *should not*, must not be rejected; (4) she will *never* be accepted by any desirable partner; (5) she is a *worthless person* because one lover has rejected her; and (6) she *deserves to be damned* for being so worthless. Such common covert hypotheses are nonsensical. . . . They can be easily elicited and demolished by any scientist worth his or her salt; and the rational-emotive therapist is exactly that: an exposing and non-sense-annihilating scientist.

Does this sound like the opposite of the warm, caring, reflective acceptance of feelings expressed by Carl Rogers? It very nearly is. Ellis intends to "make mincemeat" of people's illogical ideas—that we must be loved by everyone, that we must be thoroughly competent and successful at everything, that it is a disaster when things do not go as we wish. Change people's thinking by revealing the "absurdity" of their self-defeating ideas, he believes, and you will change their self-defeating feelings and actions. Let's eavesdrop as tart-tongued Ellis exhibits his confrontational style with a 25-year-old female client who suffers feelings of guilt, unworthiness, and depression (1989, p. 219):

Ellis: *The same crap! It's always the same crap. Now if you would look at the crap—instead of "Oh, how stupid I am! He hates me! I think I'll kill myself!"—then you'd get better right away.*

Client: *You've been listening! (laughs)*

Ellis: *Listening to what?*

Client: *(laughs) Those wild statements in my mind, like that, that I make.*

Ellis: *That's right! Because I know that you have to make those statements—because I have a good theory. And according to my theory, people couldn't get upset unless they made those nutty statements to themselves. . . . Even if I loved you madly, the next person you talk to is likely to hate you. So I like brown eyes and he likes blue eyes, or something. So you're then dead! Because you really think: "I've got to be accepted! I've got to act intelligently!" Well, why?*

rational-emotive therapy A confrontational cognitive therapy, developed by Albert Ellis, that vigorously challenges people's illogical, self-defeating attitudes and assumptions. Also recently called *rational-emotive behavior therapy* by Ellis, emphasizing a behavioral "homework" component.

Client: (*very soberly and reflectively*) *True.*

Ellis: *You see?*

Client: *Yes.*

Ellis: *Now, if you will learn that lesson, then you've had a very valuable session. Because you don't have to upset yourself. As I said before: If I thought you were the worst [expletive] who ever existed, well that's my opinion. And I'm entitled to it. But does it make you a turd?*

Client: (*reflective silence*)

Ellis: *Does it?*

Client: *No.*

Ellis: *What makes you a turd?*

Client: *Thinking that you are.*

Ellis: *That's right! Your belief that you are. That's the only thing that could ever do it. And you never have to believe that. See? You control your thinking. I control my thinking—my belief about you. But you don't have to be affected by that. You always control what you think.*

Cognitive Therapy for Depression

Like Ellis, cognitive therapist Aaron Beck was originally trained in Freudian techniques. As Beck analyzed his depressed patients' dreams, he found recurring negative themes of loss, rejection, and abandonment that extended into their waking thoughts. So in his form of cognitive therapy, Beck and his colleagues (1979) seek to reverse clients' catastrophizing beliefs about themselves, their situations, and their futures. Beck shares with Ellis the goal of getting depressed people to take off the dark glasses through which they view life. But his technique is a kinder, gentler questioning that aims to help people discover their irrationalities (Beck & others, 1979, pp. 145–146):

> **Patient:** *I agree with the descriptions of me but I guess I don't agree that the way I think makes me depressed.*
>
> **Beck:** *How do you understand it?*
>
> **Patient:** *I get depressed when things go wrong. Like when I fail a test.*
>
> **Beck:** *How can failing a test make you depressed?*
>
> **Patient:** *Well, if I fail I'll never get into law school.*
>
> **Beck:** *So failing the test means a lot to you. But if failing a test could drive people into clinical depression, wouldn't you expect everyone who failed the test to have a depression? . . . Did everyone who failed get depressed enough to require treatment?*
>
> **Patient:** *No, but it depends on how important the test was to the person.*
>
> **Beck:** *Right, and who decides the importance?*
>
> **Patient:** *I do.*
>
> **Beck:** *And so, what we have to examine is your way of viewing the test (or the way that you think about the test) and how it affects your chances of getting into law school. Do you agree?*
>
> **Patient:** *Right.*
>
> **Beck:** *Do you agree that the way you interpret the results of the test will affect you? You might feel depressed, you might have trouble sleeping, not feel like eating, and you might even wonder if you should drop out of the course.*
>
> **Patient:** *I have been thinking that I wasn't going to make it. Yes, I agree.*
>
> **Beck:** *Now what did failing mean?*
>
> **Patient:** (*tearful*) *That I couldn't get into law school.*
>
> **Beck:** *And what does that mean to you?*
>
> **Patient:** *That I'm just not smart enough.*

Beck: *Anything else?*

Patient: *That I can never be happy.*

Beck: *And how do these* thoughts *make you feel?*

Patient: *Very unhappy.*

Beck: *So it is the meaning of failing a test that makes you very unhappy. In fact, believing that you can never be happy is a powerful factor in producing unhappiness. So, you get yourself into a trap—by definition, failure to get into law school equals "I can never be happy."*

A newer variety of cognitive therapy builds on the finding that depressed people do not exhibit the self-serving bias common in nondepressed people (page 431). Instead, they often attribute their failures to themselves and attribute their successes to external circumstances. Thus, Adele Rabin and her colleagues (1986) explained to 235 depressed adults the advantages of interpreting events as nondepressed people do. She then trained them to reform their habitually negative patterns of thinking and labeling. For example, she gave the patients homework assignments that required them to record each day's positive events and to write down how they contributed to each. Compared with depressed people who remained on a waiting list, those who went through the positive thinking exercises became much less depressed (Figure 13–5). Changed thinking after cognitive therapy also reduces the risk of relapse (Hollon & others, 1992).

The more people change their negative thinking styles, the more their depression lifts (Seligman, 1989). Cognitive therapists often combine the reversal of self-defeating thinking with efforts to modify behavior. *Cognitive behavior therapy* aims to make people aware of their irrational negative thinking, to replace it with new ways of thinking and talking, *and* to practice the more positive approach in everyday settings.

Because we often think in words, getting people to change what they say to themselves is an effective way to change their thinking. Perhaps you can identify with the anxious students who before an exam make matters worse with self-defeating thoughts: "This exam is probably going to be impossible. All these other students seem so relaxed and self-confident. I wish I were better prepared. Anyhow, I'm so nervous I'll forget everything." To change such negative patterns, Donald Meichenbaum (1977, 1985) trains people to restructure their thinking in stressful situations. Sometimes it may be enough simply to say more positive things to oneself: "Relax. The exam may be hard, but it will be hard for everyone else, too. I studied harder than most people. Besides, I don't need a perfect score to get a good grade."

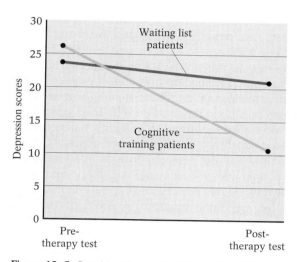

Figure 13–5 Cognitive Therapy for Depression *After undergoing a program that trained them to think more like nondepressed people—by noticing and taking personal credit for good events and by not taking blame for or overgeneralizing from bad events—patients' depression dropped dramatically. (From Rabin & others, 1986.)*

family therapy   Therapy that treats the family as a system. Views an individual's unwanted behaviors as influenced by or directed at other family members; encourages family members toward positive relationships and improved communication.

Group Therapies

5. In what group contexts do people receive therapy?

Except for traditional psychoanalysis, the therapies we have considered may also occur in therapist-led small groups. Although it does not provide the same degree of therapist involvement with each client, group therapy saves therapists' time and clients' money. More important, the social context allows people both to discover that others have problems similar to their own and to try out new ways of behaving. As you have perhaps experienced, receiving honest feedback—being reassured that you look poised even though you feel anxious and self-conscious, for example—can be very helpful. And it can be a relief to find that you are not alone—to learn that others, despite their seeming composure, share your problems and your feelings of loneliness, inadequacy, or anger.

Such has been the experience of a wide range of people, from cancer patients to dieters to recovering alcoholics (Yalom, 1985). Many participate in *self-help* and *support groups*—for substance abusers, divorced people, gamblers, the bereaved, and those simply seeking personal growth. In an individualistic age, with more and more people living or feeling alone, the popularity of support groups also reflects a longing for community and connectedness. More than 100 million Americans belong to small religious, interest, or self-help groups that meet regularly—and nine in ten report that group members "support each other emotionally" (Gallup, 1994). The grandparent of self-help groups, Alcoholics Anonymous (AA), reportedly has 60,000 chapters in 112 countries. Its famous 12-step strategy, emulated by many other self-help groups, asks members to admit their powerlessness, to seek help from a higher power and from one another, and (the twelfth step) to take the message to others in need of it.

One special type of group interaction, **family therapy**, assumes that no person is an island. We live and grow in relation to others, especially our families. We struggle to differentiate ourselves from our families but we also need to connect with them emotionally. Some of our problem behaviors arise from the tension between these two tendencies, which often creates family stress. Thus, patients often come to therapists seeking help in their relationships with family members.

Unlike most psychotherapy, which focuses on what happens inside the person's own skin, family therapists work with family groups to heal relationships and to mobilize family resources. Their aim is to help family members discover the role they play within their family's social system. A child's rebellion, for example, affects and is affected by other family tensions. Family therapists also attempt—usually with some success, research suggests (Hazelrigg & others, 1987; Shadish & others, 1993)—to open up communication within the family or to help family members discover new ways of preventing or resolving conflicts.

Family Therapy *This type of therapy often acts as a preventive mental health strategy. The therapist helps family members understand how the ways they relate to each other create problems. The treatment emphasis is not on changing the individuals but rather on changing their relationships and interactions.*

! *Rehearse It*

5. Behavior therapies apply learning principles to the treatment of problems such as sexual dysfunction, phobias, and alcoholism. In treating people with these problems, the goal of the behavior therapist is to

a. identify and treat the underlying causes of dysfunction.
b. improve learning and insight.
c. eliminate the unwanted behavior.
d. improve communication and social sensitivity.

6. Behavior therapists assume that phobias and other maladaptive behaviors are conditioned responses. Behaviorists attempt either to extinguish these responses or to countercondition a client by conditioning a new response to stimuli that trigger maladaptive or unwanted responses. Two counterconditioning techniques are systematic desensitization and

a. positive reinforcement.
b. aversive conditioning.
c. rational-emotive therapy.
d. token economy.

7. The technique of systematic desensitization, developed by Joseph Wolpe, teaches people to relax in the presence of progressively more anxiety-provoking stimuli. Systematic desensitization has been found to be especially effective in the treatment of

a. phobias.
b. depression.
c. alcoholism.
d. bedwetting.

8. In institutions such as homes for the mentally retarded or the delinquent, a token economy may be used to shape behavior. Tokens, which may later be exchanged for other rewards, are given when a person displays a desired behavior or takes a step in the right direction. The token economy is an application of

a. classical conditioning.
b. counterconditioning.
c. cognitive therapy.
d. operant conditioning.

9. Cognitive therapists assume that our internal beliefs and characteristic ways of thinking strongly influence our responses to events. They treat emotional problems by teaching people new, more constructive ways of thinking. An example of a cognitive therapy is rational-emotive therapy, which was developed by

a. Carl Rogers.
b. Joseph Wolpe.
c. Albert Ellis.
d. Aaron Beck.

10. A new form of cognitive therapy teaches people to stop attributing failures to personal inadequacy and success to external circumstances. This form of cognitive therapy has been shown to be especially effective in treating

a. mental retardation.
b. phobias.
c. alcoholism.
d. depression.

11. Psychotherapy is in large part an individual process, although most therapies may occur in therapist-led small groups. The social context of this group therapy tells people that others have problems similar to theirs and allows them to act out alternative behaviors. One type of group therapy, family therapy, serves as a

a. source of psychoanalysis.
b. preventive mental health strategy.
c. self-help group.
d. source of emotional support.

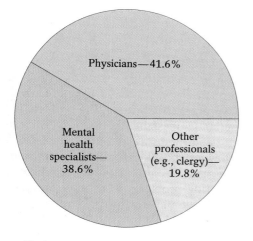

Figure 13–6 To Whom Do People Turn? *The National Institute of Mental Health reports that 19 million Americans a year seek help for psychological difficulties. About 2 in 5 seek out a mental health worker, such as a psychologist or psychiatrist. (Data from Regier & others, 1993.)*

Evaluating Psychotherapies

6. What does research on psychotherapy reveal about its effectiveness?

Advice columnist Ann Landers frequently advises her troubled letter writers to get professional help. One response urged the writer "not to give up. Hang in there until you find [a psychotherapist] who fills the bill. It's worth the effort." She advised the same day's second letter writer, "There are many excellent mental health facilities in your city. I urge you to make an appointment at once" (Farina & Fisher, 1982). Many people share Ann Landers' confidence in psychotherapy's effectiveness. The National Institute of Mental Health estimates that 15 percent of Americans seek help for psychological and addictive disorders each year (Figure 13–6).

Before 1950, the main mental health providers were psychiatrists. Since then the demand has outgrown the psychiatric profession, and most psychotherapy is now done by clinical and counseling psychologists; clinical social workers; pastoral, marital, abuse, and school counselors; and psychiatric nurses. Much of it is done through *community mental health* programs, which provide outpatient therapy, crisis phone lines, and halfway houses for those making the transition from hospitalization to independent living. Is the faith that Ann Landers and millions of other Americans have placed in these therapists justified?

Is Psychotherapy Effective?

The question, though simply put, is not simply answered. For one thing, measuring therapy's effectiveness is not like taking your body's temperature. If you and I were to undergo psychotherapy, how would we gauge its effectiveness? By how we feel about our progress? How our therapist feels about it? How our friends and family feel about it? How our behavior has changed?

Clients' Perceptions

If clients' testimonials were the only yardstick, we could strongly affirm the effectiveness of psychotherapy. Three out of four clients report themselves satisfied, and one in two say they are "very satisfied" (Lebow, 1982). We have their word for it—and who should know better?

We should not dismiss these testimonials lightly. People enter therapy because they are suffering, and most leave feeling better about themselves. But there are several reasons why client testimonials do not persuade psychotherapy's skeptics:

- **People often enter therapy in crisis.** When, with the normal ebb and flow of events, the crisis passes, people may attribute their improvement to the therapy.

- **Clients may need to believe the therapy was worth the effort.** To admit investing time and money in something ineffective is like admitting to having one's car serviced repeatedly by a mechanic who never fixed it. Self-justification is a powerful human motive.

- **Clients generally like their therapists and speak kindly of them.** Even if the clients' problems remain, say the therapy critics, "they work hard to find something positive to say. The therapist had been very understanding, the client had gained a new perspective, he learned to communicate better, his mind was eased, anything at all so as not to have to say treatment was a failure" (Zilbergeld, 1983, p. 117).

Clinicians' Perceptions

If clinicians' perceptions accurately reflected their own therapeutic effectiveness, we would have even more reason to celebrate. Case studies of successful treatment abound. Furthermore, every therapist treasures compliments from clients as they say goodbye or later express their gratitude. The problem is that clients justify entering psychotherapy by emphasizing their woes, justify leaving therapy by emphasizing their well-being, and stay in touch only if satisfied. Therapists are aware of failures, but they are mostly the failures of *other* therapists—those whose clients, having experienced only temporary relief, are now seeking a new therapist for their recurring problems. Thus, the same person with the same recurring difficulty—the same old weight problem, depression, or marital difficulty—may represent "success" stories in several therapists' files.

Because people enter therapy when they are extremely unhappy, and usually leave when they are less extremely unhappy, most therapists as well as clients testify to therapy's success—regardless of the treatment. Although "treatments" have varied widely, from chains to counseling, every generation views its own approach as more enlightened. Testimonies, therefore, do not prove effectiveness.

Outcome Research

How, then, can we objectively measure the effectiveness of psychotherapy? What types of people and problems are best helped, and by what type of psychotherapy? The questions have both academic and personal relevance. If you or someone you care about feels anxious or depressed, or suffers some psychological disorder, how likely is it that psychotherapy will help?

In hopes of better assessing psychotherapy's effectiveness, psychologists have turned to controlled research studies. Similar research in the 1800s transformed medicine from concocted treatments (bleeding, purging, infusions of plant and metal substances) into a science. The transformation occurred when skeptical physicians began to realize that many patients got better on their own, that most of the fashionable treatments were doing no good, and that sorting sense from nonsense required closely following illnesses—with and without a particular treatment. Typhoid fever patients, for example, often improved after a treatment such as bleeding. That convinced most physicians that the treatment worked. It was not until a control group was given mere bed rest—and 70 percent were observed to improve after 5 weeks of fever—that physicians were shocked to learn that their treatments were, at best, worthless (Thomas, 1992).

In psychology, the opening volley in what became a spirited debate over such research was fired by British psychologist Hans Eysenck (1952). He summarized studies showing that after undergoing psychotherapy, two-thirds of those suffering nonpsychotic disorders improve markedly. To this day, no one disputes that optimistic estimate.

So why are we still debating psychotherapy's effectiveness? Because Eysenck also reported similar improvement among *untreated* persons, such as those who were on waiting lists. With or without psychotherapy, he said, roughly two-thirds improved noticeably. Time was a great healer.

The avalanche of criticism prompted by Eysenck's conclusions revealed shortcomings in his analyses. Also, Eysenck could find only 24 studies of psychotherapy outcomes to analyze in 1952. Today, there are hundreds. The best of these studies randomly assign people on a waiting list to alternative treatments or to no treatment. Afterward, researchers evaluate.

In the first statistical digest of these studies, Mary Lee Smith and her colleagues (1980) combined the results of 475 investigations. For psychotherapists, the welcome result was that "the evidence overwhelmingly supports the efficacy of psychotherapy" (p. 183). Figure 13–7 depicts their finding—that the average therapy client ends up better off than 80 percent of the untreated individuals on waiting lists. The claim is more modest than it first appears—by definition, about 50 percent of untreated people also are better off than the

> *"Fortunately, [psycho]analysis is not the only way to resolve inner conflicts. Life itself still remains a very effective therapist."*
>
> Karen Horney
> *Our Inner Conflicts,* 1945

Figure 13–7 Treatment Versus No Treatment *These two normal distribution curves based on data from 475 studies show the improvement of untreated people and psychotherapy clients. The outcome for the average therapy client surpassed that for 80 percent of the untreated people. (Adapted from Smith & others, 1980.)*

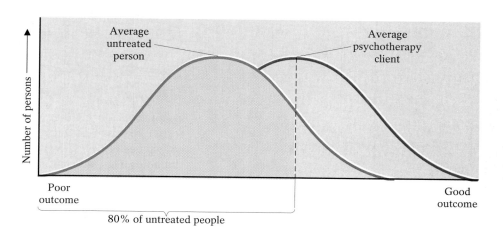

average untreated person. Nevertheless, Smith and her collaborators concluded that "psychotherapy benefits people of all ages as reliably as schooling educates them, medicine cures them, or business turns a profit" (p. 183).

Newer research summaries confirm this optimism (Lipsey & Wilson, 1993). The most ambitious of the new psychotherapy studies is a National Institute of Mental Health evaluation of three depression treatments: cognitive therapy, interpersonal therapy (which focuses on social relations), and a standard drug therapy. Twenty-eight experienced therapists at research sites in Norman, Oklahoma; Washington, DC; and Pittsburgh, Pennsylvania, were trained in one of the three methods and randomly assigned their share of the 239 depressed patients who participated. Patients in all three groups improved more than did those in a control group who received merely an inert medication and supportive attention, encouragement, and advice. Among patients who completed a full 16-week treatment program, the depression had lifted for slightly more than half of those in each treatment group—but only for 29 percent of those in the control group (Elkin & others, 1989). This verdict echoes the results of the earlier outcome studies: *Those not undergoing therapy improved, but those undergoing therapy improved more.*

Often, however, the improvement was not permanent. Only 1 in 4 patients undergoing psychotherapy and 1 in 6 undergoing drug therapy both recovered and experienced no relapse within 18 months (Shea & others, 1992). So, extravagant expectations that psychotherapy will transform your life and personality seem unwarranted. Still, Eysenck's pessimism also seems unwarranted. *On the average*, psychotherapy is somewhat effective—and is also cost-effective compared with the greater costs of medical care for psychologically related ailments (Turkington, 1987). The annual cost of psychological disorders and substance abuse is staggering—in the United States, $273 billion annually in crime, accidents, and lost productivity, says the Alcohol, Drug Abuse, and Mental Health Administration (1990). Just as an investment in prenatal and well-baby care *reduces* long-term costs, so will an investment in almost any effective treatment for psychological problems. Anything that boosts employees' psychological well-being will reduce medical costs, improve work efficiency, and diminish absenteeism. Studies by health insurers show that mental health treatment can more than pay for itself with reduced medical costs (American Psychological Association, 1991).

But note that "on the average" refers to no one therapy in particular. It is like saying, "Surgery is somewhat effective," or like reassuring lung-cancer patients that "on the average" medical treatment of health problems is effective. What people want to know is not the effectiveness of therapy in general but the effectiveness of particular treatments for their particular problems.

In general, therapy is most effective when the problem is clear-cut and specific (Singer, 1981). Those who suffer phobias, who are unassertive, or who are frustrated by sexual performance problems can hope for improvement. Those who suffer chronic schizophrenia or who wish to change their whole personality are unlikely to benefit from psychotherapy alone (Zilbergeld, 1983).

The Relative Effectiveness of Different Therapies

People considering therapy want to know *which* psychotherapy will be most effective for their problem. The analysis conducted by Mary Lee Smith and her colleagues (1977, 1980) allowed a comparison of the effectiveness of different therapies. Despite claims of superiority by advocates of different types of therapy, Smith's comparison of therapies revealed no clear winner. No one type of therapy proved consistently superior. Moreover—and more astonishing—it made no discernible difference whether the therapy was group or individual,

"Different sores have different salves."

English proverb

whether many or few sessions were offered, or how well trained and experienced the therapist was. It seemed as though the dodo bird in *Alice in Wonderland* was right: "Everyone has won and all must have prizes."

Some therapies are, however, well suited to particular disorders. With specific behavior problems such as phobias, compulsions, or sexual dysfunctions, behavioral conditioning therapies achieve especially favorable results (Bowers & Clum, 1988; Giles, 1983). With depression, the cognitive therapies prove most successful (Dobson, 1989; Shapiro & Shapiro, 1982). Just as physicians offer particular treatments for specific problems rather than treating every complaint with the same drug or surgical procedure, so psychotherapists increasingly offer particular treatments for specific problems (Stiles & others, 1986).

Commonalities Among Psychotherapies

Some clinicians suggest a reason why no one therapeutic method proves generally superior or inferior to another. Despite their differences, each therapy's effectiveness may derive from underlying commonalities. Jerome Frank (1982), Marvin Goldfried (Goldfried & Padawer, 1982), and Hans Strupp (1986) studied common ingredients of various therapies and suggested that they all offer at least three benefits: hope for demoralized people; a new perspective on oneself and the world; and an empathic, trusting, caring relationship. These "nonspecific" factors aren't all that therapy offers (Barker & others, 1988; Jones & others, 1988), but they are important aspects. They are part of what the growing numbers of self-help and support groups offer their members. And they have been part of what traditional healers offer (Jackson, 1992). Healers—special people to whom others disclose their suffering—have for centuries listened to understand and to empathize, reassure, advise, console, interpret, or explain.

Hope for Demoralized People

People who seek therapy typically feel anxious, depressed, devoid of self-esteem, and incapable of turning things around. What any therapy offers is the expectation that, with commitment from the patient, things can and will get better. Apart from the particular therapeutic technique, this belief may itself promote improved morale, new feelings of self-efficacy, and diminished symptoms (Prioleau & others, 1983). This benefit of a person's belief in a treatment is the *placebo effect*. As we saw in Chapter 1, a placebo is an inert treatment often used as a control treatment in drug experiments. The placebo has no effect apart from a person's belief in it. In psychotherapy experiments, the placebo treatment may be listening to inspirational tapes, attending group discussions, or taking a fake pill.

The finding that placebo-treated people improve more than do untreated people, although not as much as do those receiving actual psychotherapy, suggests that one reason therapies help is that they offer hope. Said differently, therapy outcomes vary with the client's attitude—the client's motivation, confidence, and commitment. Each therapy, in its individual way, may harness the client's own healing powers. And that, says psychiatrist Jerome Frank, helps us understand why all sorts of treatments—including some folk healing rites known to be powerless apart from the patient's belief—may in their own time and place produce cures.

A New Perspective

Every therapy offers people a plausible explanation of their symptoms and an alternative way of looking at themselves or responding to their worlds. Therapy also offers new experiences that help people change their views of themselves

"I utilize the best from Freud, the best from Jung, and the best from my Uncle Marty, a very smart fellow."

and their behaviors. Armed with a believable fresh perspective, they may approach life with a new attitude.

An Empathic, Trusting, Caring Relationship

To say that all therapies are about equally effective is not to say all *therapists* are equally effective. Regardless of their therapeutic technique, effective therapists are empathic people who seek to understand another's experience; whose care and concern the client feels; and whose respectful listening, reassurance, and advice earn the client's trust and respect. Indeed, some believe that warmth and empathy are hallmarks of healers everywhere, whether psychiatrists, witch doctors, or shamans (Torrey, 1986).

A Caring Relationship   *Effective therapists form a bond of trust with their patients.*

The notion that all therapies offer *hope* through the *fresh perspective* offered by a *caring person* gains support from a digest of 39 studies. Each study compared treatment offered by professional therapists with treatment offered by laypeople. These laypeople included friendly professors, people who have had a few hours of training in empathic listening skills, and college students supervised by a professional clinician. The result? The "paraprofessionals," as we call these briefly trained people, typically proved as effective as the professionals (Christensen & Jacobson, 1994). Though most of the problems they treated were mild, trained paraprofessionals were—believe it or not—as effective as professionals even when dealing with more disturbed adults, such as those diagnosed as seriously depressed.

To recap, people who seek help usually improve. So do many of those who do not undergo psychotherapy, and that is a tribute to our human resourcefulness and to our capacity to care for one another. Nevertheless, though it appears not to matter much which type of therapy is practiced, how long it lasts, or how experienced the therapist is, those who receive some psychotherapy usually improve more than those who do not. Mature, articulate people with specific emotional or behavior problems often improve the most.

Part of what all therapies offer is hope, a fresh way of looking at life, and an empathic, caring relationship. That may explain why the empathy and friendly counsel of paraprofessionals are so often as helpful as professional psychotherapy. And that may also explain why people who feel supported by close relationships—who enjoy the fellowship and friendship of caring people—are less likely to need or seek therapy (Frank, 1982; O'Connor & Brown, 1984).

Culture and Values in Psychotherapy

All therapies offer hope, and nearly all therapists attempt to enhance their clients' sensitivity, openness, personal responsibility, and sense of purpose (Jensen & Bergin, 1988). But on certain matters of moral and cultural diversity they may differ from one another and from their clients (Kelly, 1990). In Canada and the United States, for example, about 1 in 25 people—but (depending on the survey) one-fifth to one-half of psychiatrists and clinical psychologists—declare themselves atheist or agnostic (Gallup, 1993; Jensen & Bergin, 1988; Lukoff & others, 1992). That raises an issue: What values prevail in psychotherapy? What values *should* prevail?

Albert Ellis, the rational-emotive therapist, and Allen Bergin, co-editor of the *Handbook of Psychotherapy and Behavior Change*, illustrate how sharply values can differ. Ellis (1980) assumes that "no one and nothing is supreme," that "self-gratification" should be encouraged, and that "unequivocal love, commitment, service, and...fidelity to any interpersonal commitment, especially marriage, leads to harmful consequences." Bergin (1980) assumes the opposite—that "because God is supreme, humility and the acceptance of divine authority are virtues," that "self-control and committed love and self-sacrifice

A Consumer's Guide to Psychotherapists

When should a person consider seeking the help of a mental health professional? Life for everyone is marked by a mix of serenity and stress, blessing and bereavement, good moods and bad. It is only when troubling thoughts and emotions interfere with normal living that we should consider talking to a professional. The American Psychological Association includes the following on its list of common trouble signals.

- Feelings of hopelessness
- Deep and lasting depression
- Self-destructive behavior such as alcohol and drug abuse
- Disruptive fears
- Sudden mood shifts
- Thoughts of suicide
- Compulsive rituals such as hand washing
- Sexual difficulties

If you are looking for a therapist, you may wish to shop around by having a preliminary consultation with two or three therapists. You can describe your problem and learn each therapist's treatment approach. You can ask questions about the therapists' values, credentials, and fees. And, you can assess your feelings about each therapist.

Type	Description
Psychiatrists	Physicians who specialize in the treatment of psychological disorders. Not all psychiatrists have had extensive training in psychotherapy, but as M.D.s they can prescribe medications. Thus, they tend to see those with the most serious problems. Many have a private practice.
Clinical psychologists	Most are psychologists with Ph.D.s and expertise in research, assessment, and therapy, usually supplemented by a supervised internship. About half work in agencies and institutions, half in private practice.
Clinical or psychiatric social workers	A 2-year Master of Social Work graduate program plus postgraduate supervision prepares some social workers to offer psychotherapy, mostly to people with everyday personal and family problems. About half have earned the National Association of Social Workers' designation of clinical social worker.
Counselors	Marriage and family counselors specialize in problems arising from family relations. Pastoral counselors, some certified by the American Association of Pastoral Counselors, provide counseling to countless people. Abuse counselors work with substance abusers, spouse and child abusers, and their victims.

are to be encouraged," and that "infidelity to any interpersonal commitment, especially marriage, leads to harmful consequences." Bergin and Ellis disagree more radically than most therapists regarding what values are healthiest. In so doing, however, they illustrate what they agree on: that psychotherapists' personal beliefs and values influence their practice, and that therapists should divulge their values more openly.

Value differences may become significant when a therapist from one culture meets a client from another. In North America, Europe, and Australia, for example, most therapists reflect their culture's individualism (by giving priority to personal desires and identity). Clients who are immigrants from Asian countries, which expect people to be mindful of others' expectations, may therefore have difficulty with therapies that require them to think independently. Such differences help explain the reluctance of some minority populations to use mental health services (Sue, 1990). Recognizing that therapists and clients may differ in values, in communication styles, and in language, many therapy training programs are now providing training in cultural sensitivity and recruiting members of underrepresented culture groups.

Rehearse It

12. The question "Is psychotherapy effective?" has been the subject of hundreds of scientific studies and innumerable personal accounts. The most enthusiastic or optimistic view of psychotherapy comes from

a. outcome research.
b. psychologist Hans Eysenck.
c. reports of clinicians and clients.
d. a government study of treatment for depression.

13. On average, troubled people who undergo therapy are more likely to improve than those who do not, and therapy tends to be most effective when the problem is clear-cut and specific. Studies show that _____ therapy is most effective overall.

a. behavior
b. humanistic
c. individual as opposed to group
d. no one type of

14. Psychologists have observed that people's belief that a treatment will help them is often sufficient to cause some improvement. When a neutral treatment, such as an inert pill, results in improved morale and diminished symptoms, psychologists call this

a. a placebo effect.
b. preventive mental health.
c. an empathic perspective.
d. clinical treatment.

The Biomedical Therapies

Psychotherapy is one way to treat psychological disorders. The other is physically changing the brain's functioning—by altering its electrochemical transmissions with drugs, by overloading its circuits with electroconvulsive shock, or by disconnecting its circuits through psychosurgery.

Drug Therapies

7. What are the most common forms of drug therapy?

By far the most widely used biomedical treatments today are the drug therapies. When introduced in the 1950s, drug therapy greatly reduced the need for psychosurgery or hospitalization. Discoveries in **psychopharmacology** (the study of drug effects on mind and behavior) revolutionized the treatment of severely disordered people, liberating hundreds of thousands from confinement in mental hospitals. Thanks to drug therapy—and to political and legal efforts to minimize involuntary hospitalization and to return hospitalized people to their communities, aided by community mental health programs—the resident population of state and county mental hospitals in the United States today is but 20 percent of what it was 40 years ago (Figure 13–8).

For those still unable to care for themselves, however, release from hospitals has meant not liberation but homelessness. If home is the place where, as poet Robert Frost said, when you go there, they have to take you in, then some 200,000 disordered Americans have no place to call home (Leshner, 1992). Studies suggest that about one-third of the homeless suffer disabling psychological disorders (Fischer & Breakey, 1991; Levine & Rog, 1990; McCarty & others, 1991). And that doesn't include alcohol or drug abuse, which also plague about 1 in 3 homeless people. Unlike the homeless on the 1950s' skid rows in major cities, 3 percent of whom were female, 25 percent of today's homeless are female (Rossi, 1990).

With almost any new treatment, including drug therapy, there is a first wave of enthusiasm as many people apparently improve. But that enthusiasm often diminishes after researchers subtract the rate of (1) normal recovery among untreated persons and (2) recovery due to the placebo effect, which arises from

> *"The mentally ill were out of the hospital, but in many cases they were simply out on the streets, less agitated but lost, still disabled but now uncared for."*
>
> Lewis Thomas
> *Late Night Thoughts on Listening to Mahler's Ninth Symphony,* 1983

Figure 13–8 The Emptying of U.S. Mental Hospitals
After the widespread introduction of antipsychotic drugs, starting in about 1955, the number of residents in state and county mental hospitals declined sharply. But in the rush to deinstitutionalize the mentally ill, many people who were ill-equipped to care for themselves were left homeless on city streets. (Data from the National Institute of Mental Health and Bureau of the Census, 1993.)

the positive expectations of patients and mental health workers alike. So, to evaluate the effectiveness of any new drug, researchers use the *double-blind technique*. Half the patients receive the drug, the other half a similar-appearing placebo. Neither the staff nor the patients know who gets which. In double-blind studies, several types of drugs have proved useful in treating psychological disorders.

Antipsychotic Drugs

The revolution in drug therapy for psychological disorders began when it was accidentally discovered that certain drugs, used for other medical purposes, also calmed psychotic patients. These antipsychotic drugs, such as chlorpromazine (sold as Thorazine), provide most help to people experiencing the positive symptoms of auditory hallucinations and paranoia, by dampening their responsiveness to irrelevant stimuli (Lenzenweger & others, 1989). Schizophrenia patients with the negative symptoms of apathy and withdrawal often do not respond well to these antipsychotic drugs. A newer drug, clozapine (marketed as Clozaril), does sometimes enable "awakenings" in such people. It also sometimes helps those with positive symptoms who haven't responded to other drugs. Although clozapine has a toxic effect on white blood cells in 1 or 2 percent of cases—thus necessitating regular blood tests—it is currently regarded as the most effective schizophrenia treatment. In 1994 the patent expired on this very expensive drug, permitting competitive pricing that now makes clozapine affordable to more people. Researchers are testing possible cousin drugs that would offer the same benefits without the blood problem.

The molecules of antipsychotic drugs are similar enough to molecules of the neurotransmitter dopamine to occupy its receptor sites and block its activity (Pickar & others, 1984). (Clozapine also blocks serotonin activity.) This finding—that most antipsychotic drugs block dopamine receptors—reinforces the idea that, as psychopharmacologist Solomon Snyder (1984) put it, "Dopamine systems in the brain are closely related to whatever is fundamentally abnormal in schizophrenic brains—either an excess of dopamine formation or perhaps a supersensitivity of dopamine receptors."

Antipsychotics such as Thorazine are powerful drugs that can produce sluggishness, tremors, and twitches similar to those of Parkinson's disease, which is marked by too little dopamine (Kaplan & Saddock, 1989). (Clozapine, thankfully, has few such side effects.) What is an effective dose for some people may be an overdose for others. Asians, for example, seem to require lower doses than Caucasians (Holden, 1991). By carefully monitoring the dosage and its effects, therapist and patient tread the fine line between relieving the symptoms and causing extremely unpleasant side effects. In this way, and with the help of

psychopharmacology The study of the effects of drugs on mind and behavior.

Herself Renewed *Thanks to clozapine, Daphne Moss went "from hating the sunshine in the morning to loving it." No longer suffering from the paranoid delusion that her parents were witches, Moss began teaching school and living independently.*

1993 worldwide sales (Sleek, 1994):
Prozac—$1 billion
Zoloft—$460 million
Paxil—$225 million

Figure 13–9 Biology of Antidepressants *After neurotransmitters carry a message across a synapse (a), the sending nerve cell normally reabsorbs excess neurotransmitters (a process called reuptake) (b). Prozac blocks reuptake of the neurotransmitter serotonin. The extra serotonin therefore remains in the synapse, enhancing its mood-lifting effects (c).*

supportive people, hundreds of thousands of schizophrenia patients who had been consigned to the back wards of mental hospitals have returned to jobs and to near-normal lives.

Antianxiety Drugs

Among the most heavily prescribed and abused drugs are the antianxiety agents, such as Valium and Librium. Like alcohol, these drugs depress central nervous system activity. Because they reduce tension and anxiety without causing excessive sleepiness, they have been prescribed even for minor emotional stresses. Used in combination with other therapy, an antianxiety drug can help a person learn to cope successfully with frightening situations and fear-triggering stimuli.

The criticism sometimes made of the behavior therapies—that they reduce symptoms without resolving underlying problems—is also made of antianxiety drugs. Unlike the behavior therapies, they may even be used as a continuing treatment. Routinely "popping a Valium" at the first sign of tension can produce psychological dependence on the drug. When heavy users stop taking the drug, they may experience increased anxiety and insomnia, driving them back to the drug for relief.

Antidepressant Drugs

As the antianxiety drugs calm anxious people down, the antidepressants sometimes lift depressed people up. Most of these drugs increase the availability of the neurotransmitters norepinephrine or serotonin, which elevate arousal and mood and appear to be scarce during depression. For example, the antidepressant fluoxetine (marketed as Prozac, the most widely prescribed psychiatric drug) blocks the reabsorption and removal of serotonin from synapses (Figure 13–9). (Prozac, and its cousins Zoloft and Paxil, are therefore called serotonin-reuptake-inhibitor drugs.) Other antidepressants work by blocking the reabsorption of both norepinephrine and serotonin or by inhibiting an enzyme that breaks down neurotransmitters such as serotonin. These drugs, however, have more potential side effects, such as dry mouth, weight gain, or dizzy spells.

Patients who begin taking antidepressants do not wake up the next day singing "Oh, what a beautiful morning!" Although the influence of antidepressants on neurotransmission occurs within hours, their full psychological effect

Message is sent across synaptic gap.

Message is received; excess neurotransmitters are reabsorbed by sending neuron.

Prozac blocks normal reuptake of the neurotransmitter serotonin; excess serotonin in synapse enhances its mood-lifting effect.

Sending neuron

Vesicles containing neurotransmitters

Action potential

Synaptic gap

Neurotransmitter

Receptor

Receiving neuron

Reuptake

Prozac

Serotonin

(a)   (b)   (c)

lithium A chemical that provides an effective drug therapy for the mood swings of bipolar (manic-depressive) disorders.

electroconvulsive therapy (ECT) Shock treatment. A biomedical therapy for severely depressed patients in which a brief electric current is sent through the brain of the anesthetized patient.

The medical use of electricity is an ancient practice. Physicians treated the Roman Emperor Claudius (10 B.C.–A.D. 54) for headaches by pressing electric eels to his temples.

Electroconvulsive Therapy *Although ECT is controversial, it is the preferred treatment for depression that does not respond to drug therapy.*

often requires 4 weeks, sometimes aided by cognitive therapy to help the patient reverse a now-habitual negative thinking style. Moreover, the effect of these drugs—beyond that of natural recovery and the placebo effect—is often modest (Greenberg & others, 1992, 1994). Although the effects are less exciting than some news stories would have us believe, they also are less frightening than other stories have suggested. Although some people taking Prozac, for example, have committed suicide, their numbers seem fewer than we would expect from millions of depressed people if not taking the medication.

For those suffering the manic-depressive mood swings of a bipolar disorder, the simple salt **lithium** can be an effective mood stabilizer. An Australian physician, John Cade, discovered this in the 1940s when he administered lithium to a severely manic patient. Although his reason for doing so was misguided—he thought lithium had calmed excitable guinea pigs when actually it made them sick—Cade found that in less than a week the patient became perfectly well (Snyder, 1986). With continued lithium use, the emotional highs and lows typically level off. After suffering mood swings for years, many people find relief with a daily dose of this cheap salt.

Electroconvulsive Therapy

8. How effective are electroconvulsive therapy and psychosurgery?

A more controversial brain manipulation occurs through shock treatment, or **electroconvulsive therapy (ECT)**. When ECT was first introduced in 1938, the wide-awake patient was strapped to a table and jolted with roughly 100 volts of electricity to the brain, producing racking convulsions and brief unconsciousness. ECT therefore gained a barbaric image that lingers to the present. Today, however, patients first receive a general anesthetic so they are not conscious, and a muscle relaxant to prevent injury from convulsions. Then a psychiatrist electrically shocks the unconscious patient's brain for one twenty-fifth of a second. Within 30 minutes the patient awakens and remembers nothing of the treatment or of the hours preceding it.

Psychiatrists usually limit ECT to severely depressed patients. (It is usually ineffective in treating other psychological disorders.) After three such treatments a week for 2 to 4 weeks, 80 percent or more of depressed people improve markedly and without discernible brain damage (Bergsholm & others, 1989; Coffey, 1993). "A miracle had happened in 2 weeks," reported noted research psychologist Norman Endler (1982) after ECT alleviated his deep depression. A 1985 panel of the National Institutes of Health, as well as newer research reviews, report that for many others, too, ECT is an effective treatment for severe depression that has not responded to drug therapy (Consensus Conference, 1985; Parker & others, 1992). Thus, reports the American Psychiatric Association (1990), ECT has regained respectability as a "major treatment" for depression.

How does ECT work? After more than 50 years, no one knows for sure (Kapur & Mann, 1993). Perhaps electrical shock increases the release of norepinephrine. Or perhaps the shock-induced seizures cause the brain to react by calming neural centers where overactivity produces depression.

Although ECT is credited with saving many from suicide, its Frankenstein-like image continues. No matter how impressive the results, the idea of electrically shocking people into convulsions still strikes many as barbaric, especially given our ignorance about why ECT works. Moreover, ECT-treated patients, like other formerly depressed patients, are vulnerable to relapse. Nevertheless, electroconvulsive therapy is, in the minds of many psychiatrists and patients, a lesser evil than depression's misery, anguish, and risk of suicide.

psychosurgery Surgery that removes or destroys brain tissue in an effort to change behavior.

lobotomy A now-rare psychosurgical procedure once used to calm uncontrollably emotional or violent patients. In this procedure, the nerves that connect the frontal lobes to the emotion-controlling centers of the inner brain are cut.

Mind-Body Interaction *The biomedical therapies assume that mind and body are a unit: Affect one and you will affect the other.*

Psychosurgery

Because its effects are irreversible, **psychosurgery**—surgery that removes or destroys brain tissue to change behavior—is the most drastic and the least-used biomedical intervention. In the 1930s, Portuguese physician Egas Moniz developed what became the best known psychosurgical operation: the **lobotomy**. Moniz found that cutting the nerves connecting the frontal lobes with the emotion-controlling centers of the inner brain calmed uncontrollably emotional and violent patients. After shocking the patient into a coma, a neurosurgeon would hammer an icepick-like instrument through each eye socket into the brain, then wiggle it to sever connections running up to the front lobes. If a bit crude, the whole procedure was at least easy and cheap, taking only about 10 minutes. During the 1940s and 1950s, tens of thousands of severely disturbed people were *lobotomized*, and Moniz was honored with a Nobel prize (Valenstein, 1986).

Although the intention was simply to disconnect emotion from thought, the effect was often more drastic: The lobotomy produced a permanently lethargic, immature, impulsive personality. During the 1950s, after some 35,000 people had been lobotomized in the United States alone, calming drugs became available and psychosurgery was largely abandoned. Today, lobotomies are almost never performed. Other psychosurgery is used only in extreme cases. For example, if a patient suffers uncontrollable seizures, surgeons can deactivate the specific nerve clusters that cause or transmit the convulsions. Because such beneficial operations are irreversible, however, neurosurgeons perform them only as a last resort.

The effectiveness of the biomedical therapies reminds us of a fundamental lesson: We find it convenient to talk of separate psychological and biological influences, but everything psychological is biological. Every thought and feeling depends on the functioning brain. Every creative idea, every moment of joy or anger, every period of depression emerges from the electrochemical activity of the living brain.

Preventing Psychological Disorders

9. What is the rationale for preventive mental health programs?

Psychotherapies and biomedical therapies tend to locate the cause of psychological disorders within the disordered person. We infer that people who act cruelly must be cruel and that people who act "crazy" must be "sick." We attach labels to such people, thereby distinguishing them from "normal" folks. It follows, then, that we try to treat "abnormal" people by giving them insight into their problems, by changing their thinking, or by controlling them with drugs.

There is an alternative viewpoint: We could interpret many psychological disorders as understandable responses to a disturbing and stressful society. According to this view, it is not just the person who needs treatment, but also the person's social context. Better to prevent a problem by reforming a sick situation than to wait for a problem to arise and then treat it.

A story about the rescue of a drowning person from a rushing river illustrates the need for prevention. Having successfully administered first aid, the rescuer spots another struggling person and pulls her out, too. After a half

> *"It is better to prevent than to cure."*
>
> Peruvian folk wisdom

> *"Mental disorders arise from physical ones, and likewise physical disorders arise from mental ones."*
>
> *The Mahabharata,* c. A.D. 200

dozen repetitions, the rescuer suddenly turns and starts running away while the river sweeps yet another floundering person into view. "Aren't you going to rescue that fellow?" asks a bystander. "Heck no," the rescuer replies. "I'm going upstream to find out what's pushing all these people in."

Preventive mental health is upstream work. It seeks to prevent psychological casualties by identifying and alleviating the conditions that cause them. George Albee (1986) believes there is abundant evidence that poverty, meaningless work, constant criticism, unemployment, racism, and sexism undermine people's sense of competence, personal control, and self-esteem. Such stresses increase their risk of depression, alcoholism, and suicide.

Albee contends that those who care about preventing psychological casualties should therefore support programs that alleviate poverty, discrimination, and other demoralizing situations. We eliminated smallpox not by treating the afflicted but by inoculating the unafflicted. We conquered yellow fever by controlling mosquitos. Prevention of psychological problems means empowering those who have learned an attitude of helplessness, changing environments that breed loneliness, renewing the disintegrating family, and bolstering parents' and teachers' skills at nurturing children's self-esteem. Indeed, "Everything aimed at improving the human condition, at making life more fulfilling and meaningful, may be considered part of primary prevention of mental or emotional disturbance" (Kessler & Albee, 1975, p. 557).

Albee reminds us again of another of this book's themes: A human being is an integrated bio-psycho-social system. For years we have trusted our bodies to physicians and our minds to psychiatrists and psychologists. That neat separation no longer seems valid. Chemical imbalances can produce schizophrenia and depression. And anger, depression, and stress, as Chapter 10 showed, can threaten our physical health. *"Mens sana in corpore sano,"* says an ancient Latin adage: A healthy mind in a healthy body.

! Rehearse It

15. Certain antipsychotic drugs are used to calm schizophrenia patients so that they can live outside the hospital. The drugs often bring relief from auditory hallucinations and other troubling symptoms. However, they can have unpleasant side effects, most notably

a. hyperactivity.
b. convulsions and momentary memory loss.
c. sluggishness, tremors, and twitches.
d. paranoia.

16. Valium and Librium, which depress central nervous system activity, are among the most heavily prescribed and abused drugs. These drugs are referred to as _____ drugs.

a. antipsychotic
b. antianxiety
c. antidepressant

17. The antidepressant drugs seem to increase the availability of the neurotransmitters norepinephrine or serotonin, which appear to be scarce during depression. One antidepressant drug that often brings relief to patients suffering the manic-depressive mood swings of a bipolar disorder is

a. dopamine.
b. Librium.
c. lithium.
d. Valium.

18. Two controversial biomedical therapies are electroconvulsive therapy (shock treatment) and lobotomy (a type of psychosurgery). Lobotomy, once used to treat uncontrollably violent patients, is no longer an accepted treatment. Electroconvulsive therapy, however, remains in use as a treatment for

a. depression.
b. severe depression.
c. schizophrenia.
d. anxiety disorders.

19. Being poor or unemployed undermines a person's self-esteem and sense of competence. An approach that seeks to alleviate poverty and other demoralizing situations that put people at high risk for developing psychological disorders is

a. biomedical therapy.
b. the humanistic approach.
c. empathy and active listening.
d. preventive mental health.

Reviewing *Therapy*

Treatment for psychological disorders encompasses both the psychological therapies, involving structured interactions, and the biomedical therapies, which alter neural functions. The major psychotherapies derive from the familiar psychoanalytic, humanistic, behavioral, and cognitive perspectives on psychology.

The Psychological Therapies

1.   What are the aims and methods of psychoanalysis?

Psychoanalysts try to help people gain insight into the unconscious origins of their disorders and to work through the accompanying feelings. To do so, an analyst draws on techniques such as free association and the interpretation of patients' dreams, resistances, and transference to the therapist of long-repressed feelings. Like psychoanalytic theory, psychoanalysis is criticized for after-the-fact interpretations and for being time-consuming and costly. Although traditional psychoanalysis is not practiced widely, its influence can be seen in the work of therapists who explore childhood experiences, who assume that defense mechanisms repress emotion-laden information, and who seek to help their clients achieve insight into the root of their problems.

2.   What are the basic themes of humanistic therapy, such as Rogers' person-centered approach?

Unlike psychoanalysts, humanistic therapists focus on clients' current conscious feelings and on their taking responsibility for their own growth. Carl Rogers, in his person-centered therapy, used active listening to express genuineness, acceptance, and empathy.

3.   What are the assumptions and techniques of the behavior therapies?

Behavior therapists worry less about promoting self-awareness and more about directly modifying problem behaviors. Thus, they may countercondition behaviors through systematic desensitization or aversive conditioning. Or they may apply operant conditioning principles with behavior modification techniques such as, in institutional settings, token economies.

4.   What are the goals and techniques of the cognitive therapies?

The newer cognitive therapies, such as Ellis's rational-emotive therapy and Beck's cognitive therapy for depression, aim to change self-defeating thinking by training people to look at themselves in new, more positive ways. Cognitive-behavior therapy also engages clients in regular practice of new ways of thinking and talking.

5.   In what group contexts do people receive therapy?

Many therapeutic techniques can also be applied in a group context. Self-help and support groups, such as AA, engage many millions of people. Family therapy treats the family as an interactive system from which problems may arise.

Evaluating Psychotherapies

6.   What does research on psychotherapy reveal about its effectiveness?

Because the positive testimonials of clients and therapists cannot prove that therapy is actually effective, psychologists have conducted hundreds of studies of the outcomes of psychotherapy. These studies indicate that (1) people who remain untreated often improve; (2) those who receive psychotherapy are somewhat more likely to improve, regardless of what kind of therapy they receive and for how long; (3) mature, articulate people with specific behavior problems often receive the greatest benefits from therapy; but (4) placebo treatments or the sympathy and friendly counsel of "paraprofessionals" also tend to produce more improvement than occurs in untreated people. Different types of psychotherapy offer certain commonalities, such as new hope, a fresh perspective, and an empathic, caring relationship. Therapists do, however, differ in the values that influence their aims.

The Biomedical Therapies

7.   What are the most common forms of drug therapy?

Drugs are the most widely used biomedical therapy. Antipsychotic drugs, used in treating schizophrenia, block dopamine activity; antianxiety drugs depress central nervous system activity; antidepressant drugs increase availability of serotonin and norepinephrine; and lithium is a mood stabilizer prescribed for those with bipolar disorder.

8.   How effective are electroconvulsive therapy and psychosurgery?

Although controversial, a growing body of evidence indicates that ECT is an effective treatment for many severely depressed people who do not respond to drug therapy. Brain surgery has been found to alleviate specific problems, but the effects of radical psychosurgical procedures such as lobotomy are irreversible and potentially drastic. Thus, psychosurgery is seldom performed.

Preventing Psychological Disorders

9.   What is the rationale for preventive mental health programs?

Advocates of preventive mental health argue that many psychological disorders could be prevented. Their aim is to change oppressive, esteem-destroying environments into more benevolent, nurturing environments that foster individual growth and self-confidence.

Terms and Concepts to Remember

psychotherapy, p. 449

eclectic approach, p. 450

psychoanalysis, p. 450

resistance, p. 451

interpretation, p. 451

transference, p. 451

person-centered therapy, p. 453

active listening, p. 453

behavior therapy, p. 455

counterconditioning, p. 455

systematic desensitization, p. 455

aversive conditioning, p. 457

token economy, p. 458

cognitive therapy, p. 458

rational-emotive therapy, p. 459

family therapy, p. 462

psychopharmacology, p. 470

lithium, p. 473

electroconvulsive therapy (ECT), p. 473

psychosurgery, p. 474

lobotomy, p. 474

Rehearse It Answer Key

1. a.   **2.** a.   **3.** d.   **4.** c.   **5.** c.   **6.** b.   **7.** a.   **8.** d.   **9.** c.

10. d.   **11.** b.   **12.** c.   **13.** d.   **14.** a.   **15.** c.   **16.** b.   **17.** c.   **18.** b.

19. d.

Critical Thinking Exercise

Now that you have read and reviewed Chapter 13, take your learning a step further by testing your critical thinking skills on the following passage.

Deborah is very satisfied with the large amount of time and money she has invested in psychotherapy. When she began therapy, her life was in crisis and she was desperate for help in overcoming her depressed, pessimistic attitude. After shopping around, she finally found an understanding cognitive therapist who made her feel hopeful she could get her life back on track. After 3 months of psychotherapy, Deborah is once again enjoying her life and attributes her recovery to the psychotherapy.

Vincent is a middle-aged manager of an auto parts store. He is under a lot of pressure at work, has a very pessimistic attitude toward life, and "blows up" frequently at minor family annoyances. Although he admits that he is depressed and complains to his family a lot, he doesn't feel there is anything wrong with him. His family disagrees and is concerned that he is increasingly showing signs of psychologically disordered behavior. At their insistence, Vincent reluctantly agrees to see a psychotherapist. He picks a name at random from the phone book and grudgingly endures several weeks of "overpriced gibberish" to appease his family. Despite the good efforts of the psychotherapist, who attempts to countercondition Vincent's maladaptive behaviors, Vincent shows no improvement following psychotherapy.

1. Assuming that their initial problems were equally serious, what could account for Deborah's and Vincent's very different experiences with psychotherapy?

2. Deborah now swears by cognitive therapy, while Vincent is very critical of behavior therapy. Are their recommendations acceptable as scientific evidence regarding the effectiveness of psychotherapy? Why or why not?

Check your progress on becoming a critical thinker by comparing your answers with the sample answers found in Appendix B.

Social Psychology

Social Thinking

Attributing Behavior to Persons or to Situations

Attitudes and Actions

Social Influence

Conformity and Obedience

Group Influence

Cultural Influences

Social Relations

Prejudice

Aggression

Conflict

Attraction

Altruism

Peacemaking

"We cannot live for ourselves alone," remarked the novelist Herman Melville, for "our lives are connected by a thousand invisible threads." **Social psychologists** explore these connections by scientifically studying how we *think about, influence,* and *relate* to one another.

Social Thinking

Especially when the unexpected occurs, we analyze and discuss why people act as they do. Does her warmth reflect romantic interest in me, or is that how she relates to everyone? Does his absenteeism signify laziness or an oppressive work atmosphere?

Attributing Behavior to Persons or to Situations

1. How do we tend to explain others' behavior? How do we explain our own behavior?

After studying how people explain others' behavior, Fritz Heider (1958) proposed an **attribution theory**. Heider noted that people usually attribute others' behavior either to their internal dispositions or to their external situations. A teacher, for example, may wonder whether a child's hostility reflects an aggressive personality (*a dispositional attribution*) or whether the child is reacting to stress or abuse (*a situational attribution*).

In class, we notice that Julie doesn't say much; over coffee, Jack talks nonstop. Attributing their behaviors to their personal dispositions, we decide that Julie is shy and Jack is outgoing. Because people do have enduring personality traits, such attributions are sometimes valid. However, we often overestimate the influence of personality and underestimate the influence of situation. In class, Jack may be as quiet as Julie. Catch Julie at a party and you may hardly

social psychology   The scientific study of how we think about, influence, and relate to one another.

attribution theory   The theory that we tend to give a causal explanation for someone's behavior, often by crediting either the situation or the person's disposition.

fundamental attribution error The tendency for observers, when analyzing another's behavior, to underestimate the impact of the situation and to overestimate the impact of personal disposition.

recognize your quiet classmate. Underestimating situational influences is known as the **fundamental attribution error**.

An experiment by David Napolitan and George Goethals (1979) illustrates the phenomenon. They had Williams College students talk, one at a time, with a young woman who acted either aloof and critical or warm and friendly. Beforehand, they told half the students the woman's behavior would be spontaneous. They told the other half the truth—that she had been instructed to *act* friendly (or unfriendly). What effect do you suppose this information had?

None. The students disregarded the information. If the woman acted friendly, they inferred she really was a warm person. If she acted unfriendly, they inferred she really was a cold person. In other words, they attributed her behavior to her personal disposition *even when told that her behavior was situational*—that she was merely acting that way for purposes of the experiment.

Knowing about the fundamental attribution error is helpful, yet committing it is almost irresistible. In a high school play I attended recently, a talented 16-year-old girl convincingly played the part of a bitter old woman—so convincingly that, although I reminded myself of the fundamental attribution error, I still assumed that the young actress was typecast because she was well-suited for the part. Meeting her later at a cast party, I discovered she actually has a very pleasant disposition. I then remembered that several months earlier I had seen her play the part of a charming 10-year-old in *The Sound of Music*. Leonard Nimoy of "Star Trek" fame would not have been surprised by my error. He titled one of his books *I Am Not Spock*.

You, too, have surely committed the fundamental attribution error. In judging, say, whether your psychology instructor is shy or outgoing, you have perhaps by now inferred that he or she has an outgoing personality. But you know your instructor only from the classroom, a situation that demands outgoing behavior. Catch the instructor in a different situation and you might be surprised (as some of my students are when confronting me in a pick-up basketball game). Outside their assigned roles, professors seem less professorial, presidents less presidential, servants less servile.

The instructor, on the other hand, observes his or her own behavior in many different situations—in the classroom, in meetings, at home—and so might say, "Me, outgoing? It all depends on the situation. In class or with good friends, yes, I'm outgoing. But at conventions I'm really rather shy."

So, when explaining *our own* behavior, we are sensitive to how our behavior changes with the situations we encounter. When explaining *others'* behavior, particularly after observing them in only one type of situation, we often commit the fundamental attribution error: We disregard the situation and leap to unwarranted conclusions about their personality traits. We do so partly because we have learned to focus our attention more on the person than on the situational context. Meanwhile, the person's own attention focuses more on the situation to which he or she is reacting. Reverse the perspectives of actor and observer—by having each view a videotape replay of the situation from the other's perspective—and this reverses the attributions (Lassiter & Irvine, 1986; Storms, 1973). By seeing the world from the actor's perspective, the observers better appreciate the situation. Given an observer's point of view, the actors better appreciate their own initiative and personal style.

Recall from Chapter 11 that personality psychologists study the enduring, inner determinants of behavior that help to explain why different people act differently in a given situation. Social psychologists study the social influences that help explain why the same person will act differently in different situations.

The Effects of Attribution

In everyday life we often struggle to explain others' actions. To what should we attribute them? A jury must decide whether a shooting was malicious or in self-defense. An unhappy wife and husband each ponder why the other behaves so selfishly. An interviewer must judge whether the applicant's geniality is genuine. When making such judgments, our attributions—either to the person or to the situation—have important consequences (Fincham & Bradbury,

attitude A belief and feeling that predisposes one to respond in a particular way to objects, people, and events.

1993; Fletcher & others, 1990). Happily married couples attribute their spouse's tart-tongued remark to a temporary situation ("She must have had a bad day at work"). Unhappily married persons attribute the same remark to a mean disposition ("Why did I marry such a hostile person?").

Or consider the political effects of attribution: How do you explain poverty or unemployment? Researchers in Britain, India, Australia, and the United States (Furnham, 1982; Pandey & others, 1982; Wagstaff, 1982; Zucker & Weiner, 1993) report that political conservatives tend to attribute such social problems to the personal dispositions of the poor and unemployed themselves: "People generally get what they deserve. Those who don't work are often free-loaders. People who take initiative can still get ahead." Political liberals are more likely to blame past and present situations: "If you or I had to live with the same poor education, lack of opportunity, and discrimination, would we be any better off?"

In evaluating employees, managers must also make attributions. They are likely to attribute the poor performance of workers to personal factors, such as low ability or lack of motivation. Workers who are doing poorly on a job recognize situational influences: inadequate supplies, poor working conditions, difficult co-workers, impossible demands (Rice, 1985).

The practical point to remember: Our attributions—to individuals' dispositions or to their situations—have real consequences.

Attitudes and Actions

Social psychology's single most important concept has been that of *attitudes*. **Attitudes** are beliefs and feelings that predispose our reactions to objects, people, and events. If we *believe* that someone is mean, we may *feel* dislike for the person and *act* unfriendly. "Change the way people think," said South African civil rights martyr Steve Biko, "and things will never be the same."

Do Our Attitudes Guide Our Actions?

2. Under what conditions do our attitudes guide our behavior?

Although most persuasive appeals assume that changed attitudes can indeed change behavior, dozens of studies during the 1960s challenged this idea (Wicker, 1971). Moreover, studies of people's attitudes and behaviors regarding cheating, the church, and racial minorities revealed that folks often talk and act a different game. "Thinking is easy," said the German poet Goethe (1749–1832), "acting difficult, and to put one's thoughts into action, the most difficult thing in the world."

But the seeming hypocrisy did startle social psychologists, most of whom shared Biko's belief that there is a close connection between thought and action, character and conduct, private words and public deeds. So they conducted many follow-up studies during the 1970s and 1980s (Kraus, 1991). These studies reveal that our attitudes *will* guide our actions if:

- ▸ *Outside influences on what we say and do are minimal.* Social pressures may blur the underlying connection between our attitudes and actions by affecting either what we say or what we do (Figure 14–1). In 1990, 4 weeks before a congressional election, President Bush and political leaders from both parties asked members of the U.S. House of Representatives to pass a compromise deficit-reducing budget. Privately, most members of Congress agreed that the painful cuts and tax increases were essential to the nation's health: Among those retiring or unopposed for reelection and thus facing little external pressure, 86 percent voted for the bill. For others, voting their privately held attitudes was more difficult. Among the 36 representa-

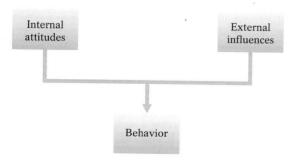

Figure 14–1 Attitudes, External Influences, and Actions
Our behavior is affected by our inner attitudes as well as by external social influences.

When Attitudes Drive Action   *Attitudes can inspire re-markable actions if we know what we believe and if our beliefs are relevant to our behavior. Here New York City police talk to a Greenpeace member as she protests a magazine's use of chlorine-treated paper.*

tives who were about to face angry voters in close races back home, there were no profiles in courage: All 36 voted against it.

⟩ ***The attitude is specifically relevant to the behavior.*** People readily profess *general* attitudes that are inconsistent with their behavior. They proclaim love while yelling at their mate, cherish honesty while cheating on their income tax returns, and value good health while smoking and not exercising. Attitudes about the specific act do, however, guide action. Attitudes toward exercise predict exercising behavior.

⟩ ***We are keenly aware of our attitudes.*** When we mindlessly follow habit or social expectations, our attitudes lie dormant. If something makes us self-conscious or reminds us of how we feel, we are truer to our convictions. For example, Martha Powell and Russell Fazio (1984) report that repeating an attitude makes it come to mind more quickly. Moreover, attitudes that come quickly to mind are more likely to guide our behavior (Fazio, 1990). When we know what we believe and are conscious of its implications for our actions, we are true to ourselves.

Do Our Actions Affect Our Attitudes?

3. Under what conditions does our behavior affect our attitudes?

So, people will stand up for what they believe under certain circumstances: when other influences are minimal, when the attitude is specific to the behavior, and when mindful of their attitudes. Attitudes will affect behavior. Now consider a more surprising principle: People also come to believe in what they have stood up for. Many streams of evidence confirm that *attitudes follow behavior.* Here are two.

The Foot-in-the-Door Phenomenon   During the Korean War, many captured American soldiers were imprisoned in war camps run by Chinese communists. Without using brutality, the captors secured their prisoners' collaboration in activities ranging from running errands and accepting favors to making radio appeals and false confessions to informing on fellow prisoners and divulging military information. When the war ended, 21 prisoners chose to stay with the communists. Many others returned home "brainwashed"—convinced that communism was a good thing for Asia.

A key ingredient of the Chinese "thought-control" program was its effective use of the **foot-in-the-door phenomenon**—a tendency for people who agree to a small request to comply later with a larger one. The Chinese harnessed this phenomenon by gradually escalating their demands on the prisoners, beginning with harmless requests (Schein, 1956). Having "trained" the prisoners to speak or write trivial statements, the communists then asked them to copy or create something more important, noting, perhaps, the flaws of capitalism. The prisoners then participated in group discussions, wrote self-criticisms, or uttered public confessions. Once they did so, perhaps to gain privileges, the prisoners then often adjusted their beliefs toward consistency with their public acts.

Research studies show that the foot-in-the-door tactic also helps boost charitable contributions, blood donations, and product sales. In one experiment, researchers posing as safety-drive volunteers asked Californians to permit the installation of a large, poorly lettered "Drive Carefully" sign in their front yards. Only 17 percent consented. Other home owners were first approached with a small request: Would they display a 3-inch high "Be a Safe Driver" sign? Nearly all readily agreed. When reapproached 2 weeks later to allow the large, ugly sign in their front yards, 76 percent consented (Freedman & Fraser, 1966).

foot-in-the-door phenomenon The tendency for people who have first agreed to a small request to comply later with a larger request.

role A set of expectations about a social position, defining how those in the position ought to behave.

"If the King destroys a man, that's proof to the King it must have been a bad man."

Thomas Cromwell in Robert Bolt's
A Man for All Seasons, 1960

Social Roles Are Powerful *Initially both the obedient recruit and the abusive sergeant may have consciously adopted the behavior expected of them. But in time they may become the characters they are playing.*

The moral is simple, says Robert Cialdini (1993): To get people to agree to something big, "Start small and build." And be wary of those who would exploit you with the tactic. This chicken-and-egg spiral of actions feeding attitudes feeding actions enables behavior to escalate. A trifling act makes the next act easier. Succumb to a temptation and you will find the next temptation harder to resist.

Dozens of experiments have simulated part of the war prisoners' experience, by coaxing people into acting against their attitudes or violating their moral standards. The nearly inevitable result: Most subjects begin to rationalize their behavior by persuading themselves that they were justified in saying or doing what they did. If induced to speak or write on behalf of a point of view they have doubts about, they begin to believe their own words. Saying becomes believing. Similarly, subjects induced to harm an innocent victim—by making cutting comments or by delivering electric shocks—typically begin to disparage their victim.

Fortunately, the attitudes-follow-behavior principle works as well for good deeds as for bad. In the years immediately following the introduction of school desegregation and the passage of the Civil Rights Act of 1964, white Americans expressed diminishing racial prejudice. And as Americans in different regions came to act more alike—thanks to more uniform national standards against discrimination—they began to think more alike. Experiments confirm that moral action has positive effects on the actor, and that doing favors for another person often leads to greater liking of the person. We love people for the good we do them as well as for the good they do us. Evil acts shape the self, but so do moral acts.

Role Playing Affects Attitudes In psychology, as in the theater, a **role** refers to a cluster of prescribed actions—the behaviors we expect of those who occupy a particular social position. When you adopt a new role—when you become a college student, marry, or begin a new job—you strive to follow the social prescriptions. At first, the behaviors may feel phony, because you are *acting* the role. The first weeks in the military feel artificial—as if one is pretending to be a soldier. The first weeks of a marriage may feel like "playing house." Before long, however, your behavior no longer feels forced. What began as play-acting in the theater of life becomes *you*.

Researchers have confirmed this effect by assessing people's attitudes before and after they adopt a new role. Sometimes this occurs in laboratory situations, sometimes in everyday situations, such as before and after taking a job. In one laboratory study, college students volunteered to spend time in a simulated prison devised by psychologist Philip Zimbardo (1972). Some he randomly designated as guards; he gave them uniforms, billy clubs, and whistles and instructed them to enforce certain rules. The remainder became prisoners; they were locked in barren cells and forced to wear humiliating outfits. After a day or two of self-consciously "playing" their roles, the simulation became real—too real. Most of the guards developed disparaging attitudes and some devised cruel and degrading routines. One by one the prisoners either broke down, rebelled, or became passively resigned, causing Zimbardo to call the study off after only 6 days.

Meanwhile, in real life, the military junta then in power in Greece was training another group of men to become torturers (Staub, 1989). The men's indoctrination into their roles occurred in small steps. First, the trainee stood guard outside the interrogation cells—the "foot in the door." Next, he stood guard inside. Only then was he ready to become actively involved in the questioning and torture. As the nineteenth-century writer Nathaniel Hawthorne noted, "No man, for any considerable period, can wear one face to himself and another to the multitude without finally getting bewildered as to which may be true." Behavior affects attitudes. What we do, we gradually become.

cognitive dissonance theory The theory that we act to reduce the discomfort (dissonance) we feel when two of our thoughts (cognitions) are inconsistent— as when we respond to our having acted contrary to our attitudes by changing those attitudes.

"Sit all day in a moping posture, sigh, and reply to everything with a dismal voice, and your melancholy lingers. . . . If we wish to conquer undesirable emotional tendencies in ourselves, we must . . . go through the outward movements of those contrary dispositions which we prefer to cultivate."

William James
Principles of Psychology, 1890

Why Do Our Actions Affect Our Attitudes? Without doubt, then, actions can affect attitudes, sometimes turning prisoners into collaborators, doubters into believers, or mere acquaintances into friends. But why? One explanation is that we feel motivated to justify our actions. When aware that our thoughts and actions don't coincide, we experience tension, called *cognitive dissonance*. To relieve this tension, according to the **cognitive dissonance theory** proposed by Leon Festinger, people often bring their attitudes into line with their actions. It's as if people rationalize, "If I chose to do it (or say it), I must believe in it." The less coerced and more responsible we feel for a troubling act, the more dissonance we feel. The more dissonance we feel, the more motivated we are to find consistency, such as by changing our attitudes to help justify the act.

Dozens of experiments have confirmed cognitive dissonance by making people feel responsible for behavior that has foreseeable consequences. As a subject in one of these experiments, you might agree for a measly $2 to help a researcher by writing an essay that supports something you don't believe in (perhaps a tuition increase). Feeling responsible for the statements (which are inconsistent with your attitudes), you likely would feel dissonance, especially if you thought an administrator would be reading your essay. How would you reduce the uncomfortable dissonance? One way would be to start believing your phony words. Let your pretense become your reality.

The attitudes-follow-behavior principle has some heartening implications. Although we cannot directly control all our feelings, we can influence them by altering our behavior. If we are unloving, we can become more loving by behaving as if we were so—by doing thoughtful things, expressing affection, giving affirmation. If we are down in the dumps, we can do as cognitive therapists advise and talk in more positive, self-accepting ways with fewer self put-downs. *The moral:* We can act ourselves into a way of thinking just about as easily as we can think ourselves into a way of acting.

! *Rehearse It*

1. In explaining a person's behavior we tend to make the fundamental attribution error—we overestimate the impact of internal factors (such as disposition, or personality) and underestimate the impact of the situation in which the behavior occurs. Thus, if we encounter a cocaine addict, we might attribute the person's behavior to

a. moral weakness or an addictive personality.
b. peer pressure.
c. the easy availability of the drug on city streets.
d. society's acceptance of drug use.

2. Whether or not our actions are really guided by our attitudes depends on several factors. For example, attitudes that are specifically relevant to a behavior are most

likely to predict that behavior. Thus we could best predict whether or not someone will vote in a mayoral election if we knew the person's attitude on

a. the value of democracy.
b. the benefits of efficient city government.
c. corruption in municipal affairs.
d. the importance of this particular election.

3. During the Korean War, the Chinese "brainwashed" soldiers to think that communism was a good thing for Asia. A key ingredient in their "thought-control" program was their ability to make use of the tendency of people who have first agreed to a small request to comply later with a larger request. This tendency is called

a. the fundamental attribution error.
b. the foot-in-the-door phenomenon.

c. the behavior-follows-attitudes principle.
d. role playing.

4. When we are aware that there is a discrepancy between our attitudes and our behavior, cognitive dissonance theory predicts that we will act to reduce the discomfort or dissonance we feel. The theory explains why

a. people who act against their attitudes tend to change their attitudes.
b. attitudes predict actions when social pressures are minimized.
c. changing an attitude—through persuasion—often fails to result in behavioral changes.
d. people are hypocritical, talking one way and acting another.

conformity Adjusting one's behavior or thinking to coincide with a group standard.

Social Influence

Social psychology's great lesson is the enormous power of social influence on our attitudes, beliefs, decisions, and actions. This influence can be seen in our conformity, compliance, and group behavior. Suicides, bomb threats, airplane hijackings, and UFO sightings all have a curious tendency to come in clusters. Armed with principles of social influence, advertisers and salespeople aim to sway our decisions to buy, to donate, to vote. Isolated with others who share their grievances, dissenters may gradually become rebels and rebels may become terrorists. During a lengthy stay in another part of the the world, we may struggle with the new cultural norms. Let's examine these potent social forces.

Conformity and Obedience

4. What do experiments on conformity and compliance reveal about the power of social influence?

Behavior is contagious. One person giggles, coughs, or yawns, and others in the group are soon doing the same. A cluster of people stands gazing upward, and passersby pause to do likewise. Laughter, even canned laughter, can be infectious. Bartenders and street musicians know to "seed" their tip cups with money to suggest that others have given.

Sometimes the effects of suggestibility are more serious. Sociologist David Phillips and his colleagues (1985, 1989) found that known suicides increase following a highly publicized suicide. So do fatal auto accidents and private airplane crashes (some of which disguise suicides)—and they do so only in areas where the suicide is publicized. Following film star Marilyn Monroe's suicide on August 6, 1962, the number of August suicides in the United States exceeded the usual count by 200. In Germany and the United States, suicide increases have also followed fictional suicides on soap operas and on dramas dealing with suicide (Gould & Shaffer, 1986; Hafner & Schmidtke, 1989; Phillips, 1982). Such copycat suicides help explain the clusters of teenage suicides that occasionally occur in some communities.

Group Pressure and Conformity

Suggestibility is a subtle type of **conformity**—adjusting our behavior or thinking to bring it into line with some group standard. To study conformity, Solomon Asch (1955) devised a simple test. As one of his subjects, you arrive at the experiment location in time to take a seat at the end of a row where four people are already seated. The experimenter asks which of three comparison lines is identical to a standard line (Figure 14–2). You see clearly that the answer is line 2 and await your turn to say so after the others. Your boredom with this experiment begins to show when the next set of lines proves equally easy.

Figure 14–2 Asch's Conformity Experiments *Which of the three comparison lines is equal to the standard line? What do you suppose most people would say after hearing four others say, "Line 3"? In this photo from one of Asch's experiments, the subject (center) shows the severe discomfort that comes from disagreeing with the responses of other group members.*

Standard line   Comparison lines

normative social influence Influence resulting from a person's desire to gain approval or avoid disapproval.

norms Understood rules for accepted and expected behavior. Norms prescribe "proper" behavior.

informational social influence Influence resulting from one's willingness to accept others' opinions about reality.

"'The way to get along,' I was told when I entered Congress, 'is to go along.'"

John F. Kennedy
Profiles in Courage, 1956

Now comes the third trial, and the correct answer seems just as clear-cut, but the first person gives what strikes you as a wrong answer: "Line 3." When the second person and then the third give the same wrong answer, you sit up straight and squint. When the fourth person agrees with the first three, you feel your heart begin to pound. The experimenter then looks to you for your answer. Torn between the unanimity of your four fellow subjects and the evidence of your own eyes, you feel tense and much less sure of yourself than you were moments ago. You hesitate before answering, wondering whether you should suffer the discomfort of being viewed as an oddball. What answer do you give?

In the experiments conducted by Asch and others after him, thousands of college students have experienced this conflict. Answering such questions alone, they erred less than 1 percent of the time. But it was a different story when several others—confederates working for the experimenter—answered incorrectly. Asch reports that his "intelligent and well-meaning" college subjects were then "willing to call white black" more than one-third of the time by going along with the group.

Conditions That Strengthen Conformity Asch's procedure became the model for later investigations. Although experiments have not always found such a high degree of blind conformity, they reveal that conformity increases when:

- we are made to feel incompetent or insecure.
- the group has at least three people. (Further increases in the group size yield not much more conformity.)
- the group is unanimous. (The support of a single fellow dissident greatly increases our social courage.)
- we admire the group's status and attractiveness.
- we have made no prior commitment to any response.
- others in the group observe our behavior.
- our culture strongly encourages respect for social standards.

Thus, we might predict the behavior of Joe, an eager but insecure new member of a prestigious fraternity: Noting that the 40 other members appear unanimous in their plans for an upcoming fund-raiser, Joe is unlikely to voice his dissent.

Reasons for Conforming Why do we clap when others clap, eat as others eat, believe what others believe, even see what others see? Frequently, it is to avoid rejection or to gain social approval. In such cases, we are responding to what social psychologists call **normative social influence**. We are sensitive to social **norms**—understood rules for accepted and expected behavior—because the price we pay for being different may be severe. Marco Lokar knows. During the 1991 Persian Gulf War, Lokar, an Italian, was the only Seton Hall University basketball player who chose not to display an American flag on his uniform. As the team traveled about, the fans' abusive responses to his nonconforming behavior became unbearable, so he quit the team and returned to Italy.

But there is another reason we may conform: The group may provide valuable information. Only a stubborn person will never listen to others. When we accept others' opinions about reality, we are responding to **informational social influence**. "Those who never retract their opinions love themselves more than they love truth," observed Joseph Joybert, an eighteenth-century French essayist.

As these reasons for conformity suggest, we perceive social influence as negative or positive according to the situation and our own unique attitudes and experiences. When influence supports what we approve, we applaud those who are "open-minded" and "sensitive" enough to be "responsive." When influence supports what we disapprove, we scorn the "submissive conformity" of those who comply with others' wishes. As we saw in Chapter 11, cultures vary in the value they place on independence versus responsiveness to others. Western Europeans and those in most English-speaking countries tend to prize individualism more than conformity and obedience. In experiments conducted in 14 countries, conformity rates have been lower in individualistic cultures than in more group-centered cultures (Bond & Smith, 1994).

Obedience

Social psychologist Stanley Milgram (1974) knew that people often comply with social pressures. But how would they respond to outright commands? To find out, he undertook what have become social psychology's most famous and controversial experiments. Imagine yourself as one of the nearly 1000 participants in Milgram's 20 experiments.

Stanley Milgram (1933–1984) *The late social psychologist's obedience experiments now "belong to the self-understanding of literate people in our age" (Sabini, 1986).*

Responding to an advertisement, you come to Yale University's psychology department to participate in an experiment. Professor Milgram's assistant explains that the study concerns the effect of punishment on learning. You and another subject draw slips out of a hat to see who will be the "teacher" (which your slip says) and who will be the "learner." The learner is then led to an adjoining room and strapped into a chair that is wired through the wall to an electric shock machine. You sit down in front of the machine, which has switches labeled with voltages. Your task: to teach and then test the learner on a list of word pairs. You are to punish the learner for wrong answers by delivering brief electric shocks, beginning with a switch labeled "15 Volts—Slight Shock." After each error by the learner, you are to move up to the next higher voltage. With each flick of a switch, lights flash, relay switches click on, and an electric buzzing fills the air.

If you comply with the experimenter's instructions, you hear the learner grunt when you flick the third, fourth, and fifth switches. After you activate the eighth switch (labeled "120 Volts—Moderate Shock"), the learner shouts that the shocks are painful. After the tenth switch ("150 Volts—Strong Shock"), he cries, "Experimenter, get me out of here! I won't be in the experiment anymore! I refuse to go on!" You draw back when you hear these pleas, but the experimenter prods you: "Please continue—the experiment requires that you continue." If you still resist, he insists, "It is absolutely essential that you continue," or "You have no other choice, you *must* go on."

If you obey, you hear the learner's protests escalate to shrieks of agony as you continue to raise the shock level with each succeeding error. After the 330-volt level, the learner refuses to answer and soon falls silent. Still, the experimenter pushes you toward the final, 450-volt switch, ordering you to ask the questions and, if a correct answer is not given, to administer the next shock level.

How far do you think you would follow the experimenter's commands? When Milgram surveyed people before conducting the experiment, most declared they would stop playing such a sadistic role soon after the learner first indicated pain and certainly before he shrieked in agony. This also was the prediction made by each of 40 psychiatrists whom Milgram asked to guess the outcome. When Milgram actually conducted the experiment with men aged 20 to 50, he was astonished to find that 63 percent complied fully—right up to the last switch.

Did the "teachers" figure out the hoax—that no shock was being delivered? Did they guess that the learner was a confederate who only pretended to feel the shocks? Did they realize that the experiment was really testing their willingness to comply with commands to inflict punishment? No, the teachers typically displayed genuine agony: They sweated, trembled, laughed nervously, and bit their lips. In defense of his use of deception, Milgram pointed out that, after the subjects learned of the deception and actual research purposes, virtually none regretted participating. When 40 of the subjects who had agonized most were later interviewed by a psychiatrist, none appeared to be suffering emotional aftereffects.

Perhaps the subjects obeyed because the learners' protests were not convincing. To preclude this possibility, Milgram repeated the experiment, with 40 new teachers. This time his confederate mentioned a "slight heart condition" while being strapped into the chair, and then complained and screamed more intensely as the shocks became more punishing. Still, 65 percent of the new teachers complied fully (Figure 14–3).

Figure 14–3 Milgram's Follow-Up Obedience Experiment *In a repeat of the earlier experiment, 65 percent of the adult male subjects fully obeyed the experimenter's commands to continue. This was despite the victim's "heart condition" and despite hearing cries of protest after 150 volts and agonized protests after 330 volts. (Data from Milgram, 1974.)*

In later experiments, Milgram discovered that subtle details of a situation powerfully influence people. When he varied the social conditions, the proportion of fully compliant subjects varied from 0 to 93 percent. Obedience was highest when:

- the person giving the orders was close at hand and perceived to be a legitimate authority figure.

- the authority figure was supported by a prestigious institution. (Milgram got somewhat less compliance when he dissociated his experiments from Yale University.)

- the victim was depersonalized or at a distance, even in another room. (Similarly, in combat with an enemy they can see, many soldiers either do not fire their rifles or do not aim them properly. Such refusals to kill are rare among those who operate the more distant weapons of artillery or aircraft [Padgett, 1989].)

- there were no role models for defiance; that is, no other subjects were seen disobeying the experimenter.

The power of legitimate, close-at-hand authorities is dramatically apparent in stories of those who complied with orders to carry out the atrocities of the Holocaust, and those who didn't. In the summer of 1942 nearly 500 middle-aged German reserve police officers were dispatched to Jozefow, Poland, in German-occupied territory. On July 13, the group's visibly upset commander informed his recruits, mostly family men, that they had been ordered to round up the village's Jews, who were said to be aiding the enemy.

Standing Up for Democracy *Some individuals—roughly one in three in Milgram's experiments—resist social coercion, as did this unarmed man in Beijing, by single-handedly challenging an advancing line of tanks the day after the 1989 Tiananmen Square uprising was crushed.*

Able-bodied men were to be sent to work camps and all the rest were to be shot on the spot. Given a chance to refuse participation in the executions, only about a dozen immediately refused. Within 17 hours, the remaining 485 officers killed 1500 helpless women, children, and elderly by shooting them in the back of the head as they lay face down, gruesomely spraying their skulls and brains. Faced with the pleadings of the victims, and seeing the gruesome results, some 20 percent of the officers did eventually dissent, managing either to miss their victims or to wander away and hide until the slaughter was over (Browning, 1992). But, as in Milgram's experiments, the disobedient were the minority.

Meanwhile, in the French village of Le Chambon, French Jews destined for deportation to Germany were being sheltered by villagers who openly defied orders to cooperate with the "New Order." The villagers' ancestors had themselves been persecuted and their pastors had been teaching them to "resist whenever our adversaries will demand of us obedience contrary to the orders of the Gospel" (Rochat, 1993). Ordered by police to give a list of sheltered Jews, the head pastor modeled defiance: "I don't know of Jews, I only know of human beings." Without realizing how long and terrible the war would be, or how much punishment and poverty they would suffer, the resisters made an initial commitment to resist. Supported by their beliefs, their role models, their interaction with one another, and their own initial acts, they remained defiant to the war's end.

Lessons From the Conformity and Obedience Studies

What do these experiments teach us about ourselves? How does judging the length of a line or flicking a shock switch relate to everyday social behavior? Recall from Chapter 1 that psychological experiments aim not to re-create the literal behaviors of everyday life but to capture and explore the underlying processes that shape those behaviors. Asch and Milgram devised experiments in which the subjects had to choose between holding to their own standards and being responsive to others, a dilemma we all face frequently.

In Milgram's experiments, subjects were also torn between what they should respond to—the pleas of the victim or the orders of the experimenter. Their moral sense warned them not to harm another, but it also prompted them to obey the experimenter and to be a good subject. With kindness and obedience on a collision course, obedience usually won.

These experiments demonstrate that social influences can be strong enough to make people conform to falsehoods or capitulate to cruelty. "The most fundamental lesson of our study," Milgram noted, is that "ordinary people, simply doing their jobs, and without any particular hostility on their part, can become agents in a terrible destructive process" (1974, p. 6). Milgram entrapped his subjects not by asking them first to zap "learners" with enough electricity to make their hair stand on end. Rather, he exploited the foot-in-the-door effect, beginning with a little tickle of electricity and escalating step by step. In the subjects' minds, the little action became justified, making the next act tolerable. In Jozefow, in Le Chambon, and in Milgram's experiments, those who resisted often did so early. With the first acts of compliance or resistance, attitudes began to follow and justify behavior.

So it happens when people succumb, gradually, to evil. In any society, great evils sometimes grow out of people's compliance with little evils. The Nazi leaders suspected that most German civil servants would resist shooting or gassing Jews directly, but they found them surprisingly willing to handle the paperwork of the Holocaust (Silver & Geller, 1978). Likewise, when Milgram asked 40 men to administer the learning test while someone else did the shocking, 93 percent complied. Contrary to our images of devilish villains, evil doesn't require monstrous evil characters; it's enough to have ordinary people corrupted by an evil situation.

"Drive off the cliff, James, I want to commit suicide."

"I was only following orders."

Adolf Eichmann, director of Nazi deportation of Jews to concentration camps

Group Influence

How do groups affect our behavior? To find out, social psychologists study the various influences that operate in the simplest of groups—one person in the presence of another—and those that operate in more complex groups, such as families, teams, and committees.

Individual Behavior in the Presence of Others

5. In what ways are we affected by the mere presence of others?

Appropriately, social psychology's first experiments focused on the simplest questions about social behavior: How are we influenced by the mere presence of others—by people watching or joining us as we engage in various activities?

Social Facilitation Having noticed that cyclists' racing times were faster when they competed against each other than when competing with a clock, Norman Triplett (1898) guessed that the presence of others boosts performance. To test his hypothesis, Triplett had adolescents wind a fishing reel as rapidly as possible. He discovered that they wound faster in the presence of someone who worked simultaneously on the same task. This stronger performance in the presence of others is known as **social facilitation**. For example, after a light turns green, drivers take about 15 percent less time to travel the first 100 yards when another car is beside them at the intersection than when they are alone (Towler, 1986). But on tougher tasks (learning nonsense syllables or solving complex multiplication problems), people perform less well when observers or others working on the same task are present.

Further studies revealed why the others' presence sometimes helps and sometimes hinders performance (Guerin, 1986; Zajonc, 1965). When observed by others, people become aroused. This arousal strengthens the most likely response—the correct one on an easy task, an incorrect one on a difficult task. Thus, when observed, people perform well-learned tasks more quickly and accurately and unmastered tasks less quickly and accurately. James Michaels and his associates (1982) found that expert pool players who made 71 percent of their shots when alone made 80 percent when four people came to watch them. Poor shooters, who made 36 percent of their shots when alone, made only 25 percent when watched. The energizing effect of an enthusiastic audience likely contributes to the home advantage enjoyed by various sports teams. Studies of more than 80,000 college and professional athletic events in Canada, the United States, and England reveal that home teams win about 6 in 10 games (somewhat fewer for baseball and football, somewhat more for basketball and soccer).

The moral: What you do well, you are likely to do even better in front of an audience, especially a friendly audience; what you normally find difficult may seem impossible when others are watching.

Social facilitation also helps explain a funny effect of crowding: Comedy records that are mildly amusing to people in an uncrowded room seem funnier to people in a densely packed room (Aiello & others, 1983; Freedman & Perlick, 1979). As comedians and actors know, a "good house" is a full one. The arousal triggered by crowding amplifies other reactions, too. If sitting close, experimental subjects like a friendly person more, an unfriendly person less (Schiffenbauer & Schiavo, 1976; Storms & Thomas, 1977).

Social Loafing The social facilitation experiments test the effect of others' presence on *individual* effort in tasks ranging from winding fishing reels to

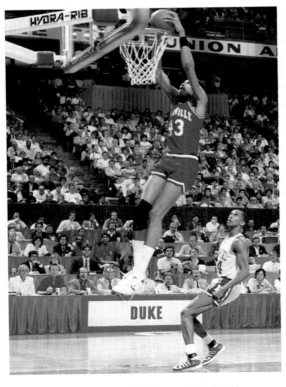

Social Facilitation *Skilled athletes often find they are "on" before an audience. What they do well, they do even better when people are watching.*

social facilitation Improved performance of tasks in the presence of others; occurs with simple or well-learned tasks but not with tasks that are difficult or not yet mastered.

social loafing The tendency for people in a group to exert less effort when pooling their efforts toward attaining a common goal than when individually accountable.

deindividuation The loss of self-awareness and self-restraint occurring in group situations that foster arousal and anonymity.

shooting pool. But what happens in situations that require a *team* effort to achieve a common goal? In a team tug-of-war, for example, do you suppose the effort people individually put forth would be more than, less than, or the same as the effort they would exert in a one-on-one tug-of-war?

To find out, Alan Ingham and his fellow researchers (1974) asked blindfolded University of Massachusetts students to "pull as hard as you can" on a rope. When Ingham fooled the students into believing three others were also pulling behind them, they exerted only 82 percent as much effort as when they knew they were pulling alone.

To describe the diminished effort by those submerged in a group, Bibb Latané and his colleagues (1981; Jackson & Williams, 1988) coined the term social loafing. In 78 experiments conducted in the United States, India, Thailand, Japan, China, and Taiwan, **social loafing** occurred on various tasks, though especially among men in individualistic cultures (Karau & Williams, 1993). For example, blindfolded subjects seated in a group clapped or shouted as loud as they could while listening through headphones to the sound of loud clapping or shouting. When told they were doing it with the others, the subjects produced about one-third less noise than when they thought their individual efforts were identifiable.

Why? First, people acting as part of a group feel less accountable and therefore worry less about what others think. Second, they may view their contribution as dispensable (Harkins & Szymanski, 1989; Kerr & Bruun, 1983). As many leaders of organizations know, if group members share equally in the group's benefits regardless of how much they contribute, they may slack off and "free-ride" on the other group members' efforts.

Deindividuation   So, the presence of others can arouse people (as in the social facilitation experiments) or can diminish their feelings of responsibility (as in the social loafing experiments). Sometimes the presence of others both arouses people *and* diminishes their sense of responsibility. The result can be uninhibited behavior ranging from a food fight in the dining hall or screaming at a basketball referee to vandalism or rioting. Abandoning normal restraints to the power of the group is termed **deindividuation**. To be deindividuated is to be less self-conscious and less restrained when in a group situation.

Deindividuation often occurs when group participation makes people feel aroused and anonymous. In one experiment, New York University women dressed in depersonalizing Ku Klux Klan-style hoods delivered twice as much electric shock to a victim as did identifiable women (Zimbardo, 1970). (As in all such experiments, the "victim" did not actually receive the shocks.) Similarly, tribal warriors who depersonalize themselves with face paints or masks are more likely than those with exposed faces to kill, torture, or mutilate captured enemies (Watson, 1973). Whether in a mob, at a rock concert, at a dance, or at worship, to lose self-consciousness (to become deindividuated) is to become more responsive to the group experience.

Effects of Group Interaction

6. What are group polarization and groupthink?

We have examined the conditions under which the presence of others can make easy tasks easier and difficult tasks harder; tempt people to free-ride on the efforts of others and motivate them to cycle faster; enhance humor and fuel mob violence. Research shows how group interaction, too, can have both bad and good effects.

Figure 14–4 Group Polarization *If a group is like-minded, discussion strengthens its prevailing opinions. Talking over racial issues increased prejudice in a high-prejudice group of high school students and decreased it in a low-prejudice group. (Data from Myers & Bishop, 1970.)*

Group Polarization   Educational researchers have noted that, over time, initial differences between groups of college students often grow. If the first-year students at College *X* tend to be more intellectually oriented than those at College *Y*, chances are their difference will be amplified by the time they are seniors. Similarly, if the political conservatism of students who join fraternities and sororities is greater than that of students who do not, the gap in the political attitudes of the two groups will probably widen as they progress through college (Wilson & others, 1975).

This enhancement of a group's prevailing tendencies—called **group polarization**—occurs when people within a group discuss attitudes that most of them favor or oppose. For example, one study discovered that when highly prejudiced high school students discussed racial issues, their attitudes became more prejudiced. When low-prejudice students discussed the same issues, they became more tolerant (Figure 14–4).

Group polarization can have beneficial results, as when it amplifies a sought-after spiritual awareness or strengthens the resolve of those in a self-help group. But it can also have dire consequences. From their analysis of terrorist organizations around the world, psychologists Clark McCauley and Mary Segal (1987) note that the terrorist mentality does not erupt suddenly. Rather, it arises among people who have come together because of a grievance and who become more and more extreme as they interact in isolation from moderating influences.

Groupthink   Does group interaction ever distort important group decisions? Social psychologist Irving Janis thought so when he first read historian Arthur M. Schlesinger, Jr.'s, account of how President John F. Kennedy and his advisers blundered into an ill-fated plan to invade Cuba with 1400 CIA-trained Cuban exiles. When the invaders were easily captured and soon linked to the U.S. government, Kennedy wondered aloud, "How could we have been so stupid?"

To find out, Janis (1982) studied the decision-making procedures that led to the fiasco. He discovered that the high morale of the recently elected President and his advisers fostered a sense that the plan would succeed. To preserve the good group feeling, dissenting views were suppressed or self-censored, especially after the President voiced his enthusiasm for the scheme. Since no one spoke sharply against the idea, everyone assumed there was consensus support for it. To describe this harmonious but unrealistic group thinking, Janis coined the term **groupthink**.

Janis and others then examined other historical fiascos—the failure to anticipate the Pearl Harbor attack, the escalation of the Vietnam War, the Watergate cover-up, the Chernobyl reactor accident (Reason, 1987), and the space shuttle *Challenger* explosion (Esser & Lindoerfer, 1989). They discovered that in these cases, too, groupthink was fed by overconfidence, conformity, self-justification, and group polarization. Buoyed by a string of successful space shuttle launches, the NASA management team approached the 1986 *Challenger* mission brimming with confidence but frustrated by launch delays. When the rocket booster's engineers opposed the launch because of dangers posed by freezing temperatures, group pressures to go ahead effectively silenced their warnings. Unless the engineers could *prove* that the rocket seals would not hold, the management group would not agree to another delay. Moreover, managers shielded the NASA executive who made the final "go" decision from information about the warnings. Wrongly assuming that support was unanimous, he launched the *Challenger* on its one-way flight to annihilation.

"*One's impulse to blow the whistle on this nonsense was simply undone by the circumstances of the discussion.*"

Arthur M. Schlesinger, Jr. (1965, p. 255)

group polarization The enhancement of a group's prevailing attitudes through discussion within the group.

groupthink The mode of thinking that occurs when the desire for harmony in a decision-making group overrides a realistic appraisal of alternatives.

Despite such fiascos and tragedies, Janis also knew that, with some types of problems, two heads are better than one. So he also studied instances in which U.S. presidents and their advisers collectively made good decisions. Examples were the Truman administration's formulation of the Marshall Plan for getting Europe back on its feet after World War II and the Kennedy administration's actions to keep the Soviets from installing missiles in Cuba. In such instances—and in the business world, too, Janis believed—groupthink is prevented by a leader who welcomes various opinions, invites experts' critiques of developing plans, or even assigns people to identify possible problems. As the suppression of dissent bends a group toward bad decisions, so open debate often shapes good decisions.

In affirming the power of social influence, we must not overlook our power as individuals. *Social control* (the power of the situation) and *personal control* (the power of the individual) interact. People aren't billiard balls. When feeling pressured, we may react by doing the opposite, thereby reasserting our sense of freedom (Brehm & Brehm, 1981). Moreover, many of the situations that influence us are ones we helped create. If we expect people to be uncooperative and hostile, we may treat them in ways that elicit such behavior. Thus, our expectations may be self-fulfilling. In one experiment, men talked more charmingly by phone to women they believed to be beautiful. This led the women to respond more warmly—confirming the men's idea that attractive people are likeable (Snyder & others, 1977).

Minority Influence

7. Can a minority sway a majority?

The power of committed individuals also appears in their influence over their groups. Social history is often made by a minority that sways the majority. Were this not so, communism would be an obscure theory, Christianity would be a small Middle Eastern sect, and Rosa Parks's refusal to sit at the back of the bus would not have ignited the civil rights movement. Technological history, too, is often made by innovative minorities who overcome the majority's resistance to change. To many folks, the railroad was a nonsensical idea; some farmers feared that train noise would prevent hens from laying eggs. People derided Robert Fulton's steamboat as "Fulton's Folly." As Fulton later said, "Never did a single encouraging remark, a bright hope, a warm wish, cross my path." Much the same reaction greeted the printing press, the telegraph, the incandescent lamp, and the typewriter (Cantril & Bumstead, 1960).

To better understand how minorities can sway majorities, European social psychologists led by Serge Moscovici (1985) have investigated groups in which one or two individuals consistently express a controversial attitude or an unusual perceptual judgment. They have repeatedly found that a minority that unswervingly holds to its position is far more successful in swaying the majority than is a minority that waffles. Holding consistently to a minority opinion will not make you popular, but it may make you influential. This is especially so if your self-confidence stimulates others to consider why you react as you do. Although people often follow the majority view publicly, they may privately develop sympathy for the minority view. Even when a minority's influence is not yet visible, it may be persuading some members of the majority to rethink their views (Wood & others, 1994). Thus, the combined powers of social thinking and social influence are enormous; but so are the powers of the committed individual.

> *"Truth springs from argument among friends."*
> Philosopher David Hume, 1711–1776

Gandhi *As the life of Mahatma Gandhi powerfully testifies, a consistent and persistent minority voice can sometimes sway the majority. The nonviolent appeals and fasts of the Hindu nationalist and spiritual leader were instrumental in winning India's independence from Britain in 1947.*

culture The enduring behaviors, ideas, attitudes, and traditions shared by a large group of people and transmitted from one generation to the next.

personal space The buffer zone we like to maintain around our bodies.

gender role A set of expected behaviors for males and for females.

Cultural Influences

8. How do cultural norms and roles affect our behavior?

The effects of our **culture** also exert a powerful, long-lasting influence on our behavior. We learn these behaviors, ideas, attitudes, and traditions from the group with which we identify most. Riding along with a unified culture is like riding a bike with the wind: As the wind carries us along, we hardly notice it's there. When we try riding *against* it we feel its force, as when moving to or visiting another part of the world. Face-to-face with a different culture, people become aware of the cultural winds. Visiting Europe, most North Americans are struck by the smallness of the cars, the left-handed use of the fork, the uninhibited attire on the beaches. Stationed in Saudi Arabia, European and American soldiers alike realized the liberality of their home cultures. Visiting North America, visitors from some cultures struggle to understand why people wear their dirty *street* shoes in the house, or why people find it fun to eat a picnic lunch out in the bush amid flies and ants.

Cultural Norms

All cultural groups evolve norms—their rules for accepted and expected behavior. Muslims use only the right hand's fingers for eating. The Japanese have norms for taking shoes off, for giving and opening gifts, and for showing respect to one's social superiors. Sometimes social expectations seem oppressive. "Why should it matter how I dress?" However, norms also grease the social machinery. Prescribed, well-learned behaviors free us from self-preoccupation. When we know when to clap or bow, which fork to pick up first at the dinner party, and what sorts of gestures and compliments are appropriate, we can relax and enjoy one another without fear of embarrassment or insult. Likewise, having a well-understood norm for greeting people in one's culture—by shaking hands or kissing each cheek—precludes awkward moments deciding whether to lead with one's hand or cheek.

When cultures collide, their differing norms often bemuse or befuddle. If someone invades our **personal space**—the portable buffer zone we like to maintain around our bodies—we feel uncomfortable. Scandinavians, most Americans, and the British prefer more personal space than do Latin Americans, Arabs, and the French (Sommer, 1969). At a social gathering, a Mexican seeking a comfortable conversation distance may waltz around a room with a backpedaling American. (You can demonstrate this at a party by playing space invader as you talk with someone.) To the American, the Mexican may seem intrusive; to the Mexican, the American may seem cold and standoffish.

Cultures also vary in their expressiveness. People whose roots are in northern European culture often perceive people from Mediterranean cultures as warm and charming, but inefficient. The Mediterraneans, in turn, see the northern Europeans as efficient, but cold and preoccupied with punctuality (Triandis, 1981).

Cultures vary in their pace of life, too. The British businessperson may feel frustrated by a Latin American client who arrives 30 minutes late for lunch. People from time-conscious Japan—where bank clocks keep exact time, pedestrians walk briskly, and postal clerks fill requests speedily—may find themselves growing impatient when visiting Indonesia, where clocks keep less exact time and the pace of life is slower (Levine, 1990). In adjusting to their host countries, U.S. Peace Corps volunteers reported that two of their greatest cul-

An Exercise in Culture *People in individualist Western cultures sometimes see the Japanese as straitjacketed by their culture's norms. But from the Japanese perspective the same tradition expresses a "serenity that comes to people who know exactly what to expect from each other" (Weisz & others, 1984).*

Culture Influences Personal Space *Behavior that is seen as appropriate in one culture may violate the norms of another group. In Arab countries, such as Morocco, people typically require less personal space than do members of some European and North American groups.*

ture shocks, after the language difference, were the slower pace of life and the differing punctuality of the people (Spradley & Phillips, 1972).

Gender Roles

A whole set of norms defines our culture's expectations for its **gender roles**—its expectations about the way men and women behave. Traditionally, men initiate dates, drive the car, and pick up the check; women cook the meals, buy the children's clothes, and do the laundry. Such formulas smooth social relations, saving awkward decisions about who does what. But they do so at a cost. When deviating from social convention, as when a woman negotiates a car repair, we may feel anxious (Green & Sandos, 1983).

Gender roles vary across cultures and over time. Different societies socialize children for varying gender roles. In nomadic societies of food-gathering people, there is little division of labor by sex. Thus, boys and girls receive much the same upbringing. In agricultural societies, women stay close to home, working in the fields and with the children; men roam more freely. Such societies typically socialize children into distinct gender roles (Segall & others, 1990; Van Leeuwen, 1978).

Even among the industrialized countries, gender roles vary. Women fill 48 percent of managerial positions in Switzerland, 28 percent in Austria, 17 percent in the United States, 3 percent in Ghana, and 2 percent in South Korea (Triandis, 1994). In North America, medicine and dentistry are predominantly male occupations; in Russia, most medical doctors are women, as are most dentists in Denmark.

Gender roles vary over time as well as across cultures. In 1938, only 1 in 5 Americans approved of "a married woman earning money in business or industry if she has a husband capable of supporting her"; by 1988, 4 in 5 approved (Niemi & others, 1989). In the flick of an apron, the number of American college women hoping to be full-time homemakers plunged during the late 1960s and early 1970s (Figure 14-5). Cultural influences are huge, but cultures can change.

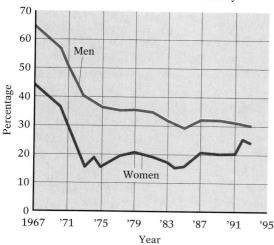

Figure 14–5 Changing Attitudes About Gender Roles *American college students' endorsement of the traditional view of women's role has declined dramatically. Men's and women's attitudes have also converged. (From Astin & others, 1993; Dey & others, 1991.)*

! *Rehearse It*

5. Conformity involves adjusting our thinking and behavior toward others in the group. Conformity studies have found that a person is most likely to conform to a group if

a. the group members have diverse opinions.
b. the person feels competent and secure.
c. the group consists of at least three people.
d. other group members will not observe the person's behavior.

6. In a classic experiment on obedience, Stanley Milgram tested his subjects' willingness to comply with a command to deliver painful high-voltage shocks to another person. Although no shocks were given, the subjects believed they were—and more than 60 percent complied with the experimenter's instruction to deliver stronger and stronger shocks. In subsequent experiments, Milgram's obedience studies showed that the rate of compliance was highest when

a. the victim was at a distance.
b. the experimenter was in another room.
c. other subjects refused to go along with the experimenter.
d. the subjects believed the victim had a heart condition.

7. In the presence of others we become aroused: Before an audience, a swimmer swims faster. Social facilitation—improved performance in the presence of others—occurs with

a. any physical task.
b. new learning.
c. a well-learned task.
d. competitive sports or activities only.

8. When people are part of a group working toward a common goal, their individual efforts are diminished. Latané and his colleagues called this

a. deindividuation.
b. social facilitation.
c. social loafing.
d. group polarization.

9. In a group situation that fosters arousal and anonymity, a person sometimes loses self-consciousness and self-control. This phenomenon, called deindividuation, is best illustrated by

a. improved performance in front of an audience.
b. unrestrained behavior at a mass rally.
c. evasion of responsibility in a group clean-up effort.
d. denial of one's own perceptions in the face of an opposing consensus.

10. If a group is like-minded, discussion strengthens its prevailing opinion. This effect is called

a. groupthink.
b. minority influence.

c. group polarization.
d. social facilitation.

11. Group interaction has the potential of distorting important group decisions. For example, when a group's desire for harmony overrides its realistic appraisal of alternatives, _____ has occurred.

a. group polarization
b. groupthink
c. social facilitation
d. deindividuation

12. In psychology, personal space refers to the portable buffer zone we like to maintain around our bodies. This space varies according to cultural norms. Which of the following prefer *less* personal space than the others?

a. Americans
b. British
c. Arabs
d. Scandinavians

13. Gender roles vary across cultures and over time. "Gender role" refers to our

a. sense of being male or female.
b. expectations about the way men and women behave.
c. biological sex.
d. beliefs about how men and women should earn a living.

Social Relations

Having sampled how we *think* about and *influence* one another, we come finally to social psychology's third focus—how we *relate* to one another. We will ponder the bad and the good: prejudice, aggression, and conflict; and attraction, altruism, and peacemaking.

Prejudice

prejudice An unjustifiable (and usually negative) attitude toward a group and its members. Prejudice generally involves stereotyped beliefs, negative feelings, and a predisposition to discriminatory action.

stereotype A generalized (often overgeneralized) belief about a group of people.

Prejudice means prejudgment. It is an unjustifiable and usually negative attitude toward a group—typically a different cultural, ethnic, or gender group. Like all attitudes, **prejudice** is a mixture of beliefs (often overgeneralized and

Does Perception Change With Race? *The Italian clothing manufacturer Benetton asked this question with altered photographs in their company magazine.*

Courtesy of COLORS Magazine.

called **stereotypes**), emotions (hostility, envy, or fear), and predispositions to action (to discriminate). To *believe* that overweight people are gluttonous, to *feel* antipathy for an overweight person, and to be hesitant to hire or date an overweight person is to be prejudiced.

Like other forms of prejudgment, prejudices are schemas that influence how we notice and interpret events. In one study, most whites perceived a white man shoving a black man as "horsing around." The same shove by the black man to the white was more often seen as "violent" (Duncan, 1976). Our preconceived ideas about people bias our impressions of their behavior. Prejudgments color perceptions.

How prejudiced are people? To find out, we can assess what they say and what they do. To judge by what Americans say, racial and gender attitudes have changed dramatically in the last half-century (Figure 14–6). Nearly everyone agrees that children of all races should attend the same schools and that women and men should receive the same pay for the same job.

Despite these more accepting attitudes, prejudice persists. In socially intimate settings (dating, dancing, marrying), many people admit they would feel uncomfortable with someone of another race. This fact helps explain why, in a survey of students at 390 colleges and universities, 53 percent of African-

Gallup Poll (1993): "In your view, does the increasing diversity that immigrants bring to this country mostly *improve* American culture or mostly *threaten* American culture?"

Mostly improve   35%
Mostly threaten   55%
Other response   10%

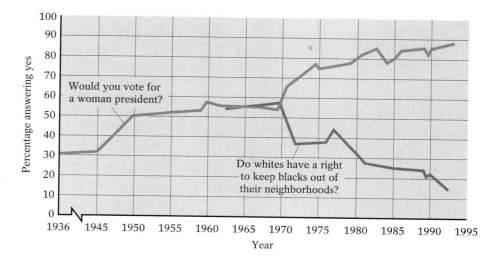

Figure 14–6 Prejudice Over Time *Americans today express much less racial and gender prejudice than they did two and three decades ago. (Niemi & others, 1989; T. Smith, 1994.)*

American students felt excluded from school activities (Hurtado & others, 1994). (Similar feelings were reported by 24 percent of Asian-Americans, 16 percent of Mexican-Americans, and 6 percent of European-Americans.) On N.B.A. basketball teams, where 81 percent of the 1995 players and all the top twenty scorers were African-American, a similar majority/minority dynamic can lead some white minority players to feel lonely or disrespected (Schoenfeld, 1995).

Since the late 1980s, prejudice has occasionally resurfaced in public settings as well. European and North American cities and campuses have experienced significant increases in "hate crimes" (slurs, vandalism, and physical violence) against immigrants, African-Americans, and homosexuals (Herek, 1989, 1990; Levine, 1990). Elsewhere, hate has raged openly—between Israel's Palestinians and Jews, Bosnia's Serbs and Muslims, Rwanda's Tutsis and Hutus.

Around the world, gender prejudice and discrimination persist, too. Worldwide, two-thirds of children without basic schooling are girls. Thus, there are some 350 million illiterate men and 600 million illiterate women (United Nations, 1991, 1993). In the Sudan, a woman may not leave the country without the permission of her husband, father, or brother (Beyer, 1990). In Saudi Arabia, women are not allowed to drive. In Western countries, we pay more to those (usually men) who take care of our garbage than to those (usually women) who take care of our children.

Nowhere are female infants left out on a hillside to die of exposure, as was the practice in ancient Greece. Yet even today boys are often valued more than their sisters. During the 1970s Bangladesh famine, preschool girls were more malnourished than boys, and in many developing countries death rates are higher for girls than boys (Bairagi, 1987). In South Korea, where testing often reveals the sex of an abortable fetus, male births exceed female births by 14 percent. In China, male births during 1992 exceeded female births by 18 percent. In five of China's provinces there are now 120 boys for every 100 girls (Kristof, 1993). Sex-selective neglect and abortions have resulted in China and India together having 76 million fewer females than they should have (Klasen, 1994). (You read that right: 76 million "missing women.")

Why does prejudice arise? Inequalities, social divisions, and emotional scapegoating are partly responsible. But so are the natural cognitive mechanisms by which we simplify our worlds.

Social Inequalities

9. What are the social and emotional roots of prejudice?

When some people have money, power, and prestige and others do not, the "haves" usually develop attitudes that justify things as they are. In the extreme case, slave owners perceived slaves as lazy, ignorant, and irresponsible—as having the very traits that "justified" enslaving them. More commonly, women are perceived as unassertive but sensitive and therefore suited for the caretaking tasks they often perform (Hoffman & Hurst, 1990). In short, prejudice rationalizes inequalities.

Discrimination also increases prejudice through the reactions it provokes in its victims, a phenomenon called the *self-fulfilling prophecy*. In his classic 1954 book, *The Nature of Prejudice*, Gordon Allport noted that being a victim of discrimination can produce either self-blame or anger. Both reactions may create new grounds for prejudice through the classic *blame-the-victim* dynamic. If the circumstances of ghetto life breed a higher crime rate, someone can then use the higher crime rate to justify continuing the discrimination that helped to create the ghetto.

"You cannot oppress people for over three centuries and then say it is all over and expect them to put on suits and ties and become decent attaché-carrying citizens and go to work on Wall Street."

Shelby Steele
"The New Segregation," 1992

ingroup bias The tendency to favor one's own group.

scapegoat theory The theory that prejudice provides an outlet for anger by providing someone to blame.

"All good people agree,
And all good people say
All nice people, like us, are We
And everyone else is They.
But if you cross over the sea
Instead of over the way
You may end by (think of it)
* looking on We*
As only a sort of They."

Rudyard Kipling
"We and They," 1926

"If the Tiber reaches the walls, if the Nile does not rise to the fields, if the sky doesn't move or the earth does, if there is famine, if there is plague, the cry is at once: `The Christians to the lion!'"

Tertullian
Apologeticus, A.D. 197

Us and Them: Ingroup and Outgroup

The social definition of who you are—your ethnicity, gender, religion, academic major—also implies who you are not. Mentally drawing a circle that defines "us" excludes "them." Such group identifications typically promote an **ingroup bias**—a favoring of one's own group. Even an arbitrary us-them distinction—created by grouping people with the toss of a coin—leads people to show favoritism to their own group when dividing rewards (Tajfel, 1982; Wilder, 1981).

The urge to distinguish enemies from friends predisposes prejudice against strangers. To Greeks of the classical era, all non-Greeks were "barbarians." Most citizens in the coalition of countries fighting in the 1991 Persian Gulf War felt more pain over the few hundred dead Allied soldiers than over the reported 100,000 Iraqi dead. In Africa, where some 700 traditional societies cluster into fewer than 50 nations, people typically like and admire their own group and direct their hostility toward other groups (Segall & others, 1990). Most children believe their school is better than the other schools in town. Even chimpanzees have been seen to wipe clean the spot where they were touched by a chimp from another group (Goodall, 1986).

Scapegoating

Prejudice springs not only from the divisions of society but also from the passions of the heart. Prejudice may express anger: When things go wrong, finding someone to blame can provide an outlet. Evidence for this **scapegoat theory** of prejudice comes from high prejudice levels among economically frustrated people and from experiments in which a temporary frustration intensifies prejudice. Nazi leader Hermann Rausching once explained the Nazis' need to scapegoat: "If the Jew did not exist, we should have to invent him" (quoted by Koltz, 1983). Passions produce prejudice.

In addition to providing a handy emotional outlet for anger, despised outgroups can also boost ingroup members' self-esteem. In experiments, students who experience failure or are made to feel insecure will often restore their self-esteem by disparaging a rival school or another person (Cialdini & Richardson, 1980; Crocker & others, 1987). To boost our own sense of status, it helps to have others to denigrate. For this reason, a rival's misfortune sometimes provides a twinge of pleasure.

Cognitive Roots of Prejudice

10. What are the cognitive roots of prejudice?

Prejudice springs from the divisions of society, the passions of the heart, and also from the mind's natural workings. Stereotyped beliefs are a by-product of how we cognitively simplify the world.

Categorization   One way we simplify our world is to categorize things. A chemist classifies molecules as organic and inorganic. A mental health professional classifies people's psychological disorders by types. In categorizing people into groups we often stereotype them. Although we view ourselves as individuals, we overestimate the similarity of people within groups other than our own. "They"—the members of some other group—seem to look and act alike, but "we" are diverse (Bothwell & others, 1989). To us on the outside, the members of fraternity X are jocks and those in fraternity Y are intellectuals. Members of each fraternity see their own diversity. To those in one ethnic group, members of another often seem more alike in appearance, personality, and attitudes than they are.

Vivid Cases   As noted in Chapter 8's discussion of the availability heuristic, we often judge the frequency of events by instances that readily come to mind. If asked whether blacks run faster than whites, many people may think of Leroy Burrell and Florence Griffith Joyner. From such vivid but exceptional cases they overgeneralize that "yes, blacks run faster."

In an experiment with University of Oregon students, Myron Rothbart and his colleagues (1978) showed how we overgeneralize from vivid, memorable cases. They divided the students into two groups and showed them information about 50 men. The first group's list included 10 men arrested for nonviolent crimes, such as forgery. The second group's list included 10 men arrested for violent crimes, such as assault. When both groups later recalled how many men on their list had committed any sort of crime, the second group overestimated how many there were. Vivid (violent) cases, being readily available to memory, influence our judgments of a group.

The Just-World Phenomenon   We noted earlier that people often justify their prejudice by blaming its victims. Bystanders may also blame victims, by assuming the world is just and that people get what they deserve. In experiments, merely observing someone receive painful shocks has led many people to think less of the victim (Lerner, 1980). This **just-world phenomenon** reflects an idea we commonly teach our children—that good is rewarded and evil is punished. From this it is a short leap to assume that those who succeed must be good and those who suffer must be bad. Such reasoning enables the rich to see their own wealth, and the poor's misfortune, as justly deserved. As one German civilian is said to have remarked when visiting the Bergen-Belsen concentration camp shortly after World War II, "What terrible criminals these prisoners must have been to receive such treatment."

Hindsight bias is also at work here (Carli & Leonard, 1989). Have you ever heard people say that rape victims, abused spouses, or people with AIDS got what they deserved? An experiment by Ronnie Janoff-Bulman and her collaborators (1985) illustrates victim-blaming. When given an account of a date that ended with the woman's being raped, people perceived the woman as partly to blame. In hindsight, they thought, "She should have known better." (Victim-blaming also reassures people that it couldn't happen to them.) Others who were given the same account, without the rape, did not perceive the woman as inviting rape. Only when victimized was she faulted for her behavior.

Do People of Another Race Look Alike?   *Balinese masseuses wear identifying numbers on their hats, enabling foreign sunbathers to recognize them easily.*

Drawing by Mankoff; © 1981 *The New Yorker* Magazine, Inc.

Aggression

The most destructive force in our social relations is aggression. In psychology, *aggression* has a more precise meaning than it does in everyday usage. The assertive, persistent salesperson is not aggressive. Nor is the dentist who makes you wince with pain. But the person who passes along a vicious rumor about you and the attacker who mugs you are aggressive. **Aggression** is any physical or verbal behavior intended to hurt or destroy, whether done out of hostility or as a calculated means to an end. Some of the 24,526 murders and 1,135,099 assaults recorded in the United States during 1993 were cool, calculated, aggressive acts, but more were hostile outbursts.

A rising tide of violence, especially violence by youth, plagues many countries. Most readers living outside the United States can, however, take comfort that their risk of being murdered is *much* lower than for Americans—for example, one-fourth as much for Canadians and Australians, one-fifth as much for New Zealanders, and, on average, one-sixth as much for Europeans (United Nations, 1992).

Why are some countries, and some individuals, so violence-prone? And why have violence rates increased in so many countries?

Time and again, we have seen that behavior emerges from the interaction of biology and experience. Research on aggression reinforces that theme. For a gun to fire, the trigger must be pulled; with some people, as with hair-trigger guns, it doesn't take much to trip an explosion. Let us look first at biological factors that influence our thresholds for aggressive behavior. Then we will examine the psychological factors that pull the trigger.

The Biology of Aggression

> *11. What biological factors influence aggressive behavior?*

According to one view, argued by Sigmund Freud and others, our species has a volcanic potential to erupt in aggression. Freud thought that, along with positive survival instincts, we harbor a self-destructive "death instinct" that we usually displace toward others as aggression or release in socially approved activities such as painting or sports.

Although aggression varies too widely from culture to culture and person to person to be considered an unlearned instinct, biology does influence aggression. Stimuli that influence aggressive behavior operate through our biological system. We can look for biological influences at three levels—genetic, neural, and biochemical. Our genes engineer our individual nervous systems, which operate electrochemically.

Genetic Influences Animals have been bred for aggressiveness—sometimes for sport, sometimes for research. Twin studies suggest that genes influence human aggression as well (Rushton & others, 1986). If one identical twin admits to "having a violent temper," the other twin will often independently admit the same. Fraternal twins are much more likely to have different responses.

Neural Influences Animal and human brains have neural systems that produce aggressive behavior when stimulated (Moyer, 1983). Consider:

⟩ The domineering leader of a caged monkey colony has a radio-controlled electrode implanted in a brain area that, when stimulated, inhibits aggression. When researchers place the button that activates the electrode in the colony's cage, one small monkey learns to push it every time the boss becomes threatening.

In the last 25 years in the United States, guns have caused 800,000 suicidal, homicidal, and accidental deaths. Compared with people of the same sex, race, age, and neighborhood, those who keep a gun in the home (often for protection) are 2.7 times more likely to be murdered—nearly always by a family member or close acquaintance (Kellermann & others, 1993).

just-world phenomenon The tendency of people to believe the world is just and that people therefore get what they deserve and deserve what they get.

aggression Any physical or verbal behavior intended to hurt or destroy.

> A mild-mannered woman has an electrode implanted in her brain's limbic system (in the amygdala) by neurosurgeons seeking to diagnose a disorder. Because the brain has no sensory receptors, she cannot feel stimulation. But at the flick of a switch she snarls, "Take my blood pressure. Take it now," and then stands up and begins to strike the doctor.

> Intensive evaluation of 15 death-row inmates reveals that all 15 have suffered severe head injury. Researcher Dorothy Lewis and her colleagues (1986) infer that many condemned criminals suffer unrecognized neurological disorders.

So, does the brain have a "violence center" that produces aggression when stimulated? Actually, no one spot in the brain controls aggression, because aggression is a complex behavior that occurs in particular contexts. Rather, the brain has neural systems that facilitate aggression, making it more likely, given provocation and no deterrents.

Biochemical Influences   Hormones, alcohol, and other substances in the blood influence the neural systems that control aggression. A raging bull will become a gentle Ferdinand when castration reduces its testosterone level. The same is true of castrated mice. When injected with testosterone, the castrated mice again become aggressive. However, the traffic between hormones and behavior is two-way. Testosterone heightens dominance and aggressiveness, but dominating or defeating behavior also boosts testosterone levels (Gladue & others, 1989).

Although humans are less sensitive to hormonal changes, violent criminals tend to be muscular young males with lower than average intelligence scores and higher than average testosterone levels (Dabbs, 1992; Wilson & Herrnstein, 1985). Drugs that sharply reduce their testosterone levels subdue their aggressive tendencies. Among the normal range of teenage boys and adult men, high testosterone levels correlate with delinquency, hard drug use, and aggressive, bullying responses to provocation (Berman & others, 1993; Dabbs & Morris, 1990; Olweus & others, 1988).

For both biological and psychological reasons, alcohol unleashes aggressive responses to provocation (Bushman, 1993; Taylor & Chermack, 1993). (Just *thinking* you've imbibed alcohol has some effect; but so, too, does unknowingly

> "He that is naturally addicted to Anger, let him Abstain from Wine; for it is but adding Fire to Fire."
>
> Seneca
> *De Ira*, A.D. 49

Deindividuation + Competition + Alcohol = Aggression
A 1985 riot at a soccer game in Brussels left 38 dead and 437 injured. Aroused by the competition and loaded with alcohol, English fans lost all restraint when provoked by Italian fans. They attacked the Italians, who retreated and were then crushed against a wall.

frustration-aggression principle The principle that frustration—the blocking of an attempt to achieve some goal—creates anger, which can generate aggression.

So Near, But . . . *Being blocked from achieving a goal can trigger aggression—against other humans and their surrogates. This is especially likely when the frustration can be blamed on the "other."*

ingesting alcohol slipped into a drink.) Police data and prison surveys reinforce conclusions from experiments on alcohol and aggression. Aggression-prone people are more likely to drink and to become violent when intoxicated (White & others, 1993). People who have been drinking commit about 50 percent of rapes and other violent crimes (Abbey & others, 1993; Reiss & Roth, 1993).

The Psychology of Aggression

12. What psychological factors influence aggressive behavior?

Biological factors influence the ease with which the aggression trigger pulls. But what psychological factors do the pulling?

Aversive Events Although suffering sometimes builds character, it may also bring out the worst in us. Studies in which animals or humans experience unpleasant events reveal that those made miserable often make others miserable (Berkowitz, 1983, 1989).

Being blocked short of a goal also increases people's readiness to aggress. This phenomenon we know as the **frustration-aggression principle**: Frustration creates anger, which may in some people generate aggression, especially in the presence of an aggressive cue, such as a gun. Frustrations are instances of aversive events. Like frustration, physical pain, personal insults, foul odors, hot temperatures, cigarette smoke, and a host of other aversive stimuli can also evoke hostility (Figure 14–7).

Learning to Express and Inhibit Aggression Aggression may be a natural response to aversive events, but learning can alter natural reactions. Animals naturally eat when they are hungry. But if appropriately rewarded or punished, they can be taught either to overeat or to starve.

Aggressive reactions are more likely in situations where experience has taught us that aggression pays. Children whose aggression successfully intimidates other children may become more aggressive. Violent demonstrations that provide demonstrators with desired attention may recur.

Aggressive behavior can be learned through direct rewards. Animals that have fought successfully to get food or mates become increasingly ferocious. It can also be learned through observation. Children who grow up observing ag-

Figure 14–7 Uncomfortably Hot Weather and Aggressive Reactions *Violent crime and spouse abuse occur more in summer than winter, in hot years than in cooler years, in hot cities than in cooler cities, and on hotter days than on colder days (Anderson, 1989). For example, between 1980 and 1982 in Houston, murders and rapes were more common on days over 91°F, as shown in the graph. This finding is consistent with those from laboratory experiments in which people working in a hot room react to provocations with greater hostility. (From Anderson & Anderson, 1984.)*

gressive models often imitate the behaviors they see. Parents of delinquent youngsters typically discipline with beatings, thus modeling aggression as a method of dealing with problems (Patterson & others, 1982).

Different cultures model, reinforce, and evoke differing tendencies toward violence. For example, crime rates are higher in countries marked by a great disparity between rich and poor (Triandis, 1994). Richard Nisbett (1993) showed how cultures can also differ within a country. He analyzed violence among whites in southern American towns settled by Scottish-Irish herders whose tradition emphasized "manly honor" and the use of arms to protect one's flock. To this day, their cultural descendants have triple the homicide rates of whites in New England towns settled by Puritan, Quaker, and Dutch farmer-artisans. They also are more supportive of physically punishing children, of warfare initiatives, and of uncontrolled gun ownership.

Social influence also appears in high violence rates among cultures and families that experience minimal father care (Triandis, 1994). For example, the U.S. Bureau of Justice Statistics reports that 70 percent of imprisoned juveniles did not grow up with two parents (Beck & others, 1988). (Because an absent parent is usually a father, most grew up with minimal father care.) The correlation between father absence and violence holds for all races, income levels, and locations (Prothrow-Stith, 1991; Staub, 1993). The correlation also appears over time. In the United States in 1960, barely over 1 in 10 children did not live with two parents, and only 16,000 juveniles were arrested for violent crime. In 1992, nearly 3 in 10 children did not live with two parents, and a similar-sized juvenile population produced 96,000 arrests for violent crime.

That many individuals lead gentle, even heroic, lives amid social stresses reminds us that individuals differ. The person matters. That people differ over time and place reminds us that environments differ. Situations matter. Aggressive behavior, like all behavior, arises from the interaction of persons and situations.

Once established, however, aggressive behavior patterns are difficult to change. To foster a kinder, gentler world we had best model and reward sensitivity and cooperation from an early age, perhaps by training parents how to discipline without modeling violence. Often, modeling violence—screaming and hitting—is precisely what exasperated parents do. Parent-training programs usually advise a more positive approach. They encourage parents to reinforce desirable behaviors and to frame statements positively ("When you finish loading the dishwasher you can go play," rather than "If you don't load the dishwasher there'll be no playing.") One "aggression-replacement program" that brought down re-arrest rates of juvenile offenders and gang members taught the youth and their parents communication skills, trained them in how to control anger, and raised their level of moral reasoning (Goldstein & Glick, in press).

Television Watching and Aggression   Parents are hardly the only aggression models. During their first 18 years, most children spend more time watching television than they spend in school. In urban homes across the world, including those of South America and Asia, television is now commonplace. In Beijing, for example, the percentage of homes with television skyrocketed from 32 percent in 1980 to 95 percent by the end of the decade (Lull, 1988). With more than 1 billion TV sets now in homes around the world, CNN reaching 150 countries, and MTV videos seen from Alaska to Bangladesh, television is creating a global pop culture (Lippman, 1992). One can watch American programs in Perth or Prague and hear Madonna and Pearl Jam from New Delhi to Newfoundland. But television does not reflect the world we live in. On evening dramas broadcast in the United States during the 1980s and early

THE FAR SIDE

In the days before television

TV's greatest effect may stem from what it displaces. Children and adults who spend 4 hours a day watching television spend 4 fewer hours in active pursuits—talking, studying, playing, reading, or socializing with friends. What would you have done with your extra time if you had never watched television, and how might you therefore be different?

"Thirty seconds worth of glorification of a soap bar sells soap. Twenty-five minutes worth of glorification of violence sells violence."

U.S. Senator Paul Simon
Remarks to the Communitarian Network, 1993

1990s and often exported to the rest of the world, only one-third of the characters were women. Fewer than 3 percent were visibly old. One percent were Hispanic. Only 1 in 10 was married (Gerbner, 1993).

In 1993, U.S. network programs offered about 3 violent acts per hour during prime time, and 18 per hour during children's Saturday morning programs (Gerbner & others, 1994). During the last 20 years the average child has viewed some 8000 TV murders and 100,000 other acts of violence before finishing elementary school (Huston & others, 1992). If one includes cable programming and video rentals, the violence numbers escalate. (Popular rental films like *Die Hard*, with its 264 deaths, are much more violent than major network programs.) This is life as rendered by a rather peculiar storyteller, one who reflects the culture's mythology but not its reality. In U.S. action-oriented crime shows (the shows most often exported to the world market), TV cops fire their guns in almost every episode; in Chicago, the average police officer fires a gun once every 27 years (Radecki, 1989).

Does viewing televised aggression influence some people to commit aggression? Was the judge who in 1993 tried two British 10-year-olds for their murder of a 2-year-old right to suspect that one possible influence was their exposure to "violent video films"? To answer such questions, researchers have conducted correlational and experimental studies (Hearold, 1986; Wood & others, 1991).

Correlational studies link young children's viewing of violence and their combativeness as teenagers and young adults (Eron, 1987; Turner & others, 1986). In the United States and Canada, a doubling of homicide rates between 1957 and 1974 coincided with the introduction and spread of television. Moreover, census regions that acquired television late showed the homicide jump correspondingly later. Among white South Africans, who were first introduced to television in 1975, a similar near-doubling of the homicide rate did not begin until after 1975 (Centerwall, 1989). "There is absolutely no doubt," concluded the 1993 American Psychological Association Commission on Violence and Youth, "that higher levels of viewing violence on television are correlated with increased acceptance of aggressive attitudes and increased aggressive behavior."

But as we know from Chapter 1, correlation does not imply causation. So these correlational studies do not prove that viewing violence *causes* aggression (Freedman, 1988; McGuire, 1986). Maybe aggressive children prefer violent programs. Maybe children of neglectful or abusive parents are both more aggressive and more often left in front of the TV. Or maybe television simply reflects, rather than affects, violent trends.

To pin down causation, experimenters have randomly assigned some viewers to view violence and others to view entertaining nonviolence. Does viewing murder and mayhem make people react more cruelly when irritated? "The consensus among most of the research community," reported the National Institute of Mental Health (1982), "is that violence on television does lead to aggressive behavior by children and teenagers who watch the programs." The violence effect stems from a combination of factors—from *arousal* by the violent excitement, from the strengthening of violence-related *ideas*, from the erosion of one's *inhibitions*, and from *imitation* (Geen & Thomas, 1986). One research team observed a seven-fold increase in violent play immediately after children viewed the "Power Rangers" (Boyatzis & others, in press). Boys' aggressive acts often precisely imitated the characters' flying karate kicks and other violent acts.

Television's unreal world, in which acts of aggression greatly outnumber acts of affection, can also affect our thinking about the real world. Those who avidly watch prime-time crime regard the world as more dangerous (Gerbner & others, 1993; Heath & Petraitis, 1987; Singer & Singer, 1986). Prolonged expo-

Stayskal/Tampa Tribune.

sure to violence also desensitizes viewers; they become more indifferent to it when later viewing a brawl, whether on TV or in real life (Rule & Ferguson, 1986). Indeed, suggest Edward Donnerstein and his co-researchers (1987), an evil psychologist could hardly imagine a better way to make people indifferent to brutality than to expose them to a graded series of scenes, from fights to killings to the mutilations in slasher movies.

Sexual Aggression and the Media   A woman's risk of rape has varied across cultures and times (Koss & others, 1994). Over the last 30 years, America's reported rape rate has quadrupled. Recent surveys of both women and men reveal that unreported rapes, most committed by dates or acquaintances, greatly outnumber those reported. In other surveys, about one-fifth of women report that a man has forced them to do something sexually, about half of women report some form of unwanted sexual coercion, and most report experiencing verbal sexual harassment (Craig & others, 1989; Koss & Burkhart, 1989; Laumann & others, 1994; Sandberg & others, 1985).

What factors might explain the modern epidemic of sexual aggression? Alcohol consumption—often linked with aggression—has not increased. Might changes in the media contribute?

Coinciding with the increase in sexual aggression has been, thanks to the home video business, easier access to R-rated "slasher films" and X-rated films. Content analyses reveal that X-rated films mostly depict quick, casual sex between strangers, but that scenes of rape and sexual exploitation of women by men are also common (Cowan & others, 1988; NCTV, 1987; Yang & Linz, 1990).

Most men are not sexually aroused (as measured by a "penile plethysmograph") while viewing rape depictions. But convicted rapists are. So are normal men if they have been drinking or if, after being aroused by exercise, a woman's insults anger them (Barbaree & Marshall, 1991). Rape scenes often portray the victim at first fleeing and resisting her attacker, then becoming aroused and finally driven to ecstasy. In less graphic form, the same unrealistic script—she resists, he persists, she melts—is commonplace in TV scenes and in romance novels. The woman who first thwarts the insistent man ends up passionately kissing him. In *Gone with the Wind*, Scarlett O'Hara is carried to bed screaming and wakes up singing. Most rapists accept this "rape myth"—the idea that some women invite or enjoy rape and get "swept away" while being "taken" (Brinson, 1992).

Pornography means different things to different people. Following Webster's dictionary, some define pornography as erotic depictions intended to excite sexual arousal. Others define it as sexual materials that exploit, degrade, or subordinate women.

In follow-up studies, Zillmann (1989) found that after massive exposure to X-rated sexual films, men and women became more accepting of extramarital sex, of women's sexual submission to men, and of a man's seducing a 12-year-old girl. As people heavily exposed to televised crime perceive the world as more dangerous, so people heavily exposed to pornography see the world as more sexual.

Hillary Rodham Clinton and others have worried that the media model an "impulsive sexuality" that encourages uncommitted sex (a predictor of sexual violence) and father-absent families (a predictor of juvenile violence).

Do such films and other similar materials influence sexual aggression? When interviewed, Canadian and U.S. sex offenders (rapists, child molesters, and serial killers) do report a greater-than-usual appetite for sexually explicit and sexually violent materials—materials typically labeled as "pornography" (Marshall, 1989; Ressler & others, 1988). For example, the Los Angeles Police Department reports that pornography was "conspicuously present" or used in 62 percent of its extrafamilial child sexual abuse cases during the 1980s (Bennett, 1991). But are the sexual offenders merely, as sex researcher John Money (1988) suspects, using pornography "as an alibi to explain to themselves and their captors what otherwise is inexplicable"?

Laboratory experiments reveal that repeated viewing of X-rated films (even if nonviolent) makes one's own partner seem less attractive (page 314), makes women's friendliness seem more sexual, and makes sexual aggression seem less serious (Harris, 1994). In one such experiment, Dolf Zillmann and Jennings Bryant (1984) showed undergraduates six brief, sexually explicit films a week for 6 weeks. A control group viewed nonerotic films during the same 6-week period. Three weeks later, both groups read a newspaper report about a man convicted but not yet sentenced for raping a hitchhiker. When asked to suggest an appropriate prison term, those who had viewed sexually explicit films recommended sentences half as long as those recommended by the control group.

In search of possible media effects on men's willingness to aggress against women, experimenters examined the effect of film viewing on men's acceptance of the rape myth. Neil Malamuth and James Check (1981) compared University of Manitoba men who were shown either two nonsexual movies or two movies depicting a man sexually overpowering a woman. A week later, when surveyed by a different experimenter, those who had seen the films with mild sexual violence were more accepting of violence against women and reported themselves a little more likely to rape if assured they could get away with it. Further experiments showed that viewing slasher movies, such as *The Texas Chainsaw Massacre*, can also lead viewers to trivialize rape.

Experiments have also explored the effect of violent versus nonviolent films on men's willingness to deliver supposed electric shocks to women who earlier provoked them. (Although such experiments cannot study actual sexual violence, they can assess a man's willingness to hurt a woman.) These experiments suggest that it's not eroticism but depictions of sexual *violence* (whether in R-rated slasher films or X-rated films) that most directly affect men's acceptance and performance of aggression against women. A 1986 conference of 21 social scientists, including many of the researchers who conducted these experiments, produced a consensus that "pornography that portrays sexual aggression as pleasurable for the victim increases the acceptance of the use of coercion in sexual relations." Contrary to much popular opinion, viewing such depictions does not provide an outlet for bottled-up impulses. Rather, "in laboratory studies measuring short-term effects, exposure to violent pornography increases punitive behavior toward women" (Surgeon General, 1986).

TV Violence, Pornography, and Society Significant behaviors such as violence usually have many determinants, making any single explanation an oversimplification. Asking what causes violence is therefore like asking what causes cancer. Those who study, say, the effects of asbestos exposure on cancer rates may remind us that asbestos is indeed a cancer cause, but only one among many. Likewise, report Neil Malamuth and his colleagues (1991), several factors can create a predisposition to sexual violence; they include not only the media but also child abuse, hostility, dominance motives, and disinhibition by

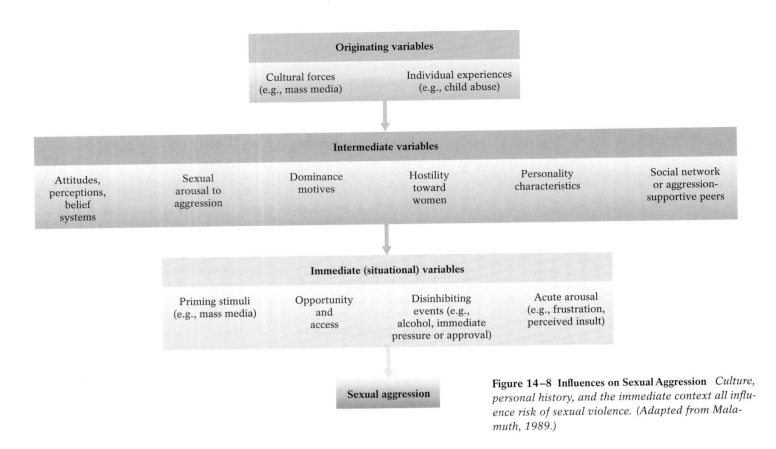

Figure 14–8 Influences on Sexual Aggression *Culture, personal history, and the immediate context all influence risk of sexual violence. (Adapted from Malamuth, 1989.)*

> "If we expect families to teach children not to solve their problems with guns and violence, we need cultural and media signals and public policies that demonize rather than glamorize and support violence."
>
> Children's Defense Fund, 1992

> "What we're trying to do is raise the level of awareness of violence against women and pornography to at least the level of awareness of racist and Ku Klux Klan literature."
>
> Gloria Steinem (1988)

alcohol (Figure 14–8). Still, if media depictions of violence can disinhibit and desensitize, if viewing sexual violence fosters attitudes and behaviors that degrade women, and if viewing pornography can lead viewers to trivialize rape and devalue their partners, then media violence is not a minor issue.

Social psychologists attribute the media's influence partly to the *social scripts* they provide. When we find ourselves in new situations, uncertain how to act, we rely on social scripts provided by our culture. After so many episodes of Power Rangers, followed by Clint Eastwood, Sylvester Stallone, and Arnold Schwarzenegger action films, youngsters may acquire a script—a mental tape for how to act—that gets played when they face real-life conflicts. Challenged, they may "act like a man" by intimidating or eliminating the threat. Likewise, after viewing 15 sexual innuendoes and acts per prime-time TV hour—nearly all involving impulsive, short-term relationships—youths may acquire sexual scripts they later enact in real-life relationships (Sapolsky & Tabarlet, 1991).

Might public consciousness be raised by making people aware of the information you have just been reading? In the 1940s, movies often depicted African-Americans as childlike, superstitious buffoons. Today, such images are offensive. In the 1960s and 1970s, entertainment from Beatles' music to movies such as *Easy Rider* glamorized drug use. No longer. Responding to a tidal change in cultural attitudes, the entertainment industry now portrays drugs as dangerous. Even gratuitous cigarette smoking has largely disappeared. Responding to growing public concern about violence and the media, television violence levels declined in the early 1990s (Gerbner & others, 1993). The growing sensitivity to violence has raised hopes that, without violating artistic freedom, society might someday look back with embarrassment on the days when movies "entertained" people with scenes of torture, mutilation, and sexual coercion.

conflict   A perceived incompatibility of actions, goals, or ideas.

social traps   Situations in which the conflicting parties, by each rationally pursuing their self-interest, become caught in mutually destructive behavior.

Conflict

13. What social processes fuel conflict?

We live in surprising times. With astonishing speed, democratic movements have swept away totalitarian rule in Eastern European countries, and hopes for a new world order have displaced the Cold War chill. Yet world spending for arms and armies continues to drain $2 billion per day from spending for housing, nutrition, education, and health care. Knowing that, as the UNESCO motto declares, wars begin in human minds, psychologists have wondered what causes destructive conflicts? How might the perceived threats of social diversity be replaced by a spirit of cooperation?

To a social psychologist, a **conflict** is a seeming incompatibility of actions, goals, or ideas. The elements of conflict are much the same at all levels, from nations in an arms race to cultural disputes within a society to individuals in marital strife. In each situation, people become enmeshed in a destructive social process that produces results no one wants. Among these destructive processes are social traps and distorted perceptions.

Social Traps   In some situations, we can enhance our collective well-being by pursuing our personal interests. As capitalist Adam Smith wrote in *The Wealth of Nations* (1776), "It is not from the benevolence of the butcher, the brewer, or the baker that we expect our dinner, but from their regard to their own interest." In other situations, the parties involved may become caught up in mutually harmful behavior as they pursue their own ends. Such situations are **social traps**.

Consider the simple game matrix in Figure 14–9, which is similar to those used in experiments with thousands of people. In this game, *both* sides can win or lose, depending on the players' individual choices. Pretend that you are person 1, and that you and person 2 will each receive the amount shown after you separately choose either *A* or *B*. (You might invite someone to look at the matrix with you and take the role of person 2.) Which do you choose—*A* or *B*?

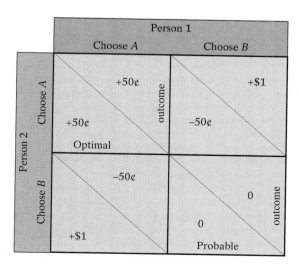

Figure 14–9   Social Trap Game Matrix   *By pursuing our self-interest and not trusting others, we can end up losers. To illustrate this, imagine playing the game above. The pink triangles show the outcomes for person 1, which depend on the choices made by both persons. If you were person 1, would you choose A or B? (This game is called a "non-zero-sum game" because the outcomes need not add up to zero; both sides can win or both can lose.)*

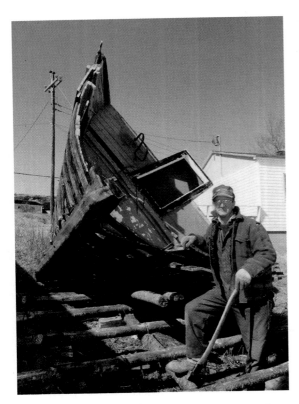

A Social Trap *In the Atlantic waters off Newfoundland, those who fished knew that their individual catch was their livelihood and, by itself, hardly depleted the whole fish population. Such reasoning by everyone, including outsiders, depleted fish stocks. The result: Newfoundland's fishing fleet sits idle and an economy is in ruins during a 1990s fishing moratorium. This unemployed fisherman has been forced to use his boat for firewood.*

"Why do you see the speck that is in your brother's eye, but do not notice the log that is in your own eye?"

Jesus
Luke 6:41–42

As you ponder the game, you will discover that you and person 2 are caught in a dilemma. If you both choose *A* you both benefit, making 50 cents each. Neither of you benefits if you both choose *B*, for neither of you make anything. Nevertheless, on any single trial you serve your own interests if you choose *B*: You can't lose, and you might make $1. But the same is true for the other person. Hence, the social trap: As long as you both pursue your own immediate best interest and choose *B*, you will both end up with nothing—the typical result—when you could have made 50 cents.

Many real-life situations similarly pit people's individual interests against their communal well-being. Individual whalers reason that the few whales they take will not threaten the species and that if they didn't take them others would anyway. The result: A species of whales becomes endangered. The individual car owner and home owner reasons, "It would cost me comfort or money to buy a more fuel-efficient car and furnace. Besides, the fossil fuels I burn don't noticeably add to the greenhouse gases." When others reason similarly, the collective result threatens disaster—global warming.

Social traps challenge us to find ways of reconciling our right to pursue our personal well-being with our responsibility for the well-being of all. Psychologists are therefore exploring ways to convince people to cooperate for their mutual betterment—through agreed-upon *regulations*, through better *communication*, and through promoting *awareness* of our responsibilities toward community, nation, and the whole of humanity (Dawes, 1980; Linder, 1982; Sato, 1987). Under such conditions, people more often cooperate, whether playing laboratory games or playing the real game of life.

Enemy Perceptions   Psychologists have noted a curious tendency for those in conflict to form diabolical images of each other. These distorted images are so similar that we call them *mirror-image perceptions*: As we see them—as untrustworthy and evil intentioned—so they see us. Thus, during the early 1980s, the U.S. government viewed the Communist support of guerrillas trying to overthrow the government of El Salvador as evidence of an "evil empire" at work. Meanwhile, the Soviets saw the U.S. support of guerrillas trying to overthrow the government of Nicaragua as the work of "imperialist warmongers." As enemies change, so do perceptions. In American minds and media, the "bloodthirsty, cruel, treacherous" Japanese of World War II later became our "intelligent, hardworking, self-disciplined, resourceful allies" (Gallup, 1972).

We have considered the psychological roots of biased perceptions. The *self-serving bias* leads each party to accept credit for good deeds and to shuck the blame for bad deeds. Although two nations admit to a buildup of military forces, the *fundamental attribution error* leads each to see the other's actions as arising from its aggressive disposition but to view its own buildup as necessary self-defense. Information about one another's actions is then filtered, interpreted, and remembered through preconceived *stereotypes*. Group interaction among like-minded policymakers may *polarize* these tendencies, leading to *groupthink* that sees one's own group as more moral, thereby justifying one's retaliation. In Soviet-U.S. relations, such biases resulted in the social perceptions that fueled the arms race: Both sides (1) wished for mutual arms reduction, but (2) wanted above all to avoid disarming while the other armed, and (3) perceived the other side as wanting above all to gain an arms advantage (Plous, 1993).

Another result of such perceptions is a vicious cycle of hostility. If Victor believes Samantha is annoyed with him, he may snub her, causing her to act in ways that justify his perception. As with individuals, so with countries. Perceptions confirm themselves by influencing the other country to react in ways that seem to justify them. The self-fulfilling prophecy rides again.

Now that we've pondered the bad side of our social relations—prejudice, aggression, and conflict—let's focus on the positive side of social relations—attraction, altruism, and peacemaking.

! *Rehearse It*

14. Experiments show that when people are temporarily frustrated, they express more intense prejudice. When things go wrong, prejudice provides an outlet for our anger—and gives us someone to blame. This effect is best described by

a. ingroup bias.
b. scapegoat theory.
c. Freud's theory on the death instinct.
d. the just-world phenomenon.

15. Stereotypes are a natural by-product of our usual ways of thinking. For example, we tend to judge the frequency of events in terms of cases that come readily to memory. Thus, if several well-publicized murders are committed by members of a particular group, we tend to react with fear and suspicion toward all members of the group. In other words, we

a. blame the victim.
b. overgeneralize from vivid, memorable cases.
c. create a scapegoat.
d. categorize people incorrectly.

16. Aggression is physical or verbal behavior that is intended to hurt someone. We find biological influences on aggression at three levels: the genetic, the neural, and the biochemical. Evidence of a biochemical influence on aggression is the finding that

a. aggressive behavior varies widely from culture to culture.
b. animals can be bred for aggressiveness.
c. stimulation of an area of the brain's limbic system produces aggressive behavior.
d. a higher than average level of the hormone testosterone is associated with violent behavior in males.

17. Studies show that delinquent young people tend to have parents who relied on beatings to enforce discipline. This demonstrates that aggression can be

a. learned through direct rewards.
b. learned through observation of aggressive models.
c. triggered by exposure to violent media.
d. caused by hormone changes at puberty.

18. There is considerable controversy about the effects of heavy exposure to violent television programming. However, most experts would agree that repeated viewing of television violence

a. makes all viewers significantly more aggressive.
b. has little effect on viewers.
c. dulls the viewer's sensitivity to violence.
d. makes viewers angry and frustrated.

19. A conference of social scientists who studied the effects of pornography on ordinary adults generally agree that violent pornography

a. has little effect on most viewers.
b. is the primary cause of reported and unreported rapes.
c. leads viewers to be more accepting of coercion in sexual relations.
d. has no short-term effects, other than arousal and entertainment.

20. Conflicts often arise from destructive social processes. In many situations, individuals, in rationally pursuing their self-interests, get caught up in a behavior that harms both themselves and others. This destructive social process is called

a. gameplaying.
b. mirror-image perception.
c. a social trap.
d. the fundamental attribution error.

Attraction

Pause a moment and think about your relationships with two people—a close friend, and someone who has stirred in you feelings of romantic love. What factors lead to friendship and romance? What factors help us sustain these relationships?

We endlessly wonder how we can win others' affection and what makes our own affections flourish or fade. Do birds of a feather flock together, or do opposites attract? Does familiarity breed contempt or liking? Does absence make the heart grow fonder, or is out of sight out of mind? Social psychology provides some answers.

mere exposure effect   The phenomenon that repeated exposure to novel stimuli increases liking of them.

Familiarity Breeds Acceptance   *When this rare white penguin was born in the Sydney, Australia, zoo, his tuxedoed peers ostracized him. To gain his acceptance, zookeepers thought they would need to dye him black. But after 3 weeks of contact, the other penguins came to accept him.*

The Mere Exposure Effect   *The mere exposure effect applies even to ourselves. Because the human face is not perfectly symmetrical, the face we see in the mirror is not the same as the one our friends see. Most of us prefer the familiar mirror image, while our friends like the reverse (Mita & others, 1977). The Prime Minister Paul Keating whom Australians know is shown at left. The person Keating sees in the mirror each morning is shown at right, and that's the photo he would probably prefer.*

"*Personal beauty is a greater recommendation than any letter of introduction.*"

Aristotle
Apothegems, 330 B.C.

The Psychology of Attraction

14. What psychological factors promote attraction?

What is the psychological chemistry that binds two people together in that special sort of friendship that helps one cope with all other relationships? Consider three ingredients of our liking for one another.

Proximity   Before friendships become close, they must begin. Proximity—geographic nearness—is perhaps the most powerful predictor of friendship. Proximity provides opportunities for aggression, but much more often it instigates liking. Study after study reveals that people are most likely to like, and even to marry, those who live in the same neighborhood, who sit nearby in class, who work in the same office, who share the same parking lot. Look around.

Why is proximity so conducive to liking? Obviously, part of the answer is the greater availability of those we often meet. But there is more to it than that. For one thing, repeated exposure to novel stimuli—be they nonsense syllables, musical selections, geometric figures, Chinese characters, human faces, or the letters of our own name—increases our liking for them (Moreland & Zajonc, 1982; Nuttin, 1987). This phenomenon, which is now exploited by advertisers, we call the **mere exposure effect**. Within certain limits (Bornstein, 1989), familiarity breeds fondness. Richard Moreland and Scott Beach (1992) demonstrated this by having four equally attractive women silently attend a 200-student class for 0, 5, 10, or 15 class sessions. Shown slides of each woman at the end of the class, the students rated the ones they'd seen the most as most attractive. The phenomenon will come as no surprise to the young Taiwanese man who wrote over 700 letters to his girlfriend, urging her to marry him. She did marry—the mail carrier (Steinberg, 1993).

Physical Attractiveness   Once proximity affords you contact, what most affects your first impressions: the person's sincerity? intelligence? personality? Hundreds of experiments reveal that it is likely something more superficial: appearance.

For people taught that "beauty is only skin deep" and that "appearances can be deceiving," the power of physical attractiveness is unnerving. In one early study, Elaine Hatfield and her co-workers (Walster & others, 1966) randomly matched new University of Minnesota students for a "Welcome Week" dance. Before the dance, all took a battery of personality and aptitude tests. On the night of the blind date, the couples danced and talked for more than 2 hours and then took a brief intermission to rate their dates. What determined whether they liked each other? So far as the researchers could determine, only one thing mattered: physical attractiveness (which had been rated by the researchers beforehand). Both the men and the women liked good-looking dates best. Although women are more likely than men to *say* that another's looks don't affect them, a man's looks do affect women's behavior (Feingold, 1990; Sprecher, 1989; Woll, 1986).

People's physical attractiveness has wide-ranging effects. It predicts their dating frequency, their feelings of popularity, and others' initial impressions of their personalities. We perceive attractive people, even children and those of our own sex, to be happier, more sensitive, more successful, and more socially skilled, though not more honest or compassionate (Eagly & others, 1991; Feingold, 1992; Hatfield & Sprecher, 1986). Attractive and well-dressed people are more likely to make a favorable impression on potential employers (Cash & Janda, 1984; Solomon, 1987). To judge from their gazing times, even babies prefer attractive over unattractive faces (Langlois & others, 1987).

That looks are important may seem unfair and unenlightened. Two thousand years ago the Roman statesman Cicero felt the same way: "The final good and the supreme duty of the wise person is to resist appearance." Cicero might be reassured by two other findings about attractiveness.

First, people's attractiveness is surprisingly unrelated to their self-esteem (Major & others, 1984). One reason may be that, except after comparing themselves with superattractive people, few people view themselves as unattractive (Thornton & Moore, 1993). (Thanks, perhaps, to the mere exposure effect, most of us become accustomed to our face.) Another reason is that strikingly attractive people are sometimes suspicious that praise may be simply a reaction to their looks. When less attractive people are praised for their work, they are more likely to accept it as sincere (Berscheid, 1981).

Cicero might also find comfort in knowing that attractiveness judgments are relative. They depend first on the accepted standards of beauty in one's place and time. Hoping to look attractive, people in different cultures have pierced their noses, lengthened their necks, bound their feet, dyed their skin and hair, eaten to achieve a full figure or liposuctioned fat to achieve a slim one, strapped on leather garments to prevent their breasts from growing or stuffed their breasts with silicone to make them bigger. (The standards by which judges crown "Miss Universe" hardly even apply to the whole planet.) In North America, the ultra-thin ideal of the Roaring Twenties gave way to the soft, voluptuous Marilyn Monroe ideal of the 1950s, to be replaced by the lean, athletic ideal of the 1990s.

"Love comes in at the eye."

William Butler Yeats
"A Drinking Song," 1909

In the Eye of the Beholder *Conceptions of attractiveness vary by culture and across time. What may be deemed attractive in one culture may seem strange or unattractive in another. And the current concept of beauty in Kenya, Morocco, and the United States may well change in the future.*

Figure 14–10 Worldwide Mating Preferences *David Buss and an international team of collaborators surveyed the mating preferences of 10,047 people in 37 countries. Men everywhere preferred attractive physical features suggesting youth and health—and reproductive potential. Women everywhere preferred men with resources and social status. (From Buss, 1994b.) This gender difference, evolutionary psychologists believe, is the result of natural selection favoring those whose choices help perpetuate their genes.*

"Love is a dirty trick played on us to achieve the continuation of the species."

Novelist W. Somerset Maugham, 1874–1965

"Love has ever in view the absolute loveliness of that which it beholds."

George MacDonald
Unspoken Sermons, 1867

Some aspects of attractiveness, however, cross place and time. It comes as no surprise to evolutionary psychologists that men in 37 cultures, from Australia to Zambia, judge women as more attractive if they have a youthful appearance (Figure 14–10). Evolutionary psychologists say that men drawn to healthy, fertile-appearing women have stood a better chance of sending their genes into the future. From yesterday's Stone Age figurines to today's *Playboy* centerfolds and Miss America winners—and regardless of cultural variations in ideal weight—men feel most attracted to women whose waists are roughly a third narrower than their hips—a sign of youthful fertility (Singh, 1993). To women, men seem more attractive if they appear mature and dominant. This connotes, say the evolutionary psychologists, a capacity to support and protect (Buss, 1994a).

Cultural differences and similarities aside, attractiveness also depends on our feelings about the person. In a Rodgers and Hammerstein musical, Prince Charming asks Cinderella, "Do I love you because you're beautiful, or are you beautiful because I love you?" Chances are it is both. As we discover someone's similarities to us, see them again and again, and come to like them, their physical imperfections grow less noticeable and their attractiveness grows more apparent (Beaman & Klentz, 1983; Gross & Crofton, 1977). As Shakespeare put it in *A Midsummer Night's Dream*, "Love looks not with the eyes, but with the mind." Until you got to know him, E.T. was as ugly as Darth Vader.

Similarity   Let's say that proximity has brought you into contact with someone and that your appearance has made a favorable first impression. What now influences whether acquaintances develop into friends? For example, as you get to know someone better, is the chemistry better if you are opposites or if you are alike?

It makes a good story—extremely different types living in harmonious union: Rat, Mole, and Badger in *The Wind in the Willows*, Frog and Toad in Arnold Lobel's books. The stories delight us by expressing what we seldom experience, for we tend *not* to like dissimilar people (Rosenbaum, 1986). In real life, opposites retract. Birds that flock together usually *are* of a feather. Friends and couples are far more likely to share common attitudes, beliefs, and interests (and, for that matter, age, religion, race, education, intelligence, smoking behavior, and economic status) than are randomly paired people. Moreover, the greater their likeness, the more their liking will endure (Byrne, 1971). Journalist Walter Lippmann was right to suppose that love is best sustained "when the lovers love many things together, and not merely each other." Similarity breeds content.

passionate love An aroused state of intense positive absorption in another, usually present at the beginning of a love relationship.

"Pardon me, but I can't help noticing that we share similar tastes in tropical-fruit-flavored chewing gum."

Proximity, attractiveness, and similarity are not the only determinants of attraction. We also like those who like us, especially when our self-image is low. When we believe someone likes us, we respond to them more warmly, which leads them to like us even more (Curtis & Miller, 1986). To be liked is powerfully rewarding.

Indeed, a simple reward theory of attraction—that we will like those whose behavior is rewarding to us and that we will continue relationships that offer more rewards than costs—can explain all the findings we have considered so far. When a person lives or works in close proximity with someone else, it costs less time and effort to develop the friendship and enjoy its benefits. Attractive people are aesthetically pleasing, and associating with them can be socially rewarding. Those with similar views reward us by validating our own.

Romantic Love

15. What is the distinction between passionate and companionate love?

Occasionally, people progress quickly from initial impressions to friendship to the more intense, complex, and mysterious state of romantic love. Elaine Hatfield (1988) distinguishes two types of love: temporary passionate love and a more enduring companionate love.

Passionate Love Noting that arousal is a key ingredient of **passionate love**, Hatfield suggests that the two-factor theory of emotion (page 353) can help us understand this intense positive absorption in another. The theory assumes that (1) emotions have two ingredients—physical arousal plus cognitive appraisal—and (2) arousal from any source can enhance one emotion or another, depending on how we interpret and label the arousal.

In tests of this theory, college men have been aroused by fright, by running in place, by viewing erotic materials, or by listening to humorous or repulsive monologues. They are then introduced to an attractive woman and asked to rate her (or their girlfriend). Unlike unaroused men, those who are stirred up attribute some of their arousal to the woman or girlfriend and feel more attracted to her (Carducci & others, 1978; Dermer & Pyszczynski, 1978; White & Kight, 1984).

Outside the laboratory, Donald Dutton and Arthur Aron (1974, 1989) went to two bridges across British Columbia's rocky Capilano River. One was a swaying footbridge 230 feet above the rocks; the other was a low, solid bridge. An attractive young female accomplice intercepted men coming off each bridge, sought their help in filling out a short questionnaire, and then offered her phone number in case they wanted to hear more about her project. Far more of those who had just crossed the high bridge—which left their hearts pounding—accepted the number and later called the woman. To be revved up and to associate some of that arousal with a desirable person is to feel the pull of passion. As lovers who take a thrilling roller coaster ride together know, adrenaline makes the heart grow fonder.

Companionate Love Inevitably, the passion of romantic love subsides. The intense absorption in the other, the thrill of the romance, the giddy "floating on a cloud" feeling fades. JUST MARRIED becomes just married. Recognizing the short duration of passionate love, some societies have deemed such feelings an irrational reason for marrying. Better, such cultures say, to choose (or have someone choose for you) a partner with compatible backgrounds and interests.

So, are the French correct in saying that "love makes the time pass and time makes love pass"? Or can friendship and commitment keep a relationship

"When two people are under the influence of the most violent, most insane, most delusive, and most transient of passions, they are required to swear that they will remain in that excited, abnormal, and exhausting condition continuously until death do them part."

George Bernard Shaw
Man and Superman, 1903

Drawing by Maslin; © 1992 The New Yorker Magazine, Inc.

Passionate Love to Companionate Love *The quality of love changes as a relationship matures from passionate absorption to affectionate attachment.*

"When a match has equal partners then I fear not."

Aeschylus
Prometheus Bound, 478 B.C.

companionate love The deep affectionate attachment we feel for those with whom our lives are intertwined.

equity A condition in which people receive from a relationship in proportion to what they give to it.

self-disclosure Revealing intimate aspects of oneself to others.

altruism Unselfish regard for the welfare of others.

going after the passion cools? Hatfield notes that if love matures it becomes a steadier **companionate love**—a deep, affectionate attachment. There may be adaptive wisdom to this change from passion to affection. Passionate love often produces children, whose survival is aided by the parents' waning obsession with one another. Social psychologist Ellen Berscheid and her colleagues (1984) note that the failure to appreciate passionate love's limited half-life can doom a relationship: "If the inevitable odds against eternal passionate love in a relationship were better understood, more people might choose to be satisfied with the quieter feelings of satisfaction and contentment."

One key to a gratifying and enduring relationship is **equity**: Both partners receive in proportion to what they give. When equity exists—when both partners freely give and receive, when they share decision making—their chances for sustained and satisfying companionate love are good (Gray-Little & Burks, 1983; Van Yperen & Buunk, 1990). Mutually sharing self and possessions, giving and getting emotional support, promoting and caring about one another's welfare, are at the core of every type of loving relationship (Sternberg & Grajek, 1984). It's true for lovers, for parent and child, and for intimate friends.

Another vital ingredient of loving relationships is intimacy. A strong friendship or marriage permits **self-disclosure**, a revealing of intimate details about ourselves—our likes and dislikes, our dreams and worries, our proud and shameful moments. "When I am with my friend," noted the Roman statesman Seneca, "me thinks I am alone, and as much at liberty to speak anything as to think it." Self-disclosure grows as a relationship deepens. As one person reveals a little, the other reciprocates, the first person reveals more, and on and on, as friends or lovers move to deeper intimacy. Given self-disclosing intimacy plus mutually supportive equality, the odds favor enduring companionate love.

Altruism

Altruism—an unselfish regard for others' welfare—is another powerful example of positive social interactions. Altruism became a major concern of social psychologists after an especially vile act of sexual violence. A knife-wielding stalker repeatedly stabbed Kitty Genovese, then raped her as she lay dying outside her Queens, New York, apartment at 3:30 A.M. on March 13, 1964. "Oh, my God, he stabbed me!" Genovese screamed into the early-morning stillness. "Please help me!" Windows opened and lights went on as 38 of her neighbors heard her screams. Her attacker fled and then returned to stab her eight more times and rape her again. Not until he departed for good did anyone so much as call the police, at 3:50 A.M.

> *"Probably no single incident has caused social psychologists to pay as much attention to an aspect of social behavior as Kitty Genovese's murder."*
>
> R. Lance Shotland (1984)

Bystander Intervention

16. What is the bystander effect?

Reflecting on the Genovese murder and other such tragedies, most commentators lamented the bystanders' "apathy" and "indifference." Rather than blaming them, social psychologists John Darley and Bibb Latané (1968b) attributed onlooker inaction to an important situational factor—the presence of others. Given the right circumstances, they suspected, most of us might behave similarly.

After staging emergencies under various conditions, Darley and Latané assembled their findings into a decision scheme: We will help only if the situation enables us first to *notice* the incident, then to *interpret* it as an emergency, and finally to *assume responsibility* for helping (Figure 14–11).

Figure 14–11 The Decision-Making Process for Bystander Intervention *Before helping, one must first notice, then correctly interpret an emergency, and then feel responsible. (From Darley & Latané, 1968b.)*

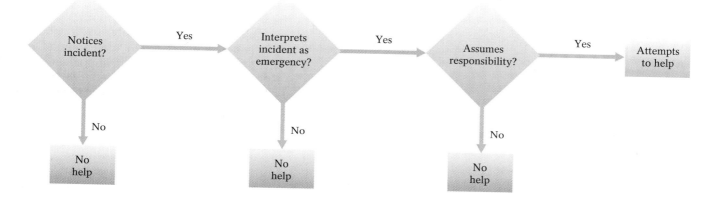

At each step, the presence of other bystanders turns people away from the path that leads to helping. In the laboratory and on the street, people in groups of strangers are more likely than solitary individuals to keep their eyes on what they are doing or where they are going. If they notice an unusual situation, they may infer from the blasé reactions of the other passersby that the situation is not an emergency. "The person lying on the sidewalk must be drunk," they think, and move on.

But sometimes, as with the Genovese murder, the emergency is unambiguous and people still fail to help. The witnesses looking out through their windows noticed the incident, correctly interpreted the emergency, yet failed to assume responsibility. To find out why, Darley and Latané (1968a) simulated a physical emergency in their laboratory. University students participated in a discussion over an intercom. Each student was in a separate cubicle, and only the person whose microphone was switched on could be heard. One of the students was an accomplice of the experimenters. When his turn came, he called for help and made sounds as though he were having an epileptic seizure.

How did the other students react? As Figure 14–12 shows, those who believed they were the only one who could hear the victim—and therefore thought they bore total responsibility for helping—usually went to his aid. Those who thought others could also hear were more likely to react as did Kitty Genovese's neighbors. When more people shared responsibility for helping, any single listener was less likely to help.

In hundreds of additional experiments, psychologists have studied the factors that influence bystanders' willingness to relay an emergency phone call, aid a stranded motorist, donate blood, pick up dropped books, contribute

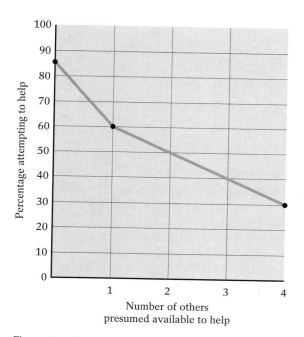

Figure 14–12 Responses to a Simulated Physical Emergency *When people thought they alone heard an epileptic seizure victim calling for help, they usually helped. But when they thought four others were hearing it too, fewer than a third responded. (From Darley & Latané, 1968a.)*

The Bystander's Dilemma *When passing someone slumped on a city sidewalk, we may wonder, "Is this person sick? If I offer help, what will the reaction be? What can I do anyway?" Yet sometimes we do offer help. What circumstances prompt our doing so?*

money, and give time. For example, Latané, James Dabbs (1975), and 145 collaborators took 1497 elevator rides in three cities and "accidentally" dropped coins or pencils in front of 4813 fellow passengers. The women coin-droppers were more likely to receive help than were the men—a gender difference often reported by other researchers (Eagly & Crowley, 1986). But the major finding was the **bystander effect**—any particular bystander was less likely to give aid with other bystanders present. When one other person was on the elevator, those who dropped the coins were helped 40 percent of the time. When there were six passengers, help came less than 20 percent of the time.

From their observations of behavior in tens of thousands of such "emergencies," altruism researchers have discerned some additional patterns. The odds of our helping someone are best when:

- we have just observed someone else being helpful.
- we are not in a hurry.
- the victim appears to need and deserve help.
- the victim is in some way similar to us.
- we are in a small town or rural area.
- we are feeling guilty.
- we are focused on others and not preoccupied.
- we are in a good mood.

This last result, that happy people are helpful people, is one of the most consistent findings in all of psychology. No matter how people are cheered—whether by being made to feel successful and intelligent, by thinking happy thoughts, by finding money, or even by receiving a posthypnotic suggestion—they become more generous and more eager to help (Carlson & others, 1988).

The Psychology of Helping

17. What other factors influence helping?

Why do we help? One widely held view is that self-interest underlies all human interactions: Our constant goal is to maximize rewards and minimize costs. Accountants call it cost–benefit analysis. Philosophers call it utilitarianism. Social psychologists call it **social exchange theory**. If you are pondering whether to donate blood, you may weigh the costs of doing so (time, discomfort, and anxi-

Bonding With a Boarder Baby *Volunteers are motivated to help if the rewards, whether psychological or social, are greater than the costs. This man finds satisfaction in comforting boarder babies, infants born to mothers who cannot care for them.*

ety) against the benefits (reduced guilt, social approval, good feelings). If the anticipated rewards of helping exceed the anticipated costs, you help.

Social expectations also influence helping. They prescribe how we ought to behave, often to our mutual benefit. Through socialization, we learn the *reciprocity norm*, the expectation that we should return help, not harm, to those who have helped us. In our relations with others of similar status, the reciprocity norm compels us to give (in favors, gifts, or social invitations) about as much as we receive. With young children and others who cannot give as much as they receive, we also learn a *social responsibility norm*—that we should help those who need our help, even if the costs outweigh the benefits. In repeated Gallup surveys, people who each week attend church or synagogue services often exhibit the social responsibility norm: They report volunteering more than twice as many hours in helping the poor and infirm than do those who rarely or never attend (Hodgkinson & Weitzman, 1992). They also give away three times as much money.

Peacemaking

18. What circumstances facilitate the resolution of conflict?

How can we transform antagonisms fed by prejudice, aggression, and various conflicts into constructive attitudes that promote peace? Such transformations are most likely in situations characterized by cooperation, communication, and conciliation.

Cooperation

Does it help to put two conflicting parties into close contact so they might get to know and like each other? It depends. When the contact is noncompetitive and between parties of equal status, such as fellow store clerks, it may help. Initially prejudiced co-workers of different races have, in such circumstances, usually learned to accept one another (Pettigrew, 1969). However, mere contact is sometimes not enough. In most desegregated junior high schools, whites and blacks resegregate themselves in the lunchrooms and on the school grounds (Schofield, 1986).

Mere contact was not enough to defuse intense conflicts instigated by researcher Muzafer Sherif (1966). He placed 22 Oklahoma City boys in two separate areas of a Boy Scout camp. He then put the two groups through a series of competitive activities, with prizes going to the victors. Before long, each group became intensely proud of itself and hostile to the other group's "sneaky," "smart-alecky stinkers." Food wars broke out during meals. Cabins were ransacked. Fistfights had to be broken up by members of the camp staff. When Sherif brought the two groups together, they avoided one another, except to taunt and threaten.

Nevertheless, within a few days Sherif transformed these young enemies into jovial comrades by giving them **superordinate goals**—shared goals that overrode their differences and that could only be achieved through cooperation. A planned disruption of the camp water supply necessitated that all 22 boys work together to restore water. Renting a movie in those pre-VCR days required their pooled resources. A truck stalled until all the boys pulled and pushed together to get it moving. Having used isolation and competition to make strangers into enemies, Sherif used shared predicaments and goals to reconcile the enemies and make them friends. What reduced conflict was not contact itself, but *cooperative* contact.

Extending these findings, Samuel Gaertner and his co-workers (1989) re-

Empathy: Feeling What Another Feels *When we see others in trouble, we sometimes feel their pain. This can motivate helping designed to relieve our own distress and the victims' suffering.*

"*You cannot shake hands with a clenched fist.*"
Indira Gandhi (1971)

bystander effect The tendency for any given bystander to be less likely to give aid if other bystanders are present.

social exchange theory The theory that our social behavior is an exchange process, the aim of which is to maximize benefits and minimize costs.

superordinate goals Shared goals that override differences among people and require their cooperation.

port that cooperation has especially positive effects when it leads people to define a new, inclusive group that dissolves their former subgroups. Seat the members of two groups not on opposite sides, but alternately around the table. Give them a new, shared name. Have them work together. Such experiences change "us" and "them" into "we." People once perceived as in another group now are part of one's own group.

During the 1970s, several teams of educational researchers simultaneously wondered: If cooperative contacts between members of rival groups encourage positive attitudes, could we apply this principle in multicultural schools? Could we promote interracial friendships by replacing competitive classroom situations with cooperative ones? And could cooperative learning maintain or even enhance student achievement? Many experiments confirm that in all three cases, the answer is yes (Johnson & Johnson, 1989, 1994; Slavin, 1989). Members of interracial groups who work together on projects and play together on athletic teams typically come to feel friendly toward those of the other race. So do those who engage in cooperative classroom learning. So encouraging are these results that more than 25,000 teachers have introduced interracial cooperative learning into their classrooms (Kohn, 1987). Working with fellow students in all their diversity sets the stage, declared the Carnegie Council on Adolescent Development (1989), for "adult work life and for citizenship in a multicultural society."

Superordinate Goals Overrode Differences   *Cooperative efforts to achieve shared goals are an effective way to break down social barriers.*

"I am prepared this day to declare myself a citizen of the world, and to invite everyone everywhere to embrace this broader vision of our interdependent world, our common quest for justice, and ultimately for Peace on Earth."

Father Theodore Hesburgh
The Human Imperative, 1974

The power of cooperative activity to make friends of former enemies has led psychologists to urge increased international exchange and cooperation (Klineberg, 1984). As we engage in mutually beneficial trade, as we work to protect our common destiny on this fragile planet, and as we become more aware that our hopes and fears are shared, we can change misperceptions into a solidarity based on common interests.

Communication

In the social trap game matrix we considered earlier, people usually are distrustful and pursue their individual interests as a defense against exploitation. But when allowed to discuss the dilemma and negotiate, cooperation increases (Jorgenson & Papciak, 1981).

When conflicts become intense, a third-party mediator—a marriage counselor, labor mediator, diplomat, community volunteer—may facilitate communication (Rubin & others, 1994). Mediators help each party to voice its viewpoint and to understand the other's. By helping each side think about one another's underlying needs and goals, the mediator aims to replace a competitive *win-lose* orientation with a cooperative *win-win* orientation that aims at a mutually beneficial resolution. A classic example concerns the two friends who, after quarreling over an orange, agreed to split it, whereupon one squeezed his

GRIT Graduated and Reciprocated Initiatives in Tension-Reduction—a strategy designed to decrease international tensions.

half for juice while the other used the peel from her half to make a cake. If only the two had understood each other's motives, they could have hit on the win-win solution of one having all the juice, the other all the peel.

Such understanding and cooperative resolution is most needed, yet least likely, in times of anger or crisis (Bodenhausen & others, 1994; Tetlock, 1988). When conflicts intensify, images become more stereotyped, communication becomes more difficult, and judgments become more rigid. Iraq's President Saddam Hussein, America's friend while attacking Iran in the 1980s, became to George Bush "another Hitler" after attacking oil-producing Kuwait in 1990. To Hussein, Bush became "Satan in the White House."

Neutral third parties may also suggest proposals that would be dismissed if offered by either side. People often "reactively devalue" a concession offered by an adversary ("if they're willing to give that up, they must not value it"); the same concession may seem less like a token gesture when suggested by a third party. Lee Ross and Constance Stillinger (1991) showed how this works. They found that a nuclear disarmament proposal that Americans dismissed when attributed to the Soviet Union seemed more acceptable when attributed to a neutral third party.

Conciliation

When tension and suspicion peak, cooperation and communication may become impossible. Each party is likely to threaten, coerce, or retaliate. In the weeks before the Persian Gulf War, President Bush threatened, in the full glare of publicity, to "kick Saddam's ass." Saddam Hussein communicated in kind, threatening to make Americans "swim in their own blood."

Under such conditions, is there an alternative to war or surrender? Social psychologist Charles Osgood (1962, 1980) advocates a strategy of "Graduated and Reciprocated Initiatives in Tension-Reduction," nicknamed **GRIT**. In applying GRIT, one side first announces its recognition of mutual interests and its intent to reduce tensions. It then initiates one or more small, conciliatory acts. Without weakening one's retaliatory capability, this modest beginning opens the door for reciprocation by the other party. Should the enemy respond with hostility, one reciprocates in kind. But so, too, with any conciliatory response. Thus, President Kennedy's gesture of stopping atmospheric nuclear tests began a series of reciprocated conciliatory acts that culminated in the atmospheric test-ban treaty.

In laboratory experiments, GRIT is the most effective strategy known for increasing trust and cooperation (Lindskold & others, 1978–1988). Even during intense personal conflict, when communication has been nonexistent, a small conciliatory gesture—a smile, a touch, a word of apology—may work wonders. Conciliations allow both parties to begin edging down the tension ladder to a safer rung where communication and mutual understanding can begin.

And how good that such can happen, for civilization advances not by cultural isolation—maintaining walls around ethnic enclaves—but by tapping the knowledge, the skills, and the arts that are each culture's legacy to the whole human race. Thomas Sowell (1991) notes that, thanks to cultural sharing, every modern society is enriched by a cultural mix. We have China to thank for paper and printing, and for the magnetic compass that opened the great explorations. We have Egypt to thank for trigonometry. We have the Islamic world and India's Hindus to thank for our Arabic numerals, which, except for numbering kings, queens, and Superbowls, really are superior to the Roman numerals they replaced. While celebrating and claiming these cultural legacies, we can also welcome the enrichment of today's social diversity. We can view ourselves as individual instruments in a human orchestra. And we can therefore affirm our own culture's heritage while building bridges of communication, understanding, and cooperation across cultural traditions.

Drawing by W. Miller; © 1983 *The New Yorker* Magazine, Inc.

"To begin with, I would like to express my sincere thanks and deep appreciation for the opportunity to meet with you. While there are still profound differences between us, I think the very fact of my presence here today is a major breakthrough."

! *Rehearse It*

21. Repeated exposure to a stimulus—including a new human face—increases our liking of the stimulus. This *mere exposure effect* helps explain why proximity is a powerful predictor of friendship and marriage, and why, for example, people tend to marry someone

a. about as attractive as themselves.
b. who lives or works nearby.
c. of similar religious or ethnic background.
d. who has similar attitudes and habits.

22. Male subjects who are aroused by various stimuli and then introduced to an attractive woman tend to attribute their arousal to the woman, and to report positive feelings toward her. This supports the two-factor theory of emotion, which assumes that emotions such as passionate love consist of physical arousal plus

a. a reward.
b. our interpretation of that arousal.
c. proximity.
d. companionate love.

23. Companionate love is described as a deep, affectionate attachment. Vital to the maintenance of such loving relationships is (are)

a. physical attraction.
b. equity and self-disclosure.
c. intense positive absorption.
d. proximity and similarity.

24. Psychologists have studied the factors that determine whether or not a bystander will come to the aid of a stranger in an "emergency." They have found that people who are in a good mood are most likely to extend their help. Perhaps the most important finding, though, is the bystander effect, which states that a particular bystander is less likely to give aid if

a. the victim is similar to him or her in appearance.
b. there is no one else present.
c. other bystanders are present.
d. the incident occurs in a deserted or rural area.

25. Social exchange theory contends that all social behavior is aimed at maximizing benefits and minimizing costs. Social expectations also influence helping. For example, through socialization, we are taught that we should help those who need our help. This is called

a. the reciprocity norm.
b. altruism.
c. the social responsibility norm.
d. bystander intervention.

26. Social psychologists have attempted to define the circumstances that facilitate conflict resolution. One way of fostering cooperation is by providing contentious groups with superordinate goals, which are

a. the goals of friendly competition.
b. shared goals that override differences.
c. goals for winning at negotiations.
d. goals for reducing conflict through increased contact.

Reviewing *Social Psychology*

Social psychologists study how people think about, influence, and relate to one another.

Social Thinking

1. How do we tend to explain others' behavior? How do we explain our own behavior?

We generally explain people's behavior by attributing it either to internal dispositions or to external situations. In accounting for others' actions, we tend to underestimate the influence of the situation, thus committing the fundamental attribution error. When we explain our own behavior, however, we more often point to the situation and not to ourselves.

2. Under what conditions do our attitudes guide our behavior?

Attitudes predict behavior only under certain conditions, as when other influences are minimized, when the attitude is specific to the behavior, and when people are aware of their attitudes.

3. Under what conditions does our behavior affect our attitudes?

Studies of the foot-in-the-door phenomenon and of role playing reveal that our actions can also modify our attitudes, especially when we feel responsible for those actions. Cognitive dissonance theorists explain that behavior shapes attitudes because people feel discomfort when their actions go against their feelings and beliefs; they reduce the discomfort by bringing their attitudes more into line with what they have done.

Social Influence

4. What do experiments on conformity and compliance reveal about the power of social influence?

Solomon Asch and others learned that under certain conditions people will conform to a group's judgment even when it is clearly incorrect. In Milgram's famous experiments, people who were torn between obeying an experimenter and responding to another's pleas usually chose to obey orders, even though obedience appeared to involve harming another person. These classic experiments demonstrate the potency of social forces, and they highlight the fact that we conform either to gain social approval (normative social influence) or because we depend on the information that others provide (informational social influence).

5. **In what ways are we affected by the mere presence of others?**

Experiments on social facilitation indicate that the presence of others can arouse individuals, slightly boosting their performance on easy tasks but hindering it on difficult ones. When people pool their efforts toward a group goal, social loafing may occur as individuals free-ride on others' efforts. When people are aroused and made anonymous by a group, they may become less self-aware and self-restrained, a psychological state known as deindividuation.

6. **What are group polarization and groupthink?**

Discussions with like-minded others often produce group polarization, an enhancement of the group's prevailing attitudes. This is one cause of groupthink, the tendency for harmony-seeking groups to make unrealistic decisions after suppressing unwelcome information.

7. **Can a minority sway a majority?**

The power of the group is great, but so can be the power of a minority, especially when its views are expressed consistently.

8. **How do cultural norms and roles affect our behavior?**

Cultural rules for accepted and expected behavior vary in ways that befuddle people. Cultures differ, for example, in their requirements for personal space, their expressiveness, their pace of life, and the strength of their role expectations. They also differ in their gender roles—the behaviors expected of males and females.

Social Relations

9. **What are the social and emotional roots of prejudice?**

Prejudice often arises as those who enjoy social and economic superiority attempt to justify the status quo. Even the temporary assignment of people to groups can cause an ingroup bias. Once established, the inertia of social influence can help maintain prejudice. Prejudice may also serve the emotional functions of draining off the anger caused by frustration and of boosting self-esteem.

10. **What are the cognitive roots of prejudice?**

Newer research reveals how our ways of processing information—for example, by overestimating similarities when we categorize people or by noticing and remembering vivid cases—work to create stereotypes. In addition, favored social groups often rationalize their higher status by the just-world phenomenon.

11. **What biological factors influence aggressive behavior?**

Aggressive behavior, like all behavior, is a product of nature and nurture. Although psychologists dismiss the idea that aggression is instinctual, aggressiveness is genetically influenced. Moreover, certain areas of the brain, when stimu-

lated, activate or inhibit aggression, and these neural areas are biochemically influenced.

12. **What psychological factors influence aggressive behavior?**

A variety of psychological factors also influence aggression. Aversive events heighten people's hostility. Such stimuli are especially likely to trigger aggression in those rewarded for their own aggression or those who have learned aggression from role models or have repeatedly observed violent media portrayals of aggressive models. Such factors desensitize people to cruelty and prime them to behave aggressively when provoked.

13. **What social processes fuel conflict?**

Conflicts between individuals and cultures often arise from malignant social processes. These include social traps, in which each party, by protecting and pursuing its self-interest, creates an outcome that no one wants. The spiral of conflict also feeds and is fed by distorted mirror-image perceptions, in which each party views itself as moral and the other as untrustworthy and evil-intentioned.

14. **What psychological factors promote attraction?**

Three factors are known to influence our liking for one another. *Proximity*—geographical nearness—is conducive to attraction, partly because mere exposure to novel stimuli enhances liking. *Physical attractiveness* influences social opportunities and the way one is perceived. As acquaintanceship moves toward friendship, *similarity* of attitudes and interests greatly increases liking.

15. **What is the distinction between passionate and companionate love?**

Passionate love can be viewed as a temporary, aroused state that we cognitively label as love. The strong affection of companionate love, which often emerges as a relationship matures, is enhanced by an equitable relationship and by intimate self-disclosure.

16. **What is the bystander effect?**

In response to incidents of bystander nonintervention in emergencies, social psychologists undertook experiments that revealed a bystander effect: Any given bystander is less likely to help if others are present. The bystander effect is especially apparent in situations where the presence of others inhibits one's noticing the event, interpreting it as an emergency, or assuming responsibility for helping. Many factors, including mood, also influence willingness to help someone in distress.

17. **What other factors influence helping?**

Social exchange theory proposes that our social behaviors—even our helpful acts— maximize our benefits (which may include our own good feelings) and minimize our costs. Our desire to help is also affected by social norms, which prescribe reciprocating the help we have received and being socially responsible toward those in need.

18. **What circumstances facilitate the resolution of conflict?**

Enemies sometimes become friends, especially when the circumstances favor cooperation to achieve superordinate goals, understanding through communication, and reciprocated conciliatory gestures.

Terms and Concepts to Remember

social psychology, p. 479

attribution theory, p. 479

fundamental attribution error, p. 480

attitude, p. 481

foot-in-the-door phenomenon, p. 482

role, p. 483

cognitive dissonance theory, p. 484

conformity, p. 485

normative social influence, p. 486

norms, p. 486

informational social influence, p. 486

social facilitation, p. 490

social loafing, p. 491

deindividuation, p. 491

group polarization, p. 492

groupthink, p. 492

culture, p. 494

personal space, p. 494

gender role, p. 495

prejudice, p. 496

stereotype, p. 497

ingroup bias, p. 499

scapegoat theory, p. 499

just-world phenomenon, p. 500

aggression, p. 501

frustration-aggression principle, p. 503

conflict, p. 509

social traps, p. 509

mere exposure effect, p. 512

passionate love, p. 515

companionate love, p. 516

equity, p. 516

self-disclosure, p. 516

altruism, p. 516

bystander effect, p. 518

social exchange theory, p. 518

superordinate goals, p. 519

GRIT, p. 520

Rehearse It Answer Key

1. a.   2. d.   3. b.   4. a.   5. c.   6. a.   7. c.   8. c.   9. b.

10. c.   11. b.   12. c.   13. b.   14. b.   15. b.   16. d.   17. b.   18. c.

19. c.   20. c.   21. b.   22. b.   23. b.   24. c.   25. c.   26. b.

Critical Thinking Exercise

Now that you have read and reviewed Chapter 14, take your learning a step further by testing your critical thinking skills on the following passage.

When Mary and Kathy met as college roommates, they discovered they had a lot in common and quickly became close friends. They spent many hours discussing their innermost feelings and were pleased to find they shared a dislike of all forms of prejudice. At the beginning of their sophomore year, they pledged with different sororities. Despite Mary's protests, Kathy pledged with a sorority that had a reputation for being elitist and somewhat prejudiced against minority groups, including Mary's. Although initially Kathy was concerned about her sorority's reputation, she felt after the first meeting with her new sorority sisters her concern was undeserved and went on to become a full member of the sorority. As weekly meetings continued, however, the discussions at Kathy's sorority became increasingly tinged with bigotry. Kathy gradually found herself thinking more and more like her sorority sisters and even openly making a few contemptuous remarks about minority groups. Although she sometimes felt troubled by her behavior, Kathy had worked so hard to become a member of the sorority that she decided she must really have felt this way about minority groups all along.

Being immersed in their separate sororities, Kathy and Mary did not see each other for several months, until their sororities met at an intramural softball game. Running over to greet her friend, Mary was hurt by Kathy's cool, almost haughty manner toward her and other minority members of Mary's sorority. In the midst of her sorority sisters, Kathy seemed a different person altogether. Later that evening, Mary confided in her journal that she must have initially misjudged Kathy as sharing her beliefs and that Kathy had finally displayed her true personality as a very prejudiced person.

1. What social psychological principles might help explain why Mary and Kathy became friends?

2. What social psychological principles might help explain why Mary and Kathy grew apart?

3. Did Mary initially misjudge Kathy's personality?

Check your progress on becoming a critical thinker by comparing your answers with the sample answers found in Appendix B.

For Further Information

For further information in this text on culture and multicultural experience, see:

Adolescence, pp. 87, 96–97
Aging, p. 98
Alcoholism, p. 416
Anger, p. 345
Attachment, pp. 82–83
Behavioral effects of culture, p. 23
Bilingualism, pp. 272–273
Child-rearing, pp. 85–86
Cognitive development, p. 91
Culture shock (in learned helplessness), p. 404
Depression, p. 429
Dieting, pp. 304, 308
Divorce, pp. 104–105
Eating disorders, p. 304

Experiencing emotion, p. 344
Expressing emotion, pp. 340–341
Happiness, p. 348
Intelligence, pp. 289–290
Kinship, p. 25
Language, pp. 272–273
Management style, p. 327
Math performance, p. 289
Menopause, p. 98
Moral development, p. 91
Obesity, pp. 305–306, 308
Participative management, p. 328
Perception, p. 153
Personality dimensions, p. 389
Physiology of emotion, p. 338

Premarital sex, p. 95
Psychological disorders, pp. 413, 416, 422–423, 429, 431–432
Schizophrenia, p. 434, 437
Self-serving bias, p. 397
Social clock, p. 104
Somatoform disorders, pp. 422–423
Study time, p. 289
Suicide, p. 428
Taste preferences, p. 303
Teen sexuality, pp. 95–96
Temperament, p. 82
Weight concern, pp. 305–306, 309
Work-related values, p. 104

For further information in this text on the psychology of women and men, see:

Abortion stress, p. 359
Adult development, pp. 98, 103–104
Alcoholism, pp. 429, 442
Body image, p. 306
Bonding, pp. 81–83
Breast cancer therapy, p. 365
Breast-feeding, p. 81
Depression, pp. 429, 431, 442
Dieting, pp. 306, 308
Dreams, pp. 172, 315
Early versus late maturation, p. 89
Eating disorders, p. 304
Emotion detection, p. 339
Employment of women, p. 106

Empty nest, p. 105
Freud's views, pp. 380–381, 383, 385
Gender typing, p. 86
Generic pronoun "he," pp. 272–273
Happiness, p. 350
Heart disease, pp. 361–362
Help-receiving, p. 518
Hormones
    sexual behavior, pp. 313–314
    sexual development, pp. 71, 88–89
Intelligence, p. 290
Intimacy and identity, pp. 93–94
Leadership, pp. 427–428
Math performance, p. 290
Menarche, p. 88

Menopause, p. 98
Moral development, p. 91
Personality disorder, pp. 440–442
Pornography, p. 314
Self-concept, pp. 398–399, 431
Sensitivity to smells, p. 137
Sexual abuse, p. 372
Sexual coercion, p. 182
Sexual development, p. 89
Sexual dysfunction, pp. 315–316
Sexual orientation, pp. 317–320
Sexuality, p. 316–317
Social connectedness, p. 94
Suicide, p. 428

Statistical Reasoning

Describing Data

Distributions

Central Tendencies

Variation

Correlation

Statistical Inference

When Is It Safe to Generalize From a Sample?

When Is a Difference Significant?

Science fiction writer H. G. Wells predicted that "statistical thinking will one day be as necessary for efficient citizenship as the ability to read and write." That day has arrived. Today's statistics are tools that help us see and interpret what the unaided eye might miss.

percentile rank The percentage of the scores in a distribution that fall below a given score.

Describing Data

Researchers or not, we all make observations or gather data that we must organize and interpret. Let's see how we might effectively do this.

Distributions

Laura is a college admissions officer. Attempting to predict which currently enrolled students succeed at her school, she sorts through their high school grades, aptitude scores, biographical statements, recommendation letters, and subsequent college grades. But there is too much information to remember. Moreover, she knows that impressions are swayed by remembered information, often the vivid or extreme instances. So she starts by laying out the basic data on a small random sample of students (Table A–1).

She is first interested in how these students did in high school. She therefore displays the applicants' precollege grade point averages as a bar graph (Figure A–1). By showing the number of GPAs within a particular interval as a bar, Laura can see approximately where any particular student's GPA falls relative to the others. She can also express any student's ranking as a **percentile rank**, which states the percentage of scores that fall below a particular score. A student whose percentile rank is 99 has a GPA that exceeds those of 99 percent of all the students. (You can never have a percentile rank of 100. Your score can never exceed those of 100 percent of the people because you are one of them.)

A note of caution: Take care when reading statistical graphs (Figure A–2). Depending on what people want to emphasize, they can design the graph to make the same difference look small or big.

Figure A–2 Read the Scale Labels *An American truck manufacturer offered graph (a)—with actual brand names included—to suggest the much greater durability of its trucks. Note, however, how the apparent difference shrinks as the vertical scale changes in graph (b).*

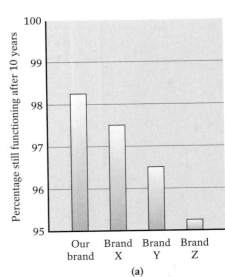

(a)

The moral: When looking at statistical graphs in books and magazines and on television ads and news broadcasts, think critically. Always read the scale labels and note their range.

TABLE A–1

Laura's Sample Data

Student	Precollege GPA	College GPA	SAT	Family Income	Student	Precollege GPA	College GPA	SAT	Family Income
Andrea	2.1	1.6	950	$ 15,000	Mark	3.6	4.0	1370	$45,000
Bubba	2.9	2.8	720	20,000	Nicole	2.9	2.2	875	35,000
Cindy	3.7	3.6	1350	30,000	Nobuyuki	3.2	2.1	1180	25,000
Dang Cho	3.1	3.9	1100	20,000	Ralph	2.7	2.8	1065	35,000
Ezekiel	3.4	3.1	1100	40,000	Renae	3.9	3.3	1130	20,000
Fiona	2.9	2.6	775	20,000	Rochelle	2.3	2.5	725	30,000
Gamal	2.7	3.3	750	25,000	Rowland	2.8	2.5	700	40,000
Hope	2.0	2.4	800	45,000	Tammy	3.0	3.5	1270	20,000
Huong	3.5	2.7	1010	70,000	Tiffany	3.1	2.7	810	25,000
Jae-Min	3.9	3.5	1375	475,000	Timothy	3.5	2.9	900	90,000
Kraig	3.4	3.7	820	30,000	Todd	3.8	3.2	940	20,000
Larry	3.1	2.5	1105	15,000	Wilbur	2.6	2.1	750	30,000
Malachi	3.4	3.3	800	50,000	Xandria	3.5	3.3	1020	20,000
Manuel	3.3	3.3	1120	25,000	Xin	4.0	3.8	1400	45,000
Maria	3.5	3.6	900	710,000	Yolanda	3.1	2.8	900	30,000

(b)

Figure A–1 Bar Graph *High school GPAs of 30 students.*

"The poor are getting poorer, but with the rich getting richer it all averages out in the long run."

Drawing by Mirachi; © 1988 *The New Yorker Magazine, Inc.*

Central Tendencies

Laura wonders: What are typical precollege grades and family income levels among her college's students? That is, what is a representative or *central tendency*? For any distribution of scores there are three commonly used measures of the central tendency. The simplest is the **mode**, the most frequently occurring score. The most commonly reported is the **mean**, or arithmetic average—the total sum of all the scores divided by the number of scores. (From calculating your grade point average, you are familiar with the mean.) The **median** is the middle score—the 50th percentile; if you arrange all the scores in order from the highest to the lowest, half will be above the median and half will be below it.

The moral: Always note which measure of central tendency is reported, and consider: If it is a mean, could a few atypical scores be distorting it?

Such measures of central tendency neatly summarize data. Laura can report, for example, that her student sample has a mean precollege GPA of 3.16. But consider what happens to the mean when a distribution is lop-sided or *skewed* (rather than symmetrical). As Figure A–3 shows with the family income data, the mode, median, and mean tell different stories. This is because the mean is biased by a few extreme scores (in this case, the two families with very high income). To say her students have a mean family income of $70,000 is true but misleading. (Understanding this, you can see how a British newspaper could accurately run the headline "Income for 62% Is Below Average" [Waterhouse, 1993]. Because the bottom half of British income earners receive only a quarter of the national income cake, most British people, like most people everywhere, make less than the mean.)

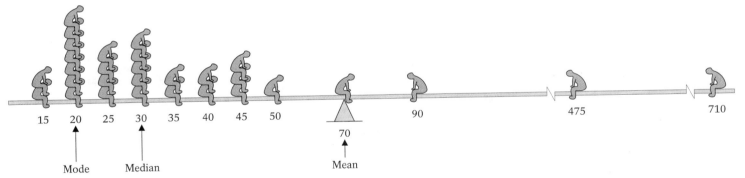

Mode — 20
Median — 30
Mean — 70

15 20 25 30 35 40 45 50   70   90   475   710

One family

Income per family in thousands of dollars

Figure A–3 A Skewed Distribution *This graphic representation of the distribution of incomes illustrates the three measures of central tendency—mode, median, and mean. Note how just a few high incomes make the mean—the fulcrum point that balances the incomes above and below—deceptively high.*

Variation

Knowing the value of an appropriate measure of central tendency can tell us a great deal. But it also helps to know how similar or diverse the scores are. Thus, Laura wonders: How much do my students vary from one another?

Averages derived from scores with low variability are more reliable than averages based on scores with high variability. If a basketball player scored between 13 and 17 points in each of her first 10 games in a season, we would be

mode The most frequently occurring score in a distribution.

mean The arithmetic average of a distribution, obtained by adding the scores and then dividing by the number of scores.

median The middle score in a distribution; half the scores are above it and half are below it.

range The difference between the highest and lowest scores in a distribution.

standard deviation A measure of score variability; computed by (1) calculating the deviation of each score from the mean, (2) squaring those deviations, (3) finding their average, and (4) finding the square root of this average.

normal curve (normal distribution) A symmetrical, bell-shaped curve that describes the distribution of many types of data; most scores fall near the mean (68 percent fall within 1 standard deviation of it) and fewer and fewer near the extremes.

more confident that she would score near 15 points in her next game than if her scores had varied from 5 to 25 points.

The **range** of scores—the gap between the lowest and highest score—provides only a crude estimate of variation because just one extreme score in an otherwise uniform group will create a deceptively large range. The $695,000 income range in Laura's sample ($710,000–$15,000) is misleadingly large because all but the two highest incomes range between $15,000 and $90,000.

The more standard measure of how much scores deviate from one another is the **standard deviation**. It better gauges whether scores are packed together or dispersed, because it uses information from each score. The standard deviation is important and not hard to compute: (1) calculate the difference, or deviation, between each score and the mean; (2) square these deviations; (3) find their average; and (4) find the square root of this average.

As an example, consider Peter, the punter on his college football team. To keep track of his progress, he records the distance of each of his punts. He does not trust his gut-level impression of how consistent his punting is. After his first football game, Peter therefore calculates the standard deviation for his four punts (Table A–2).

TABLE A–2		
Standard Deviation		
Punting Distance	**Deviation From Mean (40 Yards)**	**Deviation Squared**
36	−4	16
38	−2	4
41	+1	1
45	+5	25

Mean = 160/4 = 40   Sum of (deviations)^2 = 46

$$\text{Standard deviation} = \sqrt{\frac{\text{Sum of (deviations)}^2}{\text{Number of scores}}} = \sqrt{\frac{46}{4}} = 3.4 \text{ yards}$$

Figure A–4 The Normal Curve *Data often form a normal, or bell-shaped, curve in which 68 percent of the cases fall within 1 standard deviation of the mean and 95 percent fall within 2 standard deviations. For example, on an IQ test such as the WAIS, we assign the mean a value of 100 and 1 standard deviation we call 15 points; therefore 68 percent of the scores fall between 85 and 115, and 95 percent fall between 70 and 130.*

To grasp the meaning of this statistic, Peter would need to understand how scores tend to be distributed. In nature, large numbers of data—heights, weights, intelligence scores, grades, punt distances (though not incomes)—often form a roughly symmetrical, bell-shaped distribution. Most cases fall near the mean, and fewer cases fall near either extreme. This bell-shaped distribution is so typical that we call the curve it forms the **normal curve**.

As Figure A–4 shows, a useful property of the normal curve is that roughly 68 percent of the cases fall within 1 standard deviation on either side of the mean (in Peter's case, within 3.4 yards of his 40-yard average). About 95 percent of cases fall within 2 standard deviations. Thus, Chapter 8, Thinking, Language, and Intelligence, notes that about 68 percent of people taking an intelligence test will score within ±15 IQ points of 100. About 95 percent will score within ±30 points.

(a)

(b)

Figure A–5 Scatterplots *Plot (a) shows the relationship between total SAT scores (verbal plus mathematical) and college GPAs, and plot (b) the closer relationship between precollege and college GPAs, for 30 college students. Each point represents the data for one student.*

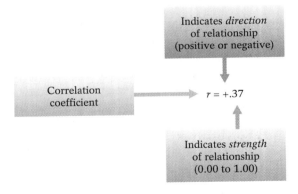

How to Read a Correlation Coefficient

scatterplot A graphed cluster of dots, each of which represents the values of two variables (such as a student's high school and college GPAs). The slope of the points suggests the degree and direction of the relationship between the two variables. (Also called a *scattergram* or *scatter diagram*.)

Correlation

In this book we often ask how much two things relate: How closely related are the personality scores of identical twins? How well do intelligence test scores predict achievement? How often does stress lead to disease? To get a feel for whether one set of scores relates to a second set, we can display the data as a **scatterplot**. Figure A–5a depicts the actual relationship between SAT scores and college GPAs for Laura's 30 students. Each point on the graph represents these two numbers for one student. Figure A–5b is a scatterplot of the relationship between these students' precollege and college GPAs.

The **correlation coefficient** is a statistical measure of how strongly related any two sets of scores are. It can range

- from +1.00, which means that one set of scores increases in direct proportion to the other's increase

- through 0.00, meaning that the scores are unrelated

- to −1.00, which means that one set of scores goes up precisely as the other goes down.

(Note that a correlation's being negative has nothing to do with its strength or weakness; a negative correlation means two things relate inversely. A weak correlation, indicating little or no relationship, is one that has a coefficient near zero.) Now look again at the scatterplots in Figure A–5. Do the correlations look positive or negative?

In each scatterplot in Figure A–5, the upward, oval-shaped slope of the cluster of points as one moves to the right shows that the two sets of scores tend to rise together. This means the correlations are positive: +.50 for the SAT–college GPA relationship shown in Figure A–5a, and a stronger +.69 for the precollege GPA–college GPA relationship shown in Figure A–5b. High SAT scores and, especially, high precollege grades predict high college grades. (The high school–college GPA relationship, incidentally, illustrates the common finding that the best predictor of people's future behavior is usually their behavior in similar situations in the past. The best predictor of future grades is past grades, which reflect both aptitude and motivation. Still, people do sometimes change.)

Perfect positive correlation (+1.00)

No relationship (0.00)

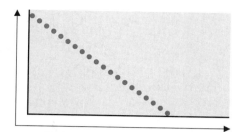

Perfect negative correlation (−1.00)

TABLE A–3

Height and Temperament of Twenty Men

Subject	Height in Inches	Temperament
1	80	75
2	63	66
3	61	60
4	79	90
5	74	60
6	69	42
7	62	42
8	75	60
9	77	81
10	60	39
11	64	48
12	76	69
13	71	72
14	66	57
15	73	63
16	70	75
17	63	30
18	71	30
19	68	84
20	70	39

correlation coefficient A statistical measure of the extent to which two factors vary together and thus how well either factor predicts the other. Scores with a *positive correlation coefficient* go up and down together (as with high school and college GPAs). A *negative correlation coefficient* indicates that one score falls as the other rises (as in the relationship between self-esteem and depression).

regression toward the mean The tendency for extremes of unusual scores to fall back (regress) toward the average.

Statistics can help us see what the naked eye sometimes misses. To demonstrate this for yourself, try to discern what relationship, if any, exists between two sets of scores not yet organized into a scatterplot. Alessandra wonders whether men's heights correlate with their temperaments. She measures the heights of 20 men, has someone else independently assess their temperaments (from zero for extremely calm to 100 for highly reactive), and obtains the data in Table A–3.

With all the relevant data right in front of you, can you tell whether there is (1) a positive correlation between height and reactive temperament, (2) very little or no correlation, or (3) a negative correlation?

Comparing the columns in Table A–3, most people detect very little relationship between height and temperament. In fact, the correlation in this imaginary example is moderately positive, +.57, as you could see if you made a scatterplot of the data. If we fail to see a relationship when data are presented as systematically as in this table, how much less likely are we to notice them in everyday life? To see what is right in front of us, we sometimes need statistical illumination. People can easily see evidence of gender discrimination when given statistically summarized information about job level, seniority, performance, gender, and salary. But they often see no discrimination when the same information dribbles in, case by case (Twiss & others, 1989).

The moral: Although the correlation coefficient tells us nothing about cause and effect, it *can* help us see the world more clearly by revealing the actual extent to which two things relate.

Correlations not only make visible relationships that we might otherwise miss, they also restrain our "seeing" nonexistent relationships. As Chapter 1 explained, perceived correlation that does not really exist is an *illusory correlation.* When we *believe* there is a relationship between two things, we are likely to *notice* and *recall* instances that confirm our belief. If we believe that dreamt events are forecasts of actual events, we may notice and recall confirming instances more than disconfirming instances. The result is an illusory correlation.

Illusory correlations feed an *illusion of control*—that chance events are subject to our personal control. Gamblers, remembering their lucky rolls, may come to believe they can influence the roll of the dice by again throwing gently for low numbers and hard for high numbers. The illusion that uncontrollable events correlate with our actions is also fed by a statistical phenomenon called **regression toward the mean**. Average results are more typical than extreme results. Thus, after an unusual event, things tend to return toward their average level; extraordinary happenings tend to be followed by more ordinary ones.

Examples are abundant: Basketball players who make or miss all their shots in the first half of the game are likely to "regress" (fall back) to their more usual performance level during the second half. Students who score much lower or higher on an exam than they usually do are likely, when retested, to regress toward their average. Unusual ESP subjects who defy chance when first tested nearly always lose their "psychic powers" when retested (a phenomenon parapsychologists have called the "decline effect").

The point may seem obvious, yet we regularly miss it. Thus, we sometimes attribute what may be a normal statistical regression (the expected falling back to normal) to something we have done:

▶ After a sudden crime wave, the town council initiates a "stop crime" drive and the crime rate then returns to previous levels. The drive may therefore appear more successful than it was.

▶ Coaches who yell at their players after an unusually bad first half may feel rewarded for having done so when the team's performance improves (returns to normal) during the second half.

▶ Scientists who win a Nobel prize often have diminished accomplishments thereafter, leading some to wonder whether winning a Nobel hinders creativity.

▶ Some people also believe there is a "*Sports Illustrated* jinx"—that athletes whose peak performances get them on the cover of the magazine will then suffer a decline in their performance.

In each of these cases, it is possible that the effect is genuine. It is more likely, however, that these represent the natural tendency for behavior to regress from the unusual to the more usual.

Failure to recognize regression is the source of many superstitions and of some ineffective practices as well. When day-to-day behavior has a large element of chance fluctuation, we may notice that others' behavior improves (regresses toward average) after we criticize them for very bad performance, and that it worsens (regresses toward average) after we warmly praise them for an exceptionally fine performance. Ironically, then, regression toward the average can mislead us into feeling rewarded for having criticized others and into feeling punished for having praised them (Tversky & Kahneman, 1974).

The moral: When a fluctuating behavior returns to normal, there is no need to invent fancy explanations for why it does so. Regression toward the mean is probably at work.

Statistical Inference

Data are "noisy." One group's average score (women's salaries) could conceivably differ from another's (men's salaries) not because of any real difference but merely due to chance fluctuation in the people sampled. So how confidently can we infer that an observed difference is reliable?

When Is It Safe to Generalize From a Sample?

In deciding whether to generalize from our samples, three principles are worth keeping in mind. Let's look at each in turn.

1. ***Representative Samples Are Better Than Biased Samples***. As Chapter 1 explained, the best basis for generalizing is not from the exceptional, memorable cases one finds at the extremes but from a representative sample of cases. No research involves a representative sample of the whole human population. Thus, it pays to keep in mind what population a study has sampled.

2. ***Less-Variable Observations Are More Reliable Than Those That Are More Variable***. As we noted in the example of the basketball player whose scores were consistent, an average is more reliable when it comes from scores with low variability.

3. ***More Cases Are Better Than Fewer.*** An eager high school senior visits two college campuses, each for a day. At the first, the student randomly attends three classes and discovers each instructor to be witty and engaging. At the next campus, the three sampled instructors seem dull and uninspiring. Returning home, the student tells friends about the "great teachers" at the first school, and the "bores" at the second school. Again, we know it but we ignore it: Small samples provide less reliable estimates of the average than do large samples. The proportion of heads in samples of 10 coin tosses varies more than in samples of 100 tosses.

Said differently, *averages based on more cases are more reliable* (less variable) than averages based on only a few cases. Knowing this, answer a question posed by Christopher Jepson, David Krantz, and Richard Nisbett (1983) to University of Michigan introductory psychology students:

> The registrar's office at the University of Michigan has found that usually about 100 students in Arts and Sciences have a 4.00 GPA at the end of their first term at the University. However, only about 10–15 students graduate with a 4.00 GPA. What do you think is the most likely explanation for the fact that there are more 4.00 GPAs after one term than at graduation?

Most of the students came up with plausible causes for the drop in GPA, such as, "Students tend to work harder at the beginning of their college careers than toward the end." Fewer than a third recognized the statistical phenomenon clearly at work: Averages based on fewer courses are more variable, which guarantees a greater number of extremely low and high GPAs at the end of the first term.

The moral: Don't be overly impressed by a few anecdotes. Generalizations based on only a few cases are unreliable.

When Is a Difference Significant?

We can have most confidence when generalizing from samples that (1) are representative of the population we wish to study, (2) give us consistent rather than highly variable data, and (3) are large rather than small. These principles extend to the inferences we make about differences between groups—as when we generalize from a gender difference in grades in our sample to the whole campus population.

Statistical tests help us decide by indicating the reliability of differences. You needn't understand how they are computed to understand the logic behind them: When *averages* from two samples are each *reliable* measures of their respective populations (as when each is based on many observations that have small variability), then the difference between the samples is likely to be reliable as well. When the *difference* between the averages for the two samples is *large*, we have even more confidence that the difference between them reflects a real difference in their populations.

In short, *when the sample averages are reliable and the difference between them is large*, we say the difference has **statistical significance**. This simply means that the difference probably reflects a real difference and is not due to chance variation between the samples. In judging statistical significance, psychologists are conservative. They are like judges who assume innocence unless guilt is proven, because they would rather risk setting a guilty person free than risk convicting an innocent person. For psychologists, proof beyond a reasonable doubt means not making much of a finding unless the odds of its occurring by chance are less than 5 percent (an arbitrary but agreed-upon criterion).

When reading about research, you should remember that, given large enough or homogeneous enough samples, a difference between them may be "statistically significant" yet have little practical significance. For example,

statistical significance A statistical statement of how likely it is that an obtained result occurred by chance.

PEANUTS

when comparing the intelligence test scores among several hundred-thousand first-born and later-born individuals, we find a highly significant tendency for first-born individuals within a family to have higher average scores than their later-born siblings—but only by one or two IQ points (Zajonc & Markus, 1975).

The moral: Statistical significance indicates the likelihood that a result will happen by chance. It does not indicate a result's importance.

Reviewing *Statistical Reasoning*

To be an educated person today is to be able to apply simple statistical principles to everyday reasoning. One needn't remember complicated formulas to think more clearly and critically about data.

From our consideration of how we can organize and describe data—by constructing distributions and computing measures of central tendency, variation, correlation, and statistical significance—we derived six practical morals for statistical reasoning:

1. When looking at statistical graphs in books and magazines and on TV ads and news broadcasts, think critically: Always read the scale labels and note their range.

2. Always note which measure of central tendency is reported, and consider: If it is a mean, could a few atypical scores be distorting it?

3. Although the correlation coefficient tells us nothing about cause and effect, it *can* help us see the world more clearly by revealing the actual extent to which two things relate.

4. When a fluctuating behavior returns to normal, there is no need to invent fancy explanations for why it does so. Regression toward the mean is probably at work.

5. Don't be overly impressed by a few anecdotes. Generalizations based on only a few cases are unreliable.

6. Statistical significance indicates the likelihood that a result will occur by chance. It does not indicate a result's importance.

Terms and Concepts to Remember

percentile rank, p. 526

mode, p. 528

mean, p. 528

median, p. 528

range, p. 529

standard deviation, p. 529

normal curve (normal distribution), p. 529

scatterplot, p. 530

correlation coefficient, p. 530

regression toward the mean, p. 531

statistical significance, p. 533

Appendix B

Sample Answers to Critical Thinking Exercises

Most psychology courses have two major goals: (1) to help you acquire a basic understanding of psychology's knowledge base, and (2) to help you learn to think like a psychologist. The second goal—learning to think like a psychologist—involves critical thinking. Critical thinking can be regarded as a special set of "thinking skills that promote conscious, purposeful, and active involvement of the thinker with new ideas" (Halonen, 1994). Included among these skills are careful observation, asking questions, seeing connections among ideas, and the ability to analyze arguments and the evidence on which they are based.

The critical thinking exercises in this textbook have been designed to help you develop your ability to think critically as you learn about psychology.[1] Each exercise emphasizes one of six categories of critical thinking: *pattern recognition, practical problem solving, creative problem solving, scientific problem solving, psychological reasoning*, and *perspective taking*.

As the foundation for all other forms of critical thinking, *pattern recognition* is the ability to use psychological concepts to describe behavior patterns and events, especially when there are discrepancies between your expectations of what is normal in a certain situation and what actually occurs.

When events or behavior are unexpected, they may constitute a problem. *Practical problem solving* is the ability to use psychological concepts to develop a plan of action that will lead to the problem's solution.

Creative problem solving is the ability to make novel connections between previously unrelated ideas. This type of critical thinking often leads to new insights about behavior and mental phenomena.

Psychologists employ the scientific method to develop comprehensive and systematic explanations of behavior and mental phenomena. At the heart of this is *scientific problem solving*, which seeks to uncover relationships among the many factors, or variables, involved in producing behavior.

[1]The model for these exercises comes from J. S. Halonen (1994), *Critical thinking companion for introductory psychology*. New York: Worth Publishers, Inc.

Psychological information is transmitted through persuasive arguments that state a relationship between some aspect of behavior, such as intelligence, and another factor, such as age. *Psychological reasoning* is thinking critically about such arguments, especially the evidence on which they are based.

The final category of critical thinking is *perspective taking*, which refers to the ability to recognize the ways in which each person's thinking is shaped by his or her values and past experiences.

You should now be ready to expand your critical thinking skills by completing the exercises prepared for each chapter of your textbook. For some chapters, the exercise presents a hypothetical situation that you will need to think through. For others, you will be asked to evaluate arguments that are derived from actual psychological research. And for still other chapters, your understanding of psychological concepts will be tested by asking you to apply them to a new situation. Carefully read the passage for each exercise and then answer the questions that follow.

Polish your critical thinking skills by applying them to each of your college courses, and to other aspects of life as well. Learn to think critically about advertising, political speeches, and the material presented in popular periodicals.

Chapter 1 Introduction: Thinking Critically With Psychology

1. *Behavior of interest:* Reading ability among first-graders.

2. *Hypothesis:* Children who watch *Sesame Street* develop greater reading ability than children who watch cartoons.

3. *Independent variable:* Type of television program (educational versus cartoon).

4. *Dependent variable:* Reading test score.

5. *Controlled variables:*

   (a) Television program content (educational versus noneducational) during the daily, 1-hour period of exposure.

   (b) Ages of subjects.

   (c) Reading ability measured over the same time period.

6. *Uncontrolled variables:*

   (a) Absence of random assignment leaves alternative explanations for reading improvement in the educational television group. As volunteers, the *Sesame Street* subjects may have been more highly motivated to have their children succeed in reading than the cartoon subjects, who were drafted.

   (b) Reading ability of subjects in the two groups was not measured *before* the experiment began. At the outset, the *Sesame Street* subjects may have had higher reading scores than the cartoon subjects.

   (c) Knowledge of the teacher's hypothesis (by both students and their parents) may have influenced the results so that the experimental group outperformed the control group.

   (d) Other daily activities, such as reading to parents or watching other television programs, might have differentially influenced the reading skills in the two groups.

7. *Valid test of hypothesis?* No. Since so many variables were not controlled, virtually nothing can be concluded from this study. A more valid test would have *randomly assigned* volunteers, who were *not informed* of the teacher's hypothesis and who had been pretested and matched for comparable reading ability in the two groups.

Chapter 2 Neuroscience and Behavior

Lower Level Structures	How the Structures Are Involved in Musical Performance
1. Medulla	This structure controls heartbeat and breathing, which keep the musician's body functioning while he or she plays.
2. Reticular formation	By helping to control arousal, this structure is crucial in maintaining the musician's attention to the task.
3. Thalamus	By routing sensory information from the musician's eyes, ears, and fingertips to higher brain regions, this structure facilitates the musician's seeing, hearing, touching, decision making, and coordination.
4. Amygdala	This structure plays a role in fear, so it may have an effect if the musician is nervous because he or she has to play in front of an audience.
5. Hypothalamus	This structure houses the brain's pleasure mechanisms, which may become responsive during the performance, helping maintain the musician's motivation.
6. Cerebellum	This structure helps coordinate voluntary movements involved in playing the instrument.

Structures of the Cerebral Cortex	How the Structures Are Involved in Musical Performance
1. Motor cortex	This area is involved in organizing the body movements necessary for playing the instrument.
2. Sensory cortex	This area is involved in processing incoming sensory information from the musician's fingertips.
3. Association areas	These areas are involved in the judging and planning inherent in reading music and playing the instrument.
4. Corpus callosum	This area is involved in combining information processed by the left and right hemispheres so that the performance reflects the integrated activity of both sides of the brain.

Chapter 3 The Developing Person

1. Mary's argument is that her father is suffering from Alzheimer's disease, which is causing his occasional memory lapses and his thinking to be uncharacteristically slow.

2. The evidence for Mary's argument comes from her daily observations of her father's behavior and the memory "experiment" she conducted.

3. Mary's evidence in not trustworthy for at least three reasons. *First*, informal observations of this type are subjective and unreliable. Since she recently read an article on Alzheimer's disease, Mary may be looking too hard for symptoms of this disorder. Her expectations may bias her observations. *Second*, Mary is comparing her father's performance on the memory "experiment" only with her recollection of his former quick thinking and excellent

memory. To be a valid test, Mary would need to have actual data on how her father would have performed on this test *before* he began to display the memory symptoms that are the basis for her concern. *Third*, even if Bentley's thinking ability has changed recently, the cause of the change has not been pinpointed. True experiments rule out the potential effects of other variables. It may be that Bentley's uncharacteristically poor performance is the result of his generally poor health, the medication he is taking for his muscle tremors (which is known to produce Alzheimer's-like symptoms), or his lack of physical and intellectual stimulation since retiring.

(By the way, the answer to Mary's brain teaser—an expanding alphabetical sequence—is *m*.)

Chapter 4 Sensation and Perception

1. Your roommate asserts that ESP, defined as perception that occurs outside of normal sensory experiences, actually occurs. She also asserts that she has psychic ability, including the ability to perceive future events (precognition) and to read your mind (telepathy).

2. Your roommate bases her belief on: (1) her ability to predict what you will say and do in certain situations, (2) her having known that something awful would happen to you a week before your automobile accident, and (3) her identifying the suit of a playing card you randomly selected. None of these constitutes trustworthy evidence that would support her assertion. (1) When we have known someone for many years, we often are able to predict what that person will say and do simply because we have observed him or her in similar situations in the past. (2) It is common for close friends to fear that bad things may happen to one another. Occasionally an unlikely event (such as an automobile accident) occurs, and what had been a vague feeling of dread is interpreted after the fact as a precognitive experience. (3) Although empirical, the telepathy "experiment" is not based on solid research. Since there are only four suits in a deck of playing cards, by chance 1 guess in 4 should be correct. Based on only 1 guess, it is impossible to determine whether your friend's accuracy was greater than chance. Had the "experiment" continued, it is likely that your friend's guesses would be correct about 25 percent of the time.

3. a. Your roommate believes that her precognitive "visions" and her ability to predict what you will say and do in certain situations can only be the result of paranormal phenomena, including extrasensory perception.

   b. The explanation provided does not verify the existence of extrasensory perception, nor does it rule out alternative explanations for your roommate's experiences.

   c. An alternative explanation is that your roommate's experiences are the result of perfectly normal phenomena. Being predisposed to believe that ESP exists, it is likely your roommate selectively recalls those few predictions that later "come true" and discounts (or just plain forgets) those that do not. Her occasional ability to predict your thoughts and actions is not necessarily anything more than familiarity with you in past situations. And finally, her accuracy in identifying the suit of one card you selected at random is not necessarily greater than chance.

Chapter 5 States of Consciousness

1. Geraldo asserts that hypnotists have the power to trigger specific behaviors, perceptions, and memories in people because hypnosis induces an

altered state of consciousness involving unique physiological and psychological changes. He further claims that hypnotic age regression allows people to relive earlier experiences and that posthypnotic suggestions can erase memories from the brain. Hypnosis is defined as a state of apparently heightened suggestibility. Age regression is defined as the reliving of earlier experiences, such as in early childhood. Posthypnotic amnesia is defined as the supposed inability of subjects to recall events experienced under hypnosis.

2. The research is not trustworthy for several reasons. First, Geraldo's belief in the power of hypnosis prevents him from being an objective and unbiased experimenter. His expectations of what people will do when hypnotized could bias the outcome of his "experiment." Second, enrollment in a hypnosis course signifies belief in its effectiveness. So the beliefs of the "volunteers" could also affect the outcome. Finally, because there is no control group of fully conscious subjects who are given the same suggestions as the hypnotized volunteers, this is not a true experiment.

3. a. The hypnotist's explanation for the subjects' childlike behavior is that the altered state of hypnosis allows subjects to "relive" earlier experiences. Posthypnotic amnesia is explained as due to the power of hypnosis to erase memories from the brain.

   b. The explanation provided does not prove that hypnosis involves a unique state of consciousness, nor does it rule out alternative explanations for the hypnotized subjects' behavior. No actual evidence of physiological change in the hypnotized subjects was presented. Nor was evidence presented that the behaviors attributed to age regression and posthypnotic amnesia could not be induced in fully conscious subjects or in those who do not have a preexisting belief in the power of hypnosis.

   c. An alternative explanation is that hypnotic phenomena may be nothing more than an extension of everyday social behavior. It is possible that the "hypnotized" people were merely acting the role of "good hypnotic subjects" as they confirmed the hypnotist's and their own, beliefs about hypnotic behavior.

   d. A more valid test of hypnosis must control for the possibility that the subjects' and the hypnotist's beliefs could influence the results. One way of doing so would be to pretest volunteers by asking them whether they believe that hypnosis "works" and whether it involves a unique state of consciousness. "Believers" and "non-believers" would then undergo hypnosis. Another, more valid test of hypnosis would compare the suggestibility of unhypnotized subjects with that of hypnotized subjects given the same "hypnotic suggestions."

Chapter 6 Learning

1. The assertion is that children are classically conditioned to wake up when their bladders are full. Classical conditioning is learning through the association of different events.

2. For children who learn to wake up without special training, the sensation of a wet bed or diaper functions as a UCS that elicits awakening, which is the UCR. Bladder tension (unless painful) is an initially neutral stimulus that becomes associated with the UCS. Over time, bladder tension becomes a CS and will cause the child to awaken before the bed or diaper is wet. This learned awakening is the CR. For children who are trained with the sheet and bell, the UCS is the bell which causes them to wake up, the

UCR is waking up in response to the bell, the CS is bladder tension, and the CR is waking up in response to bladder tension.

3. a. The explanation of how children learn to control their bladders during sleep is that waking up is a classically conditioned response to bladder tension, which has naturally been associated with the unconditioned stimulus of a wet bed or diaper.

b. The explanation appears to make sense based on the evidence. It is clear that bladder tension, unless painful, is not an unconditioned stimulus that automatically awakens a sleeping child. From the evidence cited, it is also clear that a bell can be made sufficiently loud to function as a UCS and elicit awakening as a UCR. Because the pairing of bladder tension (a neutral stimulus) with an effective UCS (the bell) eventually results in the child waking up before the bed is wet (or the bell rings), the criteria of classical conditioning have been satisfied.

c. Although the classical conditioning explanation for this example makes sense based on the evidence, an explanation based on operant conditioning is also possible. Although in very young children waking up is naturally a reflexive act (and therefore subject to classical conditioning), in older children it can be considered a *nonreflexive* act (and therefore subject to operant conditioning). Children may learn to wake up because this behavior *operates* on the environment to produce rewarding stimuli, such as the pleasurable sensation of relieving one's bladder.

Chapter 7 Memory

1. Danny was probably unable to identify the gunman shortly after seeing him run from the store because his fleeting glimpse of the man did not allow him to encode the details of the man's appearance. It is also possible that the confusion of the moment prevented Danny from rehearsing his mental image of the perpetrator so that his memory quickly decayed. Moreover, seeing hundreds of mug book photographs so soon after the crime could have retroactively interfered with whatever real memory Danny had of the gunman's appearance. Finally, the mug book may not actually have contained the gunman's photograph.

2. The misleading questioning and repeated exposure to Raymond's photograph may have caused Danny to misremember the actual event and to reconstruct his memory of it to include Raymond's involvement. Seeing the line-up of men several weeks later, Danny may have been unable to discriminate his eyewitness memory from his memory of the mug book photographs. This would also account for Danny's new-found confidence in the accuracy of his memory.

Chapter 8 Thinking, Language, and Intelligence

The correct answers are: 1. a; 2. b; 3. b; 4. b; 5. a; 6. b; 7. a; 8. b; 9. b; 10. a. Determine the percentage of questions you answered correctly by dividing the number correct by 10 and multiplying this figure by 100. Compare this percentage with your average confidence level. Were you more confident than correct? More correct than confident?

If your confidence level exceeded your accuracy, your thinking may be plagued by overconfidence. Overconfidence in the correctness of knowledge that is wrong hinders critical thinking, interferes with your ability to learn new information, and lowers academic performance. High-achieving students who are not fully realizing their academic potential often consider only evidence that supports their belief that an answer is correct and ignore reasons why it might be wrong. Simply becoming aware of this tendency will help you think more critically about your own knowledge and reasoning. This should improve the accuracy of your confidence judgments and help you make better decisions.

You can train yourself to think more critically by imagining that you will have to explain to other students why you have made a particular decision or have chosen an answer to a question such as those in this exercise. Researchers have shown that this helps to reduce overconfidence and eventually becomes a spontaneous approach to decision making.

Chapter 9 Motivation

1. Since Janet's parents are both obese, it is likely that she inherited a genetic predisposition toward obesity and possibly a lower metabolic rate than Sheila. Janet may also have a higher body weight set point than Sheila.

2. Because her parents are of normal weight, it is likely that Sheila herself is genetically predisposed to be of normal body weight. It is also likely that Sheila has a lower body weight set point and a higher metabolic rate than Janet.

3. The diet Janet and Sheila chose was effective, but more effective for Sheila due to her genetic background. Janet and her parents are all obese, so it is likely that her body has a higher percentage of fat than does Sheila's. Because fat tissue has a low metabolic rate (and therefore takes less food energy to maintain), Janet's body probably requires fewer calories to maintain its weight than does Sheila's. There is no reason to believe that Janet cheated on her diet for lack of willpower. Those genetically predisposed to obesity can eat the same foods, do the same amount of exercising, and still not lose weight as easily as those of normal body weight.

Chapter 10 Emotions, Stress, and Health

1. The James-Lange theory proposes that the experience of emotion derives from our awareness of our physiological responses to emotion-arousing stimuli. It also equates different emotions with specific body states. Assuming that sexual excitement can be triggered by the physical changes induced by exercise, this theory would predict greater reported feelings of sexual excitement during the first two phases of exercise recovery, when the subjects were actually physically aroused, than during the third phase, when the subjects were no longer aroused. The fact that sexual excitement was low during the first phase of recovery, when physical arousal was high, seems to conflict with the theory.

2. The Cannon-Bard theory proposes that an emotion-arousing stimulus simultaneously triggers physical arousal and the subjective experience of emotion. Assuming that the film was an emotion-arousing stimulus, this theory would predict greater reported feelings of sexual excitement during all three phases of the experiment because subjects viewed the film in each phase. However, this explanation is inconsistent with the finding that subjects reported being sexually excited only during the second phase of the experiment. The theory offers no explanation of why the emotional experiences of subjects during phases one and two differed.

3. According to Schachter's two-factor theory, to experience emotion one must be physically aroused and cognitively label that arousal as an emo-

tion. Of the three theories, this one seems to explain the results of the experiment most fully. During the first phase, subjects were physically aroused, and a potential "emotional" explanation for their arousal (the film) was available. Because they *perceived* that they were still aroused from the exercise, however, subjects during this phase attributed their arousal to the exercise rather than to sexual excitement. By the third phase, the subjects had fully recovered from the exercise and lacked the physical arousal necessary to trigger the emotion-attribution process. In phase two, the subjects were physically aroused but did not subjectively perceive this arousal. According to the two-factor theory, this unexplained arousal was attributed to sexual excitement.

Chapter 11 Personality

1. The psychoanalyst has made several assertions regarding Darren's behavior and attitude: (1) The roots of Darren's problems are in unresolved childhood conflicts; (2) Darren was orally overindulged as a child; (3) Darren's personality development is fixated in the oral stage of psychosexual development; and (4) Darren is rationalizing his academic failure and projecting his own self-hatred onto his professors. Rationalization is defined as the ego's attempt to protect itself from anxiety by offering a self-justifying explanation ("the test was unfair") in place of the real, more threatening reason for failure ("I was unprepared"). Projection is defined as a defense mechanism in which a threatening impulse ("I hate myself") is disguised and attributed to others ("they hate me"). The psychoanalyst's views also imply that unconscious forces are a part of personality and that children pass through a series of psychosexual stages as their personalities are formed.

2. There really is no evidence for the various assertions made by the psychoanalyst. Dr. Roitman's conclusions are based entirely on a psychoanalytic interpretation of the behaviors and attitudes Darren displays during counseling. Although many of these behaviors are observable, they do not constitute empirical evidence for the *specific* assertions made. For this reason the evidence is not trustworthy.

3. a. The theoretical explanation for Dr. Roitman's assertion is derived from Freud's psychoanalytic theory. According to this view, Darren's problems are attributed to unresolved oral conflict during his childhood. Believing that Darren was overindulged during this stage of psychosexual development, Dr. Roitman maintains that Darren's personality became fixated. Darren's self-justifying explanation for his failure and his feeling that his professors dislike him are explained as his ego's protective method of coping with unresolved conflict by unconsciously distorting reality.

b. As is generally true of psychoanalytic theory, Dr. Roitman's explanation can neither be proved nor disproved. This is because after-the-fact explanations of behavior are not based on *objective* observations and do not offer testable hypotheses. To someone who accepts psychoanalytic theory, Dr. Roitman's explanation would make sense based on the evidence; to a critically thinking scientist, however, the evidence does not necessarily support the explanation nor rule out alternative explanations.

c. Several alternative explanations can be found in the other personality theories discussed in this chapter. Humanistic theorists might explain Darren's pessimism and sarcastic manner as a result of low self-esteem. Darren's insecure feelings about his parents might mean that these caregivers did not provide him with unconditional positive regard. Humanistic theorists might also suggest that Darren has a negative self-concept because the self he dreams of becoming (a successful college student) differs from the self he fears becoming (an academic failure). Darren's unwillingness to accept responsibility for his failure might be described as a self-serving bias.

According to the social-cognitive perspective, Darren's personal/cognitive factors and behavior interacted with environmental influences to shape his personality. Darren's attitude about the world and unwillingness to accept responsibility for failure indicate that he perceives himself as being controlled by, rather than controlling, his environment.

Chapter 12 Psychological Disorders

1. Phyllis's daughter may be wrongfully attributing to old age what is really psychologically disordered behavior. Mental health workers label behavior as psychologically disordered when they judge it atypical, disturbing, maladaptive, and unjustifiable. Phyllis's behavior would certainly satisfy the first three of these criteria. Furthermore, although her hopeless attitude was triggered by the stress of her divorce, it has persisted too long and is too extreme to be considered a normal, justifiable response to a stressful event. Phyllis's daughter also hasn't realized that there is evidence of biological factors in her mother's condition—her grandmother had similar symptoms, and the antidepressant drug prescribed by her mother's psychiatrist had been effective.

2. Phyllis is showing many classic symptoms of major depressive disorder—including poor appetite, insomnia, lethargy, feelings of worthlessness, and loss of interest in family and friends. Furthermore, these symptoms have persisted much longer than would normally be expected following a stressful event.

3. Psychoanalysts would attribute Phyllis's behavior to early childhood experiences and unconscious impulses. They might suggest, for example, that the loss of her husband evoked feelings associated with troubling losses she experienced in childhood.

   Two pieces of evidence suggest the existence of biological factors in Phyllis's depression: (1) Since her mother seems to have suffered depression as well, Phyllis may have a genetic predisposition to this condition; and (2) the fact that an antidepressant drug made her feel less depressed suggests Phyllis's depression may be caused by a biochemical imbalance.

   According to the social-cognitive perspective, Phyllis may be caught in a vicious cycle of overgeneralized, self-focused negative thinking that is fueling her depression. Like many depressed people, Phyllis has explained a stressful experience (her divorce) in terms that are *stable* and *global* ("Everything I have ever done, or will do, is worthless") and *internal* ("The divorce is my fault"). The result of these self-blaming attributions is a depressing sense of hopelessness that has elicited social rejection, hampered her behavior and thinking, and is likely to lead to further negative experiences.

Chapter 13 Therapy

1. There are several possible reasons psychotherapy was apparently effective for Deborah, but not for Vincent. One is that cognitive therapies, such as Deborah's, have proven most successful in treating depression. Behavior therapies, such as the counterconditioning Vincent experienced, have proven to be more effective in treating specific behavior problems, such as phobias, compulsions, or sexual dysfunctions. A second reason is that Deb-

orah actively sought and entered therapy at a time of personal crisis, while Vincent felt that there was nothing unusual about his behavior or attitude. Deborah's depression may have lifted partly as a result of the passage of time and the lessening of the crisis. A third reason is that Deborah chose her therapist carefully, and she worked with someone who offered hope that things would improve. Vincent picked his therapist randomly, maintained a skeptical attitude throughout therapy, and never admitted he needed help. Thus, Deborah's belief in her treatment could have created a powerful placebo effect that harnessed her own healing powers and led to improvement. Finally, Deborah invested considerably more time and money in her therapy than Vincent did. This would probably result in a stronger need to justify the therapy and, thus, in a more favorable evaluation of its effectiveness.

2. Clients' perceptions of the effectiveness of psychotherapy are not acceptable as scientific evidence. One reason is that people often improve whether or not they receive treatment. Psychotherapy clients who would have improved anyway might misattribute their improvement to therapy. Furthermore, people who go into therapy with the expectation that it will be effective may fall victim to the confirmation bias and remember only information that confirms their expectation.

Chapter 14 Social Psychology

1. Several principles of social psychology help explain why Mary and Kathy became friends. Through the mere exposure effect, their proximity in the dormitory would have encouraged their friendship. Their similarity in attitudes, beliefs, interests, and education probably helped cement their fondness for one another.

2. The strongest factor in the disintegration of Mary and Kathy's friendship was probably the social influence of Kathy's sorority on her attitudes and behavior. Being a sorority sister created a role with specific norms that Kathy strived to adopt. This role included an expectation that she would harbor prejudiced attitudes toward minority groups. Although Kathy was initially troubled by these attitudes, she experienced normative social influence as her desire to gain the approval of her sorority sisters created pressure to conform to their expectations. Over time the hateful attitudes became more acceptable (through mere exposure), and Kathy found herself going along with the group—feeling more and more comfortable in her new role. Kathy probably also experienced cognitive dissonance when she first joined the sorority, as her beliefs and actions conflicted. She may have been inclined to change her beliefs regarding minority groups in order to reduce this dissonance. The weekly meetings of the like-minded sorority sisters also may have contributed to both groupthink and group polarization. This would help explain the increasingly hateful attitudes of both Kathy and her sorority sisters. Finally, Kathy's cool attitude toward Mary at the softball game may have been the result of a loss of self-awareness and self-restraint (deindividuation) in the presence of her sorority sisters.

3. It is difficult to say whether Kathy's changed behavior is the result of her true beliefs surfacing or the situational influence of the sorority. Mary may be making the fundamental attribution error by attributing Kathy's behavior at the softball game to an inner disposition of bigotry. That is, she may be underestimating the situational influence of Kathy's sorority sisters at the time of their reunion.

Glossary

absolute threshold   The minimum stimulation needed to detect a particular stimulus. (p. 119)

accommodation   The process by which the eye's lens changes shape to focus the image of near objects on the retina. (p. 125)

acetylcholine [ah-seat-el-KO-leen] **(ACh)**   A neurotransmitter that, among its functions, triggers muscle contraction. (p. 39)

achievement motivation   A desire for significant accomplishment: for mastery of things, people, or ideas; for attaining a high standard. (p. 323)

achievement tests   Tests designed to assess what a person has learned. (p. 276)

acquisition   The initial stage of learning, during which a response is established and gradually strengthened. In classical conditioning, the phase in which a stimulus comes to evoke a conditioned response. In operant conditioning, the strengthening of a reinforced response. (p. 200)

action potential   A neural impulse; a brief electrical charge that travels down an axon. (p. 36)

active listening   Empathic listening in which the listener echoes, restates, and clarifies. A feature of Rogers' person-centered therapy. (p. 453)

adaptation-level principle   Our tendency to form judgments (of sounds, of lights, of income) relative to a "neutral" level defined by our prior experience. (p. 346)

adolescence   The transition period from childhood to adulthood, extending from puberty to independence. (p. 87)

adrenal [ah-DREEN-el] **glands**   A pair of endocrine glands just above the kidneys. The adrenals secrete the hormones epinephrine (adrenaline) and norepinephrine (noradrenaline), which help to arouse the body in times of stress. (p. 44)

aerobic exercise   Sustained exercise that increases heart and lung fitness; may also alleviate depression and anxiety. (p. 368)

age regression   In hypnosis, the supposed reliving of earlier experiences, such as those of early childhood; greatly susceptible to false recollections. (p. 177)

aggression   Any physical or verbal behavior intended to hurt or destroy. (p. 501)

algorithm   A methodical, logical rule or procedure that guarantees solving a particular problem; may be contrasted with the usually speedier but also more error-prone use of *heuristics*. (p. 257)

alpha waves   The relatively slow brain waves of a relaxed, awake state. (p. 167)

altruism   Unselfish regard for the welfare of others. (p. 516)

Alzheimer's disease   A progressive and irreversible brain disorder characterized by gradual deterioration of memory, reasoning, language, and, finally, physical functioning. (p. 100)

amnesia   Loss of memory. Dissociative amnesia is selective memory loss often brought on by extreme stress. (pp. 223, 423)

amphetamines   Drugs that stimulate neural activity, causing speeded-up body functions and associated energy and mood changes. (p. 184)

amygdala [ah-MIG-dah-la]   Two almond-shaped neural centers in the limbic system that are linked to emotion. (p. 49)

anal stage   The second of Freud's psychosexual stages, from about 18 months to 3 years, during which pleasure focuses on bowel and bladder elimination, retention, and control. (p. 380)

anorexia nervosa   An eating disorder in which a normal-weight person (usually an adolescent female) diets and becomes significantly (15 percent or more) underweight, yet, still feeling fat, continues to starve herself. (p. 304)

antisocial personality   A personality disorder in which the person (usually a man) exhibits a lack of conscience for wrongdoing, even toward friends and family members. May be aggressive and ruthless or a clever con artist. (p. 440)

anxiety disorders   Psychological disorders characterized by distressing, persistent anxiety or maladaptive behaviors that reduce anxiety. (p. 418)

aphasia   Impairment of language, usually caused by left hemisphere damage either to Broca's area (impairing speaking) or to Wernicke's area (impairing understanding). (p. 55)

applied research   Scientific study that aims to solve practical problems. (p. 6)

aptitude tests   Tests designed to predict a person's future performance; aptitude is the capacity to learn. (p. 276)

association areas   Areas of the cerebral cortex that are not involved in primary motor or sensory functions; rather, they are involved in higher mental functions such as learning, remembering, thinking, and speaking. (p. 54)

associative learning   Learning that certain events occur together. The events may be two stimuli (as in classical conditioning) or a response and its consequences (as in operant conditioning). (p. 196)

attachment   An emotional tie with another person; shown in young children by their seeking closeness to the caregiver and showing distress on separation. (p. 81)

attitude   A belief and feeling that predisposes one to respond in a particular way to objects, people, and events. (p. 481)

attribution theory   The theory that we tend to give a causal explanation for someone's behavior, often by crediting either the situation or the person's disposition. (p. 479)

audition   The sense of hearing. (p. 131)

automatic processing   Unconscious encoding of incidental information, such as space, time, and frequency, and of well-learned information, such as word meanings. (p. 226)

autonomic [aw-tuh-NAHM-ik] **nervous system**   The part of the peripheral nervous system that controls the glands and the muscles of the internal organs (such as the heart). Its sympathetic division arouses; its parasympathetic division calms. (p. 42)

availability heuristic   A rule of thumb for estimating the likelihood of events based on their availability in memory; if instances come readily to mind (perhaps because of their vividness), we presume such events are likely. (p. 260)

aversive conditioning   A type of counterconditioning that associates an unpleasant state (such as nausea) with an unwanted behavior (such as drinking alcohol). (p. 457)

axon   The extension of a neuron, ending in branching terminal fibers, through which messages are sent to other neurons or to muscles or glands. (p. 36)

babbling stage   Beginning at 3 to 4 months, the stage of speech development in which the infant spontaneously utters various sounds at first unrelated to the household language. (p. 265)

barbiturates   Drugs that depress the activity of the central nervous system, reducing anxiety but impairing memory and judgment. (p. 184)

basic research   Pure science that aims to increase the scientific knowledge base. (p. 6)

basic trust   According to Erik Erikson, a sense that the world is predictable and trustworthy; said to be formed during infancy by appropriate experiences with responsive caregivers. (p. 84)

behavior therapy   Therapy that applies learning principles to the elimination of unwanted behaviors. (p. 455)

behavioral medicine   An interdisciplinary field that integrates and applies behavioral and medical knowledge to health and disease. (p. 356)

behaviorism   The view that psychology (1) should be an objective science that (2) studies behavior without reference to mental processes. Most research psychologists today agree with (1) but not (2). (p. 198)

belief perseverance   Clinging to one's initial conceptions after the basis on which they were formed has been discredited. (p. 262)

binocular cues   Depth cues, such as retinal disparity and convergence, that depend on the use of two eyes. (p. 142)

biofeedback   A system for electronically recording, amplifying, and feeding back information regarding a subtle physiological state, such as blood pressure or muscle tension. (p. 369)

biological psychology   A branch of psychology concerned with the links between biology and behavior. (Some biological psychologists call themselves *behavioral neuroscientists, neuropsychologists, physiological psychologists,* or *biopsychologists.*) (p. 36)

bipolar disorder   A mood disorder in which a person alternates between the hopelessness and lethargy of depression and the overexcited state of mania. (p. 426)

blind spot   The point at which the optic nerve leaves the eye, creating a "blind" spot because no receptor cells are located there. (p. 126)

brainstem   The oldest part and central core of the brain, beginning where the spinal cord swells as it enters the skull; it is responsible for automatic survival functions. (p. 45)

Broca's area   An area of the left frontal lobe that directs the muscle movements involved in speech. (p. 55)

bulimia nervosa   An eating disorder characterized by private, "binge-purge" episodes of overeating, usually of highly caloric foods, followed by vomiting or laxative use. (p. 304)

bystander effect   The tendency for any given bystander to be less likely to give aid if other bystanders are present. (p. 518)

Cannon-Bard theory   The theory that an emotion-arousing stimulus simultaneously triggers (1) physiological responses and (2) the subjective experience of emotion. (p. 352)

case study   An observation technique in which one person or group is studied in depth in the hopes of revealing universal principles. (p. 11)

CAT (computerized axial tomograph) scan   A series of x-ray photographs taken from different angles and combined by computer into a composite three-dimensional representation of a slice through the body. (p. 47)

catharsis   Emotional release. In psychology, the catharsis hypothesis maintains that "releasing" aggressive energy (through action or fantasy) relieves aggressive urges. (p. 345)

central nervous system (CNS)   The brain and spinal cord. (p. 41)

cerebellum [sehr-uh-BELL-um]   The "little brain" attached to the rear of the brainstem; it helps coordinate voluntary movement and balance. (p. 48)

cerebral [seh-REE-bruhl] **cortex**   The intricate fabric of interconnected neural cells that covers the cerebral hemispheres; the body's ultimate control and information-processing center. (p. 51)

chromosomes   Threadlike structures made of DNA molecules that contain the genes. (p. 70)

chunking   Organizing items into familiar, manageable units; often done automatically. (p. 230)

circadian [ser-KAY-dee-an] **rhythm**   The biological clock; regular bodily rhythms (for example, of temperature and wakefulness) that occur on a 24-hour cycle. (p. 165)

classical conditioning   A type of learning in which an organism comes to associate events. A neutral stimulus that signals an unconditioned stimulus (UCS) begins to produce a response that anticipates and prepares for the unconditioned stimulus. (Also known as *Pavlovian conditioning*.) (p. 198)

clinical psychology   A branch of psychology involving the assessment and treatment of psychological disorders. (p. 6)

closure   The perceptual tendency to fill in gaps, thus enabling one to perceive disconnected parts as a whole object. (p. 141)

cochlea [KOHK-lee-uh]   A coiled, bony, fluid-filled tube in the inner ear through which sound waves trigger nerve impulses. (p. 132)

cognition   All the mental activities associated with thinking, knowing, remembering, and communicating information. (pp. 76, 256)

cognitive dissonance theory   The theory that we act to reduce the discomfort (dissonance) we feel when two of our thoughts (cognitions) are inconsistent—as when we respond to our having acted contrary to our attitudes by changing those attitudes. (p. 484)

cognitive map   A mental representation of the layout of one's environment. For example, after exploring a maze, rats act as if they have learned a cognitive map of it. (p. 213)

cognitive therapy   Therapy that teaches people new, more adaptive ways of thinking and acting; based on the assumption that thoughts intervene between events and our emotional reactions. (p. 458)

collective unconscious   Carl Jung's concept of a shared, inherited reservoir of memory traces from our species' history. (p. 383)

collectivism   Giving priority to the goals of one's group (often one's extended family or work group) and defining one's identity accordingly. (p. 398)

color constancy   Perceiving familiar objects as having consistent color, even if changing illumination alters the wavelengths reflected by the objects. (p. 130)

companionate love   The deep affectionate attachment we feel for those with whom our lives are intertwined. (p. 516)

concept   A mental grouping of similar objects, events, or people. (p. 256)

concrete operational stage   In Piaget's theory, the stage of cognitive development (from about 6 or 7 to 11 years of age) during which children gain the mental operations that enable them to think logically about concrete events. (p. 79)

conditioned response (CR)   In classical conditioning, the learned response to a previously neutral conditioned stimulus (CS). (p. 199)

conditioned stimulus (CS)   In classical conditioning, an originally neutral stimulus that, after association with an unconditioned stimulus (UCS), comes to trigger a conditioned response. (p. 199)

cones   Receptor cells concentrated near the center of the retina that function in daylight or in well-lit conditions. The cones detect fine detail and give rise to color sensations. (p. 126)

confirmation bias   A tendency to search for information that confirms one's preconceptions. (p. 258)

conflict   A perceived incompatibility of actions, goals, or ideas. (p. 509)

conformity   Adjusting one's behavior or thinking to coincide with a group standard. (p. 485)

connectedness   The perceptual tendency to perceive features, such as dots, as a single unit when uniform and linked. (p. 141)

consciousness   Our awareness of ourselves and our environment. (p. 164)

conservation   The principle (which Piaget believed to be a part of concrete operational reasoning) that properties such as mass, volume, and number remain the same despite changes in the forms of objects. (p. 78)

continuity   The perceptual tendency to group stimuli into smooth, continuous patterns. (p. 140)

continuous reinforcement   Reinforcing the desired response every time it occurs. (p. 210)

control condition   The condition of an experiment that contrasts with the experimental treatment and serves as a comparison for evaluating the effect of the treatment. (p. 19)

convergence   A binocular cue for perceiving depth; the extent to which the eyes turn inward when looking at an object. (p. 142)

conversion disorder   A rare somatoform disorder in which a person experiences very specific, genuine physical symptoms for which no physiological basis can be found. (p. 423)

coronary heart disease   The clogging of the vessels that nourish the heart muscle. (p. 361)

corpus callosum [KOR-pus kah-LOW-sum]   The largest bundle of neural fibers connecting and carrying messages between the two brain hemispheres. (p. 59)

correlation   A statistical measure that indicates the extent to which two factors vary together and thus how well either factor predicts the other. (p. 14)

correlation coefficient   A statistical measure of the extent to which two factors vary together and thus how well either factor predicts the other. Scores with a *positive correlation coefficient* go up and down together (as with high school and college GPAs). A *negative correlation coefficient* indicates that one score falls as the other rises (as in the relationship between self-esteem and depression). (p. 530)

counterconditioning   A behavior therapy procedure that conditions new responses to stimuli that trigger unwanted behaviors; based on classical conditioning. (p. 455)

creativity   The ability to produce novel and valuable ideas. (p. 282)

critical period   An optimal period shortly after birth when an organism's exposure to certain influences produces proper development. (p. 82)

critical thinking   Thinking that does not blindly accept arguments and conclusions. Rather, it examines assumptions, discerns hidden values, evaluates evidence, and assesses conclusions. (p. 7)

cross-sectional study   A study in which people of different ages are tested or observed at the same point in time. (p. 101)

crystallized intelligence   One's accumulated knowledge and verbal skills; tends to increase with age. (p. 102)

culture   The enduring behaviors, ideas, attitudes, and traditions shared by a large group of people and transmitted from one generation to the next. (p. 494)

defense mechanisms   In psychoanalytic theory, the ego's protective methods of reducing anxiety by unconsciously distorting reality. (p. 381)

deindividuation   The loss of self-awareness and self-restraint occurring in group situations that foster arousal and anonymity. (p. 491)

déjà vu   (A French expression meaning "already seen.") That eerie sense that "I've experienced this before." Cues from the current situation may subconsciously trigger retrieval of an earlier experience. (p. 241)

delta waves   The large, slow brain waves associated with deep sleep. (p. 167)

delusions   False beliefs, often of persecution or grandeur, that may accompany schizophrenia. (p. 435)

dendrite   The bushy, branching extension of a neuron that receives messages and conducts impulses toward the cell body. (p. 36)

dependent variable   The experimental factor—in psychology, the behavior or mental process—that is being measured; the variable that may change in response to manipulations of the independent variable. (p. 19)

depressants   Drugs (such as alcohol, barbiturates, and opiates) that reduce neural activity and slow body functions. (p. 182)

depth perception   The ability to see objects in three dimensions although the images that strike the retina are two-dimensional; allows us to judge distance. (p. 141)

developmental psychology   A branch of psychology that studies physical, cognitive, and social change throughout the life span. (p. 69)

difference threshold   The minimum difference that a subject can detect between two stimuli 50 percent of the time. We experience the difference threshold as a just noticeable difference (jnd). (p. 121)

discrimination   In classical conditioning, the ability to distinguish between a conditioned stimulus and similar stimuli that do not signal an unconditioned stimulus. In operant conditioning, responding differently to stimuli that signal a behavior will be reinforced or will not be reinforced. (p. 201)

displacement   In psychoanalytic theory, the defense mechanism that shifts sexual or aggressive impulses toward a more acceptable or less threatening object or person, as when redirecting anger toward a safer outlet. (p. 382)

dissociation   A split in consciousness, which allows some thoughts and behaviors to occur simultaneously with others. (p. 178)

dissociative disorders   Disorders in which conscious awareness becomes separated (dissociated) from previous memories, thoughts, and feelings. (p. 423)

dissociative identity disorder   A rare dissociative disorder in which a person exhibits two or more distinct and alternating personalities. Also called *multiple personality disorder.* (p. 424)

DNA (deoxyribonucleic acid)   A complex molecule containing the genetic information that makes up the chromosomes. (p. 71)

double-blind procedure   An experimental procedure in which both the subject and the research staff are ignorant (blind) about whether the subject has received the treatment or a placebo. Commonly used in drug evaluation studies. (p. 21)

Down syndrome   A condition of retardation and associated physical disorders caused by an extra chromosome in one's genetic makeup. (p. 283)

drive-reduction theory   The idea that a physiological need creates an aroused tension state (a drive) that motivates an organism to satisfy the need. (p. 298)

DSM-IV   The American Psychiatric Association's *Diagnostic and Statistical Manual of Mental Disorders (Fourth Edition)*, a widely used system for classifying psychological disorders. (p. 417)

echoic memory   A momentary sensory memory of auditory stimuli; if attention is elsewhere, sounds and words can still be recalled within 3 or 4 seconds. (p. 233)

eclectic approach   An approach to psychotherapy that takes advantage of techniques from the various forms of therapy, depending on the client's problems. (p. 450)

effortful processing   Encoding that requires attention and conscious effort. (p. 226)

ego   The largely conscious, "executive" part of personality that, according to Freud, mediates among the demands of the id, superego, and reality. (p. 379)

egocentrism   In Piaget's theory, the inability of the preoperational child to take another's point of view. (p. 78)

electroconvulsive therapy (ECT)   Shock treatment. A biomedical therapy for severely depressed patients in which a brief electric current is sent through the brain of the anesthetized patient. (p. 473)

electroencephalogram (EEG)   An amplified recording of the waves of electrical activity that sweep across the brain's surface. These waves are measured by placing electrodes on the scalp. (p. 46)

embryo   The developing human organism from about 2 weeks after fertilization through the second month. (p. 72)

emotion   A response of the whole organism, involving (1) physiological arousal, (2) expressive behaviors, and (3) conscious experience. (p. 335)

empirically derived test   A test (such as the MMPI) developed by testing a pool of items and then selecting those that discriminate groups of interest. (p. 390)

encoding   The processing of information into the memory system, for example by extracting meaning. (p. 225)

endocrine [EN-duh-krin] **system**   The body's "slow" chemical communication system; a set of glands that secrete hormones into the bloodstream. (p. 43)

endorphins [en-DOR-fins]   "Morphine within"—natural, opiatelike neurotransmitters linked to pain control and to pleasure. (p. 39)

equity   A condition in which people receive from a relationship in proportion to what they give to it. (p. 516)

estrogen   A sex hormone, secreted in greater amounts by females than by males. In nonhuman female mammals, estrogen levels peak during ovulation, promoting sexual receptivity. (p. 313)

experiment   A research method in which the investigator manipulates one or more factors (independent variables) to observe their effect on some behavior or mental process (the dependent variable) while holding other factors constant. (p. 18)

experimental condition   The condition of an experiement that exposes subjects to the treatment. (p. 19)

explicit memory   Memory of facts and experiences that one can consciously know and "declare." (Also called *declarative memory*.) (p. 238)

external locus of control   The perception that chance or outside forces beyond one's personal control determine one's fate. (p. 403)

extinction   The diminishing of a response when, in classical conditioning, an unconditioned stimulus (UCS) does not follow a conditioned stimulus (CS); or when, in operant conditioning, a response is no longer reinforced. (p. 200)

extrasensory perception (ESP)   Perception that occurs without sensory input. A controversial notion, said to include telepathy, clairvoyance, and precognition. (p. 153)

extrinsic motivation   A desire to perform a behavior due to promised rewards or threats of punishment. (p. 324)

false consensus effect   The tendency to overestimate the extent to which others share our beliefs and behaviors. (p. 12)

family therapy   Therapy that treats the family as a system. Views an individual's unwanted behaviors as influenced by or directed at other family members; encourages family members toward positive relationships and improved communication. (p. 462)

feature detectors   Nerve cells in the brain that respond to specific features of the stimulus, such as movement, angle, or shape. (p. 127)

feel-good, do-good phenomenon   People's tendency to be helpful when already in a good mood. (p. 346)

fetal alcohol syndrome (FAS)   Physical and cognitive abnormalities in children caused by a pregnant woman's heavy drinking. In severe cases, symptoms include noticeable facial misproportions. (p. 72)

fetus   The developing human organism from 9 weeks after conception to birth. (p. 72)

figure-ground   The organization of the visual field into objects (the *figures*) that stand out from their surroundings (the *ground*). (p. 140)

fixation   1. The inability to see a problem from a new perspective; an impediment to problem solving. 2. According to Freud, a linger-

ing focus of pleasure-seeking energies at an earlier psychosexual stage, where conflicts were unresolved. (pp. 258, 380)

fixed-interval schedule   In operant conditioning, a schedule of reinforcement that reinforces the first response after a specified time. (p. 211)

fixed-ratio schedule   In operant conditioning, a schedule of reinforcement that reinforces a response only after a specified number of responses. (p. 210)

flashbulb memory   A clear memory of an emotionally significant moment or event. (p. 224)

fluid intelligence   One's ability to reason speedily and abstractly; tends to decrease during late adulthood. (p. 102)

foot-in-the-door phenomenon   The tendency for people who have first agreed to a small request to comply later with a larger request. (p. 482)

formal operational stage   In Piaget's theory, the stage of cognitive development (normally beginning about age 12) during which people begin to think logically about abstract concepts. (p. 79)

framing   The way an issue is posed; how an issue is framed can significantly affect decisions and judgments. (p. 262)

fraternal twins   Twins who develop from separate zygotes (fertilized eggs); who are genetically no closer than brothers and sisters, but shared the same fetal environment. (p. 108)

free association   In psychoanalysis, a method of exploring the unconscious in which the person relaxes and says whatever comes to mind, no matter how trivial or embarrassing. (p. 378)

frequency   The number of complete wavelengths that pass a point in a given time (for example, per second). (p. 132)

frontal lobes   The portion of the cerebral cortex lying just behind the forehead; involved in speaking and muscle movements and in making plans and judgments. (p. 52)

frustration-aggression principle   The principle that frustration—the blocking of an attempt to achieve some goal—creates anger, which can generate aggression. (p. 503)

fugue [fewg]   A dissociative disorder in which flight from one's home and identity accompanies amnesia. (p. 424)

functional fixedness   The tendency to think of things only in terms of their usual functions; an impediment to problem solving. (p. 259)

fundamental attribution error   The tendency for observers, when analyzing another's behavior, to underestimate the impact of the situation and to overestimate the impact of personal disposition. (p. 480)

gate-control theory   Melzack and Wall's theory that the spinal cord contains a neurological "gate" that blocks or allows pain signals to pass on to the brain. The "gate" is opened by the activity of pain signals traveling up small nerve fibers and closed by activity in larger fibers or by information coming from the brain. (p. 134)

gender   The social definition of male and female. (p. 86)

gender identity   One's sense of being male or female. (p. 86, 380)

gender role   A set of expected behaviors for males and for females. (p. 495)

gender schema theory The theory that children learn from their culture a concept of what it means to be male and female and that they adjust their behavior accordingly. (p. 86)

gender-typing The acquisition of a masculine or feminine gender identity and role. (p. 86)

general adaptation syndrome (GAS) Selye's concept of the body's adaptive response to stress as composed of three stages—alarm, resistance, exhaustion. (p. 357)

general intelligence (g) A general underlying intelligence factor believed by Spearman and others to be measured by every task on an intelligence test. (p. 281)

generalization The tendency, once a response has been conditioned, for stimuli similar to the conditioned stimulus to evoke similar responses. (p. 201)

generalized anxiety disorder An anxiety disorder in which a person is continually tense, apprehensive, and in a state of autonomic nervous system arousal. (p. 418)

genital stage The last of Freud's psychosexual stages, beginning in puberty, during which sexuality matures and the person seeks pleasure through sexual contact with others. (p. 380)

gestalt An organized whole. Gestalt psychologists emphasize our tendency to integrate pieces of information into meaningful wholes. (p. 139)

glucose The form of sugar that circulates in the blood and provides the major source of energy for body tissues. When its level is low, we feel hunger. (p. 302)

GRIT Graduated and Reciprocated Initiatives in Tension-Reduction—a strategy designed to decrease international tensions. (p. 520)

group polarization The enhancement of a group's prevailing attitudes through discussion within the group. (p. 492)

grouping The perceptual tendency to organize stimuli into coherent groups. (p. 140)

groupthink The mode of thinking that occurs when the desire for harmony in a decision-making group overrides a realistic appraisal of alternatives. (p. 492)

hallucinations False sensory experiences, such as seeing something without any external visual stimulus. (p. 186)

hallucinogens Psychedelic ("mind-manifesting") drugs, such as LSD, that distort perceptions and evoke sensory images in the absence of sensory input. (p. 182)

health psychology A subfield of psychology that provides psychology's contribution to behavioral medicine. (p. 356)

heritability The proportion of variation among individuals that we can attribute to genes. The heritability of a trait may vary, depending on the range of populations and environments studied. (p. 286)

heuristic A rule-of-thumb strategy that often allows us to make judgments and solve problems efficiently; usually speedier but also more error-prone than *algorithms*. (p. 257)

hierarchy of needs Maslow's pyramid of human needs, beginning at the base with physiological needs that must first be satisfied before higher-level safety needs and then psychological needs become active. (p. 300)

hindsight bias The tendency to believe, after learning an outcome, that one would have foreseen it. (Also known as the *I-knew-it-all-along phenomenon*.) (p. 8)

hippocampus A neural center located in the limbic system that helps process explicit memories for storage. (p. 238)

homeostasis A tendency to maintain a balanced or constant internal state; the regulation of any aspect of body chemistry, such as the level of glucose sugar in the blood, around a particular level. (p. 298)

hormones Chemical messengers, mostly those manufactured by the endocrine glands, that are produced in one tissue and affect other tissues. (p. 43)

hue The dimension of color that is determined by the wavelength of light; what we know as the color names "blue," "green," and so forth. (p. 124)

hypnosis An apparently heightened suggestibility in which some people narrow their focus of attention and claim to experience imaginary happenings as if they were real. (p. 175)

hypochondriasis A somatoform disorder in which a person misinterprets normal physical sensations as symptoms of a disease. (p. 423)

hypothalamus [hi-po-THAL-uh-muss] A neural structure lying below (*hypo*) the thalamus; it directs several maintenance activities (eating, drinking, body temperature), helps govern the endocrine system via the pituitary gland, and is linked to emotion. (p. 50)

hypothesis A testable prediction, often implied by a theory. (p. 10)

iconic memory A momentary sensory memory of visual stimuli; a photographic or picture-image memory lasting no more than a few tenths of a second. (p. 233)

id A reservoir of unconscious psychic energy that, according to Freud, strives to satisfy basic sexual and aggressive drives. (p. 379)

identical twins Twins who develop from a single zygote that splits in two, creating two genetic replicas. (p. 108)

identification The process by which, according to Freud, children incorporate their parents' values into their developing superegos. (p. 380)

identity One's sense of self; according to Erikson, the adolescent's task is to solidify a sense of self by testing and integrating various roles. (p. 93)

illusory correlation The perception of a relationship where none exists. (p. 14)

imagery Mental pictures; a powerful aid to effortful processing, especially when combined with a meaningful context. (p. 229)

implicit memory Retention without conscious recollection (of skills, preferences, and dispositions). (Also called *nondeclarative memory*.) (p. 238)

imprinting The process by which certain animals form attachments during a critical period very early in life. (p. 82)

incentives Positive or negative environmental stimuli that motivate behavior. (p. 299)

independent variable   The experimental factor that is manipulated; the variable whose effect is being studied. (p. 19)

individualism   Giving priority to one's own goals over group goals, and defining one's identity in terms of personal attributes rather than group identifications. (p. 398)

industrial/organizational psychology   A subfield of psychology that studies and advises on workplace behavior. Industrial/organizational (I/O) psychologists help organizations select and train employees, boost morale and productivity, and design products and assess responses to them. (p. 325)

informational social influence   Influence resulting from one's willingness to accept others' opinions about reality. (p. 486)

ingroup bias   The tendency to favor one's own group. (p. 499)

inner ear   The innermost part of the ear, containing the cochlea, semicircular canals, and vestibular sacs. (p. 132)

insight   A sudden and often novel realization of the solution to a problem; it contrasts with strategy-based solutions. (p. 257)

insomnia   A sleep disorder involving recurring problems in falling or staying asleep. (p. 170)

instinct   A complex behavior that is rigidly patterned throughout a species and is unlearned. (p. 298)

intelligence   The capacity for goal-directed and adaptive behavior; involves the abilities to profit from experience, solve problems, reason, and successfully meet challenges and achieve goals. (p. 275)

intelligence quotient (IQ)   Defined originally as the ratio of mental age (ma) to chronological age (ca) multiplied by 100 (thus, IQ = ma/ca × 100). On contemporary intelligence tests, the average performance for a given age is assigned a score of 100. (p. 277)

intensity   The amount of energy in a light or sound wave, which we perceive as brightness or loudness, as determined by the wave's amplitude. (p. 124)

interaction effect   A result in which the effect of one factor (such as genes) depends on the level of another (such as experience). (p. 110)

internal locus of control   The perception that one controls one's own fate. (p. 403)

interneurons   Central nervous system neurons that intervene directly between the sensory inputs and motor outputs. (p. 41)

interposition   A monocular cue for perceiving distance; nearby objects partially block our view of more distant objects. (p. 143)

interpretation   In psychoanalysis, the analyst's assisting the patient to note and understand resistances and other significant behaviors in order to promote insight. (p. 143, 451)

intimacy   In Erikson's theory, the ability to form close, loving relationships; a primary developmental task in late adolescence and early adulthood. (p. 93)

intrinsic motivation   A desire to perform a behavior for its own sake and to be effective. (p. 324)

iris   A ring of muscle tissue that forms the colored portion of the eye around the pupil and controls the size of the pupil opening. (p. 125)

James-Lange theory   The theory that our experience of emotion is our awareness of our physiological responses to emotion-arousing stimuli. (p. 352)

just noticeable difference (jnd)   See *difference threshold*. (p. 121)

just-world phenomenon   The tendency of people to believe the world is just and that people therefore get what they deserve and deserve what they get. (p. 500)

kinesthesis [kin-ehs-THEE-sehs]   The system for sensing the position and movement of individual body parts. (p. 138)

language   Our spoken, written, or gestured words and the ways we combine them to communicate meaning. (p. 264)

latency stage   The fourth of Freud's psychosexual stages, from about age 6 to puberty, during which sexual impulses are repressed. (p. 380)

latent content   According to Freud, the underlying but censored meaning of a dream (as distinct from its manifest content). Freud believed that a dream's latent content functions as a safety valve. (p. 172)

latent learning   Learning that occurs but is not apparent until there is an incentive to demonstrate it. (p. 213)

learned helplessness   The hopelessness and passive resignation learned when an animal or human is unable to avoid repeated aversive events. (p. 404)

learning   A relatively permanent change in an organism's behavior due to experience. (p. 195)

lens   The transparent structure behind the pupil that changes shape to focus images on the retina. (p. 125)

lesion [LEE-zhuhn]   To cause tissue destruction. A brain lesion is a naturally or experimentally caused destruction of brain tissue. (p. 46)

limbic system   A doughnut-shaped system of neural structures at the border of the brainstem and cerebral hemispheres; associated with emotions such as fear and aggression and drives such as those for food and sex. (p. 49)

linear perspective   A monocular cue for perceiving distance; we perceive the converging of what we know to be parallel lines as indicating increasing distance. (p. 143)

linguistic relativity   Whorf's hypothesis that language determines the way we think. (p. 272)

lithium   A chemical that provides an effective drug therapy for the mood swings of bipolar (manic-depressive) disorders. (p. 473)

lobotomy   A now-rare psychosurgical procedure once used to calm uncontrollably emotional or violent patients. In this procedure, the nerves that connect the frontal lobes to the emotion-controlling centers of the inner brain are cut. (p. 474)

long-term memory   The relatively permanent and limitless storehouse of the memory system. (p. 225)

long-term potentiation (LTP)   An increase in a synapse's firing potential after brief, rapid stimulation. Believed to be a neural basis for learning and memory. (p. 236)

longitudinal study   Research in which the same people are restudied and retested over a long time period. (p. 102)

LSD (*lysergic acid diethylamide*)   A powerful hallucinogenic drug; also known as "acid." (p. 186)

lymphocytes   The two types of white blood cells that are part of the body's immune system: one type releases antibodies that fight bacterial infections; the other attacks cancer cells, viruses, and foreign substances, among other duties. (p. 363)

major depressive disorder   A mood disorder in which a person, for no apparent reason, experiences 2 or more weeks of depressed moods, feelings of worthlessness, and diminished interest or pleasure in most activities. (p. 426)

mania   A mood disorder marked by a hyperactive, wildly optimistic state. (p. 427)

manifest content   According to Freud, the remembered story line of a dream (as distinct from its latent content). (p. 172)

maturation   Biological growth processes that enable orderly changes in behavior, relatively uninfluenced by experience. (p. 74)

mean   The arithmetic average of a distribution, obtained by adding the scores and then dividing by the number of scores. (p. 528)

median   The middle score in a distribution; half the scores are above it and half below it. (p. 528)

medical model   The concept that diseases have physical causes that can be diagnosed, treated, and, in most cases, cured. When applied to psychological disorders, the medical model assumes that these "mental" illnesses can be diagnosed on the basis of their symptoms and cured through therapy, which may include treatment in a psychiatric hospital. (p. 416)

medulla [muh-DUL-uh]   The base of the brainstem; controls heartbeat and breathing. (p. 45)

memory   The persistence of learning over time via storage and retrieval of information. (p. 223)

menarche [meh-NAR-key]   The first menstrual period. (p. 88)

menopause   The time of natural cessation of menstruation; also refers to the biological changes experienced during a woman's years of declining ability to reproduce. (p. 98)

mental age   A measure of intelligence test performance devised by Binet; the chronological age that most typically corresponds to a given level of performance. Thus, a child who does as well as the average 8-year-old is said to have a mental age of 8. (p. 276)

mental retardation   A condition of limited mental ability, as indicated by an intelligence score below 70, that produces difficulty in adapting to the demands of life; varies from mild to profound. (p. 283)

mere exposure effect   The phenomenon that repeated exposure to novel stimuli increases liking of them. (p. 512)

metabolic rate   The body's base rate of energy expenditure. (p. 303)

middle ear   The chamber between the eardrum and cochlea containing three tiny bones (hammer, anvil, and stirrup) that concentrate the vibrations of the eardrum on the cochlea's oval window. (p. 132)

Minnesota Multiphasic Personality Inventory (MMPI)   The most widely researched and clinically used of all personality tests. Originally developed to identify emotionally troubled people (still considered its most appropriate use), this test is now used for many other screening purposes. (p. 390)

misinformation effect   After witnessing an event and receiving misleading information about it, incorporating the "misinformation" into one's memory of the event. (p. 243)

mnemonics [nih-MON-iks]   Memory aids, especially those techniques that use vivid imagery and organizational devices. (p. 229)

mode   The most frequently occurring score in a distribution. (p. 528)

modeling   The process by which a behavior is observed and imitated. (p. 217)

monocular cues   Distance cues, such as linear perspective and interposition, available to either eye alone. (p. 142)

mood-congruent memory   The tendency to recall experiences that are consistent with one's current good or bad mood. (p. 242)

mood disorders   Psychological disorders characterized by emotional extremes. (p. 426)

motivation   A need or desire that energizes and directs behavior. (p. 297)

motor cortex   An area at the rear of the frontal lobes that controls voluntary movements. (p. 52)

motor neurons   The neurons that carry outgoing information from the central nervous system to the muscles and glands. (p. 41)

MRI (magnetic resonance imaging)   A technique that uses magnetic fields and radio waves to produce computer-generated images that distinguish among different types of soft tissue; this allows us to see structures within the brain. (p. 47)

myelin [MY-uh-lin] **sheath**   A layer of fatty cells segmentally encasing the fibers of many neurons; makes possible a vastly greater transmission speed of neural impulses. (p. 36)

narcolepsy   A sleep disorder characterized by uncontrollable sleep attacks in which the sufferer lapses directly into REM sleep, often at inopportune times. (p. 170)

naturalistic observation   Observing and recording behavior in naturally occurring situations without trying to manipulate and control the situation. (p. 13)

nature-nurture issue   The long-standing controversy over the relative contributions of genes and experience to the development of psychological traits and behaviors. (p. 3)

near-death experience   An altered state of consciousness reported after a close brush with death (such as through cardiac arrest); often similar to drug-induced hallucinations. (p. 186)

need to belong   A motivation to form and maintain enduring, close personal relationships. (p. 328)

nerves   Neural "cables" containing many axons. These bundled axons, which are part of the peripheral nervous system, connect the central nervous system with muscles, glands, and sense organs. (p. 41)

nervous system   The body's speedy, electrochemical communication system, consisting of all the nerve cells of the peripheral and central nervous systems. (p. 41)

neuron   A nerve cell; the basic building block of the nervous system. (p. 36)

neurotransmitters   Chemical messengers that traverse the synaptic gaps between neurons.   When released by the sending neuron, neurotransmitters travel across the synapse and bind to receptor sites on the receiving neuron, thereby influencing whether it will generate a neural impulse. (p. 38)

night terrors   A sleep disorder characterized by high arousal and an appearance of being terrified; unlike nightmares, night terrors occur during Stage 4 sleep, within 2 or 3 hours of falling asleep, and are seldom remembered. (p. 171)

normal curve   The symmetrical bell-shaped curve that describes the distribution of many physical and psychological attributes in a group of people. Most intelligence scores fall near the average, and fewer and fewer scores lie near the extremes. (pp. 279, 529)

normative social influence   Influence resulting from a person's desire to gain approval or avoid disapproval. (p. 486)

norms   Understood rules for accepted and expected behavior. Norms prescribe "proper" behavior. (p. 486)

object permanence   The awareness that things continue to exist even when not perceived. (p. 77)

observational learning   Learning by observing and imitating the behavior of others. (p. 217)

obsessive-compulsive disorder   An anxiety disorder characterized by unwanted repetitive thoughts (obsessions) and/or actions (compulsions). (p. 418)

occipital [ahk-SIP-uh-tuhl] **lobes**   The portion of the cerebral cortex lying at the back of the head; includes the visual areas, each of which receives visual information from the opposite visual field. (p. 52)

Oedipus [ED-uh-puss] **complex**   According to Freud, a boy's sexual desires toward his mother and feelings of jealousy and hatred for the rival father. According to some other psychoanalysts, a parallel Electra complex occurs in girls. (p. 380)

one-word stage   The stage in speech development, from about age 1 to 2, during which a child speaks mostly in single words. (p. 266)

operant behavior   Behavior that operates on the environment, producing consequences. (p. 206)

operant conditioning   A type of learning in which behavior is strengthened if followed by reinforcement or diminished if followed by punishment. (p. 206)

operational definition   A statement of the procedures (operations) used to define research variables. (p. 19)

opiates   Opium and its derivatives, such as morphine and heroin; they depress neural activity, temporarily lessening pain and anxiety. (p. 184)

opponent-process theory   The theory that opposing retinal processes (red-green, yellow-blue, white-black) enable color vision. For example, some cells are stimulated by green and inhibited by red; others are stimulated by red and inhibited by green. (p. 130)

optic nerve   The nerve that carries neural impulses from the eye to the brain. (p. 126)

oral stage   The first of Freud's psychosexual stages, from birth to about 18 months, during which sensual pleasure centers on the mouth through sucking, biting, and chewing. (p. 380)

overconfidence   The tendency to be more confident than correct—to overestimate the accuracy of one's beliefs and judgments. (p. 261)

panic attack   An anxiety disorder marked by a minutes-long episode of intense dread in which a person experiences terror and accompanying chest pain, choking, or other frightening sensations. (p. 419)

parallel processing   Information processing in which several aspects of a problem are processed simultaneously. The brain's natural mode of information processing for many functions, including vision; contrasts with the step-by-step (serial) processing of most computers and of conscious problem solving. (p. 128)

parapsychology   The study of paranormal phenomena including ESP and psychokinesis. (p. 154)

parasympathetic nervous system   The division of the autonomic nervous system that calms the body, conserving its energy. (p. 42)

parietal [puh-RYE-uh-tuhl] **lobes**   The portion of the cerebral cortex lying at the top of the head and toward the rear; includes the sensory cortex. (p. 52)

partial reinforcement   Reinforcing a response only part of the time; results in slower acquisition of a response but much greater resistance to extinction than does continuous reinforcement. (p. 210)

passionate love   An aroused state of intense positive absorption in another, usually present at the beginning of a love relationship. (p. 515)

percentile rank   The percentage of the scores in a distribution that fall below a given score. (p. 526)

perception   The process of organizing and interpreting sensory information, enabling us to recognize meaningful objects and events. (p. 117)

perceptual adaptation   In vision, the ability to adjust to an artificially displaced or even inverted visual field. (p. 149)

perceptual constancy   Perceiving objects as unchanging (having consistent lightness, color, shape, and size) even as illumination and retinal images change. (p. 145)

perceptual set   A mental predisposition to perceive one thing and not another. (p. 150)

peripheral nervous system (PNS)   The neurons that connect the central nervous system to the rest of the body.   It consists of the sensory neurons, which carry messages to the central nervous system from the body's sense receptors, and the motor neurons, which carry messages from the central nervous system to the muscles and glands. (p. 41)

person-centered therapy   A humanistic therapy, developed by Carl Rogers, in which the therapist uses techniques such as active listening within a genuine, accepting, empathic environment to facilitate clients' growth. (p. 453)

personal control   Our sense of controlling our environments rather than feeling helpless. (p. 403)

personal space   The buffer zone we like to maintain around our bodies. (p. 494)

personality   An individual's characteristic pattern of thinking, feeling, and acting. (p. 377)

personality disorders   Psychological disorders characterized by inflexible and enduring behavior patterns that impair social functioning. (p. 440)

personality inventory   A questionnaire (often with true-false or agree-disagree items) on which people respond to items designed to gauge a wide range of feelings and behaviors; used to assess selected personality traits. (p. 390)

PET (positron emission tomograph) scan   A visual display of brain activity that detects where a radioactive form of glucose goes while the brain performs a given task. (p. 47)

phallic stage   The third of Freud's psychosexual stages, from about ages 3 to 6, during which the pleasure zone is the genitals and sexual feelings arise toward the parent of the other sex. (p. 380)

phobic disorder   An anxiety disorder marked by a persistent, irrational fear of a specific object or situation. (p. 418)

physical dependence   A physiological need for a drug, with unpleasant withdrawal symptoms when use is discontinued. (p. 182)

pitch   A tone's highness or lowness; depends on frequency. (p. 132)

pituitary gland   The endocrine system's most influential gland. The pituitary regulates growth and controls other endocrine glands. (p. 44)

placebo [plu-see-bo]   An inert substance or condition that may be administered instead of a presumed active agent, such as a drug, to see if it triggers the effects believed to characterize the active agent. (p. 21)

plasticity   The brain's capacity for modification, as evident in brain reorganization following damage (especially in children) and in experiments on the effects of experience on brain development. (p. 58)

pleasure principle   The id's demand for immediate gratification. (p. 379)

polygraph   A machine, commonly used in attempts to detect lies, that measures several of the physiological responses accompanying emotion (such as perspiration, heart rate, blood pressure, and breathing changes). (p. 337)

population   A whole group under study, from which samples may be drawn. (p. 12)

posthypnotic amnesia   Supposed inability to recall what one experienced during hypnosis; induced by the hypnotist's suggestion. (p. 178)

posthypnotic suggestion   A suggestion, made during a hypnosis session, to be carried out after the subject is no longer hypnotized; used by some clinicians to help control the symptoms of certain ailments. (p. 178)

preconscious   A store of information that is not conscious, but is retrievable into conscious awareness. (p. 378)

prejudice   An unjustifiable (and usually negative) attitude toward a group and its members. Prejudice generally involves stereotyped beliefs, negative feelings, and a predisposition to discriminatory action. (p. 496)

preoperational stage   In Piaget's theory, the stage (from about 2 to 6 or 7 years of age) during which a child learns to use language but does not yet comprehend the mental operations of concrete logic. (p. 78)

primary reinforcer   An innately reinforcing stimulus, such as one that satisfies a biological need. (p. 209)

primary sex characteristics   The body structures (ovaries and testes) that make sexual reproduction possible. (p. 88)

priming   The activation, often unconscious, of particular associations in memory. (p. 240)

proactive interference   The disruptive effect of prior learning on the recall of new information. (p. 246)

projection   In psychoanalytic theory, the defense mechanism by which people disguise their own threatening impulses by attributing them to others. (p. 382)

projective tests   Personality tests, such as the Rorschach and TAT, that provide ambiguous stimuli designed to trigger projection of one's inner dynamics. (p. 384)

prosocial behavior   Positive, constructive, helpful behavior. The opposite of antisocial behavior. (p. 218)

prototype   The best example of a category; matching new items to the prototype provides a quick and easy method for including items in a category (as when comparing feathered creatures to a prototypical bird, such as a robin). (p. 256)

proximity   The perceptual tendency to group together visual and auditory events that are near each other. (p. 140)

psychiatry   A branch of medicine dealing with psychological disorders; practiced by physicians and sometimes involving medical (for example, drug) treatments as well as psychological therapy. (p. 6)

psychoactive drug   A chemical substance that alters mood and perceptions. (p. 181)

psychoanalysis   Freud's technique of treating psychological disorders by seeking to expose and interpret unconscious tensions. The patient's free associations, resistances, dreams, and transferences—and the therapist's interpretations of them—release previously repressed feelings, allowing the patient to gain self-insight. Freud's psychoanalytic theory of personality sought to explain what he observed during psychoanalysis. (p. 378, 450)

psychological dependence   A psychological need to use a drug, such as to relieve negative emotions. (p. 182)

psychological disorder   A condition in which behavior is judged atypical, disturbing, maladaptive, and unjustifiable. (p. 415)

psychology   The science of behavior and mental processes. (p. 3)

psychopharmacology   The study of the effects of drugs on mind and behavior. (p. 470)

psychophysics   The study of relationships between the physical characteristics of stimuli and our psychological experience of them. (p. 118)

psychophysiological illness   Literally, "mind–body" illness; any stress-related physical illness, such as hypertension, ulcers, and headaches. Note: This is distinct from hypochondriasis—misinterpreting normal physical sensations as symptoms of a disease. (p. 363)

psychosexual stages   The childhood stages of development (oral, anal, phallic, latency, genital) during which, according to Freud, the id's pleasure-seeking energies focus on distinct erogenous zones. (p. 380)

psychosurgery   Surgery that removes or destroys brain tissue in an effort to change behavior. (p. 474)

psychotherapy   An emotionally charged, confiding interaction between a trained therapist and someone who suffers a psychological difficulty. (p. 449)

puberty   The time of sexual maturation, when one first becomes capable of reproducing. (p. 88)

punishment   An aversive event that *decreases* the behavior it follows. (p. 211)

pupil   The adjustable opening in the center of the eye through which light enters. (p. 125)

random assignment   Assigning subjects to experimental and control conditions by chance, thus minimizing preexisting differences between those assigned to the different groups. (p. 19)

random sample   A sample that fairly represents a population because each member has an equal chance of inclusion. (p. 12)

range   The difference between the highest and lowest scores in a distribution. (p. 529)

rational-emotive therapy   A confrontational cognitive therapy, developed by Albert Ellis, that vigorously challenges people's illogical, self-defeating attitudes and assumptions. Also recently called *rational-emotive behavior therapy* by Ellis, emphasizing a behavioral "homework" component. (p. 459)

rationalization   In psychoanalytic theory, a defense mechanism that offers self-justifying explanations in place of the real, more threatening, unconscious reasons for one's actions. (p. 382)

reaction formation   In psychoanalytic theory, a defense mechanism by which the ego unconsciously switches unacceptable impulses into their opposites. Thus, people may express feelings that are the opposite of their anxiety-arousing unconscious feelings. (p. 381)

reality principle   The ego's tendency to satisfy the id's desires in ways that will realistically bring pleasure rather than pain. (p. 379)

recall   A measure of memory in which the person must retrieve information learned earlier, as on a fill-in-the-blank test. (p. 240)

reciprocal determinism   The interacting influences between personality and environmental factors. (p. 402)

recognition   A measure of memory in which the person need only identify items previously learned, as on a multiple-choice test. (p. 240)

reflex   A simple, automatic, inborn response to a sensory stimulus, such as the knee-jerk response. (p. 42)

refractory period   A resting period after orgasm, during which a man cannot achieve another orgasm. (p. 312)

regression   In psychoanalytic theory, an individual's retreat, when faced with anxiety, to a more infantile psychosexual stage where some psychic energy remains fixated. (p. 381)

regression toward the mean   The tendency for extremes of unusual scores to fall back (regress) toward the average. (p. 531)

rehearsal   The conscious repetition of information, either to maintain it in consciousness or to encode it for storage. (p. 226)

reinforcer   In operant conditioning, any event that *strengthens* the behavior it follows. (p. 208)

relative brightness   A monocular cue for perceiving distance; dimmer objects appear more distant. (p. 144)

relative deprivation   The perception that one is worse off relative to those with whom one compares oneself. (p. 349)

relative height   A monocular cue for perceiving distance; higher objects appear more distant. (p. 143)

relative motion   A monocular cue for perceiving distance; when we move, objects at different distances change their relative positions in our visual image, with those closest moving fastest. (p. 143)

relative size   A monocular cue for perceiving distance; when we assume two objects are the same size, the one that produces the smaller image appears more distant. (p. 142)

relearning   A memory measure that assesses the amount of time saved when relearning previously learned information. (p. 240)

reliability   The extent to which a test yields consistent results, as assessed by the consistency of scores on two halves of the test, on alternative forms of the test, or on retesting. (p. 279)

REM rebound   The tendency for REM sleep to increase following REM sleep deprivation (created by repeated awakenings during REM sleep). (p. 174)

REM sleep   Rapid eye movement sleep; a recurring sleep stage during which vivid dreams commonly occur. Also known as paradoxical sleep because the muscles are relaxed (except for minor twitches) but other body systems are active. (p. 166)

replication   Repeating the essence of a research study, usually with different subjects in different situations, to see whether the basic finding generalizes to other subjects and circumstances. (p. 11)

representativeness heuristic   A rule of thumb for judging the likelihood of things in terms of how well they seem to represent, or match, particular prototypes; may lead one to ignore other relevant information. (p. 259)

repression   In psychoanalytic theory, the basic defense mechanism that banishes anxiety–arousing thoughts, feelings, and memories from consciousness. (p. 247)

resistance   In psychoanalysis, the blocking from consciousness of anxiety-laden material. (p. 451)

respondent behavior   Behavior that occurs as an automatic response to some stimulus; Skinner's term for behavior learned through classical conditioning. (p. 206)

reticular formation   A nerve network in the brainstem that plays an important role in controlling arousal. (p. 48)

retina   The light-sensitive inner surface of the eye, containing the receptor rods and cones plus layers of neurons that begin the processing of visual information. (p. 125)

retinal disparity   A binocular cue for perceiving depth; the greater the disparity (difference) between the two images the retina receives of an object, the closer the object is to us. (p. 142)

retrieval   The process of getting information out of memory storage. (p. 225)

retroactive interference   The disruptive effect of new learning on the recall of old information. (p. 246)

rods   Retinal receptors that detect black, white, and gray; necessary for peripheral and twilight vision, when cones don't respond. (p. 126)

role   A set of expectations about a social position, defining how those in the position ought to behave. (p. 483)

rooting reflex   A baby's tendency, when touched on the cheek, to open the mouth and search for the nipple. (p. 73)

Rorschach inkblot test   The most widely used projective test, a set of 10 inkblots, designed by Hermann Rorschach; seeks to identify people's inner feelings by analyzing their interpretation of the blots. (p. 384)

savant syndrome   A condition in which a person otherwise limited in mental ability has an amazing specific skill, such as in computation or drawing. (p. 281)

scapegoat theory   The theory that prejudice provides an outlet for anger by providing someone to blame. (p. 499)

scatterplot   A graphed cluster of dots, each of which represents the values of two variables (such as a student's high school and college GPAs). The slope of the points suggests the degree and direction of the relationship between the two variables. Also called a *scatter-gram* or *scatter diagram*. (p. 530)

schema   A concept or framework that organizes and interprets information. (p. 76)

schizophrenia   A group of severe disorders characterized by disorganized and deluded thinking, disturbed perceptions, and inappropriate emotions and actions. (p. 434)

secondary reinforcer   A conditioned reinforcer; a stimulus that gains its reinforcing power by association with a primary reinforcer. (p. 209)

secondary sex characteristics   Nonreproductive sexual characteristics, such as female breasts and hips, male voice quality, and body hair. (p. 88)

selective attention   The focusing of conscious awareness on a particular stimulus, as in the *cocktail party effect*. (p. 164)

self-actualization   According to Maslow, the ultimate psychological need that arises after basic physical and psychological needs are met and self-esteem is achieved; the motivation to fulfill one's potential. (p. 394)

self-concept   All our thoughts and feelings about ourselves, in answer to the question, "Who am I?" (p. 395)

self-disclosure   Revealing intimate aspects of oneself to others. (p. 516)

self-esteem   One's feelings of high or low self-worth. (p. 396)

self-serving bias   A readiness to perceive oneself favorably. (p. 396)

sensation   The process by which our sense receptors and nervous system receive and represent stimulus energies from our environment. (p. 117)

sensorimotor stage   In Piaget's theory, the stage (from birth to about 2 years of age) during which infants know the world mostly in terms of their sensory impressions and motor activities. (p. 76)

sensory adaptation   Diminished sensitivity that is a consequence of constant stimulation. (p. 122)

sensory cortex   The area at the front of the parietal lobes that registers and processes body sensations. (p. 53)

sensory interaction   The principle that one sense may influence another, as when the smell of food influences its taste. (p. 136)

sensory memory   The immediate, initial recording of sensory information in the memory system. (p. 233)

sensory neurons   Neurons that carry incoming information from the sense receptors to the central nervous system. (p. 41)

serial position effect   Our tendency to recall best the last and first items in a list. (p. 227)

set point   The point at which an individual's "weight thermostat" is supposedly set. When the body falls below this weight, an increase in hunger and a lowered metabolic rate may act to restore the lost weight. (p. 302)

sexual dysfunction   A problem that consistently impairs sexual arousal or functioning. (p. 315)

sexual orientation   An enduring sexual attraction toward members of either one's own gender (homosexual orientation) or the other gender (heterosexual orientation). (p. 317)

sexual response cycle   The four stages of sexual response described by Masters and Johnson—excitement, plateau, orgasm, and resolution. (p. 312)

shaping   An operant conditioning procedure in which reinforcers guide behavior toward closer and closer approximations of a desired goal. (p. 207)

short-term memory   Activated memory that holds a few items briefly, such as the seven digits of a phone number while dialing, before the information is stored or forgotten. (p. 225)

similarity   The perceptual tendency to group together similar elements. (p. 140)

skeletal nervous system   The division of the peripheral nervous system that controls the body's skeletal muscles. (p. 41)

Skinner box   A chamber containing a bar or key that an animal can manipulate to obtain a food or water reinforcer, with attached devices to record the animal's rate of bar pressing or key pecking. Used in operant conditioning research. (p. 207)

sleep apnea   A sleep disorder characterized by temporary cessations of breathing during sleep and consequent momentary reawakenings. (p. 171)

social clock   The culturally preferred timing of social events such as marriage, parenthood, and retirement. (p. 104)

social exchange theory   The theory that our social behavior is an exchange process, the aim of which is to maximize benefits and minimize costs. (p. 518)

social facilitation   Improved performance of tasks in the presence of others; occurs with simple or well-learned tasks but not with tasks that are difficult or not yet mastered. (p. 490)

social leadership   Group-oriented leadership that builds teamwork, mediates conflict, and offers support. (p. 327)

social learning theory   The theory that we learn social behavior by observing and imitating and by being rewarded or punished. (p. 86)

social loafing   The tendency for people in a group to exert less effort when pooling their efforts toward attaining a common goal than when individually accountable. (p. 491)

social psychology   The scientific study of how we think about, influence, and relate to one another. (p. 479)

social traps   Situations in which the conflicting parties, by each rationally pursuing their self-interest, become caught in mutually destructive behavior. (p. 509)

social-cognitive perspective   Applies interactive principles of social learning and cognition to study how the environment shapes people's behavior and beliefs, and how these in turn influence people's situations. (p. 402)

somatoform disorders   Psychological disorders in which the symptoms take a somatic (bodily) form without apparent physical cause. (p. 422)

spacing effect   The tendency for distributed study or practice to yield better long-term retention than is achieved through massed study or practice. (p. 227)

split brain   A condition in which the two hemispheres of the brain are isolated by cutting the connecting fibers (mainly those of the corpus callosum) between them. (p. 59)

spontaneous recovery   The reappearance, after a rest period, of an extinguished conditioned response. (p. 201)

SQ3R   A study method incorporating five steps: *Survey, Question, Read, Rehearse, Review.* (p. 29)

standard deviation   A measure of score variability; computed by (1) calculating the deviation of each score from the mean, (2) squaring those deviations, (3) finding their average, and (4) finding the square root of this average. (p. 529)

standardization   Defining meaningful scores by comparison with the performance of a pretested "standardization group." (p. 279)

Stanford-Binet   The widely used American revision (by Terman at Stanford University) of Binet's original intelligence test. (p. 277)

stereotype   A generalized (often overgeneralized) belief about a group of people. (p. 497)

stimulants   Drugs (such as caffeine, nicotine, and the more powerful amphetamines and cocaine) that excite neural activity and speed up body functions. (p. 182)

storage   The retention of encoded information over time. (p. 225)

stranger anxiety   The fear of strangers that infants commonly display, beginning by about 8 months of age. (p. 81)

stress   The process by which we perceive and respond to certain events, called stressors, that we appraise as threatening or challenging. (p. 357)

sublimation   In psychoanalytic theory, the defense mechanism by which people rechannel their unacceptable impulses into socially approved activities. (p. 382)

subliminal   Below one's absolute threshold for conscious awareness. (p. 119)

superego   The part of personality that, according to Freud, represents internalized ideals and provides standards for judgment (the conscience) and for future aspirations. (p. 380)

superordinate goals   Shared goals that override differences among people and require their cooperation. (p. 519)

survey   A technique for ascertaining self-reported attitudes or behaviors of people, usually by questioning a representative, random sample of them. (p. 12)

sympathetic nervous system   The division of the autonomic nervous system that arouses the body, mobilizing its energy in stressful situations. (p. 42)

synapse [SIN-aps]   The junction between the axon tip of the sending neuron and the dendrite or cell body of the receiving neuron. The tiny gap at this junction is called the *synaptic gap* or cleft. (p. 37)

systematic desensitization   A type of counterconditioning that associates a pleasant relaxed state with gradually increasing anxiety-triggering stimuli. Commonly used to treat phobias. (p. 455)

task leadership   Goal-oriented leadership that sets standards, organizes work, and focuses attention on goals. (p. 327)

telegraphic speech   Early stage of speaking in which the child's speech is like a telegram—"go car"—using mostly nouns and verbs and omitting "auxiliary" words. (p. 266)

temperament   A person's characteristic emotional reactivity and intensity. (p. 82)

temporal lobes   The portion of the cerebral cortex lying roughly above the ears; includes the auditory areas, each of which receives auditory information primarily from the opposite ear. (p. 52)

teratogens   Agents, such as chemicals and viruses, that can reach the embryo or fetus during prenatal development and cause harm. (p. 72)

testosterone   The most important of the male sex hormones. Both males and females have it, but the additional testosterone in males stimulates the growth of the male sex organs in the fetus and the development of the male sex characteristics during puberty. (p. 71)

thalamus [THAL-uh-muss]   The brain's sensory switchboard, located on top of the brainstem; it directs messages to the sensory receiving areas in the cortex and transmits replies to the cerebellum and medulla. (p. 48)

THC   The major active ingredient in marijuana; triggers a variety of effects, including mild hallucinations. (p. 187)

Thematic Apperception Test (TAT)   A projective test in which people express their inner feelings and interests through the stories they make up about ambiguous scenes. (p. 384)

theory   An explanation using an integrated set of principles that organizes and predicts observations. (p. 10)

threshold   The level of stimulation required to trigger a neural impulse. (p. 37)

token economy   An operant conditioning procedure that rewards desired behavior. A patient exchanges a token of some sort, earned for exhibiting the desired behavior, for various privileges or treats. (p. 458)

tolerance   The diminishing of a drug's effect with regular use of the same dose, requiring the user to take larger and larger doses before experiencing the drug's effect. (p. 182)

trait   A characteristic pattern of behavior or conscious motive; assessed by self-report inventories and peer reports. (p. 387)

transference In psychoanalysis, the patient's transfer to the analyst of emotions linked with other relationships (such as love or hatred for a parent). (p. 451)

two-factor theory Schachter's theory that to experience emotion one must (1) be physically aroused and (2) cognitively label the arousal. (p. 353)

two-word stage Beginning about age 2, the stage in speech development during which a child speaks mostly two-word statements. (p. 266)

Type A Friedman and Rosenman's term for competitive, hard-driving, impatient, verbally aggressive, and anger-prone people. (p. 362)

Type B Friedman and Rosenman's term for easygoing, relaxed people. (p. 362)

unconditional positive regard According to Rogers, an attitude of total acceptance toward another person. (p. 394)

unconditioned response (UCR) In classical conditioning, the unlearned, naturally occurring response to the unconditioned stimulus (UCS), such as salivation when food is in the mouth. (p. 199)

unconditioned stimulus (UCS) In classical conditioning, a stimulus that unconditionally—naturally and automatically—triggers a response. (p. 199)

unconscious According to Freud, a reservoir of mostly unacceptable thoughts, wishes, feelings, and memories. According to contemporary research psychologists, information processing of which we are unaware. (p. 378)

validity The extent to which a test measures or predicts what it is supposed to. (p. 280)

variable-interval schedule In operant conditioning, a schedule of reinforcement that reinforces a response at unpredictable time intervals. (p. 211)

variable-ratio schedule In operant conditioning, a schedule of reinforcement that reinforces a response after an unpredictable number of responses. (p. 210)

vestibular sense The sense of the head's movement and position, including the sense of balance. (p. 138)

visual capture The tendency for vision to dominate the other senses; we perceive voices in films as coming from the screen we see rather than from the projector behind us. (p. 131)

visual cliff A laboratory device for testing depth perception in infants and young animals. (p. 141)

wavelength The distance from the peak of one light or sound wave to the peak of the next. Electromagnetic wavelengths vary from the long pulses of radio transmission to the short blips of cosmic rays. (p. 124)

Weber's law The principle that, to be perceived as different, two stimuli must differ by a constant minimum percentage (rather than a constant amount). (p. 121)

Wechsler Adult Intelligence Scale (WAIS) The current revision (WAIS-R) is the most widely used intelligence test; contains verbal and performance (nonverbal) subtests. (p. 277)

Wernicke's area An area of the left temporal lobe involved in language comprehension. (p. 55)

withdrawal The discomfort and distress that follow the discontinued use of addictive drugs. (p. 182)

X chromosome The sex chromosome found in both men and women. Females have two X chromosomes; males have one. An X chromosome from each parent produces a female. (p. 71)

Y chromosome The sex chromosome found only in males. Paired with an X sex chromosome from the mother, it produces a male child. (p. 71)

Young-Helmholtz trichromatic (three-color) theory The theory that the retina contains three diferent color receptors—one most sensitive to red, one to green, one to blue—which when combined can produce the perception of any color. (p. 129)

zygote The fertilized egg; it enters a 2-week period of rapid cell division and develops into an embryo. (p. 71)

References

Aas, H., & Klepp, K-I. (1992). Adolescents' alcohol use related to perceived norms. *Scandinavian Journal of Psychology, 33,* 315–325. (p. 190)

Abbey, A. (1987). Misperceptions of friendly behavior as sexual interest: A survey of naturally occurring incidents. *Psychology of Women Quarterly, 11,* 173–194. (p. 316)

Abbey, A. (1991). Acquaintance rape and alcohol consumption on college campuses: How are they linked? *Journal of American College Health, 39,* 165–169. (p. 182)

Abbey, A., Ross, L. T., & McDuffie, D. (1993). Alcohol's role in sexual assault. In R. R. Watson (Ed.), *Drug and alcohol abuse reviews. Vol. 5: Addictive behaviors in women.* Totowa, NJ: Humana Press. (p. 503)

ABC News. (1993). "Hello, tele-psychic," a "Primetime Live" program summarized by *Skeptical Briefs,* March, 1993, p. 8. (p. 154)

Abrams, D. (1991). AIDS: What young people believe and what they do. Paper presented at the British Association for the Advancement of Science conference. (p. 405)

Abrams, D. B., & Wilson, G. T. (1983). Alcohol, sexual arousal, and self-control. *Journal of Personality and Social Psychology, 45,* 188–198. (p. 183)

Abramson, L. Y., Metalsky, G. I., & Alloy, L. B. (1989). Hopelessness depression: A theory-based subtype. *Psychological Review, 96,* 358–372. (p. 431)

Adelmann, P. K., Antonucci, T. C., Crohan, S. F., & Coleman, L. M. (1989). Empty nest, cohort, and employment in the well-being of midlife women. *Sex Roles, 20,* 173–189. (p. 105)

Ader, R., & Cohen, N. (1985). CNS-immune system interactions: Conditioning phenomena. *Behavioral and Brain Sciences, 8,* 379–394. (p. 366)

Adler, N. E., David, H. P., Major, B. N., Roth, S. H., Russo, N. F., & Wyatt, G. E. (1990). Psychological responses after abortion. *Science, 248,* 41–44. (p. 359)

Advertising Age (1958, February 10). "Phone now," said CBC subliminally—but nobody did. p. 8. (p. 121)

Affleck, G., Tennen, H., Urrows, S., & Higgins, P. (1994). Person and contextual features of daily stress reactivity: Individual differences in relations of undesirable daily events with mood disturbance and chronic pain intensity. *Journal of Personality and Social Psychology, 66,* 329–340. (p. 347)

Aiello, J. R., Thompson, D. D., & Brodzinsky, D. M. (1983). How funny is crowding anyway? Effects of room size, group size, and the introduction of humor. *Basic and Applied Social Psychology, 4,* 193–207. (p. 490)

Ainsworth, M. D. S. (1973). The development of infant-mother attachment. In B. Caldwell & H. Ricciuti (Eds.), *Review of child development research* (Vol. 3). Chicago: University of Chicago Press. (p. 82)

Ainsworth, M. D. S. (1979). Infant-mother attachment. *American Psychologist, 34,* 932–937. (p. 83)

Ainsworth, M. D. S. (1989). Attachments beyond infancy. *American Psychologist, 44,* 709–716. (p. 82)

Albee, G. W. (1986). Toward a just society: Lessons from observations on the primary prevention of psychopathology. *American Psychologist, 41,* 891–898. (p. 475)

Alcock, J. E. (1981). *Parapsychology: Science or magic?* Oxford: Pergamon. (p. 241)

Alcock, J. E. (1985, Spring). Parapsychology: The "spiritual" science. *Free Inquiry,* pp. 25–35. (p. 157)

Alcohol, Drug Abuse, and Mental Health Administration. (1990). Economic costs of alcohol and drug abuse and mental illness: 1985. Rockville, MD: National Clearinghouse for Alcohol and Drug Information. (p. 446)

Aldrich, M. S. (1989). Automobile accidents in patients with sleep disorders. *Sleep, 12,* 487–494. (p. 170)

Aldridge-Morris, R. (1989). *Multiple personality: An exercise in deception.* Hillsdale, NJ: Erlbaum. (p. 425)

Alexander, C. N., Cranson, R. W., Boyer, R. W., & Orme-Johnson, D. W. (1987). Transcendental consciousness: A fourth state of consciousness beyond sleep, dreaming and waking. In J. Gackenbach (Ed.), *Sleep and dreams: A source-book.* New York: Garland Press. (p. 175)

Alexander, C. N., Langer, E. J., Newman, R. I., Chandler, H. M., & Davies, J. L. (1989). Transcendental meditation, mindfulness, and longevity: An experimental study with the elderly. *Journal of Personality and Social Psychology, 57,* 950–964. (p. 370)

Alkon, D. L., Amaral, D. G., Baer, M. F., Black, J., Carew, T. J., Cohen, N. J., Disterhoft, J. F., Eichenbaum, H., Golski, S., Gorman, L. K., Lynch, G., McNaughton, B. L., Mishkin, M., Moyer, J. R., Jr., Olds, J. L., Olton, D. S., Otto, T., Squire, L. R., Staubli, U., Thompson, L. T., & Wible, C. (1991). Learning and memory. *Brain Research Reviews, 16,* 193–220. (p. 236)

Allard, F., & Burnett, N. (1985).   Skill in sport. *Canadian Journal of Psychology, 39,* 294–312. (p. 230)

Allen, L. S., & Gorski, R. A. (1992).   Sexual orientation and the size of the anterior commissure in the human brain. *Proceedings of the National Academy of Sciences, 89,* 7199–7202. (p. 319)

Allman, A. L. (1989).   Subjective well-being of students with and without disabilities. Paper presented at the Midwestern Psychological Association convention. (p. 347)

Allport, G. W. (1967).   Gordon W. Allport. In E. G. Boring & G. Lindzey (Eds.), *A history of psychology in autobiography* (Vol. V). New York: Appleton-Century-Crofts. (p. 387)

Allport, G. W., & Odbert, H. S. (1936).   Trait-names: A psycho-lexical study. *Psychological Monographs, 47*(1).   (p. 388)

Alwin, D. F. (1990).   Historical changes in parental orientations to children. In N. Mandell (Ed.), *Sociological studies of child development* (Vol. 3).   Greenwich, CT: JAI Press. (p. 85)

Amabile, T. M. (1983).   *The social psychology of creativity.* New York: Springer-Verlag. (p. 396)

Amabile, T. M. (1987).   The motivation to be creative. In S. Isaksen (Ed.), *Frontiers in creativity: Beyond the basics.* Buffalo, NY: Bearly Limited. (p. 396)

Amabile, T. M. (1988).   From individual creativity to organizational innovation. In K. Gronhaug & G. Kaufmann (Eds.), *Innovation: A crossdisciplinary perspective.* Oslo: Norwegian University Press. (p. 396)

Amabile, T. M., & Hennessey, B. A. (1992).   The motivation for creativity in children. In A. K. Boggiano & T. S. Pittman (Eds.), *Achievement and motivation: A social-developmental perspective.* New York: Cambridge University Press. (p. 284)

Ambady, N., & Rosenthal, R. (1992).   Thin slices of expressive behavior as predictors of interpersonal consequences: A meta-analysis. *Psychological Bulletin, 111,* 256–274. (p. 392)

Ambady, N., & Rosenthal, R. (1993).   Half a minute: Predicting teacher evaluations from thin slices of nonverbal behavior and physical attractiveness. *Journal of Personality and Social Psychology, 64,* 431–441. (p. 392)

American Psychiatric Association. (1990).   *The practice of ECT: Recommendations for treatment, training, and privileging.* Washington, DC: American Psychiatric Press. (p. 473)

American Psychiatric Association. (1994).   *Diagnostic and statistical manual of mental disorders* (4th ed.). Washington, DC: American Psychiatric Press. (p. 283)

American Psychological Association. (1991).   Medical cost offset. Washington, DC: American Psychological Association Practice Directorate. (p. 466)

American Psychological Association. (1992).   Ethical principles of psychologists and code of conduct. *American Psychologist, 47,* 1597–1611. (p. 27)

Anda, R., Williamson, D., Jones, D., Macera, C., Eaker, E., Glassman, A., & Marks, J. (1993).   Depressed affect, hopelessness, and the risk of ischemic heart disease in a cohort of U.S. adults. *Epidemiology, 4,* 285–294. (p. 363)

Andersen, B. L. (1983).   Primary orgasmic dysfunction: Diagnostic considerations and review of treatment. *Psychological Bulletin, 93,* 105–136. (p. 315)

Andersen, B. L. (1989).   Health psychology's contribution to addressing the cancer problem: Update on accomplishments. *Health Psychology, 8,* 683–703. (p. 364)

Anderson, C. A. (1989).   Temperature and aggression: Ubiquitous effects of heat on occurrence of human violence. *Psychological Bulletin, 106,* 74–96. (p. 503)

Anderson, C. A., & Anderson, D. C. (1984).   Ambient temperature and violent crime: Tests of the linear and curvilinear hypotheses. *Journal of Personality and Social Psychology, 46,* 91–97. (p. 503)

Anderson, C. A., Lepper, M. R., & Ross, L. (1980).   Perseverance of social theories: The role of explanation in the persistence of discredited information. *Journal of Personality and Social Psychology, 39,* 1037–1049. (p. 263)

Anderson, D. R., & Jose, W. S., II (1987, December).   Employee lifestyle and the bottom line: Results from the StayWell evaluation. *Fitness in Business,* pp. 86–91. (p. 368)

Anderson, J. R. (1983).   Retrieval of information from long-term memory. *Science, 220,* 25–30. (p. 240)

Anderson, V. E. (1994).   Genes, behavior, and responsibility: Research perspectives. In M. S. Frankel & A. H. Teich (Eds.), *The genetic frontier: Ethics, law, and policy.* Washington, DC: American Association for the Advancement of Science. (p. 438)

Andreasen, N. C., Arndt, S., Swayze, V., II, Cizadlo, T., Flaum, M., O'Leary, D., Ehrhardt, J. C., & Yuh, W. T. C. (1994).   Thalamic abnormalities in schizophrenia visualized through magnetic resonance image averaging. *Science, 266,* 294–296. (p. 437)

Angoff, W. H. (1987).   The nature-nurture debate, aptitudes, and group differences. Presidential address to American Psychological Association Division 5. (p. 291)

Antoni, M. H., LaPerriere, A., Schneiderman, N., & Fletcher, M. A. (1991).   Stress and immunity in individuals at risk for AIDS. *Stress Medicine, 7,* 35–44. (p. 364)

Antony, M. M., Brown, T. A., & Barlow, D. H. (1992).   Current perspectives on panic and panic disorder. *Current Directions in Psychological Science, 1,* 79–82. (p. 421)

Antrobus, J. (1991).   Dreaming: Cognitive processes during cortical activation and high afferent thresholds. *Psychological Review, 98,* 96–121. (p. 173)

Aries, E. (1987).   Gender and communication. In P. Shaver & C. Henrick (Eds.), *Review of Personality and Social Psychology, 7,* 177–200. (p. 327)

Arnold, R. B. (1991, October 7).   A star cries incest. *People,* pp. 84–88. (p. 248)

Asch, S. E. (1955).   Opinions and social pressure. *Scientific American, 193,* 31–35. (p. 485)

Aserinsky, E. (1988, January 17).   Personal communication. (p. 166)

Associated Press. (1993, June 17).   'We deserve the money we make,' doctors say. *Grand Rapids Press,* p. A9. (p. 349)

Astin, A., Korn, W. S., & Riggs, E. R. (1993).   *The American freshman: National norms for Fall 1993.* Los Angeles: Higher Education Research Institute, Graduate School of Education, UCLA. (p. 495)

Astin, A. W., Green, K. C., & Korn, W. S. (1987).   *The American freshman: Twenty year trends.* (A report of the Cooperative Institutional Research Program sponsored by the American Council on Education.) Los Angeles, CA: Higher Education Research Institute, Graduate School of Education, UCLA. (p. 188)

Astin, A. W., Korn, W. S., Sax, L. J., & Mahoney, K. M. (1994).   *The American freshman: National norms for fall 1994.* Higher Education Research Institute, Graduate School of Education & Information Studies, UCLA. (pp. 188, 316, 347)

Atkinson, R. (1988). *The teenage world: Adolescent self-image in ten countries.* New York: Plenum Press. (p. 85)

Atwell, R. H. (1986, July 28). Drugs on campus: A perspective. *Higher Education & National Affairs*, p. 5. (p. 183)

Averill, J. R. (1969). Autonomic response patterns during sadness and mirth. *Psychophysiology, 5*, 399–414. (p. 338)

Averill, J. R. (1983). Studies on anger and aggression: Implications for theories of emotion. *American Psychologist, 38*, 1145–1160. (p. 344)

Averill, J. R. (1993). William James's other theory of emotion. In M. E. Donnelly (Ed.), *Reinterpreting the legacy of William James.* Washington, DC: American Psychological Association. (p. 353)

Avery, R. D., & 51 others (1994, December 13). Mainstream science on intelligence. *Wall Street Journal*, editorial page. (p. 289)

Ax, A. F. (1953). The physiological differentiation of fear and anger in humans. *Psychosomatic Medicine, 15*, 433–442. (p. 338)

Babad, E., Bernieri, F., & Rosenthal, R. (1991). Students as judges of teachers' verbal and nonverbal behavior. *American Educational Research Journal, 28*, 211–234. (p. 339)

Bachevalier, J., Landis, L. S., Walker, L. C., Brickson, M., Mishkin, M., Price, D. L., & Cork, L. C. (1991). Aged monkeys exhibit behavioral deficits indicative of widespread cerebral dysfunction. *Neurobiology of Aging, 12*, 99–111. (p. 101)

Bachevalier, J., & Mishkin, M. (1992). Ontogenetic development and decline of memory functions in nonhuman primates. In I. Kostovic (Ed.), *Neurodevelopment, aging, and cognition.* Boston: Birkhauser. (p. 101)

Backus, J. (1977). *The acoustical foundations of music* (2nd ed.). New York: Norton. (p. 132)

Baddeley, A. D. (1982). *Your memory: A user's guide.* New York: Macmillan. (p. 227)

Bahrick, H. P. (1984). Semantic memory content in permastore: 50 years of memory for Spanish learned in school. *Journal of Experimental Psychology: General, 111*, 1–29. (pp. 234, 235)

Bahrick, H. P., Bahrick, P. O., & Wittlinger, R. P. (1975). Fifty years of memory for names and faces: A cross-sectional approach. *Journal of Experimental Psychology: General, 104*, 54–75. (p. 240)

Bahrick, H. P., & Hall, L. K. (1991). Lifetime maintenance of high school mathematics content. *Journal of Experimental Psychology: General, 120*, 20–33. (p. 227)

Bailey, J. M., Bobrow, D., Wolfe, M., & Mikach, S. (1995). Sexual orientation of adult sons of gay fathers. *Developmental Psychology, 31*, 124–129. (p. 319)

Bailey, J. M., & Pillard, R. C. (1991). A genetic study of male sexual orientation. *Archives of General Psychiatry, 48*, 1089–1096. (p. 320)

Bailey, J. M., & Pillard, R. C. (1994, January). The innateness of homosexuality. *Harvard Mental Health Letter*, pp. 4–6. (p. 320)

Bailey, J. M., Pillard, R. C., Neale, M. C., & Agyei, Y. (1993). Heritable factors influence sexual orientation in women. *Archives of General Psychiatry, 50*, 217–223. (p. 320)

Bailey, J. M., & Zucker, K. J. (1995). Childhood sex-typed behavior and sexual orientation: A conceptual analysis and quantitative review. *Developmental Psychology, 31*, 43–55. (p. 317)

Baillargeon, R. (1992). The object concept revisited. In C. Granrud (Ed.), *Visual perception and cognition in infancy. Carnegie-Mellon Symposia on Cognition* (Vol. 23). Hillsdale, NJ: Erlbaum. (p. 77)

Bairagi, R. (1987). Food crises and female children in rural Bangladesh. *Social Science, 72*, 48–51. (p. 498)

Baker, E. L. (1987). The state of the art of clinical hypnosis. *International Journal of Clinical and Experimental Hypnosis, 35*, 203–214. (p. 178)

Baldwin, E. (1993). The case for animal research in psychology. *Journal of Social Issues, 49*(1), 121–131. (p. 27)

Ball, W., & Tronick, E. (1971). Infant responses to impending collision: Optical and real. *Science, 171*, 818–820. (p. 142)

Baltes, P. B. (1993). The aging mind: Potential and limits. *The Gerontologist, 33*, 580–594. (p. 102)

Bandura, A. (1977). *Social learning theory.* Englewood Cliffs, NJ: Prentice-Hall. (p. 218)

Bandura, A. (1986). *Social foundations of thought and action: A social-cognitive theory.* Englewood Cliffs, NJ: Prentice-Hall. (p. 402)

Bandura, A., Blanchard, E. B., & Ritter, B. (1969). Relative efficacy of desensitization and modeling approaches for inducing behavioral, affective, and attitudinal changes. *Journal of Personality and Social Psychology, 13*, 173–199. (p. 456)

Bandura, A., Ross, D., & Ross, S. A. (1961). Transmission of aggression through imitation of aggressive models. *Journal of Abnormal and Social Psychology, 63*, 575–582. (p. 218)

Barbaree, H. E., & Marshall, W. L. (1991). The role of male sexual arousal in rape: Six models. *Journal of Consulting and Clinical Psychology, 59*, 621–630. (p. 506)

Barinaga, M. (1995). "Obese" protein slims mice. *Science, 269*, 475–476. (p. 308)

Barker, S. L., Funk, S. C., & Houston, B. K. (1988). Psychological treatment versus nonspecific factors: A meta-analysis of conditions that engender comparable expectations for improvement. *Clinical Psychology Review, 8*, 579–594. (p. 467)

Baron, R. A. (1987). Interviewer's mood and reaction to job applicants: The influence of affective states on applied social judgments. *Journal of Applied Social Psychology, 17*, 911–926. (p. 346)

Baron, R. A. (1988). Negative effects of destructive criticism: Impact on conflict, self-efficacy, and task performance. *Journal of Applied Psychology, 73*, 199–207. (p. 215)

Baruch, G. K., & Barnett, R. (1986). Role quality, multiple role involvement, and psychological well-being in midlife women. *Journal of Personality and Social Psychology, 51*, 578–585. (p. 106)

Bass, E., & Davis, L. (1988). *The courage to heal.* New York: Harper & Row. (p. 248)

Bass, L. E., & Kane-Williams, E. (1993). Stereotype or reality: Another look at alcohol and drug use among African American children. U.S. Department of Health and Human Services, *Public Health Reports, 108* (Supplement 1), 78–84. (p. 189)

Baum, A., & Fleming, I. (1993). Implications of psychological research on stress and technological accidents. *American Psychologist, 48*, 665–672. (p. 358)

Baumann, L. J., & Leventhal, H. (1985). "I can tell when my blood pressure is up, can't I?" *Health Psychology, 4*, 203–218. (p. 317)

Baumeister, R. F. (1989). The optimal margin of illusion. *Journal of Social and Clinical Psychology, 8*, 176–189. (p. 262, 398)

Baumeister, R. F. (1993). Understanding the inner nature of low self-esteem: Uncertain, fragile, protective, and conflicted. In R. F. Baumeister (Ed.), *Self-esteem: The puzzle of low self-regard.* New York: Plenum. (p. 396)

Baumeister, R. F., & Leary, M. R. (1995). The need to belong: Desire for interpersonal attachment as a fundamental human motivation. *Psychological Bulletin, 117*, 497–529. (p. 328)

Baumeister, R. F., Stillwell, A., & Wotman, S. R. (1990). Victim and perpetrator accounts of interpersonal conflict: Autobiographical narratives about anger. *Journal of Personality and Social Psychology, 59,* 994–1005. (p. 346)

Baumeister, R. F., & Tice, D. M. (1986). How adolescence became the struggle for self: A historical transformation of psychological development. In J. Suls & A. G. Greenwald (Eds.), *Psychological perspectives on the self* (Vol. 3). Hillsdale, NJ: Erlbaum. (p. 87)

Baumeister, R. F., Tice, D. M., & Hutton, D. G. (1989). Self-presentational motivations and personality differences in self-esteem. *Journal of Personality, 57,* 547–579. (p. 396)

Baumgardner, A. H. (1990). To know oneself is to like oneself: Self-certainty and self-affect. *Journal of Personality and Social Psychology, 58,* 1062–1072. (p. 93)

Baumgardner, A. H., Kaufman, C. M., & Levy, P. E. (1989). Regulating affect interpersonally: When low esteem leads to greater enhancement. *Journal of Personality and Social Psychology, 56,* 907–921. (p. 396)

Baumrind, D. (1982). Adolescent sexuality: Comment on Williams' and Silka's comments on Baumrind. *American Psychologist, 37,* 1402–1403. (p. 321)

Beaman, A. L., & Klentz, B. (1983). The supposed physical attractiveness bias against supporters of the women's movement: A meta-analysis. *Personality and Social Psychology Bulletin, 9,* 544–550. (p. 514)

Beardsley, L. M. (1994). Medical diagnosis and treatment across cultures. In W. J. Lonner & R. Malpass (Eds.), *Psychology and culture.* Boston: Allyn & Bacon. (p. 416)

Beauchamp, G. K. (1987). The human preference for excess salt. *American Scientist, 75,* 27–33. (p. 303)

Beck, A. J., Kline, S. A., & Greenfeld, L. A. (1988). Survey of youth in custody, 1987 (U.S. Department of Justice, Bureau of Justice Statistics Special Report). (p. 504)

Beck, A. T., Rush, A. J., Shaw, B. F., & Emery, G. (1979). *Cognitive therapy of depression.* New York: Guilford Press. (p. 460)

Beck, A. T., & Steer, R. A. (1989). Clinical predictors of eventual suicide: A 5– to 10–year prospective study of suicide attempters. *Journal of Affective Disorders, 17,* 203–209. (p. 428)

Beck, A. T., & Young, J. E. (1978, September). College blues. *Psychology Today,* pp. 80–92. (pp. 427, 433)

Begg, I. M., Needham, D. R., & Bookbinder, M. (1993). Do backward messages unconsciously affect listeners? No. *Canadian Journal of Experimental Psychology, 47,* 1–14. (p. 120)

Beitman, B. D., Goldfried, M. R., & Norcross, J. C. (1989). The movement toward integrating the psychotherapies: An overview. *American Journal of Psychiatry, 146,* 138–147. (p. 450)

Bell, A. P. (1982, November/December). Sexual preference: A postscript (SIECUS Report, 11, No. 2). *Church and Society,* pp. 34–37. (p. 319)

Bell, A. P., Weinberg, M. S., & Hammersmith, S. K. (1981). *Sexual preference: Its development in men and women.* Bloomington: Indiana University Press. (p. 318)

Beloff, J. (1985, Spring). Science, religion and the paranormal. *Free Inquiry,* pp. 36–41. (p. 157)

Belsher, G., & Costello, C. G. (1988). Relapse after recovery from unipolar depression: A critical review. *Psychological Bulletin, 104,* 84–96. (p. 429)

Belsky, J., Lang, M., & Huston, T. L. (1986). Sex typing and division of labor as determinants of marital change across the transition to parenthood. *Journal of Personality and Social Psychology, 50,* 517–522. (p. 105)

Bem, D. J., & Honorton, C. (1994). Does psi exist? Replicable evidence for an anomalous process of information transfer. *Psychological Bulletin, 115,* 4–18. (p. 157)

Bem, S. (1993). *The lenses of gender.* New Haven, CT: Yale University Press. (p. 86)

Bem, S. L. (1987). Masculinity and femininity exist only in the mind of the perceiver. In J. M. Reinisch, L. A. Rosenblum, & S. A. Sanders (Eds.), *Masculinity/femininity: Basic perspectives.* New York: Oxford University Press. (p. 86)

Benassi, V. A., Sweeney, P. D., & Dufour, C. L. (1988). Is there a relation between locus of control orientation and depression? *Journal of Abnormal Psychology, 97,* 357–367. (p. 403)

Benbow, C. P. (1988). Sex differences in mathematical reasoning ability in intellectually talented preadolescents: Their nature, effects, and possible causes. *Behavioral and Brain Sciences, 11,* 169–182. (p. 290)

Bennett, R. (1991, February). Pornography and extrafamilial child sexual abuse: Examining the relationship. Unpublished manuscript, Los Angeles Police Department Sexually Exploited Child Unit. (p. 507)

Benson, H., & Klipper, M. Z. (1976). *The relaxation response.* New York: Morrow. (p. 370)

Benson, H., & Proctor, W. (1984). *Beyond the relaxation response: How to harness the healing power of your personal beliefs.* New York: Times Books. (p. 370)

Benson, H., & Proctor, W. (1987). *Your maximum mind.* New York: Times Books/Random House. (p. 370)

Benson, P. L. (1992, Spring). Patterns of religious development in adolescence and adulthood. *Psychologists Interested in Religious Issues Newsletter,* 2–9. (pp. 94, 370)

Benson, P. L., Sharma, A. R., & Roehlkepartain, E. C. (1994, June). New study identifies strengths of adoptive families. *Search Institute Source,* pp. 1–3. (pp. 79, 110)

Bergin, A. E. (1980). Psychotherapy and religious values. *Journal of Consulting and Clinical Psychology, 48,* 95–105. (p. 468)

Bergin, A. E. (1991). Values and religious issues in psychotherapy and mental health. *American Psychologist, 46,* 394–403. (p. 325)

Bergsholm, P., Larsen, J. L., Rosendahl, K., & Holsten, F. (1989). Electroconvulsive therapy and cerebral computed tomography. *Acta Psychiatrica Scandinavia, 80,* 566–572. (p. 473)

Berkowitz, L. (1983). Aversively stimulated aggression: Some parallels and differences in research with animals and humans. *American Psychologist, 38,* 1135–1144. (p. 503)

Berkowitz, L. (1989). Frustration-aggression hypothesis: Examination and reformulation. *Psychological Bulletin, 106,* 59–73. (p. 503)

Berkowitz, L. (1990). On the formation and regulation of anger and aggression: A cognitive-neoassociationistic analysis. *American Psychologist, 45,* 494–503. (p. 344)

Berman, M., Gladue, B., & Taylor, S. (1993). The effects of hormones, Type A behavior pattern, and provocation on aggression in men. *Motivation and Emotion, 17,* 125–138. (p. 502)

Berndt, T. J. (1992). Friendship and friends' influence in adolescence. *Current Directions in Psychological Science, 1,* 156–159. (p. 94)

Berry, D. S., & McArthur, L. Z. (1986). Perceiving character in faces: The impact of age-related craniofacial changes on social perception. *Psychological Bulletin, 100,* 3–18. (p. 201)

Berscheid, E. (1981). An overview of the psychological effects of physical attractiveness and some comments upon the psychological effects of knowledge of the effects of physical attractiveness. In G. W. Lucker, K. Ribbens, & J. A. McNamara (Eds.), *Psychological aspects of facial form* (Craniofacial growth series). Ann Arbor: Center for Human Growth and Development, University of Michigan. (p. 513)

Berscheid, E. (1985). Interpersonal attraction. In G. Lindzey & E. Aronson (Eds.), *The handbook of social psychology.* New York: Random House. (p. 329)

Berscheid, E., Gangestad, S. W., & Kulakowski, D. (1984). Emotion in close relationships: Implications for relationship counseling. In S. D. Brown & R. W. Lent (Eds.), *Handbook of counseling psychology.* New York: Wiley. (p. 516)

Beyer, L. (1990, Fall issue on women). Life behind the veil. *Time,* p. 37. (p. 498)

Beyerstein, B., & Beyerstein, D. (Eds.). (1992). *The write stuff: Evaluations of graphology.* Buffalo, NY: Prometheus Books. (p. 406)

Bhatt, R. S., Wasserman, E. A., Reynolds, W. F., Jr., & Knauss, K. S. (1988). Conceptual behavior in pigeons: Categorization of both familiar and novel examples from four classes of natural and artificial stimuli. *Journal of Experimental Psychology: Animal Behavior Processes, 14,* 219–234. (p. 207)

Binet, A., & Simon, T. (1905; reprinted 1916). New methods for the diagnosis of the intellectual level of subnormals. In A. Binet & T. Simon, *The development of intelligence in children.* Baltimore: Williams & Wilkins. (p. 276)

Binitie, A. (1975). A factor-analytical study of depression across cultures (African and European). *British Journal of Psychiatry, 127,* 559–563. (p. 423)

Bishop, G. D. (1991). Understanding the understanding of illness: Lay disease representations. In J. A. Skelton & R. T. Croyle (Eds.), *Mental representation in health and illness.* New York: Springer-Verlag. (p. 257)

Bjork, R. A. (1978). The updating of human memory. In G. H. Bower (Ed.), *The psychology of learning and motivation* (Vol. 12). New York: Academic Press. (p. 231)

Bjorklund, D. F., & Green, B. L. (1992). The adaptive nature of cognitive immaturity. *American Psychologist, 47,* 46–54. (p. 79)

Blackmore, S. (1991, Fall). Near-death experiences: In or out of the body? *Skeptical Inquirer,* pp. 34–45. (p. 186)

Blackmore, S. (1993). *Dying to live.* Amherst, NY: Prometheus Books. (p. 186)

Blom, J. M. C., Tamarkin, L., Shiber, J. R., & Nelson, R. J. (1994). *Learned conditioned immunosuppression is associated with increased risk of chemically-induced tumors.* Unpublished manuscript, Department of Psychology, Johns Hopkins University. (p. 366)

Bloom, B. S. (Ed.). (1985). *Developing talent in young people.* New York: Ballantine. (p. 324)

Bloom, F. E. (1993, January/February). What's new in neurotransmitters. *Brain Work,* pp. 7–9. (p. 38)

Bodenhausen, G. V., Sheppard, L. A., & Kramer, G. P. (1994). Negative affect and social judgment: The differential impact of anger and sadness. *European Journal of Social Psychology, 24,* 45–62. (p. 521)

Bolger, N., DeLongis, A., Kessler, R. C., & Schilling, E. A. (1989). Effects of daily stress on negative mood. *Journal of Personality and Social Psychology, 57,* 808–818. (p. 347)

Bond, C. F., Jr., Pitre, U., & Van Leeuwen, M. D. (1991). Encoding operations and the next-in-line effect. *Personality and Social Psychology Bulletin, 17,* 435–441. (p. 227)

Bond, M. H. (1988). Finding universal dimensions of individual variation in multi-cultural studies of values: The Rokeach and Chinese values surveys. *Journal of Personality and Social Psychology, 55,* 1009–1015. (p. 85)

Bond, R., & Smith, P. B. (1994). Culture and conformity: A meta-analysis of studies using the Asch-type perceptual judgment task. *British Psychological Society 1994 Proceedings,* p. 41. (p. 487)

Bonner, E. (1990, May 4). Missing-child study: Relative often to blame. *Chicago Tribune.* (p. 261)

Boring, E. G. (1930). A new ambiguous figure. *American Journal of Psychology, 42,* 444–445. (p. 150)

Bornstein, M. H. (1989). Stability in early mental development: From attention and information processing in infancy to language and cognition in childhood. In M. G. Bornstein & N. A. Krasnegor (Eds.), *Stability and continuity in mental development: Behavioral and biological perspectives.* Hillsdale, NJ: Erlbaum. (p. 82)

Bornstein, M. H., Tal, J., Rahn, C., Galperin, C. Z., Pecheux, M-G., Lamour, M., Toda, S., Azuma, H., Ogino, M., & Tamis-LeMonda, C. S. (1992a). Functional analysis of the contents of maternal speech to infants of 5 and 13 months in four cultures: Argentina, France, Japan, and the United States. *Developmental Psychology, 28,* 593–603. (p. 86)

Bornstein, M. H., Tamis-LeMonda, C. S., Tal, J., Ludemann, P., Toda, S., Rahn, C. W., Pecheux, M-G., Azuma, H., & Vardi, D. (1992b). Maternal responsiveness to infants in three societies: The United States, France, and Japan. *Child Development, 63,* 808–821. (p. 86)

Bornstein, R. F. (1989). Exposure and affect: Overview and meta-analysis of research, 1968–1987. *Psychological Bulletin, 106,* 265–289. (p. 512)

Bornstein, R. F., Galley, D. J., Leone, D. R., & Kale, A. R. (1991). The temporal stability of ratings of parents: Test-retest reliability and influence of parental contact. *Journal of Social Behavior and Personality, 6,* 641–649. (p. 242)

Bothwell, R. K., Brigham, J. C., & Malpass, R. S. (1989). Cross-racial identification. *Personality and Social Psychology Bulletin, 15,* 19–25. (p. 500)

Bothwell, R. K., Deffenbacher, K. A., & Brigham, J. C. (1987). Correlation of eyewitness accuracy and confidence: Optimality hypothesis revised. *Journal of Applied Psychology, 72,* 691–695. (p. 244)

Bouchard, T. J., Jr. (1982). Twins—Nature's twice told tale. In *1983 Yearbook of science and the future.* Chicago: Encyclopaedia Britannica. (p. 285)

Bouchard, T. J., Jr. (1993). The genetic architecture of human intelligence. In P. A. Vernon (Ed.), *Biological approaches to the study of human intelligence.* Norwood, NJ: Ablex. (p. 285)

Bouchard, T. J., Jr., & Segal, N. L. (1988). Heredity, environment, and IQ. In *Instructor's Resource Manual* to accompany G. Lindzey, R. Thompson, & B. Spring, Psychology (3rd ed.). New York: Worth Publishers. (p. 286)

Bouchard, T. J., Lykken, D. T., McGue, M., Segal, N. L., & Tellegen, A. (1990). Sources of human psychological differences: The Minnesota study of twins reared apart. *Science, 250,* 223–228. (p. 109)

Bower, G. H. (1983). Affect and cognition. *Philosophical Transaction: Royal Society of London, Series B, 302,* 387–402. (p. 241)

Bower, G. H. (1986). Prime time in cognitive psychology. In P. Eelen (Ed.), *Cognitive research and behavior therapy: Beyond the conditioning paradigm.* Amsterdam: North Holland Publishers. (p. 240)

Bower, G. H., & Clark, M. C. (1969). Narrative stories as mediators for serial learning. *Psychonomic Science, 14,* 181–182. (p. 229)

Bower, G. H., Clark, M. C., Lesgold, A. M., & Winzenz, D. (1969). Hierarchical retrieval schemes in recall of categorized word lists. *Journal of Verbal Learning and Verbal Behavior, 8,* 323–343. (p. 230)

Bower, G. H., & Morrow, D. G. (1990).   Mental models in narrative comprehension. *Science, 247,* 44–48. (p. 228)

Bowers, K. S. (1984).   Hypnosis. In N. Endler & J. M. Hunt (Eds.), *Personality and behavioral disorders* (2nd ed.). New York: Wiley. (p. 176)

Bowers, K. S. (1990).   Unconscious influences and hypnosis. In J. E. Singer (Ed.), *Repression and dissociation: Implications for personality theory, psychopathology, and health.* Chicago: University of Chicago Press. (p. 180)

Bowers, T. G., & Clum, G. A. (1988).   Relative contribution of specific and nonspecific treatment effects: Meta-analysis of placebo-controlled behavior therapy research. *Psychological Bulletin, 103,* 315–323. (p. 467)

Bowlby, J. (1979).   *The making and breaking of affectional bonds.* London: Tavistock. (p. 82)

Boyatzis, C. J., Matillo, G. M., & Nesbitt, K. M. (in press).   Effects of "The Mighty Morphin Power Rangers" on children's aggression with peers. *Child Study Journal.* (p. 505)

Boynton, R. M. (1979).   *Human color vision.* New York: Holt, Rinehart & Winston. (p. 129)

Braden, J. P. (1994).   *Deafness, deprivation, and IQ.* New York: Plenum. (p. 289)

Bradley, D. R., Dumais, S. T., & Petry, H. M. (1976).   Reply to Cavonius. *Nature, 261,* 78. (p. 139)

Brannon, L. A., & Brock, T. C. (1994).   Perilous underestimation of sex partners' sexual histories in calculating personal AIDS risk. Paper presented to the American Psychological Society convention. (p. 321)

Bransford, J. D., & Johnson, M. K. (1972).   Contextual prerequisites for understanding: Some investigations of comprehension and recall. *Journal of Verbal Learning and Verbal Behavior, 11,* 717–726. (p. 228)

Braskamp, L. A. (1987).   Spectrum: Utility for educational selection and organizational development. Paper presented at the American Psychological Association convention. (p. 326)

Bray, D. W., & Byham, W. C. (1991, Winter).   Assessment centers and their derivatives. *Journal of Continuing Higher Education,* pp. 8–11. (p. 407)

Bray, G. A. (1969).   Effect of caloric restriction on energy expenditure in obese patients. *Lancet, 2,* 397–398. (p. 307)

Brehm, S., & Brehm, J. W. (1981).   *Psychological reactance: A theory of freedom and control.* New York: Academic Press. (p. 493)

Breland, K., & Breland, M. (1961).   The misbehavior of organisms. *American Psychologist, 16,* 661–664. (p. 214)

Brennan, P. A., & Mednick, S. A. (1993).   Genetic perspectives on crime. *Acta Psychiatrica Scandinavia, 370*(Suppl.), 19–26. (p. 441)

Brenner, M. (1973).   The next-in-line effect. *Journal of Verbal Learning and Verbal Behavior, 12,* 320–323. (p. 227)

Brewer, W. F. (1977).   Memory for the pragmatic implications of sentences. *Memory and Cognition, 5,* 673–678. (p. 228)

Brewin, C. F. (1989).   Cognitive change processes in psychotherapy. *Psychological Review, 96,* 379–394. (p. 459)

Brickman, P., Coates, D., & Janoff-Bulman, R. J. (1978).   Lottery winners and accident victims: Is happiness relative? *Journal of Personality and Social Psychology, 36,* 917–927. (p. 347)

Briere, J., & Runtz, M. (1993).   Childhood sexual abuse: Long-term sequelae and implications for psychological assessment. *Journal of Interpersonal Violence, 8,* 312–330. (p. 244)

Bril, B. (1986).   Motor development and cultural attitudes. In H. T. A. Whiting & M. G. Wade (Eds.), *Themes in motor development.* Dordrecht, Netherlands: Martinus Nijhoff. (p. 75)

Brinson, S. L. (1992).   The use and opposition of rape myths in prime-time television dramas. *Sex Roles, 27,* 359–375. (p. 506)

Brislin, R. (1993).   *Understanding culture's influence on behavior.* Fort Worth, TX: Harcourt Brace. (p. 416)

British Psychological Society. (1993).   Ethical principles for conducting research with human participants. *The Psychologist: Bulletin of the British Psychological Society, 6,* 33–36. (p. 27)

British Psychological Society. (1993).   *Graphology in personnel assessment.* Leicester, England: British Psychological Society. (p. 406)

Brockner, J., & Hulton, A. J. B. (1978).   How to reverse the vicious cycle of low self-esteem: The importance of attentional focus. *Journal of Experimental Social Psychology, 14,* 564–578. (p. 396)

Brooks, K., & Siegal, M. (1991).   Children as eyewitnesses: Memory, suggestibility, and credibility. *Australian Psychologist, 26,* 84–88. (p. 244)

Brooks-Gunn, J. (1989).   Adolescents as daughters and as mothers: A developmental perspective. In I. Sigel & G. Brody (Eds.), *Family research.* Hillsdale, NJ: Erlbaum. (p. 88)

Brooks-Gunn, J., & Furstenberg, F. F., Jr. (1989).   Adolescent sexual behavior. *American Psychologist, 44,* 249–257. (p. 96)

Brothers, J. (1990, February 18).   Why wives have affairs. *Parade,* pp. 4–7. (p. 311)

Brown, E. L., & Deffenbacher, K. (1979).   *Perception and the senses.* New York: Oxford University Press. (p. 133)

Brown, J. D. (1991).   Accuracy and bias in self-knowledge. In C. R. Snyder & D. F. Forsyth (Eds.), *Handbook of social and clinical psychology: The health perspective.* New York: Pergamon Press. (pp. 396, 398)

Brown, J. D. (1991).   Staying fit and staying well: Physical fitness as a moderator of life stress. *Journal of Personality and Social Psychology, 60,* 555–561. (p. 368)

Brown, R. (1986).   Linguistic relativity. In S. H. Hulse & B. F. Green, Jr. (Eds.), *One hundred years of psychological research in America.* Baltimore: Johns Hopkins University Press. (p. 272)

Brown, R., & Kulik, J. (1982).   Flashbulb memories. In U. Neisser (Ed.), *Memory observed.* San Francisco: Freeman. (p. 224)

Brownell, K. D. (1991).   Dieting and the search for the perfect body: Where physiology and culture collide. *Behavior Therapy, 22,* 1–12. (p. 308)

Brownell, K. D., & Jeffery, R. W. (1987).   Improving long-term weight loss: Pushing the limits of treatment. *Behavior Therapy, 18,* 353–374. (p. 308)

Brownell, K. D., & Rodin, J. (1994).   The dieting maelstrom: Is it possible and advisable to lose weight? *American Psychologist, 49,* 781–791. (p. 309)

Brownell, K. D., & Wadden, T. A. (1991).   The heterogeneity of obesity: Fitting treatments to individuals. *Behavior Therapy, 22,* 153–177. (p. 309)

Brownell, K. D., & Wadden, T. A. (1992).   Etiology and treatment of obesity: Understanding a serious, prevalent, and refractory disorder. *Journal of Consulting and Clinical Psychology, 60,* 505–517. (pp. 307, 309)

Browning, C. (1992).   *Ordinary men: Reserve police battalion 101 and the final solution in Poland.* New York: HarperCollins. (p. 489)

Brownmiller, S. (1975).   *Against our will: Men, women, and rape.* New York: Simon & Schuster. (p. 315)

Buck, L., & Axel, R. (1991).   A novel multigene family may encode odorant receptors: A molecular basis for odor recognition. *Cell, 65,* 175–187. (p. 137)

Bugelski, B. R., Kidd, E., & Segmen, J. (1968).   Image as a mediator in one-trial paired-associate learning. *Journal of Experimental Psychology, 76*, 69–73. (p. 230)

Bugental, D. B. (1986).   Unmasking the "polite smile": Situational and personal determinants of managed affect in adult-child interaction. *Personality and Social Psychology Bulletin, 12*, 7–16. (p. 339)

Bullough, V. (1990).   The Kinsey scale in historical perspective. In D. P. McWhirter, S. A. Sanders, & J. M. Reinisch (Eds.), *Homosexuality/heterosexuality: Concepts of sexual orientation.* New York: Oxford University Press. (p. 317)

Buquet, R. (1988).   Le reve et les deficients visuels [Dreams and the visually-impaired]. *Psychanalyse-a-l'Universite, 13*, 319–327. (p. 172)

Bureau of the Census. (1993).   *Statistical abstract of the United States 1993.* Washington, DC: U.S. Government Printing Office. (pp. 428, 471)

Bureau of the Census. (1994).   *Statistical abstract of the United States 1994.* Washington, DC: U.S. Government Printing Office.

Burger, J. M. (1987).   Increased performance with increased personal control: A self-presentation interpretation. *Journal of Experimental Social Psychology, 23*, 350–360. (p. 327)

Burger, J. M., & Burns, L. (1988).   The illusion of unique invulnerability and the use of effective contraception. *Personality and Social Psychology Bulletin, 14*, 264–270. (p. 405)

Burish, T. G., & Carey, M. P. (1986).   Conditioned aversive responses in cancer chemotherapy patients: Theoretical and developmental analysis. *Journal of Counseling and Clinical Psychology, 54*, 593–600. (p. 203)

Burke, K. C., Burke, J. D., Regier, D. A., & Rae, D. S. (1990).   Age at onset of selected mental disorders in five community populations. *Archives of General Psychiatry, 47*, 511–518. (p. 420)

Burns, D. D. (1980).   *Feeling good: The new mood therapy.* New York: Signet. (p. 431)

Burros, M. (1994, July 17).   Despite awareness of risks, more in U.S. are getting fat. *New York Times*, pp. 1, 18. (p. 309)

Bushman, B. J. (1993).   Human aggression while under the influence of alcohol and other drugs: An integrative research review. *Current Directions in Psychological Science, 2*, 148–152. (p. 502)

Buss, A. H. (1989).   Personality as traits. *American Psychologist, 44*, 1378–1388. (pp. 95, 392)

Buss, D. (1994a).   *The evolution of desire.* New York: Basic Books. (p. 514)

Buss, D. (1994b).   The strategies of human mating. *American Scientist, 82*, 238–249. (p. 514)

Buss, D. M. (1991).   Evolutionary personality psychology. *Annual Review of Psychology, 42*, 459–491. (p. 25)

Butcher, J. N. (1990).   *The MMPI-2 in psychological treatment.* New York: Oxford University Press. (p. 391)

Butler, A. C., Hokanson, J. E., & Flynn, H. A. (1994).   A comparison of self-esteem lability and low trait self-esteem as vulnerability factors for depression. *Journal of Personality and Social Psychology, 66*, 166–177. (p. 432)

Butler, R. A. (1954, February).   Curiosity in monkeys. *Scientific American*, pp. 70–75. (p. 299)

Byne, W., & Parsons, B. (1993).   Human sexual orientation: The biologic theories reappraised. *Archives of General Psychiatry, 50*, 228–239. (p. 320)

Byrne, D. (1971).   *The attraction paradigm.* New York: Academic Press. (p. 514)

Byrne, D. (1982).   Predicting human sexual behavior. In A. G. Kraut (Ed.), *The G. Stanley Hall Lecture Series* (Vol. 2).   Washington, DC: American Psychological Association. (pp. 200, 313, 315)

Byrne, R. W. (1991, May/June).   Brute intellect. *The Sciences*, pp. 42–47. (p. 269)

Byrnes, G., & Kelly, I. W. (1992).   Crisis calls and lunar cycles: A twenty-year review. *Psychological Reports, 71*, 779–785. (p. 430)

Cameron, P., & Biber, H. (1973).   Sexual thought throughout the life-span. *Gerontologist, 13*, 144–147. (p. 175)

Campbell, D. T. (1975).   On the conflicts between biological and social evolution and between psychology and moral tradition. *American Psychologist, 30*, 1103–1126. (p. 348)

Campbell, D. T., & Specht, J. C. (1985).   Altruism: Biology, culture, and religion. *Journal of Social and Clinical Psychology, 3*(1), 33–42. (p. 400)

Campbell, S. (1986).   *The Loch Ness monster: The evidence.* Willingborough, Northamptonshire, England: Acquarian Press. (p. 150)

Campos, J. J., Bertenthal, B. I., & Kermoian, R. (1992).   Early experience and emotional development: The emergence of wariness and heights. *Psychological Science, 3*, 61–64. (pp. 142, 421)

Cannon, T. D., & Marco, E. (1994).   Structural brain abnormalities as indicators of vulnerability to schizophrenia. *Schizophrenia Bulletin, 20*, 89–101. (p. 437)

Cannon, W. B. (1929).   *Bodily changes in pain, hunger, fear, and rage.* New York: Branford. (p. 301)

Cannon, W. B., & Washburn, A. (1912).   An explanation of hunger. *American Journal of Physiology, 29*, 441–454. (p. 301)

Cantor, N., & Norem, J. K. (1989).   Defensive pessimism and stress and coping. *Social Cognition, 7*, 92–112. (p. 405)

Cantril, H., & Bumstead, C. H. (1960).   *Reflections on the human venture.* New York: New York University Press. (p. 493)

Carducci, B. J., Cosby, P. C., & Ward, D. D. (1978).   Sexual arousal and interpersonal evaluations. *Journal of Experimental Social Psychology, 14*, 449–457. (p. 515)

Carey, G. (1990).   Genes, fears, phobias, and phobic disorders. *Journal of Counseling and Development, 68*, 628–632. (p. 422)

Carli, L. L., & Leonard, J. B. (1989).   The effect of hindsight on victim derogation. *Journal of Social and Clinical Psychology, 8*, 331–343. (p. 500)

Carlson, M., Charlin, V., & Miller, N. (1988).   Positive mood and helping behavior: A test of six hypotheses. *Journal of Personality and Social Psychology, 55*, 211–229. (p. 518)

Carlson, R. (1984).   What's social about social psychology? Where's the person in personality research? *Journal of Personality and Social Psychology, 47*, 1304–1309. (p. 407)

Carlson, S. (1985).   A double-blind test of astrology. *Nature, 318*, 419–425. (p. 406)

Carnegie Council on Adolescent Development. (1989, June).   *Turning points: Preparing American youth for the 21st century* (Report of the Task Force on Education of Young Adolescents).   New York: Carnegie Corporation. (p. 520)

Carson, R. C., Butcher, J. N., & Coleman, J. C. (1988).   *Abnormal psychology and modern life* (8th ed.). Glenview, IL: Scott, Foresman. (p. 416)

Cartwright, R. D. (1978).   *A primer on sleep and dreaming.* Reading, MA: Addison-Wesley. (p. 167)

Case, R. B., Moss, A. J., Case, N., McDermott, M., & Eberly, S. (1992). Living alone after myocardial infarction: Impact on prognosis. *Journal of the American Medical Association, 267*, 515–519. (p. 372)

Cash, T., & Janda, L. H. (1984, December). The eye of the beholder. *Psychology Today*, pp. 46–52. (p. 513)

Caspi, A., & Moffitt, T. E. (1991). Individual differences are accentuated during periods of social change: The sample case of girls at puberty. *Journal of Personality and Social Psychology, 61*, 157–168. (p. 89)

Cattell, R. B. (1963). Theory of fluid and crystallized intelligence: A critical experiment. *Journal of Educational Psychology, 54*, 1–22. (p. 102)

Cavalli-Sforza, L., Menozzi, P., & Piazza, A. (1994). *The history and geography of human genes*. Princeton, NJ: Princeton University Press. (p. 289)

Ceci, S. J. (1993). Cognitive and social factors in children's testimony. Master lecture, American Psychological Association convention. (pp. 244, 245)

Ceci, S. J., & Bruck, M. (1993a). Child witnesses: Translating research into policy. *Social Policy Report* (Society for Research in Child Development), 7(3), 1–30. (pp. 244–245)

Ceci, S. J., & Bruck, M. (1993b). Suggestibility of the child witness: A historical review and synthesis. *Psychological Bulletin, 113*, 403–439. (pp. 244–245)

Ceci, S. J., Huffman, M. L. C., Smith, E., & Loftus, E. F. (1994). Repeatedly thinking about a non-event: Source misattributions among preschoolers. *Consciousness and Cognition, 3*, 388–407. (p. 245)

Ceci, S. J., & Liker, J. K. (1986). A day at the races: A study of IQ, expertise, and cognitive complexity. *Journal of Experimental Psychology: General, 115*, 255–266. (pp. 338, 374)

Centers for Disease Control. (1983). Behavioral risk factor prevalence surveys—United States. Reported in *Behavior Today Newsletter*, October 29, 1984, p. 7. (p. 183)

Centers for Disease Control. (1989). Results from the national adolescent student health survey. *Morbidity and Mortality Weekly Report, 38*(9), 147–150. (p. 428)

Centers for Disease Control. (1991). Body-weight perceptions and selected weight-management goals and practices of high school students—United States, 1990. *Morbidity and Mortality Weekly Report, 40*, 741, 747–750. (p. 309)

Centers for Disease Control. (1992, January 3). Sexual behavior among high school students—United States, 1990. *Morbidity and Mortality Weekly Report, 40*(51, 52), 885–888. (p. 96)

Centers for Disease Control. (1992, September 16). Serious mental illness and disability in the adult household population: United States, 1989. Advance Data No. 218 from *Vital and Health Statistics*, National Center for Health Statistics. (p. 442)

Centers for Disease Control. (1992, November 20). HIV instruction and selected HIV-risk behaviors among high school students—United States, 1989–1991. *Morbidity and Mortality Weekly Report, 41*(46), 866–867. (p. 92)

Centers for Disease Control Vietnam Experience Study. (1988). Health status of Vietnam veterans. *Journal of the American Medical Association, 259*, 2701–2709. (p. 360)

Centerwall, B. S. (1989). Exposure to television as a risk factor for violence. *American Journal of Epidemiology, 129*, 643–652. (p. 505)

Cerella, J. (1985). Information processing rates in the elderly. *Psychological Bulletin, 98*, 67–83. (p. 99)

Chase, W. G., & Simon, H. A. (1973). Perception in chess. *Cognitive Psychology, 4*, 55–81. (p. 230)

Chassin, L., Presson, C. C., Sherman, S. J., & McGrew, J. (1987). The changing smoking environment for middle and high school students: 1980–1983. *Journal of Behavioral Medicine, 10*, 581–593. (p. 190)

Chaves, J. F. (1989). Hypnotic control of clinical pain. In N. P. Spanos & J. F. Chaves (Eds.), *Hypnosis: The cognitive-behavioral perspective*. Buffalo, NY: Prometheus Books. (p. 179)

Cheek, J. M., & Melchior, L. A. (1990). Shyness, self-esteem, and self-consciousness. In H. Leitenberg (Ed.), *Handbook of social and evaluation anxiety*. New York: Plenum. (pp. 85, 433)

Cherfas, J. (1990). Two bomb attacks on scientists in the U.K. *Science, 248*, 1485. (p. 27)

Chess, S., & Thomas, A. (1987). *Know your child: An authoritative guide for today's parents*. New York: Basic Books. (p. 82)

Chi, M. T. H. (1976). Short-term memory limitations in children: Capacity or processing deficits. *Memory & Cognition, 4*, 559–572. (p. 234)

Chomsky, N. (1959). [Review of B. F. Skinner's *Verbal behavior*.] *Language, 35*, 26–58. (p. 266)

Chomsky, N. (1972). *Language and mind*. New York: Harcourt Brace Jovanovich. (p. 264)

Chomsky, N. (1987). Language in a psychological setting (Sophia Linguistic Working Papers in Linguistics, No. 22). Sophia University, Tokyo. (pp. 266, 267)

Christensen, A., & Jacobson, N. S. (1994). Who (or what) can do psychotherapy: The status and challenge of nonprofessional therapies. *Psychological Science, 5*, 8–14. (p. 468)

Christianson, S. A. (1992). Emotional stress and eyewitness memory: A critical review. *Psychological Bulletin, 112*, 284–309. (p. 249)

Christophersen, E. R., & Edwards, K. J. (1992). Treatment of elimination disorders: State of the art 1991. *Applied & Preventive Psychology, 1*, 15–22. (p. 457)

Chwalisz, K., Diener, E., & Gallagher, D. (1988). Autonomic arousal feedback and emotional experience: Evidence from the spinal cord injured. *Journal of Personality and Social Psychology, 54*, 820–828. (p. 347)

Cialdini, R. B. (1993). *Influence: Science and practice* (3rd ed.). New York: HarperCollins. (p. 483)

Cialdini, R. B., & Richardson, K. D. (1980). Two indirect tactics of image management: Basking and blasting. *Journal of Personality and Social Psychology, 39*, 406–415. (p. 499)

Clark, R. D., III (1990). The impact of AIDS on gender differences in willingness to engage in casual sex. *Journal of Applied Social Psychology, 20*, 771–782. (p. 316)

Clark, R. D., III, & Hatfield, E. (1989). Gender differences in willingness to engage in casual sex. *Journal of Psychology and Human Sexuality, 2*, 39–55. (p. 316)

Coe, W. C. (1989a). Posthypnotic amnesia: Theory and research. In N. P. Spanos & J. F. Chaves (Eds.), *Hypnosis: The cognitive-behavioral perspective*. Buffalo, NY: Prometheus Books. (p. 176)

Coe, W. C. (1989b). Hypnosis: The role of sociopolitical factors in a paradigm clash. In N. P. Spanos & J. F. Chaves (Eds.), *Hypnosis: The cognitive-behavioral perspective*. Buffalo, NY: Prometheus Books. (p. 180)

Coffey, C. E. (Ed.). (1993). *Clinical science of electroconvulsive therapy*. Washington, DC: American Psychiatric Press. (p. 473)

Coffey, C. E., Wilkinson, W. E., Weiner, R. D., Parashos, I. A., Djang, W. T., Webb, M. C., Figiel, G. S., & Spritzer, C. E. (1993). Quantitative cerebral anatomy in depression: A controlled magnetic resonance imaging study. *Archives of General Psychiatry, 50,* 7–16. (p. 430)

Cohen, S. (1988). Psychosocial models of the role of social support in the etiology of physical disease. *Health Psychology, 7,* 269–297. (p. 372)

Cohen, S., Doyle, W. J., Skoner, D. P., Fireman, P., Gwaltney, Jr., J. M., & Newson, J. T. (1995). State and trait negative affect as predictors of objective and subjective symptoms of respiratory viral infections. *Journal of Personality and Social Psychology, 68,* 159–169. (p. 364)

Cohen, S., Kaplan, J. R., Cunnick, J. E., Manuck, S. B., & Rabin, B. S. (1992). Chronic social stress, affiliation, and cellular immune response in nonhuman primates. *Psychological Science, 3,* 301–304. (p. 363)

Cohen, S., Tyrrell, D. A. J., & Smith, A. P. (1991). Psychological stress and susceptibility to the common cold. *New England Journal of Medicine, 325,* 606–612. (p. 364)

Cohen, S., Tyrrell, D. A. J., & Smith, A. P. (1993). Negative life events, perceived stress, negative affect, and susceptibility to the common cold. *Journal of Personality and Social Psychology, 64,* 131–140. (p. 364)

Cohen, S., & Williamson, G. M. (1991). Stress and infectious disease in humans. *Psychological Bulletin, 109,* 5–24. (p. 364)

Coile, D. C., & Miller, N. E. (1984). How radical animal activists try to mislead humane people. *American Psychologist, 39,* 700–701. (p. 26)

Coleman, J. C. (1980). *The nature of adolescence.* London: Methuen. (p. 88)

Coleman, P. D., & Flood, D. G. (1986). Dendritic proliferation in the aging brain as a compensatory repair mechanism. In D. F. Swaab, E. Fliers, M. Mirmiram, W. A. Van Gool, & F. Van Haaren (Eds.), *Progress in brain research* (Vol. 20). New York: Elsevier. (p. 100)

Colombo, J. (1982). The critical period concept: Research, methodology, and theoretical issues. *Psychological Bulletin, 91,* 260–275. (p. 82)

Colon, E. A., Callies, A. L., Popkin, M. K., & McGlave, P. B. (1991). Depressed mood and other variables related to bone marrow transplantation survival in acute leukemia. *Psychosomatics, 32,* 420–425. (pp. 364, 372)

Consensus Conference. (1985). Electroconvulsive therapy. *Journal of the American Medical Association, 254,* 2103–2108. (p. 473)

Conway, M., & Ross, M. (1984). Getting what you want by revising what you had. *Journal of Personality and Social Psychology, 47,* 738–748. (p. 247)

Cook, E. W., III, Hodes, R. L., & Lang, P. J. (1986). Preparedness and phobia: Effects of stimulus content on human visceral conditioning. *Journal of Abnormal Psychology, 95,* 195–207. (p. 203)

Cook, M., & Mineka, S. (1991). Selective associations in the origins of phobic fears and their implications for behavior therapy. In P. Martin (Ed.), *Handbook of behavior therapy and psychological science: An integrative approach.* New York: Pergamon Press. (p. 217)

Coon, P. M., Bowman, E. S., & Milstein, V. (1988). Multiple personality disorder: A clinical investigation of 50 cases. *Journal of Nervous and Mental Disease, 176,* 519–527. (p. 426)

Cooper, W. H. (1983). An achievement motivation nomological network. *Journal of Personality and Social Psychology, 44,* 841–861. (p. 323)

Coren, S. (1993). *The left-hander syndrome: The causes and consequences of left-handedness.* New York: Vintage Books. (p. 64)

Corina, D. P., Vaid, J., & Bellugi, U. (1992). The linguistic basis of left hemisphere specialization. *Science, 255,* 1258–1260. (p. 62)

Costa, P. T., Jr., & McCrae, R. R. (1989). Personality continuity and the changes of adult life. In M. Storandt & G. R. VandenBos (Eds.), *The adult years: Continuity and change.* Washington, DC: American Psychological Association. (p. 112)

Courtney, J. G., Longnecker, M. P., Theorell, T., & de Verdier, M. G. (1993). Stressful life events and the risk of colorectal cancer. *Epidemiology, 4,* 407–414. (p. 364)

Cousins, N. (1989). *Head first: The biology of hope.* New York: Dutton. (p. 398)

Covington, M. V., & Omelich, C. L. (1988). I can resist anything but temptation: Adolescent expectations for smoking cigarettes. *Journal of Applied Social Psychology, 18,* 203–227. (p. 190)

Cowan, N. (1988). Evolving conceptions of memory storage, selective attention, and their mutual constraints within the human information-processing system. *Psychological Bulletin, 104,* 163–191. (p. 233)

Cowan, N. (1994). Mechanisms of verbal short-term memory. *Current Directions in Psychological Science, 3,* 185–189. (p. 234)

Cowart, B. J. (1981). Development of taste perception in humans: Sensitivity and preference throughout the life span. *Psychological Bulletin, 90,* 43–73. (p. 136)

Craig, M. E., Kalichman, S. C., & Follingstad, D. R. (1989). Verbal coercive sexual behavior among college students. *Archives of Sexual Behavior, 18,* 421–434. (p. 506)

Craik, F. I. M., & Watkins, M. J. (1973). The role of rehearsal in short-term memory. *Journal of Verbal Learning and Verbal Behavior, 12,* 599–607. (p. 228)

Crandall, C. S. (1988). Social contagion of binge eating. *Journal of Personality and Social Psychology, 55,* 588–598. (p. 304)

Crandall, J. E. (1984). Social interest as a moderator of life stress. *Journal of Personality and Social Psychology, 47,* 164–174. (p. 400)

Crocker, J., Thompson, L. L., McGraw, K. M., & Ingerman, C. (1987). Downward comparison, prejudice, and evaluation of others: Effects of self-esteem and threat. *Journal of Personality and Social Psychology, 52,* 907–916. (p. 499)

Crook, T. H., & West, R. L. (1990). Name recall performance across the adult life-span. *British Journal of Psychology, 81,* 335–340. (p. 100)

Cross-National Collaborative Group. (1992). The changing rate of major depression. *Journal of the American Medical Association, 268,* 3098–3105. (p. 429)

Crowell, J. A., & Waters, E. (1994). Bowlby's theory grown up: The role of attachment in adult love relationships. *Psychological Inquiry, 5,* 1–22. (p. 82)

CSICOP (1994, December). Psychics fail once again. *Skeptical Briefs,* p. 9. (p. 155)

Csikszentmihalyi, M. (1990). *Flow: The psychology of optimal experience.* New York: Harper & Row. (pp. 259, 350)

Curtis, R. C., & Miller, K. (1986). Believing another likes or dislikes you: Behaviors making the beliefs come true. *Journal of Personality and Social Psychology, 51,* 284–290. (p. 515)

Cutler, B. L., & Penrod, S. D. (1989). Forensically relevant moderators of the relation between eyewitness identification accuracy and confidence. *Journal of Applied Psychology, 74,* 650–652. (p. 244)

Dabbs, J. M., Jr. (1992). Testosterone measurements in social and clinical psychology. *Journal of Social and Clinical Psychology, 11,* 302–321. (p. 502)

Dabbs, J. M., Jr., & Morris, R. (1990). Testosterone, social class, and antisocial behavior in a sample of 4,462 men. *Psychological Science, 1,* 209–211. (p. 502)

Dabbs, J. M., Jr., Ruback, R. B., & Besch, N. F. (1987). Male saliva testosterone following conversations with male and female partners. Paper presented at the American Psychological Association convention. (p. 313)

Damasio, H., Grabowski, T., Frank, R., Galaburda, A. M., & Damasio, A. R. (1994). The return of Phineas Gage: Clues about the brain from the skull of a famous patient. *Science, 264,* 1102–1105. (p. 55)

Darley, J. M., & Latané, B. (1968a). Bystander intervention in emergencies: Diffusion of responsibility. *Journal of Personality and Social Psychology, 8,* 377–383. (p. 517)

Darley, J. M., & Latané, B. (1968b, December). When will people help in a crisis? *Psychology Today,* pp. 54–57, 70–71. (p. 517)

Darrach, B., & Norris, J. (1984, August). An American tragedy. *Life,* pp. 58–74. (p. 441)

Davey, G. C. L. (1992). Classical conditioning and the acquisition of human fears and phobias: A review and synthesis of the literature. *Advances in Behavior Research and Therapy, 14,* 29–66. (p. 203)

Davidson, R. J. (1992). Emotion and affective style: Hemispheric substrates. *Psychological Science, 3,* 39–43. (pp. 338, 430)

Davidson, R. J., Ekman, P., Saron, C. D., Senulis, J. A., & Friesen, W. V. (1990). Approach-withdrawal and cerebral asymmetry: Emotional expression and brain physiology I. *Journal of Personality and Social Psychology, 58,* 330–341. (p. 338)

Davies, D. R., Matthews, G., & Wong, C. S. K. (1991). Aging and work. *International Review of Industrial and Organizational Psychology, 6,* 149–211. (p. 104)

Dawes, R. M. (1980). Social dilemmas. *Annual Review of Psychology, 31,* 169–193. (p. 510)

Dawes, R. M. (1994). *House of cards: Psychology and psychotherapy built on myth.* New York: Free Press. (p. 385)

Dean, G. A., Kelly, I. W., Saklofske, D. H., & Furnham, A. (1992). Graphology and human judgment. In B. Beyerstein & D. Beyerstein (Eds.), *The write stuff: Evaluations of graphology.* Buffalo, NY: Prometheus Books. (p. 406)

Deardorff, J. (1994, July 28). 'It feels like there's a beast inside me.' *Chicago Tribune,* p. 1. (p. 304)

Deary, I. J., & Matthews, G. (1993). Personality traits are alive and well. *The Psychologist: Bulletin of the British Psychological Society, 6,* 299–311. (p. 392)

de Boysson-Bardies, B., Halle, P., Sagart, L., & Durand, C. (1989). A cross linguistic investigation of vowel formats in babbling. *Journal of Child Language, 16,* 1–17. (p. 265)

Deci, E. L., & Ryan, R. M. (1985). *Intrinsic motivation and self-determination in human behavior.* New York: Plenum Press. (p. 324)

Deci, E. L., & Ryan, R. M. (1987). The support of autonomy and the control of behavior. *Journal of Personality and Social Psychology, 53,* 1024–1037. (p. 325)

Deci, E. L., & Ryan, R. M. (1992). The initiation and regulation of intrinsically motivated learning and achievement. In A. K. Boggiano & T. S. Pittman (Eds.), *Achievement and motivation: A social-developmental perspective.* New York: Cambridge University Press. (p. 324)

de Cuevas, J. (1990, September-October). "No, she holded them loosely." *Harvard Magazine,* pp. 60–67. (p. 266)

de Jong-Gierveld, J. (1987). Developing and testing a model of loneliness. *Journal of Personality and Social Psychology, 53,* 119–128. (p. 433)

Delgado, J. M. R. (1969). *Physical control of the mind: Toward a psychocivilized society.* New York: Harper & Row. (p. 53)

DeLoache, J. S. (1987). Rapid change in the symbolic functioning of very young children. *Science, 238,* 1556–1557. (p. 78)

Dement, W. (1990). In the PBS film, *Sleep alert.* Quoted by *Behavior Today,* March 12, p. 8. (p. 169)

Dement, W. C. (1978). *Some must watch while some must sleep.* New York: Norton. (pp. 166, 167, 170)

Dement, W. C., & Wolpert, E. A. (1958). The relation of eye movements, body mobility, and external stimuli to dream content. *Journal of Experimental Psychology, 55,* 543–553. (p. 172)

Dempster, F. N. (1988). The spacing effect: A case study in the failure to apply the results of psychological research. *American Psychologist, 43,* 627–634. (p. 227)

Denton, K., & Krebs, D. (1990). From the scene to the crime: The effect of alcohol and social context on moral judgment. *Journal of Personality and Social Psychology, 59,* 242–248. (p. 183)

D'Eon, J. L. (1989). Hypnosis in the control of labor pain. In N. P. Spanos & J. F. Chaves (Eds.), *Hypnosis: The cognitive-behavioral perspective.* Buffalo, NY: Prometheus Books. (p. 179)

Dermer, M., Cohen, S. J., Jacobsen, E., & Anderson, E. A. (1979). Evaluative judgments of aspects of life as a function of vicarious exposure to hedonic extremes. *Journal of Personality and Social Psychology, 37,* 247–260. (p. 350)

Dermer, M., & Pyszczynski, T. A. (1978). Effects of erotica upon men's loving and liking responses for women they love. *Journal of Personality and Social Psychology, 36,* 1302–1309. (p. 515)

Deutsch, J. A. (1972, July). Brain reward: ESP and ecstasy. *Psychology Today,* pp. 46–48. (p. 51)

Deutsch, M. (1991). Egalitarianism in the laboratory and at work. In R. Vermunt & H. Steensma (Eds.), *Social justice in human relations.* New York: Plenum. (p. 215)

Dey, E. L., Astin, A. W., & Korn, W. S. (1991). *The American freshman: Twenty-five year trends.* Los Angeles: Higher Education Research Institute, UCLA. (pp. 347, 495)

Diaconis, P., & Mosteller, F. (1989). Methods for studying coincidences. *Journal of the American Statistical Association, 84,* 853–861. (p. 16)

Diamond, J. (1986). Variation in human testis size. *Nature, 320,* 488–489. (p. 108)

Diamond, J. (1989, May). The great leap forward. *Discover,* pp. 50–60. (p. 264)

Diamond, R. (1993). Genetics and male sexual orientation (letter). *Science, 261,* p. 1258. (p. 320)

Diener, E. (1984). Subjective well-being. *Psychological Bulletin, 95,* 542–575. (p. 349)

Diener, E. (1993). Most Americans are happy. Unpublished manuscript, University of Illinois. (p. 397)

Dietz, W. H., Jr., & Gortmaker, S. L. (1985). Do we fatten our children at the television set? Obesity and television viewing in children and adolescents. *Pediatrics, 75,* 807–812. (p. 309)

DiLalla, L. F., & Gottesman, I. I. (1991). Biological and genetic contributors to violence—Widom's untold tale. *Psychological Bulletin, 109,* 125–129. (p. 441)

Dindia, K., & Allen, M. (1992). Sex differences in self-disclosure: A meta-analysis. *Psychological Bulletin, 112,* 106–124. (p. 94)

Dinges, N. G., & Hull, P. (1992).   Personality, culture, and international studies. In D. Lieberman (Ed.), *Revealing the world: An interdisciplinary reader for international studies.* Dubuque, IA: Kendall-Hunt. (p. 272)

Dion, K. K., & Dion, K. L. (1993).   Individualistic and collectivistic perspectives on gender and the cultural context of love and intimacy. *Journal of Social Issues, 49,* 53–69. (p. 399)

Dixon, B. (1986, April).   Dangerous thoughts: How we think and feel can make us sick. *Science, 86,* pp. 63–66. (p. 364)

Dobson, K. S. (1989).   A meta-analysis of the efficacy of cognitive therapy for depression. *Journal of Consulting and Clinical Psychology, 57,* 414–419. (p. 467)

Dohrenwend, B., Pearlin, L., Clayton, P., Hamburg, B., Dohrenwend, B. P., Riley, M., & Rose, R. (1982).   Report on stress and life events. In G. R. Elliott & C. Eisdorfer (Eds.), *Stress and human health: Analysis and implications of research* (A study by the Institute of Medicine/National Academy of Sciences).   New York: Springer. (p. 358)

Dohrenwend, B. P., Levav, I., Shrout, P. E., Schwartz, S., Naveh, G., Link, B. G., Skodol, A. E., & Stueve, A. (1992).   Socioeconomic status and psychiatric disorders: The causation-selection issue. *Science, 255,* 946–952. (p. 443)

Domjan, M. (1992).   Adult learning and mate choice: Possibilities and experimental evidence. *American Zoologist, 32,* 48–61. (p. 200)

Donaldson, M. (1979, March).   The mismatch between school and children's minds. *Human Nature,* pp. 60–67. (p. 78)

Donnerstein, E., Linz, D., & Penrod, S. (1987).   *The question of pornography.* New York: Free Press. (p. 506)

Doty, R. L., Shaman, P., Applebaum, S. L., Giberson, R., Siksorski, L., & Rosenberg, L. (1984).   Smell identification ability: Changes with age. *Science, 226,* 1441–1443. (p. 99)

Draguns, J. G. (1990a).   Normal and abnormal behavior in cross-cultural perspective: Specifying the nature of their relationship. *Nebraska Symposium on Motivation 1989, 37,* 235–277. (pp. 413, 422, 432)

Draguns, J. G. (1990b).   Applications of cross-cultural psychology in the field of mental health. In R. W. Brislin (Ed.), *Applied cross-cultural psychology.* Newbury Park, CA: Sage. (pp. 413, 416)

Drucker, P. F. (1982, December).   A conversation with Peter F. Drucker. *Psychology Today,* pp. 60–67. (p. 386)

Druckman, D., & Bjork, R. A. (1991).   *In the mind's eye: Enhancing human performance.* Washington, DC: National Academy Press. (p. 388)

Druckman, D., & Swets, J. A. (Eds.). (1988).   *Enhancing human performance: Issues, theories, and techniques.* Washington, DC: National Academy Press. (pp. 156, 274)

Duclos, S. E., Laird, J. D., Sexter, M., Stern, L., & Van Lighten, O. (1989).   Emotion-specific effects of facial expressions and postures on emotional experience. *Journal of Personality and Social Psychology, 57,* 100–108. (p. 342)

Duggan, J. P., & Booth, D. A. (1986).   Obesity, overeating, and rapid gastric emptying in rats with ventromedial hypothalamic lesions. *Science, 231,* 609–611. (p. 302)

Duncan, B. L. (1976).   Differential social perception and attribution of intergroup violence: Testing the lower limits of stereotyping of blacks. *Journal of Personality and Social Psychology, 34,* 590–598. (p. 497)

Duncan, G. J., Hill, M. S., & Hoffman, S. D. (1988).   Welfare dependence within and across generations. *Science, 239,* 467–471. (p. 260)

Duncker, K. (1945).   On problem solving. *Psychological Monographs, 58* (Whole no. 270). (pp. 258, 260)

Dunn, J., & Plomin, R. (1990).   *Separate lives: Why siblings are so different.* New York: Basic Books. (p. 110)

Dunnett, S. B. (1989).   Neural transplantation: Normal brain function and repair after damage. *The Psychologist, 1,* 4–8. (p. 58)

Dunning, D., Griffin, D. W., Milojkovic, J. D., & Ross, L. (1990).   *Journal of Personality and Social Psychology, 58,* 568–581. (p. 261)

Dutton, D. G., & Aron, A. (1989).   Romantic attraction and generalized liking for others who are sources of conflict-based arousal. *Canadian Journal of Behavioural Sciences, 21,* 246–257. (p. 515)

Dutton, D. G., & Aron, A. P. (1974).   Some evidence for heightened sexual attraction under conditions of high anxiety. *Journal of Personality and Social Psychology, 30,* 510–517. (p. 515)

Dweck, C. S., & Elliott, E. S. (1983).   Achievement motivation. In P. Mussen & E. M. Hetherington (Eds.), *Handbook of child psychology* (Vol. IV).   New York: Wiley. (p. 324)

Eagles, J. M. (1991).   Is schizophrenia disappearing? *British Journal of Psychiatry, 158,* 834–835. (p. 437)

Eagly, A. H., Ashmore, R. D., Makhijani, M. G., & Kennedy, L. C. (1991).   What is beautiful is good, but . . .: A meta-analytic review of research on the physical attractiveness stereotype. *Psychological Bulletin, 110,* 109–128. (p. 513)

Eagly, A. H., & Crowley, M. (1986).   Gender and helping behavior: A meta-analytic review of the social psychological literature. *Psychological Bulletin, 100,* 283–308. (p. 518)

Eagly, A. H., & Johnson, B. T. (1990).   Gender and leadership style: A meta-analysis. *Psychological Bulletin, 108,* 233–256. (p. 327)

Eagly, A. H., & Karau, S. J. (1991).   Gender and the emergence of leaders: A meta-analysis. *Journal of Personality and Social Psychology, 60,* 685–710. (p. 328)

Ebbesen, E. B., Duncan, B., & Konecni, V. J. (1975).   Effects of content of verbal aggression on future verbal aggression: A field experiment. *Journal of Experimental Social Psychology, 11,* 192–204. (p. 4345

Ebbinghaus, H. (1885).   *Über das Gedachtnis.* Leipzig: Duncker & Humblot. Cited in R. Klatzky (1980), *Human memory: Structures and processes.* San Francisco: Freeman. (p. 235)

Eccles, J. S., Jacobs, J. E., & Harold, R. D. (1990).   Gender role stereotypes, expectancy effects, and parents' socialization of gender differences. *Journal of Social Issues, 46,* 183–201. (p. 290)

Eckensberger, L. H. (1994).   Moral development and its measurement across cultures. In W. J. Lonner & R. Malpass (Eds.), *Psychology and culture.* Boston: Allyn and Bacon. (p. 91)

Eckert, E. D., Heston, L. L., & Bouchard, T. J., Jr. (1981).   MZ twins reared apart: Preliminary findings of psychiatric disturbances and traits. In L. Gedda, P. Paris, & W. D. Nance (Eds.), *Twin research: Vol. 3. Pt. B. Intelligence, personality, and development.* New York: Alan Liss. (p. 422)

Edwards, C. P. (1981).   The comparative study of the development of moral judgment and reasoning. In R. H. Munroe, R. L. Munroe, & B. B. Whiting (Eds.), *Handbook of cross-cultural human development.* New York: Garland Press. (p. 91)

Edwards, C. P. (1982).   Moral development in comparative cultural perspective. In D. A. Wagner & H. W. Stevenson (Eds.), *Cultural perspectives on child development.* San Francisco: Freeman. (p. 91)

Ehrlichman, H., & Halpern, J. N. (1988).   Affect and memory: Effects of pleasant and unpleasant odors on retrieval of happy and unhappy memories. *Journal of Personality and Social Psychology, 55,* 769–779. (p. 138)

Eibl-Eibesfeldt, I. (1971). *Love and hate: The natural history of behavior patterns.* New York: Holt, Rinehart & Winston. (p. 341)

Eich, E. (1990). Learning during sleep. In R. B. Bootzin, J. F. Kihlstrom, & D. L. Schacter (Eds.), *Sleep and cognition.* Washington, DC: American Psychological Association. (p. 172)

Eich, J. E. (1980). The cue-dependent nature of state-dependent retrieval. *Memory and Cognition, 8,* 157–173. (p. 183)

Eisenberg, N., & Lennon, R. (1983). Sex differences in empathy and related capacities. *Psychological Bulletin, 94,* 100–131. (p. 94)

Ekman, P. (1994). Strong evidence for universals in facial expressions: A reply to Russell's mistaken critique. *Psychological Bulletin, 115,* 268–287. (p. 340)

Ekman, P., Davidson, R. J., & Friesen, W. V. (1990). The Duchenne smile: Emotional expression and brain physiology II. *Journal of Personality and Social Psychology, 58,* 342–353. (p. 342)

Ekman, P., & Friesen, W. V. (1975). *Unmasking the face.* Englewood Cliffs, NJ: Prentice-Hall. (p. 340)

Ekman, P., Friesen, W. V., O'Sullivan, M., Chan, A., Diacoyanni-Tarlatzis, I., Heider, K., Krause, R., LeCompte, W. A., Pitcairn, T., Ricci-Bitti, P. E., Scherer, K., Tomita, M., & Tzavaras, A. (1987). Universals and cultural differences in the judgments of facial expressions of emotion. *Journal of Personality and Social Psychology, 53,* 712–717. (p. 340)

Ekman, P., Levenson, R. W., & Friesen, W. V. (1983). Autonomic nervous system activity distinguishes among emotions. *Science, 221,* 1208–1210. (p. 343)

Elkin, I., Shea, T., Watkins, J. T., Imber, S. D., Sotsky, S. M., Collins, J. F., Glass, D. R., Pilkonis, P. A., Leber, W. R., Docherty, J. P., Fiester, S. J., & Parloff, M. B. (1989). National Institute of Mental Health treatment of depression collaborative research program. *Archives of General Psychiatry, 46,* 971–983. (p. 466)

Elkind, D. (1970). The origins of religion in the child. *Review of Religious Research, 12,* 35–42. (p. 90)

Ellis, A. (1962). *Reason and emotion in psychotherapy.* Secaucus, NJ: Citadel Press. (p. 459)

Ellis, A. (1980). Psychotherapy and atheistic values: A response to A. E. Bergin's "Psychotherapy and religious values." *Journal of Consulting and Clinical Psychology, 48* 635–639. (p. 468)

Ellis, A. (1984). Rational-emotive therapy. In R. J. Corsini (Ed.), *Current psychotherapies* (3rd ed.). Itasca, IL: Peacock. (p. 459)

Ellis, A. (1987). The impossibility of achieving consistently good mental health. *American Psychologist, 42,* 364–375. (p. 459)

Ellis, A. (1989). Rational-emotive therapy. In R. J. Corsini & D. Wedding (Eds.), *Current psychotherapies* (4th ed.). Itasca, IL: Peacock. (p. 459)

Ellis, A. (1993). Changing rational-emotive therapy (RET) to rational emotive behavior therapy (REBT). *The Behavior Therapist, 16,* 257–258. (p. 459)

Ellis, A., & Becker, I. M. (1982). *A guide to personal happiness.* North Hollywood, CA: Wilshire Book Co. (p. 205)

Ellis, H. C., & Ashbrook, P. W. (1989). The "state" of mood and memory research: A selective review. *Journal of Social Behavior and Personality, 4,* 1–21. (p. 241)

Ellis, L., & Ames, M. A. (1987). Neurohormonal functioning and sexual orientation: A theory of homosexuality-heterosexuality. *Psychological Bulletin, 101,* 233–258. (p. 320)

Emde, R. N., Plomin, R., Robinson, J., Corley, R., DeFries, J., Fulker, D. W., Reznick, J. S., Campos, J., Kagan, J., & Zahn-Waxler, C. (1992). Temperament, emotion, and cognition at fourteen months: The MacArthur Longitudinal Twin Study. *Child Development, 63,* 1437–1455. (p. 82)

Empson, J. A. C., & Clarke, P. R. F. (1970). Rapid eye movements and remembering. *Nature, 227,* 287–288. (p. 173)

Endler, N. S. (1982). *Holiday of darkness: A psychologist's personal journey out of his depression.* New York: Wiley. (p. 473)

Engen, T. (1987). Remembering odors and their names. *American Scientist, 75,* 497–503. (p. 138)

Epstein, S. (1983a). Aggregation and beyond: Some basic issues on the prediction of behavior. *Journal of Personality, 51,* 360–392. (p. 392)

Epstein, S. (1983b). The stability of behavior across time and situations. In R. Zucker, J. Aronoff, & A. I. Rabin (Eds.), *Personality and the prediction of behavior.* San Diego: Academic Press. (p. 392)

Epstein, S. (1984). Controversial issues in emotions. In P. Shaver (Ed.), *Review of Personality and Social Psychology.* Beverly Hills, CA: Sage. (p. 338)

Erber, R., & Tesser, A. (1992). Task effort and the regulation of mood: The absorption hypothesis. *Journal of Experimental Social Psychology, 28,* 339–359. (p. 459)

Erdelyi, M. H. (1985). *Psychoanalysis: Freud's cognitive psychology.* New York: Freeman. (p. 385)

Erikson, E. H. (1963). *Childhood and society.* New York: Norton. (p. 92)

Eron, L. D. (1987). The development of aggressive behavior from the perspective of a developing behaviorism. *American Psychologist, 42,* 435–442. (p. 505)

Esser, J. K., & Lindoerfer, J. S. (1989). Groupthink and the space shuttle *Challenger* accident: Toward a quantitative case analysis. *Journal of Behavioral Decision Making, 2,* 167–177. (p. 492)

ETS (1992). Three reports shed new light on gender differences in testing. *ETS Developments, 37*(3), 4–7. (p. 290)

Evans, C. R., & Dion, K. L. (1991). Group cohesion and performance: A meta-analysis. *Small Group Research, 22,* 175–186. (p. 327)

Evans, G. W., Palsane, M. N., Lepore, S. J., & Martin, J. (1989). Residential density and psychological health: The mediating effects of social support. *Journal of Personality and Social Psychology, 57,* 994–999. (p. 371)

Evans, R. I., Dratt, L. M., Raines, B. E., & Rosenberg, S. S. (1988). Social influences on smoking initiation: Importance of distinguishing descriptive versus mediating process variables. *Journal of Applied Social Psychology, 18,* 925–943. (p. 190)

Exner, J. E., Jr. (1986). *The Rorschach: A comprehensive system. Volume 1: Basic Foundations* (2nd ed.). New York: Wiley. (p. 385)

Eysenck, H. J. (1952). The effects of psychotherapy: An evaluation. *Journal of Consulting Psychology, 16,* 319–324. (p. 465)

Eysenck, H. J. (1990, April 30). An improvement on personality inventory. *Current Contents: Social and Behavioral Sciences, 22*(18), 20. (p. 389)

Eysenck, H. J. (1992). Four ways five factors are *not* basic. *Personality and Individual Differences, 13,* 667–673. (p. 389)

Eysenck, H. J., & Grossarth-Maticek, R. (1991). Creative novation behaviour therapy as a prophylactic treatment for cancer and coronary heart disease: Part II—Effects of treatment. *Behaviour Research and Therapy, 29,* 17–31. (p. 371)

Eysenck, M. W., MacLeod, C., & Mathews, A. (1987). Cognitive functioning and anxiety. *Psychological Research, 49,* 189–195. (p. 403)

Eysenck, S. B. G., & Eysenck, H. J. (1963). The validity of questionnaire and rating assessments of extraversion and neuroticism, and their factorial stability. *British Journal of Psychology, 54,* 51–62. (p. 389)

Faber, N. (1987, July). Personal glimpse. *Reader's Digest,* p. 34. (p. 282)

Fagan, J. F., III (1992). Intelligence: A theoretical viewpoint. *Current Directions in Psychological Science, 1,* 82–86. (p. 290)

Falbo, T., & Polit, D. F. (1986). Quantitative review of the only child literature: Research evidence and theory development. *Psychological Bulletin, 100,* 176–189. (p. 324)

Fantz, R. L. (1961, May). The origin of form perception. *Scientific American,* pp. 66–72. (p. 72)

Farina, A. (1982). The stigma of mental disorders. In A. G. Miller (Ed.), *In the eye of the beholder.* New York: Praeger. (pp. 415, 443)

Farina, A., & Fisher, J. D. (1982). Beliefs about mental disorders: Findings and implications. In G. Weary & H. L. Mirels (Eds.), *Integrations of clinical and social psychology.* New York: Oxford University Press. (p. 463)

Farrell, P. A., Gates, W. K., Maksud, M. G., & Morgan, W. P. (1982). Increases in plasma beta-endorphin/beta-lipotropin immunoreactivity after treadmill running in humans. *Journal of Applied Physiology, 52,* 1245–1249. (p. 39)

Farrington, D. P. (1991). Antisocial personality from childhood to adulthood. *The Psychologist: Bulletin of the British Psychological Society, 4,* 389–394. (p. 440)

Fava, M., Copeland, P. M., Schweiger, U., & Herzog, D. B. (1989). Neurochemical abnormalities of anorexia nervosa and bulimia nervosa. *American Journal of Psychiatry, 146,* 963–971. (p. 304)

Fazio, R. H. (1990). Multiple processes by which attitudes guide behavior: The MODE model as an integrative framework. In M. P. Zanna (Ed.), *Advances in experimental social psychology* (Vol. 23). San Diego, CA: Academic Press. (p. 482)

Feder, H. H. (1984). Hormones and sexual behavior. *Annual Review of Psychology, 35,* 165–200. (p. 313)

Feeney, D. M. (1987). Human rights and animal welfare. *American Psychologist, 42,* 593–599. (p. 26)

Feeney, J. A., & Noller, P. (1990). Attachment style as a predictor of adult romantic relationships. *Journal of Personality and Social Psychology, 58,* 281–291. (p. 84)

Fehr, B., & Russell, J. A. (1991). The concept of love viewed from a prototype perspective. *Journal of Personality and Social Psychology, 60,* 425–438. (p. 256)

Fein, R. (1992, November). Health care reform. *Scientific American,* pp. 46–53. (p. 371)

Feingold, A. (1990). Gender differences in effects of physical attractiveness on romantic attraction: A comparison across five research paradigms. *Journal of Personality and Social Psychology, 59,* 981–993. (p. 513)

Feingold, A. (1992). Gender differences in mate selection preferences: A test of the parental investment model. *Psychological Bulletin, 112,* 125–139. (p. 513)

Fenton, W. S., & McGlashan, T. H. (1991). Natural history of schizophrenia subtypes: II. Positive and negative symptoms and long-term course. *Archives of General Psychiatry, 48,* 978–986. (p. 436)

Fenton, W. S., & McGlashan, T. H. (1994). Antecedents, symptom progression, and long-term outcome of the deficit syndrome in schizophrenia. *American Journal of Psychiatry, 151,* 351–356. (p. 436)

Fernandez, E., & Turk, D. C. (1989). The utility of cognitive coping strategies for altering pain perception: A meta-analysis. *Pain, 38,* 123–135. (p. 135)

Fichter, M. M., & Noegel, R. (1990). Concordance for bulimia nervosa in twins. *International Journal of Eating Disorders, 9,* 255–263. (p. 304)

Fiedler, F. E. (1981). Leadership effectiveness. *American Behavioral Scientist, 24,* 619–632. (p. 327)

Fiedler, F. E. (1987, September). When to lead, when to stand back. *Psychology Today,* pp. 26–27. (p. 327)

Field, T. M. (1987, May). Baby research comes to age. *Psychology Today,* p. 46. (p. 73)

Field, T. M., Schanberg, S. M., Scafidi, F., Bauer, C. R., Vega-Lahr, N., Garcia, R., Nystrom, J., & Kuhn, C. M. (1986). Tactile/kinesthetic stimulation effects on preterm neonates. *Pediatrics, 77,* 654–658. (pp. 74–75)

Fincham, F. D., & Bradbury, T. N. (1993). Marital satisfaction, depression, and attributions: A longitudinal analysis. *Journal of Personality and Social Psychology, 64,* 442–452. (pp. 480–481)

Findley, M. J., & Cooper, H. M. (1983). Locus of control and academic achievement: A literature review. *Journal of Personality and Social Psychology, 44,* 419–427. (p. 403)

Fineberg, H. V. (1988). Education to prevent AIDS: Prospects and obstacles. *Science, 239,* 592–596. (p. 317)

Finucci, J. M., & Childs, B. (1981). Are there really more dyslexic boys than girls? In A. Ansara, N. Geschwind, A. Galaburda, M. Albert, & N. Gartrell (Eds.), *Sex differences in dyslexia.* Towson, MD: The Orton Dyslexia Society. (p. 290)

Fischer, P. J., & Breakey, W. R. (1991). The epidemiology of alcohol, drug, and mental disorders among homeless persons. *American Psychologist, 46,* 1115–1128. (p. 470)

Fischhoff, B. (1982). Debiasing. In D. Kahneman, P. Slovic, & A. Tversky (Eds.), *Judgment under uncertainty: Heuristics and biases.* New York: Cambridge University Press. (p. 262)

Fischhoff, B., Slovic, P., & Lichtenstein, S. (1977). Knowing with certainty: The appropriateness of extreme confidence. *Journal of Experimental Psychology: Human Perception and Performance, 3,* 552–564. (p. 261)

Fisher, H. E. (1993, March/April). After all, maybe it's biology. *Psychology Today,* pp. 40–45. (p. 104)

Fisher, H. T. (1984). Little Albert and Little Peter. *Bulletin of the British Psychological Society, 37,* 269. (p. 455)

Fisher, R. P., Geiselman, R. E., & Amador, M. (1989). Field test of the cognitive interview: Enhancing the recollection of actual victims and witnesses of crime. *Journal of Applied Psychology, 74,* 722–727. (p. 244)

Fisher, R. P., Geiselman, R. E., & Raymond, D. S. (1987). Critical analysis of police interview techniques. *Journal of Police Science and Administration, 15,* 177–185. (p. 244)

Fleming, I., Baum, A., & Weiss, L. (1987). Social density and perceived control as mediator of crowding stress in high-density residential neighborhoods. *Journal of Personality and Social Psychology, 52,* 899–906. (p. 361)

Fleming, J. H., & Scott, B. A. (1991). The costs of confession: The Persian Gulf War POW tapes in historical an theoretical perspective. *Contemporary Social Psychology, 15,* 127–138. (p. 340)

Fletcher, G. J. O., Fitness, J., & Blampied, N. M. (1990). The link between attributions and happiness in close relationships: The roles of depression and explanatory style. *Journal of Social and Clinical Psychology, 9*, 243–255. (pp. 480–481)

Floderus-Myrhed, B., Pedersen, N., & Rasmuson, I. (1980). Assessment of heritability for personality, based on a shortform of the Eysenck Personality Inventory: A study of 12,898 twin pairs. *Behavior Genetics, 10*, 153–162. (p. 108)

Foa, E. B., & Kozak, M. J. (1986). Emotional processing of fear: Exposure to corrective information. *Psychological Bulletin, 99*, 20–35. (p. 456)

Fong, G. T., Frantz, D. H., & Nisbett, R. E. (1986). The effects of statistical training on thinking about everyday problems. *Cognitive Psychology, 18*, 253–292. (p. 22)

Fontana, A., Rosenheck, R., & Brett, E. (1992). War zone traumas and posttraumatic stress disorder symptomatology. *Journal of Nervous and Mental Disease, 180*, 748–755. (p. 360)

Forer, B. R. (1949). The fallacy of personal validation: A classroom demonstration of gullibility. *Journal of Abnormal and Social Psychology, 44*, 118–123. (p. 406)

Foreyt, J. P., & Goodrick, G. K. (1994). Attributes of successful appraoches to weight loss and control. *Applied and Preventive Psychology, 3*, 209–215. (p. 309)

Forgas, J. P., Bower, G. H., & Krantz, S. E. (1984). The influence of mood on perceptions of social interactions. *Journal of Experimental Social Psychology, 20*, 497–513. (p. 241)

Fouts, R. S. (1992). Transmission of a human gestural language in a chimpanzee mother-infant relationship. *Friends of Washoe, 12/13*, pp. 2–8. (p. 271)

Fouts, R. S., & Bodamer, M. (1987). Preliminary report to the National Geographic Society on: "Chimpanzee intrapersonal signing." *Friends of Washoe, 7*(1), 4–12. (p. 271)

Fowler, M. J., Sullivan, M. J., & Ekstrand, B. R. (1973). Sleep and memory. *Science, 179*, 302–304. (p. 246)

Fowler, R. C., Rich, C. L., & Young, D. (1986). San Diego suicide study: II. Substance abuse in young cases. *Archives of General Psychiatry, 43*, 962–965. (p. 428)

Fowler, R. D. (1986, May). Howard Hughes: A psychological autopsy. *Psychology Today*, pp. 22–33. (p. 420)

Fowles, D. C. (1992). Schizophrenia: Diathesis-stress revisited. *Annual Review of Psychology, 43*, 303–336. (p. 436)

Fox, J. L. (1984). The brain's dynamic way of keeping in touch. *Science, 225*, 820–821. (p. 54)

Fozard, J. L., & Popkin, S. J. (1978). Optimizing adult development: Ends and means of an applied psychology of aging. *American Psychologist, 33*, 975–989. (p. 99)

Frank, J. D. (1982). Therapeutic components shared by all psychotherapies. In J. H. Harvey & M. M. Parks (Eds.), *The Master Lecture Series: Vol. 1. Psychotherapy research and behavior change*. Washington, DC: American Psychological Association. (pp. 449, 467, 468)

Frank, M. G., & Gilovich, T. (1988). The dark side of self and social perception: Black uniforms and aggression in professional sports. *Journal of Personality and Social Psychology, 54*, 74–85. (pp. 18, 19)

Frank, S. J. (1988). Young adults' perceptions of their relationships with their parents: Individual differences in connectedness, competence, and emotional autonomy. *Developmental Psychology, 24*, 729–737. (p. 95)

Frankel, A., & Prentice-Dunn, S. (1990). Loneliness and the processing of self-relevant information. *Journal of Social and Clinical Psychology, 9*, 303–315. (p. 433)

Frankel, A., Strange, D. R., & Schoonover, R. (1983). CRAP: Consumer rated assessment procedure. In G. H. Scherr & R. Liebmann-Smith (Eds.), *The best of The Journal of Irreproducible Results*. New York: Workman Publishing. (p. 390)

Frankenburg, W., Dodds, J., Archer, P., Shapiro, H., & Bresnick, B. (1992). The Denver II: A major revision and restandardization of the Denver Developmental Screening Test. *Pediatrics, 89*, 91–97. (p. 75)

Freedman, J. L. (1978). *Happy people*. San Diego: Harcourt Brace Jovanovich. (p. 106)

Freedman, J. L. (1988). Television violence and aggression: What the evidence shows. In S. Oskamp (Ed.), *Television as a social issue*. Newbury Park, CA: Sage. (p. 505)

Freedman, J. L., & Fraser, S. C. (1966). Compliance without pressure: The foot-in-the-door technique. *Journal of Personality and Social Psychology, 4*, 195–202. (p. 482)

Freedman, J. L., & Perlick, D. (1979). Crowding, contagion, and laughter. *Journal of Experimental Social Psychology, 15*, 295–303. (p. 490)

Freeman, W. J. (1991, February). The physiology of perception. *Scientific American*, pp. 78–85. (p. 128)

Freud, S. (1931; reprinted 1961). Female sexuality. In J. Strachey (Trans.), *The standard edition of the complete psychological works of Sigmund Freud*. London: Hogarth Press. (pp. 380, 383)

Freud, S. (1935; reprinted 1960). *A general introduction to psychoanalysis*. New York: Washington Square Press. (p. 104)

Friedman, H. S., Tucker, J. S., Schwartz, J. E., Tomlinson-Keasey, C., Martin, L. R., Wingard, D. L., & Criqui, M. H. (1995). Psychosocial and behavioral predictors of longevity: The aging and death of the "Termites." *American Psychologist, 50*, 69–78. (p. 372)

Friedman, M., & Ulmer, D. (1984). *Treating Type A behavior—and your heart*. New York: Knopf. (pp. 361, 371)

Frieze, I. H., Parsons, J. E., Johnson, P. B., Ruble, D. N., & Zellman, G. L. (1978). *Women and sex roles: A social psychological perspective*. New York: Norton. (p. 385)

Fritsch, G., & Hitzig, E. (1870; reprinted 1960). On the electrical excitability of the cerebrum. In G. Von Bonin (Trans.), *Some papers on the cerebral cortex*. Springfield, IL: Charles C. Thomas. (p. 52)

Fromkin, V., & Rodman, R. (1983). *An introduction to language* (3rd ed.). New York: Holt, Rinehart & Winston. (p. 266)

Fulker, D. W., DeFries, J. C., & Plomin, R. (1988). Genetic influence on general mental ability increases between infancy and middle childhood. *Nature, 336*, 767–769. (p. 286)

Fuller, M. J., & Downs, A. C. (1990). Spermarche is a salient biological marker in men's development. Poster presented at the American Psychological Society convention. (p. 88)

Funder, D. C., & Block, J. (1989). The role of ego-control, ego-resiliency, and IQ in delay of gratification in adolescence. *Journal of Personality and Social Psychology, 57*, 1041–1050. (p. 91)

Furnham, A. (1982). Explanations for unemployment in Britain. *European Journal of Social Psychology, 12*, 335–352. (p. 481)

Furnham, A. (1993). A comparison between psychology and non-psychology students' misperceptions of the subject. *Journal of Social Behavior and Personality, 8*, 311–322. (p. 177)

Furnham, A., & Baguma, P. (1994). Cross-cultural differences in the evaluation of male and female body shapes. *International Journal of Eating Disorders, 15,* 81–89. (p. 305)

Furnham, A., & Taylor, L. (1990). Lay theories of homosexuality: Aetiology, behaviours, and 'cures.' *British Journal of Social Psychology, 29,* 135–147. (p. 320)

Furstenberg, F. F., Jr., Moore, K. A., & Peterson, J. L. (1985). Sex education and sexual experience among adolescents. *American Journal of Public Health, 75,* 1331–1332. (p. 321)

Gabarino, J. (1991). *No place to be a child: Growing up in a war zone.* Lexington, MA: Lexington Books. (p. 360)

Gabarino, J. (1992). *Children in danger: Coping with the consequences of community violence.* San Francisco: Jossey-Bass. (p. 360)

Gabbay, F. H. (1992). Behavior-genetic strategies in the study of emotion. *Psychological Science, 3,* 50–55. (p. 82)

Gaertner, S. L., Mann, J., Murrell, A., & Dovidio, J. F. (1989). Reducing intergroup bias: The benefits of recategorization. *Journal of Personality and Social Psychology, 57,* 239–249. (p. 519)

Galambos, N. L. (1992). Parent-adolescent relations. *Current Directions in Psychological Science, 1,* 146–149. (p. 95)

Galanter, E. (1962). Contemporary psychophysics. In R. Brown, E. Galanter, E. H. Hess, & G. Mandler (Eds.), *New directions in psychology.* New York: Holt, Rinehart & Winston. (p. 119)

Gallup, G. G., Jr., & Suarez, S. D. (1985). Alternatives to the use of animals in psychological research. *American Psychologist, 40,* 1104–1111. (p. 26)

Gallup, G. H. (1972). *The Gallup poll: Public opinion 1935–1971* (Vol. 3). New York: Random House. (p. 510)

Gallup, G. H., Jr. (October, 1994). Millions finding care and support in small groups. *Emerging Trends,* pp. 2–5. (p. 462)

Gallup, G. H., Jr., & Newport, F. (1991, Winter). Belief in paranormal phenomena among adult Americans. *Skeptical Inquirer,* pp. 137–146. (p. 153)

Gallup Organization. (1993). Other hemsipheres may think our religion is alien and exotic. *PRRC Emerging Trends, 15,* 1–3. (p. 468)

Gallup Poll Monthly (1992, October). The first presidential debate: Perot makes best impression; Bush falls short. p. 11. (p. 151)

Gallup Poll Monthly (1993, July). Americans feel threatened by new immigrants. pp. 2–16. (p. 497)

Gallup Poll Monthly (1993, September). The Gallup Poll of teenagers, p. 42. (p. 95)

Gallup Report. (1989, March/April). Commercial aviation. pp. 32–33. (p. 261)

Garcia, J., & Koelling, R. A. (1966). Relation of cue to consequence in avoidance learning. *Psychonomic Science, 4,* 123–124. (p. 202)

Gardner, H. (1983). *Frames of mind: The theory of multiple intelligences.* New York: Basic Books. (p. 281)

Gardner, H. (1993). Multiple intelligences: The theory in practice. New York: Basic Books. (p. 281)

Gardner, M. (1983). Lessons of a landmark PK hoax. *The Skeptical Inquirer, 7,* 16–19. (p. 155)

Gardner, R. A., & Gardner, B. I. (1969). Teaching sign language to a chimpanzee. *Science, 165,* 664–672. (p. 269)

Garfield, C. (1986). *Peak performers: The new heroes of American business.* New York: Morrow. (p. 274)

Garner, D. M., & Wooley, S. C. (1991). Confronting the failure of behavioral and dietary treatments for obesity. *Clinical Psychology Review, 11,* 729–780. (p. 308)

Garnets, L., & Kimmel, D. (1990). Lesbian and gay dimensions in the psychological study of human diversity. Master lecture, American Psychological Association convention. (p. 317)

Gash, D. M., Notter, M. F. D., Okawara, S. H., Kraus, A. L., & Joynt, R. J. (1986). Amniotic neuroblastoma cells used for neural implants in monkeys. *Science, 233,* 1420–1421. (p. 58)

Gawin, F. H. (1991). Cocaine addiction: Psychology and neurophysiology. *Science, 251,* 1580–1586. (p. 185)

Gazzaniga, M. S. (1967, August). The split brain in man. *Scientific American,* pp. 24–29. (pp. 59, 60)

Gazzaniga, M. S. (1988). *Mind matters: How mind and brain interact to create our conscious lives.* Boston: Houghton Mifflin. (p. 61)

Geen, R. G. (1984). Human motivation: New perspectives on old problems. In A. M. Rogers & C. J. Scheirer (Eds.), *The G. Stanley Hall Lecture Series* (Vol. 4). Washington, DC: American Psychological Association. (p. 323)

Geen, R. G., & Quanty, M. B. (1977). The catharsis of aggression: An evaluation of a hypothesis. In L. Berkowitz (Ed.), *Advances in experimental social psychology* (Vol. 10). New York: Academic Press. (p. 345)

Geen, R. G., & Thomas, S. L. (1986). The immediate effects of media violence on behavior. *Journal of Social Issues, 42*(3), 7–28. (p. 505)

Geiwitz, J. (1980). *Psychology: Looking at ourselves* (2nd ed.). Boston: Little, Brown. (p. 101)

Geldard, F. A. (1972). *The human senses* (2nd ed.). New York: Wiley. (p. 129)

Gelman, D. (1989, May 15). Voyages to the unknown. *Newsweek,* pp. 66–69. (p. 341)

Gelman, R. (1979). Preschool thought. *American Psychologist, 34,* 900–905. (p. 78)

Geranios, N. K. (1993, September 26). Chimps learn to sign, and in the process, teach humans a little. Associated Press release in *Grand Rapids Press,* p. A18. (p. 269)

Gerard, R. W. (1953, September). What is memory? *Scientific American,* pp. 118–126. (p. 236)

Gerbner, G. (1985). Dreams that hurt: Mental illness in the mass media. Keynote address to the First Rosalynn Carter Symposium on Mental Health Policy, Emory University School of Medicine, Atlanta. (p. 444)

Gerbner, G. (1990). Stories that hurt: Tobacco, alcohol, and other drugs in the mass media. In H. Resnik (Ed.), *Youth and drugs: Society's mixed messages.* Rockville, MD: Office for Substance Abuse Prevention, U.S. Department of Health and Human Services. (p. 189)

Gerbner, G. (1993, June). Women and minorities on television: A study in casting and fate. A report to the Screen Actors Guild and the American Federation of Radio and Television Artists. (p. 505)

Gerbner, G., Morgan, M., & Signorielli, N. (1993). Television violence profile No. 16: The turning point from research to action. Annenberg School for Communication, University of Pennsylvania. (pp. 505, 508)

Gerrard, M., & Luus, C. A. E. (1995). Judgments of vulnerability to pregnancy: The role of risk factors and individual differences. *Personality and Social Psychology Bulletin, 21,* 160–171. (p. 96)

Geschwind, N. (1979, September). Specializations of the human brain. *Scientific American*, pp. 180–199. (p. 56)

Gfeller, J. D., Lynn, S. J., & Pribble, W. E. (1987). Enhancing hypnotic susceptibility: Interpersonal and rapport factors. *Journal of Personality and Social Psychology, 52*, 586–595. (p. 180)

Giambra, L. M. (1974). Daydreaming across the life span: Late adolescent to senior citizen. *Aging and Human Development, 5*, 115–140. (p. 175)

Gibbons, A. (1992). Databasing the brain. *Science, 258*, 1872–1873. (p. 47)

Gibbons, F. X. (1986). Social comparison and depression: Company's effect on misery. *Journal of Personality and Social Psychology, 51*, 140–148. (p. 350)

Gibson, E. J., & Walk, R. D. (1960, April). The "visual cliff." *Scientific American*, pp. 64–71. (p. 141)

Giles, T. R. (1983). Probable superiority of behavioral interventions—II: Empirical status of the equivalence of therapies hypothesis. *Journal of Behavior Therapy and Experimental Psychiatry, 14*, 189–196. (p. 467)

Gilligan, C. (1982). *In a different voice: Psychological theory and women's development.* Cambridge, MA: Harvard University Press. (pp. 94, 103)

Gilligan, C., Lyons, N. P., & Hanmer, T. J. (Eds.). (1990). *Making connections: The relational worlds of adolescent girls at Emma Willard School.* Cambridge, MA: Harvard University Press. (p. 94)

Gilling, D., & Brightwell, R. (1982). *The human brain.* New York: Facts on File. (p. 456)

Gilovich, T. (1991). *How we know what isn't so: The fallibility of human reason in everyday life.* New York: Free Press. (pp. 14–15)

Gilovich, T., Vallone, R., & Tversky, A. (1985). The hot hand in basketball: On the misperception of random sequences. *Cognitive Psychology, 17*, 295–314. (p. 16)

Gist, R., & Welch, Q. B. (1989). Certification change versus actual behavior change in teenage suicide rates, 1955–1979. *Suicide and Life Threatening Behavior, 19*, 277–288. (p. 428)

Gjerde, P. F. (1983). Attentional capacity dysfunction and arousal in schizophrenia. *Psychological Bulletin, 93*, 57–72. (p. 435)

Gladue, B. A. (1990). Hormones and neuroendocrine factors in atypical human sexual behavior. In J. R. Feierman (Ed.), *Pedophilia: Biosocial dimensions.* New York: Springer-Verlag. (p. 320)

Gladue, B. A. (1994). The biopsychology of sexual orientation. *Current Directions in Psychological Science, 3*, 150–154. (pp. 319, 320)

Gladue, B. A., Boechler, M., & McCaul, K. D. (1989). Hormonal response to competition in human males. *Aggressive Behavior, 15*, 409–422. (p. 502)

Glenn, N. D. (1975). Psychological well-being in the postparental stage: Some evidence from national surveys. *Journal of Marriage and the Family, 37*, 105–110. (p. 105)

Glenn, N. D. (1991). The recent trend in marital success in the United States. *Journal of Marriage and the Family, 53*, 261–270. (p. 104)

Glick, P., Gottesman, D., & Jolton, J. (1989). The fault is not in the stars: Susceptibility of skeptics and believers in astrology to the Barnum effect. *Personality and Social Psychology Bulletin, 15*, 572–583. (p. 406)

Godden, D. R., & Baddeley, A. D. (1975). Context-dependent memory in two natural environments: On land and underwater. *British Journal of Psychology, 66*, 325–331. (p. 241)

Goff, D. C. (1993). Reply to Dr. Armstrong. *Journal of Nervous and Mental Disease, 181*, 604–605. (p. 425)

Goff, D. C., & Simms, C. A. (1993). Has multiple personality disorder remained consistent over time? *Journal of Nervous and Mental Disease, 181*, 595–600. (pp. 425, 426)

Gold, M., & Yanof, D. S. (1985). Mothers, daughters, and girlfriends. *Journal of Personality and Social Psychology, 49*, 654–659. (p. 95)

Goldberg, J., True, W. R., Eisen, S. A., & Henderson, W. G. (1990). A twin study of the effects of the Vietnam War on posttraumatic stress disorder. *Journal of the American Medical Association, 263*, 1227–1232. (p. 360)

Goldberg, L. R. (1993). The structure of phenotypic personality traits. *American Psychologist, 48*, 26–34. (p. 389)

Goldfried, M. R., & Padawer, W. (1982). Current status and future directions in psychotherapy. In M. R. Goldfried (Ed.), *Converging themes in psychotherapy: Trends in psychodynamic, humanistic, and behavioral practice.* New York: Springer. (p. 467)

Goldstein, A. P., & Glick, B. (1994). Aggression replacement training: Curriculum and evaluation. *Simulation and Gaming, 25*, 9–26. (p. 504)

Goleman, D. (1980, February). 1,528 little geniuses and how they grew. *Psychology Today*, pp. 28–53. (pp. 283, 324)

Golomb, J., de Leon, M. J., Kluger, A., George, A. E., Tarshish, C., & Ferris, S. H. (1993). Hippocampal atrophy in normal aging: An association with recent memory impairment. *Archives of Neurology, 50*, 967–973. (p. 238)

Golomb, J., Kluger, A., de Leon, M. J., Ferris, S. H., Convit, A., Mittelman, M. S., Cohen, J., Rusinek, H., De Santi, S., & George, A. E. (1994). Hippocampal formation size in normal human aging: A correlate of delayed secondary memory performance. *Learning & Memory, 1*, 45–54. (p. 238)

Golub, S. (1983). *Menarche: The transition from girl to woman.* Lexington, MA: Lexington Books. (p. 88)

Gonsiorek, J. C. (1982). Summary and conclusions. In W. Paul, J. D. Weinrich, J. C. Gonsiorek, & M. E. Hotvedt (Eds.), *Homosexuality: Social, psychological, and biological issues.* Beverly Hills, CA: Sage. (p. 318)

Goodall, J. (1986). *The chimpanzees of Gombe: Patterns of behavior.* Cambridge, MA: Harvard University Press. (p. 499)

Goodchilds, J. (1987). Quoted by Carol Tavris, Old age is not what it used to be. *The New York Times Magazine: Good Health Magazine*, September 27, pp. 24–25, 91–92. (p. 98)

Goodhart, D. E. (1986). The effects of positive and negative thinking on performance in an achievement situation. *Journal of Personality and Social Psychology, 51*, 117–124. (p. 405)

Goodman, L. A., Koss, M. P., & Russo, N. F. (1993). Violence against women: Mental health effects. Part II. Conceptualizations of posttraumatic stress. Applied & Preventive Psychology, 2, 123–130. (p. 360)

Goodman, T. R., & Koenig, L. J. (1992). Sex differences in depression: Explaining the absence in college populations. Paper presented to the American Psychological Association convention. (p. 429)

Goodwin, C. J. (1991). Misportraying Pavlov's apparatus. *American Journal of Psychology, 104*, 135–141. (p. 199)

Gopnik, A., & Meltzoff, A. N. (1986). Relations between semantic and cognitive development in the one-word stage: The specificity hypothesis. *Child Development, 57*, 1040–1053. (p. 273)

Goranson, R. E. (1978). *The hindsight effect in problem solving.* Unpublished manuscript, cited by G. Wood (1984), Research methodology:

A decision-making perspective. In A. M. Rogers & C. J. Scheirer (Eds.), *The G. Stanley Hall Lecture Series*, vol. 4. Washington, DC: American Psychological Association. (p. 9)

Gore, A., Jr. (1992). *Earth in the balance: Ecology and the human spirit.* Boston: Houghton-Mifflin. (p. 260)

Gorsuch, R. L. (1988). Psychology of religion. *Annual Review of Psychology, 39,* 201–222. (p. 325)

Gortmaker, S. L., Must, A., Perrin, J. M., Sobol, A. M., & Dietz, W. H. (1993). Social and economic consequences of overweight in adolescence and young adulthood. *New England Journal of Medicine, 329,* 1008–1012. (p. 306)

Gotlib, I. H. (1992). Interpersonal and cognitive aspects of depression. *Current Directions in Psychological Science, 1,* 149–154. (p. 397)

Gotlib, I. H., & Hammen, C. L. (1992). *Psychological aspects of depression: Toward a cognitive-interpersonal integration.* New York: Wiley. (p. 432)

Gottesman, I. I. (1991). *Schizophrenia genesis: The origins of madness.* New York: Freeman. (p. 438)

Gottesman, I. I. (1993). The origins of schizophrenia: Past as prologue. In R. Plomin & G. E. McClearn (Eds.), *Nature, nurture, and psychology.* Washington, DC: American Psychological Association. (p. 438)

Gottman, J. (1994). *Why marriages succeed or fail.* New York: Simon & Schuster. (p. 105)

Gould, M. S., & Shaffer, D. (1986). The impact of suicide in television movies: Evidence of imitation. *New England Journal of Medicine, 315,* 690–694. (p. 485)

Gould, S. J. (1981). *The mismeasure of man.* New York: Norton. (p. 276)

Gould, S. J. (1981). *The panda's thumb: More reflections in natural history.* New York: Norton. (pp. 154, 285)

Graf, P. (1990). Life-span changes in implicit and explicit memory. *Bulletin of the Psychonomic Society, 28,* 353–358. (p. 101)

Graham, J. W., Marks, G., & Hansen, W. B. (1991). Social influence processes affecting adolescent substance use. *Journal of Applied Psychology, 76,* 291–298. (p. 190)

Gray-Little, B., & Burks, N. (1983). Power and satisfaction in marriage: A review and critique. *Psychological Bulletin, 93,* 513–538. (p. 516)

Greeley, A. M. (1991). *Faithful attraction.* New York: Tor Books. (p. 311)

Green, S. K., & Sandos, P. (1983). Perceptions of male and female initiators of relationships. *Sex Roles, 9,* 849–852. (p. 495)

Greenberg, R. P., Bornstein, R. F., Greenberg, M. D., & Fisher, S. (1992). A meta-analysis of antidepressant outcome under "blinder" conditions. *Journal of Consulting and Clinical Psychology, 60,* 664–669. (p. 473)

Greenberg, R. P., Bornstein, R. F., Zborowski, M. J., Fisher, S., & Greenberg, M. D. (1994). A meta-analysis of fluoxetine outcome in the treatment of depression. *Journal of Nervous and Mental Disease, 182,* 547–551. (p. 473)

Greene, R. L. (1987). Effects of maintenance rehearsal on human memory. *Psychological Bulletin, 102,* 403–413. (p. 228)

Greenwald, A. G. (1992). New look 3: Unconscious cognition reclaimed. *American Psychologist, 47,* 766–779. (p. 385)

Greenwald, A. G. (1992). Subliminal semantic activation and subliminal snake oil. Paper presented to the American Psychological Association Convention, Washington, DC. (p. 21)

Greenwald, A. G., & Banaji, M. R. (1995). Implicit social cognition: Attitudes, self-esteem, and stereotypes. *Psychological Review, 102,* 4–27. (p. 164)

Greenwald, A. G., Spangenberg, E. R., Pratkanis, A. R., & Eskenazi, J. (1991). Double-blind tests of subliminal self-help audiotapes. *Psychological Science, 2,* 119–122. (p. 21)

Greenwood, M. R. C. (1989). Sexual dimorphism and obesity. In A. J. Stunkard & A. Baum (Eds.). *Perspectives in behavioral medicine: Eating, sleeping, and sex.* Hillsdale, NJ: Erlbaum. (p. 306)

Greer, G. (1984, April). The uses of chastity and other paths to sexual pleasures. *MS,* pp. 53–60, 96. (p. 314)

Gregory, R. L. (1968, November). Visual illusions. *Scientific American,* pp. 66–76. (p. 146)

Gregory, R. L. (1978). *Eye and brain: The psychology of seeing* (3rd ed.). New York: McGraw-Hill. (p. 149)

Gregory, R. L., & Gombrich, E. H. (Eds.). (1973). *Illusion in nature and art.* New York: Charles Scribner's Sons. (p. 153)

Greif, E. B., & Ulman, K. J. (1982). The psychological impact of menarche on early adolescent females: A review of the literature. *Child Development, 53,* 1413–1430. (p. 88)

Grilo, C. M., & Pogue-Geile, M. F. (1991). The nature of environmental influences on weight and obesity: A behavior genetic analysis. *Psychological Bulletin, 110,* 520–537. (p. 308)

Grobstein, C. (1979, June). External human fertilization. *Scientific American,* pp. 57–67. (p. 71)

Gross, A. E., & Crofton, C. (1977). What is good is beautiful. *Sociometry, 40,* 85–90. (p. 514)

Grossman, M., & Wood, W. (1993). Sex differences in intensity of emotional experience: A social role interpretation. *Journal of Personality and Social Psychology, 65,* 1010–1022. (p. 94)

Gruder, C. L. (1977). Choice of comparison persons in evaluating oneself. In J. M. Suls & R. L. Miller (Eds.), *Social comparison processes.* New York: Hemisphere. (p. 349)

Guerin, B. (1986). Mere presence effects in humans: A review. *Journal of Personality and Social Psychology, 22,* 38–77. (p. 490)

Gulevich, G., Dement, W., & Johnson, L. (1966). Psychiatric and EEG observations on a case of prolonged (264 hours) wakefulness. *Archives of General Psychiatry, 15,* 29–35. (p. 169)

Gur, R. E., Mozley, D., Resnick, S. M., Shtasel, D., Kohn, M., Zimmerman, R., Herman, G., Atlas, S., Grossman, R., Erwin, R., Gur, R. C. (1991). Magnetic resonance imaging in schizophrenia. *Archives of General Psychiatry, 48,* 407–412. (p. 437)

Gustavson, C. R., Garcia, J., Hankins, W. G., & Rusiniak, K. W. (1974). Coyote predation control by aversive conditioning. *Science, 184,* 581–583. (p. 203)

Gustavson, C. R., Kelly, D. J., & Sweeney, M. (1976). Prey-lithium aversions I: Coyotes and wolves. *Behavioral Biology, 17,* 61–72. (p. 203)

Gutierres, S. E., Kenrick, D. T., & Goldberg, L. (1985). *Adverse influence on exposure to popular erotica: Effects on judgments of others and judgments of one's spouse.* Paper presented at the meeting of the Midwestern Psychological Association. (p. 314)

Haber, R. N. (1970, May). How we remember what we see. *Scientific American,* pp. 104–112. (p. 224)

Hackel, L. S., & Ruble, D. N. (1992). Changes in the marital relationship after the first baby is born: Predicting the impact of expectancy disconfirmation. *Journal of Personality and Social Psychology, 62,* 944–957. (p. 105)

Hafner, H., & Schmidtke, A. (1989). Do televised fictional suicide models produce suicides? In D. R. Pfeffer (Ed.), *Suicide among youth: Perspectives on risk and prevention.* Washington, DC: American Psychiatric Press. (p. 485)

Halaas, J. L., Gajiwala, K. S., Maffei, M., Cohen, S. L., Chait, B. T., Rabinowitz, D., Lallone, R. L., Burley, S. K., & Friedman, J. M. (1995). Weight-reducing effects of the plasma protein encoded by the *obese* gene. *Science, 269,* 543–546. (p. 308)

Haldeman, D. C. (1994). The practice and ethics of sexual orientation conversion therapy. *Journal of Consulting and Clinical Psychology, 62,* 221–227. (p. 318)

Hall, C. S., Dornhoff, W., Blick, K. A., & Weesner, K. E. (1982). The dreams of college men and women in 1950 and 1980: A comparison of dream contents and sex differences. *Sleep, 5,* 188–194. (p. 172)

Hall, C. S., & Lindzey, G. (1978). *Theories of personality* (2nd ed.). New York: Wiley. (p. 386)

Hall, C. S., & Van de Castle, R. L. (1966). *The content analysis of dreams.* New York: Appleton-Century-Crofts. (p. 172)

Hall, G. S. (1904). *Adolescence: Its psychology and its relations to physiology, anthropology, sex, crime, religion and education* (Vol. I). New York: Appleton-Century-Crofts. (p. 88)

Hall, J. A. (1987). On explaining gender differences: The case of nonverbal communication. In P. Shaver & C. Hendrick (Eds.), *Review of Personality and Social Psychology, 7,* 177–200. (pp. 94, 328)

Hall, N. R., & Goldstein, A. L. (1986, March/April). Thinking well: The chemical links between emotions and health. *The Sciences,* pp. 34–40. (p. 365)

Hall, T. (1987, September 27). Cravings: Does your body know what it needs? *The New York Times Magazine: Good Health Magazine,* pp. 23, 62–65. (p. 302)

Halonen, J. S. (1994). *Critical thinking companion for introductory psychology.* New York: Worth Publishers. (p. 537)

Halpern, D. F. (1986). *Sex differences in cognitive abilities.* Hillsdale, NJ: Erlbaum. (p. 290)

Halpern, D. F. (1991). *Cognitive sex differences: Why diversity is a critical research issue.* Paper presented to the American Psychological Association convention. (p. 290)

Hamid, A. (1992). The developmental cycle of a drug epidemic: The cocaine smoking epidemic of 1981–1991. *Journal of Psychoactive Drugs, 24,* 337–348. (p. 185)

Hamill, R., Wilson, T. D., & Nisbett, R. E. (1980). Insensitivity to sample bias: Generalizing from atypical cases. *Journal of Personality and Social Psychology, 39,* 578–589. (p. 260)

Hamilton, M. C. (1988). Using masculine generics: Does generic "he" increase male bias in the user's imagery? *Sex Roles, 19,* 785–799. (p. 273)

Hamilton, V. L., Hoffman, W. S., Broman, C. L., & Rauma, D. (1993). Unemployment, distress, and coping: A panel study of autoworkers. *Journal of Personality and Social Psychology, 65,* 234–247. (p. 432)

Hammersmith, S. K. (1982, August). *Sexual preference: An empirical study from the Alfred C. Kinsey Institute for Sex Research.* Paper presented at the meeting of the American Psychological Association, Washington, DC. (p. 318)

Hansel, C. E. M. (1980). *ESP and parapsychology: A critical reevaluation.* Buffalo, NY: Prometheus. (p. 385)

Hansen, C. H., & Hansen, R. D. (1988). Finding the face-in-the-crowd: An anger superiority effect. *Journal of Personality and Social Psychology, 54,* 917–924. (p. 339)

Hardin, C., & Banaji, M. R. (1993). The influence of language on thought. *Social Cognition, 11,* 277–308. (p. 272)

Hare, R. D. (1975). Psychophysiological studies of psychopathy. In D. C. Fowles (Ed.), *Clinical applications of psychophysiology.* New York: Columbia University Press. (p. 441)

Harkins, S. G., & Szymanski, K. (1989). Social loafing and group evaluation. *Journal of Personality and Social Psychology, 56,* 934–941. (p. 491)

Harlow, H. F., Harlow, M. K., & Suomi, S. J. (1971). From thought to therapy: Lessons from a primate laboratory. *American Scientist, 59,* 538–549. (p. 81)

Harrington, D. M., Block, J. H., & Block, J. (1987). Testing aspects of Carl Rogers's theory of creative environments: Child-rearing antecedents of creative potential in young adolescents. *Journal of Personality and Social Psychology, 52,* 851–856. (p. 395)

Harris, B. (1979). Whatever happened to Little Albert? *American Psychologist, 34,* 151–160. (p. 204)

Harris, L. (1987). *Inside America.* New York: Random House. (p. 359)

Harris, R. J. (1994). The impact of sexually explicit media. In J. Brant & D. Zillmann (Eds.), *Media effects: Advances in theory and research.* Hillsdale, NJ: Erlbaum. (p. 507)

Harriston, K. A. (1993, December 24). 1 shakes, 1 snoozes; both win $45 million. *Washington Post* release in *Tacoma News Tribune,* pp. A1, A2. (p. 407)

Hartmann, E. (1981, April). The strangest sleep disorder. *Psychology Today,* pp. 14, 16, 18. (p. 170)

Hartmann, E. (1984). *The nightmare: The psychology and biology of terrifying dreams.* New York: Basic Books. (p. 171)

Harvey, S. M. (1987). Female sexual behavior: Fluctuations during the menstrual cycle. *Journal of Psychosomatic Research, 31,* 101–110. (p. 313)

Haskins, R. (1989). Beyond metaphor: The efficacy of early childhood education. *American Psychologist, 44,* 274–282. (p. 288)

Hassan, R., & Carr, J. (1989). Changing patterns of suicide in Australia. *Australian and New Zealand Journal of Psychiatry, 23,* 226–234. (p. 428)

Hatfield, E. (1988). Passionate and companionate love. In R. J. Sternberg & M. L. Barnes (Eds.), *The psychology of love.* New Haven: Yale University Press. (p. 515)

Hatfield, E., & Sprecher, S. (1986). *Mirror, mirror . . . The importance of looks in everyday life.* Albany: State University of New York Press. (p. 513)

Hathaway, S. R. (1960). *An MMPI Handbook* (Vol. 1, Foreword). Minneapolis: University of Minnesota Press. (Revised edition, 1972). (p. 390)

Hayes, J. R. (1981). *The complete problem solver.* Philadelphia: Franklin Institute Press. (p. 240)

Hazelrigg, M. D., Cooper, H. M., & Borduin, C. M. (1987). Evaluating the effectiveness of family therapies: An integrative review and analysis. *Psychological Bulletin, 101,* 428–442. (p. 462)

Hearold, S. (1986). A synthesis of 1043 effects of television on social behavior. In G. Comstock (Ed.), *Public communication and behavior.* New York: Academic Press. (p. 505)

Heath, A. C., Eaves, L. J., & Martin, N. G. (1989). The genetic structure of personality: III. Multivariate genetic item analysis of the EPQ scales. *Personality and Individual Differences, 10,* 877–888. (p. 189)

Heath, A. C., Jardine, R., Eaves, L. J., & Martin, N. G. (1989). The genetic structure of personality: II. Genetic item analysis of the EPQ. *Personality and Individual Differences, 10,* 615–624. (p. 189)

Heath, L., & Petraitis, J. (1987). Television viewing and fear of crime: Where is the mean world? *Basic and Applied Social Psychology, 8,* 97–123. (p. 505)

Heatherton, T. F., & Baumeister, R. F. (1991). Binge eating as escape from self-awareness. *Psychological Bulletin, 110,* 86–108. (p. 304)

Hebb, D. O. (1980). *Essay on mind.* Hillsdale, NJ: Erlbaum. 9–16. (p. 335)

Hedges, L. V., & Nowell, A. (1995). Sex differences in mental test scores, variability, and numbers of high-scoring individuals. *Science, 269,* 41–45. (p. 290)

Heider, F. (1958). *The psychology of interpersonal relations.* New York: Wiley. (p. 479)

Heiman, J. R. (1975, April). The physiology of erotica: Women's sexual arousal. *Psychology Today,* 90–94. (p. 314)

Heller, W. (1990, May/June). Of one mind: Second thoughts about the brain's dual nature. *The Sciences,* pp. 38–44. (p. 62)

Hellige, J. B. (1993). Unity of thought and action: Varieties of interaction between the left and right cerebral hemispheres. *Current Directions in Psychological Science, 2,* 21–25. (p. 64)

Helmreich, W. B. (1992). *Against all odds: Holocaust survivors and the successful lives they made in America.* New York: Simon & Schuster. (pp. 249, 360)

Helmreich, W. B. (1994). Personal correspondence. Department of Sociology, City University of New York. (p. 249)

Hembree, R. (1988). Correlates, causes, effects, and treatment of test anxiety. *Review of Educational Research, 58,* 47–77. (p. 336)

Henley, N. M. (1989). Molehill or mountain? What we know and don't know about sex bias in language. In M. Crawford & M. Gentry (Eds.), *Gender and thought: Psychological perspectives.* New York: Springer-Verlag. (p. 272)

Henninger, P. (1992). Conditional handedness: Handedness changes in multiple personality disordered subject reflect shift in hemispheric dominance. *Consciousness and Cognition, 1,* 265–287. (p. 425)

Henry, J. P., & Stephens, P. M. (1977). *Stress, health, and the social environment.* New York: Springer-Verlag. (p. 359)

Herbert, T. B., & Cohen, S. (1993). Depression and immunity: A meta-analytic review. *Psychological Bulletin, 113,* 472–486. (p. 364)

Herek, G. M. (1989). Hate crimes against lesbians and gay men: Issues for research and policy. *American Psychologist, 44,* 948–955. (p. 498)

Herek, G. M. (1990). The context of anti-gay violence: Notes on cultural and psychological heterosexism. *Journal of Interpersonal Violence, 5,* 316–333. (p. 498)

Herman, C. P., & Polivy, J. (1980). Restrained eating. In A. J. Stunkard (Ed.), *Obesity.* Philadelphia: Saunders. (p. 309)

Herrmann, D. (1982). Know thy memory: The use of questionnaires to assess and study memory. *Psychological Bulletin, 92,* 434–452. (p. 250)

Herrnstein, R. J., & Loveland, D. H. (1964). Complex visual concept in the pigeon. *Science, 146,* 549–551. (p. 207)

Hershenson, M. (1989). *The moon illusion.* Hillsdale, NJ: Erlbaum. (p. 146)

Hesburg, T. M. (1974). *The humane imperative: A challenge for the year 2000.* New Haven, CT: Yale University Press. (p. 520)

Hess, D. J. (1993). *Science in the new age: The paranormal, its defenders and debunkers, and American culture.* Madison: University of Wisconsin Press. (p. 156)

Hess, E. H. (1956, July). Space perception in the chick. *Scientific American,* pp. 71–80. (p. 149)

Hetherington, E. M., & Clingempeel, W. G. (1992). Coping with marital transitions: A family systems perspective. *Society for Research in Child Development Monographs, 57,* 1–242. (p. 84)

Hetherington, E. M., Stanley-Hagan, M., & Anderson, E. R. (1989). Marital transitions: A child's perspective. *American Psychologist, 44,* 303–312. (p. 84)

Higgins, E. T. (1987). Self-discrepancy: A theory relating self and affect. *Psychological Review, 94,* 319–340. (p. 396)

Hilgard, E. R. (1986). *Divided consciousness: Multiple controls in human thought and action.* New York: Wiley. (p. 180)

Hilgard, E. R. (1992). Dissociation and theories of hypnosis. In E. Fromm & M. R. Nash (Eds.), *Contemporary hypnosis research.* New York: Guilford. (p. 180)

Hines, M., & Green, R. (1991). Human hormonal and neural correlates of sex-typed behaviors. *Review of Psychiatry, 10,* 536–555. (p. 71)

Hintzman, D. L. (1978). *The psychology of learning and memory.* San Francisco: Freeman. (p. 230)

Hinz, L. D., & Williamson, D. A. (1987). Bulimia and depression: A review of the affective variant hypothesis. *Psychological Bulletin, 102,* 150–158. (p. 304)

Hirst, W., Neisser, U., & Spelke, E. (1978, June). Divided attention. *Human Nature,* pp. 54–61. (p. 181)

Hirt, E. R., Zillmann, D., Erickson, G. A., & Kennedy, C. (1992). Costs and benefits of allegiance: Changes in fans' self-ascribed competencies after team victory versus defeat. *Journal of Personality and Social Psychology, 63,* 724–738. (p. 432)

Hobfoll, S. E. (1989). Conservation of resources: A new attempt at conceptualizing stress. *American Psychologist, 44,* 513–524. (p. 357)

Hobfoll, S. E., Lomranz, J., Eyal, N., Bridges, A., & Tzemach, M. (1989). Pulse of a nation: Depressive mood reactions of Israelis to the Israel-Lebanon war. *Journal of Personality and Social Psychology, 56,* 1002–1012. (p. 429)

Hobson, J. A. (1988). *The dreaming brain.* New York: Basic Books. (p. 173)

Hodgkinson, V. A., & Weitzman, M. S. (1992). *Giving and volunteering in the United States.* Washington, DC: Independent Sector. (p. 519)

Hoebel, B. G., & Teitelbaum, P. (1966). Effects of forcefeeding and starvation on food intake and body weight in a rat with ventromedial hypothalamic lesions. *Journal of Comparative and Physiological Psychology, 61,* 189–193. (p. 302)

Hoffman, C., & Hurst, N. (1990). Gender stereotypes: Perception or rationalization? *Journal of Personality and Social Psychology, 58,* 197–208. (p. 498)

Hofstede, G. (1980). *Culture's consequences: International differences in work-related values.* Beverly Hills: Sage. (p. 398)

Hogan, J. (1989).   Personality correlates of physical fitness. *Journal of Personality and Social Psychology, 56,* 284–288. (p. 368)

Hohmann, G. W. (1966).   Some effects of spinal cord lesions on experienced emotional feelings. *Psychophysiology, 3,* 143–156. (p. 352)

Hokanson, J. E., & Edelman, R. (1966).   Effects of three social responses on vascular processes. *Journal of Personality and Social Psychology, 3,* 442–447. (p. 345)

Holden, C. (1980a).   Identical twins reared apart. *Science, 207,* 1323–1325. (p. 109)

Holden, C. (1980b, November).   Twins reunited. *Science, 80,* 55–59. (p. 109)

Holden, C. (1986a).   Days may be numbered for polygraphs in the private sector. *Science, 232,* 705. (p. 337)

Holden, C. (1986b).   Researchers grapple with problems of updating classic psychological test. *Science, 233,* 1249–1251. (p. 400)

Holden, C. (1991).   Alcoholism gene: Coming or going? *Science, 254,* 200. (p. 189)

Holden, C. (1991).   New center to study therapies and ethnicity. *Science, 251,* 748. (p. 471)

Holden, C. (1993).   Wake-up call for sleep research. *Science, 259,* 305. (p. 169)

Hollon, S. D., DeRubeis, R. J., & Seligman, M. E. P. (1992).   Cognitive therapy and the prevention of depression. *Applied & Preventive Psychology, 1,* 89–95. (p. 461)

Holmes, D. (1990).   The evidence for repression: An examination of sixty years of research. In J. Singer (Ed.), *Repression and dissociation: Implications for personality theory, psychopathology, and health.* Chicago: University of Chicago Press. (p. 249)

Holmes, D. S. (1978).   Projection as a defense mechanism. *Psychological Bulletin, 85,* 677–688. (p. 385)

Holmes, D. S. (1981).   Existence of classical projection and the stress-reducing function of attributive projection: A reply to Sherwood. *Psychological Bulletin, 90,* 460–466. (p. 385)

Holmes, D. S. (1984).   Meditation and somatic arousal reduction: A review of the experimental evidence. *American Psychologist, 39,* 1–10. (p. 175)

Holmes, D. S. (1994).   Is there evidence for repression? No. (Unexpurgated version on an article which was rewritten by the *Harvard Mental Health Letter* and published as "Is there evidence for repression? Doubtful," June, 1994, pp. 4–6.) (pp. 247, 249, 385)

Holzman, P. S., & Matthysse, S. (1990).   The genetics of schizophrenia: A review. *Psychological Science, 1,* 279–286. (p. 122)

Hooper, J., & Teresi, D. (1986).   *The three-pound universe.* New York: Macmillan. (p. 51)

Hooykaas, R. (1972).   *Religion and the rise of modern science.* Grand Rapids, MI: Eerdmans. (p. 7)

Horn, J. L. (1982).   The aging of human abilities. In J. Wolman (Ed.), *Handbook of developmental psychology.* Englewood Cliffs, NJ: Prentice-Hall. (p. 102)

Horne, J. A. (1989).   Sleep loss and "divergent" thinking ability. *Sleep, 11,* 528–536. (p. 169)

Horney, K. (1945) *Our inner conflicts: A constructive theory of neurosis.* New York: Norton. (p. 465)

House, J. S., Landis, K. R., & Umberson, D. (1988).   Social relationships and health. *Science, 241,* 540–545. (p. 372)

House, R. J., & Singh, J. V. (1987).   Organizational behavior: Some new directions for I/O psychology. *Annual Review of Psychology, 38,* 669–718. (p. 328)

Howe, M. L., & Courage, M. L. (1993).   On resolving the enigma of infantile amnesia. *Psychological Bulletin, 113,* 305–326. (p. 74)

Hoyer, G., & Lund, E. (1993).   Suicide among women related to number of children in marriage. *Archives of General Psychiatry, 50,* 134–137. (p. 428)

Hubel, D. H. (1979, September).   The brain. *Scientific American,* pp. 45–53. (p. 122)

Hubel, D. H., & Wiesel, T. N. (1979, September).   Brain mechanisms of vision. *Scientific American,* pp. 150–162. (p. 127)

Hucker, S. J., & Bain, J. (1990).   Androgenic hormones and sexual assault. In W. Marshall, R. Law, & H. Barbaree (Eds.), *The handbook on sexual assault.* New York: Plenum. (p. 313)

Hugick, L. (1989, July).   Women play the leading role in keeping modern families close. *Gallup Report,* No. 286, pp. 27–34. (p. 94)

Hull, J. G., & Bond, C. F., Jr. (1986).   Social and behavioral consequences of alcohol consumption and expectancy: A meta-analysis. *Psychological Bulletin, 99,* 347–360. (p. 183)

Hull, J. G., Young, R. D., & Jouriles, E. (1986).   Applications of the self-awareness model of alcohol consumption: Predicting patterns of use and abuse. *Journal of Personality and Social Psychology, 51,* 790–796. (p. 183)

Hulme, C., & Tordoff, V. (1989).   Working memory development: The effects of speech rate, word length, and acoustic similarity on serial recall. *Journal of Experimental Child Psychology, 47,* 72–87. (p. 234)

Humphrey, N., & Dennett, D. C. (1989, Summer).   Speaking for ourselves: An assessment of multiple personality disorder. *Raritan: A Quarterly Review, 9,* 68–98. (p. 425)

Hunt, J. M. (1982).   Toward equalizing the developmental opportunities of infants and preschool children. *Journal of Social Issues, 38*(4), 163–191. (p. 287)

Hunt, M. (1974).   *Sexual behavior in the 1970s.* Chicago: Playboy Press. (p. 315)

Hunt, M. (1990).   *The compassionate beast: What science is discovering about the humane side of humankind.* New York: William Morrow. (p. 3)

Hunt, M. (1993).   *The story of psychology.* New York: Doubleday. (pp. 91, 92, 204, 283)

Hunter, S., & Sundel, M. (Eds.). (1989).   *Midlife myths: Issues, findings, and practice implications.* Newbury Park, CA: Sage. (p. 103)

Hurtado, S., Dey, E. L., & Trevino, J. G. (1994).   Exclusion or self-segregation? Interaction across racial/ethnic groups on college campuses. Paper presented at the American Educational Research Association annual meeting. (p. 498)

Huston, A. C., Donnerstein, E., Fairchild, H., Feshbach, N. D., Katz, P. A., & Murray, J. P. (1992).   *Big world, small screen: The role of television in American society.* Lincoln, NE: University of Nebraska Press. (p. 505)

Hyde, J. S. (1983, November).   *Bem's gender schema theory.* Paper presented at GLCA Women's Studies Conference, Rochester, IN. (p. 242)

Hyde, J. S. (1984, July).   Children's understanding of sexist language. *Developmental Psychology, 20*(4), 697–706. (p. 272)

Hyde, J. S., Fennema, E., & Lamon, S. J. (1990).   Gender differences in mathematics performance: A meta-analysis. *Psychological Bulletin, 107,* 139–155. (p. 290)

Hyde, J. S., & Linn, M. C. (1988).   Gender differences in verbal ability: A meta-analysis. *Psychological Bulletin, 104,* 53–69. (p. 290)

Hyler, S., Gabbard, G. O., & Schneider, I. (1991).   Homicidal maniacs and narcissistic parasites: Stigmatization of mentally ill persons in the movies. *Hospital and Community Psychiatry, 42,* 1044–1048. (p. 444)

Hyman, R. (1981).   Cold reading: How to convince strangers that you know all about them. In K. Frazier (Ed.), *Paranormal borderlands of science.* Buffalo, NY: Prometheus. (p. 406)

Hyman, R. (1986).   Maimonides dream-telepathy experiments. *Skeptical Inquirer, 11,* 91–92. (p. 156)

Hyman, R. (1994).   Anomaly or artifact? Comments on Bem and Honorton. *Psychological Bulletin, 115,* 19–24. (p. 157)

Iacono, W. G., & Grove, W. M. (1993).   Schizophrenia reviewed: Toward an integrative genetic model. *Psychological Science, 4,* 273–276. (p. 436)

Ingham, A. G., Levinger, G., Graves, J., & Peckham, V. (1974).   The Ringelmann effect: Studies of group size and group performance. *Journal of Experimental Social Psychology, 10,* 371–384. (p. 491)

Inglehart, M. R., Markus, H., & Brown, D. R. (1989).   The effects of possible selves on academic achievement—A panel study. In J. P. Forgas & J. M. Innes (Eds.), *Recent advances in social psychology: An international perspective.* New York: Elsevier Science Publishers. (p. 395)

Inglehart, R. (1990).   *Culture shift in advanced industrial society.* Princeton, NJ: Princeton University Press. (pp. 12, 105, 106, 330, 404)

Insel, P. M., & Roth, W. T. (1976).   *Health in a changing society.* Palo Alto, CA: Mayfield. (p. 98)

Isen, A. M., & Means, B. (1983).   The influence of positive affect on decision-making strategy. *Social Cognition, 2,* 28–31. (p. 346)

Isham, W. P., & Kamin, L. J. (1993).   Blackness, deafness, IQ, and *g. Intelligence, 17,* 37–46. (p. 273)

Izard, C. E. (1977).   *Human emotions.* New York: Plenum Press. (pp. 340, 344)

Izard, C. E. (1994).   Innate and universal facial expressions: Evidence from developmental and cross-cultural research. *Psychological Bulletin, 115,* 288–299. (p. 340)

Jackson, D., & Rothstein, M. (1993).   Evaluating personality testing in personnel selection. *The Psychologist: Bulletin of the British Psychological Society, 6,* 8–11. (p. 392)

Jackson, J. M., & Williams, K. D. (1988).   Social loafing: A review and theoretical analysis. Unpublished manuscript, Fordham University, New York. (p. 491)

Jackson, S. W. (1992).   The listening healer in the history of psychological healing. *American Journal Psychiatry, 149,* 1623–1632. (p. 467)

Jacobs, B. L. (1987).   How hallucinogenic drugs work. *American Scientist, 75,* 386–392. (p. 186)

Jacobs, W. J., & Nadel, L. (1985).   Stress-induced recovery of fears and phobias. *Psychological Bulletin, 92,* 512–531. (p. 421)

James, W. (1890).   *The principles of psychology* (Vol. 2).   New York: Holt. (pp. 134, 181, 231, 250, 342, 351, 395, 484)

James, W. (1902/1958).   *Varieties of religious experience.* New York: Mentor Books. (p. 346)

Jameson, D. (1985).   Opponent-colors theory in light of physiological findings. In D. Ottoson & S. Zeki (Eds.), *Central and peripheral mechanisms of color vision.* New York: Macmillan. (p. 130)

Jamison, K. R. (1993).   *Touched with fire: Manic-depressive illness and the artistic temperament.* New York: Free Press. (p. 427)

Jamison, K. R. (1995, February).   Manic-depressive illness and creativity. *Scientific American,* pp. 62–67. (p. 427)

Janis, I. L. (1982).   *Groupthink: Psychological studies of policy decisions and fiascoes.* Boston: Houghton Mifflin. (p. 492)

Janis, I. L. (1986).   Problems of international crisis management in the nuclear age. *Journal of Social Issues, 42*(2), 201–220. (p. 259)

Janis, I. L. (1989).   *Crucial decisions: Leadership in policymaking and crisis management.* New York: Free Press. (p. 258)

Janoff-Bulman, R., Timko, C., & Carli, L. L. (1985).   Cognitive biases in blaming the victim. *Journal of Experimental Social Psychology, 21,* 161–177. (p. 500)

Jarvik, L. F. (1975).   Thoughts on the psychobiology of aging. *American Psychologist, 30,* 576–583. (p. 100)

Jeffery, R. W., & Wing, R. R. (1983).   Recidivism and self-cure of smoking and obesity: Data from population studies. *American Psychologist, 38,* 852. (p. 310)

Jemmott, J. B., III, & Locke, S. E. (1984).   Psychosocial factors, immunologic mediation, and human susceptibility to infectious diseases: How much do we know? *Psychological Bulletin, 95,* 78–108. (p. 363)

Jemmott, J. B., III, & Magloire, K. (1988).   Academic stress, social support, and secretory immunoglobulin A. *Journal of Personality and Social Psychology, 55,* 803–810. (p. 364)

Jenish, D. (1993, October 11).   The king of porn. *Maclean's,* pp. 52–64. (p. 316)

Jenkins, J. G., & Dallenbach, K. M. (1924).   Obliviscence during sleep and waking. *American Journal of Psychology, 35,* 605–612. (p. 246)

Jensen, J. P., & Bergin, A. E. (1988).   Mental health values of professional therapists: A national interdisciplinary survey. *Professional Psychology: Research and Practice, 19,* 290–297. (p. 468)

Jepson, C., Krantz, D. H., & Nisbett, R. E. (1983).   Inductive reasoning: Competence or skill. *The Behavioral and Brain Sciences, 3,* 494–501. (p. 533)

Jervis, R. (1985, April 2).   Quoted in D. Goleman, Political forces come under new scrutiny of psychology. *The New York Times,* pp. C1, C4. (p. 265)

John, O. P. (1990).   The "big five" factor taxonomy: Dimensions of personality in the natural language and in questionnaires. In L. A. Pervin (Ed.), *Handbook of personality: Theory and research.* New York: Guilford Press. (p. 389)

Johnson, C. B., Stockdale, M. S., & Saal, F. E. (1991).   Persistence of men's misperceptions of friendly cues across a variety of interpersonal encounters. *Psychology of Women Quarterly, 15,* 463–475. (p. 316)

Johnson, D. (1990).   Animal rights and human lives: Time for scientists to right the balance. *Psychological Science, 1,* 213–214. (p. 27)

Johnson, D., & Drenick, E. J. (1977).   Therapeutic fasting in morbid obesity. Long-term follow-up. *Archives of Internal Medicine, 137,* 1381–1382. (p. 308)

Johnson, D. W., & Johnson, R. T. (1989).   *Cooperation and competition: Theory and research.* Edina, MN: Interaction Book. (p. 520)

Johnson, D. W., & Johnson, R. T. (1994).   Constructive conflict in the schools. *Journal of Social Issues, 50*(1), 117–137. (p. 520)

Johnson, E. J., & Tversky, A. (1983).   Affect, generalization, and the perception of risk. *Journal of Personality and Social Psychology, 45,* 20–31. (p. 346)

Johnson, J. S., & Newport, E. L. (1989).   Critical period effects in second language learning: The influence of maturational state on the acquisition of English as a second language. *Cognitive Psychology, 21,* 60–99. (p. 267)

Johnson, M. H. (1992).   Imprinting and the development of face recognition: From chick to man. *Current Directions in Psychological Science, 1,* 52–55. (p. 82)

Johnston, L. D. (1994, December 8).   Drug use continues to climb among American teen-agers. University of Michigan News and Information Services press release. (pp. 185, 188, 189, 190)

Johnston, L. D., O'Malley, P., & Bachman, J. (1994, January 27). Drug use rises among American teen-agers. Ann Arbor: News and Information Services, University of Michigan. (pp. 185, 188, 189)

Jones, E. E., Cumming, J. D., & Horowitz, M. J. (1988).   Another look at the nonspecific hypothesis of therapeutic effectiveness. *Journal of Consulting and Clinical Psychology, 56,* 48–55. (p. 467)

Jones, L. (1985–86).   CSICOP's international conference in London: Investigation and belief, past lives and prizes. *Skeptical Inquirer, 10,* 98–104. (p. 156)

Jones, M. C. (1924).   A laboratory study of fear: The case of Peter. *Journal of Genetic Psychology, 31,* 308–315. (p. 455)

Jones, M. C. (1957).   The later careers of boys who were early or late maturing. *Child Development, 28,* 113–128. (p. 89)

Jones, S. S., Collins, K., & Hong, H-W. (1991).   An audience effect on smile production in 10–month-old infants. *Psychological Science, 2,* 45–49. (p. 341)

Jones, W. H., Carpenter, B. N., & Quintana, D. (1985).   Personality and interpersonal predictors of loneliness in two cultures. *Journal of Personality and Social Psychology, 48,* 1503–1511. (p. 24)

Jorgenson, D. O., & Papciak, A. S. (1981).   The effects of communication, resource feedback, and identifiability on behavior in a simulated commons. *Journal of Experimental Social Psychology, 17,* 373–385. (p. 520)

Jorm, A. F., Korten, A. E., & Henderson, A. S. (1987).   The prevalence of dementia: A quantitative integration of the literature. *Acta Psychiatrica Scandinavica, 76,* 465–479. (p. 100)

Joseph, J. G., Montgomery, S. B., Emmons, C-A., Kirscht, J. P., Kessler, R. C., Ostrow, D. G., Wortman, C. B., O'Brien, K., Eller, M., & Eshleman, S. (1987).   Perceived risk of AIDS: Assessing the behavioral and psychosocial consequences in a cohort of gay men. *Journal of Applied Social Psychology, 17,* 231–250. (p. 317)

Kagan, J. (1976).   Emergent themes in human development. *American Scientist, 64,* 186–196. (p. 83)

Kagan, J. (1984).   *The nature of the child.* New York: Basic Books. (p. 81)

Kagan, J. (1989).   *Unstable ideas: Temperament, cognition, and self.* Cambridge, MA: Harvard University Press. (pp. 112, 385, 388)

Kagan, J., Snidman, N., & Arcus, D. M. (1992).   Initial reactions to unfamiliarity. *Current Directions in Psychological Science, 1,* 171–174. (p. 82)

Kahneman, D. (1985, June).   Quoted by K. McKean, Decisions, decisions. *Discover,* pp. 22–31. (p. 532)

Kahneman, D., Fredrickson, B. L., Schreiber, C. A., & Redelmeier, D. A. (1993).   When more pain is preferred to less: Adding a better end. *Psychological Science, 4,* 401–405. (p. 135)

Kahneman, D., Knetsch, J. L., & Thaler, R. (1986).   Fairness as a constraint on profit seeking: Entitlements in the market. *American Economic Review, 76,* 728–741. (p. 262)

Kahneman, D., & Tversky, A. (1972).   Subjective probability: A judgment of representativeness. *Cognitive Psychology, 3,* 430–454. (p. 15)

Kail, R. (1991).   Developmental change in speed of processing during childhood and adolescence. *Psychological Bulletin, 109,* 490–501. (p. 99)

Kalin, N. H. (1993, May).   The neurobiology of fear. *Scientific American,* pp. 94–101. (p. 338)

Kandel, D. B., & Raveis, V. H. (1989).   Cessation of illicit drug use in young adulthood. *Archives of General Psychiatry, 46,* 109–116. (p. 190)

Kandel, E. R., & Schwartz, J. H. (1982).   Molecular biology of learning: Modulation of transmitter release. *Science, 218,* 433–443. (p. 236)

Kanekar, S., & Nazareth, A. (1988).   Attributed rape victim's fault as a function of her attractiveness, physical hurt, and emotional disturbance. *Social Behaviour, 3,* 37–40. (p. 316)

Kann, L., Warren, W., Collins, J. L., Ross, J., Collins, B., Kolbe, L. J. (1993).   Results from the national school-based 1991 Youth Risk Behavior Survey and progress toward achieving related health objectives for the nation. U.S. Department of Health and Human Services, *Public Health Reports, 108* (Supplement 1), 47–55. (pp. 95, 189)

Kapitza, S. (1991, August).   Antiscience trends in the U.S.S.R. *Scientific American,* pp. 32–38. (p. 157)

Kaplan, H. I., & Saddock, B. J. (Eds.). (1989). *Comprehensive textbook of psychiatry, V.* Baltimore, MD: Williams and Wilkins. (p. 471)

Kaplan, H. S. (1979).   *Disorders of sexual desire.* New York: Brunner/Mazel. (p. 313)

Kaprio, J., Koskenvuo, M., & Rita, H. (1987).   Mortality after bereavement: A prospective study of 95,647 widowed persons. *American Journal of Public Health, 77,* 283–287. (p. 359)

Kapur, S., & Mann, J. J. (1993).   Antidepressant action and the neurobiologic effects of ECT: Human studies. In C. E. Coffey (Ed.), *The clinical science of electroconvulsive therapy.* Washington, DC: American Psychiatric Press. (p. 473)

Karacan, I., Aslan, C., & Hirshkowitz, M. (1983).   Erectile mechanisms in man. *Science, 220,* 1080–1082. (p. 168)

Karacan, I., Goodenough, D. R., Shapiro, A., & Starker, S. (1966). Erection cycle during sleep in relation to dream anxiety. *Archives of General Psychiatry, 15,* 183–189. (p. 168)

Karau, S. J., & Williams, K. D. (1993).   Social loafing: A meta-analytic review and theoretical integation. *Journal of Personality and Social Psychology, 65,* 681–706. (p. 491)

Karni, A., & Sagi, D. (1994).   Dependence on REM sleep of overnight improvement of perceptual skills. *Science, 265,* 679–682. (p. 173)

Karno, M., Golding, J. M., Sorenson, S. B., & Burnam, A. (1988).   The epidemiology of obsessive-compulsive disorder in five US communities. *Archives of General Psychiatry, 45,* 1094—1099. (p. 420)

Karr, B. (1993, March).   Challenge awards. *Skeptical Briefs,* p. 6. (p. 156)

Kashima, Y., Siegal, M., Tanaka, K., & Kashima, E. S. (1992).   Do people believe behaviours are consistent with attitudes? Towards a cultural psychology of attribution processes. *British Journal of Social Psychology, 31,* 111–124. (p. 398)

Kaufman, A. S., Reynolds, C. R., & McLean, J. E. (1989).   Age and WAIS-R intelligence in a national sample of adults in the 20- to 74-year age range: A cross-sectional analysis with educational level controlled. *Intelligence, 13,* 235–253. (p. 102)

Kaufman, J., & Zigler, E. (1987).   Do abused children become abusive parents? *American Journal of Orthopsychiatry, 57,* 186–192. (p. 84)

Kaufman, L., & Rock, I. (1962). The moon illusion I. *Science, 136,* 953–961. (p. 146)

Kaylor, J. A., King, D. W., & King, L. A. (1987). Psychological effects of military service in Vietnam: A meta-analysis. *Psychological Bulletin, 102,* 257–271. (p. 360)

Keesey, R. E., & Corbett, S. W. (1983). Metabolic defense of the body weight set-point. In A. J. Stunkard & E. Stellar (Eds.), *Eating and its disorders.* New York: Raven Press. (p. 302)

Kellerman, J., Lewis, J., & Laird, J. D. (1989). Looking and loving: The effects of mutual gaze on feelings of romantic love. *Journal of Research in Personality, 23,* 145–161. (p. 339)

Kellermann, A. L., Rivara, F. P., Rushforth, N. B., Banton, H. G., Feay, D. T., Francisco, J. T., Locci, A. B., Prodzinski, J., Hackman, B. B., & Somes, G. (1993). Gun ownership as a risk factor for homicide in the home. *New England Journal of medicine, 329,* 1084–1091. (p. 501)

Kelling, S. T., & Halpern, B. P. (1983). Taste flashes: Reaction times, intensity, and quality. *Science, 219,* 412–414. (p. 136)

Kelly, I. W., Laverty, W. H., & Saklofske, D. H. (1990). Geophysical variables and behavior: LXIV. An empirical investigation of the relationship between worldwide automobile traffic disasters and lunar cycles: No relationship. *Psychological Reports, 67,* 987–994. (p. 440)

Kelly, T. A. (1990). The role of values in psychotherapy: A critical review of process and outcome effects. *Clinical Psychology Review, 10,* 171–186. (p. 468)

Kempe, R. S., & Kempe, C. C. (1978). *Child abuse.* Cambridge, MA: Harvard University Press. (p. 84)

Kendall-Tackett, K. A., Williams, L. M., & Finkelhor, D. (1993). Impact of sexual abuse on children: A review and synthesis of recent empirical studies. *Psychological Bulletin, 113,* 164–180. (pp. 84, 248)

Kendler, K. S., Neale, M. C., Kessler, R. C., Heath, A. C., & Eaves, L. J. (1992). Generalized anxiety disorder in women: A population-based twin study. *Archives of General Psychiatry, 49,* 267–272. (p. 422)

Kendler, K. S., Neale, M., Kessler, R., Heath, A., & Eaves, L. (1993). A twin study of recent life events and difficulties. *Archives of General Psychiatry, 50,* 789–796. (p. 432)

Kennedy, S., & Over, R. (1990). Psychophysiological assessment of male sexual arousal following spinal cord injury. *Archives of Sexual Behavior, 19,* 15–27. (p. 43)

Kenrick, D. T., & Funder, D. C. (1988). Profiting from controversy: Lessons from the person-situation debate. *American Psychologist, 43,* 23–34. (p. 392)

Kenrick, D. T., & Gutierres, S. E. (1980). Contrast effects and judgments of physical attractiveness: When beauty becomes a social problem. *Journal of Personality and Social Psychology, 38,* 131–140. (p. 314)

Kenrick, D. T., & Trost, M. R. (1987). A biosocial theory of heterosexual relationships. In K. Kelly (Ed.), *Females, males, and sexuality.* Albany: State University of New York Press. (p. 316)

Kerr, N. L., & Bruun, S. E. (1983). Dispensability of member effort and group motivation losses: Free-rider effects. *Journal of Personality and Social Psychology, 44,* 78–94. (p. 491)

Kessler, M., & Albee, G. (1975). Primary prevention. *Annual Review of Psychology, 26,* 557–591. (p. 475)

Kessler, R. C., Foster, C., Joseph, J., Ostrow, D., Wortman, C., Phair, J., & Chmiel, J. (1991). Stressful life events and symptom onset in HIV infection. *American Journal of Psychiatry, 148,* 733–738. (p. 365)

Keys, A., Brozek, J., Henschel, A., Mickelsen, O., & Taylor, H. L. (1950). *The biology of human starvation.* Minneapolis: University of Minnesota Press. (p. 301)

Kiecolt-Glaser, J. K., Malarkey, W. B., Chee, M., Newton, T., Cacioppo, J. T., Mao, H-Y., & Glaser, R. (1993). Negative behavior during marital conflict is associated with immunological down-regulation. *Psychosomatic Medicine, 55,* 395–409. (p. 364)

Kihlstrom, J. F. (1985). Hypnosis. *Annual Review of Psychology, 36,* 385–418. (p. 176)

Kihlstrom, J. F. (1990). Awareness, the psychological unconscious, and the self. Address to the American Psychological Association convention. (pp. 247, 385)

Kihlstrom, J. F. (1990). The psychological unconscious. In L. A. Pervin (Ed.), *Handbook of personality: Theory and research.* New York: Guilford Press. (p. 247)

Kihlstrom, J. F. (1994). The social construction of memory. Paper presented to the American Psychological Society convention. (p. 244)

Kihlstrom, J. F., & McConkey, K. M. (1990). William James and hypnosis: A centennial reflection. *Psychological Science, 1,* 174–177. (p. 181)

Kimball, M. M. (1989). A new perspective on women's math achievement. *Psychological Bulletin, 105,* 198–214. (p. 290)

Kimble, G. A. (1956). *Principles of general psychology.* New York: Ronald Press. (p. 202)

Kimble, G. A. (1981). *Biological and cognitive constraints on learning.* In L. T. Benjamin, Jr. (Ed.), *The G. Stanley Hall Lecture Series* (Vol. 1). Washington, DC: American Psychological Association. (p. 202)

Kimzey, S. L. (1975). The effects of extended spaceflight on hematologic and immunologic systems. *Journal of the American Medical Women's Association, 30*(5), 218–232. (p. 364)

Kimzey, S. L., Johnson, P. C., Ritzman, S. E., & Mengel, C. E. (1976, April). Hematology and immunology studies: The second manned Skylab mission. *Aviation, Space, and Environmental Medicine,* pp. 383–390. (p. 364)

King, D. W., & King, L. A. (1991). Validity issues in research on Vietnam veteran adjustment. *Psychological Bulletin, 109,* 107–124. (p. 360)

King, N. J., & Montgomery, R. B. (1980). Biofeedback-induced control of human peripheral temperature: A critical review of the literature. *Psychological Bulletin, 88,* 738–752. (p. 370)

King, P. (1991, March 18). Bawl players. *Sports Illustrated,* pp. 14–17. (p. 349)

Kinsey, A. C., Pomeroy, W., & Martin, C. (1948). *Sexual behavior in the human male.* Philadelphia: Saunders. (p. 311)

Kinsey, A. C., Pomeroy, W., Martin, C., & Gebhard, P. (1953). *Sexual behavior in the human female.* Philadelphia: Saunders. (p. 311)

Kirkpatrick, L. A. (1994). The role of attachment in religious belief and behavior. *Advances in Personal Relationships, 5,* 239–265. (p. 82)

Kitayama, S., & Markus, H. R. (in press). Construal of the self as cultural frame: Implications for internationalizing psychology. In J. D'Arms, R. G. Hastie, S. E. Hoelscher, & H. K. Jacobson (Eds.), *Becoming more international and global: Challenges for American higher education.* Ann Arbor: University of Michigan Press. (p. 339)

Kite, M. E., & Johnson, B. T. (1988). Attitudes toward older and younger adults: A meta-analysis. *Psychology and Aging, 3,* 233–244. (p. 100)

Klasen, S. (1994). "Missing women" reconsidered. *World Development, 22,* 1061–1071. (p. 498)

Klayman, J., & Ha, Y-W. (1987). Confirmation, disconfirmation, and information in hypothesis testing. *Psychological Review, 94,* 211–228. (p. 258)

Kleinke, C. L. (1986).   Gaze and eye contact: A research review. *Psychological Bulletin, 100*, 78–100. (p. 339)

Kleinmuntz, B., & Szucko, J. J. (1984).   A field study of the fallibility of polygraph lie detection. *Nature, 308*, 449–450. (p. 337)

Kleitman, N. (1960, November).   Patterns of dreaming. *Scientific American*, pp. 82–88. (p. 166)

Klemm, W. R. (1990).   Historical and introductory perspectives on brainstem-mediated behaviors. In W. R. Klemm & R. P. Vertes (Eds.), *Brainstem mechanisms of behavior.* New York: Wiley. (p. 45)

Kline, D., & Schieber, F. (1985).   Vision and aging. In J. E. Birren & K. W. Schaie (Eds.), *Handbook of the psychology of aging.* New York: Van Nostrand Reinhold. (p. 99)

Kline, N. S. (1974).   *From sad to glad.* New York: Ballantine Books. (p. 433)

Klineberg, O. (1938).   Emotional expression in Chinese literature. *Journal of Abnormal and Social Psychology, 33*, 517–520. (p. 340)

Klineberg, O. (1984).   Public opinion and nuclear war. *American Psychologist, 39*, 1245–1253. (p. 520)

Kluft, R. P. (1991).   Multiple personality disorder. In A. Tasman & S. M. Goldfinger (Eds.), *Review of Psychiatry*, vol. 10. Washington, DC: American Psychiatric Press. (pp. 425, 426)

Klüver, H., & Bucy, P. C. (1939).   Preliminary analysis of functions of the temporal lobes in monkeys. *Archives of Neurology and Psychiatry, 42*, 979–1000. (p. 49)

Kohlberg, L. (1981).   *The philosophy of moral development: Essays on moral development* (Vol. I).   San Francisco: Harper & Row. (p. 90)

Kohlberg, L. (1984).   *The psychology of moral development: Essays on moral development* (Vol. II).   San Francisco: Harper & Row. (p. 90)

Köhler, W. (1925; reprinted 1957).   *The mentality of apes.* London: Pelican. (p. 257)

Kohn, A. (1987, October).   It's hard to get left out of a pair. *Psychology Today*, pp. 53–57. (p. 520)

Kohn, P. M., & Macdonald, J. E. (1992).   The survey of recent life experiences: A decontaminated hassles scale for adults. *Journal of Behavioral Medicine, 15*, 221–236. (p. 359)

Kolata, G. (1986).   Youth suicide: New research focuses on a growing social problem. *Science, 233*, 839–841. (p. 428)

Kolata, G. (1987).   Metabolic catch-22 of exercise regimens. *Science, 236*, 146–147. (p. 309)

Kolb, B. (1989).   Brain development, plasticity, and behavior. *American Psychologist, 44*, 1203–1212. (p. 58)

Kolers, P. A. (1975).   Specificity of operations in sentence recognition. *Cognitive Psychology, 7*, 289–306. (p. 226)

Kolominsky, Y., & Parkhomenko, V. (1993).   Realization of sociopsychological assistance to children and youth of Chernobyl in the Republic of Belarus. Unpublished manuscript, Byelorussian Research Institute for Education, 16 Karolya Street, Minsk. (p. 358)

Koltz, C. (1983, December).   Scapegoating. *Psychology Today*, pp. 68–69. (p. 499)

Konishi, M. (1993, April).   Listening with two ears. *Scientific American*, pp. 66–73. (p. 133)

Koslowsky, M., & Babkoff, H. (1992).   Meta-analysis of the relationship between total sleep deprivation and performance. *Chronobiology International, 9*, 132–136. (p. 169)

Koss, M. P., & Burkhart, B. R. (1989).   A conceptual analysis of rape victimization. *Psychology of Women Quarterly, 13*, 27–40. (p. 506)

Koss, M. P., Heise, L., & Russo, N. F. (1994).   The global health burden of rape. *Psychology of Women Quarterly, 18*, 509–537. (p. 506)

Kotva, H. J., & Schneider, H. G. (1990).   Those "talks"—general and sexual communication between mothers and daughters. *Journal of Social Behavior and Personality, 5*, 603–613. (p. 96)

Kraft, C. (1978).   A psychophysical approach to air safety: Simulator studies of visual illusions in night approaches. In H. L. Pick, H. W. Leibowitz, J. E. Singer, A. Steinschneider, & H. W. Stevenson (Eds.), *Psychology: From research to practice.* New York: Plenum Press. (p. 152)

Kramer, M. (1993, March 8).   Getting smart about Head Start. *Time*, p. 43. (p. 288)

Kraus, S. J. (1991).   Attitudes and the prediction of behavior. Doctoral dissertation, Harvard University. (p. 481)

Kraut, R. E., & Johnston, R. E. (1979).   Social and emotional messages of smiling: An ethological approach. *Journal of Personality and Social Psychology, 37*, 1539–1553. (p. 341)

Krauthammer, C. (1993, July 24–25).   Science ought to stay out of the gay-rights fight. *International Herald Tribune*, p. 6. (p. 320)

Kristof, N. (1993, July 22).   China faces huge surplus of males as scans hold key to missing girls. *The Guardian* (England), p. 22. (p. 498)

Krosnick, J. A., & Alwin, D. F. (1989).   Aging and susceptibility to attitude change. *Journal of Personality and Social Psychology, 57*, 416–425. (p. 112)

Krosnick, J. A., Betz, A. L., Jussim, L. J., & Lynn, A. R. (1992).   Subliminal conditioning of attitudes. *Personality and Social Psychology Bulletin, 18*, 152–162. (p. 120)

Krupa, D. J., Thompson, J. K., & Thompson, R. F. (1993).   Localization of a memory trace in the mammalian brain. *Science, 260*, 989–991. (p. 239)

Kuhl, P. K., & Meltzoff, A. N. (1982).   The bimodal perception of speech in infancy. *Science, 218*, 1138–1141. (p. 265)

Kulik, J. A., Kulik, C. C., & Bangert-Drowns, R. L. (1985).   Effectiveness of computer-based education in elementary schools. *Computers in Human Behavior, 1*, 59–74. (p. 215)

Kulik, J. A., Kulik, C. C., & Cohen, P. A. (1980).   Effectiveness of computer-based college teaching: A meta-analysis of findings. *Review of Educational Research, 50*, 525–544. (p. 215)

Kurtz, P. (1983, Spring).   Stars, planets, and people. *The Skeptical Inquirer*, pp. 65–68. (p. 406)

Kutas, M. (1990).   Event-related brain potential (ERP) studies of cognition during sleep: Is it more than a dream? In R. R. Bootzin, J. F. Kihlstrom, & D. Schacter (Eds.), *Sleep and cognition.* Washington, DC: American Psychological Association. (p. 167)

Kwong, K. K., & 12 others (1992).   Dynamic magnetic resonance imagine of human brain activity during primary sensory stimulation. *Proceedings of the National Academy of Sciences, 89*, 5675–5679. (p. 47)

Labbe, R., Firl, A., Jr., Mufson, E. J., & Stein, D. G. (1983).   Fetal brain transplants: Reduction of cognitive deficits in rats with frontal cortex lesions. *Science, 221*, 470–472. (p. 47) (p. 58)

Labouvie-Vief, G., & Schell, D. A. (1982).   Learning and memory in later life. In B. B. Wolman (Ed.), *Handbook of developmental psychology.* Englewood Cliffs, NJ: Prentice-Hall. (p. 101)

Ladd, G. T. (1887). *Elements of physiological psychology*. New York: Scribner's. (p. 163)

Lagerweij, E., Nelis, P. C., van Ree, J. M., & Wiegant, V. M. (1984). The twitch in horses: A variant of acupuncture. *Science, 225,* 1172–1174. (p. 39)

Laird, J. D. (1974). Self-attribution of emotion: The effects of expressive behavior on the quality of emotional experience. *Journal of Personality and Social Psychology, 29,* 475–486. (p. 341)

Laird, J. D. (1984). The real role of facial response in the experience of emotion: A reply to Tourangeau and Ellsworth, and others. *Journal of Personality and Social Psychology, 47,* 909–917. (p. 341)

Laird, J. D., Cuniff, M., Sheehan, K., Shulman, D., & Strum, G. (1989). Emotion specific effects of facial expressions on memory for life events. *Journal of Social Behavior and Personality, 4,* 87–98. (p. 341)

Lambert, W. E. (1992). Challenging established views on social issues: The power and limitations of research. *American Psychologist, 47,* 533–542. (p. 273)

Lambert, W. E., Genesee, F., Holobow, N., & Chartrand, L. (1993). Bilingual education for majority English-speaking children. *European Journal of Psychology of Education, 8,* 3–22. (p. 273)

Lancioni, G. (1980). Infant operant conditioning and its implications for early intervention. *Psychological Bulletin, 88,* 516–534. (p. 73)

Landauer, T. K. (1986). How much do people remember? Some estimates of the quantity of learned information in long-term memory. *Cognitive Science, 10,* 477–493. (p. 234)

Landers, A. (1969, April 8). Syndicated newspaper column. Cited by L. Berkowitz, The case for bottling up rage. *Psychology Today,* September, 1973, pp. 24–31. (p. 345)

Landfield, P., Cadwallader, L. B., & Vinsant, S. (1988). Quantitative changes in hippocampal structure following long-term exposure to Delta-9–tetrahydrocannabinol: Possible mediation by glucocorticoid systems. *Brain Research,* Vol. 443, 47–62. (p. 187)

Langer, E. J. (1983). *The psychology of control*. Beverly Hills, CA: Sage. (p. 404)

Langer, E. J., & Abelson, R. P. (1974). A patient by any other name . . . : Clinician group differences in labeling bias. *Journal of Consulting and Clinical Psychology, 42,* 4–9. (p. 443)

Langer, E. J., & Imber, L. (1980). The role of mindlessness in the perception of deviance. *Journal of Personality and Social Psychology, 39,* 360–367. (p. 443)

Langlois, J. H., Roggman, L. A., Casey, R. J., Ritter, J. M., Rieser-Danner, L. A., & Jenkins, V. Y. (1987). Infant preferences for attractive faces: Rudiments of a stereotype? *Developmental Psychology, 23,* 363–369. (p. 513)

Larsen, R. J., Kasimatis, M., & Frey, K. (1992). Facilitating the furrowed brow: An unobtrusive test of the facial feedback hypothesis applied to unpleasant affect. *Cognition and Emotion, 6,* 321–338. (p. 342)

Larson, R. W., & Bradney, N. (1988). Precious moments with family members and friends. In R. M. Milardo (Ed.), *Families and social networks*. Newbury Park, CA: Sage. (p. 95)

Lashley, K. S. (1950). In search of the engram. In *Symposium of the Society for Experimental Biology* (Vol. 4). New York: Cambridge University Press. (pp. 59, 236)

Lassiter, G. D., & Irvine, A. A. (1986). Video-taped confessions: The impact of camera point of view on judgments of coercion. *Journal of Personality and Social Psychology, 16,* 268–276. (p. 480)

Latané, B. (1981). The psychology of social impact. *American Psychologist, 36,* 343–356. (p. 491)

Latané, B., & Dabbs, J. M., Jr. (1975). Sex, group size and helping in three cities. *Sociometry, 38,* 180–194. (p. 518)

Lau, S., & Gruen, G. E. (1992). The social stigma of loneliness: Effect of target person's and perceiver's sex. *Personality and Social Psychology Bulletin, 18,* 182–189. (p. 433)

Laudenslager, M. L., & Reite, M. L. (1984). Losses and separations: Immunological consequences and health implications. *Review of Personality and Social Psychology, 5,* 285–312. (p. 360)

Laumann, E. O., Gagnon, J. H., Michael, R. T., & Michaels, S. (1994). *The social organization of sexuality: Sexual practices in the United States*. Chicago: University of Chicago Press. (pp. 311, 316, 317, 506)

Laurence, J-R., & Perry, C. (1988). *Hypnosis, will and memory: A psycho-legal history*. New York: Guilford. (p. 177)

Layton, B. D., & Turnbull, B. (1975). Belief, evaluation, and performance on an ESP task. *Journal of Experimental Social Psychology, 11,* 166–179. (p. 154)

Lazarus, R. S. (1984). On the primacy of cognition. *American Psychologist, 39,* 124–129. (p. 354)

Lazarus, R. S. (1990). Theory-based stress measurement. *Psychological Inquiry, 1,* 3–13. (p. 359)

Lazarus, R. S. (1991). Progress on a cognitive-motivational-relational theory of emotion. *American Psychologist, 46,* 352–367. (p. 354)

Leach, P. (1993). Should parents hit their children? *The Psychologist: Bulletin of the British Psychological Society, 6,* 216–220. (p. 212)

Leach, P. (1994). *Children first*. New York: Knopf. (p. 212)

Lebow, J. (1982). Consumer satisfaction with mental health treatment. *Psychological Bulletin, 91,* 244–259. (p. 464)

LeDoux, J. (1994, June). Emotion, memory and the brain. *Scientific American,* pp. 50–57. (p. 354)

Lee, G. R., Seccombe, K., & Shehan, C. L. (1991). Marital status and personal happiness: An analysis of trend data. *Journal of Marriage and the Family, 53,* 839–844. (p. 105)

Lefcourt, H. M. (1982). *Locus of control: Current trends in theory and research*. Hillsdale, NJ: Erlbaum. (p. 403)

Lehman, D. R., Lempert, R. O., & Nisbett, R. E. (1988). The effects of graduate training on reasoning: Formal discipline and thinking about everyday-life events. *American Psychologist, 43,* 431–442. (p. 22)

Lehman, D. R., & Nisbett, R. E. (1985). Effects of higher education on inductive reasoning. Unpublished manuscript, University of Michigan. (p. 405)

Lehman, D. R. Wortman, C. B., & Williams, A. F. (1987). Long-term effects of losing a spouse or child in a motor vehicle crash. *Journal of Personality and Social Psychology, 52,* 218–231. (p. 106)

Leibowitz, H. W. (1985). Grade crossing accidents and human factors engineering. *American Scientist, 73,* 558–562. (p. 143)

Leigh, B. C. (1989). In search of the seven dwarves: Issues of measurement and meaning in alcohol expectancy research. *Psychological Bulletin, 105,* 361–373. (p. 183)

Leigh, B. C., Temple, M. T., & Trocki, K. F. (1993). The sexual behavior of US adults: Results from a national survey. *American Journal of Public Health, 83,* 1400–1408. (p. 311)

Lenneberg, E. H. (1967). *Biological foundations of language*. New York: Wiley. (p. 74)

Lenzenweger, M. F., Dworkin, R. H., & Wethington, E. (1989). Models of positive and negative symptoms in schizophrenia: An empirical evaluation of latent structures. *Journal of Abnormal Psychology, 98,* 62–70. (p. 471)

Lerner, M. J. (1980). *The belief in a just world: A fundamental delusion.* New York: Plenum Press. (p. 500)

Leshner, A. I. (1992). *Outcasts on main street: Report of the federal task force on homelessness and severe mental illness.* Washington, DC: Interagency Council on the Homeless, Office of the Programs for the Homeless Mentally Ill, National Institute of Mental Health. (p. 470)

LeVay, S. (1991). A difference in hypothalamic structure between heterosexual and homosexual men. *Science, 253,* 1034–1037. (p. 319)

LeVay, S. (1994, March). Quoted in D. Nimmons, Sex and the brain. *Discover,* pp. 64–71. (p. 319)

Levenson, R. W. (1992). Autonomic nervous system differences among emotions. *Psychological Science, 3,* 23–27. (p. 338)

Levenson, R. W., Ekman, P., Heider, K., & Friesen, W. V. (1991). Emotion and autonomic nervous system activity in an Indonesian culture. Unpublished manuscript, University of California, Berkeley. (p. 338)

Levenson, R. W., Ekman, P., Heider, K., & Friesen, W. V. (1992). Emotion and autonomic nervous system activity in the Minangkabau of West Sumatra. *Journal of Personality and Social Psychology, 62,* 972–988. (p. 340)

Lever, J. (1978). Sex differences in the complexity of children's play and games. *American Sociological Review, 43,* 471–483. (p. 94)

Levin, I. P., & Gaeth, G. J. (1988). How consumers are affected by the framing of attribute information before and after consuming the product. *Journal of Consumer Research, 15,* 374–378. (p. 262)

Levin, I. P., Schnittjer, S. K., & Thee, S. L. (1988). Information framing effects in social and personal decisions. *Journal of Experimental Social Psychology, 24,* 520–529. (p. 262)

Levine, A. (1990, May 7). America's youthful bigots. *U.S. News and World Report,* pp. 59–60. (pp. 494, 498)

Levine, B., Roehrs, T., Zorick, F., & Roth, T. (1988). Daytime sleepiness in young adults. *Sleep, 11,* 39–46. (p. 168)

Levine, I. S., & Rog, D. J. (1990). Mental health services for homeless mentally ill persons: Federal initiatives and current service trends. *American Psychologist, 45,* 963–968. (p. 470)

Levinson, D. J. (1986). A conception of adult development. *American Psychologist, 41,* 3–13. (p. 103)

Levinson, D. J., Darow, C. N., Klein, E. B., Levinson, M. H., & McKee, B. (1978). *The seasons of a man's life.* New York: Knopf. (p. 103)

Levitt, E. E. (1986). Coercion, voluntariness, compliance and resistance: The essence of hypnosis twenty-seven years after Orne. Invited address to the American Psychological Association convention. (p. 178)

Levy, J. (1985, May). Right brain, left brain: Fact and fiction. *Psychology Today,* pp. 38–44. (p. 64)

Lewicki, P., Hill, T., & Czyzewska, M. (1992). Nonconscious acquisition of information. *American Psychologist, 47,* 796–801. (p. 385)

Lewinsohn, P. M., Hoberman, H., Teri, L., & Hautziner, M. (1985). An integrative theory of depression. In S. Reiss & R. Bootzin (Eds.), *Theoretical issues in behavior therapy.* Orlando, FL: Academic Press. (pp. 429, 433)

Lewinsohn, P. M., & Rosenbaum, M. (1987). Recall of parental behavior by acute depressives, remitted depressives, and nondepressives. *Journal of Personality and Social Psychology, 52,* 611–619. (p. 242)

Lewis, D. O., Pincus, J. H., Bard, B., Richardson, E., Prichep, L. S., Feldman, M., & Yeager, C. (1988). Neuropsychiatric, psychoeducational, and family characteristics of 14 juveniles condemned to death in the United States. *American Journal of Psychiatry, 145,* 584–589. (p. 84)

Lewis, D. O., Pincus, J. H., Feldman, M., Jackson, L., & Bard, B. (1986). Psychiatric, neurological, and psychoeducational characteristics of 15 death row inmates in the United States. *American Journal of Psychiatry, 143,* 838–845. (p. 502)

Lewis, M. (1992). Commentary. *Human Development, 35,* 44–51. (p. 242)

Lewontin, R. (1982). *Human diversity.* New York: Scientific American Library. (pp. 25, 289)

Licata, A., Taylor, S., Berman, M., & Cranston, J. (1993). Effects of cocaine on human aggression. *Pharmacology Biochemistry and Behavior, 45,* 549–552. (p. 186)

Lichtman, S. W., Pisarska, K., Berman, E. R., Pestone, M., Dowling, H., Offenbacher, E., Weisel, H., Heshka, S., Matthews, D. E., & Heymsfield, S. B. (1992). Discrepancy between self-reported and actual caloric intake and exercise in obese subjects. *New England Journal of Medicine, 327,* 1893–1898. (p. 307)

Life (1991, January). Barbie fashion doll proportions. p. 78. (p. 308)

Lifton, R. J. (1986). *The Nazi doctors.* New York: Basic Books. (p. 183)

Light, K. C., Koepke, J. P., Obrist, P. A., & Willis, P. W., Jr. (1983). Psychological stress induces sodium and fluid retention in men at high risk for hypertension. *Science, 220,* 429–431. (p. 363)

Linder, D. (1982). Social trap analogs: The tragedy of the commons in the laboratory. In V. J. Derlega & J. Grzelak (Eds.), *Cooperative and helping behavior: Theories and research.* New York: Academic Press. (p. 510)

Lindskold, S. (1978). Trust development, the GRIT proposal, and the effects of conciliatory acts on conflict and cooperation. *Psychological Bulletin, 85,* 772–793. (p. 521)

Lindskold, S. (1986). GRIT: Reducing distrust through carefully introduced conciliation. In S. Worchel & W. G. Austin (Eds.), *Psychology of intergroup relations* (2nd ed.). Chicago: Nelson-Hall. (p. 521)

Lindskold, S., & Han, G. (1988). GRIT as a foundation for integrative bargaining. *Personality and Social Psychology Bulletin, 14,* 335–345. (p. 521)

Lindskold, S., Han, G., & Betz, B. (1986). Repeated persuasion in interpersonal conflict. *Journal of Personality and Social Psychology, 51,* 1183–1188. (p. 521)

Lindskold, S., Walters, P. S., & Koutsourais, H. (1983). Cooperators, competitors, and response to GRIT. *Journal of Conflict Resolution, 27,* 521–532. (p. 521)

Linn, M. C., & Hyde, J. S. (1991). Trends in cognitive and psychosocial gender differences. In R. M. Lerner, A. C. Petersen, & J. Brooks-Gunn (Eds.), *The encyclopedia of adolescence.* New York: Garland Publishing. (p. 291)

Linn, M. C., & Peterson, A. C. (1986). A meta-analysis of gender differences in spatial ability: Implications for mathematics and science achievement. In J. S. Hyde & M. C. Linn (Eds.), *The psychology of gender: Advances through meta-analysis.* Baltimore: Johns Hopkins University Press. (p. 290)

Linville, P. W., Fischer, G. W., & Fischhoff, B. (1992). AIDS risk perceptions and decision biases. In J. B. Pryor & G. D. Reeder (Eds.), *The social psychology of HIV infection.* Hillsdale, NJ: Erlbaum. (p. 262)

Lippman, J. (1992, October 25). Global village is characterized by a television in every home. *Grand Rapids Press (Los Angeles Times Syndicate),* p. F9. (p. 504)

Lipsey, M. W., & Wilson, D. B. (1993). The efficacy of psychological, educational, and behavioral treatment: Confirmation from meta-analyses. *American Psychologist, 48,* 1181–1209. (p. 466)

Livingstone, M., & Hubel, D. (1988). Segregation of form, color, movement, and depth: Anatomy, physiology, and perception. *Science, 240,* 740–749. (p. 128)

Lock, M., Kaufert, P., & Gilbert, P. (1988). Cultural construction of the menopausal syndrome: The Japanese case. *Maturitas, 10,* 317–332. (p. 98)

Locke, E. A., & Latham, G. P. (1990). Work motivation and satisfaction: Light at the end of the tunnel. *Psychological Science, 1,* 240–246. (p. 327)

Loehlin, J. C., & Nichols, R. C. (1976). *Heredity, environment, and personality.* Austin: University of Texas Press. (pp. 108, 285)

Loewenstein, G., & Furstenberg, F. (1991). Is teenage sexual behavior rational? *Journal of Applied Social Psychology, 21,* 957–986. (p. 210)

Loftus, E. F. (1992). When a lie becomes memory's truth: Memory distortion after exposure to misinformation. *Current Directions in Psychological Science, 1,* 121–123. (pp. 243, 249)

Loftus, E. F. (1995, March/April). Remembering dangerously. *Skeptical Inquirer,* pp. 20–29. (pp. 247, 248)

Loftus, E. F., & Coan, D. (in press). The construction of childhood memories. In D. Peters (Ed.), *The child witness in context: Cognitive, social and legal perspectives.* New York: Kluwer. (p. 249)

Loftus, E. F., & Ketcham, K. (1994). *The myth of repressed memory.* New York: St. Martin's Press.

Loftus, E. F., Levidow, B., & Duensing, S. (1992). Who remembers best? Individual differences in memory for events that occurred in a science museum. *Applied Cognitive Psychology, 6,* 93–107. (p. 244)

Loftus, E. F., & Loftus, G. R. (1980). On the permanence of stored information in the human brain. *American Psychologist, 35,* 409–420. (p. 236)

Loftus, E. F., & Palmer, J. C. (1974). Reconstruction of automobile destruction: An example of the interaction between language and memory. *Journal of Verbal Learning and Verbal Behavior, 13,* 585–589. (p. 243)

London, P. (1970). The rescuers: Motivational hypotheses about Christians who saved Jews from the Nazis. In J. Macaulay & L. Berkowitz (Eds.), *Altruism and helping behavior.* New York: Academic Press. (p. 218)

LoPiccolo, J. L., & Stock, W. E. (1986). Treatment of sexual dysfunction. *Journal of Consulting and Clinical Psychology, 54,* 158–167. (p. 316)

Lord, C. G., Lepper, M. R., & Preston, E. (1984). Considering the opposite: A corrective strategy for social judgment. *Journal of Personality and Social Psychology, 47,* 1231–1247. (p. 263)

Lord, C. G., Ross, L., & Lepper, M. (1979). Biased assimilation and attitude polarization: The effects of prior theories on subsequently considered evidence. *Journal of Personality and Social Psychology, 37,* 2098–2109. (p. 263)

Lorenz, K. (1937). The companion in the bird's world. *Auk, 54,* 245–273. (p. 82)

Lovaas, O. I. (1987). Behavioral treatment and normal educational and intellectual functioning in young autistic children. *Journal of Consulting and Clinical Psychology, 55,* 3–9. (p. 458)

Lu, Z.-L., Williamson, S. J., & Kaufman, L. (1992). Behavioral lifetime of human auditory sensory memory predicted by physiological measures. *Science, 258,* 1668–1670. (p. 233)

Lubart, T. I. (1990). Creativity and cross-cultural variation. *International Journal of Psychology, 25,* 39–59. (p. 282)

Lubin, B., Larsen, R. M., & Matarazzo, J. D. (1984). Patterns of psychological test usage in the United States: 1935–1982. *American Psychologist, 39,* 451–454. (p. 384)

Lubinski, D., & Benbow, C. P. (1992). Gender differences in abilities and preferences among the gifted: Implications for the math-science pipeline. *Current Directions in Psychological Science, 1,* 61–66. (p. 290)

Lukoff, D., Lu, F., & Turner, R. (1992). Toward a more culturally sensitive DSM-IV: Psychoreligious and psychospiritual problems. *Journal of Nervous and Mental Disease, 180,* 673–682. (p. 468)

Lull, J. (Ed.). (1988). *World families watch television.* Newbury Park, CA: Sage. (p. 504)

Lummis, M., & Stevenson, H. W. (1990). Gender differences in beliefs and achievement: A cross-cultural study. *Developmental Psychology, 26,* 254–263. (p. 290)

Lumsden, C. J., & Wilson, E. O. (1983). *Promethean fire: Reflections on the origin of mind.* Cambridge, MA: Harvard University Press. (p. 217)

Luria, A. M. (1968). In L. Solotaroff (Trans.), *The mind of a mnemonist.* New York: Basic Books. (p. 223)

Lykken, D. T. (1982, September). Fearlessness: Its carefree charm and deadly risks. *Psychology Today,* pp. 20–28. (p. 441)

Lykken, D. T. (1983, April). Polygraph prejudice. *APA Monitor,* p. 4. (p. 337)

Lykken, D. T. (1991). Science, lies, and controversy: An epitaph for the polygraph. Invited address upon receipt of the Senior Career award for Distinguished Contribution to Psychology in the Public Interest, American Psychological Association convention. (p. 337)

Lykken, D. T., McGue, M., Tellegen, A., & Bouchard, T. J., Jr. (1992). Emergenesis: Genetic traits that may not run in families. *American Psychologist, 47,* 1565–1577. (p. 110)

Lynch, G., & Staubli, U. (1991). Possible contributions of long-term potentiation to the encoding and organization of memory. *Brain Research Reviews, 16,* 204–206. (p. 237)

Lynn, M. (1988). The effects of alcohol consumption on restaurant tipping. *Personality and Social Psychology Bulletin, 14,* 87–91. (p. 182)

Lynn, R. (1987). Japan: Land of the rising IQ. A reply to Flynn. *Bulletin of the British Psychological Society, 40,* 464–468. (p. 291)

Lynn, R. (1991). The evolution of racial differences in intelligence. *The Mankind Quarterly, 32,* 99–145. (p. 289)

Lynn, S. J., & Rhue, J. W. (1986). The fantasy-prone person: Hypnosis, imagination, and creativity. *Journal of Personality and Social Psychology, 51,* 404–408. (p. 177)

Lynn, S. J., Rhue, J. W., & Weekes, J. R. (1990). Hypnotic involuntariness: A social cognitive analysis. *Psychological Review, 97,* 169–184. (p. 180)

Lytton, H., & Romney, D. M. (1991). Parents' differential socialization of boys and girls: A meta-analysis. *Psychological Bulletin, 109,* 267–296. (p. 86)

Lyubomirsky, S., & Nolen-Hoeksema, S. (1994). The effects of depressive rumination on thinking and problem solving. Unpublished manuscript, Stanford University. (p. 459)

Maccoby, E. E. (1990). Gender and relationships: A developmental account. *American Psychologist, 45,* 513–520. (p. 94)

MacDonald, N. (1960). Living with schizophrenia. *Canadian Medical Association Journal, 82,* 218–221. (p. 435)

MacDonald, T. K., Zanna, M. P., & Fong, G. T. (1994a). Intoxication decreases condom use among males who typically use condoms. Paper presented to the American Psychological Society convention. (p. 183)

MacDonald, T. K., Zanna, M. P., & Fong, G. T. (1994b). The effects of alcohol on intentions to use condoms. Paper presented to the American Psychological Association convention. (p. 183)

MacFarlane, A. (1978, February). What a baby knows. *Human Nature*, pp. 74–81. (p. 73)

Macfarlane, J. W. (1964). Perspectives on personality consistency and change from the guidance study. *Vita Humana, 7*, 115–126. (pp. 88, 112)

MacKay, D. G. (1983). Prescriptive grammar and the pronoun problem. In B. Thorne, C. Kramarae, & N. Henley (Eds.), *Language, gender and society.* Rowley, MA: Newbury House. (p. 273)

MacKinnon, D. W., & Hall, W. B. (1972). Intelligence and creativity. *Proceedings, XVIIth International Congress of Applied Psychology* (Vol. 2, pp. 1883–1888). Brussels: Editest. (p. 282)

MacLeod, C., & Campbell, L. (1992). Memory accessibility and probability judgments: An experimental evaluation of the availability heuristic. *Journal of Personality and Social Psychology, 63*, 890–902. (p. 260)

Maehr, M. L., & Braskamp, L. A. (1986). *The motivation factor: A theory of personal investment.* Lexington, MA: Lexington Books. (p. 326)

Magnusson, D. (1990). Personality research—challenges for the future. *European Journal of Personality, 4*, 1–17. (p. 441)

Major, B., Carrington, P. I., & Carnevale, P. J. D. (1984). Physical attractiveness and self-esteem: Attribution for praise from an other-sex evaluator. *Personality and Social Psychology Bulletin, 10*, 43–50. (p. 513)

Major, B., Cozzarelli, C., Sciacchitano, A. M., Cooper, M. L., Testa, M., & Mueller, P. M. (1990). Perceived social support, self-efficacy, and adjustment to abortion. *Journal of Personality and Social Psychology, 59*, 452–463. (p. 359)

Major, B., Schmidlin, A. M., & Williams, L. (1990). Gender patterns in social touch: The impact of setting and age. *Journal of Personality and Social Psychology, 58*, 634–643. (p. 328)

Malamuth, N. M. (1989). Sexually violent media, thought patterns, and antisocial behavior. In G. Comstock (Ed.), *Public communication and behavior* (Vol. 2). San Diego, CA: Academic Press. (p. 508)

Malamuth, N. M., & Check, J. V. P. (1981). The effects of media exposure on acceptance of violence against women: A field experiment. *Journal of Research in Personality, 15*, 436–446. (p. 507)

Malamuth, N. M., Sockloskie, R. J., Koss, M. P., & Tanaka, J. S. (1991). Characteristics of aggressors against women: Testing a model using a national sample of college students. *Journal of Consulting and Clinical Psychology, 59*, 670–681. (p. 507)

Malinosky-Rummell, R., & Hansen, D. J. (1993). Long-term consequences of childhood physical abuse. *Psychological bulletin, 114*, 68–79. (p. 84)

Malkiel, B. (1985). *A random walk down Wall Street* (4th ed.). New York: Norton. (p. 261)

Malloy, E. A. & others (1994, June 7). Report of the Commission on Substance Abuse at Colleges and Universities, reported by *Associated Press.* (p. 183)

Malmquist, C. P. (1986). Children who witness parental murder: Post-traumatic aspects. *Journal of the American Academy of Child Psychiatry, 25*, 320–325. (p. 249)

Malone, T. W., & Lepper, M. R. (1986). Making learning fun: A taxonomy of intrinsic motivations for learning. In R. E. Snow & M. J. Farr (Eds.), *Aptitude, learning, and instruction: III. Cognitive and affective process analysis.* Hillsdale, NJ: Erlbaum. (p. 325)

Mandel, D. (1983, March 13). One man's holocaust: Part II. The story of David Mandel's journey through hell as told to David Kagan. *Wonderland Magazine* (Grand Rapids Press), pp. 2–7. (p. 297)

Manning, W. G., Keefer, E. B., Newhouse, J. P., Sloss, E. M., & Wasserman, J. (1989). The taxes of sin: Do smokers and drinkers pay their way? *Journal of the American Medical Association, 261*, 1604–1609. (p. 184)

Marks, D. F. (1986). Investigating the paranormal. *Nature, 320*, 119–124. (p. 156)

Markus, H., & Kitayama, S. (1991). Culture and the self: Implications for cognition, emotion, and motivation. *Psychological Review, 98*, 224–253. (pp. 272, 341, 344, 399)

Markus, H., & Nurius, P. (1986). Possible selves. *American Psychologist, 41*, 954–969. (p. 395)

Marlatt, G. A. (1991). Substance abuse: Etiology, prevention, and treatment issues. Master lecture, American Psychological Association convention. (pp. 183, 210)

Marschark, M., Richman, C. L., Yuille, J. C., & Hunt, R. R. (1987). The role of imagery in memory: On shared and distinctive information. *Psychological Bulletin, 102*, 28–41. (p. 229)

Marsh, H. W., & Parker, J. W. (1984). Determinants of student self-concept: Is it better to be a relatively large fish in a small pond even if you don't learn to swim as well? *Journal of Personality and Social Psychology, 47*, 213–231. (p. 350)

Marshall, W. L. (1989). Pornography and sex offenders. In D. Zillmann & J. Bryant (Eds.), *Pornography: Research advances and policy considerations.* Hillsdale, NJ: Erlbaum. (p. 507)

Marteau, T. M. (1989). Framing of information: Its influences upon decisions of doctors and patients. *British Journal of Social Psychology, 28*, 89–94. (p. 262)

Martin, R. J., White, B. D., & Hulsey, M. G. (1991). The regulation of body weight. *American Scientist, 79*, 528–541. (p. 303)

Martin, S. J., Kelly, I. W., & Saklofske, D. H. (1992). Suicide and lunar cycles: A critical review over 28 years. *Psychological Reports, 71*, 787–795. (p. 440)

Martinsen, E. W. (1987). The role of aerobic exercise in the treatment of depression. *Stress Medicine, 3*, 93–100. (p. 369)

Martyna, W. (1978). What does "he" mean? Use of generic masculine. *Journal of Communication, 28*(1), 131–138. (p. 273)

Maslow, A. H. (1970). *Motivation and personality* (2nd ed.). New York: Harper & Row. (pp. 300, 394)

Maslow, A. H. (1971). *The farther reaches of human nature.* New York: Viking Press. (p. 300)

Masters, W. H., & Johnson, V. E. (1966). *Human sexual response.* Boston: Little, Brown. (p. 312)

Matarazzo, J. D. (1983). Computerized psychological testing. *Science, 221*, 323. (p. 390)

Matheny, A. P., Jr. (1989). Children's behavioral inhibition over age and across situations: Genetic similarity for a trait during change. *Journal of Personality, 57*, 215–235. (p. 108)

Matsumoto, D. (1994). *People: Psychology from a cultural perspective.* Pacific Grove, CA: Brooks/Cole. (p. 272)

Matsumoto, D., Kudoh, T., Scherer, K., & Wallbott, H. (1988). Antecedents of and reactions to emotions in the United States and Japan. *Journal of Cross-Cultural Psychology, 19,* 267–286. (pp. 341, 344)

Matt, G. E., Vazquez, C., & Campbell, W. K. (1992). Mood-congruent recall of affectively toned stimuli: A meta-analytic review. *Clinical Psychology Review, 12,* 227–255. (p. 241)

Matthews, K. A. (1988). CHD and Type A behaviors: Update on and alternative to the Booth-Kewley and Friedman quantitative review. *Psychological Bulletin, 104,* 373–380. (p. 362)

Matthews, K. A. (1992). Myths and realities of the menopause. *Psychosomatic Medicine, 54,* 1–9. (p. 98)

Maurer, D., & Maurer, C. (1988). *The world of the newborn.* New York: Basic Books. (p. 73)

May, C. P., Hasher, L., & Stoltzfus, E. R. (1993). Optimal time of day and the magnitude of age differences in memory. *Psychological Science, 4,* 326–330. (p. 101)

May, P. A. (1986). Alcohol and drug misuse prevention programs for American Indians: Needs and opportunities. *Journal of Studies on Alcohol, 47,* 187–195. (p. 416)

May, R. (1982). The problem of evil: An open letter to Carl Rogers. *Journal of Humanistic Psychology, 22,* 10–21. (p. 401)

McBurney, D. H., & Collings, V. B. (1984). *Introduction to sensation and perception* (2nd ed.). Englewood Cliffs, NJ: Prentice-Hall. (pp. 147, 148)

McBurney, D. H., & Gent, J. F. (1979). On the nature of taste qualities. *Psychological Bulletin, 86,* 151–167. (p. 135)

McCall, R. B. (1994). Academic underachievers. *Current Directions in Psychological Science, 3,* 15–19. (p. 323)

McCall, R. B., Evahn, C., & Kratzer, L. (1992). High school underachievers. Newbury Park, CA: Sage. (p. 290)

McCann, I. L., & Holmes, D. S. (1984). Influence of aerobic exercise on depression. *Journal of Personality and Social Psychology, 46,* 1142–1147. (p. 368)

McCarthy, P. (1986, July). Scent: The tie that binds? *Psychology Today,* pp. 6, 10. (p. 136)

McCartney, K., Harris, M. J., & Bernieri, F. (1990). Growing up and growing apart: A developmental meta-analysis of twin studies. *Psychological Bulletin, 107,* 226–237. (p. 109)

McCarty, D., Argeriou, M., Huebner, R. B., & Lubran, B. (1991). Alcoholism, drug abuse, and the homeless. *American Psychologist, 46,* 1139–1148. (p. 470)

McCaul, K. D., & Malott, J. M. (1984). Distraction and coping with pain. *Psychological Bulletin, 95,* 516–533. (p. 135)

McCauley, C. R., & Segal, M. E. (1987). Social psychology of terrorist groups. In C. Hendrick (Ed.), *Group processes and intergroup relations.* Beverly Hills, CA: Sage. (p. 492)

McCloskey, M., Wible, C. G., & Cohen, N. J. (1988). Is there a special flashbulb-memory mechanism? *Journal of Experimental Psychology: General, 117,* 171–181. (p. 224)

McConkey, K. M. (1992). The effects of hypnotic procedures on remembering: The experimental findings and their implications for forensic hypnosis. In E. Fromm & M. R. Nash (Eds.), *Contemporary hypnosis research.* New York: Guilford Press. (p. 177)

McConnell, R. A. (1991). National Academy of Sciences opinion on parapsychology. *Journal of the American Society for Psychical Research, 85,* 333–365. (p. 154)

McCormick, C. M., & Witelson, S. F. (1991). A cognitive profile of homosexual men compared to heterosexual men and women. *Psychoneuroendocrinology, 16,* 459–473. (p. 320)

McCrae, R. R., & Costa, P. T., Jr. (1990). *Personality in adulthood.* New York: Guilford. (pp. 103, 104)

McCrae, R. R., & Costa, P. T., Jr. (1994). The stability of personality: Observations and evaluations. *Current Directions in Psychological Science, 3,* 173–175. (pp. 112, 392)

McFarland, C., & Ross, M. (1987). The relation between current impressions and memories of self and dating partners. *Psychological Bulletin, 13,* 228–238. (p. 244)

McGhee, P. E. (1976). Children's appreciation of humor: A test of the cognitive congruency principle. *Child Development, 47,* 420–426. (p. 79)

McGrath, J., Welham, J., & Pemberton, M. (1994). Month of birth, hemisphere of birth and schizophrenia. Unpublished (submitted) manuscript, Wolston Park Hospital, Brisbane, Australia. (p. 437)

McGrath, M. J., & Cohen, D. G. (1978). REM sleep facilitation of adaptive waking behavior: A review of the literature. *Psychological Bulletin, 85,* 24–57. (p. 173)

McGue, M., Bouchard, T. J., Jr., Iacono, W. G., & Lykken, D. T. (1993). Behavioral genetics of cognitive ability: A life-span perspective. In R. Plomin & G. E. McClearn (Eds.), *Nature, nurture and psychology.* Washington, DC: American Psychological Association. (p. 286)

McGue, M., Pickens, R. W., & Svikis, D. S. (1992). Sex and age effects on the inheritance of alcohol problems: A twin study. *Journal of Abnormal Psychology, 202,* 3–17. (p. 189)

McGuire, W. J. (1986). The myth of massive media impact: Savings and salvagings. In G. Comstock (Ed.), *Public communication and behavior.* Orlando, FL: Academic Press. (p. 505)

McHugh, P. R., & Moran, T. H. (1978). Accuracy of the regulation of caloric ingestion in the rhesus monkey. *American Journal of Physiology, 235,* R29–34. (p. 302)

McKinlay, J. B., McKinlay, S. M., & Brambilla, D. J. (1987a). Health status and utilization behavior associated with menopause. *American Journal of Epidemiology, 125,* 110–121. (p. 98)

McKinlay, J. B., McKinlay, S. M., & Brambilla, D. (1987b). The relative contributions of endocrine changes and social circumstances to depression in mid-aged women. *Journal of Health and Social Behavior, 28,* 345–363. (p. 98)

McNally, R. J. (1987). Preparedness and phobias: A review. *Psychological Bulletin, 101,* 283–303. (p. 217)

Meador, B. D., & Rogers, C. R. (1984). Person-centered therapy. In R. J. Corsini (Ed.), *Current psychotherapies* (3rd ed.). Itasca, IL: Peacock. (p. 454)

Meaney, M. J., Aitken, D. H., Van Berkel, C., Bhatnagar, S., & Sapolsky, R. M. (1988). Effect of neonatal handling on age-related impairments associated with the hippocampus. *Science, 239,* 766–768. (p. 75)

Medawar, P. (1982). *Pluto's republic.* New York: Oxford University Press. (p. 386)

Mednick, S. A., Huttunen, M. O., & Machon, R. A. (1994). Prenatal influenza infections and adult schizophrenia. *Schizophrenia Bulletin, 20,* 263–267. (p. 437)

Meichenbaum, D. (1977). *Cognitive-behavior modification: An integrative approach.* New York: Plenum Press. (p. 461)

Meichenbaum, D. (1985). *Stress inoculation training.* New York: Pergamon. (p. 461)

Meier, R. P. (1991).   Language acquisition by deaf children. *American Scientist, 79*, 60–70. (p. 268)

Meltzoff, A. N. (1988a).   Infant imitation and memory: Nine-month-olds in immediate and deferred tests. *Child Development, 59*, 217–225. (p. 217)

Meltzoff, A. N. (1988b).   Infant imitation after a 1–week delay: Long-term memory for novel acts and multiple stimuli. *Developmental Psychology, 24*, 470–476. (p. 217)

Meltzoff, A. N. (1988c).   Imitation of televised models by infants. *Child Development, 59*, 1221–1229. (p. 217)

Melzack, R. (1984).   The myth of painless childbirth. *Pain, 19*, 321–337. (p. 135)

Melzack, R. (1992, April).   Phantom limbs. *Scientific American*, pp. 120–126. (p. 134)

Melzack, R., & Wall, P. D. (1965).   Pain mechanisms: A new theory. *Science, 150*, 971–979. (p. 134)

Melzack, R., & Wall, P. D. (1983).   *The challenge of pain*. New York: Basic Books. (p. 134)

Mendolia, M., & Kleck, R. E. (1993).   Effects of talking about a stressful event on arousal: Does what we talk about make a difference? *Journal of Personality and Social Psychology, 64*, 283–292. (p. 373)

Mento, A. J., Steel, R. P., & Karren, R. J. (1987).   A meta-analytic study of the effects of goal setting on task performance: 1966–1984. *Organizational Behavior and Human Decision Processes, 39*, 52–83. (p. 327)

Merskey, H. (1992).   The manufacture of personalities: The production of multiple personality disorder. *British Journal of Psychiatry, 160*, 327–340. (p. 425)

Merton, R. K. (1938; reprinted 1970).   *Science, technology and society in seventeenth-century England*. New York: Fertig. (p. 7)

Merton, R. K., & Kitt, A. S. (1950).   Contributions to the theory of reference group behavior. In R. K. Merton & P. F. Lazarsfeld (Eds.), *Continuities in social research: Studies in the scope and method of the American soldier*. Glencoe, IL: Free Press. (p. 349)

Mesquita, B., & Frijda, N. H. (1992).   Cultural variations in emotions: A review. *Psychological Bulletin, 112*, 179–204. (p. 340)

Messer, W. S., & Griggs, R. A. (1989).   Student belief and involvement in the paranormal and performance in introductory psychology. *Teaching of Psychology, 16*, 187–191. (p. 155)

Metalsky, G. I., Joiner, T. E., Jr., Hardin, T. S., & Abramson, L. Y. (1993). Depressive reactions to failure in a naturalistic setting: A test of the hopelessness and self-esteem theories of depression. *Journal of Abnormal Psychology, 102*, 101–109. (p. 432)

Meuwissen, I., & Over, R. (1992).   Sexual arousal across phases of the human menstrual cycle. *Archives of Sexual Behavior, 21*, 101–119. (p. 313)

Michaels, J. W., Bloomel, J. M., Brocato, R. M., Linkous, R. A., & Rowe, J. S. (1982). Social facilitation and inhibition in a natural setting. *Replications in Social Psychology, 2*, 21–24. (p. 490)

Middlebrooks, J. C., & Green, D. M. (1991).   Sound localization by human listeners. *Annual Review of Psychology, 42*, 135–159. (p. 133)

Mikulincer, M., Babkoff, H., Caspy, T., & Sing, H. (1989).   The effects of 72 hours of sleep loss on psychological variables. *British Journal of Psychology, 80*, 145–162. (p. 169)

Milan, R. J., Jr., & Kilmann, P. R. (1987).   Interpersonal factors in premarital contraception. *Journal of Sex Research, 23*, 289–321. (p. 96)

Milgram, S. (1974).   *Obedience to authority*. New York: Harper & Row. (pp. 487, 488, 489)

Miller, G. A. (1956).   The magical number seven, plus or minus two: Some limits on our capacity for processing information. *Psychological Review, 63*, 81–97. (p. 234)

Miller, G. A. (1962).   *Psychology: The science of mental life*. New York: Harper & Row. (p. 378)

Miller, G. A., & Gildea, P. M. (1987, September).   How children learn words. *Scientific American*, pp. 94–99. (p. 265)

Miller, K. I., & Monge, P. R. (1986).   Participation, satisfaction, and productivity: A meta-analytic review. *Academy of Management Journal, 29*, 727–753. (p. 404)

Miller, N. E. (1983).   Value and ethics of research on animals. Paper presented at the meeting of the American Psychological Association. (p. 26)

Miller, N. E. (1985, February).   Rx: biofeedback. *Psychology Today*, pp. 54–59. (p. 370)

Miller, N. E., & Brucker, B. S. (1979).   A learned visceral response apparently independent of skeletal ones in patients paralyzed by spinal lesions. In N. Birbaumer & H. D. Kimmel (Eds.), *Biofeedback and self-regulation*. Hillsdale, NJ: Erlbaum. (p. 369)

Miller, P. C., Lefcourt, H. M., Holmes, J. G., Ware, E. E., & Saleh, W. E. (1986). Marital locus of control and marital problem solving. *Journal of Personality and Social Psychology, 51*, 161–169. (p. 403)

Mills, M., & Melhuish, E. (1974).   Recognition of mother's voice in early infancy. *Nature, 252*, 123–124. (p. 73)

Mineka, S. (1985).   The frightful complexity of the origins of fears. In F. R. Brush & J. B. Overmier (Eds.), *Affect, conditioning and cognition: Essays on the determinants of behavior*. Hillsdale, NJ: Erlbaum. (p. 217)

Mineka, S., & Sutton, S. K. (1992).   Cognitive biases and the emotional disorders. *Psychological Science, 3*, 65–69. (p. 421)

Mirin, S. M., & Weiss, R. D. (1989).   Genetic factors in the development of alcoholism. *Psychiatric Annals, 19*, 239–242. (p. 189)

Mischel, W. (1968).   *Personality and assessment*. New York: Wiley. (p. 392)

Mischel, W. (1981).   Current issues and challenges in personality. In L. T. Benjamin, Jr. (Ed.), *The G. Stanley Hall Lecture Series* (Vol. 1). Washington, DC: American Psychological Association. (p. 407)

Mischel, W. (1984).   Convergences and challenges in the search for consistency. *American Psychologist, 39*, 351–364. (p. 392)

Mischel, W., Shoda, Y., & Peake, P. K. (1988).   The nature of adolescent competencies predicted by preschool delay of gratification. *Journal of Personality and Social Psychology, 54*, 687–696. (p. 91)

Mischel, W., Shoda, Y., & Rodriguez, M. L. (1989).   Delay of gratification in children. *Science, 244*, 933–938. (pp. 91, 209)

Mita, T. H., Dermer, M., & Knight, J. (1977).   Reversed facial images and the mere-exposure hypothesis. *Journal of Personality and Social Psychology, 35*, 597–601. (p. 512)

Monaghan, P. (1992, September 23).   Professor of psychology stokes a controversy on the reliability and repression of memory. *Chronicle of Higher Education*, pp. A9–A10. (p. 249)

Monahan, J. (1992).   Mental disorder and violent behavior: Perceptions and evidence. *American Psychologist, 47*, 511–521. (p. 444)

Money, J. (1987).   Sin, sickness, or status? Homosexual gender identity and psychoneuroendocrinology. *American Psychologist, 42*, 384–399. (pp. 319, 320)

Money, J. (1988). *Gay, straight, and in-between.* New York: Oxford University Press. (p. 507)

Money, J., Berlin, F. S., Falck, A., & Stein, M. (1983). *Antiandrogenic and counseling treatment of sex offenders.* Baltimore: Department of Psychiatry and Behavioral Sciences, The Johns Hopkins University School of Medicine. (p. 313)

Moody, R. (1976). *Life after life.* Harrisburg, PA: Stackpole Books. (p. 186)

Mook, D. G. (1983). In defense of external invalidity. *American Psychologist, 38,* 379–387. (p. 23)

Moorcroft, W. (1993). *Sleep, dreaming, and sleep disorders: An introduction* (2nd ed.). Landam, MD: University Press of America. (pp. 167, 169)

Moore, D. W. (1993, April). Public polarized on gay issue. *Gallup Poll Monthly,* pp. 30–34. (p. 320)

Moreland, R. L., & Beach, S. R. (1992). Exposure effects in the classroom: The development of affinity among students. *Journal of Experimental Social Psychology, 28,* 255–276. (p. 512)

Moreland, R. L., & Zajonc, R. B. (1982). Exposure effects in person perception: Familiarity, similarity, and attraction. *Journal of Experimental Social Psychology, 18,* 395–415. (p. 512)

Morelli, G. A., Rogoff, B., Oppenheim, D., & Goldsmith, D. (1992). Cultural variation in infants' sleeping arrangements: Questions of independence. *Developmental Psychology, 26,* 604–613. (p. 85)

Morris, N. M., Udry, J. R., Kahn-Dawood, F., & Dawood, M. Y. (1987). Marital sex frequency and midcycle female testosterone. *Archives of Sexual Behavior, 16,* 27–37. (p. 313)

Morrison, D. M. (1985). Adolescent contraceptive behavior: A review. *Psychological Bulletin, 98,* 538–568. (p. 96)

Morton, G. E. (1994). Personal communication, 525 E. Mission, Spokane, Washington 99202. (p. 10)

Moruzzi, G., & Magoun, H. W. (1949). Brain stem reticular formation and activation of the EEG. *Electroencephalography and Clinical Neurophysiology, 1,* 455–473. (p. 48)

Moscovici, S. (1985). Social influence and conformity. In G. Lindzey & E. Aronson (Eds.), *The handbook of social psychology,* 3rd ed. Hillsdale, N.J.: Erlbaum. (p. 493)

Mosher, D. L., & Anderson, R. D. (1986). Macho personality, sexual aggression, and reactions to guided imagery of realistic rape. *Journal of Research in Personality, 20,* 77–94. (p. 182)

Moss, A. J., Allen, K. F., Giovino, G. A., & Mills, S. L. (1992, December 2). Recent trends in adolescent smoking, smoking-update correlates, and expectations about the future. *Advance Data* No. 221 (from Vital and Health Statistics of the Centers for Disease Control and Prevention). (p. 190)

Moss, H. A., & Susman, E. J. (1980). Longitudinal study of personality development. In O. G. Brim, Jr., & J. Kagan (Eds.), *Constancy and change in human development.* Cambridge, MA: Harvard University Press. (p. 112)

Moyer, K. E. (1983). The physiology of motivation: Aggression as a model. In C. J. Scheier & A. M. Rogers (Eds.), *G. Stanley Hall Lecture Series* (Vol. 3). Washington, DC: American Psychological Association. (p. 501)

Muehlenhard, C. L. (1988). Misinterpreted dating behaviors and the risk of date rape. *Journal of Social and Clinical Psychology, 6,* 20–37. (p. 316)

Murphy, G. E., & Wetzel, R. D. (1990). The lifetime risk of suicide in alcoholism. *Archives of General Psychiatry, 47,* 383–392. (p. 428)

Murphy, S. T., & Zajonc, R. B. (1993). Affect, cognition, and awareness: Affective priming with optimal and suboptimal stimulus exposures. *Journal of Personality and Social Psychology, 64,* 723–739. (p. 120)

Murphy, T. N. (1982). Pain: Its assessment and management. In R. J. Gatchel, A. Baum, & J. E. Singer (Eds.), *Handbook of psychology and health: Vol. I. Clinical psychology and behavioral medicine: Overlapping disciplines.* Hillsdale, NJ: Erlbaum. (p. 135)

Murray, C., & Herrnstein, R. J. (1994, October 31). Race, genes and I.Q.—An apologia. *New Republic,* pp. 27–37. (p. 289)

Murray, H. (1938). *Explorations in personality.* New York: Oxford University Press. (p. 323)

Murray, H. A. (1933). The effect of fear upon estimates of the maliciousness of other personalities. *Journal of Social Psychology, 4,* 310–329. (p. 384)

Murray, H. A., & Wheeler, D. R. (1937). A note on the possible clairvoyance of dreams. *Journal of Psychology, 3,* 309–313. (p. 155)

Murray, R., Jones, P., O'Callaghan, E., Takei, N., & Sham, P. (1992). Genes, viruses, and neurodevelopmental schizophrenia. *Journal of Psychiatric Research, 26,* 225–235. (p. 437)

Myers, D. G. (1993). *Social psychology* (4th ed.). New York: McGraw-Hill. (pp. 346, 396)

Myers, D. G. (1993). *The pursuit of happiness.* New York: Avon Books. (pp. 346, 350)

Myers, D. G. (1994). Society in the balance: America's social recession and renewal. Unpublished manuscript, Hope College, Holland, MI. (p. 96)

Myers, D. G., & Bishop, G. D. (1970). Discussion effects on racial attitudes. *Science, 169,* 778–779. (p. 492)

Myers, D. G., & Diener, E. (1995). Who is happy? *Psychological Science, 6,* 10–19. (p. 350)

Myers, I. B. (1987). *Introduction to type: A description of the theory and applications of the Myers-Briggs Type Indicator.* Palo Alto, CA: Consulting Psychologists Press. (p. 388)

Napolitan, D. A., & Goethals, G. R. (1979). The attribution of friendliness. *Journal of Experimental Social Psychology, 15,* 105–113. (p. 480)

Nash, M. (1987). What, if anything, is regressed about hypnotic age regression? A review of the empirical literature. *Psychological Bulletin, 102,* 42–52. (p. 177)

National Academy of Sciences, Institute of Medicine. (1982). *Marijuana and health.* Washington, DC: National Academy Press. (p. 187)

National Academy of Sciences. (1984). *Bereavement: Reactions, consequences, and cure.* Washington, DC: National Academy Press. (pp. 363, 364)

National Academy of Sciences. (1991). *Science, medicine, and animals.* Washington, DC: National Academy Press. (p. 26)

National Center for Health Statistics. (1990, October 1). Child care arrangements. *Advance data from vital and health statistics of the National Center for Health Statistics,* Report No. 187. (p. 99)

National Center for Health Statistics. (1991). Family structure and children's health: United States, 1988. *Vital and health statistics,* Series 10, No. 178, DHHS Publication No. PHS 91–1506 by Deborah A. Dawson. (pp. 84, 317)

National Institute of Mental Health. (1982). *Television and behavior: Ten years of scientific progress and implications for the eighties.* Washington, DC: U.S. Government Printing Office. (p. 505)

National Institute on Drug Abuse. (1991). *National household survey on drug abuse: Population estimates 1991.* Rockville, MD: Alcohol, Drug Abuse, and Mental Health Administration. (p. 185)

National Opinion Research Center. (1985, October/November). Images of the world. *Public Opinion,* p. 38. (p. 400)

National Research Council. (1987). *Risking the future: Adolescent sexuality, pregnancy, and childbearing.* Washington, DC: National Academy Press. (p. 96)

National Research Council. (1990). *Human factors research needs for an aging population.* Washington, DC: National Academy Press. (p. 99)

National Safety Council. (1991). *Accident facts.* Chicago: National Safety Council. (p. 261)

Naylor, T. H. (1990). Redefining corporate motivation, Swedish style. *Christian Century, 107,* 566–570. (p. 328)

NCTV News. (1987, July-August). More research links harmful effects to non-violent porn. National Coalition on Television Violence, p. 12. (p. 506)

Needles, D. J., & Abramson, L. Y. (1990). Positive life events, attributional style, and hopefulness: Testing a model of recovery from depression. *Journal of Abnormal Psychology, 99,* 156–165. (p. 432)

Neese, R. M. (1991, November/December). What good is feeling bad? The evolutionary benefits of psychic pain. *The Sciences,* pp. 30–37. (pp. 134, 203, 427)

Neisser, U. (1981). John Dean's memory: A case study. *Cognition, 9,* 1–22. (pp. 224, 241)

Neisser, U., & Harsch, N. (1992). Phantom flashbulbs: False recollections of hearing the news about *Challenger.* In E. Winograd & U. Neisser (Eds.), *Affect and accuracy in recall: Studies of "flashbulb" memories.* New York: Cambridge University Press. (pp. 224, 243)

Neisser, U., Winograd, E., & Weldon, M. S. (1991). Remembering the earthquake: "What I experienced" vs. "How I heard the news." Paper presented to the Psychonomic Society convention. (p. 237)

Neitz, J., Geist, T., & Jacobs, G. H. (1989). Color vision in the dog. *Visual Neuroscience, 3,* 119–125. (p. 129)

Nelson, K. (1973). Structure and strategy in learning to talk. *Monographs of the Society for Research in Child Development, 38*(1 & 2, Serial No. 149). (p. 266)

Nelson, K. (1993). The psychological and social origins of autobiographical memory. *Psychological Science, 4,* 7–13. (p. 74)

Nelson, N. (1988). *A meta-analysis of the life-event/health paradigm: The influence of social support.* Unpublished doctoral dissertation, Temple University, Philadelphia. (p. 372)

Neugarten, B. L. (1974). The roles we play. In American Medical Association, *Quality of life: The middle years.* Acton, MA: Publishing Sciences Group. (p. 105)

Nevin, J. A. (1988). Behavioral momentum and the partial reinforcement effect. *Psychological Bulletin, 103,* 44–56. (p. 210)

Newcomb, M. D., & Bentler, P. M. (1988). Impact of adolescent drug use and social support on problems of young adults: A longitudinal study. *Journal of Abnormal Psychology, 97,* 64–75. (p. 187)

Newcomb, M. D., & Harlow, L. L. (1986). Life events and substance use among adolescents: Mediating effects of perceived loss of control and meaninglessness in life. *Journal of Personality and Social Psychology, 51,* 564–577. (p. 189)

Newell, A. (1988, March 9). Quoted in D. L. Wheeler, From years of work in psychology and computer science, scientists build theories of thinking and learning. *Chronicle of Higher Education,* pp. A4, A6. (p. 10)

Newport, E. L. (1990). Maturational constraints on language learning. *Cognitive Science, 14,* 11–28. (p. 268)

Ng, S. H. (1990). Androcentric coding of man and his in memory by language users. *Journal of Experimental Social Psychology, 26,* 455–464. (p. 273)

Nickerson, R. S., & Adams, M. J. (1979). Long-term memory for a common object. *Cognitive Psychology, 11,* 287–307. (pp. 231, 232)

Nicol, S. E., & Gottesman, I. I. (1983). Clues to the genetics and neurobiology of schizophrenia. *American Scientist, 71,* 398–404. (p. 438)

Nicolaus, L. K., Cassel, J. F., Carlson, R. B., & Gustavson, C. R. (1983). Taste-aversion conditioning of crows to control predation on eggs. *Science, 220,* 212–214. (p. 203)

Niemi, R. G., Mueller, J., & Smith, T. W. (1989). *Trends in public opinion: A compendium of survey data.* New York: Greenwood Press. (pp. 348, 495, 497)

Nigro, G. (1984). Cited in U. Neisser, The role of invariant structures in the control of movement. In M. Frese & J. Sabini (Eds.), *Goal directed behavior: The concept of action in psychology.* Hillsdale, NJ: Erlbaum. (p. 274)

Nisbett, R. E. (1993). Violence and U.S. regional culture. *American Psychologist, 48,* 441–449. (p. 504)

Nisbett, R. E., & Borgida, E. (1975). Attribution and the psychology of prediction. *Journal of Personality and Social Psychology, 32,* 932–943. (p. 263)

Nisbett, R. E., & Ross, L. (1980). *Human inference: Strategies and shortcomings of social judgment.* Englewood Cliffs, NJ: Prentice-Hall. (p. 259)

Nisbett, R., & Ross, L. (1991). *The person and the situation.* New York: McGraw-Hill. (p. 328)

Noble, E. P. (1993). The D2 dopamine receptor gene: A review of association studies in alcoholism. *Behavior Genetics, 23,* 119–129. (p. 189)

Noel, J. G., Forsyth, D. R., & Kelley, K. N. (1987). Improving the performance of failing students by overcoming their self-serving attributional biases. *Basic and Applied Social Psychology, 8,* 151–162. (p. 404)

Nolen-Hoeksema, S. (1990). *Sex differences in depression.* Stanford, CA: Stanford University Press. (pp. 429, 431)

Nolen-Hoeksema, S., & Morrow, J. (1991). A prospective study of depression and post-traumatic stress symptoms following a natural disaster: The 1989 Loma Prieta earthquake. *Journal of Personality and Social Psychology, 61,* 115–121. (p. 432)

Noller, P., Law, H., & Comrey, A. L. (1987). Cattell, Comrey, and Eysenck personality factors compared: More evidence for the five robust factors? *Journal of Personality and Social Psychology, 53,* 1208–1217. (p. 389)

NORC. (1993, March/April). National Opinion Research Center surveys on homosexuality reported in *American Enterprise,* pp. 82–83. (p. 320)

Norman, D. A. (1988). *The psychology of everyday things.* New York: Basic Books. (p. 152)

Norris, P. A. (1986). On the status of biofeedback and clinical practice. *American Psychologist, 41,* 1009–1010. (p. 369)

Notarius, C., & Markman, H. (1993). *We can work it out.* New York: Putnam. (p. 105)

Nuttin, J. M., Jr. (1987). Affective consequences of mere ownership: The name letter effect in twelve European languages. *European Journal of Social Psychology, 17*, 381–402. (p. 512)

O'Connor, P., & Brown, G. W. (1984). Supportive relationships: Fact or fancy? *Journal of Social and Personal Relationships, 1*, 159–175. (p. 468)

Oetting, E. R., & Beauvais, F. (1987). Peer cluster theory, socialization characteristics, and adolescent drug use: A path analysis. *Journal of Counseling Psychology, 34*, 205–213. (p. 190)

Oetting, E. R., & Beauvais, F. (1990). Adolescent drug use: Findings of national and local surveys. *Journal of Consulting and Clinical Psychology, 58*, 385–394. (p. 190)

Oettingen, G., & Seligman, M. E. P. (1990). Pessimism and behavioural signs of depression in East versus West Berlin. *European Journal of Social Psychology, 20*, 207–220. (p. 404)

Offer, D., Ostrov, E., Howard, K. I., & Atkinson, R. (1988). *The teenage world: Adolescents' self-image in ten countries.* New York: Plenum. (p. 95)

Olds, J., & Milner, P. (1954). Positive reinforcement produced by electrical stimulation of the septal area and other regions of rat brain. *Journal of Comparative and Physiological Psychology, 47*, 419–427. (p. 50)

Oliner, S. P., & Oliner, P. M. (1988). *The altruistic personality: Rescuers of Jews in Nazi Europe.* New York: Free Press. (p. 218)

Oliver, M. B., & Hyde, J. S. (1993). Gender differences in sexuality: A meta-analysis. *Psychological Bulletin, 114*, 29–51. (p. 316)

Olweus, D., Mattsson, A., Schalling, D., & Low, H. (1988). Circulating testosterone levels and aggression in adolescent males: A causal analysis. *Psychosomatic Medicine, 50*, 261–272. (p. 502)

O'Malley, P. M., & Bachman, J. G. (1983). Self-esteem: Change and stability between ages 13 and 23. *Developmental Psychology, 19*, 257–268. (p. 93)

O'Neill, M. J. (1993). The relationship between privacy, control, and stress responses in office workers. Paper presented to the Human Factors and Ergonomics Society convention. (p. 360)

Orne, M. T. (1982, April 28). Affidavit submitted to State of Pennsylvania. (p. 179)

Orne, M. T., & Evans, F. J. (1965). Social control in the psychological experiment: Antisocial behavior and hypnosis. *Journal of Personality and Social Psychology, 1*, 189–200. (p. 178)

Osgood, C. E. (1962). *An alternative to war or surrender.* Urbana: University of Illinois Press. (p. 521)

Osgood, C. E. (1980). *GRIT: A strategy for survival in mankind's nuclear age?* Paper presented at the Pugwash Conference on New Directions in Disarmament. (p. 521)

OSS Assessment Staff. (1948). *The assessment of men.* New York: Rinehart. (p. 405)

Ostfeld, A. M., Kasl, S. V., D'Atri, D. A., & Fitzgerald, E. F. (1987). *Stress, crowding, and blood pressure in prison.* Hillsdale, NJ: Erlbaum. (p. 361)

Padgett, V. R. (1989). Predicting organizational violence: An application of 11 powerful principles of obedience. Paper presented to the American Psychological Association convention. (p. 488)

Paffenbarger, R. S., Jr., Hyde, R. T., Wing, A. L., & Hsieh, C-C. (1986). Physical activity, all-cause mortality, and longevity of college alumni. *New England Journal of Medicine, 314*, 605–612. (p. 368)

Page, S. (1977). Effects of the mental illness label in attempts to obtain accommodation. *Canadian Journal of Behavioral Science, 9*, 84–90. (p. 443)

Paikoff, R. L., & Brooks-Gunn, J. (1991). Do parent-child relationships change during puberty? *Psychological Bulletin, 110*, 47–66. (p. 94)

Paivio, A. (1986). *Mental representations: A dual coding approach.* New York: Oxford University Press. (p. 229)

Palace, E. M., & Gorzalka, B. B. (1990). The enhancing effects of anxiety on arousal in sexually dysfunctional and functional women. *Journal of Abnormal Psychology, 99*, 403–411. (p. 354)

Palladino, J. J., & Carducci, B. J. (1983). *"Things that go bump in the night": Students' knowledge of sleep and dreams.* Paper presented at the meeting of the Southeastern Psychological Association. (p. 165)

Palmer, S., Schreiber, C., & Box, C. (1991). Remembering the earthquake: "Flashbulb" memory for experienced vs. reported events. Paper presented to the Psychonomic Society convention. (p. 237)

Palumbo, S. R. (1978). *Dreaming and memory: A new information-processing model.* New York: Basic Books. (p. 173)

Pandey, J., Sinha, Y., Prakash, A., & Tripathi, R. C. (1982). Right-left political ideologies and attribution of the causes of poverty. *European Journal of Social Psychology, 12*, 327–331. (p. 481)

Panksepp, J. (1982). Toward a general psychobiological theory of emotions. *Behavioral and Brain Sciences, 5*, 407–467. (p. 338)

Parducci, A. (1995). *Happiness pleasure, and judgement: The contextual theory and its applications.* Hillsdale, NJ: Erlbaum. (p. 348)

Parker, G., Roy, K., Hadzi, P. D., & Pedic, F. (1992). Psychotic (delusional) depression: A meta-analyis of physical treatments. *Journal of Affective Disorders, 24*, 17–24. (p. 473)

Parloff, M. B. (1987, February). Psychotherapy: An import from Japan. *Psychology Today*, pp. 74–75. (p. 449)

Pate, J. E., Pumariega, A. J., Hester, C., & Garner, D. M. (1992). Cross-cultural patterns in eating disorders: A review. *Journal of the American Academy of Child and Adolescent Psychiatry, 31*, 802–809. (p. 304)

Paton, D. (1992). Disaster research: The Scottish dimension. *The Psychologist: Bulletin of the British Psychological Society, 5*, 535–538. (p. 358)

Patterson, F. (1978, October). Conversations with a gorilla. *National Geographic*, pp. 438–465. (p. 269)

Patterson, G. R., Chamberlain, P., & Reid, J. B. (1982). A comparative evaluation of parent training procedures. *Behavior Therapy, 13*, 638–650. (p. 504)

Patterson, R. (1951). *The riddle of Emily Dickinson.* Boston: Houghton Mifflin. (p. 433)

Pauls, D. L., Morton, L. A., & Egeland, J. A. (1992). Risks of affective illness among first-degree relatives of bipolar I old-order Amish probands. *Archives of General Psychiatry, 49*, 703–708. (p. 430)

Pavlov, I. P. (1927). In G. V. Anrep (Trans.), *Conditioned reflexes.* London: Oxford University Press. (pp. 198, 201)

Pedersen, N. L., Plomin, R., McClearn, G. E., & Friberg, L. (1988). Neuroticism, extraversion, and related traits in adult twins reared apart and reared together. *Journal of Personality and Social Psychology, 55*, 950–957. (p. 109)

Pekkanen, J. (1982, June). Why do we sleep? *Science, 82*, p. 86. (p. 169)

Pelham, B. W. (1993). On the highly positive thoughts of the highly depressed. In R. F. Baumeister (Ed.), *Self-esteem: The puzzle of low self-regard*. New York: Plenum. (p. 396)

Penfield, W. (1969). Consciousness, memory, and man's conditioned reflexes. In K. Pigram (Ed.), *On the biology of learning*. New York: Harcourt, Brace & World. (p. 235)

Pennebaker, J. (1990). *Opening up: The healing power of confiding in others*. New York: W. Morrow. (p. 372)

Pennebaker, J. W., Barger, S. D., & Tiebout, J. (1989). Disclosure of traumas and health among Holocaust survivors. *Psychosomatic Medicine, 51*, 577–589. (p. 372)

Pennebaker, J. W., & Harber, K. D. (1993). A social stage model of collective coping: The Loma Prieta earthquake and the Persian Gulf war. *Journal of Social Issues, 49*, 125–145. (p. 373)

Pennebaker, J. W., & O'Heeron, R. C. (1984). Confiding in others and illness rate among spouses of suicide and accidental death victims. *Journal of Abnormal Psychology, 93*, 473–476. (p. 372)

Peplau, L. A. (1982). Research on homosexual couples: An overview. *Journal of Homosexuality, 8*(2), 3–8. (p. 318)

Perkins, K. A., Dubbert, P. M., Martin, J. E., Faulstich, M. E., & Harris, J. K. (1986). Cardiovascular reactivity to psychological stress in aerobically trained versus untrained mild hypertensives and normotensives. *Health Psychology, 5*, 407–421. (p. 369)

Perlmutter, M. (1983). Learning and memory through adulthood. In M. W. Riley, B. B. Hess, & K. Bond (Eds.), *Aging in society: Selected reviews of recent research*. Hillsdale, NJ: Erlbaum. (p. 101)

Persky, V. W., Kempthorne-Rawson, J., & Shekelle, R. B. (1987). Personality and risk of cancer: 20–year follow-up of the Western Electric study. *Psychosomatic Medicine, 49*, 435–449. (p. 364)

Persons, J. B. (1986). The advantages of studying psychological phenomena rather than psychiatric diagnoses. *American Psychologist, 41*, 1252–1260. (p. 443)

Pert, C. B., & Snyder, S. H. (1973). Opiate receptor: Demonstration in nervous tissue. *Science, 179*, 1011–1014. (p. 39)

Peschel, E. R., & Peschel, R. E. (1987). Medical insights into the castrati in opera. *American Scientist, 75*, 578–583. (p. 313)

Peters, T. J., & Waterman, R. H., Jr. (1982). *In search of excellence: Lessons from America's best-run companies*. New York: Harper & Row. (p. 215)

Petersen, A. C. (1987, September). Those gangly years. *Psychology Today*, pp. 28–34. (p. 89)

Peterson, C., & Barrett, L. C. (1987). Explanatory style and academic performance among university freshmen. *Journal of Personality and Social Psychology, 53*, 603–607. (p. 404)

Peterson, C., Peterson, J., & Skevington, S. (1986). Heated argument and adolescent development. *Journal of Social and Personal Relationships, 3*, 229–240. (p. 90)

Peterson, L. R., & Peterson, M. J. (1959). Short-term retention of individual verbal items. *Journal of Experimental Psychology, 58*, 193–198. (pp. 233, 234)

Peterson, R. (1978). Review of the Rorschach. In O. K. Buros (Ed.), *The eighth mental measurements yearbook* (Vol. I). Highland Park, NJ: Gryphon Press. (p. 384)

Petitto, L. A., & Marentette, P. F. (1991). Babbling in the manual mode: Evidence for the ontogeny of language. *Science, 251*, 1493–1496. (pp. 265, 267)

Peto, R., Lopez, A. D., Boreham, J., Thun, M., & Heath, C., Jr. (1992). Mortality from tobacco in developed countries: Indirect estimation from national vital statistics. *Lancet, 339*, 1268–1278. (p. 184)

Peto, R., & others (1994). *Mortality from smoking in developed countries, 1950–2000: Indirect estimates from national vital statistics*. New York: Oxford University Press. (p. 184)

Petruzzello, S. J., Landers, D. M., Hatfield, B. D., Kubitz, K. A., & Salazar, W. (1991). A meta-analysis on the anxiety-reducing effects of acute and chronic exercise. *Sports Medicine, 11*, 143–182. (p. 368)

Pettigrew, T. F. (1969). Racially separate or together? *Journal of Social Issues, 25*, 43–69. (p. 519)

Pettingale, K. W., Morris, T., Greer, S., & Haybittle, J. L. (1985, March 30). Mental attitudes to cancer: An additional prognostic factor. *Lancet*, p. 750. (p. 365)

Pfeiffer, E. (1977). Sexual behavior in old age. In E. W. Busse & E. Pfeiffer (Eds.), *Behavior and adaptation in late life* (2nd ed.). Boston: Little, Brown. (p. 100)

Phillips, D. P. (1982). The impact of fictional television stories on U.S. adult fatalities: New evidence on the effect of the mass media on violence. *American Journal of Sociology, 87*, 1340–1359. (p. 485)

Phillips, D. P. (1985). Natural experiments on the effects of mass media violence on fatal aggression: Strengths and weaknesses of a new approach. In L. Berkowitz (Ed.), *Advances in experimental social psychology* (Vol. 19). Orlando, FL: Academic Press. (p. 485)

Phillips, D. P., Carstensen, L. L., & Paight, D. J. (1989). Effects of mass media news stories on suicide, with new evidence on the role of story content. In D. R. Pfeffer (Ed.), *Suicide among youth: Perspectives on risk and prevention*. Washington, DC: American Psychiatric Press. (p. 485)

Phillips, D., & Stipek, D. (1993). Early formal schooling: Are we promoting achievement or anxiety? *Applied and Preventive Psychology, 2*, 141–150. (p. 287)

Phillips, J. L. (1969). *Origins of intellect: Piaget's theory*. San Francisco: Freeman. (p. 78)

Phillips, M. R., Wolf, A. S., & Coons, D. J. (1988). Psychiatry and the criminal justice system: Testing the myths. *American Journal of Psychiatry, 145*, 605–610. (p. 444)

Piaget, J. (1930). *The child's conception of physical causality*. London: Routledge & Kegan Paul. (p. 75)

Piaget, J. (1932). *The moral judgment of the child*. New York: Harcourt, Brace & World. (p. 90)

Piccione, C., Hilgard, E. R., & Zimbardo, P. G. (1989). On the degree of stability of measured hypnotizability over a 25–year period. *Journal of Personality and Social Psychology, 56*, 289–295. (p. 177)

Pickar, D., Labarca, R., Linnoila, M., Roy, A., Hommer, D., Everett, D., & Payl, S. M. (1984). Neuroleptic-induced decrease in plasma homovanillic acid and antipsychotic activity in schizophrenic patients. *Science, 225*, 954–957. (p. 471)

Pike, K. M., & Rodin, J. (1991). Mothers, daughters, and disordered eating. *Journal of Abnormal Psychology, 100*, 198–204. (p. 304)

Pinel, J. P. J. (1993). *Biopsychology* (2nd ed.). Boston: Allyn & Bacon. (p. 302)

Pinker, S. (1990, September-October). Quoted in J. de Cuevas, "No, she holded them loosely." *Harvard Magazine*, pp. 60–67. (p. 264)

Piotrowski, C., & Keller, J. W. (1989). Psychological testing in outpatient mental health facilities: A national study. *Professional Psychology: Research and Practice, 20*, 423–425. (pp. 384, 390)

Planned Parenthood Federation of America. (1986, December 15). Sex education for parents. *USA Today*, p. 11A. (p. 96)

Pleck, J. H., Sonenstein, F. L., & Ku, L. C. (1993). Masculinity ideology: Its impact on adolescent males' heterosexual relationships. *Journal of Social Issues, 49,* 11–29. (p. 316)

Pliner, P. (1982). The effects of mere exposure on liking for edible substances. *Appetite: Journal for Intake Research, 3,* 283–290. (p. 303)

Pliner, P., Pelchat, M., & Grabski, M. (1993). Reduction of neophobia in humans by exposure to novel foods. *Appetite, 20,* 111–123. (p. 303)

Pliner, P., & Pelchat, M. L. (1991). Neophobia in humans and the special status of foods of animal origin. *Appetite, 16,* 205–218. (p. 303)

Plomin, R., McClearn, G. E., Pedersen, N. L., Nesselroade, J. R., & Bergeman, C. S. (1988). Genetic influence on childhood family environment perceived retrospectively from the last half of the life span. *Developmental Psychology, 24,* 37–45. (p. 111)

Plomin, R., & Rende, R. (1991). Human behavioral genetics. *Annual Review of Psychology, 42,* 161–190. (p. 286)

Plous, S. (1993). Psychological mechanisms in the human use of animals. *Journal of Social Issues, 49*(1), 11–52. (p. 26)

Plous, S. (1993). The nuclear arms race: Prisoner's dilemma or perceptual dilemma? *Journal of Peace Research, 30,* 163–179. (p. 510)

Polivy, J., & Herman, C. P. (1985). Dieting and binging: A causal analysis. *American Psychologist, 40,* 193–201. (p. 309)

Polivy, J., & Herman, C. P. (1987). Diagnosis and treatment of normal eating. *Journal of Personality and Social Psychology, 55,* 635–644. (p. 309)

Pollard, R. (1992). 100 years in psychology and deafness: A centennial retrospective. Invited address to the American Psychological Association convention, Washington, DC. (p. 273)

Pomerleau, O. F., & Pomerleau, C. S. (1984). Neuroregulators and the reinforcement of smoking: Towards a biobehavioral explanation. *Neuroscience and Biobehavioral Reviews, 8,* 503–513. (p. 185)

Pomeroy, W. B. (1972). *Dr. Kinsey and the Institute for Sex Research.* New York: Harper & Row. (p. 311)

Poole, D. A., & Lindsay, D. S. (1995). Interviewing preschoolers: Effects of nonsuggestive techniques, parental coaching and leading questions on reports of nonexperienced events. *Journal of Experimental Child Psychology,* in press. (p. 243)

Poole, D. A., Lindsay, D. S., Memon, A., & Bull, R. (1994). Psychotherapy and the recovery of memories of childhood sexual abuse: U.S. and British practitioners' opinions, practices, and experiences. *Journal of Consulting and Clinical Psychology, 63,* 426–437. (p. 248)

Poon, L. W. (1987). Myths and truisms: Beyond extant analyses of speed of behavior and age. Address to the Eastern Psychological Association convention. (p. 99)

Popenoe, D. (1993). The evolution of marriage and the problem of stepfamilies: A biosocial perspective. Paper presented at the National Symposium on Stepfamilies, Pennsylvania State University. (p. 399)

Porter, D., & Neuringer, A. (1984). Music discriminations by pigeons. *Journal of Experimental Psychology: Animal Behavior Processes, 10,* 138–148. (p. 207)

Posner, M. I., & Carr, T. H. (1992). Lexical access and the brain: Anatomical constraints on cognitive models of word recognition. *American Journal of Psychology, 105,* 1–26. (p. 57)

Powell, J. (1989). *Happiness is an inside job.* Valencia, CA: Tabor. (p. 397)

Powell, K. E., Thompson, P. D., Caspersen, C. J., & Kendrick, J. S. (1987). Physical activity and the incidence of coronary heart disease. *Annual Review of Public Health, 8,* 253–287. (p. 368)

Powell, M. C., & Fazio, R. H. (1984). Attitude accessibility as a function of repeated attitudinal expression. *Personality and Social Psychology Bulletin, 10,* 139–148. (p. 482)

Pratkanis, A. R. (1992). The cargo-cult science of subliminal persuasion. *Skeptical Inquirer, 16,* 260–272. (p. 119)

Prentice, D. A., & Miller, D. T. (1993). Pluralistic ignorance and alcohol use on campus: Some consequences of misperceiving the social norm. *Journal of Personality and Social Psychology, 64,* 243–256. (p. 190)

Presley, C. A., & Meilman, P. W. (1992). *Alcohol and drugs on American college campuses: Report to college presidents.* Carbondale, IL: Student Health Program, Southern Illinois University. (p. 183)

Prevention (1995). Prevention index survey by *Prevention* magazine, summarized by Associated Press, March 6 (*Grand Rapids Press,* p. A1). (p. 368)

Prioleau, L., Murdock, M., & Brody, N. (1983). An analysis of psychotherapy versus placebo studies. *The Behavioral and Brain Sciences, 6,* 275–310. (p. 467)

Pritchard, R. M. (1961, June). Stabilized images on the retina. *Scientific American,* pp. 72–78. (p. 122)

Project on Redefining the Meaning and Purpose of Baccalaureate Degrees. (1985). *Integrity in the college curriculum.* Washington, DC: Association of American Colleges. (p. 22)

Prothrow-Stith, D. (1991). *Deadly consequences.* New York: HarperCollins. (p. 504)

Psychic Abscam. (1983, March). *Discover,* p. 10. (p. 155)

Public Opinion. (1984, August/September). Phears and Phobias, p. 32. (p. 419)

Public Opinion. (1984, August/September). Tradeoffs, p. 36. (p. 12)

Public Opinion. (1985, February/March). Defining woman's place, p. 40. (p. 12)

Public Opinion. (1987, May/June). Teen angels (report of University of Michigan survey), p. 32. (p. 88)

Pugh, G. E. (1977). *The biological origin of human values.* New York: Basic Books. (p. 63)

Pulver, A. E., Liang, K-Y., Brown, C. H., Wolyniec, P., McGrath, J., Adler, L., Tam, D., Carpenter, W. T., & Childs, B. (1992). Risk factors in schizophrenia: Season of birth, gender, and familial risk. *British Journal of Psychiatry, 160,* 65–71. (p. 437)

Putnam, F. W. (1991). Recent research on multiple personality disorder. *Psychiatric Clinics of North America, 14,* 489–502. (p. 425)

Pyszczynski, T., Hamilton, J. C., Greenberg, J., & Becker, S. E. (1991). Self-awareness and psychological dysfunction. In C. R. Snyder & D. O. Forsyth (Eds.), *Handbook of social and clinical psychology: The health perspective.* New York: Pergamon. (p. 432)

Qualls, P. J., & Sheehan, P. W. (1981). Electromyograph biofeedback as a relaxation technique: A critical appraisal and reassessment. *Psychological Bulletin, 90,* 21–42. (p. 370)

Rabin, A. S., Kaslow, N. J., & Rehm, L. P. (1986). Aggregate outcome and follow-up results following self-control therapy for depression. Paper presented at the American Psychological Association convention. (p. 461)

Radecki, T. (1989, February-March). On picking good television and film entertainment. *NCTV News, 10*(1–2), p. 5. (p. 505)

Ramey, S. L., & Ramey, C. T. (1992). Early educational intervention with disadvantaged children—To what effect? *Applied and Preventive Psychology, 1,* 131–140. (p. 287)

Rand, C. S. W., & Macgregor, A. M. C. (1990). Morbidly obese patients' perceptions of social discrimination before and after surgery for obesity. *Southern Medical Journal, 83,* 1390–1395. (p. 306)

Rand, C. S. W., & Macgregor, A. M. C. (1991). Successful weight loss following obesity surgery and the perceived liability or morbid obesity. *Internal Journal of Obesity, 15,* 577–579. (p. 306)

Randi, J. (1983a, Summer). The Project Alpha experiment: Part 1. The first two years. *The Skeptical Inquirer,* pp. 24–33. (p. 155)

Randi, J. (1983b, Fall). The Project Alpha experiment: Part 2. Beyond the laboratory. *The Skeptical Inquirer,* pp. 36–45. (p. 155)

Rapoport, J. L. (1989, March). The biology of obsessions and compulsions. *Scientific American,* pp. 83–89. (pp. 420, 422)

Rauch, S. L., & Jenike, M. A. (1993). Neurobiological models of obsessive-compulsive disorder. *Psychomatics, 34,* 20–32. (p. 422)

Ray, O., & Ksir, C. (1990). *Drugs, society, and human behavior* (5th ed.). St. Louis: Times Mirror/Mosby. (p. 185)

Reason, J. (1987). The Chernobyl errors. *Bulletin of the British Psychological Society, 40,* 201–206. (p. 492)

Reason, J., & Mycielska, K. (1982). *Absent-minded? The psychology of mental lapses and everyday errors.* Englewood Cliffs, NJ: Prentice-Hall. (p. 151)

Reisenzein, R. (1983). The Schachter theory of emotion: Two decades later. *Psychological Bulletin, 94,* 239–264. (p. 354)

Reiser, M. (1982). *Police psychology.* Los Angeles: LEHI. (p. 155)

Reiss, A. J., Jr., & Roth, J. A. (Eds.) (1993). *Understanding and preventing violence.* Washington, DC: National Academy Press. (p. 503)

Remley, A. (1988, October). From obedience to independence. *Psychology Today,* pp. 56–59. (p. 85)

Renner, M. J., & Rosenzweig, M. R. (1987). Enriched and impoverished environments: Effects on brain and behavior. New York: Springer-Verlag. (p. 74)

Rescorla, R. A., & Wagner, A. R. (1972). A theory of Pavlovian conditioning: Variations in the effectiveness of reinforcement and nonreinforcement. In A. H. Black & W. F. Perokasy (Eds.), *Classical conditioning II: Current theory.* New York: Appleton-Century-Crofts. (p. 202)

Resnick, S. M. (1992). Positron emission tomography in psychiatric illness. *Current Directions in Psychological Science, 1,* 92–98. (p. 422)

Ressler, R. K., Burgess, A. W., & Douglas, J. E. (1988). *Sexual homicide patterns.* Boston: Lexington Books. (p. 507)

Retterstøl, N. (1993). *Suicide: A European perspective.* New York: Cambridge University Press. (p. 428)

Reveen, P. J. (1987–88). Fantasizing under hypnosis: Some experimental evidence. *The Skeptical Inquirer, 12,* 181–183. (p. 179)

Rheingold, H. L. (1985). Development as the acquisition of familiarity. *Annual Review of Psychology, 36,* 1–17. (p. 82)

Rhodes, S. R. (1983). Age-related differences in work attitudes and behavior: A review and conceptual analysis. *Psychological Bulletin, 93,* 328–367. (p. 99)

Rice, B. (1985, September). Performance review: The job nobody likes. *Psychology Today,* pp. 30–36. (p. 481)

Rice, M. E., & Grusec, J. E. (1975). Saying and doing: Effects on observer performance. *Journal of Personality and Social Psychology, 32,* 584–593. (p. 218)

Richardson, J. (1993). The curious case of coins: Remembering the appearance of familiar objects. *The Psychologist: Bulletin of the British Psychological Society, 6,* 360–366. (p. 232)

Rieff, P. (1979). *Freud: The mind of a moralist* (3rd ed.). Chicago: University of Chicago Press. (p. 386)

Ring, K. (1980). *Life at death: A scientific investigation of the near-death experience.* New York: Coward, McCann & Geoghegan. (p. 186)

Ring, K. (1992). *The omega project: Near death experiences, UFO encounters, and mind at large.* New York: Morrow. (p. 187)

Roberts, L. (1988). Beyond Noah's ark: What do we need to know? *Science, 242,* 1247. (p. 361)

Roberts, T-A. (1991). Gender and the influence of evaluations on self-assessments in achievement settings. *Psychological Bulletin, 109,* 297–308. (p. 94)

Robins, L., & Regier, D. (Eds.). (1991). *Psychiatric disorders in America.* New York: Free Press. (pp. 413, 442, 443)

Robinson, J. L., Kagan, J., Reznick, J. S., & Corley, R. (1992). The heritability of inhibited and uninhibited behavior: A twin study. *Developmental Psychology, 28,* 1030–1037. (p. 82)

Rochat, F. (1993). How did they resist authority? Protecting refugees in Le Chambon during World War II. Paper presented at the American Psychological Association convention. (p. 489)

Rock, I., & Palmer, S. (1990, December). The legacy of Gestalt psychology. *Scientific American,* pp. 84–90. (p. 140)

Rodin, J. (1979). *Obesity theory and behavior therapy: An uneasy couple?* Paper presented at the meeting of the Association for the Advancement of Behavior Therapy. (p. 309)

Rodin, J. (1984, December). A sense of control [interview]. *Psychology Today,* pp. 38–45. (p. 305)

Rodin, J. (1985). Insulin levels, hunger and food intake: An example of feedback loops in body weight regulation. *Health Psychology, 4,* 1–18. (p. 309)

Rodin, J. (1986). Aging and health: Effects of the sense of control. *Science, 233,* 1271–1276. (pp. 360, 361, 404)

Rodin, J., & Slochower, J. (1976). Externality in the non-obese: Effects of environmental responsiveness on weight. *Journal of Personality and Social Psychology, 33,* 338–344. (p. 305)

Roediger, H. L., III, Wheeler, M. A., & Rajaram, S. (1993). Remembering, knowing, and reconstructing the past. In D. L. Medin (Ed.), *The psychology of learning and motivation: Advances in research and theory* (Vol. 30). Orlando, FL: Academic Press. (p. 243)

Roemer, M. I. (1991). *National health systems of the world: Vol. I. The countries.* New York: Oxford University Press. (p. 371)

Rogers, C. R. (1958). Reinhold Niebuhr's *The self and the dramas of history:* A criticism. *Pastoral Psychology, 9,* 15–17. (p. 396)

Rogers, C. R. (1961). *On becoming a person: A therapist's view of psychotherapy.* Boston: Houghton Mifflin. (p. 453)

Rogers, C. R. (1980). *A way of being.* Boston: Houghton Mifflin. (pp. 394, 453)

Rogers, C. R. (1981). Notes on Rollo May. *Perspectives, 2*(1), 16. (p. 401)

Rogers, S. (1992–1993, Winter).   How a publicity blitz created the myth of subliminal advertising. *Public Relations Quarterly*, pp. 12–17. (p. 119)

Rogers, S. (1994).   Subliminal advertising: Grand scam of the 20th century. Paper presented to the American Academy of Advertising convention. (p. 119)

Rogers, S. M., & Turner, C. F. (1991).   Male-male sexual contact in the U.S.A.: Findings from five sample surveys, 1970–1990. *Journal of Sex Research, 28*, 491–519. (p. 317)

Rohner, R. P. (1986).   *The warmth dimension: Foundations of parental acceptance-rejection theory.* Newbury Park, CA: Sage. (p. 86)

Rook, K. S. (1984).   Promoting social bonding: Strategies for helping the lonely and socially isolated. *American Psychologist, 39*, 1389–1407. (p. 433)

Rosch, E. (1974).   Linguistic relativity. In A. Silverstein (Ed.), *Human communication: Theoretical perspectives.* New York: Halsted Press. (p. 272)

Rosch, E. (1978).   Principles of categorization. In E. Rosch & B. L. Lloyd (Eds.), *Cognition and categorization.* Hillsdale, NJ: Erlbaum. (p. 256)

Rose, G. A., & Williams, R. T. (1961).   Metabolic studies on large and small eaters. *British Journal of Nutrition, 1*, 1–9. (p. 307)

Rose, R. J., Koskenvuo, M., Kaprio, J., Sarna, S., & Langinvainio, H. (1988).   Shared genes, shared experiences, and similarity of personality: Data from 14,228 adult Finnish co-twins. *Journal of Personality and Social Psychology, 54*, 161–171. (p. 108)

Rosenbaum, M. (1986).   The repulsion hypothesis: On the nondevelopment of relationships. *Journal of Personality and Social Psychology, 51*, 1156–1166. (p. 514)

Rosenstein, M. J., Milazzo-Sayre, L. J., & Manderscheid, R. W. **(1989).** Care of persons with schizophrenia: A statistical profile. *Schizophrenia Bulletin, 15*, 45–58. (p. 413)

Rosenthal, R., Hall, J. A., Archer, D., DiMatteo, M. R., & Rogers, P. L. (1979).   The PONS test: Measuring sensitivity to nonverbal cues. In S. Weitz (Ed.), *Nonverbal communication* (2nd ed.). New York: Oxford University Press. (p. 339)

Rosenzweig, M. R. (1984).   Experience, memory, and the brain. *American Psychologist, 39*, 365–376. (p. 74)

Ross, H. (1975, June 19).   Mist, murk, and visual perception. *New Scientist*, pp. 658–660. (p. 144)

Ross, L., Greene, D., & House, P. (1977).   The false consensus effect: An egocentric bias in social perception and attribution process. *Journal of Experimental Social Psychology, 13*, 279–301. (p. 12)

Ross, L., & Stillinger, C. (1991).   Barriers to conflict resolution. *Negotiation Journal, 7*, 389–404. (p. 521)

Ross, M., McFarland, C., & Fletcher, G. J. O. (1981).   The effect of attitude on the recall of personal histories. *Journal of Personality and Social Psychology, 40*, 627–634. (p. 247)

Rossi, A. S., & Rossi, P. H. (1993).   *Of human bonding: Parent-child relations across the life course.* Hawthorne, NY: Aldine de Gruyter. (p. 94)

Rossi, P. J. (1968).   Adaptation and negative aftereffect to lateral optical displacement in newly hatched chicks. *Science, 160*, 430–432. (p. 149)

Roth, T., Roehrs, T., Zwyghuizen-Doorenbos, A., Stpeanski, E., & Witting, R. (1988). Sleep and memory. In I. Hindmarch & H. Ott (Eds.), *Benzodiazepine receptor ligans, memory and information processing.* New York: Springer-Verlag. (p. 172)

Rothbart, M., Fulero, S., Jensen, C., Howard, J., & Birrell, P. (1978). From individual to group impressions: Availability heuristics in stereotype formation. *Journal of Experimental Social Psychology, 14*, 237–255. (p. 500)

Rothblum, E. D. (1990).   Women and weight: Fad and fiction. *Journal of Psychology, 124*, 5–24. (p. 309)

Rothstein, W. G. (1980).   The significance of occupations in work careers: An empirical and theoretical review. *Journal of Vocational Behavior, 17*, 328–343. (p. 105)

Rotton, J., & Kelly, I. W. (1985).   Much ado about the full moon: A meta-analysis of lunar-lunacy research. *Psychological Bulletin, 97*, 286–306. (p. 440)

Roviaro, S., Holmes, D. S., & Holmsten, R. D. (1984).   Influence of a cardiac rehabilitation program on the cardiovascular, psychological, and social functioning of cardiac patients. *Journal of Behavioral Medicine, 7*, 61–81. (p. 369)

Rowe, D. C. (1990).   As the twig is bent? The myth of child-rearing influences on personality development. *Journal of Counseling and Development, 68*, 606–611. (p. 110)

Rowe, D. C., Vazsonyi, A. T., & Flannery, D. J. (1994).   No more than skin deep: Ethnic and racial similarity in developmental process. *Psychological Review, 101*, 396–413. (p. 291)

Rozin, P. (1976).   The selection of food by rats, humans and other animals. In J. Rosenblatt, R. A. Hinde, C. Beer, & E. Shaw (Eds.), *Advances in the study of behavior* (Vol. 6).   New York: Academic Press. (p. 303)

Ruback, R. B., Carr, T. S., & Hopper, C. H. (1986).   Perceived control in prison: Its relation to reported crowding, stress, and symptoms. *Journal of Applied Social Psychology, 16*, 375–386. (p. 404)

Rubin, J. Z., Pruitt, D. G., & Kim, S. H. (1994).   *Social conflict: Escalation, stalemate, and settlement.* New York: McGraw-Hill. (p. 520)

Rubin, Z. (1970).   Measurement of romantic love. *Journal of Personality and Social Psychology, 16*, 265–273. (p. 339)

Rubonis, A. V., & Bickman, L. (1991).   Psychological impairment in the wake of disaster: The disaster-psychopathology relationship. *Psychological Bulletin, 109*, 384–399. (p. 358)

Ruchlis, H. (1990).   *Clear thinking: A practical introduction.* Buffalo, NY: Prometheus Books. (p. 257)

Ruffin, C. L. (1993).   Stress and health—little hassles vs. major life events. *Australian psychologist, 28*, 201–208. (p. 359)

Rule, B. G., & Ferguson, T. J. (1986).   The effects of media violence on attitudes, emotions, and cognitions. *Journal of Social Issues, 42*(3), 29–50. (p. 506)

Rumbaugh, D. M. (1977).   *Language learning by a chimpanzee: The Lana project.* New York: Academic Press. (p. 269)

Rumbaugh, D. M. (1994, February 15).   Remarks on "Nova: Can chimps talk?" Public Broadcasting Service. (p. 271)

Rumbaugh, D. M., & Savage-Rumbaugh, S. (1978).   Chimpanzee language research: Status and potential. *Behavior Research Methods & Instrumentation, 10*, 119–131. (p. 271)

Rumbaugh, D. M., & Savage-Rumbaugh, S. (1994, January/February). Language and apes. *Psychology Teacher Network*, pp. 2–5, 9. (p. 271)

Rushton, J. P. (1975).   Generosity in children: Immediate and long-term effects of modeling, preaching, and moral judgment. *Journal of Personality and Social Psychology, 31*, 459–466. (p. 218)

Rushton, J. P. (1990).   Race differences, r/K theory, and a reply to Flynn. *The Psychologist: Bulletin of the British Psychological Society, 5*, 195–198. (p. 289)

Rushton, J. P., Fulker, D. W., Neale, M. C., Nias, D. K. B., & Eysenck, H. J. (1986). Altruism and aggression: The heritability of individual differences. *Journal of Personality and Social Psychology, 50*, 1192–1198. (p. 501)

Russell, B. (1930/1985). *The conquest of happiness.* London: Unwin Paperbacks. (p. 349)

Russell, J. A. (1991). Culture and the categorization of emotions. *Psychological Bulletin, 110*, 426–450. (p. 340)

Russell, J. A., Lewicka, M., & Niit, T. (1989). A cross-cultural study of a circumplex model of affect. *Journal of Personality and Social Psychology, 57*, 848–856. (p. 344)

Russo, N. F. (1992). Abortion, childbearing, and women's well-being. *Professional Psychology: Research and Practice, 23*, 269–280. (p. 359)

Rutter, M. (1979). Maternal deprivation, 1972–1978: New findings, new concepts, new approaches. *Child Development, 50*, 283–305. (p. 84)

Ryan, E. D. (1980). Attribution, intrinsic motivation, and athletics: A replication and extension. In C. H. Nadeau, W. R. Halliwell, K. M. Newell, & G. C. Roberts (Eds.), *Psychology of motor behavior and sport—1979.* Champaign, IL: Human Kinetics Press. (p. 324)

Ryckman, R. M., Robbins, M. A., Kaczor, L. M., & Gold J. A. (1989). Male and female raters' stereotyping of male and female physiques. *Personality and Social Psychology Bulletin, 15*, 244–251. (p. 306)

Rzewnicki, R., & Forgays, D. G. (1987). Recidivism and self-cure of smoking and obesity: An attempt to replicate. *American Psychologist, 42*, 97–100. (p. 310)

Sabini, J. (1986). Stanley Milgram (1933–1984). *American Psychologist, 41*, 1378–1379. (p. 487)

Sacks, O. (1985). *The man who mistook his wife for a hat.* New York: Summit Books. (pp. 60, 138, 237)

Sacks, O. (1990). *Seeing voices: A journey into the world of the deaf.* New York: HarperCollins. (p. 273)

Sacks, O. (1995, January 9). Prodigies. *New Yorker*, pp. 44–65. (p. 281)

Sagan, C. (1979a). *Broca's brain.* New York: Random House. (p. 45)

Sagan, C. (1979b). *Dragons of Eden.* New York: Random House. (p. 44)

Sagan, C. (1987, February 1). The fine art of baloney detection. *Parade.* (p. 156)

Sagan, C. (1994, March). Basketball's lessons for science: There is theory behind those magical stars and streaks. *CSICOP Newsletter*, p. 3. (p. 16)

Sagan, C., & Druyan, A. (1992). *Shadows of forgotten ancestors: A search for who we are.* New York: Random House. (p. 269)

Salovey, P. (1990, January/February). Interview. *American Scientist*, pp. 25–29. (p. 346)

Salthouse, T. A. (1992). *Mechanisms of age-cognition relations in adulthood.* Hillsdale, NJ: Erlbaum. (pp. 99, 234)

Samuels, S., & McCabe, G. (1989). Quoted in P. Diaconis & F. Mosteller, Methods for studying coincidences. *Journal of the American Statistical Association, 84*, 853–861. (p. 16)

Sandberg, G. G., Jackson, T. L., & Petretic-Jackson, P. (1985). *Sexual aggression and courtship violence in dating relationships.* Paper presented at the meeting of the Midwestern Psychological Association. (p. 506)

Sanders, B., & Soares, M. P. (1986). Sexual maturation and spatial ability in college students. *Developmental Psychology, 22*, 199–203. (p. 290)

Sapolsky, B. S., & Tabarlet, J. O. (1991). Sex in primetime television: 1979 versus 1989. *Journal of Broadcasting and Electronic Media, 35*, 505–516. (pp. 96, 508)

Sarnoff, I., & Sarnoff, S. (1989). *Love-centered marriage in a self-centered world.* New York: Hemisphere. (p. 312)

Sartorius, N. R. (1994). Description of WHO's mental health programme. In W. J. Lonner & R. Malpass (Eds.), *Psychology and culture.* Boston: Allyn & Bacon. (pp. 356, 413)

Sato, K. (1987). Distribution of the cost of maintaining common resources. *Journal of Experimental Social Psychology, 23*, 19–31. (p. 510)

Savage-Rumbaugh, E. S., Murphy, J., Sevcik, R. A., Brakke, K. E., Williams, S. L., & Rumbaugh, D. M., with commentary by Bates, E. (1993). Language comprehension in ape and child. *Monographs of the Society for Research in Child Development, 58* (no. 233), 1–254. (p. 271)

Sayre, R. F. (1979). The parents' last lessons. In D. D. Van Tassel (Ed.), *Aging, death, and the completion of being.* Philadelphia: University of Pennsylvania Press. (p. 100)

Scarr, S. (1984, May). What's a parent to do? [Conversation with E. Hall.] *Psychology Today*, pp. 58–63. (p. 287)

Scarr, S. (1989). Protecting general intelligence: Constructs and consequences for interventions. In R. J. Linn (Ed.), *Intelligence: Measurement, theory, and public policy.* Champaign: University of Illinois Press. (pp. 282, 286)

Scarr, S. (1990). Back cover comments on J. Dunn & R. Plomin (1990). *Separate lives: Why siblings are so different.* New York: Basic Books. (p. 111)

Scarr, S., & McCartney, K. (1983). How people make their own environments: A theory of genotype _ environment effects. *Child Development, 54*, 424–435. (p. 111)

Schab, F. R. (1990). Odors and the remembrance of things past. *Journal of Experimental Psychology: Learning, Memory, and Cognition, 16*, 648–655. (p. 138)

Schab, F. R. (1991). Odor memory: Taking stock. *Psychological Bulletin, 109*, 242–251. (p. 138)

Schachter, S. (1982). Recidivism and self-cure of smoking and obesity. *American Psychologist, 37*, 436–444. (p. 309)

Schachter, S., & Singer, J. E. (1962). Cognitive, social and physiological determinants of emotional state. *Psychological Review, 69*, 379–399. (p. 353)

Schacter, D. L. (1992). Understanding implicit memory: A cognitive neuroscience approach. *American Psychologist, 47*, 559–569. (p. 238)

Schaie, K. W. (1989). Perceptual speed in adulthood: Cross-sectional and longitudinal studies. *Psychology and Aging, 4*, 443–453. (p. 99)

Schaie, K. W. (1994). The life course of adult intellectual abilities. *American Psychologist, 49*, 304–313. (p. 102)

Schaie, K. W., & Geiwitz, J. (1982). *Adult development and aging.* Boston: Little, Brown. (p. 102)

Scheerer, M. (1963, April). Problem solving. *Scientific American*, pp. 118–128. (pp. 258, 260)

Scheier, M. F., & Carver, C. S. (1992). Effects of optimism on psychological and physical well-being: Theoretical overview and empirical update. *Cognitive Therapy and Research, 16*, 201–228. (p. 360)

Schein, E. H. (1956). The Chinese indoctrination program for prisoners of war: A study of attempted brainwashing. *Psychiatry, 19*, 149–172. (p. 482)

Schiavi, R. C., & Schreiner-Engel, P. (1988).   Nocturnal penile tumescence in healthy aging men. *Journal of Gerontology: Medical Sciences, 43*, M146–150. (p. 168)

Schiffenbauer, A., & Schiavo, R. S. (1976).   Physical distance and attraction: An intensification effect. *Journal of Experimental Social Psychology, 12*, 274–282. (p. 490)

Schleifer, S. J., Keller, S. E., McKegney, F. P., & Stein, M. (1979).   *The influence of stress and other psychosocial factors on human immunity.* Paper presented at the 36th annual meeting of the American Psychosomatic Society. (p. 364)

Schlesinger, A. M., Jr. (1965).   *A thousand days.* Boston: Houghton Mifflin. (p. 492)

Schnaper, N. (1980).   Comments germane to the paper entitled "The reality of death experiences" by Ernst Rodin. *Journal of Nervous and Mental Disease, 168*, 268–270. (p. 186)

Schoeneman, T. J. (1994).   *Individualism.* In V. S. Ramachandran (Ed.), *Encyclopedia of Human Behavior.* San Diego: Academic Press. (p. 400)

Schoenfeld, B. (1995, May 14).   The loneliness of being white in the N.B.A. *New York Times*, pp. 34–37. (p. 498)

Schofield, J. W. (1986).   Black-white contact in desegregated schools. In M. Hewstone & R. Brown (Eds.), *Contact and conflict in intergroup encounters.* Oxford: Blackwell. (p. 519)

Schonfield, D., & Robertson, B. A. (1966).   Memory storage and aging. *Canadian Journal of Psychology, 20*, 228–236. (p. 101)

Schooler, J. W., Gerhard, D., & Loftus, E. F. (1986).   Qualities of the unreal. *Journal of Experimental Psychology: Learning, Memory, and Cognition, 12*, 171–181. (p. 243)

Schuckit, M. A. (1994).   Low level of response to alcohol as a predictor of future alcoholism. *American Journal of Psychiatry, 151*, 184–189. (p. 189)

Schulenberg, J., Bachman, J. G., O'Malley, P. M., & Johnston, L. D. (1994).   High school educational success and subsequent substance use: A panel analysis following adolescents into young adulthood. *Journal of Health and Social Behavior, 35*, 45–62. (p. 190)

Schwartz, B. (1984).   *Psychology of learning and behavior* (2nd ed.). New York: Norton. (pp. 204, 421)

Schwarz, N., & Clore, G. L. (1983).   Mood, misattribution, and judgments of well-being: Informative and directive functions of affective states. *Journal of Personality and Social Psychology, 45*, 513–523. (p. 346)

Schwarz, N., Strack, F., Kommer, D., & Wagner, D. (1987).   Soccer, rooms, and the quality of your life: Mood effects on judgments of satisfaction with life in general and with specific domains. *European Journal of Social Psychology, 17*, 69–79. (p. 242)

Scott, C., & Pepperell, P. (1992).   Exercise and depression: A meta-analysis. Paper presented at the Southwestern Psychological Association convention. (p. 368)

Scott, W. A., Scott, R., & McCabe, M. (1991).   Family relationships and children's personality: A cross-cultural, cross-source comparison. *British Journal of Social Psychology, 30*, 1–20. (p. 86)

Seeman, P., Guan, H-C., & Van Tol, H. H. M. (1993).   Dopamine D4 receptors elevated in schizophrenia. *Nature, 365*, 441–445. (p. 437)

Segall, M. H., Dasen, P. R., Berry, J. W., & Poortinga, Y. H. (1990).

Human behavior in global perspective: An introduction to cross-cultural psychology. New York: Pergamon. (pp. 80, 316, 495, 499)

Segerstrom, S. C., McCarthy, W. J., Caskey, N. H., Gross, T. D., & Jarvik, M. E. (1993). Optimistic bias among cigarette smokers. *Journal of Applied Social Psychology, 23*, 1606–1618. (p. 405)

Segrin, C., & Dillard, J. P. (1992).   The interactional theory of depression: A meta-analysis of the research literature. *Journal of Social and Clinical Psychology, 11*, 43–70. (p. 432)

Self, E. A. (1994).   Pluralistic ignorance of alcohol attitudes and use among both sexes. Paper presented at the American Psychological Association convention. (p. 190)

Seligman, M. E. P. (1974, May).   Submissive death: Giving up on life. *Psychology Today*, pp. 80–85. (p. 336)

Seligman, M. E. P. (1975).   *Helplessness: On depression, development and death.* San Francisco: Freeman. (p. 404)

Seligman, M. E. P. (1988, October).   Boomer blues. *Psychology Today*, pp. 50–55. (p. 399)

Seligman, M. E. P. (1989).   Explanatory style: Predicting depression, achievement, and health. In M. D. Yapko (Ed.), *Brief therapy approaches to treating anxiety and depression.* New York: Brunner/Mazel. (p. 461)

Seligman, M. E. P. (1991).   *Learned optimism.* New York: Knopf. (pp. 163, 404, 431, 432)

Seligman, M. E. P., & Schulman, P. (1986).   Explanatory style as a predictor of productivity and quitting among life insurance sales agents. *Journal of Personality and Social Psychology, 50*, 832–838. (p. 404)

Seligman, M. E. P., & Yellen, A. (1987).   What is a dream? *Behavior Research and Therapy, 25*, 1–24. (pp. 166, 174)

Selye, H. (1936).   A syndrome produced by diverse nocuous agents. *Nature, 138*, 32. (p. 357)

Selye, H. (1976).   *The stress of life.* New York: McGraw-Hill. (p. 357)

Service, R. F. (1994).   Will a new type of drug make memory-making easier? *Science, 266*, 218–219. (p. 237)

Shadish, W. R., Montgomery, L. M., Wilson, P., Wilson, M. R., Bright, I., & Okwumabua, T. (1993).   Effects of family and marital psychotherapies: A meta-analysis. *Journal of Consulting and Clinical Psychology, 61*, 992–1002. (p. 462)

Shamir, B., House, R. J., & Arthur, M. B. (1993).   The motivational effects of charismatic leadership: A self-concept based theory. *Organizational Science, 4*, 577–594. (p. 328)

Shanks, D. (1993, 30 January).   Breaking Chomsky's rules. *New Scientist*, pp. 26–29. (p. 267)

Shapiro, D. A., & Shapiro, D. (1982).   Meta-analysis of comparative therapy outcome studies: A replication and refinement. *Psychological Bulletin, 92*, 581–604. (p. 467)

Shaver, P. R., & Hazan, C. (1993).   Adult romantic attachment: Theory and evidence. In D. Perlman & W. Jones (Eds.), *Advances in personal relationships*, Vol. 4. Greenwich, CT: JAI. (p. 84)

Shaw, H. L. (1989–90).   Comprehension of the spoken word and ASL translation by chimpanzees (Pan troglodytes). *Friends of Washoe, 9*(1/2), 8–19. (p. 271)

Shea, M. T., Elkin, I., Imber, S. D., Sotsky, S. M., Watkins, J. T., Collins, J. F., Pilkonis, P. A., Beckham, E., Glass, D. R., Dolan, R. T., & Parloff, M. B. (1992).   Course of depressive symptoms over follow-up: Findings from the National Institute of mental Health Treatment of Depression Collaborative Research Program. *Archives of General Psychiatry, 49*, 782–787. (p. 466)

Sheehan, S. (1982).   *Is there no place on earth for me?* Boston: Houghton Mifflin. (p. 434)

Sheehan, S. (1995, February 20 and 27).   The last days of Sylvia Frumkin. *New Yorker,* pp. 200–211. (p. 434)

Shenton, M. E., Kiknis, R., Jolesz, F. A., & others (1992).   Abnormalities of the left temporal lobe and thought disorder in schizophrenia: A quantitative magnetic resonance imaging study. *New England Journal of Medicine, 327,* 604–612. (p. 437)

Shepard, R. N. (1981).   Psychophysical complementarity. In M. Kubovy & J. R. Pomerantz (Eds.), *Perceptual organization.* Hillsdale, NJ: Erlbaum. (p. 145)

Shepard, R. N. (1990).   *Mind sights.* New York: Freeman. (pp. 27, 146, 150, 151)

Shepherd, C., Kohut, J. J., & Sweet, R. (1990).   *More news of the weird.* New York: Penguin/Plume Books. (p. 441)

Sherif, M. (1966).   *In common predicament: Social psychology of intergroup conflict and cooperation.* Boston: Houghton Mifflin. (p. 519)

Sherry, D., & Vaccarino, A. L. (1989).   Hippocampus and memory for food caches in black-capped chickadees. *Behavioral Neuroscience, 103,* 308–318. (p. 238)

Shettleworth, S. J. (1973).   Food reinforcement and the organization of behavior in golden hamsters. In R. A. Hinde & J. Stevenson-Hinde (Eds.), *Constraints on learning.* London: Academic Press. (p. 213)

Shettleworth, S. J. (1993). Where is the comparison in compative cognition? Alternative research programs. *Psychological Science, 4,* 179–184. (p. 234)

Shneidman, E. (1987, March).   At the point of no return. *Psychology Today,* pp. 54–58. (p. 428)

Shontz, F. C., & Green, P. (1992).   Trends in research on the Rorschach: Review and recommendations. *Applied and Preventive Psychology, 1,* 149–156. (p. 385)

Shotland, R. L. (1989).   A model of the causes of date rape in developing and close relationships. In C. Hendrick (Ed.), *Review of Personality and Social Psychology* (Vol. 10). Newbury Park, CA: Sage. (pp. 316, 517)

Showers, C. (1992).   The motivational and emotional consequences of considering positive or negative possibilities for an upcoming event. *Journal of Personality and Social Psychology, 63,* 474–484. (p. 405)

Shrout, P. E., Link, B. G., Dohrenwend, B. P., Skodol, A. E., Stueve, A., & Mirotznik, J. (1989).   Characterizing life events as risk factors for depression: The role of fateful loss events. *Journal of Abnormal Psychology, 98,* 460–467. (p. 429)

Shulruff, L. I. (1990, August 10).   In sex case, focus is on multiple personalities. *New York Times.* (p. 425)

Siegel, J. M. (1990).   Stressful life events and use of physician services among the elderly: The moderating role of pet ownership. *Journal of Personality and Social Psychology, 58,* 1081–1086. (p. 371)

Siegel, L. S., & Hodkin, B. (1982).   The garden path to the understanding of cognitive development: Has Piaget led us into the poison ivy? In S. Modgil & C. Modgil (Eds.), *Jean Piaget: Consensus and controversy.* New York: Praeger. (p. 78)

Siegel, R. K. (1977, October).   Hallucinations. *Scientific American,* pp. 132–140. (p. 186)

Siegel, R. K. (1980).   The psychology of life after death. *American Psychologist, 35,* 911–931. (p. 186)

Siegel, R. K. (1984, March 15).   Personal communication. (p. 186)

Siegel, R. K. (1990).   *Intoxication.* New York: Pocket Books. (pp. 183, 185, 186, 187)

Siegel, R. K. Quoted by J. Hooper (1982, October), Mind tripping. *Omni,* pp. 72–82, 159–160. (p. 186)

Silva, A. J., Stevens, C. F., Tonegawa, S., & Wang, Y. (1992).   Deficient hippocampal long-term potentiation in alpha-calcium-calmodulin kinase II mutant mice. *Science, 257,* 201–206. (p. 237)

Silva, C. E., & Kirsch, I. (1992).   Interpretive sets, expectancy, fantasy proneness, and dissociation as predictors of hypnotic response. *Journal of Personality and Social Psychology, 63,* 847–856. (p. 177)

Silver, M., & Geller, D. (1978).   On the irrelevance of evil: The organization and individual action. *Journal of Social Issues, 34,* 125–136. (p. 489)

Silverman, K., Evans, S. M., Strain, E. C., & Griffiths, R. R. (1992). Withdrawal syndrome after the double-blind cessation of caffeine consumption. *New England Journal of Medicine, 327,* 1109–1114. (p. 184)

Silverman, P. S., & Retzlaff, P. D. (1986).   Cognitive stage regression through hypnosis: Are earlier cognitive stages retrievable? *International Journal of Clinical and Experimental Hypnosis, 34,* 192–204. (p. 177)

Silverton, L. (1988).   Crime and the schizophrenia spectrum: A study of three Danish cohorts. In T. E. Moffitt & S. A. Mednick (Eds.), *Biological contributions to crime causation.* New York: Martinus-Nijhoff. (p. 444)

Simmons, R. G., & Blyth, D. A. (1987).   *Moving into adolescence: The impact of pubertal change and school context.* New York: Aldine De Gruyter. (p. 89)

Simonton, D. K. (1988).   Age and outstanding achievement: What do we know after a century of research? *Psychological Bulletin, 104,* 251–267. (p. 103)

Simonton, D. K. (1990).   Creativity in the later years: Optimistic prospects for achievement. *The Gerontologist, 30,* 626–631. (p. 103)

Simonton, D. K. (1992).   The social context of career success and course for 2,026 scientists and inventors. *Personality and Social Psychology Bulletin, 18,* 452–463. (p. 284)

Simonton, D. K. (1994).   *Greatness: Who makes history and why.* New York: Guilford Press. (p. 324)

Simpson, J. A., Rholes, W. S., & Nelligan, J. S. (1992).   Support seeking and support giving within couples in an anxiety-provoking situation: The role of attachment styles. *Journal of Personality and Social Psychology, 62,* 434–446. (p. 84)

Sinclair, R. C., Hoffman, C., Mark, M. M., Martin, L. L., & Pickering, T. L. (1994). Construct accessibility and the misattribution of arousal: Schachter and Singer revisited. *Psychological Science, 5,* 15–18. (p. 354)

Singer, J. L. (1975).   Navigating the stream of consciousness: Research in daydreaming and related inner experience. *American Psychologist, 30,* 727–738. (p. 175)

Singer, J. L. (1976, July).   Fantasy: The foundation of serenity. *Psychology Today,* pp. 32–37. (p. 175)

Singer, J. L. (1981).   Clinical intervention: New developments in methods and evaluation. In L. T. Benjamin, Jr. (Ed.), *The G. Stanley Hall Lecture Series* (Vol. 1).   Washington, DC: American Psychological Association. (p. 466)

Singer, J. L. (1986).   Is television bad for children? *Social Science, 71,* 178–182. (p. 175)

Singer, J. L., & Singer, D. G. (1986).   Family experiences and television viewing as predictors of children's imagination, restlessness, and aggression. *Journal of Social Issues, 42*(3), 7–28. (p. 505)

Singh, D. (1993). Adaptive significance of female physical attractiveness: Role of waist-to-hip ratio. *Journal of Personality and Social Psychology, 65,* 293–307. (p. 514)

Sjöstrom, L. (1980). Fat cells and body weight. In A. J. Stunkard (Ed.), *Obesity.* Philadelphia: Saunders. (p. 307)

Skinner, B. F. (1953). *Science and human behavior.* New York: Macmillan. (p. 210)

Skinner, B. F. (1956). A case history in scientific method. *American Psychologist, 11,* 221–233. (p. 211)

Skinner, B. F. (1957). *Verbal behavior.* Englewood Cliffs, NJ: Prentice-Hall. (p. 266)

Skinner, B. F. (1961, November). Teaching machines. *Scientific American,* pp. 91–102. (pp. 210, 211)

Skinner, B. F. (1983, September). Origins of a behaviorist. *Psychology Today,* pp. 22–33. (pp. 214, 432)

Skinner, B. F. (1985). *Cognitive science and behaviorism.* Unpublished manuscript, Harvard University. (p. 266)

Skinner, B. F. (1986). What is wrong with daily life in the western world? *American Psychologist, 41,* 568–574. (p. 215)

Skinner, B. F. (1988). The school of the future. Address to the American Psychological Association convention. (p. 215)

Skinner, B. F. (1989). Teaching machines. *Science, 243,* 1535. (p. 215)

Skinner, B. F. (1990). Address to the American Psychological Association convention. (p. 213)

Sklar, L. S., & Anisman, H. (1981). Stress and cancer. *Psychological Bulletin, 89,* 369–406. (p. 364)

Skov, R. B., & Sherman, S. J. (1986). Information-gathering processes: Diagnosticity, hypothesis-confirmatory strategies, and perceived hypothesis confirmation. *Journal of Experimental Social Psychology, 22,* 93–121. (p. 258)

Slavin, R. E. (1989). Cooperative learning and student achievement. In R. E. Slavin (Ed.), *School and classroom organization.* Hillsdale, NJ: Erlbaum. (p. 520)

Sleek, S. (1994, April). Could Prozac replace demand for therapy? *APA Monitor,* p. 28. (p. 472)

Slovic, P. (1987). Perception of risk. *Science, 236,* 280–285. (p. 261)

Slovic, P., & Fischhoff, B. (1977). On the psychology of experimental surprises. *Journal of Experimental Psychology: Human Perception and Performance, 3,* 544–551. (p. 8)

Smart, R. G., Adlaf, E. M., & Walsh, G. W. (1991). The Ontario student drug use survey: Trends between 1977 and 1991. Toronto: Addiction Research Foundation. (p. 188)

Smith, A. (1983). Personal correspondence. (p. 437)

Smith, A. (1987). Personal communication. (p. 58)

Smith, A., & Sugar, O. (1975). Development of above normal language and intelligence 21 years after left hemispherectomy. *Neurology, 25,* 813–818. (p. 58)

Smith, D. (1982). Trends in counseling and psychotherapy. *American Psychologist, 37,* 802–809. (p. 450)

Smith, M. B. (1978). Psychology and values. *Journal of Social Issues, 34,* 181–199. (p. 400)

Smith, M. L., & Glass, G. V. (1977). Meta-analysis of psychotherapy outcome studies. *American Psychologist, 32,* 752–760. (p. 466)

Smith, M. L., Glass, G. V., & Miller, R. L. (1980). *The benefits of psychotherapy.* Baltimore: Johns Hopkins Press. (pp. 465, 466)

Smith, P. B., & Tayeb, M. (1989). Organizational structure and processes. In M. Bond (Ed.), *The cross-cultural challenge to social psychology.* Newbury Park, CA: Sage. (p. 328)

Smith, T. W. (1990). Adult sexual behavior in 1989: Number of partners, frequency, and risk. General Social Survey Topic Report No. 18, National Opinion Research Center, University of Chicago. (p. 311)

Smith, T. W. (1994). Attitudes towards sexual permissiveness: Trends and correlates. In A. S. Rossi (Ed.), *Sexuality across the life course.* Chicago: University of Chicago Press. (p. 311)

Smith, T. W. (1994). Personal correspondence. Data from General Social Survey, National Opinion Research Center, University of Chicago. (pp. 348, 497)

Snarey, J. (1987, June). A question of morality. *Psychology Today,* pp. 6–7. (p. 91)

Snarey, J. R. (1985). Cross-cultural universality of social-moral development: A critical review of Kohlbergian research. *Psychological Bulletin, 97,* 202–233. (p. 91)

Snodgrass, M. A. (1987). The relationships of differential loneliness, intimacy and characterological attributional style to duration of loneliness. *Journal of Social Behavior and Personality, 2,* 173–186. (p. 433)

Snyder, M. (1984). When belief creates reality. In L. Berkowitz (Ed.), *Advances in experimental social psychology* (Vol. 18). New York: Academic Press. (p. 444)

Snyder, M., Tanke, E. D., & Berscheid, E. (1977). Social perception and interpersonal behavior: On the self-fulfilling nature of social stereotypes. *Journal of Personality and Social Psychology, 35,* 656–666. (p. 493)

Snyder, S. H. (1984). Neurosciences: An integrative discipline. *Science, 225,* 1255–1257. (pp. 37, 471)

Snyder, S. H. (1986). *Drugs and the brain.* New York: Scientific American Library. (p. 473)

Sokhadze, E. M., & Shtark, M. B. (1991). Scientific and clinical biofeedback in the USSR. *Biofeedback and Self-Regulation, 16,* 253–260. (p. 370)

Sokoll, G. R., & Mynatt, C. R. (1984). *Arousal and free throw shooting.* Paper presented at the meeting of the Midwestern Psychological Association. (p. 336)

Solomon, M. (1987, December). Standard issue. *Psychology Today,* pp. 30–31. (p. 513)

Solomon, Z. (1990). Does the war end when the shooting stops? The psychological toll of war. *Journal of Applied Social Psychology, 20,* 1733–1745. (p. 360)

Sommer, R. (1969). *Personal space.* Englewood Cliffs, NJ: Prentice-Hall. (p. 494)

Sonenstein, F. L. (1992). Condom use. *Science, 257,* 861. (p. 96)

Sontag, S. (1978). *Illness as metaphor.* New York: Farrar, Straus, & Giroux. (p. 365)

Sowell, T. (1991, May/June). Cultural diversity: A world view. *American Enterprise,* pp. 44–55. (p. 521)

Spanos, N. P. (1986). Hypnosis, nonvolitional responding, and multiple personality: A social psychological perspective. *Progress in Experimental Personality Research, 14,* 1–62. (p. 425)

Spanos, N. P. (1987–88). Past-life hypnotic regression: A critical view. *The Skeptical Inquirer, 12,* 174–180. (p. 179)

Spanos, N. P. (1991). Hypnosis, hypnotizability, and hypnotherapy. In C. R. Snyder & D. R. Forsyth (Eds.), *Handbook of social and clinical psychology: The health perspective.* New York: Pergamon Press. (p. 178)

Spanos, N. P. (1994).   Multiple identity enactments and multiple personality disorder: A sociocognitive perspective. *Psychological Bulletin, 116,* 143–165. (p. 425)

Spanos, N. P. (1994).   Multiple identity enactments and multiple personality disorder: A sociocognitive perspective. *Psychological Bulletin, 116,* 143–165. (p. 180)

Spanos, N. P., & Coe, W. C. (1992).   A Social-psychological approach to hypnosis. In E. Fromm & M. R. Nash (Eds.), *Contemporary hypnosis research.* New York: Guilford. (p. 180)

Spanos, N. P., Menary, E., Gabora, N. J., DuBreuil, S. C., & Dewhirst, B. (1991). Secondary identity enactments during hypnotic past-life regression: A sociocognitive perspective. *Journal of Personality and Social Psychology, 61,* 308–320. (p. 179)

Spanos, N. P., Radtke, L., & Bertrand, L. D. (1985).   Hypnotic amnesia as a strategic enactment: Breaching amnesia in highly susceptible subjects. *Journal of Personality and Social Psychology, 47,* 1155–1169. (p. 176)

Spector, P. E. (1986).   Perceived control by employees: A meta-analysis of studies concerning autonomy and participation at work. *Human Relations, 39,* 1005–1016. (p. 327)

Spelke, E. S., Breinlinger, K., Macomber, J., & Jacobson, K. (1992). Origins of knowledge. *Psychological Review, 99,* 605–632. (p. 77)

Sperling, G. (1960).   The information available in brief visual presentations. *Psychological Monographs, 74* (Whole No. 498). (p. 233)

Sperry, R. W. (1964).   *Problems outstanding in the evolution of brain function.* James Arthur Lecture, American Museum of Natural History, New York. Cited by R. Ornstein (1977), *The psychology of consciousness* (2nd ed.). New York: Harcourt Brace Jovanovich. (p. 61)

Sperry, R. W. (1968).   Hemisphere deconnection and unity in conscious awareness. *American Psychologist, 23,* 723–733. (p. 60)

Sperry, R. W. (1985).   Changed concepts of brain and consciousness: Some value implications. *Zygon, 20,* 41–57. (p. 128)

Spiegel, D. (1993).   Social support: How friends, family, and groups can help. In D. Goleman & J. Gurin (Eds.), *Mind-body medicine: How to use your mind for better health.* Yonkers, NY: Consumer Reports Books. (p. 365)

Spiegel, D., Bloom, J. R., Kraemer, H. C., & Gottheil, E. (1989, October 14).   Effect of psychosocial treatment on survival of patients with metastatic breast cancer. *The Lancet,* pp. 888–891. (p. 365)

Spielberger, C., & London, P. (1982).   Rage boomerangs. *American Health, 1,* 52–56. (p. 362)

Spiess, W. F. J., Greer, J. H., & O'Donohue, W. T. (1984).   Premature ejaculation: Investigation of factors in ejaculatory latency. *Journal of Abnormal Psychology, 93,* 242–245. (p. 315)

Spitzberg, B. H., & Hurt, H. T. (1987).   The relationship of interpersonal competence and skill to reported loneliness across time. *Journal of Social Behavior and Personality, 2,* 157–172. (p. 433)

Spitzer, R. L. (1975).   On pseudoscience in science, logic in remission, and psychiatric diagnosis: A critique of Rosenhan's "On being sane in insane places." *Journal of Abnormal Psychology, 84,* 442–452. (p. 444)

Spitzer, R. L., Gibbon, M., Skodol, A. E., Williams, J. B. W., & First, M. B. (1989). *DSM-III-R casebook.* Washington, DC: American Psychiatric Press. (p. 423)

Spradley, J. P., & Phillips, M. (1972).   Culture and stress: A quantitative analysis. *American Anthropologist, 74,* 518–529. (p. 495)

Sprecher, S. (1989).   The importance to males and females of physical attractiveness, earning potential, and expressiveness in initial attraction. *Sex Roles, 21,* 591–607. (p. 513)

Sprecher, S., & Sedikides, C. (1993).   Gender differences in perceptions of emotionality: The case of close heterosexual relationships. *Sex Roles, 28,* 511–530. (p. 94)

Springer, S. P., & Deutsch, G. (1985).   *Left brain, right brain.* San Francisco: Freeman. (p. 62)

Squire, L. R. (1987).   *Memory and brain.* New York: Oxford University Press. (p. 237, 238)

Sroufe, L. A., Fox, N. E., & Pancake, V. R. (1983).   Attachment and dependency in developmental perspective. *Child Development, 54,* 1615–1627. (p. 83)

Stack, S. (1992).   Marriage, family, religion, and suicide. In R. Maris, A. Berman, J. Maltsberger, & R. Yufit (Eds.), *Assessment and prediction of suicide.* New York: Guilford Press. (p. 428)

Stattin, H., & Magnusson, D. (1990).   *Pubertal maturation in female development.* Hillsdale, NJ: Erlbaum. (p. 89)

Staub, E. (1989).   *The roots of evil: The psychological and cultural sources of genocide.* New York: Cambridge University Press. (p. 483)

Staub, E. (1993).   Societal-cultural, familial and psychological origins of youth violence. Paper presented at the American Psychological Association convention. (p. 504)

Steele, C. (1990a, May).   A conversation with Claude Steele. *APS Observer,* pp. 11–17. (p. 289)

Steele, C. M., & Josephs, R. A. (1990).   Alcohol myopia: Its prized and dangerous effects. *American Psychologist, 45,* 921–933. (p. 183)

Stein, J. A., Newcomb, M. D., & Bentler, P. M. (1986).   Stability and change in personality: A longitudinal study from early adolescence to young adulthood. *Journal of Research In Personality, 20,* 276–291. (p. 112)

Steinberg, L. (1987, September).   Bound to bicker. *Psychology Today,* pp. 36–39. (p. 95)

Steinberg, N. (1993, February).   Astonishing love stories (from an earlier United Press International report).   *Games,* p. 47. (p. 512)

Stengel, E. (1981).   Suicide. In *The new encyclopaedia britannica, macropaedia* (Vol. 17, pp. 777–782). Chicago: Encyclopaedia Britannica. (p. 428)

Stephens, T. (1988).   Physical activity and mental health in the United States and Canada: Evidence from four population surveys. *Preventive Medicine, 17,* 35–47. (p. 368)

Sternberg, R. J. (1988).   Applying cognitive theory to the testing and teaching of intelligence. *Applied Cognitive Psychology, 2,* 231–255. (p. 282)

Sternberg, R. J., & Grajek, S. (1984).   The nature of love. *Journal of Personality and Social Psychology, 47,* 312–329. (p. 516)

Sternberg, R. J., & Lubart, T. I. (1991).   An investment theory of creativity and its development. *Human Development,* 1–31. (p. 282)

Sternberg, R. J., & Lubart, T. I. (1992).   Buy low and sell high: An investment approach to creativity. *Psychological Science, 1,* 1–5. (p. 282)

Sternberg, R. J., & Salter, W. (1982).   Conceptions of intelligence. In R. J. Sternberg (Ed.), *Handbook of human intelligence.* New York: Cambridge University Press. (p. 275)

Sternberg, R. J., & Wagner, R. K. (1993).   The g-ocentric view of intelligence and job performance is wrong. *Current Directions in Psychological Science, 2,* 1–5. (p. 282)

Stevenson, H. W. (1992, December). Learning from Asian schools. *Scientific American*, pp. 70–76. (p. 289)

Stice, E., & Shaw, H. E. (1994). Adverse effects of the media portrayed thin-ideal on women and linkages to bulimic symptomatology. *Journal of Social and Clinical Psychology, 13*, 288–308. (p. 308)

Stiles, W. B., Shapiro, D. A., & Elliott, R. (1986). "Are all psychotherapies equivalent?" *American Psychologist, 41*, 165–180. (p. 467)

Stockton, M. C., & Murnen, S. K. (1992). Gender and sexual arousal in response to sexual stimuli: A meta-analytic review. Presented at the American Psychological Society convention. (p. 314)

Stoll, A. L., Tohen, M., Baldessarini, R. J., Goodwin, D. C., Stein, S., Katz, S., Geenens, D., Swinson, R. P., Goethe, J. W., & McGlashan, T. (1993). Shifts in diagnostic frequencies of schizophrenia and major affective disorders at six North American psychiatric hospitals, 1972–1988. *American Journal of Psychiatry, 150*, 1668–1673. (p. 430)

Stone, A. A., Cox, D. S., Valdimarsdottir, H., Jandor, L., & Neale, J. M. (1987). Evidence that secretory IgA antibody is associated with daily mood. *Journal of Personality and Social Psychology, 52*, 988–993. (p. 364)

Stone, A. A., & Neale, J. M. (1984). Effects of severe daily events on mood. *Journal of Personality and Social Psychology, 46*, 137–144. (p. 347)

Stoppard, J. M., & Gruchy, C. D. G. (1993). Gender, context, and expression of positive emotion. *Personality and Social Psychology Bulletin, 19*, 143–150. (p. 94)

Storms, M. D. (1973). Videotape and the attribution process: Reversing actors' and observers' points of view. *Journal of Personality and Social Psychology, 27*, 165–175. (p. 480)

Storms, M. D. (1981). A theory of erotic orientation development. *Psychological Review, 88*, 340–353. (p. 319)

Storms, M. D. (1983). *Development of sexual orientation.* Washington, DC: Office of Social and Ethical Responsibility, American Psychological Association. (p. 318)

Storms, M. D., & Thomas, G. C. (1977). Reactions to physical closeness. *Journal of Personality and Social Psychology, 35*, 412–418. (p. 490)

Strack, F., Martin, L., & Stepper, S. (1988). Inhibiting and facilitating conditions of the human smile: A nonobtrusive test of the facial feedback hypothesis. *Journal of Personality and Social Psychology, 54*, 768–777. (p. 342)

Strack, S., & Coyne, J. C. (1983). Social confirmation of dysphoria: Shared and private reactions to depression. *Journal of Personality and Social Behavior, 44*, 798–806. (p. 432)

Strange, S. L., & Forsyth, D. R. (1993). Long-term benefits of adolescent peer groups. Paper presented at the Eastern Psychological Association convention. (p. 93)

Stratton, G. M. (1896). Some preliminary experiments on vision without inversion of the retinal image. *Psychological Review, 3*, 611–617. (p. 150)

Straub, R. O., Seidenberg, M. S., Bever, T. G., & Terrace, H. S. (1979). Serial learning in the pigeon. *Journal of the Experimental Analysis of Behavior, 32*, 137–148. (p. 270)

Straus, M. A., & Gelles, R. J. (1980). *Behind closed doors: Violence in the American family.* New York: Anchor/Doubleday. (p. 212)

Streissguth, A. P., LaDue, R. A., & Randels, S. P. (1988). *A manual on adolescents and adults with fetal alcohol syndrome with special reference to American Indians.* Department of Psychiatry and Behavioral Sciences, University of Washington. (p. 72)

Strentz, H. (1986, January 1). Become a psychic and amaze your friends! *Atlanta Journal*, p. 15A. (p. 155)

Striegel-Moore, R. H., Silberstein, L. R., & Rodin, J. (1993). The social self in bulimia nervosa: Public self-consciousness, social anxiety, and perceived fraudulence. *Journal of Abnormal Psychology, 102*, 297–303. (p. 304)

Strupp, H. H. (1986). Psychotherapy: Research, practice, and public policy (How to avoid dead ends). *American Psychologist, 41*, 120–130. (p. 467)

Stunkard, A. J., Harris, J. R., Pedersen, N. L., & McClearn, G. E. (1990). A separated twin study of the body mass index. *New England Journal of Medicine, 322*, 1483–1487. (p. 308)

Suddath, R. L., Christison, G. W., Torrey, E. F., Casanova, M. F., & Weinberger, D. R. (1990). Anatomical abnormalities in the brains of monozygotic twins discordant for schizophrenia. *New England Journal of Medicine, 322*, 789–794. (p. 439)

Sue, D. W. (1990). Culture-specific strategies in counseling: A conceptual framework. *Professional Psychology: Research and Practice, 21*, 424–433. (p. 469)

Suedfeld, P., & Mocellin, J. S. P. (1987). The "sensed presence" in unusual environments. *Environment and Behavior, 19*, 33–52. (p. 187)

Suinn, R. M. (1986). *Seven steps to peak performance.* Toronto: Hogrefe. (p. 274)

Sulloway, F. J. (1990). Orthodoxy and innovation in science: The influence of birth order in a multivariate context. Paper delivered at the American Association for the Advancement of Science annual meeting. (p. 324)

Suls, J. M., & Tesch, F. (1978). Students' preferences for information about their test performance: A social comparison study. *Journal of Experimental Social Psychology, 8*, 189–197. (p. 349)

Sundstrom, E., De Meuse, K. P., & Futrell, D. (1990). Work teams: Applications and effectiveness. *American Psychologist, 45*, 120–133. (p. 328)

Suomi, S. J. (1986). Anxiety-like disorders in young nonhuman primates. In R. Gettleman (Ed.), *Anxiety disorders of childhood.* New York: Guilford Press. (p. 422)

Suomi, S. J. (1987). Genetic and maternal contributions to individual differences in rhesus monkey biobehavioral development. In N. A. Krasnegor & others (Eds.), *Perinatal development: A psychobiological perspective.* Orlando, FL: Academic Press. (pp. 82, 108, 381)

Suppes, P. Quoted by R. H. Ennis (1982). Children's ability to handle Piaget's propositional logic: A conceptual critique. In S. Modgil & C. Modgil (Eds.), *Jean Piaget: Consensus and controversy.* New York: Praeger. (p. 79)

Surgeon General. (1986). *The Surgeon General's workshop on pornography and public health*, June 22–24. Report prepared by E. P. Mulvey & J. L. Haugaard and released by Office of the Surgeon General on August 4, 1986. (p. 507)

Sweat, J. A., & Durm, M. W. (1993). Psychics: Do police departments really use them? *Skeptical Inquirer, 17*, 148–158. (p. 155)

Swerdlow, N. R., & Koob, G. F. (1987). Dopamine, schizophrenia, mania, and depression: Toward a unified hypothesis of cortico-stiato-pallido-thalamic function (with commentary). *Behavioral and Brain Sciences, 10*, 197–246. (p. 437)

Szasz, T. (1984). *The therapeutic state: Psychiatry in the mirror of current events.* Buffalo, NY: Prometheus. (p. 416)

Szasz, T. (1987). *Insanity: The idea and its consequences.* New York: Wiley. (p. 416)

Taha, F. A. (1972).   A comparative study of how sighted and blind perceive the manifest content of dreams. *National Review of Social Sciences, 9*(3), p. 28. (p. 172)

Tajfel, H. (Ed.). (1982).   *Social identity and intergroup relations.* New York: Cambridge University Press. (p. 499)

Tannen, D. (1990).   *You just don't understand: Women and men in conversation.* New York: Morrow. (p. 94)

Tanner, J. M. (1978).   *Fetus into man: Physical growth from conception to maturity.* Cambridge, MA: Harvard University Press. (p. 88)

Tassinary, L. G., & Cacioppo, J. T. (1992).   Unobservable facial actions and emotion. *Psychological Science, 3*, 28–33. (p. 339)

Tatarkiewicz, W. (1976).   *Analysis of happiness.* The Hague: Martinus Nijhoff. (p. 347)

Tavris, C. (1982, November).   Anger defused. *Psychology Today,* pp. 25–35. (p. 346)

Tavris, C. (1993, January 3).   Beware the incest-survivor machine. *New York Times Book Review,* pp. 1, 16–18. (p. 248)

Taylor, S. E. (1989).   *Positive illusions.* New York: Basic Books. (pp. 262, 371, 398)

Taylor, S. P., & Chermack, S. T. (1993).   Alcohol, drugs and human physical aggression. *Journal of Studies on Alcohol,* Supplement No. 11, 78–88. (p. 502)

Teevan, R. C., & McGhee, P. E. (1972).   Childhood development of fear of failure motivation. *Journal of Personality and Social Psychology, 21*, 345–348. (p. 324)

Teghtsoonian, R. (1971).   On the exponents in Stevens' law and the constant in Ekman's law. *Psychological Review, 78*, 71–80. (p. 121)

Terrace, H. S. (1979, November).   How Nim Chimpsky changed my mind. *Psychology Today,* pp. 65–76. (p. 270)

Tetlock, P. E. (1988). Monitoring the integrative complexity of American and Soviet policy rhetoric: What can be learned? *Journal of Social Issues, 44*, 101–131. (p. 521)

Thatcher, R. W., Walker, R. A., & Giudice, S. (1987).   Human cerebral hemispheres develop at different rates and ages. *Science, 236*, 1110–1113. (p. 111)

Thayer, R. E. (1987).   Energy, tiredness, and tension effects of a sugar snack versus moderate exercise. *Journal of Personality and Social Psychology, 52*, 119–125. (p. 368)

Thayer, R. E. (1993).   Mood and behavior (smoking and sugar snacking) following moderate exercise: A partial test of self-regulation theory. *Personality and Individual Differences, 14*, 97–104. (p. 368)

Thomas, A., & Chess, S. (1986).   The New York Longitudinal Study: From infancy to early adult life. In R. Plomin & J. Dunn (Eds.), *The study of temperament: Changes, continuities, and challenges.* Hillsdale, NJ: Erlbaum. (p. 112)

Thomas, G. V., & Blackman, D. (1991).   Are animal experiments on the way out? *The Psychologist, 14*, 208–212. (p. 26)

Thomas, L. (1974).   *The lives of a cell.* New York: Viking Press. (p. 137)

Thomas, L. (1983).   *The youngest science: Notes of a medicine watcher.* New York: Viking Press. (p. 39)

Thomas, L. (1992).   *The fragile species.* New York: Maxwell Macmillan. (p. 465)

Thompson, C. P., Frieman, J., & Cowan, T. (1993).   Rajan's memory. Paper presented to the American Psychological Society convention. (p. 234)

Thompson, J. K., Jarvie, G. J., Lahey, B. B., & Cureton, K. J. (1982). Exercise and obesity: Etiology, physiology, and intervention. *Psychological Bulletin, 91*, 55–79. (p. 309)

Thorndike, A. L., & Hagen, E. P. (1977).   Measurement and evaluation in psychology and education. New York: Macmillan. (p. 278)

Thornton, B., & Moore, S. (1993).   Physical attractiveness contrast effect: Implications for self-esteem and evaluations of the social self. *Personality and Social Psychology Bulletin, 19*, 474–480. (p. 513)

Tiggemann, M., & Rothblum, E. D. (1988).   Gender differences in social consequences of perceived overweight in the United States and Australia. *Sex Roles, 18*, 75–86. (p. 309)

Timberlake, W., & Farmer-Dougan, V. A. (1991).   Reinforcement in applied settings: Figuring out ahead of time what will work. *Psychological Bulletin, 110*, 379–391. (p. 208)

Tinbergen, N. (1951).   *The study of instinct.* Oxford: Clarendon. (p. 298)

Tirrell, M. E. (1990).   Personal communication. (p. 200)

Tolchin, M. (1994, April 17).   Major airlines go two years without a fatality. *New York Times* report in *Grand Rapids Press,* p. A10. (p. 261)

Tolstoy, L. (1904).   *My confessions.* Boston: Dana Estes. (p. 5)

Torrey, E. F. (1986).   *Witchdoctors and psychiatrists.* New York: Harper & Row. (p. 468)

Torrey, E. F., Torrey, B. B., & Peterson, M. A. (1977).   Seasonality of schizophrenic births in the United States. *Archives of General Psychiatry, 34*, 1065–1070. (p. 437)

Toufexis, A. (1993, May 24).   Sex has many accents. *Time,* p. 66. (p. 95)

Towler, G. (1986).   From zero to one hundred: Coaction in a natural setting. *Perceptual and Motor Skills, 62*, 377–378. (p. 490)

Treisman, A. (1987).   Properties, parts, and objects. In K. R. Boff, L. Kaufman, & J. P. Thomas (Eds.), *Handbook of perception and human performance.* New York: Wiley. (p. 140)

Triandis, H. C. (1981).   Some dimensions of intercultural variation and their implications for interpersonal behavior. Paper presented at the American Psychological Association convention. (p. 494)

Triandis, H. C. (1989a).   The self and social behavior in differing cultural contexts. *Psychological Review, 96*, 506–520. (p. 398)

Triandis, H. C. (1989b).   Cross-cultural studies of individualism and collectivism. In J. J. Berman (Ed.), *Nebraska symposium on motivation 1989* (Vol. 37). Lincoln, NE: University of Nebraska Press. (p. 398)

Triandis, H. C. (1994).   *Culture and social behavior.* New York: McGraw-Hill. (pp. 85, 341, 398, 404, 495, 504)

Triandis, H. C., Brislin, R., & Hui, C. H. (1988).   Cross-cultural training across the individualism-collectivism divide. *International Journal of Intercultural Relations, 12*, 269–289. (p. 399)

Trickett, P. K., & Putnam, F. W. (1993).   Impact of child sexual abuse on females: Toward a developmental, psychobiological integration. *Psychological Science, 4*, 81–87. (p. 244)

Trimble, J. E. (1994).   Cultural variations in the use of alcohol and drugs. In W. J. Lonner & R. Malpass (Eds.), *Psychology and culture.* Boston: Allyn & Bacon. (p. 189)

Triplett, N. (1898).   The dynamogenic factors in pacemaking and competition. *American Journal of Psychology, 9*, 507–533. (p. 490)

Trolier, T. K., & Hamilton, D. L. (1986).   Variables influencing judgments of correlational relations. *Journal of Personality and Social Psychology, 50*, 879–888. (p. 14)

True, R. M. (1949).   Experimental control in hypnotic age regression states. *Science, 110,* 583–584. (p. 179)

Tsang, Y. C. (1938).   Hunger motivation in gastrectomized rats. *Journal of Comparative Psychology, 26,* 1–17. (p. 302)

Tsuang, M. T., & Faraone, S. V. (1990).   *The genetics of mood disorders.* Baltimore, MD: Johns Hopkins University Press. (p. 430)

Tubbs, M. E. (1986).   Goal setting: A meta-analytic examination of the empirical evidence. *Journal of Applied Psychology, 71,* 474–483. (p. 327)

Turk, D. C., Meichenbaum, D. H., & Berman, W. H. (1979).   Application of biofeedback for the regulation of pain: A critical review. *Psychological Bulletin, 86,* 1322–1338. (p. 370)

Turkheimer, E. (1991).   Individual and group differences in adoption studies of IQ. *Psychological Bulletin, 110,* 392–405. (p. 286)

Turkington, C. (1987, August).   Help for the worried well. *Psychology Today,* pp. 44–48. (p. 466)

Turner, C. W., Hesse, B. W., & Peterson-Lewis, S. (1986).   Naturalistic studies of the long-term effects of television violence. *Journal of Social Issues, 42*(3), 7–28. (p. 505)

Tversky, A. (1985, June).   Quoted in K. McKean, Decisions, decisions. *Discover,* pp. 22–31. (p. 259)

Tversky, A., & Kahneman, D. (1974).   Judgment under uncertainty: Heuristics and biases. *Science, 185,* 1124–1131. (pp. 259, 532)

Twiss, C., Tabb, S., & Crosby, F. (1989).   Affirmative action and aggregate data: The importance of patterns in the perception of discrimination. In F. Blanchard & F. Crosby (Eds.), *Affirmative action: Social psychological perspectives.* New York: Springer-Verlag. (p. 531)

Ulrich, R. E. (1991).   Animal rights, animal wrongs and the question of balance. *Psychological Science, 2,* 197–201. (p. 26)

Underwood, B. J. (1957).   Interference and forgetting. *Psychological Review, 64,* 49–60. (p. 246)

United Nations (1991).   *The world's women 1970–1990: Trends and statistics.* New York: United Nations. (p. 498)

United Nations (1992).   *1991 demographic yearbook.* New York: United Nations. (pp. 104, 501)

United Nations (1993).   Children: A basic focus in IYF. *The Family,* No. 3., pp. 1–2. (p. 498)

Urbany, J. E., Bearden, W. O., & Weilbaker, D. C. (1988).   The effect of plausible and exaggerated reference prices on consumer perceptions and price search. *Journal of Consumer Research, 15,* 95–110. (p. 262)

Valenstein, E. S. (1986).   *Great and desperate cures: The rise and decline of psychosurgery.* New York: Basic Books. (p. 474)

Vallone, R. P., Griffin, D. W., Lin, S., & Ross, L. (1990).   Overconfident prediction of future actions and outcomes by self and others. *Journal of Personality and Social Psychology, 58,* 582–592. (pp. 9, 261)

Vance, E. B., & Wagner, N. N. (1976).   Written descriptions of orgasm: A study of sex differences. *Archives of Sexual Behavior, 5,* 87–98. (p. 312)

van den Boom, D. (1990).   Preventive intervention and the quality of mother-infant interaction and infant exploration in irritable infants. In W. Koops, H. J. G. Soppe, J. L. van der Linden, P. C. M. Molenaar, & J. J. F. Schroots (Eds.), *Developmental psychology behind the dikes: An outline of developmental psychology research in The Netherlands.* The Netherlands: Uitgeverij Eburon. Cited by C. Hazan & P. R. Shaver (1994). Deeper into attachment theory. *Psychological Inquiry, 5,* 68–79. (p. 83)

Van Dyke, C., & Byck, R. (1982, March).   Cocaine. *Scientific American,* pp. 128–141. (p. 186)

Van Horn, J. D., & McManus, I. C. (1992).   Ventricular enlargement in schizophrenia: A meta-analysis of studies of the ventricular:brain ratio (VBR). *British Journal of Psychiatry, 160,* 687–697. (p. 437)

van IJzendoorn, M. H., & Kroonenberg, P. M. (1988).   Cross-cultural patterns of attachment: A meta-analysis of the strange situation. *Child Development, 59,* 147–156. (p. 82)

Van Leeuwen, M. S. (1978).   A cross-cultural examination of psychological differentiation in males and females. *International Journal of Psychology, 13,* 87–122. (p. 495)

Van Leeuwen, M. S. (1982).   IQism and the just society: Historical background. *Journal of the American Scientific Affiliation, 34,* 193–201. (p. 279)

Van Yperen, N. W., & Buunk, B. P. (1990).   A longitudinal study of equity and satisfaction in intimate relationships. *European Journal of Social Psychology, 20,* 287–309. (p. 516)

Vaughn, K. B., & Lanzetta, J. T. (1981).   The effect of modification of expressive displays on vicarious emotional arousal. *Journal of Experimental Social Psychology, 17,* 16–30. (p. 343)

Vaux, A. (1988).   Social and personal factors in loneliness. *Journal of Social and Clinical Psychology, 6,* 462–471. (p. 433)

Vekassy, L. (1977).   Dreams of the blind. *Magyar Pszichologiai Szemle, 34,* 478–491. (p. 172)

Vemer, E., Coleman, M., Ganong, L. H., & Cooper, H. (1989).   Marital satisfaction in remarriage: A meta-analysis. *Journal of Marriage and the Family, 51,* 713–725. (p. 104)

Venn, J. (1986).   Hypnosis and the Lamaze method: A reply to Wideman and Singer. *American Psychologist, 41,* 475–476. (p. 178)

Vokey, J. R., & Read, J. D. (1985).   Subliminal messages: Between the devil and the media. *American Psychologist, 40,* 1231–1239. (pp. 120, 151)

von Senden, M. (1932; reprinted 1960).   In P. Heath (Trans.), *Space and sight: The perception of space and shape in the congenitally blind before and after operation.* Glencoe, IL: Free Press. (p. 149)

Vygotsky, L. S. (1932, reprinted 1962).   *Thought and language* (E. Haufmann & G. Vaker, Eds. & trans.). Cambridge, MA: MIT Press. (p. 79)

Waddington, J. L. (1993).   Neurodynamics of abnormalities in cerebral metabolism and structure in schizophrenia. *Schizophrenia Bulletin, 19,* 55–69. (p. 437)

Wagstaff, G. (1982).   Attitudes to rape: The "just world" strikes again? *Bulletin of the British Psychological Society, 13,* 275–283. (p. 481)

Wahl, O. F. (1992).   Mass media images of mental illness: A review of the literature. *Journal of Community Psychology, 20,* 343–352. (p. 444)

Wakefield, J. C. (1987).   The semantics of success: Do masturbation exercises lead to partner orgasm? *Journal of Sex and Marital Therapy, 13,* 3–14. (p. 316)

Wakefield, J. C. (1992).   The concept of mental disorder: On the boundary between biological facts and social values. *American Psychologist, 47,* 373–388. (p. 414)

Wallach, M. A., & Wallach, L. (1983).   *Psychology's sanction for selfishness: The error of egoism in theory and therapy.* New York: Freeman. (p. 400)

Wallach, M. A., & Wallach, L. (1985, February).   How psychology sanctions the cult of the self. *Washington Monthly,* pp. 46–56. (p. 400)

Wallis, C. (1983, June 6).   Stress: Can we cope? *Time*, pp. 48–54. (p. 359)

Walster (Hatfield), E., Aronson, V., Abrahams, D., & Rottman, L. (1966). Importance of physical attractiveness in dating behavior. *Journal of Personality and Social Psychology, 4*, 508–516. (p. 512)

Ward, C. (1994).   Culture and altered states of consciousness. In W. J. Lonner & R. Malpass (Eds.), *Psychology and culture*. Boston: Allyn & Bacon. (p. 184)

Warr, P., & Payne, R. (1982).   Experiences of strain and pleasure among British adults. *Social Science and Medicine, 16*, 1691–1697. (p. 371)

Wason, P. C. (1960).   On the failure to eliminate hypotheses in a conceptual task. *Quarterly Journal of Experimental Psychology, 12*, 129–140. (p. 258)

Wason, P. C. (1981).   The importance of cognitive illusions. *The Behavioral and Brain Sciences, 4*, 356. (p. 9)

Wasserman, E. A. (1993).   Comparative cognition: Toward a general understanding of cognition in behavior. *Psychological Science, 4*, 156–161. (p. 207)

Waterhouse, R. (1993, July 19).   Income for 62 percent is below average pay. *The Independent*, p. 4. (p. 528)

Waterman, A. S. (1988).   Identity status theory and Erikson's theory: Commonalities and differences. *Developmental Review, 8*, 185–208. (p. 93)

Watkins, J. G. (1984).   The Bianchi (L. A. Hillside Strangler) case: Sociopath or multiple personality? *International Journal of Clinical and Experimental Hypnosis, 32*, 67–101. (p. 424)

Watson, J. B. (1913).   Psychology as the behaviorist views it. *Psychological Review, 20*, 158–177. (pp. 163, 198)

Watson, J. B., & Rayner, R. (1920).   Conditioned emotional reactions. *Journal of Experimental Psychology, 3*, 1–14. (p. 204)

Watson, R. I., Jr. (1973).   Investigation into deindividuation using a cross-cultural survey technique. *Journal of Personality and Social Psychology, 25*, 342–345. (p. 491)

Weaver, J. B., Masland, J. L., & Zillmann, D. (1984).   Effect of erotica on young men's aesthetic perception of their female sexual partners. *Perceptual and Motor Skills, 58*, 929–930. (p. 314)

Webb, W. B. (1992).   *Sleep: The gentle tyrant*. Bolton, MA: Anker Publishing. (pp. 168, 170)

Webb, W. B., & Campbell, S. S. (1983).   Relationships in sleep characteristics of identical and fraternal twins. *Archives of General Psychiatry, 40*, 1093–1095. (p. 170)

Wechsler, D. (1972).   "Hold" and "Don't Hold" tests. In S. M. Chown (Ed.), *Human aging*. New York: Penguin. (p. 101)

Wechsler, H., Davenport, A., Dowdall, G., Moeykens, B., & Castillo, S. (1994).   Health and behavioral consequences of binge drinking in college. *Journal of the American Medical Association, 272*, 1672–1677. (p. 183)

Weinberg, M. S., & Williams, C. (1974).   *Male homosexuals: Their problems and adaptations*. New York: Oxford University Press. (p. 318)

Weinberg, R. A., Scarr, S., & Waldman, I. D. (1992).   The Minnesota transracial adoption study: A follow-up of IQ test performance at adolescence. *Intelligence, 16*, 117–135. (p. 289)

Weingartner, H., Rudorfer, M. V., Buchsbaum, M. S., & Linnoila, M. (1983).   Effects of serotonin on memory impairments produced by ethanol. *Science, 221*, 472–473. (p. 237)

Weinstein, N. D. (1980).   Unrealistic optimism about future life events. *Journal of Personality and Social Psychology, 39*, 806–820. (p. 405)

Weinstein, N. D. (1982).   Unrealistic optimism about susceptibility to health problems. *Journal of Behavioral Medicine, 5*, 441–460. (p. 405)

Weiss, J. M. (1977).   Psychological and behavioral influences on gastrointestinal lesions in animal models. In J. D. Maser & M. E. P. Seligman (Eds.), *Psychopathology: Experimental models*. San Francisco: Freeman. (p. 361)

Weisse, C. S. (1992).   Depression and immunocompetence: A review of the literature. *Psychological Bulletin, 111*, 475–489. (p. 364)

Weissman, M. M., Merikangas, K. R., Wickramaratne, P., Kidd, K. K., Prusoff, B. A., Leckman, J. F., & Pauls, D. L. (1986).   Understanding the clinical heterogeneity of major depression using family data. *Archives of General Psychiatry, 43*, 430–434. (p. 430)

Weisz, J. R., Rothbaum, F. M., & Blackburn, T. C. (1984).   Standing out and standing in: The psychology of control in America and Japan. *American Psychologist, 39*, 955–969. (p. 494)

Wellman, H. M., & Gelman, S. A. (1992).   Cognitive development: Foundational theories of core domains. *Annual Review of Psychology, 43*, 337–375. (p. 77)

Wells, G. L. (1981).   Lay analyses of causal forces on behavior. In J. Harvey (Ed.), *Cognition, social behavior and the environment*. Hillsdale, NJ: Erlbaum. (p. 196)

Wells, G., & Murray, D. M. (1984).   Eyewitness confidence. In G. L. Wells & E. F. Loftus (Eds.), *Eyewitness testimony: Psychological perspectives*. New York: Cambridge University Press. (p. 244)

Wender, P. H., Kety, S. S., Rosenthal, D., Schulsinger, F., Ortmann, J., & Lunde, I. (1986).   Psychiatric disorders in the biological and adoptive families of adopted individuals with affective disorders. *Archives of General Psychiatry, 43*, 923–929. (p. 430)

Wener, R., Frazier, W., & Farbstein, J. (1987, June).   Building better jails. *Psychology Today*, pp. 40–49. (p. 404)

Werker, J. F. (1989).   Becoming a native listener. *American Scientist, 77*, 54–59. (p. 265)

West, P. D. B., & Evans, E. F. (1990).   Early detection of hearing damage in young listeners resulting from exposure to amplified music. *British Journal of Audiology, 24*, 89–103. (p. 132)

Westefeld, J. S., & Furr, S. R. (1987).   Suicide and depression among college students. *Professional Psychology: Research and Practice, 18*, 119–123. (p. 428)

Whelan, J. P., Mahoney, M. J., & Meyers, A. W. (1991).   Performance enhancement in sport: A cognitive behavioral domain. *Behavior Therapy, 22*, 307–327. (p. 274)

White, G. L., & Kight, T. D. (1984).   Misattribution of arousal and attraction: Effects of salience of explanations for arousal. *Journal of Experimental Social Psychology, 20*, 55–64. (p. 515)

White, H. R., Brick, J., & Hansell, S. (1993).   A longitudinal investigation of alcohol use and aggression in adolescence. *Journal of Studies on Alcohol*, Supplement No. 11, 62–77. (pp. 14, 503)

White, K. M. (1983).   Young adults and their parents: Individuation to mutuality. *New Directions for Child Development, 22*, 61–76. (p. 95)

White, L., & Edwards, J. (1990).   Emptying the nest and parental well-being: An analysis of national panel data. *American Sociological Review, 55*, 235–242. (p. 105)

Whiting, B. B., & Edwards, C. P. (1988).   *Children of different worlds: The formation of social behavior*. Cambridge, MA: Harvard University Press. (p. 85)

Whitley, B. E., Jr. (1990). The relationships of heterosexuals' attributions for the causes of homosexuality to attitudes toward lesbians and gay men. *Personality and Social Psychology Bulletin, 16,* 369–377. (p. 320)

Whorf, B. L. (1956). Science and linguistics. In J. B. Carroll (Ed.), *Language, thought, and reality: Selected writings of Benjamin Lee Whorf.* Cambridge, MA: MIT Press. (p. 272)

Wickelgren, W. A. (1977). *Learning and memory.* Englewood Cliffs, NJ: Prentice-Hall. (p. 229)

Wicker, A. W. (1971). An examination of the "other variables" explanation of attitude-behavior inconsistency. *Journal of Personality and Social Psychology, 19,* 18–30. (p. 481)

Widom, C. S. (1989a). Does violence beget violence? A critical examination of the literature. *Psychological Bulletin, 106,* 3–28. (p. 84)

Widom, C. S. (1989b). The cycle of violence. *Science, 244,* 160–166. (p. 84)

Wiens, A. N., & Menustik, C. E. (1983). Treatment outcome and patient characteristics in an aversion therapy program for alcoholism. *American Psychologist, 38,* 1089–1096. (p. 457)

Wiesel, T. N. (1982). Postnatal development of the visual cortex and the influence of environment. *Nature, 299,* 583–591. (p. 149)

Wigdor, A. K., & Garner, W. R. (1982). *Ability testing: Uses, consequences, and controversies.* Washington, DC: National Academy Press. (p. 291)

Wilder, D. A. (1981). Perceiving persons as a group: Categorization and intergroup relations. In D. L. Hamilton (Ed.), *Cognitive processes in stereotyping and intergroup behavior.* Hillsdale, NJ: Erlbaum. (p. 499)

Williams, C. L., & Berry, J. W. (1991). Primary prevention of acculturative stress among refugees. *American Psychologist, 46,* 632–641. (p. 358)

Williams, J. E. (1992). Culture and behavior: Sense and nonsense. Presidential address to the Southeastern Psychological Association convention. (p. 18)

Williams, J. E., & Best, D. L. (1990). *Measuring sex stereotypes: A multination study.* Newbury Park, CA: Sage. (p. 327)

Williams, L. M. (in press). Recall of childhood trauma: A prospective study of women's memories of child sexual abuse. *Journal of Consulting and Clinical Psychology, 62,* 1167–1176. (p. 248)

Williams, R. (1989). *The trusting heart: Great news about Type A behavior.* New York: Random House. (p. 362)

Williams, R. (1993). *Anger kills.* New York: Times Books. (p. 362)

Williams, R. B., Barefoot, J. C., Califf, R. M., Haney, T. L., Saunders, W. B., Pryor, D. B., Hlatky, M. A., Siegler, I. C., Mark, D. B. (1992). Prognostic importance of social and economic resources among medically treated patients with angiographically documented coronary artery disease. *Journal of the American Medical Association, 267,* 520–524. (p. 372)

Williams, S. L. (1987). Self-efficacy and mastery-oriented treatment for severe phobias. Paper presented to the American Psychological Association convention. (p. 456).

Willmuth, M. E. (1987). Sexuality after spinal cord injury: A critical review. *Clinical Psychology Review, 7,* 389–412. (p. 315)

Wilson, J. P., Harel, Z., & Kahana, B. (1988). *Human adaptation to extreme stress: From the Holocaust to Vietnam.* New York: Plenum Press. (p. 360)

Wilson, J. Q., & Herrnstein, R. J. (1985). *Crime and human nature.* New York: Simon and Schuster. (p. 502)

Wilson, R. C., Gaft, J. G., Dienst, E. R., Wood, L., & Bavry, J. L. (1975). *College professors and their impact on students.* New York: Wiley. (p. 492)

Wilson, R. S. (1979). Analysis of longitudinal twin data: Basic model and applications to physical growth measures. *Acta Geneticae medicae et Gemellologiae, 28,* 93–105. (p. 75)

Wilson, S. C., & Barber, T. X. (1983). The fantasy-prone personality: Implications for understanding imagery, hypnosis, and parapsychological phenomena. In A. A. Sheikh (Ed.), *Imagery: Current theory, research, and applications.* New York: Wiley. (p. 187)

Windholz, G. (1989, April-June). The discovery of the principles of reinforcement, extinction, generalization, and differentiation of conditional reflexes in Pavlov's laboratories. *Pavlovian Journal of Biological Science, 26,* 64–74. (p. 201)

Wing, R. R., & Jeffery, R. W. (1979). Outpatient treatments of obesity: A comparison of methodology and clinical results. *International Journal of Obesity, 3,* 261–279. (p. 308)

Winkelstein, W., Jr., Samuel, M., Padian, N. S., & Wiley, J. A. (1987). Selected sexual practices of San Francisco heterosexual men and risk of infection by the human immunodeficiency virus. *Journal of the American Medical Association, 257,* 1470. (p. 317)

Witelson, S. F. (1985). The brain connection: The corpus callosum is larger in left-handers. *Science, 229,* 665–667. (p. 62)

Wixted, J. T., & Ebbesen, E. B. (1991). On the form of forgetting. *Psychological Science, 2,* 409–415. (p. 234)

Wolf, N. (1991). *The beauty myth: How images of beauty are used against women.* New York: Morrow. (p. 308)

Woll, S. (1986). So many to choose from: Decision strategies in video-dating. *Journal of Social and Personal Relationships, 3,* 43–52. (p. 513)

Wolpe, J. (1958). *Psychotherapy by reciprocal inhibition.* Stanford, CA: Stanford University Press. (p. 455)

Wolpe, J. (1982). *The practice of behavior therapy.* New York: Pergamon. (p. 455)

Wong, D. F., & associates. (1986). Positron emission tomography reveals elevated D2 dopamine receptors in drug-naive schizophrenics. *Science, 234,* 1588–1563. (p. 437)

Wong, M. M., & Csikszentmihalyi, M. (1991). Affiliation motivation and daily experience: Some issues on gender differences. *Journal of Personality and Social Psychology, 60,* 154–164. (p. 94)

Wood, G. (1979). The knew-it-all-along effect. *Journal of Experimental Psychology: Human Perception and Performance, 4,* 345–353. (p. 8)

Wood, J. M., Bootzin, R. R., Kihlstrom, J. F., & Schacter, D. L. (1992). Implicit and explicit memory for verbal information presented during sleep. *Psychological Science, 3,* 236–239. (pp. 172, 227)

Wood, J. V., Saltzberg, J. A., & Goldsamt, L. A. (1990). Does affect induce self-focused attention? *Journal of Personality and Social Psychology, 58,* 899–908. (p. 432)

Wood, J. V., Saltzberg, J. A., Neale, J. M., Stone, A. A., & Rachmiel, T. B. (1990). Self-focused attention, coping responses, and distressed mood in everyday life. *Journal of Personality and Social Psychology, 58,* 1027–1036. (p. 432)

Wood, W. (1987). Meta-analytic review of sex differences in group performance. *Psychological Bulletin, 102,* 53–71. (p. 327)

Wood, W., Lundgren, S., Ouellette, J. A., Busceme, S., & Blackstone, T. (1994). Minority influence: A meta-analytic review of social influence processes. *Psychological Bulletin, 115,* 323–345. (p. 493)

Wood, W., Wong, F. Y., & Chachere, J. G. (1991). Effects of media violence on viewers' aggression in unconstrained social interaction. *Psychological Bulletin, 109,* 371–383. (p. 505)

Woodruff-Pak, D. S. (1989). Aging and intelligence: Changing perspectives in the twentieth century. *Journal of Aging Studies, 3,* 91–118. (p. 101)

Woods, N. F., Dery, G. K., & Most, A. (1983). Recollections of menarche, current menstrual attitudes, and premenstrual symptoms. In S. Golub (Ed.), *Menarche: The transition from girl to woman.* Lexington, MA: Lexington Books. (p. 88)

Wooley, S., & Wooley, O. (1983). Should obesity be treated at all? *Psychiatric Annals, 13*(11), 884–885, 888. (p. 304)

World Health Organization.(1979). *Schizophrenia: An international follow-up study.* Chicester, England: Wiley. (p. 436)

Worthington, E. L., Jr. (1989). Religious faith across the life span: Implications for counseling and research. *The Counseling Psychologist, 17,* 555–612. (p. 90)

Wortman, C. B., & Silver, R. C. (1989). The myths of coping with loss. *Journal of Consulting and Clinical Psychology, 57,* 349–357. (p. 107)

Wright, P., & Murray, R. M. (1993). Schizophrenia: Prenatal influenza and autoimmunity. *Annals of Medicine, 25,* 497–502. (p. 437)

Wu, T-C., Tashkin, D. P., Djahed, B., & Rose, J. E. (1988). Pulmonary hazards of smoking marijuana as compared with tobacco. *New England Journal of Medicine, 318,* 347–351. (p. 187)

Wulff, D. (1991). *The psychology of religion.* New York: Wiley. (p. 325)

Wyatt, J. K., & Bootzin, R. R. (1994). Cognitive processing and sleep: Implications for enhancing job performance. *Human Performance, 7,* 119–139. (p. 227)

Wynn, K. (1992). Addition and subtraction by human infants. *Nature, 358,* 749–759. (p. 77)

Wysocki, C. J., & Gilbert, A. N. (1989). *National Geographic* survey: Effects of age are heterogeneous. *Annals of the New York Academy of Sciences, 561,* 12–28. (p. 137)

Yalom, I. D. (1985). *The theory and practice of group psychotherapy* (3rd ed.). New York: Basic Books. (p. 462)

Yang, N., & Linz, D. (1990). Movie ratings and the content of adult videos: The sex-violence ratio. *Journal of Communication, 40*(2), 28–42. (p. 506)

Yapko, M. D. (1994). Suggestibility and repressed memories of abuse: A survey of psychotherapists' beliefs. *American Journal of Clinical Hypnosis, 36,* 163–171. (p. 178)

Yarnell, P. R., & Lynch, S. (1970, April 25). Retrograde memory immediately after concussion. *Lancet,* pp. 863–865. (p. 237)

Yates, A. (1989). Current perspectives on the eating disorders: I. History, psychological and biological aspects. *Journal of the American Academy of Child and Adolescent Psychiatry, 28,* 813–828. (p. 304)

Yates, A. (1990). Current perspectives on the eating disorders: II. Treatment, outcome, and research directions. *Journal of the American Academy of Child and Adolescent Psychiatry, 29,* 1–9. (p. 304)

Zajonc, R. B. (1965). Social facilitation. *Science, 149,* 269–274. (p. 490)

Zajonc, R. B. (1980). Feeling and thinking: Preferences need no inferences. *American Psychologist, 35,* 151–175. (p. 354)

Zajonc, R. B. (1984a). On the primacy of affect. *American Psychologist, 39,* 117–123. (p. 354)

Zajonc, R. B. (1984b, July 22). Quoted by D. Goleman, Rethinking IQ tests and their value. *The New York Times,* p. D22. (p. 278)

Zajonc, R. B., & Markus, G. B. (1975). Birth order and intellectual development. *Psychological Review, 82,* 74–88. (p. 534)

Zajonc, R. B., Murphy, S. T., & Inglehart, M. (1989). Feeling and facial efference: Implications of the vascular theory of emotions. *Psychological Review, 96,* 395–416. (p. 342)

Zeidner, M. (1990). Perceptions of ethnic group modal intelligence: Reflections of cultural stereotypes or intelligence test scores? *Journal of Cross-Cultural Psychology, 21,* 214–231. (p. 289)

Zelnick, M., & Kim, Y. J. (1982). Sex education and its association with teenage sexual activity, pregnancy, and contraceptive use. *Family Planning Perspectives, 14*(3), 117–126. (p. 321)

Zhang, S-D., & Odenwald, W. F. (1995). Misexpression of the white (*w*) gene triggers male—male courtship in *Drosophila. Proceedings of the National Academy of Sciences, 92,* 5525–5529. (p. 320)

Zigler, E. F. (1987). Formal schooling for four-year-olds? No. *American Psychologist, 42,* 254–260. (p. 287)

Zigler, E. F., & Muenchow, S. (1992). *Head start: The inside story of a great American experiment.* New York: Basic Books. (p. 288)

Zilbergeld, B. (1983). *The shrinking of America: Myths of psychological change.* Boston: Little, Brown. (pp. 464, 466)

Zillmann, D. (1986). *Effects of prolonged consumption of pornography.* Background paper for The Surgeon General's workshop on pornography and public health, June 22–24. Report prepared by E. P. Mulvey & J. L. Haugaard and released by Office of the Surgeon General on August 4, 1986. (pp. 338, 354)

Zillmann, D. (1989). Effects of prolonged consumption of pornography. In D. Zillmann & J. Bryant (Eds.), *Pornography: Research advances and policy considerations.* Hillsdale, NJ: Erlbaum. (pp. 314, 507)

Zillmann, D., & Bryant, J. (1984). Effects of massive exposure to pornography. In N. Malamuth & E. Donnerstein (Eds.), *Pornography and sexual aggression.* Orlando, FL: Academic Press. (p. 507)

Zimbardo, P. G. (1970). The human choice: Individuation, reason, and order versus deindividuation, impulse, and chaos. In W. J. Arnold & D. Levine (Eds.), *Nebraska Symposium on Motivation, 1969.* Lincoln, NE: University of Nebraska Press. (p. 491)

Zimbardo, P. G. (1972, April). Pathology of imprisonment. *Transaction/Society,* pp. 4–8. (p. 483)

Zoglin, R. (1992, November 23). Can anybody work this thing? *Time,* p. 67. (p. 152)

Zucker, G. S., & Weiner, B. (1993). Conservatism and perceptions of poverty: An attributional analysis. *Journal of Applied Social Psychology, 23,* 925–943. (p. 481)

Zuckerman, M. (1979). *Sensation seeking: Beyond the optimal level of arousal.* Hillsdale, NJ: Erlbaum. (p. 299)

Illustration Credits

Chapter 1

Opener Adam McCauley; **p. 2** (*left*) Sally Cassidy/The Picture Cube; (*center*) Joe Carini/The Image Works; (*right*) Robert Caputo/Stock, Boston; **p. 3** Laura Dwight Photography; **p. 4** (*top*)Laura Dwight Photography; (*bottom*)Topham/The Image Works; **p. 5** (*left*) Richard Howard; (*center and right*) Treë; **p. 7** Bob Kinmonth; **p. 8** AP/Wide World Photos; **p. 12** (*top*) Susan Kuklin/Photo Researchers, Inc.; (*bottom*) Elsa Peterson/Design Conceptions; **p. 14** Courtesy of David S. Wilkie; **Fig. 1-2** Reprinted with the permission of The Free Press, an imprint of Simon & Schuster Inc. From *How we know what isn't so: The fallibility of human reason in everyday life* by Thomas Gilovich. Copyright © 1991 by Thomas Gilovich.; **Fig. 1-3** Barry Ross/© 1987 *Discover* Magazine.; **p. 18** Movie Still Archives; **Fig. 1-5** Frank, M. G. & Gilovich, T. (1988). The dark side of self and social perception: Black uniforms and aggression in professional sports. *Journal of Personality and Social Psychology, 54,* 74-85. Copyright © 1988 by the American Psychological Association. Reprinted with permission.; **p. 20** (*top*) Movie Still Archives; (*bottom*) Susan Kuklin/Photo Researchers, Inc.; **p. 24** Mark S. Wexler/Woodfin Camp & Associates; **p. 26** Jim Amos/Science Source/Photo Researchers, Inc.; **p. 27** From: *Mind sights* by Shepard. Copyright © 1990 by Roger N. Shepard. Used with permission of W.H. Freeman and Company. Used with permission.

Chapter 2

Opener p. 34 Bonnie Hofkin; **p. 37** Hank Morgan/Science Source/Photo Researchers, Inc.; **p. 44** Bettina Cirone/Photo Researchers, Inc.; **p. 45** A. Glauberman/Photo Researchers, Inc.; **p. 46** Alexander Tsiaras/Stock, Boston; **p. 47** (*top*) Daniel R. Weinberger, M.D., CBDB, NIMH; (*bottom*) Hank Morgan/Rainbow; **p. 50** (*left*) Scott Camazine/Science Source/Photo Researchers, Inc.; (*right*) Frank Siteman/Stock, Boston; **p. 54** Courtesy of Drs. Jack Belliveau & Bruce Rosen, Massachusetts General Hospital, NMR Center; **p. 55** Hanna Damasis, M.D., University of Iowa and Science; **p. 59** Martin M. Rotker; **Figs. 2-24 and 2-25** Gazzaniga, M. S. (1983). Right hemisphere language following brain bisection: A 20-year perspective. *American Psychologist, 38,* 525-537.; **p. 62** Courtesy of Drs. Michael E. Phelps & John Mazziotta, UCLA School of Medicine

Chapter 3

Opener p. 68 Bart Goldman; **p. 70** Ralph Domingez/Globe Photos; **p. 71** (*top*) Lennart Nilsson/Bonnier Fakta Bokforlag; (*bottom*) Lennart Nilsson/Bonnier Fakta Bokforlag; **p. 72** (*a-c*) Petit Format/Science Source/Photo Researchers, Inc.; (*d*) Donald Yeager/Camera MD Studios; **p. 73** Enrico Ferorelli; **Fig. 3-3** Conel, J. L. (1939-1963). *The postnatal development of the human cerebral cortex* (Vols. I-VI). Reprinted by permission of Harvard University Press.; **Fig. 3-4** "Brain changes in response to experience" by M. R. Rosenzweig, E. L. Bennett, & M. C. Diamond.

Copyright © 1972 Scientific American, Inc. All rights reserved.; **p. 75** (*top*) Laura Dwight; (*bottom*) Bill Anderson/Monkmeyer Press Photos; **p. 76** (*left*) Patti Putnam/The Stock Market; (*right*) David M. Grossman; (*bottom*) Joel Gordon; **p. 77** (*left, center, and right*) Doug Goodman/Monkmeyer Press Photos; **Fig. 3-5** Wynn, K. (1992). Addition and subtraction by human infants. *Nature, 358,* 749-759. Reprinted by permission of *Nature.* Copyright © 1992 Macmillan Magazines Limited.; **p. 78** (*left and right*) Ontario Science Center; **p. 81** *and* 83 Harlow Primate Laboratory, University of Wisconsin; **Fig. 3-8** Kagan, J. (1976). Emergent themes in human development. *American Scientist, 64,* 186-196.; **p. 85** (*top*) Laura Dwight; (*bottom*) Sybil Shackman/Monkmeyer Press Photos; **Fig. 3-11** Tanner, J. M. (1978). *Fetus into man: Physical growth from conception to maturity.* Reprinted by permission of Harvard University Press.; **p. 88** Bob Daemmrich/Stock, Boston; **p. 90** (*left*) Bob Daemmrich/The Image Works; (*right*) Vanessa Vick/Photo Researchers, Inc.; **p. 91** UPI/The Bettmann Archive; **p. 92** Bob Daemmrich/The Image Works; **p. 93** (*left*) David Vance/The Image Bank; (*right*) David Delossy/The Image Bank; **p. 95** Joel Gordon; **Fig. 3-13** Data for National Center for Health Statistics; Bureau of the Census, 1993, Table 1380; and British Central Statistical Office, 1993.; **p. 98** Peter Southwick/Stock, Boston; **Fig. 3-14** Adapted from Insel, P. M. & Roth, W. T. (1976). *Health in a changing society,* p. 98. Mountain View, CA: Mayfield.; **Fig. 3-15** Adapted from Doty, R. L., et al. (1984). Smell identification ability: Changes with age. *Science, 226,* 1441-1443. Copyright © 1984 by the American Association for the Advancement of Science.; **p. 99** David Wells/The Image Works; **Fig. 3-16** Jorm, A. F., Korten, A. E., & Henderson, A. S. (1987). The prevalence of dementia: A quantitative integration of the literature. *Acta Psychiatrica Scandinivica, 76,* 465-479. Copyright © 1987 Munksgaard International Publishers Ltd., Copenhagen Denmark.; **Fig. 3-17** Data from Crook, P. H., & West, R. L. (1990). Name and recall performance across the adult life-span. *British Journal of Psychology, 81,* 335-349.; **Fig. 3-18** Schonfield, D. & Robertson, B. A. (1966). Memory storage and aging. *Canadian Journal of Psychology, 20,* 228-236. Copyright © 1966 Canadian Psychological Association. Reprinted with permission.; **Fig. 3-19** Geiwitz, J. (1980). *Psychology: Looking at ourselves.* Boston: Little, Brown, & Co.; **Fig. 3-20** Schaie, K. W. (1994). The life course of adult intellectual abilities. *American Psychologist, 49,* 304-313.; **Fig. 3-21** Adapted from Kaufman, A. S., Reynolds, C. R. & McLean, J. E. (1989). Age and WAIS-R intelligence in a national sample of adults in the 20 to 74 year age range: A cross-sectional analysis with educational level controlled. *Intelligence, 13,* 235-253. Reprinted with permission from Ablex Publishing Corporation.; **p. 103** Henley & Savage/Stock, Boston; **Fig. 3-22** McCrae, R. R. & Costa, P. T., Jr. (1990). *Personality in adulthood.* Figure 6, p. 149. New York: Guilford Press. Copyright 1990 by the Guilford Press.; **p. 105** (*top*) Joe McNally; (*center*) Bob Daemmrich/The Image Works; (*bottom*) Charles Harbutt/Actuality; **p. 106** Bob Woodward/The Stock Market; **Fig. 3-23** Data from Inglehart, R. (1990). *Culture shift in advanced industrial society.* Princeton, NJ: Princeton University Press.; **p. 107** Andrew Lichtenstein/Impact Visuals; **p. 109** Bob Sacha/Black Star; **p. 110** Kathleen Marie Menke/Crystal Images/Monkmeyer Press Photos

Chapter 4

Opener p. 116 Robert Goldstrom; **p. 118** Detail "The Forest Has Eyes" by Bev Doolittle/The Greenwich Workshop, Inc., Trumbull, CT.; **p. 119** (*left and right*) Thomas Eisner; **p. 121** (*left*) Marvin Lyons/The Image Bank; (*right*) Geoff Tompkinson/Science Photo Library/Photo Reasearchers, Inc.; **Fig. 4-2** "Stabilized images on the retina" by R. M. Pritchard. Copyright © 1961 Scientific American, Inc. All rights reserved.; **p. 126** E. R. Lewis, Y. Y. Zeevi, & F. S. Werblin, 1969; **Fig. 4-8** Adapted from Frisby, J. P. (1980). *Seeing: Illusion, brain and mind* (p. 157). London, Roxby Press. Reprinted by permission of the publisher.; **p. 128** Fritz Goro/*Life* Magazine ©1971 Time Warner, Inc.; **p. 128** Edward S. Gazsi © National Geographic Society; **p. 129** (*top*) Fritz Goro/*Life* Magazine ©1944 Time Warner, Inc.; (*bottom*) From Richmond Products, Boca Raton, FL.; **Fig 4-14** From Albers, J. (1975). *The interaction of color.* (revised pocket edition) (Plate VI-3). New Haven, CT: Yale University Press. Photo courtesy of the Josef Albers Foundation.; **p. 132** Nilsson, L. (1974) Behold Man/Boston: Little, Brown. Photo courtesy of Bonnier Fakta; **p. 134** (*top*) James Carroll; (*bottom*) Community News, Christchurch, New Zealand. Courtesy *The skeptical inquirer*; **Fig. 4-18** Wysocki, C. J., & Gilbert, A. N. (1989). In C. Murphy & W. S. Cain (Eds.), Proceedings of the conference on nutrition and the chemical senses in aging. *Annals of the New York Academy of Sciences,* Vol. 561, New York: New York Academy of Sciences.; **Fig. 4-19** Bradley, D. R., et al. (1976). Reply to Cavonius. *Nature, 261,* 78. Reprinted by permission from *Nature.* Copyright © 1976 by Macmillan Journals Limited.; **p. 141** (*top*) Walter Wick; (*bottom*) Enrico Ferorelli; **p. 142** Otto Greule, Jr./Allsport USA; **p. 143** (*top*) Ron Watts/Black Star; (*center*) Rick Friedman/Black Star; (*bottom*) Rainer Grosskopf/Tony Stone Images; **p. 144** (*top*) Photos courtesy Helen E. Ross from Ross, H. E., (1975). Mist, murk, and visual perception. *New Scientist, 66,* 658-660; (*bottom*) City Art Gallery, Bristol/The Bridgeman Art Library, Superstock; **Fig. 4-25** Shepard, R. N. (1981). Psychophysical. In M. Kubovky & J. R. Pomerantz (Eds.), *Perceptual organization* (pp. 279-341). Hillsdale, NJ: Lawrence Erlbaum. Copyright © 1981 by Lawrence Erlbaum Associates.; **126 Fig. 4-27(a)** *Mind sights* by Shepard. Copyright © 1990 by Roger N. Shepard. Used with permission of W.H. Freeman and Company.; **p. 146** Alan Choisnet/The Image Bank; **p. 147** S. Schwartzenberg/The Exploratorium; **p. 149** Walter Wick; **p. 151** (*left*) Frank Searle/Photo supplied by Steuart Campbell; (*right*) Dick Ruhl; **Fig. 4-33** *Mind sights* by Shepard. Copyright © 1990 by Roger N. Shepard. Used with permission of W.H. Freeman and Company.; **p. 152** *The psychology of everyday things* by D. A. Norman, p. 209. Copyright © 1988 by BasicBooks, Inc. Reprinted by permission of BasicBooks, a division of HarperCollins Publishers, Inc.; **Fig. 4-34** Kraft, C. (1978). A psychological approach to air safety: Simulator studies of visual illusions in night approaches. In H. L. Pick, H. W. Leibowitz, J. E. Singer, A. Steinschneider, & H. W. Stevenson (Eds.), *Psychology: From research to practice.* New York: Plenum Press.; **p. 153** Adapted from Gregory, R. L., & Gombrich, E. H. (Eds.), (1974). *Illusion in nature and art.* New York: Charles Scribner's Sons. Copyright © 1973 by C. Blakemore, J. D. Deregowski, E. H. Gombrich, R. L. Gregory, H. P. Hinton, & R. Primrose. Reprinted by permission of Gerald Duckworth & Co., Ltd.; **p. 157** Alva Bernadine

Chapter 5

Opener p. 162 Tim Lewis; **p. 164** Will & Deni McIntyre/Photo Researchers, Inc.; **p. 165** Carl Weinberg/The Image Bank; **p. 166** Allan Hobson/Photo Researchers, Inc.; **Figs. 5-1 and 5-2** Dement, W. (1972). *Some must watch while some must sleep.* Stanford, CA: Portable Stanford Book Series, 1972. Reprinted by permission of the Stanford Alumni Association, Stanford University; **Fig. 5-3** Cartwright, R. D. (1978). *A primer on sleep and dreaming.* Reading, MA: Addison-Wesley.; **Fig. 5-4** Webb, W. B. (1992). *Sleep: The gentle tyrant.* (2nd ed.) Bolton, MA: Anker Publishing.; **Fig. 5-5** Hartmann, E. (1994). *The nightmare: The psychology and biology of terrifying dreams.* New York: BasicBooks. Copyright © 1984 by Ernest Hartmann. Reprinted by permission of BasicBooks, Inc., a division of HarperCollins Publishers, Inc.; **p. 172** National Gallery of Art, Washington, Rosenwald Collection; **Fig. 5-6** Snyder, F. & Scott, J. (1972). The psychophysiology of sleep. In N. S. Greenfield and R. A. Steinback (Eds.), *Handbook of psychophysiology.* New York: Holt, Rine-

hart and Winston.; **p. 175** Peter Turnley/Black Star; **p. 176** (*top*) James Wilson/Woodfin Camp & Associates; (*bottom*) Mimi Forsyth/Monkmeyer Press Photos; **p. 177** The Bettmann Archive; **p. 178** Joel Gordon; **p. 180** Courtesy of News and Publications Service, Stanford University; **p. 183** UPI/The Bettmann Archive; **Fig. 5-9** "Hallucinations" by R. K. Siegel. Copyright © 1977 Scientific American, Inc. All rights reserved.; **Fig. 5-10** Johnston, L. D., O'Malley, P. M., & Bachman, J. G. (1995). National survey results on drug use from the Monitoring the Future Study, 1975-1994. Volume I, Secondary School Students (Dhhs Pub. No. (ADM) 95-4026). Rockville, MD: National Institute on Drug Abuse.; **p. 190** Joel Gordon

Chapter 6

Opener p. 194 Jason Dowd; **p. 197** Lawrence Migdale/Stock, Boston; **p. 198** Sovfoto; **Fig. 6-3** Adapted from Goodwin, C. J. (1991). Misportraying Pavlov's apparatus. *American Journal of Psychology, 104,* 135-141. Copyright © 1991 by the Board of Trustees of the University of Illinois Press.; **p. 203** Courtesy of UCLA Media; **p. 204** Brown Brothers; **p. 207** Richard Wood/The Picture Cube; **p. 208** Fred Bavendam/Peter Arnold, Inc.; **p. 209** Jim Corwin/Photo Researchers, Inc.; **Fig. 6-8** Adapted from "Teaching machines" by B. F. Skinner. Copyright © 1961 Scientific American, Inc. All rights reserved.; **p. 212** Joan Liftin/Actuality; **p. 213** Courtesy Animal Behavior Enterprises; **p. 214** Joe McNally; **p. 215** Joel Gordon; **p. 216** Lawrence Migdale/Stock, Boston; **p. 217** From Meltzoff, A. N. (1988). Imitation of televised models by infants. *Child Development, 59,* 1221-1229. Photos courtesy of A. N. Meltzoff & M. Hanak; **p. 218** Courtesy of Albert Bandura, Stanford University; **p. 219** Bob Daemmrich/The Image Works

Chapter 7

Opener p. 222 Elsa Warnick; **p. 224** Courtesy of Hersh & Treadgold, Inc., Desktop Paging Software, Inc., & NEC, Inc.; **p. 225** Fred Ward/Black Star; **p. 226** (*left*) Erika Stone; (*right*) Bob Daemmrich/Stock, Boston; **Fig. 7-2** Data from H. Ebbinghaus, 1885. Graph from Baddeley, A. D. (1982). *Your memory: A user's guide.* New York: Macmillan. Copyright © 1982 Macmillan Publishing Co., Inc. Reprinted by permission.; **Fig. 7-3** Craik, F. I. M. & Watkins, M. J. (1973). The role of rehearsal in short-term memory. *Journal of Verbal Learning and Verbal Behavior, 12,* 599-607. Reprinted by permission of Academic Press, Inc.; **Fig. 7-4** From *The psychology of learning and memory* by Douglas L. Hintzman. Copyright © 1978 by W.H. Freeman and Company. Reprinted with permission.; **Fig. 7-7** Nickerson, R. S. & Adams, M. J. (1979). Long-term memory for a common object. *Cognitive Psychology, 11,* 287-307.; **Fig. 7-9** Peterson, L. R. & Peterson, M. J. (1959). Short-term retention of individual verbal items. *Journal of Experimental Psychology, 58,* 193-198. ; **p. 234** R. J. Erwin/Photo Researchers, Inc.; **Fig. 7-10** Adapted from Ebbinghaus, E. (1885). Über das Gedächtnis. Leipzig: Dunker. Cited in R. Klatkzy (1980). *Human memory: Structures and processes.* Copyright © 1980 by W.H. Freeman and Company. All rights reserved.; **Fig. 7-11** Adapted from Bahrick, H. P. (1984). Semantic memory content in permastore: 50 years of memory for Spanish learned in school. *Journal of Experimental Psychology: General, 113,* 1-29. Copyright © 1984 American Psychological Association. Adapted by permission.; **p. 237** Lynn Johnson/Black Star; **p. 240** Seth Poppel/Yearbook Archives; **Fig. 7-14** Adapted from Bower, G. H. (1986). Prime time in cognitive psychology. In P. Eelen (Ed.), *Cognitive research and behavior therapy: Beyond the conditioning paradigm.* Amsterdam: North Holland Publishers.; **Fig. 7-15** Adapted from Godden, D. R. & Baddeley, A. D. (1975). Context-dependent memory in two natural environments: On land and under water. *British Journal of Psychology, 66,* 325-331.; **Fig. 7-16** Loftus, E. F. (1979). The malleability of human memory: *American Scientist, 67,* 313-320. Reprinted with permission of *American Scientist,* Journal of Sigma Xi, the Scientific Research Society.; **Fig. 7-18** Jenkins, J. G. & Dallenbach, K. M. (1924). Obliviscence during sleep and waking. *American Journal of Psychology, 35,* 605-612. Copyright © 1924 by the Board of Trustees and the University of Illinois Press.; **p. 249** Courtesy Elizabeth Loftus, University of Washington; **p. 251** Flip Chalfant/The Image Bank

Chapter 8

Opener p. 254 Michael Bonilla/Stockworks; **p. 256** (*top*) Ron Sanford/Black Star; (*bottom*) J. Messerschmidt/The Picture Cube; **Fig. 8-1** "Problem Solving" by M. Scheerer. Copyright © 1963 by Scientific American, Inc. All rights reserved.; **Fig. 8-2** Duncker, K. (1945). On problem solving. *Psychological Monographs, 58* (Whole no. 270), pp. 329-330.; **Fig. 8-3** "Problem Solving" by M. Scheerer. Copyright © 1963 by Scientific American, Inc. All rights reserved.; **Fig. 8-4** Duncker, K. (1945). On problem solving. *Psychological Monographs, 58* (Whole no. 270), pp. 329-330.; **p. 261** Diedra Laird/*The Charlotte Observer;* **p. 263** Stanley Rowin/The Picture Cube; **p. 264** M. & E. Bernheim/Woodfin Camp & Associates; **Fig. 8-5** Adapted from Werker, J. F. (1989). Becoming a native listener. *American Scientist, 77* 54-59. Reprinted by permission of *American Scientist,* Journal of Sigma Xi, the Scientific Research Society. Photos courtesy of Peter McCleod, Acadia University; **Fig. 8-7** Johnson, J. S. & Newport, E. L. (1989). Critical period effects in second language learning: the influence of maturational state on the acquisition of English as a second language. *Cognitive Psychology, 21,* 60-99.; **p. 268** (*top*) Elizabeth Crews; (*bottom*) George Ancona in Ancona, G., & Beth, M. © 1989 *The handtalk zoo.* NY: Macmillan Publishing; **p. 269** (*left*) Language Research Center, Yerkes Regional Primate Research Center; (*right*) Paul Fusco/Magnum Photos; **p. 271** From Savage-Rumbaugh, E. S., Murphy, J., Sevcik, R. A., Brakke, K. E., Williams, S. L., & Rumbaugh, D. M., with commentary by Bates, E. (1993). Language comprehension in ape and child. *Monographs of the Society for Research in Child Development, 58* (no. 233), 1-254. ; **p. 272** Elizabeth Crews/ The Image Works; **p. 273** Stephen Dunn/Allsport; **p. 274** Tony Freeman/Photo Edit; **p. 276** National Library of Medicine; **p. 277** (*left*) Lew Merrim/Monkmeyer Press Photos; (*right*) Will & Deni McIntyre/Photo Researchers, Inc.; **Fig. 8-9** Thorndike, et al. *Measurement and evaluation in psychology and education,* 5/e, © 1990, p. 364. Reprinted by permission of Prentice Hall, Upper Saddle River, New Jersey.; **p. 281** From Wiltshire, S. 1991 *Floating cities.* London: Michael Joseph, Ltd.; **Table 8-2** American Psychiatric Association: *Diagnostic and statistical manual of mental disorders, (*4th ed.). Washington DC, American Psychiatric Association, 1994.; **p. 283** Tony Mendoza/The Picture Cube; **Fig. 8-12** Bouchard, T. J., Jr. (1982). Twins—Nature's twice-told tale. In *1983 Yearbook of Science and the Future.* Chicago: Encyclopaedia Britannica. Reprinted with permission from *Britannica book of the year, 1983* © 1982 Encyclopaedia Britannica, Inc.; **Fig. 8-13** Fulker, D. W., DeFries, J. C., & Plomin, R. (1988). Genetic influence on general mental ability increases between infancy and middle childhood. *Nature, 336,* 767-769. Reprinted by permission of *Nature.* Copyright © 1988 Macmillan Magazines Limited.; **p. 288** (*left*) Jacques Chenet/Woodfin Camp & Associates; (*right*) Susan Lapides/Design Conceptions; **Fig. 8-14** Reprinted with permission of authors and publishers from: Vandenberg, S. G. & Kuse, A. R. Mental rotations, a group test of three-dimensional spacial visualization. *Perceptual and Motor Skills, 47,* 599-604, Fig. 1. Copyright © *Perceptual and Motor Skills,* 1978.

Chapter 9

Opener p. 296 Mehosh Photography; **p. 298** (*top*) Tony Brandenburg/Bruce Coleman, Inc.; (*bottom*) Bob Daemmrich/The Image Works; **p. 299** (*left*) George Ancona/International Stock Photo; (*right*) Harlow Primate Laboratory, University of Wisconsin; **Fig. 9-1** Maslow, A. H. (1970). *Motivation and personality* (2nd ed.). New York: Harper & Row. Copyright © 1970 by Abraham H. Maslow. Reprinted by permission of HarperCollins Publishers, Inc.; **Fig. 9-2** Adapted from Cannon, W. B. (1929). *Bodily changes in pain, hunger, fear, and rage.* New York: Branford.; **p. 303** (*top*) Richard Howard; (*bottom*) Richard Olsenius/Black Star; **p. 304** Kansas City Star/Sipa Press; **p. 305** Lincoln Russell/Stock, Boston; **p. 306** (*top left*) *The Garden of Love,* (*detail*) Peter Paul Rubens, The Prado, Madrid/The Bridgeman Art Library, Superstock; (*top right*) J. Baes/Photo Researchers, Inc.; (*bottom left*) Steve Chenn/Westlight; (*bottom right*) Mercury Archive/The Image Bank; **Fig. 9-4** Bray, G. A. (1969). Effect of caloric restriction on energy expenditure in obese patients. *Lancet, 2,* 397-398.; **p. 308** Joseph Neumayer/Design Conceptions; **Fig. 9-5** Adapted from Brownell, K. D., & Jeffrey, R. W. (1987). Improving long-term weight loss: Pushing the limits of treatment. *Behavior Therapy, 18,* 353-374. Copyright © 1987 Association for the Advancement of Behavior Therapy. Reprinted by permission of the publisher and the authors.; **Fig. 9-6** Dietz, W. H. Jr. & Gortmaker, S. L. (1985). Do we fatten our children at the television set? Obesity and television viewing children and adolescents. Reproduced by permission of *Pediatrics,* Vol. 75; p. 807, copyright 1985.; **p. 311** Photo by Dellenbeck. Reprinted by permission of the Kinsey Institute for Research in Sex, Gender, and Reproduction, Inc.; **Fig. 9-7** Byrne, D. (1982). Predicting human sexual behavior. In A. G. Kraut, *The G. Stanley Hall Lecture Series* (Vol. 2). Copyright © 1982 by the American Psychological Association. Reprinted by permission of the author and publisher.; **p. 317** David Kryszak/Black Star; **p. 319** Cynthia Johnson/*Time* Magazine; **p. 321** Dorothy Littel Greco/Stock, Boston; **p. 323** (*top*) The Bettmann Archive; (*bottom*) McClelland, D.C., et al. (1953). *The achievement motive.* NY:

Appleton-Century-Crofts. Reprinted by permission of Irvington Publishers, New York. ; **p. 325** The Bettman Archive; **p. 326** Fujifotos/The Image Works; **p. 327** Ted Thai/*Time* Magazine; **p. 329** Walter Hodges/Westlight

Chapter 10

Opener p. 334 Terry Shoffner; **p. 337** Bernard Gottfryd/Woodfin Camp & Associates; **Fig. 10-3** Kleinmuntz, B & Szucko, J. J. (1984). A field study of the fallibility of polygraph lie detection. *Nature, 308,* 449-450. Reprinted by permission of *Nature.* Copyright © 1984 Macmillan Journals Limited.; **p. 339** Four types of smiles, courtesy of Dr. Paul Ekman, University of California at San Fransisco.; **p. 340** (*top*) Culver Pictures; (*bottom*) Set of 6 emotions from Ekman, P., & Friesen, W. V. *Unmasking the face,* 1975, copyright Paul Ekman, 1975.; **p. 341** (*left*) Willie L. Hill, Jr./Stock, Boston; (*center*) Sally Cassidy/The Picture Cube; (*right*) Lawrence Migdale/Stock, Boston; **p. 342** Courtesy Louis Schakel; **p. 343** Michael Kausman/The New York Times Pictures; **p. 344** Courtesy of Professor Carroll Izard, University of Delaware; **p. 345** Wolfgang Kaehler; **Fig. 10-8** From Astin, et al., *The American freshman: National Norms for 91–94.* Los Angeles: Higher Education Research Institute, UCLA and Dey, E. L., et al. (1991). *The American freshman: Twenty-five year trends.* Los Angeles: Higher Education Research Institute, UCLA.; **p. 349** William Johnson/Stock, Boston; **p. 350** (*top*) Robert Deutsch/*USA Today;* (*bottom*) Sally Cassidy/The Picture Cube; **Fig. 10-13** Adapted from Joseph LeDoux, "Emotion, Memory, and the Brain," June 1994, p. 56. Copyright © 1994 by Scientific American, Inc. All rights reserved.; **p. 356** (*left*) Andy Levin/Photo Researchers, Inc.; (*right*) Arlene Collins/Monkmeyer Press Photo Service; **p. 359** Michael Salas/The Image Bank; **Fig. 10-17** Weiss, J. M. (1977). Psychological and behavioral influences on gastrointestinal lesions in animal models. From: *Psychopathology: Experimental models* by Maser & Seligman. Copyright © 1977 by Martin E.P. Seligman & Jack Maser. Used with permission of W.H. Freeman and Company.; **p. 363** Lennart Nilsson/Boehringer Ingelheim International GmbH; **p. 365** Paul Fusco/Magnum Photos; **Fig. 10-20** Adapted from McCann, I. L. & Holmes, D. S. (1984). Influence of aerobic exercise on depression. *Journal of Personality and Social Psychology, 46,* 1142-1147. Copyright © 1984 by the American Psychological Association. Adapted by permission of the authors.; **p. 369** Dan McCoy/Rainbow; **p. 370** Steve Liss/*Time* Magazine; **Fig. 10-22** From *Treating type A behavior and your heart* by Meyer Friedman & Diane Ulmer. Copyright © 1984 by Meyer Friedman. Reprinted by permission of Alfred A. Knopf, Inc.; **p. 372** Bob Krist/Black Star

Chapter 11

Opener p. 376 Paula Pertile; **p. 378** Culver Pictures; **Fig. 379** Adapted from Freud, S. (1933). *New introductory lectures on psychoanalysis.* New York: Carlton House, p. 111.; **p. 381** (*left*) Rick Friedman/Black Star; (*right*) Harlow Primate Lab, University of Wisconsin; **p. 382** Edmund Engelman; **p. 383** (*left*) National Library of Medicine; (*center*) The Bettman Archive; (*right*) Archives of the History of American Psychology; **p. 384** (*top and bottom*) Lew Merrim/Monkmeyer Press Photos; **p. 388** AP/Wide World Photos; **Fig. 11-2** Eysenck, S. B. G. & Eysenck, H. J. (1963). The validity of questionnaire and rating assessments of extraversion and neuroticism, and their factorial stability. *British Journal of Psychology, 54,* 51-62, Fig. 1.; **Table 11-1** Adapted from McCrae, R. & Costa, P. T. Jr. (1986). Clinical assessment can benefit from recent advances in personality psychology. *American Psychologist, 41,* 1002. Copyright © 1986 American Psychological Association. Adapted by permission.; **p. 389** Peter Southwick/Stock, Boston; **Fig. 11-3** Adapted from Butcher, J. N. (1990). *The MMPI-2 in psychological treatment.* Figures 1-3 and 1-4, pp. 13-14. New York: Oxford University Press.; **p. 394** Ted Polumbaum/*Life* Magazine © 1968 Time Warner Inc.; **p. 395** (*top*) Mark Antman/The Image Works; (*bottom*) Sybil Shackman/Monkmeyer Press Photos; **p. 399** D. Cannon/Allsport USA; **Fig. 11-4** Adapted from Bandura, A. (1978). The self-system in reciprocal determinism. *American Psychologist, 33,* 344-358. Copyright © 1978 by the American Psychological Association. Adapted by permission of the author.; **p. 402** Stephen Wade/Allsport USA; **p. 404** Joe McNally; **p. 408** AP/Wide World Photos

Chapter 12

Opener p. 412 John Paul Genzo; **p. 414** Tony Ray Jones/Magnum Photos; **p. 415** J. Otis Wheelock/Courtesy of Department of Library Services, American Musuem of Natural History; **Fig. 12-2** Roper report 84-3, February 11-25, 1984. *Public Opinion,* August/September, 25. Reprinted with permission of American Enterprise Institute for Public Policy Research, Washington, D. C.; **Table 12-1** Adapted from Rapoport, J. L. (1989, March). The biology of obsessions and compulsions. *Scientific American,* pp. 83-89.; **p. 422** (*top*) John Coletti/Stock, Boston; (*bottom*) Baxter, L. R., et al. © 1987 Local cerebral glucose metabolic rates in obsessive-compulsive disorder. *Archives of General Psychology, 44* (3), 211-218. American Medical Association; **p. 424** AP/Wide World Photos; **p. 430** (*top*) AP/Wide World Photos; (*bottom*) Stephen P. Allen/Gamma Liaison; **p. 431** Courtesy Drs. Lewis Baxter & Michael E. Phelps/UCLA School of Medicine; **Fig. 12-8** Adapted from Lewinsohn, P. M., et al. (1985). An integrative theory of depression. In S. Reiss and R. Bootzin (Eds.), *Theoretical issues in behavior therapy.* Orlando, FL: Academic Press.; **p. 435** (*left*) Berthold, L., *Untitled.* The Prinzhorn Collection, University of Heidelberg; (*right*) August Natterer, *Witch's Head.* The Prinzhorn Collection, University of Heidelberg. Photos: Krannert Museum, University of Illinois at Urbana-Champaign; **Fig. 12-9** From: *Schizophrenia genesis* by Gottesman. Copyright © 1991 by Irving I. Gottesman. Used with permission of W.H. Freeman and Company.; **p. 439** (*top*) NSC from Suddath, Richard L., et al. (1990) Anatomical abnormalities in the brains of monozygotic twins discordant for schizophrenia. *The New England Journal of Medicine, 322,* 12. © 1990 Massachusetts Medical Society. Photo courtesy Daniel R. Weinberger, M.D., NIH-NIMH; (*bottom*) Courtesy Genain Family; **Fig. 12-10** Adapted from Magnusson, D. (1990). Personality research—challenges for the future. *European Journal of Personality, 4,* 1-17. Copyright © 1990, reprinted by permission of John Wiley & Sons, Ltd.; **p. 442** Comstock

Chapter 13

Opener p. 448 Paul Schulenburg/Stockworks; **p. 449** Culver Pictures; **p. 450** (*left*) The Granger Collection; (*right*) The Bettmann Archive; **p. 451** Paul Meredith/Tony Stone Images; **p. 452** Steve Goldberg/Monkmeyer Press Photos; **p. 453** Michael Rougier/*Life* Magazine, © Time Warner, Inc; **Fig. 13-1** Gilling, D. & Brightwell, R. (1982). *The human brain.* New York: Facts on File. Reprinted by permission of Little, Brown & Co. (UK).; **Fig. 13-5** Rabin, A. S., et al. (1986). Aggregate outcome and follow-up results following self-control therapy for depression. Paper presented at the American Psychological Association convention.; **p. 462** Stacy Pick/Stock, Boston; **Fig. 13-7** Adapted from Smith, M. L., et al. (1980). *The benefits of psychotherapy.* Baltimore, MD: Johns Hopkins University Press, p.88. Reprinted by permission of Johns Hopkins University Press.; **p. 468** Mark Antman/The Image Works; **p. 471** Lee Snider/The Image Works; **p. 472** Lynn Johnson/Black Star; **p. 473** James Wilson/Woodfin Camp & Associates

Chapter 14

Opener p. 478 Elsa Warnick/Stockworks; **p. 482** The Bettman Archive; **p. 483** Thomas Hopker/Magnum Photos; **p. 485** William Vandivert/*Scientific American*; **p.** **487** Courtesy of CUNY Graduate School and University Center; **Fig. 14-3** Milgram, S. (1974). *Obedience to authority.* New York: Harper & Row Publishers, Inc. Copyright © 1974 by Stanley Milgram. Reprinted by permission of HarperCollins Publishers.; **p. 489** AP/Wide World Photos; **p. 490** Focus on Sports; **Fig. 14-4** Reprinted with permission from Myers, D. G. & Bishop, G. D. (1970). Discussion effects on racial attitudes. *Science, 169,* 778-779. Copyright © 1970 American Association for the Advancement of Science.; **p. 493** Margaret Bourke-White/*Life* Magazine © 1946 Time Warner, Inc.; **p. 494** Fujifotos/The Image Works; **p. 495** Gary Rogers/The Image Bank; **Fig. 14-5** Astin, et al. *The American freshman: National norms for 91–94.* Los Angeles: Higher Education Research Institute, UCLA and Dey, E. L., et al. (1991). *The American freshman: Twenty-five year trends.* Los Angeles: Higher Education Research Institute, UCLA.; **Fig. 14-6** Niemi, et al., *Trends in public opinion* (Greenwood Press, Westport, CT, 1989). Reprinted with permission.; Smith, T.W. (1994). Personal correspondence. Data from General Social Survey, National Opinion Research Center, University of Chicago.; **p. 500** Michael S. Yamashita/Woodfin Camp & Associates; **p. 502** Presse-Sports; **p. 503** Dion Ogust/The Image Works; **Fig. 14-7** Anderson, C. A. & Anderson, D. C. (1984). Ambient temperature and violent crime: Tests of the linear and curvilinear hypotheses. *Journal of Personality and Social Psychology, 46,* 91-97. Copyright © 1984 American Psychological Association. Reprinted by permission of the author.; **Fig. 14-8** Adapted from Malamuth, N. M. (1989). Sexually violent media, thought patterns, and anti-social behavior, in G. Comstock (Ed.), *Public communication and behavior, Vol. 2.* San Diego, CA: Academic Press.; **p. 510** Keith Gosse/The Evening Telegram; **p. 512** (*top*) Rex USA; (*bottom*) Cynthia Johnson/Gamma Liaison; **p. 513** (*left*) Margaret Gowan/Tony Stone Images; (*center*) Victor Englebert/Photo Researchers, Inc.; (*right*) John P. Kelly/The Image Bank; **Fig. 14-10** Buss, D. (1994). *The evolution of desire.* New York: BasicBooks. Copyright © 1994 by David M. Buss. Reprinted by permission of BasicBooks, a division of HarperCollins Publishers, Inc.; **p. 516** (*left*) Barros & Barros/The Image Bank; (*right*) Martin Hooper/The Image Bank; **Fig. 14-11** Darley J. M. & Latane, B. (1968b, December). When will people help in a crisis? *Psychology Today,* 54-57, 70-71. Reprinted with permission from *Psychology Today* Magazine. Copyright © 1968 (Sussex Publishers, Inc.).; **Fig. 14-12** Darley J. M. & Latane, B. (1968a). Bystander intervention in emergencies: Diffusion of responsibility. *Journal of Personality and Social Psychology, 8,* 377-383. Copyright © 1968 by the American Psychological Association. Reprinted by permission.; **p. 518** (*top*) Akos Szilvasi/Stock, Boston; (*bottom*) Joel Gordon; **p. 519** Brian A. Potts; **p. 520** Bob Daemmrich/Stock, Boston

Name Index

Aas, H., 190
Abbey, A., 182, 316, 503
Abelson, R. P., 443
Abrahams, D., 512
Abrams, D., 405
Abrams, D. B., 183
Abramson, L. Y., 431, 432
Acton, W., 414
Adams, E. M., 15
Adams, M. J., 231, 232
Adelmann, P. K., 105
Ader, R., 366
Adlaf, E. M., 188
Adler, A., 383, 393, 409
Adler, L., 437
Adler, N. E., 359
Aeschylus, 516
Affleck, G., 347
Agyei, Y., 320
Aiello, J. R., 490
Ainsworth, M. D. S., 82, 83
Aitken, D. H., 75
Albee, G. W., 475
Albers, J., 130
Alcock, J. E., 157, 241
Aldrich, M. S., 170
Aldridge-Morris, R., 425
Alexander, C. N., 175, 370
Alexander the Great, 349, 400
Alkon, D. L., 236
Allard, F., 230
Allen, K. F., 190
Allen, L. S., 319
Allen, M., 94
Allen, W., 170, 444, 452
Allman, A. L., 347
Alloy, L. B., 431
Allport, G. W., 387, 388, 393, 395, 498, 387
Alwin, D. F., 85, 112
Amabile, T. M., 284, 396
Amador, M., 244
Amaral, D. G., 236
Ambady, N., 392
Ames, A., 147
Ames, M. A., 320

Anda, R., 363
Andersen, B. L., 315, 364
Anderson, C. A., 263, 503
Anderson, D. C., 503
Anderson, D. R., 368
Anderson, E. A., 350
Anderson, E. R., 84
Anderson, J. R., 240
Anderson, R. D., 182
Anderson, V. E., 438
Andreason, N. C., 437
Angoff, W. H., 291
Anisman, H., 364
Antoni, M. H., 364
Antonucci, T. C., 105
Antony, M. M., 421
Antrobus, J., 173
Applebaum, S. L., 99
Appleton, J., 257
Archer, D., 339
Archer, P., 75
Arcus, D. M., 82
Argeriou, M., 470
Aries, E., 327
Aristotle, 196, 512
Arndt, S., 437
Arnold, R. B., 248
Aron, A., 515
Aronson, V., 512
Arthur, M. B., 328
Asch, S. E., 485, 486, 489
Aserinksy, E., 166
Aserinsky, A., 166
Ashbery, J., 435
Ashbrook, P. W., 241
Ashmore, R. D., 513
Aslan, C., 168
Astin, A. W., 188, 316, 347, 495
Atkinson, J., 323
Atkinson, R., 85, 95
Atlas, S., 437
Atwell, R. H., 183
Averill, J. R., 338, 344, 353
Avery, R. D., 289
Ax, A. F., 338

Axel, R., 137
Azuma, H., 86

Babad, E., 339
Babkoff, H., 169
Bach, J. S., 207
Bachevalier, J., 101
Bachman, J. G., 93, 185, 188, 189, 190
Backus, J., 132
Bacon, F., 258, 260
Baddeley, A. D., 227, 241
Baer, M. F., 236
Baguma, P., 305
Bahrick, H. P., 227, 234, 235, 240
Bahrick, P. O., 240
Bailey, J. M., 317, 319, 320
Baillargeon, R., 77
Bain, J., 313
Bairagi, R., 498
Baker, E. L., 178
Baldessarini, R. J., 430
Baldwin, E., 27
Ball, W., 142
Baltes, P. B., 102
Banaji, M. R., 164, 272
Bandura, A., 218, 219, 402, 408, 456
Bangert-Drowns, R. L., 215
Banton, H. G., 501
Barbaree, H. E., 506
Barber, T. X., 187
Bard, B., 84, 502
Bard, P., 352, 353, 374
Barefoot, J. C., 372
Barger, S. D., 373
Barinaga, M., 308
Barker, S. L., 467
Barlow, D. H., 421
Barnett, R., 106
Barnum, P. T., 406, 407
Baron, R. A., 215, 346
Barrett, L. C., 404
Barry, D., 134
Baruch, G. K., 106
Bass, E., 248

Bass, L. E., 189
Bates, E., 271
Bauer, C. R., 74
Baum, A., 358, 361
Baumann, L. J., 317
Baumeister, R. F., 87, 262, 304, 328, 346, 396, 398
Baumgardner, A. H., 93, 396
Baumrind, D., 321
Bavry, J. L., 492
Baxter, L., 431
Beach, S. R., 512
Beaman, A. L., 514
Bearden, W. O., 262
Beardsley, L. M., 416
Beauchamp, G. K., 303
Beauvais, F., 190
Beck, A. J., 504
Beck, A. T., 427, 428, 433, 460, 461, 463, 476
Becker, I. M., 205
Becker, S. E., 432
Beckham, E., 466
Beecher, H. W., 272
Begg, I., 120
Beitman, B. D., 450
Bell, A. P., 318, 319
Bellugi, U., 62
Beloff, J., 157
Belsher, G., 429
Belsky, J., 105
Bem, D. J., 157
Bem, S. L., 86
Benassi, V. A., 403
Bennett, E. L., 74
Bennett, R., 507
Benson, H., 175, 370
Benson, P. L., 79, 110, 94, 110
Bentler, P. M., 112, 187
Bergeman, C. S., 111
Bergin, A.
Bergin, A. E., 325, 468, 469
Bergsholm, P., 473
Berk, L. E., 79
Berkowitz, L., 344, 503
Berlin, F. S., 313
Berman, E. R., 307
Berman, M., 186, 502
Berman, W. H., 370
Berndt, T. J., 94
Bernieri, F., 109, 339
Berra, Y., 13
Berry, D. S., 201
Berry, J. W., 80, 316, 358, 495, 499
Berscheid, E., 329, 493, 513, 516
Bertenthal, B. I., 142, 421
Bertrand, L. D., 176
Besch, N. F., 313
Best, D. L., 327
Betz, A. L., 120
Betz, B., 521
Bever, T. G., 270
Beyer, L., 498
Beyerstein, B., 406
Beyerstein, D., 406
Bhatnagar, S., 75
Bhatt, R. S., 207
Bianchi, K., 424, 425
Biber, H., 175
Bickman, L., 358
Biko, S., 481
Binet, A., 276, 277, 284, 291, 292, 293
Bintie, A., 423
Bird, L., 16
Birrell, P., 500

Bishop, G. D., 257, 492
Bjork, R. A., 231, 388
Bjorklund, D. F., 79
Black, J., 236
Blackburn, T. C., 494
Blackman, D., 26
Blackmore, S., 186
Blackstone, T., 493
Blair, R., 71
Blampied, N. M., 481
Blanchard, E. B., 456
Blick, K. A., 172
Block, J., 81, 395
Block, J. H., 395
Blom, J. M. C., 366
Bloom, B. S., 324
Bloom, F. E., 38
Bloom, J. R., 365
Bloomel, J. M., 490
Blyth, D. A., 89
Bobrow, D., 319
Bodamer, M., 271
Bodenhausen, G. V., 521
Boechler, M., 502
Bogen, J., 59
Bolger, N., 347
Bolt, R., 483
Bonaparte, N., 349, 400
Bond, C. F., Jr., 183, 227
Bond, M. H., 85
Bond, R., 487
Bonner, E., 261
Bookbinder, M., 120
Booth, D. A., 302
Bootzin, R. R., 172, 227
Borduin, C. M., 462
Boreham, J., 184
Borgida, E., 263
Boring, E. G., 150
Bornstein, M. H., 82, 86
Bornstein, R. F., 242, 473, 512
Bothwell, R. K., 244, 500
Bouchard, T., 108
Bouchard, T. J., Jr., 109, 110, 285, 286, 422
Bower, G. H., 228, 229, 230, 240, 241
Bowers, K. S., 176, 180
Bowers, T. G., 467
Bowlby, J., 82
Bowman, E. S., 426
Box, C., 237
Boyatzis, C. J., 505
Boynton, R. M., 129
Bradbury, T. N., 480-481
Braden, J. P., 289
Bradley, D. R., 139
Bradney, N., 95
Brakke, K. E., 271
Brambilla, D. J., 98
Brannon, L. A., 321
Bransford, J. D., 228
Braskamp, L. A., 326
Bray, D. W., 407
Bray, G. A., 307
Breakey, W. R., 470
Brehm, J. W., 493
Brehm, S., 493
Breinlinger, K., 77
Breland, K., 214
Breland, M., 214
Brennan, P. A., 441
Brenner, M., 227
Bresnick, B., 75
Brett, E., 360
Brewer, W. F., 228

Brewin, C. F., 459
Brick, J., 503
Brickman, P., 347
Brickson, M., 101
Bridges, A., 429
Briere, J., 244
Briggs, K., 388
Brigham, J. C., 244, 500
Bright, I., 462
Brightwell, R., 456
Bril, B., 75
Brislin, R., 399, 416
Broca, P., 55
Brocato, R. M., 490
Brock, T. C., 321
Brockner, J., 396
Brody, N., 467
Brodzinsky, D. M., 490
Broman, C. L., 432
Brontë, E., 427
Brooks, K., 244
Brooks-Gunn, J., 88, 94, 96
Brothers, J., 311
Brown, C., 347
Brown, C. H., 437
Brown, D. R., 395
Brown, E. L., 133
Brown, G. W., 468
Brown, J. D., 368, 396, 398
Brown, R., 224, 272
Brown, T. A., 421
Brownell, K. D., 307, 308, 309
Browning, C., 489
Brownmiller, S., 315
Brozek, J., 301
Bruck, M., 244, 245
Brucker, B. S., 369
Bruun, S. E., 491
Bryant, J., 507
Buchan, J., 211
Buchsbaum, M. S., 237
Buck, L., 137
Bucy, P., 49
Buddha, 344
Bugelski, B. R., 230
Bugental, D. B., 339
Bukowski, C., 359
Bull, R., 248
Bullough, V., 317
Bumstead, C. H., 493
Buquet, R., 172
Burger, J. M., 327, 405
Burgess, A. W., 507
Burish, T. G., 203
Burke, J. D., 420
Burke, K. C., 420
Burkhart, B. R., 506
Burks, N., 516
Burley, S. K., 308
Burnam, A., 420
Burnett, N., 230
Burns, D. D., 431
Burns, G., 99
Burns, L., 405
Burrell, L., 500
Burros, M., 309
Burson, J., 135
Busceme, S., 493
Bush, G., 152, 481, 521
Bushman, B. J., 502
Buss, A. H., 95, 392
Buss, B. M., 25
Buss, D., 514
Butcher, J. N., 391, 416

Butler, A. C., 432
Butler, R. A., 299
Buunk, B. P., 516
Byck, R., 186
Byham, W. C., 407
Byne, W., 320
Byrne, D., 200, 313, 315, 514
Byrne, R. W., 14, 269
Byrnes, G., 440

Cacioppo, J. T., 339, 364
Cade, J., 473
Cadwallader, L. B., 187
Caesar, 349
Califf, R. M., 372
Callies, A. L., 364, 372
Cameron, P., 175
Campbell, D. T., 348, 400
Campbell, J., 134
Campbell, L., 260
Campbell, P. A., 109
Campbell, S., 150
Campbell, S. S., 170
Campbell, W. K., 241
Campos, J. J., 82, 142, 421
Cannon, T. D., 437
Cannon, W., 352, 353, 357
Cannon, W. B., 301, 357, 367, 374
Canseco, J., 349
Cantor, N., 405
Cantril, H., 493
Carducci, B. J., 165, 515
Carew, T. J., 236
Carey, G., 422
Carey, M. P., 203
Carli, L. L., 500
Carlson, M., 518
Carlson, R., 407
Carlson, R. B., 203
Carlson, S., 406
Carnevale, P. J. D., 513
Carpenter, B. N., 24
Carpenter, W. T., 437
Carr, J., 428
Carr, T. H., 57
Carr, T. S., 404
Carrington, P. I., 513
Carroll, L., 120
Carson, R. C., 416
Carstenson, L. L., 485
Cartwright, R. D., 167
Carver, C. S., 360
Casanova, M. F., 439
Case, N., 372
Case, R. B., 372
Casey, R. J., 513
Cash, T., 513
Caskey, N. H., 405
Caspersen, C. J., 368
Caspi, A., 89
Caspy, T., 169
Cassel, J. F., 203
Castillo, S., 183
Cato, 344
Cattell, R. B., 102
Cavalli-Sforza, L., 289
Ceci, S. J., 244, 245, 282
Centerwall, B. S., 505
Cerella, J., 99
Chachere, J. G., 505
Chait, B. T., 308
Chamberlain, P., 212, 504
Chan, A., 340

Chandler, H. M., 175, 370
Charles, R., 262
Charlin, V., 518
Chartrand, L., 273
Chassin, L., 190
Chaves, J. F., 179
Check, J. V. P., 507
Chee, M., 364
Cheek, J. M., 85, 433
Chekhov, 427
Cherfas, J., 27
Chermack, S. T., 502
Chess, S., 82, 112
Chesterton, G. K., 86
Chi, M. T. H., 234
Childs, B., 290, 437
Chimpsky, N., 12
Chimsky, N., 270
Chmiel, J., 365
Chomsky, N., 264, 266, 267, 268, 275, 293
Christensen, A., 468
Christianson, S. A., 249
Christie, A., 7, 25
Christison, G. W., 439
Christophersen, E. R., 457
Churchill, W., 433
Chwalisz, K., 347
Cialdini, R. B., 483, 499
Cicero, 223, 290, 513
Cizadlo, T., 437
Clark, M. C., 229, 230
Clark, R. D., III, 316
Clarke, P. R. F., 173
Claudius, 473
Clayton, P., 358
Clingempeel, W. G., 84
Clinton, B., 96
Clinton, H. R., 507
Clore, G. L., 346
Close, F., 156
Clum, G. A., 467
Coan, D. J., 249
Coates, D., 347
Coe, W. C., 176, 180
Coffey, C. E., 430, 473
Cohen, D. G., 173
Cohen, J., 238
Cohen, N., 366
Cohen, N. J., 224, 236
Cohen, P. A., 215
Cohen, S., 363, 364, 372
Cohen, S. J., 350
Cohen, S. L., 308
Coile, C., 26
Coleman, J. C., 88, 416
Coleman, L. M., 105
Coleman, M., 105
Coleman, P. D., 100
Collings, V. B., 147, 148
Collins, B., 95, 189
Collins, J. F., 466
Collins, J. L., 95, 189
Collins, K., 341
Colombo, J., 82
Colon, E. A., 364, 372
Comrey, A. L., 389
Confucius, 24, 262
Conklin, C., 340
Convit, A., 238
Conway, M., 247
Cook, E. W., III, 203
Cook, M., 217
Coon, P. M., 426
Coons, D. J., 444

Cooper, H., 105
Cooper, H. M., 403, 462
Cooper, M. L., 359
Cooper, W. H., 323
Copeland, P. M., 304
Corbett, S. W., 302
Coren, S., 64
Corina, D. P., 62
Cork, L. C., 101
Corley, R., 82
Cosby, P. C., 515
Costa, P. T., Jr., 103, 104, 112, 392
Costello, C. G., 429
Costello, L., 434
Courage, M. L., 74
Courtney, J. G., 364
Cousins, N., 398
Covington, M. V., 190
Cowan, G., 506
Cowan, N., 233, 234
Cowan, T., 234
Cowart, B. J., 136
Cox, D. S., 364
Coyne, J. C., 432
Cozzarelli, C., 359
Craig, M. E., 506
Craik, F. I. M., 228
Crandall, C. S., 304
Crandall, J. E., 400
Cranston, J., 186
Criqui, M. H., 372
Crocker, J., 499
Crofton, C., 514
Crohan, S. F., 105
Cromwell, T., 483
Crook, T. H., 100
Crosby, F., 531
Crowell, J. A., 82
Crowley, M., 518
Csikszentmihalyi, M., 94, 259, 350
Cumming, J. D., 467
Cuniff, M., 342
Cunnick, J. E., 363
Cureton, K. J., 309
Curtis, R. C., 515
Cutler, B. L., 244
Czyzewska, M., 385

D'Atri, D. A., 361
D'Eon, J. L., 179
Dabbs, J. M., Jr., 313, 502, 518
Dallenbach, K. M., 246
Damasio, A. R., 55
Damasio, H., 55
Dante, 103
Darley, J. M., 517
Darow, C. N., 103
Darrach, B., 441
Darwin, C., 135, 202, 203, 206, 298, 331, 341, 342, 345
Dasen, P. R., 80, 316, 495, 499
Davenport, A., 183
Davey, G. C. L., 203
David, H. P., 359
Davidson, R. J., 338, 340, 342, 430
Davies, D. R., 104
Davies, J. L., 175, 370
Davis, L., 248
Dawes, R. M., 385, 510
Dawood, M. Y., 313
Dean, G. A., 406
Dean, J., 224, 225, 228, 241, 244
Deardorff, J., 304

Deary, I. J., 392
de Beauvoir, S., 28
DeBoer, J., 297
de Boysson-Bardies, B., 265
Deci, E. L., 324, 325
de Cuevas, J., 266
Deffenbacher, K., 133
Deffenbacher, K. A., 244
DeFries, J., 82
DeFries, J. C., 286
de Goya, F., 172
de Jong-Gierveld, J., 433
de Leon, M. J., 238
Delgado, J. M. R., 53
DeLoache, J., 78
DeLongis, A., 347
Dement, W. C., 166, 167, 169, 170, 172
De Meuse, K. P., 328
de Montaigne, M., 391
Dempster, F. N., 227
Dennett, D. C., 202, 425
Denton, K., 183
Dermer, M., 350, 512, 515
DeRubeis, R. J., 461
Dery, G. K., 88
DeSanti, S., 238
Descartes, 271
Deutsch, G., 62
Deutsch, J. A., 51
Deutsch, M., 215
de Verdier, M. G., 364
Dewhirst, B., 179
Dey, E. L., 347, 495, 498
Diaconis, P., 16
Diacoyanni-Tarlatzis, I., 340
Diamond, J., 108, 264
Diamond, M. C., 74
Diamond, R., 320
DiBiasi, P., 109
Dickinson, E., 433
Diener, E., 347, 349, 350, 397
Dienst, E. R., 492
Dietz, W. H., 306
Dietz, W. H., Jr., 309
DiLalla, L. F., 441
Dillard, A., 243
Dillard, J. P., 432
DiMatteo, M. R., 339
Dindia, K., 94
Dinges, N. G., 272
Dion, K. K., 399
Dion, K. L., 327, 399
Disterhoft, J. F., 236
Dix, D., 301, 449
Dixon, B., 364
Djahed, B., 187
Djang, W. T., 430
Dobson, K. S., 467
Docherty, J. P., 466
Dodds, J., 75
Dohrenwend, B., 358
Dohrenwend, B. P., 429, 443
Dolan, R., 466
Dolezal, H., 150
Domjan, M., 200
Donaldson, M., 78
Donders, K., 243
Donnerstein, E., 505, 506
Doolittle, B., 118
Dornhoff, W., 172
Dostoevsky, F., 427
Doty, R. L., 99
Douglas, J. E., 507
Dovidio, J. F., 519

Dowdall, G., 183
Dowling, H., 307
Downs, A. C., 88
Doyle, A. C., 49, 123, 234
Doyle, W. J., 364
Draguns, J. G., 413, 416, 422, 432
Drake, T., 196
Dratt, L. M., 190
Drenick, E. J., 308
Drucker, P. F., 386
Druckman, D., 156, 274, 388
Druyan, A., 269
Dubbert, P. M., 369
DuBreuil, S. C., 179
Duchess of Windsor, 304
Duclos, S. E., 342
Duensing, S., 244
Dufour, C. L., 403
Duggan, J. P., 302
Duke, P., 430
Dumais, S. T., 139
Duncan, B. L., 345, 497
Duncan, G. J., 260
Duncker, K., 258, 260
Dunn, J., 110
Dunnett, S. B., 58
Dunning, D., 261
Durand, C., 265
Durm, M. W., 155
Dutton, D. G., 515
Dweck, C. S., 324
Dworkin, R. H., 471

Eagles, J. M., 437
Eagleton, T., 443
Eagly, A. H., 327, 328, 513, 518
Eaker, E., 363
Eastwood, C., 508
Eaves, L. J., 189, 422, 432
Ebbesen, E. B., 234, 345
Ebbinghaus, H., 227, 229, 232, 234, 235, 239, 246, 247
Eccles, J. S., 290
Eckensberger, L. H., 91
Eckert, E. D., 422
Edelman, R., 345
Edkenazi, J., 21
Edwards, C. P., 85, 91
Edwards, J., 105
Edwards, K. J., 457
Edwards, M., 155
Efe, 14
Egeland, J. A., 430
Ehrhardt, J. C., 437
Ehrlichman, H., 138
Eibl-Eibesfeldt, I., 341
Eich, E., 172
Eich, J. E., 183
Eichenbaum, H., 236
Eichmann, A., 489
Eisen, S. A., 360
Eisenberg, N., 94
Ekman, P., 338, 339, 340, 341, 342, 343
Ekstrand, B. R., 246
El Greco, 427
Eliot, C., 30
Eliot, T. S., 255
Elkin, I., 466
Elkind, D., 90
Eller, M., 317
Elliot, R., 467
Elliott, E. S., 324

Ellis, A., 205, 458, 459, 460, 463, 468, 469, 476
Ellis, H. C., 241
Ellis, L., 320
Emde, R. N., 82
Emerson, R. W., 413
Emery, G., 460
Emmons, C-A., 317
Emmons, S., 440
Empson, J. A. C., 173
Endler, N. S., 473
Engen, T., 138
Epstein, S., 338, 392
Erber, R., 459
Erdelyi, M. H., 385
Erickson, G. A., 432
Erikson, E., 92, 84, 93, 104, 107, 111, 114
Eron, L. D., 505
Erwin, R., 437
Eshleman, S., 317
Esser, J. K., 492
Evahn, C., 290
Evans, C. R., 327
Evans, E. F., 132
Evans, F. J., 178
Evans, G. W., 371
Evans, R. I., 190
Evans, S. M., 184
Everette, D., 471
Everly, S., 372
Exner, J. E., Jr., 385
Eyal, N., 429
Eysenck, H. J., 371, 389, 393, 465, 466, 470, 501
Eysenck, M. W., 403
Eysenck, S. B. G., 389, 393

Faber, N., 282
Fagan, J. F., III, 290
Fairchild, H., 505
Falbo, T., 324
Falck, A., 313
Fantz, R. L., 72
Faraone, S. V., 430
Farbstein, J., 404
Farina, A., 415, 443, 463
Farmer-Dougan, V. A., 208
Farr, S., 414
Farrell, P. A., 39
Farrington, D. P., 440
Faulkner, W., 377, 391, 392
Faulstich, M. E., 369
Fava, M., 304
Fazenda, L., 340
Fazio, R. H., 482
Feay, D. T., 501
Feder, H. H., 313
Feeney, D., 26
Feeney, J. A., 84
Fehr, B., 256
Fein, R., 371
Feingold, A., 513
Feldman, M., 84, 502
Fennema, E., 290
Fenton, W. S., 436
Ferguson, T. J., 506
Fernandez, E., 135
Ferris, S. H., 238
Feshbach, N. D., 505
Festinger, L., 484
Feynman, R., 282
Fichter, M. M., 304
Fiedler, F. E., 327
Field, T. M., 73, 74
Fiester, S. J., 466

Figiel, G. S., 430
Fincham, F. D., 480, 481
Findley, M. J., 403
Fineberg, H. V., 317
Finkelhor, D., 84, 248
Finucci, J. M., 290
Fireman, P., 364
Firl, A., Jr., 58
First, M. B., 423
Fischer, G. W., 262
Fischer, P. J., 470
Fischhoff, B., 8, 261, 262
Fisher, H. E., 104
Fisher, H. T., 455
Fisher, J. D., 463
Fisher, R. P., 244
Fisher, S., 473
Fitness, J., 481
Fitzgerald, E. F., 361
Flannery, D. J., 291
Flaum, M., 437
Fleming, I., 358, 361
Fleming, J. H., 340
Fletcher, G. J. O., 247, 480-481
Fletcher, M. A., 364
Floderus-Myrhed, B., 108
Flood, D. G., 100
Flynn, H. A., 432
Foa, E. B., 456
Foerster, O., 53
Follingstad, D. R., 506
Fong, G. T., 22, 183
Fontana, A., 360
Ford, H., 385
Foreyt, J. P., 309
Forgas, J. P., 241
Forgays, D. G., 310
Forrestal, J., 414
Forsyth, D. R., 93, 404
Foster, C., 365
Fouts, R. S., 271
Fowler, M. J., 246
Fowler, R. C., 428
Fowler, R. D., 420
Fowles, D. C., 436
Fox, J. L., 54
Fox, N. E., 83
Fox, R., 213
Fozard, J. L., 99
Francisco, J. T., 501
Frank, A., 93
Frank, J. D., 449, 467, 468
Frank, M. G., 18, 19, 20
Frank, R., 55
Frank, S. J., 95
Frankel, A., 390, 433
Frankenburg, W., 75
Frantz, D. H., 22
Fraser, S. C., 482
Frazier, W., 404
Fredrickson, B. L., 135
Freedman, J. L., 106, 482, 490, 505
Freeman, W. J., 128
Freud, S., 2, 11, 104, 106, 107, 172, 173, 174,
  235, 247, 250, 377, 378, 379, 380, 381, 382,
  383, 384, 385, 386, 387, 393, 399, 409, 418,
  419, 421, 423, 424, 430, 450, 451, 501
Frey, K., 342
Friberg, L., 109
Friedman, H. S., 372
Friedman, J. M., 308
Friedman, M., 361, 362, 367, 370, 371
Frieman, J., 234
Friesen, M. V., 343

Friesen, W. V., 338, 340, 342
Frieze, I. H., 385
Frijda, N. H., 340
Fritsch, G., 52
Fromkin, V., 266
Frost, R., 470
Fulero, S., 500
Fulker, D. W., 82, 286, 501
Fuller, M. J., 88
Fuller, T., 344
Fulton, R., 493
Funder, D. C., 91, 392
Funk, S. C., 467
Furnham, A., 177, 305, 320, 406, 481
Furr, S. R., 428
Furstenberg, F., 210
Furstenberg, F. F., Jr., 96, 321
Futrell, D., 328

Gabbard, G. O., 444
Gabbay, F. H., 82
Gabora, N. J., 179
Gaertner, S. L., 519
Gaeth, G. J., 262
Gaft, J. G., 492
Gage, P., 55
Gagnon, J. H., 311, 317, 316, 506
Gajiwala, K. S., 308
Galaburda, A. M., 55
Galambos, N. L., 95
Galanter, E., 119
Gall, F., 35
Gallagher, D., 347
Galley, D. J., 242
Gallup, G., Jr., 26
Gallup, G. H., 510
Gallup, G. H., Jr., 153, 462
Galperin, C. Z., 86
Galton, F., 70
Gandhi, I., 519
Gandhi, M., 27, 218, 493
Gangestad, S. W., 516
Ganong, L. H., 105
Garbarino, J., 360
Garcia, J., 202, 203, 206, 212
Garcia, R., 74
Gardner, B. I., 269
Gardner, H., 281, 282, 284
Gardner, M., 155
Gardner, R., 169
Gardner, R. A., 269
Garfield, C., 274
Garner, D. M., 304, 308
Garner, W. R., 291
Garnets, L., 317
Gash, D. M., 58
Gates, W. K., 39
Gauguelin, M., 406
Gawin, F. H., 185
Gazzaniga, M. S., 59, 60, 61
Gebhard, P., 311
Geen, R. G., 323, 345, 505
Geenens, D., 430
Geiselman, R. E., 244
Geiser, C., 440
Geist, T., 129
Geiwitz, J., 101, 102
Geldard, F. A., 129
Geller, D., 489
Gelles, R. J., 211
Gelman, D., 341
Gelman, R., 78
Gelman, S. A., 77

Genain, H., 439
Genain, I., 439
Genain, M., 439
Genain, N., 439
Genesee, F., 273
Genovese, K., 516, 517
Gent, J. F., 135
George, A. E., 238
Gerard, R. W., 236
Gerbner, G., 189, 444, 505, 508
Gerhard, D., 243
Gernios, N. K., 269
Gerrard, M., 96
Geschwind, N., 56
Gfeller, J. D., 180
Giambra, L. M., 175
Gibbon, M., 423
Gibbons, A., 47
Gibbons, F. X., 350
Giberson, R., 99
Gibson, E. J., 141, 148
Gilbert, A. N., 137
Gilbert, P., 98
Gildea, P. M., 265
Giles, T. R., 467
Gill, C., 407
Gilligan, C., 94, 103
Gilling, D., 456
Gilovich, T., 14, 15, 16, 18, 19, 20
Giovino, G. A., 190
Gist, R., 428
Giudice, S., 111
Gjerde, P. F., 435
Gladue, B. A., 319, 320, 502
Glaser, R., 364
Glass, D. R., 466
Glass, G. V., 465, 466
Glassman, A., 363
Glenn, N. D., 104, 105
Glick, B., 504
Glick, P., 406
Godden, D. R., 241
Goethals, G. R., 480
Goethe, 90, 481
Goethe, J. W., 430
Goff, D. C., 425, 426
Gold, J. A., 306
Gold, M., 95
Goldberg, J., 360
Goldberg, L., 314
Goldberg, L. R., 389
Goldberg, W., 388
Goldfried, M. R., 450, 467
Golding, J. M., 420
Goldsamt, L. A., 432
Goldstein, A. L., 365
Goldstein, A. P., 504
Goleman, D., 283, 324
Golomb, J., 238
Golski, S., 236
Golub, S., 88
Gombrich, E. H., 153
Gonsiorek, J. C., 318
Gonzales, A., 297
Goodall, J., 499
Goodchilds, J., 98
Goodenough, D. R., 168
Goodhart, D. E., 405
Goodman, L. A., 360
Goodman, T. R., 429
Goodrick, G. K., 309
Goodwin, C. J., 199
Goodwin, D. C., 430
Gopnik, A., 273

Goranson, R. E., 9
Gorbachev, M., 295
Gore, A., Jr., 260
Gore, T., 152
Gorman, L. K., 236
Gorski, R. A., 319
Gorsuch, R. L., 325
Gortmaker, S. L., 306, 309
Gorzalka, B. B., 354
Gotlib, I. H., 397, 432
Gottesman, D., 406
Gottesman, I. I., 438, 439, 441
Gottheil, E., 365
Gottman, J., 105
Gould, M. S., 485
Gould, S. J., 154, 156, 276, 285
Grabowski, T., 55
Grabski, M., 303
Gracián, B., 247
Graf, P., 101
Graham, J. W., 190
Grajek, S., 516
Graves, J., 491
Gray-Little, B., 516
Greely, A. M., 311
Green, B. L., 79
Green, D. M., 133
Green, K. C., 188
Green, P., 385
Green, R., 71
Green, S. K., 495
Greenberg, M. D., 473
Greenberg, R. P., 473
Greenburg, J., 432
Greene, D., 12
Greene, R. L., 228
Greenfeld, L. A., 504
Greenwald, A. G., 21, 164, 385
Greenwood, M. R. C., 306
Greer, G., 314
Greer, J. H., 315
Greer, S., 365
Gregory, R. L., 146, 149, 153
Gregory of Nyssa, 427
Gregory of Sinai, 370
Greif, E. B., 88
Griffin, D. W., 9, 261
Griffiths, R. R., 184
Griggs, R. A., 155
Grillo, C. M., 308
Grobstein, C., 71
Gross, A. E., 514
Gross, T. D., 405
Grossarth-Maticek, R., 371
Grossman, M., 94
Grossman, R., 437
Grove, W. M., 436
Gruchy, C. D. G., 94
Gruder, C. L., 349
Gruen, G. E., 433
Grusec, J. E., 218
Guan, H-C., 437
Guerin, B., 490
Gulevich, G., 169
Gur, R. E., 437
Gustavson, C. R., 203
Gutierres, S. E., 314

Ha, Y-W., 258
Haber, R. N., 224
Hackel, L. S., 105
Hackman, B. B., 501
Hadzi, P. D., 473

Hafner, H., 485
Hagen, E. P., 278
Halaas, J. L., 308
Haldane, J. B. S., 122
Haldeman, D. C., 318
Haldeman, R., 224
Hall, C. S., 172, 386
Hall, G. S., 88
Hall, J. A., 94, 328, 339
Hall, L. K., 227
Hall, N. R., 365
Hall, T., 302
Hall, W. B., 282
Halle, P., 265
Halonen, J. S., 537
Halpern, B. P., 136
Halpern, D. F., 290
Halpern, J. N., 138
Hamburg, B., 358
Hamid, A., 185
Hamill, R., 260
Hamilton, D. L., 14
Hamilton, J. C., 432
Hamilton, M. C., 273
Hamilton, V. L., 432
Hammen, C. L., 432
Hammersmith, S. K., 318
Hammerstein, O., 352, 514
Han, G., 521
Handel, G. F., 427
Haney, T. L., 372
Hankins, W. G., 203
Hanmer, T. J., 94
Hansel, C. E. M., 385
Hansell, S., 503
Hansen, C. H., 339
Hansen, D. J., 84
Hansen, R. D., 339
Hansen, W. B., 190
Harber, K. D., 373
Hardin, C., 272
Hardin, T. S., 432
Hare, R. D., 441
Harel, Z., 360
Harkins, S. G., 491
Harlow, H. F., 81, 83, 84
Harlow, L. L., 189
Harlow, M. K., 81
Harold, R. D., 290
Harrington, D. M., 395
Harris, B., 204
Harris, J. K., 369
Harris, J. R., 308
Harris, L., 359
Harris, M. J., 109
Harris, R. J., 507
Harriston, K. A., 407
Harsch, N., 224, 243
Hartmann, E., 171
Hartshorne, H., 392
Harvey, S. M., 313
Hasher, L., 101
Haskins, R., 288
Hassan, R., 428
Hatfield, B. D., 368
Hatfield, E., 316, 512, 513, 515
Hathaway, S. R., 390
Hautziner, M., 429, 433
Hawthorne, N., 483
Haybittle, J. L., 365
Hayes, J. R., 240
Hazan, C., 84
Hazelrigg, M. D., 462
Hazlitt, W., 398

Hearold, S., 505
Heath, A., 432
Heath, A. C., 189, 422
Heath, C., Jr., 184
Heath, L., 505
Heatherton, T. F., 304
Hebb, D. O., 335
Heckman, M., 317
Hedges, L. V., 290
Heider, F., 479
Heider, K., 338, 340
Heiman, J. R., 314
Heise, L., 506
Heller, W., 62
Hellige, J. B., 64
Helmreich, W. B., 249, 360
Hembree, R., 336
Henderson, A. S., 100
Henderson, R., 16, 349
Henderson, W. G., 360
Henley, N. M., 272
Hennessey, B. A., 284
Henninger, P., 425
Henrich, C., 304
Henry, J. P., 359
Henschel, A., 301
Herbert, T. B., 364
Herek, G. M., 498
Hering, E., 129, 130
Herman, C. P., 309
Herman, G., 437
Herrmann, D., 250
Herrnstein, R. J., 207, 289, 502
Hershenson, M., 146
Herzog, D. B., 304
Hesburgh, T. M., 520
Heshka, S., 307
Hess, D. J., 156
Hess, E. H., 149
Hesse, B. W., 505
Hester, C., 304
Heston, L. L., 422
Hetherington, E. M., 84
Heymsfield, S. B., 307
Higgins, E. T., 396
Higgins, P., 347
Hilgard, E. R., 177, 180, 181
Hill, M. S., 260
Hill, T., 385
Hines, M., 71
Hintzman, D. L., 230
Hinz, L. D., 304
Hippocrates, 357
Hirshkowitz, M., 168
Hirst, W., 181
Hirt, E. R., 432
Hitler, A., 521
Hitzig, E., 52
Hlatky, M. A., 372
Hoberman, H., 429, 433
Hobfoll, S. E., 357, 429
Hobson, J. A., 173
Hodes, R. L., 203
Hodgkinson, V. A., 519
Hodkin, B., 78
Hoebel, B. G., 302
Hoffman, C., 498
Hoffman, H. G., 243
Hoffman, S. D., 260
Hoffman, W. S., 432
Hofmann, A., 186
Hofstede, G., 398
Hogan, J., 368
Hogarth, W., 450

Hohmann, G. W., 352
Hokanson, J. E., 345, 432
Holden, C., 109, 169, 189, 337, 400, 471
Hollon, S. D., 461
Holmes, D. S., 175, 249, 247, 368, 369, 385
Holmes, J. G., 403
Holmes, O. W., 261, 415
Holmsten, R. D., 369
Holobow, N., 273
Holsten, F., 473
Holzman, P. S., 122
Hommer, D., 471
Hong, H-W., 341
Honorton, C., 157
Hooper, J., 51
Hooykaas, R., 7
Hopkin, A., 444
Hopper, C. H., 404
Horace, 229, 344
Horn, J. L., 102
Horne, J. A., 169
Horney, K., 383, 409, 465
Horowitz, M. J., 467
House, J. S., 372
House, P., 12
House, R. J., 328
Houston, B. K., 467
Houston, C., 70
Houston, W., 70
Howard, J., 500
Howard, K. I., 95
Howe, M. L., 74
Hoy, W., 273
Hoyer, G., 428
Hsieh, C-C., 368
Hubel, D. H., 122, 127, 128, 131
Huberty, J. O., 414, 415
Hucker, S. J., 313
Huebner, R. B., 470
Huffman, M. L. C., 245
Hughes, H., 420
Hugick, L., 94
Hui, C. H., 399
Hull, J. G., 183
Hull, P., 272
Hulme, C., 234
Hulsey, M. G., 303
Hulton, J. B., 396
Hume, D., 493
Humphrey, N., 425
Hunt, J. M., 287
Hunt, M., 3, 91, 92, 204, 284, 315
Hunt, R. R., 229
Hunter, S., 103
Hurst, N., 498
Hurt, H. T., 433
Hurtado, S., 498
Hussein, S., 155, 521
Huston, A. C., 505
Huston, T. L., 105
Hutton, D. G., 396
Huttunen, M. O., 437
Huxley, T. H., 443
Hyde, J., 272, 273
Hyde, J. S., 242, 290, 290, 291, 316
Hyde, R. T., 368
Hyler, S., 444
Hyman, R., 156, 157, 406, 407

Iacono, W. G., 286, 436
Imber, L., 443
Imber, S. D., 466
Ingerman, C., 499

Ingham, A. G., 491
Inglehart, M., 342
Inglehart, M. R., 395
Inglehart, R., 12, 105, 106, 330, 404
Insel, P. M., 98
Irvine, A. A., 480
Isen, A. M., 346
Isham, W. P., 273
Izard, C., 340
Izard, C. E., 344

Jackson, D., 392
Jackson, J., 325
Jackson, J. M., 491
Jackson, L., 502
Jackson, M., 155
Jackson, S. W., 467
Jackson, T. L., 506
Jacobs, B. L., 186
Jacobs, G. H., 129
Jacobs, J. E., 290
Jacobs, W. J., 421
Jacobsen, E., 350
Jacobson, K., 77
Jacobson, N. S., 468
James, W., 2, 30, 134, 181, 231, 251, 342, 346, 351, 353, 374, 395, 413, 484
Jameson, D., 130
Jamison, K. R., 427
Janda, L. H., 513
Jandor, L., 364
Janis, I. L., 258, 259, 492, 493
Janoff-Bulman, R., 500
Janoff-Bulman, R. J., 347
Jardine, R., 189
Jarvie, G. J., 309
Jarvik, L. F., 100
Jarvik, M. E., 405
Jefferson, T., 394
Jeffrey, R. W., 308, 310
Jemmott, J. B., III., 363, 364
Jenike, M. A., 422
Jenish, D., 316
Jenkins, J. G., 246
Jenkins, V. Y., 513
Jennings, J. R., 362
Jennings, P., 152
Jensen, C., 500
Jensen, J. P., 468
Jepson, C., 533
Jervis, R., 263
Jesus, 370, 440, 510
John, O. P., 389
Johnson, B. T., 100, 327
Johnson, C. B., 316
Johnson, D., 27, 308
Johnson, D. W., 520
Johnson, E. J., 346
Johnson, J. S., 267
Johnson, L., 169
Johnson, M. H., 82
Johnson, M. K., 228
Johnson, P. B., 385
Johnson, P. C., 364
Johnson, R. T., 520
Johnson, V. E., 312, 315, 322, 414
Johnston, L. D., 185, 188, 189, 190
Johnston, R. E., 341
Joiner, T. E., Jr., 432
Jolesz, F. A., 437
Jolton, J., 406
Jones, D., 363
Jones, E. E., 467

Jones, L., 156
Jones, M., 441
Jones, M. C., 89, 455
Jones, P., 437
Jones, S. S., 341
Jones, W. H., 24
Jordan, M., 43, 75
Jorgenson, D. O., 520
Jorm, A. F., 100
Jose, W. S., II., 368
Joseph, J., 365
Joseph, J. G., 317
Josephs, R. A., 183
Joubert, J., 217
Jouriles, E., 183
Joybert, J., 486
Joyner, F. G., 500
Joynt, R. J., 58
Jung, C., 83, 107, 382, 383, 387, 409
Jussim, L. J., 120
Juvenal, 98

Kaczor, L. M., 306
Kagan, J., 81, 82, 83, 112, 385, 388, 389
Kahana, B., 360
Kahn-Dawood, F., 313
Kahneman, D., 15, 135, 259, 262, 532
Kail, R., 99
Kale, A. R., 242
Kalichman, S. C., 506
Kalin, N. H., 338
Kamin, L. J., 273
Kandel, D. B., 190
Kandel, E. R., 236
Kane-Williams, E., 189
Kanekar, S., 316
Kann, L., 95, 189
Kant, I., 148
Kanzi, 271
Kapitza, S., 157
Kaplan, H. I., 471
Kaplan, H. S., 313
Kaplan, J. R., 363
Kaprio, J., 108, 359
Kapur, S., 473
Karacan, I., 168
Karau, S. J., 328, 491
Karmarck, T., 362
Karni, A., 173
Karno, M., 420
Karr, B., 156
Karren, R. J., 327
Kashima, E. S., 398
Kashima, Y., 398
Kasimatis, M., 342
Kasl, S. V., 361
Katz, P. A., 505
Katz, S., 430
Kaufert, P., 98
Kaufman, A. S., 102
Kaufman, C. M., 396
Kaufman, J., 84
Kaufman, L., 146, 233
Kaylor, J. a., 360
Keefer, E. B., 184
Keesey, R. E., 302
Keillor, G., 397
Keller, H., 74
Keller, J. W., 384, 390
Keller, S. E., 364
Kellerman, A. L., 501
Kellerman, J., 339

Kelley, K. N., 404
Kelling, S. T., 136
Kelly, D. J., 203
Kelly, I. W., 406, 440
Kelly, T. A., 468
Kempe, C. C., 84
Kempe, R. S., 84
Kempthorne-Rawson, J., 364
Kendell-Tackett, K. A., 248
Kendler, K. S., 422, 432
Kendrick, J. S., 368
Kennedy, C., 432
Kennedy, J. F., 224, 486, 492, 493, 521
Kennedy, L. C., 513
Kennedy, S., 43
Kenrick, D. T., 314, 316, 392
Kermoian, R., 142, 421
Kern, P., 109
Kerr, N. L., 491
Kessler, M., 475
Kessler, R., 432
Kessler, R. C., 347, 317, 365, 422
Kety, S. S., 430
Keys, A., 301, 305
Kidd, E., 230
Kidd, K. K., 430
Kiecolt-Glaser, J. K., 364
Kierkegaard, S., 8
Kight, T. D., 515
Kihlstrom, J. F., 172, 176, 181, 227, 244, 247,
     385
Kiknis, R., 437
Kilmann, P. R., 96
Kim, S. H., 520
Kim, Y. J., 321
Kimball, M. M., 290
Kimble, G. A., 202, 206
Kimmel, D., 317
Kimura, D., 64
Kimzey, S. L., 364
King, D. W., 360
King, L. A., 360
King, M. L., Jr., 91, 218
King, N. J., 370
King, P., 349
King Henry VIII, 179
Kinsey, A. C., 311, 312, 322
Kipling, R., 499
Kirpatrick, L. A., 82
Kirsch, I., 177
Kirscht, J. P., 317
Kitayama, S., 272, 341, 345, 399
Kite, M. E., 100
Kitt, A. S., 349
Klasen, S., 498
Klayman, J., 258
Kleck, R. E., 373
Klein, E. B., 103
Kleinke, C. L., 339
Kleinmuntz, B., 337
Kleitman, N., 166
Klemm, W. R., 45
Klentz, B., 514
Klepp, K-I., 190
Kline, D., 99
Kline, N. S., 433
Kline, S. A., 504
Klineberg, O., 340, 520
Klipper, M. Z., 370
Kluft, R. P., 425, 426
Kluger, A., 238
Klüver, H., 49
Knauss, K. S., 207
Knetsch, J. L., 262

Knight, J., 512
Knotts, D., 434
Koelling, R. A., 202, 203, 206
Koenig, L. J., 429
Koepke, J. P., 363
Koestler, A., 154
Kohlberg, L., 90, 91, 111, 113
Köhler, W., 257
Kohn, A., 520
Kohn, M., 437
Kohn, P. M., 359
Kohut, J. J., 441
Koko, 269
Kolata, G., 309, 428
Kolb, B., 58
Kolbe, L. J., 95, 189
Kolers, P. A., 226
Kolominsky, Y., 358
Koltz, C., 499
Kommer, D., 242
Konecni, V. J., 345
Konishi, M., 133
Koob, G. F., 437
Korn, W. S., 188, 316, 347, 495
Korten, A. E., 100
Koskenvuo, M., 108, 359
Koslowsky, M., 169
Koss, M. P., 360, 506, 507
Kotva, H. J., 96
Koutsourais, H., 521
Kozak, M. J., 456
Kraemer, H. C., 365
Kraft, C., 152
Kramer, G. P., 521
Kramer, M., 288
Krantz, D. H., 533
Krantz, S. E., 241
Kratzer, L., 290
Kraus, A. L., 58
Krause, R., 340
Krause, S. J., 481
Kraut, R. E., 341
Krauthammer, C., 320
Krebs, D., 183
Krishnamurti, 416
Kristof, N., 498
Kroonenberg, P. M., 82
Krosnick, J. A., 112, 120
Krupa, D., 239
Ksir, C., 185
Ku, L. C., 316
Kubitz, K. A., 368
Kudoh, T., 341, 344
Kuhl, P. K., 265
Kuhn, C. M., 74
Kulakowski, D., 516
Kulik, C. C., 215
Kulik, J., 224
Kulik, J. A., 215
Kung, L. C., 273
Kurtz, P., 7, 406
Kutas, M., 167
Kwong, K. K., 47

L'Engle, M., 8, 292, 427
Labarka, R., 471
Labbe, R., 58
Labouvie-Vief, G., 101
Ladd, G. T., 163
LaDue, R. A., 72
Lagerweij, E., 39
Lahey, B. B., 309
Laird, J. D., 339, 342

Lallone, R. L., 308
Lambert, W. F., 273
Lamon, S. J., 290
Lamour, M., 86
Lana, 269
Lancioni, G., 73
Landauer, T. K., 234
Landers, A., 345, 463, 464
Landers, D. M., 368
Landfield, P., 187
Landis, K. R., 372
Landis, L. S., 101
Lang, E., 350
Lang, M., 105
Lang, P. J., 203
Lange, C., 352, 353, 374
Langer, E. J., 175, 370, 404, 443
Langinvainio, H., 108
Langlois, J. H., 513
Lanzetta, J. T., 343
LaPerriere, A., 364
Larsen, J. L., 473
Larsen, R. J., 342
Larsen, R. M., 384
Larson, R. W., 95
Lashley, K., 59
Lashley, K. S., 236
Lassiter, G. D., 480
Latané, B., 491, 496, 517, 518
Latham, G. P., 327
Lau, S., 433
Laudenslager, M. L., 360
Laumann, E. O., 311, 316, 317, 506
Laurence, J-R., 177
Laverty, W. H., 440
Lavoisier, A., 272
Law, H., 389
Lawford, P., 434
Layton, B. D., 154, 156, 157
Lazarus, R. S., 354, 355, 359, 374
Leach, P., 211
Leary, M. R., 328
Leber, W. R., 466
Lebow, J., 464
Leckman, J. F., 430
LeCompte, W. A., 340
LeDoux, J., 354
Lee, C., 506
Lee, G. R., 105
Lefcourt, H. M., 403
Lehman, D. R., 22, 106, 405
Leibowitz, H. W., 143
Leigh, B. C., 183, 311
Lempert, R. O., 22
Lenneberg, E. H., 74
Lennon, J., 372
Lennon, R., 94
Lenzenweger, M. F., 471
Leonard, J. B., 500
Leonardo da Vinci, 382, 444
Leone, D. R., 242
Lepore, S. J., 371
Lepper, M. R., 263, 325
Lerner, M. J., 500
Leshner, A. I., 470
Levav, I., 443
LeVay, S., 319, 322
Levenson, R. W., 338, 340, 343
Leventhal, H., 317
Lever, J., 94
Levey, G., 109
Levidow, B., 244
Levin, I. P., 262

Levine, A., 494, 498
Levine, B., 168
Levine, I. S., 470
Levinger, G., 491
Levinson, D. J., 103, 111, 114
Levinson, M. H., 103
Levitt, E. E., 178
Levy, D., 506
Levy, J., 64
Levy, P. E., 396
Lewicka, M., 344
Lewicki, P., 385
Lewin, K., 328
Lewinsohn, P. M., 242, 429, 433
Lewis, B., 109
Lewis, C., 395
Lewis, C. S., 231, 329, 338, 386, 396
Lewis, D. O., 84, 502
Lewis, J., 109, 339
Lewis, L., 109
Lewis, M., 242
Lewontin, R., 25, 289
Liang, K-Y., 437
Licata, A., 186
Lichtenstein, S., 261
Lichtman, S. W., 307
Liddy, G. G., 224
Lifton, R. J., 183
Light, K. C., 363
Liker, J. K., 282
Lin, S., 9, 261
Lincoln, A., 394, 433
Lindbergh, C., 156
Linder, D., 510
Lindoerfer, J. S., 492
Lindsay, D. S., 243, 248
Lindskold, S., 521
Lindzey, G., 386
Link, B. G., 429, 443
Linkous, R. A., 490
Linn, M. C., 290, 291
Linnoila, M., 237, 471
Linville, P. W., 262
Linz, D., 506
Lippman, J., 504
Lippmann, W., 514
Lipsey, M. W., 466
Little Albert, 204, 205, 206, 455
Little Hans, 421
Livingstone, D., 39
Livingstone, M., 128
Lobel, A., 514
Locci, A. B., 501
Lock, M., 98
Locke, E. A., 327
Locke, J., 148, 149
Locke, S. E., 363
Loehlin, J. C., 108, 285
Loewenstein, G., 210
Loftus, E. F., 236, 243, 244, 245, 247, 248, 249
Loftus, G. R., 236
Lokar, M., 486
Lombardi, V., 325-326
Lomranz, J., 429
London, P., 218, 362
Longnecker, M. P., 364
Lopez, A. D., 184
LoPiccolo, J. L., 316
Lord, C. G., 263
Lorenz, K., 82
Lott, J., 441
Loulis, 271
Lovaas, O. I., 458
Loveland, D. H., 207

Low, H., 502
Lu, F., 468
Lu, Z-L., 233
Lubart, T. I., 282
Lubin, B., 384
Lubinski, D., 290
Lubran, B., 470
Lucas, G., 96
Lucas, H. L., 441
Ludeman, P., 86
Lukoff, D., 468
Lull, J., 504
Lummis, M., 290
Lumsden, C. J., 217
Lund, E., 428
Lunde, I., 430
Lungren, S., 493
Luria, A. M., 223
Luus, C. A. E., 96
Lykken, D. T., 109, 110, 286, 337, 441
Lynch, G., 236, 237
Lynch, S., 237
Lynn, A. R., 120
Lynn, M., 182
Lynn, R., 289, 291
Lynn, S. J., 177, 180
Lyons, N. P., 94
Lytton, H., 86
Lyubomirsky, S., 459

Maccoby, E. E., 94
MacDonald, G., 242, 514
Macdonald, J. E., 359
MacDonald, N., 435
MacDonald, T. K., 183
Macera, C., 363
MacFarlane, A., 73
Macfarlane, J. W., 88, 112
Macgregor, A. M. C., 306
Machon, R. A., 437
MacKay, D. G., 273
MacKinnon, D. W., 282
MacLaine, S., 415
MacLeod, C., 260, 403
Macomber, J., 77
Madonna, 240, 504
Maehr, M. L., 326
Maffei, M., 308
Magloire, K., 364
Magnusson, D., 89, 441
Magoun, H. W., 48
Mahadevan, R., 234
Mahoney, K. M., 188, 316, 347
Mahoney, M. J., 274
Major, B., 328, 359, 513
Major, B. N., 359
Makhijani, M. G., 513
Maksud, M. G., 39
Malamuth, N. M., 507, 508
Malan, D., 452
Malarkey, W. B., 364
Malinosky-Rummell, R., 84
Malkiel, B., 261
Mallory, G., 299
Malloy, E. A., 183
Malmquist, C. P., 249
Malone, T. W., 325
Malott, J. M., 135
Malpass, R. S., 500
Mandel, D., 297
Mandela, N., 55
Mann, J., 519
Mann, J. J., 473

Manning, W. G., 184
Manuck, S. B., 363
Mao, H-Y., 364
Marco, E., 437
Marentette, P. F., 265, 267, 268
Mark, D. B., 372
Markman, H., 105
Marks, D. F., 156
Marks, G., 190
Marks, J., 363
Markus, G. B., 534
Markus, H. R., 272, 341, 345, 395, 399
Marlatt, G. A., 183, 210
Marschark, M., 229
Marsh, H. W., 350
Marshall, W. L., 506, 507
Marteau, T. M., 262
Martin, C., 311
Martin, J., 371
Martin, J. E., 369
Martin, L., 342
Martin, L. R., 372
Martin, N. G., 189
Martin, R. J., 303
Martin, S. J., 440
Martinsen, E. W., 369
Martyna, W., 273
Masland, J. L., 314
Maslow, A. H., 300, 322, 331, 393, 394, 395, 396, 400, 401, 409
Mason, M., 436
Masters, W. H., 312, 315, 322, 414
Matarazzo, J. D., 384, 390
Matheny, A. P., Jr., 108
Mathews, A., 403
Matillo, G. M., 505
Matsumoto, D., 272, 341, 344
Matt, G. E., 241
Matthews, D. E., 307
Matthews, G., 104, 392
Matthews, K. A., 98, 362
Matthysse, S., 122
Mattsson, A., 502
Maugham, W. S., 514
Maurer, C., 73
Maurer, D. C., 73
May, C. P., 101
May, M., 392
May, P. A., 416
May, R., 401
Mayne, T. J., 458
McArthur, L. Z., 201
McBurney, D. H., 135, 147, 148
McCabe, G., 16
McCabe, M., 86
McCall, R. B., 290, 323
McCann, I. L., 368
McCarthy, P., 136
McCarthy, W. J., 405
McCartney, K., 109, 111
McCartney, P., 372
McCarty, D., 470
McCaul, K. D., 135, 502
McCauley, C. R., 492
McClearn, G. E., 109, 111, 308
McClelland, D., 323
McCloskey, M., 224
McClure, J., 260
McConkey, K. M., 177, 181
McConnell, R. A., 154
McCormick, C. M., 320
McCrae, R. R., 103, 104, 112, 392
McDermott, M., 372
McDonald, R., 169

McDuffie, D., 503
McFarland, C., 244, 247
McGhee, P. E., 79, 324
McGlasham, T., 430
McGlashan, T. H., 436
McGlave, P. B., 364, 372
McGrath, J., 437
McGrath, M. J., 173
McGraw, K. M., 499
McGrew, J., 190
McGue, M., 109, 110, 189, 286
McGuire, W. J., 505
McHugh, P. R., 302
McKee, B., 103
McKegney, F. P., 364
McKinlay, J. B., 98
McKinlay, S. M., 98
McLean, J. E., 102
McManus, I. C., 437
McNally, R. J., 217
McNaughton, B. L., 236
Meador, B. D., 454
Meaney, M. J., 75
Means, B., 346
Medawar, P., 386
Mednick, S. A., 437, 441
Meichenbaum, D., 461
Meichenbaum, D. H., 370
Meier, R. P., 268
Meilman, P. W., 183
Melchior, L. A., 85, 433
Melhuish, E., 73
Meltzoff, A. N., 217, 265, 273
Melville, H., 479
Melzack, R., 134, 135
Memon, A., 248
Menary, E., 179
Mendolia, M., 373
Mengel, C. E., 364
Menozzi, P., 289
Mento, A. J., 327
Menustik, C. E., 457
Merikangas, K. R., 430
Merskey, H., 425
Merton, R. K., 7, 349
Mesmer, F. A., 177
Mesquita, B., 340
Messer, W. S., 155
Metalsky, G. I., 431, 432
Meuwissen, I., 313
Meyers, A. W., 274
Michael, R. T., 311, 316, 317, 506
Michaels, J. W., 490
Michaels, S., 311, 316, 317, 506
Michelangelo, 97
Mickelsen, O., 301
Middlebrooks, J. C., 133
Mikachi, S., 319
Mikulincer, M., 169
Milan, R. J., Jr., 96
Milgram, S., 487, 488, 489, 496, 522
Miller, D. T., 190
Miller, G. A., 234, 265, 378
Miller, K., 515
Miller, K. I., 404
Miller, N., 518
Miller, N. E., 26, 369, 370, 373
Miller, P. C., 403
Miller, R. L., 465, 466
Millman, L., 201
Mills, M., 73
Mills, S. L., 190
Milner, P., 50
Milojkovic, J. D., 261

Milstein, V., 426
Mineka, J., 421
Mineka, S., 217
Mirin, S. M., 189
Mirotznik, J., 429
Mischel, W., 91, 209, 392, 407
Mishkin, M., 101, 236
Mita, T. H., 512
Mittelman, M. S., 238
Mocellin, J. S. P., 187
Moeykens, B., 183
Moffitt, T. E., 89
Molyneux, W., 149
Monaghan, P., 249
Monahan, J., 444
Money, J., 313, 319, 320, 507
Monge, P. R., 404
Moniz, E., 474
Monroe, M., 485, 513
Montaigne, 90
Montgomery, L. M., 462
Montgomery, R. B., 370
Montgomery, S. B., 317
Moody, R., 186
Mook, D. G., 23
Moorcroft, W., 167, 169
Moore, D. W., 320
Moore, K. A., 321
Moore, S., 513
Moran, T. H., 302
Moreland, R. L., 512
Morelli, G. A., 14, 85
Morgan, M., 505, 508
Morgan, W. P., 39
Morris, N. M., 313
Morris, R., 502
Morris, T., 365
Morrison, D. M., 96
Morrow, D. G., 228
Morrow, J., 432
Morton, G. E., 10
Morton, L. A., 430
Moruzzi, G., 48
Moscovici, S., 493
Moses, 7
Moses, G., 102
Mosher, D. L., 182
Moss, A. J., 190, 372
Moss, D., 472
Moss, H. A., 112
Most, A., 88
Mosteller, F., 16
Mowrer, O. H., 457
Moyer, J. R., Jr., 236
Moyer, K. E., 501
Mozart, W. A., 427
Mozley, D., 437
Muehlenhard, C. L., 316
Mueller, J., 348, 495, 497
Mueller, P. M., 359
Muenchow, S., 288
Mufson, E. J., 58
Müller-Lyer, F., 146
Murdock, M., 467
Murnen, S. K., 314
Murphy, G. E., 428
Murphy, J., 271
Murphy, S. T., 120, 342
Murphy, T. N., 135
Murray, C., 289
Murray, D. M., 244
Murray, H., 323, 393
Murray, H. A., 155, 384
Murray, J. P., 505

Murray, R., 437
Murray, R. M., 437
Murrell, A., 519
Must, A., 306
Mycielska, K., 151
Myers, A., 247
Myers, C., 247
Myers, D. G., 96, 346, 350, 396, 492
Myers, I. B., 388
Myers, L., 79, 247
Myers, P., 247
Myers, R., 59
Mynatt, C. R., 336

Nadel, L., 421
Napolitan, D. A., 480
Nash, M., 177
Naveh, G., 443
Naylor, T. H., 328
Nazareth, A., 316
Neale, J. M., 347, 364, 432
Neale, M., 432
Neale, M. C., 320, 422, 501
Needham, D. R., 120
Needles, D. J., 432
Neese, R. M., 134, 203, 427
Neisser, U., 181, 224, 237, 241, 243
Neitz, J., 129
Nelis, P. C., 39
Nelligan, J. S., 84, 354
Nelson, K., 74, 266
Nelson, N., 372
Nelson, R. J., 366
Nemeroff, C., 201
Nesbitt, K. M., 505
Nesselroade, J. R., 111
Neugarten, B. L., 105
Neuringer, A., 207
Nevin, J. A., 210
Newcomb, M. D., 112, 187, 189
Newell, A., 10
Newhouse, J. P., 184
Newkirk, I., 27
Newman, M., 109
Newman, P., 240
Newman, R. I., 175, 370
Newport, E. L., 267, 268
Newport, F., 153
Newson, J. T., 364
Newton, I., 129, 444
Newton, T., 364
Ng, S. H., 273
Nias, D. K. B., 501
Nichols, R. C., 108, 285
Nickerson, R. S., 231, 232
Nicklaus, J., 274
Nicodemus, N., 377
Nicol, S. E., 438, 439
Nicolaus, L. K., 203
Niebuhr, R., 365, 405
Niemi, R. G., 348, 495, 497
Nigro, G., 274
Niit, T., 344
Nimoy, L., 480
Nisbett, R., 328
Nisbett, R. E., 22, 259, 260, 263, 405, 504, 533
Nixon, R. M., 224, 225, 227, 228, 340
Noble, E. P., 189
Noegel, R., 304
Noel, J. G., 404
Nolen-Hoeksema, S., 429, 431, 432, 459
Noller, P., 84, 389
Norcross, J. C., 450, 458

Norem, J. K., 405
Norman, D. A., 152
Norris, J., 441
Norris, P. A., 369
Northall, G. F., 203
Nostradamus, 155
Notarius, C., 105
Notter, M. F. D., 58
Nowell, A., 290
Nurius, P., 395
Nuttin, J. M., Jr., 512
Nystrom, J., 74

O'Brien, K., 317
O'Callaghan, E., 437
O'Connor, P., 468
O'Donohue, W. T., 315
O'Heeron, R. C., 372
O'Leary, D., 437
O'Malley, P. M., 93, 185, 188, 189, 190
O'Neill, M. J., 360
O'Sullivan, M., 340
Obrist, P. A., 363
Odbert, H. S., 388
Odenwald, W. F., 320
Oetting, E. R., 190
Oettingen, G., 404
Offenbacher, E., 307
Offer, D., 95
Ogino, M., 86
Okawara, S. H., 58
Okwumabua, T., 462
Olds, J., 50
Olds, J. L., 236
Oliner, P. M., 218
Oliner, S. P., 218
Oliver, M. B., 316
Olton, D. S., 236
Olweus, D., 502
Omelich, C. L., 190
Openheim, D., 85
Orne, M. T., 178, 179
Ortmann, J., 430
Orwell, G., 247
Osgood, C. E., 521
Ostfeld, A. M., 361
Ostrov, E., 95
Ostrow, D. G., 317, 365
Otto, T., 236
Ouellette, J. A., 493
Over, R., 43, 313
Owens, J., 395

Padawer, W., 467
Padgett, V. R., 488
Padian, N. S., 317
Paffenbarger, R. S., Jr., 368
Page, S., 443
Paight, D. J., 485
Paikoff, R. L., 94
Paivio, A., 229
Palace, E. M., 354
Palladino, J. J., 165
Palmer, J. C., 243
Palmer, S., 140, 237
Palsane, M. N., 371
Palumbo, S. R., 173
Pancake, V. R., 83
Pandey, J., 481
Panksepp, J., 338

Papciak, A. S., 520
Parashos, I. A., 430
Parducci, A., 348
Parker, G., 473
Parker, J. W., 350
Parkhomenko, V., 358
Parks, R., 493
Parloff, M. B., 449, 466
Parsons, B., 320
Parsons, J. E., 385
Pasteur, L., 26, 282
Pate, J. E., 304
Paton, D., 358
Patterson, F., 269
Patterson, G. R., 211, 504
Patterson, R., 433
Paulos, J. A., 317
Pauls, D. L., 430
Pavlov, I. P., 2, 198, 200, 201, 202, 204, 206, 212, 219, 220, 221, 455
Payl, S. M., 471
Payne, R., 371
Peake, P. K., 91
Pearlin, L., 358
Pecheux, M-G., 86
Peckham, V., 491
Pedersen, N. L., 108, 109, 111, 308
Pedic, F., 473
Pekkanen, J., 169
Pelchat, M. L., 303
Pelham, B. W., 396
Pemberton, M., 437
Penfield, W., 53, 235, 236
Pennebaker, J. W., 372, 373
Penrod, S. D., 244, 506
Peplau, L. A., 318
Pepperell, P., 368
Perkins, K. A., 369
Perlick, D., 490
Perlmutter, M., 101
Perrin, J. M., 306
Perry, C., 177
Perry, N., 75
Persky, V. W., 364
Persons, J. B., 443
Pert, C. B., 39
Peschel, E. R., 313
Peschel, R. E., 313
Pestone, M., 307
Peters, T. J., 215
Petersen, A. C., 89
Peterson, A. C., 290
Peterson, C., 90, 404
Peterson, J., 90
Peterson, J. L., 321
Peterson, L. R., 233
Peterson, M. A., 437
Peterson, M. J., 233
Peterson, R., 384
Peterson-Lewis, S., 505
Petitto, L. A., 265, 267, 268
Peto, R., 184
Petraitis, J., 505
Petretic-Jackson, P., 506
Petruzzello, S. J., 368
Petry, H. M., 139
Pettigrew, T. F., 519
Pettingale, K. W., 365
Pfeiffer, E., 100
Phair, J., 365
Phelps, M. E., 431
Phillips, D., 287
Phillips, D. P., 485
Phillips, J. L., 78

Phillips, M., 495
Phillips, M. R., 444
Piaget, J., 2, 11, 75, 76, 77, 78, 79, 80, 90, 111, 113, 114, 243, 283
Piazza, A., 289
Piccione, C., 177
Pickar, D., 471
Pickens, R. W., 189
Piercy, M., 315
Pike, K. M., 304
Pilkonis, P. A., 466
Pillard, R. C., 320
Pincus, J. H., 84, 502
Pinel, J. P. J., 302
Pinel, P., 415, 418, 449
Pinker, S., 264
Piotrowski, C., 384, 390
Pirandello, L., 391
Pirsig, R., 532
Pisarska, K., 307
Pitcairn, T., 340
Pitre, U., 227
Plato, 188
Pleck, J. H., 316
Pliner, P., 303
Plomin, R., 82, 109, 110, 111, 286
Plous, S., 26, 510
Pogue-Geile, M. F., 308
Polit, D. F., 324
Polivy, J., 309
Pollard, R., 273
Pomerleau, C. S., 185
Pomerleau, O. F., 185
Pomeroy, W. B., 311
Poole, D. A., 243, 248
Poon, L. W., 99
Poortinga, Y. H., 80, 316, 495, 499
Popenoe, D., 399
Popkin, M. K., 364, 372
Popkin, S. J., 99
Porter, S., 207
Posner, M. I., 57
Powell, J., 397
Powell, K. E., 368
Powell, M. C., 482
Prakash, A., 481
Pratkanis, A. R., 21, 119
Prentice, D. A., 190
Prentice-Dunn, S., 433
Presley, C. A., 183
Presley, L. M., 155
Presson, C. C., 190
Preston, E., 263
Pribble, W. E., 180
Price, D. L., 101
Prichep, L. S., 84
Pridgen, P. R., 407
Priestly, J., 20
Prioleau, L., 467
Pritchard, R. M., 122
Proctor, W., 370
Prodzinski, J., 501
Prothrow-Stith, D., 504
Proust, M., 138
Pruitt, D. G., 520
Prusoff, B. A., 430
Pryor, D. B., 372
Publilius Syrus, 419
Pugh, E. M., 63
Pugh, G. E., 63
Pulver, A. E., 437
Pumariega, A. J., 304
Putnam, F. W., 244, 425
Pyszczyski, T. A., 432, 515

Qualls, P. J., 370
Quanty, M. B., 345
Queen Elizabeth, 155
Quintana, D., 24

Rabin, A. S., 461
Rabin, B. S., 363
Rabinowitz, D., 308
Rachmiel, T. B., 432
Radecki, T., 505
Radtke, L., 176
Rae, D. S., 420
Rahn, C. W., 86
Raines, B. E., 190
Rajaram, S., 243
Ramey, C. T., 287
Ramey, S. L., 287
Ramón y Cajal, S., 37
Rand, C. S. W., 306
Randels, S. P., 72
Randi, J., 7, 155, 156
Rapoport, J. L., 420, 422
Rasmuson, I., 108
Rauch, S. L., 422
Rauma, D., 432
Rausching, H., 499
Raveis, V. H., 190
Rawlings, J., 89
Ray, O., 185
Raymond, D. S., 244
Rayner, R., 204, 205
Read, J. D., 120, 151
Reason, J., 151, 492
Redelmeier, D. A., 135
Reeves, J., 169
Regier, D., 413, 442, 443
Rehm, L. P., 461
Reid, J. B., 212, 504
Reiger, D. A., 420
Reisenzein, R., 354
Reiser, M., 155
Reiss, A. J., Jr., 503
Reite, M. L., 360
Remley, A., 85
Rende, R., 286
Renner, M. J., 74
Rescorla, R. A., 202
Resenberg, S. D.
Resnick, S. M., 422, 437
Ressler, R. K., 507
Rettersøl, N., 428
Retzlaff, P. D., 177
Reveen, P. J., 179
Reynolds, C. R., 102
Reynolds, W. F., Jr., 207
Reznick, J. S., 82
Rheingold, H. L., 82
Rhodes, S. R., 99
Rholes, W. S., 84, 354
Rhue, J. W., 177, 180
Ricci-Bitti, P. E., 340
Rice, B., 481
Rice, M. E., 218
Rich, C. L., 428
Richardson, E., 84
Richardson, J., 232
Richardson, K. D., 499
Richman, C. L., 229
Rieff, P., 386
Rieser-Danner, L. A., 513
Riggs, E. R., 495
Riley, M., 358
Ring, K., 186, 187

Rita, H., 359
Ritter, B., 456
Ritter, J. M., 513
Ritzman, S. E., 364
Rivara, F. P., 501
Robaum, F. M., 494
Robbins, M. A., 306
Roberts, L., 361
Roberts, T-A., 94
Robertson, B. A., 101
Robins, L., 413, 442, 443
Robinson, J. L., 82
Rochat, F., 489
Rock, I., 140, 146
Rock, J., 102
Rockefeller, J. D., Sr., 400
Rodgers, R., 352, 514
Rodin, J., 304, 305, 309, 360, 361, 404
Rodman, R., 266
Rodriguez, M. L., 91, 209
Roediger, H. L., III, 243
Roehlkepartain, E. C., 79, 110
Roehrs, T., 168, 172
Roemer, M. I., 371
Rog, D. J., 470
Rogers, C. R., 393, 394, 395, 396, 400, 401, 409,
   453, 454, 459, 463
Rogers, P. L., 339
Rogers, S., 119
Rogers, S. M., 317
Roggman, L. A., 513
Rogoff, B., 85
Rohner, R. P., 86
Romney, D. M., 86
Rook, K. S., 433
Roosevelt, E., 112, 394
Roosevelt, F. D., 237
Rorschach, H., 384, 385, 387
Rosch, E., 256, 272
Rose, G. A., 307
Rose, J. E., 187
Rose, R., 358
Rose, R. J., 108
Rosenbaum, M., 242, 514
Rosenberg, L., 99
Rosenberg, S. S., 190
Rosendahl, K., 473
Rosenheck, R., 360
Rosenman, R., 361, 362, 367
Rosenthal, D., 430
Rosenthal, R., 339, 392
Rosenzweig, M. R., 74
Ross, B., 16
Ross, H., 144
Ross, J., 95, 189
Ross, L., 9, 12, 328, 521
Ross, L. D., 259, 261, 263
Ross, L. T., 503
Ross, M., 244, 247
Ross, O., 218
Ross, S. A., 218
Rossi, A. S., 94
Rossi, P. H., 94
Rossi, P. J., 149
Roth, J. A., 503
Roth, S. H., 359
Roth, T., 168, 172
Roth, W. T., 98
Rothbart, M., 500
Rothblum, E. D., 309
Rothstein, M., 392
Rothstein, W. G., 105
Rotter, J., 403
Rottman, L., 512

Rotton, J., 440
Roviario, S., 369
Rowe, D. C., 110, 291
Rowe, J. S., 490
Roy, A., 471
Roy, K., 473
Rozin, P., 201, 303
Ruback, R. B., 313, 404
Rubin, J. Z., 520
Rubin, Z., 339
Ruble, D. N., 105, 385
Rubonis, A. V., 358
Ruchlis, H., 257
Rudner, R., 165
Rudorfer, M. V., 237
Ruffin, C. L., 359
Rule, B. G., 506
Rumbaugh, D. M., 269, 271
Runtz, M., 244
Rush, A. J., 460
Rush, B., 450
Rushforth, N. B., 501
Rushton, J. P., 218, 289, 501
Rusinek, H., 238
Rusiniak, K. W., 203
Russell, B., 172, 349
Russell, J. A., 256, 340, 344
Russo, N. F., 359, 360, 506
Rutter, M., 84
Ryan, E. D., 324
Ryan, R. M., 324, 325
Ryckman, R. M., 306
Rzewnicki, R., 310

Saal, F. E., 316
Sabini, J., 487
Sacks, O., 60, 138, 237, 273, 281
Saddock, B. J., 471
Sadi, 134
Sagan, C., 7, 16, 45, 16, 130, 156, 269, 414
Sagart, L., 265
Sagi, D., 173
Saklofske, D. H., 406, 440
Salazar, W., 368
Saleh, W. E., 403
Salovey, P., 346
Salter, W., 275
Salthouse, T. A., 99, 234
Saltzberg, J. A., 432
Samuel, M., 317
Samuels, S., 16
Sandberg, G. G., 506
Sanders, B., 290
Sandos, P., 495
Sapolsky, B. S., 96, 508
Sapolsky, R. M., 75
Sarna, S., 108
Sarnoff, I., 312
Sarnoff, S., 312
Saron, C. D., 338
Sartorius, N. R., 356, 413
Sartre, J-P., 371
Sato, K., 510
Saunders, W. B., 372
Savage-Rumbaugh, S., 271
Sax, L. J., 188, 316, 347
Sayette, M. A., 458
Sayre, R. F., 100
Scafidi, F., 74
Scarr, S., 111, 282, 286, 287, 289
Schab, F. R., 138
Schachter, S., 309, 310
Schacter, D. L., 172, 227, 238

Schacter, S., 353, 354, 374, 375
Schaie, K. W., 99, 102
Schalling, D., 502
Schanberg, S. M., 74
Scheerer, M., 258, 260
Scheier, M. F., 360
Schein, E. H., 482
Schell, D. A., 101
Scherer, K., 340, 341, 344
Schiavi, R. C., 168
Schiavo, R. S., 490
Schieber, F., 99
Schiffenbauer, A., 490
Schilling, E. A., 347
Schleifer, S. J., 364
Schlesinger, A. M., Jr., 492
Schloredt, B., 144
Schmidlin, A. M., 328
Schmidtke, A., 485
Schnaper, N., 186
Schneider, H. G., 96
Schneider, I., 444
Schneiderman, N., 364
Schnittjer, S. K., 262
Schoeneman, T. J., 400
Schoenfeld, B., 498
Schofield, J. W., 519
Schonfield, S., 101
Schooler, J. W., 243
Schoonover, R., 390
Schreiber, C. A., 135, 237
Schreiner-Engel, P., 168
Schuckit, M. A., 189
Schulenberg, J., 190
Schulman, P., 404
Schulsinger, F., 430
Schwartz, B., 204, 421
Schwartz, J. E., 372
Schwartz, J. H., 236
Schwartz, S., 443
Schwarz, N., 242, 346
Schwarzenegger, A., 508
Schweiger, U., 304
Sciacchitano, A. M., 359
Scott, B. A., 340
Scott, C., 368
Scott, R., 86
Scott, W. A., 86
Seccombe, K., 105
Sedgwick, J., 9
Sedikides, C., 94
Seeman, P., 437
Segal, N. L., 109, 286
Segall, M. H., 80, 316, 495, 499
Segerstrom, S. C., 405
Segmen, J., 230
Segrin, C., 432
Seidenberg, M. S., 270
Seigel, R. K., 189
Self, E. A., 190
Seligman, M. E. P., 163, 166, 174, 336, 399, 404,
    405, 408, 431, 432, 432, 461, 492
Selye, H., 356, 357, 367, 374
Seneca, 98, 227, 348, 404, 502, 516
Senulis, J. A., 338
Service, R. F., 237
Seuss, Dr., 135
Sevcik, R. A., 271
Sexter, M., 342
Shadish, W. R., 462
Shaffer, D., 485
Shakespeare, W., 157, 216, 255, 339, 344, 426,
    427, 428
Sham, P., 437

Shaman, P., 99
Shamir, B., 328
Shanks, D., 267
Shapiro, A., 168
Shapiro, D. A., 467
Shapiro, H., 75
Sharma, A. R., 79, 110
Shase, W. G., 230
Shaughnessey, J. J., 22
Shaver, P. R., 84
Shaw, B. F., 460
Shaw, G. B., 515
Shaw, H. E., 308
Shaw, H. L., 271
Shaw, S., 155
Shea, M. T., 466
Shea, T., 466
Sheehan, K., 342
Sheehan, P. W., 370
Sheehan, S., 434
Shehan, C. L., 105
Shekelle, R. B., 364
Shenton, M. E., 437
Shepard, R. N., 27, 145, 146, 150, 151
Shepherd, C., 441
Sheppard, L. A., 521
Shereshevskii, 223, 231
Sherif, M., 519
Sherman, S. J., 190, 258
Sherry, D., 238
Shettleworth, S. J., 213, 234
Shiber, J. R., 366
Shneidman, E., 428
Shoda, Y., 91, 209
Shontz, F. C., 385
Shotland, R. L., 316, 517
Showers, C., 405
Shrout, P. E., 429, 443
Shtark, M. B., 370
Shtasel, D., 437
Shulman, D., 342
Shulruff, L. I., 425
Siegal, M., 244, 398
Siegel, J. M., 371
Siegel, L. S., 78
Siegel, R. K., 183, 185, 186, 187
Siegler, I. C., 372
Sigmund, B. B., 365
Signorielli, N., 505, 508
Siksorski, L., 99
Silberstein, L. R., 304
Silva, A. J., 237
Silva, C. E., 177
Silver, M., 489
Silver, R. C., 107
Silverman, K., 184
Silverman, P. S., 177
Silverton, L., 444
Simmons, R. G., 89
Simon, H. A., 230
Simon, P., 505
Simon, T., 276, 293
Simonton, D. K., 103, 284, 324
Simpson, J. A., 84
Simpson, O. J., 155
Sims, C. A., 425, 426
Sinclair, R. C., 354
Sing, H., 169
Singer, D. G., 505
Singer, J. E., 353, 354
Singer, J. L., 175, 466, 505
Singh, D., 514
Singh, V. J., 328
Sinha, Y., 481

Sjöstrum, L., 307
Skevington, S., 90
Skinner, B. F., 207, 208, 210, 211, 212, 213, 214,
    215, 219, 220, 266, 268, 275, 431
Sklar, L. S., 364
Skodol, A. E., 423, 429, 443
Skoner, D. P., 364
Skov, R. B., 258
Slavin, R. E., 520
Sleek, S., 472
Slochower, J., 305
Sloss, E. M., 184
Slovic, P., 8, 261
Smart, R. G., 188
Smith, A., 58, 437, 509
Smith, A. P., 364
Smith, D., 450
Smith, E., 245
Smith, G., 424
Smith, M. B., 400
Smith, M. L., 465, 466
Smith, P. B., 328, 487
Smith, T. W., 311, 348, 495, 497
Snarey, J. R., 91
Snidman, N., 82
Snodgrass, M. A., 433
Snyder, D., 506
Snyder, M., 444
Snyder, S. H., 37, 39, 471, 473
Soares, M. P., 290
Sobol, A. M., 306
Sockloskie, R. J., 507
Sokhadze, E. M., 370
Sokoll, G. R., 336
Solomon, M., 513
Solomon, Z., 360
Somes, G., 501
Sommer, R., 494
Sonenstein, F. L., 96, 316
Sontag, S., 365
Sorenson, S. B., 420
Sotsky, S. M., 466
Sowell, T., 521
Spangenberg, E. R., 21
Spanos, N. P., 176, 178, 179, 180, 425
Spearman, C., 184, 280, 281
Specher, S., 94
Specht, J. C., 400
Spector, P. E., 327
Spelke, E., 77, 181
Sperling, G., 233
Sperry, R., 59, 60, 61, 64, 128
Spiegel, D., 365
Spielberger, C., 362
Spiess, W. F. J., 315
Spitzberg, B. H., 433
Spitzer, R. L., 423, 444
Spradley, J. P., 495
Sprecher, S., 513
Springer, B., 109
Springer, J., 109
Springer, L., 109
Springer, S. P., 62
Spritzer, C. E., 430
Squire, L. R., 236, 237, 238
Sroufe, L. A., 83
St. John, 427
Stack, S., 428
Stagg, A. A., 102
Stallone, S., 508
Stanley-Hagan, M., 84
Starker, S., 168
Stattin, H., 89
Staub, E., 483, 504

Staubli, U., 236, 237
Steel, R. P., 327
Steele, C. M., 183, 289
Steele, S., 25, 498
Steer, R. A., 428
Stein, D. G., 58
Stein, J. A., 112
Stein, M., 313, 364
Stein, S., 430
Steinberg, L., 95
Steinberg, N., 512
Steinem, G., 508
Stengel, E., 428
Stephens, P. M., 359
Stephens, T., 368
Stepper, S., 342
Stern, L., 342
Stern, W., 277
Sternberg, R. J., 275, 282, 516
Stevens, C. F., 237
Stevenson, H. W., 289, 290
Stevenson, R. L., 424
Stice, E., 308
Stiles, W. B., 467
Stillinger, C., 521
Stillwell, A., 346
Stipek, D., 287
Stock, W. E., 316
Stockdale, M. S., 316
Stockton, M. C., 314
Stoll, A. L., 430
Stoltzfus, E. R., 101
Stone, A. A., 347, 364, 432
Stoppard, J. M., 94
Storms, M. D., 318, 319, 480, 490
Stpeanski, E., 172
Strack, F., 242, 342
Strack, S., 432
Strain, E. C., 184
Strange, D. R., 390
Strange, S. L., 93
Stratton, G. M., 150
Straub, R. O., 30, 33, 270
Straus, M. A., 212
Stravinsky, I., 207
Streissguth, A. P., 72
Strentz, H., 155
Strickland, F., 441
Striegel-Moore, R. H., 304
Strum, G., 342
Strupp, H. H., 467
Stueve, A., 429, 443
Stunkard, A. J., 308
Suarez, S. D., 26
Suddarth, R. L., 439
Sue, D. W., 469
Suedfeld, P., 187
Sugar, O., 58
Suinn, R. M., 274
Sullivan, A., 74
Sullivan, M. J., 246
Sulloway, F. J., 324
Suls, J. M., 349
Sultan, 257
Sundel, M., 103
Sundstrom, E., 328
Suomi, S. J., 81, 82, 108, 381, 422
Suppes, P., 79
Susman, E. J., 112
Sutton, S. K., 421
Svikis, D. S., 189
Swayze, V., II., 437
Sweat, J. A., 155
Sweeney, M., 203

Sweeney, P. D., 403
Sweet, R., 441
Swerdlow, N. R., 437
Swets, J. A., 156, 274
Swinson, R. P., 430
Szasz, T., 416
Szucko, J. J., 337
Szymanski, K., 491

Tabarlet, J. O., 96, 508
Tabb, S., 531
Taha, F. A., 172
Taj, J., 86
Tajfel, H., 499
Takei, N., 437
Tam, D., 437
Tamarkin, L., 366
Tamis-LeMonda, C. S., 86
Tanaka, J. S., 507
Tanaka, K., 398
Tanke, E. D., 493
Tannen, D., 24, 94
Tanner, J. M., 88
Tarshish, C., 238
Tashkin, D. P., 187
Tassinary, L. G., 339
Tatarkiewicz, W., 347
Tatro, M., 319
Tavris, C., 248, 346
Tayeb, M., 328
Taylor, H. L., 301
Taylor, L., 320
Taylor, S., 186, 502
Taylor, S. E., 262, 371, 397, 398
Taylor, S. P., 502
Tchaikovsky,, 273
Teevan, R. C., 324
Teghtsoonian, R., 121
Teitelbaum, P., 302
Tellegen, A., 109, 110
Temple, M. T., 311
Tennen, H., 347
Teresi, D., 51
Teri, L., 429, 433
Terman, L., 276, 277, 279, 283, 284, 293
Terrace, H., 12
Terrace, H. S., 270
Tertullian, 499
Tesch, F., 349
Tesser, A., 459
Testa, M., 359
Tetlock, P. E., 521
Thaler, R., 262
Thatcher, R. W., 111
Thayer, R. E., 368
Thee, S. L., 262
Theorell, T., 364
Thomas, A., 82, 112
Thomas, G. C., 490
Thomas, G. V., 26
Thomas, L., 39, 69, 137, 465, 470
Thomas, S. L., 505
Thompson, C. P., 234
Thompson, D. D., 490
Thompson, J. K., 239, 309
Thompson, L. L., 499
Thompson, L. T., 236
Thompson, P. D., 368
Thompson, R. F., 239
Thoreau, H. D., 311
Thorndike, A. L., 278
Thorndike, E. L., 207, 212
Thornton, B., 513

Thun, M., 184
Tice, D. M., 87, 396
Tichener, E. B., 45
Tiebout, J., 373
Tiger, L., 213
Tiggemann, M., 309
Timberlake, W., 208
Timko, C., 500
Tinbergen, N., 298
Tirrell, M. E., 200, 201
Toda, S., 86
Tohen, M., 430
Tolchin, M., 261
Tolstoy, L., 5, 104, 427, 444
Tomita, M., 340
Tomlinson-Keasey, C., 372
Tonegawa, S., 237
Toole, E., 441
Tordoff, V., 234
Torrey, B. B., 437
Torrey, E. F., 437, 439, 468
Toufexis, A., 95
Towler, G., 490
Treadgold, A., 224
Treadgold, L., 224
Trevino, J. G., 498
Triandis, H. C., 341, 398, 399, 404, 494, 495, 504
Trickett, P. K., 244
Triesman, A., 140
Trimble, J. E., 189
Trindis, H. C., 85
Tripathi, R. C., 481
Triplett, N., 490
Trocki, K. F., 311
Troilier, T. K., 14
Tronick, E., 142
Trost, M. R., 316
True, R. M., 179
True, W. R., 360
Truman, H. S., 237, 493
Tsang, Y. C., 302
Tsuang, M. T., 430
Tubbs, M. E., 327
Tucker, J. S., 372
Turk, D. C., 135, 370
Turkheimer, F., 286
Turkington, C., 466
Turnbull, B., 154, 156, 157
Turner, C. F., 317
Turner, C. W., 505
Turner, R., 468
Tversky, A., 15, 16, 259, 346, 532
Twain, M., 90, 214, 287, 396
Twiss, C., 531
Tyrell, D. A. J., 364
Tzavaras, A., 340
Tzemach, M., 429

Udry, J. R., 313
Ulman, K. J., 88
Ulmer, D., 361, 371
Ulrich, R., 26
Umberson, D., 372
Underwood, B. J., 246
Urbany, J. E., 262
Urrows, S., 347

Vaccarino, A. L., 238
Vachon, R., 16
Vaid, J., 62
Valdimardottir, H., 364
Valenstein, E. S., 474

Vallone, R. P., 9, 16, 261
Van Berkel, C., 75
Vance, E. B., 312
Van de Castle, R. L., 172
van den Boom, D., 83
Vander Stoep, S. W., 22
Van Dyke, C., 186
Van Horn, J. D., 437
van IJzendoorn, M. H., 82
Van Leeuwen, M. D., 227
Van Leeuwen, M. S., 279, 495
Van Lighten, O., 342
van Ree, J. M., 39
Van Tol, H. H. M., 437
Van Yperen, N. W., 516
Vardi, D., 86
Vaughn, K. B., 343
Vaux, A., 433
Vazquez, C., 241
Vazsonyi, A. T., 291
Vega-Lahr, N., 74
Vekassy, L., 172
Vemer, E., 105
Venn, J., 178
Virgil, 18, 324, 344
Visant, S., 187
Vlassidis, M. C., 319
Vogel, P., 59
Vokey, J. R., 120, 151
Voltaire, 64
von Ebner-Eschenbach, M., 102
von Senden, M., 149
Vygotsky, L., 79

Wadden, T. A., 307, 309
Waddington, J. L., 437
Wagner, A. R., 202
Wagner, D., 242
Wagner, N. N., 312
Wagner, R. K., 282
Wagstaff, G., 481
Wahl, O. F., 444
Wakefield, J. C., 316, 414
Waldman, I. D., 289
Walk, R. D., 141, 148
Walker, L. C., 101
Walker, R. A., 111
Wall, P. D., 134, 135
Wallace, M., 430
Wallace, R. K., 175
Wallach, L., 400
Wallach, M. A., 400
Wallbott, H., 341, 344
Wallis, C., 359
Walsh, G. W., 188
Walster, E., 512
Walters, B., 152
Walters, P. S., 521
Wang, Y., 237
Ward, A., 9
Ward, C., 183
Ward, D. D., 515
Ware, E. E., 403
Warr, P., 371
Warren, W., 95, 189
Warwick, D., 70
Washburn, A. L., 301
Washoe, 269, 270, 271
Wason, P. C., 9, 258
Wasserman, E. A., 207
Wasserman, J., 184
Waterhouse, R., 528
Waterman, A. S., 93

Waterman, R. H., Jr., 215
Waters, E., 82
Watkins, J. G., 424-425
Watkins, J. T., 466
Watkins, M. J., 228
Watson, J., 430
Watson, J. B., 163, 198, 202, 204, 205, 206, 212, 219, 220, 455
Watson, R. I., Jr., 491
Watson, T., 215
Weaver, J. B., 314
Webb, M. C., 430
Webb, W. B., 168, 170
Weber, E., 121
Wechsler, D., 101, 277, 293
Wechsler, H., 183
Weekes, J. R., 180
Weesner, K. E., 172
Weilbaker, D. C., 262
Weinberg, M. S., 318
Weinberg, R. A., 289
Weinberger, D. R., 439
Weiner, R. D., 430
Weingartner, H., 237
Weinstein, N. D., 405
Weisel, H., 307
Weiss, J. M., 361
Weiss, L., 361
Weiss, R. D., 189
Weissman, M. M., 430
Weisz, J. R., 494
Weitzman, M. S., 519
Welch, Q. B., 428
Weldon, M. S., 237
Welham, J., 437
Wellman, H. M., 77
Wells, B. L., 315
Wells, G. L., 196, 244
Wells, H. G., 526
Wender, P. H., 430
Wener, R., 404
Werker, J. F., 265
Wernicke, K., 55
West, P. D. B., 132
West, R. L., 100
Westefeld, J. S., 428
Wethington, E., 471
Wetzel, R. D., 428
Wheeler, D. R., 155
Wheeler, M. A., 243
Whelan, J. P., 274
White, B. D., 303
White, G. L., 515
White, H. R., 503
White, K. M., 95
White, L., 105
Whitehead, A. N., 346
Whiten, A., 14
Whiting, B. B., 85
Whitley, B. E., Jr., 320
Whitman, C., 338
Whitman, W., 36
Whorf, B. L., 272, 275
Wible, C. G., 224, 236
Wickelgren, W. A., 229
Wicker, A. W., 481
Wickramaratne, P., 430
Widom, C. S., 84
Wiegant, V. M., 39
Wiens, A. N., 457
Wiesel, T. N., 127, 128, 131, 149
Wigdor, A. K., 291
Wilde, O., 396
Wilder, D. A., 499

Wiley, J. A., 317
Wilkinson, W. E., 430
Williams, A. F., 106
Williams, C., 318
Williams, C. L., 358
Williams, J. B. W., 423
Williams, J. E., 18, 327
Williams, K. D., 491
Williams, L., 328
Williams, L. M., 84, 248, 248
Williams, R., 362
Williams, R. B., 372
Williams, R. T., 307
Williams, S. L., 271, 456
Williamson, D., 363
Williamson, D. A., 304
Williamson, G. M., 364
Williamson, S. J., 233
Willis, P. W., Jr., 363
Willmuth, M. E., 315
Wilson, D. B., 466
Wilson, E. O., 217
Wilson, G. T., 183
Wilson, J. P., 360
Wilson, J. Q., 502
Wilson, M. R., 462
Wilson, P., 462
Wilson, R. C., 492
Wilson, R. S., 75
Wilson, S. C., 187
Wilson, T. D., 260
Wiltshire, S., 281
Windholz, G., 201
Winfrey, O., 155, 310, 323
Wing, A. L., 368
Wing, R. R., 308, 310
Wingard, D. L., 372
Winkelstein, W., Jr., 317
Winograd, E., 237
Winzenz, D., 230
Witelson, S. F., 62, 320
Witting, R., 172
Wittlinger, R. P., 240
Wixted, J. T., 234
Wolf, A. S., 444
Wolf, N., 308
Wolfe, M., 319
Woll, S., 513
Wolpe, J., 455, 463
Wolpert, E. A., 172
Wolyniec, P., 437
Wong, C. S. K., 104
Wong, D. F., 437
Wong, F. Y., 505
Wong, M. M., 94
Wood, G., 8
Wood, J. M., 172, 227
Wood, J. V., 432
Wood, L., 492
Wood, W., 94, 327, 493, 505
Woodruff-Pak, D. S., 101
Woods, N. F., 88
Woodyard, D., 208
Wooley, O., 304
Wooley, S., 304
Wooley, S. C., 308
Worthington, E. L., Jr., 90
Wortman, C. B., 106, 107, 317, 365
Wotman, S. R., 346
Wright, F. L., 102
Wright, P., 437
Wu, T-C., 187
Wulff, D., 325
Wundt, W., 2, 31

Wyatt, G. E., 359
Wyatt, J. K., 172, 227
Wynn, K., 77
Wysocki, C. J., 137

Yalom, I. D., 462
Yang, N., 506
Yanof, D. S., 95
Yapko, M. D., 178
Yarnell, P. R., 237
Yates, A., 304
Yeager, C., 84
Yeats, W. B., 513
Yellen, A., 166, 174

Yeltsin, B., 295
Young, D., 428
Young, J. E., 427, 433
Young, R. D., 183
Yuh, W. T. C., 437
Yuille, J. C., 229

Zahn-Waxler, C., 82
Zajonc, R. B., 120, 278, 342, 354, 355, 374, 490,
    512, 534
Zanna, M. P., 183
Zborowski, M. J., 473
Zeidner, M., 289
Zellman, G. L., 385

Zelnik, M., 321
Zeno, 453
Zhang, S-D., 320
Zigler, E. F., 84, 287, 288
Zilbergeld, B., 464, 466
Zillmann, D., 314, 338, 354, 432, 507
Zimbardo, P. G., 177, 483, 491
Zimmerman, R., 437
Zoglin, R., 152
Zorick, F., 168
Zucker, G. S., 481
Zuckerman, M., 299
Zuker, K. J., 317
Zwyghuizen-Doorenbos, A., 172

Subject Index

Abnormal behavior. *See* Psychological disorders
Absolute thresholds, 119
Abuse, of children, repressed memories of, 248–249
Acceptance, in person-centered therapy, 394, 453
Accommodation (of lens), 125
Accuracy, of memories, 242–245
Acetylcholine (ACh), 39
Achievement, 104
Achievement motivation, 323–328
  identifying, 323–324
  intrinsic versus extrinsic motivation and, 324–326
  motivating people and, 325–328
  sources of, 324
Achievement tests, 276
Acquired immunodeficiency syndrome (AIDS), 106
Acquisition, 200
ACT (American College Testing) exam, 278
Action potential, 36
Active listening, in person-centered therapy, 453, 454
Acute schizophrenia, 436
Adaptation
  to environment, learning and, 203
  perceptual, 149–150
  sensory, 122–123
Adaptation-level principle, 348–349
Adolescence, 87–97
  cognitive development during, 89–91
  personality development during, 380

physical development during, 88–89
  sexuality during, 95–97
  social development during, 92–97
Adoption studies, 110
  of intelligence, 286
  of obesity, 307–308
  of schizophrenia, 438
Adrenal glands, 44
Adrenaline, 44
  arousal and, 336
  stress response and, 357
Adulthood, 97–107
  cognitive changes during, 100–103
  personality development during, 380–381
  physical changes during, 98–100
  social changes during, 103–107
Aerobic exercise, for stress management, 368–369
Affect, flat, in schizophrenia, 436
Affiliation, 104
Afterimages, 129–130
Age. *See also* Aging; *specific age groups, e.g.,* Adolescence
  mental, 276
  suicide rates and, 428
Age regression, hypnosis and, 177–178, 179
Aggression, 501–508
  aversive events and, 503
  biology of, 501–503
  learning to express and inhibit, 503–504
  sexual, 205, 248–249, 506–507
  television watching and, 504–508

Aging
  intelligence and, 101–103
  memory and, 100–101
Agoraphobia, 420
AIDS (acquired immunodeficiency syndrome), 106
Alarm reaction, 357
Alcohol, 182–183, 188
  adolescent pregnancy and, 96
  aggression and, 502–503
  fetal alcohol syndrome and, 72
  reasons for use of, 188, 189
Algorithms, for problem solving, 257
All-or-none response, 37
Alpha waves, 167
Altruism, 516–519
  bystander intervention and, 517–518
  reciprocity norm and, 519
  social exchange theory of, 518–519
  social responsibility norm and, 519
Alzheimer's disease, 100, 237
American College Testing (ACT) exam, 278
Amnesia, 223
  dissociative, 423–424
  infantile, 249
  posthypnotic, 176
Amphetamines, 184
Amygdala, 49–50
Anal expulsive personality, 381
Anal retentive personality, 381
Anal stage, 380
Anger, 344–346

heart disease and, 362
physiological states accompanying, 338
Animal research
ethics of, 26–27
on language, 268–271
on problem solving, 257
reasons for, 24
Anorexia nervosa, 304
Antianxiety drugs, 472
Antidepressant drugs, 472–473
Antipsychotic drugs, 471–472
Antisocial personality disorder, 440–441
Anvil (bone), 132
Anxiety. *See also* Fears
defense mechanisms and, 381–382
drug therapy for, 472
stranger, 81
Anxiety disorders, 418–422
biological perspective on, 422
drug therapy for, 472
generalized, 418–419
learning perspective on, 421–422
obsessive-compulsive, 418, 420
phobic, 418, 419–420
psychoanalytic perspective on, 421
Apes
language in, 269–271
problem solving by, 257
Aphasia, 55
Applied research, 6
Aptitude tests, 276
Arousal
emotions and, 335–336
sexual, physiological states accompanying, 338
Arousal theory of motivation, 299
Association, free, 378
Association areas, 54–55
Associative learning, 196–198. *See also* Classical conditioning; Operant conditioning
Astrology, 406–407
Attachment, 81–85, 104
deprivation of, 84
divorce and, 84–85
effects of, 83–85
origins of, 81–83
Attention
conscious, 165
selective, 164
Attitudes, 481–484. *See also* Beliefs; Prejudice
effect of behavior on, 482–484
effect on behavior, 481–482
roles and, 483
scientific, 7
sexual, 316
Attraction, 511–516. *See also* Love
physical attractiveness and, 512–514
proximity and, 512
romantic love and, 515–516
similarity and, 514–515
Attribution, 479–481
of blame, mood disorders and, 431
conflict and, 510
effects of, 480–481
individualistic vs. collectivistic values concerning, 398
Attribution theory, 479
Audition. *See* Hearing
Automatic processing, 226
Autonomic nervous system, 42
arousal and, 336
Autonomy, 92
Availability heuristic, 260
Aversive conditioning, 455, 457
Aversive events, aggression and, 503

Awareness, conscious, 164
Axons, 36

Babbling stage, 265
Backward messages, 120
Barbiturates, 184
Basic research, 6
Basic trust, 84
Basilar membrane, 132
Behavior
abnormal. *See* Psychological disorders
assessment of, social-cognitive perspective on personality and, 405–407
attitudes affecting, 481–482
cultural factors and, 23–24
definition of, 3
effect on attitudes, 482–484
gender and, 24
mood disorders and, 429
operant, 206–207
sexual. *See* Sexual behavior
social. *See* Social development; Social psychology
Behavioral medicine, 356
Behavioral perspective, 4. *See also* Classical conditioning; Learning; Operant conditioning
on language development, 266
Behaviorism, 163, 198
Behavior therapies, 455–458
classical conditioning techniques, 455–457
operant conditioning techniques, 457–458
Beliefs
perseverance of, decision making and, 262–263
self-defeating, mood disorders and, 431
Belonging, need for, 328–330
Bias
confirmation, 258
hindsight, 8–9
ingroup, 499
in intelligence tests, 291–292
self-serving, 396–398, 510
Big Five theory of personality, 389
Binocular cues, 142
Biochemical influences. *See* Drugs; Hormones
Biofeedback, for stress management, 369–370
Biological perspective, 4, 67. *See also* Biological predispositions; Genetic factors; Nature-nurture issue; Physiology
on aggression, 501–503
on anxiety disorders, 422
on mood disorders, 430
on sexual orientation, 319–320
Biological predispositions
classical conditioning and, 202–203
operant conditioning and, 213–214
Biological psychologists, 6, 36
Biomedical therapies, 470–474
drug therapies, 470–473
electroconvulsive therapy, 473
psychosurgery, 474
Bipolar cells, 126
Bipolar disorder, 426, 427, 429
drug therapy for, 473
Birth control, 96
Blame-the-victim dynamic, 498
Blindness, color, 129
Blind spot, 126
Blood-brain barrier, 40
Body chemistry, hunger and, 302
Body contact, attachment and, 81–82
Body position sense, 138
Body weight. *See also* Obesity

dieting and, 308–310
metabolic rate and, 303, 307
set point for, 302–303, 307
Bones, of ear, 132
Borderline personality disorder, 440
Bottom-up processing, 117
Brain, 45–63, 255. *See also* Amygdala; Brainstem; Cerebral cortex; Corpus callosum; Hippocampus; Hypothalamus; Limbic system
Alzheimer's disease and, 100
depression and, 430
development of, 74–75
hemispheres of, 58–64
hunger and, 302–303
imaging of, 47
left. *See* Hemispheric specialization
lesions in, 46, 55
lower level structures of, 45, 48–51
memory and, 235–239
recording electrical activity of, 46
reflexes and, 43
reorganization of, 58
right. *See* Hemispheric specialization
schizophrenia and, 437
sexual orientation and, 319
Brainstem, 45, 48
Brightness, relative, as monocular cue, 144
Brightness constancy, 147–148
Broca's area, 55
Bulimia nervosa, 304
Bystander effect, 517–518

Cancer, stress and, 364–365
Cannon-Bard theory of emotion, 352–353
Case study method, 11–12
Catastrophes, stress and, 358
Catatonia, 436
Categorization, prejudice and, 500
Catharsis, 345
CAT (computerized axial tomograph) scans, 47
Causation, correlation and, 17
Central nervous system, 41, 42–43. *See also* Brain
Central tendencies, 528
Cerebellum, 48–49
Cerebral cortex, 51–57
association areas of, 54–55
functions of, 52–57
motor areas of, 52–53
sensory areas of, 53–54
structure of, 51–52
Change. *See* Stability/change issue
Childhood. *See also* Adolescence; Infancy
cognitive development during, 75–76, 78–80
eyewitness recall during, 244–245
intelligence testing during, 277
language development during, 265–268
parenting during. *See* Parenting
personality development during, 380
physical development during, 74–75
Project Head Start and, 288
social development during, 84–87
Child-rearing. *See* Parenting
Chimpanzees
language in, 269–271
problem solving by, 257
Chlorpromazine (Thorazine), 471
Chromosomes, 70–71
sex, 71
Chronic schizophrenia, 436
Chunking, 230
Cigarette smoking. *See* Nicotine
Circadian rhythm, 165–166

Clairvoyance, 154
Clarification, for active listening, 454
Classical conditioning, 196, 197, 198–206
    acquisition and, 200
    applications of, 204–205
    in behavior therapy, 455–457
    biological predispositions and, 202–203
    cognitive processes and, 202
    discrimination and, 201
    extinction and, 200
    generalization and, 201
    of immune system, 365–367
    operant conditioning compared with, 216
    Pavlov's experiments in, 198–201
    rape as, 205
    spontaneous recovery and, 201
Clinical psychologists, 6
Closure, perceptual grouping and, 141
Clozapine (Clozaril), 471
Cocaine, 185–186, 188
Cochlea, 132
Cocktail party effect, 164
Cognition, 76, 256. See also Information processing; Intelligence; Thinking
    classical conditioning and, 202
    emotion and, 353–355
    mood disorders and, 429
    operant conditioning and, 213
    prejudice and, 500
Cognitive behavior therapy. See Cognitive therapies
Cognitive development
    during adolescence, 89–91
    during adulthood, 100–103
    during childhood, 75–76, 78–80
    during infancy, 75–77
    Piaget's theory of, 75–80, 90
Cognitive dissonance theory, 484
Cognitive maps, 213
Cognitive perspective, 4. See also Social-cognitive perspective on mood disorders; Social-cognitive perspective on personality
    on language development, 267–268
Cognitive psychologists, 256
Cognitive therapies, 458–461
    for depression, 460–461
    rational-emotive therapy, 459–460
Collective unconscious, 383–384
Collectivism, 389–399
Color blindness, 129
Color constancy, 130
Color vision, 129–130
    color constancy and, 130
Commitment, 104
Common sense, 8
Communication. See also Language; Language development
    neural, 37–40. See also Neurotransmitters
    nonverbal, 339–341
    peacemaking and, 520–521
Community mental health programs, 463–464
Companionate love, 515–516
Competence, 92, 104
Compulsions, in obsessive-compulsive disorder, 420
Computerized axial tomograph (CAT) scans, 47
Concepts, 256–257
Conciliation, peacemaking and, 521
Concrete operational stage, 79
Conditioned response (CR), 199
Conditioned stimulus (CS), 199, 200, 201
Conditioning, 196–197. See also Classical conditioning; Operant conditioning
    aversive, 455, 457
Cones (retinal), 126

Confirmation bias, 258
Conflict, 509–511
    enemy perceptions and, 510
    resolving. See Peacemaking
    social traps and, 509–510
Conformity, 485–487, 489
    group pressure and, 485–487
    obedience and, 487–489
Connectedness, perceptual grouping and, 141
Conscience, 380
Consciousness, 163–192. See also Dreams; Hypnosis; Sleep
    daydreams and, 175
    drugs and. See Psychoactive drugs
    levels of information processing and, 164–165
    meditation and, 175
    selective attention and, 164
    study of, 163–165
Conservation principle, 78–79
Constancy, perceptual, 145–148
    lightness, 147–148
    shape and size, 145–147
Context effects
    perceptual set and, 151, 153
    retrieval and, 241
Continuity, perceptual grouping and, 140
Continuity/stages issue, 69, 111
Continuous reinforcement, 210
Control
    locus of, external versus internal, 403
    perceived, stress and, 360–361
    personal. See Personal control
    social, 493
Control condition, 19
Conventional morality, 91
Convergence, as binocular cue, 142
Conversion disorder, 423
Cooperation, peacemaking and, 519–520
Coping, with stress. See Stress management
Coronary heart disease. See Heart disease
Corpus callosum, 59
Correlation, 14–17, 20, 530–532
    causation and, 17
    illusory, 14–15
    random events and, 15–16
    reliability and, 279–280
Correlation coefficient, 530–531
Cortex. See Cerebral cortex
Counterconditioning, 455
CR (conditioned response), 199
Creative intelligence, 282
Creativity, 282, 284
Criminals, antisocial personality disorder and, 440–441
Critical periods, attachment and, 82
Critical thinking, 7. See also Research
    about extrasensory perception, 156–157
    about humanistic perspective on personality, 399–401
    about psychoanalytic perspective, 385–386
    about social-cognitive perspective on personality, 407
    about trait perspective on personality, 391–393
Cross-sectional studies, of intellectual decline, 101
Crystallized intelligence, 102
CS (conditioned stimulus), 199, 200, 201
Cues
    binocular, 142
    monocular, 142–144
    retrieval, 240–242
Cultural sharing, peacemaking and, 521
Cultural similarities and differences, 494–495
    in attractiveness, 514
    behavior and, 23–24

    child-rearing and, 85–86
    drug use and, 189
    in emotional expression, 340–341
    gender roles and, 495
    hunger and, 303
    in intelligence, 289–290
    norms and, 494–495
    in perception of psychological disorders, 416
    psychotherapy and, 468–469
    self and, 389–399
    somatoform disorders and, 422–423
    in standards for acceptability of behaviors, 414, 416
    in suicide rates, 428
    thinking and, 272–273

Daily hassles, stress and, 359
Daydreams, 175
Death and dying, 106–107
Decibels, 132
Decision making, 259–263
    belief perseverance and, 262–263
    framing and, 262
    heuristics and, 259–261
    overconfidence and, 261–262
    risk perception and, 261
Declarative memory, 237–239
Defense mechanisms, 378, 381–382, 385
Deindividuation, 491
Déjà vu, 241
Delayed reinforcers, 209–210
Delta waves, 167
Delusions, in schizophrenia, 435
Dendrites, 36
Deoxyribonucleic acid (DNA), 71
Dependence, on drugs, 182
Dependent variable, 19
Depressants, 182–184, 188
    alcohol, 182–183, 188
    barbiturates (tranquilizers), 184
    opiates, 184, 188
Depression, 347. See also Mood disorders
    in bipolar (manic depressive) disorder, 426, 427
    cognitive therapy for, 460–461
    drug therapy for, 472–473
    heart disease and, 363
    major depressive disorder and, 426, 427
    physiological states accompanying, 338
    suicide and, 428
    vicious cycle of, 432
Deprivation
    of attachment, 84
    relative, happiness and, 349–350
Depth perception, 141–144
    binocular cues and, 142
    monocular cues and, 142–144
Descriptive research, 11–14, 20
    case study method for, 11–12
    naturalistic observation for, 13–14
    survey method for, 12–13
Descriptive statistics, 526–532
    central tendencies and, 528
    correlation and, 530–532
    distributions and, 526–527
    variation and, 528–529
Development, 69–112
    cognitive, 75–80, 89–91, 100–103
    continuity and stages and, 69, 111
    gender differences in, 86–87
    of language, 264–268
    nature-nurture issue and, 69, 108–111. See also Nature-nurture issue

of newborn, 72–73
physical, 74–75, 88–89, 98–100
prenatal, 70–72, 320
social, 80–87, 92–97, 103–107
stability and change and, 70, 101–103, 112
Developmental psychologists, 6, 69
Diagnostic and Statistical Manual of Mental Disorders (Fourth Edition) (DSM-IV), 417
Dieting, 308–310
hints for, 309
Difference thresholds, 121
Dipositional attribution, 479
Direct relationship, 14
Discrimination, in classical conditioning, 201
Disease. *See* Illness; Psychological disorders
Displacement, 382
Dissociated consciousness, hypnosis as, 180–181
Dissociation, 178
Dissociative disorders, 423–426
amnesia, 423–424
fugue, 424
identity, 424–426
Distance, size-distance relationship and, 145–147
Distributions, 526–527
Diversity, 525. *See also* Cultural similarities and differences; Gender similarities and differences
communication as response to, 520–521
conciliation as response to, 521
conflict as response to, 509–510
cooperation as response to, 519–520
kinship and, 25
prejudice as response to, 496–500
Divided-consciousness theory of hypnosis, 180–181
Divorce, 105
children and, 84–85
DNA (deoxyribonucleic acid), 71
Dopamine, 40
schizophrenia and, 437, 471
Double-blind procedure, 21
Down syndrome, 283
Dreams, 171–174
content of, 172
daydreams and, 175
functions of, 172–174
psychoanalytic perspective on, 172–173
Drive-reduction theory of motivation, 298
Drug addiction, 184–187
fetal alcohol syndrome and, 72
influences on, 188–190
neurotransmission and, 39–40
withdrawal and, 182
Drugs
aggression and, 502–503
neurotransmission and, 39–40
psychoactive. *See* Psychoactive drugs
Drug therapies, 470–473
antianxiety drugs and, 472
antidepressant drugs and, 472–473
antipsychotic drugs and, 471–472
DSM-IV (*Diagnostic and Statistical Manual of Mental Disorders [Fourth Edition]*), 417
Dying, 106–107

Ear
equilibrium and, 138
hearing and, 132–133
Eardrum, 132
Eating disorders, 304
Echoic memory, 233
Eclectic approach, 450
ECT (electroconvulsive therapy), 473
Education. *See also* Learning; Schools

operant conditioning in, 214–215
EEG (electroencephalogram), 46
Effortful processing, 226–228
Ego, 379
Egocentrism, 78
Ego defense mechanisms, 378, 381–382, 385
Ejaculation, premature, 315
Electra complex, 380
Electroconvulsive therapy (ECT), 473
Electroencephalogram (EEG), 46
during sleep, 167
Electromagnetic spectrum, 124
Embryo, 72
Emotion, 335–355. *See also specific emotions, e.g.,* Anger
amygdala, 49–50
arousal and, 335–337
cognition and, 353–355
cultural differences in expression of, 340–341
experiencing, 344–351
expressing, 338–343
facial expressions and, 339–343
in infants, 344
lie detection and, 337
negative, heart disease and, 362–363
physiology of, 335–338
reflection of, for active listening, 454
in schizophrenia, 436
theories of, 351–355
Emotional stability-instability dimension of personality, 389
Empathy, in psychotherapy, 394, 468
Empirical derivation of test items, 390
Employee participation, motivation and, 328
Empty nest syndrome, 105
Encoding, 226–232
automatic processing and, 226
effortful processing and, 226–228
forgetting as failure of, 231–232
of imagery, 229–230
of meaning, 228–229
organizing information for, 230–231
Endocrine system, 43–44. *See also* Hormones
Endorphins, 39
Enemies, perceptions of, 510
Environmental factors. *See also* Nature-nurture issue
creativity and, 284
in intelligence, 287–288
psychological disorders and, 416
Epinephrine, 44
arousal and, 366
stress response and, 357
Equilibrium, 138
Equity, companionate love and, 516
Erikson's stage theory, 92, 104–106
Erogenous zones, 380
ESP. *See* Extrasensory perception (ESP)
Estrogen, sexual behavior and, 313
Ethics, of research, 26–27
Ethnicity. *See* Cultural similarities and differences; Prejudice
Evolution
of brain, 45
of language, 266
of learning, 202–203
of motivation, 298
Excitement phase of sexual response cycle, 312
Exercise, aerobic, for stress management, 368–369
Exhaustion stage of general adaptation syndrome, 357
Experience
brain development and, 74–75
peak, 394

prior, happiness and, 348–349
Experiment(s), 18–22
ethics in, 26–27
relationship to everyday life, 23
Experimental condition, 19
Expertise, creativity and, 282, 284
Explicit memory, 237–239
Expressiveness, cultural similarities and differences in, 340–341
External incentives, hunger and, 305
External locus of control, 403
Extinction, 200
resistance to, 210
Extrasensory perception (ESP), 153–158
claims of, 154
skepticism about, 155–157
Extraversion, 388
Extraversion-introversion dimension of personality, 389
Extrinsic motivation, 324–325
Eye, 125–127. *See also* Vision
Eyewitness recall, of children, 244–245
Eysenck Personality Questionnaire, 389

Facial expressions, 339–343
cultural similarities and differences in, 340–341
effect on emotions, 342–343
emotion and, 339–341
Factor analysis
intelligence and, 281–282
of personality traits, 388
False consensus effect, 12
Familiarity, attachment and, 82
Families. *See* Divorce; Marriage; Parent(s); Parenting
Family therapy, 462
Fantasies, sexual behavior and, 315
FAS (fetal alcohol syndrome), 72
Fast MRI, 47
Fat cells, obesity and, 307
Fatness. *See* Obesity
Fears
phobic disorders and, 418, 419–420
physiological states accompanying, 338
systematic desensitization for, 455–457
Feature detectors, 127–128
Feel-good, do-good phenomenon, 346
Feelings. *See* Emotion
Females. *See* Gender similarities and differences; Sexual behavior; Women
Fetal alcohol syndrome (FAS), 72
Fetus, 72
Figure-ground relationship, 140
Fixation
as obstacle to problem solving, 258–259
psychoanalytic theory of, 380–381
Fixed-interval schedules, 211
Fixed-ratio schedules, 210
Flashbulb memories, 224
Flat affect, in schizophrenia, 436
Fluid intelligence, 102–103
Fluoxetine (Prozac), 472
Foot-in-the-door phenomenon, 482
Forgetting, 223–224. *See also* Amnesia
as encoding failure, 231–232
motivated, 247–249
as retrieval failure, 245–249
Formal operational stage, 79, 90
Form perception, 140–141
figure and ground and, 140
grouping and, 140–141
Framing, decision making and, 262

Fraternal twins, 108
Free association, 378
Frequency, of sound, 132
Freudian theory. *See* Psychoanalysis; Psychoanalytic perspective
Frontal lobes, 52
  damage to, 55
  lobotomy and, 474
Frustration-aggression principle, 503
Fugue, 424
Functional fixedness, 259
Functional MRI, 47
Fundamental attribution error, 480, 510

Ganglion cells, 126
GAS (general adaptation syndrome), 357
Gate-control theory of pain, 134–135
Gender, 86. *See also* Gender similarities and differences; Sexual behavior
  gender identity and, 86, 380
  gender roles and, 495
  gender-typing and, 86
Gender identity, 86
  psychoanalytic theory of, 380
Gender roles, 495
Gender schema theory, 86–87
Gender similarities and differences, 525
  behavior and, 24
  in development, 86–87
  in intelligence, 290–291
  prenatal development and, 71
  puberty and, 88–89
  in sexual attitudes and behaviors, 316
  social connectedness and, 94
  in suicide rates, 428
  in vulnerability to mood disorders, 429
Gender-typing, 86
General adaptation syndrome (GAS), 357
General intelligence (g) factor, 281
Generalization, 201
  from samples, 532–533
Generalized anxiety disorder, 418–419
Generativity, 104
Genetic factors. *See also* Nature-nurture issue
  in aggression, 501
  in drug use, 189
  in intelligence, 285–287
  in mood disorders, 430
  in obesity, 307–308
  in schizophrenia, 438
  in sexual orientation, 320
Genital stage, 380
Genuineness, in person-centered therapy, 394, 453
Gestalt, 139
g (general intelligence) factor, 281
Glands, endocrine, 44
Glucose, hunger and, 302
Goals
  superordinate, diversity and, 519
  in workplace, 327
Graduated and Reciprocated Initiatives in Tension-Reduction (GRIT), 521
GRIT (Graduated and Reciprocated Initiatives in Tension-Reduction), 521
Group(s)
  differences among, 25. *See also* Cultural similarities and differences; Gender similarities and differences
  influence of. *See* Group influence
  ingroups and outgroups and, 499
  need to belong to, 328–330
  support, 462
Group influence, 490–493

deindividuation and, 491
group polarization and, 492
groupthink and, 492–493
of minority, 493
social facilitation and, 490
social loafing and, 490–491
Grouping, form perception and, 140–141
Group polarization, 492
  conflict and, 510
Group pressure, conformity and, 485–487
Group therapy, 462
Groupthink, 492–493
Guilt, adolescent pregnancy and, 96
Guilty knowledge test, 337

Hair cells, of ear, 132–133
Hallucinations, 186
  in schizophrenia, 435–436
Hallucinogens, 182, 186–188, 188
  LSD (lysergic acid diethylamide), 186–187
  marijuana, 187–188
Hammer (bone), 132
Happiness, 346–351
  adaptation-level principle and, 348–349
  predictors of, 350
  relative deprivation principle and, 349–350
Health, 356–373. *See also* Illness; Psychological disorders
  hypochondriasis and, 423
  during late adulthood, 99–100
  need to belong and, 330
  promoting, 368–373, 475
  stress and. *See* Stress
Health promotion, 368–373
  preventive mental health and, 475
Health psychology, 356. *See also* Stress
Hearing, 131–133
  ear and, 132–133
  sound localization and, 133
  sound waves and, 132
Heart disease
  personality and, 361–363
  prevention of, 370–371
Height, relative, as monocular cue, 143
Helping. *See* Altruism; Bystander effect
Helplessness, learned, 404
  mood disorders and, 431
Hemispheric specialization, 58–64
  split-brain studies of, 59–61
  studying in intact brain, 62–63
Heritability. *See also* Genetic factors; Nature-nurture issue
  of intelligence, 285–287
Heroin, 184, 188
Heterosexuality, 317–320
Heuristics
  decision making and, 259–261
  for problem solving, 257
Hierarchies
  encoding and, 230–231
  of needs, 299–300, 394
Hindsight bias, 8–9
Hippocampus, 49
  memory and, 238–239
Histrionic personality disorder, 440
Home, operant conditioning and, 216
Homeostasis, 298
Homosexuality, 317–320
Hormones, 43–44
  aggression and, 502
  arousal and, 336
  depression and, 430
  sex, 71
  sexual behavior and, 313–314

sexual orientation and, 320
  stress response and, 357
Hue, of light, 124
Human factors psychologists, 152
Humanistic perspective on personality, 393–401
  assessment of self and, 395–399
  evaluating, 399–401
  person-centered, 394–395
  self-actualization and, 394
Humanistic psychologists, 393
Humanistic therapies, 394, 453–454
Human research, ethics of, 27
Humility, 7
Hunger, 301–310
  body chemistry and, 302
  culture and, 303
  eating disorders and, 304
  external incentives and, 305
  obesity and, 305–310
  set point and, 302–303
Hypnosis, 175–181
  age regression and, 177–178, 179
  as divided consciousness, 180–181
  inducement to act against one's will by, 178
  recall of forgotten events and, 177–178
  as social phenomenon, 180
  susceptibility to, 176–177
  therapeutic use of, 178–179
Hypochondriasis, 423
Hypothalamus, 50–51
  hunger and, 302
  sexual behavior and, 314
Hypotheses, 10–11

ICD-10 (*International Classification of Diseases*), 417
Iconic memory, 233
Id, 379
Identical twins, 108
Identification, psychoanalytic theory of, 380
Identity
  development of, 93
  gender, 86
Ignorance, adolescent pregnancy and, 96
I-knew-it-all-along phenomenon, 8–9
Illness
  cancer, 364–365
  heart disease, 361–363, 370–371
  mental. *See* Psychological disorders
Illusions, 146–147
Illusory correlation, 14–15
Imagery, encoding, 229–230
Imagination, sexual behavior and, 315
Imaginative thinking skills, 284
Imaging, of brain, 47
Immediate reinforcers, 209–210
Immune system
  classical conditioning of, 365–367
  stress and, 363–364
Implicit memory, 237–239
Impotence, 315
Imprinting, 82
Incentive theory of motivation, 299
Independent variable, 19
Individual differences, 25
Individualism, 85, 389–399, 487
Industrial/organizational psychologists, 6
Industrial/organizational psychology, 325–328, 333
  attending to people's motives and, 326
  cultivating intrinsic motivation and, 325–326
  goal setting and, 327
  leadership style and, 327–328
Infancy
  cognitive development during, 75–77

depth perception and, 141
emotions during, 344
language development during, 265
personality development during, 380
physical development during, 74–75
social development during, 80–84
Infantile amnesia, 249
Inference, statistical, 532–534
generalization from samples and, 532–533
statistical significance and, 533–534
Influence. *See* Social influence
Informational social influence, 486–487
Information processing
dreams as, 173
levels of, 164–165
memory as, 225. *See also* Encoding; Retrieval;
Storage
visual, 127–128
Ingroup bias, 499
Initiative, 92
Inner ear, 132
Insecure attachment, 82
Insight, 257
in psychoanalysis, 451
Insomnia, 170
Instinct theory of motivation, 298
Insulin, hunger and, 302
Integrity, 107
Intelligence, 275–292
aging and, 101–103
assessment of. *See* Intelligence tests
creativity and, 282, 284
crystallized, 102
environmental influences on, 287–288
extremes of, 281, 283
fluid, 102
gender differences in, 290–291
general intelligence factor and, 280–281
genetic influences on, 285–287
group differences in, 288–292
heritability of, 286–287
multiple intelligences and, 281–282
Intelligence quotient (IQ), 276–277. *See also*
Intelligence tests
Intelligence tests, 275–280
American College Testing exam, 278
bias and, 291–292
group differences in scores on, 288–292
IQ and, 276–277
origins of, 276–278
reliability of, 279–280
Scholastic Assessment Test, 278, 291
standardization of, 279
Stanford-Binet, 277
validity of, 280
Wechsler Adult Intelligence Scale–Revised,
277–278
Wechsler Intelligence Scale for Children,
277
Intensity, of light, 124
Interaction
of nature and nurture, 111. *See also*
Nature-nurture issue
sensory, 136
Interference, retrieval and, 246
Internal locus of control, 403
International Classification of Diseases
(ICD-10), 417
Interneurons, 41
Interpersonal relationships. *See also* Aggression;
Altruism; Attraction; Intimacy
depression and, 432–433
need to belong and, 329–330
Interposition, as monocular cue, 143
Interpretations, in psychoanalysis, 451–452

Intimacy, 104. *See also* Love; Sexual behavior
development of, 93–95
Intrinsic motivation, 324–326
creativity and, 284
Intuition, 8
Inverse relationship, 14
IQ (intelligence quotient), 276–277. *See also*
Intelligence tests
Iris, 125

James-Lange theory of emotion, 351–353
jnd (just noticeable difference), 121
Just noticeable difference (jnd), 121
Just-world phenomenon, prejudice and, 500

Kinesthesis, 138
Kinship, diversity and, 25

Labeling, 443–444
Language, 264–275
in animals, 268–271
brain and, 55–57
cultural differences in, 273
development of. *See* Language development
hemispheric specialization and, 62
thinking and, 272–274
Language development, 264–268
acquisition in, 265–266
explanations of, 266–268
Late adulthood, physical changes during, 98–100
Latency stage, 380
Latent content of dreams, 172–173
Latent learning, 213
Lateral hypothalamus (LH), hunger and, 302
Law of effect, 207
L-Dopa, 40
Leadership style, motivation and, 327–328
Learned helplessness, 404
mood disorders and, 431
Learning, 195–221
adaptation and, 203
anxiety disorders and, 421–422
associative, 196–198. *See also*
Classical conditioning; Operant conditioning
to express and inhibit aggression, 503–504
latent, 213
observational, 217–219
relearning and, 240
during sleep, 227
social learning theory and gender identity and,
86
Left brain. *See* Hemispheric specialization
Lens (of eye), 125
Lesions, in brain, 46, 55
LH (lateral hypothalamus), hunger and, 302
Librium, 472
Lie detection, 337
Life events, stress and, 358–359
Light, 124–125
lightness constancy and, 147–148
as monocular cue, 144
Light energy, 124
Lightness constancy, 147–148
Limbic system, 49–51. *See also* Hippocampus;
Hypothalamus
amygdala and, 49–50
Linear perspective, as monocular cue, 143
Linguistic perspective, on language development,
266–267
Linguistic relativity hypothesis, 272
Listening, active, in person-centered therapy, 453,
454

Loafing, social, 490–491
Lobotomy, 474
Locus of control, external versus internal, 403
Loneliness, 433
Longitudinal studies, of intellectual stability, 102
Long-term memory, 225, 234–235
Long-term potentiation (LTP), 236–237
Loudness, 132
Love
during adulthood, 104–105
romantic, 515–516
LSD (lysergic acid diethylamide), 186–187
LTP (long-term potentiation), 236–237
Luminance, relative, 147
Lymphocytes, 363
Lysergic acid diethylamide (LSD), 186–187

Magnetic resonance imaging (MRI), 47
Mainstreaming, 283
Major depressive disorder, 426, 427
Males. *See* Gender similarities and differences;
Sexual behavior
Management. *See* Industrial/organizational psy-
chologists; Industrial/organizational psychology
Mania, in bipolar (manic depressive) disorder,
426, 427
Manic depressive disorder, 426, 427, 429
drug therapy for, 473
Manifest content of dreams, 172
Marijuana, 187–188
Marriage, 105
divorce and, 84–85, 105
sexual behavior and, 311
Maslow's hierarchy of needs, 299–300, 394
Maturation, 74
early, 89
Mean, 528
regression toward, 531–532
Meaning, encoding, 228–229
Media
adolescent pregnancy and, 96
aggression and, 504–508
Median, 528
Medical perspective. *See also* Biomedical therapies
on psychological disorders, 415–416
Medicine. *See also* Biomedical therapies; Health;
Illness; Psychological disorders
behavioral, 356
Meditation, 175
Medulla, 45
Memory, 223–252. *See also* Amnesia; Forgetting
aging and, 100–101
Alzheimer's disease and, 100, 237
echoic, 233
explicit (declarative), 237–239
flashbulb, 224
forgetting and, 223–224, 231–232
forming memories and, 224–225
hypnosis and, 176, 177–178, 179
iconic, 233
implicit (nondeclarative), 237–239
improving, 250–251
as information processing, 225. *See also* Encoding; Retrieval; Storage
long-term, 225, 234–235
mood-congruent, 242
odors and, 138
of pain, 135
sensory, 233
short-term (working), 225, 233–234
state-dependent, 241–242
Men. *See* Gender similarities and differences;
Sexual behavior

Menarche, 88
Menopause, 98
Mental age, 276
Mental illness, 415–416. *See* Psychological disorders
Mental processes, definition of, 3
Mental retardation, 283
    savant syndrome and, 281
Mere exposure effect, 512
Metabolic rate, body weight and, 303, 307
Middle adulthood, physical changes during, 98
Middle ear, 132
Midlife crises, 103–104
Minnesota Multiphasic Personality Inventory (MMPI), 390–391
Minorities. *See* Cultural similarities and differences; Prejudice
Minority influence, 493
Mirror-image perceptions, 510
Misinformation effect, 243
MMPI (Minnesota Multiphasic Personality Inventory), 390–391
Mnemonic devices, 229–230
Mode, 528
Modeling, 217–219
Monocular cues, 142–144
Mood(s), 347. *See also specific moods, e.g.,* Happiness
    memories and, 241–242
Mood disorders, 426–434
    biological perspective on, 430
    bipolar (manic depressive) disorder, 426, 427, 429
    loneliness and, 433
    major depressive disorder, 426, 427
    psychoanalytic perspective on, 430
    social-cognitive perspective on, 431–433
    suicide and, 428
Moon illusion, 146
Moral development, 90–91
Motion
    perception of, 138
    relative, as monocular cue, 143
Motivated forgetting, 247–249
Motivation, 297–332
    achievement. *See* Achievement motivation
    creativity and, 284
    extrinsic, 324–325
    hunger and. *See* Hunger
    intrinsic, 324–326
    need to belong and, 328–330
    sexual. *See* Sexual behavior
    theories of, 298–300
    in workplace, 327–328
Motor cortex, 52–53
Motor development, during infancy, 75
Motor neurons, 41
Movement sense, 138
MRI (magnetic resonance imaging), 47
Müller-Lyer illusion, 146
Multiple intelligences, 281–282
Multiple personality. *See* Dissociative identity disorder
Myelin sheath, 36
Myers-Briggs Type Indicators, 388

Narcissistic personality disorder, 440
Narcolepsy, 170
Naturalistic observation, 13–14
Nature-nurture issue, 3–4, 69, 108–111. *See also* Environmental factors; Genetic factors
    adoption studies and, 110
    intelligence and, 285–292
    motor development and, 75

obesity and, 307–308
    in prenatal development, 72
    schizophrenia and, 438–439
    twin studies and, 108–110
Near-death experiences, 186
Needs
    to belong, 328–330
    hierarchy of, 299–300, 394
Negative correlation, 14
Negative symptoms, of schizophrenia, 436
Neo-Freudian theory, 383–384
Nerves, 41
    optic, 126
Nervous system, 41–43. *See also* Brain
    autonomic, 42, 336
    central, 41, 42–43
    parasympathetic, 42, 336
    peripheral, 41–42
    skeletal, 41
    sympathetic, 42, 336
Neural communication, 36–40
    alteration by drugs, 39–40
    process of, 37–38
Neural factors, in aggression, 501–502
Neural processing
    bottom-up, 117
    parallel, 128
    top-down, 117
Neurons, 36–40
    communication by, 37–38. *See also* Neurotransmitters
    interneurons, 41
    motor, 41
    sensory, 41
Neurotransmitters, 38–40. *See also* Acetylcholine (ACh); Epinephrine; L-Dopa; Norepinephrine; Serotonin
    depression and, 44, 472
    diet and, 302
    drug alteration of neurotransmission and, 39–40
    endorphins, 39
    physical storage and, 236–237
    schizophrenia and, 437, 471
Newborns, capabilities of, 72–73
Next-in-line effect, 227
Nicotine, 184–185, 188
    reasons for use of, 190
Night terrors, 171
Nondeclarative memory, 237–239
Nondirective therapy, 394, 453–454
Nonverbal communication, 339–341. *See also* Facial expressions
Norepinephrine (noradrenaline), 44
    arousal and, 336
    depression and, 472
    stress response and, 357
Norm(s)
    conformity and, 486–487
    cultural, 494–495
    reciprocity, 519
    social responsibility, 519
Normal curve, 279, 529
Normal distribution, 279
Normative social influence, 486–487
Nutrition. *See* Dieting; Eating disorders

Obedience, 487–489
Obesity, 305–310
    physiology of, 307–308
    weight loss and, 308–310
Object permanence, 77
Observation, naturalistic, 13–14
Observational learning, 217–219

of aggression, 504–508
    applications of, 218–219
    Bandura's research in, 218
Obsessive-compulsive disorder, 418, 420
Occipital lobes, 52
Odors, 136–138
Oedipus complex, 380
Olfaction, 136–138
One-word stage, 266
Operant behavior, 206–207
Operant conditioning, 196, 197, 206–216
    applications of, 214–216
    in behavior therapy, 457–458
    biological predispositions and, 213–214
    classical conditioning compared with, 216
    cognition and, 213
    punishment and, 211–212
    reinforcement and, 208–211
    shaping and, 207–208
    Skinner's experiments in, 207–212
Operational definitions, 19
Opiates, 184, 188
Opponent-process theory of color vision, 130
Optic nerve, 126
Optimism, personal control and, 404–405
Oral stage, 380
Organization
    for encoding, 230–231
    perceptual, 139–149
Organizational psychology. *See* Industrial/organizational psychologists; Industrial/organizational psychology
Orgasm, 312
    orgasmic dysfunction and, 315
Oval window, 132
Overconfidence, 9
    decision making and, 261–262

Pain, 134–135
    control of, 135, 178–179
Pain reflex, 43
Palm reading, 406–407
Panic attacks, 419
Paradoxical sleep, 171–174
Parallel processing, visual, 128
Paranoid schizophrenia, 435
Paranormal phenomena. *See* Extrasensory perception (ESP)
Paraphrasing, for active listening, 454
Parapsychologists, 154
Parapsychology. *See* Extrasensory perception (ESP)
Parasympathetic nervous system, 42
    arousal and, 336
Parent(s), separating from, 94–95
Parenting
    culture and, 85–86
    gender and, 86–87
    responsive, attachment and, 83
Parietal lobes, 52
Parkinsonian symptoms, antipsychotic drugs and, 471
Parkinson's disease, 40
Partial reinforcement, 210
Passionate love, 515
Pavlovian conditioning. *See* Classical conditioning
Paxil, 472
Peacemaking, 519–521
    communication and, 520–521
    conciliation and, 521
    cooperation and, 519–520
Peer influence, drug use and, 189–190

Perceived control, stress and, 360–361
Percentile rank, 526
Perception, 117–118, 139–158. *See also* Hearing;
    Sensation; Vision
    adaptation of, 149–150
    constancy of, 145–148
    of depth, 141–144
    of enemies, 510
    extrasensory, 153–158
    of form, 140–141
    interpretation of, 148–153
    of movement, 138
    organization of, 139–148
    perceptual set and, 150–151, 153
    of risk, 261
    in schizophrenia, 435–436
    selective attention and, 164
    sensory restriction and, 149
Perceptual adaptation, 149–150
Perceptual constancy, 145–148
    lightness, 147–148
    shape and size, 145–147
Perceptual set, 150–151, 153
    context effects and, 151, 153
Peripheral nervous system, 41–42
Personal control, 403–405
    learned helplessness and, 404
    locus of, 403
    optimism and, 404–405
    social influence and, 493
Personality, 377–410
    assessing, 384–385
    creativity and, 284
    development of, 380–381
    disorders of, 424–426, 440–441
    heart disease and, 361–363
    humanistic perspective on. *See* Humanistic
        perspective on personality
    multiple (dissociative identity disorder),
        424–426
    psychoanalytic perspective on. *See* Psychoana-
        lytic perspective
    social-cognitive perspective on. *See* Social-cog-
        nitive perspective on personality
    structure of, 379–380
    trait perspective on. *See* Trait perspective on
        personality
    Type A and B, 362, 388
Personality disorders, 424–426, 440–441
Personality inventories, 390–391
Personality psychologists, 6
Personal space, 494
Person-centered perspective on personality,
    394–395
Person-centered therapy, 394, 453–454
Perspective, linear, as monocular cue, 143
Perspectives of psychology, 3–5. *See also specific
    perspectives, e.g.,* Psychoanalytic perspective
Persuasion, subliminal, 119–121
Pessimism
    depression and, 432
    personal control and, 404–405
PET (positron emission tomograph) scans, 47, 56
Phallic stage, 380
Phobic disorders, 418, 419–420
Phrenology, 35
Physical attractiveness, attraction and, 512–514
Physical dependence, on drugs, 182
Physical development
    during adolescence, 88–89
    during adulthood, 98–100
    during childhood, 74–75
    during infancy, 74–75
Physical storage, 235–239

implicit and explicit memories in, 237–239
    synaptic changes in, 236–237
Physiology. *See also* Biological perspective; Bio-
    logical predispositions; Genetic factors;
    Nature-nurture issue
    of emotion, 335–338
    of hunger, 301–303
    of obesity, 307–308
    of sex, 312–314
    of sexual behavior, 319–320
Piaget's theory of cognitive development, 75–80,
    90
Pitch, 132
Pituitary gland, 44
Placebo, 21
Placebo effect
    drug therapies and, 470–471, 473
    psychotherapy and, 467
Plasticity, of brain, 58
Plateau phase of sexual response cycle, 312
Pleasure centers, of brain, 50–51
Pleasure principle, 379
Polygraph, 337
Population (in research), 12
Pornography, aggression and, 507–508
Positive correlation, 14
Positive regard, unconditional, 394
    in person-centered therapy, 394, 454
Positive symptoms, of schizophrenia, 436
Positive transfer, 246
Positron emission tomograph (PET) scans, 47, 56
Postconventional morality, 91
Posthypnotic amnesia, 176
Posthypnotic suggestions, 178
Post-traumatic stress disorder (PTSD), 360
Practical intelligence, 282
Precognition, 154
Preconscious, 378
Preconventional morality, 91
Prediction
    correlation and, 14
    of future behavior, 407
    by tests, 280
Pregnancy. *See also* Prenatal development
    during adolescence, 95–97
Prejudice, 496–500
    cognitive roots of, 500
    ingroup bias and, 499
    scapegoating and, 499
    social inequalities and, 498
Premature ejaculation, 315
Prenatal development, 70–72
    sexual orientation and, 320
Preoperational stage, 78–79
Preventive mental health, 475
Primary reinforcers, 209
Primary sex characteristics, 88
Priming, 240–241
Proactive interference, 246
Problem solving, 257–259
    assessment of, 282
    obstacles to, 258–259
Processing. *See* Encoding; Information process-
    ing; Retrieval; Storage
Process schizophrenia, 436
Productivity, 104
Project Head Start, 288
Projection, 382
Projective tests, 384–385
Prosocial models, 218
Prosopagnosia, 117–118
Prototypes, 256–257
Proximity
    attraction and, 512

perceptual grouping and, 140
Prozac (fluoxetine), 472
Psychedelics. *See* Hallucinogens
Psychiatrists, 6
Psychoactive drugs, 181–190
    depressants, 182–184, 188
    hallucinogens (psychedelics), 182, 186–188
    influences on use of, 188–190
    stimulants, 182, 184–186, 188
Psychoanalysis, 378, 450–452
    aims of, 450
    methods of, 450–452
Psychoanalytic perspective, 4, 378–387
    on anxiety disorders, 421
    assessment and, 384–385
    defense mechanisms and, 381–382
    on dreams, 172–173
    evaluating, 385–386
    on mood disorders, 430
    neo-Freudian, 383–384
    on personality development, 380–381
    on personality structure, 379–380
    as scientific theory, 386
    unconscious and, 378–384
Psychokinesis, 154
Psychological dependence, on drugs, 182
Psychological disorders, 413–446
    anxiety, 418–422
    classification of, 417
    defining, 414–415
    dissociative, 423–426
    labeling and, 443–444
    medical perspective on, 415–416
    mood, 426–434. *See also* Depression
    personality, 440–441
    preventing, 474–475
    rates of, 442–443
    schizophrenia, 434–440
    social-cultural perspectives on, 416
    somatoform, 422–423
    therapies for. *See* Biomedical therapies; Psy-
        choanalysis; Psychotherapy
Psychological factors, in schizophrenia, 439
Psychology
    perspectives of, 3–5. *See also specific perspec-
        tives, e.g.,* Psychoanalytic perspective
    power of, 28
    roots of, 2–3
    study of, 6–9
    subfields of, 5–6. *See also specific subfields,
        e.g.,* Industrial/organizational psychology
    tips for studying, 29–30
Psychopaths, 440–441
Psychopharmacology, 470. *See also* Drug thera-
    pies
Psychophysics, 118. *See also* Thresholds
Psychophysiological illnesses, 363
Psychosexual stages, 380–381
Psychosocial tasks, 92–93
Psychosomatic disorders, 363
Psychosurgery, 474
Psychotherapy, 449–470. *See also* Psychoanalysis
    behavior therapies, 455–458
    cognitive, 458–461
    commonalities among, 467–468
    culture and values in, 468–469
    eclectic approach to, 450
    effectiveness of, 464–467
    group, 462
    humanistic, 394, 452–454
    psychoanalysis, 450–452
    therapists and, 6, 469
PTSD (post-traumatic stress disorder), 360
Puberty, 88–89

Punishment, 211–212
Pupil (of eye), 125

Questions, wording of, for surveys, 12

Race. *See also* Cultural similarities and differences; Prejudice
  intelligence test scores and, 289–290
Rage, physiological states accompanying, 338
Random assignment, 19
Random events, 15–16
Random sample, 12–13
Range, 529
Rape
  as classical conditioning, 205
  television watching and, 506–507
Rapid eye movement (REM) sleep, 171–174
Rational-emotive therapy, 459–460
Rationalization, 382
Reaction formation, 381–382
Reactive schizophrenia, 436
Reality principle, 379
Reasoning
  development of, 90
  moral, 90–91
Recall, 240
  eyewitness, of children, 244–245
  hypnosis and, 177–178
Reciprocal determinism, 402–403
Reciprocity norm, 519
Recognition, 240
Reflection, for active listening, 454
Reflexes, 42–43, 73
Refractory period, 312–313
Regression
  age, hypnosis and, 177–178, 179
  as defense mechanism, 381
Regression toward the mean, 531–532
Rehearsal, 226–228
Reinforcement, 208–211
  immediate and delayed reinforcers and, 209–210
  primary and secondary reinforcers and, 209
  schedules of, 210–211
Reinforcers, 208–210
Relationships
  direct and inverse, 14
  figure-ground, 140
  interpersonal. *See* Aggression; Altruism; Attraction; Interpersonal relationships; Intimacy; Love
  size-distance, 145–147
Relative brightness, as monocular cue, 144
Relative deprivation, happiness and, 349–350
Relative height, as monocular cue, 143
Relative luminance, 147
Relative motion, as monocular cue, 143
Relative size, as monocular cue, 142
Relaxation, for stress management, 370–371
Relearning, 240
Reliability, of tests, 279–280
Religion
  and adolescence, 90
  confession in, 372
  and depression, 431
  and minority influence, 493
  and motivation, 325
  pastoral counseling in, 463
  as predictor of life satisfaction, 350
  and psychotherapy, 468
  and social support, 372
  and Type A behavior, 371
REM rebound, 174

REM (rapid eye movement) sleep, 171–174
Replication, 11
Representativeness heuristic, 259–260
Repression, 247–249, 378, 381, 385
Research
  adoption studies. *See* Adoption studies
  animal, 24
  applied, 6
  Bandura's research in observational learning, 218
  basic, 6
  correlational, 20
  correlation and, 14–17
  cross-sectional, 101
  descriptive, 11–14, 20
  ethics of, 26–27
  experimental, 18–22, 23
  on hemispheric specialization, 59–63
  longitudinal, 102
  on outcomes of psychotherapy, 465–466
  Pavlov's experiments in classical conditioning, 198–201
  psychoanalytic perspective and, 385–386
  replication of, 11
  scientific method and, 10–11
  on self, 395–398
  on sex, 321–322
  Skinner's experiments in operant conditioning, 207–212
  statistics and. *See* Statistics
  trait perspective on personality and, 391–393
  twin studies. *See* Twin studies
Resistance, in psychoanalysis, 451
Resistance stage of general adaptation syndrome, 357
Resolution phase of sexual response cycle, 312–313
Respondent behavior, 206
Response
  all-or-none, of neurons, 37
  conditioned, 199
  relaxation, 370
  sexual, cycle of, 312
  unconditioned, 199
Responsive parenting, attachment and, 83
Retention. *See* Storage
Reticular formation, 48
Retina, 125–127
Retinal disparity, 142
Retrieval, 225, 240–250
  children's eyewitness recall and, 244–245
  context effects and, 241
  cues for, 240–242
  forgetting as failure of, 245–249
  memory construction and, 241–245
  moods and, 241–242
Retroactive interference, 246
Reward centers, of brain, 50–51
Right brain. *See* Hemispheric specialization
Risk, perception of, 261
Rods (retinal), 126
Role(s), gender, 495
Role playing, attitudes and, 483
Romantic love, 515–516
  companionate, 515–516
  passionate, 515
Rooting reflex, 73
Rorschach inkblot test, 384–385

Sadness. *See* Depression; Mood disorders
Sampling, 12–13
  generalization from samples and, 532–533
SAT (Scholastic Assessment Test), 278, 291
Savant syndrome, 281

Scapegoat theory of prejudice, 499
Scatterplots, 530
Schachter's two-factor theory of emotion, 353–354
Schemas
  cognitive development and, 75–76
  gender schema theory and, 86–87
Schizophrenia, 434–440
  brain abnormalities and, 437
  drug therapy for, 471–472
  experiencing, 440
  genetic factors in, 438
  psychological factors in, 439
  symptoms of, 434–436
  types of, 436
Scholastic Assessment Test (SAT), 278, 291
Schools, operant conditioning in, 214–215
Science, psychology as, 3
Scientific attitude, 7
Scientific method, 10–11
Secondary reinforcers, 209
Secondary sex characteristics, 88
Secure attachment, 82
  social competence and, 83–84
Selective attention, 164
Self. *See also* Humanistic perspective on personality
  individualist versus collectivist views of, 389–399
  research on, 395–398
Self-actualization, 394
Self-concept, personality and, 395
Self-defeating beliefs, mood disorders and, 431
Self-disclosure, companionate love and, 516
Self-esteem, benefits of, 396
Self-fulfilling prophecy, 498
Self-help groups, 462
Self-serving bias, 396–398, 510
Semicircular canal, 138
Sensation, 117, 118–139
  abilities during late adulthood, 99
  equilibrium and, 138
  hearing and, 131–133
  kinesthesis and, 138
  pain and, 134–135
  sensory adaptation and, 122–123
  smell sense and, 136–138
  taste sense and, 135–136
  thresholds and, 118–121
  touch sense and, 133–134
  vision and, 123–130
Sensorimotor stage, 76–77
Sensory adaptation, 122–123
Sensory cortex, 53–54
Sensory interaction, 136
Sensory memory, 233
Sensory neurons, 41
Sensory restriction, 149
Separation, from parents, 94–95
Serial position effect, 227–228
Serotonin
  depression and, 472
  diet and, 302
Set point, for body weight, 302–303, 307
Sex characteristics, primary and secondary, 88
Sex chromosomes, 71
Sex hormones, 71
Sex research, 321–322
Sexual abuse. *See also* Rape
  repressed memories of, 248–249
Sexual aggression. *See* Rape; Sexual abuse
Sexual arousal, physiological states accompanying, 338
Sexual behavior, 311–322

during adolescence, 95–97
external stimuli and, 314
gender differences in, 316
hormones and, 313–314
imaginative stimuli and, 315
sexual dysfunctions and therapy and, 315–316
sexual orientation and, 317–320
sexual response cycle and, 312
values and, 321–322
Sexual dysfunctions, 315–316
Sexual orientation, 317–320
explanations of, 318–320
Sexual response cycle, 312
Shape constancy, 145
Shaping, 207–208
Shock treatments, 473
Short-term memory, 225, 233–234
Significance, statistical, 533–534
Sign language
hemispheric specialization and, 62
use by chimpanzees, 269–271
use by deaf people, 268, 273
Similarity
attraction and, 514–515
perceptual grouping and, 140
Situational attribution, 479–480
Size, relative, as monocular cue, 142
Size constancy, 145–147
size-distance relationship and, 145–147
Skeletal nervous system, 41
Skepticism, 7
Skinner box, 207
Sleep, 165–174. *See also* Dreams
disorders of, 170–171
functions of, 168–169
reasons for, 168–169
REM (rapid eye movement), 166–168, 171–174
rhythm of, 165–168
Sleep apnea, 171
Sleep learning, 227
Sleep spindles, 167
Smell sense, 136–138
Smoking. *See* Nicotine
Social acceptance, need to belong and, 329
Social clock, 104
Social-cognitive perspective on mood disorders, 431–433
Social-cognitive perspective on personality, 402–408
behavior assessment and, 405–407
evaluating, 407
personal control and, 403–405
reciprocal determinism and, 402–403
Social competence, secure attachment and, 83–84
Social connectedness, gender and, 94
Social control, 493
Social-cultural perspective, 4
on psychological disorders, 416
Social development
during adolescence, 92–97
during adulthood, 103–107
during childhood, 84–87
Erikson's theory of, 84, 92–93, 104, 107
during infancy, 80–84
Social exchange theory, 518–519
Social facilitation, 490
Social inequalities, prejudice and, 498
Social influence
conformity and, 485–487, 489
cultural, 494–495
drug use and, 189
group, 490–493
of minorities, 493

obedience and, 487–489
Social influence theory of hypnosis, 180
Social leadership, 327
Social learning theory, gender identity and, 86
Social loafing, 490–491
Social phobia, 420
Social psychology, 479–523
attitudes and, 481–484
attribution and, 479–481
influence and. *See* Conformity; Group influence; Obedience
relations and. *See* Aggression; Altruism; Attraction; Conflict; Interpersonal relationships; Intimacy; Love; Peacemaking; Prejudice
Social responsibility norms, 519
Social scripts, media influence and, 508
Social support, for stress management, 371–373
Social traps, 509–510
Sociopaths, 440–441
Somatoform disorders, 422–423
Sound, localization of, 133
Sound waves, 132
Spacing effect, 227
Spectrum, electromagnetic, 124
Speech. *See also* Communication; Language; Language development
telegraphic, 266
Spinal cord, reflexes and, 42–43
Split-brain studies, 59–61
Split-half reliability, 280
Spontaneous recovery, 201
SQ3R study technique, 29, 250
Stability/change issue, 70, 112
intelligence and, 101–103
Stages, continuity/stages issue and, 69, 153
Standard deviation, 529
Standardization, of tests, 279
Stanford-Binet test, 277
State-dependent memory, 241–242
Statistical significance, 533–534
Statistics, 526–534
descriptive, 526–532
inference and, 532–534
Stereotypes, 497
conflict and, 510
Stimulants, 182, 184–186, 188
cocaine, 185–186, 188
nicotine, 184–185, 188
Stimulation
brain development and, 74–75
sexual behavior and, 314–315
subliminal, 119–121
Stimulus
conditioned, 199, 200, 201
light, 124–125
sound, 132
unconditioned, 199, 200, 201
Stirrup (bone), 132
Storage, 225, 233–239
brain and, 235–239
of implicit and explicit memories, 237–239
long-term, 225, 234–235
sensory, 233
short-term, 225, 233–234
synaptic changes and, 236–237
Stranger anxiety, 81
Stress, 356–367
arousal and, 336
cancer and, 364–365
coping with. *See* Stress management
immune system and, 363–364, 365–367
mood disorders and, 429
perceived control and, 360–361
personality and heart disease and, 361–363

post-traumatic stress disorder and, 360
resistance to disease and, 363–367
response system and, 357–358
stressors and, 356–361
Stress management, 368–373
aerobic exercise for, 368–369
biofeedback for, 369–370
relaxation for, 370–371
social support for, 371–373
Stressors, 356–361
life events as, 358–359
Study tips, 29–30, 250–251
Sublimation, 382
Subliminal stimulation, 119–121
Suicide, 428
suggestibility and, 485
Superego, 380
Superordinate goals, 519
Support, social, for stress management, 371–373
Support groups, 462
Surgery, for psychological disorders, 474
Survey method, 12–13
sampling and, 12–13
wording effects and, 12
Survival, need to belong and, 328–329
Sympathetic nervous system, 42
arousal and, 336
Synapses, 37
memory and, 236–237
Synaptic gap, 37
Systematic desensitization, 455–457

Task leadership, 327
Taste sense, 135–136
cultural preferences in, 303
TAT (Thematic Apperception Test), 384
Telegraphic speech, 266
Telepathy, 154
Television watching, aggression and, 504–508
Temperament, attachment and, 82
Temporal lobes, 52
Teratogens, 72
Test(s)
achievement, 276
aptitude, 276
construction of, 279–280
intelligence. *See* Intelligence tests
lie detector, 337
personality, 390–391
projective, 384–385
taking, 30
Testosterone, 71
aggression and, 502
sexual behavior and, 313, 314
sexual orientation and, 320
Test-retest reliability, 280
Thalamus, 48
schizophrenia and, 437
THC, 187
Thematic Apperception Test (TAT), 384
Theory, 10
Therapists, 6
perceptions of effectiveness of psychotherapy, 464
selecting, 469
Therapy, 449–476
biomedical. *See* Biomedical therapies
psychoanalytic. *See* Psychoanalysis
psychological. *See* Psychotherapy
for sexual dysfunctions, 315–316
Thinking, 256–264. *See also* Cognition; Cognitive development; Information processing; Intelligence; Reasoning

concepts and, 256–257
critical. *See* Critical thinking; Research
decision making and, 259–263
groupthink and, 492–493
imaginative, 284
linguistic influences on, 272–273
negative, depression and, 432
problem solving and, 257–259
in schizophrenia, 434–435
without language, 273–274
Thorazine (chlorpromazine), 471
Thresholds, 37, 118–121
absolute, 119
difference, 121
subliminal stimulation and, 119–121
Tip of the tongue phenomenon, 245
Tobacco. *See* Nicotine
Token economies, 458
Tolerance, to drugs, 182
Top-down processing, 117
Touch sense, 133–134
Trait perspective on personality, 387–393
assessing traits and, 390–391
evaluating, 391–393
traits and, 387–389
Tranquilizers, 184
Transfer, positive, 246
Transference, in psychoanalysis, 451
Trauma, posttraumatic stress disorder and, 360
Treatment. *See* Biomedical therapies; Psycho-
analysis; Psychotherapy; Therapy
Trust, basic, 84
Twin studies, 108–110
of intelligence, 285–286
of obesity, 307–308
of schizophrenia, 438
of separated twins, 108–110
Two-factor theory of emotion, 353–354
Two-word stage, 266
Type A and B personality, 362, 388

UCR (unconditioned response), 199
UCS (unconditioned stimulus), 199, 200, 201

Unconditional positive regard, in person-centered
therapy, 394, 454
Unconditioned response (UCR), 199
Unconditioned stimulus (UCS), 199, 200, 201
Unconscious, 378–384. *See also* Psychoanalytic
perspective
assessing, 384–385
collective, 383–384
Unhappiness. *See* Depression; Mood disorders

Validity, 280
Valium, 472
Value(s)
psychotherapy and, 468–469
sex research and, 321–322
Value judgments, 27–28
Variable(s), 19
Variable-interval schedules, 211
Variable-ratio schedules, 210
Variation, 528–529
Ventromedial hypothalamus (VMH), hunger and,
302
Vestibular sense, 138
Vicious cycle of depression, 432
Violence. *See* Aggression
Vision, 123–131
color, 129–130
depth perception and, 142–144
eye and, 125–127
information processing and, 127–128
light energy and, 124–125
restored, 149
Visual capture, 131
Visual cliff, 141–142
Visual illusions, 146–147
Visual imagery. *See* Imagery
Visual information processing, 127–128
feature detection and, 127–128
parallel, 128
VMH (ventromedial hypothalamus), hunger and,
302

WAIS-R (Wechsler Adult Intelligence Scale–Re-
vised), 277–278
Wavelength, of light, 124
Weber's law, 121
Wechsler Adult Intelligence Scale–Revised
(WAIS-R), 277–278
Wechsler Intelligence Scale for Children (WISC),
277
Weight. *See* Body weight; Obesity
Well-being. *See also* Health
across life span, 106
stress and, 259
Wernicke's area, 55
WISC (Wechsler Intelligence Scale for Children),
277
Withdrawal, from drugs, 182
Women. *See also* Gender similarities and differ-
ences; Sexual behavior
menopause and, 98
Wording, of survey questions, 12
Word salad, in schizophrenia, 435
Work. *See also* Industrial/organizational psychol-
ogists; Industrial/organizational psychology
during adulthood, 105–106
operant conditioning and, 215
Working memory, 225, 233–234

X chromosomes, 71

Y chromosomes, 71
Young-Helmholtz trichromatic theory, 129

Zoloft, 472
Zygotes, 71–72